RIVERS & LOCHS
OF SCOTLAND

Bruce Sandison

MERLIN UNWIN BOOKS

First published in Britain by Merlin Unwin Books, 1997
Second edition published in 2001

ISBN 1 873674 430

Text copyright © Bruce Sandison

All rights reserved. No part of this publication may be reproduced, stored in a retrieval system or transmitted in any form or by any means, electronic, mechanical, photocopying, recording or otherwise, without the prior permission of Merlin Unwin Books.

Published by
Merlin Unwin Books
Palmers House, 7 Corve Street, Ludlow
Shropshire SY8 1DB

The author asserts his moral right to be identified as the author of this work.

British Library Cataloguing-in-Publication Data:
A catalogue record for this book is available from the British Library.

Designed and typeset in Sabon by David Aldred.
Printed in Great Britain by Biddles Ltd, Guildford, UK.

Contents

OS Map No	Map Name	Page
1.	Shetland - Yell & Unst	1
2.	Shetland - Whalsay	5
3.	Shetland - North Mainland	6
4.	Shetland - South Mainland	20
5.	Orkney - Northern Isles	23
6.	Orkney - Mainland	25
7.	Orkney - Pentland Firth	28
8.	Stornoway & North Lewis	29
9.	Cape Wrath, Durness & Scourie	52
10.	Strathnaver	74
11.	Thurso & Dunbeath	93
12.	Thurso, Wick & surrounding area	96
13.	West Lewis & North Harris	107
14.	Tarbert & Loch Seaforth	125
15.	Loch Assynt & surrounding area	145
16.	Lairg, Loch Shin & surrounding area	173
17.	Strath of Kildonan	182
18.	Sound of Harris & St Kilda	186
19.	Gairloch, Ullapool & Loch Maree	195
20.	Beinn Dearg & surrounding area	209
21.	Dornoch, Alness & Invergordon area	213
22.	Benbecula & South Uist	217
23.	North Skye	230
24.	Raasay, Applecross & Loch Torridon	235
25.	Glen Carron & surrounding area	241
26.	Inverness & Strathglass area	249
27.	Nairn & Forres, River Findhorn	255
28.	Elgin, Dufftown & surrounding area	258
29.	Banff & surrounding area	261
30.	Fraserburgh, Peterhead & District	262
31.	Barra & South Uist, Vatersay & Eriskay	264

OS Map No	Map Name	Page
32.	South Skye	268
33.	Loch Alsh, Glen Shiel & surrounding area	274
34.	Fort Augustus & Glen Albyn area	277
35.	Kingussie & Monadhliath Mountains	284
36.	Grantown, Aviemore & Cairngorm area	287
37.	Strathdon & surrounding area	290
38.	Aberdeen, Inverurie & Pitmedden	291
39.	Rhum & Eigg	294
40.	Loch Shiel, Mallaig & Glenfinnan	294
41.	Ben Nevis, Fort William & surrounding area	299
42.	Glen Garry & Loch Rannoch area	302
43.	Braemar & Blair Atholl	305
44.	Ballater, Glen Clova & surrounding area	308
45.	Stonehaven & Banchory	310
46.	Coll & Tiree	311
47.	Tobermory & North Mull	313
48.	Iona & West Mull, Ulva	315
49.	Oban & East Mull	316
50.	Glen Orchy & surrounding area	323
51.	Loch Tay & surrounding area	326
52.	Pitlochry to Crieff	329
53.	Blairgowrie & surrounding area	334
54.	Dundee to Montrose	338
55.	Lochgilphead & Loch Awe	341
56.	Loch Lomond & Inveraray	347
57.	Stirling & The Trossachs area	351
58.	Perth & Kinross	355
59.	St Andrews, Kirkcaldy & Glenrothes	360
60.	Islay	362
61.	Jura & Colonsay	367
62.	North Kintyre area	370
63.	Firth of Clyde area	371
64.	Glasgow, Motherwell & Airdrie	377
65.	Falkirk & Linlithgow, Dunfermline	379
66.	Edinburgh, Penicuik & North Berwick	382
67.	Duns, Dunbar & Eyemouth area	386
68.	South Kintyre & Campbeltown	388
69.	Isle of Arran	390
70.	Ayr, Kilmarnock & surrounding area	391

OS Map No	Map Name	Page
71.	Lanark & Upper Nithsdale area	394
72.	Upper Clyde Valley	395
73.	Peebles, Galashiels & surrounding area	397
74.	Kelso & Coldstream, Jedburgh & Duns	400
75.	Berwick-upon-Tweed & surrounding area	402
76.	Girvan, Ballantrae & Barrhill	402
77.	New Galloway & Glen Trool	405
78.	Nithsdale & Annandale area	408
79.	Hawick & Eskdale area	412
80.	Cheviot Hills & Kielder Forest area	416
81.	Alnwick, Morpeth & surrounding area	416
82.	Stranraer & Glen Luce, The Rhins	416
83.	Newton Stewart & Kirkcudbright, Gatehouse of Fleet	419
84.	Dumfries & Castle Douglas	423
85.	Carlisle & Solway Firth, Gretna Green	424

For Ann

'Will the bees come, the wild bees with their white noses?'

Introduction to the Second Edition

I would like to thank, from the bottom of my wellies, everyone who has helped make this book possible; riparian owners, angling clubs and individual anglers whose courtesy and consideration in support of my work has been a constant joy. If I have made errors, I apologise, but in a book of this nature it is almost impossible to be entirely accurate. Please let me have any revisions you would like to suggest (see page xiv) and I will try to include them in future editions.

This new edition is being published at a critical time for game fishing in Scotland. Our well-loved sport is under increasing pressure from a number of circumstances over which we anglers have little control.

May I record here my thanks to Allan Berry of Cannich in Inverness-shire. Allan has fought tirelessly on our behalf for many years. He, above all, has argued the scientific case for adopting a precautionary approach to the development of sea cage fish farming. His Petition to the Scottish Parliament (PE96) calling for an independent public inquiry into the industry was a major step forward. May I also record my appreciation of the work done on this subject by Don Staniford, Friends of the Earth (Scotland). We owe them both a huge debt of gratitude.

Bruce Sandison, Hysbackie
Tongue, Sutherland

Sketch map of Scotland showing the positions of the OS maps.
See pages iii–v for complete list of map names.

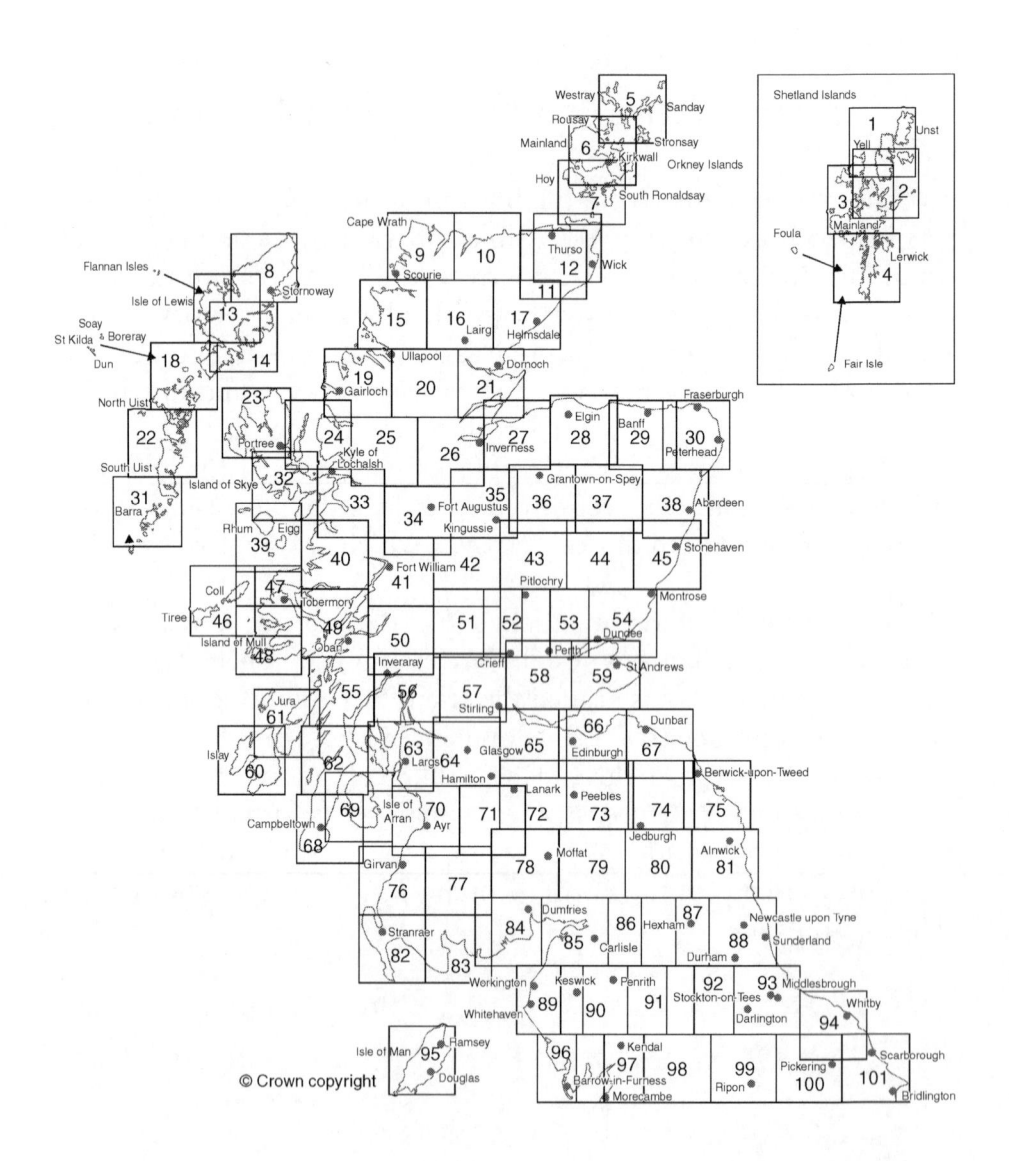

Publisher's Note

In Scots law, trout fishing rights are inseparable from the land upon which the loch or river lies. These rights, unlike salmon fishing rights, cannot be sold separately from the land.

All fishing in Scotland is therefore the legal property of riparian owners and, as such, all fishing in Scotland is private. You will be committing either a civil or criminal offence if you so much as wet a line without permission to do so from the relevant fishery owner.

The publisher and the author and all others associated with the production of this book have made every effort to ensure that the content of this book is accurate at the time of going to press. They have, prior to the publication of this book and in so far as they have been able to do so, invited comment and correction of the text from bodies such as local angling clubs, sporting rights agents and fishery owners.

An entry in this book does not imply in any way that the owner of the fishing described in that entry will either give, or refuse to give, members of the public a right to fish in the waters described in that entry. The right of fishing remains solely with the owner of the fishing concerned and it is the responsibility of all anglers, prior to fishing, to ensure that they have proper permission to do so from the owner of the fishery in question.

In as much as all fishing in Scotland is the property of riparian owners, all fishing in Scotland is private. Where the term 'private' is used in this book it means only that the owner does not allow or encourage public access specifically to the entries described in the book as being private. The absence of the word 'private' in connection with the other entries in the book does not imply that members of the public have any right to fish these waters.

The information contained in this book is to be used solely within the limitations of the provisions noted in the foregoing paragraphs. The publisher and the author and all others associated with the production of this book will not accept responsibility for any inaccuracies in the text or for any action under any circumstances whatsoever that may result from the use of the book.

The Scottish Tourist Boards

The following list shows the principal regional Tourist Offices. They are always willing to help the visiting angler in any way they can.

The Scottish Tourist Board, 23 Ravelston Terrace, EDINBURGH EH4 3EU. Tel: 0131 332 2433; Fax: 0131 343 1513.

The Scottish Tourist Board, Thistle House, Beechwood Park North, INVERNESS IV2 3ED. Tel: 01463 716996; Fax: 01463 717233.

Aberdeen and Grampian Tourist Board, Migvie House, North Silver Street, ABERDEEN AB10 1RJ. Tel: 01224 632727; Fax: 01224 639836.

Angus & City of Dundee Tourist Board, 4 City Square, DUNDEE DD1 3BA. Tel: 01382 434664; Fax: 01382 434665.

Argyll, The Isles, Loch Lomond, Stirling and Trossachs Tourist Board, Old Town Jail, St John Street, STIRLING FK8 1EA. Tel: 01786 445222; Fax: 01786 471301/446325.

Ayrshire & Arran Tourist Board, Burns House, Burns Statue Square, AYR KA7 1UP. Tel: 01292 288688; Fax: 01292 288686.

Dumfries and Galloway Tourist Board, Campbell House, Bankend Road, DUMFRIES DG1 4TH. Tel: 01387 250434; Fax: 01387 250462.

Edinburgh & Lothians Tourist Board, 4 Rothesay Terrace, EDINBURGH EH3 7RY. Tel: 0131 226 6800; Fax: 0131 226 6805.

Greater Glasgow & Clyde Valley Tourist Board, 11 George Square, GLASGOW G2 1DY. Tel: 0141 2044480; Fax: 0141 2044772.

The Highlands of Scotland Tourist Board, Peffery House, STRATHPEFFER IV14 9HA. Tel: 01997 421160; Fax: 01997 421168.

Kingdom of Fife Tourist Board, 7 Hanover Court, North Street, GLENROTHES KY7 5BS. Tel: 01592 750066; Fax: 01592 611180.

Orkney Tourist Board, 6 Broad Street, Kirkwall, ORKNEY KW15 1NX. Tel: 01856 872856; Fax: 01856 875056.

Perthshire Tourist Board, Lower City Mills, West Mill Street, PERTH PH1 5QP. Tel: 01738 627958; Fax: 01738 630416.

Scottish Borders Tourist Board, Shepherds Mills, Whinfield Road, SELKIRK TD7 5DT. Tel: 01750 20555; Fax: 01750 21886.

Shetland Island Tourism, Market Cross, Lerwick, SHETLAND ZE1 0LU. Tel: 01595 693434; Fax: 01595 695807.

Western Isles Tourist Board, 26 Cromwell Street, STORNOWAY, Isle of Lewis HS1 2DD. Tel: 01851 703088; Fax: 01851 705244.

How To Use This Book

This book is based on the Landranger Ordnance Survey map series (Scale 1:5000). The 'chapters' reflect the 85 maps which cover Scotland. If you are unsure about the map numbers and the regions to which they relate, please consult the Location Map on page viii and the accompanying list of map numbers and region names on page iii.

There are two ways of using this reference book:
If you already know the loch or river you are interested in, you can find it in the index at the back of the book, which will give you a page reference.
If you have a more general interest in the fishing opportunities in a particular region, then you must identify the relevant OS Map number (see page viii). The OS Maps are presented in numerical order throughout the book (OS 1–85). Within each OS Map chapter all the rivers and lochs of the region are listed alphabetically.

OS Map reference numbers are used to pin-point locations. If you are not familiar with the convention of grid references, this is how they work. Take, for example, **Sandavat, Loch (Brenish)** on the Isle of Lewis at grid reference 13/006270. This is on OS Map 13 (the first numerals). After the diagonal slash, the first three numerals (006) indicate the horizontal scale on the map, and the following three numerals (270) indicate the vertical scale. By following the lines of these two axes to their meeting point you will be able to locate the water in question.

If there is a name in brackets after the water name (in this case 'Brenish') this is to distinguish it from another loch with an identical name. In this instance, for example, there is another Loch Sandavat just two miles to the north.

Salmon Fisheries - the open season

The following dates indicate the varying opening and closing dates for salmon fishing on the major systems in Scotland. Please always remember, it is a criminal offence to fish for salmon or sea-trout in Scotland without the written permission of the owner of the fishing rights concerned. Fishing for salmon or sea-trout on a Sunday in Scotland is prohibited.

11 January - 30 September
Carron (Easter Ross)
Helmsdale
Oykle
Shin
Thurso (ends 5 October)

12 January - 30 September
Borgie
Halladale
Naver
Hope
Strathy

15 January - 15 October
Tay
Ness

26 January - 30 September
Conon

1 February - 30 September
Dee (Aberdeenshire)
Brora (ends 15 October)
Croe (ends 31 October)
Tweed (ends 30 November)

5 February - 31 October
Eden

11 February - 15 October
Awe
Beauly
Berridale
Dunbeath
Findhorn (ends 6 October)
Inver
Kirkaig
Nairn (ends 7 October)

11 February - 16 October
Creed
South Uist

11 February - 31 October
Ailort
Aline
Alness
Arinsdale
Ayr
Baa
Badachro
Balgay
Bladnoch
Broom
Carron (Wester Ross)
Clyde
Coladoir
Creran
Dee (Kirkcudbrightshire)
Deveron
Dionard
Don
Doon
Ewe
Forss
Gruinard
Gruinard (Little)
Kishorn
Laxford
Inchard
Kanaird
Kerry
Lewis (ends 30 September)
Moidart
Morar
Mull
Lochy
Shiel
Shieldaig
Skye
Torridon

Ullapool
Wick
Ythan
Spey (ends 30 September)

16 February - 31 October
Add
Eachaig
Esk (North)
Esk (South)
Fyne
Ruel
Ugie

25 February - 31 October
Arran
Bervie
Carradale
Fleet (Kirkcudbrightshire)
Fleet (Sutherland)
Girvan

Islay
Lossie
Luce
North Uist
Stincher

25 February - 15 November
Annan
Applecross
Irvine

25 February - 30 November
Urr
Nith

1 February - 31 October
Earn
Forth

1 March - 14 October
Cree

Trout Fisheries - the law and the open season

It is a civil offence to fish for brown trout in Scotland without the written permission of the owner of the fishing rights concerned. In areas covered by a Protection Order, fishing without the permission of the owner is a criminal offence.

Brown trout fishing in Scotland begins on 15 March and ends on 5 October. However, some fisheries delay the start of the season until 1 April and, in a few cases, until the 1 May. These differences are sometimes noted in the text but you should check specific dates with the owner of the fishery when making a booking.

In some areas, particularly in the Highlands and in the Hebridean Islands, Sunday is traditionally a non-fishing day. You should respect the local custom. You should also, as a matter of courtesy, ask permission from the owner of croft lands if you have to cross them in order to access a fishing location.

There is no close season for fishing for rainbow trout and most put-and-take rainbow trout fisheries remain open all year round. However, some do close in October. Check specific dates with the owner of the fishery when making a booking.

Please Keep Us Informed

In a work of this size and nature some mistakes will inevitably creep in. If you do spot such errors please help us to correct them. Alternatively you may know some essential information that we may have omitted unintentionally. Your help in this respect will be invaluable to us in preparing the text for subsequent editions and it will certainly be much appreciated. Kindly make your corrections on a photocopy of the blank form below and return it to: Merlin Unwin Books, Palmers House, 7 Corve Street, Ludlow, Shropshire SY8 1DB.

OS Map number and name:

Water name:

Location & access (OS map reference)

Commentary:

Fish:

Tactics & Flies:

Permission & Charges:

OS Map 1

Shetland – Yell & Unst

BASTA, Loch
Location & Access 1/506950 Park on the A968 at 1/511950 where the Burn of Basta cross the main road. Follow the burn west to reach the loch after a walk of about ten mins.
Commentary Two small lochs here: Loch of Basta, with Trona Water (1/500959) to the north - the rationale for an afternoon walking the moorlands by Trollakeldas Houlla (120m) and Hill of Colvister (110m). Outstanding birdlife and wild flowers.
Fish Trout average in the region of 10oz. Loch Basta may receive seatrout from August onwards.
Flies & Tactics Loch of Basta is about four acres in extent, Trona water about eight. Easily covered from the bank. After fishing Loch of Basta, walk north-west for half a mile to reach Trona Water. Flies: Loch Ordie, March Brown, Silver Butcher.
Permission & Charges See Loch of Ulsta (OS Map 3).

BELMONT, Loch
Location & Access 1/562010 To the east of the car park at the pier. Approach from along Wick of Belmont beach, or from near the ruins of Belmont House, abandoned in 1914.
Commentary Easily accessible, shallow, 20 acres in extent and as interesting for Hoga Ness Broch as it is for its fishing. The broch (BC200-AD300), which was originally 60ft in diameter, 30ft high, with double walls 15ft thick, is still impressive and well worth a visit.
Fish Excellent quality brown trout which average 12oz, with good numbers of fish of up to and over 2lb.
Flies & Tactics Bank fishing and reasonably comfortable wading. Trout are taken from all round the shore and no one place is substantially better than any other. Flies: Loch Ordie, Ke-He, Alexandra.
Permission & Charges David McMillan, Secretary, Unst Angling Association, Rockfield, Haroldswick, Unst. Tel: (01957) 711544. An all lochs season ticket costs £10.

BIRKA Water
Location & Access 1/317874 Park half a mile north of Loch of Housetter (1/363854 - small fish) at Midastew (1/363862) on the A970 road. Walk down the hill to the west and climb the saddle on the ridge of Beorgs of Skelberry (196m) to gain the edge of North Roe Moor. A seven mile walk on North Roe visiting 16 unnamed lochs and unnamed lochans.
Commentary This is a long day out so make an early start. You will need stout walking boots and plenty of stamina. A compass and map are essential. Should a mist descend you will need it. The first loch, Roer Water (1/337862), is the largest, half a mile long by up to quarter of a mile wide, and you should fish the north shore. Also have a cast on the tiny, unnamed lochan at 1/343864 to the north of Roer Water. Maadle Swankie, (1/331868) joined to Roer Water, is next. After Maadle Swankie, angle north west to the unnamed lochan at 1/323875, known locally as The Loch of the Grey Ewe. Birka Water, one of the most beautiful lochs in Shetland, is ten minutes further west. The exit stream from Birka Water flows steeply into Lang Clodie Loch (1/311878), before tumbling over the cliffs into the sea. There is a spectacular waterfall at the south end of Birka Water. Climb this to reach the Moshella Lochs (1/315869), a series of three lochans above Birka Water. Follow the inlet burn of the largest of the Moshella Lochs to reach the Loch of Many Crooks (1/313862) and Swabie Water (1/310854) ten minutes further south on the north slopes of Ronas hill. Now walk west to island-clad Sandy Water (1/305865), and return via the Loch of Many Crooks to fish the Loch of Had (1/319860). Return to the car by the south shore of Roer Water. This is one of the great Shetland fishing adventures, with wonderful wildlife and scenery throughout, including red-throated diver and Arctic skua.
Fish Trout average in the region of 8oz, but many of these lochs and lochans contain much larger specimens. Fish of up to 3lb are taken from Swabie Water and Sandy Water. Birka and the Moshella Lochs can produce trout of up to 2lb and more.
Flies & Tactics Bank fishing all the way. Wading is generally unnecessary and largely dangerous. In such a remote location it is foolish to take chances. Stay on the shore at all times. To do these lochs, and the beauty of the surrounding scenery, full justice, pack a tent and camp out on the beach near the waterfall on Birka Water. Also pack: Black Pennell, Loch Ordie, Soldier Palmer, Ke-He, March Brown, Greenwell's Glory, Dunkeld, Silver Butcher.
Permission & Charges Shetland Tourist Information Centre, Market Cross, Lerwick. Tel: (01595) 693434 or Rod & Line, Harbour Street, Lerwick. Tel: (01595) 695055. Costs: £5 per rod per day, £20 per season.
BIRRIER, Loch 1/541888. See Loch of Vatsetter.
BIRRIESGIRT, Loch 1/441910. See Sand Water, Mid Yell.
BRECKSIE, Loch 1/593030. See Easter Loch.

BROUGH, Loch
Location & Access 1/530030 Approach from Greenbank on the B9083 at 1/538042. Follow the minor road south to reach the north end of the loch.
Commentary The lochs of North Yell, including Loch of Brough and Loch of Cullivoe (OS1/533022) can be very dour, but contain some of the largest trout on the island. They are easily accessible and offer challenging sport in attractive surroundings.
Fish Trout in both lochs average 10oz, but there are also a number of fish of up to 3lb in weight.
Flies & Tactics These small lochs are best fished from the bank, indeed wading can be downright dangerous. Stay ashore, the fish lie close. If Loch of Brough is unyielding, walk south-east for ten minutes to wrestle with Loch of Cullivoe. Mid-summer evenings offer the best opportunity of tempting the brutes. Try: Loch Ordie, Black Zulu, Ke-He.
Permission & Charges See Loch of Ulsta (OS Map 3).

CLIFF, Loch of
Location & Access OS1/600120 Easy access from the B9086 at Burrafirth to the north end of the loch, or

1

Shetland - Yell & Unst
OS Map 1

from Baliasta (1/600099) to the south end.
Commentary One of the most exciting lochs in Shetland, over two miles north/south, narrow, but with a north-east arm extending for half a mile to near Quoys (1/615128). North from the loch is the Hermaness National Nature Reserve, home to thousands of sea birds: puffin, gannet, kittiwake, guillemot, razorbill, Arctic skua and 800 breeding pairs of great skua.
Fish Loch of Cliff trout average 10oz with a good number of fish over 1lb. The heaviest trout caught in recent years weighed 10lb. Seatrout arrive from mid-August onwards and average 1lb 8oz.
Flies & Tactics Boats may be available on Loch of Cliff (enquire Unst Angling Association 01957-711544), and fishing from a boat generally brings best results. as well as being a most convenient method of exploring this large loch. If bank fishing, do not wade. The west shore, where six feeder streams enter, is a productive drift for brown trout. Best sport with seatrout is found at the south end of the loch. Weed becomes a problem as the season advances. Seatrout may also be caught, throughout the season, in the sea, at Burra Firth. There are two small lochans in the hills to the west of Loch of Cliff: North Water (1/583132) and Heimar Water (1/583216)., both of which hold small trout. Offer: Ke-He, Greenwell's Glory, Alexandra.
Permission & Charges see Loch of Belmont entry.

CRO Waters
Location & Access 1/450937 Leave the A968 at the south end of Whale Sound (1/482914). Follow the minor road and take the first left to Efstigarth (1/461928). Park, and walk north-west to reach the Cro Waters within 40 mins.
Commentary There are five lochs here, from The Herra, north to Stuis of Graveland. Visiting them will take all day and involve you in a round trip of approximately four miles over some pretty tough country. The reward is absolute peace and the chance to see skuas, red-throated diver and golden plovers amidst splendid surroundings.
Fish Good numbers of 8oz trout with the chance of a few larger fish, particularly in the Cro Waters.
Flies & Tactics From the first of the Cro Waters (1/453931), walk north up the outlet stream to Virdi Water (1/453938), then west to the larger of the Cro Waters. Go north to tiny Hulk Water (1/448945), then north-east to reach Houlls Water (1/455952). Return south, stopping along the way for a cast in the unnamed lochan at 1/459943, via The Herra and Grommond. Bank fishing, and a compass and map are essential. Flies to try: Black Zulu, Soldier Palmer, Alexandra.
Permission & Charges See Loch of Ulsta (OS Map 3).

CULLIVOE, Loch 1/533022. See Loch of Brough.
DAM Loch (Unst) 1/595020. See Easter Loch.

EASTER Loch
Location & Access 1/599014 At Uyeasound, easily accessible and separated from the sea by a narrow isthmus.
Commentary Visit the Clivocast Standing Stone (Circa 3000BC) at 1/605005 and the remains of Gletna Church (1/599020), the 'unfinished' church. The devil is reputed to have removed at night that which had been built during the day.
Fish Easter Loch, along with Dam Loch (1/595020), is the principal seatrout system on Unst although all the lochs contain good brown trout as well. Loch of Brecksie (1/593030) and the unnamed lochan at 1/594039, approached from the A968, also receive seatrout. Brown trout average 8-10oz, seatrout average 1lb.
Flies & Tactics Bank fishing, with all the water easily covered from the shore. Use: Black Pennell, Greenwell's Glory, Silver Butcher.
Permission & Charges See Loch of Belmont.
EVRA Loch 1/490975. See Lochs of Lumbister.

FLUGARTH, Loch
Location & Access 1/363904 From North Roe (1/367899) take the minor road leading to the sea at Sandvoe. The loch is adjacent to the west of the road. Loch of Flugarth is half a mile long by up to 200yds wide, joined to the sea in Sand Voe by a shore stream.
Commentary Easy access and a good place to take little ones.
Fish Brown trout which average 8oz, but a few larger specimens as well. From August onwards, the possibility of seatrout, both in loch and in Sand Voe.
Flies & Tactics A boat would be a good idea, but otherwise, bank fish with confidence: fish are taken from all round the shore. Flies that tempt: Loch Ordie, March Brown, Peter Ross.
Permission & Charges See Birka Water (OS Map 3).

FUGLA Water 1/491013. See Gossa Water.
GARTH, Loch
Location & Access 1/545005 Close to the B9082, but give it a miss. To the best of my knowledge, it is fishless.
GLOUP Lochs 1/515035. See Kussa Waters.

GLOUP VOE Sea Loch
Location & Access 1/504035 Continue along the minor road which is an extension of the B9083 at Greenbank. Park at Gloup, the end of the road, and follow the track south down the Easter Lee of Gloup.
Commentary A long, narrow, steep-sided sea loch, culminating in Mare's Pool, at the south end.
Fish Seatrout which average 1lb in weight, but always the chance of a few larger specimens.
Flies & Tactics See Hamna Voe, Yell.
Permission & Charges See Hamna Voe, Yell (OS Map 3).
GOSSA Water (Unst) 1/579058. See Loch of Watlee.

GOSSA Water (Yell)
Location & Access 1/490000 Park near the head of Basta Voe at 1/510992 on the A968. Follow the Burn of Gossawater north-west for approx. 40 mins to reach the loch.
Commentary A good day out fishing and exploring the lochs and lochans between Basta Voe and Yell Sound. You will cover some four miles over rough

OS Map 1

Shetland - Yell & Unst

country and should go well prepared with compass and map. Hike out to Grud Waters (1/486014) and Fugla Water (1/491013), lochans to the north of Gossa Water, and visit Mirka Water (1/498993), to the south-east; fish Sandy Water (1/488988) and its unnamed satellite lochan on the return journey.
Fish Gossa Water trout average three-to-the-pound but there are occasional surprises with the odd fish of up to 3lb. The other waters hold fish which vary in size between 6oz and 2lb.
Flies & Tactics Gossa Water covers almost 180 acres and is the largest and most productive of these lochs. Wading is relatively comfortable, but as always it is better to stay ashore. Fish are taken from all round the bank and no one place is substantially better than any other. The lochans are easily covered. Don't forget to have an experimental cast in the two small, unnamed waters (1/490992 and 1/485994) immediately to the south of Gossa Water. Flies to try: Loch Ordie, Greenwell's Glory, Silver Butcher.
Permission & Charges See Loch of Ulsta (OS Map 3)

GREY EWE, Loch of the 1/323875. See Birka Water.
GRUD Waters 1/486014. See Gossa Water, Yell.

GUTCHER, Loch
Location & Access 1/548998 By the ferry pier at Gutcher and the penultimate break in the A968 before Unst.
Commentary A small loch, separated from the sea and the Wick of Gutcher by a narrow isthmus.
Fish Small brown trout averaging 8oz, but a good seatrout loch from August onwards.
Flies & Tactics Bank fishing, and easily covered. Do not wade. Use: Black Pennell, March Brown, Silver Butcher.
Permission & Charges See Loch of Ulsta (OS Map 3).

HADD, Loch 1/319860. See Birka Water.

HELLIERS Water
Location & Access 1/610049 Leave the A968 at 1/604061 and drive south to the end of the minor road at the north end of the loch.
Commentary An ideal beginners' loch, easily accessible, and the principal water supply for the island.
Fish Not glass case country, but good sport with brown trout which average about 6-8oz.
Flies & Tactics Bank fishing only, and the most productive area is at the south end where the two feeder burns enter. Offer them: Black Pennell, Grouse & Claret, Alexandra.
Permission & Charges See Loch of Belmont.

HEVDADALE Water 1/312894. See Inniscord Lochs.
HOULLS Water (Yell) 1/455952. See Cro Waters.
HOUSETTER, Loch 1/363854. See Birka Water.

HOVERSTA, Loch
Location & Access 1/608025 In Uyeasound, follow the minor road between Dam Loch and Easter Loch and park at the end at Mailand (1/605018). Walk north-east for 15 mins to reach Loch of Hoversta.

Also fish Loch of Vatnagarth (1/609028), immediately to the north.
Commentary The ideal place to spend a warm, midsummer day. One of the most beautiful Shetland beaches lies a few minutes to the east at Sand Wick. Above the beach are a series of ruined buildings of the Viking era, whilst on the hill to the north of the beach is the ruined 12th century Chapel of Eastings.
Fish Brown trout which average 12oz, with Loch of Hoversta occasionally producing fish of over 2lb in weight. Both lochs receive seatrout from the Dam Loch system and sport with seatrout is the principal interest here from August onwards.
Flies & Tactics These small, clear-water lochs are best fished from the shore. Wading is dangerous and only frightens the fish. Offer them: Loch Ordie, Invicta, Peter Ross.
Permission & Charges See Loch of Belmont.

HULK Water 1/448945. See Cro Waters.
INNIS Loch 1/382707. See Inniscord Lochs.

INNISCORD Lochs
Location & Access 1/322898 Park at Greenfield (1/365698) in North Roe on the A970. A track leads south-west then west, out into the hills, following the north slope of Beorgs of Skelberry (196m) and Beorgs of Uyea (174m).
Commentary A long day out. You will cover a distance of some seven miles over rough country, fishing nine named and unnamed lochs and lochans along the way. Golden plover country, and the opportunity of seeing Arctic skua performing their spectacular tumbling display flight.
Fish As far as size is concerned, just about everything, from bright little 6oz trout right up to fish of over 3lb.
Flies & Tactics A compass and map are essential. Tell someone where you are going and when you expect to return. Fish Pettadale Water (1/341899) first which has trout of up to 1lb; return to the track and continue to Mill Loch (1/331901) where trout average 10oz and there are fish of up to 2lb. Walk north, having a look at the two unnamed lochans to the east of Mill Loch, to reach Innis Loch (1/382707) after ten mins. Tramp south-west for one mile, by Hamara Field, to see the waterfall by Red Geo, then south to fish Hevdadale Water (1/312894). Walk north-north-east now to reach the straggle of Inniscord Lochs where trout of 1lb may be encountered. Follow the inlet burn from Inniscord Lochs over to Moosa Water, which has smaller fish. From Moosa, return north-east, round the side of the hill, to pick up the Burn of Sandvoe which leads to the track. Turn right and walk back to the start point at Greenfield. Throughout, stay on the bank and do not wade. Flies: Loch Ordie, March Brown, Silver Butcher.
Permission & Charges See Birka Water (OS Map 3).

KIRK Loch 1/534048. See Loch of Papil, Yell.

KUSSA Waters
Location & Access OS1/519029 Park as for Loch of Brough and, after a couple of casts, follow the track

3

Shetland - Yell & Unst

OS Map 1

down the west bank. At the inlet burn, head due west across the moor to reach Kussa Waters after a tramp of about 15 mins.
Commentary The chance of some nice fish, starting at Loch of Brough and ending at Muskra Loch (OS1/523021), returning to Loch of Brough by a convenient peat track. Kussa Waters consist of two small lochans, each about ten acres in extent with, for further entertainment, to the north, tiny Gloup Lochs (OS1/515035) and Sand Water (OS1/519033).
Fish Brown trout which average 8-10oz with the possibility of one for the glass case from Muskra.
Flies & Tactics Stay on the bank. Do not wade. The water is easily covered from the shore and fish tend to lie close. Flies: Ke-He, Invicta, Peter Ross.
Permission & Charges see Loch of Ulsta. (OS Map 3).

LANG CLODIE Loch 1/311878. See Birka Water.
LITTLE LUNGA Water 1/320881. See Muckle Lunga Water.
LONGA Water 1/585070. See Loch of Watlee.

LOWER SETTER, Loch
Location & Access 1/369922 Park at Isbister, at the end of the A970, and follow the peat track due north round the west side of Lanchestoo Hill (130m), to reach the Lower Loch of Setter after a walk of about 20 mins. Upper Loch of Setter (1/375921) lies to the east. Walk the inlet burn from the east shore of the lower loch to find its higher brother. Another convenient peat track eases the way south, back to Isbister. Turn left by the cemetery near Houll and walk out to have a further cast in the unnamed lochan (1/379910) on the cliffs overlooking Yell Sound.
Fish Nothing vast, but accommodating trout averaging 6-8oz.
Flies & Tactics Both lochs are only a few acres in extent and offer easy bank fishing. Flies to try: Black Zulu, Ke-He, Dunkeld.
Permission & Charges See Birka Water (OS Map 3)

LUMBISTER, Loch
Location & Access OS1/485967 Park at 1/509974 on the A968 near Colvister. Follow the outlet burn upstream for half a mile to reach Loch of Colvister (1/498970). Continue west along the north shore of Colvister to find the first and largest of the Lochs of Lumbister after three quarters of an hour.
Commentary The Lochs of Lumbister are owned by the Royal Society for the Protection of Birds. Anglers should avoid disturbing nesting species and observe the countryside code. This is a magical land, full of the sound of piping golden plover and shy greenshank. After fishing the first loch, which covers an area of almost 150 acres, walk north, following the inlet stream via the tiny lochan at 1/485972, to reach the second of the Lumbister lochs at 1/482976; butterfly-shaped and about 20 acres in extent. Now, walk west to the last of the lochs as 1/482976, lying on the cliffs by Gorset Hill (83m). There are two, one of ten acres and a smaller neighbour. Return to the start point along the north shore of the butterfly loch, to have a cast in little Evra Loch (OS1/490975) before heading home.

Fish On Loch of Colvister and the main loch of Lumbister, expect great sport with fine little trout averaging 6-8oz and the odd larger fish of up to 1lb. The other lochs contain similar sized fish, and a few surprises. Be prepared. Loch of Colvister may also receive seatrout, from August onwards.
Flies & Tactics A marvellous day out in the hills, bank fishing and exploring. Wear stout walking boots and take a compass and map. The south shore of Loch of Colvister is best, and you should concentrate most of your efforts on the main Lumbister loch at the south-west end, amongst the small islands. The remaining waters are easily covered. Weed can be a problem as the season advances, so visit during June and July. Flies to use: Black Pennell, Soldier Palmer, Peter Ross.
Permission & Charges See Loch of Ulsta. (OS Map 3).

LUNGA Water (Mid Yell) 1/460900. See Sand Water, Mid Yell.
MAADLE SWANKIE Water See Birka Water.
MAEA Water See Sand Water.
MANY CROOKS Loch See Birka Water.
MILL Loch (Mid Yell) 1/449902. See Sand Water, Mid Yell.
MILL Loch (North Roe) See Inniscord Lochs.
MILL LOCHS OF SANDVOE See Muckle Lunga Water.
MIRKA Water See Gossa Water, Yell.
MOOSA Water See Inniscord Lochs.
MOSHELLA Lochs See Birka Water.

MUCKLE LUNGA Water
Location & Access 1/329883 Start from Greenfield (1/365898) in North Roe on the A970 road. Walk south-west, then west along a good peat track leading out into the moor by Beorgs of Skelberry (196m) and Beorgs of Uyea (174m). At 1/348894, turn south and follow the line of Burn of Sandvoe for three quarters of a mile to Mill Lochs of Sandvoe (1/341881).
Commentary A day out exploring nine named and unnamed lochs and lochans on North Roe. Be prepared for all kinds of weather, tell someone where you are going and when you expect to return. Take a compass and map. This is rough country and it is easy to become disorientated should a mist descend.
Fish Muckle Lunga Water has the largest fish, up to and over 3lb, but they are dour and hard to tempt. The other lochs and lochans all contain brown trout which vary in size from 6oz up to fish of 2lb and more.
Flies & Tactics Have a cast in the three lochs which constitute the Mill Lochs of Sandvoe, then walk due south to Sandy Lochs (1/339872). Then head west to Tonga Water (1/331873) where the best sport is to be had along the south shore. North, now, to Muckle Lunga Water where you should thoroughly explore the north bay. Continue west again to Little Lunga Water (1/320881), a narrow loch which fishes best from the east shore. Sae Waters (1/310888) comprise three small lochans to the north-east of Little Lunga Water. Wading in any of these lochs is not advisable. Stay safe ashore. Trout tend to lie close and are easily covered from the bank. Offer them: Black Zulu, Soldier Palmer, Silver Butcher.

OS Maps 1-2 — Shetland - Whalsay

Permission & Charges See Birka Water. (OS Map 3)

MUCKLE VANDRA Water
Location & Access 1/496893 Approach from the A986 at Setter (1/491914). Follow the Burn of Setter south between Hill of Halsagarth and Hill of Setter until it turns south-west. At this point, angle south-east for ten minutes to reach the loch.
Commentary A small loch in a remote setting, covering an area of about 15 acres and reached after a stiff walk of some one and a half miles.
Fish Pretty, well-shaped, 8oz trout, with a few of up to 1lb. Possibility of seatrout after July.
Flies & Tactics Can be dour, but generally manages to send you home with a brace for supper. Bank fishing, and the water is easily covered using: Black Pennell, Soldier Palmer, Silver Butcher.
Permission & Charges See Loch of Ulsta. (OS Map 3)

MUSKRA Loch 1/523021. See Kussa Waters.

PAPIL, Loch of (Yell)
Location & Access 1/541041 Behind the school at Greenbank and easily accessible from the B9083 via a track along the south shore.
Commentary A beginners' loch, just about right for a few casts before dinner. For more strenuous action, and to properly test your skill, visit Kirk Loch (1/534048), a mile north, near Brough.
Fish In Loch of Papil, good stocks of trout which average three to the pound. In Kirk Loch, dour monsters of up to 5lb in weight.
Flies & Tactics Both lochs are fished from the bank. Loch of Papil becomes very weedy as the season advances but there is generally room for a cast or two. Which should include: Loch Ordie, Soldier Palmer, Black Pennell.
Permission & Charges See Loch of Ulsta (OS Map 3)

PAPIL Water (Fetlar)
Location & Access 1/603905 By ferry from Gutcher on the Island of Yell, thence via the B9088. Turn right by the phone box at Southdale then, just before the sea, turn right again to park by the old church at 1/608905.
Commentary For the angler/naturalist, a paradise: wild flowers in abundance, marvellous birdlife, chambered cairns, brochs and standing stones. Three lochs to visit: Papil Water, Loch of Funzie (1/655899) and Loch of Winyadepla (1/640930), all of which contain good trout. A fourth loch, Skutes Water, is not fished as it lies within a Royal Society for the Protection Birds sanctuary.
Fish Papil Water contains trout which average 10oz and a few fish of up to 2lb. Loch of Funzie has 8oz trout. Winyadepla, dour and difficult, has fish of up to and over 3lb in weight.
Flies & Tactics Park any non-fishing members of your party on the beach at Papil Water. Wading is comfortable and most of the water is easily covered. If you really wish a physical and angling challenge, walk out to Winyadepla, a stern three mile round-trip from Setter (1/626915). Upon no account attempt to wade in Winyadepla.
Permission & Charges See Birka Water. (OS Map 3)

PETTADALE Water 1/341899. See Inniscord Lochs.
QUOY, Loch 1/570063. See Loch of Watlee.
ROER Water 1/337862. See Birka Water.

SAND Water (Mid Yell)
Location & Access 1/465901 Park near the sand pit on the A968 road at 1/460900. Sand Water is 5 mins to the south of the road.
Commentary This is one of a number of small lochans around West Sandwick, all of which hold fish and offer good sport in pleasant surroundings. After fishing Sand Water, have a few casts in Lunga Water (1/460900), then return to the car and drive down to Loch of Scattland (1/451890), contained within the old and new roads. There are two further lochs in the parish worth visiting, reached from the end of the minor road at Harkland (1/445895) by following a good track north. This brings you to Mill Loch (1/449902). Next, angle north-west across the moor to reach Loch of Birriesgirt (1/441910) after 20 mins, on the cliffs near Sweina Stack. Noteworthy here is a settlement site, perched on a promontory overlooking Yell Sound.
Fish Nothing monstrous, but good fun with hard-fighting little trout averaging 6-8oz.
Flies & Tactics Bank fishing, with good sport all round. Keep back from the cliff edge when visiting Loch of Birriesgirt and resist the temptation to explore the settlement site. Flies to try: Black Zulu, Soldier Palmer, Peter Ross.
Permission & Charges See Loch of Ulsta. (OS Map 3).

SCATTLAND, Loch 1/451890. See Sand Water, Mid Yell.
VIRDI Water 1/453938. See Cro Waters.

Shetland - Whalsay

EAST LOCH OF SKAW 2/595665. See Loch Vats-Houll
FETLAR FISHING LOCATIONS See OS MAP 1

HOULL, Loch
Location & Access 2/558640 To the south and east of Brough, accessible from a track near the post office in the village which leads to the north end of the loch.
Commentary A large (80 acres), shallow and easily easily accessible water.
Fish Brown trout which average 8-10oz, along with a number of fish of up to and over 2lb in weight.
Flies & Tactics Boat fishing brings best results and a boat might be available from the angling association. Otherwise bank fishing. The south shore is most productive, and, if things are quiet, walk over to have a cast in the small lochans to the south, at 2/557635 and 2/563635. Flies that do the damage: Loch Ordie, Woodcock & Hare-lug, Peter Ross.
Permission & Charges See Loch of Huxter

5

Shetland - North Mainland
OS Maps 2-3

HUXTER, Loch
Location & Access 2/559622 Drive anti-clockwise round the island to find the loch to the east of the road, one mile from the Symbister Harbour.
Commentary The most productive loch on Whalsay, covering an area of some 80 acres. Loch of Livister (OS2/559630), a smaller neighbour, is a few minutes walk to the north, on the other side of the road.
Fish The largest trout taken in recent years weighed 9lb 4oz, although the average size is more in the region of 8oz. Nevertheless, most seasons produce fish of up to and over 3lb in weight. Loch of Livister also has some seriously large trout, but they do not give themselves up easily.
Flies & Tactics Boats may be available on Loch of Huxter, but bank fishing can be just as productive and fish are taken from all round the shore. Bank fishing only on Loch of Livister and do not wade on either water. Flies: Loch Ordie, Woodcock & Hare-lug, Peter Ross.
Permission & Charges Brian Polson, Whalsay Angling Association, Sheardaal, Huxter, Whalsay. Tel: (01806) 566472. Visitor Membership: £10.00.

ISBISTER, Loch
Location & Access 2/576643 Just to the north of the village of Isbister and easily accessible from the road.
Commentary Loch Isbister lies on The Leans in the north of Whalsay and offers excellent sport. Nuckro Water, midway between Loch of Huxter and Isbister Loch, to the west of the road, is also worth a cast or two.
Fish Good quality brown trout which average 10-12oz in weight with the chance of fish of up to 3lb. Nickro trout average 8oz, with a few fish of up to 1lb in weight.
Flies & Tactics Boat fishing brings best results on Isbister Loch and a boat may be available through the angling association. Otherwise, bank fishing, but difficult wading. Flies to offer: Loch Ordie, March Brown, Kingfisher Butcher.
Permission & Charges See Loch of Huxter

LIVISTER, Loch 2/559630. See Loch of Huxter
MAINLAND FISHING LOCATIONS See OS MAP 1
NUCKRO WATER See Isbister Loch

VATS-HOULL, Loch
Location & Access 2/571658 One mile north from Brough, adjacent and to the right of the road.
Commentary A very attractive loch covering an area of some 20 acres, shallow and easily accessible. There are two lochans to the north, West Loch of Skaw (2/580661), and East Loch of Skaw (2/595665) near the airstrip, which are also worth a quick look.
Fish Some nice brown trout of up to 3lb in weight, as well as good numbers of fish averaging 8oz.
Flies & Tactics Boat fishing is best on Loch Vats-Houll, and a boat may be available through the angling association. Otherwise, bank fishing with reasonably comfortable wading. Fish these lochs early in the season (April/May). They weed up thereafter. Offer the residents: Loch Ordie, March Brown, Dunkeld.

Permission & Charges See Loch of Huxter

WEST LOCH OF SKAW 2/580661. See Loch Vats-Houll
YELL FISHING LOCATIONS See OS MAP 1.

Shetland - North Mainland

AITHSNESS, Loch
Location & Access 3/329584 Drive north from Aith (3/341558) along the minor road to Vementry. Loch of Aithsness is just past Braewick, on the left of the road.
Commentary Easily accessible from the road, and from a good track along the south shore. Approximately 35ft deep and relatively comfortable wading, apart from the east shore where you should stay on the bank.
Fish Brown trout averaging 8oz with the chance of seatrout after August.
Flies & Tactics Best fished from a boat, if you have one, but good bank fishing as well, particularly along the south shore. Weed can be a problem as the season advances. Try: Loch Ordie, Invicta, Alexandra.
Permission & Charges Shetland Tourist Information Centre, Market Cross, Lerwick. Tel: 01595 693434. Season ticket, £20.00; Day ticket, £5.00. Use of five angling club boats, £20.00.

BARDISTER, Loch OS3/238501 See Loch of Kirkigarth.

BAYS Water
Location & Access 3/334673 Park at Mavis Grind (3/340684) on the A970 Isbister road. Follow the south shore of the Voe, west along the side of Cliva Hill (97m). After 15 mins, bear south up the Ness of Culseter, following the outlet stream to the loch.
Commentary A very attractive loch in a wonderful setting. There are pre-historic settlement sites and a chambered cairn close to the east shore of the loch. After fishing Bays Water, walk north-east to have a cast in Houlls (OS3/340676) before returning to the start point.
Fish Fine quality, silvery trout, which average 10oz, but also a few fish of over 2lb. Seatrout sometimes reach the loch from late July onwards.
Flies & Tactics Bays Water covers about 40 acres and the banks shelve steeply. Stay ashore. Do not wade. Weed can be a problem as the season advances. Begin on the west shore, then try the area of the two inlet burns on the east bank. Offer them: Loch Ordie, Greenwell's Glory, Silver Butcher.
Permission & Charges See Aithsness Loch.

BELLISTER, Loch
Location & Access 3/469582 On the west side of the B9075 road in North Nesting. Park at Kirk Ward

OS Map 3 — Shetland - North Mainland

(3/481584). The loch is by the roadside. Use this as a starting point for a visit to Black Water (3/466574), on the south side of Bow Field Hill, a walk of some 20 minutes from Loch of Bellister.
Commentary A very pleasant afternoon on the hill amidst splendid scenery. Guaranteed seclusion.
Fish Nothing for the glass case, but enough for breakfast. Attractive trout which average 6-8oz.
Flies & Tactics Easy bank fishing with: Soldier Palmer, March Brown, Dunkeld.
Permission & Charges See Aithsness Loch.

BENSTON, Loch
Location & Access OS3/463535 Easily accessible from the B9075. Turn right at 3/415540 and drive south-east for one mile to reach the loch by Vassa (3/465534).
Commentary Perhaps the best loch on Shetland, certainly one of the most popular and lovely. Half a mile long by up to quarter of a mile wide, with a delightful scrub and yellow flag-clad island in the north-east corner.
Fish Super, hard-fighting brown trout averaging 1lb in weight, with frequent fish of up to and over 3lb. Chance of the odd seatrout from August onwards.
Flies & Tactics This is a shallow, clear water loch with an average depth of 7ft. Boat fishing generally brings best results and the Association have one for hire to visitors. Tackle Benston early in the season. Weed becomes a problem later on. When bank fishing, avoid the south-west end of the loch which has a soft bottom. Flies: Loch Ordie, Woodcock & Hare-lug, Black Pennell.
Permission & Charges See Aithsness Loch.

BERRARUNIES, Loch OS3/320500 See Loch of Semblister.
BLACK Loch OS3/428492 See Loch of Vatster.
BLACK Water OS3/466574 See Loch of Bellister.
BORDIGARTH, Loch OS3/427738 See Sand Water.

BRECK, Loch
Location & Access OS3/212484 Drive west from Walls and turn left towards Burrastow. Park at 3/217483. Loch of Breck is a 5-minute walk to your right.
Commentary A day out round Mucklure, Hill of Scarvister and The Hamar, to be enjoyed as much for the sea-scape scenery as for the fishing. Walk south from Loch of Breck to reach Loch of Quinnigeo (3/212473) after 30 mins. Have a few casts and then visit Rusna Stacks (3/209470) and The Peak Stack near Uskie Geo. In windy weather stay well back from the cliff edge. From The Peak, walk over the hill to reach the Lochs of Littlure (3/204482). Return via Hill of Scarvister to the start point at Loch of Breck.
Fish Not 'glass case' country, but you should catch something for supper.
Flies & Tactics Easy bank fishing all the way with no need to wade. Wear stout walking boots. Flies: Loch Ordie, March Brown, Silver Butcher.
Permission & Charges Burrastow House Hotel, Walls. Tel: 01595 809307. Free to residents, day permits when available, £5.00 per rod.

BRECKON, Loch OS3/214779 See West Loch.

BREI Water (Lunnasting)
Location & Access OS3/505646 At the end of the B9071 road in Lunnasting, follow the minor road across Vidlin Voe. At the road junction, bear left and park near Gardin (3/485655). This is the start point for a visit to the lochs of Fora Dale and Hamna Dale which lie to the east of Gardin.
Commentary A day out exploring five lovely lochs between Vidlin Voe and Lunning Sound. Outstanding birdlife. Take compass and map in case of a change in the weather, and keep back from the cliff edge.
Fish Good stocks of brown trout which average about 8-10oz, and a few larger specimens as well.
Flies & Tactics Follow a track north-east to reach the first two lochs: Geria Water (3/491660) and Lorga Water (3/496657). Walk south up Fora Dale from Lorga Water to reach Brei Water. Now north to little Mirka Water (3/502652) in Hamna Dale, and north again to reach the last loch, Mill Loch, at 3/503660. Flies: Loch Ordie, Greenwell's Glory, Black Pennell.
Permission & Charges See Aithsness Loch.

BREI Water (Mangaster)
Location & Access OS3/319712 Leave the A970 Brae/Isbister road at 3/333716 and follow the minor road south-west to Mangaster. Park at the end of the road and follow a good track west to Punds of Mangaster (3/322704) then walk the stream uphill, past Lungawater (3/319708), unnamed on the map, to Brei Water.
Commentary There are more than a dozen lochs here, between the A970 and the sea, on Fellsa Moors, and they all contain trout. It takes two days to do them proper justice and day one starts at Lungawater, followed by Brei Water. Next, tramp north-west to fish Punds Lochs (OS3/310716), then follow the inlet stream on the east shore to Brei Water of Nibon (OS3/316719) and its northern satellite lochan. Finally, descend from Fellsa Moors by way of Punds Water (OS3/325715), also fishing the unnamed lochan at OS3/328720, before returning to the car at Mangaster. The walking is fairly rugged, but the rewards are outstanding. Quite apart from trout, there is a good chance of seeing golden plover, red-throated diver (Shetland 'rain geese') and Arctic and great skua.
Fish Some excellent fish of up to and over 2lb in weight, along with good numbers of their smaller brethren.
Flies & Tactics Do not wade these lochs, stay safely ashore and let the fish come to you. Unhappily, they do so reluctantly, for these waters can be dour. Try them with: Loch Ordie, March Brown, Silver Butcher, and crossed fingers.
Permission & Charges See Aithsness Loch.

BREI Water of Nibon OS3/316719 See Brei Water (Mangaster).

BROUSTER, Loch of
Location & Access OS3/261513 The A971 Bridge of Walls/Walls road crosses Voe of Browland and the

7

Shetland - North Mainland — OS Map 3

north section of the voe is known as Loch of Brouster. The loch is immediately adjacent to the A971 and is easily accessible.
Commentary Loch of Brouster is brackish and being so close to the road it is somewhat public. Nevertheless, well worth a few casts on the way north to its neighbours, Upper Loch of Brouster (3/261520) and Loch of Voxterby (3/260532). A few minutes to the east of Upper Loch of Brouster, and joined to it by a small stream, is Skula Water (3/267521); sheltered by Ward of Browland Hill (100m), a useful bolt-hole when the wind blows.
Fish Loch of Brouster has some decent-sized 'slob' trout and can offer opportunities for sport with seatrout from July onwards. Upper Loch of Brouster has brown trout averaging 8oz and seatrout towards the end of the season; Loch of Voxterby holds brown trout in the order of 8-10oz, as well as seatrout. Skula Water trout average 6-8oz.
Flies & Tactics Fish from the bank on Loch of Brouster, wade with care on the west shore of Upper Loch of Brouster, elsewhere stay out of the water. The north and west shore is best on Loch of Brouster; on the Upper loch, fish the south-east corner and the extreme north end where the burn enters from Loch of Voxterby. Loch of Voxterby is the largest of the three, being almost one mile north/south by a quarter of a mile wide across the south bay. Fish may be taken from all round the shore, but the north section is perhaps the most productive area, particularly in the vicinity of promontories and islands. Try them with: Loch Ordie, March Brown, Alexandra.
Permission & Charges See Aithsness Loch.

BROUSTER, Upper Loch OS3/261520 See Loch of Brouster.

BURGA Water, Lunnasting
Location & Access OS3/481641 At the end of the B9071 in Lunnasting, drive east along the minor road across Vidlin Voe. Turn south at Orgill (3/482652). Burga Water is a further one mile south, to the west of the road.
Commentary Visit Burga Water in conjunction with a trip to Ollas Water (3/491646), a ten minute walk east from Burga Water. Burga has the remains of a Broch site off the south-west shore.
Fish Nice trout which average 8oz and a few larger fish. After August, Ollas can hold seatrout.
Flies & Tactics Few problems, provided you stay on the bank. All the water is easily covered from the shore. Try: Loch Ordie, Grouse & Claret, Black Pennell.
Permission & Charges See Aithsness Loch.

BURGA Water, Mousa Vords
Location & Access OS3/233540 Burga Water is to the east of the A971 Bridge of Walls/Norby road. Park at 3/228536 and walk north-east for five mins to reach the loch.
Commentary This is a straggling water, quarter of a mile east/west and quarter of a mile north/south. The small island off the south shore contains the ruins of a 2000 year old fortified dwelling (dun) and there is a Neolithic cairn just to the north of where the Burn of Cattikismires enters the loch.
Fish Brown trout average 8oz and seatrout arrive from August onwards. Some of the surrounding lochans hold larger fish.
Flies & Tactics Start on Burga Water and, depending upon wind direction, continue the day by making a circular tour of other lochs: Loch of Whitebrigs (3/243534) and its satellite, Galta Water (3/249544) and, finally, Daney's Loch (3/241547). Tempt them with: Ke-He, Invicta, Dunkeld.
Permission & Charges See Aithsness Loch.

BURKI Waters OS3/311642 See Gilsa Water.
BURNATWATT, Loch OS3/251511 See Loch of Flatpunds.

BURRALAND, Loch
Location & Access OS3/340748 Turn east from the A970 Brae/Isbister road at 3/332748. The loch lies to the south of the track.
Commentary Loch of Burraland is nearly half a mile east/west by up to 400 yds north/south. In spite of being exposed and often windy, this shallow, peaty loch is always worth a visit, especially around midsummer's night. Weed becomes a serious problem later in the season.
Fish Nice brown trout which average 8oz and the chance of a few larger specimens up to 1lb. Seatrout run the Seali Burn from The Houlb and may be encountered from August onwards.
Flies & Tactics Best fished from a boat, otherwise, stay ashore and do not wade. Fish are taken from all round the loch. Start at the north-east corner and work round to the south-west bay. Show them: Ke-He, Grouse & Claret, Black Pennell.
Permission & Charges See Aithsness Loch.

BURRALAND, Loch OS3/221498 See Loch of Kirkigarth.

CLINGS Water
Location & Access OS3/310560 Leave the B9071 road at 3/330530 and drive north through Twatt to Clousta. Bear left before Clousta and park on a farm track south of Ponton.
Commentary Clings Water is a large, circular loch, 50ft deep and easily accessible. It provides shelter when strong winds blow being protected by surrounding hills. If Clings Water trout are 'difficult' trudge south, over the hill, to visit Forse Water (OS3/300550).
Fish Very attractive trout which average 10oz and a few larger specimens as well. The small, unnamed lochan on the right of the road is a beginners water, full of bright little fish. Forse Water has trout averaging 8-10oz, and a chance of seatrout after August.
Flies & Tactics Bank fishing and the east shore brings best results. Wading here is comfortable but avoid wading anywhere else. On Forse Water, concentrate on the south-west arm. Flies: Loch Ordie, Black Pennell, Silver Butcher.
Permission & Charges See Aithsness Loch.

OS Map 3 — Shetland - North Mainland

CLODIS Water
Location & Access OS3/512842 Drive north from Burravoe on the B9081 and park at Holligarth (3/521839). Walk north-west up the hill to reach the loch after a tramp of about 15 mins.
Commentary Clodis Water is a small loch lying between Hill of Holligarth to the north and Hill of Canisdale (159m) to the south. This is golden plover and curlew country.
Fish Bright little trout which average 6-8oz.
Flies & Tactics Very easily fished from the shore but can be weedy as the season advances. Try: Black Pennell, March Brown, Dunkeld
Permission & Charges See Aithsness Loch.

CLOUSTA, Loch
Location & Access OS3/315580 Approach from the minor road from Aith to Vementry in the north at 3/320590, or from Clousta in the south at 3/312574.
Commentary Loch of Clousta is three quarters of a mile long by up to quarter of a mile wide, over 30ft deep in the south bay, shallower in the island-scattered north bay. A great day out, with the opportunity of walking over to fish the Loch of Vaara (3/325568), a similar size to Loch of Clousta.
Fish Mainly 8oz trout, but a good chance of larger fish, particularly in Loch of Vaara.
Flies & Tactics On Loch of Clousta, concentrate on the north bay. When fishing Loch of Vaara, begin along the north shore. Avoid wading in either water. Offer the inhabitants: Loch Ordie, Greenwell's Glory, Silver Butcher.
Permission & Charges See Aithsness Loch.

CLUBBA Water OS3/440683 See Mill Loch, Muckla Moor.

COLLASTER, Loch (Twatt)
Location & Access OS3/315547 Approach from the south end of Loch of North-house at 3/324547 on the minor road between Twatt and Clousta. Follow a peat road west to reach the loch in approx 15 mins.
Commentary Loch of Collaster drains south through Kirkhouse Water (3/312537) via the Burn of Twatt. The loch covers an area of some 30 acres and lies on the moorlands of Sneuan.
Fish Excellent brown trout averaging 10oz in weight, with larger fish of up to and over 2lb. Weed can be a problem as the season advances.
Flies & Tactics They do not give themselves up easily. Keep trying, from the bank, particularly in the vicinity of the inlet burn in the north-west corner and where the loch exits to Kirkhouse Water in the south. Try: Loch Ordie, Grouse & Claret, Peter Ross.
Permission & Charges See Aithsness Loch.

CRO WATER, South Yell
Location & Access OS3/462844 Drive north from Ulsta on the A968 road towards West Sandwick. Park at the tiny lochan on the right of the road at 3/454846. Follow the inlet burn up the hill to reach Cro Water after a 20 minute hike.
Commentary Cro Water lies on Evra Houll (164m) and gives wonderful views west to Ronas Hill on Mainland, and north towards Unst. A step north from Cro Water is Gossa Water (3/463849), also worth a few casts before returning to the car.
Fish These lochs are rarely fished from one season to the next, and offer splendid sport with trout which average 8oz.
Flies & Tactics Easily covered from the bank and no need to wade. Fish are taken from all round the shore and no one place is substantially better than another. First cast: Loch Ordie, Woodcock & Hare-lug, Peter Ross.
Permission & Charges See Aithsness Loch.

CULTERYIN, Loch OS3/286542 See Grass Water.
CUPPA Water OS3/421527 See Hill of Girlsta Lochs.
CURE Water OS3/311753 See Punds Water.
DALSA Waters OS3/234553 See Loch Mousavord.
DANEY'S, Loch OS3/241547 See Burga Water.
DJUBA Water, Longa OS3/274573 See Longa Water.
DJUBA Water, Norby OS3/234553 See Loch Mousavord.
EAST YELL, Loch OS3/531820 See Loch of Neapaback.

EELA Water
Location & Access OS3/330785 Lies immediately to the west of the A970 Brae/Isbister road.
Commentary This is the largest loch in the north of Mainland, circular and approximately half a mile across. Often windy, exposed to public view, but worth a few hours on a good day.
Fish Eela Water trout average 8oz, with some larger fish of over 1lb in weight.
Flies & Tactics A relatively deep loch (over 10m), and best fished from a boat. Avoid wading if bank fishing and concentrate around the north-west corner, working south down the west shore to where Burn of Eelwater exits to the sea in Hamar Voe. Try: Black Zulu, Soldier Palmer, Silver Invicta.
Permission & Charges See Aithsness Loch. Boat available for hire from Shetland Angling Association.

ELVISTER, Loch OS3/227496 See Loch of Kirkigarth.

FLATPUNDS, Loch
Location & Access OS3/245620 Flatpunds is easily accessible, adjacent and to the north of the A971 Bridge of Walls/Melby road.
Commentary Loch of Flatpunds drains north-east via Twatt Burn into Loch of Voxterby. To the north, at 3/247528, is an unnamed lochan which should also be explored, as should be Mousa Water, to the south as 3/251518, and little Loch of Burnatwatt at 3/251511.
Fish Nothing glass-case-sized, but plenty of sport with trout which average 8-10oz, and perhaps the chance of the odd fish of around 1lb in weight.
Flies & Tactics Wading is dangerous. On Loch of Flatpunds, try the west shore, north from the inlet burn, and the bay to the south of the inlet burn promontory. The other lochs are all easily covered. Use: Wickham's Fancy, Ke-He, Silver Butcher.

Shetland - North Mainland   OS Map 3

Permission & Charges See Aithsness Loch.

FORSE Water OS3/300550 See Clings Water.
FRAMGORD, Loch OS3/209785 See West Loch.
FREESTER, Loch OS3/453539 See Loch of Houlland, South Nesting.

FUGLA Water
Location & Access OS3/510719 At the end of the B9071 in Lunnasting (3/474653), continue north on the minor road to Lunna and Outrabister. Park at 3/503722. Walk east for 10 mins to reach Fugla Water.
Commentary A splendid day out exploring the little lochans on the Lunna Ness Peninsula, with fine views north to Yell and Feltar, and east and south to the Out Skerries and Whalsay. Fugla Water is the largest loch, the other waters include: Mill Loch North (OS3/510731), South Loch Stofast (OS3/510714), Mill Loch South (OS3/500704), and Loch of Grutwick (OS3/502708).
Fish Plenty of fun with trout averaging 6-8oz.
Flies & Tactics Take care near the cliffs, and avoid wading in the lochs. Apart from Fugla, the others can be easily covered from terra firma. Use: Loch Ordie, March Brown, Black Pennell.
Permission & Charges See Aithsness Loch.

GALTA Water OS3/249544 See Burga Water.
GERDIE, Loch OS3/206782 See West Loch.
GERIA Water OS3/491660 See Brei Water.

GILSA Water
Location & Access OS3/308632 Turn south from the A970 Isbister road at 3/358676 and follow the minor road past Busta House Hotel on the west shore of Busta Voe. Cross Roe Sound and park at the end of the road at Little-ayre. Walk west over the south shoulder of Muckla Field Hill (120m) to reach the loch in 30 mins.
Commentary A compass-and-map day out, fishing remote lochs and lochans on Muckle Roe. Total distance covered, approx. five miles; lochs fished, eight. After Gilsa Water, follow the outlet burn north to Muckla Water (3/305638). Continue north along the west slope of Muckla Field, past Giffords Hill, to reach Lairds Loch (3/300650). Now walk north-north-east across Green Hill for 20 mins to reach Town Loch (3/304660) and lunch. After lunch, view the cliffs and sea-stacks in the bay of North Ham. Track the inlet stream from the north-east corner of Town Loch up the glen to Mill Loch (3/315657), sheltered by The Chubb (100m), North Ward (150m) and South Ward (169m). Leave Mill Loch at the south end, climbing south-west over The Cooses to find Burki Waters: two, delightful, interconnected lochs, at 3/311642. A track leads south from East Burki, past the last of the lochs in the series, Mill Lochs, tiny lochans at 3/319637. At the road, turn right and walk back to the start point at Little-ayre.
Fish These lochs are infrequently fished and although the average size of trout is in the order of 6-8oz, there are much larger fish as well.
Flies & Tactics Stout walking boots, wet weather gear, and a good knowledge of map reading are essential. Stay well back from the cliff edges, particularly after rain and in strong wind. Bank fishing, using Loch Ordie, Soldier Palmer, Alexandra. Mill Loch is always interesting.
Permission & Charges See Aithsness Loch.

GIRLSTA, Loch
Location & Access OS3/433520 Adjacent to the east of the A970 Lerwick/Hillside road.
Commentary Loch of Girsta is one and a half miles long by up to almost half a mile wide and nearly 80ft deep. A cairn on the west shore marks the spot where the fishing tackle of an angler, wading the loch, was found. The angler himself never was, so be warned. Nevertheless, one of the best lochs on Mainland, particularly down the east shore where a long under-water promontory can be waded with care.
Fish Good stocks of excellent quality brown trout which average 10oz. Much larger fish are taken most seasons and this loch holds the record for Shetland trout, a fish of over 10lb. Also Arctic char, and a chance of seatrout from July onwards.
Flies & Tactics Boat fishing brings best results when you should engineer a drift down the east shore, some ten yards out from the bank. When bank fishing, concentrate your efforts along the north-east shore-line, tempting them with: Loch Ordie, Soldier Palmer, Black Pennell.
Permission & Charges See Aithsness Loch.

GIRSIE, Loch OS3/421519 See Hill of Girlsta Lochs.

GLUSS Water
Location & Access OS3/256810 Leave the A970 Brae/Hillswick road at 3/290778 and follow the B9078. Immediately before Braewick (3/246790), turn right and follow the minor road towards Hamnaovoe. Park at 3/245804 and take the track north, to reach the loch after a walk of about 20 mins.
Commentary Gluss Water is half a mile by up to 300 yds wide and lies to the north of Esha Ness by Scora Field. North and east from Gluss Water, there are a further 12 lochs, all of which contain trout. These lochs are very remote, lying on the north shore of Ronas Voe, overlooked by Ronas Hill, the highest point on Shetland. They involve a long hike, but if you appreciate Shetland scenery at its finest, then head for Gossa Waters (3/258838), Lergeo Water (3/254849) and the Mill Lochs of Okran (3/249843).
Fish Gluss Water contains some excellent trout. The only trouble is getting them out, but fish of up to and over 3lb are sometimes taken and the average weight is in the order of 10-12oz. The more distant lochs are rarely fished and hold a few surprises for those prepared to make the effort involved in getting there.
Flies & Tactics Persevere, and fish hopefully, from the bank, on Gluss Water. Keep back from the edge, since fish tend to lie close. The north end, where a number of feeder streams enter, is a good place to start. With: Black Zulu, Soldier Palmer, Silver Butcher.
Permission & Charges See Aithsness Loch.

OS Map 3

Shetland - North Mainland

GLUSSDALE Water OS3/334333 See Moor Waters.

GONFIRTH, Loch
Location & Access OS3/385623 To the north of the B9071 between Voe and Gonfirth.
Commentary An easily accessible roadside loch, circular in shape and covering an area of approximately 40 acres.
Fish Brown trout averaging 8oz with a few larger fish as well.
Flies & Tactics Easy bank fishing, but stay on the bank. Wading is difficult. The best area is at the west end of the loch, by the small island, and north from that point. First cast: Loch Ordie, Greenwell's Glory, Alexandra.
Permission & Charges See Aithsness Loch.

GOSSA Water, Burraview OS3/244563 See Hamari Water.

GOSSA Water (North Nesting)
Location & Access OS3/436606 Park near the Bridge of Atler at 3/457610 on the B9075 in North Nesting. Follow the burn west up the hill until it swings north at 3/447611 and then bear south-west to reach the loch after a walk of some 30 minutes.
Commentary A lovely loch of some 40 acres in the heart of North Nesting, between Mossy Hill and West Hill of Grunnafirth. After fishing Gossa Water, a good route home would be to walk south to fish Long Loch (3/449598), then east to take in a few casts on Quinni Loch (3/438598) before striking north-east to Bridge of Atler. Quinni Loch is an ideal place for a quiet picnic.
Fish Brown trout average about 8oz. Gossa Water is connected to the sea by the Laxo Burn and, from August onwards, there is the chance of seatrout.
Flies & Tactics Weed can be a problem as the season advances and high winds discolour the shallow water. Do not wade. Approach with caution. Fish lie close to the shore. The north-east bank produces best results, but also explore the area round the promontory on the south shore and inlet burns at the south corner. Long Loch, which is in fact tiny, and Quinni Loch hold very pretty little fish. Use: Ke-He, Soldier Palmer, Black Pennell.
Permission & Charges See Aithsness Loch.

GOSSA Water, Yell
Location & Access OS3/463859 See Cro Water, South Yell. *Permission & Charges* Nisbet, D., Altona, Mid Yell, Shetland, Tel: (01957) 702037.
GOSSA Waters, Mus Wells OS3/258838 See Gluss Water.
GOSTER, Loch OS3/174514 See Loch of Kirkigarth.

GRASS Water
Location & Access OS3/283535 Turn north from the A971 Lerwick/Bridge of Walls road at 3/279526 and follow the minor road to Unifirth. Park at 3/279538 and walk east for five mins to reach the loch.
Commentary Half a mile long, draining north to the sea through Culeryin Loch (3/286542) to Marlee Loch (sea loch) and The Vadills. On the west side of the road is Heilia Water (3/273532), linked to Grass Water by Merki Burn, which is also worth a cast.
Fish Expect brown trout averaging 8oz and, later in the season, the possibility of seatrout.
Flies & Tactics Bank fishing. Start at the north end of Grass Water, in the wide, island-scattered bay. Stay on the shore. On Heilia Water, fish the west bank by the two inlet burns and the narrow north arm. Try: Loch Ordie, Ke-He, Black Pennell.
Permission & Charges See Aithsness Loch.

GRUNNAVOE, Loch
Location & Access OS3/258492 Turn south, at the end of the A971 road at the village of Walls, and follow the minor road to Vadlure. Park at 3/249488 and follow the outlet burn up to the loch, a walk of about 10 mins.
Commentary Loch of Grunnavoe is a large water, some half a mile east/west by up to a quarter of a mile north/south. Outlines of Viking field systems and settlements may be found nearby at 3/260498, overlooking Voe of Browland and there are pre-historic burial chambers to the south of Grunivoe.
Fish The loch contains excellent trout which average 10oz in weight as well as a few fish of over 1lb. Grunnivoe is connected to the sea by The Houb in Vaila Sound and there is always the chance of seatrout after August.
Flies & Tactics Uncomfortable wading and best to stay ashore. The east end of the loch generally produces best results, particularly round the little island, but fish may be encountered almost anywhere. Offer them: Loch Ordie, March Brown, Peter Ross
Permission & Charges See Aithsness Loch.

GRUTING, Loch
Location & Access OS3/294502 Turn south on the A971 Lerwick/Bridge of Walls road at Roadside (3/300524) and follow the minor road for two miles. Loch of Gruting is on the left.
Commentary A small, accessible roadside loch joined to the sea by the Burn of Scuta Voe. At the south end of the loch, to the west of the road, are the remains of an early settlement with clearly identifiable field patterns.
Fish Good brown trout which average 8oz and, from August onwards, the chance of seatrout.
Flies & Tactics The water is easily covered from the bank. The bottom of the loch consists of mud-covered rocks and wading is not recommended. As the season advances, weed becomes a problem. Use: Ke-He, March Brown, Peter Ross.
Permission & Charges See Aithsness Loch.

GRUTWICK, Loch OS3/502708 See Fugla Water.
HAGGRISTER, Loch OS3/338704 See Loch of Lunnister.

HAMARI Water
Location & Access OS3/250555 Leave the A971 Lerwick/Walls road at 3/279526 and follow the minor road north through Unifirth. Turn south to Fogrigarth at 3/256560 and park at the end of the road. Walk south-west for ten mins to reach the loch.

Shetland - North Mainland
OS Map 3

Commentary An attractive loch in a moorland setting with some shelter from prevailing winds, provided by Smiths Hamar and Kellister Hills. After fishing Hamari, walk west to explore the Loch of Kellister (OS3/241560). Lunch at Voe of Snarraness, on the beach adjacent to the north shore of the loch. Gossa Water (OS3/244563), north-east, is also worth a cast on the way home.
Fish Good stocks of trout averaging 8oz, plus some fish of up to 1lb.
Flies & Tactics Bank fishing and stay ashore. Wading is dangerous. The north and west shore of Hamari Water is most productive. The other lochs are small and easily covered from the bank. Offer them: Loch Ordie, Greenwell's Glory, Silver Butcher.
Permission & Charges See Aithsness Loch.

HAMARSLAND, Loch OS3/ See Loch of Vatster.

HAMNA VOE, Estuary, South Yell
Location & Access OS3/486805 Easy access from the B9081.
Commentary A wide estuary, guarded by the island of the Ness of Galtagarth, into which flow Cada Burn, Burn of Arisdale and Burn of Hamnavoe. Outstanding birdlife and wild flowers.
Fish Seatrout, although, sadly, not in any great numbers now, but still worth a look.
Flies & Tactics The promontory at Salt Ness (3/486804) is the best of the west bank fishing and around Whirly (3/491804) for the east bank. Spinning or flyfishing can produce results. Flies to try: Soldier Palmer, Black Pennell, Teal Blue & Silver.
Permission & Charges See Aithsness Loch.

HEILIA Water, Bridge of Walls OS3/273532 See Grass Water.

HELLISTER, Loch
Location & Access OS3/390500 Located by the east side of the A971 Lerwick/Walls road by the village of Hellister.
Commentary Half a mile long by almost quarter of a mile wide, brackish and very much in public view. The east shore is backed by the steep crags of Hill of Hellister (120m).
Fish Small brown trout and the chance of seatrout towards the end of the season.
Flies & Tactics Don't wade, and concentrate your activity along the north bank and in the area of the promontory half-way down the east shore. Offer: Black Pennell, Soldier Palmer, Silver Butcher.
Permission & Charges See Aithsness Loch.

HILL OF GIRLSTA Lochs
Location & Access OS3/425515 On the hill to the west of Loch of Girlsta (3/434525), easily accessible from the A970 Lerwick road. Park at 3/430515 and follow the outlet burn west up the hill for ten minutes to reach the first loch.
Commentary There are four small waters: Longnecked Loch (3/423514), Girsie Loch (3/421519) and its adjoining partner, and Cuppa Water (3/421527). If things are stiff on Girlsta, tramp up and explore these delightful little waters.
Fish Brown trout which average 8oz, but some larger fish as well
Flies & Tactics Approach with caution, the fish lie close. Easily covered from the shore and no need to wade. Try: Ke-He, Invicta, Silver Butcher.
Permission & Charges See Aithsness Loch.

HOLLORIN, Loch
Location & Access OS3/275558 Loch of Hollorin lies to the south of Unifirth and is approached from 3/278555 where it is possible to park in a small quarry. Walk north-west to reach the loch after about ten minutes. Also worth a cast are the two small lochs to the east of the road, near Newton, Quassawall Loch (3/279550) and Mill Loch (3/281550), and the Smalla Waters (3/270548) to the west.
Commentary This is a splendid day out exploring a series of delightful lochs and lochans where there is something for everyone, beginner and expert alike. The unnamed loch at 3/269555 is known locally as Robbie Glen's Loch and is ideal for beginners.
Fish Loch of Hollorin has the largest fish, averaging 12-14oz and a few of up to 2lb. Robbie Glen's Loch trout average 6oz. The Smalla Waters hold some good fish although they are hard to catch.
Flies & Tactics All bank fishing. Begin on Loch of Hollorin and work south to the Smalla Waters, then east across the road to Quassawall and Mill lochs before returning to the quarry. First cast: Soldier Palmer, Loch Ordie, Alexandra.
Permission & Charges See Aithsness Loch.

HORSE Water OS3/526815 See Loch of Neapaback.

HOSTIGATES, Lochs
Location & Access OS3/312593 Drive north from Aith (3/341558) along the minor road to Vementry. The Lochs of Hostigates are at the end of this road.
Commentary A small, deep loch to the south of the road, linked to an even smaller companion to the north, draining into Uyea Sound.
Fish Brown trout averaging 8oz, with a few fish of up to 1lb.
Flies & Tactics Do not wade. All the water is easily covered from the bank. Offer: Loch Ordie, Invicta, Black Pennell.
Permission & Charges See Aithsness Loch.

HOULLAND, Loch OS3/215792 See West Loch.

HOULLAND, Loch (South Nesting)
Location & Access OS3/454543 Close to the north side of the B9075 road between Catfirth and Brettabister.
Commentary Easily accessible and generally fished in conjunction with its neighbour, Loch of Freester (3/453539), to the south of the B9705. Weed becomes a problem as the season advances.
Fish Loch of Houlland has the largest fish, brown trout which average 10oz, but Freester sometimes holds seatrout during August and September.

OS Map 3

Shetland - North Mainland

Flies & Tactics Neither water is deep, but wading is not advised. On Houlland, try the north-west corner where the water is deeper, and on Freester, fish the east end. First cast: Black Pennell, Greenwell's Glory, Peter Ross.
Permission & Charges See Aithsness Loch.

HOULLS Water OS3/? See Bays Water.
HOULMA Water OS3/266576 See Longa Water.

HOUSTER, Loch
Location & Access OS3/343553 Close to Aith and the B9071 Bixter/Burrafirth road.
Commentary Easily accessible from Aith and ideal for a few casts before setting out to explore the lochs on North Mid Field Hill (see Lamba Water entry).
Fish Brown trout which average 8oz.
Flies & Tactics Easy bank fishing. Do not wade. Fish are taken from all round the shore of this pleasant little loch. Flies: Soldier Palmer, March Brown, Silver Butcher.
Permission & Charges See Aithsness Loch.

HULMA Water
Location & Access OS3/295528 Hulma Water lies immediately to the north of the A971 Lerwick/Bridge of Walls road.
Commentary An easily accessible, very pretty loch, one mile east/west by some 300yds north/south. A boat is useful, if available, otherwise excellent bank fishing. Also visit Sand Water (3/297538), to the north of Hulma, where trout for breakfast is guaranteed.
Fish Nothing huge, but plenty of sport with hard-fighting, little trout averaging 8oz. There are larger specimens as well, and fish of over 1lb are not uncommon.
Flies & Tactics The water is peat-stained and it is best to avoid wading. On Hulma, concentrate your efforts at the west end, near the small islands, and in the large bay at the north-west corner. Fish may be taken from all round the shore on Sand Water. Tempt them with: Black Pennell, Soldier Palmer, Silver Butcher.
Permission & Charges See Aithsness Loch.

JOHNNIE MANN'S Loch OS3/332729 See Moora Waters.
KELLISTER, Loch OS3/241560 See Hamari Water.

KETTLESTER, Loch
Location & Access OS3/513807 To the north of Littlester on the B9081 Ferry/Burravoe road.
Commentary An attractive, shallow loch, easily accessible and covering an area of approx. 40 acres.
Fish Excellent quality brown trout averaging 8-10oz with the chance of a few larger fish and seatrout from August onwards.
Flies & Tactics Wade with caution. The north end of the loch is best, and unusual in that the two principal feeder streams are separated by only a few yards from the outlet burn. Offer trout: Loch Ordie, March Brown, Peter Ross.
Permission & Charges See Aithsness Loch.

KILKA Water
Location & Access OS3/335656 On Muckle Roe. Turn south from the A970 Hillside/Isbister road at 3/358676 and follow the minor road past Busta House Hotel on the west shore of Busta Voe. After crossing Roe Sound, turn right to Glen. The loch is a couple of minutes walk south from the end of the road.
Commentary Kilka Water and nearby Orwick Water (3/340648) are the most easily accessible of the Muckle Roe lochs, being close to the only road on the peninsula.
Fish Very pretty fish in both lochs, averaging 10oz and great fun to catch.
Flies & Tactics Kilka Water is the largest of the pair, approx. 40 acres, and both lochs are fished from the bank. Do not wade. The water is coloured and dark, bushy flies work best. Offer them: Black Zulu, Soldier Palmer, Black Pennell.
Permission & Charges See Aithsness Loch.

KIRKABISTER, Loch
Location & Access OS3 See Loch of Stavaness entry.

KIRKHOUSE Water
Location & Access OS3/312536 Lies to the north of the A971 Lerwick/Bridge of Walls road. Approach from Park Hall (3/311527) along a track to Turdale Water (3/306530), thence north-east for ten minutes to reach Kirkhouse Loch.
Commentary Have a look at the Chambered Cairn site on Ara Clett hill along the way, and spare time for a cast or two in Turdale Water which holds some nice trout.
Fish Kirkhouse trout average 10-12oz and there are larger fish of up to 3lb as well. From August onwards there is the chance of seatrout.
Flies & Tactics Kirkhouse Water is a dour, unforgiving loch. Stay on the bank and avoid wading. The best sport is generally at the north end, on either side of the promontory where the loch narrows in the north-east corner, and down the north-west bank. First cast: Black Zulu, Loch Ordie, Peter Ross.
Permission & Charges See Aithsness Loch.

KIRKIGARTH, Loch
Location & Access OS3/237497 North of the village of Walls, behind the school, easily accessible and ideal for a few casts if time is limited.
Commentary An attractive loch, joined by a feeder stream to Loch Bardister (3/238501) to the north. West from Walls, along the minor road towards Sung, are a number of other small lochs which are all easily fished during the course of a day: Elvister (3/227496), Burraland (3/221498), Loch of Sung (3/192501), Loch of Watsness (3/175505), and Loch of Goster (3/174514).
Fish Brown trout averaging 8oz in most of these lochs, but with one or two surprises along the way.
Flies & Tactics No problems, provided you avoid wading. Don't waste too much time if fish are not rising. Stow the rod and drive along to the next water. The viewpoint at Swinister (3/179510) is a marvellous place for lunch. Try: Blue Zulu, Invicta, Peter Ross.
Permission & Charges See Aithsness Loch.

13

Shetland - North Mainland
OS Map 3

LAIRDS, Loch OS3/300650 See Gilsa Water.

LAMBA Water
Location & Access OS3/382560 One of a series of five lochs on North Mid Field Hill (147m), approached from Aith (3/346557) on the B9071 Bixter/Burrafirth road.
Commentary Start from Aith by following the track past the burial ground south-east up the hill. Whitelaw Loch (3/359540) is ten minutes south-east from the end of the track. Three quarters of a mile north-east brings you to Truggles Water (3/371546), joined north to Maa Water (3/378553) by a small stream. A step further north is Lamba Water, and, finally, half a mile north again, Loch of Lunklet (3/379570).
Fish All these water contain stocks of 8oz fish and good numbers of larger trout as well.
Flies & Tactics This is a splendid day out fishing a great variety of waters in lovely surroundings. Spend most time on Maa Water and Lamba Water. On Maa Water, work round the south and east shore, finishing by the islands at the north corner. On Lamba, concentrate on the north-east and north shore. Do not wade in any of the lochs. Tempt them with: Ke-He, Loch Ordie, Black Pennell.
Permission & Charges See Aithsness Loch.

LANG, Loch OS3/271588 See Longa Water.

LAXO Water
Location & Access OS3/444650 Park near Laxo at 3/441636 on the B9071. Walk north, following the burn on the right up to the loch, a comfortable 15 minutes.
Commentary A narrow, half-mile long water with a wide north-east bay. The water is peat-strained.
Fish Good stocks of brown trout which average 6oz. There are a few larger fish, but rarely of more than 1lb. Seatrout may reach Laxo Water towards the end of the season.
Flies & Tactics It is dangerous to wade. The north end of the loch, on Yella Moor, is the most productive area, particularly on either side of the inlet burn. Offer them: Blue Zulu, Invicta, Peter Ross.
Permission & Charges See Aithsness Loch.

LERGEO Water OS3/254849 See Gluss Water.

LITTLESTER, Loch
Location & Access OS3/512797 Immediately adjacent to the south of the B9081 Ferry/Burravoe road.
Commentary One of the most productive lochs on Yell, easily accessible and covering an area of approximately 50 acres.
Fish Brown trout average 1lb with good numbers of fish of up to and over 2lb in weight. The largest trout caught in recent years (1991) weighed 8lb 8oz. Also the chance of seatrout from August onwards.
Flies & Tactics A boat may be available but bank fishing is every bit as productive. Wading is not advisable, and Littlester is best fished early in the season before weed growth becomes a problem. The south shore and roadside north shore are productive areas, but start at the south-east corner, where the outlet burn leaves the loch. Offer them: Loch Ordie, March Brown, Black Pennell.
Permission & Charges Boat from: J. C. Wilson, The Manor House, Yell. Tel: (01957) 722233 at £15 per day. See Loch of Ulsta for other details.

LITTLURE, Loch OS3/204482 See Loch of Breck.
LONG, Loch See Gossa Water, North Nesting.

LONGA Water, West Burrafirth
Location & Access OS3/265569 Leave the A971 Lerwick/Walls road at 3/279526 and follow the minor road north through Unifirth. Longa Water lies immediately adjacent to the north of the road, near West Burrafirth.
Commentary The first of a series of excellent trout lochs lying amidst the hills and moorlands of Oxna Field and Neeans. The walking is tough, particularly after rain, but this is a perfect get-away-from-it-all circuit. Start at Longa Water, then walk north to fish Houlma Water (3/266576). North again to reach Maw Loch (3/266585) and its neighbour to the north-west, Lang Loch (3/271588). On the return, have a cast in the unnamed lochan at 3/275587 before walking due south to finish on Djuba Water (3/274573).
Fish Generally 8-10oz trout, but also larger fish, particularly in Djuba and Houlma Waters, where trout of up to and over 1lb 8oz are not unknown.
Flies & Tactics Bank fishing all the way and wading is dangerous. Stay ashore. Houlma Water probably holds the best trout. Try the north-east corner, just where the loch begins to narrow. First cast: Ke-He, March Brown, Silver Invicta.
Permission & Charges See Aithsness Loch.

LONGNECKED, Loch OS3/423514 See Hill of Girlsta Lochs.
LORGA Water 3/496657 See Brei Water, Lunnasting.

LUNGA Water
Location & Access OS3/235527 Immediately adjacent and to the west of the A971 Bridge of Walls/Melby road, an easily accessible and popular loch.
Commentary Lunga Water is the public water supply for the local community. Shetland Angling Association have permission to use outboards on this reservoir. If things are too restful on Lunga Water, there are three further lochs, to the west, known as the Sma Lochs (3/228522) which are also worth a cast.
Fish Trout average about 10oz, but there are fish of up to and over 2lb in weight.
Flies & Tactics Wading is dangerous and really unnecessary: fish lie close to the shore. Lunga Water fishes well in a good wind - a not infrequent occurrence in Shetland - and the best sport is had at the north end where an inlet stream enters, and along the south shore. First cast: Black Pennell, Grouse & Claret, Alexandra.
Permission & Charges See Aithsness Loch.

OS Map 3 — Shetland - North Mainland

LUNGAWATER, Loch 3/319708 See Brei Water.
LUNKLET, Loch 3/379570 See Lamba Water entry.

LUNNISTER, Loch
Location & Access OS3/346715 Leave the A970 Brae/Isbister road at 3/339693 and follow the minor road east to Lunnister (3/347714). The loch is to the west of the road.
Commentary An easily accessible loch on the west shore of Sullom Voe, half a mile north/south by approx. 300 yds wide. Three further lochs in the vicinity are worth cast or two: Loch of Haggrister (OS3/338704), a long, straggling water close to the A970, and, to the north, Scora Water (OS3/338719) and Stanes Water (OS3/337712). These are best approached from the A970, rather than from Lunnister.
Fish Loch of Lunnister has the best trout, fish which average 8-10oz and the odd trout of over 2lb. There is a chance of seatrout after August. The other lochs contain smaller trout and all the lochs tend to weed up as the season advances.
Flies & Tactics Boat fishing produces best results on Loch of Lunnister, but you have to bring your own. Otherwise, stay on the bank, wading is not recommended. Flies to try: Loch Ordie, Black Zulu, Soldier Palmer.
Permission & Charges See Aithsness Loch.

MAA Water, Loch 3/378553 See Lamba Water entry.
MAAMIE of Garth, Loch 3/219560 See Loch Mousavord.
MARROFIELD Water, Loch 3/387593 See Smerla Water entry.
MAW, Loch 3/266585 See Longa Water.
MILL, Loch 3/315657 See Gilsa Water.
MILL, Loch (Lunnasting) 3/503660 See Brei Water entry.

MILL Loch (Muckla Moor)
Location & Access OS3/449690 Leave the A968 Hillside/Toft road at Garth of Susetter (3/410660) and follow the minor road to its conclusion at Collafirth (3/431689). Park carefully. Climb steeply, east-south-east, for 15 mins, to reach the top of Collafirth Hill (150m). From the summit, Mill Loch is a further 30 minute walk east.
Commentary Mill Loch, along with its neighbour, Clubba Water (3/440683), is infrequently visited and the setting is spectacular. Hard walking, but worth every step.
Fish Expect brown trout averaging 8oz in weight.
Flies & Tactics Begin with Clubba Water and follow the outlet stream north-east to Mill Loch. Concentrate your effort on where the stream enters Mill Loch, then work round the west shore to the outlet burn in the north corner. Offer them: Ke-He, Loch Ordie, Black Pennell.
Permission & Charges See Aithsness Loch.
MILL, Loch (Unifirth) 3/281550 See Loch of Hollorin.
MILL, Lochs 3/319637 See Gilsa Water.
MILL, Lochs of Okran 3/249843 See Gluss Water.
MILL, North Loch (Lunna Ness) 3/510731 See Fugla Water.
MILL, South Loch (Lunna Ness) 3/500704 See Fugla Water.
MIRKA Water, Loch 3/502652 See Brei Water entry.
MOO Water, Loch 3/457555. See Loch of Skellister entry.

MOORA Waters
Location & Access OS3/325726 Leave the A970 Brae/Isbister road between Johnnie Mann's Loch (3/332729) and Glusdale Water (3/334333), both of which deserve a cast, and park at 3/329734. Follow the outlet stream south up the hill to reach the first of the Moora Lochs after a 10 minute walk.
Commentary This is a day-out circuit of six lochs around Flangna Field and Moo Field, starting with the two Moora Waters. After fishing them, continue west to the unnamed lochan at 3/321792, before fishing Soolmisvird Water (3/318729), the largest loch in the group, and the unnamed lochan to the south at 3/317725. End the day by walking north-east, crossing the road to fish little Trolladale Water (3/326736), before returning to your car.
Fish There are some good fish waiting, up to and over 2lb in weight, but the average is more like 8-10oz.
Flies & Tactics These are clear water lochs and they do not give up their riches easily. Be prepared to work hard for your breakfast brace. Stay on the bank and cast hopefully, using: Black Pennell, Invicta, Alexandra.
Permission & Charges See Aithsness Loch.

MOUSA Water 3/251518 See Loch of Flatpunds.

MOUSAVORD, Loch
Location & Access OS3/224554 Park near Loch Stanevatstoe (OS3/216545), which is worth a cast, on the A971 Bridge of Walls/Norby road at OS3/215552. The loch is a ten minute walk, downhill to the east.
Commentary Loch Mousavord is roughly circular and covers an area of approx. 80 acres. There are a number of adjacent water which should be visited whilst in the 'parish': Dalsa Waters (3/234553), a group of four small lochans, three unnamed lochans to the north-west at 3/230555, Djuba Water (3/226563), and Maamie of Garth (3/219560), a tiny pool to the north of Mousavord.
Fish Trout average 8oz, although a few larger specimens are taken from time to time, particularly from the more remote waters.
Flies & Tactics High banks and deep water make wading uncomfortable on Mousavord. Stay ashore. Fish the south bank of Mousavord before walking, in an anti-clockwise direction, round the other waters. Finish by thrashing the north-east shore of Mousavord, which is probably the most productive fishing area. Try: Black Zulu, Greenwell's Glory, Peter Ross.
Permission & Charges See Aithsness Loch.

MUCKLA Water 3/305638 See Gilsa Water.

Shetland - North Mainland
OS Map 3

MURRASTER, Loch
Location & Access OS3/279522 Loch of Murraster lies at the east of the A971 road between Bridge of Twatt and Bridge of Walls. Park by the gravel pit at 3/276524.
Commentary A bit public, but fine for a few casts if time is limited. If things are quiet on Murraster, visit Heilia Water (3/273533) to the north. Park at 3/279534 and walk west following the Merki Burn up to the loch.
Fish Small brown trout and the odd seatrout in Loch of Murraster. Heilia Water fish average 8-10oz, with a few fish over 1lb in weight.
Flies & Tactics Bank fishing and it is best to avoid wading. Loch of Murraster is easily covered and the south-east shore produces good results. On Heilia Water, concentrate along the west shore down to the south-west corner. Flies: Soldier Palmer, Woodcock & Hare-lug, Peter Ross.
Permission & Charges See Aithsness Loch.

MUSSEL, Loch
Location & Access OS3/473788 From the ferry, turn right at Fluke Hole and follow the minor road east to park at 3/472795. Walk the inlet burn south to reach the loch after about 10 mins.
Commentary A wonderful little loch on the cliffs above the sea at Wester Wick of Copister, close to the sea-pool known as Tangi Loch at 3/469785.
Fish Trout in Mussel Loch average 10-12oz and are of excellent quality. Sea-trout in Tangi Loch most times of the year.
Flies & Tactics Reasonably safe wading at the south-east end of the loch but, elsewhere, inadvisable. The south shore, near the outlet stream is a good place to launch your attack, as is the north-east shore. Offer them: Loch Ordie, Grouse & Claret, Silver Butcher.
Permission & Charges See Loch of Ulsta.

NEAPABACK, Loch
Location & Access OS3/525807 From the B9081 at 3/519802 via a track leading east to Upper Neapaback. Park considerately at 3/526803 and walk over to the loch, which is on your left.
Commentary This small loch is one of a series of waters lying on the cliffs between B9081 and the sea. After exploring Neapaback, return to the track and walk north to reach Horse Water (3/526815), then angle north-east to Loch of East Yell (3/531820), perched above Revri Geo.
Fish Nothing too heavy to carry home, but almost certainly something for breakfast.
Flies & Tactics A good cast could reach the far bank in most cases, so stay on the shore, well back from the edge and avoid wading. Tempt them with: Loch Ordie, Ke-He, Silver Butcher.
Permission & Charges See Loch of Ulsta.

NESHION Water 3/425753 See Sand Water.

NORTH-HOUSE, Loch
Location & Access OS3/325552 Approach from the B9071 road at 3/330530. Drive north through the village of Twatt. The loch is on the right of the road, after two miles.
Commentary A roadside loch, three quarters of a mile long by up to a quarter of a mile wide, joined to the sea by the Burn of Twatt. The north end is a narrow arm of the main body of the water.
Fish Brown trout averaging 8-10oz with a few seatrout after August.
Flies & Tactics Wading is not recommended. The east shore produces best results, particularly the large bay mid-way up the loch, and the far north-east corner. Offer them: Black Pennell, Greenwell's Glory, Silver Butcher.
Permission & Charges See Aithsness Loch.

OLLAS Water, Loch 3/491646 See Burga Water entry.
ORWICK Water 3/340648 See Kilka Water.

PETTA Water
Location & Access OS3/428590 Easily accessible, adjacent to the west side of the A970 Lerwick/Hillside road in Petta Dale.
Commentary Quarter of a mile long by up to 200 yards wide, enclosed between East Kame Hill (160m) and Mid Kame Hill (170m).
Fish Can be dour, but contains trout which average 8oz and a few larger fish of up to and over 1lb in weight.
Flies & Tactics Fish are taken all over the loch, but the west shore is probably the best. Stay on the shore. Do not wade. Temp them with: Loch Ordie, Greenwell's Glory, Alexandra.
Permission & Charges See Aithsness Loch.

PUNDS, Lochs 3/310716 See Brei Water.

PUNDS Water
Location & Access OS3/327757 Punds Water lies immediately to the west of the A970 Brae/Isbister road and is easily accessible from the A970, and from convenient tracks which border the north and south shores.
Commentary Exposed to public view, but a pleasant place for a few casts. More attractive sport lies west, on the lochs of The Vaava Runs and Ness of Hamar: Cure Water (3/311753), the unnamed loch at 3/312748, West Mill Loch of Hamar (3/300756) and Stubba Water (3/317755).
Fish Expect 8oz trout, with a few larger fish of up to and over 1lb in weight, particularly from Punds Water and Cure Water.
Flies & Tactics Boat fishing is best on Punds Water, otherwise, do not wade, anywhere. The long finger-like west shore promontory is a good place to begin, before heading west into the hills. Cure Water is a very pretty loch and the ideal half-way house for lunch. Flies: Loch Ordie, March Brown, Gold Butcher.
Permission & Charges See Aithsness Loch.

PUNDS Water 3/325715 See Brei Water.
QUASSAWALL, Loch 3/279550 See Loch of Hollorin.
QUINNI, Loch See Gossa Water, North Nesting.
QUINNIGEO, Loch 3/212473 See Loch of Breck.

OS Map 3 — Shetland - North Mainland

ROBBIE GLEN'S, Loch 3/269555 See Loch of Hollorin.
RONAS Hill Lochs Loch of the Hadd, Loch of Many Crooks, Swabie Water, Sandy Water, Moshella Lochs, Maadle Swankie Water, Clubbi Shuns, Loch of Housetter. See OS Map 1.
SAE Water, Loch 3/423629 See Loch of Voe entry.

SALT WATER SEATROUT FISHING LOCATIONS

Bixter Voe (3/331520); Seli Voe (3/337480); Olas Voe (3/287470); Voe of Snarraness (3/239560); The Vadills (3/291546); Club of Mulla (3/393648); Olna Firth (3/402638); Gunnister Voe (3/319742); Hamar Voe (3/314765); Ura Firth (3/310787); Orr Wick (3/333813); Gluss Voe (3/358775); The Vadill (3/401756); Dales Voe (3/412689); Colla Firth (3/430690); Boatsroom Voe (3/497707); Ayre of Dury (3/462604); Quoys of Catfirth (3/443540).

The best time for seatrout fishing in the voes and firths is from July onwards, when the main runs start. Nevertheless, seatrout are present throughout most of the year and may be caught from as early as March onwards. Recent years have seen a decline in the numbers of seatrout caught, as well as a general decline in the average weight, down to about 1lb, although larger specimens are sometimes taken. Spinning is the most popular method of salt water seatrout fishing, but flyfishing can be just as effective, particularly Ke-He, Black Pennell, Silver Invicta, Soldier Palmer, Peter Ross, Teal Blue & Silver. Be aware of the dangers involved of fishing the voes. Sudden tide surges, unexpected waves, unstable shores, slippery rocks all wait to catch the unwary. Be alert at all times and take the greatest possible care. Seek local advice in every instance, prior to setting out.

SAND Water

Location & Access OS3/423745. Park at 3/433745 on the A968 Hillside/Boath of Toft road. Sand Water lies to the west, reached after a 20 minute walk up the hill.
Commentary A very pleasant loch in a bright, moorland setting on the Hill of Crooksetter (110m). A few minutes north lies Neshion Water (3/425753), whilst to the south is Loch of Bordigarth (3/427738), both of which are worth a visit.
Fish Sand Water holds the largest fish, with trout averaging 12oz and a few fish of up to and over 2lb 8oz in weight. Neshion Water and Loch of Bordigarth trout are more modest in size. There is also the chance of seatrout from August onwards.
Flies & Tactics Wading is uncomfortable and it is best to stay on the shore. The north end of Sand Water is the most productive area. The other lochs are easily covered and fish can be taken from all round the bank. Flies to try: Black Zulu, Ke-He, Black Pennell.
Permission & Charges See Aithsness Loch.

SAND Water, Lamba Scord

Location & Access OS3/417547 Sand Water loch lies adjacent to the west of the A970 Lerwick/Hillside road, and is bounded on the north by the B9075 road to Weisdale.
Commentary Easily accessible, covering an area of half a mile north/south by up to quarter of a mile east/west. Shallow and exposed to every gale that blows, which churns up the bottom mightily making it impossible to fish. On calm days, worth a few casts, but given the proximity of much more interesting waters, don't spend too long here.
Fish The chance of seatrout from July onwards, with fish of up to 2lb in weight. Brown trout average 8oz, with the odd larger specimen of up to and over 1lb.
Flies & Tactics Most seatrout are encountered in the middle of the loch, so a boat would be useful. For brown trout, concentrate along the east shore, particularly in the bays separated by the headland. Offer them: Ke-He, Greenwell's Glory, Peter Ross.
Permission & Charges See Aithsness Loch.

SAND Water, Loch (Garderhouse)

Location & Access OS3/318478 Park south of Garderhouse on the B9071 Effirth/Easter Skeld road at 3/331476. A track leads west to reach Sand Water after a walk of about 15 mins.
Commentary An attractive little loch in a remote setting between Gruting and Seli Voe. Rarely fished and sheltered by Sand Field hill (133m) to the north and Aulins Glen to the south.
Fish Brown trout averaging 8-10oz, with the chance of the odd larger fish.
Flies & Tactics Easily covered from the bank and fish may be taken from all round the shore.
Permission & Charges See Aithsness Loch.

SAND Water, Loch (Hulma) 3/297538 See Hulma Water.
SCORA Water 3/338719 See Loch of Lunnister.

SEMBLISTER, Loch

Location & Access OS3/336496 To the east of the B9071 Effirth/Easter Skeld road.
Commentary Borders the road. A convenient track also gives access to the east shoreline. Whilst in the parish, it is worth walking out to have a cast in Loch Berrarunies (3/320500) which lies to the south of Hagmark Hill (80m).
Fish Not glass-case country, but good sport with 8oz brown trout and the chance of seatrout in the autumn.
Flies & Tactics Loch of Semblister is a shallow, narrow water, almost half a mile long. Stay on the bank. The south end gives best sport. Flies: Loch Ordie, Soldier Palmer, Alexandra.
Permission & Charges See Aithsness Loch.

SKELLISTER, Loch

Location & Access OS3/460562. Park near Newing at 3/467557 on the B9075 road in South Nesting. A rough track leads north-west up the hill to reach Loch of Skellister after ten minutes.
Commentary Loch of Skellister is owned by the Shetland Angling Association and covers an area of about fifty acres. Easily accessible and should be linked with a visit to Moo Water (3/457555), a small, dour lochan to the south.
Fish Good numbers of trout which average 8oz, but look out for a few specimen fish of up to 4lb in

Shetland - North Mainland   OS Map 3

weight. Moo Water is reputed to hold some larger trout as well.
Flies & Tactics Avoid wading on Loch of Skellister, other than from the shallow, north-west shore. Even here, take great care on the shingle/sand raised beaches, where the best sport is generally had. Moo Water is easily covered from the shore. Attack them with: Loch Ordie, Woodcock & Hare-lug, Silver Butcher.
Permission & Charges See Aithsness Loch.

SKULA Water 3/267521 See Loch of Brouster.
SMA, Lochs 3/228522 See Loch of Lunga.
SMALLA Waters 3/270548 See Loch of Holorin.

SMERLA Water, Loch
Location & Access OS3/383608 Park at the Loch of Gonfirth (3/385623) and walk south for half a mile. Smerla Water lies in a hollow surrounded by Snelda, Bratta and Marro Field hills.
Commentary A very attractive loch in a perfect setting. Also visit Marrofield Water (3/387593), a further half-mile south from Smerla Water round the west shoulder of Bratta Field Hill (220m).
Fish Pretty, hard fighting trout which average about 8oz, but larger specimens as well.
Flies & Tactics Smerla Water is almost half a mile long by up to 300 yards wide. Bank fishing only and it is safest not to wade. The west shore fishes best. Fish can be taken everywhere on Marrofield Water, but the east shore, by the island, is a good place to start. Flies: Loch Ordie, Greenwell's Glory, Black Pennell.
Permission & Charges See Aithsness Loch.

SOOLMISVIRD Water
Location & Access 3/318729 See Moora Waters.
SOUTH STOFAST, Loch
Location & Access 3/510714 See Fugla Water.
STANES Water
Location & Access 3/337712 See Loch of Lunnister.
STANEVATSTOE, Loch
Location & Access 3/216545 See Loch Mousavord.

STAVANESS, Loch
Location & Access OS3/500597 Follow the B9075 road to Brettabister (3/481575) and turn east on the minor road to Kirkabister. Park at the end of the road at Neap (3/501581). Stavaness is to the north, reached after an easy walk of 15 minutes over Northbanks Hill.
Commentary Loch of Stavaness is almost half a mile long by up to 150 yards wide, 'pinched' at the north end by narrows. The loch exits onto a beach to the sea in The Groot, a perfect little cove. After fishing Stavaness, return to Neap and have a cast in Loch of Kirkabister, a small, scattered loch close to the road.
Fish Brown trout average 8oz, but the principal interest here is seatrout which arrive towards the end of August. Look out also for sea fish in this brackish water, including saithe. Loch of Kirkabister trout average 8oz.
Flies & Tactics Dangerous to wade. Concentrate your activities from the shore, along the south bank, and near to the north side of the narrows. Try: Loch Ordie, Black Pennell, Peter Ross.

Permission & Charges See Aithsness Loch.

STROM, Loch
Location & Access OS3/403490 The A971 Lerwick/Walls road crosses the south end of the loch and a minor road at 3/390482 gives easy access to the west shore. There is also a track along the first half mile of the east shore as far as West Hamarsland (3/400479).
Commentary Loch of Strom is two and a half miles long by up to quarter of a mile wide, 'pinched' into two sections between Quoyness, west, and Hamarsland, east. The loch is tidal, the south end being sea-water, mingling north into clear, brackish shallows. The east shore is crowded by the steep slopes of the Hill of Hamarsland (150m).
Fish Something for everyone; good brown trout which average 10-12oz, slob trout and seatrout, which arrive from July onwards.
Flies & Tactics The best sport with brown trout is had at the north end, particularly along the east shore between the inlet burns and the head of the loch. Seatrout are best attacked from a boat, if you happen to have one with you, otherwise, cast hopefully from the shore. Upon no account wade. Flies: Black Pennell, Ke-He, Alexandra.
Permission & Charges See Aithsness Loch.
STUBBA Water
Location & Access 3/317755 See Punds Water.

SULMA Water
Location & Access OS3/260550 Leave the A971 Lerwick/Walls road at 3/279526 and follow the minor road north through Unifirth. Turn south to Fogrigarth at 3/256560. The loch is on your left. Alternatively, park in the quarry at 3/276555 and walk south-west for 40 mins to reach the south end of Sulma Water.
Commentary The loch is one mile long, with a narrow north section, widening into a half a mile wide south bay. Midway down the west shore, at 3/258552, is a homestead site dating from the 7th century. A dramatic place for lunch.
Fish Sulma Water trout average 8oz and tend to be dark gold in colour. There are a few larger fish over 1lb in weight and the chance of seatrout after August.
Flies & Tactics The large south bay is the most productive fishing area, particularly in the vicinity of the island off the north-east shore and round the promontory in the east bay, where the feeder burn enters from Smalla Waters. At the narrow north end of the loch, try the area of the feeder burn from the Lochs of Sulma-ness (3/262559). The lochs themselves are also worth a cast. Stay ashore. The water is peaty and wading dangerous. Offer them: Black Pennell, Grouse & Claret, Dunkeld.
Permission & Charges See Aithsness Loch.

SULMA-NESS, Loch 3/262559 See Sulma Water.
SUNG, Loch 3/192501 See Loch of Kirkigarth.
TANGI, Loch 3/469785 See Mussel Loch.
TOWN, Loch 3/304660 See Gilsa Water.
TROLLADALE Water 3/326736 See Moora Waters.
TRUDALE Water 3/306530 See Kirkhouse Water.

OS Maps 3

Shetland - North Mainland

TRUGGLES Water 3/371546 See Lamba Water.

ULSTA, Loch of
Location & Access OS3/472813 Follow the B9081 from the ferry towards Burravoe. Park at 3/475810. The loch is a 5 minute walk north from the road.
Commentary A good introduction to Yell trout fishing, easily accessible and the perfect place to take a beginner.
Fish Lots of bright little 6oz trout which fight well and the possibility of seatrout from August onwards.
Flies & Tactics This small loch is easily covered from the bank and there is no need to wade. Offer them: Loch Ordie, Soldier Palmer, Black Pennell.
Permission & Charges Visitors are advised to join the Shetland Anglers Association and Mr David Nisbet of Altona on Mid Yell will be happy to advise anglers about game fishing on the island. Contact David on (01957) 702037.

VAARA, Loch 3/325568 See Loch of Clousta entry.

VATSTER, Loch
Location & Access OS3/429482 Adjacent to the east of the new road, Lerwick/Girlsta road, eight miles north of Lerwick.
Commentary Tucked below The Snuckle (80m), a small, shallow, scattered, peaty loch. To the south-west, a walk of some 15 minutes, is Longa Water (3/418477) which is also worth visiting. Whilst in the vicinity, step over to the tiny lochans of Whirls Water (3/412476) then north to Loch of Hamarsland (3/412481) before returning to the start point. Also visit the Black Loch (3/428492), on the other side of the A970 road before calling it a day.
Fish Nothing for the glass case but most certainly something for breakfast. Trout average 8oz.
Flies & Tactics Bank fishing, stay ashore and do not wade. The water is easily covered. Offer: Loch Ordie, Grouse & Claret, Black Pennell.
Permission & Charges See Aithsness Loch.

VOE, Loch
Location & Access OS3/426628 The Loch of Voe is near Hillside, enclosed by the A970 to the west, the B9071 to the south and Tagon Hill (140m) to the north.
Commentary Easily accessible, covering an area of some 30 acres and joined to the sea in Olna Firth. Sae Water (3/423629), approximately eight acres, lies to the east, on the south side of the B9071.
Fish Moderate-sized brown trout, averaging 6oz, in both Voe and Sae.
Flies & Tactics Bank fishing only and safest to stay ashore. Try the north bank to the east of the promontory.
Permission & Charges See Aithsness Loch.

VOXTERBY, Loch 3/260532 See Loch of Brouster.
WATSNESS, Loch 3/175505 See Loch of Kirkigarth.

WEST Loch
Location & Access OS3/218779 Leave the A970 Brae/Hillswick road at 3/290778 and follow the B9078 to West Heogaland and Stenness. West Loch is to the left of the road, on the junction to Esha Ness church and burial ground.
Commentary West Loch, and its five neighbours, are amongst the best trout lochs on Mainland Shetland, although it must be noted that they can be heart-breakingly dour. Nevertheless, they are a 'must' for visiting anglers. After West Loch, fish the unnamed loch at 3/214779, known locally as Breckon Loch. Return to the car and drive along to the viewpoint at 3/210785. From here, fish Loch of Framgord (3/209785), to the south of the road and, further south, Loch of Gerdie (3/206782). Lunch by the viewpoint and then attack Loch of Houlland (3/215792), which lies in a hollow on the cliff-top to the north of Loch of Framgord. The cliffs here, known as The Villians of Ure, are spectacular, but should be approached with great caution. Marvel from afar, rather than risk a terminal tumble.
Fish All the lochs have a high pH and, consequently, contain excellent quality trout. Houlland trout average 1lb. Fish of over 2lb are not infrequently taken from most of these waters.
Flies & Tactics All bank fishing, with some cautious, uncomfortable wading. Best advice is to stay ashore, regardless of temptation. These small waters are easily covered and, from the shore, there is far less chance of alerting the residents to your evil intent. Flies to offer: Loch Ordie, Woodcock & Hare-lug, Peter Ross.
Permission & Charges See Aithsness Loch.

WEST MILL LOCH OF HAMAR 3/300756 See Punds Water.

WESTER Water
Location & Access OS3/336764 Park at the north end of Punds Water (3/326761) and walk east for 20 mins to reach the lochs.
Commentary Two small, inter-linked lochans and an even smaller satellite, sheltered by the south slopes of Hamara Scord Hill and Yamna Field (150m), draining south into Loch of Burraland (3/340748).
Fish Trout average 8oz, but there are a few larger fish which are mostly encountered towards the end of the season.
Flies & Tactics All the water is easily covered from the shore. Offer them: Loch Ordie, Wickham's Fancy, Peter Ross.
Permission & Charges See Aithsness Loch.

WHIRLS Water, Loch 3/412476 See Loch of Vatster entry.
WHITEBRIGS, Loch 3/243534 See Burga Water.
WHITELAW, Loch 3/359540 See Lamba Water entry.

Shetland - South Mainland

OS Map 4

Shetland - South Mainland

AITH, Loch 4/510428. See Loch of Setter.

ASTA, Loch
Location & Access 4/412415. Adjacent to and east of the B9074 in the Tingwall Valley.
Commentary A very attractive loch to fish, joined to its more famous neighbour, Loch of Tingwall, by a small stream. Loch of Asta is half a mile north/south by up to 200 yards wide, clear water with a high pH. Some shelter from the surrounding slopes, Hill of Steinswall to the east, Hill of Houlland to the west.
Fish Brown trout which average 8-10oz, and a few seatrout from August onwards.
Flies & Tactics Bank fishing, and if you want to launch a boat, seek permission at Asta Farm before doing so. Wading requires great care. Fish are taken from all round the shore, but the east bank is probably the most productive. First cast: Black Pennell, Greenwell's Glory, Peter Ross.
Permission & Charges Contact: Shetland Tourist Information Centre, Market Cross, Lerwick. Tel: 01595 693434. Season ticket: £20.00. Day ticket: £5.00. Use of five angling club boats: £20.00 per season.

BEOSETTER, Lochs of
Location & Access 4/490437. By ferry from Lerwick, then drive north. Walk the last quarter of a mile.
Commentary A group of four lochs at the north of the Island of Bressay, to the west of Gunnista: Mill Loch (4/490437), Loch of Cruester (4/488433), Gunnista Lochs (4/493430 and 4/492433). A challenging day out, involving a good tramp over broken moorland.
Fish A good chance of specimen trout, although they do not give themselves up easily. Anticipate fish of up to 4lb amongst good stocks of 12oz trout.
Flies & Tactics Wading is dangerous so all the lochs should be fished from the bank. The water is coloured and Mill Loch becomes weedy as the season advances. Try: Black Pennell, Greenwell's Glory, Dunkeld.
Permission & Charges See Loch Asta.

BRINDISTER, Loch
Location & Access 4/433370. Six miles south from Lerwick, to the west of the A970 road to Sumburgh and adjacent to the road.
Commentary A circular loch with a small island containing the site of a Dun, sheltered to the west by Virda Law and Staba Field. Outboard engines are allowed.
Fish Principal interest is high quality brown trout which average 12oz.
Flies & Tactics Bank fishing only, and easy access from a good peat track along the south shore. Concentrate your effort where the inlet stream enters, near the end of the track, and in the north-east corner, opposite the Dun. Clear water and wading is comfortable, but dangerous along the north shore. First cast: Ke-He, Woodcock & Hare-lug, Silver Butcher.

Permission & Charges See Loch Asta.
BROCH OF CUSTWICK Loch
Location & Access 4/255447. See Ward of Custwick.
BROO Loch
Location & Access 4/403442. See Loch of Griesta.

BROUGH, Loch
Location & Access 4/512408. On the Island of Bressay, accessible by ferry from Lerwick. Drive west towards the Island of Noss to reach the loch, adjacent to the road, within two miles.
Commentary Accessible from the road and easily combined with a visit to Loch of Grimsetter (4/518398), due south. Whilst in the parish, consider walking south again to fish Sand Vatn Loch (4/513372), two rugged moorland miles south from the road end.
Fish Loch of Brough has the reputation of being dour, but it contains trout which average 10oz and a few much larger specimen fish. Loch of Grimsetter and Sand Vatn have similar fish.
Flies & Tactics All bank fishing and generally comfortable wading, although, as always, caution is required. On Loch of Brough, start along the north shore, working down the west bank. The north shore of Loch of Grimsetter is productive and on Sand Vatn, try the area of the two inlet burns at the north end of the loch. Flies: Soldier Palmer, Grouse & Claret, Peter Ross.
Permission & Charges See Loch Asta.

BURWICK, Loch 4/393411. See Loch of Griesta.

CLUMLIE, Loch
Location & Access 4/405174. To the east of the A970 Sumburgh/Lerwick road, adjacent to Troswickness (4/406172) on a minor ring road.
Commentary Easily accessible little loch covering approximately 20 acres with some shelter from west winds. The water is shallow, peaty, and wading is unsafe. Stay ashore.
Fish Attractive fish which average 12oz in weight.
Flies & Tactics Bank fishing only and an early visit is likely to be most productive since weed can become a problem as the season advances.
Permission & Charges See Loch Asta.

CRUESTER, Loch 4/488433. See Lochs of Beosetter.
GARTH, Loch 4/402422. See Loch of Griesta.
GERSHON, Loch 4/380327. See Loch of Sandwick.

GOSSA Water
Location & Access 4/303460. Easily accessible from the B9071 and from Stump Farm (4/310455) where a track leads to the west shore of the loch.
Commentary Gossa Water is half a mile long by up to quarter of a mile wide, in a shallow hollow between Too Field Hill and Hestinsetter Hill to the west and Stump Hill to the east. The remains of a Neolithic chambered cairn can be found on the highest point of Hestinsetter Hill.
Fish Pretty brown trout which average 10oz in weight with a few larger specimens as well.
Flies & Tactics Bank fishing only and great care is

OS Map 4

Shetland - South Mainland

required when wading. There are rocks and boulders, particularly along the south and west shore. Commence your attack on the west shore, in the vicinity of the five small inlet streams. Offer: Loch Ordie, Soldier Palmer, Dunkeld.
Permission & Charges See Loch Asta.

GRIESTA, Loch of
Location & Access 4/410440. To the west of Loch of Tingwall (4/415427) and accessible from the B9074 via tracks at the north-west of the loch and from South Setter Farm. An easy 15 minute walk.
Commentary The ideal start point for a day out exploring the lochs between Tingwall and Whiteness Voe. There are seven other waters: Broo Loch (4/403442), Ustaness (4/400434), Jamie Cheyne's Loch (4/400428), Maggie Black's Loch (4/397424), Loch of Garth (4/402422), Loch of Houlland (4/400417), and Loch of Burwick (4/393411). Compass and map essential, as are stout boots. Splendid scenery, wild flowers and birds.
Fish Brown trout in all the lochs, and, after July, the chance of seatrout in Loch of Griesta, Loch of Burwick and Loch of Houlland. Trout average 10oz, but there are much larger fish, particularly in the smaller lochans.
Flies & Tactics Most important tactic is to arrange lunch at the south-east corner of Loch of Ustaness: a perfect green promontory by a tumbled sheep fold. Otherwise, great bank fishing all the way. Stay ashore, there is really no need to wade and it is dangerous to do so in most of these waters. Flies: Loch Ordie, Woodcock & Hare-lug, Black Pennell.
Permission & Charges See Loch Asta.

GRIMSETTER, Loch 4/518393. See Loch of Brough.
GUNNISTA Lochs 4/494430 and 4/492433. See Lochs of Beosetter.
HOULLAND, Loch 4/400417. See Loch of Griesta.

HOUSA Water
Location & Access 4/287442. Lies to the south of the B9071 road near Hestinsetter (4/292451). Approach from Wester Skeld (4/296439), a moorland walk west of about ten minutes. Lunga Water (4/289449), to the north, is reputed to be fishless.
Commentary If things are quiet on Housa Water, decamp south to explore Scarf Water (4/290436) and its larger neighbour, Loch of Westerwick (4/284432), both of which are well worth a visit.
Fish Housa Water contains good numbers of 10oz trout and also a few fish of up to and over 2lb in weight. The lochs to the south have very pretty trout which average 8-10oz.
Flies & Tactics All bank fishing, and the best policy when fishing Shetland lochs is to stay on the shore. Wading is dangerous. On Housa Water, concentrate on the south-west shore, east from the inlet stream; on Loch of Westerwick, the north and west shore give best results. Tempt them with: Loch Ordie, March Brown, Black Pennell.
Permission & Charges See Loch Asta.

JAMIE CHEYNE'S Loch 4/400428. See Loch of Griesta.

KEBISTER, Loch
Location & Access 4/457446. Approach from Gremista (4/461432), one mile north of Lerwick. Follow a peat track north, then over the hill for about 20 minutes to reach the loch.
Commentary A small lochan in a hollow between Hill of Gremista and the Banks of the Lees above Dales Voe; rarely visited and sheltered in high winds. Stocked with fingerling trout in 1996.
Fish Trout average 8oz and fight well.
Flies & Tactics Bank fishing and the water is easily covered from the shore. Trout rise and are taken from all round the bank. Offer them: Loch Ordie, March Brown, Peter Ross.
Permission & Charges See Loch Asta.

LUNGA Water See Housa Water.
MAGGIE BLACK'S Loch 4/397424. See Loch of Griesta.
MILL Loch 4/490437. See Lochs of Beosetter.
MILL POND Loch 4/386334. See Loch of Sandwick.
RUFF, Loch 4/362319. See Loch of Sandwick.
SAND VATN Loch 4/513372. See Loch of Brough.
SAND Water (Culswick) See Ward of Culswick Lochs.

SANDWICK, Loch
Location & Access 4/364328. Approach from between Blythoit and Scalloway, the ancient capital of Shetland, at the head of East Voe of Scalloway (4/408400). Follow the minor road south across Trondra towards Hamnavoe on West Burra, turning left at Meal (4/376358) for Bridge End (4/370331). The loch lies to the west of Bridge End, south of the end of a peat road.
Commentary Loch of Sandwick is a tiny, clear water loch with a reputation of being dour. Whilst in the vicinity, visit a number of other Burra waters which also have good trout: Ruff Loch (4/362319) a short walk west to Ukna Skerry, Mill Pond (4/386334), Loch of Gershon (4/380327) and Loch of Houss (4/380321) on East Burra.
Fish Trout average 12oz with some fish of up to and over 1lb.
Flies & Tactics No need to wade in these waters, all of which can be covered from the shore. As the season progresses, weed becomes a problem. Best fished in May and June. Flies: Ke-He, March Brown, Black Pennell.
Permission & Charges See Loch Asta.

SANDY, Loch
Location & Access 4/450404. To the north of the A970 road, two miles south from Lerwick.
Commentary One mile long by quarter of a mile wide, exposed and sometimes windy. The main public water supply for Lerwick. Permission from Water Board to launch a boat. Engines are allowed.
Fish Rainbow trout were once stocked in years past (none survived) but Loch of Sandy still contains good stocks of brown trout which average 8oz. There are

21

Shetland - South Mainland

OS Map 4

also a few fish of up to and over 2lb.
Flies & Tactics There are peat tracks along the east and north shore and the best flyfishing areas are in the north-west corner, the west shore, where a feeder burn enters, and the south shore. Wading is dangerous. Use: Black Pennell, March Brown, Alexandra.
Permission & Charges See Loch Asta.

SCARF Water 4/290436. See Housa Water.

SETTER, Loch
Location & Access 4/514417. By ferry from Lerwick to Bressay, thence north-west to Setter via Clodisdale (4/505416), a distance of two miles. The loch is to the south, at the end of the road.
Commentary A small, shallow loch by Voe of Cullingsburgh on Bressay, close to the site of St Mary's Church and a cliff-side broch on Ander Hill. Loch of Aith (4/510428), by Bruntland, lies one mile north and is also worth a cast or two.
Fish Brown trout averaging 8oz and the occasional fish of up to 1lb.
Flies & Tactics Can be dour, and best fished from the middle bay in early evening. Crystal clear water, easily covered from the bank. The north-west shore is best, in the vicinity of the inlet stream. Do not wade. Offer: Loch Ordie, Soldier Palmer, Black Pennell.
Permission & Charges See Loch Asta.

SOTERSTA, Loch 4/261450. See Ward of Culswick.

SPIGGIE, Loch
Location & Access 4/373168. At Littleness (4/369169) and from the B9122 road.
Commentary Loch of Spiggie is owned by the Royal Society for the Protection of Birds (RSPB) and leased by the Shetland Angling Association. Lying north /south for nearly one and a half miles, by up to half a mile wide, Spiggie is a clear water loch, as famous for the quality of its birdlife as for its trout fishing.
Fish Brown trout, and seatrout from August onwards. Brown trout average 10oz, with a few fish of up to 2lb; seatrout average 1lb with fish of up to 3lb.
Flies & Tactics Strictly fly only and no outboard motors allowed. Boat fishing bring best results and anglers must read the rules regarding RSPB restricted fishing areas before setting out. Bank fishing is also productive and wading is generally on shallow/sandy ground. Although good sport is had in most areas, the west and north-east shores are the best places to begin.
Flies: Loch Ordie, March Brown, Silver Butcher.
Permission & Charges See Loch Asta.

STRAND, Loch
Location & Access 4/431460. Lies to the north of Gott on the line of the old A970 Bridge of Fitch/Voe road, immediately adjacent to the road.
Commentary Bounded on two sides by the main road and very public but still worth fishing. The loch is joined to the sea and is affected by the tide. The water is brackish and peaty.
Fish The principal interest is seatrout, which average 1-2lb and arrive from June onwards. There are also brown trout which average 8-10oz.
Flies & Tactics Very easy to cover this small water from the bank and there is no need to wade. The east shore produces best results. Flies: Black Pennell, Grouse & Claret, Peter Ross.
Permission & Charges See Loch Asta.

TINGWALL, Loch
Location & Access 4/416427. Easily accessible from the B9074 which margins the west shore of the loch.
Commentary One of the best lochs on Shetland and one of the most attractive to fish. Site of Viking Parliament at north end at 'Law Ting Holm'. Loch of Tingwall is one mile long, hour-glass-pinched in the middle by Holm of Setter. The north section tends to be coloured and weedy towards the end of the season. The south section is crystal clear.
Fish Hard fighting brown trout throughout, averaging 10oz, with good numbers of larger fish, and the chance of seatrout from August onwards.
Flies & Tactics Boat fishing brings best results and the best drift in the north section is from the inlet burn in the north-east corner directly back to the boathouse and mooring bay on the west shore. In the south section, drift down the east bank, about five yards out. Bank fishing can be good and wading is reasonably comfortable; but there are unsuspected holes in both sections of the loch, on the east side. Flies: Wickham's Fancy, Black Pennell, Silver Butcher. Association boat available for hire.
Permission & Charges See Loch Asta.

TREBISTER, Loch
Location & Access 4/454394. Easily accessible, to the south of the A970, near the Geophysical Laboratory, two miles south of Lerwick.
Commentary A small loch of approximately 20 acres, ideal for a few evening casts, with protection from east winds by the ridge of Tansie Knowes.
Fish Stocked with rainbow trout some years ago, (none now survive) there are still excellent brown trout which average 10oz and the odd fish of up to 1lb.
Flies & Tactics Deep water along the east shore and generally dangerous wading. Best to stay on the bank. Concentrate your efforts, from the bank, along the north and west shore. Fish are easily covered. Offer them: Loch Ordie, Greenwell's Glory, Cinnamon & Gold.
Permission & Charges See Loch Asta.

TURRI Water 4/276459. See Ward of Custwick.
USTANESS, Loch 4/400434. See Loch of Griesta.

VATSETTER, Loch
Location & Access 4/377234. Leave the B9122 at Williamsetter (4/387215) and follow the minor road north for two miles to reach the loch.
Commentary An easily accessible loch, lying close to the road, Loch of Vatsetter is half a mile north/south by 100 yards wide. May Wick Bay, a mile further north, is a good lunch spot.
Fish Brown trout which average 10oz in weight with a few fish of up to 1lb.

OS Maps 4-5 — Orkney & Northern Isles

Flies & Tactics A peaty loch and bank fishing only. Stay on the shore. Wading is dangerous. Fish lie in the deep water close to the bank, so approach with caution. Offer them: Black Zulu, Greenwell's Glory, Alexandra.
Permission & Charges See Loch Asta.

VIVILIE Loch 4/261459. See Ward of Custwick.

VOE AND BEACH SEATROUT FISHING

LOCATIONS
Location & Access Olas Voe 4/288468; Stead of Culswick 4/271444; Wester Wick 4/284426; Sil Wick 4/295419; Skelda Voe 4/313441; Bur Wick 4/395408; East Voe of Scalloway 4/404395; West Voe of Quarff 4/404350; Voe of North Ho 4/378315; Banna Minn 4/365304; May Wick 4/376247; Bay of Scousburgh 4/373181; Muckle Sound Bay 4/367178
Commentary Take great care at all times when fishing voes and beaches. Danger is never far distant, from sudden tide surges, waves, slippery rocks and unstable bottoms. Always tell someone where you are going and when you expect to return. Better safe than sorry. If in doubt, don't.
Fish Seatrout at most times of the season. Average weight 1lb with heavier fish as well. Best from July onwards.
Flies & Tactics Seatrout in the sea have soft mouths and are hard to hook, but when hooked look out for spectacular sport. Both fly and spinning. Flies: Black Pennell, Greenwell's Glory, Peter Ross; lures: black, red, copper, and silver toby's and spinners; also use Stewart tackle with live bait. Remember to wash you tackle at the end of the day. Sea-water is not tackle user-friendly.
Permission & Charges See Loch Asta.

WARD OF CULSWICK Lochs
Location & Access 4/266460. A group of six small lochs to the west and north of Culswick: Turri Water (4/276459), Vivilie Loch (4/261459), Broch of Custwick Loch (4/255447), Loch of Sotersta (4/261450), the small unnamed lochan at 4/263446 and Sand Water (4/269447).
Commentary A wonderful day out exploring a series of rarely fished waters in a remote setting. Start from Brigalee (OS4/275457) and walk north to reach Turri Water in five minutes, then west over Ward of Culswick to Vivilie Loch; now south and east to find the others.
Fish Nothing monstrous, but great fun with good, trout which fight well and average 8-10oz, and the chance of the odd fish of up to 1lb in weight as well.
Flies & Tactics Be well prepared for every type of weather and take a compass and map and wear stout boots. Arrange matters to arrive at the Broch site on the cliff above Gruting Voe for lunch. Bank fishing and no need to wade. Best flies: Loch Ordie, Greenwell's Glory, Black Pennell.
Permission & Charges See Loch Asta.

WESTERWICK, Loch
Location & Access 4/284432. See Housa Water.

WORMADALE, Water
Location & Access 4/410455. To the south of the A971 Bridge of Fitch/Walls road. Park near Catwalls (4/417453) and follow a peat track north-west to reach the lochs in ten minutes.
Commentary Two small lochans to the north of the Hill of Griesta.
Fish Some nice brown trout which average 10oz.
Flies & Tactics Very easy bank fishing. Stay back from the shore to avoid 'spooking' the fish. Offer them: Ke-He, Greenwell's Glory, Black Pennell.
Permission & Charges See Loch Asta.

Orkney - Northern Isles

BALACLAVA, Loch See Lairo Water
BAYWEST, Loch See Meikle Water, Stronsay

BEA Loch
Location & Access OS5/655400 A few minutes' drive north from the pier on the Island of Sanday, to the west of the B9068 road.
Commentary The most productive of the Sanday lochs, easily accessible and set amidst attractive surroundings. Wonderful wild flowers and bird life and probably one the best trout lochs in Scotland.
Fish Excellent quality brown trout which average 12-14oz in weight. Trout of 6lb and 4lb 4oz have been caught, and the largest fish landed in recent years weighed 8lb.
Flies & Tactics Boats are available, but bank fishing can be just as rewarding. Fish are taken all round the loch and no one place is better than another. Bea Loch is best fished early in the season (late April/May) because weed becomes a problem from July onwards. Try: Loch Ordie, Soldier Palmer, Silver Invicta.
Permission & Charges From Boat: £12 per day. Bank fishing: £6 per day. Mr E. Groundwater, Castlehill, Sanday. Tel: (01857) 600285.

BOSQUOY, Loch
Location & Access OS6/305186 From the A896 near Madras House, or from the minor road through Russland to the west on the shores of Loch Harray.
Commentary A small, shallow water, joined to the Loch Harray and prone to drying up during summer months.
Fish Used to hold good numbers of trout but, because of low water levels, few fish remain and those still there are highly educated.
Flies & Tactics Worth a few casts, from the bank, and easily covered in a couple of hours. Try: Black Zulu, March Brown, Silver Butcher.
Permission & Charges See Lairo Water.

BRUE, Loch See North Loch
BURNESS, Loch See Loch of Swartmill

CLUMMLY, Loch
Location & Access OS6/254164 Easily accessible and immediately adjacent to the A967 Stromness/Twatt road.

Orkney & Northern Isles
OS Map 5

Commentary A small water covering an area of approximately twenty acres, near to Skara Brae and Bay of Skail (see Loch of Skail,). There is a Broch site at the south-west corner of the loch, and, to the east, across the main road, the Stones of Via (OS6/261160).
Fish Like nearby Loch of Skail, a little loch with a big reputation where trout average 1lb 8oz and larger fish lurk.
Flies & Tactics Bank fishing only, from the north shore, where wading is, with care, possible. Fish Clummly early in the season. The water level often drops drastically during summer months and weed can be a problem. Flies to try: Black Zulu, Soldier Palmer, Silver Invicta.
Permission & Charges See Lairo Water.

DOOMY, Loch See Island of Eady
EADY, Island There are two lochs on the island: Loch of Doomy (5/558342) and Mill Loch (5/565368). Loch of Doomy disappears during dry weather and Mill Loch is reputed to be fishless. However, don't let that stop you paying Eady a visit. Eady is one of the most lovely of the Northern Isles, with splendid beaches, cliff walks, bird life, wild flowers and ancient monuments.
EGILSAY, Island There are three small lochs on the island: Loch of Welland (5/477315), Loch of Watten (5/479310), and Manse Loch (5/478299). To the best of my knowledge, they are fishless. Manse Loch and Loch of Welland, during high tides, are invaded by the sea.

LAIRO Water
Location & Access OS5/510190 Lies to the north of the B9058 on the Island of Shapinsay. Approach from Swartaquoy (5/515190). Ask permission first from Miss M. Groat, Skenstoft, Shapinsay, Orkney. Tel: 01856 711281.
Commentary The only trout loch on the island, close to the sea by Ling Holm and the The Ouse in Veantrow Bay. The other loch marked out on OS Map 5 on Shapinsay, near Balaclava (5/485175), was a mill loch and has been drained. It is a fishless swamp and RSPB bird reserve.
Fish Stocked in recent years and trout average 10oz. Larger fish of up to and over 1lb 8oz are also caught.
Flies & Tactics Lairo Water is a small, shallow loch fished from the bank. The bottom is soft and wading requires care. Fish may be taken from all round the shore. Try: Blue Zulu, Invicta, Silver Butcher.
Permission & Charges Traditionally, trout fishing in Orkney, with some exceptions, is free of charge. However, as a matter of courtesy, anglers should seek permission from the landowner before crossing his ground. Where fishing permission is required this is noted in the text. Visiting anglers should join the local angling association to obtain the best advice and for the use of the association's facilities.
LANGAMAY, Loch See North Loch
LEA SHUN Loch
Location & Access See Meikle Water, Stronsay
MANSE Loch, Egilsay
Location & Access See Island of Egilsay

MEIKLE Water, Stronsay
Location & Access OS5/665244 Lies to the east of the B9060 on the Island of Stronsay.
Commentary The most productive Stronsay trout loch, easily accessible from the B9060 and surrounding minor roads. Meikle Water (pronounced Muckle locally) is best approached from Greenfield (5/667248) at the north-east end. The loch is shallow, covering some 40 acres. Lea Shun Loch (5/662214), by Ward of Houseby, was stocked with 2,000 brown trout in 1993 and contains fish averaging 8-10oz; Mill Bay Loch (5/669295), on the island of Papa Stronsay, has a few fish, but Baywest Loch (5/626242), near Rothiesholm at the south end of the island, is reputed to be fishless.
Fish Meikle Water holds excellent quality brown trout which average 14oz, and good numbers of fish of up to 3lb.
Flies & Tactics Stronsay is well-endowed with beaches for the bucket-and-spade brigade whilst you attack the trout. Bank fishing only and the muddy bottom makes wading uncomfortable. The best fishing is approached via Greenfield (see above), where there is a rocky shoreline. Wade with caution on both Meikle Water and Lea Shun Loch. Flies: Soldier Palmer, Greenwell's Glory, Peter Ross.
Permission & Charges See Lairo Water. Further advice and information from Stronsay Hotel, Stronsay, Orkney Islands. Tel: (018576) 616213.

MILL Loch, Island of Eady See Island of Eady

NORTH Loch, Sanday
Location & Access OS5/754458 Turn right from the B9068 a mile north of the pier on Sanday, and follow the B9069 to Northwall. At the end of the road, turn north along the minor road to Galilee (5/768459). The loch is adjacent to the road.
Commentary The largest loch on the Island of Sanday, three quarters of a mile north/south by almost half a mile east/west. North Loch is shallow and often windy, but the setting is superb. Nearby, are a number of other, smaller waters, rarely fished, but also offering sport with small, hard-fighting brown trout: Loch of Rummie (5/758450), Loch of Brue (5/766444), Loch of Langamay (5/745445), Westyre Loch (5/726443).
Fish Good fish in North Loch, not particularly large, but well-shaped and pink-fleshed, averaging 10oz. Seatrout as well, in the sea to the north in Bay of Sandquoy (5/740447).
Flies & Tactics Bank fishing all round, with care and caution. On North Loch, concentrate your efforts along the west shoreline. Even greater caution when seatrout fishing. Watch out for sudden waves and remember to freshwater wash your tackle at the end of play.
Permission & Charges See Bea Loch

NORTH RONALDSAY, Island There are four lochs on North Ronaldsay: Hooking Loch (5/766533), Loch of Garso (5/772554), Ancum Loch (5/763544) and Loch of Gretchen (5/749529). None contain trout, at the moment, but there are proposals to stock Ancum Loch. Further information may be obtained from the Orkney Trout Fishing Association.

OS Maps 5-6 — Orkney Mainland

ROOS Loch
Location & Access OS5/657447 Drive north from the pier on the Island of Sanday along the B9068 and turn left at 5/670435 along the minor road to Bellevue (5/656444). The loch is immediately adjacent to the road.
Commentary Roos Loch covers an area of approx. 40 acres and lies close to the sea at Roos Wick. The loch is easily accessible and offers great sport in dramatic surroundings.
Fish Not for the faint-hearted, but some large trout inhabit this lovely little loch. Even better, seatrout are present throughout most of the year, in Roos Wick, and to the east by Quoys Banks and Hucklinsower (5/675460).
Flies & Tactics Cautious bank fishing in Roos Water, but most of the loch is easily covered from the shore. Take great care in the sea and seek advice regarding tide times (from Ernie Groundwater) before mounting your assault. For both trout and seatrout, use: Black Pennell, Invicta, Alexandra.
Permission & Charges See Bea Loch

ROUSAY, Island See OS Map 6
RUMMIE, Loch See North Loch
SAINTEAR, Loch See Loch of Swartmill

ST. TREDWELL, Loch
Location & Access OS5/495510 The only loch on the Island of Papa Westray, easily accessible and lying to the east of Backaskaill.
Commentary Loch of St. Tredwell is a shallow water, joined to the sea at the north end by a small burn. The loch is three quarters of a mile north/south by up to 300 yds east/west and divided into two sections by a farm road at the south end. The larger, northern part, has a muddy bottom, whilst the smaller, southern section, is sandy. They are joined together during winter months and after heavy rainfall. A promontory on the north-east shore contains the ruins of the 13th century St. Tredwell's Chapel, as well as the remains of a broch (BC300-AD100), and evidence of even earlier habitation dating back to Neolithic times.
Fish An enigmatic water which contains some excellent trout. In July 1994 experimental netting in the north section, in one sweep, produced nine trout, including a fish weighing 5lb. Fish in the southern section are of better quality and have deep-red flesh. At the end of the 1980s, 5,000 seatrout fry were introduced, and in 1992, 2,000 brown trout. In 1995 the loch was netted at night by poachers and it is not known how badly this damaged stocks.
Flies & Tactics There is one boat on the loch and bank fishing is also available. Trout rarely rise and tend to be bottom feeders. This is a challenging loch where blank days are the rule, rather than the exception, but there is always the chance of 'one for the glass case'. Use traditional patterns: Loch Ordie, Black Pennell, Ke-He. Crossing the fingers also helps.
Permission & Charges For permission to fish and the possibility of boat hire, contact the owner, John Rendall, Holland Farm, Papa Westray, Orkney. Tel: (01857) 644151. A small charge is made for the hire of the boat.

SWARTMILL, Loch
Location & Access OS5/478458 Easily accessible and to the north of the B9066 road.
Commentary The principal loch on the Island of Westray and the best trout fishery. Swartmill is a shallow water of approx. 60 acres, often windy, but great fun to fish. A minor road and a farm track encircles the loch making access easy. Ask permission first, before crossing farm land to the lochside.
Fish The loch has been regularly stocked over years, with brown trout reared in Mainland. Trout are of exceptional quality and average 12-14oz in weight. Fish of up to 3lb are taken regularly. The other two lochs on the island, Loch of Saintear (5/439474) and Loch of Burness (5/430481), have also been stocked in the past, but they contain few, if any fish.
Flies & Tactics A boat may be available from Lochside Farm, but bank fishing is just as productive; indeed, it is possible, "for a tall man", to wade from one side of the loch to the other. Whilst doing so, offer the inhabitants: Ke-He, March Brown, Black Pennell.
Permission & Charges See Lairo Water entry. Boat hire: John Hewison, Lochside, Westray. Tel: (01857) 677439 at 50p per hour.

WATTEN, Loch, Egilsay See Egilsay, Island
WELLAND, Loch See Egilsay, Island
WESTYRE Loch See North Loch

Orkney Mainland

BOARDHOUSE, Loch
Location & Access OS6/270260 Easily accesssible from the A967 Twatt/Birsay road, or from the minor road which runs close the east shoreline.
Commentary This shallow loch is two miles north/south by up to three quarters of a mile wide. Boardhouse is divided into two sections by a substantial "waist".
Fish Trout average in the order of 10oz-12oz but there are good numbers of larger trout as well. Fish of over 3lb in weight have been taken in recent years.
Flies & Tactics Boardhouse is best fished from the boat and fish rise are are caught everywhere, from the margins to the middle. As the season advances, weed can become a problem, particularly at the south end where a large patch of weed grows in the centre of the bay. Carefully fish the edge of this weed patch. Flies: Ke-He, Loch Ordie, Silver Butcher.
Permission & Charges Traditionally, trout fishing in Orkney, with some exceptions, is free. Where permission is required, this is noted in the text. However, most visiting anglers join the Orkney Trout Fishing Association. The association work hard to preserve and maintain the quality of game fishing in Orkney and the season ticket, at £15.00, is a small price to pay to help them do so. Contact: W S Sinclair, Tackle Shop, 27 John St. Stromness. Tel: 01856 850469

BOSQUOY, Loch
Location & Access OS6/305186. From the A896 near

Orkney Mainland — OS Map 6

Madras House, or from the minor road through Russland to the west on the shore of Loch Harray.
Commentary A small, shallow water, joined to Loch Harray but prone to drying up during hot summer months.
Fish Used to hold good numbers of fish. Those that remain are reputed to be large but "dour".
Flies & Tactics Worth a few casts. Try: Black Zulu, March Brown, Silver Butcher.
Permission & Charges See Loch of Boardhouse entry.

BROCKAN, Loch OS6/395190 To the north of Isbister. Not regarded as a serious fishery, although there are some small trout in the loch.

CLUMMLY, Loch
Location & Access OS6/254164 Easily accessible and adjacent to the A967 Stromness/Twatt road.
Commentary Clummly covers an area of approximately 20 acres and lies close to the famous Neolithic site of Skara Brae.
Fish Like nearby Loch of Skail, Clummly is a little loch with a big reputation. Trout average 1lb 8oz and there are much larger fish as well.
Flies & Tactics Bank fishing only, from the north shore where wading is, with care, possible. The water level drops during the summer months when weed becomes a problem, so fish Clummly early in the season. Try: Black Zulu, Greenwell's Glory, Silver Invicta.
Permission & Charges See Loch of Boardhouse entry.

HARRAY, Loch
Location & Access OS6/290170 Loch of Harray lies to the north of Stromness and is easily accessible from public roads; including the B9055 on the west shore and from minor roads branching off the A986 on the east shore.
Commentary Loch of Harray has a long-established reputation for producing high-quality sport. The loch is five miles north/south by up to one and a half miles wide across the north bay. Harray is strewn with skerries (barely submerged rocky outcrops) and it covers an area of 2,500 acres. Three important Neolithic monuments lie close to the loch: Maeshowe (6/315128), Ring of Brogar (6/295134) and the Standing Stones of Stenness (6/311125).
Fish Loch of Harray trout are exceptional, well-formed, silver, pink fleshed. The average weight is 12oz and good baskets are the rule, rather than the exception. Fish of over 4lb in weight are sometimes caught. Sea-trout may also be caught, mostly at the south end where Harray is linked to Loch of Stenness (6/304126).
Flies & Tactics Boat fishing is preferred, but bank fishing can be just as productive. Generally, the margins of the loch and in the vicinity of the skerries is the place to concentrate. At the north end, drift towards Scarrataing (6/276178), then south to Whilliastane (6/280170). From the Merkister Hotel, drift south by Burrian Broch (6/296186) down to Kirk Quoy (6/294178). Ballarat House shore is also good (6/298164), as is rocky Ling Holms Bay (6/290155) on the west shore. When afloat, hasten slowly and keep a sharp lookout for skerries. Try: Soldier Palmer, March Brown, Silver Invicta.
Permission & Charges See Loch of Boardhouse entry. Also from Merkister Hotel, Harray, Orkney. Tel: (01856) 77366

HUNDLAND, Loch
Location & Access OS6/295260 Approach from the minor road from Twatt (6/273241) or via the minor road through Hillside from the B9057 at 6/224235.
Commentary A shallow, peaty loch, one mile north/south by up to half a mile east/west. Excellent wildlife and wild flowers.
Fish Good quality brown trout which average 10oz-12oz in weight. Also the chance of fish of up to and over 3lb.
Flies & Tactics Boat fishing produces best results, although bank fishing can also give good sport. However, the bottom of the loch is soft and wading is uncomfortable. The early months are best. As the season advances weed becomes a problem. The best fishing areas tend to be at the north and south ends of the loch when even on a bright sunny day, Hundland can produce fish.
Permission & Charges See Loch of Boardhouse entry.

ISBISTER, Loch
Location & Access OS6/257237 Approach from either the A967 at 6/269224, or from the B9056 at 6/244236 via Knowe of Holland.
Commentary This is a small, shallow water covering an area of approximately 40 acres. An old airfield borders the east margin of the loch whilst the land to the north is part of an RSPB nature Reserve.
Fish Dour, but good quality trout which average 1lb in weight.
Flies & Tactics Bank fishing only. Stay on the bank, because wading is dangerous. Begin along the south shore, paying particular attention to the burn mouth and the two small islands, then work north up the west bank. Fishes well early in the season. Try: Ke-He, March Brown, Alexandra.
Permission & Charges See Loch of Boardhouse entry.

KIRBISTER, Loch
Location & Access OS6/370080 The loch lies to the north of the A964 Stromness/Kirkwall road. A minor road margins the west shore whilst a convenient track gives easy access to the east shoreline.
Commentary Loch of Kirbister is shallow, one mile in length and up to half a mile wide. An ideal beginners water.
Fish There are excellent stocks of good quality trout which average about 10oz in weight. Fish of over 2lb are occasionally caught and towards the end of the season there is a possibility of sea-trout.
Flies & Tactics Boat fishing is best, but bank fishing can be productive, particularly along the north-west shoreline and in the south-east corner of the loch. Offer: Loch Ordie, Invicta, Kingfisher Butcher.
Permission & Charges See Loch of Boardhouse entry.

MUCKLE WATER, Rousay

OS Map 6 — Orkney Mainland

Location & Access OS6/395300 The loch is approached from Gue (6/383291) at the end of the B9064. Follow the peat track which runs north between Ward Hill (210m) and Swarta Fiold (141m). Perrie Water (6/400295) is reached after 15 minutes, Muckle Water is a short step further north.
Commentary Muckle Water is the most productive of the Rousay trout lochs. It is one mile east/west by up to 250yds wide.
Fish Trout average 12oz in weight. There are larger speciments as well.
Permission & Charges These lochs are currently preserved by the owner and are not available to the general public.

PERRIE WATER, Mainland

Location & Access OS6/335272 Leave the A966 road at Costa (6/335282) and follow the farm road to Hewin. The loch is immediately to the south.
Commentary An attractive little loch covering approximately 15 acres. Outstanding wildflowers and birdlife.
Fish Excellent beginners loch, well-filled with small trout averaging 6oz-8oz in weight.
Flies & Tactics Easily covered from the shore and the trout are not fussy about which flies they take.
Permission & Charges See Loch of boardhouse entry.

PERRIE WATER, Rousay See Muckle Water, Rousay. See also Loch of Swartmill.

SEA-TROUT FISHING LOCATIONS

Location & Access Mar Wick OS6/228248 Bridge of Waithe OS6/282110 Swanbister Bay OS6/352050 Skaith OS6/377063 Scapa Bay OS6/434088 Graemshall OS6/491017 Sandside Bay OS6/590068 Bay of Suckquoy OS6/522044 Grimsquoy OS6/476087 Bay of Isbister OS6/391182 Wood Wick OS6/382240 Sands of Evie OS6/376263
Commentary The majority of sea-trout are caught in the sea, fishing from the shore, although they may be caught in Loch of Stenness, Loch of Harray and Loch of Kirbister. Sadly, however, since the advent of fish farming in Orkney, wild sea-trout are now all but extinct.
Fish Season runs from 25th February to the end of October. Best time, March and April.
Flies & Tactics Bait and lure fishing is the preferred angling method, but sea-trout may also be tempted by Black Pennell, Ke-He, Soldier Palmer, Teal Blue & Silver, Peter Ross and Invicta. Take great care wading. Check tide times and seek local advice before setting out.

SHAPINSAY, Island See OS Map 5

SKAIL, Loch

Location & Access OS6/240180 Easy access from the B9056 which margins the north shore of the loch.
Commentary One of the most attractive and exciting Orkney lochs, close to the famous Neolithic village of Skara Brae.
Fish Loch of Skail has wonderful trout of exceptional quality. Average weight, 2lb, but, be warned, they are "dour".
Flies & Tactics The loch is three quarters of a mile east/west by up to half a mile wide. Best results come from boat fishing. Begin with a drift down the west shore. Pay particular attention to the mouth of the inlet stream at the south-west corner. Try: Black Pennell, Invicta, Alexandra.
Permission & Charges See Loch of Boardhouse entry.

STENNESS, Loch

Location & Access OS6/280130 Loch of Stenness lies to the north of Stromness and is easily accessible from public roads round the loch.
Commentary This is the most "difficult" of Orkney lochs but it can also be one of the most rewarding. The setting is majestic, with the hills of Hoy as a backdrop and the nearby dramatic Neolithic Ring of Brogar. Outstanding wildflowers and birdlife as well.
Fish One of the largest UK brown trout came from Loch of Stenness and weighed 29lb 8oz. A cast of this fish may be seen in Kirkwall and another is at the Freshwater Fisheries Lab in Pitlochry. Stenness trout are bright silver and their flesh is red. They average about 1lb in weight, but fish of up to and over 7lb are sometimes caught - as well as sea-trout, mullet, saithe, herring, flounders and cod.
Flies & Tactics Best results come from fishing close to the shore, boat or bank. June and July are the most productive months and you should mount your attack on a rising tide. Offer: Black Pennell, Soldier Palmer, Silver Invicta.
Permission & Charges See Loch of Boardhouse entry. Also, Standing Stones Hotel, Stenness, Orkney. Tel: 01856 850449

STROMNESS, Loch

Location & Access OS6/239106 Approach from the minor road from Stromness to Glenfield.
Commentary This is an artifical loch and the public water supply for Stromness.
Fish Some really excellent brown trout. Fish of up to and over 4lb in weight have been caught in recent years.
Flies & Tactics Fishing from the dam wall is not allowed. The rest of the loch is easily covered from the bank. Try: Ke-He, March Brown, Silver Invicta.
Permission & Charges Apply to Orkney Island Council, Council Offices, Kirkwall. Tel: 01856 873535.

SWANNAY, Loch

Location & Access OS6/310280 The loch lies in the north of Mainland. The west shore is approached from the minor road from Twatt (6/273241) on the A986 via the road to Loudenhill Farm (6/303278). The east shore is approached from the A966 at Chrismo (6/316288) to Dale (6/319277).
Commentary Loch of Swannay is a shallow loch, often windy, and covers an area of some 670 acres, being two miles long by up to half a mile wide. The south end is graced by Muckle Holm Island.
Fish The average weight of Swannay trout is in the order of 14oz, but each season produces good numbers of fish of over 2lb. Trout of 4lb in weight are not uncommon.

Pentland Firth — OS Maps 6-7

Flies & Tactics Boat fishing is best, but bank fishing can also be very productive, particularly during the early months of the season. Take care wading, because the bottom is rocky. The most productive drifts are in the vicinity of Muckle Holm Island; down the Loudenhill shore about ten yards out from the bank, and the south-east corner where the Burn of Eitheriegoe enters. When boat fishing, hasten slowly, there are skerries and barely submerged rocks. Take spare sheer pins for the outboard motor. Always have a Black Pennell on your cast.
Permission & Charges See Loch of Boardhouse entry.

TANKERNESS, Loch Looks inviting, but to all intents and purposes, fishless.

WABISTER, Loch
Location & Access OS6/397333 Loch of Wabister, known locally as Wester Loch, lies in the north of the Island of Rousay to the north of the school at Quoyostray.
Commentary Visit Rousay as much for its wealth of Neolithic monuments as for its fishing.
Fish Excellent quality brown trout, pink fleshed and averaging about 10oz in weight.
Flies & Tactics Comfortable bank fishing all round the loch. Start in the vicinity of the promontory on the east shore. Try: Black Pennell, Ke-He, Alexandra.
Permission & Charges Contact Trumland Estate, Rousay, Orkney. Tel: 01856 821340

WASDALE, Loch
Location & Access OS6/343149 Loch of Wasdale lies to the east of the A986 road near Finstown. It is easily accessible from Refuge (6/339153).
Commentary This is a narrow, peaty loch, half a mile north/south by 150yds wide, shletered by Cuiffie Hill (145m).
Fish Substantial numbers of traditional brown trout which average 6loz in weight.
Flies & Tactics Bank fishing only and stay ashore. Wading is dangerous. Offer: Black Pennell, Soldier Palmer, Silver Butcher.
Permission & Charges Contact: M Gray, Wasdale, Firth, Orkney. Tel: 01856 761298.

Pentland Firth

GRAEMSHALL LOCH See St Mary's Loch.
GRAEMSTON LOCH See South Ronaldsay.

HELDALE WATER
Location & Access 7/255922 Drive south from Moness Pier on the B9047, the only road on Hoy. Park at Heldale (7/283912) and follow a peat track leading north-west up the hill. Heldale Water is a ten minute walk beyond the end of the track.
Commentary Heldale Water, and its two neighbours, Sands Water (7/248939) to the north and Hoglinns Water (7/250913) to the south, are amongst the most remote and least visited trout lochs in Scotland. Their setting is magnificent, above the red cliffs of the Island of Hoy, with Ward Hill towering to the north. The moor is home to hen harrier, great skua, golden plover, dunlin and greenshank and a wide variety of wild flowers: orchid, tormentil, bog ashpodel, butterwort, milkwort.
Fish Not many, dour, but large. Trout of up to and over 5lb in Heldale Water and Hoglinns Water, smaller fish in Sands Water.
Flies & Tactics Bank fishing only. Heldale is largest loch. Sands Water is one mile north, over Bakingstone Hill (152m), Hoglinns Water lies quarter of a mile south over Skird Hill (164m). Be prepared for serious tramping. Flies: Black Pennell, March Brown, Silver Invicta.
Permission & Charges Permission to visit should be obtained from the landowner, prior to setting out. Contact: H. Seatter, Melsetter Farm, Hoy, Orkney. Tel: (01856) 791308

HOGLINNS WATER See Heldale Water.
LYTHE, Loch See South Ronaldsay.
SANDS WATER, Hoy See Heldale Water.

SANDY WATER
Location & Access 7/219030 A small loch on the Island of Hoy, approached from Moness Pier by driving west past the Outdoor Centre and Orgil church (7/233036).
Commentary Sandy Water lies adjacent to the footpath out to Rackwick on the west coast of Hoy, sheltered to the south by Ward Hill (479m) and to the north by Cuilags Hill (433m). The loch is infrequently visited and makes an exciting change from fishing Mainland.
Fish Not many, and dour with it, but some excellent trout of considerable size.
Flies & Tactics Easy bank fishing and approach with caution to avoid 'spooking' the fish. Offer them: Black Zulu, Invicta, Alexandra.
Permission & Charges The loch lies within a RSPB reserve. Details from: RSPB Office, Smyril, Stenness, Orkney. Tel: (01856) 850176.

SEATROUT FISHING LOCATIONS See OS Map 6 for general details and season opening and closing dates. Bay of Creekland 7/236047, Bay of Quoys 7/242033, Lyrawa Bay 7/291988, Pegal Bay 7/297978, Mill Bay 7/300955, Ore Bay 7/305939, Heldale 7/284912, Saltness 7/278899, Myre Bay 7/328910.

SOUTH RONALDSAY, Island There are a number of small lochs on South Ronaldsay, including Graemston Loch (7/540846), Trena Loch (7/467852), and Loch of Lythe (7/442858), but they have no game fishing significance.

ST MARY'S LOCH 7/470012 In Holm, close to the village of St Mary's and the Churchill Barreirs. In days past, a useful seatrout loch, but now of little game fishing interest. The same applies to Graemshall Loch (7/488020), to the east of St Mary's, although some seatrout are still caught after August.

TRENA LOCH See South Ronaldsay.

OS Map 8 — Stornoway & North Lewis

Stornoway and North Lewis

Isles of Lewis and Harris Introduction
No matter where you fish in Lewis and Harris, permission must be obtained before doing so. At times, it is difficult to establish who owns the fishing rights and whether or not access is available. The best place to seek advice is: Sportsworld, 1 Francis Street, Stornoway. Tel: (01851) 705464. You should also, always, seek permission from the local crofter before crossing his land to reach a fishing location. Where access information is known, it is noted in the appropriate text. However, please double-check this information before fishing as details may change.

A'BHAILE, Loch See Loch an Duna.
A'BHAILE, Loch (Tolsta Chaolais) See Loch Chulain.
A'BHLAR BHUIDE, Loch See Loch Buaile Bhig.
A'BHRAGHAIL, Loch See OS Map 13.
A'BHUNA, Loch See Loch Breugach.
A'CHAIRN, Loch See Loch Grinnavat (Gress)
A'CHAPHAIL, Loch See OS Map 13.
A'CHITEAR, Loch See Loch Mor a'Ghoba.
A'CHLACHAIN, Loch See Loch an Fheoir.
A'CHLACHAIN, Loch (Creed) See River Creed.
A'CHNOIC DUIBHE, Loch See Loch Breugach.
A'GHAINMHICH, Loch See Lochan a'Sgeil.
A'GHILLE RUAIDH, Lochan See Loch Tana.

A'LEADHARAIN, Loch
Location & Access 8/387336 An easy five minute walk to the south of the A858 Stornoway/Garynahine road, two miles from town.
Commentary Not over-fished, probably because of the attraction and quality of so many other lochs in the area. Nevertheless, if time is limited, this little loch on Sidhean Mor could provide breakfast.
Fish Trout average 10-12oz.
Flies & Tactics Very easily fished from the shore with Blue Zulu, March Brown, Silver Butcher.
Permission & Charges The best place to seek advice is: Sportsworld, 1 Francis Street, Stornoway. Tel: (01851) 705464.

A'SGAIL, Loch See Loch na Muilne (Bosta)

A'SGEIL, Lochan
Location & Access 8/434435 Park on the A857 Stornoway/Barvas at 8/395430. Follow the north bank of the Roundogro burn east.
Commentary A five mile outing to fish ten named and unnamed lochs on the headwaters of the Roundogro burn and the River Coll. Loch a'Ghainmhich (8/420427) is first, reached after a stiff walk of 45 mins. After fishing Loch a'Ghainmhich, head due north over rising moorland, aiming for the top of the hill (122m). Find Loch an Tuim (8/425435) to the the east side of the summit. Turn east, now, to explore the three unnamed lochs around 8/430428 before walking over to fish Lochan a'Sgeil. Leave Lochan a'Sgeil at the south end and follow the inlet burn to the shielings at 8/431429. Angle south-west now to find Loch an Fheoir Bheag (8/425420) after a walk of half a mile. Loch an Fheoir Mhoir lies immediately to the west. A possible diversion here could include a visit to two good little lochs, 15 mins south from Loch an Fheoir Bheag: the unnamed loch at 8/428414, and Loch nam Breac at 8/424413. After fishing Loch an Fheoir Mhoir, walk north-west to find the Roundogro burn. Follow it back to the A857.
Fish A variety of good quality trout of 6oz to over 3lb in weight.
Flies & Tactics Be prepared for heavy going over rough ground, particularly after rain. Bank fishing. Do not wade. The north shore of Loch a'Ghainmhich, which is almost half a mile east/west, fishes best. Loch an Tuim and its surrounding lochs will provide great fun, and dinner. Lochan a' Sgeil, a challenging clear water loch, has a big-fish reputation, but they are hard to tempt. Concentrate on the west shore. The other lochs are rarely fished and could hold some surprises. Offer: Black Pennell, Grouse & Claret, Silver Butcher all round.
Permission & Charges The best place to seek advice is: Sportsworld, 1 Francis Street, Stornoway. Tel: (01851) 705464.

ABHAINN GEIRAHA (River Garry) See Loch Vatacolla.
AHAVAT BEAG, Loch See Loch an Duna.
AHAVAT MOR, Loch See Loch an Duna.
AIRD, Loch (Grimersta) See OS Map 13.
AIRIGH AN SGAIRBH, Loch See Loch Buaile Bhig.
AIRIGH AN T-SAGAIRT, Loch, Orasay See Loch Orasay.
AIRIGH CHONNICH, Loch See Loch Mor a'Ghoba.
AIRIGH MHIC FHIONNLAIDH, Loch See Loch Ceann Allavat.

AIRIGH NA LIC, Loch
Location & Access 8/400342. A mile west of Stornoway and immediately to the north of the A858 Stornoway/Garynahine road.
Commentary Not one of the most beautiful lochs in the world - litter-marred and close to the Stornoway refuse tip at the north-west end. Both shores are easily accessible and the loch carries the Glen River from Ben Hulabie (150m) to the sea in Stornoway Harbour.
Fish The brown trout are small and, given the quality of other North Lewis Lochs, Airigh na Lic is not an attractive option. Its main claim to fame, however, is as a seatrout fishery and, with good rain, from July to September it can provide excellent sport. There is also the possibility of the odd salmon.
Flies & Tactics Wading is comfortable and is required to reach the best lies which are generally at the east and west end of his half-mile long loch. Flies to try: Black Zulu, Soldier Palmer, Peter Ross.
Permission & Charges See Isles of Lewis and Harris introduction.

AIRIGH NAN GLEANN, Loch See Loch Buaile Bhig.

Stornoway & North Lewis — OS Map 8

AIRIGH RIABHACH, Loch See Loch Breugach.

AIRIGH SEIBH, Loch
Location & Access 8/260387 Park at 8/246388 on the Pentland road where the River Ohagro crosses to enter Loch Laxavat Ard (8/245380). Walk north-east up the hill to find the outlet stream from Loch Airigh Seibh and follow it round the north shoulder of the hill to find the loch after 30 mins.
Commentary A large, shallow water, three quarters of a mile north/south by over 300yds wide. Loch Airigh Seibh is sheltered from most winds and it is generally possible to find a suitable place to fish.
Fish Lots of hard fighting brown trout which average 8oz in weight and a few of up to 1lb. At the end of the season, and after very heavy rain, there is also the possibility of salmon and seatrout.
Flies & Tactics The north end is a good starting point. Fish the area of the outlet burn then work the west shore, by the two inlet streams and down to the island. The south-west corner can also be very productive; if you are going to encounter salmon or seatrout, then this is where they will be. Flies: Blue Zulu, Woodcock & Hare-lug, Silver Invicta.
Permission & Charges See Isles of Lewis & Harris introduction.

ALLAVAT, Loch See Loch nan Lea (Clistul).

ALMAISTEAN, Loch
Location & Access 8/219396 Park on the Pentland road at 8/224403 and climb south into the hills. Follow the outlet stream up to the loch which is reached after a walk of approx. 15 mins.
Commentary Loch Fionnacleit (8/215395), to the west of Loch Almaistean, is also worth a visit as are the two unnamed lochans in the hill to the south at 8/223388.
Fish Trout average about 8oz and there are a few larger specimens as well.
Flies & Tactics Bank fishing with good sport from all round the shores of these delightful lochs. Picnic at Loch Fionnacleit, by the islands at the north end. Offer trout: Ke-He, Greenwell's Glory, Dunkeld.
Permission & Charges See Isles of Lewis and Harris introduction

AMAR SINE, Loch See Loch Laxavat (Iorach).
AMHASTAR, Loch See Loch an Tuim, Pentland Road.

AN DAIMH, Loch, Aird Skapraid
Location & Access 8/275275 Park at 8/274305 at the east end of the commercial forest block on the A858 Stornoway/Garynahine road. Follow the edge of the plantation south. Loch Daimh is reached after a walk of some two miles.
Commentary Loch an Daimh is a lovely loch in a remote setting. There are three other lochs to fish along the way, the first being little Loch Sgriachach (8/271296). Work the west shore then continue south to fish the west shore of Loch Lochavat (8/270286). Five minutes south-east from the south end of Loch Lochavat brings you to Loch Tana (8/271280). Again, fish the west shore before crossing south to island-clad Loch an Daimh, the ideal place for lunch. Return to the start point along the east shores of the lochs to complete a splendid day out in the hills.
Fish A wide variety of trout, none of which will break the scales, but they fight well and give great sport. The average weight is about 8oz with a few fish of up to 1lb, particularly in Loch Lochavat.
Flies & Tactics Bank fishing, and stay banked. The north shore of Loch Lochavat, amongst the corners and bays, can be very productive. On Loch Tana expect action all round the loch. The west shore of Loch an Daimh, in the vicinity of the islands, should provide lunch. Tempt them with: Blue Zulu, Soldier Palmer, Silver Butcher.
Permission & Charges See Isles of Lewis and Harris introduction.

AN DUIN, Loch
Location & Access 8/394542 Adjacent to the A857 Barvas/Ness road between Upper and Lower Shader.
Commentary The dun which gives the loch its name is the most impressive aspect of this easily accessible water. There are various other ancient monuments nearby (see Loch Bacavat, Shader) which are also well worth visiting. South from Loch an Duin, and approached by a good peat track from the south end of the loch at 8/395549, is another, excellent, easily accessible water, Loch Maravat (8/403537) which covers an area of some 25 acres. If Loch an Duin trout are uncooperative, despair not - head for Loch Maravat.
Fish Good quality brown trout in Loch an Duin, averaging 10oz in weight. Loch Maravat holds trout of similar quality which average 12-14oz.
Flies & Tactics Wade with care on Loch an Duin and concentrate your attack along the west shore; fish rise and are taken all round Loch Maravat. Offer them: Soldier Palmer, Grouse & Claret, Silver Butcher.
Permission & Charges See Isles of Lewis and Harris introduction.

AN DUIN, Loch, Aird See Eye Peninsula.

AN DUIN, Loch (Carloway)
Location & Access 8/189408 Leave the A858 Breasclete/Carloway road at 8/195411 and drive west through the township of Doune Carloway. The loch is to the south of the road.
Commentary The most spectacular aspect of this loch is the magnificent broch on the hill to the north, one of the best preserved brochs in Europe. The lower part of the structure is still largely intact, clearly showing the entrance and double-wall construction. After visiting the broch and fishing Loch an Duin, follow the track at the west end of the loch which leads south to little Loch Honagro (8/185402) which is worth an hour or so, particularly during September.
Fish Loch an Duin trout average 8oz, but there are a few fish of up to and over 1lb in weight as well. Loch Honagro trout are smaller.
Flies & Tactics Bank fishing only on this 25 acre loch and the north shoreline produces best results. Loch Honagro is easily covered from the shore.

OS Map 8 — Stornoway & North Lewis

Permission & Charges See Loch Laxavat Ard.

AN DUIN, Loch (Lower Bayble) See Eye Peninsula.

AN DUNA, Loch
Location & Access 8/283472 Loch an Duna borders the A858 Barvas/Carloway road between Bragar and North Shawbost.
Commentary Somewhat public, but dominated by the marvellous ruin of the Broch on a promontory at the north-east corner. To the west, behind the school at Bragar, lies Loch Grinavat (8/295474). Also easily accessible from Loch an Duna are a number of other waters, all of which offer the chance of sport. These include the unnamed lochan at 8/276473, and, to the north of the A858, Loch na Muilne, North Shawbost and Loch a'Bhaile, close to the sea at 8/255473. To the east lies Loch Ordais (8/283487), by Labost and Port Mhor Bragar. Good peat roads run south from Bragar and Loch an Duna and these give easy access to four more remote lochs, lying on the northern slopes of Beinn Bragar (261m) and Beinn Choinnich (210m): Loch Uanalair (8/288464), Loch Ahavat Mor (8/277457), Loch Ahavat Beag (8/278452) and Loch Nighean Shomhairle (8/285451).
Fish Loch Ordais holds the largest trout, fish of up to and over 3lb in weight, but they are difficult to tempt. Loch an Duna has excellent trout which average 8-10oz, and larger fish as well. The other waters contain trout of between 6oz and 2lb. Seatrout may be caught in the sea near Loch Ordais and Loch a' Bhaile.
Flies & Tactics Bank fishing and best to avoid wading. The south shore on Loch an Duna is the most productive area; on Loch Ordais, which can be brackish, concentrate your effort along the west bank; Loch Grinavat fishes well all round, as do the other lochs noted. As the season advances, weed can become a problem, so plan your visit during May and June. Flies: Ke-He, March Brown, Alexandra.
Permission & Charges See Isles of Lewis & Harris introduction.

AN DUNA, Loch (Orasay) See Loch Crogovat (Orasay).
AN DUNAIN, Loch See Loch Chulain.
AN EARBALL, Loch See OS Map 13.
AN EILEAN CHUBHRAIDH, Loch See Loch an Fhada Bhig.
AN EILEIN, Loch See Loch an Tobhair.

AN FHADA BHIG, Loch
Location & Access 8/251267 Park at 8/274305 at the east end of the forest block on the A858 Stornoway/Garynahine road. Follow the edge of the plantation south, then west to the north end of Loch an Culaidhean (8/264290), the first loch of the day.
Commentary Loch an Fhada Bhig is the most southerly loch in a series of 12 named and unnamed lochs and lochans which, if taken together, offer one of the best fishing expeditions on North Lewis. You will cover more than six miles, over rough country, so be well prepared. A compass and map are essential. Loch nan Culaidhean is one mile long. Fish the east bank as you walk south. Follow the inlet burn uphill from the south end of Loch nan Culaidhean to find Loch Skapraid (8/267277). Climb the glen and inlet burn at the south end of Loch Skapraid to explore tiny Loch Tana (8/269265), working west across broken ground to the unnamed lochan at 8/263262; then north for five minutes to reach the large, unnamed, loch at 8/260266, known locally as Loch an Eilean Chubraidh. Climb over Fada Beag (60m), to arrive at Loch an Fhada Bhig, the perfect place for lunch. Before leaving Loch and Fhada Bhig, detour west to have a cast in the unnamed lochan at 8/245268. Now cross north-east to Loch Gobhlaich, then north-west to visit narrow Loch an Tairbeart. Climb north now, over South Cleitshal (106m), and descend to the south shore of Loch an Tuim Aird. Fish the west bank. Return to the start point by the north-west shore of Loch nan Culaidhean.
Fish Loch Culaidhean and Loch Tuim Aird are part of the headwater system of the Blackwater river and consequently, after heavy rain and towards the end of the season, there is always the chance of encountering salmon and seatrout. Brown trout average 8oz in the other lochs. Loch an Fhada Bhig has the largest fish. All the trout are of excellent quality.
Flies & Tactics Stay on the bank, all round, do not wade. The east shoreline of Loch Skapraid is the most productive area, although casting is complicated by the steep bank. The other hill lochs are easily understandable and easily covered. On Loch an Tuim Aird, concentrate on the west shore and the north-west bay. Flies: Loch Ordie, Black Zulu, Kingfisher Butcher.
Permission & Charges For Loch nan Culaidhean and Loch an Tuim Aird, contact: Malcolm MacPhail, Head Keeper, Garynahine Estate, Estate Office, Garynahine, Isle of Lewis. Tel: 01851-621383 (evenings). For the other waters, see Isles of Lewis and Harris introduction.

AN FHEOIR, Loch See Loch Mor Soval (Arnish).
AN FHEOIR BHEAG, Loch See Lochan a'Sgeil.

AN FHEOIR, Loch
Location & Access 8/467521 Start from High Borve on the A857 Barvas/Ness road. A peat road runs east along the south bank of the Borve River. At the end of the track, continue east, following the course of the river to where it branches into two streams. Leave the river and continue due east over rising ground to the top of Beinn Sheunta (140m). Descend for one mile to reach the loch; a long, hard tramp, and a round trip of some eight miles.
Commentary There are four lochs. Fish Loch a'Chlachain (8/461526) first, then its neighbouring, unnamed loch at 8/465526. Walk south for ten minutes to reach Loch an Fheoir, then south-west for half a mile to find Loch Eileatier (8/459515). This is a glorious, compass-and-map day out and these little waters are very rarely fished from one season to the next.
Fish Reports, from time to time, of some specimen trout, but mostly fish which average 8-10oz in weight.
Flies & Tactics Hearty lungs and strong legs are a prerequisite of visiting these remote lochs. Fish them care-

Stornoway & North Lewis
OS Map 8

fully from the bank. Stay back to avoid spooking fish. The unnamed loch should be thoroughly investigated. Offer: Soldier Palmer, March Brown, Silver Butcher.
Permission & Charges See Isles of Lewis and Harris introduction.

AN FHEOIR, Loch See Loch an Tobair.
AN FHEOIR MHOIR, Loch See Lochan a'Sgeil.
AN FHIR MHAOIL, Loch See OS Map 13.
AN FHRAOICH, Loch See Loch Ceann Allavat.
AN LAOIGH, Loch, Beinn Ghreinaval See Loch an Tuim, Pentland Road.
AN LAOIGH, Loch, Pentland Road See Loch an Tuim, Pentland Road.
AN LOCHAIN, Loch See Loch Foisnavat.
AN OIS GHUIRM, Loch See Loch Cleit Steirmeis.
AN OIS, Loch (Beinn Tulagaval) See Loch Suainagadail.
AN OIS, Loch (River Creed) See River Creed.
AN SGEIREACH MHOIR, Loch See Loch Suainagadail.
AN T- SIDHEIN, Loch See Eye Peninsula.
AN TAIRBEART, Loch (South Cleitshal) See Loch an Fhada Bhig.
AN TAIRBEART NAN CLEITICHEAN, Loch See Loch an Tuim, Pentland Road.
AN TIUMPAN, Loch See Eye Peninsula.

AN TOBAIR, Loch
Location & Access 8/435456 Drive north from Stornoway on the B895 to the village of Back. 100yds past the church, turn left and then, after one mile, right at 8/480414 onto the peat road that margins the south bank of the River Gress. Park at 8/467428.
Commentary One of the great 'Heather Isles' fishing adventures, walking eight miles over very rough terrain to visit a series of ten lochs at the heart of North Lewis. From the peat road, walk north-west to Loch Ullavat a'Deas (8/458430), then via the inlet stream at the north end to Loch Ullavat a'Clith. Head west from Loch Ullavat a'Clith for ten minutes to reach Loch an Eilein (8/445436), the source of the River Coll. Follow the inlet burn at the north shore of Loch an Eilein north to scattered Loch Fada Caol (8/435443). Also fish the unnamed loch, joined to Loch Fada Caol, at 8/440446. Now find the inlet burn at the extreme north-east corner of the loch and follow it north to Loch an Tobair, a walk of some 15 mins. After exploiting Loch an Tobair, step over to narrow Loch an Fheoir (8/441460), before turning south again to explore tiny Loch nan Leac (8/445458) and then over the rise to Loch na Fola (8/443454). The last loch in the series is little Loch na Ciste (8/451451), half a mile south-east from Loch na Fola. Have a few casts before continuing east to cross the Gress River and pick up a good track back to the start point. In spate conditions, simply walk the south bank of the river to Sithean Airigh Mhurchaidh (8/463444) where you will meet the same track.
Fish The chance of specimen fish of up to and over 3lb in weight; also good numbers of trout averaging 6-8oz as well as numerous fish of between 10 and 12oz.
Flies & Tactics These lochs are infrequently fished,

particularly the more distant waters, Loch an Tobair and Loch an Fheoir, and Loch nan Leac and Loch na Fola. On Loch Ullavat a' Deas, concentrate in the vicinity of the two inlet burns at the north-west corner. Loch an Eilein can hold seatrout and salmon after August, given heavy rain. Look for them in the south-west bay and at the north end of the loch. Trout rise and are taken everywhere on Loch Fada Caol. On Loch an Tobair, try the south-east corner and the east bank. The other waters are easily covered. Flies: Blue Zulu, Soldier Palmer, Dunkeld. It is worth noting here that the Gress River and Coll River can offer sport with salmon and sea-trout towards the end of the season, provided there has been a lot of rain. Indeed, the Gress River was, in days past, one of the best salmon streams on the island. Seatrout may also be caught at the mouth of the two streams; from Gress Sands (OS8/491413); the camp site by Coll Sands at OS8/461385 which is the mouth of the Allt an t-Sniomh burn; and at the mouth of the Coll River (OS8/469394).
Permission & Charges See Isles of Lewis and Harris introduction.

AN TUIM AIRD, Loch See Loch an Fhada Bhig.
AN TUIM, Loch See Lochan a'Sgeil.

AN TUIM, Loch (Pentland Road)
Location & Access 8/255358 Easily accessible and immediately to the south of the Breasclete/Pentland road.
Commentary This is the largest of a series of lochs which lie adjacent to the south side of the road. Loch an Tuim is almost half a mile north/south and covers an area of some 50 acres. The other waters are: Loch an Laoigh, Pentland Road (8/269359), Loch an Tairbeart nan Cleitichean (8/264360), Loch Amhastar (8/240358), Loch na Gainmhich, Breasclete (8/233356), Loch na Beinne Bige (8/224353), Loch na Ba Riabhaich (8/247349), Loch na Leamhain (8/247344), Loch an Laoigh, Bein Ghreinaval (8/237342).
Fish All these waters contain good stocks of small trout which average 6-8oz. Loch na Leamhain and Loch na Ba Riabhaich are the headwaters of the River Breasclete and in spate conditions there is the possibility of seatrout. There is also the chance of sport with seatrout at the mouth of the stream at 8/217347.
Flies & Tactics Bank fishing, and best to stay ashore. Loch an Tuim in particular is a dangerous loch to wade. If fate is unkind and the fish dour, then resort to the unnamed lochan at 8/247358. First cast: Black Spider, Soldier Palmer, Black Pennell.
Permission & Charges See Isles of Lewis and Harris introduction.

AN UMHLAICH, Loch See Loch nan Leac (Clistul).
AORAIDH, Loch See Loch Dubh Gormilevat.
ARD A'GHILLE A'RUAIDH, Loch See Loch Orasay.

ARNOL, Loch
Location & Access 8/300489 Leave the A858 at 8/314483 and drive north through the township of

OS Map 8 — Stornoway & North Lewis

Arnol. At the telephone kiosk bear left and follow the minor road out to the beach to park at 8/303492. Loch Arnol is on your left.
Commentary A small loch covering an area of some 20 acres, close to the sea and a good place for a family day out.
Fish In days past, Loch Arnol and the Arnol river used to produce good numbers of salmon and seatrout. Sadly, the river has fallen into disrepair and the few fish that make the effort are generally taken by nets.
Flies & Tactics After heavy rain, and towards the end of the season, there is always the chance of a fish or two, but sport now is principally with brown trout which average 8oz. Easy bank fishing all round with: Black Pennell, Grouse & Claret, Alexandra. Seatrout may also be caught in the sea from the beach.
Permission & Charges See Isles of Lewis & Harris introduction.

ARNOL, River See Loch Arnol.
BACAVAT ARD, Loch See Lochan Hatravat.
BACAVAT CROSS, Loch See Lochan Hatravat.
BACAVAT IORACH, Loch See Lochan Hatravat.
BACAVAT, Loch, Barvas Moor See Loch Dubh Gormilevat.
BACAVAT, Loch (Gress) See Loch Grinnavat (Gress).

BACAVAT, Loch (Shader)
Location & Access 8/398552 Conveniently adjacent to the A857 road between Lower Shader and Five Penny Borve.
Commentary Significant pre-historic monuments nearby, worth exploring: Clach Stei Lin church (8/397547), Dun (8/393544), Steinacleit (8/396541), Teampull Pheadair 12th century church ruins (8/380550).
Fish Small and lots of them. A few of up to 12oz.
Flies & Tactics The loch is easily covered from the shore. The inhabitants are not too particular, but the best flies are probably: Black Pennell, Greenwell's Glory, Silver Butcher.
Permission & Charges See Isles of Lewis and Harris introduction.

BARAVAT, Loch
Location & Access 8/462597 A roadside loch, adjacent to the A857 Barvas/Ness road, one mile north from Galson Lodge (8/455591).
Commentary Rather public and exposed, but a good place to stop for a few casts and, possibly, one for the glass case.
Fish Trout average 10oz but there are reputed to be fish of up to and over 5lb as well.
Flies & Tactics This shallow water is easily covered from the bank. Fish fine and far off, with: Black Pennell, March Brown, Silver Butcher.
Permission & Charges See Isles of Lewis and Harris introduction.

BARVAS River
Location & Access Source 8/357404 Outflow 8/340508 The Barvas River, approximately nine miles in length and the longest river in Lewis, rises from Loch na Scaravat (8/357404) and after two miles flows parallel to the A875 Stornoway/Barvas road to reach the sea through Loch Mor Barvas (8/345500) at Goile Chroic (8/340508), south of the Army Range.
Commentary Fishing is limited to the lower reaches and on Loch Mor Barvas. There are two pools below the dam at the west end of the loch, and these are netted by the estate. Some fish escape and, given the right conditions, good sport is frequently had to rod and line anglers. The river is stocked on a regular basis.
Fish Barvas salmon are not large and average in the region of 6-7lb, although a few bigger fish are taken most seasons. The number caught depends very much upon weather conditions and varies from between 30 and 100 salmon each year.
Flies & Tactics Being in the right place at the right time is the name of the game. After stormy weather, when the sea floods into Loch Mor Barvas, sport can be particularly good, on both loch and river. Use light tackle and be prepared to stalk your fish. Offer standard pattern trout flies such as: Soldier Palmer, Black Pennell, Grouse & Claret, Greenwell's Glory, March Brown, Silver Invicta, varying the size according to prevailing water conditions.
Permission & Charges Day tickets and boat hire may be available at £10 per rod per day from Mrs Graham. Tel: (01851) 840206. For further details, contact The Keeper, The Cottage, Barvas Lodge, Lower Barvas, Isle of Lewis. Tel: (01851) 840469.

BEAG A'CHOCAIR, Loch See Loch Mor a'Chocair.
BEAG A'GHRIANAIN, Loch See Loch Buaile Bhig.
BEAG AN STAIRR, Loch See Loch Mor an Stairr.

BEAG CNOC A CHOILICH, Loch
Location & Access 8/390316 Easily accessible and two and a half miles south from Stornoway on the A859 Stornoway/Balallan road. Park at 8/394314 and walk north-west for ten minutes to reach the loch.
Commentary Loch Cnoc a Choilich, the loch nearest to the road at 8/397318, is reputed to be troutless, but a visit to Loch Beag Cnoc a Choilich can be usefully combined with an assault on Loch Briodag (8/385311) to the south.
Fish Pretty trout which average 8oz and a few larger ones as well.
Flies & Tactics Both lochs are approx. 500yds east/west, covering an area of some 15-18 acres, so there is plenty of water to explore. Bank fishing, and on Loch Beag Cnoc a Choilich concentrate your effort along the north shore towards the island at the west end. Loch Briodag is a narrow water easily covered from the bank. Offer the inhabitants: Black Zulu, Soldier Palmer, Alexandra.
Permission & Charges See Isles of Lewis and Harris introduction.

BEAG EILEAVAT, Loch See Loch Tana.
BEAG GAINEAMHAICH, Loch See Loch Vatacolla.
BEAG LEIG TADH, Loch See Loch Mor Leig Tadh.
BEAG, Loch (Arnish) See Loch Mor Soval (Arnish).

Stornoway & North Lewis — OS Map 8

BEAG NA CRAOIBHE, Loch (Orasay)
Location & Access 8/378293. Close to the A859 Stornoway/Balallan road. Park at 8/377298 and follow the peat road east to reach the north end of the loch in five minutes.
Commentary A pleasant loch for a few casts, easily accessible from the main road. If things are quiet on Loch Beag na Craoibhe, drive south to explore another attractive roadside loch, Loch Sandavat at 8/363278.
Fish Both can provide good sport on their day, but the fish are often hard to move. Expect trout of about 8oz in weight, and a few larger specimens of up to 14oz.
Flies & Tactics Loch Sandavat is probably the most productive of these waters, half a mile east/west by up to 300yds wide at the east end. Work the south shore with: Black Pennell, Grouse & Claret, Dunkeld.
Permission & Charges See Isles of Lewis and Harris introduction.

BEAG SANDAVAT, Loch See Loch Tana.
BEAG SGEIREACH, Loch See Loch Vatacolla.
BEAG THOMA DHUIBHE, Loch See Loch Gil Speireig.
BEALACH NA SGAIL, Loch See Loch Borasdale.
BEIG NA BEISTE, Loch See OS Map 13.
BEINN BHREAC, Loch (Arnish) See Loch Mor Soval (Arnish).
BEINN IOBHEIR, Loch See Loch Grinnavat (Gress).
BEINN NA GAINMHEICH, Loch (Orasay) See Loch Orasay.
BEINN NAN SGALAG, Loch See Loch Laxavat Iorach.

BEINN NAN SGALAG, Loch (West)
Location & Access 8/224365. Turn east towards the Pentland road in Breasclete and park where the first stream crosses under the road at 8/227356. Walk north up the glen, following the stream, to reach the loch in ten minutes.
Commentary An attractive, easily accessible, little loch with small islands at either end, often offering welcome shelter when strong winds howl. Immediately to the west is Loch Dubh (8/218367) and its satellite lochan, both of which merit a cast or three whilst you are in the vicinity.
Fish Nothing monstrous, but fun with bright 6-8oz trout which fight hard.
Flies & Tactics Bank fishing and all these small waters are easily covered from the shore. Try: Black Zulu, March Brown, Silver Butcher.
Permission & Charges See Isles of Lewis and Harris introduction.

BHREAGLEIT, Loch See Loch Milleho.
BHRUTHADAIL, Loch See Loch Urrahag.

BLACKWATER, River
Location & Access Source 8/277390 Outflow 8/234314 The Blackwater river has three principal feeder systems: from Loch Ceann Allavat (8/277390) in the north, Loch Uraval (8/305328) to the north-east, and from Loch Tuim an Aird (8/257293) to the east.
Commentary These streams meet six miles from the sea to form the main flow of the river, where there are 23 named pools, including Big Round, Shipton, and the famous Major's Pool and Sea Pools. Apart from the river, there are 40 lochs on the Garynahine Estate, many of which are linked to the river system and which can, in times of high water, offer sport with salmon and seatrout. The two principal salmon and seatrout lochs are Loch Mhic Leoid and Loch an Tairbeart, and there is a boat on each loch. The other lochs are all fished from the bank. Access is by way of well-maintained tracks to the principal fishings, and by a vigorous moorland tramp to the more remote waters.
Fish Blackwater salmon average 7-8lb, although fish of up to 18lb have been landed. Seatrout average 1lb. The seasonal average is 57 salmon and 57 seatrout
Flies & Tactics Although the Blackwater is a spate river, it differs from the majority of such streams in that the system holds salmon from June to October. The long, tidal pools, invariably produce sport under most conditions, with fresh shoals of salmon and seatrout on successive tides. The river is divided into two, two-rod beats, over three miles of double bank fishing, with rods changing at 1pm each day. A light, single-handed salmon rod is adequate for most situations and wading is not necessary. The lochs provide angling for four rods. Flies: Goat's Toe, General Practitioner, Munro Killer, Garry Dog, Willie Gunn, Thunder & Lightning, Hairy Mary, Green Highlander. For seatrout, and on the lochs, use standard patterns such as: Black Pennell, Kate Maclaren, Soldier Palmer, March Brown, Peter Ross.
Permission & Charges Details from Malcolm Mac Phail, Head Keeper, Estate Manager, Garynahine Estate, Garynahine, Isle of Lewis. Tel: 01851 621383 (evenings). The estate let Garynahine Lodge, including fishing, to parties of up to 12 anglers. The estate also offer shooting for grouse, woodcock, snipe, geese and wildfowl.

BORASDALE, Loch
Location & Access 8/213409 Turn south in Carloway, just past the school, and park at 8/210418, the start point for a rugged tramp round four lochs to the south of the village.
Commentary A good introduction to the wilds of the Heather Isles and hard going. Loch Fasgro (8/204414) is on your right, but ignore it for the time being and walk south up the peat track to Loch Borasdale, a journey of about 15 mins. Leave Loch Borasdale by the crags at the south-west corner and climb to Loch Cliasam Creag (8/206404). Immediately to the west of Loch Cliasam Creag, below Buailaval Mor (97m), is an unnamed loch at 8/202404, know locally as Loch Bealach na Sgail. The outlet burn from Loch Bealach na Sgail, at the north end, leads back down to Loch Fasgro, the water supply for Carloway. Fish the south shore of the loch, back to the start point.
Fish Trout average 8oz, but a few larger fish are occasionally taken, particularly from Loch Fasgro.
Flies & Tactics Wading is uncomfortable all round and down-right dangerous in Loch Fasgro. Stay

OS Map 8

Stornoway & North Lewis

ashore. Trout may be taken from all round the shore on these lochs. Flies: Loch Ordie, Soldier Palmer, Silver Butcher.
Permission & Charges See Isles of Lewis & Harris introduction.

BORVE River See Loch Glinnavat.
BRANAHUIE, Loch See Eye Peninsula.
BREASCLETE, River See Loch an Tuim, Pentland Road.

BREIVAT, Loch
Location & Access 8/330455 Approach from the A858 on the same route for Loch Spealdravat Mor, 8/329473. Walk south from Loch Spealdravat Mor for half a mile over rising ground to reach the north shore of the loch.
Commentary A first class loch and the ideal place for a family day out; far, but not too far for little legs, and in a most attractive setting. Adventure further south for five minutes to explore Loch Muavat (8/332444) and the tiny unnamed loch with the island at 8/328443.
Fish Great fun with trout which average 10oz, and reasonable numbers of fish of up to 1lb.
Flies & Tactics This is a large, circular loch, half a mile across and covering more than 200 acres. The water is shallow and wading is safe and comfortable, perfect for beginners. The south and south-west seem to be best, although fish can be taken anywhere, as is the case on Loch Muavat. First cast: Black Pennell, Grouse & Claret, Alexandra.
Permission & Charges See Isles of Lewis & Harris introduction.

BREIVAT, Loch (Carloway) See Loch na h-Airde.

BREUGACH, Loch
Location & Access 8/375300 Four miles south from Stornoway on the A859 Stornoway/Balallan road. Park at 8/377300, just past the junction with the A897.
Commentary Although close to Stornoway and relatively easily accessible, Loch Breugach and the surrounding waters require a fair bit of tramping over rough ground. Druim Fada moor can be hard work, particularly after heavy rain, so be prepared. There are 12 lochs between the A859 and the A858 Stornoway/Garynahine road: Loch Breugach, the unnamed loch at 8/367300, Loch nan Sgiath (8/362303), Loch Faoileag (8/359298), Loch Leiniscal (8/366294), Loch a'Chnoic Duibhe (8/362288), Loch a'Bhuna (8/348305), Loch Druim nan Sgorach (8/360309), Loch Speireag (8/360314), Loch Uisg an t-Soluis (8/373310) and Loch Airigh Riabhach (8/378306). The best approach is to divide the series into two days out, attacking from both north and south in order to more easily cover all the waters. The route from the north starts on the A858 road at 8/340312, near the ruined shielings. Walk south round the east shoulder of Beinn a'Bhuna (149m) to reach the first water, Loch a'Bhuna, after about ten minutes.
Fish A diversity of trout which range from 6oz up to fish of over 2lb in weight. Loch Uisg an t-Soluis is connected to the River Creed and after heavy rain, particularly towards the end of the season, there is the possibility of salmon and seatrout.
Flies & Tactics The Stornoway Angling Association have boats for hire on Loch Breugach and this half-mile long loch is best fished from the boat. The rest of these waters are fished from the shore. On Loch Leiniscal, a very attractive, long, straggling water, work the north shore, round the islands. Loch nan Sgiath does not give up its residents easily, anywhere, and on its neighbour, Loch Faoileag, fish the north-east shore. Loch a'Bhuna is a large, circular water, some 400yds across, and fish are taken from all round the shore. The headland on the east bank, near the outlet stream, is particularly productive. On Loch Druim nan Sgorach ply the north shore, on Loch Uisg an t-Soluis concentrate on the west bay, by the inlet stream, and along the south and east bank. Loch Airigh Riabhach can be dour, but it contains some very nice trout which average 8-10oz. Offer them: Blue Zulu, Invicta, Black Pennell.
Permission & Charges Sportsworld, 1 Francis Street, Stornoway, Isle of Lewis. Tel: (01851) 705464.

BRIODAG, Loch See Loch Beag Cnoc a Choilich.

BUAILE BHIG, Loch
Location & Access 8/421293 Lies two miles east of the A859 Stornoway/Balallan road. Approach from 8/393310 via the peat road at the north end of Loch Lathamul (8/392308) which is reputed to be troutless.
Commentary The furthermost loch east in a series of lochs lying on Arnish Moor, south of Stornoway. Fishing them involves a rough, five-mile hike over tough, broken country and a compass and map is essential to find your way around. You may shorten the journey by tackling only a few of these waters, when an alternative approach may be made from the north, via the peat road out to Arnish which leaves the A859 Stornoway/Balallan road at OS8/403324, just south of where the road crosses the River Creed.
Fish Expect brown trout which average 8oz. Loch Airigh nan Gleann has larger fish, including trout of up to and over 2lb. Under certain conditions, high tides, after heavy rain, seatrout may be encountered in Loch Buaile Bhig which hurries the River Leiravay to the sea at Tob Leiravay (8/423297).
Flies & Tactics Begin at Loch Lathamul (difficult to resist a cast, but don't delay), and hike north-east to Loch Beag a'Ghrianain (8/402304), unnamed on the OS Map, and larger Loch Mor a'Ghrianain (8/404308). Fish the two unnamed waters immediately to the north of Loch Mor a'Ghrianain before moving on to Loch Airigh an Sgairbh (8/409310), known locally as 'Piper Loch'. From Loch Airigh an Sgairbh tramp south, following the outlet burn down past two unnamed lochans to Loch Mor a'Chrotaich (8/410303), known locally as 'The Frying Pan'. Now angle east over the hill towards the coast to find Loch Arnish (8/423302), then south to lunch at Tob Leiravay. Walk the stream up to Loch Buaile Bhig and onto the ridge above the south shore of the loch to

35

Stornoway & North Lewis   OS Map 8

have look at little Loch nan Deareag (8/421289) and Loch nan Starr (8/415290). Descend north over rough ground to reach the River Leiravay again and the unnamed loch at 8/410299. A hard half-mile west brings you to Loch a'Bhair Bhuidhe, stopping along the way for a throw in the super little unnamed lochan at 8/400300. The last loch in the circuit, and perhaps the best, is Loch Airigh nan Gleann (8/398306). Walk back to the car from the north end of the loch. Flies: Blue Zulu, Soldier Palmer, Silver Invicta.
Permission & Charges See Isles of Lewis and Harris introduction.
CAM NAN EILIDEAN, Loch See Loch Rahacleit.
CAOL DUIN OTHAIL, Loch See Loch Sgeireach na Creige Brist.

CARLOWAY, River
Location & Access Source 8/245380 Outflow 8/205426 Easily accessible throughout its length from the Pentland road.
Commentary In days past, River Carloway used to produce good numbers of salmon, and, given the right water conditions, still can. However, there are few reports of salmon numbers.
Fish Typical Hebridean salmon which average 7-8lb in weight, and some seatrout.
Flies & Tactics Best chance of a fish is after very heavy rain, and the place to look is in headwater lochs, particularly Loch Laxavat Ard (8/245380). Use trout flies: Ke-He, Soldier Palmer, Peter Ross.
Permission & Charges See Loch Laxavat Ard.

CARTACH, Loch See Loch Mor an Stairr.
CASGRO, Loch See Loch Spealdravat.

CEANN ALLAVAT, Loch
Location & Access 8/276390 The Pentland road joins the A858 from Carloway in the west to Loch Vatandip at 8/362338 in the east, and gives convenient access to a wide number of lochs on the west side of North Lewis. Begin this expedition from the Pentland road at 8/261370.
Commentary This is a major, nine mile, adventure over featureless, rough terrain. A compass and map are essential, as is wet weather gear and food for the journey. To properly explore the 11 lochs in the series, camp out at Loch Ceann Allavat in one of the ruined shielings at the north end of the loch. From the Pentland road, climb north-east over the obvious shoulder to the left of Cleitichean Beag to reach the first loch, Loch nan Cleitichean (8/271371). Loch nam Breac (8/281370), Fionn Allt Beag is next, half a mile east. Find the inlet burn on the east side of Loch nam Breac, by the island, and follow it north-east for 45 mins to reach Loch na Moineach (8/293384). Walk north-east again over gently rising ground for half a mile to find Loch nam Breac (8/330390). Descend due west for one and a half miles, passing little Loch an Fhraoich at 8/288391, to locate Loch Ceann Allavat. If you are staying overnight, consider a sortie further north to visit Loch nan Leac (8/279399), Ceann Allavat, and one of the most remote of the North Lewis waters, Loch Galavat (8/285405) one mile north from Loch Ceann Allavat. Return south, following the outlet stream from Loch Ceann Allavat, to little Loch Airigh Mhic Fhionnlaidh Dhuibh (8/279380) and its larger neighbour, Loch nan Caorach (8/275381). The outlet burn on the south-west shore of Loch nan Caorach will direct you to the last loch, Loch Mor Ghrianain (8/265376). At the first stream-junction, walk north-west up the hill to locate the loch. Descend half a mile to the Pentland road and the start point.
Fish These lochs are infrequently visited, particularly the small waters furthest out, and few see an artificial fly from one season to the next. The average weight of trout is about 8oz, but there are much larger fish as well. Loch Ceann Allavat has the best fish, averaging 10oz, but it also has a reputation of holding trout of over 4lb in weight. Towards the end of the season, after heavy rain, seatrout are sometimes encountered in Loch nam Breac, Loch Airigh Mhic Fhionnlaidh and in Loch Ceann Allavat. They run the Allt Fionn Beag burn after a hazardous, six-mile journey from the Abhainn Dhubh near Garynahine (8/234314).
Flies & Tactics Stay on the bank, not only from the point of view of safety, but also because fish tend to lie close to the margins, feeding. Wading only scares them out into the middle of the loch. On Loch Nam Breac, Allt Fionn Beag, fish the south end, by the inlet streams and round to the island. Do the same on Loch Ceann Allavat. The east shore is best on Loch nan Caorach. The other, smaller waters are easily covered from the bank and fish may be taken anywhere. Flies: Loch Ordie, Soldier Palmer, Blue Zulu.
Permission & Charges See Isles of Lewis and Harris introduction.

CHEARASAIDH, Loch See Loch Ruisavat.
CHOIN, Loch (Allt na Muilne) See Loch Cleit Steirmeis.

CHULAIN, Loch
Location & Access 8/184396 Approach from the A858 Breasclete/Carloway road at 8/202385. Follow the minor road west round the north end of Loch a'Bhaile (8/197383). Park at 8/190391 and climb north-west for 15 mins to reach the loch.
Commentary Rough going over broken moorland, but worth the effort. Also have a cast in the little lochan immediately to the north of Loch Chulain. On the way back to the car, and towards the end of the season, look out for seatrout in Loch Shader at 8/190389. Loch a'Bhaile can also provide sport with seatrout. Closer to the main road, by the Doune Braes Hotel, is Loch an Dunain (8/199400), ideal for a quick, passing cast. Whilst in the parish, also visit Loch na Muilne (8/205379) on the west side of the A858, and the three unnamed lochs which drain into Loch na Muilne on the moor to the east of the main road at 8/210377.
Fish Brown trout average 8oz, but larger fish are present and trout of over 1lb in weight are not uncommon, particularly on Loch a' Bhaile. Seatrout average approx. 1lb 8oz.
Flies & Tactics Bank fishing on all these lochs. The sea

OS Map 8 — Stornoway & North Lewis

floods into Loch a'Bhaile on high tides and this is the time to search for seatrout, particularly at the narrow, north-east end where the burn enters and down the north-east shore. Fish Loch a'Bhaile early in the season to avoid the weed growth of later months.
Flies: Loch Ordie, Soldier Palmer, Peter Ross.
Permission & Charges See Loch Laxavat Ard.

CHULAPUILL, Loch See Loch Grinnavat (Gress).
CLACHARAN, Loch See Loch Laxavat Ard.

CLEIT EIRMIS, Loch
Location & Access 8/243277 Begin from 8/234314 on the B8011 Garynahine/Timsgarry road. Walk the south bank of the Blackwater river to reach the first, unnamed, loch in the series at 8/242295. Loch Cleit Eirmis is a further one and a half miles south.
Commentary A round trip of seven lochs to the east of the B8011, covering some five miles across rough country where a compass and map, and knowing how to use them, are essential. From the first water, climb south-west to an unnamed lochan at 8/238291. Follow the outlet burn at the south-east corner to another, unnamed lochan, dominated by a small island, at 8/241288. Now climb south-west again to reach Loch na Cleith (8/237285) on the east side of Neipaval (90m). Descend south-east down the glen, passing a tiny lochan along the way, to arrive at the south end of Loch Cleit Eirmis after a walk of about 15 mins. Lunch. Have a cast in the satellite lochan at 8/239275 before exploring Loch Cleit Eirmis, working the east shore, north to the narrow, island-clad, pan-handle at the north end. Follow the outlet burn from Loch Cleit Eirmis down to the last loch in the walk, Loch Crogach (8/247290). Return to the start point via the south bank of the Blackwater river.
Fish Trout average about 6-8oz, but there are a few larger specimens as well. Loch Crogach is joined to the Blackwater river and there is always a chance of salmon and seatrout after heavy rain.
Flies & Tactics Few problems, other than finding your way round. The lochans are easily covered from the shore. In high winds, South Cleitshal (106m) to the east and Neipaval (90m) to the west can offer welcome shelter whilst fishing Loch Cleit Eirmis. The steep east bank of Loch Cleit Eirmis and the north narrows are the most productive fishing areas. Offer: Black Pennell, Grouse & Claret, Peter Ross.
Permission & Charges Details from The Garynahine Estate (see Loch an Fhada Bhig) and The Grimersta Estate, Callanish, Isle of Lewis. Tel: 01851 621358; Fax: 01851 621389. See also Isles of Lewis and Harris introduction.

CLEIT STEIRMEIS, Loch
Location & Access 8/230269 Park at 8/227297 on the B8011 Garynahine/Timsgarry road and walk south-east up the burn towards the west side of Neipaval (90m). Loch Cleit Steirmeis is two miles distant, reached after a walk of about one hour.
Commentary Loch Cleit Steirmeis lies in wild country and is shaped like a vast letter 'j'; with a one and a half mile north/south arm and wide leg at the south end which projects westward for half a mile. There are three other lochs which may be included in a visit, as well as a number of unnamed, largely unexplored, lochans to the south. The first water reached is Loch Choin (8/229285), in a natural gully on the hill with, a few minutes further south, the narrow north end of Loch Cleit Steirmeis. Fish down the east shore of Cleit Steirmeis, then explore the south shoreline. Work the north-west shore and locate the outlet burn by the promontory. Follow this north to reach Loch an Ois Ghuirm (8/227278) which is just under half a mile north/south by 300yds wide. Climb steeply west from Loch an Ois Ghuirm to fish Loch nam Fiasgan (8/219285). Return down the Allt na Muilne burn.
Fish The trout in these lochs vary in size and quality and average about 8oz. However, there are a few much larger specimens and fish of up to 7lb have been taken here. Be prepared.
Flies & Tactics This is a taxing hike but well worth the effort involved. Wading is not advisable. Trout may be taken from all round the shores of these waters, but the south and north banks of the west 'leg' of Loch Cleit Steirmeis are the most productive areas. Try: Blue Zulu, Soldier Palmer, Invicta.
Permission & Charges Details from the Grimersta Estate, Callanish, Isle of Lewis. Tel 01851 621358; Fax: 01851 621389.

CLIASAM CREAG, Loch See Loch Borasdale.
CNOC CHOILICH, Loch See Loch Beag Cnoc a Choilich.
COLL, River See Loch an Tobair.
COLLAVAL, Loch See OS Map 13.
CORRASAVAT, Loch See Loch Grinnavat, Gress.

CREED, River
Location & Access Source 8/342374 Outflow 8/420318 From the Stornoway/Balallan road at the bridge at 8/405326 where there are well-maintained paths. Access to the upper river is from the same point, or from the A858 Stornoway/Garynahine road at the bridge at 8/357324 for the upper river, and for the principal headwater lochs, Loch a'Chlachain (8/364324) and Loch an Ois (8/340328).
Commentary The River Creed is available to both local and visiting anglers alike. When Lord Leverhume, the one-time owner of Harris and Lewis, sold his estates early in the twentieth century, he bequeathed a large part of them - including the River Creed - in perpetuity, to the islanders. This inheritance is managed by the Stornoway Trust who let the salmon fishing on the River Creed and its lochs on a daily basis throughout the season. The river is divided into three, two-rod, rotating, beats, with two beats on each loch fishing from boats. The principal fishing is between the sea and these lochs, five miles of double bank with 13 main pools including: Junction, Long Pool, Falls Pool, Peatstack, Bridge Pool, Sheriff, Bend Pool, and, amongst the best pools, Dam and Bothy on Beat 2.
Fish A few salmon and seatrout are caught through-out the season, depending, as always, upon reasonable water levels. The 2000 season produced 34 salmon and 42 sea-trout. Salmon average 7-8lb, sea-trout 2lb.

37

Stornoway & North Lewis
OS Map 8

Flies & Tactics The river produces better sport than the lochs, although, in low water conditions, the lochs are generally more productive. The river is easily accessible and easily fished, without much need for wading. The upper river is narrow, changing to slower moving water between Loch a' Chlachain and the A859. From the road bridge, the river flows swiftly through a narrow gorge to reach the sea at Greeta Island. The lochs are shallow, approx. 45 acres each, and fish may be encountered almost anywhere. However, the best fishing areas are by the island and along the south shore on Loch a' Chlachain, and in the south and north bays on Loch an Ois. The most productive flies include: Stoat's Tail, Hairy Mary, Munro Killer, Silver Doctor, Thunder & Lightning, Ally's Shrimp, Black Pennell, Soldier Palmer, Kate Maclaren, Peter Ross.
Permission & Charges The Stornoway Trust, Estate Office, Stornoway, Isle of Lewis. Tel: 01851 702002. Prices for 1994 were: per rod per day, £12; boat fishing, with two rods fishing, £32 per day; evening fishing, half price.

CROSS REFERENCES See OS 13 for the following: Grimersta River; Loch an Earball; Loch na Plaide; Loch Faoghail Charrasan; Loch Ruadh Gheure Dubh Mhor; Loch an Fhir Mhaoil; Loch Sgaire; Loch Speireag; Loch Beag na Beiste; Loch na Beiste (Grimersta); Loch a'Bhraghad; Loch Aird (Grimersta); Loch na Faing; Loch a'Chaphail; Loch Collaval; Loch Smuaisaval; Loch na Muilne (Grimersta); Loch Mharcoil; Loch na Craobhaigh; Loch Gobhlach.

CUILC, Loch See Eye Peninsula.
DA LOCHAN FHEIDH, Loch See Loch Spealdravat.
DA LOCH FUAIMAVAT See Loch Tana.
DALBEG, Loch See Loch Raoinavat.
DELL River See Loch Dibadle.

DIBADALE, Loch
Location & Access 8/480613 Close to the village of South Dell and easily accessible.
Commentary A perfect little machair loch near two delightful bays, Dell Sands (8/489626) at the mouth of the Dell River, and Cross Sands (8/494628) by Airnistean. A track leads south-west from Loch Dibadale to Loch Drollavat, which is also a good trout fishery. The Dell River has no significant salmon or seatrout fishing interest other than the chance of an odd seatrout at the mouth of the river.
Fish Loch Dibadale has been stocked in recent years by the local angling association and it contains excellent quality trout which average 10-12oz, and some much larger fish. Loch Drollavat has trout of similar quality.
Flies & Tactics Both lochs are shallow but offer comfortable, safe wading. Use a long leader and fish fine and far off with: Black Pennell, Black Spider, Dunkeld. To extend the day, also visit Loch Leinavat (8/481600) and Loch Shiavat (8/476593), which is on the moor to the east of the A857. If Dibadale and Drollavat have been 'dour', these delightful little lochs will soon restore your confidence.

Permission & Charges See Isles of Lewis and Harris introduction.

DRIDEAN, Loch See Loch Vatacolla.
DROLLAVAT, Loch See Loch Dibadale.
DRUIM A'GHRIANAIN, Loch See Loch Mor Connaidh.
DRUIM NAN SGORACH, Loch See Loch Breugach.
DUBH A'CHLEITE, Loch See Loch Raoinavat.
DUBH AN DUINE, Loch See Loch na Scaravat.

DUBH GORMILEVAT, Loch
Location & Access 8/365435 Park at 8/389453 on the A857 Stornoway/Barvas road, by the bridge where the Cliastul burn passes under the road to join the Barvas River.
Commentary A five-mile hike round nine named and unnamed lochs on Barvas Mor and Druim Eidhbhat (100m) starting with a stiff uphill haul. From the car, follow the Cliastul burn down to the river. Cross, and walk 100yds upstream to where a burn enters at the right. Climb the north arm of this burn. The first water, Loch Bacavat (8/366450), is half a mile due west from the end of the burn. Ten minutes north-west from Loch Bacavat brings you to Loch Aoraidh (8/360455). Walk SSW now, for one mile to find Loch Kearstavat (8/350435). Locate the inlet stream on the east shore of Loch Kearstavat and follow it east, stopping for a glance at two unnamed lochans on the way at 8/356435 and 8/362435, to reach Loch Dubh Gormilevat (8/365435). Do not attempt to cross the outflow. From Loch Dubh Gormilevat, step south to have a cast in little Loch Eidhbhat (8/369430). End the day by tramping north-east, through the obvious saddle on the hill, and descend to Loch Eagasgro (8/373442). Track the outlet stream from Loch Eagasgro downhill to the Barvas river and your car.
Fish Lots of trout which average 6-8oz in weight.
Flies & Tactics Dangerous wading throughout the whole area. Avoid trouble and stay ashore. These lochs are infrequently visited and you should have little problem providing breakfast. Offer them: Black Zulu, Soldier Palmer, Alexandra.
Permission & Charges See Isles of Lewis and Harris introduction.

DUBH, Loch (Breasclete) See Loch Beinn nan Sgalag (West).
DUBH, Loch (Stornoway) See Loch Mor an Stairr.
DUBH SKIASGRO, Loch See Loch Mor a'Ghoba.
DUBH THURTAIL, Loch See Loch Tana.
DUBH A'GHOBHA, Loch See Loch Tana.
EAGASGRO, Loch See Loch Dubh Gormilevat.
EIDHBHAT, Loch See Loch Dubh Gormilevat.
EILASTER, Loch See Loch Laxavat Iorach.
EILEATIER, Loch See Loch an Fheoir.
EILEAVAT, Loch See Loch Glinnavat.
EILLAGVAL, Loch See Loch Sgeireach na Creige Brist.

ERERAY, Loch
Location & Access 8/328507 Leave the A858 road at 8/341489 and drive north through Brue (8/340496) to park at the end of the road (8/332505). Loch Ereray is immediately to your left.

OS Map 8 — Stornoway & North Lewis

Commentary A very attractive loch, close to the sea by the rocks of Sliegeag. Loch Mor Barvas (8/345500) lies to the east and this is a good point for an attack on both waters. Loch na Muilne (8/318496) is nearby, accessible from the Black House at 8/310493.
Fish Trout average 8oz and fight well. From time to time, larger specimens are taken, but they are the exception rather than the rule.
Flies & Tactics Comfortable wading on these shallow lochs, but approach with caution to avoid spooking the residents. Loch na Muilne has larger trout and both waters are easily covered from the shore. On Loch Ereray, concentrate at the south end where the River Ereray enters.
Permission & Charges See Isles of Lewis & Harris introduction.

ERERAY, River See Loch Ereray.
ERRAID, Loch See Loch Mor Connaidh.

EYE PENINSULA, Lochs
Location & Access 8/520330 The Eye Peninsula lies to the east of Stornoway along the A868, over the narrow Branahuie Banks causeway by St. Columba's Church to Knock and Aird.
Commentary There are nine small lochs on the Eye Peninsula and they are very rarely visited, given the attractions of the other North Lewis waters. This in itself makes them worth vistiting and all are easily accessible.
Fish Brown trout of modest proportions and the chance of seatrout from the sea on the north side of Branahuie Banks, Swordale Bay (8/489313), and Rubh an t-Sean Eich (8/493327).
Flies & Tactics The Eye Peninsula lochs are: Loch Branahuie (8/474324), Loch Swordale (8/502311) and its southern satellite, Loch Cuilc (8/507294), Loch an Duin (8/517303) by Lower Bayble, Loch Innis (8/549324) and Loch and t-Sidhein (8/546330) at Sheshader, Loch a Duin (8/556360) and Loch an Tiumpan (8/568370) near Aird. Flies: Black Zulu, Soldier Palmer, Silver Invicta.
Permission & Charges See Isles of Lewis and Harris introduction.

FAD ORAM, Loch See Loch Vatacolla.
FADA CAOL, Loch See Loch an Tobair.
FADA NAM FAOILEAG, Loch See Loch Mor Leig Tadh.
FAOGHAIL CHARRASAN, Loch See OS Map 13.
FAOILEAG, Loch See Loch Breugach.
FASGRO, Loch See Loch Borasdale.
FEATH LOCH GLEAHARAN See Loch Mor Connaidh.
FHRAOICH, Loch See Loch Laxavat.
FIONNACLEIT, Loch See Loch Almaistean.

FOISNAVAT, Loch
Location & Access 8/431507 Leave the A857 Barvas/Ness road at Loch an Duin in Shader (8/389543) and park at the end of the track (8/404530). Walk south-east for two miles to reach the loch after approximately one hour.

Commentary A wonderful day out in the hills, exploring Glen Shader and fishing Loch Keartavat (8/418523) and two small lochs along the way: Loch an Lobain (8/414529) and Loch Sgeireach, North Lewis (8/425515). The glen is scattered with the ruins of shielings where, in days past, whole families used to spend summer months grazing sheep and cattle on the heather and rough moorland grass.
Fish Nothing for the glass case but almost certainly plenty for breakfast.
Flies & Tactics The main lochs are perfect for beginners, both to trout fishing and to hill and moorland walking. They are generally safe to wade and fish rise and are taken from all round the shore. The smaller waters have room for a couple of exploratory casts on the way by. Offer them: Loch Ordie, March Brown, Peter Ross.
Permission & Charges See Isles of Lewis and Harris introduction.

FRYING PAN, Loch See Loch Buaile Bhig.
GAINEAMHAICH, Loch See Loch Vatacolla.

GAINMHEACH NAM FAOILEAG, Loch
Location & Access 8/316380. Park on the Pentland Road at 8/320351.
Commentary This is the start point for a visit to a group of seven lochs lying on the moorland between Beinn Mhaol Stacashal (171m), Stacashal (216m) and Druim a'Botha Clach (173m) to the west, and Beinn Chailein (231m), Beinn a'Sgridhe (268m), and Beinn Bhearnach (278m) to the east. Difficult walking conditions, particularly after rain, and it is best to try, as far as it is possible, to keep to the firmer, higher ground. Begin by contouring the east shoulder of Beinn Mhaol Stacashal to reach the first loch, Loch nan Stearnag (8/320370), after one mile. Leave from the north-east side and walk up to fish Loch Dubh nan Stearnag (8/326374) and Loch nan Steall (8/329377), the headwater lochs of the River Creed. A step north-west brings you to Loch nan Gainmhich (8/321380). On the way, stop for an investigative cast in the unnamed lochan at 8/326379. Now hike north-east for 15 mins to explore little Loch Leitir (8/33385), one of the headwater lochs of the River Arnol. A hard, 30 min. walk west brings you to the north end of Loch Gainmheach nam Faoileag, the principle source of the River Arnol. After fishing Loch Gainmheach nam Faoileag, and the west shore of Loch nan Stearnag, climb between Stacashal and Beinn Mhaol Stacashal to visit Loch nan Geadh (8/305363). Return to the car by walking SSW over the gully on Beinn Mhaol Stacashal.
Fish Good brown trout which average 8-10oz and the chance of larger fish of up to and over 1lb in weight. There is also the possibility of the odd salmon or seatrout, but only after very heavy rain and towards the end of the season.
Flies & Tactics There is a lot of fishing here. Loch nan Stearnag and Loch Gainmheach nam Faoileag are both half a mile long by up to 300yds wide and Loch na Gainmhich covers an area of approx. 40 acres. The east shore of Loch nan Stearnag is most productive,

39

Stornoway & North Lewis — OS Map 8

and there is a most convenient, long, promontory at the north end which gives easy access to a wide area. On Loch na Gainmhich, thrash the south-west shore and the long east shore on Loch Gainmheach nam Faoileag. The other waters noted above are more manageable and are comfortably covered from the shore. Flies: Black Pennell, March Brown, Silver Butcher.
Permission & Charges See Isles of Lewis and Harris introduction.

GALAVAT, Loch See Loch Ceann Allavat.
GARVAIG, Loch See Loch Mor a'Chocair.

GIL SPEIREIG MHOR, Loch
Location & Access 8/328304 Immediately to the north of the A858 Stornoway/Garynahine road.
Commentary One of a group of small lochs close to the main road and easily accessible. Lying between Beinn a'Bhuna (149m) to the south and Beinn nan Surrag (200m) and Eitshal (223m) to the north, they can provide shelter during strong winds. There are six lochs: Loch Gil Speireig, Loch nan Eilean (8/332305), Loch Beag Thoma Dhuibhe (8/338311), Loch na Linne (8/334302), Loch Tana (8/336297) and Loch nan Ramh (8/327300).
Fish With the exception of Loch nan Ramh, where trout of up to and over 2lb can be taken, not very large but lots of them.
Flies & Tactics These lochs are ideal for introducing beginners to flyfishing. They are easily fished from the shore and trout rise positively to: Black Pennell, Greenwell's Glory, Silver Butcher.
Permission & Charges See Isles of Lewis and Harris introduction.

GLINNAVAT, Loch
Location & Access 8/412545 Turn right in Five Penny Borve (8/409560), immediately after the church, and follow the peat road east to reach the loch.
Commentary A small loch covering an area of approximately eight acres, easily accessible. A few minutes walk east from Loch Glinnavat brings you to another good water of similar size, Loch Eileavat (8/419546). The Borve River, which drains Loch Eileavat, offers sport with the occasional seatrout where the stream enters the sea (8/408570).
Fish Good quality brown trout averaging 10oz.
Flies & Tactics Comfortable bank fishing and don't forget to have a cast in the little satellite loch attached to the north of Loch Glinnavat. Offer them: Ke-He, Soldier Palmer, Silver Invicta.
Permission & Charges See Isles of Lewis and Harris introduction.

GOBHLAICH, Loch See Loch an Fhada Bhig.
GOBLACH, Loch See OS Map 13.
GORMAG MOR, Loch See Loch Ionadargo.
GRASSAVAT, Lochan See Loch Ruisavat.
GRESS, Loch See Loch nan Leac (Clistul).
GRESS, River See Loch an Tobair.
GRINAVAT, Loch See Loch an Duna.
GRINNAVAT, Loch See Loch Raoinavat.

GRINNAVAT, Loch (Gress)
Location & Access 8/473450 Drive north from Stornoway on the B895 through Back and Gress and park at 8/506439. This is the start point for a visit to nine named and unnamed lochs lying to the north of the Gress River.
Commentary From the car, follow the outlet burn to the first water, Loch Bacavat (8/502442), which is reached after five minutes. Head north-west from Loch Bacavat to find its neighbour, Loch Corrasavat (8/498447). Walk the inlet burn from the south-west corner of Loch Corrasavat up to the unnamed loch at 8/491448, and then north over the hill to the unnamed water at 8/491452 which drains into Loch Sgeireach Mor (8/490457) - see Loch Mor a'Ghoba. Now head south-west for quarter of a mile to fish Loch Langavat (8/483446), and then north-west for half a mile to find Loch Grinnavat, which drains into the Gress River and is the mid-point of the expedition. Leave Loch Grinnavat at the south end and walk ten minutes south-east to little Loch a'Chairn. Continue south-east for half a mile to Loch Chulapuill (8/485439). Descend from Loch Chulapuill, cross the burn, and climb to the last water in the series, Loch Beinn Iobheir (8/495436), before returning to the car.
Fish In times past, when the Gress River was 'managed', salmon and seatrout could reach Loch Grinnavat and Loch a'Chairn and, indeed, even Loch Langavat, but their main interest today is as trout fisheries. Expect pretty brown trout from all these lochs, averaging 8oz, with a few larger fish of up to and over 1lb in weight.
Flies & Tactics A glorious day out, but you will need compass and map to navigate round. Bank fishing, with the chance of great sport all round. First cast: Ke-He, Invicta, Black Pennell.
Permission & Charges See Isles of Lewis and Harris introduction.

GRINNAVAT, Loch, Stornoway See Loch Mor an Stairr.
GROGACH, Loch See Loch Cleit Eirmis.
GROSAVAT, Loch See Loch Ionadargo.

GRUNAVAT, Loch (Leurbost)
Location & Access 8/377261 Approach from Leurbost on OS Map 14 at 14/378259. The loch is to the left of the school.
Commentary An easily accessible loch with a good track running along the east shoreline. From the north end of the loch, leave the track and walk west to visit tiny Loch Ta (8/371263) and its larger neighbour, Loch na Buaile Gharbha (8/367263).
Fish Supper-sized trout.
Flies & Tactics Easy bank fishing with the best chance of sport coming from the west end of Loch na Buaile Gharbha. Show them: Blue Zulu, Grouse & Claret, Alexandra.
Permission & Charges Contact Sportsworld, 1 Francis Street, Stornoway, Isle of Lewis. Tel: (01851) 705464.

GUNNA, Loch
Location & Access 8/405415 Adjacent to the A857

OS Map 8

Stornoway & North Lewis

Stornoway/Barvas road. Park at 8/398414 by the small plantation and walk east to reach the loch in five minutes.
Commentary An easily accessible loch, quarter of a mile long, covering an area of some 20 acres. To the west of the A857, and about ten mins up the hill above Gleann Airigh na Faing, is another good little loch which also offers sport: Loch an Brathan Mor at OS8/390418. If things are dull on Loch Gunna, make for Loch na Brathan Mor.
Fish Trout average 6-8oz, but plenty of them to keep the interest up.
Flies & Tactics Wading is uncomfortable and largely unnecessary on Gunna and fish rise and are taken all round the loch. The east end, by the three inlet burns, is perhaps the most productive area. Little Loch na Brathan Mor is easily covered from the bank. Try: Black Pennell, Grouse & Claret, Peter Ross.
Permission & Charges See Isles of Lewis and Harris introduction.

HATRAVAT, Lochan
Location & Access 8/533554 Approach from the A857 at Lionel (8/530635). Drive south-east along the B8015 on to a good peat road and park at Cuiashader Shielings (8/540582). Walk SSW by the stream to reach Loch Bacavat Cross (8/532570). Continue south on the line of the same stream to reach Lochan Hatravat after a hike of about one hour.
Commentary Lochan Hatravat is a local water supply and is joined in the west to Loch Neil Bhain (OS8/529555). Both waters cover an area of some 40 acres and lie in a remote, moorland setting, surrounded by a number of ruined shielings. Return to Cuiashader via little Loch Bacavat Ard (OS8/559557) and Loch Bacavat Iorach (OS8/559564), which lie on the cliffs above Cellar Head.
Fish Loch Bacavat Cross contains trout which average 6-8oz, as do Loch Bacavat Ard and the main body of Lochan Hatravat. Loch Bacavat Iorach has larger trout, but the best fishing is to be found at the south end of Loch Hatravat and in adjoining Loch Neil Bhain where trout of up to and over 3lb may be caught.
Flies & Tactics Rarely visited and good bank fishing. Stay on the bank and avoid wading. Concentrate your effort along the south-west shore of Lochan Hatravat, offering them: Black Pennell, Wickham's Fancy, Silver Butcher.
Permission & Charges See Isles of Lewis and Harris introduction.

HATRAVAT, Lower Loch
Location & Access 8/377516 Leave the A857 Barvas/Ness road in Upper Barvas at 8/366512. Park on the peat road and follow the track out to Lower Loch Hatravat, an easy walk of 15 mins.
Commentary After fishing Lower Loch Hatravat, visit Upper Loch Hatravat (8/383510) which lies a quarter of a mile to the south-east. Follow the inlet stream at the north-east corner of Lower Loch Hatravat to reach its neighbour after about ten minutes. To extend the day, continue south-east for a quarter of a mile to fish Loch Niosavat (8/390507), then on again to visit Loch na Craoibhe (8/401500) and Loch Sleitir (8/409498) at the head of Glen Ordale. The more remote lochs are very rarely visited but were an important grazing area in days gone by. Families would spend the warm summer months here, tending their livestock, and the ruins of more than twenty shielings scatter the moor.
Fish The Hatravats contain good stocks of bright little trout which average 8oz. Loch Niosavat, Loch na Craoibhe and Loch Sleitir contain larger trout, a few of which weigh over 1lb.
Flies & Tactics Wading requires care on the Hatravats due to the soft, muddy bottom. Indeed, it is better to stay safely ashore whilst fishing all these waters; trout lie close to the bank and wading only scares them out into the middle of the loch. Pay particular attention to the east shore of Loch na Craoibhe. Offer them: Blue Zulu, Wickham's Fancy, Peter Ross.
Permission & Charges See Isles of Lewis and Harris introduction.

HATRAVAT, Upper Loch See Hatravat, Lower Loch.
HONAGRO, Loch See Loch an Duin (Carloway).
INNIS, Loch See Eye Peninsula.
INNSEAG, Loch See Loch Tom an Fheidh.
IOBHAIR, Loch See Loch Tom an Fheidh.

IONADAGRO, Loch
Location & Access 8/511465 Drive north from Stornoway along the B895 to North Tolsta. At 8/534480, turn left on the peat road and after crossing the Allt na Muilne burn, park at 8/525481.
Commentary A tramp round a series of seven easily accessible lochs to the west of the village of North Tolsta, scattered amidst heather moorland and small glens. The first water, Loch Lingavat Beag (OS8/522481) is five minutes from the car. A long, narrow unnamed loch is next at OS8/522474, followed by Loch na Muilne (OS8/522471) and Loch Tanavat (OS8/521469). Now walk south-west from Loch Tanavat for ten minutes to reach Loch Ionadagro. Return via the south shore of Loch Tanavat to fish Loch Grosavat (OS8/525470) which is conveniently surrounded by a good peat track. North now to explore Loch Gormag Mor (OS8/527475), the highest point of the walk (118m), before returning to the car. Wonderful views over North Tolsta to the Minch. Also, a superb one and a half mile long beach between Tolsta Head and the site of Caisteal a' Mhorair fort, where the Allt na Muilne enters the sea.
Fish All these lochs hold good stocks of brown trout which average 6-8oz in weight. There are a few larger specimens but fish of over 1lb are rare. Nevertheless, great fun and the place to take beginners.
Flies & Tactics Comfortable bank fishing. By the little island on the north shore of Loch Lingavat Beag is a good place to start, but trout rise and are caught from all round the shores of all these lochs so cast with confidence. Try: Black Zulu, Wickham's Fancy, Peter Ross. Seatrout may be encountered at the mouth of the Allt na Muilne burn, off Traigh Mhor beach, particularly after heavy rain.

Stornoway & North Lewis OS Map 8

Permission & Charges See Isles of Lewis and Harris introduction.

KEARSAVAT, Loch See Loch Rumsagro.
KEARSTAVAT, Loch See Loch Dubh Gormileavat.
KEARTAVAT, Loch See Loch Foisnavat.

LANGAVAT, Loch (Carloway)
Location & Access 8/216438 Leave the A858 Carloway/Barvas road at 8/226431, at the bend in the road, and drive north towards Dalmore to park at 8/221441. Walk west up the hill for ten minutes to reach the loch.
Commentary A long, narrow water extending south/north for almost half a mile. If things are quiet on Loch Langavat, walk north-west for a further ten minutes to find Loch Skorashal (OS8/207444), just as delightful to fish and sometimes very rewarding indeed.
Fish Glass case country, at least as far as Loch Langavat is concerned, but they are very hard to tempt. Hope for trout of up to and over 4lb in weight.
Flies & Tactics Bank fishing and start at the south end where a convenient, long, finger-like promontory points north. The area round the little island off the north-west shore should also be fished. Little Loch Skorashal is easily covered from the bank. Offer them: Black Zulu, Grouse & Claret, Peter Ross.
Permission & Charges See Isles of Lewis and Harris introduction.

LANGAVAT, Loch (Gress) See Loch Grinnavat (Gress).
LANGAVAT, Loch (North Lewis) See Loch Sgeireach na Creige Brist.
LATHAMUL, Loch See Loch Buaile Bhig.

LAXAVAT ARD, Loch
Location & Access 8/245380 Immediately adjacent and to the south of the Pentland Road. Park at 8/245388 where the River Ohagro enters the north end of the loch.
Commentary One of the principal lochs on the headwaters of the Carloway River, shallow, scattered with islands, and covering an area of some 60 acres. The loch is divided into two sections, and offers a wonderful day out in the rugged hills between the Pentland Road and the A858 Breasclete/Carloway road to the west. This is rough country, so be well-shod and ready for some hard walking. The more adventurous might care to explore the smaller lochs to the south: Loch na Beiste (OS8/250373), Loch na Braiste (OS8/253370) and Loch Sandavat (OS8/250370); and further west, Loch Clacharan (OS8/243367) and little Loch an Fhraoich (OS8/238364). They can also be reached from OS8/262370 on the Pentland Road by climbing the hill directly to the west of the road and following the inlet burn down to Loch na Braiste. Loch Clacharan and Loch an Fhraoich are best attacked from the minor road which links the Pentland Road to Breasclete. If approaching from Loch Laxavat Ard, climb from the south end of the loch to reach the other waters noted.
Fish Trout average 6-8oz.
Flies & Tactics Bank fishing, and it is safest to stay ashore. The south bay on Loch Laxavat Ard is first-class, as is the area around the islands off the promontory which almost divides the loch in two. The other waters are adequately covered from the shore. Flies: Blue Zulu, Soldier Palmer, Peter Ross.
Permission & Charges Fishing is managed by the Carloway Angling Club and permits should be purchased at Carloway Post Office, prior to fishing. The lochs are open to residents and visitors staying in the Carloway area. Day ticket: £3; Weekly: £5. Contact Carloway Post Office for details. Tel: (01851) 643388.

LAXAVAT IORACH, Loch
Location & Access 8/230390 Park on the Pentland Road at the north end of the loch at 8/229388. Little Loch Earraid is on your left.
Commentary Loch Laxavat Iorach extends north/south for a distance of almost one mile and is up to 350yds wide. The loch is easily accessible from the Pentland Road and offers good sport in very lovely surroundings. Even nicer, is to tramp off into the hills and explore the lochs to the south and west of Loch Laxavat Iorach; hard walking over rough terrain, but superb, away-from-it-all fishing. A compass and map are essential to find your way round this series of seven named and unnamed waters. At the south end of Loch Laxavat Iorach, follow the inlet stream up the glen to Loch Beinn nan Sgalag (8/228370), a distance of half a mile. Have a careful look at the lochan to the south of Loch Beinn nan Sgalag at 8/227369 whilst you are there. Now, locate the outlet stream at the north end and march north to reach Loch Amar Sine, having a cast along the way in the lochan before fishing Loch Amar Sine at 8/225374. Loch Eilaster (8/225387) is next, five minutes north again from Loch Amar Sine. Leave from the north end of Loch Eilaster through the gully to the north-east, to find two good unnamed lochans at 8/225387 and 8/223398. Rejoin the west shore of Loch Laxavat Iorach and fish back to the start point and the Pentland Road.
Fish Lots of fun with very pretty trout which average 6-8oz, and, in the smaller lochs, the chance of some larger fish. Always the possibility of encountering salmon and seatrout in Loch Laxavat Iorach, which is on the headwaters of the Carloway River.
Flies & Tactics On Loch Laxavat Iorach work the east shore. The first promontory and the island bay is generally kind, and pay particular attention as you move further south to the large island which guards the Leig Mhuthoir, the inlet burn from Loch Laxavat Ard (8/227369). You will quickly get the feel of the other, smaller waters, and on Loch Eilaster, which is nearly half a mile long, concentrate your effort along the east shoreline and the shallow north bay. Flies to try: Ke-He, March Brown, Black Pennell.
Permission & Charges See Loch Laxavat Ard.

LEINAVAT, Loch See Loch Dibadale.
LEINISCAL, Loch See Loch Breugach.

OS Map 8 — Stornoway & North Lewis

LEIRAVAY, River See Loch Buaile Bhig.
LEISAVAT, Loch See Loch Rumsagro.
LEITIR, Loch See Loch Gainmheach nam Faoileag.
LINGAVAT BEAG, Loch See Loch Ionadargo.
LINGAVAT MOR, Loch See Loch Vatacolla.
LOCHAVAT, Loch See Loch an Daimh (Aird Skapraid).
MARAVAT, Loch See Loch an Duin.
MEADHONACH, Lochan See Loch Sgeireach na Creige Brist.
MHARCOIL, Loch See OS Map 13.

MILLEHO, Loch
Location & Access 8/422390 Park by Loch Dubh (8/410383) - small trout averaging 6oz - walk NNE up the hill for 30 mins to reach the loch.
Commentary Visit Milleho as much for the vista as for the fishing. The loch lies on the top of the hill at about 100m, giving a splendid, panoramic view of the island. A step further on is Loch Bhreagleit (8/429396), which is just as much fun to visit. To complete your enjoyment, walk north-west to explore the little unnamed lochs and lochans at 8/421401, the largest of which is a secondary source of the Coll River.
Fish Nothing for the glass case, but almost certainly something for supper.
Flies & Tactics Tough going, particularly after rain. Approach with caution and fish carefully from the shore. Do not wade. Tempt them with: Soldier Palmer, March Brown, Silver Invicta.
Permission & Charges See Isles of Lewis and Harris introduction.
MOR A'CHROTAICH, Loch See Loch Buaile Bhig.

MOR A'GHOBA, Loch
Location & Access 8/485471 Drive north from Stornoway along the B895 through Back and Gress and park in Glen Tolsta at 8/520458. Follow the peat track that heads due west onto the moor and begin this expedition at Loch Tarstavat (8/508459), a walk of 15 mins from the car.
Commentary Make an early start for this long day out in the hills. You will climb to 110m, covering seven miles through wonderful moorland scenery, fishing 12 named and unnamed lochs along the way. Compass and map country, so be well prepared. After Loch Tarstavat, continue north-west to its neighbour, Loch Sandavat (8/505461). Cross the inlet stream at the north end and walk north-west again for half a mile to reach an unnamed loch at 8/501469. Skirt the south shore of Loch Beag Sgeireach at 8/497471 (see Loch Vatacolla) and after a further half mile, reach Loch Mor a'Ghoba. Explore Loch Mor a'Ghoba, and its little satellite loch to the north, before walking the inlet stream west to Loch a'Chitear (8/480470) and its small neighbour, unnamed, at 8/481468. Now head south-west over the moor for ten minutes to Loch Dubh Skiasgro (8/469465) which drains into the Gress River. Leave Loch Dubh Skiasgro along the inlet burn at the south-east corner to visit the unnamed loch at 8/478459. Then walk north-east to Loch nan Geadh (8/483463), and Loch Airigh Choinnich (8/489466). After fishing Loch Airigh Choinnich, turn south, stopping for a cast in the unnamed loch at 8/490461, to examine Loch Sgeireach Mor (8/490457), the largest loch in the group covering 40 acres. There are also two further unnamed lochs within striking distance, at 8/495465 and at 8/498461, which can be rewarding. For non-fishing members of your party, there are lovely beaches nearby: at Traigh Mor and Giordale Sands at North Tolsta, and, more remote, Shielavig Mor (8/514431).
Fish Good sport all the way with the chance of some really nice trout; particularly in the unnamed loch at 8/501469 and the little unnamed loch to the south of Loch a'Chitear. For the rest, expect good fun with hard fighting fish which average 6-8oz.
Flies & Tactics Hard going over rough ground but comfortable bank fishing all round. Avoid wading, it only scares the fish. Stay ashore and offer them: Black Pennell, Grouse & Claret, Kingfisher Butcher.
Permission & Charges See Isles of Lewis and Harris introduction.

MOR A'CHOCAIR, Loch
Location & Access 8/347344
Commentary Loch Mor a'Chocair is a small loch which lies immediately adjacent and to the north of the Pentland Road. It drains through its neighbour, Loch Beag a'Chocair (8/342347) into the River Creed. Little Loch na Cairteach (8/342349), to the north of Loch Beag a'Chocair, also feeds the system. Two further waters, to the east, Loch nan Caorann (8/360351) and Lock Garvaig (8/375353) drain east into the River Laxdale.
Fish Small brown trout which average 8oz in weight.
Flies & Tactics Bank fishing. Park at 8/345344 to visit Mor a'Chocair, Beag a'Chocair and Loch na Cairteach. Park at 8/360339 to visit the other waters noted. Try: Ke-He, March Brown and Silver Butcher.
Permission & Charges Sportsworld, Francis St, Stornoway, Isle of Lewis. Tel: 01851 705464.

MOR A'GHRIANAIN, Loch See Loch Buaile Bhig.

MOR CONNAIDH, Loch
Location & Access 8/251398 From the Pentland road (see Loch Ceann Allavat) at 8/245388, at the north end of Loch Laxavat Ard (8/245380). Park where the River Ohagro crosses under the road.
Commentary A splendid day out in the hills to the north of the Pentland road fishing eight named and unnamed lochs. You will cover four and a half miles over rugged ground. Follow the River Ohagro north and at the first junction, walk north-east over the hill to drop down to Loch Mor Connaidh. From Loch Mor Connaidh, hike north-west via the little unnamed lochan at 8/249399 to reach Loch Sandavat at 8/246403. At the north end of Loch Sandavat, tramp the inlet burn to Feath Loch Gleaharan (8/243411). Walk west now for half a mile to locate little Loch Tom Liavrat (8/233413) as you descend the hill. A one-mile walk due south brings you back to the Pentland road via two small, productive lochs: Loch Druim a'Ghrianain (8/237400) and Loch Erraid (8/229399). Turn left down the Pentland road to reach your car.

43

Stornoway & North Lewis   OS Map 8

Fish Excellent numbers of bright little trout which average 8oz in weight as well as good numbers of larger fish over 1lb. At the end of the season, and after heavy rain, look out for seatrout and the odd salmon which can enter from the River Carloway.

Flies & Tactics Bank fishing, and all these waters are easily covered from the shore. For an extra challenge, consider climbing the hill to the east of Loch Sandavat to have a cast in the unnamed lochan on the top at 8/256406. Years pass without residents ever seeing an artificial fly. Try: Black Zulu, Ke-He, Silver Invicta.

Permission & Charges Contact: Sportsworld, 1 Francis Street, Stornoway, Isle of Lewis. Tel: (01851) 705464.

MOR EILEAVAT, Loch See Loch Tana.
MOR GHRIANAIN, Loch See Loch Ceann Allavat.

MOR LEIG TADH, Loch

Location & Access 8/498518 Approach as for Loch Tana.

Commentary A four mile round trip to visit a series of named and unnamed lochs to the north of the Abhainn Geiraha (River Garry). The first water, Loch Sgeireach a'Ghlinn Mhoir (8/517510), the largest, is reached after a walk of 15 mins from the end of the peat track. Fish the north shore as you pass. Continue north-west to reach Loch Tana Nan Leac (8/513516). Quarter of a mile further north-west is little Loch Fada nam Faoileag (8/504519). Now walk due west for ten minutes to reach Loch Mor Leig Tadh, the mid-point of your journey. Immediately to the south of Loch Mor Leig Tadh is Loch Beag Leig Tadh (8/496515). Fish this and then walk east for half a mile to reach a group of three unnamed lochans at 8/505515. Return south-east to the start point, fishing the south shore of Loch Sgeireach a'Ghlinn Mhoir along the way.

Fish Some really good fish of up to and over 2lb in weight, but mostly hard fighting little trout which average 8oz.

Flies & Tactics All the waters are easily covered from the bank and there is really no need to wade. Offer the residents a choice of: Black Zulu, Soldier Palmer, Silver Invicta.

Permission & Charges See Isles of Lewis and Harris introduction.

MOR, Loch See Loch Tana.
MOR SANDAVAT, Loch (Clistul) See Loch nan Leac (Clistul).
MOR SANDAVAT, Loch (Tolsta) See Loch Tana.
MOR SGEIREACH, Loch See Loch Vatacolla.

MOR SOVAL, Loch (Arnish)

Location & Access 8/423276 Drive south from Stornoway on the A859 and turn left on the B897 to Crossbost. Turn left again at 8/393275 on the minor road to Grimshader and park at 8/403260. Walk north-east on the peat road to the north of Ben Casgro.

Commentary A wonderful day out on South Arnish Moor, fishing a series of named and unnamed lochs and lochans. You will require a compass and map and accurate navigation to find your way around, over rough country. Loch nan Capull (8/411264) is first, reached a few minutes' walk after the end of the peat road. Follow the inlet stream at the north shore of the loch up to two unnamed lochans at 8/414268 and 8/415266. Ten minutes further east is Lochan nan Cnamh (8/420266), which is really two adjacent waters. Walk north now for a quarter of a mile to find Loch an Fheoir (8/415273). Follow the inlet stream from Loch an Fheoir north, past the unnamed lochan at 8/420273, to locate Loch Mor Soval. Lunch by the loch then head north-west to reach Loch na h-Earaig (8/419281). Now walk south-west to lovely Loch nan Eilean (8/415276) and south-west again to tiny Loch Beinn Bhreac at 8/408271. Visit Loch nan Cnamh (8/403270), the best loch of them all, before returning to the start point via little Loch Beag (8/405267) and Loch na Cois (8/411263).

Fish You will enjoy good sport with fine trout which average 6-8oz, with the chance of the odd fish of up to 14oz.

Flies & Tactics On a clear day, one of the most splendid fishing walks in the world; marvellous scenery, wildlife, and exciting bank fishing all the way. The lochs are easily covered from the shore and the best flies include: Ke-He, Grouse & Claret, Silver Butcher.

Permission & Charges See Isles of Lewis and Harris introduction.

MOR AN STAIRR, Loch

Location & Access 8/395387 Approach via the line of the disused railway which leaves the A857 Stornoway/Barvas road two miles north from Stornoway at 8/414374.

Commentary Loch Mor an Stairr is the Stornoway water supply, one mile long by up to quarter of a mile wide, and it lies at the centre of a group of ten lochs between the A857 and Ben Barvas (180m) and Beinn Mholach (292m); all within easy distance of town, and all offering good sport. Follow the inlet burn at the north end of Loch Mor an Stairr to reach Loch Beag an Stairr (8/395387), and then ten minutes north-west to reach Loch nan Clach (8/384400). Immediately to the south and west of Loch Mor an Stairr, there are five unnamed lochs, passed on the way out to Loch na Cartach (8/378386) on the lower slopes of Ben Barvas. The most remote loch is Loch nam Breac (8/382376), half a mile south from Loch na Cartach. Whilst there, have a cast in the unnamed loch immediately to the east at 8/386376. More easily accessible, and to the south of the track out to Loch Mor an Stairr, is Loch Sgeireach (8/402371). Further south again, and approached by a good track from Grianan (8/419358), is Loch Grinnavat (8/406362). Loch Roisnavat (8/400398), by the side of the A857 road, is now a private rainbow trout fishery. To the east, its tiny neighbours, Loch Tom an Rishal (8/403399) and Loch Dubh (8/410383).

Fish Loch Mor an Stairr holds the best trout which average 10-12oz with good numbers of fish of over 1lb as well. Loch Beag an Stairr can also produce good quality trout, as does Loch nam Breac.

OS Map 8 — Stornoway & North Lewis

Flies & Tactics All these lochs are attacked from the bank. Fish the south and west shore of Loch Mor an Stairr, and the north end, where the burn enters from Loch Cartach. The other waters are easily explored and covered and fish may be taken from all round the shorelines. You will not go home empty-handed. First cast: Ke-He, Soldier Palmer, Peter Ross.
Permission & Charges See Isles of Lewis & Harris introduction.

MUAVAT, Loch See Loch Breivat.
NA BA RIABHAICH, Loch See Loch an Tuim (Pentland Road).
NA BEINNE BIGE, Loch See Loch an Tuim (Pentland Road).
NA BEISTE, Loch (Carloway) See Loch Laxavat Ard.
NA BEISTE, Loch (Grimersta) See OS Map 13.
NA BRAISTE, Loch See Loch Laxavat Ard.
NA BRATHAN MOR, Loch See Loch Gunna.
NA BUAILE GHARBHA, Loch See Loch Grunavat, Leurbost
NA CAIRTEACH, Loch See Loch Mor a'Chocair.
NA CISTE, Loch See Loch an Tobair.
NA CLEITH, Loch See Loch Cleit Eirmis.
NA CLOICH, Loch See Loch Vatacolla.
NA COIS, Loch See Loch Mor Soval (Arnish).
NA CRAOBHAIG, Loch See OS Map 13.
NA CRAOIBHE, Loch (Glen Ordale) See Hatravat (Lower Loch).
NA CREIGE GUIRME, Loch See Loch na Craoibhe.
NA EILEAN, Loch, Arnish See Loch Mor Soval (Arnish).
NA FAING, Loch See Loch nan Leac (Clistul).
NA FOLA, Loch See Loch an Tobair.
NA GAINMHICH, Loch See Loch Gainmheach nam Faoileag.
NA GAINMHICH, Loch (Achmore). See Loch na Craoibhe.
NA GAINMHICH, Loch (Breasclete) See Loch an Tuim (Pentland Road).
NA GEADH, Loch See Loch Mor a'Ghoba.

NA H-AIRDE, Loch
Location & Access 8/175427 In Carloway (8/206427), follow the minor road north towards Garenin (8/191442) and park at 8/200434.
Commentary Start point for a wildlife/angling hike of three miles out to the Berie Lighthouse at Aird Laimishader (115m), exploring a series of five named and unnamed lochs along the way. Rough going with numerous ups and downs, but nothing too serious. Leave the car and fish the loch immediately to the west at 8/197434. Exit from the west bank to reach Loch Breivat (8/194434). A further ten minutes WNW towards the coast brings you to a little unnamed lochan at 8/196436. Now walk the cliff line south-west for twenty minutes to Loch Runageo (8/179433), then follow the glen round the west side of Aird Laimishader to Loch na h-Airde. Return the same way, catching the ones that got away on the outward journey.
Fish Nothing large, but good sport with trout which average 6-8oz.

Flies & Tactics The bay at Garenin is the place to park those not inclined to hike, but this expedition is a good place to introduce little ones to hill walking and hill loch fishing. Bank fishing, and all the waters are easily covered from the shore. Tempt them with: Soldier Palmer, Grouse & Claret, Alexandra.
Permission & Charges See Isles of Lewis and Harris introduction.

NA H-AIRIGH UISGE, Loch See Loch Nisreaval.
NA H-EARAIG, Loch See Lor Mor Soval (Arnish).
NA LEAC, Loch (Beinn Tulagaval) See Loch Suainagadail.
NA LEAMHAIN, Loch See Loch an Tuim (Pentland Road).
NA LINNE, Loch See Loch Gil Speireig.
NA MOINEACH, Loch See Loch Ceann Allavat.
NA MUILNE, Loch See Loch Lonadargo.
NA MUILNE, Loch (Arnol) See Loch Ereray.
NA MUILNE, Loch (Grimersta) See OS Map 13.
NA MUILNE, Loch (North Shawbost) See Loch an Duna.
NA MUILNE, Loch (South Shawbost) See Loch Raoinavat.
NA MUILNE, Loch (Stiapavat) See Loch Stiapavat.
NA MUILNE, Loch (Tolsta Chaolais) See Loch Chulain.
NA PLAIDE, Loch See OS Map 13.

NA SCARAVAT, Loch
Location & Access 8/357405. Park on the A857 Stornoway/Barvas road at 8/398425. Walk west, keeping Loch na Brathan Mor, 8/390428, to the north, to reach the first loch in this expedition, Loch Sgaravat Beag (8/360415), after an arduous two mile tramp over rough, rising ground.
Commentary A tough walk of some eight miles, visiting five remote lochs lying to the north of Ben Barvas (280m) and Beinn Mholach (292m). Choose a good, dry, day because the moor becomes very wet and soggy after rain. Pack compass and map. You will need them. After fishing Loch Sgaravat Beag, walk south for half a mile to find the north end of Loch na Scaravat. Work round the west shore, stepping west to explore Loch Dubh an Duine (OS8/352406) as you go, and then strike south-west for 20 mins to reach the most distant water, Loch nan Caorann (OS8/343495). Return to fish the east shoreline of Loch na Scaravat and then walk east to find an unnamed lochan at OS8/370407. An hour further east, descending through Gleinn Airigh na Faing, brings you back to Loch na Brathan Mor and the main road.
Fish Worth the effort involved and the chance of some really nice trout which average 8-10oz and larger specimens as well.
Flies & Tactics Stay on the bank. Loch Sgaravat Beag is a long, narrow water, almost half a mile in length and wind direction will dictate which shore you fish. The east bank of Loch na Scaravat is perhaps the most productive, particularly the south bay and the north east bay. On Loch Dubh an Duine and Loch nan Caorann, cast with confidence everywhere. Flies: Black Zulu, Invicta, Dunkeld.

45

Stornoway & North Lewis — OS Map 8

Permission & Charges See Isles of Lewis and Harris introduction.

NAM BREAC, Loch (Druim a'Botha Chlach) See Loch Ceann Allavat.
NAM BREAC, Loch (Fionn Allt Beag) See Loch Ceann Allavat.
NAM BREAC, Loch (Stornoway) See Lochan a'Sgeil.
NAM BREAC, Loch (Stornoway) See Loch Mor an Stairr.
NAM FALCAG, Loch See Loch na Craoibhe.
NAM FIASGAN, Loch See Loch Cleit Steirmeis.
NAN CAORACH, Loch See Loch Ceann Allavat.
NAN CAORANN, Loch See Loch Tana.
NAN CAORANN, Loch (Ben Hulabie) See Loch Mor a'Chocair.
NAN CAORANN, Loch (Ben Mholach) See Loch na Scaravat.
NAN CAPULL, Loch See Loch Mor Soval (Arnish).

NAN CLABAN, Loch
Location & Access 8/525586. Approach as for Lochan Hatravat. At Cuiashader walk north-west for one mile to reach the loch.
Commentary A pleasant, infrequently visited, loch covering an area of four acres.
Fish Contains brown trout which average 6oz and a few larger specimens.
Flies & Tactics Easy bank fishing all round.
Permission & Charges See Isles of Lewis and Harris introduction.

NAN CLACH, Loch (Stornoway) See Loch Mor an Stairr.
NAN CLEITICHEAN, Loch See Loch Ceann Allavat.
NAN CNAMH, Loch See Loch Mor Soval (Arnish).
NAN CULAIDHEAN, Loch See Loch an Fhada Bhig.
NAN DEAREAG, Loch (Arnish) See Loch Buaile Bhig.
NAN EILEAN, Loch (Achmore). See Loch Gil Speireig
NAN GEADH, Loch (Stacashal). See Loch Gainmheach nam Faoileag.
NAN LAOGH, Loch (Orasay) See Loch Orasay.
NAN LEAC, Loch (Ceann Allavat) See Loch Ceann Allavat.

NAN LEAC, Loch (Cliastul)
Location & Access 8/430483. Park on the A857 Stornoway/Barvas road at 8/389453 by the bridge where the Cliastul burn crosses the road.
Commentary This is the start point for a major fishing expedition; walking seven miles over rough, featureless terrain, visiting ten lochs and lochans along the way. A compass and map are essential. Set off north-east over gently rising ground for two miles to find the first loch, Loch Taravat (8/425463). Exit south. The north end is boggy. Ten minutes' walk brings you to the largest water, Loch Mor Sandavat (8/435467), three quarters of a mile long, covering an area of 50 acres, divided into two sections. From Loch Mor Sandavat, head north to Lochan Sandavat (8/432475), then north again to find Loch nan Leac. There are two smaller waters to the north of Loch nan Leac which are also worth a visit: Loch Allavat (8/431489) and Loch an Umhlaich (8/435488). At this point, decide if you wish to continue north-east for one mile to fish Loch Gress (8/450502), one of the most distant of the North Lewis lochs; or, from Loch nan Leac, walk west for ten minutes to explore Loch na Faing (8/423487). Return to the start point by retracing your steps, catching the ones you missed on the way out; or walk smartly south-west over Gleann Euscleit, which is lined with ruined summer shielings, to fish the little unnamed lochan with the island at 8/414477 and shallow Loch nan Stearnag (8/405475). From Loch nan Stearnag, descend from the moor to the main road and your car.
Fish Trout of between 6oz and over 3lb in weight.
Flies & Tactics Loch nan Leac is the 'premier' water where trout average 14oz in weight; just under half a mile north/south and covering an area of more than 30 acres. Begin your attack at the south end, working carefully up the east shore. Stay on the bank. Wading only spooks the fish. The other lochs in the series have trout which average 8oz (Loch Gress, 6oz), but there are a few surprises along the way. Loch na Faing has specimen fish, but they are hard to tempt; Loch Mor Sandavat has excellent quality trout, which although modest in size, always provide good sport. May and June are the best time to fish these lochs, preferably when there is a good breeze to disguise evil intent. Most patterns of fly produce results. Begin with: Ke-He, Soldier Palmer, Black Pennell.
Permission & Charges See Isles of Lewis & Harris introduction.

NAN LEAC, Loch (Gress) See Loch an Tobair.
NAN LUIG, Loch See Loch Sgeireach na Creaige Brist.
NAN SGIATH, Loch See Loch Breugach.
NAN STARR, Loch See Loch Buaile Bhig.
NAN STEALL, Loch See Loch Gainmheach nam Faoileag.
NAN STEARNAG, Loch See Loch nan Leac (Cliastul).
NAN STEARNAG, Loch (Stacashal) See Loch Gainmheach nam Faoileag.
NAN UIDHEAN, Loch (Garynahide) See Airigh nan Sloc.
NEADAVAT, Loch See Loch Rahacleit.
NEIL BHAIN, Loch See Lochan Hatravat.
NIC DHOMHNUIL, Loch See Loch Vatacolla.
NIGHEAN SHOMHAIRLE, Loch See Loch an Duna.
NIOSAVAT, Loch See Hatravat (Lower Loch).

NISREAVAL, Loch
Location & Access 8/335264 Drive south from Stornoway on the A859 Stornoway/Balallan road. After six miles, park at 8/349274. Walk up the glen to your right, over the south shoulder of Nisreaval (95m), to reach the loch after 15 mins.
Commentary Loch Nisreaval lies between Nisreaval (95m) and Steishal (100m), and covers an area of 70 acres, being half a mile north/south by up to almost half a mile wide across the north bay. Make a visit to

OS Map 8

Stornoway & North Lewis

Loch Nisreaval part of a longer expedition by including Loch Cnoc na h-Iolaire (8/321261), Loch na h-Airigh Uisge (8/310261), return via tiny Loch na Cairteach at 8/318271.

Fish Beginners' country and good sport with bright little trout which average 6-8oz, but also the chance of a few larger specimens of up to 1lb in weight.

Flies & Tactics Bank fishing all the way and best to stay ashore. Start at the south end of Loch Nisreaval, working round the steep south-west bank, then cross over (ten minutes west) to Loch Cnoc na h-Iolaire. Follow the inlet burn from Loch Cnoc na h-Iolaire west to Loch na h-Airigh Uisge, a long (three quarters of a mile), narrow water. The west bay, and by the two islands, is a productive area to fish. Walk north-east for 15 mins, over damp, rising ground, to find Loch na Cairteach which is easily covered from the shore. Now, south-east to return to the north shore of Loch Nisreaval. Concentrate your effort down the east shoreline, particularly in the narrow fjord-like inlets, before returning with supper to the car. Flies: Blue Zulu, Soldier Palmer, Alexandra.

Permission & Charges See Isles of Lewis and North Harris.

NORTH GALSON, River See Loch Ruisavat.
OICHEAN, Loch See Loch Crogavat (Orasay).

ORASAY, Loch
Location & Access 8/390280 Easy accessible and immediately to the west of the B897 Stornoway/Crossbost road.

Commentary Loch Orasay is almost one mile north/south by up to half a mile wide and covers an area of more than 100 acres. The loch is dominated by Eilean Mor, a large central island 70m high and to the west are several other waters which are worth a visit. They are: Loch Beinn na Gainmheich (8/379280) which flows into the south end of Loch Orasay; Loch Airigh an t-Sagairt (8/380286) and its small subsidiary water, Loch nan Laogh (8/380288); and Loch Ard Airigh Ghille a'Ruaidh (8/373284), two small corrie lochs ten minutes walk west.

Fish Loch Orasay has the best trout, fish which average about 8-10oz, as well as occasional trout of up to 3lb; but the other lochs noted all hold good trout, and a few surprises.

Flies & Tactics Bank fishing, and on Loch Orasay pay particular attention to the north and north-east island-scattered bay. The south-west bay, where the inlet stream enters from Loch Beinn na Gainmheich, is also productive. The smaller waters are easily covered from the shore. Flies: Black Zulu, Grouse & Claret, Silver Invicta.

Permission & Charges See Isles of Lewis & Harris introduction.

ORDAIS, Loch See Loch an Duna.
PIPER, Loch See Loch Buaile Bhig.

RAHACLEIT, Loch
Location & Access 8/256420 Park on the peat road to the east of the A858 Carloway/Barvas road where the Dalbeg Burn crosses at 8/236447.

Commentary A splendid day out, visiting five excellent lochs to the south of Dalbeg. Good chance of seeing golden eagle, buzzard and moorland birds such as golden plover and greenshank. Stiff walking, covering five miles, and a compass and map are essential. From the peat road, follow the Dalbeg Burn up to the first loch, Loch Neadavat (8/237435). Continue from the south end of Loch Neadavat, along up the inlet burn to find Loch Risord (8/241427) on the west shoulder of Ben Horshader (130m). Decision time. Either contour south-east round Ben Horshader, or go over the top, having a cast in the unnamed lochan near the summit at 8/244430 before descending to Loch Rahacleit. From the north end of Loch Rahacleit, follow the line of the crags round Ben Horshader, rising north-west to locate Loch Cam nan Eilidean (8/243440). Descend from here to the start point at the A858.

Fish Trout which average 8oz, but larger fish as well of up to and over 1lb in weight.

Flies & Tactics Comfortable bank fishing. Loch Neadavat is long and narrow and wind direction will dictate which bank you fish. Loch Risord is smaller, but easily covered from the shore. Loch Rahacleit is the largest water, three quarters of a mile north/south by up to 250yds across the south bay, which is the best fishing area. Loch Rahacleit is sheltered in windy conditions by Ben Horshader to the west and the dramatic heights of Beinn Rahacleit (249m) and Beinn Bragar (216m) to the east. Loch Cam nan Eilidean is in fact a series of three, interlinked waters, draining north-east by the Binasgro Burn. There are some good fish here, but they are hard to tempt. Try with: Loch Ordie, Soldier Palmer, Black Pennell.

Permission & Charges See Isles of Lewis and Harris introduction.

RAOINAVAT, Loch
Location & Access 8/236460 Easily accessible and adjacent to the north of the A858 Carloway/Barvas road, west from South Shawbost.

Commentary A large, shallow loch, extending to three quarters of a mile east/west by up to a quarter of mile wide and covering an are of 70 acres. North-east over the hill from Loch Raoinavat is Loch na Muilne, South Shawbost at 8/243476, and, immediately to the south of the A858, little Loch Grinnavat (8/251460). A peat road runs south on the west shore of Loch Grinnavat, leading to a delightful, unnamed, smaller water (8/250454) with an island. In Shawbost, turn south through New Shawbost to reach Loch Tuamister (8/265455) which is also worth a look. To the west of Loch Raoinavat are two further lochs which could be included in an expedition: Loch Dalbeg (8/228458) and, on the top of the hill, Loch Dubh a'Chleite (8/229447). Plenty to do for non-fishing members whilst you angle. There are good beaches at Dalbeg Bay (8/227459) where there is a caravan site, and at Loch Shawbost (8/285476) and Dalmore Bay (8/215452).

Fish Trout of between 6oz and over 1lb in weight and the chance of seatrout, fishing from the various beaches noted above.

47

Stornoway & North Lewis — OS Map 8

Flies & Tactics Easy bank fishing all round and Loch Raoinavat is the most productive water with the best trout. The north shore, in the vicinity of the small islands, is a good place to start. On Loch na Muilne, fish the south shore. The other lochs are small and are readily covered from terra firma. Flies: Ke-He, March Brown, Silver Butcher.

Permission & Charges See Isles of Lewis and Harris introduction.

RISORD, Loch See Loch Rahacleit.
ROISNAVAT, Loch See Loch Mor an Stairr.
RUADH GHEURE DUBH MHOR, Loch See OS Map 13.
RUAIDH EITSEAL BHEAG, Loch See Loch Airigh nan Sloc.
RUIGLAVAT, Loch See Loch Rumsagro.

RUISAVAT, Loch
Location & Access 8/482569 Two miles south-east from Galson Lodge (8/455591) on the A857 Barvas/Ness road. A hard tramp up the line of the North Galson river to Gleann Mor. After a walk of one hour, and before the shielings, bear south to reach the loch. The North Galson River has no significance as a fishery, other than the chance of a few seatrout where the river enters the sea.
Commentary This small loch (ten acres) can be one of the most exciting of the North Lewis lochs and is well worth the long hike out. Brighten the day by returning via Lochan Grassavat (8/485580), two tiny waters surrounded by boggy ground, and Loch Chearasaidh (8/467582).
Fish Loch Ruisavat has the best trout, averaging 10oz as well as fish of over 1lb. Lochan Grassavat has smaller trout. To complete your enjoyment, at the end of the day, Loch Chearasaidh will welcome you with hard-fighting fish which average 12oz, and the chance of the odd larger specimen.
Flies & Tactics All these lochs are easily covered from the bank so avoid wading. Fish tend to lie close to the shore and wading only chases them into the middle of the loch. Fish them early in the season - May/June. First cast: Black Zulu, Wickham's Fancy, Alexandra.
Permission & Charges See Isles of Lewis and Harris introduction.

RUMSAGRO, Loch
Location & Access 8/463559 In South Galson (8/439583), turn right immediately after the post office and follow the peat road south. Park at the Water Tower at 8/441574 on Tom a'Mhile (72m).
Commentary Loch Rumsagro is the midway point of a day out in the hills fishing five lochs along the way. From the Water Tower, walk south-west for ten minutes to reach the first water, Loch Leisavat (8/435572); now walk due south for one and a half miles to find Loch Striamavat (8/447554), the largest of the group and covering an area of some eighteen acres. After fishing Loch Striamavat, tramp south-east for half a mile to reach Loch Kearsavat (8/457552), then north-east for half a mile to find Loch Ruiglavat (8/468557). The final water, Loch Rumsagro itself, is a few minutes north-west from Loch Ruiglavat. Total distance covered: five miles.
Fish Loch Leisavat trout average 10oz and are of excellent quality; Loch Striamavat and Loch Kearsavat have lots of 6-8oz fish; Loch Ruiglavat is the best loch in the series, with trout averaging 12oz and good numbers of fish of over 1lb; expect break-fast-sized trout in Loch Rumsagro.
Flies & Tactics Bank fishing all the way and it is best to stay on terra firma. Let the fish come to you. On Loch Ruiglavat, mount your attack along the south shore. Offer residents: Soldier Palmer, Black Pennell, Silver Invicta.
Permission & Charges See Isles of Lewis and Harris introduction.

RUNAGEO, Loch See Loch na h-Airde.
SANDAVAT, Loch (Carloway) See Loch Laxavat Ard.
SANDAVAT, Loch (Glen Tolsta) See Loch Mor a'Ghoba.
SANDAVAT, Loch (Orasay) See Loch Beag na Craoibhe (Orasay).
SANDAVAT, Loch (Pentland Road) See Loch Mor Connaidh.
SANDAVAT, Lochan See Loch nan Leac (Cliastul).
SCARRASDALE, Loch See Loch Vatacolla.
SGAIRE, Loch See OS Map 13.
SGARAVAT BEAG, Loch See Loch na Scaravat.
SGEIREACH A'GHLINN MHOIR, Loch See Loch Mor Leig Tadh.
SGEIREACH, Loch (North Lewis) See Loch Foisnavat.
SGEIREACH, Loch (Springcorrie) See Loch Mhurchaidh.
SGEIREACH, Loch (Stornoway) See Loch Mor an Stairr.
SGEIREACH MOR, Loch See Loch Mor a'Ghoba.

SGEIREACH NA CREIGE BRIST, Loch
Location & Access 8/546535. Approach as for Loch Tana, but at the junction in the peat track, continue north to cross the Abhainn na Cloich burn. At the end of the track, pant due north for two miles to reach the loch.
Commentary Hard going, but a super cliff walk with sea-bird cry all the way and a good chance of spotting moorland birds such as golden plover and dunlin. Make a round trip of the expedition, starting with Loch Caol Duin Othail (8/537525), then Loch Sgeireach na Creige Brist, returning west via the unnamed loch (8/542540), Lochan Meadhonach (8/536538) and its three satellite lochans. After fishing Loch Meadhonach, walk west again to explore Loch Langavat (8/725545), the largest of the North Lewis lochs, and full of trout which average 6oz. Now walk south to the unnamed loch at 8/531531, and south-west again for half a mile to find two excellent, unnamed lochs at 8/524528; now south-east for ten minutes to find Loch Eillagval (8/530524) and little loch Loch nan Luig (8/531515) before returning to the peat road by the waterfall at Bun Abhain na Cloich.
Fish Quality brown trout, particularly in Loch

OS Map 8 — Stornoway & North Lewis

Sgeireach na Creige Brist where fish of over 5lb have been taken in recent years. The average weight of trout in these lochs is in the region of 10oz, but there are fish up to and over 2lb as well.
Flies & Tactics Bank fishing all round and these lochs can be dour and unrelenting, so do not expect large baskets. On Loch Sgeireach na Creige Brist, concentrate your effort along the ragged east shore. Pay particular attention to the smaller of the two unnamed lochs at 8/530524; and, if all else fails, you should catch supper off the promontory on the north-west shore of Loch Eillagval. Tempt them with: Loch Ordie, Soldier Palmer, Alexandra.
Permission & Charges See Isles of Lewis and Harris introduction.

SGRIACHACH, Loch (Aird Skapraid) See Loch an Daimh (Aird Skapraid).
SHADER, Loch See Loch Chulain.
SHIAVAT, Loch See Loch Dibadale.
SKAPRAID, Loch See Loch an Fhada Bhig.
SKAVAT, Loch See Loch Crogavat (Orasay).
SKORASHAL, Loch See Loch Langavat (Carloway).
SLEITIR, Loch See Hatravat (Lower Loch).

SMINIG, Loch
Location & Access 8/365528 Loch Sminig lies to the west of the A857 Barvas/Ness road. Park on the main road at 8/368524 and follow the stream over the moor to reach the loch after a walk of ten minutes.
Commentary There are two sections to Loch Sminig, both of which cover an area of approximately eight acres. The southern section has a small island and the lochs are joined by a narrow stream.
Fish Nothing spectacular, but good stocks of trout which average 8oz.
Flies & Tactics Easy bank fishing and comfortable. Ideal beginners' water. Flies: Black Pennell, Grouse & Claret, Silver Butcher.
Permission & Charges See Isles of Lewis and Harris introduction.

SMUAISAVAL, Loch See OS Map 13.

SPEALDRAVAT MOR, Loch
Location & Access 8/329473 Approach from the A858 Barvas/Carloway road via a peat road at 8/330485. The loch is half a mile south from the main road.
Commentary Loch Spealdravat Mor is 400yds north/south by up to 200yds wide and covers an area of approx. 30 acres. Step over to examine little Da Loch an Fheidh (OS8/334480) on the way out and, after thoroughly thrashing Loch Spealdravat, walk east to spend some time on Loch Casgro (OS8/340472). Have a cast in the unnamed lochans at OS8/331471, OS8/335475 and OS8/336473 as you go.
Fish Good stocks of pretty trout which average 8-10oz and a few larger fish as well. Loch Casgro drains into Loch Mor Barvas (8/345500) and there is always the chance of encountering salmon and seatrout towards the end of the season and after heavy rain.
Flies & Tactics Bank fishing all the way and relatively comfortable wading. The east side and south end of Loch Spealdravat are most productive. On Loch Casgro, work carefully round the six little inlet streams. Offer them: Loch Ordie, March Brown, Silver Butcher.
Permission & Charges See Isles of Lewis & Harris introduction.

SPEALTRAVAT, Loch See Loch Urrahag.
SPEIREACH, Loch See Loch Breugach.
SPEIREAG, Loch See OS Map 13.
STIAPAVAT, Loch OS8/530642 Between the B8013 and B8014 near Five Penny Ness. Limited fishing interest. Almost dries up during hot summer weather. This also applies to Loch na Muilne (8/515619), south of Swainbost. However, there are other attractions in the area, particularly if you have to 'park' non-fishing members of the tribe whilst you set off over the moor. Wonderful beaches at Eoropie, Traigh Sands (8/511645) and at Swainbost, Swainbost Sands (8/505638), the dramatic, restored 12th century Teampull Moluidh church at 8/519651 and a visit to the lighthouse at the Butt of Lewis (8/510606); superb wild flowers on the machair fields bordering the sea; fine quality Harris Tweed on sale in Eoropie.

STRIAMAVAT, Loch
Location & Access See Loch Rumsagro.

SUAINAGADAIL, Loch
Location & Access 8/325416 In Bragar, on the A858 Barvas/Carloway road, mid-way between Lochan Duna and the school, turn south along the peat road and park at the end.
Commentary Prepare yourself for a long walk in the wilds of North Lewis, fishing a series of remote lochs which lie in the hills around Glen Bragar and the course of the Arnol river. The moor is scattered with the remains of summer shielings and the best course is to pack a tent and camp out overnight in one of the ruins. At the end of the peat road, descend south over Gleann Almagro, then, keeping to the high ground, skirt the east shoulder of Choinnich (210m). After one and a half miles, you will find Loch an Sgeireach Mhoir (8/294430). Walk east to the River Arnol and follow the stream south past its junction with Gleann Torradail at 8/304410 by the ruined shielings. Cross the river and ascend the right-hand shoulder of Beinn Tulagaval (121m) to reach Loch nan Leac (8/316405). Climb east from Loch nan Leac to locate Loch an Ois (8/328405) after half a mile. After fishing Loch nan Leac, follow the outlet burn from the south end of the loch down to Loch Suainagadail and the unnamed lochan to the east at 8/331417 on the slopes of Roishal Mor (174m). Camp at Loch Suainagadail. Fish Loch Suainagadail and the small unnamed lochans to the west in Gleann Ioagro (8/320414) before tramping WNW for 15 mins to reach Loch Tulagaval (8/312420). Return to the peat road by walking north-west for two miles.
Fish Excellent sport in all these lochs with trout which average 8oz. There are larger fish as well, particularly in Loch Suainagadail and Loch an Ois.

49

Stornoway & North Lewis
OS Map 8

Flies & Tactics First essential is a compass and map and the knowledge to use them. Also make sure you let someone know where you are going and when you expect to return. This is a tough journey and should not be undertaken lightly, or by inexperienced hill walkers. On Loch an Sgeireach Mor, fish the south-west corner where four streams enter. In spate conditions, good trout are sometimes taken from the River Arnol, to the east. Loch Tulagavat is easily covered from the shore, as is Loch nan Leac and Loch an Ois. Fish by the small islands on Loch Suainagadail and in the vicinity of the inlet stream on the east shore. The lochans nearby also hold good trout. Start with: Black Zulu, Grouse & Claret, Peter Ross. The scenery along the way is splendid, with fine views south-east across the moor to Beinn Mholach (292m) and Ben Barvas (280m).
Permission & Charges See Isles of Lewis & Harris introduction.

SWORDALE, Loch See Eye Peninsula.
TA, Loch See Loch Grunavat (Leurbost).

TANA, Loch
Location & Access 8/492547 One of the most remote of the North Lewis lochs, and a stiff walk of about two hours over rough ground. Drive north from Stornoway along the B895 through Gress and North Tolsta and New Tolsta. Continue north along the minor road and park at 8/531500. Follow the peat track, crossing the Abhainn Geiraha (River Garry), branching left at 8/534504, and walk north-west along the line of the Abhainn na Cloich burn. Keep Da Loch Fuaimavat (small trout averaging 6-8oz) to your right and hike past Tom Vataleois (133m) also on your right, and Loch Mor Sandavat Tolsta (8/499525) and Loch Beag Sandavat (8/499530) on your left. Pass between the west end of Loch Mor at 8/495544 and the unnamed loch immediately on your left, to find Loch Tana ten minutes further north. There are ruined shielings on the west shore and the loch is sheltered by Scrihaval (162m) to the west.
Commentary Not for the faint-hearted, but an utterly splendid day amidst the heather moors of North Lewis. Make an early start. Even better, take a tent and camp overnight by the shielings at Loch Tana. This allows you to explore the Sandavat lochs and Loch na nCaorann (8/492521), Lochan a'Ghille Ruaidh (8/494528) and Loch Dubh Thurtail (8/491534) on the way out to Loch Tana and Loch Mor. On the way home, fish the unnamed loch at 8/504543, before walking ESW to the Vataleois lochs: Loch Beag Eileavat (8/511540), East Loch Beag Eileavat (8/514540, unnamed on the OS Map, Lochan Vataleois (OS8/517537), the two lochs to the north at 8/521541 and OS8/524540, Loch Mor Eileavat (8/513534), and the surrounding, satellite lochs between Lochan Vataleois and Loch Dubh a'Ghobha (8/528537).
Fish Some of the best trout in Lewis lie in these lochs. Loch Tana and Loch Mor have produced fish of over 5lb in weight; East Loch Beag Eileavat has trout of up to and over 2lb. The other lochs all contain excellent stocks of trout which vary in size from 6oz up to 2lb. The smaller of the Sandavat lochs also hold a few specimen trout.
Flies & Tactics Take compass, map and whistle. Make sure you let someone know where you are going and when you expect to return. Stay ashore and attack from the bank. Loch Tana is small (eight acres) and easily covered. Concentrate in the vicinity of the islands at the west end of Loch Mor. Elsewhere, expect good sport from all round the shores. Best flies: Black Pennell, Soldier Palmer, Silver Invicta.
Permission & Charges See Isles of Lewis and Harris introduction.

TANA, Loch See Loch Gil Speireig.
TANA, Loch (Aird Skapraid) See Loch an Daimh (Aird Skapraid).
TANA, Loch (Garynahine) See Loch Airigh nan Sloc.
TANA, Loch (Skapraid) See Loch an Fhada Bhig.
TANA NAN LEAC, Loch See Loch Mor Leig Tadh.
TANAVAT, Loch See Loch Ionadagro.
TARAVAT, Loch See Loch nan Leac (Cliastul).
TARSTAVAT, Loch See Loch Mor a'Ghoba.

THOTA BRIDEIN, Loch
Location & Access 8/336275 Turn right from the A859 Stornoway/Balallan road five miles south from Stornoway at Cameron Terrace (8/355274). Drive west towards Achmore. After two miles, the loch is on your left by the roadside. Park at the north end.
Commentary A shallow, easily accessible loch covering an area of 70 acres, half a mile north/south by up to 400yds wide. Some shelter is provided from the prevailing south-west winds by Oidraval (107m) and Nisreaval (95m).
Fish Good quality brown trout which average about 8-10oz, but fish of up to and over 1lb as well.
Flies & Tactics The loch has been used for fish farming in the past, and the vicinity of the old cages at the north end can be productive. However, the west and south shore is best, particularly by the inlet streams in the south-west corner and the outlet burn (Abhainn Ghlas) to the south-east. Bank fishing, although it is possible to launch a boat. Wading is reasonably comfortable, but fish tend to lie close to the shore. Start well back, before wetting a toe. A good wind generally brings best results and the bigger the wind, the bigger the fly. Offer them: Black Zulu, Soldier Palmer, Dunkeld.
Permission & Charges Contact: Sportsworld, 1 Francis Street, Stornoway, Isle of Lewis. Tel: (01851) 705464.

TOM AN FHEIDH, Loch
Location & Access 8/414284 Three miles south from Stornoway on the A859 road, turn left on the B897 to Crossbost. Park at 8/394280 by Loch Orasay.
Commentary A day out on Arnish Moor visiting three attractive lochs. Total distance covered is four miles and the going is rugged. From the car, walk east over Druim Linuisg (64m) for ten minutes and descend to little Loch Iobhair (8/400280). Loch Innseag is immediately to the east and is the largest water, half a mile

OS Maps 8 — Stornoway & North Lewis

north/south by up to quarter of a mile across. From Loch Innseag, continue east for a further ten minutes to find Loch Tom an Fheidh, a narrow, scattered water, over half a mile east/west and covering an area of some thirty acres.
Fish Small trout in Loch Iobhair and Loch Innseag, averaging 8oz, but the chance of a few larger fish of up to 2lb in Loch Tom an Fheidh.
Flies & Tactics The east shore of Loch Innseag is lined with small bays and promontories which make bank fishing easy. The most productive area is at the south end in the vicinity of the small islands. Loch Tom an Fheidh winds in and out through narrows and bays and you will tramp a fair way in order to explore the whole loch. Concentrate your best effort at the east end of the loch. Offer: Black Zulu, Grouse & Claret, Alexndra.
Permission & Charges See Isles of Lewis and Harris introduction.

TOM AN RISHAL, Loch See Loch Mor an Stairr.
TOM LIAVRAT, Loch See Loch Mor Connaidh.
TOM, Loch (Springcorrie) See Loch Mhurchaidh.
TOM NAN AIGHEAN, Loch See Loch na Craoibhe.
TOMA DUBHA, Loch See Loch an Tairbeart (Garynahine).
TUAMISTER, Loch See Loch Raoinavat.
TULAGAVAL, Loch See Loch Suainagadail.
UANALAIR, Loch See Loch an Duna.
UISG AN T-SOLUIS, Loch See Loch Breugach.
ULLAVAT A'CLITH, Loch See Loch an Tobair.
ULLAVAT A'DEAS See Loch an Tobair.
URAVAL, Loch (Garynahine). See Loch Airigh nan Sloc.

URRAHAG, Loch
Location & Access 8/324480 Near the township of Arnol and easily accessible from the A858 Barvas/Carloway road. There are several access points: immediately adjacent to the road at the north end of the loch at 8/323486; for the west shore, from peat roads at 8/314483 and 8/309480; for the east shore, from a peat road at 8/330485.
Commentary Loch Urrahag is linked to its neighbour, Loch Bhruthadail (8/316460), and together they form a loch extending north/south for almost two miles, being half a mile east/west across the northern bay. A bridge spans the lochs at 8/318466 allowing the opportunity to easily cross to fish the east shore of Loch Bhruthadail. Immediately to the south of Loch Bhrutadail lies little Loch Spealtravat (8/312463) which is also worth a few casts.
Fish Average weight of trout is about 8oz in all these lochs, but there are larger fish of up to and over 1lb in weight.
Flies & Tactics Frustrating bank fishing, with plenty of time to watch fish rising well outwith casting distance; but, nevertheless, great sport and the ideal place to introduce beginners to the gentle art of flyfishing. On Loch Urrahag, fish the west shore, paying particular attention to where the little burn enters at 8/320471, and the north-east bay where the stream enters from Loch Spealdravat Mor (8/329473). The south end of Loch Bhruthadail is most productive, where the inlet streams enter, and fish rise and are taken from the shore all round Loch Spealtravat. A good wind helps matters along and you should start with: Soldier Palmer, Woodcock & Hare-lug, Peter Ross.
Permission & Charges See Isles of Lewis & Harris introduction.

VATACOLLA, Loch
Location & Access 8/485485 Drive north from Stornoway to New Tolsta. At the end of the B895, take the peat road that runs west (8/542486), crossing the Allt na Muilne burn. this track leads to the first of our lochs for the day, Loch Dridean at 8/517487.
Commentary A visit to ten lochs to the west of New Tolsta on Cleith Mhor (133m) and Muirneag (248m). This is a major expedition involving a walk of some eight miles over rough ground and you will most certainly require a compass and map to find your way around. Fish the south-east shore of Loch Dridean and then its near neighbour, Loch Lingavat Mor (8/515481). Follow the inlet stream from Loch Lingavat Mor south to Loch Gaineamhaich (8/510475), fishing the north shore. Pick up the inlet burn at the west end and move on to little Loch Beag Gaineamhaich (8/503475). Loch Beag Gaineamhaich is linked south-west to Loch Beag Sgeireach (8/497471), the last of the chain of lochs draining north into the Allt na Muilne burn. Now walk north-west for ten minutes to find Loch Mor Sgeireach (8/491477). Continue north-west, aiming for the high-point of Muirneag, to locate Loch Vatacolla, which drains into the Abhainn Geirha (River Garry). Walk the outlet stream on the east side of the loch down to Loch Nic Dhomhnuill (8/491490), with Cleith Mhor on your right. Then north-west again to find remote Loch Fad Oram (8/488494). Angle north-east, now, and walk for three quarters of a mile to Loch Scarrasdale (8/502498). Ten minutes south from Loch Scarrasdale is the last of the lochs, Loch na Cloich. Return to the start point, east from Loch na Cloich, fishing along the north shore of Loch Dridean as you go. For those with strong legs and a strong constitution, consider, somewhere along the route, walking to the middle of the circle to fish the unnamed loch at 8/501483. The reward for doing so could be considerable.
Fish Trout average about 6-8oz with larger fish in Loch Mor Sgeireach and Loch Gaineamhaich. After August, and after heavy rain, there is always the possibility of salmon and seatrout in Loch Scarrasdale, Loch Vatacolla and Loch Dhomhnuill, from the River Garry. The river itself is of little fishing interest other than towards the end of the season (September), when a few pools in the lower section can provide sport.
Flies & Tactics Be well prepared for changes in the weather and take spare clothing. Bank fishing all the way and it is best to stay ashore. The fish lie close in and most of these waters are easily covered from the bank. Flies: Black Pennell, Soldier Palmer, Alexandra.
Permission & Charges See Isles of Lewis and Harris introduction.

Cape Wrath — OS Map 8-9

VATALEIOS, Lochan See Loch Tana.

VATANDIP, Loch
Location & Access 8/354337 An easily accessible loch lying close to the Pentland road and to the A858 Stornoway/Garynahine road.
Commentary Loch Vatandip is a long, narrow water, extending one mile east/west and covering an area of some 60 acres.
Fish The average weight of trout is about 8oz, but there are larger fish as well and trout of over 2lb are not uncommon. Loch Vatandip drains into the River Creed and during September there is always the possibility of seatrout.
Flies & Tactics There are no longer boats for hire on this loch. First cast: Ke-He, Grouse & Claret, Dunkeld.
Permission & Charges See Isles of Lewis and Harris introduction.

Cape Wrath

A'BHAGH GHAINMHICH, Loch
Location & Access 9/193458 Enfolded in a bend of the A838 Scourie/Lairg road.
Commentary I confess that I have never seen anyone fishing here. It is very public.
Fish Small trout which average 6-8oz.
Flies & Tactics Because of its proximity to the main road, only the south shore is really worth fishing; otherwise you are liable to hook a passing caravan on the back cast. If you do have a go, offer them traditional patterns of flies.
Permission & Charges Scourie Hotel, Scourie, by Lairg, Sutherland. Tel: (01971) 502396. £5 per rod per day for bank fishing.

A'CHAM ALTAIN, Loch
Location & Access 9/283447 Via the stalkers path from Stack Lodge (9/270437). After about one mile, the track skirts the west end of the loch.
Commentary Make this part of an extended expedition, including Loch Airigh a'Bhaird (9/288453) and Loch an Nighe Leathaid (9/290449). After fishing a'Chaim Altain, walk south to fish Coal Lochan (9/284440) and Loch Grosvenor (9/281434) on the way home.
Fish Large stocks of breakfast-sized trout and an ideal place for beginners.
Flies & Tactics Easy bank fishing and trout are not too particular about flies. Offer them: Blue Zulu, Invicta, Peter Ross.
Permission & Charges Also for Loch An Nigh Leathaid: Reay Forest Estate Office, Achfary, by Lairg, Sutherland. Tel: (01971) 500221.

A'CHREAGAIN THET, Loch
9/167423 To the east of the A894 Scourie/Ullapool road, three miles south from Scourie at Lower Badcall. Used as the water supply for the Eddrachilles Hotel and not really a fishing loch. For any further information, contact: Eddrachilles Hotel, Badcall Bay, Scourie, by Lairg, Sutherland. Tel: (01971) 502080. This also applies to the little lochan at 9/169418, known locally as the 'Ice Loch'.

A'GHARBH-BHAID BEAG, Loch
Location & Access 9/267500 Easily accessible via the track along the east bank of the Rhiconich River from the A838 at 9/245521.
Commentary Three quarters of a mile long and up to 200 yards wide, often windy. The favourite loch of General Osborne who bought Rhiconich Estate in 1943. Boat house and boat at north end. Mount your attack during July or August, after praying for rain.
Fish Depending upon water levels, a'Gharbh-bhaid Beag can produce outstanding sport with salmon and seatrout, but the loch is particularly renowned as a salmon fishery. Salmon average 7-8lb, seatrout 1lb 8oz.
Flies & Tactics Because the loch is so narrow, bank fishing can often be as productive as fishing from the boat; and has the added attraction of allowing the angler to 'stalk' the fish, cautiously from the shore. However, some of the water, particularly at the south end, is best covered from the boat. Best flies: Hairy Mary Double, Stoats Tail Double and Muddler.
Permission & Charges The Rhiconich Hotel, Rhiconich, by Lairg, Sutherland. Tel: (01971) 521224. This controls all the fishing on the loch. They sub-let one day to Scourie Hotel, Scourie, by Lairg, Sutherland. Tel: (01971) 502396. Boat fishing: £25 per day. Bank fishing: £10 per day.

A'GHARBH-BHAID MOR, Loch
Location & Access 9/276480 No easy way into this remote loch. Approach from Rhiconich (9/245521) and Loch a'Gharbh-bhaid Beag (9/267500), a long tramp of three miles; or attack from Stack Lodge (9/270437) along the stalkers path round the west shoulder of Arkle (787m), longer, but more user-friendly because of the track.
Commentary Part of the Rhiconich River system, more than one mile long by up to 250 yards wide. Splendid scenery, curtained by Arkle and Foinaven (908m).
Fish Salmon and seatrout, from the Rhiconich River, arrive in late June, depending upon rainfall, and sport can be excellent during July and August. It all depends upon the weather. a'Gharbh-bhaid Mor is more productive as a seatrout fishery. They don't hang about and run straight from the sea at Loch Inchard, through a'Gharbh-bhaid Beag, into Mor. Salmon average 7-8lb, seatrout 1lb 8oz.
Flies & Tactics Boat fishing brings best results, but bank fishing can also be productive. A gillie is a great help, to keep the boat on station, close to the shore. Concentrate your effort at the south end of the loch, by the four feeder streams. First cast: Black Pennell, Soldier Palmer, Peter Ross.
Permission & Charges The Rhiconich Hotel, Rhiconich, by Lairg, Sutherland. Tel: (01971) 521224. Scourie Hotel, Scourie, by Lairg, Sutherland. Tel (01971) 502396. Boat fishing: £25 per day. Bank fishing: £10 per day.

OS Map 9   Cape Wrath

A'GHEODHA RUAIDH, Loch
Location & Access 9/247674 Approach via the Kyle of Durness ferry from 9/378662. Take the Cape Wrath lighthouse bus to Inshore (9/326694). Walk south west across the southern shoulder of Maovally (299m), crossing the Kearvaig River (a small burn) after one hour. At Loch Keisgaig, (40 minutes later) follow the south shore round the slopes of the hill to reach to loch after a further 30 minutes. Check RAF activity also, the area is part of a bombing range.
Commentary A long, long walk through the wilderness. Take a tent and fish Keisgaig along the way, camping overnight at Keisgaig bay (9/249695), one of the most perfect beaches in all Scotland.
Fish Don't expect any monsters, but you will certainly have good sport and catch your supper. Trout average 8-10oz in weight.
Flies & Tactics Blue Zulu, Invicta, Peter Ross.
Permission & Charges The Cape Wrath Hotel, Keodale, Durness, by Lairg, Sutherland. Tel: (01971) 511212; Fax: (01971) 511313. Free to hotel guests, day lets may be available at £10 per rod per day.

A'MHILL DHEIRG, Loch
Location & Access 9/152433 Approach by a short track, right from the A894 Scourie/Ullapool road, one mile south of the village by the old manse on the hill.
Commentary Was used as a grilse fishery until recently, but now a traditional brown trout fishery. Easily accessible and ideal for those with limited time.
Fish Some good trout of up to and over 1lb.
Flies & Tactics Comfortable bank fishing and the water is readily covered from the shore.
Permission & Charges Scourie Hotel, Scourie, by Lairg, Sutherland. Tel: (01971) 502396. £5 per rod per day.

A'MHUILINN, Loch
Location & Access 9/208630 Leave the car at Blairmore (9/195601) and walk north towards Sandwood Bay.
Commentary Visit a'Mhuilinn as part of a round tour, fishing Loch na Gainimh (9/204614), Lochain nan Sac (9/198625) on the way out, and then, after fishing a'Mhuilinn, Loch Meadhonach (9/210635), Loch Clais nan Coinneal (9/213639), Sandwood Loch (9/230640), Strath Shinary (9/240620), and Loch Mor a'Chraisg (9/230602) on the way home.
Fish Trout average 6-8oz.
Flies & Tactics Easy bank fishing and comfortable wading. Try: Ke-He, Woodcock & Hare-lug, Silver Butcher.
Permission & Charges See Sandwood Loch.

A'MHUINEAN, Lochs
Location & Access 9/158475 Approach from Tarbet (9/165488), south down a coastal peat track, a walk of some 30 minutes. The loch is to the west of the track.
Commentary The first in a series of six lochans to the south of Tarbet, fished consecutively as part of a day out. After Loch a'Mhuinean, continue south to fish the small lochans by Clais Bhan (9/155470), then return north-east to 9/162471, and 9/169476 by Mullach na Creige Deirge and, lastly, 9/168481.
Fish User-friendly brown trout, but can be dour in mid-summer. You should go home with breakfast.
Flies & Tactics These lochs are rarely visited so watch out for the odd larger fish. Remember to keep back from the bank as trout lie close to in some of these lovely little waters. Try: Blue Zulu, Grouse & Claret, Alexandra.
Permission & Charges Sec. Mrs R Mackay, Scourie Angling Club, 12 Park Terrace, Scourie. Tel: (01971) 502425 or at the village shop. £5 per rod per day for bank fishing.

A'MHUIRT, Loch
Location & Access 9/203448 Park on the A838 Scourie/Lairg road at 9/191454 and walk over the moor towards the obvious saddle on the hill. Loch a 'Mhuirt lies south-east and is reached within 15 minutes.
Commentary The 'Murder Loch'. In the Middle Ages, a man living on the main island was killed by an arrow shot from the shore. Lord Reay, who gave the order, coveted the man's wife but she refused his advances: "whilst my husband lives". Reay presented the lady with her husband's head, on a platter. Keep a sharp lookout whilst fishing.
Fish Packed with pretty little fish which average 6-8oz. For the chance of something larger, over 3lb, visit the unnamed lochan at OS9/204449, to the north, and the lochans at OS9/200445 and OS9/203444 to the south.
Flies & Tactics Bank fishing is productive, although the shoreline is uncomfortably rocky in places. Most flies work. Start with: Ke-He, March Brown, Kingfisher Butcher.
Permission & Charges Scourie Hotel, Scourie, by Lairg, Sutherland. Tel: (01971) 502396. Bank fishing: £5 per rod per day.

A'PHREASAIN CHALLTUINE, Loch
Location & Access 9/188468 Adjacent to the minor road from Claisfearn (9/191460) on the A838 out to Tarbet (9/164490).
Commentary A small, easily accessible lochan that will tempt you to stop for a cast on the way to Loch nan Brac (9/180480).
Fish Small, breakfast-sized trout, but plenty of them.
Flies & Tactics Bank fishing and most patterns bring results. Start with: Ke-He, March Brown, Silver Butcher.
Permission & Charges Sec. Mrs R Mackay, Scourie Angling Club, 12 Park Terrace, Scourie. Tel: (01971) 502425 or at the village shop. £5 per rod per day bank fishing.

A'PHREASAN CHAILLTEAN, Loch
Location & Access 9/213534 The easiest way to reach a'Phreasan Chailltean is by boat via Loch Crocach (see Loch Crocach - Rhiconich). Moor the boat at 9/215530 and walk west for five minutes to the loch.
Commentary Utter peace and seclusion amidst spectacular scenery and a good place to introduce children

53

Cape Wrath — OS Map 9

to the delights of hill loch fishing, without over-much strain on little legs. Whilst there, also fish Loch Eileanach, OS9/209534, a brief step west.
Fish Generally plenty of them, trout, averaging 8oz, but can be dour in mid-summer.
Flies & Tactics Bank fishing and most of the water is easily covered. Lots of bays and inviting casting points. The south shore is best, depending upon wind direction, but fish can be taken all round the loch.
Permission & Charges The Rhiconich Hotel, Rhiconich, by Lairg, Sutherland. Tel: (0971) 521224. Bank fishing: £5 per day.

A'PHUILL BHUIDHE, Loch
Location & Access 9/269632 A hard hike. Start at 9/205596 along the track north past Loch Mor a'Chraisg (9/220602), crossing the River Shinary to Strathan (9/248612). Climb north over the first shoulder of An Grianan (467m) and follow the Allt na Rainich burn up the glen, east of An Grianan to reach the loch; a walk of about two and a half hours.
Commentary Few more wonderful places to fish. Utterly isolated, amidst magnificent scenery, worth every step of the way; sheltered to the north by Creag Riabhach (485m) and to the south by An Grianan.
Fish They do not give themselves up easily, but good brown trout averaging 10oz and a few larger fish as well.
Flies & Tactics Loch a'Phuill Buidhe covers an area of some 25 acres and fish are taken from all round the shore. The south end, by the inlet burn, is particularly productive. First cast: Black Pennelll, March Brown, Kingfisher Butcher.
Permission & Charges The Cape Wrath Hotel, Keodale, Durness, by Lairg, Sutherland. Tel: (01971) 511212. Fax: (01971) 511313. Fishing on the Cape Wrath Hotel hill lochs is free to guests. Day lets may be available at £10 pe rod per day.

A'BHADAIDH DARAICH, Loch
Location & Access 9/165445 On the north of the A894 Laxford Bridge/Scourie road, just before entering the village of Scourie.
Commentary Over one mile long by up to half a mile wide, deep, dark and windy. Rarely fished.
Fish Loch a'Bhaidaidh Daraich is connected to the sea at Scourie Bay and some years ago the Angling Association expended considerable energy in improving the outlet stream. A few seatrout are taken, and, no doubt, salmon and grilse also enter on high water, but they are not often caught. Being more than 100ft deep, the loch will also contain ferox trout.
Flies & Tactics For a challenge, bank fish the north shore, concentrating your effort at the shallow west and east end of the loch, particularly below the wood at the north east corner.
Permission & Charges Sec. Mrs R Mackay, Scourie Angling Club, 12 Park Terrace, Scourie. Tel: (01971) 502425. Tickets may be obtained from the village shop at £5 per rod per day.

A'BHUIC, Loch
See Loch Meadie entry, OS Map 16.

AIRIGH A'BHAIRD, Loch
Location & Access 9/288453 An easy walk out from Stack Lodge (9/270437) along a good stalkers path. Reach the loch after about one and a half miles, as the track swings north between Airigh a'Bhaird and Loch an Nighe Leathaid (9/290449).
Commentary Make this part of an extended expedition, including Loch an Nighe Leathaid (9/290449). After fishing Loch An Nighe Leathaid, walk back down the track to Loch a'Cham Altain (9/283447), then south over the moor to fish Coal Lochan (9/284440) and Loch Grosvenor (9/281434) on the way home.
Fish Large stocks of breakfast-sized trout and an ideal place for beginners and a beautiful loch to fish.
Flies & Tactics Easy bank fishing. Try: Black Pennell, Greenwell's Glory, Silver Butcher.
Permission & Charges Also for Loch An Nigh Leathaid: Reay Forest Estate, Estate Office, Achfary, by Lairg, Sutherland. Tel: (01971) 500421.

AIRIGH NA BEINNE, Loch
Location & Access 9/326663 From Keodale (9/378662) via the ferry across the Kyle of Durness. Take the Cape Wrath lighthouse bus to Daill (9/358682). Follow the course of the Daill River south west, past Loch Bad an Fheur-loch (9/339672) to the loch, a walk of about 50 minutes. Check ferry sailing times at Cape Wrath Hotel. Part of the area is a bombing range, so also check that the RAF is not busy.
Commentary A lonely moorland loch in the heart of the Cape Wrath peninsular. Take a tent and stay out, visiting Loch Bad an Fheur-loch (see above), Loch na Gainmhich (OS9/307658), Loch na Glaic Tarsuinn (OS9/297663) and Loch na Glaimhaichd (OS9/290667). Airigh na Beinne lies to the east of Fashven (457m), the highest peak on the peninsula. It is the source of the River Diall, shallow, three quarters of a mile long by up to quarter of a mile wide. The largest area is the south bay, then the loch narrows northwards.
Fish A dense population of beautiful little trout which average in the order of 6-8oz, although there a few larger specimens. There is also the possibility of encountering salmon.
Flies & Tactics Wonderful bank fishing, all round the loch, and in the small satellite lochan to the east. Large baskets are the rule and trout rise readily to most patterns of fly. Begin with: Black Pennell, March Brown, Alexandra.
Permission & Charges The Cape Wrath Hotel, Keodale, Durness, by Lairg, Sutherland. Tel: (01971) 511212; Fax: (01971) 511313. Fishing on the Cape Wrath hill lochs is free to hotel guests. Day lets may be available at £10 per rod per day.

AISIR, Loch
Location & Access 9/199603 Close to the track out to Sandwood bay at Blairmore (9/200600).
Commentary An easily accessible, little roadside loch covering ten acres.
Fish Modest trout averaging 6-8oz.
Flies & Tactics Worth a few casts on the way back from fishing the lochs further north. Use: Black

OS Map 9 — Cape Wrath

Pennell, Grouse & Claret, Silver Butcher.
Permission & Charges See Sandwood Loch.

AISIR MOR, Loch
Location & Access 9/215590 Via a track which leads out to the loch from the Oldshoremore caravan park (9/211585).
Commentary Aisir covers about 100 acres, easily accessible and somewhat exposed, both from the point of view of weather and tourists, but fun to fish nevertheless.
Fish Brown trout which average 10-12oz in weight and the chance of larger fish of up to 1lb and over.
Flies & Tactics Boat fishing brings best results. Concentrate in the vicinity of the inlet burns along the north shore. First cast: Black Pennell, Soldier Palmer, Kingfisher Butcher.
Permission & Charges The Rhiconich Hotel, Rhiconich, by Lairg, Sutherland. Tel: (01971) 521224. Boat fishing: £10 per day. Bank fishing: £5 per rod per day.

ALLTNASUILEIG, Lochs
Location & Access 9/238446 From Alltnasuileig (9/255454), climb south-west up the hill towards the two groups of trees. The first of the Alltnasuileig lochs is on the other side of the ridge.
Commentary Ideal for guests staying in the estate cottages at Alltnasuileig. After fishing 9/238446, walk further south to 9/235444, not forgetting to have a few casts on 9/230443 as well. A shorter expedition can also be made to explore the two lochans on Cnoc nan Cro (9/245460), to the north-west of Alltnasuileig.
Fish Decent trout averaging 8oz and the occasional larger fish.
Flies & Tactics Bank fishing and all the waters are easily covered. Try: Blue Zulu, Invicta, Peter Ross.
Permission & Charges Reay Forest Estate, Estate Office, Achfary by Lairg, Sutherland. Tel: (01971) 500221.

AN DAIMH MOR, Loch
Location & Access 9/160430 Immediately adjacent and to the west of the A894 Scourie/Ullapool road, two miles south from Scourie.
Commentary Divided by the minor road out to Upper Badcall and very public. The east shore margins the road and is steep-sided and difficult to fish. The west shoreline is accessible.
Fish Habitat improvement work was carried out a few years ago by the Freshwater Fishery Laboratory and Loch an Daimh Mor holds good stocks of trout which average 8-12oz, as well a a few larger fish of up to and over 2lb. A few salmon run into this water, lying off the sand banks to the south-east of the loch.
Flies & Tactics Concentrate your efforts along the west shoreline, from the bank, rather than wading. The fish tend to lie close. Try: Black Zulu, Greenwell's Glory, Alexandra.
Permission & Charges Sec. Mrs R Mackay, Scourie Angling Club, 12 Park Terrace, Scourie. Tel: (01971) 502425. Tickets may be obtained from the village shop at £5 per rod per day.

AN DUBH, Loch
Location & Access 9/355460 A remote loch involving a long, tough hike out from Lone (9/309422) at the east end of Loch Stack. Not for the faint-hearted, but breath-taking scenery. Follow the stalkers path skirting Creagan Meall Horn (792m). The loch lies to the south of this track.
Commentary An all day hill-walking and fishing expedition. Allow eight hours for the round trip. After visiting An Dubh, walk south to Lochan Ulbha (9/358454) and Loch na Seilge (9/370446). After Na Seilge, continue south between Sabhal Mor (703m) and Sabhal Beag (729m) to a track down Strath Luib na Seillich which leads back to Lone.
Fish This delightful little loch has good stocks of wild trout which average 8-10oz and fight well.
Flies & Tactics Fish rise all round the loch. First cast: Soldier Palmer, Grouse & Green, Dunkeld. Bank fishing only.
Permission & Charges Reay Forest Estate, Estate Office, Achfary, by Lairg, Sutherland. Tel: (01971) 500221.

AN EAS GHAIRBH, Loch
Location & Access 9/269525 A few minutes' walk up the hill, east from the A838 Durness/Rhiconich road. Start at 9/267529.
Commentary East Ghairbh is the western section of Loch na Claise Carnaich (9/280527) and is a maze of narrow channels and small bays.
Fish A few surprises, but generally traditional highland brown trout which average 8-10oz.
Flies & Tactics Bank fishing only but the water is easily covered. Carefully check the wind direction before deciding which bank to fish, otherwise, it is a long walk round.
Permission & Charges Rhiconich Hotel, Rhiconich, by Lairg, Sutherland. Tel: (01971) 521224. Bank fishing: £5 per day.

AN EASAIN UAINE, Loch
Location & Access 9/325464 A long walk, but a good track most of the way. Start from Stack Lodge (9/270438), skirting the west shoulder of Arkle (757m) to Loch na Tuadh (9/310472). Follow the inlet burn from Na Tuadh to An Easain Uaine (the loch of the green waterfall). Allow a full day for the expedition.
Commentary A beautiful corrie loch lying between two of Scotland's most famous mountains, Arkle and Foinaven (908m). From a distance, Easain Uaine seems to have a gold-sand beach. Close acquaintance discloses smooth pebbles.
Fish Excellent stocks of small trout which average in the order of 8oz, with a few larger fish.
Flies & Tactics The water is clear, but fish are not easily 'spooked' and rise well to most patterns of fly. Begin with: Ke-He, Grouse & Claret, Silver Invicta. Bank fishing.
Permission & Charges Scourie Hotel, Scourie, by Lairg, Sutherland. Tel: (01971) 502396. Charges in the order of £5 per rod per day.

Cape Wrath — OS Map 9

AN FHEIDH, Lochan
Location & Access 9/201478 Park at the east end of Loch Claise Fearna (OS9/204470) on the A838 Lairg/Scourie road and walk north for 15 minutes to reach Loch an Fheidh.
Commentary Splendid little lochan in a delightful, remote setting on the hill above Loch Laxford, draining into Claise Fearna.
Fish Excellent stocks of small trout which give a good account of themselves.
Flies & Tactics Easy bank fishing with action all round the shore. The islands at either end are a good place to concentrate. Offer. Black Zulu, March Brown, Silver Butcher.
Permission & Charges Scourie Hotel, Scourie, by Lairg, Sutherland. Tel: (01971) 502396. £5 per rod per day for bank fishing.

AN NIGHE LEATHAID, Loch
Location & Access 9/290449 An easy walk out from Stack Lodge (9/270437) along a good stalkers path. Reach the loch after about one and a half miles, as the track swings north between Airigh a'Bhaird and Loch an Nighe Leathaid (9/290449).
Commentary Make this part of an extended expedition, including Loch Airigh a'Bhaird. After fishing Loch Airigh a'Bhaird and Loch an Nighe Leathaid, walk back down the track to Loch a'Cham Altain (9/283447), then south over the moor to fish Coal Lochan (9/284440) and Loch Grosvenor (9/281434) on the way home.
Fish Salmon, seatrout and brown trout. The Estate have banned all seatrout fishing in an attempt to give the species a chance to recover from its present state of decline. Any caught, therefore, should be carefully returned.
Flies & Tactics Bank fishing and don't build up your hopes, this is a very dour loch. Try: Black Pennell, Greenwell's Glory, Silver Butcher.
Permission & Charges For Loch An Nigh Leathaid: Reay Forest Estate, Estate Office, Achfary, by Lairg, Sutherland. Tel: (01971) 50221. The Scourie Hotel, Scourie, by Lairg, Sutherland. Tel: (01971) 502396. £5 per rod per day.

AN T-SEANA PHUILL, Loch
Location & Access 9/210458 Park by Loch Claise Fearna at 9/203467 and follow the inlet stream south up the hill past the unnamed loch at 9/209465. Loch an-Seana Phuill (also known as Mrs Little's Loch) is ten minutes further south.
Commentary Wonderful setting with Ben Stack (721m) in the background. Greenshank country and great sport.
Fish Both lochs have good stocks of trout which average 8oz, but there are much larger fish, of up to and over 2lb in weight, particularly in the unnamed loch. Can be dour in high-summer.
Flies & Tactics Bank fishing only, but safe wading on An t-Seana Phuill, along the north shore. Start by the rocky beach by the inlet burn (9/212459). Flies: Blue Zulu, March Brown, Peter Ross.
Permission & Charges Scourie Hotel, Scourie, by Lairg, Sutherland. Tel: (01971) 502396. £5 per rod per day for bank fishing.

AN TIGH SHELG, Loch
Location & Access 9/297484 Start from Stack Lodge (9/270438), skirting the west shoulder of Arkle (757m). After three and half miles, as the track descends, An Tigh Shelg lies to the north of the path.
Commentary A splendid, beautiful place, dominated by the vast bulk of Foinaven (908m), towering north. The loch has a sandy beach at the south end, near to the inlet burn; perfect for lunch and an after-lunch snooze.
Fish An Tigh Shelg trout average 10-12oz and fight hard. Expect at least a brace or two for breakfast.
Flies & Tactics Bank fishing. The south end has a sandy bottom with easy wading, particularly in the vicinity of the inlet burn. The east and west shore are rocky, stumbling country. Take care. Also fish the satellite lochans - some hold much larger fish. Cast: Soldier Palmer, March Brown, Silver Butcher.
Permission & Charges Scourie Hotel, Scourie, by Lairg, Sutherland. Tel: (01971) 502396. Charges in the order of £5 per rod per day.

BAD AN FHEUR-LOCH, Loch
Location & Access 9/339672 From Keodale (9/378662) via the ferry across the Kyle of Durness. Take the Cape Wrath lighthouse bus to Daill (9/358682). Follow the course of the Daill River south west to the loch, a walk of about 30 minutes. Check ferry sailing times at Cape Wrath Hotel. Part of the area is a bombing range, so also check that the RAF is not busy.
Commentary A small moorland loch on the Cape Wrath peninsular. Take a tent and stay out, visiting Loch Airigh na Beinne (9/327664), Loch na Gainmhich (9/307658), Loch na Glaic Tarsuinn (9/297663) and Loch na Glaimhaichd (9/290667). On the course of the River Daill and extending to approximately six acres.
Fish Trout average in the order of 6-8oz and there is a good possibility of encountering salmon, particularly during July and August.
Flies & Tactics Easy bank fishing all round the loch and trout rise readily to most patterns of fly. Begin with: Black Pennell, March Brown, Alexandra.
Permission & Charges The Cape Wrath Hotel, Keodale, Durness, by Lairg, Sutherland. Tel: (01971) 511212; Fax: (01971) 511313. Fishing on the Cape Wrath hill lochs is free to hotel guests. Day lets may be available at £10 per rod per day.

BAD AN T-SEABHAIG, Loch
Location & Access 9/232457 Park near Badnabay (9/220468) and follow the track that skirts the south edge of the forestry plantation to reach the loch in about 15 minutes.
Commentary A very attractive, easily accessible loch, sheltered on three sides by mature conifers. Escape here in stormy weather.
Fish Trout average 8oz and fight well, but can be dour at times.

OS Map 9 — Cape Wrath

Flies & Tactics Bank fishing, and begin along the north shore, near the island, working east amongst the small bays. The area of the inlet burn can also provide breakfast. Offer them: Ke-He, Greenwell's Glory, Silver Butcher.
Permission & Charges Scourie Hotel, Scourie, by Lairg, Sutherland. Tel: (01971) 502396. £5 per rod per day.

BAD NA H-ACHLAISE, Loch
Location & Access 9/385520 Approach from the A838 Bettyhill/Durness road at Polla (9/387547). Walk south from Polla, following the west bank of the Polla River. The loch lies to the west of the river after a walk of about 30 minutes.
Commentary A remote loch in Strath Beag, bounded on the west shore by high crags leading to Conamheall (482m).
Fish Modest brown trout and sea trout to keep you busy should water conditions in the River Polla prove difficult.
Flies & Tactics Easy bank fishing and trout rise to most patterns: Blue Zulu, Greenwell's Glory, Alexandra.
Permission & Charges Charles Marsham, Rispond & Polla Estate, Durness, by Lairg, Sutherland. Tel: (01971) 511224.

BAD NAM MULT, Loch
Location & Access 9/172413 Immediately adjacent to the A894 Scourie/Ullapool road. Park by the shepherd's hut at Geisgeil (9/171411).
Commentary A roadside loch, exposed and often very windy. Worth a few casts, but much more rewarding sport lies in the hills to the east.
Fish Trout average 6-8oz.
Flies & Tactics Easy bank fishing all round the shore. Use: Black Zulu, Greenwell's Glory, Silver Invicta.
Permission & Charges Scourie Estate, Dr Jean Balfour, Kirkforthar House, MacKinch, Glenrothes, Fife. Tel: (01592) 752233.

BEALACH AN EILEIN, Lochs
Location & Access 9/158462 Approach from the peat track at 9/160453 to the north of Scourie Bay, a walk of about 20 minutes.
Commentary A great day out hill walking and fishing, visiting Loch Bealach an Eilein and a series of eight further, unnamed lochs and lochans lying to the north and south of Cnoc Mhichie (208m). Start at Bealach an Eilein, then fish 9/154465, 9/161466, 9/166467, 9/169468, now walk south to 9/168462, 9/170459, 9/174459 and return south-west to a peat track at 9/160453 which leads back to Scourie Village.
Fish Sometimes dour, but generally lots of fun with trout which average 8-10oz in weight. Some of these lochs also contain much larger fish.
Flies & Tactics Splendid bank fishing with all the lochs easily covered. Remember that on many of these waters trout often lie close to the shore, so approach with caution. Tempt them with: Soldier Palmer, Invicta, Kingfisher Butcher.
Permission & Charges Sec. Mrs R Mackay, Scourie Angling Club, 12 Park Terrace, Scourie. Tel: (01971) 502425 or at the village shop. £5 per rod per day bank fishing.

BLARLOCH MOR, Loch
Location & Access 9/285495 Approach from Rhiconich (9/255521) along the east bank of the Rhiconich River. The track ends at 9/267503 by Loch a'Gharb-bhaid Beag (9/267503). Walk on, and, after crossing the Carbh Allt burn, head south east up the hill to reach Blarloch Mor within twenty minutes.
Commentary Blarloch Mor is a straggling, narrow water of over a mile in length. A classic hill loch in ideal surroundings. May also be fished from Stack Lodge (9/270438) as part of an expedition to Loch Tigh an Shelg (9/298482) and Loch Cul Uidh an Tuim (9/291491). Either way, a fair hike, but great sport at the end of the road.
Fish Average weight of trout is in the order of 10oz, but there are larger fish and trout of up to 2lb are sometimes taken.
Flies & Tactics The loch lies north/south making it an ideal location for windy days and fish are taken from all round the shore. Stumbling wading, so be careful. Don't miss the substantial inlet stream from Loch an Tigh Shelg. Good fish are caught here. Start with: Ke-He, Invicta, Alexandra.
Permission & Charges The Reay Forest Estate, Estate Office, Achfary, by Lairg, Sutherland. Tel: (01971) 500221. Charges in the order of £5 per rod per day.

BORRALIE, Loch
Location & Access 9/383670 Easy access from behind the Cape Wrath Hotel (9/381662). A 10 minute walk over a firm grass field.
Commentary A magnificent, exciting loch in lovely surroundings. One of the best in Scotland. A classic, crystal-clear, limestone loch, approximately three quarters of a mile long by a quarter of a mile wide, dropping to a depth of over 100ft to the west of the island. Superb wild flowers (abundant mushrooms) and birdlife.
Fish Borralie contains some huge brown trout as well as good sized Arctic char. Trout average 1lb in weight, char approximately 8-10oz. A few years ago, divers surveying the biological diversity of the bottom of the loch, reported seeing trout of enormous size, but they are difficult to tempt to surface flies.
Flies & Tactics Both boat and bank fishing produce good results. From the boat, concentrate your efforts immediately to the south and east of the island, staying in fairly deep water, and also through the narrow channel between the island and the east shore. From the bank, attack in the evening, as darkness is falling, from half-way north down the west shore. The water deepens quickly and fish often cruise in to feed. Small flies are best, size 16-18, on light tackle. Try: Black Pennell, Woodcock & Hare-lug, Silver Butcher.
Permission & Charges Jack Watson, the Cape Wrath Hotel, Keodale, Durness, by Lairg, Sutherland. Tel: (01971) 511212; Fax: (01971) 511313. A week's full board and fishing costs in the order of £450 per person. Daily lets may be available at £15 per person.

Cape Wrath — OS Map 9

CALADAIL, Loch
Location & Access 9/395667 Caladail lies close to the A838 Durness/Laxford Bridge road. Park at the cottage at 9/395671. Walk down the field to the boat mooring bay.
Commentary One of the finest wild brown trout lochs in Europe. Caladail was formed during the early 1920s and is shallow and lime-rich. The water is crystal clear with excellent feeding for fish. The southern end of the loch has extensive weed growth and the surrounding land hosts a wide variety of rare wild flowers (orchids, mountain aven, mountain everlasting) and exciting birdlife.
Fish Outstanding quality trout averaging just over 1lb in weight. Trout of over 4lb are frequently taken (two at 4lb 8oz last season) and even larger fish are not uncommon.
Flies & Tactics To preserve water quality, outboard motors are not allowed. The best drift is from the headland on the north shore, directly down the middle of the loch towards the island at the south end. Hot spot: 50 yards north of the island. Having said which, trout may be caught all over the loch and, if it is too windy to launch the boat, bank fish with confidence, particularly from the east shore. Fine-and-far-off is the key to success, using small flies, size 16-18. The water is so clear that fish are easily 'spooked' and every bad cast is instantly punished. Expect to work hard for success, but the rewards can be spectacular. First cast: Black Pennell, March Brown, Dunkeld. Dry fly, during the evening, is often productive.
Permission & Charges Jack Watson, the Cape Wrath Hotel, Keodale, Durness, by Lairg, Sutherland. Tel: (01971) 511212; Fax: (01971) 511313. A week's full board and fishing costs in the order of £450 per person. Daily lets may be available at £15 per person.

CARN MHARASAID, Loch
Location & Access 9/237584 Approach from a peat track at 9/211584 near the caravan site at Oldshoremore. The walk out to the loch takes about 30 minutes.
Commentary A very pretty loch, not too far, and therefore a good place to introduce youngsters to hill loch fishing.
Fish Lots of small trout average 6oz in weight.
Flies & Tactics Safe bank fishing and action all round the shore. First cast: Loch Ordie, Greenwell's Glory, Dunkeld.
Permission & Charges Mr C Morrison, 200 Kinlochbervie, by Lairg, Sutherland, IV27 4RP. Tel: (01971) 521240. £5 per rod per day.

CLAIS NAN COINNEAL, Loch
Location & Access 9/214639 Leave the car at Blairmore (9/195601) and walk north towards Sandwood Bay.
Commentary Visit Loch Clais nan Coinneal as part of a round tour, fishing Loch na Gainimh (9/204614), Lochain nan Sac (9/198625), Loch a'Mhuilinn (9/207630 and Loch Meadhonach (9/210635) on the way out, and then, after Loch Clais nan Coinneal (9/214639), Sandwood Loch (9/230640), Strath Shinary (9/240620), and Loch Mor a'Chraisg (9/230602) on the way home.
Fish Three to the pound sport with bright little trout.
Flies & Tactics Room for a few casts on the way north. Try: Ke-He, Woodcock & Hare-lug, Silver Butcher.
Permission & Charges See Sandwood Loch.

CLAR LOCH MOR, Loch
Location & Access 9/210427 No easy way in. Park on the A838 Scourie/Lairg road at 9/191454. Walk over the moor and up the glen to the obvious 'saddle'. Continue south-east, past Loch a'Mhuirt (9/203448) to Loch Gorm (9/211442). Now angle south-east, past Loch Eilean na Craoibhe Moire (9/209447) to Clar Loch Mor. A journey of about an hour.
Commentary Along the way, have a cast in the unnamed lochans at 9/215433 and after fishing Clar Loch Mor, return exploring Lochain a'Chaorainn, a series of ten unnamed lochans which lie to the west. You need accurate map reading to find your way back to the road from Lochain a'Chaorainn (9/196427). Best bet is to aim for between Loch na h-Airigh Sleibhe and Loch na Mnatha at 9/192438, then north to the top of the saddle.
Fish Wonderful sport with trout averaging 8oz, but some of these lochans contain much larger fish of up to and over 5lb in weight. Finding where they lie is one of the great joys of fishing amidst these lonely hills.
Flies & Tactics All day bank fishing and walking. Don't stop too long in any one place, keep moving, and keep watching for that tell-tale, huge swirl. First cast: Loch Ordie, Greenwell's Glory, Silver Butcher.
Permission & Charges Scourie Hotel, Scourie, by Lairg, Sutherland. Tel: (01971) 502396. £5 per rod per day.

CLAR, Loch, Scourie
Location & Access 9/186474 Adjacent to the minor road from Claisfearn (9/191460) on the A838 out to Foindle (9/190484).
Commentary A small, easily accessible lochan that will tempt you to sop for a cast on the way to Loch nan Brac (9/180480).
Fish Small, breakfast-sized trout, but plenty of them.
Flies & Tactics Bank fishing and most patterns bring results. Start with : Ke-He, March Brown, Silver Butcher.
Permission & Charges Sec. Mrs R Mackay, Scourie Angling Club, 12 Park Terrace, Scourie. Tel: (01971) 502425 or at the village shop. £5 per rod per day bank fishing.

CNOC THORMAID, Lochs
Location & Access 9/188422 Start from Geisgeil (9/171411). Follow the east shore of Loch Bad nam Mult to the inlet burn at the north end. Keep the crags on your right and walk up the burn, bearing slightly right at the top to reach the first loch in this series at 9/184425.
Commentary Wild country and hard walking, exploring the lochans on the hill above Loch nan Uidh (9/194417). After 9/184425, walk over to 9/188422,

OS Map 9 — Cape Wrath

known locally as 'Parson's Loch', perhaps one of the most lovely lochs in all of Sutherland. Then, the final challenge, the tiny waters to the east at 9/193420 and 9/200418.

Fish Look out for fireworks from some really hard-fighting trout. Their average weight is in the order of 8-10oz, but they are magnificent. Somewhere up here, also, is the odd fish of over 6lb. Find out exactly where for yourself.

Flies & Tactics Bank fishing and be stealthy, particularly on the smaller waters. Parson's golden trout lie close, so approach quietly. The south east shore is best, near the little island. Tempt them with Soldier Palmer, Woodcock & Hare-lug, Alexandra.

Permission & Charges Scourie Hotel, Scourie, by Lairg, Sutherland. Tel: (01971) 502396. £5 per rod per day.

CNOC THULL, Lochs

Location & Access 9/249490 A series of fourteen lochs and lochans lying on the hill above the A838 Rhiconich/Laxford Bridge road. Park at 9/239495 and follow the glen south-west to reach the first loch.

Commentary There is at least two days fishing here involving some tough walking over rough country. None of the lochs are named on the OS map, so carefully note the grid references given below to find your way around. This is a splendid place to fish, the land of the red-throated diver.

Fish These lochs can be dour, but they all contain traditional, 6-8oz wild brown trout, and also some specimen fish of up to 4lb in weight. Be prepared.

Flies & Tactics Leave 9/249490 for the way home. Skirt the south shore (wet feet crossing) and follow the outlet stream over the brow of the hill. Fish 9/252493 and the deep, little satellite lochan on the hill at 9/254480. Continue east, fishing 9/257479 and boot-shaped 9/260476, where large trout lurk. Hike north-east to 9/265478, which is also glass case country, then return via 9/259482. Of the lochans to the south, have a look particularly at 9/241484 and 9/252477. Offer them: Black Pennell, Soldier Palmer, Silver Invicta. Bank fishing all the way.

Permission & Charges Scourie Hotel, Scourie, by Lairg, Sutherland. Tel: (01971) 502396. £5 per rod per day.

COAL LOCH A' MHIND, Loch

Location & Access 9/265455 Approach from the A838 Achfary/Scourie road at 9/251466 by crossing the Laxford River and following the path along the north bank. After a few hundred yards, as the river bends, you will see the outlet stream from Coal Loch a 'Mhind entering from Druim na h'Aimhne. Walk up the stream to the loch.

Commentary The first in a series of six lochs, including Loch Eileanach (9/272471), lying above the Laxford River. The setting is dramatic, but, be warned, in poor weather you will need a compass and map to find your way home. Make this a full day expedition.

Fish All the lochs contain good stocks of trout averaging in size from 6oz up to fish of 3lb and more. Finding where the big ones live is part of the adventure.

Flies & Tactics Fish the lochs in this order: Coal Loch a'Mhind first, then north to 9/267459, 9/270460, 9/276465 and north-west to Eileanach. Walk south from Eileanach, down the glen to 9/266469. If you have time, examine the small lochans on Druim na h-Aimhne at 9/260469 and 9/264463. Black Pennell country, with March Brown and Dunkeld.

Permission & Charges Scourie Hotel, Scourie, by Lairg, Sutherland. Tel: (01971) 502396. £5 per rod per day.

COAL, Lochan

Location & Access 9/284440 An easy walk, reached from the stalkers path from Stack Lodge (9/270437). After half a mile, the lochan is on your right.

Commentary Make this part of an extended expedition, starting at Loch Airight a'Bhaird (9/288453) and including Loch an Nighe Leathaid (9/290449). After fishing Loch An Nighe Leathaid, walk back down the track to Loch a'Cham Altain (9/283447), then south over the moor to fish Coal Lochan (9/284440) and Loch Grosvenor (9/281434) on the way home.

Fish Large stocks of breakfast-sized trout and an ideal place for beginners and a beautiful loch to fish.

Flies & Tactics Good bank fishing. Try: Ke-He, Greenwell's Glory, Silver Butcher.

Permission & Charges The Scourie Hotel, Scourie, by Lairg, Sutherland. Tel: (01971) 502396. £5 per rod per day. For Loch An Nigh Leathaid: Reay Forest Estate, Estate Office, Achfary, by Lairg, Sutherland. Tel: (01971) 50221.

COILL A'GHORM LOCHA, Loch
See Loch na h-Airigh Sleibhe.

CROCACH, Loch (Rhiconich)

Location & Access 9/223528 Leave the A838 at 9/247518 and follow the minor road west towards Ardmore. Park at the end and walk north for ten minutes to reach the loch.

Commentary One of the most lovely lochs in the area, one mile north/south, up to three quarters of a mile east/west. The southern end is a long, narrow arm, leading north to a splendid bay guarded by a large island and four satellite islands, the perfect place for lunch.

Fish Full of bright trout which average 8oz and a few larger specimens as well. Can be dour, particularly in mid-summer, but rarely sends you home without supper.

Flies & Tactics Boat fishing makes it easy to explore all the corners and bays, but bank fishing is just as nice. Both bring good results. Fish are caught all round the loch, but from the boat, concentrate in the vicinity of the islands. First cast: Black Zulu, March Brown, Dunkeld.

Permission & Charges The Rhiconich Hotel, Rhiconich, by Lairg, Sutherland. Tel: (01971) 521224. Boat fishing: £10 per day. Bank fishing: £5 per rod per day.

CROISPOL, Loch

Location & Access 9/391680 Approach from the road to the old manse, a walk of about five minutes.

Cape Wrath — OS Map 9

Commentary One of Scotland's brightest and best lochs offering great sport in splendid surroundings. Approximately 15 acres and mostly shallow, apart from one 40 feet deep 'hole'. Clear, lime-rich water. Sheltered bank fishing in high winds. Great wild flowers and birdlife.
Fish Croispol trout are perfectly shaped, silver and fight hard. They are not so large (average 12oz) as trout in the other Durness lochs, but they rise more readily to the fly.
Flies & Tactics Good results from boat or bank, but you will need the boat to properly explore the deep 'hole' close to the east shore at the south end. It is easily spotted, because of the different colouring of the water. Inch round the margins. A few years ago, Norman Simmonds from Edinburgh took a 4lb 8oz trout here. First cast: Ke-He, Grouse & Claret, Silver Invicta.
Permission & Charges Jack Watson, the Cape Wrath Hotel, Keodale, Durness, by Lairg, Sutherland. Tel: (01971) 511212; Fax: (01971) 511313. A week's full board and fishing costs in the order of £450 per person. Daily lets may be available at £15 per person.

CUL NA CREIGE, Lochan

Location & Access 9/280535 Approach from Clach a'Bhoineid (9/277542) on the A838 Durness/Rhiconich road, avoiding the steepest of the roadside crags. On the hill, walk south to reach the loch within 15 minutes. May also be approached, by boat, from Loch na Claise Carnaich, into which Cul na Creige drains.
Commentary Head for Cul na Creige on windy days. There is generally a sheltered corner. The loch is divided into bays, north and south, and the surrounding scenery is perfect.
Fish Nothing to fill the glass case, but plenty of sport with bright little brown trout.
Flies & Tactics Bank fishing only, but lots of exciting bays and points where fish lie. The northern section, and the bays by the narrows are the most productive areas. Offer them: Black Zulu, Grouse & Claret, Silver Invicta.
Permission & Charges Rhiconich Hotel, Rhiconich, by Lairg, Sutherland. Tel: (01971) 521224. Bank fishing: £5 per day.

CUL UIDH AN TUIM, Loch

Location & Access 9/291491 Approach from Rhiconich (9/255521). The track ends by Loch a'Gharbh-bhaid Beag (9/267503). After crossing the Garbh Allt burn, head south-east to reach Blarloch Mor (9/285495). Walk south down the west shore of Blarloch Mor to cross the Uidh an Tuim burn at 9/292487. Due north now to the loch.
Commentary This remote loch lies in a dramatic setting on the southern slopes of Foinaven (908m) and is rarely fished. May also be attacked via Stack Lodge (9/270438) as part of an expedition to Loch Tigh an Shelg (9/298482) and Blarloch Mor. A breath-taking journey, in every sense of the word.
Fish Wild brown trout which do not give themselves up easily, averaging 10-12oz, but with a few much larger specimens waiting to test your skill.

Flies & Tactics Bank fishing, and the southern end of the loch, in the vicinity of the tiny island, is a good place to start, thence carefully up the east shoreline. Offer them: Black Pennell, Grouse & Claret, Silver Invicta.
Permission & Charges The Reay Forest Estate, Estate Office, Achfary, by Lairg, Sutherland. Tel: (01971) 500221. 1994 charges in the order of £5 per rod per day.

DAILL, River

Location & Access Source 9/315664 Outflow 9/370682 Via the Kyle of Durness ferry to the Cape Wrath Peninsula (check sailing times at Cape Wrath Hotel).
Commentary A rocky, little stream flowing through rugged countryside, rarely fished. There are two lochs to explore along the way, Loch Bad an Fheur-loch (9/339671) and Loch Airigh na Beinne (9/335664).
Fish Salmon run the Daill from June onwards and grilse join them in July. Salmon are often 12lb and upwards in weight, grilse average 6lb.
Flies & Tactics Absolutely dependent upon spate conditions and even then fishable water is limited. From Loch Bad an Fheur-loch the narrow stream rushes over rocky outcrops to the Kyle. Above the loch, the river is slow moving and weedy. Loch Airigh na Beinne is probably the best place to concentrate. If salmon don't cooperate, there is always sport with brown trout. Use Ke-He, Black Pennell, Loch Ordie for both.
Permission & Charges Cape Wrath Hotel, Keodale, Durness, by Lairg, Sutherland. Tel (01971) 511212. Between £10 and £15 per rod per day depending upon the time of season.

DEIBHEADH, Loch See Loch Mor a'Chraisg.
DIONARD, Loch See River Dionard (below).

DIONARD, River

Location & Access Source 9/356490 Outflow 9/365626 The lower river is accessible from the A838 Durness/Laxford Bridge road, but at 9/352599 the Dionard parts company with the road, flowing down from Loch Dionard (9/356490) through wild, inaccessible country. An estate road has recently been built from Gualin Lodge (9/310570) out to the loch, to provide easy access for sluggards.
Commentary A productive, exciting river, set amidst dramatic scenery. There are some fifty named pools with best results coming from the lower and middle river, and from Loch Dionard. The loch is one of the most beautiful in Scotland, dominated by Foinaven (918m) to the west, Creagan Meall Horn (729m) south, and Cranstackie (800m) to the east.
Fish Salmon and seatrout enter the system from February onwards, but the main runs do not occur until late June. From then until the end of the season, depending upon water levels, sport is excellent with August being the 'prime' month. Salmon average 6.5lb, seatrout 1lb 8oz, with most seatrout being taken from Loch Dionard and from the Kyle of Durness. Accurate catch returns are not available but

OS Map 9 — Cape Wrath

my 'guesstimate' is in the order of up to 200 salmon and a similar number of seatrout each season.
Flies & Tactics The river is easily fished without wading and a light salmon rod is adequate for most situations. The river is narrow throughout most of its length and staying below the skyline is vital for success. Loch Dionard, half a mile in length, fishes best at the south end, and close to either shore. Flies to use include: Garry Dog, Silver Wilkinson, Green Highlander, Mary, Stoat's Tail, General Practitioner, Shrimp Fly, Willie Gunn.
Permission & Charges The Dionard is owned jointly by Gualin Estate, and Scottish Office Department of Fisheries who let their fishing to the Cape Wrath Hotel. Contact: Gualin Estate, Gualin, Durness, by Lairg, Sutherland. Tel: (01971) 521282; Early booking is essential and charges vary according to which part of the river you are fishing and the time of year. Approximate costs are from £300 per two rod beat up to £500 per two rod beat.

DRUIM NA COILLE, Loch
Location & Access 9/189492 Leave the A838 Lairg/Scourie road at Claisfearn (9/192460), signposted to Tarbet. Bear right at 9/184471 towards Foindle and Fangmore. Druim na Coille lies to the north of the roadside lochan at 9/187489 at Foindle.
Commentary A small lochan on the cliffs above Loch Laxford, easily accessible and rarely fished. Also have a few casts in 9/187489.
Fish Can be dour but has good stocks of trout averaging 8-10oz in weight.
Flies & Tactics Easy bank fishing. Start at the north end, by the island. Try: Black Zulu, Soldier Palmer, Dunkeld.
Permission & Charges Sec. Mrs R Mackay, Scourie Angling Club, 12 Park Terrace, Scourie. Tel: (01971) 502425. Tel: (0971) 502420, or at the village shop. £5 per rod per day bank fishing.

DUAIL, Loch
Location & Access 9/430640 From the A838 Tongue/Durness road at 9/440631. Walk north-west up Beinn Ceannabeinne (383m) to reach the loch in 30 minutes.
Commentary A long, hard hike, to a small loch about Loch Eriboll, where you will be rewarded by some of the finest views in the north of Scotland. Guaranteed peace and seclusion.
Fish Small, eager, highland trout which average three to the pound.
Flies & Tactics Room for a few casts and space and time aplenty for glorious contemplation. Use: Soldier Palmer, March Brown, Alexandra.
Permission & Charges Durness Estate - contact the agent Mr Wilson on (01786) 822161.

EILEAN NA CRAOIBHE MOIRE, Lochs
Location & Access 9/209437 Park on the A838 Scourie/Lairg road at 9/191454 and cross the moor towards the obvious saddle on the hill. Walk south-east, passing Loch a'Mhuirt at 9/203448, reaching Loch Gorm after a journey of about 30 mins. Walk south from Loch Gorm for ten mins to reach Eilean na Craoibhe Moire.
Commentary Also known as 'Hutchinson's Loch', after a retired army colonel who got lost overnight amidst this watery maze. Easily done, as I know to my cost. If the worst comes to the worst, turn your back on Ben Stack (721m) and walk in a straight line. Eventually, foot-sore and weary, you will hit the A838 Scourie/Lairg road.
Fish The chance of some really good trout, from the main loch and from the surrounding dozen or so adjacent lochans.
Flies & Tactics Bank fishing and be stealthy, the fish lies close. Also visit 9/214432 and its satellite lochans. First cast: Soldier Palmer, Grouse & Claret, Dunkeld.
Permission & Charges Scourie Hotel, Scourie, by Lairg, Sutherland. Tel: (01971) 502396. £5 per rod per day.

EILEANACH, Loch (Ardmore) See Loch a'Phreasan Chailltean.

EILEANACH, Loch (Ben Auskaird) See Feur Lochan.

EILEANACH, Loch (Ben Stack)
Location & Access 9/244425 Park by the shepherd's hut at 9/264437 on the A838 Scourie/Lairg road and climb south on the stalkers path round the west shoulder of Ben Stack (721m). Loch na Seilge is first, at 9/255435, Loch Eileanach is a further 15 minutes south.
Commentary One of the most exciting lochs in the Reay Forest, but can be difficult, particularly during high summer. The loch extends for almost one mile, west from Ben Stack, in a delightful, interconnected series of island-clad waters. Good chance of seeing, rather than just hearing, greenshank, as well as red-throated diver and peregrine.
Fish Beautiful trout which average 10oz as well as fish of up to and over 3lb.
Flies & Tactics Bank fishing. Begin on the small, unnamed lochan to the left of Eileanach at 9/247424, fishing the sandy-bottomed east shore. There are good fish here. Eileanach trout lie close, so approach with caution, otherwise all you will see are large wakes heading for the middle. The area in the vicinity of the tiny island at 9/244425 on the south shore is a 'hot-spot'. Offer: Black Pennell, Woodcock & Hare-lug, Dunkeld.
Permission & Charges Scourie Hotel, Scourie, by Lairg, Sutherland. Tel: (01971) 502396. £5 per rod per day.

EILEANACH, Loch (Druim na h-Aimhne)
Location & Access 9/272471 Same as for Coal Loch a'Mhind.
Commentary One of a series of six lochs, including Coal Loch a'Mhind (9/265455), lying above the Laxford River. The setting is dramatic.
Fish All the lochs contain good stocks of trout averaging in size from 6oz up to fish of 3lb and more. Finding where the big ones live is part of the adventure.
Flies & Tactics Fish the lochs in this order: Coal Loch a'Mhind first, then north to 9/267459, 9/270460,

Cape Wrath — OS Map 9

9/276465 and north-west to Eileanach. Walk south from Eileanach, down the glen to 9/266469. If you have time, examine the small lochans on Druim na h-Aimhne at 9/260469 and 9/264463. Black Pennell country, with March Brown and Dunkeld.
Permission & Charges Scourie Hotel, Scourie, by Lairg, Sutherland. Tel: (01971) 502396. £5 per rod per day.

EILEANACH, Loch (Rhiconich) See Loch Crocach (Rhiconich).

FANGMORE, Lochs
Location & Access 9/177496 Leave the A838 Lairg/Scourie road at Claisfearn (9/192460), signposted to Tarbet. Bear right at 9/184471 towards Foindle and Fangmore. The lochs lie to the north of Fangmore.
Commentary A series of six, unnamed, small lochans lying on the Fangmore peninsula, rarely, if ever, fished. A wonderful place to spend a day. Lunch by the cove at Acarseid Mhic Mhurchaidh Oig (9/161504).
Fish Brown trout which average 6-8oz. There are, however, reports of larger fish, but which of the tiny lochs contain them is unrecorded. Find out for yourself.
Flies & Tactics Start at 9/169502, north from Fangmore, then on to 9/165505 and the most remote loch, at 9/165509. South along the cliff now to lunch, then 9/163500 and 9/166496 and back to Fangmore. Bank fishing, using: Black Zulu, Soldier Palmer, Alexandra.
Permission & Charges Sec. Mrs R Mackay, Scourie Angling Club, 12 Park Terrace, Scourie. Tel: (01971) 502425 or at the village shop. £5 per rod per day bank fishing.

FEUR, Lochan
Location & Access 9/248415 Park by the shepherd's hut at 9/264437 on the A838 Scourie/Lairg road and climb south on the stalkers path round the west shoulder of Ben Stack (721m). Pass Loch na Seilge (9/255435), then Loch Eileanach (9/244425). At 9/246419, bear left up Strath Stack. After 100 yards, climb south to reach Feur Loch.
Commentary After fishing Feur Lochan, walk south to fish the unnamed lochs at 9/245411 and 9/240407. Continue west, crossing the stalkers path, to fish Loch Eileanach (Ben Auskaird) at 9/224409, then, finally, north on the track to fish Loch na h-Ath (9/239419).
Fish Trout average 8oz but there are also fish of over 3lb in some of these waters.
Flies & Tactics Eileanach (Ben Auskaird) is particularly productive, as are the two tiny satellite lochans adjacent to Loch na h-Ath at 9/236420 and 9/239422. Bank fishing, using Loch Ordie, Greenwell's Glory, Alexandra.
Permission & Charges Reay Forest Estate, Estate Office, Achfary, by Lairg, Sutherland. Tel: (01971) 500221.

GOBHLOCH, Loch
Location & Access 9/174143 Leave the A838 Lairg/Scourie road at Claisfearn (9/192460), signposted to Tarbet. Bear right at 9/184471 towards Foindle and Fangmore. Gobhloch Loch lies adjacent to the road south of Fangmore.
Commentary A small, easily accessible loch between Fangmore and Tarbet, easily fished from the bank and ideal for a few casts if time is limited.
Fish Can be dour. Trout average 8oz in weight.
Flies & Tactics Bank fishing and the west shore is best. Try: Loch Ordie, Greenwell's Glory, Peter Ross.
Permission & Charges Sec. Mrs R Mackay, Scourie Angling Club, 12 Park Terrace, Scourie. Tel: (01971) 502425 or at the village shop. £5 per rod per day bank fishing.

GORM, Loch
Location & Access 9/215445 Park on the A838 Scourie/Lairg road at 9/191454 and cross the moor towards the obvious saddle on the hill. Walk south-east, passing Loch a'Mhuirt at 9/203448, reaching Loch Gorm after a journey of about thirty minutes. The boat is moored at 9/211442.
Commentary A wonderful place to spend the day. The loch is divided into two main bays, joined by narrows. Carefully note the route, otherwise you might spend an inconsiderable amount of time in the north bay, rowing round and round in dangerously decreasing circles searching for the way home.
Fish Not glass case country, but full of nice trout which average 6-8oz, and the odd fish of up to 1lb. Larger specimens reside in the surrounding lochans, fish of up to and over 3lb, but they are hard to tempt. Try, particularly at 9/210444, 9/212444 and 9/221442.
Flies & Tactics You really need the boat for Gorm Loch, otherwise access is difficult. The north bay is most productive, round the main island, and by the island in the east bay. Bushy flies: Ke-He, Soldier Palmer, Black Zulu.
Permission & Charges Scourie Hotel, Scourie, by Lairg, Sutherland. Tel: (01971) 502396. £5 per rod per day.

GROSVENOR, Loch
Location & Access 9/281434 A small loch, fifteen minutes walk east from Stack Lodge (9/270437).
Commentary Make this part of an extended expedition, starting at Loch Airigh a'Bhaird (9/288453) and including Loch an Nighe Leathaid (9/290449). After fishing Loch an Nighe Leathaid, walk back down the track to Loch a'Cham Altain (9/283447), then south over the moor to fish Coal Lochan (9/284440), ending at Loch Grosvenor (9/281434).
Fish Brown trout, and the chance of salmon and seatrout. The estate have banned all seatrout fishing in an attempt to give the species a chance to recover from its present state of decline. Any caught, therefore, should be carefully returned.
Flies & Tactics Dour, and the fish are easily disturbed. Try: Loch Ordie, Soldier Palmer, Peter Ross.
Permission & Charges The Scourie Hotel, Scourie, by Lairg, Sutherland. Tel: (01971) 502396. £5 per rod per day. For Loch An Nigh Leathaid: Reay Forest Estate, Estate Office, Achfary, by Lairg, Sutherland. Tel: (01971) 50221.

OS Map 9 — Cape Wrath

GRUDIE, River
Location & Access Source 9/298633 Outflow 9/354628 Approach from the A838 Durness/Laxford Bridge road. Park near 9/366618 and cross the River Dionard by the footbridge. Walk north-west over Siathean Mor (9/357622) to the mouth of the Grudie.
Commentary A perfect little highland spate stream rising from the wilds of the Parpah Peninsula, the Viking name for Cape Wrath, meaning 'turning point'. Not often fished, the Dionard being the main attraction her, but after heavy rains, always the chance of fish.
Fish Some excellent salmon, fish of up to and over 15lb, run the stream from June onwards, with grilse appearing in July. Seatrout seem to prefer the Dionard and are rarely caught in the Grudie.
Flies & Tactics The river flows across peat moorlands before cascading down dramatic falls. Above and below the falls is where most fish are caught. This is salmon-stalking country, using a light, strong rod, and sport is entirely dependent upon there being plenty of water in the stream. Offer them: Willie Gunn, Garry Dog, Hairy Mary, Stoat's Tail.
Permission & Charges Cape Wrath Hotel, Keodale, Durness, by Lairg, Sutherland. Tel (01971) 511212. Between £15 and £25 per rod per day depending upon the time of season.

HOPE, Loch
Location & Access North End: 9/475600; Middle Bay: 9/461529; South End: 9/459513. For North End, approach directly from the A838 Tongue/Durness road at 9/476602. For South End and Middle Bay, approach from Altnaharra along the minor road which margins the east shore of the loch.
Commentary One of the most productive and most beautiful Scottish seatrout lochs. Hope lies in three, inter-connected glacial basins between Ben Hope (927m) to the east, and Fionaven (908m) to the west. The loch is six miles long by up to one mile wide across Middle Bay. North End and South End are shallow, Middle Bay drops to over 200ft in depth. The surrounding scenery is glorious.
Fish The principal interest is seatrout, although in recent years good numbers of salmon have also been taken. First fish are generally landed in June, with the peak period being July and August. Approximately 350 seatrout are caught each season averaging 2lb in weight, but with many fish of up to and over 5lb. Salmon average 6lb. In order to preserve seatrout stocks, restrictions have been placed upon the size and number of seatrout which may be killed. Gillies will advise guests of the details.
Flies & Tactics A classic dapping loch, where the daddy longlegs, natural or live, produces best results. Traditional wet flies, such as Black Pennell, Ke-He, Soldier Palmer, March Brown, Invicta, Peter Ross, Alexandra, and Silver Butcher also fish well. Bank fishing is not allowed.
On North End and Middle Bay, outboard motors are allowed, are are essential, whereas South End, which contains the three most productive fishing beats, is restricted to rowing. Fish the margins on North End. On Middle Bay, the west shore is the best fishing area (The Castle), but the long east shoreline offers a good chance of salmon. Position the boat about ten yards out from the bank. Fish the west shore on Beat 3, again, about ten yards out from the bank. On Beat 1 and Beat 2, both averaging 15ft in depth, fish may be caught anywhere. The services of a gillie greatly increase your chance of catching fish.
Permission & Charges North End: For bookings & general information about North End: Mr Ian MacDonald (Loch Keeper). Tel/Fax: (01847) 601272. For Middle Bay and South End, contact the Altnaharra Hotel, Altnaharra, by Lairg, Sutherland. Tel: (01549) 411222. Boat hire per day for Middle Bay: £31 (plus £12 for the engine). South End: £35. Gillie hire: £35. Strathmore Lodge, Altnaharra, by Lairg, Sutherland, also have one boat on South End of Hope and fishing for 2 rods on the Strathmore River. North End costs: Boat per week £138; per day £27. Outboard & fuel per week: £80; per day £16.50.

HOPE, River
Location & Access Source 9/474603 Outflow 9/479622 From the A838 Thurso/Durness road via a good track on the east bank of the river.
Commentary A very attractive little river, flowing north from Loch Hope to the sea in a distance of one and a quarter miles. Most of the pools have been created by building croys and the lower pools are tidal. Loch Hope acts as a 'reservoir', maintaining reasonable water levels in the river during much of the season.
Fish Salmon and seatrout enter the Hope throughout the season with main run commencing in June. The best fishing period is generally July and August, although September can also produce excellent results. The average weight of salmon is about 8lb, seatrout average 1lb 8oz. Catch statistics are not available, but my 'guesstimate' is up to 100 salmon and a similar number of seatrout each season.
Flies & Tactics Fishing is by fly only. Willie Gunn, Garry Dog, Munro Killer, General Practitioner, and Green Highlander work well, as do Black Pennell, Grouse & Claret, Soldier Palmer, Peter Ross, for both seatrout and salmon, in low water conditions. The lies are readily covered using a light salmon rod. Thigh waders are useful.
Permission & Charges Fishing is only rarely available, usually in September, and is let with Hope Lodge. For further information and details, contact: Mr Boileau, Braesgill Ltd, Wyaston Grove, Ashbourne, Derbyshire DE6 2DR.

INNIS NA BA BUIDHE, Loch
Location & Access 9/227565 From the B801 Rhiconich/Kinlochbervie road. A track borders the east shoreline. The north end of the loch is easily approached from the Oldshoremore road.
Commentary Innis na Ba Buidhe lies to the north of Kinlochbervie and is one mile long by up to a quarter of a mile wide. The west shore is protected by high crags, but the east shore is easily fished from the bank. Ideal for a few casts if time is limited.

Cape Wrath — OS Map 9

Fish Good sport with pretty, brown trout averaging 8oz, but there are larger fish - one of over 5lb was taken recently.
Flies & Tactics Relatively safe wading and fish are taken all round the loch. Cast with confidence, offering them: March Brown, Grouse & Claret, Alexandra.
Permission & Charges Mr C Morrison, 200 Kinlochbervie, by Lairg, Sutherland, IV27 4RP. Tel: (01971) 521240. £5 per rod per day.

INSHORE, Loch
Location & Access 9/330697 Approach via the Kyle of Durness ferry from 9/378662 and the Cape Wrath lighthouse bus. The loch is immediately adjacent to the road. Check ferry times at Cape Wrath Hotel. Check RAF activity also, the area is part of a bombing range.
Commentary Easily accessible and generally fished in conjunction with Lochan Breac Buidhe (9/337689), half a mile east to the south of the Cape Wrath/Ferry road. A delightful loch, where even the least experienced will catch fish.
Fish A lot of them, averaging 6-8oz in weight.
Flies & Tactics Easy bank fishing with trout anxious to please. Offer: Soldier Palmer, March Brown, Silver Butcher.
Permission & Charges Cape Wrath Hotel, Keodale, Durness, by Lairg, Sutherland. Tel: (01971) 511212; Fax: (01971) 511313. Fishing on the Cape Wrath lochs is free to hotel guests. Day lets may be available at £10 per rod per day.

KEARVAIG, River
Location & Access Source 9/308662 Outflow 9/290728 Via the Kyle of Durness ferry to the Cape Wrath Peninsula, thence by min-bus. Check sailing and bus times at the Cape Wrath Hotel. Leave the bus at 9/289718 where the road crosses the river.
Commentary The most northerly salmon stream on mainland Scotland, flowing into the North Sea across a splendid little beach. The river rises from Loch na Gainmhich (9/307658), to the west of Fashven (457m), flowing north across desolate moorlands for two and a half miles to Kearvaig Bay. This area is a military gunnery range and is closed to the public when in use.
Fish Given good water levels, salmon and grilse run the river from June onwards. Salmon average 10lb, grilse, 5lb.
Flies & Tactics The right time to be there is in mid-July, August or September, after heavy rain. The lower section, from the road north to the sea, has a few good pools, the upper section, narrow and often slow-moving, is more difficult to fish. Offer them seatrout flies; Black Pennell, Soldier Palmer, Grouse & Claret, Peter Ross.
Permission & Charges Cape Wrath Hotel, Keodale, Durness, by Lairg, Sutherland. Tel (01971) 511212. Between £10 and £15 per rod per day depending upon the time of season.

KEISGAIG, Loch
Location & Access OS9/267680 Approach via the Kyle of Durness ferry from 9/378662. Take the Cape Wrath lighthouse bus to Inshore (9/326694). Walk south west across the southern shoulder of Maovally (299m), crossing the Kearvaig River (a small burn) after one hour. Keisgaig is 40 minutes further west. Alternatively, approach from Daill (see Loch na Gainmhich entry). Check ferry times at Cape Wrath Hotel. Check RAF activity also, the area is part of a bombing range.
Commentary The best of the Cape Wrath lochs. Take a tent and stay out, visiting Lochan na Glamhaichd (9/290667), Loch na Gainmhich (9/307658), Loch na Glaic Tarsuinn (9/298662) and Loch a' Gheodha Ruaidh (9/247674) along the way. Approximately 600 yards east to west by 250 yards north to south, shallow and relatively sheltered by Cnoc an Daimh to the north and the slopes of Beinn Dearg to the south. The outlet burn flows into the sea in one of Scotland's most remote and lovely beaches at 9/258695.
Fish Reported as being dour in recent years, but containing superb trout of up to 2lb and over in weight; also, their similar smaller brethren, which guarantees keeping your interest alive.
Flies & Tactics Try: Ke-He, Black Zulu, Silver Butcher.
Permission & Charges The Cape Wrath Hotel, Keodale, Durness, by Lairg, Sutherland. Tel: (01971) 511212; Fax: (01971) 511313. Fishing on the Cape Wrath hill lochs is free to hotel guests. Day lets may be available at £10 per rod per day.

KINLOCH, River The Kinloch River, which flows into the Kyle of Tongue, is preserved by the owner.

KYLE OF DURNESS Sea Loch
Location & Access Head of Kyle: 9/365625 Seaward limit: 9/365685 Easy access from Keodale (9/380660).
Commentary Can offer reasonable sport, particularly when water levels in the River Dionard are low. Regardless of whether or not the fish are cooperating, this is a dramatic place to fish, the verdant fields of the Durness limestone outcrop contrasting vividly with the surrounding mountains and golden sands of the Kyle.
Fish Seatrout are the principal quarry. Salmon are rarely taken. Fish average 1lb 8oz in weight and approximately 50 are landed during the season.
Flies & Tactics Launch your assault during the period two hours before and after low tide. Spinning brings best results, perhaps simply because most people chose to spin. However, traditional wet-fly seatrout patterns also produce fish. Try: Black Pennell, Grouse & Green, Teal Blue & Silver.
Permission & Charges Jack Watson, the Cape Wrath Hotel, Keodale, Durness, by Lairg, Sutherland. Tel: (01971) 511212; Fax: (01971) 511313. He will point you to the best fishing locations on the Kyle. A weeks' full board and fishing at the Cape Wrath Hotel costs in the order of £450 per person.

LADY, Loch See Loch Sgeir a'Chadha.

OS Map 9 — Cape Wrath

LAIRCHEARD, Loch
Location & Access 9/180460 South of the minor road which leaves the A838 Lairg/Scourie road at Claisfearn (9/192459), signposted to Tarbet and Handa Island. Park at 9/188465 and walk south-west to reach the loch in ten minutes.
Commentary Laircheard is a long, straggling loch, extending south for nearly one mile with an additional arm to the south-east. There are myriad fishy points, promontories and quiet corners offering great sport. Also have a cast on the eight, unnamed satellite lochans, particularly 9/177453.
Fish Plenty of medium-sized, hard-fighting brown trout and the chance of the odd larger specimen.
Flies & Tactics The Scourie Angling Association have a boat on this fine loch, but bank fishing is just as productive. Pay particular attention to the south-east bay, and in the vicinity of the narrows leading into the main south bay. Offer them: Black Zulu, Soldier Palmer, Dunkeld.
Permission & Charges Sec. Mrs R Mackay, Scourie Angling Club, 12 Park Terrace, Scourie. Tel: (01971) 502425 or at the village shop. Bank fishing: £5 per rod per day. Boat: £4 per day.

LANLISH, Loch
Location & Access 9/386683 Approach from Balnakeil and the car park at Durness Golf Club (9/389687). Follow the track behind the club house, round the hill, to reach the loch in ten minutes.
Commentary One of the most challenging and finest little lochs in all of Scotland. A never-ending delight and a privilege to fish. Lanlish extends to approximately eight acres, is lime-rich, shallow, and the ideal habitat for trout. The west shore is now bordered by the golf course, so Lanlish is less private than it used to be, but golfers and anglers co-habit happily. Regardless of wind force or direction, there is always a sheltered fishing area. Bank fishing only.
Fish Average weight is in the region of 2lb. Fish of this size really should be returned to grow bigger and fight more furiously another day. Lanlish trout are of quite exceptional quality. In days past, fish of over 14 pounds were taken and even today, trout of 8lb and more are caught.
Flies & Tactics Crossing the fingers helps. Lanlish trout do not give themselves up easily. If you chose to wade - and it is hard to resist the temptation - stalk the water as cautiously as a hungry heron; but, invariably, you will find yourself wading where you should be fishing. During the day, offer them small flies (Nos 16/18/22): Black Spider, Black Pennell, Ke-He, Grouse & Claret, Kingfisher Butcher; after dusk, sometimes, a large, daddy longlegs, fished dry, can produce results.
Permission & Charges Jack Watson, The Cape Wrath Hotel, Keodale, Durness, by Lairg, Sutherland. Tel: (01971) 511212; Fax: (01971) 511313. A week's full board and fishing costs in the order of £450 per person. Daily lets may be available at £15 per person.

LAXFORD, River
Location & Access Source 15/347350 Outflow 9/236470 Adjacent to the A838 Lairg/Scourie Road.
Commentary One of the most attractive and most productive salmon streams in the north but don't rush, because it is very expensive and rarely available to casual rods. Nevertheless, from time time, there might be a let, so it is always worth registering your interest. The surrounding scenery alone makes this river one of the most desirable fishing locations in all of Scotland.
Fish Salmon and seatrout although, at the time of writing, because of the disastrous decline in seatrout numbers, the estate has banned all seatrout fishing for the time being. Upwards of 200 salmon are taken most years.
Flies & Tactics The principal fishing extends form Loch Stack to Loch Laxford, a distance of some three and a half miles, and the most notable pools include: Top Pool, Duke's Pool, Duchess's Pool, Ridge Pool and Cottage Pool, although fish are taken throughout the system.
Permission & Charges For full details and further information contact: The Reay Forest Estate, Estate Office, Achfary, by Lairg, Sutherland. Tel (01971) 511221.

LEATHAID NAN CRUINEACHD, Loch See Loch Sgeireach.
LOCHAIN A'CHAORAINN, Loch See Clar Loch Mor.

LOCHAIN DOMIHAIN Lochs
Location & Access 9/223430 Park on the A838 Scourie/Lairg road at 9/191454 and cross the moor towards the obvious saddle on the hill. Walk south-east, passing Loch a'Mhuirt at 9/203448, reaching Loch Gorm after a journey of about thirty minutes. Continue south-east for a further thirty minutes to Lochain Domihain.
Commentary Compass and map time. A series of seven waters known as 'Top Chain', my favourite Scourie lochs, involving an invigorating walk to reach, but utterly lovely. As you approach Lochain Domihain watch out for the principal promontory. 'Pennell Point': the first Black Pennell of the season, cast from this point, is always rewarded with a fish of 1lb.
Fish Trout vary in size from 6oz up to fish of over 3lb in weight. Treat each rise with respect.
Flies & Tactics Bank fishing. Only the west end of Loch Domihain is accessible. After fishing there, climb to 9/231430 (Aeroplane Loch), and then to 9/232432 (Boot Loch). Circle back round the east end of Loch Domihain to fish the tiny lochan at 9/227428. Now south-west to 9/219437 (Pound Loch - all the trout are 1lb in weight), then 9/219425 (Otter Loch). Take no chances, use: Black Pennell, March Brown, Silver Butcher.
Permission & Charges Scourie Hotel, Scourie, by Lairg, Sutherland. Tel: (01971) 502396. £5 per rod per day.

DUBHA, Lochain
Location & Access 9/298553 Adjacent to the A838 Durness/Rhiconich road. Walk round the south shore of Loch Tarbhaidh to reach Lochain Dubha in ten minutes.

Cape Wrath — OS Map 9

Commentary A very attractive little loch, ideal for those who can't manage long walks, and for introducing beginners to the 'gentle art'.
Fish Small, bright, hard-fighting trout which average 6-8oz.
Flies & Tactics Bank fishing only and the water is easily covered. Also have a cast in the small lochans to the east of Dubha. They contain some good trout. First cast: Black Pennell, Grouse & Green, Peter Ross.
Permission & Charges Rhiconich Hotel, Rhiconich, by Lairg, Sutherland. Tel: (01971) 521224. Bank fishing: £5 per day.

LOCHAIN NA CREIGE DUIBHE Lochs
Location & Access 9/189409 Start a step south from Geisgeil (9/171411) and follow the outlet burn up the hill, a steep hike, to reach the lochs in about 30 minutes.
Commentary Three little lochs nestling below Creag Dhubh (245m), a land of red-throated diver, raven and peregrine. Clear, clear water, absolute solitude, peace and quite with magnificent views west to the Hebrides.
Fish Brightly-marked trout which do not give themselves up easily and average 8oz in weight.
Flies & Tactics The north loch (9/189409) is most productive, the middle loch lovely, and the south loch, a stumble down a crag to reach it, is utterly beautiful. Just being there is reward enough, regardless of fish, but you should not go home empty-handed. Approach with caution, the trout lie close. Try: Loch Ordie, Soldier Palmer, Black Pennell.
Permission & Charges Mr Hugh McKay, Scourie Angling Club, 12 Park Terrace, Scourie, Sutherland. Tel: (01971) 502425. £5 per rod per day.

LOCHAIN NA CREIGE GILE, Loch
Location & Access 9/273453 Via the stalkers path from Stack Lodge (9/270437). After about one mile, at 9/279444, bear left/west and follow the burn up to the first of this series of lochs.
Commentary Seven little lochans lying in hilly country to the north of Stack Lodge, each one a special delight, different in character, but all offering the chance of great sport and a wonderful day out.
Fish Brown trout which vary in size from 6oz up to fish of over 2lb in weight.
Flies & Tactics Fish the lochs in this order: 9/273447, 9/272452, 9/272456, 9/273454, 9/277457, 9/279457, 9/279450. All bank fishing and avoid wading. Fish lie close and most of the water is easily covered. Look out for the big ones, particularly in 9/272456. Offer them: Ke-He, Grouse & Claret, Silver Invicta.
Permission & Charges Scourie Hotel, Scourie, by Lairg, Sutherland. Tel: (01971) 502396. £5 per rod per day.

MATHAIR A'GHARBH UILT
Location & Access 9/278505 Approach from Rhiconich (9/255521) via the track on the east bank of the Rhiconich River. At the end of the track, walk north-east to reach the loch in 15 minutes.
Commentary Mathair a'Gharbh is a long, straggling loch, guarded to the north by Cnoc Liath, draining into Loch a'Gharbh-Bhaid Beag and thence to the sea in Loch Inchard. This is wild country, dominated by Foinaven (908m) and Arkle (787m), where you are certain of peace and quiet, and excellent sport.
Fish Brown trout only.
Flies & Tactics Bank fishing, with care, should provide you with breakfast. Fish are taken all round the loch and in the numerous satellite lochans. The east bay, where there is a small island, is particularly productive. Offer them: Black Zulu, Invicta, Dunkeld.
Permission & Charges Rhiconich Hotel, Rhiconich, by Lairg, Sutherland. Tel: (01971) 521224. £10 per rod per day. The Reay Forest Estate also have fishing on this loch.

MEADAIDH, Loch, Durness
Location & Access 9/402645 Approach from the peat track which leaves the A838 at 9/411673.
Commentary Proposals to develop a super-quarry here would destroy this excellent loch. The super-quarry would also seriously endanger the Durness limestone lochs, Caladail, Borralie, Lanlish and Croispol. Object now, before it is too late, by writing to: The Director of Planning, Highland Regional Council, Glenurquhart Road, Inverness. A very lovely loch in a dramatic, mountain and moorland setting, three quarters of a mile long by up to three hundred yards wide at the south end.
Fish Good Stocks of wild brown trout which average 10oz in weight, and larger fish of up to 1lb and over.
Flies & Tactics Easy bank fishing with best results coming from the extended south bay. Try: Soldier Palmer, Grouse & Claret, Silver Butcher.
Permission & Charges The Cape Wrath Hotel, Keodale, Durness, by Lairg, Sutherland. Tel: (01971) 511212; Fax: (01971) 511313. Fishing on the Cape Wrath hill lochs is free to hotel guests. Day lets may be available at £10 per rod per day.

MEADHONACH, Loch
Location & Access 9/210635 Leave the car at Blairmore (9/195601) and walk north towards Sandwood Bay.
Commentary Visit Meadhonach as part of a round tour, fishing Loch na Gainimh (9/204614), Lochain nan Sac (9/198625), Loch a'Mhuilinn (9/207630) on the way out, and then, after fishing Meadhonach, Loch Clais nan Coinneal (9/213639), Sandwood Loch (9/230640), Strath Shinary (9/240620), and Loch Mor a'Chraisg (9/230602) on the way home.
Fish Three to the pound sport with bright little trout.
Flies & Tactics Room for a few casts on the way north. Try: Ke-He, Woodcock & Hare-lug, Silver Butcher.
Permission & Charges See Sandwood Loch.

MEADIE, Loch
Location & Access 9/5004005 The boat-mooring bay is at 16/500491. Approach from Altnaharra via the Hope road.
Commentary One of the most attractive lochs in Sutherland, extending north towards Ben Loyal for more than six miles. Three miles from boat bay, the

OS Map 9 — Cape Wrath

loch narrows. There is a wonderful, little island here, the ideal place for lunch.
Fish A paradise of breakfast-sized trout which rise readily to surface flies and fight with great dash and spirit. Larger specimens are sometimes taken, particularly at the north end, and a trout of 4lb was caught here recently.
Flies & Tactics Meadie trout are not particular. However, start with Black Pennell, Grouse & Claret, Silver Butcher. Bank fishing is allowed, but fishing from a boat allows you to cover more water and easily explore the north end. Take care using an outboard, there are sudden shallows and hidden rocks.
Permission & Charges Altnaharra Hotel, Altnaharra, by Lairg, Sutherland. Tel: (01549) 411222. Boat, outboard engine and fuel: approx £20 per day.

MOR A'CHRAISG, Loch
Location & Access 9/230602 Can be included in the Sandwood Bay round tour (See Sandwood Loch entry), or visited separately from a peat track at 9/205596. Walk north to reach the loch in about 40 minutes.
Commentary A main loch surrounded by seven satellite lochans, including Loch Deibheadh (OS9/225607), in a remote, wonderful moorland setting, ideal for a day out in the hills.
Fish Some good brown trout of up to and over 1lb in weight and lots of their smaller brethren.
Flies & Tactics Delightful bank fishing on Mor a'Chraisg with the added pleasure of exploring the satellite lochans. All the water is easily covered and you might tempt them with: Ke-He, March Brown, Silver Invicta.
Permission & Charges See Sandwood Loch.

NA CAILLICH, Loch
Location & Access 9/247507 See Lady Loch.
Commentary A narrow passage of water, mostly blocked off by an old stone wall, connects it with Na Thull.
Fish Na Caillich does contain some sea trout, but is no longer as good as it was 12 years ago.

NA CAISE LUACHRAICH, Loch
Location & Access 9/223493 Lies to the west of the A838 Rhiconich/Laxford Bridge road. Park at 9/239495 and on the way west fish the two un-named lochs at 9/235495 and 9/229497. After fishing Caise Luachraich, continue west to fish 9/217796 at Meall an Ulbhaidh.
Commentary A fine day out amidst dramatic scenery, fishing a delightful series of lochans above Loch Laxford. Yours for the day.
Fish Reported as dour but some large fish. A 2lb 12oz brown trout was caught in 1996.
Flies & Tactics Bank fishing, but the water is easily covered from the shore. First cast: Black Zulu, Soldier Palmer, Alexandra.
Permission & Charges The Rhiconich Hotel, Rhiconich, by Lairg, Sutherland. Tel: (01971) 521224. £5 per rod per day.

NA CLAISE CARNAICH, Loch
Location & Access 9/280527 To the east of Rhiconich, reached after a stiff moorland tramp of some 30 minutes. Boat location and details when booking.
Commentary The largest of the Rhiconich lochs and also perhaps the most lovely, with Foinaven (908m) towering to the east. Na Claise Carnaich is nearly one mile long by up to quarter of a mile wide, scattered with six tiny islands, bays and 'fishy' corners.
Fish Excellent stocks of brown trout which average 10-12oz, and larger fish as well. Well-shaped, hard-fighting trout which give a good account of themselves.
Flies & Tactics Boat and bank fishing, but the boat allows you to cover the water more easily. The northeast bay is a good place to start, by the inlet stream flowing down from Cnoc a'Mhadaidh (589m) and Ceann Garbh (901m). The bays and islands in the south-east corner also produce good results. Try: Blue Zulu, Woodcock & Hare-lug, Alexandra.
Permission & Charges Rhiconich Hotel, Rhiconich, by Lairg, Sutherland. Tel: (01971) 521224. Boat fishing: £10 per day. Bank fishing: £5 per day.

NA CLAISE FEARNA, Loch
Location & Access 9/201468 Immediately adjacent to the north of the A838 Lairg/Scourie road.
Commentary Although exposed to public view, a very pretty little loch and easily accessible. An ideal beginners' waters and often sheltered in high winds.
Fish Very large stocks of very small brown trout, but with a few larger fish of up to 1lb. Claise Fearna is, however, connected to Loch Laxford and salmon and seatrout enter the system and are occasionally caught.
Flies & Tactics Boat fishing, but bank fishing can also be rewarding. The northern part, amidst the small bays and promontories, is the best fishing area, and in the vicinity of the two islands. Try: Black Zulu, Soldier Palmer, Alexandra.
Permission & Charges Scourie Hotel, Scourie, by Lairg, Sutherland. Tel: (01971) 502396. Bank fishing: £5 per rod per day.

NA CREIGE RIABHAICH, Loch
Location & Access 9/288633 Nearly five miles from Gruide (9/362632), to the west of the A838 Durness/Laxford Bridge road. No track, rough going, compass and map essential. Follow the Grudie River into the hills, aiming for the south end of the Creag Riabhaich (485m) ridge.
Commentary Years might pass without this loch seeing an artificial fly. Definitely for the angler who likes a long walk and fishing remote places. Utterly splendid.
Fish Recent information indicates good stocks of traditional Highland brown trout, but some larger fish as well. However, be warned, this loch can be dour.
Flies & Tactics Watching and waiting helps. Don't just dash straight in. Pay particular attention to the two streams, north and south, at the west end. Offer them: Soldier Palmer, Greenwell's Glory, Black Zulu
Permission & Charges The Cape Wrath Hotel,

67

Cape Wrath — OS Map 9

Keodale, Durness, by Lairg, Sutherland. Tel: (01971) 511212. Fax: (01971) 511313. Fishing on the Cape Wrath Hotel hill lochs is free to guests. Day lets may be available at £10 per rod per day.

NA FAOILEIGE, Lochan
Location & Access 9/327449 Approach from Lone (9/310422) at the east end of Loch Stack via a good stalkers path. After two miles, at 9/334447, leave the track and walk up the hill to the loch, reaching Na Faoileige in about 15 minutes.
Commentary A wonderful little corrie lochan on the east slopes of Arkle (787m), protected by the crags of An Garbh-choire. Magnificent views to Ben Stack and Creagan Meall Horn (729m), guaranteed peace and seclusion.
Fish Small, wild brown trout which give great sport and average in the order of 6-8oz, ideal for breakfast.
Flies & Tactics Bank fishing with action all round the loch, but particularly in the east corner by the small island. Offer: Blue Zulu, March Brown, Silver Butcher.
Permission & Charges The Reay Forest Estate, Estate Office, Achfary, by Lairg, Sutherland. Tel: (01971) 500221. 1994 charges in the order of £5 per rod per day.

NA FREAGAIRT, Lochan
9/184440 See Loch na h-Airigh Sleibhe.

NA GAINIMH, Loch (Sandwood)
Location & Access 9/204614 On the track out to Sandwood Bay. Leave the car at Blairmore (9/195601) and walk north to reach the loch in 15 minutes.
Commentary The muddy track skirts the sandy south shore of this 100 acre loch but it is easy to escape Sandwood Bay traffic by walking round to the west shore where you will find bucketfulls of peace and quiet.
Fish Nothing of vast size, but great fun with very pretty little trout which average 6-8oz. Reports from time to time of larger fish, so treat every rise with respect.
Flies & Tactics Wonderful bank fishing and comfortable wading. The west and north shore produce best results. Offer them: Soldier Palmer, March Brown, Peter Ross.
Permission & Charges See Sandwood Loch.

NA GAINMHICH, Loch
Location & Access 9/307658 From Keodale (9/378662) via the ferry across the Kyle of Durness. Take the Cape Wrath lighthouse bus to Daill (9/358682). Follow the Daill River south-west, past Loch Bad an Fheur-loch (9/339672) and Loch Airigh na Beinne (9/327664). Skirt the south shore of Airigh na Beinne and climb the south shoulder of Fashven to reach the loch in a walk of approximately one hour and thirty minutes. Check ferry sailing times at Cape Wrath Hotel. The area is an RAF bombing range, so also check that they are not busy.
Commentary An excellent Cape Wrath peninsular loch. Take a tent and stay out, visiting Loch Bad an Fheur-loch, Loch Airigh na Beinne (see above), Loch na Gainmhich (9/307658), Loch na Glaic Tarsuinn (9/297663), Loch na Glamhaichd (9/290667) along the way. A substantial, shallow loch lying between Fashven to the north and Cnoc na Farsuinn to the south, extending to nearly half a mile in length by over quarter of a mile wide.
Fish Hard-fighting, little trout which average 8oz.
Flies & Tactics Exciting bank fishing all round the loch and trout rise readily to most patterns of fly. Begin with: Black Pennell, March Brown, Alexandra.
Permission & Charges The Cape Wrath Hotel, Keodale, Durness, by Lairg, Sutherland. Tel: (01971) 511212; Fax: (01971) 511313. Fishing on the Cape Wrath hill lochs is free to hotel guests. Day lets may be available at £10 per rod per day.

NA GLAIC TARSUINN, Loch
Location & Access 9/298662 Approach via the Kyle of Durness ferry from 9/378662. Take the Cape Wrath lighthouse bus to Inshore (9/326694). Walk south-west, with Maovally (299m) on your right and Fashven (457m) on your left, to reach the loch after a walk of about one hour thirty minutes. Alternatively, approach from Daill (see Loch na Gainmhich entry). Check ferry times at Cape Wrath Hotel. Check RAF activity also, the area is part of a bombing range.
Commentary A lovely, little lochan, deep in the heart of the Cape Wrath peninsular. Take a tent and stay out, visiting Loch na Gainmhich (9/307658), Loch na Galmhaichd (9/290667) along the way. A good site for base camp prior to further exploring, sheltered by the northern crags of Cnoc na Glaic Tarsuinn.
Fish The place to catch breakfast, lunch and dinner. Great sport with bright, little fish which average 8oz in weight.
Flies & Tactics Tempt them with: Black Pennell, Greenwell's Glory, Dunkeld.
Permission & Charges The Cape Wrath Hotel, Keodale, Durness, by Lairg, Sutherland. Tel: (01971) 511212; Fax: (01971) 511313. Fishing on the Cape Wrath hill lochs is free to hotel guests. Day lets may be available at £10 per rod per day.

NA GLAMHAICHD, Lochan
Location & Access 9/290667 Approach via the Kyle of Durness ferry from 9/378662. Take the Cape Wrath lighthouse bus to Inshore (9/326694). Walk south south-west, with Maovally (299m) on your right and Fashven (457m) on your left, to reach the loch after a walk of about one hour thirty minutes. Alternatively, approach from Daill (see Loch na Gainmhich entry). Check ferry times at Cape Wrath Hotel. Check RAF activity also, the area is part of a bombing range.
Commentary A remote lochan, deep in the heart of the Cape Wrath peninsular. Take a tent and stay out, visiting Loch na Gainmhich (OS9/307658), Loch na Glaic Tarsuinn (OS9/298662) along the way. Lies to the north of Beinn Dearg (423m), in a shallow hollow, extending to approximately five acres. Have a few casts on the way to Keisgaig.
Fish Trout average 8oz in weight.
Flies & Tactics Tempt them with: Black Pennell, Greenwell's Glory, Dunkeld.
Permission & Charges The Cape Wrath Hotel, Keodale, Durness, by Lairg, Sutherland. Tel: (01971) 511212; Fax: (01971) 511313. Fishing on the Cape

OS Map 9 — Cape Wrath

Wrath hill lochs is free to hotel guests. Day lets may be available at £10 per rod per day.

NA H-AIRIGH SLEIBHE, Loch
Location & Access 9/188435 Park at 9/165430 on the A894 Scourie/Ullapool road and follow the peat track east by the Chambered Cairn. The loch is 15 minutes from the end of the track.
Commentary A deep loch (30m at the north end), more than half a mile long by up to quarter of a mile wide across the south bay, in dramatic surroundings. Also visit Lochan na Fregairt (9/184440) and the unnamed lochan by Cnoc na Glaice Moire at 9/188444. On your return, stop for a cast in Loch Coill a'Ghorm Locha (9/183432).
Fish Trout here average 8oz but there is always the chance of something much larger, tempted from the depths, but can be dour, hard work. The alternative lochs noted are often far more rewarding.
Flies & Tactics Bank fishing and the west shoreline is best, particularly at the south end in the shallower water.
Permission & Charges Scourie Hotel, Scourie, by Lairg, Sutherland. Tel: (01971) 502396. £5 per rod per day.

NA H-ATH, Loch
9/239419 See Feur Lochan.

NA LAIRE DUIBHE, Loch
Location & Access 9/232524 The last in a series of four lochs lying to the west of the Rhiconich/Laxford Bridge road. Park on the minor road leading out to Ardmore at 9/245518 and follow the outlet stream up to the first, un-named loch at 9/244520.
Commentary A pleasant, easy ramble, exploring and fishing four super little lochans on Ceatlramh Garbh along the way.
Fish Traditional highland brown trout, averaging 6-8oz. Can be hard work making them rise, but great fun and they fight hard.
Flies & Tactics After fishing 9/244520, walk east to visit 9/240521, then 15 minutes west again to Na Laire Duibhe. Now south to 9/232520, then back to the Ardmore road and your car. Offer Blue Zulu, Silver Invicta, Dunkeld. Easy bank fishing.
Permission & Charges The Rhiconich Hotel, Rhiconich, by Lairg, Sutherland. Tel: (01971) 521224. £5 per rod per day.

NA LARACH, Loch
Location & Access 9/219581 An easily accessible little lochan lying adjacent to the Kinlochbervie/Oldshoremore road.
Commentary A bit public, being so close to the road, but a good place for a few casts if time is limited
Fish Brown trout which average 6-8oz.
Flies & Tactics Comfortable bank fishing and the fish are not over-particular about their diet. Offer them: Black Pennell, March Brown, Silver Butcher.
Permission & Charges Mr C Morrison, 200 Kinlochbervie, by Lairg, Sutherland, IV27 4RP. Tel: (01971) 521240. £5 per rod per day.

NA MNATHA, Loch
Location & Access 9/196440 Park on the A838 Scourie/Lairg road at 9/191454 and walk over the moor towards the obvious saddle on the hill. Walk south-west to Loch a'Mhuirt (9/203448) and at 9/200446 head south to reach Loch Na Mnatha within ten minutes.
Commentary This is the 'Woman's Loch,' given as a consolation prize to the widow of a man Lord Reay had killed on Loch a' Mhuirt during the Middle Ages (see Loch a' Mhuirt entry).
Fish Loch na Mnatha contains large stocks of bright little trout averaging 6-8oz, but the surrounding lochans contain a few surprises and should be carefully examined, particularly OS9/192442.
Flies & Tactics All bank fishing and areas of Loch na Mnatha will make you stumble. Approach the lochans very quietly, trout lie close. Begin with: Soldier Palmer, Grouse & Claret, Peter Ross.
Permission & Charges Scourie Hotel, Scourie, by Lairg, Sutherland. Tel: (01971) 502396. £5 per rod per day.

NA SEAMRAIG, Loch
Location & Access 9/280727 Approach via the Kyle of Durness ferry from 9/378662 and the Cape Wrath lighthouse bus. Leave the bus at 9/274725 and walk north for 15 minutes to reach the loch. Check ferry times at Cape Wrath Hotel. Check RAF activity also, the area is part of a bombing range.
Commentary A good location for a family day out, combined with a visit to Kearvaig beach (9/291728). A small loch on dramatic cliff near Cape Wrath, surrounded by superb scenery and close to a delightful beach.
Fish Plenty of action with small fish with average 6oz in weight.
Flies & Tactics Cast with confidence anywhere, the fish are eager to please. Start with: Solder Palmer, Grouse & Claret, Silver Butcher.
Permission & Charges The Cape Wrath Hotel, Keodale, Durness, by Lairg, Sutherland. Tel: (01971) 511212; Fax: (01971) 511313. Fishing on the Cape Wrath hill lochs is free to hotel guests. Day lets may be available at £10 per rod per day.

NA SEILG, Loch
Location & Access 9/369588 Park at 9/405572 and follow the stream north-west up the hill. The loch lies between Meall nan Cra (490m) to the north, and Carn an Righ, the most northerly outliner of Beinn Spionaidh (772m), to the south.
Commentary Fishing is of secondary importance amidst this magnificent landscape. Carrying a trout rod is simply an added benefit of a marvellous, unforgettable day out in the hills.
Fish A magical little loch with breakfast-sized trout which are great fun to catch.
Flies & Tactics Know how to use a compass and map, and if the weather closes in, come down from the hill immediately. Easy bank fishing. Use: Loch Ordie, March Brown, Silver Butcher.
Permission & Charges The Manager, Balnakiel Farm, Durness, Sutherland.

Cape Wrath   OS Map 9

NA SEILGE, Loch (Ben Stack)
Location & Access 9/255435 Park by the shepherd's hut at 9/264437 on the A838 Scourie/Lairg road. Follow the track that climbs south over the west shoulder of Ben Stack (721m). After 15 minutes you will see Loch na Seilge in a hollow at the foot of the hill.
Commentary A very pretty loch with a sandy beach and delightful island, rarely fished as most anglers head further south in search of grander things. An ideal beginners loch, in spite of the steep climb down - and back up at the end of the day.
Fish Full of lively little trout and a few fish of up to 1lb in weight.
Flies & Tactics Bank fishing only. Trout are taken from all round the shore but the west end is best.
Permission & Charges Scourie Hotel, Scourie, by Lairg, Sutherland. Tel: (01971) 502396. £5 per rod per day.

NA SEILGE, Loch (Creagan Meall Horn)
Location & Access 9/370446 A tough hike from Lone (9/309422) at the east end of Loch Stack and not for the faint-hearted. Follow the stalkers' path skirting Creagan Meall Horn (792m). The loch lies to the south of this track, past An Dubh Loch and Lochan Ulbha, in a corrie on the north-east shoulder of Sabhal Mor.
Commentary An all day hill-walking and fishing expedition. Allow eight hours for the round trip. Fish An Dubh first, then Lochan Ulbha. After Ulbha, walk south to fish and Loch na Seilge (9/370446). Continue south between Sabhal Mor (703m) and Sabhal Beag (729m) to a track down Strath Luib na Seillich which leads back to Lone.
Fish Good stocks of wild brown trout which average 8-10oz, and the chance of larger fish.
Flies & Tactics Trout are taken all round the loch. First cast: Ke-He, Woodcock & Hare-lug, Silver Butcher. Bank fishing.
Permission & Charges Grosvenor Estate (contact Reay Forest Estate Office, Achfary, by Lairg, Sutherland. Tel: 01971 500221).

NA STIOMA GILE, Loch
Location & Access 9/302492 Start from Stack Lodge (9/270438). After three and a half miles, the track descends to Loch an Tigh Shelg. Walk the right bank of An Tigh Shelg to find the outlet stream from Na Stioma Gile. Follow the stream up to the loch. From Stack Lodge, a distance of four and a half miles.
Commentary A perfect little lochan on the slopes of Foinaven (908m) at the end of a long, hard walk. Rarely fished from one season to the next. Far from the madding crowd fishing, remote and wonderful. A place to treasure.
Fish Excellent stocks of wild trout, tinged dark green with bright red spots. Average weight 10-12oz.
Flies & Tactics Weedy and fished from the bank, but easy wading. Fish rise eagerly and frequently there are two to the cast. Take a brace for breakfast. The tiny loch above Stioma Gile is also worth a cast.
Permission & Charges The Reay Forest Estate, Estate Office, Achfary, by Lairg, Sutherland. Tel: (01971) 500021. 1994 charges in the order of £5 per rod per day.

NA THULL, Loch
Location & Access 9/253500 Awkward to approach, in spite of being close to the A838 Rhiconich/Laxford Bridge road. Park south of the bend at 9/239504 and walk back to the west end, to fish the south shore. Park at 9/247507 to explore the north shore and Loch na Caillich, which is an extension of Loch na Thull.
Commentary A difficult, dour loch. The margins are bounded by the crags of Cnoc Thull on the south and fishing here involves climbing over the crags to reach the next fishable stance. The north shore is easier but is step-sided along much of the way.
Fish Brown trout, small and dark, although there are reports of large fish being hooked and lost. Thull is connected to the sea at Loch a'Chadh-fi and it is not impossible for seatrout to gain access. Indeed, some years ago, the writer took a seatrout whilst fishing the narrows at 9/246502. The loch is deep up to 100 feet in places and is a good place to troll for ferox.
Flies & Tactics Bank fishing only and stumbling country, so take great care, the crags on the south shore are dangerous. Offer the brutes Black Pennell, Soldier Palmer, Alexandra.
Permission & Charges Jointly owned by the Rhiconich Hotel, Rhiconich, by Lairg, Sutherland, IV27 4RP, Tel: (01971) 521224, and the Reay Forest Estate, Estate Office, Achfary, by Lairg, Sutherland. Tel: (01971) 500221. £5 per rod per day. The Rhiconich Hotel have a boat on this loch (£10 per day and £5 for the bank).

NA TUADH, Loch
Location & Access 9/310472 A long walk, but a good track all the way. Start from Stack Lodge (9/270438), skirting the west shoulder of Arkle (757m), to reach the loch after a four and half mile hike.
Commentary Tuadh lies between Arkle and Foinaven (908m) and is three quarters of a mile long by three hundred yards wide. The surrounding scenery is absolutely magnificent, just reward for effort.
Fish You will not return empty-handed. Tuadh has good stocks of wild trout which fight well and average 8-10oz. There are also a few larger specimens, so be alert.
Flies & Tactics Wonderful bank fishing, particularly along the north shore and into the finger-like east bay. Both outlet and inlet streams can also provide great sport and can often produce larger fish. Begin with: Black Pennell, Greenwell's Glory, Dunkeld.
Permission & Charges Scourie Hotel, Scourie, by Lairg, Sutherland. Tel: (01971) 502396. 1994 charges in the order of £5 per rod per day.

NAM BRAC, Loch
Location & Access 9/180480 Immediately adjacent to and north of the minor road which leaves the A838 Lairg/Scourie road at Claisfearn (9/192459), signposted to Tarbet and Handa Island.
Commentary This loch, with its six finger-like bays and scattered islands, is no longer fished, the trout stocks and water quality having been adversely affected by fish farm cage sewage.
Fish It used to have good quality brown trout averaging 8-10oz.

OS Map 9 — Cape Wrath

Flies & Tactics The Scourie Angling Association used to put two boats on Nam Brac.
Permission & Charges Enquiries about the current situation to: Mrs R. Mackay, The Secretary, Scourie Angling Club, 12 Park Terrace, Scourie. Tel: (01971) 502425 or at the village shop.

NAM BREAC BUIDHE, Lochan (Cape Wrath)
Location & Access 9/337689 Approach via the Kyle of Durness ferry from 9/378662 and the Cape Wrath lighthouse bus. The loch is immediately adjacent to the road. Check ferry times at Cape Wrath Hotel. Check RAF activity also, the area is part of a bombing range.
Commentary Easily accessible and generally fished in conjunction with Loch Inshore (9/330697), half a mile west to the north of the Cape Wrath/Ferry road. A small, roadside lochan, ideal for beginners and great fun to fish.
Fish A lot of them, averaging 6-8oz in weight.
Flies & Tactics Easy bank fishing with trout anxious to please. Offer: Soldier Palmer, March Brown, Silver Butcher.
Permission & Charges The Cape Wrath Hotel, Keodale, Durness, by Lairg, Sutherland. Tel: (01971) 511212; Fax: (01971) 511313. Fishing on the Cape Wrath hill lochs is free to hotel guests. Day lets may be available at £10 per rod per day.

NAN UIDH, Loch
Location & Access 9/194417 Start from Geisgeil (9/171411) by the A894 Scourie/Ullapool road. Follow the east shore of Loch Bad nam Mult (9/172413) and climb the waterfall gully (9/178418) up to the west end of Loch nan Uidh.
Commentary Loch nan Uidh is part of a long series of lochs extending two miles east, joined by a narrow stream to Loch Airigh na Beinne (9/201411) and Clar Loch Cnoc Thormaid (9/206417). There are excellent satellite lochans to the south at 9/189414 and at 9/195413. Don't miss them.
Fish Good stocks of trout averaging 6-8oz, but also occasional fish of up to 2lb.
Flies & Tactics Loch nan Uidh has a boat, but you will have to 'hoof' it to Airigh na Beinne and Clar Loch Cnoc Thormaid. Concentrate activities on Uidh in the boat mooring bay and round the island at the east end. On Clar Loch Cnoc Thormaid, fish the north east shore and the north narrows. Use: Ke-He, March Brown, Kingfisher Butcher.
Permission & Charges Scourie Hotel, Scourie, by Lairg, Sutherland. Tel: (01971) 502396. Bank fishing: £5 per rod per day.

NUMBERS Lochs
Location & Access 9/275510 Approach from Rhiconich (9/256521) and the boathouse on Loch a'Gharbh-bhaid Beag (9/265507), walking north-east up the hill to reach the lochs in about 15 minutes.
Commentary A series of seven little lochs and lochans between Cnoc a'Gharbh-bhaid Beag and Cnoc Liath (9/281516) providing a grand day out in the wilds.
Fish Plenty of sport with bright, little trout and a few surprises. Try not to be surprised. Concentrate all the time.

Flies & Tactics Bank fishing and take care not to spook the fish by towering over the water. Keep back, the trout lie close to the shore. Big, bushy flies: Ke-He, Loch Ordie, Black Zulu.
Permission & Charges The Rhiconich Hotel, Rhiconich, by Lairg, Sutherland. Tel: (01971) 521224. £5 per rod per day.

POLLA, River
Location & Access Source 9/380492 Outflow 9/391546 Approach from the A838 Thurso/Durness road at the south end of Loch Eriboll.
Commentary A modest highland spate stream flowing north from Creag Shomhairle (369m) to Loch Eriboll in a distance of six miles. The river used to be owned by Sir Reginald Rootes, the industrialist and motor car manufacturer. In recent years, a fish farm enterprise has been operating in Loch Erribol and the rather ugly rearing tanks are on the Polla, close to the sea. However, upstream, the landscape is unchanged and quite marvellous. Falls, three miles from the sea, exclude salmon from the headwaters. Only the bottom 1.5 miles is seriously fished.
Fish Mainly a salmon stream, although good seatrout are taken (Mr Brothers had a 6lb 11oz fish in 1997), particularly in the lower pools and in the estuary. Some large salmon have been caught in recent years, Angus MacArthur from Laide taking a fish of over 20lb, but the average weight is 6-7lb. Fish arrive in July, but the most productive month is September. Approximately 60-80 fish are taken most seasons.
Flies & Tactics The water in this narrow stream is gin clear. You can easily see the fish in the pools, but they can just as easily see you. Stay well back from the bank, extending line, rather than walking down the bank. Keep below the skyline. There are 15 named pools, the best of which are probably Abbas, Half Moon and Park Pool. Useful flies: Munro Killer, Silver Charm, Hairy Mary, Red Stoat's Tail.
Permission & Charges Fishing is well-booked in advance. Full details: Charles Marsham, Rispond & Polla Estate, Durness, by Lairg, Sutherland. Tel: (01971) 511224. Expect a weekly charge for two rods and accommodation for about £500-£1000, depending upon time of year.

PRIVATE WATERS NA GAINIMH, Loch (9/270564).
GENERAL'S Loch, to the north of Rhiconich and named after General Stronach who instigated the making of the loch just after the 1st World War, is private. The lochs between Rhimichie (9/237544) and Kinsaile (9/211550) are also private and not available to public fishing. The roadside lochans to the south of Gualin House (9/308560) are preserved and not available for public fishing. The following lochs are not available to the general public: three lochs to the south of Whiten Head (9/050665); the hill lochs between Ben Hope and Meallan Liath; the hill lochs between Loch Hope and Loch Eribol.

RHICONICH, River
See Loch a'Gharbh-bhaid Beag and Loch a'Gharbh-bhaid Mor.

Cape Wrath — OS Map 9

SANDWOOD, Loch
Location & Access 9/227640 Park at Blairmore (9/15601) and walk north to the loch in about two hours.
Commentary Visit Sandwood as part of a round tour, fishing Loch na Gainimh (9/204614), Lochain nan Sac (9/198625), Loch a'Mhuilinn (9/207630) Loch Meadhonach (9/210635) and Loch Clais nan Coinneal (9/213639) on the way out, and then, after Sandwood, Strath Shinary (9/240620), and Loch Mor a'Chraisg (9/230602) on the way home. Sandwood Estate is owned by the John Muir Trust, a charity dedicated to conserving wild places for nature and people. Their policy is to welcome unrestricted responsible pedestrian access but to restrict the promotion of access only to sites that have adequate carrying capacity. They make permits available locally for fishing on their properties but do not actively promote their availability. Fishing on some lochs is discouraged to prevent disturbance to sensitive wildlife.
Fish Small brown trout with a few larger specimens which lie deep and are rarely caught. Sandwood is joined to the sea and in high tides and spate conditions, salmon and seatrout enter the system, particularly in June and in August and September.
Flies & Tactics This is the largest loch on the Cape Wrath Peninsula, just over one mile in length and up to half a mile wide. Bank fishing only, and catching salmon or seatrout depends entirely upon being there at the right time. However, as far as the writer is concerned, any time is the right time to visit this most lovely of Scottish bays. First cast: Loch Ordie, Grouse & Claret, Dunkeld.
Permission & Charges Contact: Will Boyd-Wallis, Raven Cottage, 144 Oldshoremore, Rhiconich, Lairg, Sutherland IV27 4RS. Tel: 01971 521459, Charges in the order of £5 per rod per day. Salmon and seatrout fishing may be available on Sandwood at £10 per rod per day.

SGEIREACH, Lochan
Location & Access 9/166436 Approach from the peat track which leaves the A894 Scourie/Ullapool road at 9/165492. Walk east up the hill for 300 yards to pick up a path heading north to the loch. A fifteen minute walk.
Commentary Sgeireach in conjunction with little Loch Leathaid nan Cruineachd (9/161440). Both these lochs are easily accessible and close to Scourie Village. Ideal for an early morning or after dinner assault.
Fish Traditional highland trout averaging 6-8oz.
Flies & Tactics Comfortable bank fishing on both waters and fish are taken everywhere. Offer them: Black Pennell, March Brown, Silver Butcher.
Permission & Charges Scourie Hotel, Scourie, by Lairg, Sutherland. Tel: (01971) 502396. £5 per rod per day.

SGIER A'CHADHA, Loch
Location & Access 9/232510 Approach from the A838 Rhiconich/Laxford Bridge road at 9/239504, signposted to Skerricha (9/241507). The loch lies immediately to the north at the end of the road.
Commentary An easily accessible loch near to John Ridgway's Adventure School on Loch a'Chadh-Fi, an arm of Loch Laxford. Along the way, stop for a cast or two in the un-named lochans at 9/233505 and 9/238507.
Fish Salmon and seatrout, but not very productive. There is also the possibility of seatrout in 9/238507.

Flies & Tactics Boat fishing brings best results, although bank fishing can also be productive. Everything depends upon good water levels to bring seatrout into the system. Prior to fishing, pray for rain. Don't forget to have a cast in the satellite lochan at OS9/232513 which is joined to Sgeir a' Chadh by a narrow stream. Offer them: Ke-He, Grouse & Claret, Peter Ross.
Permission & Charges The Rhiconich Hotel, Rhiconich, by Lairg, Sutherland. Tel: (01971) 521224. Boat fishing: £15 per day. Bank fishing: £5 per day.

SHINARY, River
Location & Access Source 9/279620 Outflow 9/225654 Approach from Blairmore (9/196601), west of Kinlochbervie. Walk north to Sandwood Bay, a journey of approximately one and a half hours. Sandwood Loch (9/2347640), which drains the River Shinary, is to the east of the track, close to Sandwood Bay.
Commentary Possibly the most remote and most difficult to access salmon stream in Scotland, consequently rarely fished. There are other problems. The outlet from Sandwood Loch is across a golden beach and the stream is frequently silted up. However, in high tides or after heavy rain, fish can gain access to the system. Having said all of which, given the choice of a day on the Tay or a day on the Shinary, I would always choose the latter.
Fish Few details of numbers or size of fish, but salmon, grilse and seatrout are present from June onwards, depending upon water levels.
Flies & Tactics The loch should be examined first, then explore the river, from the inlet up to the footbridge at Strathan (9/248611). Look first, cast later, and keep well back from the bank. Use small flies: Willie Gunn, Garry Dog, Black Pennell, Grouse & Claret, Peter Ross. Crossing the fingers also helps.
Permission & Charges See Sandwood Loch.

SIAN, Loch
Location & Access 9/448632 On the west side of Loch Eriboll, approached by a track leading down from the A838 Bettyhill/Durness road near Laide at 9/440632.
Commentary Once a very lovely little seaside loch, now sadly disfigured by the presence of fish farming cages.
Fish Seatrout and brown trout. Seatrout enter on the tide and average 1lb 8oz, with fish of up to 4lb; brown trout are larger than adjacent lochs because of additional feeding from the cages.
Flies & Tactics Easily fished from the shore and let in conjunction with the Polla River and on a daily basis.
Permission & Charges Charles Marsham, Rispond & Polla Estate, Durness, by Lairg, Sutherland. Tel: (01971) 511318 or (01971) 511224. For charges see River Polla entry. Daily charges from £7.50 per rod.

SGAOTHAICHEAN, Lochan See Loch Meadie entry on OS Map 16.

STACK, Loch
Location & Access 9/295420 Easily accessible from A338 Lairg/Scourie road. Boats are moored at the west end of the loch.

OS Map 9 — Cape Wrath

Commentary One of Scotland's most famous and most beautiful seatrout fisheries, sadly suffering from the national decline in numbers of fish.
Fish Seatrout, salmon and some good brown trout. Seatrout average 1lb 8oz in weight, with occasional fish of up to 6lb and over. Salmon average 7-8lb. Large brown trout are caught, generally by accident, and can weigh up to 4lb and more.
Flies & Tactics Boats from Hotel will not let be without a ghillie. Outboard engines are not allowed, therefore be prepared for some heavy rowing, or engage the services of a gillie. Fish lie close to the shore over most of the loch but a gillie is almost a must if you are new to the water. First cast: Loch Ordie, Greenwell's Glory, Peter Ross.
Permission & Charges Scourie Hotel, Scourie, by Lairg, Sutherland. Tel: (01971) 502396. 1997 charges vary from £20 - £30 per day, depending upon the time of year.

STRATHMORE, River
Location & Access Source 9/382400 Outflow 9/451511 From the minor road between Altnaharra and Hope through Strath More.
Commentary The stream rises in the heart of the Reay Forest by Meall Garbh (752m) joining the Golly River at Gobernuisgach Lodge (9/437417) to become the Strathmore River. Strath More is a green, fertile glen, and the river meanders past Dun Dornaigil Broch (BC200-AD100) to enter Loch Hope at Eilean Mor (9/451511).
Fish Salmon and seatrout enter from Loch Hope, the first fish often appearing in late May, but the most productive fishing is during July, August and September. Salmon average 8lb, seatrout 1lb 8oz. Catch returns are not available but my 'guesstimate' is about 60 salmon and 100 seatrout each season.
Flies & Tactics Success is very much dependent upon spate conditions. The river is easily fished, wearing thigh waders, using a light salmon rod, although during high water a double-handed rod is best for covering some of the temporarily extended pools. The lower pools are slow-moving and the technique of 'backing up' is usefully employed. Try: Willie Gunn, General Practitioner, Garry Dog, Silver Wilkinson, Hairy Mary. In low water, come down to small seatrout flies: Black Pennell, Soldier Palmer, Peter Ross.
Permission & Charges Fishing is always well-booked in advance and the river is divided into two beats: Upper River goes with Gobernuisgach Lodge, details from Reay Forest Estate, Estate Office, Achfary, by Lairg, Sutherland. Tel: (01971) 500221; the lower river is let, with a boat on South End Loch Hope (for five weeks only) with Strathmore Lodge - details from Mrs Heather Gow, Pitscandly, Forfar, Angus DD8 3NZ. Tel: (01307) 462437.

TARBHAIDH, Loch
Location & Access 9/295555 Immediately adjacent to the A838 Durness/Rhiconich road.
Commentary A very attractive, roadside loch, half a mile long by 200 yards wide and the best brown trout loch on the Rhiconich Hotel Estate. Ideal for little ones who can't manage long walks, and for introducing beginners to the 'gentle art.'
Fish Brown trout with an average size of 12oz and plenty of 1-1.5lb fish.
Flies & Tactics Both boat and bank fishing bring good results and fish are taken from all over the loch. The small finger-like promontory on the north-east shore is a good place to start. Try: Ke-He, Greenwell's Glory, Silver Butcher.
Permission & Charges Rhiconich Hotel, Rhiconich, by Lairg, Sutherland. Tel: (01971) 521224. Boat fishing: £10 per day. Bank fishing: £5 per day.

UAMH DHADHAIDH, Loch
Location & Access 9/448631 Approach from the A838 Bettyhill/Durness road via a track at 9/445644. At the end of the track walk east to reach the loch in ten minutes.
Commentary A delightful little loch extending to about eight acres, lying on the cliff on the west shore of Loch Eriboll. Rarely fished.
Fish Small, highland brown trout which average 6oz.
Flies & Tactics Easily covered, although can be dour at times. Offer them: Ke-He, March Brown, Silver Butcher.
Permission & Charges Charles Marsham, Rispond & Polla Estate, Durness, by Lairg, Sutherland. Tel: (01971) 511224.

ULBHA, Lochan
Location & Access 9/358454 A long, tough hike from Lone (9/309422) at the east end of Loch Stack through magnificent scenery. Follow the stalkers path skirting Creagan Meall Horn (792m). The loch lies to the south of this track, above the crags at the south end of An Dubh Loch. Follow the inlet burn up to Ulbha.
Commentary An all day hill-walking and fishing expedition. Allow eight hours for the round trip. Fish An Dubh first, then climb to Lochan Ulbha. After Ulbha, walk south again to fish and Loch na Seilge (OS9/370446). Continue south between Sabhal Mor (703m) and Sabhal Beag (729m) to a track down Strath Luib na Seillich which leads back to Lone.
Fish Good stocks of wild brown trout which average 8-10oz.
Flies & Tactics Fish rise all round the loch. First cast: Loch Ordie, March Brown, Silver Butcher. Bank fishing.
Permission & Charges Grosvenor Estate (contact Reay Forest Estate Office, Achfary, by Lairg, Sutherland. Tel: 01971 500221).

WHEELHOUSE, Lochans
Location & Access 9/401611 To the west of the A838 Bettyhill/Durness road. Park in Laid at 9/413591 and follow the Allt nan Lagain up the hill to the lochans.
Commentary An adventure-hike to a series of six tiny lochans, close to the site of one of the most extensive and best preserved Pictish wheelhouses in Britain. The surrounding country is spectacular, with Foinaven (908m) and Arkle (787m) dominating the southern horizon.
Fish Small, hungry highland trout.
Flies & Tactics The lochans are spread over an area of about a mile, centred by the wheelhouse. Have a few casts in each. Try: Black Zulu, Loch Ordie, Dunkeld
Permission & Charges Enquire: Jack Watson, Cape Wrath Hotel, Durness, Sutherland.

Strathnaver

A'BHUALAIDH, Loch
Location & Access 10/538563 After crossing the Kyle of Tongue causeway, turn south down the west shore of the Kyle. Park at 10/565568 and follow the track west to the loch which will be reached after a walk of about 45 minutes.
Commentary A very attractive small, narrow, shallow loch in a wonderful moorland setting. Hill loch fishing at its finest.
Fish Hard fighting trout which average 8/10oz in weight and the chance of the odd larger fish.
Flies & Tactics Bank fishing only and comfortable wading. Begin with: Blue Zulu, Grouse & Claret, Silver Butcher.
Permission & Charges From the Ben Loyal Hotel, Tongue, by Lairg, Sutherland. Tel (01847) 611216. Charges: £3 per rod per day.

A'CHAORUINN, Loch
Location & Access 10/668601 Between Bettyhill and Tongue, north of the A836, within the 'ring road' round Skerray (10/660631).
Commentary A small, easily accessible loch worth a few casts on the way to/from Loch Skerray. Traditional highland trout fishing in a lovely setting. Outstanding beaches at Tongue, Coldbackie and Talmine; windsurfing and sailing in Kyle of Tongue; pony trekking, hill walking and climbing.
Fish Bright little trout which fight well.
Flies & Tactics Bank fishing only. Trout are taken all over the loch. Try: Ke-He, March Brown, Silver Butcher.
Permission & Charges From the Borgie Lodge Hotel, Skerray, by Thurso, Sutherland. Cost: £5 per rod per day.

A'MHUILINN, Loch
Location & Access 10/874562 Approach from the A897 Helmsdale/Melvich road, turning on to the minor road that follows the west bank of the Halladale river at 10/896524. Park at 10/899561 and walk west up the hill for 20 minutes to reach the loch.
Commentary A secluded moorland loch offering good sport. A small, shallow water which can often be windy.
Fish Trout average 6-8oz as well as a few larger trout of up to 1lb in weight.
Flies & Tactics Bank fishing, and fish rise all over the loch. Start with: Black Zulu, March Brown, Kingfisher Butcher.
Permission & Charges Dave Clements, The Dorran Bungalow, Forsinard, Strath Halladale, Sutherland. Tel: (01641) 571254. Bank fishing, £9.00 per rod per day.

A'MHUILINN, Loch (Tongue)
Location & Access 10/570608 Turn north towards Talmine after crossing the Kyle of Tongue and park at 10/580607. Follow a peat track west up the hill to the loch, which will be reached in fifteen minutes.
Commentary A'Mhuilinn is shallow and approx 70 acres in extent. Very scenic, with a small island at the south end. Splendid, isolated little loch and well worth fishing.
Fish Trout average 8oz and rise well to most patterns of fly.
Flies & Tactics Bank fishing and trout may be caught from all round the shoreline. Concentrate in the area of the major inlet burn half way down the west shore. Trout lie close in so stay ashore and keep well back. Offer them Ke-He, Woodcock & Hare-lug, Dunkeld.
Permission & Charges From the Ben Loyal Hotel, Tongue, by Lairg, Sutherland. Tel: (01847) 611216. At £3 per rod per day for bank fishing.

ACHRUGAN, Loch
Location & Access 10/825629 from the A836 Thurso/Bettyhill road by turning south at Strathy (10/844650). Park at 10/832620 and walk west, crossing the Strathy River. The loch lies ten minutes away through the forest.
Commentary Shallow, completely surrounded by commercial forestry, but the east bank is clear of trees and offers reasonable access and bank fishing. Sheltered from most winds.
Fish Bright little trout averaging 6oz.
Flies & Tactics Good baskets can be taken and most patterns of fly produce results. Try: Black Pennell, Invicta, Alexandra.
Permission & Charges Recently sold to an overseas forestry investor who does not let the fishing.

AIRIGH NA CREIGE, Loch
Location & Access 10/730583 At the bridge over the River Naver in Bettyhill, on the A836, continue south on the minor road towards Skelpick. Park at 10/715598, near the Broch site, and follow the peat track south east up the hill. Reach the loch in 20 minutes.
Commentary Excellent for beginners to both hill walking and trout fishing. A series of three, small hill lochans draining into the River Naver through Loch Duinte (10/717583).
Fish Good numbers of trout which average 8oz in weight, and a few larger fish.
Flies & Tactics Easy bank fishing with fish being taken all round the shores. The east loch has a delightful little island where you always catch fish. Offer them: Ke-He, Grouse & Claret, Silver Butcher.
Permission & Charges Robert McBain, The Skelpick Partnership, Skelpick, Betyhill, Sutherland. Tel: (01641) 521311. Bank fishing: £5 per rod per day.

ALLT LON A'CHUIL, River
Location & Access Source 10/732432 Outflow 17/756390 Easy access from the B871 Kinbrace/Syre Road. Park at the bridge over the stream at 17/739399.
Commentary A typical Sutherlandshire burn, rising amidst wild, remote moorlands and flowing south into Loch Rimsdale (17/740360). Splendid fun to fish.
Fish Allt Lon a'Chuil is a narrow, deep stream, containing surprisingly good trout, some of which undoubtedly are Loch Rimsdale fish, which can weight up to and over 2lb.

OS Map 10 Strathnaver

Flies & Tactics Very much a question of light tackle and keeping well back from the bank, below the line of vision of the fish. Crouch down, Covering the water effectively will test both your patience and skill. Use one fly: Black Pennell.
Permission & Charges Tony Henderson, Garvault Hotel, Kinbrace, Sutherland. Tel: 01431 831224. £5.00 per rod per day.

AN EILEIN, Loch
Location & Access 10/756502 Follow the B871 south down Strathnaver and park at 10/724495. Cross the River Naver and walk to Rhifail (10/730495). Skirting the north edge of the forestry plantation, climb the north shoulder of Bein Rifa-gil and walk north east to reach the loch in 40 minutes.
Commentary A delightful loch in superb surroundings. Fish it in conjuction with a visit to the Dunviden Lochs (10/748507), a few steps to the north. The headwaters of the Skelpick Burn, a tributary of the River Naver, Loch Eilein is a shallow hill loch covering an area of approx. 30 acres, in two sections, joined by narrows.
Fish Average weight of trout is in the order of 8oz with a few larger specimens of up to 1lb.
Flies & Tactics Good sport is had from all round the shore, with cooperative trout which fight well. Offer them: Soldier Palmer, Invicta, Peter Ross.
Permission & Charges See Loch Arigh na Creigh entry

AN FHEOIR, Loch
Location & Access 10/844562 Approach from the A836 Thurso/Bettyhill road. Turn south at Strathy (10/844650) and drive past Bowside Lodge to park at 10/828565. Follow the edge of the forestry plantation east, then south east for thirty minutes to the loch.
Commentary Stop for a few cast on the way to Caol loch South (see above). Visit Loch an Fheoir as part of a long day out fishing Caol Loch South (10/845572), Loch Preas an Lochan (10/845538), Lochan na Ceardaich (10/839550) and Loch Crasgach (10/835543) along the way. Excellent beaches at Melvich, golf at Reay, pony trekking in Strath Halladale and swimming pool in Thurso and Bettyhill.
Fish Trout average approx. 6/8oz.
Flies & Tactics Bank fishing all the water is easily covered. First cast: Ke-He, March Brown, Dunkeld.
Permission & Charges Jack Paterson, The Halladale Inn, Melvich, Sutherland KW14 7YJ. Tel: (01641) 531282. Charges: Bank fishing at £5 per rod per day.

AN TIGH-CHOIMHID, Loch
Location & Access 10/662608 Approach from Deepburn at 10/678602, just north from the Borgie Hotel. Walk up the hill, passing Loch a'Chaoruinn (10/668600) and Loch Skerray (10/665600) on your left. Tigh-choimhid is 10 minutes further west.
Commentary A cast along the way to a series of other, similar, delightful little Skerray hill lochans: Lochan nam Burag (10/651610), Loch na Coit (10/662614), Loch nan Cnamh (10/659618) and Lochan Blar a'Bhainne (10/670613). A rewarding, round tour of a series of remote, beautiful, small lochans lying to the west of the Borgie Hotel.

Fish All these lochans contain trout which average 6/8oz. Some have larger fish of up to and over 1lb. Discover which.
Flies & Tactics Easy bank fishing and delicate casting. Stay back from the back. Trout lie close in. Offer: Blue Zulu, March Brown, Alexandra.
Permission & Charges Peter MacGregor at the Borgie Lodge Hotel (01641 521332). Cost: £5 per rod per day.

ARBHAIR, Lochan
Location & Access 10/674572. Access at 10/679579 off Bettyhill/Borgie road. Drive down forest road for approx. half mile. When at forest, park and walk east along the fence. The loch is no more than 300 yards away. Find gate in the fence and step through to the boat.
Commentary A beautiful little loch nestling in the shelter of the surrounding hills, and Borgie forest. Only fishable from the boat as it has steep sides and wading is treacherous.
Fish Small fish, but they provide good sport in tranquil surroundings.
Flies & Tactics Try: Butcher, Pennell, Invicta.
Permission & Charges One boat and bank fishing not allowed. Cost: £15 per day from Borgie Lodge Hotel, Skerray, by Thurso, Sutherland. (01641 521332).

ARCHRIDIGILL, Loch
Location & Access 10/853614 Leave the A836 Thurso/Bettyhill road at 10/868652 and follow the road south. This turns into a rough peat track but, with care, it is possible to drive to the end. Park and walk south, keeping to the high ground along the east shoulder of Cnoc Eipteil (10/863629). Archridigill is about a 15-minute walk.
Commentary A beginner's loch in a delightful setting where large baskets may be taken. Approximately 80 acres in extent, shallow with rocky shores which makes wading difficult, but not impossible. The north shore is usefully sheltered from the wind.
Fish Small, but hard-fighting trout, brightly marked. From time to time larger fish are taken but they are the exception rather than the rule.
Flies & Tactics Bank fishing only and fish are caught from all round the shore. Start with Blue Zulu, March Brown, Alexandra.
Permission & Charges Dave Clements, The Dorran Bungalow, Forsinard, Strath Halladale, Sutherland. Tel: (01641) 571 254. Bank fishing, £9 per rod per day.

BAD A'BHOTHAIN, Loch
Location & Access 10/9185075 From the A897 Helmsdale/Melvich road at 10/900496.
Commentary Easily accessible but surrounded by commercial forestry. Best months: May, June and Sept.
Fish Trout here average 10oz and good baskets are the norm.
Flies & Tactics Fish rise readily all over this little loch and most patterns of fly will produce results.
Permission & Charges See River Halladale entry.

Strathnaver — OS Map 10

BADAIDH NA MEANA, Loch
Location & Access 10/850560 Approach from the A836 Thurso/Bettyhill road. Turn south at Strathy (10/844650) and drive past Bowside Lodge to park at 10/828583. Walk due east up the hill for approx 45 minutes to reach the loch.
Commentary Badaidh na Meana is a shallow loch in a very remote setting, covering an area of about fifteen acres. The moor north and west is very boggy. A remote loch in a perfect moorland setting. Visit Badaidh na Meana as part of a circular tour including Coal Loch North (OS10/850560) and Loch nam bo Uidhre (OS10/845572).
Fish Trout in Badaidh na Meana average approx. 8oz but there a few larger fish.
Flies & Tactics Bank fishing, and best results come from along the west shoreline and south bay, particularly by the inlet burn. Most flies tempt. Start with: Black Pennell, March Brown, Silver Butcher.
Permission & Charges Jack Paterson, The Halladale Inn, Melvich, Sutherland KW14 7YJ. Tel: (01641) 531282. Charges: bank fishing £5 per rod per day.

BALIGILL, Loch
Location & Access 10/857620 Leave the A836 Thurso/Bettyhill road at 10/868652 and follow the rough, metaled road south. This becomes a peat track but with care it can be negotiated. Park at the end of the track and walk south and west round the side of Cnoc Eipteil (10/863629). Baligill is 20 minutes distant.
Commentary A small loch, easily covered from either boat or bank. One of the dourest waters in the area but home to some seriously large trout.
Fish When fish decide to rise, Baligill produces outstanding sport. More often than not, however, they tend to sulk on the bottom. The heaviest fish taken in recent years weighed nearly 9lb. In 1997, a trout of 6lb 8oz was landed.
Flies & Tactics Both boat and bank fishing can bring results. Attack on a warm June evening, fingers crossed. Flies: a Black Pennell is statutory, then try everything else in your box.
Permission & Charges Jack Paterson, The Halladale Inn, Melvich, Sutherland KW14 7YJ. Tel: (01641) 531282. Charges: Bank fishing £5 per rod per day.

BLAR A'BHAINNE, Lochan
Location & Access 10/670613 A tiny lochan, not easy to find. Best approach is to follow an outlet burn up the hill from 10/675616, branching right along an even smaller stream as you reach the top of the gully.
Commentary A rewarding, round tour of a series of remote, beautiful, small lochans lying to the west of the Borgie Hotel. The first stop/cast along the way to a series of other, similar, delightful little Skerray Hill Lochans: Loch an Tigh-chimhid (10/662608), Lochan nam Burag (10/651610), Loch na Coit (10/662614) and Loch nan Cnamh (10/659618).
Fish All these lochans contain bright trout which average 6/8oz. Some have larger fish up to and over 1lb/ Discover which.
Flies & Tactics Careful bank fishing and delicate casting. Stay away from the bank since the trout tend to lie close in. Offer them: Blue Zulu, March Brown, Alexandra. All these lochans contain bright trout which average 6/8oz. Some have larger fish up to and over 1lb.
Permission & Charges Peter MacGregor at the Borgie Hotel, Skerray, by Thurso, Sutherland. Tel: (01641) 521332. Costs: £5 per rod per day for bank fishing.

BORGIE, River
Location & Access 10/559420 Outflow 10/681611 Via a good forestry track which leaves the A836 Bettyhill/Tongue road at 10/666586: approach the upper river by walking south from the car park at 10/654578.
Commentary The Borgie rises on the southern slopes of Ben Loyal, 'Queen of Scottish Mountains', flowing north through lochs Coulside, Loyal, Craggie and Slaim, to reach the sea in Torrisdale Bay, two miles west from the mouth of the River Naver. Although many of the pools on the river have been man-made, the Borgie remains one of the most attractive of all highland streams. The upper reaches, above the falls, are delightfully secluded, surrounded by dramatic mountain and moorland scenery. The falls consist of three distinct steps, the first of which forces the stream into a spectacular, deep, foaming cauldron. Below the falls, the river bustles busily through more gentle countryside, backed by mature woodlands. All fishing is strictly by fly only and the river is divided into four, two-rod beats. Beat 4, the upper river, is not included in the daily fishing rotation. Water is stored in Loch Slaim and released during the times of low water, particularly the summer months, when there is a useful grilse run. There are 50 named pools, the most productive being, on Beat 3: Falls Pool and Still Pool; Beat Two: Murrays and Ford; Beat 1 Upper Brecko and Foresters. Below Beat 1, the Lower River is available as day ticket water and includes some really excellent pools such as: Jimmy's and the Cruive Pool. The most productive month is July, followed by Aug and Sept.
Fish The 10 year average is in the region of 200 fish per season, although recent years have frequently produced more than 300 salmon. 1993 was an exceptional year, producing 420 salmon.
Flies & Tactics Wading is not required and a strong sea-trout or grilse rod is perfectly adequate to cover the flies. As with most modest highland streams, a cautious approach brings best results, staying well back from the bank, stalking the pools from a single point, lengthening line, rather than 'marching' down the bank. Offer them: Willie Gunn, Garry Dog, Silver Wilkinson, Stoat's Tail, General Practitioner, Hairy Mary; in low water, sea-trout and brown trout flies are best: Black Pennell, March Brown, Ke-He, Peter Ross, Dunkeld.
Permission & Charges Contact Martin Ward, Jamie & Partners, Rectory Place, Loughborough, Leicestershire LE11 1UR. Tel: Loughborough (01509) 233433; Fax: (01509) 232634. Prices vary during the season. Expect to pay, per two rod beat, in the order of £358 for an early season week, to £575 for a July or autumn week. The Ticket Water costs approx. £25 per rod per day. The Altnaharra Hotel also has six weeks of river fish-

OS Map 10 Strathnaver

ing to let and exclusive rights to Loch Coulside. Early booking is essential.

BRAIGHE, Lochan
Location & Access 10/764513 Approach from the the A836 Thurso/Bettyhill road. Turn south at Strathy and follow the forestry road out to 10/774536. Skirt the plantation, walking south then south west, to reach the loch in 15 minutes.
Commentary A long, rough drive in and then a damp hike over the moor, but well worth the effort. Make it a full day out, including an assault on Loch Nan Clach (10/770530) and a visit to the un-named lochans at 10/763519, 10/771499 and 10/7654990.
Fish A series of, small, shallow, remote lochs lying to the west of the Forsinard plantations and immediately north from Loch Strathy (10/777470). Splendid Flow Country scenery and exciting fishing.
Flies & Tactics Lochan Braighe, and the un-named adjacent loch to the east, contain some good trout of up to and over 1lb in weight. The surrounding waters are more modestly provisioned with fish averaging in the order of 6/8oz.
Permission & Charges Easy bank fishing on all these waters and trout rise to most patterns of fly. Begin with Blue Zulu, Invicta, Alexandra. Permission Jack Paterson, The Halladale Inn, Melvich, Sutherland KW14 7YJ. Tel: (01641) 531282. Cost: £5 per rod per day.

BUIDHE BEAG, Loch
Location & Access 10/774595 Approach from the A836 Thurso/Bettyhill road. Turn south at Strathy (10/844650) and drive past Bowside Lodge. Turn right at 10/831597 (Keeper's Cottage on your right), and follow the forestry road out to park at 10/802568. Walk west through the forest, then north from Loch Meala (10/789570) past Loch Buidhe Mor (10/778584) to reach Buidhe Beag after about 45 minutes.
Commentary A long drive followed by a long walk and, consequently, rarely fished. Go there. Buidhe Beag is a shallow loch, 600 yards long by up to three hundred yards wide, narrowing towards the inlet burn at the south end.
Fish Excellent quality trout which average 10/12oz. Fish of up to 4lb have been caught recently.
Flies & Tactics Bank fishing only and the most productive fishing area is along the west shoreline. Try Black Pennell, Invicta, Dunkeld.
Permission & Charges Dave Clements, The Dorran Bungalow, Strath Halladale, Sutheralnd. Tel: (01641) 571254

BUIDHE, Loch
Location & Access 10/631594 Immediately adjacent to the north of the A836 Bettyhill/Tongue road. Park at 10/634591 and follow the peat track to the loch.
Commentary Ideal for a few casts when time is limited. An attractive loch to fish in spite of being so close to the main road. Ben Blandy (187m) often offers shelter during strong westerly winds.
Fish Trout here average 8oz, with a few larger fish of up to 1lb in weight.

Flies & Tactics The west shore brings best results and wading is comfortable. As the season advances, weed-growth can be a problem. Try: Soldier Palmer, Grouse & Claret, Dunkeld
Permission & Charges Peter MacGregor at The Borgie Hotel, Skerray, by Thurso, Sutherland. Tel: (01641) 521332. Costs: £5 per rod per day for bank fishing.

BUIDHE MOR, Loch
Location & Access 10/778584 Approach from the A836 Thurso/Bettyhill road. Turn south at Strathy (10/844650) and drive past Bowside Lodge. Turn right at 10/831597 (Keeper's Cottage on your right), and follow the forestry road out to park at 10/802568. Walk west through the forest, then north from Loch Meala (10/789570), to reach Buidhe Mor after about 20 minutes.
Commentary A long drive followed by a long walk and consequently, rarely fished. Buidhe Mor is approx. half a mile long by up to quarter of a mile wide, sheltered west and east by Creag Meadie and Beinn nam Bo.
Fish Excellent quality trout which average 10/12oz. Fish of up to 4lb have been caught recently.
Flies & Tactics Bank fishing only and the most productive fishing area is along the west shoreline. Pay particular attention to where the three feeder streams enter the loch. The south bay is also good. Try Black Pennell, Invicta, Dunkeld.
Permission & Charges Forsinard Hotel, Forsinard, Sutherland, KW13 6YT. Tel: (01641) 571221. Bank fishing: £9 per rod per day.

CAOL NORTH, Loch
Location & Access 10/850560 Approach from the A836 Thurso/Bettyhill road. Turn south at Strathy (10/844650) and drive past Bowside Lodge to park at 10/828583. Walk up the hill for 25 minutes to reach the loch.
Commentary Caol is shallow, about 600 yards loch sharply narrowing towards the south, surrounded by open moorlands. A remote loch in a perfect moorland setting. Visit Caol as part of a circular tour including Loch Badaidh na Meana (OS10/855575) and Loch nam Bo Uidhre (OS10/845572).
Fish Trout in Caol average approx. 6oz and there are plenty of them, with the chance of the odd large specimen.
Flies & Tactics Bank fishing only and the best results come at the north and where wading is comfortable. Most flies tempt. Start with: Black Penel, March Brown, Silver Butcher.
Permission & Charges Contact Jack Paterson, The Halladale Inn, Melvich, Sutherland KW14 7YJ. Tel: (01641) 531282. Charges: Bank fishing at £5 per rod per day.

CAOL SOUTH, Loch
Location & Access 10/845572 Approach from the A836 Thurso/Bettyhill road. Turn south at Strathy (10/844650) and drive past Bowside Lodge to park at 10/828565. Follow the edge of the forestry plantation east, then south east for one hour to reach the loch.
Commentary Visit Caol Loch South as part of a long

77

Strathnaver OS Map 10

day out visiting Loch an Fheoir (OS10/844562), Loch Preas an Lochan (OS10/845538), Lochan na Ceardaich (OS10/839550) and Loch Crasgach (OS10/835543) along the way. Caol Loch South, three quarters of a mile long by up to one hundred yards wide, is one of the most remote lochs in the area and is surrounded by glorious moorlands.
Fish Good trout averaging approximately 6/8 oz with the chance of the odd larger fish.
Flies & Tactics Bank fishing, and fish rise and are caught all over the loch. The two inlet burns at the south west end are particularly productive. First cast: Ke-He, March Brown, Dunkeld.
Permission & Charges Jack Paterson, The Halladale Inn, Melvich, Sutherland KW14 7YJ. Tel: (01641) 531282. Bank fishing: £5 per rod per day.

CAOL-LOCH BEAG, Loch
Location & Access 10/779435 Approach from the B871 Kinbrace/Syre road and park at the Garvault Hotel 17/781387. Follow the west bank of the Garbh Allt burn north, keeping to the high ground on the side of Biod Eag hill. From the high point at the north slope of Beinn a Mhadaidh, you will see the loch about half a mile ahead.
Commentary Approximately 12 acres in extent, shallow and easy to fish. In the heart of the Flow Country. A hill walkers' loch in a glorious, peaceful setting. The amazing wild flowers and birdlife of the Flow Country is attraction enough for walking this way. Look out, particularly for greenshank.
Fish Small, well-shaped fish which average in the order of 6/8oz.
Flies & Tactics Good bank fishing and expect action anywhere on the loch. Relatively comfortable wading, but take care. Most flies bring results. Try: Soldier Palmer, March Brown, Dunkeld.
Permission & Charges From Tony Henderson, Garvault Hotel, Garvault, Kinbrace, Sutherland. Tel: (01431) 831224 Charges: £5 per rod per day bank fishing.

CAOL-LOCH CREAG NAN LAOGH
Location & Access 10/770570 Park on the A836 Melvich/Bettyhill road at 10/750620. Follow the peat track south. Walk the east shore of Loch Meadie (10/753600). Angle round the north slope of Creag Meadie to fish the Caol-loch (10/764596). Walk due south, past Loch na Glaic (10/765586). Creag nan Laogh is a further twenty minutes south.
Commentary Visit Creag nan Laogh as part of a full day expedition, fishing Loch Meadie, the Caol-loch and Loch na Glaic. A remote, narrow little lochan to the south of Loch Meadie, offering some shelter during high winds.
Fish Nothing for the glass case, but great fun.
Flies & Tactics Easy bank fishing using standard pattern flies.
Permission & Charges Forsinard Hotel, Forsinard, Sutherland, KW13 6YT. Tel: (01641) 571221. Bank fishing: £9 per rod per day.

CAOL-LOCH, Loch (Meadie)
Location & Access 10/764596 Park on the A836 Melvich/Bettyhill road at 10/750620. Follow the peat track south, then walk the east shore of Loch Meadie (10/753600). Angle round the north slope of Creag Meadie to reach Caol-loch.
Commentary Visit Caol-loch as part of a full day expedition, fishing Loch Meadie, Loch na Glaic (10/767587) and Caol-loch Creag nan Laogh (10/770570). A remote little lochan to the east of Loch Meadie, approx. 200 yards long by a cast wide.
Fish Nothing for the glass case, but great fun.
Flies & Tactics Easy bank fishing using standard pattern flies.
Permission & Charges See Loch Airgh na Creigh entry.

CAOL-LOCH MOR
Location & Access 10/782445 Approach from the B871 Kinbrace/Syre road and park at the Garvault Hotel 17/781387. Follow the west bank of the Garbh Allt burn north, keeping to the high ground on the side of Biod Eag hill. From the high point at the north slope of Beinn a Mhadaidh, you will see the loch about one mile ahead.
Commentary Approximately half a mile long by up to 200 yards wide, shallow and relatively sheltered, in the midst of the Flow Country. A hill walkers loch in a glorious, peaceful setting. The amazing wild flowers and birdlife of the Flow Country is attraction enough for walking this way. Look out, particularly, for greenshank.
Fish Small, well-shaped fish which average in the order of 6/8oz.
Flies & Tactics Great bank fishing and expect action anywhere on the loch. Relatively comfortable wading, but take care. Most flies bring results. Try: Soldier Palmer, March Brown, Dunkeld.
Permission & Charges From Tony Henderson, Garvault Hotel, Garvault, Kinbrace, Sutherland. Tel (01997) 414205. Charges at £5 per rod per day.

CLAISEIN, Loch
Location & Access 10/654600 Park on the A836 Bettyhill/Tongue road at 10/646592, by Loch Dubh Beul na Faire (10/646592). Walk north round the west shore to the head of the loch, then angle north east to reach Loch Claisein within fifteen minutes.
Commentary Although easily accessible, away-from-it-all fishing amidst superb scenery. A long (400 yards), narrow loch, in a sheltered hollow on the moor, rarely fished.
Fish Well-conditioned trout which average 8oz and a few larger specimens of up to 1lb.
Flies & Tactics Often relatively sheltered in high winds and good bank fishing. Trout are taken all round the loch. Begin with: Blue Zulu, Invicta, Peter Ross.
Permission & Charges Peter MacGregor, Borgie Hotel, Skerray, by Thurso, Sutherland. Tel: (01641) 521332. Bank fishing: £5 per rod per day.

CLAR-LOCH MOR, Loch
Location & Access 10/650586 Immediately adjacent to the A836 Bettyhill/Tongue road. Park at 10/654588

OS Map 10 — Strathnaver

and approach via a good peat track. Tiny Clar-loch Beag is to the east of this track.
Commentary Easily accessible and thus somewhat public, but, nevertheless, a pleasant loch to fish. Extend your day with a further walk south to fish Nan Gamhna (10/546581), Grian-loch Beag (10/642568), and Grian-loch Mor (10/645558). Clar-loch Mor covers approximately thirty acres whilst its neighbour, Clar-loch Beag extends to half a dozen casts. Both are shallow, with a reputation for being dour.
Fish Trout here average 6/8oz in weight.
Flies & Tactics Concentrate your efforts along the west shore of Clar-loch Mor. Stay on the bank. Wading is difficult. Try: Loch Ordie, March Brown, Silver Butcher.
Permission & Charges Peter MacGregor, Borgie Hotel, Skerray, by Thurso, Sutherland. Tel: (01641) 521332. Bank fishing: £5 per rod per day.

COIRE NAM MANG, Loch
Location & Access 10/810415 Approach from the B871 Kinbrace/Syre road at 17/787379. A good track skirts the west shoulder of Ben Griam Mor and, after a vigorous 20 minutes, leads directly to the boat house on the west shore of the loch.
Commentary Not as productive as in days past, but still one of the best lochs in the area and always worth a visit. Wonderful scenery, sheltered to the south by Ben Griam Mor and to the east by Ben Griam Beg. 'Away from it all' fishing. Climb Ben Griam Beg to view the remains of the highest pictish hill fort in Scotland.
Fish Trout average 10oz with good numbers of fish of up to and over 1lb in weight. Well shaped, excellent quality trout with pink flesh.
Flies & Tactics Boat fishing produces the best results and you should concentrate your initial efforts in the vicinity of the three small inlet streams at the south end of the loch. First cast: Black Pennell, March Brown, Silver Invicta. Dapping can also be very productive.
Permission & Charges Tony Henderson, Garvault Hotel, Kinbrace, Sutherland. Tel: (01997) 414205. Fishing is available when not required by hotel guests. Bank fishing: £5 per rod per day. Use of boat, £15.00 per day.

CORMAIC, Loch
Location & Access 10/627582 Between Bettyhill and Tongue, south of the A836. At 10/622594, turn south on the minor road and park at Dalcharn. A good track leads south east, up the hill, to the loch, a walk of about ten minutes.
Commentary This fine loch can provide sheltered fishing in strong westerly winds.
Fish Bright little trout which fight well.
Flies & Tactics Bank fishing and boat fishing both produce results. A good track margins at the east shoreline. Trout are taken all over the loch. Try: Ke-He, March Brown, Silver Butcher.
Permission & Charges From the Ben Loyal Hotel, Tongue, by Lairg, Sutherland. Tel: (01847) 611216. Charges: £3 per rod per day bank fishing; a boat costs £10 per day. No outboard motors on this loch.

COULDBACKIE Lochan
Location & Access 10/874614 Leave the A836 Thurso/Bettyhill road at 10/868652 and follow the rough, metalled road south. This becomes a peat track but with care it can be negotiated. Park at the end and walk south east past Loch Sgiathanach (10/870624) to reach the loch in forty minutes.
Commentary For the angler who likes to be alone, and could be linked in to a day out including Loch Sgiathanach (see above), Loch Achridigill (10/853614) and Loch Baligill (10/857620). A small, shallow loch, peaceful and secluded, easily fished from the bank.
Fish Hard fighting trout which average 8oz.
Flies & Tactics Stay well back from the bank and offer them standard patterns: Ke-He, Woodcock & Hare-lug, Silver Invicta.
Permission & Charges Contact: Jack Paterson, The Halladale Inn, Melvich, Sutherland KW14 7YJ. Tel: (01641) 531282. Bank fishing: £5 per rod per day.

CRAGGIE, Loch (Tongue)
Location & Access 10/615520 Easily accessible from the A836 Tongue/Altnaharra road. Park at 10/614510, in a small quarry, and walk down to the boats.
Commentary A large, clear-water loch, one and a half miles long by up to half a mile wide and 80ft deep. Can be very wild and windy, but there is generally shelter somewhere.
Fish Good stocks of brown trout averaging 8oz in weight, with a few much larger fish which are difficult to tempt. Craggie is part of the Borgie System and a few salmon are taken each year.
Flies & Tactics An outboard motor is essential and boat fishing brings best results and makes it easier to explore the loch. Nevertheless, bank fishing is also productive, particularly along the west shoreline where salmon lie close in (10/613513 to 10/614522). Salmon are encountered off the fence post on the east shore in the vicinity of 10/617522. Trolling is allowed for salmon. Flies to use: Black Pennell, Greenwell's Glory, Silver Invicta.
Permission & Charges Ben Loyal Hotel, Tongue, by Lairg, Sutherland. Tel: (01847) 611216. Bank fishing, £5 per rod per day. Use of boat, £10.00 per day. outboard motor hire, £5.00 per day. Permits also from Borgie Lodge Hotel, Skerray, by Thurso, Sutherland. Tel: (01641 521332 Altnaharra Hotel, Altnaharra, by Lairg, Sutherland. Tel: (01549) 411222.

CRAISG, Loch
Location & Access 10/599577 To the north of Tongue Village. Approach from 10/600583. Full directions will be given with permit.
Commentary A small, shallow, sheltered water extending to approximately 25 acres. Easily accessible and the place to catch breakfast.
Fish Trout average 8oz and rise well to most patterns of fly. There are a few larger fish.
Flies & Tactics Boat fishing and bank fishing and trout may be caught all over the loch, but perhaps the east shoreline is most productive. First cast: Black Pennell, Invicta, Bloody Butcher.
Permission & Charges From Ben Loyal Hotel, Tongue,

Strathnaver   OS Map 10

by Lairg, Sutherland. Tel: (01847) 611216. £3 per rod per day for bank fishing, £10 per boat per day. No outboards on this loch.

CRASGACH, Loch
Location & Access 10/835543 Approach from the A836 Thurso/Bettyhill road. Turn south at Strathy (10/844650) and drive past Bowside Lodge to park at 10/828565. Follow the edge of the forestry plantation east, then south east. Loch Crasgach lies to the west of Caol Loch South.
Commentary Visit Loch Crasgach as part of a long day out fishing Loch an Fheoir (10/844562), Caol Loch South (10/845572), Loch Preas an Lochan (10/845538) and Lochan na Ceardaich (10/839550) along the way. A very pretty little loch in a moorland setting with two small islands.
Fish Trout average approximately 8oz.
Flies & Tactics Easy bank fishing and comfortable wading. First cast: Ke-He, March Brown, Dunkeld.
Permission & Charges Jack Paterson, The Halladale Inn, Melvich, Sutherland KW14 7YJ. Tel: (01641) 531282. Bank fishing: £5 per rod per day.

CROCACH, Loch
Location & Access 10/804438 Approach from the A897 Helmsdale/Melvich road by a forestry track at 10/891436. Full directions will be given with permit.
Commentary An ideal beginners' loch in an ideal setting. It is one of the most remote and lovely lochs in Sutherland, full of interesting corners and fishy bays. The scenery is spectacular with the Ben Griam mountains providing a dramatic backdrop to the south. Being at this loch is an adventure in itself, regardless of fishing, because of the outstanding flora and fauna.
Fish Trout average 8oz and large baskets are the rule, rather than the exception. Crocach fish are very pretty and fight well - and they are the perfect size for breakfast.
Flies & Tactics Both boat and bank fishing produce results and fish rise freely to most patterns of fly. First cast: Ke-He, Greenwell's, Dunkeld.
Permission & Charges The Forsinard Hotel, Forsinard, Strath Halladale, Sutherland. Tel: (01641) 571221. Bank fishing: £9 per rod per day.

CROCACH, Loch (Strathtongue)
Location & Access 10/644592 Immediately adjacent to the A836 Bettyhill/Tongue road. Park at 10/650590.
Commentary A reputation for being dour. A pretty, road-side loch with an attractive island and fine views south west to Ben Loyal. Look out for Black-throated divers.
Fish Crocach trout average 8oz but the loch is reputed to hold some much larger fish.
Flies & Tactics Bank fishing only and wading is dangerous. The narrow, south end of the loch produces best results. Offer them: Ke-He, Grouse & Claret, Silver Butcher.
Permission & Charges Peter MacGregor at the Borgie Hotel, Skerray, by Thurso, Sutherland. Tel: (01641) 521332. Bank fishing: £5 per rod per day.

CROSS Lochs
Location & Access 10/870465 Approach from the A987 Helmsdale/Melvich Road by a forestry track at 10/896452. Full directions will be given with permit.
Commentary Dour, difficult, but the possibility of 'one for the glass case'. A series of five lochs in the heart of the flow country, surrounded by commercial forestry plantations. These lochs differ in character, the majority being peat-stained and dark, but one, known as the Jubilee Loch (10/872464), is a marl loch with crystal clear water.
Fish The Jubilee Loch was once stocked with Canadian Brook Trout, but now contains only brown trout. The loch to the south of the Jubilee has the largest fish, the average weight being about 2lb. Persuading them to rise to the fly is another matter, but fish of over 4lb are not uncommon.
Flies & Tactics Both boat and bank fishing can produce results; indeed, evening bank fishing is probably the best tactic for tempting the larger inhabitants. Wading is safe and comfortable on the Jubilee Loch, but the others should be fished from the bank without wading. First cast: Black Spider, Woodcock & Harelug, Silver Butcher.
Permission & Charges The Forsinard Hotel, Forsinard, Strath Halladale, Sutherland when not required by hotel guests. Tel: (01641) 571221. Bank fishing: £9 per rod per day. Boat fishing: use of boat, £19 per day.

DRUIM A'CHLIABHAIN, Loch
Location & Access 10/810415 Approach from the B871 Kinbrace/Syre road at 17/787379. A good track skirts the west shoulder of Ben Griam Mor leading to the boat house on the west shore of Coire nam Mang. Walk round the north shore and continue east to the boat house on Druim a'Chliabhain at 10/806407.
Commentary Can be dour, but well worth a visit. Sheltered to the south by Ben Griam Mor and to the east by Ben Briam Beg, but frequently subjected to strong winds. The loch is nearly one and a half miles long by half a mile wide, and up to 45ft deep at the south end, and to the north of the narrows. Climb Ben Griam Beg to view the remains of the highest pictish hill fort in Scotland.
Fish Trout average 12oz with good numbers of fish of over 1lb in weight. From time to time, larger trout are caught, but in recent years they have been harder to tempt.
Flies & Tactics Boat fishing produces the best results. Launch your attack along the south east shoreline, working north to the old boat house. The north west bay is also good. Position the boat about ten yards from the bank. Begin with Black Zulu, Grouse & Claret, Silver Butcher. Dapping can also be productive.
Permission & Charges Tony Henderson, Garvault Hotel, Kinbrace, Sutherland (noted in the Guinness Book of Records as the 'most remote hotel on Mainland Britain'). Tel: (01997) 414205. Fishing is available when not required by hotel guests. Bank fishing: £5 per rod per day. Use of boat: £15 per day.

OS Map 10   Strathnaver

DUBH AIRIGH, Lochan (Skelpick)
Location & Access 10/735570 At the bridge over the River Naver at Bettyhill, on the A836, follow the minor road south to Skelpick. Park at 10/72562 and walk due east, up the hill.
Commentary A series of six very attractive little hill lochans where great sport is guaranteed.
Fish Breakfast-sized trout which fight well and average 6/8oz in weight.
Flies & Tactics Comfortable bank fishing. Offer: Black Pennell, Soldier Palmer, Alexandra.
Permission & Charges See Loch Airgh na Creigh entry.

DUBH BEUL NA FAIRE
Location & Access 10/647594 Immediately adjacent to and north of the A836 Bettyhill/Tongue road. Park at 10/647591.
Commentary Public and exposed. A tiny, weedy lochan, close to the main road.
Fish Trout are few in numbers, but of good size, sereral in 2-4lb bracket.
Flies & Tactics Beul na Faire becomes very weedy as the season advances, making fishing difficult. Most flies can produce results.
Permission & Charges Peter MacGregor at the Borgie Hotel, Skerray, by Thurso, Sutherland. Tel: (01641) 521332. £5 per rod per day.

DUBH EAST, Lochan (Borgie)
Location & Access 10/665594 Park at the Borgie Hotel (10/676595) and walk due west up the hill. The Dubh Lochan is reached in fifteen minutes.
Commentary A small lochan close to the Borgie Hotel. Ideal for pre-dinner exercise or for catching breakfast. A tiny lochan on the hill. Visit it in conjunction with a longer day out exploring the other Skerray Hill lochs.
Fish Breakfast-sized trout, but great fun nonetheless.
Flies & Tactics Most of the loch can be covered with a few casts and trout will take most flies. Try: Black Pennell, March Brown, Silver Butcher.
Permission & Charges Peter MacGregor, The Borgie Hotel, Skerray, by Thurso, Sutherland. Tel: (01641) 521332. £5 per rod per day.

DUBH, Lochan
Location & Access 10/749631 From the A836 Thurso/Bettyhill road via a peat track which begins at 10/754624. After half a mile, the lochan lies to the west of the track.
Commentary An accessible little lochan in remote setting. Easily fished from the bank.
Fish Trout average in the order of 6/8oz.
Flies & Tactics Most flies tempt them. Try: Loch Ordie, Invicta, Peter Ross.
Permission & Charges Contact: Jack Paterson, The Halladale Inn, Melvich, Sutherland KW14 7YJ. Tel: (01641) 531282. £5 per rod per day, bank fishing.

DUBH WEST, Lochan (Borgie)
Location & Access 10/649599 Park on the A836 Bettyhill/Tongue road at 10/646592, by Loch Dubh Beul na Faire (10/646592). Walk north round the west shore of the loch to reach Lochan Dubh in ten minutes.

Commentary Worth a few casts as part of a longer expedition taking in Loch Claisein (10/654600) and Loch Tuirslighe (10/659592).
Fish Expect good little trout which average 6/8oz.
Flies & Tactics Bank fishing, and all the standard patterns will produce results.
Permission & Charges Peter MacGregor at the Borgie Hotel, Skerray, by Thurso, Sutherland. Tel: (01641) 521332. £5 per rod per day.

DUINTE, Loch
Location & Access 10/717583 At the bridge across the River Naver at Bettyhill, on the A836, continue south on the minor road to Skelpick. Loch Duinte is to the east, immediately adjacent to the road.
Commentary Easily accessible and ideal for beginners. There is also a well-preserved Highland Clearance Village on the hill to the north of the loch. About twenty acres, sheltered in high winds, offering good sport from either bank or boat.
Fish Trout in Duinte average in the region of 8oz.
Flies & Tactics Fish with confidence, trout are taken all over the loch. Duinte is also close to the Association Water on the River Naver, and if salmon are playing hard to get, have a few casts on Duinte instead. Start with: Soldier Palmer, Invicta, Dunkeld.
Permission & Charges Robert McBain, The Skelpick Partnership, Skelpick, Bettyhill, Sutherland. Tel: (01641) 521311

DUNVIDEN Lochs
Location & Access 10/748507 Follow the B871 south down Strathnaver and park at 10/724495. Cross the River Naver and walk to Rhifail (10/730495). Skirting the north edge of the forestry plantation, angle NNE up the hill. A hearty 40 minute hike brings you to the lochs.
Commentary Two very lovely little lochans, deep in the wilderness, which may be fished as part of a more extensive day out, including a visit to nearby Loch an Eilein at OS10/756502. These waters drain into the River Naver and lie on the moorlands to the east of Dunviden Hill (250m). The most northern loch is particularly attractive, graced with three small islands off the west shore. Both offer perfect peace and solitude.
Fish Guaranteed breakfast, and probably lunch and dinner as well. Not glass case country, but wonderful sport in wonderful surroundings.
Flies & Tactics Both the lochs are easily fished from the bank and trout respond famously to most patterns of fly. Begin with: Ke-He, Greenwell's Glory, Alexandra.
Permission & Charges See Loch Airgh na Creigh entry.

EALACH, Lochan
Location & Access 10/820651 Immediately adjacent to the A836 Thurso/Bettyhill road west of Melvich Village
Commentary Easily accessible and useful for a few casts before dinner. Shallow, weedy in places and very public.
Fish Trout average 6oz.

81

Strathnaver — OS Map 10

Flies & Tactics Good baskets may be taken from the bank and fish are caught all round the loch.
Permission & Charges Contact: Jack Paterson, The Halladale Inn, Melvich, Sutherland KW14 7YJ. Tel: (01641) 531282. Bank fishing £5 per road.

EARACHA, Loch
Location & Access 10/899608 Close to the A897 Helmsdale/Melvich road.
Commentary A useful alternative trout loch when water levels on the Halladale River make salmon fishing difficult. A small loch adjacent to the road and consequently, somewhat exposed.
Fish Large stocks of modest trout which rise readily to the fly.
Flies & Tactics Comfortably fished from the shore and most patterns of fly will produce results. Try Ke-He, Grouse & Claret, Dunkeld.
Permission & Charges Dave Clement, The Dorran Bungalow, Forsinard, Strath Halladale, Sutherland. Bank fishing £9 per rod per day.

EILEANACH, Loch
Location & Access 10/592404 Park by Loch Staing (10/580407) on the A836 Altnaharra/Tongue road. Walk due east from the south end of Staing for 20 minutes to reach Eileannach.
Commentary Eileanach is divided into two sizeable areas by narrows, scattered with small islands, interesting bays and fishy corners. Escapism at its best. Away-from-it-all fishing is absolutely splendid scenery.
Fish Trout average 6/8oz, there are plenty of them and they fight well.
Flies & Tactics Bank or boat fishing and the water is easily covered. The south west corner of the north bay is excellent, but fish are taken from all round the shore and they rise readily to most patterns of fly. Start with Black Zulu, Greenwell's Glory, Silver Butcher.
Permission & Charges From Altnaharra Hotel, Altnaharra, by Lairg, Sutherland. Tel: (01549) 411222. Charges at £20 per day for boat with two rods fishing.

EILEANACH, Loch (Bettyhill)
Location & Access 10/790608 From the A836 Thurso/Bettyhill road. Park at 10/785634 and walk south, following the general line if the Allt Beag burn, with Beinn Chuldail on your left. The loch is about one and a half miles from the road.
Commentary A splendid loch is a very remote setting, well worth the effort involved. Eileanach covers an area of approx. 30 acres and is graced with three little islands.
Fish Expect large baskets of trout which average 6/8oz, but look out for larger fish of up to and over 2lb.
Flies & Tactics Easy bank fishing with action all round the loch to most standard patterns of fly. Begin with: Ke-He, Loch Ordie, Alexandra.
Permission & Charges Contact: Jack Paterson, The Halladale Inn, Melvich, Sutherland KW14 7YJ. Tel: (01641) 531282. Bank fishing: £5 per rod per day.

FEUSAIGE, Loch
Location & Access 10/750465 Follow the B871 south down Strathnaver and park at 10/724495. Cross the River Naver and walk to Rhifail (10/730495). Skirting the north edge of the forestry plantation, climb the north shoulder of Beinn Rifa-gil. After fishing loch warander (10/764492), walk SSE for 15 minutes to fish Rifa-gil. Continue south for a further 30 minutes to reach Loch Feusaige. Also consider a detour to have a cast in two un-named lochans on Meall Bad na Cuaiche (10/760471 and 10/763470). You will probably be the first to do so for several seasons.
Commentary Fish Loch Feusaige as part of a full day expedition, in conjunction with Lochs Warender (10/746492) and Loch Rifa-gil (10/750484), returning to Rhifail via the Allt Rivigill Burn and a good track along the east bank of the River Naver.
Fish Trout average 6/8oz and plenty of them.
Flies & Tactics Most standard patterns of fly produce results and all the water is easily covered from the bank. Begin with: Black Zulu, Woodcock & hare-lug, Silver Butcher.
Permission & Charges See Loch Airgh na Creigh entry.

FHIONNAICH, Loch
Location & Access 10/555563 After crossing the Kyle of Tongue causeway, turn south down the west shore of the kyle. Park at 10/565568 and follow the track west to the loch which will be reached after a walk of about 15 minutes.
Commentary A very attractive small, narrow, shallow loch in a wonderful moorland setting, worth a visit on the way too or from Loch a'Bhualaidh (10/538563). Highly recommended for lovers of wild places.
Fish Bright little fish which average 6/8oz.
Flies & Tactics Bank fishing. Begin with: Blue Zulu, Grouse & Claret, Silver Butcher.
Permission & Charges From the Ben Loyal Hotel, Tongue, by Lairg, Sutherland. Tel: (01847) 611216. Charges: £3 per rod per day.

GAINEIMH, Loch (Bettyhill)
Location & Access 10/76510 From the A836 Thurso/Bettyhill road via a peat track which begins at 10/750620. The end of the track points south east, directly towards the loch, which you will reach in about 10 minutes.
Commentary The perfect place to spend a day, ideal for a family fishing outing. Don't ignore the small lochans to north and south as you approach Gaineimh. They also offer good sport. Gaineimh is nearly half a mile long by some 200 yards wide, shallow and easily fished from the bank.
Fish Bright little trout which average in the order of 8oz, and a few larger fish.
Flies & Tactics Expect action all round the loch to most standard patterns of fly. Begin with: Black Pennell, Soldier Palmer, Silver Butcher.
Permission & Charges Contact: Jack Paterson, The Halladale Inn, Melvich, Sutherland KW14 7YJ. Tel: (01641) 531282. Bank fishing costs: £5 per rod per day.

GAINEIMH, Loch (Forsinard)
Location & Access 10/799430 A six mile drive from

OS Map 10 — Strathnaver

10/891436 along forestry roads, west from the A897 Helmsdale/Melvich road, followed by a 20-minute walk south over the moors from Loch Crocach (10/804438). Full directions given with permit.
Commentary A small loch well worth visiting in spite of the considerable effort involved in getting to it. Rarely fished because of the long walk in. Easily covered from the bank, and safe wading.
Fish Gaineimh has the reputation of holding some really good fish of up to and over 2lb in weight.
Flies & Tactics Approach with caution and start your attack from the bank. Only after fully exploring the margins, wade in to try the deeper water.
Permission & Charges Forsinard Hotel, Forsinard, Strath Halladale, Sutherland. Tel: (01641) 571221. Bank fishing, £9 per rod per day.

GAINMNICH, Loch
Location & Access 10/811650 Immediately adjacent to the A836 Thurso/Bettyhill road west of Melvich Village.
Commentary Easily accessible and useful for a few casts before dinner. Shallow, weedy in places and very public. Dramatic cliffs and good hill walking country.
Fish Trout average 6oz.
Flies & Tactics Good baskets may be taken from the bank and fish caught all round the loch.
Permission & Charges Dave Clements, The Dorran Bungalow, Forsinard, Strath Halladale, Sutherland. Bank fishing, £9 per rod per day.

GRIAN-LOCH BEAG, Loch
Location & Access 10/642568 South of the A836 Bettyhill/Thurso road. Park at 10/654588 and follow the peat track south past Clar-loch Mor (10/650587) and Clar-loch Beag (10/654585). At the end of the track, angle south past the east end of Loch nan Gamha. Grian-loch Beag is a further twenty minute walk south.
Commentary Wonderfully remote and well worth the long walk. A small, shallow loch covering an area of approximately twenty five acres, draining through Grian-loch Mor (10/645558) into the Borgie River.
Fish Trout here average about 8oz with a few larger fish of up to 11lb in weight.
Flies & Tactics Easy bank fishing and good sport with hard-fighting fish. The south end of the loch, by the outflow burn, seems to produce best results. Try: Grouse & Claret, Woodcock & hare-lug, Peter Ross.
Permission & Charges Peter MacGregor at the Borgie Hotel, Skerray, by Thurso, Sutherland. Tel: (01641) 521332. £5 per rod per day

GRIAN-LOCH MOR, Loch
Location & Access 10/645558 South of the A836 Bettyhill/Thurso road. At 10/667587, drive south through the Borgie Forest and park at 10/659555. Walk west along a fire break to the edge of the forest. Grian-loch Mor is a ten minute walk west across the moor.
Commentary Fine fishing in a remote, lovely setting. This small lochan drains south into the River Borgie and covers an area of twenty five acres. Rarely fished and often windswept and wild.
Fish Expect good baskets of bright little trout averaging 8oz.
Flies & Tactics Non-discriminatory trout, eager to please. Start with: Black Pennell, March Brown, Silver Invicta.
Permission & Charges Peter MacGregor at the Borgie Hotel, Skerray, by Thurso, Sutherland. Tel: (01641) 521332. £5 per rod per day.

HAKEL, Loch
Location & Access 10/570530 Drive south through Tongue towards Ben Loyal. Park on the hill overlooking Lock Hakel at 10/567530. Directions to the boat mooring bay will be given with the permit.
Commentary One of the most scenic lochs in all of Scotland, guarded by Ben Loyal, 'The Queen of Scottish Mountains'. Loch Hakel always provides sport, even in the most adverse conditions, and is a 'must' for anyone visiting the area.
Fish Trout average 6/8oz but they fight like fish of twice their weight. From time to time, larger fish are taken, but regardless of size, Hakel trout are magnificent.
Flies & Tactics Bank or boat fishing and all the water is easily covered. Fish are taken from all round the loch and they rise readily to most patterns of fly. Start with Soldier Palmer, Grouse & Claret, Dunkeld.
Permission & Charges From The Ben Loyal Hotel, Tongue, by Lairg, Sutherland. Tel: (01847) 611216. Costs: £3 per rod per day for bank fishing, £10 per boat per day. No outboards on this loch.

HALLADALE, River
Location & Access Source 17/940372 (Knockfin Heights) Outflow 10/885655 (Melvich Bay) Easy access from A897 Melvich/Helmsdale road which borders the east bank of the river.
Commentary A classic Highland spate stream, greatly improved since the curtailment of netting at the river mouth. Also useful sea-trout fishing in the estuary, below the Halladale road bridge, to the sea at Melvich Bay. Strictly fly only. The Lower river is divided into four three-rod beats, containing excellent holding pools which include: Barriers, Sandy Brae, Mugs, Run Out, Victoria, Munro's, Lady Bighouse, MacBeath's, Harper's and Bridge Pool. The Upper River is narrow, one section running through a dramatic gorge, but also has a number of excellent holding pools which can be very productive, given water levels: Gracies, Devil's, Raven's Rock, MacNicholls, Forsinain Bridge, Coffin, Cross Burn, and Major's Pool. Season: 12 Jan - 30 Sept.
Fish Salmon average 10lb 8oz, grilse 6lb 8oz. Rod catch returns Lower River (River Dyke to upstream of Halladale Bridge on A836) 5 year average: 320 salmon and grilse; Upper River (Dyke River to 10/899456): approx 50 salmon and grilse each season.
Flies & Tactics A strong, single-handed rod is adequate. The character of the river varies significantly throughout its course, testing all your casting skills, although generally the river is free from obstructions. Without doubt, the most successful fly over the years has been the Garry Dog, but other useful patterns

Strathnaver — OS Map 10

include: Green Highlander, Hairy Mary, Stoat's Tail, General Practitioner.
Permission & Charges Details of River Halladale fishing from Mrs Audrey Imlach, Bunahoun, Forsinard, Strath Halladale, Sutherland. Tel: (01641) 571271. Cost: from £185 to £923 (VAT incl) for a 3 rod beat, depending on time of year.

KINLOCH, River
Location & Access Source 10/540480 Outflow 10/557529. The river, and the source loch, Loch an Dherue, is preserved by the owner and is not available to members of the public.

KYLE OF TONGUE (Sea Loch)
Location & Access 10/575575 A large, shallow, sandy, tidal loch, south of the Kyle of Tongue causeway.
Commentary Local knowledge is vital, as access to fishing hot-spots requires walking out over exposed sand. Best fishing is two hours before and after low tide. Full details given with permit. 1 Feb - 6 Oct. Excellent sea-trout fishing in a dramatic setting, overlooked by Ben Loyal to the east and Ben Hope to the west.
Fish Sea-trout average 1lb 4oz, but most seasons produce fish of up to 5lb in weight. Approximately 200/250 sea-trout are taken each season.
Flies & Tactics Traditional sea-trout patterns such as Teal Blue & Silver, Black Pennell, Peter Ross, Silver Invicta all bring results, but most fish are taken by spinning. Good areas include: 10/571575, 10/573588, 10/578568, 10/569573. Best months are March, April, Aug and Sept.
Permission & Charges From the Ben Loyal Hotel, Tongue, by Lairg, Sutherland. Tel: (01847) 611216. Charges: £4 per rod per day. Also Borgie Lodge Hotel (01641 521332).

LOYAL, Loch
Location & Access 10/620490 Bounded on the west shore by the A836 Altnaharra/Tongue road. Boat locations given with permit.
Commentary Over 200ft deep, four miles long by approximately half a mile wide, often windy, and to be treated with respect at all times. Magnificent scenery, with Ben Loyal, Queen of Scottish mountains, guarding west shoreline.
Fish Large stocks of traditional brown trout averaging 8/10oz in weight. Good numbers of larger fish in the region of 1 lb/3 lb and, in the depths, ferox trout. Largest taken in recent years, by trolling, weighed just under 10lb. Occasionally, salmon are also caught. The loch is part of the River Borgie system.
Flies & Tactics Boat fishing is best, and allows easy access to the east shoreline, which is trackless. Outboard motor is essential, as are drouge and flotation jackets. Unless trolling, stay within fifteen yards of the bank. As a general rule, if you can't see the bottom, you are too far out. Begin on the east shore at 10/630465 and work south. the extreme southern end of the loch is excellent. First cast: Black Pennell, Grouse & Claret, Silver Butcher.
Permission & Charges Contact: Ben Loyal Hotel, Tongue, by Lairg, Sutherland. Tel: (01847) 611216. Cost: £21 per day (outboard incl.), for two rods. Permits also from Altnaharra Hotel, Altnaharra, by Lairg, Sutherland. Tel: (01549) 411222 and from the Borgie Lodge Hotel, Skerray, by Thurso, Sutherland. Tel: (01641) 521332.

MEADIE, Loch
Location & Access 10/752600 From the A836 Thurso/Bettyhill road. Park at 10/750620 and walk south along a good peat track. Where the track turns south east, bear right over the moor to reach Loch Meadie within 10 minutes.
Commentary Ideal for a family outing and for introducing little ones to the 'gentle art', easily accessible and often providing shelter in wild conditions. A long (one and a half miles), narrow, straggling loch, opening out into a wide bay towards the south end. Don't miss a few casts on little Caol-loch Meadie, on the east side of Creag Meadie at 10/764595.
Fish Good baskets of trout which average 6/8oz, but look out for larger fish as well.
Flies & Tactics Easy bank fishing with action all round the loch to most standard patterns of fly, but the most productive area is at the south end. Offer them: Ke-He, Black Pennell, Silver Invicta.
Permission & Charges See Loch Airgh na Creigh entry.

MEALA, Loch
Location & Access 10/7705300 From the A836 Thurso/Bettyhill road. Turn south at Strathy (10/844650) and drive past Bowside Lodge. Turn right at 10/831597 and follow the forestry road out to park at /10/802568. Walk west through the forest to reach the loch within ten minutes.
Commentary The best of the Strathy Forest trout lochs. Loch Meala covers an area of some 80 acres and fishes well in most conditions. A good possibility of meeting an otter here.
Fish Excellent quality trout which average 8/10oz with a number of larger fish of up to 2lb in weight.
Flies & Tactics Both boat and bank fishing bring results. Bank fishing is best from the west shoreline, the north of the loch is most productive when fishing from the boat. First cast: Loch Ordie, Grouse & Claret, Dunkeld.
Permission & Charges Jack Paterson, The Halladale Inn, Melvich, Sutherland KW14 7YJ. Tel: (01641) 531282. Bank fishing: £5 per rod per day, use of a boat £10 per day.

MODSARIE, Loch
Location & Access 10/648615 Between Bettyhill and Tongue, north of the A836, within the 'ring road' through Borgie and Skerray townships, Approach from the west.
Commentary Easily accessible and good fishing in wonderful surroundings. A long, narrow loch, approx 600 yards by 150 yards, shallow which fishes well in most conditions.
Fish Excellent quality trout averaging 10oz in weight with the chance of larger fish of up to and over 1 lb.
Flies & Tactics Bank fishing only, although a boat is

OS Map 10 — Strathnaver

occasionally available. The east shoreline brings best results, particularly at the south end in the vicinity of the small island. First cast: Black Pennell, Invicta, Peter Ross.
Permission & Charges Peter MacGregor, Borgie Lodge Hotel, Skerray, by Thurso, Sutherland. Tel: (01641) 521332. Bank fishing, £5.00 per rod per day.

MOLACH, Loch
Location & Access 10/735409 Approach from the B871 Kinbrace/Syre road and park at 16/725399 near the bridge. Walk north, following the west bank of the Allt Lon a'Chuil burn. After about one mile, Molach is on your right.
Commentary A few acres, a few casts, in the heart of the Flow Country. Visit Molach as part of an exciting circular tour including Loch nam Faoileag (10/735409) and Rhifail Loch (10/720425). Wild flowers and birds of the Flow Country; look out, particularly, for greenshank.
Fish Bright little trout which fight with spirit. Average weight 6oz.
Flies & Tactics Easy bank fishing with action anywhere on the loch. Try: Black Pennell, Invicta, Silver Butcher.
Permission & Charges Tony Henderson, Garvault Hotel, Garvault, Kinbrace, Sutherland. Tel: Kinbrace (01997) 414205. Charges: £5 per rod per day.

MOR, Loch (Bettyhill)
Location & Access 10/720609 Behind the village of Bettyhill on the A836 road. Park at Dalcharn at 10/714613 and walk south. You will reach the loch in 10 minutes.
Commentary A small, shallow water covering an area of about 10 acres.
Fish Good baskets of trout which average 6/8oz and also larger fish of up to 2lb.
Flies & Tactics Easily fished from the bank with action all round the loch to most standard patterns of fly. Begin with Black Pennell, March Brown, Peter Ross.
Permission & Charges Robert McBain, The Skelpick Partnership, Skelpick, Bettyhill, Sutherland. Tel: (01641) 521311. Bank fishing, £5 per rod per day.

MOR, Loch (Melvich)
Location & Access 10/889634 Immediately adjacent to the A836 Thurso/Bettyhill road in Melvich Village.
Commentary Easily accessible and useful for a few casts before dinner. Shallow, weedy in places and very public.
Fish Trout average 6oz.
Flies & Tactics Good baskets may be taken from the bank and fish are caught all round the loch.
Permission & Charges Jack Paterson, The Halladale Inn, Melvich, Sutherland KW14 7YJ. Tel: (01641) 531282. Bank fishing: £5 per rod per day.

MOR NA CAORACH, Loch (Skelpick)
Location & Access 10/764545 At the bridge over the River Naver at Bettyhill, on the A836 road, drive south on the minor road, past Skelpick. Park at 10/727551. Follow the peat track, south east. At the end of the track, strike due east, crossing the Skelpick Burn. A further forty five minutes will bring you to the loch.
Commentary Probably the best loch in the area, from the point of size of trout. Also, a very long walk through really wild country. Mor na Caorach covers some 80 acres in extent and is surrounded by a number of smaller, satellite lochans, including Loch nan Laogh (10/758558), to the north. Take care here, the ground is very wet.
Fish Trout of up to and over 4lb are taken, including a fish of 4lb 8oz last July. They do not give themselves up easily and you will have to work hard, but they are there, waiting.
Flies & Tactics Cautious bank fishing along soggy margins. The north west shore is probably best, particularly where a tiny stream enters, and north from this point. Start with: Black Zulu, Soldier Palmer, Dunkeld.
Permission & Charges Robert McBain, The Skelpick Partnership, Skelpick, Bettyhill, Sutherland. Tel: (01641) 521311.

NA AIRIGH BIGE, Loch
Location & Access 10/550550 After crossing the Kyle of Tongue causeway, turn south down the west shore of the Kyle. Park at the waterfall at 10/555544. Walk back north up the road to the first passing place to find the track out to the loch.
Commentary A very attractive small, shallow loch in a hollow on the moor, sheltered and private.
Fish Hard fighting trout which average 8/10oz in weight. 1 April - 30 Sept highly recommended for lovers of wild places.
Flies & Tactics Bank fishing only and comfortable wading. Begin with: Blue Zulu, Grouse & Claret, Silver Butcher.
Permission & Charges The Ben Loyal Hotel, Tongue, by Lairg, Sutherland. Tel (01847) 611216. Charges £3 per rod per day.

NA CAORACH, Loch
Location & Access 10/913585 From the A897 Hemsdale/Mervich road in Strath Halladale, at 12/905600, by a new forestry road. Full directions given with permit.
Commentary Shallow, approximately one mile long, narrowing towards the south. A peaceful, secluded, 'comfortable' loch, providing excellent sport with hard-fighting trout. Best months, May, June and Sept.
Fish Good trout which vary from 8oz up to 2lb. Well shaped and pink-fleshed.
Flies & Tactics The most productive fishing areas are at the south end, particularly around the headland on the east shore. First cast: Black Pennell, Grouse & Claret, Kingfisher Butcher.
Permission & Charges Dave Clements, The Dorran Bungalow, Forsinard, Strath Halladale, Sutherland. Tel: (01641) 571254. Bank fishing, £9 per rod per day.

NA CEARDAICH, Loch
Location & Access 10/839550 Approach from the A836 Thurso/Bettyhill road. Turn south at Strathy (10/844650) and drive past Bowside Lodge to park at 10/828565. Follow the edge of the forestry plantation

Strathnaver — OS Map 10

east, then south east. Loch na Ceardaich lies to the west of Caol Loch South.
Commentary Visit Loch na Ceardaich as part of a long day out fishing Loch an Fheoir (10/844562), Caol Loch South (10/845572), Loch Preas an Lochan (10/845538) and Loch Crasgach (10/835543) along the way. A very pretty little loch in a wild moorland setting. Worth a few casts on the way home.
Fish Trout average approx. 8oz.
Flies & Tactics Easy bank fishing and comfortable wading. First cast: Ke-He, March Brown, Dunkeld.
Permission & Charges Contact: Jack Paterson, The Halladale Inn, Melvich, Sutherland KW14 7YJ. Tel: (01641) 531282. Bank fishing: £5 per rod per day.

NA COIT, Loch
Location & Access 10/662615 Approach from Deepburn at 10/678602, north from the Borgie Hotel. Walk up the hill. Loch a'Chaoruinn (10/668600) and Loch Skerray (10/665600) are on your left. At Loch Tigh-choimhid (10/662608), walk due north for ten minutes to reach the loch.
Commentary A cast along the way to a series of other, similar, delightful little Skerry Hill lochans: Loch an'Tig-choimid (10/662608), Loch nam Burag (10/658610), Loch nan Cnamh (10/659618) and Lochan Blar a'Bhainne (10/670613). A rewarding, round tour of a series of remote, beautiful, small lochans lying to the west of the Borgie Hotel.
Fish All these lochans contain trout which average 6/8oz. Some have larger fish of up to and over 1lb.
Flies & Tactics Easy bank fishing and delicate casting. Stay back from the bank. Trout lie close in. Offer: Blue Zulu, March Brown, Alexandra.
Permission & Charges Peter MacGregor at the Borgie Hotel, Skerray, by Thurso, Sutherland. Tel: (01641) 521332. £5 per rod per day.

NA CUILCE, Lochan
Location & Access 10/573536 Drive south through Tongue towards Ben Loyal. Park at 10/574535. The loch is on your right, a few yards from the road.
Commentary A small, shallow, sheltered water easily fished. Also known as Lilly Loch.
Fish Trout average 8oz and rise well to most patterns of fly. There are also a few larger specimens.
Flies & Tactics Bank fishing only and trout may be encountered all over the loch, from the margins to the middle. Try: Soldier Palmer, Grouse & Claret, Dunkeld.
Permission & Charges This loch is now preserved by the owner and is no longer available for fishing.

NA GLAIC, Loch
Location & Access 10/767587 Park on the A836 Melvich/Bettyhill road at 10/750620. Follow the peat track south, then walk the east shore of Loch Meadie (10/753600). Angle round the north slope of Creag Meadie to fish the Caol-loch (10/764596). Walk due south to reach Loch na Glaic.
Commentary Visit Loch na Glaic as part of a full day expedition, fishing Loch Meadie, the Caol-loch and Caol-loch Creag nan Laogh (10/770570). A remote little lochan to the south of Loch Meadie, extending to approximately twenty acres.
Fish Nothing for the glass case, but great fun.
Flies & Tactics Easy bank fishing using standard pattern flies.
Permission & Charges See Loch Airgh na Creigh entry.

NA H-EAGLAISE BEAG, Loch
Location & Access 10/913585 Leave the A836 Thurso/Bettyhill road at 10/868652 and drive south. This road becomes a peat track but it is negotiable. Park at the end and walk south, along the east shoulder of Cnoc Eipteil (10/863629). Eventually, you are forced on to the moor. Head due south, past the east end of Loch Achridigill, to the north end of Loch na h-Eaglaise Mor (10/861599). Follow the west shore of the loch and near the middle, angle south west over the moor. Eaglaise Beag is ten minutes further on.
Commentary This is a small, shallow loch with weed patches along the west shore, easily fished from the bank. Take care wading the west shore, because the water deepens quickly. One of the best lochs in the area, remote and peaceful and a delight to fish.
Fish Some wonderful fish of up to and over 2lb in weight along with good numbers of more modest trout, to keep you interested and alert.
Flies & Tactics At the time of writing, there is no boat on Eaglaise Beag and boat fishing produces best results. Nevertheless, good baskets are taken from the shore. Concentrate on the west shore, where a feeder burn enters, and by the weed patches. First cast: Black Pennell, Greenwell's Glory, Silver March Brown.
Permission & Charges Dave Clements, The Dorran Bungalow, Forsinard, Strath Halladale, Sutherland. Tel: (01641) 571254. Bank fishing, £9 per rod per day.

NA H-EAGLAISE MOR, Loch
Location & Access 10/861599 Leave the A836 Thurso/Bettyhill road at 10/868652 and drive south. This road soon becomes a peat track but, iwth care, it is negotiable. Park at the end and walk south, keeping to the high ground along the east shoulder of Cnoc Eipteil (10/863629). Eventually, you are forced on to the soggy moor. Head due south, past the east end of Loch Achridigill and you will find Eaglaise Mor after a further, weary, fifteen minute plodge.
Commentary A narrow loch, approximately half a mile long, in a wild, moorland setting. Can give great sport and, in spite of the hard walk, Eaglaise Mor is always welcoming.
Fish Good stocks of well-conditioned trout which average 10oz in weight.
Flies & Tactics At the time of writing, there is no boat on Eaglaise Mor and, frankly, boat fishing produces best results. Nevertheless, good baskets are taken from the shore, and, depending upon wind direction, either east or west shore should provide you with supper. Best cast: Black Pennell, Grouse & Claret, Silver Butcher.
Permission & Charges Dave Clements, The Dorran Bungalow, Forsinard, Strath Halladale, Sutherland. Tel: (01641) 571254. Bank fishing, £9 per rod per day.

OS Map 10 — Strathnaver

NA H-IMRICHE, Loch
Location & Access 10/768643 From the A836 Thurso/Bettyhill road. Park at Druimbasbie (10/771631) and walk NNW for fifteen minutes to reach the loch.
Commentary A good loch in a lovely setting, well worth a few casts. Na h-Imriche is a small loch between the main road and the sea, is easily fished from the bank. Usually visited in conjunction with Lochan Tiormachd (10/762649), to the north of Na h-Imriche.
Fish First class trout which average in the order of 12oz.
Flies & Tactics Don't wade. Evening fishing in June can be very exciting and rewarding. Offer them: Soldier Palmer, Invicta, Silver Butcher.
Permission & Charges Dave Clements, The Dorran Bungalow, Forsinard, Strath Halladale, Sutherland. Bank fishing £9 per rod per day.

NA MOINE, Loch
Location & Access 10/629518 Park at 10/616508 off the A836 Tongue/Altnaharra road. A track leads to the burn joining Loch Craggie (10/615520) and Loch Loyal (10/620490). Cross the wooden bridge. Walk east along the north shore of Loyal, then follow the track that leads up the hill. At 10/626515, walk north to reach Loch na Moine via the outlet stream.
Commentary Stunning views west to Ben Loyal and Ben Hope, and, occasionally, absolutely stunning fishing. However, expect more than your fair share of blank days. A difficult, dangerous loch to fish, because of the very boggy surrounding terrain. It is virtually impossible to circle the loch and to attempt to do so is to invite disaster. Only the south and east shoreline is accessible, and only with caution.
Fish Average weight of trout is in the order of 2lb 8oz, with much larger fish of up to 7lb, but they are very hard to catch.
Flies & Tactics The soggy margins make casting problematical and it is hard to reach the few rising fish seen. With great care, it is possible to wade a section of the east shoreline, covering a wide area of water. Try: Ke-He, Black Pennell, Silver Butcher. Crossing the fingers also helps, mightily.
Permission & Charges Ben Loyal Hotel, Tongue, by Lairg, Sutherland. Tel: (01847) 611 216. £3 per rod per day.

NA SAOBHAIDHE, Loch
Location & Access 10/800470 Approach from the A897 Helmsdale/Melvich road at 10/891437 along the forestry track, a distance of some five and a half miles. Park at 10/819471 and walk west for 20 minutes.
Commentary A very lovely loch, away-from-it-all, in a wonderful setting. Loch na Saobhaidhe lies in the heart of the Flow Country, guarded to the south by the Beinn Griam mountains. There are two small islands and inviting bays and headlands which demand attention.
Fish Large baskets of bright little trout which average 6/8oz. Breakfast is guaranteed here.
Flies & Tactics Bank fishing, and fish are taken all over the loch. Fish rise readily to most patterns of fly, but start with: Blue Zulu, Greenwells's Glory, Dunkeld.
Permission & Charges Forsinard Hotel, Forsinard, Sutherland, KW13 6YT. Tel: (01641) 571221. Bank fishing: £9 per rod per day.

NA SEILGE, Loch 11/923586 see OS Map 11.

NA SGEULACHD, BEALACH Loch
Location & Access 10/426539. Park by the telephone kiosk on the A838 Tongue/Durness road. Follow a well-marked track south, climbing steeply into the hills. Once 'up', at Gd Ref: 438550, leave the track and strike SSW over rough ground to reach the loch after a tramp of one mile.
Commentary An excellent water in a dramatic setting, surrounded by nine other smaller, unnamed waters, all of which also hold trout. There is a boat on Bealach na Sgeulachd, the others are fished from the shore. Fly fishing only, and restricted to 4 anglers on the loch at any one time. There is a bag limit of 3 fish per rod. Thereafter, fishing is catch and release.
Fish Rarely fished because of the long walk required to reach it, but fine-quality trout which average 8oz/10oz. The loch can also produce much larger fish, as can the other waters. Bank fishing is just as productive as boat fishing.
Flies & Tactics Offer: Ke-He, Invicta, Silver Butcher.
Permission & Charges Ben Loyal Hotel, Tongue, by Lairg, Sutherland. Tel: (01847) 611216. Bank fishing, £3 per rod per day. Use of boat £10 per day.

NAM BO UIDHRE, Loch
Location & Access 10/845572 Approach from the A836 Thurso/Bettyhill road. Turn south at Strathy (10/844650) and drive past Bowside Lodge to park at 10/828583. Walk ESE up the hill for approx. 25 minutes to reach the loch.
Commentary An excellent little loch. visit Loch nam Bo Uidhre as part of a circular tour including Coal Loch North (10/850560) and Loch na Meana (10/850560). Loch nam Bo Uidhre is a shallow loch in a remote moorland setting covering an area of about 20 acres. The moor surrounding the loch is very boggy.
Fish Good trout averaging approx. 8oz with larger fish of up to and over 1lb.
Flies & Tactics Bank fishing, and best results come from along the east shoreline, by the outlet burn, and in the south bay. Most flies tempt. Start with: Black Pennell, March Brown, Silver Butcher.
Permission & Charges Jack Paterson, The Halladale Inn, Melvich, Sutherland KW14 7YJ. Tel: (01641) 531282. Bank fishing: £5 per rod per day.

NAM BREAC BEAG, Loch
Location & Access 10/825629 From the A836 Thurso/Bettyhill road by turning south at Strathy (10/844650). Park near Bowside Lodge at 10/830610) and walk west, crossing the Strathy River. The loch lies 10 minutes away through the forest.
Commentary Sheltered from most winds. Shallow and now completely surrounded by commercial forestry.
Fish Sport with bright little trout averaging 6oz/8oz.
Flies & Tactics Good baskets can be taken and most

Strathnaver OS Map 10

patterns of fly produce results. Try: Black Pennell, Invicta, Alexandra. A boat is sometimes available.
Permission & Charges Dave Clements, The Dorran Bungalow, Forsinard, Strath Halladale, Sutherland. Tel: (01641) 571254. Bank fishing, £9 per rod per day.

NAM BREAC BUIDGE, Loch
Location & Access 10/650570 Between Bettyhill and Tongue, south of the A836. Park at 10/657586 on the west margin of the Borgie Forest. Follow a peat road which devolves into a track across the moor. Journey takes about thirty minutes.
Commentary Breac Buidge is approximately 600 yards long by up to 300 yards wide, with a delightful, scattered bay at the south end. Splendid views south and west to Ben Loyal and Ben Hope. One of the best lochs in the area.
Fish As the name implies, 'the loch of the golden trout', Breac Buidge fish are of excellent quality. They average 10/12oz in weight, with good numbers of large specimens of up to and over 2lb.
Flies & Tactics Bank fishing only, but most of the water is easily covered. Work south down the west shoreline, paying particular attention in the vicinity of the small island. first cast: Soldier Palmer, Woodcock & Hare-lug, Alexandra.
Permission & Charges From Ben Loyal Hotel, Tongue, by Lairg, Sutherland. Tel: Tongue (01847) 611216. Charges at £3 per rod per day.

NAM BREAC BUIDHE, Loch
Location & Access 10/618433 To the east of the A836 Altnaharra/Tongue road. Park at 10/599441 and walk the line of the forestry plantation for twenty five minutes. You will see the loch from the brow of the hill.
Commentary A small loch (approx 25 acres) on open moorland which can often be windy. One of the best little trout lochs in the area. On its day, unbeatable sport.
Fish Well-conditioned brown trout averaging 12oz in weight with a few larger fish of up to and over 2lb.
Flies & Tactics Boat fishing is best, but bank fishing can also produce good results. Fish rise and are caught all over this delightful little loch so cast with confidence. Try: Ke-He, March Brown, Peter Ross.
Permission & Charges From Altnaharra Hotel, Altnaharra, by Lairg, Sutherland. Tel: (01549) 411222. Charges: £20 per day for boat with two rods fishing.

NAM BREAC, Loch
Location & Access 10/826480 A six mile drive from 10/891436 along forestry roads, west from the A897 Helmdale/Melvich road through Strath Halladale. Full directions will be given with permit.
Commentary Rarely fished in times past because of the long walk in. Now, relatively easily accessible and still retaining a sense of remoteness, in spite of rampant forestry.
Fish Trout average 8oz, rise readily to the fly and fight well. Large baskets are the rule.
Flies & Tactics Boat fishing produces best results and fish rise and are caught all over this small, shallow loch. Start with Soldier Palmer, March Brown, Alexandra.
Permission & Charges From the Forsinard Hotel, Forsinard, Strath Halladale, Sutherland. Tel: (01641) 571221. Bank fishing £9 per rod per day.

NAM BREAC MOR, Loch
Location & Access 10/810802 From the A836 Thurso/Bettyhill road by turning south at Strathy (10/844650). Park near Bowside Lodge at 10/830610 and walk west, crossing the Strathy River. The loch lies 10 minutes away through the forest.
Commentary Sheltered from most winds. Shallow and surrounded by commercial forestry, except for the north west shore.
Fish Sport with bright little trout averaging 6/8oz.
Flies & Tactics Good baskets can be taken and most patterns of fly produce results. Try: Black Pennell, Invicta, Alexandra. A boat is sometimes available.
Permission & Charges Dave Clements, The Dorran Bungalow, Forsinard, Strath Halladale, Sutherland. Tel: (01641) 571254. Bank fishing, £9 per rod per day.

NAM BURAG, Lochan
Location & Access 10/658610 Approach from Deepburn at 10/678602, north from the Borgie Hotel. Walk up the hill. Loch a'Chaoruinn (10/668600) and Loch Skerray (10/665600) are on your left. At Loch Tigh-choimhid (10/662608), find the inlet burn at the north west end and follow it west to Lochan nam Burag.
Commentary A cast along the way to a series of other, similar, delightful little Skerray Hill lochans: Loch an'Tigh-choimhid (10/662608), Loch na Goit (10/662614), Loch nan Cnamh (10/659618) and Lochan Blar a'Bhainne (10/670613). A rewarding, round tour of a series of remote, beautiful, small lochans lying to the west of the Borgie Hotel.
Fish All these lochans contain trout which average 6/8oz. Some have larger fish of up to and over 1lb. Discover which.
Flies & Tactics Easy bank fishing and delicate casting. Stay back from the bank. Trout lies close in. Offer: Blue Zulu, March Brown, Alexandra.
Permission & Charges Peter MacGregor at the Borgie Hotel, Skerray, by Thurso, Sutherland. Tel: (01641) 521332. £5 per rod per day.

NAM FAOILEAG, Loch
Location & Access 10/735409 Approach from the B871 Kinbrace/Syre road and park at 16/725399 near the bridge. Walk north, following the line of Allt Lon a'Chuil burn for 100 yards, then angle slightly north east across the moor. Nam Faoileag is ten minutes distant.
Commentary A few acres, surrounded by scattered smaller ponds, but an attractive place to fish. Visit nam Faoileag as part of an exciting circular tour including Loch Molach (10/724420) and Rhifail Loch (10/720425). Wild flowers and birds of the Flow Country; look out, particularly, for greenshank.
Fish Bright little trout which fight with spirit. Average weight 6oz.

OS Map 10 — Strathnaver

Flies & Tactics Easy bank fishing with action anywhere on the loch. Try: Black Pennell, Invicta, Silver Butcher.
Permission & Charges Contact: Tony Henderson, Garvault Hotel, Garvault, Kinbrace, Sutherland. Tel: (01997) 414205. Charges: £5 per rod per day.

NAN CLACH, Loch
Location & Access 10/7705300 from the A836 Thurso/Bettyhill road. Turn south at Strathy (10/844650) and drive past Bowside Lodge following the forestry road for 10 miles to 10/774536. Walk west through the forest to the loch.
Commentary Because of its remote location, rarely fished and often offering shelter in high wind conditions. Loch nan Clach is surrounded by the Strath Forest and covers an area of half a mile long by up to 400 hundred yards wide.
Fish Large baskets of small trout which average 6/8oz. Breakfast is guaranteed.
Flies & Tactics Bank fishing, and fish are taken all over the loch. Fish rise readily to most patterns of fly, but start with: Soldier Palmer, Grouse & Claret, Silver Butcher.
Permission & Charges Contact: Jack Paterson, The Halladale Inn, Melvich, Sutherland KW14 7YJ. Tel: (01641) 531282. Bank fishing: £5 per rod per day.

NAN CNAMH, Loch
Location & Access 10/659618. Not easy to find. Best approach is to follow an outlet burn up the hill from 10/675616, north from the Borgie Hotel. At the top of the hill, where the stream turns south, walk on west to reach the loch in ten minutes.
Commentary A cast along the way to a series of other similar, delightful little Skerray Hill lochans: Loch an'Tigh-choimhid (10/662608), Loch nam Burag (10/658610), Loch na Coit (10/662614) and Lochan Blar a'Bhainne (10/670613). A rewarding, round tour of a series of remote, beautiful, small lochans lying to the west of the Borgie Hotel.
Fish All these lochans contain trout which average 6/8oz. Some have larger fish of up to and over 1lb. Discover which.
Flies & Tactics Easy bank fishing and delicate casting. Stay back from the bank. Trout lies close in. Offer: Blue Zulu, March Brown, Alexandra.
Permission & Charges Peter MacGregor at the Borgie Hotel, Skerray, by Thurso, Sutherland. Tel: (01641) 521332. £5 per rod per day.

NAN GALL, Loch
Location & Access 10/839550. Approach from the A897 Helmsdale/Melvich road, turning on to the minor road that follows the west bank of the Halladale River at 10/896524. Park at Upper Bighouse (10/889575). Take the track past the remains of the Broch and walk west for 25 minutes to reach the loch.
Commentary A secluded moorland loch offering good sport. Loch nan Gall lies in a hollow on the moor and is four hundred yards long by up to 200 yards wide. It exits via the Allt nan Gall burn into the Halladale River from the north end.
Fish Hard fighting fish which average 8oz as well as a few larger trout of up to and over 1lb in weight.
Flies & Tactics Bank fishing, and the south end, by the inlet burn, is a good place to start. first cast: Black Zulu, March Brown, Kingfisher Butcher.
Permission & Charges Contact: Jack Paterson, The Halladale Inn, Melvich, Sutherland KW14 7YJ. Tel: (01641) 531282. Bank fishing: £5 per rod per day.

NAN GAMHNA, Loch
Location & Access 10/646581 To the south of the A836 Bettyhill/Thurso road. Park at 10/654588 and follow the peat track south past Clar-loch Mor (10/650587) and Clar-loch Beag (10/654585). At the end of the track, angle south-east to reach Nan Gamha in ten minutes.
Commentary Combine a visit to Nan Gamhna with a more extended day out fishing Clar-loch Mor and Clar-loch Beag (see above), as well as fishing Grian-loch Beag (10/642568) and Grian-loch Mor (10/645558), further south, returning by Loch nam Breac Buidge (10/650569). A small, moorland lochan, worth a few casts on the walk south to finer things.
Fish Not glass-case country, but decent little trout which fight well.
Flies & Tactics Bank fishing. Offer them: Ke-He, Greenwell's Glory, Silver Butcher.
Permission & Charges Peter MacGregor at The Borgie Hotel, Skerray, by Thurso, Sutherland. Tel: (01641) 521332. £5 per rod per day.

NAVER, River
Location & Access Source 16/620370 Outflow 10/710602
Commentary The River Naver rises from Loch Naver amidst dramatic scenery, guarded to the east by the towering slopes of Ben Klibreck. It then flows 18 miles north to reach the sea through the wide sands of Torrisdale Bay by Bettyhill. The Upper Naver, from the Loch Naver to Syre, is typically 'Highland' in character, rocky, quick runs and delightful pools; thereafter, the Naver is bordered by wind-blown trees and grassy banks until its final rush to Torrisdale Bay. The Naver is one of the most productive and most exclusive Scottish salmon streams. Fishing is restricted to six rods per day on the main river, rotating through three beats. A system of 'man and boy' (or lady) rod is operated, with two rods per beat. Casual rods are rarely available, but a lower beat is reserved for the local angling club and visitors may obtain a days fishing on this part of the river. It often offers outstanding sport. Although most fish are taken during August and September, spring runs persist on the Naver and some superb fish are caught in Feb, March and April. Approach from the A836 Bettyhill/Tongue road, and from the B873 Bettyhill/Altnaharra road which is adjacent to the west bank of the river.
Fish Figures of rod catch returns are not generally released but a reasonable estimate would be in the order of between 500 and 800 fish most seasons.
Flies & Tactics A double-handed, 15/16ft salmon rod is best, to cover all the lies, and to control fish in heavy water. The banks of the upper river are generally

Strathnaver   OS Map 10

obstruction-free, although some of the pools below Syre will test all your casting skills. The angling club water is easily fished. Flies for the Naver include: Willie Gunn, Hairy Mary, General Practitioner, Garry Dog, Stoat's Tail, Waddingtons, Shrimp Fly, Silver Wilkinson, Green Highlander.

Permission & Charges Permission to fish on the Association Water of the River Naver is readily available from: The Store, Bettyhill, Strathnaver. Tel: (01641) 521207. Cost: £21 per rod per day. Bookings taken on a first-come-first-served basis, 24 hours before the date of fishing. Rods may be available from time to time on the Syre Fishings, let in conjunction with Syre Lodge. For details contact: Finlyson Hughes, 29 Barossa Place, Perth PH1 5 EP. Tel: (01738) 639017. Altnaharra Hotel can also sometimes arrange fishing on the river.

PALM, Loch

Location & Access 10/710410 Immediately adjacent to the B871 Kinbrace/Syre road.

Commentary Being so close to the road, a bit 'public' but a pleasant loch to fish. Very weedy as the season advances. Easily accessible and ideal for beginners or as a warm-up for a visit to Rhifail Loch (10/735409), Loch nam Faoileag (10/735409) and Loch Molach (10/735409).

Fish Bright little trout which fight with spirit. Average weight 6oz.

Flies & Tactics Easy bank fishing with action anywhere on the loch. Try: Black Pennell, Invicta, Silver Butcher.

Permission & Charges Contact: Tony Henderson, Garvault Hotel, Garvault, Kinbrace, Sutherland. Tel: (01997) 414205. Charges: £5 per rod per day.

PREAS AN LOCHAN, Loch

Location & Access 10/845538. Approch From the A836 Thurso/Bettyhill road. Turn south at Strathy (10/844650) and drive past Bowside Lodge to park at 10/828565. Follow the edge of the forestry plantation east, then south east to Caol Loch South. Loch Preas an Lochan is a further 20 minutes south.

Commentary Visit Loch Preas an Lochan as part of a long day out fishing Loch an Fheoir (10/844652), Caol Loch South (10/845572), Lochan na Ceardaich (10/839550) and Loch Crasgach (10/835543) along the way. Stop for a few casts after fishing Caol loch South (see above).

Fish Trout average approximately 6oz.

Flies & Tactics Easy bank fishing. First cast: Ke-He, March Brown, Dunkeld.

Permission & Charges Jack Paterson, The Halladale Inn, Melvich, Sutherland KW14 7YJ. Tel: (01641) 531282. Bank fishing: £5 per rod per day.

PRIVATE WATERS The lochs within grid square NW5446, NE5746, and SW5444, SE5744, and MHOID, Loch (The Plantation Loch) at (10/568410) and DIONACH-CARAIDH, Loch at (10/559402), are preserved by the owner and are not available to members of the public. The lochs within grid square NW6147, NE6947, and SW6041, SE6941 (excluding Loch Loyal), are preserved by the owner and are not available to members of the public. The lochs within grid square NW6657, NE7257, and SW6651, SE7251 are preserved by the owner and are not available to members of the public.

RHIFAIL, Loch

Location & Access 10/735409 Approach from the B871 Kinbrace/Syre road and park at 10/713425, near Palm Loch. Walk due north for one mile to reach Rhifail.

Commentary A 'boot-shaped', delightful loch with a smaller, satellite lochan to the north, well worth the walk. Visit Rhifail Loch as part of an exciting circular tour including Loch nam Faoileag (10/735409).

Fish Bright little trout which fight with spirit. Average weight 6/8 oz with the odd larger specimen.

Flies & Tactics Easy bank fishing with action anywhere on the loch. Try: Black Pennell, Invicta, Silver Butcher.

Permission & Charges Contact: Tony Henderson, Garvault Hotel, Garvault, Kinbrace, Sutherland. Tel: Kinbrace (01997) 414205. Charges: £5 per rod per day.

RIFA-GIL, Loch

Location & Access 10/750484 Follow the B871 south down Strathnaver and park at 10/724495. Cross the River Naver and walk to Rhifail (10/730495) Skirting the north edge of the forestry plantation, climb the north shoulder of Beinn Rifa-gil. After fishing Loch Warander (10/746492), walk SSE for 15 minutes to reach Rifa-gil.

Commentary Fish Loch Rifa-gil in conjunction with Loch Feusaige (10/750465), to the south, as part of a splendid moorland 'tour', returning to Rhifail via the Allt Rivigill Burn and a good track along the east bank of the River Naver. A very attractive lochan on the headwaters of the Skelpick Burn, Rifa-gil extends to some 35 acres and is infrequently fished, if at all, from one season to the next.

Fish Trout are well-shaped and average 8oz with a few large fish of up to 1lb.

Flies & Tactics Comfortable wading, with a number of useful casting points and promon tories. The bays and island at the north east corner of the loch are particularly productive. First cast: Black Pennell, Greenwell's Glory, Dunkeld.

Permission & Charges See Loch Airgh na Creigh entry.

ROSAIL, Loch

Location & Access 10/715400 Immediately adjacent to the B871 Kinbrace/Syre road. Park at 10/719402.

Commentary Very pretty little loch with a small island off the east shore. Easily accessible and ideal for beginners or as a warm-up for a visit to Rhifail Loch (10/735409), Loch nam Faoileag (10/735409) and Loch Molach (10/735409).

Fish Bright little trout which fight with spirit. Average weight 6oz and the chance of some larger trout of up to 1lb in weight.

Flies & Tactics Easy bank fishing with action anywhere on the loch. First cast: Ke-He, Grouse & Claret, Alexandra.

OS Map 10 — Strathnaver

Permission & Charges Contact: The Garvault Hotel, Garvault, Kinbrace, Sutherland. Tel: (01997) 414205. Charges: £5 per rod per day.

RUADH, Lochan
Location & Access 10/636619 Approach from the Strathan arm of Skerray 'ring road' at 10/645620. Walk west up the hill. The loch lies just to the north of Meall an Lochan Ruaidh (113m).
Commentary A very special little lochan in a remote moorland setting. Rarely fished form one season to the next, offering splendid isolation, peace and quiet.
Fish Nothing for the glass case, but plenty for breakfast.
Flies & Tactics Easily fished from the bank. Most flies will bring results. Start with: Black Pennell, Grouse & Claret, Silver Butcher.
Permission & Charges Peter MacGregor at The Borgie Hotel, Skerray, by Thurso, Sutherland. Tel: (01641) 521332. £5 per rod per day.

SGEIREADH, Loch
Location & Access 10/758432 Approach from the B871 Kinbrace/Syre road and park at the Garvault Hotel 17/781387. Walk north west from the hotel, round the south shoulder of Beinn a'Mhadaidh. Sgeireadh lies in a hollow, one mile north west from Beinn a'Mhadaidh.
Commentary A small, circular, shallow loch, edged with sandy beaches and sheltered banks, surrounded by the absolute peace of the Flow Country. One of the most attractive lochs in the north. The amazing wild flowers and birds of the Flow Country is attraction enough for walking this way. Look out, particularly for greenshank.
Fish Small, bright little trout which fight with great dash and spirit. Average weight 8oz.
Flies & Tactics Comfortable bank fishing and expect action anywhere on the loch. The north shore, where three feeder streams enter, always produces results. Try: Black Pennell, Invicta, Silver Butcher.
Permission & Charges Contact: Tony Henderson, Garvault Hotel, Garvault, Kinbrace, Sutherland. Tel: (01997) 414205. Charges: £5 per rod per day.

SGIATHANAGH, Loch
Location & Access 10/870624 Leave the A836 Thurso/Bettyhill road at 10/868652 and follow the rough, metled road south. This becomes a peat track but with care it can be negotiated . Park at the end and walk south east for 15 minutes to reach the loch.
Commentary Worth a cast on the way to Loch Couldbackie (10/874614). A tiny lochan, easily covered from the bank.
Fish Small fish are the 'norm' but the loch has a reputation for holding a few larger trout.
Flies & Tactics Stay well back from the bank and offer them standard patterns: Ke-He, Woodcock & Harelug, Silver Invicta.
Permission & Charges Contact: Jack Paterson, The Halladale Inn, Melvich, Sutherland KW14 7YJ. Tel: (01641) 531282. Bank fishing: £5 per rod per day.

SKERRAY, Loch
Location & Access 10/665600 Between Bettyhill and Tongue, north of the A836, within the 'ring road' through Borgie and Skerray townships.
Commentary Traditional highland trout fishing in a very attractive setting. A narrow, easily accessible loch which is the subject of a local conservation and environmental protection exercise.
Fish Bright little trout which fight hard with the chance of larger fish of up to and over 1lb in weight.
Flies & Tactics Bank fishing only. Trout are taken all over the loch. Try: Ke-He, March Brown, Silver Butcher.
Permission & Charges Peter MacGregor, The Borgie Lodge Hotel, Skerray, by Thurso, Sutherland. Tel: (01641) 521332

SLAIM, Loch
Location & Access 10/623535. Off A836 at 10/608547. Drive down to end of track and walk 1 mile to boat at bottom of fence.
Commentary A very attractive loch to fish in a completely remote setting. The tiny, unnamed lochan on the hill to the east is also worth a cast (10/631537). Slaim is used as a reservoir for the Borgie River and there is a dam and sluice at the north end. As the season advances, weed-growth extends over a wide area, making fishing difficult. Often sheltered when the wind rages elsewhere.
Fish Although on the headwaters of the Borgie River and undoubtedly containing salmon, in recent years at least, very few have been caught. Large stocks of brown trout averaging 8oz in weight more than adequately make up for lack of salmon. This is an ideal beginners' water and large baskets are frequently taken.
Flies & Tactics Boat fishing is best and trout rise and are caught all over the loch. The east bay is particularly productive. Start with: Loch Ordie, Grouse & Claret, Dunkeld. Dapping also brings results.
Permission & Charges The Borgie Hotel, Skerray, by Thurso, Sutherland. Tel: (01641) 521332; Altnaharra Hotel, Altnaharra, by Lairg, Sutherland. Tel: (01549) 411222. Boat fishing: £20 per day with two rods fishing. No bank fishing.

STAING, Loch
Location & Access 10/580407 Immediately adjacent to the A836 Altnaharra/Tongue road.
Commentary A small, shallow loch, easily accessible and surrounded by magnificent scenery.
Fish Not glass-case country, but ideal for beginners with good stocks of hard-fighting little fish which average 6/8oz in weight.
Flies & Tactics Boat fishing or bank fish will produce the desired results. Easy wading along the east and north shore. Most patterns of fly tempt them but start with Black Zulu, Greenwell's Glory, Silver Butcher.
Permission & Charges Altnaharra Hotel, Altnaharra, by Lairg, Sutherland. Tel (01549) 411222. Charges: £20 per day for boat with two rods fishing.

Strathnaver OS Map 10

STRATHY, Loch
Location & Access 10/777470 Turn south from the A836 Melvich/Bettyhill road at 10/842651 and follow the forestry road to Lochstrathy at 10/794490, a distance of 12 rough miles. A further one mile walk, south west across the damp moor, brings you to the loch.
Commentary A very remote loch in a glorious setting, away-from-it-all. Ideal for beginners and for those who enjoy a wild setting a long day out in the hills. Loch Strathy is approx. three quarters of a mile long by up to quarter of a mile wide. It lies in the heart of the Flow Country and is best visited early in the season, before the midges become oppressively active.
Fish Excellent stocks of well-formed, hard-fighting small brown trout which average 8oz in weight.
Flies & Tactics Bank fishing only and comfortable wading. Fish are taken all round the loch, particularly at the south end where the feeder steams enter from Gorm-loch Mor (10/782445). All standard pattern flies produce results. Start with: Black Pennell, March Brown, Silver Butcher.
Permission & Charges Robert McBain, The Skelpick Partnership, Skelpick, Bettyhill, Sutherland. Tel: (01641) 521311. £5 per rod per day.

STRATHY, River
Location & Access Source: 10/780450 Outflow: 10/834660 For the Upper River, from the A836 Thurso/Bettyhill road at 10/842650 via a good track leading south to Bowside Lodge. The Lower River is approached from the bridge over the A836 at 10/835652.
Commentary The Strathy is a small spate river. It gathers strength from the streams and lochans of Meall Bad na Cuaiche, Meall Ceann Loch Strathy and Cnoc nan Tri-chiach, then flows 15 miles north to reach the sea over Strathy Sands. In recent years, the character of the area has been altered by extensive commercial forestry planting, making the Strathy ever more reliant upon heavy rain in order to produce sport. Considerable effort has been made in the past to improve the fishing, including stocking and the construction of artificial pools. Although many of these pools have been washed out, there are still a number of good lies; including The Dye, deepish, slow-moving water, six miles up river from the sea; Rock Pool, Mann's Pool and The Forestry Pools. Most fish are caught during Aug and Sept, depending upon water levels. 10 Jan - 30 Sept
Fish Approximately 40 fish are taken during the season, depending upon water levels. Expect more grilse than salmon and they average about 6lb in weight. A fish of 16lb 8oz was caught in 1994. Jack Paterson had a brown trout weighing 5lb 4oz in 1999.
Flies & Tactics A single-handed rod is adequate. Stalk the fish, from one point, lengthening line, rather than walking down the bank. Flies: Willie Gunn, Garry Dog, Munro Killer, Stoat's Tail. In low water conditions, use trout flies.
Permission & Charges Weekly and daily lets may be available at £12.50 per rod per day through: Jack Paterson, The Halladale Inn, Melvich, Sutherland KW14 7YJ. Tel: (01641) 531282. Accommodation also available.

TIGH-CHOIMHID, Lochan
Location & Access 10/662608 Between Bettyhill and Tongue, north of the A836, within the 'ring road' through Borgie and Skerray townships.
Commentary A tiny lochan to the north of Loch Skerray (10/665600). Well worth a few casts whilst visiting Loch Skerray.
Fish Bright little trout which fight well.
Flies & Tactics Bank fishing only. Trout are taken all over the loch. Try: Ke-He, March Brown, Silver Butcher.
Permission & Charges Peter MacGregor, The Borgie Lodge Hotel, Skerray, by Thurso, Sutherland. Tel: (01641) 521332

TIORMACHD, Lochan
Location & Access 10/762649 From the A836 Thurso/Bettyhill road. Park at Druimbasbie (10/771631) and walk NNW, past Loch Na h-Imriche, (10/768643) for 40 minutes to reach the loch.
Commentary A tiny lochan in a lovely setting, well worth a few casts. Easily fished from the bank and usually visited in conjunction with Loch Na h-Imriche (see above).
Fish Good trout which average in the order of 12oz.
Flies & Tactics Offer them: Soldier Palmer, Invicta, Silver Butcher.
Permission & Charges Dave Clement, The Dorran Bungalow, Forsinard, Strath Halladale, Sutherland. Tel: (01641) 571254. Bank fishing, £9 per rod per day.

TUIRSLIGHE, Loch
Location & Access 10/658593 To the north of the A836 Bettyhill/Tongue road. Park at 10/647586, cross the road, and walk north up the hill. You will reach the loch in ten minutes.
Commentary An attractive little lochan in a remote location. Easily accessible, relatively sheltered, ideal as part of a ramble round the Skerray hill lochs.
Fish Trout are not large, averaging 6-8oz, but they rise readily and fight well.
Flies & Tactics The lochan is easily covered from the bank. Offer them: Black Pennell, Invicta, Silver Butcher.
Permission & Charges Peter MacGregor at The Borgie Hotel, Skerray, by Thurso, Sutherland. Tel: (01641) 521332. £5 per rod per day.

WARENDER, Loch
Location & Access 10/746492 Follow the B871 south down Strathnaver and park at 10/724495. Cross the River Naver and walk to Rhifail (10/730495). Skirting the north edge of the forestry plantation, climb the north shoulder of Beinn Rifa-gil. The loch is immediately below the summit.
Commentary Fish Loch Warender in conjunction with a visit to Loch Rifa-gil (10/750484) and Loch Feusaige (10/750465), to the south, as part of a splendid circular, moorland 'tour'. A tiny lochan, lying in a shallow hollow 1,000ft above Strathnaver.

OS Map 10-11 Thurso & Dunbeath

Fish Very rarely fished. average weight of trout is in the order of 6oz, but splendid fun to catch and well worth a cast or two or three on the way out to Rifa-gil and Feusaige.
Flies & Tactics Easily covered from the bank. Tempt them with Ke-He, March Brown, Silver Butcher.
Permission & Charges See Loch Airgh na Creigh entry.

Thurso & Dunbeath

AIRIGH LEATHAID, Lochan
Location & Access 11/991390 Take the unclassified road from Westerdale (12/127516), turning right onto the private forestry/estate road at 12/089471. Follow this road west past Dalnawillan Lodge (11/030408) to Dalganachan. A signpost points uphill to Airigh Leathaid. Twenty minute hike north.
Commentary There are a few more lovely places to fish in Caithness than Airigh Leathaid. There are three lochs, two of which extend to about five acres each, the third, to the north, being barely a 'guid Scots acre'.
Fish Splendid fishing for excellent quality brown trout. Airigh Leathaid is stocked with Thurso River trout. They thrive mightily in their moorland adopted home. Average weight in the region of 1 lb 2oz, but fish of up to and over 3lb are taken.
Flies & Tactics Comfortable bank fishing. The middle lochan has a sandy/rocky north shore promontory which offers excellent sport. Do not wade the smallest lochan. Keep well back from the edge. This tiny water holds fish of over 4lb. First cast: Ke-He, Woodcock & hare-lug, Dunkeld.
Permission & Charges Ulbster Arms Hotel, Bridge Street, Halkirk, Caithness. Tel: Halkirk (01847) 831206. When not required by hotel guests at £10 per day.

AKRAN, Loch
Location & Access 11/923605 From the A897 Helmsdale/Melvich road in Strath Halladale, at 10/905600, by a new forestry road. Full directions will be given with permit.
Commentary The perfect place to introduce little ones to the delights of fly-fishing. Easy access and no casting obstructions. There is a sandy picnic beach on the east shore and the water here is shallow, allowing safe wading.
Fish Akran is a traditional 'Highland' loch, full of small fish which cooperate readily. Average weight is in the order of three to the pound.
Flies & Tactics Almost any pattern will bring results, either from shore or boat. Most productive areas are along the south shoreline and in the narrow, south east bay. Keep clear of the overhead pylons which border the east shore. Best months, May, June and September.
Permission & Charges Dave Clement, The Dorran Bungalow, Forsinard, Strath Halladale, Sutherland. Tel: (01641) 571254. Bank fishing, £9 per rod per day.

BERRIEDALE Water 17/940345 See OS Map 17.

CAOL, Loch
Location & Access 11/903615 From the A897 Helmsdale/Melvich road in Strath Halladale, at 10/905600, by a new forestry road. Full directions will be given with permit.
Commentary More distant and not as heavily fished as Seilge and Akran to the south, but, nevertheless, a pleasant place to fish. Caol is a long narrow, loch in a remote setting, shallow and easily fished from the bank.
Fish Traditional 'highland' fishing for small, brightly marked brown trout which average 6oz. There are larger fish, so always be prepared for a more violent 'tug'.
Flies & Tactics The most productive fishing area is along the west shoreline, particularly in the vicinity of the outlet burn and the small island. Try Black Zulu, Grouse & Claret, Silver, Butcher. Best months: June and Sept.
Permission & Charges See Loch Akran entry.

CLAR, Loch
Location & Access OS11/954442 From the A897 Helmsdale/Melvich road north from Forsinard at 10/903485. Follow the forestry road east around the south shoulder of Sletill Hill. Follow this road to Loch Leir. Walk south to Loch Clar.
Commentary An ideal beginners loch, but a long walk. Once in a delightful moorland setting, now, sadly, surrounded by forestry. Season 1 April - 30 Sept.
Fish Breakfast-sized trout and lots of them.
Flies & Tactics Bank fishing only and trout may be caught all round the loch.
Permission & Charges The Forsinard Hotel, Forsinard, Strath Halladale, Sutherland. Tel: (01641) 571221. Bank fishing, £9 per rod per day.

CROSS REFERENCE For details and information on the following lochs, see OS Map 17: Loch Breac, Loch Dubh Glutt, Catherine's Loch, Loch Mhadadh, Loch Braigh na h-Aibhne and Loch nam Bo Riabhach.

DUNBEATH Water (River) 11/999319. See OS Map 17.

EALACH MOR, Lochan
Location & Access OS11/967482 From the A897 Helmsdale/Melvich road north from Forsinard at 10/903485. Follow the forestry road east round the south shoulder of Sletill Hill. the route to Lochan Ealach Mor is signposted.
Commentary An ideal beginner's loch, full of bright little fish. Once in a delightful moorland setting at the heart of the Flow Country, now, sadly, surrounded by commercial forestry plantations.
Fish Great sport with bright little trout.
Flies & Tactics Trout may be caught all round the loch, particularly in the vicinity of the three inlet burns, in the north, east and west. Most flies bring results. Best months are June and September.
Permission & Charges The Forsinard Hotel, Forsinard, Strath Halladale, Sutherland. Tel: (01641) 571221. Fishing is available when not required by hotel guests. Bank fishing: £9 per rod per day.

Thurso & Dunbeath — OS Map 11

EUN, Loch
Location & Access OS11/984425 Approach from Westerdale (11/128516) along the unclassified road towards Loch More. At 11/090471 bear right onto the forestry and estate road. At Dalnawillan Lodge (11/030408) turn right to Altnabreac Station. Before the station (11/003454) turn left. Past Badnaheen Cottage (11/995443), park on Cnoc Seasaimh (11/995429). A track leads to the loch. A high wheel-base vehicle is preferable.
Commentary One of the best little lochs in Caithness. A long, arduous drive, but worth the effort. This tiny loch is set amidst most attractive scenery and is the perfect place to escape from every day worries. Season 1 April - 30 September.
Fish Fine quality, pink-fleshed, hard-fighting trout which average 1 lb 8oz in weight. The heaviest fish taken in recent years weighed 3lb 4oz.
Flies & Tactics A small, intimate loch, easily covered from both bank and boat. Flies: try Cochy-bondhu, March Brown, Dunkeld.
Permission & Charges The Ulbster Arms Hotel, Bridge Street, Halkirk, Caithness. Tel: (01847) 83206. Bank fishing, £10 per day, or £15 to include the use of the boat (two anglers fishing).

GLUTT Loch 11/992374 Glutt Loch is an excellent, clear-water loch which holds superb, hard-fighting fish of up to and over 3 lb, but, sadly, it is not available for fishing at the time of writing.

LEIR, Loch
Location & Access OS11/946458 From the A987 Helmsdale/Melvich road north from Forsinard at 10/903485. Follow the forestry road east round the south shoulder of Sletill Hill. The route to Leir is signposted.
Commentary An excellent loch with a good stock of trout which rise readily to the fly. Once in a delightful moorland setting at the heart of the Flow country, now, sadly, surrounded by commercial forestry plantations. Best months, June and Sept.
Fish Trout are not as large as neighbouring Loch Sletill but they rise more readily to the fly. The average weight is in the order of 10oz but they fight as though they were twice their size.
Flies & Tactics Boat and bank fishing, with boat fishing probably bringing best results. Nevertheless, in windy conditions, bank fishing can be just as productive, particularly along the north shore where wading is comfortable. Try a cast with Ke-He, March Brown, Silver Butcher.
Permission & Charges The Forsinard Hotel, Forsinard, Strath Halladale, Sutherland. Tel: (01641) 571221. Bank fishing, £9 per rod per day. Use of boat, £19 per day.

NA CLOICHE, Loch
Location & Access 11/976474 From the A897 Helmsdale/Melvich road north from Forsinard at 10/903485. Follow the forestry road east round the south shoulder of Sletill Hill. The route to Loch na Cloiche is signposted.
Commentary An ideal beginner's loch, full of bright little fish. Once in a delightful moorland setting at the heart of the Flow country, now, sadly, surrounded by commercial forestry plantations.
Fish Do not expect one for the glass case, but do expect great sprot with very pretty little trout.
Flies & Tactics Trout may be caught all round the loch, particularly in the vicinity of the inlet burns, from Lochan Ealach Mor in the north and the burn at the south end. Most flies bring results. Best months are June and September.
Permission & Charges The Forsinard Hotel, Forsinard, Strath Halladale, Sutherland. Tel: (01641) 571221. Bank fishing, £9 per rod per day.

NA SEILGE, Loch
Location & Access 11/923586 From the A897 Helmsdale/Melvich road in Strath Halladale, at 10/905600, by a new forestry road. Full directions given with permit.
Commentary One of the most attractive and productive lochs in North Strath Halladale. The setting has altered recently through commercial afforestation, but Seilge is still a lovely place to fish, with wonderful views westwards and complete seclusion. The small island is an ideal picnic spot, with a remarkable range of wild flowers and natural vegetation.
Fish Full of excellent trout varying in size from 8oz to over 2lb. Well shaped and pink-fleshed.
Flies & Tactics Bank fishing only. The most productive fishing areas in the vicinity of the small island and the S and E shoreline. First cast: Ke-He, Greenwell's Glory, Kingfisher Butcher.
Permission & Charges See Loch Akran entry.

NAN CLACH GEALA, Lochan
Location & Access 11/935495 From the A897 Helmsdale/Melvich road at 10/903485. Full directions given with permit.
Commentary Experts' water, but undoubtedly the place to go for specimen fish. Well worth a visit. Two small moorland lochans with three satellite waters nearby. Often affected by high winds; dark, peaty water. Challenging.
Fish A long record of outstanding catches including a recent trout weighing 4lb, caught by Mr Morris Draper. Outstanding quality of fish which average 1lb 8oz. Another recent basket produced 4 trout weighing 9lb.
Flies & Tactics Expect more blank than productive days. Bank fishing only and wading can be dangerous in the main water. Start with Black Zulu, Ke-He, Silver Invicta.
Permission & Charges The Forsinard Hotel, Forsinard, Strath Halladale, Sutherland. Tel: (01641) 571221, when not required by hotel guests. Bank fishing, £9 per rod per day.

NOTTINGHAM MILL DAM, Loch
Location & Access 11/209360 From the A9 Inverness/Wick road at 11/218345, along the private road to Nottingham Mains Farm. Park at the farm and walk north to the loch.

94

OS Map 11 — Thurso & Dunbeath

Commentary An easily accessible small, man-made loch that contrives to look natural; shallow and surrounded by commercial forestry to the north. In recent years, sediment, washed out of the forestry ploughing furrows, has diminished the fishable area. Season 1 April - 30 Sept. Best months: May, June and Sept.
Fish Introduced many years ago but now breeding naturally. Trout are of excellent quality and average about 12oz - 1lb.
Flies & Tactics Bank fishing only. Use small flies, Black Pennell, Greenwell's Glory, Silver Invicta, and on calm evenings, offer dry flies of similar patterns.
Permission & Charges Ian H Sinclair, The Cottage, Nottingham Mains Farm, Latheron, Caithness. Tel: (01593) 741319. Bank fishing: £5 per rod per day.

PRIVATE WATERS The lochs and streams bounded south west by 11/9350 and south east by 11/9950 and north east by 11/9958 and north west by 11/9258 are preserved by the owners. The lochs and streams bounded by OS square SW0141 to SE0541 and NE0546 to NW0146 are also preserved by the owner.

RUMSDALE, Loch
Location & Access 11/969419 Approach from Westerdale (11/128516) along the unclassified road towards Loch More. At 11/090471 bear right onto the forestry and estate road. At Dalnawillan Lodge (11/030408) turn right to Altnabreac Station. Before the station (11/003454) turn left. Past Badnaheen Cottage (11/995443), park on Cnoc Seasaimh (11/995429). Walk west, past Loch Eun for 15 minutes to reach Rumsdale.
Commentary A long, arduous drive, followed by a good walk, but worth the effort. This tiny loch is set amidst most attractive scenery and is the perfect place to escape from every day worries. Season 1 April - 30 Sept.
Fish Full of breakfast sized trout.
Flies & Tactics Easily fished from the bank and the trout rise readily to almost any pattern of fly they are offered
Permission & Charges Ulbster Arms Hotel, Bridge Street, Halkirk, Caithness. Tel: (01847) 83206. Bank fishing, £10 per day.

RUMSDALE, Water
Location & Access Source: 11/970376. Outflow: 11/008399. Along the unclassified road from Westerdale (12/127516), turning right onto the private forestry/estate road at 12/089471. Follow this road west past Dalnawillan Lodge (11/030408) to Dalganachan where Rumsdale water enters the Thurso River.
Commentary Given a good flow, Rumsdale Water offers almost three miles of excellent burn fishing. Season 1 April - 30 Sept. Rumsdale Water flows through a wilderness of delight, with a wonderful array of wild flowers and wildlife. Good chance of seeing red deer, buzzard, hen harrier and golden plover.
Fish Brightly-marked little brown trout, with the chance of an occasional larger fish. This is a salmon spawning stream: carefully return any salmon parr caught.
Flies & Tactics Use light tackle and small (size 16-18) flies. Walk up stream and fish back down. This is trout-stalking country and Rumsdale will test all your casting skills. Most patterns of fly produce results.
Permission & Charges The Ulbster Arms Hotel, Bridge Street, Halkirk, Caithness. Tel: (01847) 83206. £10 per day.

SLEACH, Water
Location & Access Source: 11/988450. Outflow:12/074433 Approach from Westerdale (12/128517) along the unclassified road towards Loch More. At 12/091472, bear right onto the private estate and forestry road skirting the north shore of Loch More. Park at 12/072463.
Commentary This little burn is now enclosed by commercial forestry throughout much of its length but still offers sport with brown trout from where it enters Loch More, upstream to the first conifer block. Nearby are the remains of 14th century Dirlot Castle on a cliff by Thurso River at 12/127487; neolithic stone rows at 12/124485.
Fish The trout are small, about three to the pound.
Flies & Tactics Success depends upon delicate casting and a fine technique. On the lower, wider part of the stream, try dry fly. Most standard patters will produce results.
Permission & Charges The Ulbster Arms Hotel, Bridge Street, Halkirk, Caithness. Tel: (01847) 83206. Cost, £10 per day.

SLETILL, Loch
Location & Access 11/959470 From the A897 Helmsdale/Melvich road north from Forsinard at 10/903485. Follow the forestry road east round the south shoulder of Sletill Hill. The loch is a short walk from the road at 11/952473.
Commentary A shallow loch of some 100 acres. In days past, probably one of the best lochs in the area, not only because of the quality of fishing, but also for its scenic beauty. Commercial forestry has dramatically altered the landscape, but the fishing is still excellent.
Fish High-quality brown trout which average 12oz. Larger fish are frequently taken and most seasons produce trout of up to 3lb.
Flies & Tactics Trout are caught all over the loch, no one place being substantially better than another. Boat and bank fishing both bring results. Wading is safe and comfortable, particularly from the boat-mooring bay and northwards, where the bottom is sandy.
Permission & Charges The Forsinard Hotel, Forsinard, Strath Halladale, Sutherland. Tel: (01641) 571221, when not required by hotel guests. Bank fishing, £9 per day, use of the boat, £19 per day.

TALLAHEEL, Loch
Location & Access 11/955489 From the A897 Helmsdale/Melvich road north from Forsinard at 10/903485. Follow the forestry road east round the south shoulder of Sletill Hill. Follow this road to Loch Sletill. Talaheel lies to the north.

Thurso & Wick

OS Maps 11-12

Commentary A good loch with good stocks of fish. Once in a delightful moorland setting, now, sadly, surrounded by forestry. Season 1 April - 30 Sept.
Fish Talaheel can spring the occasional surprise, but the average weight of trout is about 8-10oz.
Flies & Tactics Bank and boat fishing on this small, intimate loch where large baskets are the rule, rather than the exception. Start with Black Pennell, Woodcock & hare-lug, Dunkeld.
Permission & Charges The Forsinard Hotel, Forsinard, Strath Halladale, Sutherland. Tel: (01641) 571221, when not required by hotel guests. Bank fishing, £9 per rod per day. Use of the boat, £19 per day.

THURSO, River

Location & Access Source: 11/92653. Outflow: 11/123688 Between Thurso and Halkirk, the B874; Halkirk to Westerdale (11/130528), unclassified road to the east of the river and from B870 at Westerdale; south of Westerdale, access is from Dalmore, (11/140492), Strathmore, (11/098467), and Lochmore Cottage (11/084460). The Upper Thurso River is approached from an Estate road bordering the west bank.
Commentary A classic Highland river rising from peat moorlands, flowing north through Loch More, thence down a fertile strath to the sea at Thurso Bay. A dam, sluice and fish pass, built at the outlet of Loch More in 1907, is used for river management purposes. The Thurso is divided into 13, two rod beats, both banks. An additional beat, above Westerdale, is preserved for the proprietor. Beat 1, at the mouth of the river, is fished by the Thurso Angling Association. Season 11 Jan - 5 Oct.
Fish The 10 year average rod catch return is 836 fish. One of the finest Scottish salmon streams and still producing good numbers of spring salmon. The most productive months are July, August and September. Fishing is strictly fly only. A hatchery is operated, with fry grown on to smolt stage, being released during April and May.
Flies & Tactics Use a 15ft double-handed rod. There are few riverbank obstructions to impede casting. Wading is not required, although thigh waders are advised for walking the bank and crossing the river. Gillies are available, if you are new to the river, but it is not compulsory to engage one. Useful flies: Garry Dog, General Practitioner, Stoat's Tail, Munro Killer, Green Highlander, Hairy Mary.
Permission & Charges For bookings, contact P J W Blackwood, Thurso Fisheries, Estate Office, Thurso East, Thurso, Caithness. Tel: Thurso (01847) 893134. Preference is given to those staying at The Ulbster Arms Hotel, Halkirk, Caithness. Tel: (01847) 831206. Occasional day lets might be available. Costs on application.

Thurso & Wick

A'CERACHER, Loch

Location & Access 12/133395 Approach along the unclassified road from Westerdale (12/127516). Park at Loch More Cottage (12/085460). Walk over the bridge and follow the track along the east shore of Loch More. At 12/085455, bear left along the track which leads over Druim Carn nam Muc and on to Loch Thulachan (12/106413). Behind the derelict lodge, take to the moor and walk south-east for thirty minutes to the loch.
Commentary A long, arduous walk to a tiny loch in a magical setting of wild, open moorlands. Magnificent scenery with a very good chance of seeing red deer, otter and wildcat. Outstanding wild flowers along the way. Look out for golden plover.
Fish Brightly marked, wild fish, genetically intact since the last Ice Age. Not very large and averaging perhaps four to the pound, but exciting to catch.
Flies & Tactics Easy bank fishing, from the shore, no need to lug along waders. All standard patterns of fly will produce results.
Permission & Charges The Ulbster Arms Hotel, Bridge Street, Halkirk, Caithness. Tel: (01847) 831206. Cost, £10 per day.

A'CERIGAL, Loch

Location & Access 12/100488 Approach along the unclassified road from Westerdale (12/127516). Park by Strathmore Lodge at 12/101480. Loch a'Cherigal is signposted and is a ten-minute walk north.
Commentary A small, shallow loch best fished from the boat. The west shore is very boggy and weed extends out into the loch for some distance, making bank fishing almost impossible.
Fish Excellent brown trout which average 12oz in weight and good numbers of heavier fish. Trout of over 2lb are taken most seasons. Hard-fighting fish of outstanding quality.
Flies & Tactics The best fishing area is from the east bank, from the small promontory, drifting across to the west shore. Flies: Ke-He, Woodcock & Hare-lug, Kingfisher Butcher.
Permission & Charges The Ulbster Arms Hotel, Bridge Street, Halkirk, Caithness. Tel: (01847) 831206, when not being used by hotel guests. Bank fishing: £10 per day, or, use of boat, £15 per day.

A'CHAIRN, Loch

Location & Access 12/077493 Approach along the unclassified road from Westerdale (12/127516). Park at 12/093475. Follow the western fence of the Cnoc a Bothain forest block for two miles to the loch.
Commentary A delightful little loch, somewhat apart from the commercial forests to the east and south. Set amidst a Site of Special Scientific Interest, a Chairn preserves much of what was best of the pre-afforestation Flow Country.
Fish Trout are not large, but there are a few surprises. Unstocked and quite natural.

OS Map 12 — Thurso & Wick

Flies & Tactics Easily covered from the bank and most patterns of fly will produce results.
Permission & Charges The Ulbster Arms Hotel, Bridge Street, Halkirk, Caithness. Tel: (01847) 831206. Bank fishing, £10 per day.

BANNISKIRK, Loch
Location & Access 12/176572 Approach from A895 Thurso/Latheron road at 12/156590. Follow a minor road to Banniskirk Farm. The loch is to the south.
Commentary Contains excellent trout. A small loch of about four acres on the hill behind Banniskirk Farm, surrounded by agricultural land.
Fish Stocked in past years and still containing trout which average 1lb in weight.
Flies & Tactics Bank fishing only and fish may be taken from all round the shore. Flies: Black Pennell, Ke-He, Soldier Palmer, Invicta, Greenwell's Glory, Butchers.
Permission & Charges Call at Banniskirk Farm and ask for details.

CAISE, Loch
Location & Access 12/023467 Approach from either Forsinard in Strath Halladale in Sutherland, or from 12/072463 by Loch More in Caithness, along forestry tracks. A high wheel base vehicle is preferable.
Commentary A small loch close to the railway. shallow and weedy at the north and north east end. Another small loch, joined to Caise, lies on the hill immediately to the east of Caise. This often dries out completely and is of no fishing interest. Explore a remaining segment of the Flow Country, across the railway to the north east of Loch Caise.
Fish Caise is an ideal beginners loch, easily accessible, close to the forestry road. Trout average in the region of four to the pound, rise readily and fight well.
Flies & Tactics Trout are taken all round the loch, but perhaps the north end is most productive, particularly where the tiny stream enters on the north east shore. Flies: Ke-He, March Brown, Alexandra. There is a good boat.
Permission & Charges The Forsinard Hotel, Forsinard, Strath Halladale, Sutherland. Tel: (01641) 571221. Bank fishing, £9 per rod per day. Use of boat, £19 per day.

CALDER, Loch
Location & Access OS12/075600 Two miles west from Halkirk, along a minor road which leaves the B874 Glengolly/Halkirk road at 12/130599.
Commentary Good stocks of trout but not of the same quality as the principal Caithness lochs - Watten, Heilen, and St John's. Calder is the deepest Caithness loch (120ft deep at north end) and the county water supply. The loch is two and a half miles long by up to one mile wide, and it can often be very stormy and dangerous. Wading is not recommended. Water level fluctuations make the margins unstable.
Fish Brown trout average 8oz and the loch also contains Arctic char. Some very large fish are taken and most seasons produce fish of over 3lb. Undoubtedly, there are ferox in the depths and this loch could contain double-figure fish.

Flies & Tactics This is the only Caithness loch where spinning and bait fishing is allowed. Flyfishing is just as productive, but if you are after a ferox 'you will have to troll deep. Best fishing areas are in the long, narrow, shallow bay to the south-west, and north from there amongst a series of small corners and headlands. An outboard motor is essential. Wear life-jackets at all times.
Permission & Charges Harper's Fly Fishing Services, 57 High Street, Thurso, Caithness. Tel: (01847) 893179; Mrs J Mackay, Achaguie, Scotscalder, Halkirk, Caithness. Tel: (01847) 831650. Hugo Ross, 56 High Street, Wick, Caithness. Tel: 01955 604200. Cost: £2 per rod per day for bank fishing. The use a boat is an additional £15 per day.

CAMSTER, Loch
12/263442 To the east of the minor road from Watten to Lybster. Small, peaty, troutless 'stank' of no fishing interest.

CAOL, Loch
Location & Access 12/026485 Approach from either Forsinard in Strath Halladale, or from 12/027463 by Loch More in Caithness. A high wheel-base vehicle is preferable. Park at 12/ 023467. Walk down the track past Loch Caise, cross the railway, then follow the peat track out along the west edge of a forestry block to the loch.
Commentary A finger of sanity amidst the commercial forestry, always welcoming. Caol is a narrow loch, extending into a wide, sandy bay at the north end. Unspoiled Flow Country sweeps northwards into the neighbouring, unplanted, Dorrery Estate. Marvellous views south to the Caithness mountains of Morven and the Scrabens. Explore the Flow Country to the north. There is also a wonderful get-away-from-it-all picnic site on the sandy beach at the north end of the loch.
Fish Good stocks of hard-fighting trout which average 10 oz in weight intermingled with one or two larger fish up to 2lb.
Flies & Tactics The narrow, south end is least productive, but, apart from that, trout may be caught from all round the shoreline. The east bank offers the most comfortable wading, with the west shore being rocky. When boat fishing, concentrate in the wide north bay. Flies: Loch Ordie, Soldier Palmer, Silver Butcher.
Permission & Charges Forsinard Hotel, Forsinard, Strath Halladale, Sutherland. Tel: (01641) 571 221. Bank fishing, £9 per rod per day. Use of a boat, £19 per day.

COIRE NA BEINNE, Lochan
Location & Access 12/147399 Drive south down the A895 Thurso to Latheron road. Park by the substantial ruined buildings at 12/182394 on the west side of the road. Using compass and map, tramp west across open moorland to Coire na Beinne hill (226m). The loch lies to the south-west of the summit. Allow forty-five minutes for the journey.
Commentary An adventure. A tiny, shallow loch in dramatic wilderness surroundings where you will be guaranteed complete isolation. Marvellous wildlife along the way: flowers, birds, red deer, otter and wildcat.

Thurso & Wick   OS Map 12

Fish Not much known since this lochan is rarely visited, but local tradition reports that it contains excellent trout.
Flies & Tactics Use standard pattern flies. The loch is very small and easily fished from the bank.
Permission & Charges John Anderson, Latheronwheel Estate, Latheron, Caithness. Tel: (01593) 741230. Cost, £5 per rod per day.

DUBH NAN GEODH, Loch

Location & Access 12/060477 Approach along the private forestry and estate road from 12/089471, skirting the north shore of Loch More. At 12/072464, turn right through commercial forestry and follow the signs.
Commentary A dark-water, shallow, scattered loch, with inviting promontories and corners, draining eastwards into Loch Eileanach via a small stream.
Fish Trout here average 1lb 10oz, but do not give themselves up easily. The heaviest fish taken in recent years, caught by Eddie McArthy, weighed 4lb 10oz.
Flies & Tactics Boat fishing generally brings best results, but in windy conditions cast with confidence along the north shore. Flies to offer: Coch-y-Bondhu, Soldier Palmer, Silver Butcher.
Permission & Charges The Ulbster Arms Hotel, Bridge Street, Halkirk, Caithness. Tel: (01847) 831206. Bank fishing, £10 per day, the use of a boat, £15 per day.

DUNNET HEAD, Lochs

Location & Access 12/205750. Approach from Dunnet on the A836 Thurso/John O' Groats road. Turn north on the B855 round the west shore of loch St John's, then drive to Dunnet Head. Foot-slog to the remote waters.
Commentary Stocked and managed by the Dunnet Head Angling Club. Worth a visit, particularly when wind makes other Caithness waters unfishable. Small, peaty waters, very lovely. A permit is availabe to fish Black Loch OS12/203745; Many Lochs OS12/200749; Long Loch OS12/204761; Sanders Loch (North shore only) OS12/187749 and Loch of Easter Head between May 1st and 6th October. Dunnet Head Lighthouse (OS12/202768), most northerly point on mainland Britain. Loch of Bushta (OS12/195726), during warm weather, is an excellent place for a picnic and a swim. The south end of the loch is sandy. Good chance of seeing great skua, divers and other moorland and sea birds.
Fish Trout average in the region of 1lb-3lb. West Sanders Loch is reputed to contain some very large fish but the Long Loch produces best results.
Flies & Tactics Bank fishing only. Wading is not really necessary as fish lie close to the margins. Offer: Black Pennell, Ke-He, Soldier Palmer, Invicta, Woodcock & Hare-lug, Kingfisher Butcher, Dunkeld.
Permission & Charges Northern Sands Hotel, Dunnet, Caithness. Tel: (01847) 851270. Harpers Fly Fishing Services, 57 High Street, Thurso, Caithness. Tel: 01847 893170. Hugo Ross, 56 High Street, Wick, Caithness. Tel: (01955) 604200. Day ticket, £5, evening ticket, £3. No Sunday fishing.

EILEANACH, Loch

Location & Access 12/070475 Approach along the private forestry and estate road from 12/089471, skirting the north shore of Loch More. At 12/072464, turn right through commercial forestry and follow the signs.
Commentary Eileanach belies its gaelic name, having only one tiny island at the north end, but this loch still offers a glimpse of what these waters used to look like prior to afforestation.
Fish Small, dark fish, averaging 8/10oz in weight, but plenty of them and they fight well. Occasional fish of up to 1lb are taken.
Flies & Tactics Boat and bank fishing are equally productive. The west shore is the best fishing area, where the burn enters from Lochan nan Dubh Geodh, round the island, and in the north bay. Use: Ke-He, Black Pennell, Silver Butcher.
Permission & Charges The Ulbster Arms Hotel, Bridge Street, Halkirk, Caithness. Tel: (01847) 831206. Bank fishing, £10 per day, or with the use of the boat, £15 per day.

FORSS, River

Location & Access Source: 12/000510 Outflow: 12/028702 From A836 Thurso/Bettyhill road at Bridge of Forss (12/038687) for Beat 2, below the Falls, and upstream for Beat 3. Beat 1 is approached from Crosskirk (12/030700) where it is possible to drive to the bank of the river. For Beat 4 approach from Lythmore Strath (12/046662 & 12/045665).
Commentary The Forss is a delightful stream, but sport is entirely dependent upon there being good water levels. No water, no fish. The lower three and a half miles produce the best sport and this section of the river is time-shared. The upper river is preserved. Season: 11 Feb - 31 Oct.
Fish Few fish are caught before July, but during spate conditions all the beats can produce excellent results with September being the most productive month. The average weight of salmon is in the order of 8lb, but fish of over 10lb are frequently taken. The river is divided into four beats, four rods fishing each beat, rotating at 2pm each day. Rod catch return: The five year average is 91 fiish. The best fish taken in recent years weighed 17lb and was caught in Falls Pool in 1998.
Flies & Tactics The Forss is a narrow stream and a single handed rod is adequate. Wading is not necessary; indeed, anglers should stay well back from the bank to avoid 'spooking' fish. Beat 1, which includes the sea-pools, is slow moving and 'backing-up' should be used. This beat always holds fish even in low-water conditions. Flies to offer include: Shrimp Fly, Munro Killer, Stoat's Tail, General Practitioner, Waddingtons.
Permission & Charges Jamie MacGregor, Forss House Hotel, by Thurso, Caithness. Tel: (01847) 86201. Weekly lets are generally available. Charges vary according to the time of year. Expect to pay between £100 and £250 per rod per week.

OS Map 12 — Thurso & Wick

FRESWICK, Burn
Location & Access Source: 12/315685. Outflow: 12/378672. From the A9 Wick/John O'Groats road at 12/372668.
Commentary A tiny, narrow burn that rise from the moorlands of the Battans of Brabster, flowing east to meet the sea in Freswick Bay.
Fish The only fishable section is the lower two hundred yards of the stream, between the A9 and the sea. Only worth fishing after heavy rains, and then, briefly.
Flies & Tactics The stream is so narrow that it is possible to straddle the flow, so success on Freswick Burn depends upon a fine, delicate technique, 'stalking' the river. Use one small trout fly: Black Pennell, Greenwell's Glory, Silver Invicta.
Permission & Charges Details from Freswick Farm, Freswick, by Wick, Caithness.

GAINEIMH, Loch, Westerdale
Location & Access 12/038467 Approach along the private forestry estate road from 12/089471, skirting the north shore of Loch More. At 12/072464, turn right through commercial forestry plantations.
Commentary Surrounded east and west by conifer plantations, Gaineimh is approximately half a mile long by up to five hundred yards wide. This is a shallow, peaty loch and it is often windy. Sleach Water, to the south, can provide useful trout fishing as well, particularly after heavy rain.
Fish Well provided with stocks of smaller trout which average in the order of 8oz. They rise readily to the fly and good baskets are the rule, rather than the exception.
Flies & Tactics Boat fishing is best, with trout taking all over the loch. The vicinity of the inlet stream, at the north end, and the area around the outlet stream (12/051466) are most productive. Flies: Black Zulu, Soldier Palmer, Silver Butcher.
Permission & Charges The Ulbster Arms Hotel, Bridge Street, Halkirk, Caithness. Tel: (01847) 831206. Bank fishing, £10 per day, or with use of the boat, £15 per day.

GARBH, Loch
Location & Access 12/038468 Approach from either Forsinard in Strath Halladale in Sutherland or from 12/072463 by Loch More in Caithness, along a forestry track. A high wheel base vehicle is preferable.
Commentary Good stocks of modest fish with perhaps one or two monsters still lurking in the depths. Surrounded by commercial forestry.
Fish Large Baskets are more likely than not from this dark, peat-stained loch, and trout average in the order of 8oz. However, there are consistent reports of much larger fishing being hooked - and lost.
Flies & Tactics The most productive area is down the east shore where wading is safe and comfortable. The west side is rocky and difficult. Concentrate particularly in the north east corner, where good fish might be encountered. Flies: Black Pennell, Woodcock & Harelug, Alexandra. A boat is available.
Permission & Charges The Forsinard Hotel, Forsinard, Strath Halladale, Sutherland. Tel: (01641)

571221 Bank fishing, £9 per rod per day. Use of boat, £19 per day.

HEILAN, Loch
Location & Access 12/255684. Via a good track from Greenland Mains Farm private road at 12/245685. All-weather surface. Park at lochside.
Commentary The most challenging loch in Caithness. Few waters, anywhere in the world, have wild fish of such quality. The loch covers an area of approximately 170 acres and has an average depth of 4ft. Weed is a problem as the season advances. Lime-rich, high pH. Often windy when it is unfishable because of discoloration, but settles quickly. Wonderful wild flowers: orchids and *Primula Scotica*, the rare Scottish primrose.
Fish Heilan brown trout average 2lb in weight and most seasons produce fish of up to 5lb. The heaviest fish taken in recent years weighed 8lb 9oz. Explosive, perfectly shaped and pink fleshed.
Flies & Tactics Strictly fly only. Blank days more often than not. May and June are the best when bank and boat fishing can be rewarding. Outboard motors should be used cautiously. The loch is shallow. From the boat, concentrate in the middle. Bankside 'hot spot' (where heaviest trout was taken, in May), on the south shore, by the old concrete building. Safe wading. Flies: Ke-He, Loch Ordie, Black Pennell, Soldier Palmer, Greenwell's Glory, Black Spider.
Permission & Charges Hamish T Pottinger, Greenland Mains Farm, Castletown, Caithness. Tel: (01847) 821210. Hamish Pottinger has one boat. Early booking is essential. Costs, £10 per person per day for use of boat, £8 per person per day bank fishing. Tickets also from: Harpers Fly Fishing Services, 57 High Street, Thurso, Caithness. Tel: 01847 893179

HEMPRIGGS, Loch
Location & Access 12/342470. The loch lies a mile south from Wick to the west of the A9. Park well clear of the A9.
Commentary Hempriggs has a reputation for being dour and, being close to the road, it is rather public. Surrounded by a flat and featureless terrain, exposed and often very windy. The loch covers an area of about 180 acres. The south and south-west end is peaty with dark water, other areas, margined by farmland, are less discoloured.
Fish Unconfirmed reports of occasional 'red-letter' baskets of good trout but fish tend to be small, averaging 8oz.
Flies & Tactics The problem with Hempriggs is that it is all bank fishing, and, because of the size and nature of the loch, it is reasonable to assume that the better fish lie, safe from harm, further out. Wading the east shoreline is not comfortable, but possible. Do not attempt to wade at the south end. Most patterns of fly produce results.
Permission & Charges Thrumster Garage, Thrumster, by Wick, Caithness. Tel: (01955) 651252. Hugo Ross, 56 High Street, Wick, caithness. Tel: (01955) 604200. Bank fishing: £5 per rod per day.

Thurso & Wick   OS Map 12

KILIMSTER, Loch
Location & Access 12/308560. from A9 Wick/Thurso road at 12/327568. A private estate road leads to boathouse and loch.
Commentary The only rainbow trout fishery in Caithness, strictly preserved for Ackergill Tower guests. A small (5 acres), deep, clear-water lochan lying on Moss of Killimster a few miles north from Wick. All year round fishery. A sporting holiday at Ackergill Tower is a special experience (and very expensive) including a wide range of salmon, seatrout, brown trout and sea-fishing. Also, almost every other type of outdoor sport imaginable. Ackergill Tower: an historic building, used by Cromwell's army as officers quarters when 'visiting' Caithness in the 17th century. Wonderfully restored and furnished, with dramatic antlered, baronial dining room. Ackergill Tower is a world-renowned centre of excellence.
Fish Stocked with good quality rainbow trout which are given time to 'grow on' and over-winter.
Flies & Tactics Bank fishing, from damp margins. Wading is not possible. Use traditional patterns: Black Pennell, Ke-He, Soldier Palmer and Butchers, and rainbow trout lures, if you must, such as Ace of Spades, Dog Nobblers and the like. Ackergill Tower staff will advise guests on the 'fly-of-the-moment'.
Permission & Charges Contact: Ackergill Tower, Ackergill, by Wick, Caithness. Tel: (01955) 603556; Fax: (01955) 602140 for details.

LOMASHION, Loch 12/386700 This moorland loch lies to the east of the A9 Wick/John O'Groats road. To the best of my knowledge it is fishless.

MARL, Loch
Location & Access 12/300442. Drive south from Wick on the A9 road to Thrumster (12/338452). Turn right, then, after a mile, first left. Marl Loch is two miles further on, at the end of this road.
Commentary Excellent bank fishing. Sheltered in windy conditions, easy access and ideal for a few casts before dinner. Marl Loch was formed recently by damming an inlet burn to Loch of Yarrows. The backed-up water-flooded pasture land providing excellent feeding. 1 April - 30 Sept Unique array of neolithic, Norse and Pictish remains at south end of Loch of Yarrows at OS12/305484 including chambered cairn, standing stones and a broch.
Fish Trout were stocked into Marl Loch from adjacent Loch of Yarrows. Because of the quality of feeding, trout thrived mightily, quickly attaining an average weight of 12oz, with good numbers of fish in the 1lb range.
Flies & Tactics Bank fishing. Creep up on them in thigh waders. Sunken walls poke out into the loch from the west shore. With care, they may be used as a means of access. Otherwise, expect good sport anywhere round the margins. Flies: Black Zulu, Black Spider, Black Pennell, Woodcock & Hare-lug, Greenwell's Glory, Grouse & Claret, Dunkeld.
Permission & Charges See Marl Loch entry.

MEADIE, Loch
Location & Access 12/092480 Approach along the unclassified road from Westerdale (12/127516). Park at 12/093475.
Commentary Meadie lies adjacent to the road and is nearly one mile long by up to three hundred yards wide at its widest point. There is a small sandy beach at the south end, near to where the boats are moored, ideal for the bucket-and-spade brigade.
Fish The loch is full of small fish which average 8/10oz in weight with the occasional larger specimen of over 1lb. Good baskets are frequently taken.
Flies & Tactics Both boat and bank fishing are equally productive, but boat fishing is more comfortable since the loch shallows are rocky. The best drift, relatively speaking, is from the mooring point north down the west shoreline, about ten yards out from the bank. Most patterns of fly bring results, but always have a Black Pennell on the cast.
Permission & Charges The Ulbster Arms Hotel Bridge Street, Halkirk, Caithness Tel: (01847)831206. Bank fishing, £10 per day, or, with the use of the boat, £15 per day.

MEY, Loch 12/272738 Lies to the north of the A836 Thurso/John O'Groats road. Looks inviting, but is in fact fishless. Completely dries out during warm summer months.

MORE, Loch
Location & Access 12/075458 Approach along the unclassified road from Westerdale (12/127516). Park at the end of this road by Lochmore Cottage (12/084461).
Commentary A featureless loch, surrounded to the north by commercial forestry. Loch More is two and three quarter miles long by up to half a mile wide across the north bay, shallow and sandy. The loch acts as a compensation reservoir for the Thurso River and there is a dam, sluice and fish-ladder adjacent to Lochmore Cottage.
Fish Thurso salmon pass through Loch More on their way to upstream spawning grounds and river rods have the right to fish for salmon in the loch. The most productive area for salmon is immediately to the north of Lochmore Cottage, there are also large stocks of brown trout which average 8oz in weight. They tend to be dark, white-fleshed fish.
Flies & Tactics All bank fishing and take care when water levels are low: large areas of sand are exposed, encouraging anglers to walk out, but the sand can be very soft in places. Most patterns of flies produce results.
Permission & Charges The Ulbster Arms Hotel, Bridge Street, Halkirk, Caithness. Tel: (01847) 831206. Trout fishing costs £10 per day.

NAM BREAC, Lochan
Location & Access 12/001479 Approach from either Forsinard in Strath Halladale in Sutherland, or from 12/072463 by Loch More in Caithness, along a forestry track. A high wheel base vehicle is preferable.
Commentary A delightful little lochan to the west of

OS Map 12 — Thurso & Wick

Skyline Loch, useful for restoring confidence if Skyline trout are being difficult. Bordered by forestry planting to the west, but open to the north. Ideal for beginners. Explore a fragment of the Flow Country to the north of the loch.

Fish Small, brightly marked little fish which average four to the pound and rise readily to the fly.

Flies & Tactics Easy bank fishing and wading. Almost any pattern of fly will produce results.

Permission & Charges The Forsinard Hotel, Forsinard, Strath Halladale, Sutherland. Tel: (01641) 571221. Bank fishing, £9 per rod per day.

NAN CLACHAN GEALA, Loch

Location & Access 12/002584 Approach from Halkirk and Loch Calder via Brawlbin (12/070580), or north from the unclassified Glengolly (12/101663) Reay road, turning south at Shebster (12/018639). Thence by forestry track at 12/026614 (locked gate).

Commentary Used to be an outstanding little loch containing superb trout, but was fished out some years ago. Now re-stocked from nearby Loch Saorach. Approximately four acres in extent. Bounded north, east and south by commercial forestry plantations. Broubster Village (12/034603). Ruins of cottages from which tenants were evicted during the 19th century Highland Clearances.

Fish Known as the 'white' loch, because of the clarity and purity of the water. Trout are of excellent quality and grow to a considerable size.

Flies & Tactics Bank fishing only. The water is easily covered. Use Black Pennell, Greenwell's Glory and Dunkeld.

Permission & Charges Fountain Forestry Limited, West End Garage, Lairg, Sutherland. Tel: Lairg (01549) 402274. Permits at £5 per rod per day.

OLIGINEY, Loch

Location & Access 12/090574. From the B870, north of Scotscalder at 12/096575. Call at the farm for access and permission.

Commentary Easy access, good fish, but can be very dour indeed. A circular, shallow loch of about 100 acres lying to the south of its more popular neighbour, Loch Calder. Subject to high winds which can stir up the bottom and make the loch unfishable.

Fish Stocked many years ago with trout from Loch Heilen by the indomitable Mr D Murray, who did much to improve a number of Caithness lochs. The trout are of excellent quality, darker than their ancestors, but well shaped and pink-fleshed.

Flies & Tactics Bank fishing only and comfortable wading around most of the margins. A new forestry plantation on the west shore gives some shelter. Evening fishing, particularly in June, can bring good results. Flies: Soldier Palmer, March Brown, Silver Invicta.

Permission & Charges Generally no charge, but anglers should call at the farm at OS12/0975674 and ask the riparian owner for permission to fish.

PRIVATE WATERS

Location & Access The lochs and streams bounded by OS square SW0141 to SE0541 and NE0546 to NW0146 and those contained within OS square SW0050/SE0450 and NW0056/NE0456 are preserved by the respective owners. The lochs and streams bounded by OS square SW0536 to SE0736 and NE0738 to NW0538 are also preserved by the owners.

RANGAG, Loch

Location & Access 12/177417. At Achavanich (12/180427) on the A895 Thurso to Latheron road. The loch is immediately adjacent to the main road, on the west. Safe off-road parking for vehicles.

Commentary A delightful beginners loch where it is almost impossible not to catch a fish. Although lying close to the main road, Rangag has a remote feeling, being surrounded by desolate moorlands. A small, safe, shallow, intimate water, ideal for a family picnic and giving casting instruction to little anglers. Dramatic neolithic standing stones and chambered cairn nearby at south end of Loch Stemster (12/188417). Broch and site of Greysteel's (Caithness robber-baron) Castle by lochside at 12/180417.

Fish The loch has large stocks of brightly marked small brown trout which average three to the pound. From time to time, heavier fish are taken, but they rarely reach 1lb in weight. Trout rise readily to the fly, even in adverse weather conditions.

Flies & Tactics A boat is available, but bank fishing is just as effective. Safe wading and fish are taken all round from all round the loch. Almost any flies will produce results.

Permission & Charges Hugo Ross, 56 High Street, Wick, Caithness. Tel: (01955) 604200. John Anderson, Latheronwheel Estate, Latheron, Caithness. Tel: (01593) 741230. Bank fishing, £5 per rod per day, use of the boat, £15 per day.

RUARD, Loch

Location & Access 12/142433. Drive south down the A895 Thurso to Latheron road. Park by the ruined croft buildings at 12/179436. Walk down the track to the west. Cross the Loop Burn and continue to the farm buildings at Acheraskill (12/158432). Follow the north bank of the outlet burn up to the loch.

Commentary Remote and lovely. The walk out is an easy thirty minutes. Ruard covers an area of approximately 150 acres, surrounded by wild moorlands. This is a peaty loch, shallow and scattered with weed banks, particularly at the west and south ends. The east shore, in the vicinity of the boathouse, is sandy. Blar nam Faoileag at 12/132445, to the north of Ruard, is an important Site of Special Scientific Interest, a growing peat bog: sphagnum moss, soft rush, tormentil, milkwort, marsh violet. Also, look out for otter and wildcat.

Fish Ruard contains excellent stocks of brown trout which average 8oz in weight. There are few larger fish, but the inhabitants are handsome trout which rise readily to the fly and give a good account of themselves. Loch Dubh (OS12/147425), east of Ruard, appears to be fishless.

Flies & Tactics Boat fishing produces best results, as well as being the most convenient method of travelling

Thurso & Wick OS Map 12

around the loch. The margins, particularly to the north, are very boggy. Most of the action is along the west shore, and in the north bay. Flies: Black Pennell, March Brown, Silver Butcher.
Permission & Charges See Loch Rangag entry.

SAND, Loch
Location & Access 12/106413 Approach along the unclassified road from Westerdale (12/127516). Park at Lochmore Cottage (12/085460). Walk over the bridge and follow the track along the east shore of Loch More to Backlass at 12/082423. Take to the moor and walk south east for twenty minutes to the Loch.
Commentary A magical setting of wild, open moorlands where the sky seems to go on forever and the fishing is even nicer. Joined to its neighbour, Lochan Thulachan, by a small stream at the north east end. Magnificent scenery with a very good chance of seeing otter and wildcat. Also, arctic skua, peregrine, hen harrier and divers. Outstanding wild flowers. There is a Pictish cross slab at 12/105395.
Fish Brightly marked, wild fish, genetically intact since the last Ice Age. Not very large and averaging three to the pound, but exciting to catch.
Flies & Tactics Bank fishing with comfortable wading. The west shore of the loch is boggy and best results come from the east shoreline and the south end by the inlet stream. Most standard patterns of fly will produce results.
Permission & Charges The Ulbster Arms Hotel, Bridge Street, Halkirk, Caithness. Tel: (01847) 831206. Cost, £10 per day.

SAORACH, Loch
Location & Access 12/015605 Approach from Halkirk and Loch Calder via Brawlbin (12/070580), or north from the unclassified Glengolly (12/101663) Reay road, turning south at Shebster (12/018639). Thence by forestry track at 12/026614 (locked gate).
Commentary Never noted for quality of fishing, but a wonderful day out in a moorland setting. Saorach is three quarters of a mile long up to two hundred and fifty yards wide, shallow and peaty; 1 April - 30 Sept.
Fish Large numbers of small, dark trout which average four to the pound.
Flies & Tactics Bank fishing only, with safe wading, particularly along the middle of the east shoreline, by the ruined mill and dry stane dyke. all flies produce results.
Permission & Charges Leslie Crawford, Askival, Reay, Nr Thurso, Caithness. Tel: (01847) 811470. Permit: £5 per rod per day. Tickets also from: Harpers Fly Fishing Services, 57 High Street, Thurso, Caithness. Tel: 01847 893179.

SARCLET, Loch
Location & Access 12/342427. Follow the A9 road south from Wick to Thrumster (12/338452). Turn left in the village and take the unclassified road, bearing right at the only junction, to the loch.
Commentary A few years ago, one of the finest lochs in Caithness, now with a somewhat diminished reputation. However, still well worth a visit. A small,

narrow loch, some 700 yards long by 200 yards wide on the cliffs close to the sea. High pH and generally clear water, 'muddied' during the season by the activities of the Wick Model Yacht Club who hold regattas on Sarclet.
Fish Very high quality, hard-fighting trout which average 1lb. Fish of over 5lb have been taken from Sarclet in days past and trout of over 3lb are still sometimes taken.
Flies & Tactics Wading is comfortable, with care, and the west bank brings best results. Hot spot: general area of the outlet burn at south-east corner. Flies: Black Pennell, Loch Ordie, He-He, Black Zulu, Greenwell's Glory, Butchers.
Permission & Charges See Marl Loch entry.

SCARMCLATE, Loch
Location & Access 12/190595 At Gelshfield, on the A882 Wick/Thurso Road, at 12/180584, turn north along a farm road. Cross a railway (beware of trains and shut gates) and drive to the loch. In wet weather leave the car before the railway. Walk to the loch. Access permission from Gelshfield Farm, to the right of the access road.
Commentary A splendid, productive loch containing good quality wild trout. Ideal for beginners. Approximately 150 acres, joined eastwards by a feeder stream to Loch Watten. This is a shallow loch, but wading is dangerous. Marl was dredged for fertiliser and the bottom is very soft. The loch is a Site of Special Scientific Interest with marvellous birds and wild flowers.
Fish Scarmclate fish averages 10oz in weight. They are silver, perfectly shaped, pink fleshed and fight hard. Watten trout reach Scarmclate during the spawning season and the loch acts as a nursery for its grander neighbour.
Flies & Tactics As the season advances, Scarmclate weeds up, making fishing difficult. The best time to fish is May and June. Trout are caught all over the loch with no one place being substantially better than any other. Flies: Black Pennell, Ke-He, Soldier Palmer, Greenwell's Glory, March Brown, Silver Invicta, Alexandria, Butchers. Outboard with care.
Permission & Charges Harpers Fly Fishing Services, 57 High Street, Thurso, Caithness. Tel: (01847) 893179. Boat fishing: £10 per day with two rods fishing.

SCRABSTER, Loch
Location & Access 12/088703. Take the A882 from Thurso to Scrabster and turn left by Scrabster House. Follow this road, through the housing estate, to a locked gate and a farm track. Park at the brow of the hill. The loch is on your left.
Commentary A popular fishery with easy access from Thurso. This small loch on the hill, above Scrabster Harbour, is comparatively sheltered from northern gales and is ideal for those who have only limited time to spare. Restricted fishing because of weed growth, but can provide exciting sport.
Fish Stocked in past years, Scrabster Loch contains good quality brown trout, some of which grow to considerable size. The average weight is in the order of 1lb.

OS Map 12 — Thurso & Wick

Flies & Tactics Bank fishing only with best results obtained fishing from the south shore. Hot spot: off the obvious promontory. Flies: Black Zulu, Ke-He, Invicta, Alexandra.

Permission & Charges Harpers Fly Fishing Services, 57 High Street, Thurso, Caithness. Tel: (0847) 63179. Two sessions: £8 per rod per day, and £4 per rod per evening (from 1800 hrs).

SHURRERY, Loch

Location & Access 12/045555 Approach from Halkirk and Loch Calder, via Brawlbin (12/070580), or north from the unclassified Glengolly (12/101663).

Commentary An attractive loch to fish, somewhat spoiled by the presence of the dam at the north end. Water is drawn from the loch and used for cooling purposes at Dounreay Nuclear Power Station. Loch Shurrery is one and a quarter miles long by up to quarter of a mile wide. This is a shallow loch and the principal source of the Forss River. The inlet burn, Torran Water, is an important salmon spawning stream. Ben Dorrery Hill (244m), the highest point in Caithness (OS12/064551) and Beinn Freiceadain (238m), adjacent to Ben Dorrery (OS12/060558), make a rewarding round trip walk. Start from OS12/042568 by the bridge over the Forss River. Pictish hill fort on Beinn Freiceadain.

Fish Large stocks of modest trout which average three to the pound in weight, with the possibility of a few larger fish of up to 1 lb 8oz. Salmon are undoubtedly present in Loch Shurrery. They are frequently seen but rarely caught.

Flies & Tactics Fish are taken all over the loch. All flies produce results.

Permission & Charges Fishing preserved by the owner Sir Robert Black who does not encourage visiting anglers, although access can sometimes be onbtained. Contact Head Keeper, Shurrery Estate, Halkirk, Caithness. Tel: (01847) 811252

SKYLINE, Loch

Location & Access 12/010480 Approach from either Forsinard in Strath Halladale in Sutherland, or from 12/072463 by Loch More in Caithness, along a forestry track. A high wheel base vehicle is preferable.

Commentary Skyline is one of the most challenging Caithness lochs and always worth a visit. The small lochan immediately to the south east of Skyline is of no fishing interest. A once-distant, clear-water, moorland loch now made easily accessible by a commercial forestry road. Dense planting to the west, still open moorland to the north on neighbouring Dorrery Estate.

Fish Quite outstanding quality and averaging in the region of 2lb.

Flies & Tactics Concentrate on the main body of the loch. The narrow north end, beyond the island, is not so productive. Fishing from the west bank, stay well back from the edge. The water is deep and trout lie very close to the bank. On the east shore, wading is comfortable, but again, start by fishing well back from the shore before entering the water. Flies: Loch Ordie, Invicta, Dunkeld. A boat is available.

Permission & Charges The Forsinard Hotel, Forsinard, Strath Halladale, Sutherland. Tel: (01641) 571221. Bank fishing, £9 per rod per day. Use of the boat, £19 per day.

ST JOHN'S, Loch

Location & Access 12/225723. Directly from the A836 Thurso/John O'Groats road. The loch lies to the north of the road, a few hundred yards east of the Northern Sands Hotel in Dunnet Village. Turn north in Dunnet village and follow the road round the east shore of the loch to reach the mooring bay at 12/220726.

Commentary One of the most famous northern trout lochs with a well-deserved reputation for producing high-quality sport. St John's is a shallow, lime-rich loch covering an area of approximately 175 acres. It is surrounded by farmland and somewhat protected from northern gales by Dunnet Head. Best months: May, June and September.

Fish After a number of years of declining catches, the Loch St John's Angling Improvement Association was formed in the 1970's with a view to restoring the loch and improving returns. The association achieved their objective using native stock, reared in a lochside hatchery, and trout are of exceptional quality. Average weight is in the order of 12oz/14oz. Each season generally produces fish of over 3lb.

Flies & Tactics Boat fishing only, apart from two small areas of shoreline. In late June there is a prolific mayfly hatch. Best drift: from the mooring bay, south to the old harbour. Flies: Black Pennell, Ke-He, Soldier Palmer, Greenwell's Glory, March Brown, Dunkled, Silver Butcher. An outboard motor is advisable.

Permission & Charges Hugo Ross, Fishing Tackle Shop, 56 High Street, Wick, Caithness. Tel: (01955) 604200; The Northern Sands Hotel, Dunnet, Caithness. Tel: Barrock (01847) 851270; Harpers Fly Fishing Services, 57 High Street, Thurso, Caithness. Tel: (01847) 893179. Day divided into two sessions: 0800-1800hrs: £15 for boat with two rods fishing; 1800hrs until dark, £6 for boat with two rods fishing. Same sessions for bank fishing: £3 per day, £1 for the evening. There is no Sunday fishing.

STEMSTER, Loch

Location & Access 12/190424. At Achavanich (12/180427), on the A895 Thurso to Latheron road, turn east on minor road to Lybster. Within half a mile, turn left over a cattle grid to the loch.

Commentary An easily accessible loch which fishes particularly well early in the season. Regardless of direction or force of the wind, always possible to fish. The water is slightly peaty but this does not affect fishing, and there are a number of excellent promontories and bays from which large areas may be covered. Dramatic Neolithic standing stones and chambered cairn at south end of loch at 12/188417. Wild flowers, including bog-bean in nearby pools.

Fish Good stocks of quality wild brown trout which rise well to the fly. Fish average 9oz in weight but there are fish of over 2lb as well. Pink-fleshed and fighting fit.

Flies & Tactics A boat is available, but bank fishing is just as effective. The loch deepens quickly from the

103

Thurso & Wick — OS Map 12

margins, so long casting is unnecessary. No one part is better than another and fish are taken all round the loch. Flies: Black Pennell, Ke-He, March Brown, Grouse & Claret, Butcher.
Permission & Charges See Loch Rangag entry.

STRATH, Burn
Location & Access Source: 12/2154755 Outflow: 12/370506 From the unclassified Watten/Lybster road at 12/256521 and 12/248504.
Commentary Strath Burn is one of the most delightful little streams in Caithness, flowing through glorious scenery. The stream is a major tributary of the Wick River, which it joins by the old corn mill at Milton (12/240535).
Fish The principal interest here is brown trout and the burn contains good numbers of small fish that are great fun to catch. Best results come after heavy spates and there is always the chance of an unsuspecting salmon towards the end of the season.
Flies & Tactics An 8ft rod and light tackle are required, as well as a highly developed, skilful, casting technique. Use a two fly cast: Ke-He and Greenwell's Glory.
Permission & Charges J. Mackay, Strath House, Strath, Watten, Caithness. Tel: (01955) 621210. About £8 per rod per day. Mr Mackay also has boats on Loch Watten.

THORMAID, Loch
Location & Access 12/010605 Approach from Halkirk and Loch Calder via Brawlbin (12/070580), or north from the unclassified Glengolly (12/101663) Reay road, turning south at Shebster (12/018639). Thence by forestry track at 12/026614 (locked gate).
Commentary Never noted for quality of fishing, but used to be a wonderful day out in moorland setting. Thormaid is four hundred yards long by about 100 yards wide, shallow and peaty; Thormaid is joined to Saorach by a stream exiting from the east shore. Broubster village (12/034603). Ruins of cottages from which tenants were evicted during the 19th century Highland Clearances.
Fish Large numbers of small, dark trout which average four to the pound.
Flies & Tactics Bank fishing only, with safe wading. All flies produce results.
Permission & Charges See Loch Sorach entry.

THULACHAN, Lochan
Location & Access 12/106413 Approach along the unclassified road from Westerdale (12/127516). Park at Lochmore Cottage (12/085460). Walk over the bridge and follow the track along the east shore of Loch More. At 12/085455, bear left along the track leading over Druim Carn nam Muc. A soggy twenty minutes brings you to the loch.
Commentary A magical setting of wild, open moorlands where the sky seems to go on forever and the fishing is even nicer. There is a semi-ruined lodge by the south east shore, close to the inlet stream. Magnificent scenery with a good chance of seeing otter and wildcat. Also, arctic skua, peregrine, hen harrier and divers.

Outstanding wildflowers. There is a Pictish cross slab at 12/105395.
Fish Brightly marked, wild fish, genetically intact since the last Ice Age. Not very large and averaging three to the pound, but exciting to catch.
Flies & Tactics Bank fishing with comfortable wading and good fishing all round the margins. If anything, the south shore is perhaps the most productive. Most standard patterns of fly will produce results.
Permission & Charges The Ulbster Arms Hotel, Bridge Street, Halkirk, Caithness. Tel: (01847) 831206. Bank fishing, £10 per day.

TOFTINGALL, Loch
Location & Access 12/190525 Approach from B870 Watten/Mybster road along forestry road at 17/2531. Two locked gates. Drive to lochside and boathouse.
Commentary A first class, easily accessible water. Approximately 140 acres. Good boathouse and mooring bay by inlet burn and small natural woodland of rowan and silver birch.
Fish Trout average 8oz/12oz with the occasional fish of over 2lb. Very pretty trout which fight well and are mostly pink-fleshed.
Flies & Tactics Boat or bank fishing, both are equally effective. Take care wading at north end where bottom is soft. From the boat, watch out for a barely submerged rock one hundred yards out from the west bank at the south end. There is a good mayfly hatch in June. Flies: Ke-He, Soldier Palmer, Greenwell's Glory, March Brown, Silver Invicta, Dunkeld.
Permission & Charges Hugo Ross, Fishing Tackle Shop, 56 High Street, Wick, Caithness KW1 4BP. Tel: (01955) 604200. Boat: £18 per day with two rods fishing, plus £3 per rod per fsihing permit. £5 for bank permit.

WAREHOUSE, Loch
Location & Access 12/300424 Park by Marl Loch (12/300442). Walk towards South Yarrows. On the right is Marl Loch inlet burn. Strike south west, climbing by the burn up an obvious gully. Warehouse is at the top. Easy going. Allow twenty minutes.
Commentary Infrequently visited, tiny lochan in remote setting, containing a few good fish. Warehouse lies in a gully on the Hill of Yarrows. A damaged sluice at the east end still maintains a reasonable depth of water in the loch. Neolithic, Norse and Pictish remains at South Yarrows (12/305484) and, immediately adjacent to Warehouse (12/304422), chambered cairns and a broch.
Fish Warehouse was stocked from Yarrows. Because of the nature of the terrain, fish tend to be dark/golden in colour. Small fish predominate, but there are trout of up to 2lb.
Flies & Tactics Bank fishing. It is possible to cast across the loch. The north shore is best. Stay back from the margin, fish lie close. Flies: most patterns bring results but always include a Black Pennell.
Permission & Charges See Marl Loch entry.

WATENAN, Loch
Location & Access 12/319412. South from Wick on

OS Map 12 — Thurso & Wick

A9 to Ulbster (12/320404), eight miles. At Ulbster, turn right (the only right). This narrow road leads to the loch within half a mile. Park by lochside.
Commentary Difficult fishing, but, quite simply, outstanding birdlife and wild flowers, and an amazing range of prehistoric monuments. Perfect picnic place. Two sections, joined by narrows. The north end is completely weeded and almost impossible to fish. South end has extensive fishing areas, around dense weed patches. There are more than 80 prehistoric monuments in the immediate vicinity, including Garrywhin hill fort, chambered cairn and stone rows at 12/313413. Also, Whaligoe Steps (12/3211443), 365 steps cut into the vertical face of a cliff, leading down to a tiny harbour.
Fish Fish of up to 5lb have been taken but average weight is in the region of 12oz. Golden trout which fight furiously.
Flies & Tactics From parking place, stay on the bank, well back. North, beyond the fence, wade out safely to cover open water. From east bank, start north from ruined croft and work south. Flies: Ke-He, Black Pennell, March Brown, Grouse & Claret, Peter Ross, Butchers.
Permission & Charges John Swanson, Aspen Bank, Banks Road, Watten, Caithness. Tel: (01955) 621326. Bank fishing only, £5 per rod per day.

WATTEN, Loch

Location & Access 12/230560. From Watten Village, Oldhall and Lynegar.
Commentary The most productive Caithness loch. One of the best Scottish wild trout fisheries. Approximately three miles long by up to half a mile wide. Lime-rich, high pH, shallow, with an average depth of 9ft.
Fish Outstanding quality, pink-fleshed, brown trout which average approximately 1lb in weight. Expect a basket of four fish for a day's fishing. The heaviest trout taken in recent years weighed 4lb 8oz.
Flies & Tactics Strictly fly only. Boat fishing is best and fish are caught from the margins to middle. Outboard motor and drogue essential. Hot spots: round the small island in Factors Bay (12/247558), Shearer's Pool (12/215575), Oldhall (12/214567). Flies: Black Pennell, Ke-He, Soldier Palmer, Greenwell's Glory, March Brown, Invicta, Butchers.
Permission & Charges Hugo Ross, Fishing Tackle Shop, 56 High Street, Wick, Caithness. Tel: (01955) 604200; Hugo Ross has boats, outboards and a comfortable fishing hut for use of fishing guests. John Swanson, Aspen Bank, Banks Road, Watten, Caithness. Tel: (01955) 621326; D Gunn, Watten Lodge, Watten, Caithness. Tel: (01955) 621217, Facsimile: (01955) 82390; The Loch Watten Hotel, Watten, Caithness. Tel: (01955) 621232. Boat fishing: £15 per day, two rods fishing. Outboard engine hire: £15 per day plus fuel. Bank fishing, £2 per rod per day.

WESTER, Loch

Location & Access 12/325593 Take the A9 Wick/John O'Groats road to Bridge of Wester (12/332587), then turn left, signposted to Lyth. Auckhorn Farm is at 12/327598, and access is from here, where it is possible to drive to the lochside.
Commentary An 'un-sung' hero amongst Scottish seatrout lochs, still producing excellent sport; indeed, far better than more famous waters such as Maree, Sheil or Eilt. Value-for-money seatrout fishing with a reasonable chance of salmon as well. The loch covers an area of approximately 120 acres and is very shallow. It is possible to wade across, safely, wearing chest waders. Recent afforestation along the catchment has exacerbated flash-flooding and a pipe-fabrication railway track somewhat disfigures the landscape.
Fish The loch contains good stocks of brown trout but they are small and the main interest here is seatrout and salmon. Fish run the system from February and the only difficulty they face (apart from anglers) is a sand bar at the mouth of the river which has to be cleared regularly to allow access.
Flies & Tactics Boat or bank fishing, with perhaps boat fishing bringing best results. Use an outboard motor cautiously because of the shallow nature of the loch. Hot spots: the mouth of feeder burn by the boat mooring bay is a known salmon lie (12/325595); where the Lyth Burn flows into the loch, at the west end; the vicinity of the outflow into Wester River. Flies: Black Pennell, Ke-He, Loch Ordie, Soldier Palmer, Invicta, March Brown, Teal Blue & Silver, Peter Ross.
Permission & Charges Hugo Ross, 56 High Street, Wick, Caithness. Tel: (01955) 604200 for North Bank of both river and loch. Ackergill Tower, Ackergill, by Wick, Caithness. Tel: (01955) 603556; Fax: (01955) 602140. Andrew Dunnet, Auckhorn Farm, Lyth, by Wick, Caithness. Tel: (01955) 631208. £15 per rod per day for the use of a boat, £10 per day bank fishing.

WESTER, River

Location & Access Source: 12/315645. Outflow: 12/345576. From Wester Loch (12/332587) on the A9 Wick/John O'Groats road.
Commentary Rises on moorlands north of Loch of Wester as Kirk Burn, becoming Burn of Lyth, prior to entering loch. The main river is one mile long, slow-flowing through sand dunes to the sea in Sinclair Bay.
Fish Fish the last few hundred yards before the sea, when, given good water levels, seatrout and salmon may be tempted. Good sport can also be had fly-fishing the mouth of the river, in the sea. Best seatrout in recent years weighed 9lb. Average weight of seatrout is 1.5lb to 2lb. Salmon average 7lb.
Flies & Tactics Stay well back from the river bank, casting a long line downstream using a single-handed rod. Large patterns of trout flies do best, particularly: Black Pennell, Silver Butcher, Soldier Palmer. Fish two hours either side of low tide. Fish are caught from February onwards but best months are September and October.
Permission & Charges For south bank, on application from Ackergill Tower, Ackergill, by Wick, Caithness. Tel: (01955) 603556; Fax: (01955) 602140 ; for north bank, Hugo Ross, 56 High Street, Wick, Caithness. Tel: (01955) 604200. A. Dunnet, Auckhorn Farm, Lyth, by Wick, Caithness. Tel: (01955) 631208. £10 per rod per day.

Thurso & Wick — OS Map 12

WICK, River

Location & Access Source: 12/255444. Outflow: 12/377506 To the south bank from: Stirkoke (12/321514), Bilbster (12/284536), Borgie (12/260546) on A882 Wick/Thurso road. To the north bank, on B874 from: Sibster (12/330529), Ingimster (12/298535), Bilbster (12/284536), Tarroul (12/265549).

Commentary A slow moving, spate river, which sometimes, in summer drought conditions almost disappears completely. Over a distance of eight miles, from Wattten to Wick, the gradient is only 10ft. Forestry planting in the river catchment in recent years has exacerbated flash-flooding. The Wick flows through intensively farmed, good agricultural land, joining the North Sea in the shallow waters of Wick Bay. Season: 11 Feb - 21 Oct. The river is leased and managed by the Wick Angling Association. There are no Beat divisions and the whole river is available to association members and visitors. Best sport is from Bilbster Bridge upstream, where there are excellent holding pools: The Pot, Cows, Borgie, Tarroul, Quarry Hole and Wash Pool. Downstream, try Otter Island, Dyke End and Willie's Pool.

Fish The river often produces outstanding results. The 10 year average is probably in the region of 300 fish per season.

Flies & Tactics Most salmon are taken bait fishing although there are also good stretches of fly water. A 12ft salmon rod is most useful and anglers must be prepared to 'stalk' their fish, keeping well back from the river bank. Spinning is allowed from 11th February until 15th May; Bait fishing, from 1st May until 30th September. No gaffs after 30th September. Flies to offer include: Garry Dog, Thunder & Lightening, Hugo's GP, General Practitioner, Shrimp Fly. Also use large trout flies: Black Pennell, Ke-He, Invicta.

Permission & Charges Hugo Ross, Fishing Tackle Shop, 56 High Street, Caithness. Tel: (01955) 604200. Charges: £20 per rod per day, £75 per rod per week; Juniors/OAPs £5 per rod per day, £25 per rod per week. Reductions for evening and early part of season.

WINLESS, Loch

Location & Access 12/293547. Approach from the B847, Westerseat to Watten road, at Winless Farm, 12/301541.

Commentary This is a narrow, weedy, peaty little loch of about three acres, lying close to the B847. Because of the boggy nature of the surrounding terrain, it is best fished from the north bank, via Winless Farm. This is a Site of Special Scientific Interest, rich in wild flowers and wildfowl.

Fish Large stock of small trout, three to the pound, with an occasional fish of up to 1lb in weight.

Flies & Tactics Very soggy margins, weed fringed, making wading dangerous. A long cast is required to get beyond the weeds, and flies are frequently entangled. There are a few clear areas for bank fishing on the north shore.

Permission & Charges North Winless Farm, by Wick, Caithness. Tel: (01955) 603372. Bank fishing: £5 per rod per day.

YARROWS, Loch

Location & Access 12/310440 Take the A9 south to Thrumster Village (12/338452) and turn right, then, after half a mile, first left. Park at /12307444, by a style over barbwire fence.

Commentary Very lovely setting, in spite of being water supply for the town of Wick. The loch lies in a hollow and can't really be seen from the approach road. Steep sides, difficult and dangerous to wade. Stay on the shore. Covers an area of some 70 acres. Unique array of neolithic, Norse and Pictish remains at south end of loch in the vicinity of 12/305484 including: chambered cairn, standing stones, and broch.

Fish Very large stocks of small trout which average three to the pound. Large baskets regularly taken. The most productive area is the south end of the loch, where the water is shallow

Flies & Tactics This loch should be fished from a boat (with outboard engine). Otherwise, it could be dangerous. Most flies bring results.

Permission & Charges Thrumster Garage, Thrumster, by Wick, Caithness. Tel: (01955) 651252. Boat: £8 per half day; £16 per day (two rods fishing) plus fishing permit at £4 per rod per day.

OS Map 13 — West Lewis & North Harris

West Lewis and North Harris

Isles of Lewis & Harris Introduction
No matter where you fish in Lewis and Harris, permission must be obtained before doing so. At times, it is difficult to establish who owns the fishing rights and whether or not access is available. The best place to seek advice is: Sportsworld, 1 Francis Street, Stornoway. Tel: (01851) 705464. You should also, always, seek permission from the local crofter before crossing his land to reach a fishing location. Where access information is known, it is noted in the appropriate text. However, please double-check this information before fishing as details may change.

A'BHEANNAICH, Loch (Uig) See Loch Mheacleit. Apply Uig and Hamanavay Estate - Head Keeper. Tel: (01851) 672421.

A'BHEANNAIN, Loch (Ardroil) Brown trout. Apply Uig and Hamanavay Estate - Head Keeper. Tel: (01851) 672421. See also Loch a'Phealuir entry.

A'BHRAGHAD, Loch See Loch Fhreunadail.

A'BHROMA, Loch See Loch Trealaval.

A'CHAMA, Loch See Loch Raonasgail. Apply Uig and Hamanavay Estate - Head Keeper. Tel: (01851) 672421.

A'CHAPHAIL, Loch (Scaliscro) See Loch Fhreunadail.

A'CHAS BHRAIGHE RUAIDH, Loch See Loch Raonasgail.

A'CHLEITE TUATH, Loch See Loch Morsgail.

A'CHNUIC, Loch See Loch na Muilne (Bosta).

A'CHOIN, Loch See Loch nan Eilean (Valtos).

A'FHRAOICH, Loch See Loch Raonasgail.

A'GEODHA BEAG, Loch See Loch Halladale.

A'GHARAIDH, Loch See Loch Raonasgail.

A'GHEOIDH, Loch See Loch Sgailler.

A'GHLINNE, Loch
Location & Access 13/025127 Loch a'Ghlinne may be approached from a track on the north-west shore of Loch Leosaid (14/056089) up the line of the River Leosaid, a journey of two and a half miles. Otherwise, drive to the end of the B887 at Hushinish and take the sandy road to the north, leading to the pier. Park by the pier and follow a track which leads north along the shore of Caolas an Scarp, climbing between Husival Beag (306m) to the south and Gresclett (150m) to the north, descending to Loch na Cleavag (13/095137). Walk the south shore of Loch na Cleavag, past the ruined shieling to reach the north end of Loch a'Ghlinne after a further ten minutes. Loch a'Ghlinne is one mile north/south by up to 400yds wide and exits over a superb beach into the sea in Loch Cravadale at Haranish (13/018135). On the hill to the south-east, Ceartaval (556m), is a tiny trout loch, Loch Braigh Bheagarais (13/046121), rarely, if ever, fished form one season to the next.
Commentary Loch a'Ghlinne and Loch Cleavag are utterly splendid, not only because of their fishing, but also because they are close to one of the most lovely beaches in the Outer Hebrides. Non-fishing members of your party may linger on the beach whilst you attack the things below the waves.
Fish A good chance of seatrout from August onwards, depending upon rain, and some very nice brown trout of up to 1lb in weight. Little Loch Braigh Bheagarais, the head water of the Leosaid river is very much an unknown quantity.
Flies & Tactics Loch Cleavag, the smaller of the two main lochs, is the easier to fish and the best area is along the north shore and at the west end. Loch a'Ghlinne is steep-sided and deep near the shore. Do not wade. The south end is the most productive area. Offer: Blue Zulu, Goat's Toe, Clan Chief.
Permission & Charges Contact: North Harris Estate, Amhuinnsuidhe, Harris, Western Isles. All fishing on the estate is preserved by the owner. For further information, contact the Head Keeper on Tel: (01859) 560234 or the Factor on Tel: (01859) 500329. Sporting lets are arranged through Finlyson Hughes, Lynedoch House, Barossa Place, Perth PH1 5EP. Tel: (01738) 451600.

A'GHOIRTEIN, Loch See Loch Halladale.

A'MHAIDE, Loch See Loch Strandavat (Balallan).

A'MHAIDE, Loch (Soval) See Loch Trealaval.

A'MHAIRT, Loch See Loch Tungavat.

A'MHULA, Loch See Loch Halladale.

A'PHEALUIR MOR, Loch
Location & Access 13/098300 Leave the B8011 Enaclete/Miavaig road at 13/114291 by Loch Sandavat (13/117290) and follow the peat track west. Park at the south end of Loch Croistean (13/110290) and walk the line of the River Todale up the glen to reach the south end of Loch a'Phealuir after 15 mins.
Commentary The north of the loch is guarded by the heights of Suainaval (429m), with Aineval (186m) to the north-east. Loch a' Phealuir is divided into two sections, both of which cover an area extending one mile north/south by up to 200yds wide. The round trip, fishing the west and east banks, is four miles there and back.
Fish Plenty of hard-fighting brown trout which average 8oz, and a few larger specimens of up to 1lb in weight.
Flies & Tactics Bank fishing, and stay on terra firma. The fish lie close to the shore and wading only scares them out into the depths. The north loch is probably the most productive, particularly in the vicinity of the four streams which enter from Suainaval on the west shore; but fish may be taken from all round the shoreline, so cast with confidence, everywhere. In spate conditions, the Todale River can also provide exciting sport. Offer them: Ke-He, Grouse & Claret, Silver Butcher.
Permission & Charges Apply Uig and Hamanavay Estate - Head Keeper. Tel: (01851) 672421. All fishing on the estate is preserved by the owner and permission to fish must be obtained from the Head Keeper. Sporting lets with self-catering accommodation are factored by Finlyson Hughes, Lynedoch House, Barossa Place, Perth PH1 5EOP. Tel: (01738) 451600.

West Lewis & North Harris — OS Map 13

A'ROTHAID, Loch See Loch an Duin, Scalpay.
A'SGAIL, Loch See Loch na Muilne (Bosta).
A'SGUAIR, Loch See Loch Suirstavat.
A'TUATH, Loch (Morsgail) See Loch Morsgail.
AHALTAIR, Loch See Loch Tungavat.
AIRD, Loch (Scaliscro) See Loch Fhreunadail.
AIRIGH A'BHEALAICH, Loch See Loch an Fhir Mhaoil.
AIRIGH A'GHILLE RUAIDH, Loch See Loch Strandavat, Balallan.
AIRIGH AN UISGE, Loch See Loch Coirgavat.
AIRIGH FHEARCHAIR, Loch See Loch Leathain.
AIRIGH NA CEARDAICH, Loch See Loch Trealaval.
AIRIGH NA H-AIRDE, Loch See Grimersta River.
AN ATH RUAIDH, Loch See Loch Raonasgail.
AN DEASPOIRT, Loch See Loch Dhomhnuill.
AN DRUNGA, Loch See Loch Trealaval.
AN EARBALL, Loch See Grimersta River.
AN EASA GHIL, Loch See Grimersta River.

AN EILEAN LIATH, Loch
Location & Access 13/340234 Loch an Eilean Liath lies immediately to the north of the A859 Stornoway/Tarbert road, one mile south from Soval Lodge. Park at 13/345235, at the north end of Loch Cnoc Iain Duibh (13/348225), and follow the inlet stream down to the east end of the loch.
Commentary Loch an Eilean Liath is just under half a mile east/west by 350yds wide, covering an area of approximately 33 acres. The other lochs in the vicinity are also worth a cast. Work the crooked north shoreline of Loch a Eilean Liath round to the narrow west end, then cross over to explore Loch nam Breac (13/334230). Follow the outlet burn from the south end of Loch nam Breac down to Loch Nabhar, unnamed on the OS map. Return north to Loch an Eilean Liath via the group of three unnamed lochans at 13/340229.
Fish Good numbers of trout which average 6-8oz, but always the chance of a few larger specimens. Towards the end of the season and after heavy rain, there is a possibility of seatrout and salmon in Loch Nabhar, and in the unnamed loch on the east side of the A859, near the school at 13/345224, and also in the sea at the mouth of the Abhainn Nabhar (13/344215).
Flies & Tactics Stay on the bank and do not wade. The north shore on Loch an Eilean Liath is the most productive area, particularly where the two feeder streams enter from Loch na Creige Fraoich (13/342241). The other waters noted are easily covered from the shore. Try: Loch Ordie, Grouse & Claret, Silver Invicta.
Permission & Charges See Loch Trealaval entry.

AN EILEAN, Loch (Grimersta East) See Grimersta River.
AN EILEIN CHOINNICH, Loch See Loch Coirgavat.
AN EILEIN, Loch (Scaliscro) See Loch Mohal Beag.
AN FHEOIR, Loch (Habost) See Loch na h-Inghinn.

AN FHIR MHAOIL, Loch
Location & Access 13/182260 Park on the B8011 Garynahine/Miavaig road at 13/177272 and walk south for 15 mins to reach the boathouse at the north end of the loch. Loch an Fhir Mhaoil is known locally as 'The Loch of the Bald-Headed Man'.
Commentary A very attractive loch lying to the north of Beinn a'Sgurain (170m) and Beinn a'Chuailein (153m). Loch an Fhir Mhaoil is one mile north/south, including its satellite Loch Airigh a' Bhealaich (13/185251), and up to half a mile wide across the north bay. The loch drains east through Loch an Easa Ghil (13/200253) into the Grimersta system and the sea at Loch Ceann Hulavig. A narrow stream joins Loch an Fhir Mhaoil with Loch Airigh a'Bhealaich to the south, a narrow, quarter of a mile long, east/west extension of the main water.
Fish Nothing 'bald-headed' about the fish. Good brown trout, but the principal interest is seatrout, from early July onwards, and salmon from August to the end of the season.
Flies & Tactics Bank fishing can be just as productive as boat fishing, but the boat makes it easier to get around the large expanse of water. The small bay on the north-east shore, with the island, is a good place to start. From the narrows, south, arrange a drift fairly close to the shore, about ten yards out, round the bay. Pay particular attention by the numerous islands. Offer: Ke-He, Soldier Palmer, Black Pennell.
Permission & Charges See Loch Mohal Beag entry.

AN FHORSA, Loch See Loch Fuaroil.

AN IAR, Loch
Location & Access 13/270179 Leave the A859 Stornoway/Tarbet road at 13/260194. Loch an Iar is one mile south-east on the minor road to Eishken.
Commentary Loch an Iar, with its neighbour, Loch na Muilne (13/276176), are easily accessible. There are two, linked, unnamed lochans close by at 13/280177 which are also worth a look, as is Loch Oyavat (13/279189) which lies to the north on the moor above Shiltenish.
Fish Good quality trout all round, averaging 8-10oz in weight, with the possibility of larger fish of up to and over 1lb, particularly in Loch na Muilne.
Flies & Tactics These lochs are easily fished from the bank. Wading is not necessary and not recommended. Loch na Muilne has a fish farming cage and the west shore is the most productive fishing area. Flies: Black Pennell, Grouse & Claret, Silver Butcher.
Permission & Charges All fishing is preserved by the owner and visitors must seek permission before fishing. Make local enquiries.

AN SGATH, Loch See Loch Trealaval.
AN T-SLIOS, Loch See Grimersta River.
AN TAOBH SEAR, Loch See Grimersta River.
AN TOMAIN, Loch See Loch Trealaval.

BARAVAT, Loch (Great Bernera)
Location & Access 13/156356 Park by the stream at 13/148361, south from Valasay. The loch is five minutes' walk to the east.
Commentary This is the largest water on the Island of Great Bernera, over one mile north/south, by up to

OS Map 13 — West Lewis & North Harris

300yds wide. There are four other waters nearby, all worth your attention: Loch Ionail (13/156363), Loch na Ceannamhoir (13/159355), School Loch (13/159365), unnamed on the OS map, and Lochan Sgeireach (13/151353) to the west. To properly explore them all would take about a full week, apart from exploring the other excellent lochs on Great Bernera. This is a lovely island, with plenty to do for non-fishers, including outstanding beaches at Bosta (13/137403) in the north and at Barraglom (13/175344) in the south.

Fish Trout are of good quality and average 8-12oz but there are also trout of up to and over 2lb.

Flies & Tactics Unlike the majority of Lewis lochs, Loch Baravat has safe wading down the whole of the west bank. The north-west bay is productive, as is the south bay by Hacklete. On the east bank, concentrate your activities in the vicinity of the Dun (13/156356) and in the south-east arm of the loch (13/158352). Loch Ionail, Loch na Ceannamhoir and Lochan Sgeireach are easily covered from the shore. On School Loch, work the west shore, paying particular attention to the area where the stream flows out to Loch Ionail. School Loch has the largest fish, but these lochs can be weedy as the season advances and are best visited before the end of July. Offer: Black Zulu, Loch Ordie, Black Pennell.

Permission & Charges Apply Uig and Hamanavay Estate - Head Keeper. Tel: (01851) 672421 - see Loch a'Phealuir entry.

BARAVAT, Loch (Uig) See Loch Camasord.
BEAG AIRIGH NAN LINNTEAN, Loch See Loch Langavat.
BEAG NA BEISTE, Loch (Grimersta) See Loch Sgaire.
BEAG NA MUILNE, Loch See Loch Uamasbroc.
BEAG RUADH, Loch (Gisla) See Loch Coirgavat.
BEAG SHEILABRIE, Loch See Loch Morsgail.
BENISVAL, Loch See Loch Raonasgail.
BODAVAT, Loch See Loch Raonasgail.
BRAIGH AN T-SIDHEIN, Loch See Loch Uidemul.
BRAIGH BHEAGARAIS, Loch See Loch a'Ghlinne.
BRAIGHE GRIOMAVAL, Loch See Loch Raonasgail.

BREACLETE, Loch

Location & Access 13/163365 An easily accessible loch lying to the east of the road by Breaclete. Immediately east again, over the hill, is Loch nan Geadraisean (13/168268) which can be included in the expedition.

Commentary Loch Breaclete is almost half a mile north/south and covers an area of 40 acres. The northern section of Loch nan Geadraisean is known locally as Loch na Muilne. Weed can be a problem as the season advances.

Fish Good quality trout which average about 12oz in Loch Breaclete and 8oz in Loch nan Geadraisean.

Flies & Tactics Bank fishing only. Fish the west and south shore of Loch Breaclete before working the east bank up to the two bays at 13/165366. From here, walk round the north slope of the hill to fish the northern section (Loch na Muilne) of Loch na Geadraisean. Offer: Ke-He, Invicta, Silver Butcher.

Permission & Charges Contact: Sportsworld, 1 Francis Street, Stornoway, Isle of Lewis. Tel: (01851) 705464.

BRENISH, River See Loch Clibhe. Apply Uig and Hamanavay Estate - Head Keeper. Tel: (01851) 672421.

BRINNAVAL, Loch

Location & Access 13/030295 Follow the minor road that continues south from the end of the B8011 past Uig Lodge (13/055332) and Ardroil (13/050321). Park at 13/010304. Walk east up the outlet stream to the first loch of the day, Loch Sandavat (13/013303).

Commentary A five-mile expedition over rough ground, fishing a series of nine named and unnamed lochs between the road and Brinnaval (213m). Compass and map country and magnificent scenery all the way. For those who prefer more sedentary pursuits, there are a number of tiny, isolated coves nearby, ideal for lazy family days, whilst you plodge round the hills above: Mangersta Sands (13/008308), Aird Fenish (13/995293), Camas Islivig (13/989279). Camas Islivig also has its own, unnamed trout loch to the west of the bay.

Fish Good quality brown trout which average 6-8oz in all the lochs, and the chance of a few fish of over 1lb in weight. Loch Brinnaval, Loch na Faoirbh (13/023284) and Loch na Cloich Airde (13/019299) are connected to the Stockgill River which flows into Abhainn Caslavat (known locally as the Red River), and there is always the chance of salmon, towards the end of the season and after heavy rain.

Flies & Tactics After Loch Sandavat, climb south-east to reach Loch na Cloich Airde. Follow the outlet stream at the south end, having a cast in the unnamed lochan between Loch na Cloich Airde and its neighbour, Loch na Faoirbh, the largest of the group. Fish the north-west and north shore of Loch na Faoirbh before skirting the crags north to find Loch Brinnaval. Fish clockwise round Brinnaval and return to examine the east and south-east shoreline of Loch na Faoirbh. Leave the loch at the south end and walk over the hill to the unnamed lochan at 13/012292; then descend to the last of water, Loch Melavat (13/010296). Bank fishing all the way and it is best to stay ashore. The lochs are easily covered and fish are readily taken from the bank. Loch na Faoirbh has the best trout and east bank is most productive. Offer them: Loch Ordie, Greenwell's Glory, Black Pennell.

Permission & Charges Apply Uig and Hamanavay Estate - Head Keeper. Tel: (01851) 672421 - see Loch a'Pheluir entry.

BRUICHE BREIVAT, Loch See Loch Langavat.

BUAILE MIRAVAT, Loch

Location & Access 13/149373. Loch Buaile Miravat lies to the north of Valasay on the Island of Great Bernera. Park by the sea loch at 13/153364. Walk the east shoreline north to find the outlet stream and follow it to the loch, a journey of approx. 20 mins.

Commentary A small loch on the moor above the long finger of Tob Valasay, with two, tiny, satellite lochans

109

West Lewis & North Harris — OS Map 13

immediately to the west.
Fish Bright brown trout which average 6-8oz, but the possibility of seatrout after heavy rain.
Flies & Tactics The water is easily covered from the shore and Loch Buaile Miravat often provides welcome shelter from the prevailing winds. Tempt them with: Black Zulu, Soldier Palmer, Silver Invicta.
Permission & Charges Apply Uig and Hamanavay Estate - Head Keeper, Tel: (01851) 672421 - see Loch a'Phealuir entry. For further information, contact Sportsworld, 1 Francis Street, Stornoway, Isle of Lewis. Tel: (01851) 705464.

BUAILE NAN CAORACH, Loch See Loch Camasord.
CAMASORD, Loch (Ardroil) See Loch Stacsavat.

CAMASORD, Loch (Crowlista)
Location & Access 13/034350 At the end of the B8011 Miavaig/Timsgarry road, at 13/059343, turn north. After the school, take the next left and park at 13/046349. Walk west to reach Loch Camasord.
Commentary The ideal place for a family fishing/beach outing. Uig sands, to the south, are incredibly lovely. After leaving the car, fish Loch Baravat (13/040349), the first water of four waters to the north of Crowlista (13/040340). At the west end of Loch Baravat, follow the inlet stream west for five minutes to reach Loch Camasord. The inlet burn at the south end of Loch Camasord leads to Loch Buaile nan Caorach (13/033345) and its small, unnamed, satellite lochan to the south east at 13/036343. Walk north east from this lochan to return to the south end of Loch Baravat and the start point.
Fish Trout average in the region of 8oz, but there are a few larger specimens as well.
Flies & Tactics Easy bank fishing and few problems. Stay ashore, the water is readily covered and fish lie close to the margin. Flies: Loch Ordie, Grouse & Claret, Silver Butcher.
Permission & Charges Apply Uig and Hamanavay Estate - Head Keeper. Tel: (01851) 672421. See also Loch a'Phealuir entry.

CAOL, Loch (Gisla) See Loch Fuaroil.

CAOL, Loch (Scaliscro)
Location & Access 13/156315 From Earshader at 13/165338, just before the B8059 crosses Sruth Earshader to Great Bernera. Follow the coastline west for 15 mins to find the sandy bay and inlet stream at 13/156334. This beach can be a productive seatrout fishing location.
Commentary Tough going, and a compass and map are essential. Non-fishing members of your party can linger on the fine beach whilst you head for the hills. Walk up the stream for five minutes, then angle west round the side of the hill to the ruined shieling and unnamed lochan at 13/150326. After exploring the lochan, climb south-east past the ruin, over the hill, to reach Loch Gill Breinadale (13/159323). Follow the line of the south-west inlet stream of Loch Gill Breinadale, and climb out of the glen to find Caol Loch which is sheltered from harsh winds by the heights of Ben Drovinish (185m) to the west and Ben Fuailaval (175m) to the east. Return to the south end of Loch Gill Breinadale and walk due north to little Loch Hamasord (13/160327). Follow the outlet stream from the north end of the loch down to the beach and return east to the start point.
Fish More walking and looking than 'one for the glass case' country, with nice trout which average 6-8oz and the chance of seatrout in the bay.
Flies & Tactics These little lochs are rarely fished. Approach with caution, to avoid spooking the residents, and stay ashore. Wading is not required. Tempt them with: Black Zulu, Grouse & Claret, Dunkeld.
Permission & Charges See Loch Tungavat.

CEANN HULAVIG, Sea-loch See Grimersta River.
CHAOLARTAN, Loch See Loch Grunavat. Brown trout only. Apply Uig and Hamanavay Estate - Head Keeper. Tel: (01851) 672421.
CHRAGOL, Loch See Loch na h-Inghinn.
CHOILLEIGAR, Loch See Loch Raonasgail.
CLACH NA H-IOLAIRE, Loch See Loch na Craoibhe (Shiltenish).
CLEIT DUASTAL, Loch See Loch Morsgail.
CLIBH CRACAVAL, Loch See Loch Clibhe.
CNOC NAN SLIGEAN, Loch See Loch Plocrapool.

COIRGAVAT, Loch
Location & Access 13/117265 Approach from near the power station at Gisla (13/128258). Park at 13/123277 on the B8011 Garynahine/Miavaig road and follow the peat track west, past the tiny lochan to the south of the track.
Commentary Loch Coirgavat is impounded and feeds water to the power station on the shore of Little Loch Roag. The loch is three quarters of a mile north/south by up to 300yds wide. The north end is the most attractive, scattered with four islands. There are five other waters which can be included in an expedition to the north end of Loch Coirgavat. Ten minutes due west from the end of the peat track is the first, Loch an Eilein Choinnich (13/114278), then, a step north, Loch na Graoibhaige Moire (13/109281). After fishing Loch na Graoibhaige Moire, cross to the unnamed lochan immediately south, then west to explore Loch Airigh an Uisge (13/109273). The ruined shieling on the north slope of Cleite Ghiosla (185m) is a good place for lunch. Walk south-east to Loch Coirgavat. Fish the north end, east to the large, adjacent east bay. Return north-east across the moor to the road. As an alternative, you may choose to fish the south end of Loch Coirgavat starting from Gisla. The most productive area is the south-west bay, particularly in the vicinity of where the Gisla river enters by the promontory on the south-west shore. As attractive, is to follow the inlet stream south from Loch Coirgavat for 15 mins to explore four additional lochs: Loch Beag Ruadh (13/118251) and its adjacent unnamed lochan to the east, then little Loch na Muilne (13/122249) and its satellite to the north. Follow the outlet stream from Loch na Muilne back to road at Gisla.
Fish Pretty, little, brown trout in the small lochs with

110

OS Map 13 — West Lewis & North Harris

the chance of more serious specimens in Loch Coirigavat.
Flies & Tactics The small lochs are all easily covered from the shore. On Loch Coirigavat, stay on the bank. Do not wade. Trout lie close all along the north bank. The steep-sided north-west bank can also be productive. When fishing the south end of Loch Coirigavat, concentrate your effort in the south-west bay by the large island. Offer them: Black Pennell, Grouse & Claret, Silver Invicta.
Permission & Charges Apply Uig and Hamanavay Estate - Head Keeper. Tel: (01851) 672421 See also Loch a'Phealuir entry.

COIRIGEROD, Loch See Loch Langavat.
COLLAVAL, Loch See Loch Smuaisaval.
CRAGACH, Loch (Morsgail) See Loch Morsgail. Apply Uig and Hamanavay Estate - Head Keeper. Tel: (01851) 672421.
CRAGACH, Lochanan See Loch Raonasgail.
CREAG FORTHILL, Loch See Loch na h-Airigh Uir.
CREAGACH, Loch See Loch Raonasgail.
CRIADHA, Loch See Loch Fada (Laxay).
CRO CRIOSDAIG, Loch See Loch Raonasgail.
CROCACH, Loch (Scaliscro) See Loch Tungavat.
CROISTEAN, Loch See Loch Sandavat. Brown trout only.

CROSS REFERENCES The lochs on OS Map 13 contained within the square NW230260 to NE350260 and SE350230 to SW230230 are detailed on OS Map 14. The lochs and rivers contained within the area N17/E26 and N17/E43 are noted on OS Map 8; with the exception of those waters contained within the area bounded by 8/170260 to 8/220260 and 8/170330 to 8/220330 which are noted on OS Map 13.

CUIL AIRIGH A'FLOD, Loch See Loch Trealaval.
CUTHAIG, Loch See Loch Trealaval.
DEIREADH BANAIG, Loch See Loch Sgailler.

DHOMHNUILL BHIG, Loch
Location & Access 13/293220 Park on the A895 Stornoway/Tarbert road at 13/309213 between Loch Valtos (13/315213) and Loch an Deaspoirt (13/305215). Follow the peat road north, then west, to the east shore of Loch an Deaspoirt. At the north end of Loch nan Deaspoirt, follow the inlet stream west for five minutes to reach Loch Dhomhnuill Bhig.
Commentary Loch Dhomhnuill Bhig and Loch nan Deaspoirt offer good sport in attractive surroundings. They are easily accessible from the main road and a circuit of both waters provides a full day's fishing. The lochs are approximately half a mile north/south by up to 300 yds wide and each covers an area of some 35 acres.
Fish No record breakers, but plenty of fun with bright trout which average in the order of 6oz/8oz. Loch Dhomhnuill Bhig contains very pretty, silver trout, as well as few more traditional specimens which can be much larger.
Flies & Tactics Fish the east shores on the way north and return to the start point down the west shores, fishing as you go. The narrow north arm of Loch Dhomhnuill Bhig is the most productive area. On Loch an Deaspoirt, concentrate on the area by Balallan Plantation. An early season assault is best because weed becomes a major problem as the season advances. Flies: Black Zulu, Invicta, Silver Butcher.
Permission & Charges Some good lochs in the district of Balallan are controlled by the Soval Angling Association and are available to visitors at a modest cost. Enquiries to: The Secretary, Billy, 45 Leurbost, Lochs. Tel: (home) 01851 860491 or (business) 01851 705242. For Loch Dhomhnuill Bhig enquire Head Keeper, Laxay River (01851) 830202.

DIBADALE, Loch See Loch Raonasgail.
DUBH, Loch (Habost) See Loch na h-Inghinn.
DUBH, Loch (Morsgail) See Loch Morsgail for commentary. Apply Uig and Hamanavay Estate - Head Keeper. Tel: (01851) 672421.
DUBH, Loch (Shiltenish) See Loch na Craoibhe.
DUBH Loch (Tamanavay) See Loch Raonasgail.
DUBH, Lochan (Loch Suirstavat) See Loch Suirstavat.
DUBH, Lochan (Maivaig) See Loch nan Eilean. Apply Uig and Hamanavay Estate - Head Keeper. Tel: (01851) 672421.
DUBH MAS HOLASMUL, Loch See Loch Rogavat.
DUBH SUBHAL, Loch See Loch na h-Airigh Uir.
EALAIDH, Loch See Loch na h-Inghinn.
EASTAPER, Loch See Loch na h-Airigh Uir.

FADA, Loch (Laxay)
Location & Access 13/318247 Loch Fada lies to the north and west of the A859 Stornoway/Tarbert road and is best approached from near Laxay by a peat road which runs north from 13/330220.
Commentary A three mile day, exploring five lochs, of which Loch Fada is the largest: three quarters of a mile east/west by up to 500 yds wide and covering an area of about 100 acres. Ignore Loch Ulapool (13/327225), which has miniscule trout, and is immediately adjacent to the west of the peat road. Park near Loch Criadha (13/325245). After finding Loch Criadha, walk north round the shoulder of Ben Keadrashal (120m) to reach Loch Fada. Loch Keadrashal is by far the best of these lochs to fish. Half way along the south shore of Loch Fada, climb south for ten minutes to explore Loch na Speireig (13/325245).
Fish Trout average 6oz/8oz, but there are larger fish particularly in Loch Criadha.
Flies & Tactics Bank fishing only, and it is beast to avoid wading. Loch Ulapool is not generally regarded as worth fishing. Loch Criadha is approximately 25 acres and the fish may be taken from all round the bank. The loch becomes weedy as the season advances and the west shore is the most productive area. Fish may be taken everywhere on Loch Fada, but this loch can be 'dour'. The north west bay, where Lon Ban burn enters, and the north east corner are perhaps the most productive areas. Loch na Speireig offers comfortable bank fishing and is readily covered from the shore. Offer them: Blue Zulu, Soldier Palmer, Peter Ross.
Permission & Charges See Loch Trealaval.

111

West Lewis & North Harris
OS Map 13

FADAGOA, Loch See Loch Trealaval.
FAOGHAIL AN TUIM, Loch See Grimersta River.
FAOGHAIL CHARRASAN, Loch See Grimersta River.
FAOGHAIL KIRRAVAL, Loch See Grimersta River.
FAOGHAIL NAN CAORACH, Loch See Grimersta River.

FHORSA, River
Location & Access Source Loch Suainaval 13/068290 Outflow 13/052330. A short, easily accessible salmon stream flowing into the sea over Uig Sands to the south of Timsgarry (13/056340).
Commentary A delightful little salmon river of some one and a half miles in length, flowing north from Loch Suainaval through Loch Stacsavat to reach the sea at Camas Uig. The river hosts four rods, double bank, with additional rods fishing Loch Stacsavat and Loch Suainaval. There are 15 named pools, including slow moving water and fast, turbulent runs. The key factor for success is being there at the right time, that is, after heavy rain. Otherwise, the lochs provide the best opportunity for sport, with both salmon and trout. The surrounding area is very beautiful and the fishing is let with Uig Lodge; an imposing, Victorian shooting lodge overlooking Uig Sands sleeping 16 guests. There is also a small nine hole golf course for those so afflicted, but the principal interest here is angling.
Fish Numbers caught vary according to conditions, but most seasons produce about 100 salmon which average 6-7lb in weight. Seatrout do not run the system but 40-60 seatrout are taken in the tidal waters, mostly during May and June.
Flies & Tactics The river is readily understood and easily fished with a single-handed rod. Wading is not necessary. The lower half of the river is tidal, including the famous Bruton Stream Pool (the lazy man's salmon pool - the tide does the work, bringing the fish to the angler, who may, if he so chooses, remain in the same spot). Flies: Goat's Toe, Clan Chief, Green Highlander, Hairy Mary, Garry Dog, General Practitioner, Silver Wilkinson, Black Doctor.
Permission & Charges See Loch Suainaval.

FHREUNADAIL, Loch
Location & Access 13/183326 Approach from Lundale at 13/183326 on the B8059 Grimersta/Earshader road. Loch Fhreunadail is at the end of a rough, 30 minute hike, south-west from the road. Compass and map are essential.
Commentary A very attractive loch in a remote setting, covering an area of some 40 acres, 700yds north/south by up to 300yds wide. Make Loch Fhreunadail the centre point for an expedition to include five other named and unnamed lochs and lochans along the way. Start at Loch Aird (13/180324), then have a cast in Loch na Faing to the south. Follow the inlet stream from Loch na Faing south over rising ground, with the possibility of a detour to little Loch a'Bhraghad on the hill to the east. Descend now past the ruined shieling to reach Loch Fhreunadail and the boat, which is moored at the south end of the loch. After attacking the unsuspecting inhabitants, find the outlet stream at the north-east corner of the loch and follow it down to Loch a'Chaphail (13/172329) and its attendant unnamed lochans. Walk due east from Loch a'Chaphail to return to the start point.
Fish Very pretty fish of good quality averaging 8oz in weight.
Flies & Tactics Trout rise and are taken from all round the shoreline. On Loch Fhreunadail, concentrate your efforts along the east and south shore, particularly by the small island where the feeder burn enters the loch. Flies: Blue Zulu, Soldier Palmer, Alexandra.
Permission & Charges See Loch Tungavat.

FUAROIL, Loch
Location & Access 13/123240. Park on the B8011 Garynahine/Miavaig road at 13/138240 and walk due west up the hill for 20 mins to reach the loch.
Commentary Loch Fuaroil lies between the south end of Little Loch Roag, a sea loch, to the east, and the ragged heights of Skeun (265m) and Coduinn (241m) to the west. The loch covers an area of some 40 acres and is easily fished from the shore. A further climb/hike up the glen between Skeun and Coduinn will bring you to four more small waters: the unnamed lochan at 13/118233, Caol Loch (13/110232), Loch an Fhorsa (13/118230), and Loch Gainmhich (13/129230).
Fish Great sport with bright, well marked, small brown trout which average 8oz.
Flies & Tactics Work round the north shore of Loch Fuaroil to the inlet stream on the west bank. Climb the inlet stream to reach the unnamed lochan. After exploring this lochan, walk west, crossing the inlet stream to Loch an Fhorsa, to reach Caol Loch. Return to Loch an Fhorsa, then circle round the south shoulder of Coduinn to find Loch Gainmhich. Walk due north, back to Loch Fuaroil and fish the south-west, south, and east shore. Pay particular attention to the area round the little island in the southern bay. Flies: Blue Zulu, Invicta, Silver Butcher.
Permission & Charges Apply Uig and Hamanavay Estate - Head Keeper. Tel: (01851) 672421. See Loch a'Phealuir entry.

GAINMHICH, Loch (Gisla) See Loch Fuaroil.
GEAL, Loch (Great Bernera) See Loch na Muilne (Bosta).
GILL BREINADALE, Loch See Caol Loch (Scaliscro).
GISLA, River See Loch Coirgavat.

GOBHLACH, Loch
Location & Access 13/178360. Park at 13/184360 and walk west over the hill for ten minutes to reach the loch.
Commentary Loch Gobhlach is one of three good lochs lying to the north of the township of Kirkibost on the Island of Great Bernera. The other two are Loch na Craobhaig (13/181355) and Shieling Loch (13/179358), which is unnamed on the OS Map. Further south, a couple of minutes' walk to the west of the Totarol road, is another little loch worth a cast, Loch Mharcoil (13/188344).
Fish Excellent quality trout which average about 8oz,

OS Map 13 — West Lewis & North Harris

but a few larger fish of up to 2lb as well.
Flies & Tactics Begin at the east end of Loch Gobhlach, working round the north shore, including a step west to have a cast in the unnamed lochan at 13/174362. Fish the west shore, down to Shieling Loch, paying particular attention to the stream mouth. Walk south from Shieling Loch for a couple of minutes to find Loch na Craobhaig and the tiny, unnamed, lochan to the west (13/179355). Concentrate your effort at the south end where the heaviest trout are taken. Now walk north again, fishing as you go. The east bank of Loch Gobhlach can be very productive. Drive south to fish Loch Mharcoil. Flies: Blue Zulu, Grouse & Claret, Silver Butcher.
Permission & Charges See Loch a'Phealuir entry. Further information from: Sportsworld, 1 Francis Street, Stornoway, Isle of Lewis. Tel: (01851) 705464.

GREIVAT, Loch See Loch Sandavat (Brenish). Brown trout only.

GRIMERSTA, River
Location & Access Source Loch Langavat 13/170175 Outflow Loch Ceann Hulavig (13/218300). The river crosses the B8011 Garynahine/Miavaig road at 13/214296 and there is a well maintained system of tracks leading to the principal fishing locations.
Commentary One of the most famous and exclusive salmon and seatrout systems in Europe. The river is one and three quarters of a mile long, with man-made pools and croys including: Bridge Pool, Captain's Pool, Long Pool and Battery Pool. Most sport is, however, not on the river itself, but on the lochs that form the major part of the system. They are, north to south, Loch Faoghail an Tuim (13/203280), Loch Faoghail Charrasan (13/207265), Loch Fhaoghail Kirraval (13/208255), Loch an Easa Ghil (13/200253), Loch Airigh na h-Airde (13/215235), Loch Faoghail nan Caorach (13/215222), and Loch Langavat. There are numerous lochs adjacent to the principal waters, all of which offer good sport with brown trout and a few where there is the chance of salmon as well. The principal waters in this category are: Loch an Earball (13/217265) and Loch na Plaide (13/214272). The unnamed lochans at 13/207279 and 13/211279 to the north of Loch na Plaide have good fish; Loch an t-Slios (13/213248) by Kirraval (116m); the unnamed loch at 13/210233; Loch an Taobh Sear (13/228245) to the east of Kirraval; and Loch an Eilean (13/230234), one of the most attractive lochs in the area, scattered with tiny islands.
Fish Salmon, seatrout and brown trout. Catch returns are not generally available but the annual average is probably in the region of 300 salmon and a similar number of seatrout. Salmon average 7-8lb in weight, with a few fish in the teens of pounds; seatrout average 1lb 8oz. The brown trout vary in size from 8oz to fish of up to and over 2lb in weight.
Flies & Tactics All fishing is by fly only and boats are used as 'ferries' to reach the more remote parts of the system. The estate is well-managed and gillies are available to guide guests to the most productive fishing areas. Flies: the essential patterns are Blue Elver, Muddler and Stoat's Tail. Other traditional flies here are Green Highlander, Hairy Mary, Willie Gunn, Garry Dog, General Practitioner, Goats Toe, Black Pennell, Loch Ordie, Ke-He, Soldier Palmer, Clan Chief, Kate Maclaren, Peter Ross, Alexandra.
Permission & Charges In recent years, Grimersta Lodge has been made available for let during April, May and early June. This can be a very productive period for salmon fishing and some weeks may produce up to 50 fish. There is always excellent sport to be had with brown trout. The estate encourages visitor access to trout fishing for which there is no charge. Contact: Simon Scott, Estate Manager, Grimersta Estate Office, Grimersta, Isle of Lewis. Tel: (01851) 621358; Fax: (01851) 621389. Sporting lets are also arranged through Finlyson Hughes, Lynedoch House, Barossa Place, Perth PH1 5EP. Tel: (01738) 451600.

GRUNAVAT, Loch
Location & Access 13/088275. Turn west at Gisla (13/128258) on the B8011 Garynahine/Miavaig road and follow the track up to the south end of Loch Coirgavat (13/122262). Walk round the south end of the loch to find the inlet stream (Gisla River) on the west bank at 13/117263. Walk the stream, between Cleite Ghiosla (185m) to the north and Skeun (265m) to the south, to reach Loch na Ciste (13/097262) which is an extension of Loch Grunavat.
Commentary The walk from Gisla is two miles of rough going and a compass and map are essential. Loch Grunavat is 70 ft deep, over two miles north/south and up to half a mile wide, so you will probably hike a good 8 miles during the day to complete a circuit of the whole loch; plus a diversion west to explore the lochans by Lochannan Sgeireach (13/088271) to the north of Cleite nan Caorach (172m). Further adventure may be had by combining a visit to the south end of Loch Grunavat with a visit to the remote lochs round Beinn Mheadhonach (397m) and Beinn a'Deas (351m) to the south of Loch Grunavat: Loch Scanadale (13/095238), Loch Uamasbroc (13/083240), Lochan nan Allt Ruadh (13/074235). Whilst in the parish, consider continuing west to explore two, additional, excellent lochs to the west, below the steep crags of Mula Chaolartan (354m): Loch Chaolartan (13/064247) and Loch nan Uidhean (13/069249). To complete a round trip of them all is a hard 11 mile tramp, but there is the option of camping out overnight at the sheiling at 13/067245.
Fish Loch Grunavat contains some large trout which are not easy to fool. Expect great fun with 8oz/10oz fish, but be prepared for that sudden, extra-fierce, heart-stopping tug. The other lochs contain brown trout which vary in size from 6oz to fish of up to and over 1lb.
Flies & Tactics Wading is not recommended. Stay safely ashore and let the trout come to you. The south end of Loch Grunavat always provides sport by the inlet streams and also in Loch na Ciste. The large bay to the north of Loch na Ciste is also good. Work quickly up the north east shore to concentrate on the extreme north end, then down to the promontory and bay where the burn enters at 13/084273. The south west

West Lewis & North Harris — OS Map 13

shore, as the loch shallows, can also provide nice trout. Loch Chaolartan, which is joined to Loch nan Uidhean by a useful stream, is one of the most attractive lochs in Lewis, very rarely fished and offering fine sport amidst dramatic surroundings. Take along a good supply of: Black Pennell, Grouse & Claret, Invicta, Ke-He, Soldier Palmer, March Brown, Loch Ordie, Black Zulu, Blue Zulu, Peter Ross, Alexandra, Silver Butcher.
Permission & Charges For further details and information about access, apply to the Head Keeper, Uig & Hamanavay Estate, tel. 01851 672421. See also Loch a'Phealuir entry.

HALLADALE, Loch
Location & Access 13/029087. Loch Halladale lies on the Arda Mora peninsula, immediately to the south of the B887 road, one mile west from Amhuinnsuidhe Castle.
Commentary Loch Halladale, and the River Halladale which enters the loch from the slopes of Creagan Ruadha to the north, is a good salmon seatrout system, easily accessible and great fun to fish. There is an adjacent loch, known locally as Upper Loch Halladale (13/028085), but a grid across the outlet burn prevents the entry of migratory fish. There are a number of other easily accessible lochs on Arda Mora and Arda Beaga which also offer good sport: Loch nan Sligean (13/024082), to the south of Upper Loch Halladale; Loch Langavat (13/023093), by the road; Loch Geodha Beag (13/010095), easily approached from the track to Govig; Loch a'Ghoirtein (13/014099); Loch na Beiste (13/003105) and Loch a'Mhula (13/004108), further west towards Hushinish.
Fish The brown trout here average 8oz, although there are a few fish of up to 1lb in weight as well. Seatrout may be encountered in the sea at Govig Bay, where the burn from Loch Geodha enters, and in the bay to the west at 13/005090.
Flies & Tactics Good water levels are all essential for sport with migratory fish. Given such, then sport can be fast and furious, particularly towards the end of the season when some large seatrout run the river. The loch is easily 'read' and fish may be taken all over its 20 acre area. The north shore, by the little island, where the main feeder stream enters, is a good place to begin. The other lochs are simply covered from the shore. Offer: Ke-He, Loch Ordie, Peter Ross.
Permission & Charges See Loch Voshimid.

HALLADALE, River See Loch Halladale.
HALLADALE, Upper Loch See Loch Halladale.
HAMASORD, Loch See Caol Loch (Scaliscro).
IBHEIR, Loch See Loch Trealaval.
IONAIL, Loch See Loch Baravat (Great Bernera).
LAMADALE, Loch See Loch Raonasgail.
LANGAVAT, Loch (Amhuinnsuidhe) See Loch Halladale.

LANGAVAT, Loch (Central)
Location & Access South end 13/155128; North end 13/223220. This is the largest freshwater loch in Lewis and access is controlled by a number of estates who own the fishing rights: Soval Estate, Grimersta Estate, Morsgail Estate, Aline Estate, Uig & Hamanavay Estate. Access, by prior permission from these estates, is varied; you can walk from Aline Lodge (13/198120) on the shores of Loch Seaforth to the east.
Commentary Loch Langavat is over eight miles long and rarely more than half a mile wide. It lies amidst dramatic scenery and it would take a dozen seasons to properly appreciate all this wonderful loch has to offer. There are a number of excellent lochs lying to the north, on the Grimersta Estate - see Grimersta River entry - which offer a wide variety of additional sport. These are best approached from Loch Langavat and include: Loch Beag Airigh nan Linntean (13/207215), Loch Mor Airigh nan Linntean (13/211221), Loch nan Eilean (13/157213), Loch na ciste (13/195224), Loch Bruiche Breivat (13/187217). Loch Coirigerod (13/175215), Loch Lomhain (13/164198), Loch Ruadh a'Deas (13/153209) and Loch Ruadh Meadhonach (13/157213) to the west, are on Morsgail Estate - see Loch Morsgail entry. South of Loch Langavat, is Loch Moglavat (13/199189), a small water on the Aline Estate - see Loch Tiorsdam entry - but also well worth a cast or two or three.
Fish Just about everything, in all shapes and sizes, including salmon, sea-trout and brown trout. With the exception of the lochs to the west of Loch Coirigerod, all the others are, one way or another, joined to Loch Langavat, the headwater of the famous Grimersta System.
Flies & Tactics Most salmon are taken from estate boats, largely by trolling. The south and middle sections of the loch are deepest, dropping to more than 80ft. The north end is relatively shallow and that is where most salmon and sea-trout are taken, close to the shore. Boat Bay, at the extreme north east end is much favoured in this regard; as is the north shoreline, from the exit of Loch Bruiche Breivat, west round the headland to the outlet stream from Loch Coirigerod. Trout fishing is excellent from the shore, but wading is not advised. A good place to start is exactly where the track arrives over the hill from Aline Lodge at 13/174168, a journey of one hour. A number of streams flow into Loch Langavat here and trout gather to feed at these outlets. The jagged bays to the right of the shielings, in particular, can produce some excellent fish. Loch Langavat trout average 10oz/12oz, but specimen fish of up to and over 5lb are not uncommon. The shallow south end of Loch Langavat can also produce good results and this area is best approached from the A859 Stornoway/Tarbert road at Vigadale Bay (13/188115). A track climbs steeply west between Mullach a'Ruisg (473m) north, and Mullach an Langa (614m) south, to reach Loch Langavat after a stiff, one hour tramp. The Langdale River feeds Loch Langavat here, and this stream also provides sport with salmon. Aline Estate have the fishing rights - see Loch Tiorsdam entry. The surrounding lochs are all fished from the shore and wading is generally inadvisable. Loch nan Eilean is perhaps the loveliest of the group, scattered with small islands and full of interesting corners and fishy points. The unnamed lochs immediately to the east of Loch nan Eilean should also be explored (13/210225). Loch Coirigerod deserves an expedition

OS Map 13

West Lewis & North Harris

in its own right. The loch is almost one mile long by up to 600 yds wide across the north bay and contains some excellent trout which rarely see an artificial fly from one season to the next. The north end, amidst the small islands, is the most productive area. A number of the burns flowing into Loch Langavat can also often give sport after heavy rain: in the north, the stream between Loch Langavat and Loch Faoghail nan Caorach at 13/216218; to the west, entering the north shore of Loch Langavat, Abhainn Gleann Sandig at 13/157176. This is the remote, wild landscape, and, as always, you must leave word where you are going and when you expect to return. You must also remember that heavy rain can turn the moor into a nightmare, making once easily forded streams impassable. You will enjoy every moment spent in this paradise, but even more so if you are thoroughly prepared for all contingencies. Flies to offer the beasts include: Clan Chief, Goat's Toe, Willie Gunn, General Practitioner, Silver Wilkinson, Black Pennell, Loch Ordie, Ke-He, Soldier Palmer, Grouse & Claret, March Brown, Greenwell's Glory, Peter Ross, Silver Butcher, Teal Blue & Silver.
Permission & Charges Apply to the various estates, all of which are cross-referenced in the text above. Day lets are sometimes available. Ask John Macleod, Valtos Cottage, Laxay, Lochs, Stornoway, Isle of Lewis. Tel: (01851) 830202, the Head Keeper of the Soval Estate for advice.

LANGADALE, River See Loch Langavat.

LAXAY, River

Location & Access Source: 13/285235 Outflow: 13/32521. The Laxay River crosses the Stornoway/Tarbert road at 13/316218 between the townships of Laxay and Balallan and is easily accessible from this point by a series of well-maintained riverside paths.
Commentary An excellent little salmon stream which extends over a distance of some three and a half miles, from Loch nam Faoileag to the sea in Loch Erisort. There are six principal pools; downstream from the A859 are Top, Middle and Lower Pools, above the road, Island, Rocky and S-Bend Pools. The river is divided into three beats, including Loch Valtos (13/315213) which is the most productive part of the system. Water flow is controlled by a series of dams which help to create artificial freshets during dry spells and can also be used to prolong spates. The river is careful maintained and there is a good, stone-built boat house, and three boats, on Loch Valtos. Soval Lodge and 38,000 adjacent acres, also have a 30 ft sea-going boat which is available for sea fishing expeditions. The lodge accommodates 15 guests and is let on an all-inclusive basis, staffed with a cook and two maids. The estate also offer shooting for snipe and grouse. Argo-cat transport helps to reach the more inaccessible on Lewis's largest loch, Loch Langavat (13/190200).
Fish The annual catch for the system depends very much upon water levels. It can vary from between 50 salmon and 100 sea-trout in a dry year, up to over 150 salmon and 250 sea-trout when conditions are right. Most seasons produce upwards of 1,000 brown trout, including good numbers of fish of over 1lb in weight. The main salmon and sea-trout run occurs in July and early August, but salmon and sea-trout are also taken in June. The Laxay has a reputation for producing large salmon and double figure fish are not uncommon. The largest salmon caught on the Laxay, so far, weighed 33lb 8oz and was taken in 1933 by Richard D'Oyly Carte - whose ancestor promoted Gilbert & Sullivan operas.
Flies & Tactics The river is easily accessible and readily fished using a single-handed rod. Wading is not really required. Loch Valtos, where most of the action takes place, is best fished from the boat, apart from the famous pier, known as 'The Cast', and fish are encountered throughout the 40 acre loch. Sea-trout may also be caught at the mouth of the river, in the estuary between the shore and Eilean Mor Laxay. Flies that help: Goat's Toe, General Practitioner, Hairy Mary, Green Highlander, Black Doctor, Willie Gunn, Garry Dog, Silver Watkinson. Trout flies, such as Ke-He, Black Pennell, Clan Chief, Loch Ordie, Teal Blue & Silver, Peter Ross, Grouse & Claret, Soldier Palmer can also bring results, particularly during low water conditions.
Permission & Charges Full details of charges and availability from: Richard Kershaw, Joseph Holt plc, Empire Street, Cheetham, Manchester M3 1JD. Tel: (01618) 343285.

LEATHA, Loch (Morsgail) See Loch Morsgail. Apply Uig and Hamanavay Estate - Head Keeper. Tel: (01851) 672421.

LEATHAIN, Loch

Location & Access 13/343183. A three-mile tramp round a series of eight named and unnamed lochs and lochans which lie to the south of Kershader on the B8060 Shiltenish/Gravir road. Park at 13/338199 and follow the burn south up the hill to reach the first loch of the day, Loch Airigh Fhearchair (13/343195), after an easy, ten minutes. From the inlet stream at the south end of Loch Airigh Fhearchair, walk due south over rising ground to find Loch Leathain within half a mile.
Commentary A further ten minutes south brings you to the unnamed lochan at 13/345178, the half-way point of the expedition. After exploring this lochan, climb west over the hill to the next unnamed lochan at 13/339178. Have a cast in Loch Ealaidh (13/333181) before walking north down the Abhainn Ealaidh to reach the last water, the unnamed lochan by the road at 13/337196.
Fish Trout average 6-8oz, but they are good quality and fight well. The unnamed lochans may offer a few surprises.
Flies & Tactics This is rough country, so be well shod and take along a compass and map to see you safely round. The west shore of Loch Airigh Fharchair is generally kind, whilst the north and west shore on Loch Leathain is the most productive. The unnamed lochans may all be comfortably covered from the shore. Try: Black Zulu, Soldier Palmer, Dunkeld.
Permission & Charges See Loch an Iar.

115

West Lewis & North Harris — OS Map 13

LINISH, Loch
Location & Access 13/113350 Leave the B8011 Garynahine/Enaclete at Miavaig and turn right by the doctor's surgery. Park at Reef (13/113346). The loch is five minutes walk to the north of the road.
Commentary There are five lochs between the Miavaig/Cliff road and sea, all of which can be visited during the course of a single outing. The principal waters are Loch Linish and Loch Trialavat (13/090358), the others, unnamed on the OS Map are at 13/104350, 13/099354, and 13/099359. The Reef Peninsula is perfect for the angler with a non fishing family. The long, dune-backed beach at Traigh na Beire is a golden crescent of near deserted sand. There are archaeological remains, currently being investigated, in one of the lochs; and the ruins of Norse grain mills may be found by the little stream which enters the sea at the north end of the beach.
Fish Loch Linish has the largest trout, fine fish which average in the order of 10oz/12oz in weight. Loch Trialavat was the site, some years ago, of an experimental introduction of rainbow trout and, allegedly, a few survive. Otherwise, expect nice, brightly marked 6oz/8oz trout.
Flies & Tactics Begin behind the dunes, fishing the nearest of the unnamed lochs, then follow the inlet stream at the north end up the glen to find Loch Trialavat. From the south end of Loch Trialavat, climb over the saddle on Nisa Mhor (136m) and walk round the south shoulder of the adjacent hill to find the unnamed loch with the Dun. Descend south east, now, to the unnamed loch with remains of the Broch, and finish by driving round to Reef to attack the best loch, Loch Linish. Flies to use: Black Zulu, Soldier Palmer, Peter Ross.
Permission & Charges For details, contact: Sportsworld, 1 Francis Street, Stornoway, Isle of Lewis. Tel: (01851) 705464.

LOMHAIN, Loch See Loch Langavat.
MELAVAT, Loch See Loch Brinnaval. Brown trout.
MHARCOIL, Loch See Loch Gobhlach.

MHEACLEIT, Loch
Location & Access 13/050356 At the end of the B8011 Miavaig/Timsgarry road, north at 13/059343 towards Aird Uig. After two miles, you will see Loch Mheacleit to the left of the road.
Commentary The loch is 500 yds north/south by 400 yds wide, shallow and covering an area of approximately 35 acres. It is easily accessible from the Timsgarry/Aird Uig road. If you wish to walk out to fish remote Loch Nasavig (13/041368), it is best to approach Loch Mheacleit from the peat road leading to the north end. There are two other Lochs here which are worth a look: Loch Steishal (13/047355), to the south of Loch Mheacleit, with two satellite lochans, best approached by the peat road from 13/045349 to Durim Mor (74m) at 13/045362; and, to the north, Loch a'Bheannaich on the cliffs above Gallan Beag, close to the ruins of a 13th century chapel (13/040381). Access to Loch a'Bheannaich is from the peat road in Aird Uig at 13/050380. Visit the lochs as much for their outstanding setting as for their trout. The tiny cove at Geodha Nasavig (13/035367) is sheer paradise.
Fish Not glass case country, but plenty to keep you interested all day.
Flies & Tactics Bank fishing, and on Loch Mheacleit the south end produces best results, particularly where the burn enters from Loch Steishal. The south east shoreline can also be kind. The other lochs noted above are easily covered. Offer: Ke-He, Invicta, Alexandra.
Permission & Charges Apply Uig and Hamanavay Estate - Head Keeper. Tel: (01851) 672421 See also Loch a'Phealuir entry.

MOGLAVAT, Loch
Location & Access See Loch Langavat.

MOHAL BEAG, Loch
Location & Access 13/175257. Loch Mohal Beag lies to the south of the B8011 Garynahine/Miavaig road. Park at 13/159256 near the Scaliscro Lodge track and walk north-east past Loch an Eilein (13/162257) to reach the loch after 15 mins.
Commentary Loch Mohal Beag is a shallow, scattered water, covering an area of approx. 20 acres; twisting and turning over the moor to the north of Ben Mohal (207m) and Beinn a'Sgurain (170m). It drains east through Loch an Fhir Mhaoil (13/182260) to the Grimersta System and the sea at Loch Ceann Hulavig.
Fish Brown trout which average 8oz and a few larger fish of up to and over 2lb. After heavy rain and towards the end of the season there is a good chance of seatrout and the occasional salmon.
Flies & Tactics On the way out to Loch Mohal Beag, 'test' the numerous small, unnamed lochans round Loch an Eilein. They can produce a few surprises. Fish are encountered all round the shore of the main loch, but the most productive area is probably the north bank, from the narrows, east to where the flow runs into Loch an Fhir Mhaoil. Try: Soldier Palmer, Invicta, Alexandra.
Permission & Charges Fishing is free of charge to lodge guests who have priority. Non residents pay £12 per rod per day. Apply: Scaliscro Lodge, Scaliscro, Uig, Isle of Lewis HS2 9EL. Tel: (01851) 672325; Fax: (01851) 672393.

MOR AIRIGH NAN LINNTEAN, Loch See Loch Langavat.
MOR AN FHADA MHOIR, Loch See Loch Trealaval.
MOR AN IARUINN, Loch See Loch na Craoibhe (Shiltenish).
MOR BRAIGH AN TARAIN, Loch See Loch Raonasgail.
MOR, Loch See Loch Sgailler.
MOR NA CLIBHE, Loch See Loch Raonasgail.

MORSGAIL, Loch
Location & Access 13/137220 Access is from the B8011 Garynahine/Miavaig road at the head of Little Loch Roag, south along a private estate road which parallels the Morsgail River.
Commentary Morsgail Loch is the headwater of the

OS Map 13 — West Lewis & North Harris

Morsgail River and fishing rights are owned by Morsgail Estate. Apart from the river and loch, which are the principal fisheries, there are excellent trout lochs lying to the south, in Strath Ban. The watershed is Mointeach a'Loin where another system flows south to reach the sea in Loch Resort near Kinloch Resort. The north-flowing lochs are: Loch Ruairidh (13/129220) and Loch Traighidh (13/124212), to the west of Loch Morsgail; Loch Cragach (13/124212) and its myriad surrounding lochans; Loch Dubh (13/104209), Loch a'Tuath (13/118203), Loch na Faing (13/104210) and Loch Cleit Duastal (13/099206). The waters from these lochs are gathered together by Abhainn Cleit Duastal and Allt Bo Nighean Mhuirich and join the Abhainn a'Loin which flows into the south end of Loch Morsgail. Loch Beag Sheilabrie (13/131191) and its satellite lochan at 13/128191, on the north face of Sheilabrie (210m), also flow into Abhainn a'Loin. Loch nan Creaganan Groid (13/113198) flows south to Loch Leatha (13/108188), collecting Lochan A'Chleite Tuath (13/120188) and Loch nan Faoileag (13/109181) from the west slope of Sheilabrie along the way, reaching the sea by the shieling on the north shore of Loch Resort.

Fish The Morsgail System holds salmon and sea-trout but is entirely dependent upon rain to produce sport. In a good season, upwards of 70 salmon and over 100 sea-trout may be expected; although in recent years, and probably because of the proximity of fish farms, the number of migratory fish running the system has declined. All the estate lochs contain excellent quality brown trout, fish ranging from a few ounces to fish of up to and over 3lb in weight, but the average size is in the order of 8/10oz.

Flies & Tactics The River Morsgail and Abhainn a'Loin are easily fished from the bank and wading is not required. 'Stalk' the fish, from one point, lengthening line, rather that marching down the bank in the traditional fashion. Morsgail Loch, half a mile north/south by up to 400 yds wide, is fished from the boat, although bank fishing can also produce results as salmon often lie close to the margin. Reaching the other lochs noted above requires not inconsiderable effort, but all are readily fished from the bank and offer great sport. Sea-trout may also be caught in the sea at the head of Loch Resort. Flies that work, most of the time, include: Black Pennell, Clan Chief, Goat's Toe, Willie Gunn, Hairy Mary, Loch Ordie, Ke-He, Black Zulu, Soldier Palmer, Kate McLaren, Peter Ross, Dunkeld.

Permission & Charges Robin Davidson, Morsgail Estate, Morsgail, Isle of Lewis. For Lochs Traighidh and Na Faing apply to the Head Keeper, Uig & Hamanavay Estate, tel: 01851 672421. See also Loch a'Phealuir entry.

MORSGAIL, River See Loch Morsgail.
NA BEISTE, Loch See Loch Halladale.
NA BEISTE, Loch (Grimersta) See Loch Sgaire.
NA CAILLICH, Loch See Loch Raonasgail.
NA CARTACH, Loch See Loch na h-Inghinn.
NA CEANNAMHOIR, Loch See Loch Baravat (Great Bernera).

NA CISTE, Loch (Habost) See Loch na h-Inghinn.
NA CISTE, Loch (Langavat) See Loch Langavat.
NA CISTE, Loch (Scaliscro) See Loch Ruadh (North Scaliscro).
NA CISTE, Loch (Soval) See Loch Trealaval.
NA CISTE, Loch (Uig) See Loch Grunavat.
NA CLEAVAG, Loch See Loch a'Ghlinne.

NA CLIBHE, Loch
Location & Access 13/011246 Park where the Brenish river crosses the road, one mile south of Brenish at the end of the minor road leading south from Ardroil (13/050321).
Commentary An adventure day out amidst the grandeur of the West Lewis hills. A a stiff five miles, climbing to 300m, and exploring three small lochs along the way. Park non-fishing/hiking members of your tribe on the beach at Camas a'Mhoil (13/986256) where the Brenish river enters the sea.
Fish No monsters, simply great fun with hard-fighting brown trout. However, in spate conditions, and during June, there is a chance of sport with seatrout at the mouth of the Brenish river.
Flies & Tactics Follow the Brenish river up the hill to find Loch na Clibhe which is approximately 20 acres in extent. This is a classic, horseshoe-corrie lochan, surrounded by steep hills. The north and west shores are most productive, particularly where the feeder streams enter. Fifteen minutes south, between Taireval (186m) and the west slope of Laival a'Tuath (505m), is little Loch Uladale (13/009240), the headwater of the Abhainn Hotarol burn, and always worth a cast. Having done so, return to Loch na Clibhe and locate the feeder stream at the north-west corner of the loch. Follow this stream steeply up the glen to reach Loch Clibh Cracaval (13/020254), eight acres and lying at the highest point of the expedition. Descend from here by following the outlet stream (Allt nan Easan Geala) at the north end, round the north shoulder of Snodribie (200m). This delightful, crystal-clear stream eventually joins the Brenish river and leads back to the start point. Flies: Black Zulu, Soldier Palmer, Dunkeld.
Permission & Charges Apply Uig and Hamanavay Estate - Head Keeper. Tel: (01851) 672421. See Loch a'Phealuir entry.

NA CLOICH AIRDE, Loch See Loch Brinnaval.
NA COIRNISH, Loch See Loch Raonasgail.
NA CRAOBHAIG, Loch See Loch Uamasbroc
NA CRAOBHAIG, Loch (Great Bernera) See Loch Gobhlach.
NA CRAOBHAIG, Loch (Tamanavay) See Loch Raonasgail.
NA CRAOBHAIGE MOIRE, Loch See Loch Coirgavat.

NA CRAOIBHE, Loch (Shiltenish)
Location & Access 13/300182 Loch na Craoibhe lies to the south of the B8060 Shiltenish/Gravir road. Park just after the bend in the road at 13/287191 and walk the burn east to reach the first loch of the day, Loch Dubh (13/293190) after ten minutes. Loch na Craoibhe is a further ten minutes south from Loch Dubh.

West Lewis & North Harris
OS Map 13

Commentary There are four lochs here which offer a good day out in the hills to the south of Shiltenish, the largest water being Loch na Craoibhe - almost half a mile north/south by up to 300yds wide and covering an area of 50 acres.
Fish Good brown trout in the lochs and the chance of sport with seatrout from the north shore of Loch Erisort at 13/286197, the narrow inlet to the east of Shiltenish, and further east at 13/310195.
Flies & Tactics The west, south and south-east shores of Loch na Craoibhe are most productive, particularly in the vicinity of the inlet streams. Climb to little Loch Clach na h-Iolaire (13/306182) above the east shore of Loch na Craoibhe, before exploring the north-east shoreline of the main loch. Return north to the B8060 to have a cast in Loch Mor an Iaruinn (13/300195), immediately to the north of the road, prior to considering an assault on seatrout. Best flies: Soldier Palmer, Invicta, Alexandra.
Permission & Charges See Loch an Iar.

NA CREIGE FRAOICH, Loch See Loch na h-Airigh Uir.
NA CRICHE, Loch (Scaliscro) See Loch Uamasbroc.
NA CROIBHE, Loch (Soval) See Loch Trealaval.
NA FAING, Loch (Morsgail) See Loch Morsgail.
NA FAING, Loch (Scaliscro) See Loch Fhreunadail.
NA FAOIRBH, Loch See Loch Brinnaval.
NA AIRICH, Loch See Loch Raonasgail.

NA H-INGHINN, Loch
Location & Access 13/337172 A fine day out, hill walking and fishing a series of eight named and unnamed lochs and lochans to the south of Habost on the B8060 Shiltenish/Gravir road.
Commentary You will cover up to five miles across rough country and a compass and map are essential to find your way round. Leave Habost by the peat road at 13/324196 and walk south to find the first loch, Loch na Ciste (13/320182) after 15 mins. Climb due south from Loch na Ciste to locate Loch na Cartach (13/322172). After fishing Loch na Cartach, follow the inlet stream from the east bank up to the unnamed lochan at 13/325174, then east again to examine Loch Dubh (13/332173). From Loch Dubh, descend to Loch na h-Inghinn, the half-way point and time for lunch. Walk north to find the stream to the east of Loch Dubh and follow it down to Loch Ealaidh (13/333181). Leave Loch Ealaidh at the north end, walking north-east, crossing another stream, to locate Loch Chragol (13/325184). The last loch of the day is five minutes north-east from Loch Chragol, Loch an Fheoir (13/329198). The start point is half a mile north-west.
Fish Brown trout average 8oz with the possibility of a few larger fish of up to 1lb. There is also the chance of seatrout in the sea at 13/334198, between Habost and Kershader (13/341202).
Flies & Tactics The Lochs are readily covered from the shore. Do not wade. On Loch na Ciste, try the long promontory on the north shore. On Loch Chragol, concentrate along the south bank, paying strict attention to where the feeder stream enters. The other lochs are easily understood. First cast: Ke-He, Invicta, Peter Ross.

Permission & Charges See Loch an Iar.

NA H-IOLAIRE, Loch (Soval) See Loch Trealaval.
NA H-OLA, Loch See Loch Strandavat, Balallan.
NA LEARGA, Loch See Loch Uidemul.

NA MUILNE, Loch (Bosta)
Location & Access 13/147397 Loch na Muilne is easily accessible and lies adjacent to the west side of the Breaclete/Bosta road on the Island of Great Bernera.
Commentary Loch na Muilne is one of a number of lochs close to the Breaclete/Bosta road. The others are tiny Loch Ruig Sandavat (13/155379), Loch a'Chnuic (13/150384) and its satellite lochan to the south; Loch Tana (13/152387) and Loch Geal (13/150391). Immediately to the west of Loch Geal are three unnamed lochans which are worth a visit. On the branch road right to Croir, at 13/154392, are two more lochans which should be explored. All these waters are close to the road and it is possible to visit them during the course of a day. For a longer expedition, continue west from Bosta to the car park near the cemetery. Walk south along the line of the burn through a narrow glen to reach Loch a'Sgail (13/139393). The unnamed lochan to the west at 13/133398 should also be visited.
Fish Tout average 8oz.
Flies & Tactics All these waters are readily covered from the shore. Indeed, the best policy is to stay back from the bank to avoid spooking the fish, particularly on Loch a'Sgail which has some good trout which often lie close to the margin. First cast: Soldier Palmer, Grouse & Claret, Alexandra.
Permission & Charges See Loch a'Phealuir entry. Further information from: Sportsworld, 1 Francis Street, Stornoway, Isle of Lewis. Tel: (01851) 705464.

NA MUILNE, Loch (Gisla) See Loch Coirgavat.
NA MUILNE, Loch (Grimersta) See Loch Smuaisaval.
NA MUILNE, Loch (Loch nan Geadraisean) See Loch Breaclete.
NA MUILNE, Loch (Shiltenish) See Loch an Iar.
NA MUILNE, Loch (Tamanavay) See Loch Raonasgail.
NA PLAIDE, Loch See Grimersta River.
NAM BREAC, Loch (Laxay) See Loch an Eilean Liath.
NAM FAOILEAG, Loch See Loch Trealaval.
NAN ALLT RUADH, Lochan See Loch Grunavat
NAN CREAGANAN GROID, Loch See Loch Morsgail.

NAN EILEAN, Loch
Location & Access 13/070349 Park in Glen Valtos at 13/071344 on the B8011 Miavaig/Timsgarry road. Climb steeply south, following the outlet burn uphill to reach the loch after 15 mins.
Commentary Glen Valtos is a dark, forbidding glen, banked by steep cliffs. However, once on the moor, there are super views over the surrounding countryside and the option of walking further south to explore two small lochs on the west side of Flodraval Mor (180m); Dubh Lochan at 13/073327 and Loch a'Choin at 12/066334.

# West Lewis & North Harris

Fish Some quite good trout in Loch nan Eilean, but mostly fish which average 8oz.
Flies & Tactics Loch nan Eilean covers an area of approx. 12 acres and is easily fished from the shore. Also have a cast in the adjacent lochan a short step south-west. Walk south from Loch nan Eilean, following the line of the inlet burn, and then climb the hill to find Dubh Lochan in a remote corrie. After exploring Dubh Lochan and the nearby headwater lochan of the Abhainn Dubh Bheag burn, descend north-west to Loch a'Choin. Return north-east to Loch nan Eilean and the start point in Glen Valtos. Flies: Black Pennell, March Brown, Alexandra.
Permission & Charges See Loch a'Phealuir entry. For further information, contact: Sportsworld, 1 Francis Street, Stornoway, Isle of Lewis. Tel: (01851) 705464.

NAN EILEAN, Loch (Langavat) See Loch Langavat.
NAN EILEAN, Loch (Roineval) See Loch Trealaval.
NAN FAOILEAG, Loch (Morsgail) See Loch Morsgail.
NAN GEADRAISEAN, Loch See Loch Breaclete.
NAN LEARGA, Lochan See Loch Suirstavat.
NAN RAMH, Loch (Tamanavay) See Loch Raonasgail.
NAN SLIGEAN, Loch See Loch Halladale.
NAN UIDHEAN, Loch (Tamanavay) See Loch Raonasgail.
NAN UIDHEAN, Loch (Uig) See Loch Grunavat.
NASAVIG, Loch See Loch Mheacleit.

NISHAVAT, Loch
Location & Access 13/169350. Loch Nishavat lies to the east of Barraglom but is best approached from the road from Barraglom to Kirkibost to the south. Park at 13/170345.
Commentary An easily accessible, attractive loch. The loch is approximately half a mile north/south by up to 200yds wide and surrounding hills give some protection from the prevailing winds.
Fish Brown trout which average 8oz, and the chance of seatrout and salmon towards the end of the season and after heavy rain.
Flies & Tactics Comfortable bank fishing, but weed can be a problem as the season advances. Fish may be taken throughout the length of this long, narrow water, but the north end is probably the most productive area, particularly where the inlet stream enters on the north-east shore. Offer the residents: Ke-He, Grouse & Claret, Peter Ross.
Permission & Charges Contact: Sportsworld, 1 Francis Street, Stornoway, Isle of Lewis. Tel: (01851) 705464.

OYAVAT, Loch See Loch an Iar.
RAMALACH, Loch See Loch Uidemul.

RANGAVAT, Loch (Ardroil)
Location & Access 13/042310 After passing Uig Lodge (13/055332) and the Fhorsa river, park at Ardroil (13/050321) and walk south, climbing up the burn to explore Loch Rangavat and a series of unnamed lochans on the hill along the way.
Commentary This is splendid country and there is an excellent chance of seeing golden eagle, raven and buzzard during the course of the day. These lochs are infrequently fished. Another option, if time is limited or supper demanded, is to drive west to fish Loch Scaslavat (13/025316) which lies immediately to the north of the road by Aird Mheadhonach (13/015322). This is a substantial body of water covering an area of 40 acres, close to Uig Sands and the outlet of Abhainn Caslavat burn.
Fish Large numbers of small trout in the hill lochs which average 6-8oz. Loch Scaslavat, which is over 60ft deep, has some larger fish, and there is always the possibility of seatrout at the mouth of the burn.
Flies & Tactics On the hill lochs, the most important tactic is to stay back from the bank to avoid spooking the fish. Otherwise, trout here are not particular and readily take most patterns of fly. On Loch Scaslavat, the north shore produces best results. Avoid wading. Start with: Black Zulu, Soldier Palmer, Silver Butcher.
Permission & Charges Rangavat (brown trout): apply Head keeper, Uig & Hamanavay Estate. Tel:01851 672421. Scaslavat: apply Kenny Mackay, Keepers Cottage, Uig, Isle of Lewis. Tel: (01851) 672250. See also Loch a'Phealuir entry.

RAONASGAIL, Loch
Location & Access 13/037270 A major expedition, starting from the peat road near the gravel pit by Uig Sands at 13/0353156, where Abhainn Caslavat (known locally as the Red River) flows into Camas Uig bay. At the end of the peat road, descend south to cross the Stockgill river then climb the hill to reach Loch Brinnaval (13/030295) after 30 mins. Skirt the north shore of Loch Brinnaval and, keeping to the high ground, contour round the east side of Brinnaval (213m) to find Loch Mor na Clibhe (13/034282) after 20 mins. Explore the north shore of Loch Mor na Clibhe. Loch Raonasgail is a further ten minutes south.
Commentary One of the most dramatic and exciting places to fish in West Lewis. For those who like a challenge, climb the gully between Tarain (411m) and Tahaval (515m) on the east shore of Loch Raonasgail to fish the corrie loch on the saddle, Loch Mor Braigh an Tarain (13/049270). Loch Raonasgail lies at the north end of a steep-sided glen and the path climbs south between Cracaval (514m) and Teinnasval (497m) before picking up the course of the Abhainn Cheann Chuisil burn and descending to the sea loch of the same name at 13/035214. Walk round the east shore of the sea loch to the mouth of the Tamanavay river (13/040201). Along the way south through the glen, at Loch a' Chama (13/033240), leave the track and angle steeply uphill on the west shoulder of Tamanaisval (467m), descending just as steeply to the shores of Loch Dibadale (13/052235). Loch Dibadale is half a mile north/south and 250yds wide, shallow and sheltered. From June onwards and after heavy rain, the loch can contain salmon and seatrout which enter from the Tamanavay river. The loch may also be approached, more gently, from the south, but either way it is still a long, tiring hike. To the east, on Coilleigar (90m) are a number of small hill lochs: Loch na Muilne (13/046217), Loch Coilleigar (13/044212),

West Lewis & North Harris
OS Map 13

Lochanan Cragach (13/058215), with its satellite waters - all of which hold trout. North-west, amidst the broken corries of Griomaval (497m) lie two of the most remote lochs in the Hebrides: the Dubh Loch (13/011224) and Loch Braighe Griomaval (13/017223) - both of which contain very pretty little trout. Fishing from the shore at sea loch Cheann Chuisil can be very good for seatrout, as is the mouth of the Tamanavay river. The Tamanavay River is very much a spate stream and has been well keepered for the past 15 years. The most accessible loch on the system, relatively speaking, is Loch Grunavat (13/043196) on the hill overlooking the estuary, but it holds only brown trout. In recent years the estate have improved this stream. From June onwards salmon and seatrout run the mile and a half long river to reach Loch na Craobhaig (13/065205). Loch na Craobhaig is a large, shallow water extending across the moor for a distance of one mile and almost half a mile wide. It is joined eastwards by a short stream to Loch Cro Criosdaig (13/085205), which is slightly smaller than its neighbour. The headwater loch of the system is Loch Benisval (13/087190) which is almost one mile north/south by half a mile wide. There are two small lochs on the hill to the south-west of Loch Benisval which should not be ignored: Loch a' Fhraoich (13/083182) and its neighbour to the south, Loch Creagach (13/083179). South from the Tamanavay river, between Ainneval (166m) and the long inlet of sea loch Resort, on Aird Mhor and Corcasmol (117m), there are more than a dozen named and unnamed lochans to explore. The largest of these lochs is Loch Bodavat (13/062190) which is joined north to Loch nan Ramh (13/073198) and Loch a'Gharaidh (13/073201). This system, including Loch na h-Airigh (13/063177), enters the sea on Loch Resort at Creag an Fhitich (13/062173) and there is always the possibility of a seatrout or salmon. The moor to the north of Loch Bodavat and east of Loch nan Ramh is scattered with a maze of tiny, unnamed lochans, some of which can produce surprisingly good trout - small fish, stocked from the adjacent larger waters, and left to grow. East of the outlet stream from Loch Bodavat, lies tiny Lochan Cleit an Eoin (13/057181). Loch Snehaval (13/051181) is five minutes east from Loch Cleit an Eoin and feeds a small stream which enters the sea at Mol Tealasavay. Loch na Caillich (13/049189) with its delightful scrub-covered island, and Loch an Ath Ruaidh (13/053185) are on the hill to the north of Loch Snehaval, whilst Loch Snehaval Beag (13/051174) is ten minutes south. Loch Lamadale (13/041175) and Loch a' Chas Bhraighe Ruaidh (13/043173) are a stumble west up a rough, narrow glen. The Aird Mhor lochs: Loch nan Uidhean (13/031170) and little Loch na Coirnish (13/021168) on the cliffs above Geodha nan Sgarbh, are perhaps the most inviting, not only because of their remote position, but also because of their scenic beauty. The nearby cove between Rubha Glas and Rubha nan Uan (13/025165), where a short stream enters, can produce sport with seatrout. Approach from Mol Tealasavay.
Fish Just about everything. Brown trout from 6oz up to fish of over 2lbs, seatrout from 1lb 8oz, and salmon from 6lbs upwards. There is also excellent sea fishing, both from the rocks and from numerous coves and beaches.
Flies & Tactics A compass and map are essential to find your way around, and you must make sure someone knows when you are going and where you expect to return. Flies: take along an assortment of bushy bob flies and standard patterns such as Black Pennell, Grouse & Claret, March Brown, Greenwell's Glory, Silver Butcher, Silver Invicta, Peter Ross, Dunkeld, Teal Blue & Silver.
Permission & Charges For permission apply to: the Head Keeper, Uig & Hamanavay Estate, Tel. (01851) 672421. See also Loch a'Phealuir entry.

RIBAVAT, Loch See Loch Stacsavat.
ROINEVAL, Loch See Loch Trealaval.
RUADH A'DEAS, Loch (Langavat) See Loch Langavat.

RUADH GHEURE DUBH MHOR, Loch
Location & Access 13/190273 Park on the B8011 Garynahine/Miavaig road at 13/186278 and follow the inlet stream south to reach the loch after five minutes.
Commentary An easily accessible loch, half a mile north/south, 350yds wide, covering an area of 50 acres. The surrounding hills offer some protection from the prevailing wind and the loch is joined through Loch an Fhir Mhaoil (13/182260) to the Grimersta system.
Fish Brown trout average in the order of 8-10oz, with a few larger specimens as well. After heavy rain and towards the end of the season there is always the possibility of seatrout and salmon.
Flies & Tactics Bank fishing and it is best to stay ashore. Fish tend to lie close and wading only scares them. The south end of the loch produces best results, particularly down the south-west shore in the vicinity of the island. The bay in the south-east corner is also good. Offer: Black Zulu, March Brown, Peter Ross.
Permission & Charges See Grimersta River entry.

RUADH, Loch (North Scaliscro)
Location & Access 13/139270 Immediately to the west of the Scaliscro Lodge road.
Commentary On the private estate road to Scaliscro Lodge from the B8011 Garynahine/Miavaig road. Easily accessible and hard to resist the temptation of a cast when passing. For a more vigorous temptation, hike north-east up the south slopes of Skeun (200m) to explore Loch na Ciste (13/149271) and Loch Skeun (13/149277) both of which seldom see an artificial fly from one season to the next.
Fish Expect good fun with bright little trout which average 8oz. Loch Ruadh is joined to the sea below Scariscro Lodge and, after heavy rain, can hold seatrout.
Flies & Tactics Straightforward bank fishing and all these small waters are easily covered from the shore. Offer them Black Zulu, Greenwell's Glory, Dunkeld.
Permission & Charges Scaliscro Lodge guests have priority. Bank fishing may be available at £12 per rod per day. Apply: Scaliscro Lodge, Scaliscro, Uig, Isle of

OS Map 13 — West Lewis & North Harris

Lewis HS2 9EL. Tel: (01851) 672325; Fax: (01851) 672393.

RUADH, Loch (South Scaliscro) See Loch Suirstavat.
RUADH MEADHONACH, Loch See Loch Langavat.
RUAIRIDH, Loch (Morsgail) See Loch Morsgail.
RUIG SANDAVAT, Loch See Loch na Muilne (Bosta).

SANDAVAT, Loch
Location & Access 13/117290 Loch Sandavat lies immediately adjacent to the east of the B8011 road north from the township of Enaclete (13/122283).
Commentary An easily accessible loch covering an area of approximately 20 acres. The surrounding scenery is stunning, and you should look out particularly for the 'lazy beds' (the old method of cultivation, using seaweed as fertiliser on furrow ridges) in the fields overlooking Little Loch Roag. To the north of Loch Sandavat, and adjacent to the west of the road, is another easily accessible water, Loch Croistean (13/112295), over half a mile north/south by approx 100yds wide. Loch Croistean is sheltered from the prevailing winds by Ollashal (206m) to the west, and Sheaval (120m) to the east.
Fish Something for supper, rather than for the glass case, but the chance of a few larger specimens in Loch Croistean.
Flies & Tactics Ideal for a few casts before setting off west for more serious business in the hills, but great fun. Fish may be taken from all round the shore. Fling: Black Zulu, Invicta, Peter Ross.
Permission & Charges For brown trout fishing contact the Head Keeper, Uig & Hamanavay Estate, tel: 01851 672421. See also Loch a'Phealuir entry.

SANDAVAT, Loch (Brenish)
Location & Access 13/007270 Park at Brenish (13/003264), on the minor road which leads south from Ardroil (13/050321). Walk east up the hill along the line of the Allt Geislir burn to reach the loch after 20 minutes.
Commentary An excellent loch, rarely fished and lying in a dramatic setting on the western slopes of Mealisval (574m), the highest mountain in West Lewis. The loch is generally circular, shallow, and covers an area of 35 acres. Less taxing, and more easily accessible, is another loch, Loch Greivat, to the west which is approached from a peat track north of where the Allt Geislir burn crosses the road. Both waters may be explored during the course of the day. There is the possibility of seatrout from the shore at Camas Islivig (13/988279) to the north.
Fish Trout average 8oz, but there are larger specimens, particularly in Loch Greivat.
Flies & Tactics Easy bank fishing on both lochs. Don't forget to have a cast in the unnamed lochan above Camas Islivig at 13/985278. Offer the inhabitants: Ke-He, Grouse and Claret, Kingfisher Butcher.
Permission & Charges For brown trout fishing apply: the Head Keeper, Uig & Hamanavay Estate, tel: 01851 672421. See also Loch a'Phealuir entry.

SANDAVAT, Loch (Mangersta) See Loch Brinnaval.

SCANADALE, Loch See Loch Grunavat.
SCHOOL, Loch See Loch Baravat (Great Bernera).

SGAILLER, Loch
Location & Access 13/086353 Leave the B8011 in Miavaig (13/085346) and drive north past the doctor's surgery towards the township of Cliff (13/083360). The loch is on the left of the road.
Commentary Easily accessible roadside loch, 600yds long, casting distance wide, covering about 12 acres. There are a number of unnamed lochans on the hill to the west of Loch Sgailler and these are best approached from the peat road at Cliff. This convenient peat road also gives access to good lochs on Forsnaval (205m): Loch Mor (13/072363) to the north, and Loch a'Gheoidh (13/076350) to the south. Loch Mor has a small satellite lochan which is also worth a cast on the way by. The Loch Mor peat track ends close to the most remote loch in this group, Loch Deireadh Banaig (13/065370), lying in a shallow hollow between Rubha Mor (160m) to the north and Forsnaval to the south.
Fish Expect trout averaging 8oz in Loch Sgailler with a few of up to 1lb. Loch Mor is breakfast-time fishing. Loch a'Gheoidh will test your skill and tax your patience, but has fish of up to and over 1lb in weight. The other lochs in the vicinity all provide sport with trout averaging 8-10oz.
Flies & Tactics These waters are easily fished from the bank and wading is not advised. If the fates are unkind and trout hard to move, resort to the magnificent beach at Valtos (13/084365). Splash in the shallows, but do not swim - there are dangerous currents. For the trout, offer: Loch Ordie, March Brown, Black Pennell.
Permission & Charges Apply Uig and Hamanavay Estate - Head Keeper. Tel: (01851) 672421. See also Loch a'Phealuir entry.

SGAIRE, Loch
Location & Access 13/197285 Easily accessible from either the B8011 Garynahine/Timsgarry road or from the B8059 Garynahine/Earshader road.
Commentary Loch Sgaire is used to supply freshet water to the Grimersta system through Loch Faoghail an Tuim (8/203280). The loch is three quarters of a mile north/south by up to 300yds wide, island-dressed at the narrow, south end. To the north of Loch Sgaire, and joined to it by a small stream, is Loch Speireag (13/195296), and in the hills to the west, Loch Beag na Beiste (13/185295) which is surrounded by a number of tiny, unnamed lochans, five minutes further west from Loch Beag na Beiste is Loch na Beiste (13/180297).
Fish Loch Sgaire has brown trout which average 8-10oz and good numbers of larger fish up to and over 1lb in weight. There is also a chance of seatrout and salmon. The hill lochs mentioned contain pretty, well-marked brown trout which rise readily to the fly.
Flies & Tactics Loch Sgaire is fished from the bank, although a boat may be available from time to time from the Grimersta Estate. However, bank fishing brings excellent results, particularly in the island-scattered south bay and along the west shoreline. The hill lochs are easily covered from the bank. Do not wade.

West Lewis & North Harris — OS Map 13

Offer the residents: Black Zulu, March Brown, Dunkeld.
Permission & Charges See Grimersta River entry.

SGEIREACH, Lochan (Great Bernera) See Loch Baravat (Great Bernera).
SGEIREACH, Lochanan See Loch Grunavat.
SGIBACLEIT, Loch See OS Map 14
SHIELING, Loch (Great Bernera) See Loch Gobhlach.
SKEUN, Loch See Loch Ruadh (North Scaliscro).

SMUAISAVAL, Loch
Location & Access 13/200300 Loch Smuaisaval lies between the B8059 Garynahine/Earshader road the minor road from the B8011 at Grimersta leading west to Linshader. It may be approached from either west or east. Decide which depending upon wind direction. Loch na Muilne (8/210307), immediately adjacent to the west side of the Linshader road, is also worth a few casts and is ideal for beginners to the gentle art or if fishing time is limited.
Commentary A first class loch in a delightful setting covering 70 acres; three quarters of a mile north/south by up to 400yds wide across the north bay. The loch offers ample shelter from high winds, being protected to the east by Smuaisaval (94m), and to the west by Cleite na Beiste (150m).
Fish Trout average 8-10oz and are of good quality. There are much larger fish as well, of up to and over 4lb in weight, but they are difficult to tempt.
Flies & Tactics Wind direction will dictate which bank you fish but, in general, expect sport from all round the shore. The south bay, in the vicinity of the islands, is a good place to begin, particularly where the feeder stream enters at the south-east shore. At the north end of the loch, concentrate your effort round the north-west shore, in the large bay and by the inlet stream from Loch Collaval (8/202312). Loch Collaval also offers good sport - and welcome shelter from the wind. Wading is dangerous on all these lochs. Stay ashore.
Flies: Ke-He, Black Zulu, Silver Butcher.
Permission & Charges See Grimersta River entry.

SNEHAVAL BEAG, Loch See Loch Raonasgail.
SNEHAVAL, Loch See Loch Raonasgail.
SOVAL, Loch See Os Map 14
SPAGACH, Loch See Loch Uamasbroc.
SPEIREAG, Loch See Loch Sgaire.
SPEIREIG, Loch See Loch Fada (Laxay)
SROINE MOIRE, Loch See Loch Uamasbroc.

STACSAVAT, Loch
Location & Access 13/064317 Easily accessible from the road to the south of Uig Lodge at 13/057323. The loch is at the head of the Fhorsa River.
Commentary Loch Stacsavat is the principal fishery on the Fhorsa River System and covers an area of some 60 acres. The loch is shallow, nearly half a mile north/south by up to 400 yds wide. A short stream flows in from Loch Suainaval (13/068290) to the south. Uig sands lie at the mouth of the river and the area is one of outstanding natural beauty with a wide variety of flora and fauna. The most accessible of the hill lochs lie close to the west side of the road by the Fhorsa River: Loch Camasord (13/055311) and Loch Ribavat (13/055315), with tiny Loch a'Gheoidh (13/053315) to the west. These lochs provide an non-taxing, good day out. To reach the other hill lochs, park at the south end of Loch Stacsavat and follow the track south west up the hill to an unnamed lochan at 13/061307. This is joined to another unnamed lochan five minutes south west at 13/059304. From this lochan, walk south over the moor for ten minutes to reach Loch a'Bheannain (13/058299). Three inlet streams enter Loch a'Bheannain at the south end. Follow the middle stream west and south, climbing steeply between Flodraskarve Mor (238m) and Bheannan a'Deas (252m) to find a remote, unanamed lochan at 13/061290. Retrace your route back to the start point.
Fish Loch Stacsavat is an excellent salmon fishery and generally holds fish from June to the end of the season in October. There are also brown trout which average 8oz, but some of the unnamed lochans have larger trout of up to and over 1lb in weight.
Flies & Tactics Boat fishing on Loch Stacsavat and the salmon tend to lie close to the margins. The south east bay is perhaps the best area, but the west shore can also produce results. The hill lochs are easily fished from the bank and trout are taken from all round the shore. Avoid wading, it only scares the fish out into the middle of the loch. On Loch Stacsavat, use Black Pennell, March Brown, Clan Chief, Loch Ordie, Soldier Palmer, Goat's Toe, Silver Invicta, Green Highlander, Black Doctor. For the hill lochs, Black Zulu, Grouse & Claret, Peter Ross.
Permission & Charges For casual day lets, contact Kenny Mackay, Keepers Cottage, Uig, Isle of Lewis. Tel: (01851) 672250. Trout fishing is approximately £15 per rod per day. Uig Lodge is let by Finlyson Hughes, 29 Barossa Place, Perth PH1 5EP. Tel: (01738) 30926 Fax: (01738) 39017. The lodge sleeps up to sixteen people and costs from £500 per week in May and June with trout fishing. Thereafter, the cost is from £2500 per week for the lodge with salmon and trout fishing. For brown trout fishing on Loch Ribavat apply: the Head Keeper, Uig & Hamanavay Estate, tel: 01851 672421.

STEISHAL, Loch See Loch Mheaclait.

STRANDAVAT, Loch (Balallan)
Location & Access 13/256194 Easily accessible and immediately to the north of the A859 Stornoway/Tarbert road, two and a half miles south from Balallan.
Commentary A long, narrow water, extending one and a half miles north/south by up to 250yds wide across the south bay and covering an area of some 120 acres. Step west from Loch Strandavat to have a cast in Loch Airigh a'Ghille Ruaidhe (13/242183) and its satellite lochans. If still supperless, return to the road and cross south to explore Loch a'Mhaide (13/258180), then head north to Loch na h-Ola (13/263188), approaching from the Eishken road at 13/265190.

OS Map 13 — West Lewis & North Harris

Fish Trout in Loch Strandavat and Loch Airigh a'Ghille Ruaidhe average 8oz, but there are plenty of them and a few larger specimens as well. Towards the end of the season, and after heavy rain, there is also the possibility of salmon and seatrout which enter from Loch Erisort via the Abhainn Mhor. Loch a'Mhaide trout are less cooperative, but the loch holds fish of up to and over 1lb. Loch na h-Ola generally provides a decent meal.

Flies & Tactics Bank fishing all round and on Loch Strandavat concentrate your activity down the east shore, from 13/255199 south. The south-east and south-west bank can also be productive, but the north-west shore is very shallow. The best chance of autumn salmon and seatrout is at the north end of the loch, but it is difficult to fish due to extensive weed growth. Seatrout may also be encountered in the sea, at the head of Loch Erisort (13/275197). The other waters noted above are easily covered from the shore. Offer them: Loch Ordie, Soldier Palmer, Black Pennell.

Permission & Charges See Laxay River (Head keeper 01851 830202).

SUAINAVAL, Loch

Location & Access 13/068290 Turn south from the Uig Lodge/Ardroil road at 13/057323 and follow the track for one and a half miles, past Loch Stacsavat (13/064317), to park by the wier at the north end of the loch.

Commentary Loch Suainaval is one of the largest lochs in Lewis, almost three miles north/south by up to half a mile wide across the middle bay. This is a deep loch, falling to some 200 ft, and it can be very stormy with the surrounding hills acting as a wind tunnel. Nevertheless, Loch Suainaval is a most attractive, dramatic loch to fish. The scenery is magnificent, as are Uig Sands by Camas Uig bay, exactly where to park any non-fishing members of your party. There is even a small, nine-hole golf course by the Lodge.

Fish Ferox trout in the depths, brown trout from 8oz up to and over 2lb, and the chance of salmon.

Flies & Tactics Boat fishing is most productive and helps mightily in getting round this large expanse of water. Bank fishing can also produce results, but upon no account wade. The north east bay, below Suainaval (429m), is a good place to start. The south end of the loch, where two feeder burns enter, is also excellent. Down the west shore, arrange your drift about ten yards from the bank and concentrate mightily where the ten burns enter the loch along this shoreline. Offer: Blue Zulu, Soldier Palmer, Peter Ross.

Permission & Charges For casual day lets, contact Kenny Mackay, Keepers Cottage, Uig, Isle of Lewis. Tel: (01851) 672250. Trout fishing is approximately £15 per rod per day. Uig Lodge is let by Finlyson Hughes, 29 Barossa Place, Perth PH1 5EP. Tel: (01738) 30926 Fax: (01738) 39017. The lodge sleeps up to sixteen people. Prices on application

SUIRSTAVAT, Loch

Location & Access 13/150253 Immediately adjacent to the north of the B8011 Garynahine/Miavaig road.

Commentary Loch Suirstavat is some 700yds north/south by up to 250yds east/west. For the angler who enjoys something more exciting, follow the inlet stream to Loch Suirstavat (River Suirstavat) south-east over the moor to find Loch Ruadh (13/165242), Lochan nan Learga (13/158236) and tiny Lochan Dubh (13/154236). Whilst in this wonderful parish, continue south to explore Loch a'Sguair (13/169230). This is golden eagle country, surrounded by dramatic peaks: Ben Mohal (207m) to the north, and Caultrashal Beag (226m) and Caultrashal Mor (228m) to the west and south.

Fish Seatrout in Loch Suirstavat and, possibly, after heavy rain, in Loch Ruadh. The other waters contain good brown trout which average 6-8oz, but Loch a'Sguair also contains a few larger specimens of up to and over 1lb in weight.

Flies & Tactics Fish lie close to the shore on Loch Suirstavat and the west bay, by the island, is a good starting point. From Loch Ruadh, follow the inlet stream south for 15 mins, over the watershed, to find Loch a' Sguair. Fish clockwise round Loch a' Sguair and then climb north-west to reach Lochan nan Learga and Lochan Dubh. Return to the B8011 from Lochan Dubh by skirting the north-east slopes and crags of Caultrashal Beag, descending to the River Suirstavat. In spate conditions the river can also be productive. Try: Loch Ordie, Grouse & Claret, Kingfisher Butcher.

Permission & Charges For further information, contact: Scaliscro Estate (Tel. Scaliscro Lodge 01851 672325)

SUIRSTAVAT, River See Loch Suirstavat.
TANA, Loch (Great Bernera) See Loch na Muilne (Bosta).
TANA NA GILE RUAIDHE, Loch See Loch Trealaval.
TODALE, River See Loch a'Phealuir.
TRAIGHIDH, Loch See Loch Morsgail.
TRIALAVAT, Loch (Valtos) See Loch Linish.

TREALAVAL, Loch

Location & Access 13/275235 Loch Trealaval is best approached from Balallan, by the peat road near the school which leads north from the A859 Stornoway/Arivruaich at 13/285207. Although in terms of distance it is only one and a half miles to the loch, detours are required to circumvent other waters along the way. Loch Trealaval is a complicated maze of bays, narrows and crooked corners. It extends over the moor for a distance of some three miles; linked in the west to Loch Fadagoa (13/245233), Loch Roineval (13/236224), Loch nan Eilean (13/232234) and Loch Tana na Gile Ruaidhe (13/236255). To the east, Loch Trealaval is joined to Loch nam Faoileag (13/285235) and Loch na h-Iolaire (13/287244). Loch an Drunga (13/265247), Loch a'Bhroma (13/252241), Loch Mor an Fhada Mhoir (13/256257), and Loch na Ciste (13/246253) lie to the north, between Trealaval (121m) and Fada Mor (96m). South from Loch Trealaval, and flowing into it, are Loch Cuil Airigh a'Flod (13/272223), known locally as Loch a'Mhaide, Loch Airigh na Ceardaich (13/280226), Loch Cuthaig (13/275214) and Loch Ibheir (13/275214). Loch na

West Lewis & North Harris
OS Map 13

Croibhe (13/285219), Loch an Tomain (13/259213) and Loch an Sgath (13/252214) flow south to the sea at Loch Erisort.

Commentary To properly explore all these lochs would take several seasons and a compass and map are essential to find your way round. Make sure you leave word where you are going and when you expect to return. Loch Trealaval is the source of the River Laxay and water from Trealaval and its surrounding lochs is used to provide back-up flow in dry conditions and after spates. All these lochs contain brown trout which vary in size from 4oz up to fish of over 3lb in weight. The interconnecting streams between the lochs can be difficult to ford, particularly after heavy rain, however, there are a few recognised, safe crossing places. The easiest approach to the lochs north of Loch Trealaval is by the crossing at 13/257235. There are other crossing places at 13/235228, between Loch an Eilean to the north and Loch Roineval to the south. The wide stream between Loch Roineval and Loch Fadagoa, to the east, may be crossed at 13/238228 and at 13/242231. Otherwise, you are on your own and take great care, particularly after heavy rain. Soval Estate have boats on a number of the best trout lochs, including Loch Trealaval, but the majority of these waters are fished from the bank and wading is not advisable. Stay safely ashore at all times. Fish tend to lie close and are easily covered. Loch nan Eilean is a very attractive water, scattered with delightful little islands and the north end is most productive with a good chance of trout of up to and over 1lb 8oz in weight. Loch Roineval trout average 8oz. Loch Fadagoa is two miles north/south and up to almost half a mile wide. It contains some really excellent trout, including fish of over 3lb. The narrows to the north, by the islands, and the bay leading to Loch Trealaval are the most productive areas. There are a number of unnamed lochans between Loch an Eilean and Loch Fadagoa at 13/246238 which should not be missed. This also applies to the lochans north and east from Loch a'Bhroma at 13/255242, 13/255249 and 13/256250. Loch a'Bhroma has good quality trout which average 8-10oz and a few of up to 1lb as well. Whilst visiting the north arm of Loch Trealaval, park the boat at 13/275240, by a feeder burn, and walk west for five minutes to examine an unnamed lochan at 13/272240. Further south, park again and walk over to explore the lochan at 13/276248. Both hold good trout.

Fish The lochs to the south of Loch Trealaval are the most easily accessible, relatively speaking, and all offer the chance of some nice trout. Loch na Croibhe, to the east of the Balallan peat road, has fish averaging 6-8oz, but larger trout of up to and over 1lb are sometimes caught as well. The best fish here are in Loch Cuthaig, three quarters of a mile east/west by up to 400yds wide and covering an area of approx. 90 acres. Wading is possible along the south shore which is the most productive area. The trout in the other lochs average 6-8oz.

Flies & Tactics Most flies produce results, but the best patterns include my old favourites: Black Pennell, Black Zulu, Blue Zulu, Ke-He, Loch Ordie, Soldier Palmer, Greenwell's Glory, March Brown, Grouse & Claret, Alexandra, Peter Ross, Silver Butcher, Dunkeld.

Permission & Charges See Laxay River (Head keeper 01851 830202)

TUNGAVAT, Loch

Location & Access 13/161287 Park by the roadside lochan at 13/172271 on the B8011 Garynahine/Timsgarry road. Keeping to the west side of the burn, walk north along the slopes of Ben Mocacleit (176m) to reach the loch after a walk of about 30 mins.

Commentary This is a demanding, six-mile expedition over rough ground, including some severe work on the oars, visiting seven named and unnamed lochs along the way. There are five, small unnamed lochans to the south and east of Loch Tungavat, which are worth a cast: at 13/159279, 13/163289, 13/164280, and on the hill to the west, 13/168284 and 13/170285. From the north end of Loch Tungavat, continue up the glen for ten minutes to reach Loch Ahaltair (13/155298). Fish round the east shore of Loch Ahaltair and walk north to Loch Tana (13/157303) and Loch a'Mhairt (13/160304). From Loch a'Mhairt, visit narrow Loch Crocach (13/157307) and pause for lunch. Return south from Loch Crocach, fishing the west shore of Loch Ahaltair, with a five minute detour west from the shieling for a cast in the unnamed lochan at 13/153298. Continue south along the west shore of Loch Tungavat to return to the start point.

Fish Brown trout in Loch Tungavat average 10-12oz and in the other lochs, 8oz. There are larger fish as well and the possibility of salmon and seatrout towards the end of the season.

Flies & Tactics There are boats on Loch Tungavat and Loch Ahaltair, available to guests at Scaliscro Lodge Hotel, but bank fishing can be just as productive. Loch Tungavat is the largest water, three quarters of a mile long by up to 500yds wide, and the west and north shore are best, particularly amongst the bays and little islands. Reading the other lochs mentioned above is simple and fish are taken from all round the shoreline. Offer the residents: Loch Ordie, Soldier Palmer, Peter Ross.

Permission & Charges Details from Scaliscro Lodge Hotel, Scaliscro, Uig, Isle of Lewis. Tel: (01851) 672325; Fax: (01851) 672393. cost to non residents, £12 per day.

UAMASBROC, Loch

Location & Access 13/140284 Loch Uamasbroc lies to the north-east of Scalisgro Lodge Hotel, above the shores of Little Loch Roag. Reaching the loch involves a stiff, 20 minute, uphill hike to the north of Skeun (180m), and there are eight further named and unnamed lochs which can be included to make an exciting, full-day fishing adventure.

Commentary From Loch Uamasbroc, follow the inlet stream north to fish the unnamed loch at 13/140285, known locally as Loch Beag na Muilne. Walk the inlet burn on the east shore of Loch Beinn Charnain up the glen to the tiny, unnamed lochan on Beinn Charnain (175m). Contour north round the crags to find Loch na Sroine Moire at 13/146295. After exploring Loch

OS Maps 13-14 — Tarbert & Loch Seaforth

Tarbert and Loch Seaforth

na Sroine Moire, descend to fish the unnamed lochan at 13/145293, known locally as Loch Spagach, then west again to Loch na Craobhaig (13/140293) and its small satellite lochan to the south. Continue over the hill and descend south to Loch Beag na Muilne, with the chance to catch the ones that got away on the outward journey, and a few casts in Loch na Criche (13/138286) before returning to Scaliscro. The views and wildlife along the way make this an unforgettable expedition.
Fish Excellent quality trout with Loch na Craobhaig and Loch Spagach holding fish of up to 2lb in weight. Loch Uamasbroc has smaller fish, averaging 6-8oz, but a few larger specimens of up to 1lb; whilst Loch Beag na Muilne has good numbers of hard-fighting trout in the order of 12-14oz.
Flies & Tactics A boat is available on Loch Uamasbroc, the other lochs are all comfortably fished from terra firma and easily covered from the bank. Avoid wading. Try: Black Pennell, Greenwell's Glory, Silver Invicta.
Permission & Charges See Loch Tungavat.

UAMASBROC, Loch (Uig) See Loch Grunavat.

UIDEMUL, Loch
Location & Access 13/978145. Not easy, unless you have your own boat, or are renting a holiday cottage on the Island of Scarp. Approach from the pier (13/989124) to the north of Hushinish at the end of the B887.
Commentary Loch Uidemul is the largest loch on Scarp and covers an area of approx. 20 acres. It drains Loch Rumalach (13/979147), a smaller loch to the north. There are two further Scarp lochs, both tiny and of limited fishing interest; Loch na Learga (13/966161) and Loch Braigh an t-Sidhean (13/960150). The only dwellings on the island are clustered round the landing pier. Loch Uidemul is reached by hiking over craggy Beinn fo Thuath (179m). The other lochs lie west amidst the wilderness of rocky corries round Sron Romul (308m) and Sron Udemul (250m).
Fish Modest brown trout which average 8oz in weight.
Flies & Tactics Everything about Scarp is superlative - scenery, wildlife, flora, fauna and beaches. Loch Uidemul is easily fished from the shore and the larger, north bay, is the most productive area. Begin your assault in the vicinity of the two small islands. Flies: Blue Zulu, Soldier Palmer, Alexandra.
Permission & Charges for further information, contact: Sportsworld, 1 Francis Street, Stornoway, Isle of Lewis. Tel: (01851) 705464.

ULADALE, Loch (Brenish) See Loch Na Clibhe.
ULAPOLL, Loch See Loch Fada (Laxay).
UPPER HALLADALE, Loch See Loch Halladale.
VALTOS, Loch See River Laxay.

Isles of Lewis & Harris Introduction
No matter where you fish in Lewis and Harris, permission must be obtained before doing so. At times, it is difficult to establish who owns the fishing rights and whether or not access is available. The best place to seek advice is: Sportsworld, 1 Francis Street, Stornoway. Tel: (01851) 705464. You should also, always, seek permission from the local crofter before crossing his land to reach a fishing location. Where access information is known, it is noted in the appropriate text. However, please double-check this information before fishing as details may change.

A'BHEALAICH, Loch
Location & Access See Loch Carran

A'BHEANNAN MHOIR, Loch
Location & Access 14/293093 See Loch an Eilein Bhig entry. Start from Waterfall Bridge over the Abhainn Gleann Airigh an Domhnuill burn at 14/295108, at the head of Loch Sealg.
Commentary A four mile hike round three small lochs to the south of Loch Sealg. The quickest way in is directly south, up the steep gully between Beannan Mor (242m) and Beannan Beag (190m). After catching your breath, walk south for half a mile to Loch a'Bheannan Mhoir to catch your supper. Cross east along the north shoulder of Ruadh Chleit (340m) and descend to Loch Chlachan Dearga (14/305094) after a tramp of 20 minutes. Climb north east from Loch Chlachan Dearga for half a mile to reach the last loch of the day, Cleit a'Ghuib Choille (14/311098). Waterfall Bridge is one mile to north west.
Fish See Loch an Eilein Bhig.
Flies & Tactics These small lochs are easily covered from the shore and fish may be taken from all round the bank. Try: Ke-He, Grouse & Claret, Silver Butcher.
Permission & Charges See Loch an Eilein Bhig.

A'BHOINEID, Loch See Loch Tiorsdam.
A'BHRODUINN, Loch See Loch Linngrabhaidh
A'CHAIRN, Loch See Loch Stiomrabhaigh
A'CHEIVLA, Loch See Loch Ulladale
A'CHLACHAIN, Loch See Loch Udromul.
A'CHOIN BHAIN, Loch See Loch Gaineamhaich.
A'GHARAIDH, Loch See Loch Oil entry
A'GHARAIDH, Loch (Udromul) See Loch Udromul.
A'GHEOIDH, Loch See Loch Aoghnais Mhic Fhionnlaidh.
A'GHIUTHAIS, Loch See Loch Eishken

A'GHRUAGAICH, Loch
Location & Access 14/412180. An easily accessible loch lying to the west of the minor road from Calbost to Marvig.
Commentary There are three roadside lochs here, all of which offer good fishing in splendid surroundings. The

Tarbert & Loch Seaforth

OS Map 14

other two are Lochan Sgeireach (14/414185) and Loch na Buaile Duibhe (14/415183). The latter is particularly attractive and is a good base from which to explore its neighbours. These lochs are rarely fished.
Fish Brown trout which average 8oz, with the possibility of seatrout as well. It is also worth considering a seatrout visit to 14/409191 near Marvig, and, more distant, to 14/418184 at Mol nam Braithrean.
Flies & Tactics Few problems and all these waters are easily covered from the shore. Avoid wading. Offer: Black Pennell, Greenwell's Glory, Dunkeld.
Permission & Charges Permission must be obtained before fishing any of the Tarbert and Loch Seaforth waters. Finding out from whom to obtain that permission is sometimes difficult, but, nevertheless, anglers wishing to fish must do so. Where this information is known, it is noted in the text. Otherwise, seek local advice - The Harris Hotel in Tarbert. Tel: (01859) 502154) - or, for further information, contact Sportsworld, 1 Francis Street, Stornoway, Isle of Lewis. Tel: 01851 705464. Also remember to seek permission from the owner of the land you cross on the way to the fishing location.

A'GHOBHAINN, Loch (Garyvard) See Loch Totaichean Aulaidh.
A'MHONAIDH, Loch See Horsaclett River

A'MHORGHAIN, Loch
Location & Access 14/153049. The loch is easily accessible and immediately to the south of the A859 Stornoway/Tarbert road.
Commentary Loch a'Mhorghain is the largest of a chain of three lochs which lie close to the main road, the other, smaller lochs being Loch na Ciste (14/162061) and Loch Sgeireagan Mor (14/148046). The system drains west and reaches the sea at Ceann an Ora (14/136035), to the north of the Skeaudale River.
Fish In spate conditions and towards the end of the season, there is the possibility of sea-trout and the occasional salmon, but mainly brown trout which average 8/10oz in weight.
Flies & Tactics The north, roadside, shores of these lochs are the most productive areas. The south shore is steep and backed by the slopes of Sgaoth Iosal (531m). Avoid wading. Also visit the beach at Ceann an Ora, particularly after heavy rain, to fish the mouth of the river, and the mouth of the Skeaudale River. Flies to offer them: Ke-He, Grouse & Claret, Silver Butcher.
Permission & Charges From Sammy Macleod, The Anchorage, Ardhasaig, Harris, HS3 3AJ. Tel 01859 502009.

A'PHEIRCIL, Loch See Loch Ulladale

A'SGAIL, Loch
Location & Access 14/131079. Start from Bunavoneader (14/130043) on the shores of West Loch Tarbert, near the ruins of the old whaling station. A track leads north over Creag Ghreine-brigh (150m). At the end of the track, continue north up the line of the Abhainn Loch a'Sgail to reach the loch after a further one and a half miles.
Commentary Away-from-it-all trout fishing in a remote, high loch between Usignaval Beg (729m) to the west and Mulla-fo-dheas (743m) to the east. On your return journey south from Loch a'Sgail, keep to the west of the outlet stream and traverse one mile south west, past Creag Uilisker, up the slope, to visit Loch Brunaval (14/122067). After fishing Loch Brunaval, track the outlet stream down almost to sea-level and pick up the line of Abhainn Loch a'Sgail which grows into the Abhainn Eadar river and enters the sea by the dam at Bunavoneader in Ceann an Ora. This expedition will take you on a five mile round trip across difficult country.
Fish Nothing that will break any records, but almost certainly enough for an evening meal. There is always the possibility of sea-trout in the lower reaches of the Abhainn Eadar, particularly after heavy rain.
Flies & Tactics No problems. The lochs are small and easily fished from the shore. Avoid wading. Flies: Black Zulu, March Brown, Peter Ross.
Permission & Charges See Loch Voshimid.

ABHAINN EADAR, River See Loch a'Sgail
AIGHEROIL, Loch See Loch na Sroine
AIRIGH IAIN OIG, Loch See Laxdale River.

AIRIGH THORMAID, Loch
Location & Access 14/290140 See Loch Sgibacleit. Access is either by foot or by Scaliscro Lodge argocat, south from Seaforth Head along the line of the Abhainn Sgeiravat burn which is the loch outlet stream. The journey on foot takes 30 minutes.
Commentary The loch is over half a mile long, north/south, by about 300 yds wide and lies in a wild glen surrounded by high hills: Beinn Mheadhonach (288m) to the east, Beinn na h-Uamha (389m) to the south, and Mor Mhonadh (401m) to the west.
Fish Primarily a sea-trout fishery, but salmon as well. See Loch Sgibacleit entry for catch returns.
Flies & Tactics Fish lie close to the margins of this steep-sided loch and you should concentrate your principal activity in the vicinity of the small streams that tumble in from the surrounding heights. The south west shore and south end is perhaps the most productive area. Offer: Blue Zulu, Clan Chief, Goat's Toe.
Permission & Charges See Loch Sgibacleit.

ALATAIR, Loch See OS Map 18.
ALLT NAM BEARNACH, Loch See Loch an Eilein Bhig
AN DAIMH, Loch (Marvig) See Loch Druim nam Bideannan.

AN DUIN, Loch (Scalpay)
Location & Access 14/225965 This is the largest loch on the Island of Scalpay and is reached from Tarbert via the minor road along the north shore of East Loch Tarbert.
Commentary Scalpay has five named lochs and five unnamed lochans, all of which offer a chance of sport amidst dramatic surroundings. The lochs lie to the east of the only road on the island and could be visited

OS Map 14 — Tarbert & Loch Seaforth

during the course of a single, day-long outing. The other waters are: Loch Tarsuinn 14/225962, immediately to the south of Loch an Duin; Loch Cuilceach 14/234962 and its unnamed neighbour at 14/238961, a five minute walk from the east end of Loch an Duin. Loch na Craoibhe 14/237951 and its unnamed satellite lochans to the east are probably best approached from Kennavay 14/232952, as is Loch a'Rothaid 14/226955.

Fish Modest brown trout in all the lochs, with the chance of a few larger specimens, and the possibility of sea-trout and the occasional salmon in Loch an Duin.

Flies & Tactics Loch an Duin used to have an excellent reputation as a sea-trout fishery, but water quality has declined in recent years and the loch can be dour. Nevertheless, it is worth a visit and you should concentrate your effort along the north shore, paying particular attention to the first bay which contains three small islands. The other waters listed above are smaller and are easily covered from the shore. As always, avoid wading in any of these lochs. First cast: Blue Zulu, Soldier Palmer, Silver Butcher.

Permission & Charges See Loch a'Mhorghain

AN EILEAN, Loch (Eishken) See Loch Eishken

AN EILEIN BHIG, Loch

Location & Access 14/352082. One of a group of South Eishken Estate lochs lying to the south of Loch Sealg; bounded on the west by Loch Seaforth and to east and south by the Minch. All these waters are remote and access is difficult: by foot along estate roads or by argocat tracks.

Commentary The most convenient means of approach is, more often than not, by sea, but even then, once ashore, a long, hard hike is required to reach the more distant waters. The rewards, however, are spectacular, not only from the point of view of the fishing, but also because of the wild nature of the landscape. This five-mile day out begins at Tob na Gile Moire (14/338099) on the north shore of Loch Sealg. Walk south-west up the line of the Allt Gil Mhic Phaic burn to reach the first water, Loch Braigh nan Ron (14/348089) after 30 minutes. After fishing the Loch Braigh nan Ron and its unnamed satellite at 14/344083, cross south west to Loch na Ba Ruaidhe (14/344083). From the south end, angle east over the hill to Loch an Eilein Bhig. Don't miss the small, unnamed lochan on the hill to the south east at 14/357080, reached by walking up the inlet stream at the south east corner of Loch an Eilein Bhig. Fish the east shore of Loch an Eilein Bhig north to the small island, then walk up the stream in the glen to the north-east to reach the unnamed lochan at 14/355086. Lunch by the island in the bay at the south east shore. Follow the inlet stream up the hill to the north-east and then head due east to fish Loch Allt nam Bearnach (14/364085). Track the inlet stream at the north end of Loch Allt nam Bearnach north for half a mile to the unnamed lochan at 14/361094, then climb the hill to the west to descend to the unnamed lochan at 14/355095. Climb due west now to the last lochan, unnamed, at 14/349094. The outlet stream at the north end leads you back to the start.

Fish Not much is known about these remote waters because they are very rarely fished. Some have a reputation for holding specimen trout, all contain wild brown trout of about 6-8oz in weight.

Flies & Tactics Most important is the necessity of obtaining proper permission prior to setting out. Bank fishing all the way, do not wade. Stay safely ashore at all times. You will need a compass and map, appropriate all-weather gear. Remember, this is a desolate, unpopulated area and you will have to rely entirely upon your own resources at all times. Flies: Blue Zulu, Soldier Palmer, Silver Invicta. If you approach by sea, be fully aware of the fact that a sudden change in the weather could leave you stranded, without hope of rescue, for days. In that event, you will have to find your own way home, over the hills. This is not a light undertaking so you must be experienced and well prepared for all eventualities before considering visiting these remote locations.

Permission & Charges The South Eishken Estate is factored by Messrs Strutt & Parker, Sporting Agency, 13 Hill Street, Berkeley Square, London W1X 8DL. Tel: 0207 692 7282; Fax 0207 499 1657. The Head Gillie is C. MacRae, Tel: 01851 830486. Charges on application. Eishken Estate Office: Tel 01851 672325.

AN EILEIN DUIBH, Loch (Glenside) See Loch Gaineamhaich.
AN FHEOIR, Lochan See Loch Mor (Rhenigdale)
AN FHEOIR, Lochan (Ulladale) See Loch Ulladale
AN FHEOIR, Lochan (Voshimid) See Loch Voshimid
AN RATHAID, Loch See Loch Tiorsdam
AN ROTHAID, Loch See Loch Mhic Neacail
AN TAIRBEIRT, Loch See Loch Totaichean Aulaidh.
AN TAIRBH DUINN, Loch See Loch Diraclett
AN TAIRBH, Loch See Loch Gaineamhaich.
AN TRUIM, Loch See Loch Brunaval
AN UISGE MHAITH MOR, Loch See Loch Criadha.

AOGHNAIS MHIC FHIONNLAIDH, Loch

Location & Access 14/068872. This easily accessible loch lies immediately to the south of the South Harris east coast minor road between Ardvey (14/080874) and the south end of Loch Langavat (14/054880).

Commentary Loch Aoghnais Mhic Fhionnlaidh is the principal loch in an excellent little migratory fish system which enters the sea by Finsbay at OS14/076867. The system rises in Loch Meurach (OS14/061879) and crosses under the road at OS14/065875, collecting in the flow from the unnamed lochans at OS14/058878 and OS14/061875, before joining Loch Aoghnais Mhic Fhionnlaidh. The system also drains Loch a' Gheoidh (OS14/065875), to the north of the road, and the unnamed loch at OS14/069869 by Cnoc an Sgumain (67m). To the north of Cnoc an Sgumain, close to the road, is another, separate unnamed lochan at OS14/072872, which also has a run of migratory fish and enters the sea in Loch Finsbay near the church.

Fish Seatrout, a good chance of salmon, and brown trout which average 8oz.

Flies & Tactics Easy bank fishing. All the lochs noted above can produce sport, provided there are good

127

Tarbert & Loch Seaforth

OS Map 14

water levels. Flies: Blue Zulu, Soldier Palmer, Peter Ross.
Permission & Charges See Loch Geimisgarave.

ASHAVAT, Loch See Loch Chliostair

BEAG CATISVAL, Loch
Location & Access 14/402174. Park by the bridge at 14/40517 on the Gravir/Marvig road. Follow the outlet stream north-west for ten minutes to reach the loch.
Commentary A very pretty loch in the hills to the south of Marvig, the centre of a day out exploring a series of small lochs in the vicinity, including Loch na Ba Riabhaich (OS14/400179) to the north. There are eight unnamed lochans nearby - all of which hold trout. How many you fish depends upon how active you wish to be and how accurate your map reading is. This is rough country, so be well shod and prepared.
Fish Expect great fun with trout which average 6oz, but look out for a few larger fish as well.
Flies & Tactics Fish the west shoreline of Loch Beag Catisval to the inlet stream at the north-west corner. Follow this west to visit the south bank - a chain of three little lochans. Return by the north bank of these waters and walk north for five minutes to find Loch na Ba Riabhaich. Fish clockwise round Loch na Ba Riabhaich and continue south to end the day by fishing the east shore of Loch Beag Catisval. Easy bank fishing and no need to wade. Offer them: Blue Zulu, Grouse & Claret, Peter Ross.
Permission & Charges See Loch a'Ghruagaich entry.

BEAG, Loch (Rhenigdale) See Loch Mor (Rhenigdale)
BEAG, Lochan (Eaval River) See Loch Chliostair
BEALACH STOCKLETT, Loch See Laxdale River.
BEARASTA MOR, Loch See Laxdale River.

BHREACAICH, Loch
Location & Access 14/377118 Approach from Lemreway. The loch is five minute walk west from the B8060.
Commentary A small, easily accessible loch covering an area of about 10 acres, with an attractive island at the north end. Plenty of fishy corners and promontories. There is an unnamed lochan to the south, approached from the road at 14/377110, which is also worth a few casts. The sea at 14/377110 provides an opportunity for sea-trout, as do the beaches to the west in the vicinity of Orinsay. The best loch in the area is the unnamed water at 14/371123, known locally as the Dubh Loch and approached from the north via the minor road from the B8060 to Orinsay. Also well worth a visit is Loch Mor na Muilne (14/369127), to the north of the minor road, and Loch Caol (14/361129). After fishing Loch Caol, explore its satellite lochans, particularly the one at 14/359130.
Fish The Dubh Loch has the best trout and fish of up to and over 2lb in weight are not uncommon. The other waters have more modest, but none the less desirable residents.
Flies & Tactics Stay ashore and do not wade, least of all in the Dubh Loch. Fish tend to lie close to the shore anyway, and the water is readily covered from the bank. Flies: Blue Zulu, Greenwell's Glory, Goat's Toe.
Permission & Charges See Loch a'Ghruagaich entry.

BRAIGH NA H-IMRICH, Loch
Location & Access 14/195997 Drive east from Tarbert along the north shore of East Loch Tarbert towards Scalpay and park at Carragreich (14/196987). Follow the outlet burn north, climbing past the ruined shielings, to reach the loch after half a mile.
Commentary A lovely loch in a dramatic setting, surrounded by high hills, and covering an area of some 30 acres. An excellent chance of seeing golden eagle and red-throated diver.
Fish Brown trout which average 8/10oz, with the possibility of a few fish of up to 1lb in weight.
Flies & Tactics Easily covered from the shore. Do not wade. The north end of the loch is the most productive area. Offer them: Blue Zulu, Soldier Palmer, Dunkeld.
Permission & Charges See Loch a'Mhorghain.

BRAIGH NAN RON, Loch See Loch an Eilein Bhig
BRUNAVAL, Loch (Eadar) See Loch a'Sgail

BRUNAVAL, Loch (Resort)
Location & Access 14/065158 There is no easy way into Loch Brunaval, or to the surrounding lochs and lochans. One possiblity is to follow the Loch Ulladale route (see entry), then climb from Loch Ulladale north west over the shoulder between Mas a'Chnoic-chuairtich (386m) to the south and Feadan Dirascal (230m) to the north; a distance of one mile from the north west shore of Loch Ulladale brings you to Loch Brunaval.
Commentary Less taxing, but more difficult to organise, is to approach by boat from the jetty to the north of Hushinish at 13/990124. Otherwise, one is faced with a very hard ten mile slog north and east past the island of Scarp, Rubh an Tighe (13/000147) and the glorious beach at the head of Glen Cravadale. Thereafter, compass and map work. Navigate between Sgianait (425m) south and Mas Garbh (360m) to the north and descend by Cnoc Breac Beag (13/030140) into Lon na Graidhe at 13/037137. Find the stream and follow it north, down the glen to reach Loch Uiseader (13/050150) and its unnamed satellite at 13/044149. Additional torture may be obtained by striking west to three, tiny lochans between Taran Mor (303m) and Mas Garbh (360m) known collectively as Lochan na Sgail (13/032149). Return to Loch Uiseader and, from the east end follow the outlet stream down to where the Abhainn Bearraray turns north (14/056154). Continue directly north east from this point, descending for half a mile to reach Loch Brunaval. On the hill to the north of Loch Brunaval is an excellent little trout loch, Loch nan Gillean 14/061162. To the east lie Loch nan Uidhean 14/084167 and its satellite locahan at 14/083165 and Loch an Truim 14/094170.
Fish There are good numbers of trout which average 6/8oz, a few larger specimens, and the possibility of sea-trout and salmon in the lochs which flow into Loch Resort.
Flies & Tactics You are on your own in this wilderness

OS Map 14 — Tarbert & Loch Seaforth

and entirely dependent upon your own resources. Leave word of where you are going and when you expect to return. Do not wade in these lochs, stay safely ashore. Loch Uiseader is the largest, covering an area of some 20 acres. You will be able to cast across Loch an Truim and Loch nan Uidhean. The beaches along the way are irresistable, in fine weather, and you should have seals, otters and golden eagles for company. Use: Blue Zulu, March Brown, Alexandra.
Permission & Charges See Loch Voshimid

CAOL EISHAL, Loch See Loch Mor Tanga.
CAOL A'GHARAIDH MHOIR, Loch (Glenside) See Loch Sgorr Ni Dhonnachaidh.
CAOL, Loch (Lemreway) See Loch Bhreacaich
CAOL, Loch (Tom an Fhuadain) See Loch nan Stearnag

CARRAN, Loch
Location & Access 14/083960. Loch Carran was a man-made loch and no longer exists since the outflow dam has been washed away.
Commentary The stream which enters the sea by Rubha Reamhar is worth a visit.
Fish Sea-trout, when tide and water conditions are right, and brown trout in the lochs.
Flies & Tactics Perseverence, stealth and crossed fingers are required to tempt sea-trout. For those who prefer a hike, there is a chance of sea-trout in Loch a'Bhealaich (14/095953) after heavy rain. The loch lies below Creag an Eoin (100m) and is one mile south from the estuary along a good stalkers' track. Further adventure, and sport with bright little trout, may be obtained by climbing from the sea along the line of the Abhainn Gil an Tailleir burn. Hike south for 1.5 miles, then climb south west again for ten minutes to Loch Heileasbhal (14/077946); a substantial, beautiful loch, between Heileasbhal Beag (150m) and Clunishval (280m). Flies: Ke-He, Clan Chief, Goat's Toe.
Permission & Charges see Laxdale River.

CARTACH, Loch (Lemreway) See Lochan Loch
CATISVAL, Loch See Loch Druim nam Bideannan.
CAVERSTA, River See Loch Totaichean Aulaidh.
CHLACHAN DEARGA, Loch See Loch a'Bheannan Mhoir
CHLEISTIR, Loch See Loch Voshimid

CHLIOSTAIR, Loch
Location & Access 14/070106 See Loch Ulladale.
Commentary This is the headwater loch of the River Eaval system. It is of limited interest as a salmon and sea-trout fishery because of the hydro electric generating scheme on its course. The loch is fed by Loch Ashavat (14/072119) from the north but the river below Loch Chliostair has dried out. Down stream from the power station, is Loch Leosaid (14/060085), a deep, dour water, rarely fished. This flows south into Lochan Beag (14/057078) which in turn flows into a small, weedy loch known as Ladies' Loch (14/055079). The river then flows through a rocky gorge to reach the sea over steep falls near Amhuinnsuidhe Castle. There are two small lochs, difficult of access but in splendid surroundings, in the hills above Loch Chliostair: Loch Maolaig (14/063109) to the west, and Loch Colluscarve (14/071089) to the east. To the south of the B887, is Loch nan Caor (14/064071), easily accessible, with the chance of sport in the loch and where it enters the sea in Ard Hurnish (14/067066).
Fish See Loch Voshimid.
Flies & Tactics Because of the fall, migratory fish have difficulty in running the river. Nevertheless, they gather in great numbers at the mouth as the attempt to do so. The best sport is to be had in two pools on the lower river, known locally as Castle Burn, which are Gate Pool and Gorge Pool, and in the Ladies' Loch. Few fish are taken elsewhere. The River Leosaid which enters Loch Leosaid at 14/056089 is now the major spawning area for the fish that do manage to negotiate the falls. The other lochs noted above contain brown trout which average 8oz, but there are also some very much larger specimens, particularly in Loch Leosaid. A single-handed rod and stalking tactics will bring the best results here, and hooking and playing a fresh fish in these confined waters is very exciting. Offer them: Goat's Toe, Clan Chief, Willie Gunn, General Practitioner, Hairy Mary, Stoat's Tail, Garry Dog.
Permission & Charges See Loch Voshimid.

CHROCHAIRE, Loch See Lochan Loch
CHUMRABORGH, Loch See Loch nam Faoileag.
CLAR, Loch See Loch Eishken.
CLEIT A'GHUIB CHOILLE, Loch See Loch a'Bheannan Mhoir.
CLEIT AN AISEIG, Loch See Loch Oil.
CLEIT NA STIUIRE, Loch See Loch Tiorsdam.
CNOC BERUL, Loch See Loch Keose.

CNOC IAIN DUIBH, Loch
Location & Access 14/347225. The loch lies immediately adjacent and to the east of the A859 Stornoway/Tarbert road, from which road the west shore may be reached. To explore the east bank, turn east from the A859 at 14/345224 and, after passing the school, turn north on the peat road at 14/349221.
Commentary Loch Cnoc Iain Duibh is a long, narrow water, almost three quarters of a mile north/south by up to 250yds wide. It is separated from Loch nan Ritheanan (14/355230), its neighbour to the east, by a rocky ridge. The peat road mentioned above gives easy access to both the south end of Loch Cnoc Iain Duibh and to the south-west and south-east shore Loch nan Ritheanan. The main body of Loch nan Ritheanan is to the north, where the loch is almost half a mile wide across the north bay. Access to this end is along a track which starts in the township of Keose Glebe. Turn left just after the church at 14/357217. The track continues where this road ends and reaches the north-east shore of Loch nan Ritheanan after 30 mins.
Fish Plenty of action with nice trout averaging 8oz and the chance of good numbers of fish of up to and over 1lb in weight. Seatrout in the sea along Loch Leurbost.
Flies & Tactics There is at least a week's fishing here, including little Loch na Muilne (14/361225) to the south-east of Loch nan Ritheanan, and Loch Holavat (14/357240), Loch na h-Inghinn (14/349245) and

Tarbert & Loch Seaforth — OS Map 14

Loch Soval (14/350255) to the north. The small, unnamed lochan at 14/357251 is also worth a cast. Seatrout may be encountered in the two, long inlets along the south shore of sea Loch Leurbost at 14/371240 and 14/384236. Bank fishing only and avoid wading. Flies to try include: Black Pennell, Soldier Palmer, Alexandra.

Permission & Charges Fishing is generally let to tenants of Soval Estate staying in Soval Lodge. For details and further information about the possibility of casual bookings, contact: John Macleod, Keeper, Valtos Cottage, Laxay, Lochs, Stornoway, Isle of Lewis. Tel: 01851 830202.

COILLE SHUARDAIL, Loch See Loch Keose.
COLLUSCARVE, Loch See Loch Chliostair.
CREAVAT, Loch See Loch Saile.

CRIADHA, Loch
Location & Access 14/388140 Leave the B8060 just past the school in Gravir and turn east to the head of Loch Odhairn. Follow the road along the south shore of the loch to Tom an Fhuadain (14/394146). A peat road leads south from here to 14/390143. Loch Criadha is a five minute walk south again from the end of the track and is the start point for this day-long expedition.

Commentary After fishing Loch Criadha, climb the glen by the inlet burn at the south end of the loch to find Lochan Dubh (14/384137). Fish Lochan Dubh and track the inlet stream to the unnamed lochan to the south-east at 14/386133. Fish anti-clockwise round Loch Kinneastal and walk up the inlet burn at the north east corner, stopping for a cast in the unnamed lochan on the hill at 14/411130, then descend to the north shore of long Loch an Uisge Mhaith Mor (14/394129). Fish down the west shore of the loch and at the south end, climb slowly rising ground to reach Lochan Tota Ruairidh Dhuibh (14/396120). Attack Lochan Tota Ruairidh Dhuibh anti-clockwise. At the south end, consider a ten minute sortie south to explore a rarely fished, unnamed lochan at 14/399115 to the north of Carnan Mor (143m). Return to the east shore of Lochan Tota Ruairidh Dhuibh and leave by the north-east corner. Tramp the east side of the crags to examine the three unnamed lochans at 14/399125. Follow the outlet stream of the west, island lochan, back down to Lochan Tota Ruairidh Dhuibh and continue up the east shore, with a side-cast in the unnamed adjacent lochan at the north east corner. Walk north-north-west now for twenty minutes and descend the glen to the start point at Loch Criadha.

Fish Some good trout, particularly in Loch an Uisge Mhaith Mor and Lochan Tota Ruairidh Dhuibh where fish of over 1lb may be taken. The surrounding waters hold stocks of trout which average in the order of 6/8oz.

Flies & Tactics A six mile adventure over rough, taxing ground. You will need stout boots, stout lungs, and the ability to use a compass and map. Bank fishing all round, and, as always, it is best to stay safely ashore. The waters are easily covered. Picnic at the south end of Loch un Uisge Mhaith Mor, the largest loch. Flies: Blue Zulu, Soldier Palmer, Peter Ross.

Permission & Charges See Loch a'Ghruagaich entry.

CROIS AILEIN, Loch
Location & Access OS14/385160. An easily accessible loch lying to the east of the B8060 Garyvard/Lemreway road at Gravir. The north shore is best approached from OS14/381162. For the south shore, follow the minor road from OS14/378159 east to Crois Ailein Lodge.

Commentary Loch Crois Ailein is one of the most attractive and productive lochs in the area. It is almost half a mile east/west by up to 250yds wide, covering an area of some 40 acres, divided by narrows into two sections. There is an unnamed loch (known locally as the 'Lady's Loch') to the south at OS14/387156, joined to Loch Crois Ailein, and this is also well worth a cast.

Fish Good numbers of trout which average 8-10oz and also larger fish of up to and over 2lb in weight.

Flies & Tactics Boats may be available for hire from Crois Ailein Lodge, otherwise, bank fishing will please just as well. The north shore is perhaps the most productive area, particularly the north-east corner and the east shoreline where the feeder streams enter. Flies that help: Ke-He, Invicta, Black Pennell.

Permission & Charges Crois Ailean Lodge, Gravir, Stornoway, Isle of Lewis. Tel: (01851) 880409. Boat fishing is £10 per boat per day and Crois Ailein Lodge provides first-class accommodation for visiting anglers. Fishing is free to lodge guests.

CROMORE, Loch
Location & Access 14/404205. An easily accessible loch lying immediately to the east of the township of Cromore. Loch na Beiste (14/399202), which is joined to Loch Cromore to the south, should also be carefully examined.

Commentary This is a brackish water, almost half a mile north/south by up to 700yds wide and covering an area of 50 acres. There are two unnamed lochans to the north at OS14/406214 which should be explored whilst you are in the parish. The larger can hold seatrout after heavy rain and towards the end of the season.

Fish Brown trout, seatrout and even some species of saltwater fish in Loch Cromore. Average weight of trout is 10-12oz.

Flies & Tactics Bank fishing is productive and a boat may also be available from Mr Macleod at 11 Cromore. The east bay, near the two islands, is a good place to start. The bay to the south of the ruined dun can also be productive.

Permission & Charges See Loch a'Ghruagaich entry.

CUILCEACH, Loch See Loch an Duin (Scalpay).
CUL NA BEINNE, Loch See Loch Plocrapool.

DIRACLETT, Loch
Location & Access 14/156989 An easily accessible roadside loch, half a mile south from Tarbert on the A859.

Commentary Loch Diraclett is a good start point for a day out fishing the lochs round Ceann Reamhar

OS Map 14 — Tarbert & Loch Seaforth

(4667m) and Langraclett (166m), to the west of the main road. Start the walk from 14/153990 and follow the line of the burn up the hill, having a cast in the four, small, unnamed lochans along the way. After half a mile you will reach Loch an Tairbh Duinn (14/139998), a very pretty loch covering an area of about 5 acres. The more adventurous might now choose to walk on, north-west for another half mile, to locate little Loch Stioclett (14/129004) by the remote beach at Bagh Stioclett on West Loch Tarbert. The ideal place for lunch. From the south arm of Loch an Tairbh Duinn, find the inlet burn and trace it uphill to the next loch in the series, Loch nan Caor (14/135994). Now walk due south, between the crags, to fish Loch Uamadale (14/135988). Loch Uamadale is flanked to the east by two unnamed lochans. Fish them and return down their outlet stream to the start point by Loch Diraclett.
Fish Some good quality trout, particularly in Loch Diraclett, which is managed by the local angling club.
Flies & Tactics As always, when tramping in the Outer Hebrides, a compass and map are essential. The weather is fickle and what might begin as a clear-blue-sky day can turn really nasty in seconds. The fishing is all from the bank and these lochs are easily 'read' and understood. Fish are taken from all round the shores so cast with confidence using: Black Pennell, Greenwell's Glory, Peter Ross.
Permission & Charges See Loch a'Mhorghain.

DOIMHNE, Loch See Loch Linngrabhaidh.
DRINISHADER, Loch See Horsaclett River.

DRUIM NAM BIDEANNAN, Loch
Location & Access OS14/406194. Leave the B8060 Garyvard/Lemreway road at OS14/381178 and drive east to Marvig. The loch is to the west of the minor road which runs north from Marvig.
Commentary Loch Druim nam Bideannan is one of a group of three lochs between the B8060 to the west, the Marvig road to the south, and sea loch Mharabhig to the east. The other two, to the south, are Loch Catisval (14/405187) and Loch an Daimh (14/400184). Access to the latter two lochs is from the Marvig road. For Loch Druim nam Bideannan, park at the end of the minor road, by Loch Mharabhig, and climb the hill to the west to reach the loch. There are also eight further, unnamed lochans in the area, all of which can produce sport.
Fish Good stocks of brown trout which average 8oz and also fish of up to and over 1lb in weight. Many of the smaller lochs in the area have been selectively stocked in recent years with fish from adjacent waters. They can hold surprisingly large trout. Loch Catisval has had a checkered, somewhat sad career, progressing from rainbow trout farm to rainbow fishery. It was also used as a smolt rearing location. Why anyone should want to introduce rainbow trout to the Outer Hebrides is beyond belief; worse is the prospect of a put-and-take stew pond in such a paradise.
Flies & Tactics Bank fishing, but boats may be available on Loch Catisval from Donald Maclennan at 19 Marvig. Avoid wading. First cast: Black Pennell, Soldier Palmer, Silver Butcher.
Permission & Charges See Loch a'Ghruagaich entry.

DRUIM NAN GOBAN RAINICH, Loch
Location & Access 14/255048 See Loch an Eilein Bhig. Best approach is by boat from Tarbert, landing by the shielings at the mouth of the Abhainn a'Bhaig burn enters the Sound of Shiant.
Commentary This is a five mile walk north up the peninsula, with Loch Seaforth to the west and Loch Claidh to the east. From the shielings, walk south-west to little Lochan Eich (14/267022) on the north slope of Aird a'Bhaih (112m). Hike north now, on the high ground, for half a mile to reach Loch Druim nan Caorach (14/255036). Cross north-east from Loch Druim nan Coarach to locate the Allt Bun Chorcabhig. Follow this stream up to Loch Druim nan Goban Rainich. Descend north-west fom Loch Druim nan Goban Rainich and follow the inlet stream down to Lochan Chipeagil Bheag (14/248055). This in turn leads to Loch Chipeagil Mhor (14/238059). Continue north for a further mile to reach Kenmore (14/220068) on the east shore of Loch Seaforth where, hopefully, you will have arranged to be picked up.
Fish See Loch an Eilein Bigh. A good chance of sea-trout at both the beginning and end of the expedition.
Flies & Tactics For your own safety, read carefully the Loch an Eilein entry.
Permission & Charges See Loch an Eilein.

DUBH, Lochan (Tom an Fhuadain) See Loch Criadha.

DUBH SLETTEVAL, Loch
Location & Access 14/055899 The quickest way to reach this loch, and its neighbour to the north, Loch na Moine (14/058906), is to start from the south end of Loch Langavat at 14/055880 and climb north-east over Scara Ruadh (104m). The lochs lie approximately two miles from the road, over very rough ground.
Commentary Also explore the dozen or so unnamed lochans round Leana an Fheoir (14/064895), and twin-sectioned Locha Dubha (14/073885) and its surrounding, unnamed lochans on the hill to the east of the Abhainn na Ciste burn. Attack over two days, visiting the southern section from Ardvey at 14/080874. The Abhainn na Ciste burn enters the sea here through a long, narrow, extension of the stream at 14/064883, and a substantial, productive, tidal pond at 14/077875.
Fish A full score, with the chance of salmon and sea-trout in the lower reaches and good brown trout in the surrounding and headwater lochs.
Flies & Tactics The most important 'tactic' is accurate compass and map work, sound all-weather gear, and strong lungs. Otherwise, the fishing is easily read and you should have no problems. Offer them: Black Pennell, Invicta, Silver Butcher.
Permission & Charges See Loch Geimisgarave.

DUBH, Loch (Lemreway) See Loch Bhreacaich.
EAVAL, River See Loch Chliostair.

Tarbert & Loch Seaforth — OS Map 14

EISHKEN, Loch
Location & Access 14/320125. Access to North and South Eishken Estate is by private road, east from the A859 Stornoway/Tarbert road at 14/260194. The track ends at Eishken Lodge (14/326130) on the north shore of sea-loch Sealg.
Commentary Loch Eishken drains south through the river Eishken to the sea at Tob Eishken. Loch Eishken collects the waters from several other lochs to the west via Abhainn Cheothadail, including Loch na Beirighe (14/298122), Loch Fath (14/288128) and Clar Loch (14/287143). To the north of Loch Eishken, and also draining into it, is Loch an Eilein (14/322132), with its satellite lochan at 14/320134 and little Loch a'Ghiuthais (14/325140). To the south-west, on the east shoulder of Beinn na h-Uamah (389m), is Loch Raoinabhat (14/325117) which also drains into the system through Loch na Beirighe.
Fish The principal interest here is salmon and sea-trout, although good numbers of brown trout are taken each season. Salmon average 7lb, sea-trout 1lb.
Flies & Tactics The principal lochs are fished from boats, smaller waters are attacked from the shore. The north shore of Loch Eishken, where a number of feeder streams enter, is a good place to start. The stream joining Loch Eishken to Loch na Beirighe to the west, Abhainn Cheothadail, can also offer good sport after heavy rain. The little River Eishken, given water, can also be an exciting and productive stream. Fish may be encountered from all round the shore on Loch Raoinabhat, but the area in the vicinity of the island at the north-east corner of the loch, and the east shoreline, is perhaps most productive. To reach the more remote lochs, Loch Fath and Clar Loch, tramp north along the inlet burn at the west end of Loch na Beirighe. They are easily covered from the shore. Flies that do the damage: Blue Zulu, Black Zulu, Black Pennell, Loch Ordie, Kate McLaren, Silver Butcher. The Estate gillies tell you the 'fly of the moment' and advise on the best locations for deploying it.
Permission & Charges Fishing is let in conjunction with Eishken Lodge on a fully catered basis, and there are also two excellent self-catering cottages available for rental. Prices on application. Details and bookings: Strutt & Parker, Sporting Agency, 13 Hill Street, Berkley Square, London W1X 8DL. Tel (0207) 629 7282, Fax (0207) 449 1675. Head Gillie is Mr C. MaCrae, Tel: (01851) 830486. Eishken Estate Office: Tel (01851) 672325.

EISHKEN, River See Loch Eishken.
FATH, Loch See Loch Eishken.
FEOIR, Loch See Loch nam Faoileag.

FHOIRABHAL BHEAG, Loch
Location & Access 14/225111. For access details see Loch Eishken entry. A major expedition involving a round hike of 12 miles. An alternative is to approach by boat from Aline on the west shore of Loch Seaforth landing on the beach at 14/218119 and then following the outlet stream south-east to reach the loch after 30 minutes.
Commentary Not for the faint-hearted and very rarely fished due to its remote location. But if you like an adventure, and utterly wild country, this is the expedition for you. If approaching from Eishken, you pass little Loch nam Breac (14/250110) along the way.
Fish There are no records for this loch, but it exits via a substantial stream, Abhainn Sgaladal Mhoir, to the sea at Loch Seaforth. Undoubtedly, there is an excellent possibility of sea-trout, both in the stream and in the loch.
Flies & Tactics Compass and map essential, as are strong lungs and legs. However, given that good numbers of sea-trout run Loch Shromois (14/257153) to the north, Loch Fhoirabhal Bheag should produce just as exciting results so your journey could be rewarding. From Eishken, follow the Abhainn Gleann Airigh an Domhnuill burn west from where it enters the head of Loch Sealg, climbing to a watershed between Muaithabhal (424m) to the north and Beinn Mhor (572m), the highest peak in Pairc, to the south. Golden eagle and harrier land. Descend from the watershed to Loch nam Breac. Loch Fhoirabhal Bheag is 1.5 miles due west. The outlet to the sea is two miles west-north-west, along the line of the burn. No problem covering the water from the shore. Try: Ke-He, Grouse & Claret, Kate McLaren.
Permission & Charges See Loch Eishken entry.

FINCASTLE, Loch See Laxdale River.

GAINEAMHAICH, Loch (Lemreway)
Location & Access 14/372139 An easily accessible loch lying to the west of the B8060 road between Gravir and Lemreway. Attack Loch Gaineamhaich and its neighbour to the east, Loch an Tairbh (14/392141), from the road at 14/377142.
Commentary Loch Gaineamhaich is just under half a mile east/west and covers an area of some fifteen acres. It collects in Loch an Tairbh and then exits south, finding the sea to the east of Orinsay. These can be dour waters, but in reasonable conditions they should provide breakfast. If things are quiet on Loch Gaineamhaich and Loch Tairbh, consider a moorland expedition to examine Lochan Eilein Duibh (14/364147) and its surrounding, unnamed lochans, the best of which is the long, narrow water at 14/362149. Half a mile further west brings you to Loch a'Choin Bhain (14/351149) and its satellite lochan at 14/350114. These lochs are best approached from the north. Park at the end of the Glenside road at 14/363159. Cross the Kinloch Ouirn River, into which they flow, and walk south up the outlet burn to reach Lochan Eilein Duibh after an easy twenty minutes.
Fish Brown trout which average 8oz and the chance of a few larger fish of up to 1lb in weight. Towards the end of the season and after heavy rain there is also the possibility of migratory fish.
Flies & Tactics Easy bank fishing all round, but do not wade. Flies: Blue Zulu, Greenwell's Glory, Silver Butcher.
Permission & Charges See Loch a'Ghruagaich entry.

GEIMISGARAVE, Loch
Location & Access 14/107919 Approach from near the

OS Map 14 — Tarbert & Loch Seaforth

post office at Mill (14/111904) on the South Harris east coast minor road. Follow the outlet stream from the sea north to reach the loch after a one mile tramp.
Commentary The loch exits to the sea in Loch Beacravik and is set amidst an almost lunar landscape of barren, bare rocks and wind-blown deer grass. Maoladh Mhicearraig (340m) towers to the north and then feeds the loch by a stream which enters the north east bay down Glen Lingadale.
Fish Sea-trout and the chance of an occasional salmon in high water conditions.
Flies & Tactics Heavy rainfall is required to tempt the fish up to the loch. Boat fishing is easiest, but bank fishing can be just as productive. The south and east shore line is a good place to begin, not too far out, working round anti-clockwise to the inlet stream in the north. Another stream feeds the loch at the north west corner, and this can also produce sport. There is also a chance of sport with sea-trout in the sea, at Mill, and at the head of Loch Beacravik at 14/114907; and at outflow from Loch na Cartach at 14/115909, and further east at 14/118907 Geocrab. Flies: Black Pennell, Soldier Palmer, Peter Ross.
Permission & Charges From £12 per rod per day, including boat, and from £95 per week. There is also a boat available for disabled anglers. For full details contact Mrs Mackinnon, Finsbay Loch, South Harris, Outer Hebrides. Tel: (01859) 530318. Excellent self-catering accommodation is also available, with the fishing and there are boats available for sea fishing.

GLEANN NA MOINE, Loch
Location & Access 14/064950. Loch Gleann na Moine lies to the south of Seilebost on the A895 Tarbert/Leverburgh road, at the end of a healthy, tough, one-mile hike.
Commentary The loch is approached by following the line of the Seilebost River up Glen Seilebost. Loch Gleann na Moine is in a dramatic setting in a small corrie on the east side of Airde-chlife (200m). The estuary of the river, at Faodhail Seilebost, can also provide sport with seatrout and, given high water levels, there is always the possibility of fish finding their way up to the loch. The dunes by Seilebost, to the north of the school, is an ideal picnic place, with abundant wild flowers and marvellous views to the South Harris hills.
Fish The possibility of seatrout and brown trout which average 6-8oz.
Flies & Tactics Fish for seatrout in the sea at either side of low-tide. Gleann na Moine is easily covered from the shore. Offer: Loch Ordie, Soldier Palmer, Black Pennell.
Permission & Charges See Laxdale River.

GLUMRA BEAG, Loch See Loch Saile.
GLUMRA MORE, Loch See Loch Saile.
GRANNDA, Loch See Loch Plocrapool.
GROSEBAY, Loch See Horsaclett River.
HAMARSHADER, Loch See Loch Lighigeag.
HARMASAIG, Loch See Loch Plocrapool.
HEILEASBHAL, Loch See Loch Carran.
HOLAVAT, Loch See Loch Cnoc Iain Duibh.
HOLMASAIG, Loch See Loch Huamavat.

HORSACLETT, Loch See Horsaclett River.

HORSACLETT, River
Location & Access Source: Lochanan Mora (OS14/136975); outflow: Bun Challagrich (14/152965) in sea-loch Ceann Dibig. The river crosses the A859 Tarbert/Leverburgh road two and a half miles south from Tarbert and, because it is so small, the stream may easily be missed. Horsaclett Lodge is on the right, by the shore of a small loch of the same name (14/141964).
Commentary The river is more an 'excuse' to join together the myriad named and unnamed lochs and lochans which make up the system. But it does this very well, and in doing so provides a wonderland of excellent fishing opportunities amidst dramatic surroundings. The principal waters are: Lochanan Mora (see above); Sheep Loch (14/139967), unnamed on the OS map; Loch na Larach Leithe (14/154961), and its surrounding, unnamed satellite lochans to the south of Meavag; Loch Drinishader (14/167957), the largest loch on the Horsaclett Estate. Loch a'Mhonaidh (14/160957) and the two unnamed lochans to the south at 14/159951 and 14/159949; Loch nah-Iolaire (14/150951); Loch nan Uidhean (14/146955); Loch nan Craobhag (14/148938); and Loch Grosebay (14/150930). Although a deal of tramping is required to reach most of these waters, and over rough ground, access is relatively simple from suitable points along the minor road which contains them.
Fish Those lochs which are joined to the river always offer the possibility of sport with sea-trout and salmon. All contain brown trout of varying size, from a few ounces up to fish of over 2lb in weight. Approximately 20 salmon and up to 80 sea-trout can be taken during a good season.
Flies & Tactics Water levels are all important. No water, no fish. Most of the lochs are fished from the bank, there are boats on others. On Lochanan Mora, which is almost half a mile north/south, carefully work the west shoreline, where feeder streams tumble in from Uaval More (358m). The estate keeper will advise visitors on other profitable locations, such as Loch Drinishader, which is best fished from the boat. This is one of the most attractive and productive trout lochs on South Harris. The loch is half a mile north/south by up to 300 yds wide, shallow and island scattered. Loch Drinishader trout are pink fleshed and average 8/10oz, with fish of up to and over 2lb as well. Flies that help things along include: Black Zulu, Ke-He, Loch Ordie, Invicta, Soldier Palmer, Dunkeld, Teal Blue & Silver, Peter Ross.
Permission & Charges Contact Neil Macdonald, 7 Diraclett, Tarbert, Isle of Harris, Outer Hebrides. Tel: (01859) 502464.

HOUSAY, River See Loch Ulladale.

HUAMAVAT, Loch
Location & Access 14/084885. The south end of Loch Huamavat touches the South Harris east coast road at 14/089879, half a mile south form Flodabay, and the

Tarbert & Loch Seaforth — OS Map 14

loch is easily accessible from this point.
Commentary Loch Huamavat and its neighbour, Loch Holmasaig, are the principal migratory fish lochs near Flodabay. They drain a vast area to the west and the system rises in Allt Loch an Fheoir burn on the rough crags of Heileasbhal Mor (384m). From its source to where it enters Loch Huamavat, the burn passes through a series of small, unnamed lochans on Braighnam-bagh (67m). The loch exits south through two further unnamed lochs before reaching Loch Holmasaig and the sea just to the north of Ardvey.
Fish Seatrout and a possibility of salmon. Brown trout which average 6-8oz, and a few larger specimens.
Flies & Tactics Loch Huamavat is a large, scattered water, full of promising bays and fish corners. Boat fishing brings best results and allows you to accurately cover the shoreline of the principal promontory, which is almost an island, at the north end of the loch. Three feeder streams enter from narrow bays to the north and this is a good place to begin your attack. The connecting stream and lochs to the south, including Loch Holmasaig, are all easily fished from the bank and, given good water levels, can provide sport. It things are 'quiet' on the main lochs, it is a simple matter to hike north to the unnamed lochans where supper will be assured. Flies: Blue Zulu, Soldier Palmer, Goat's Toe
Permission & Charges See Loch Geimisgarave.

ILLE CHIPAIN, Loch See Loch Tiorsdam.

KEOSE, Loch
Location & Access 14/369225. Exit south-east from the A859 Stornoway/Balallan road at 14/346324 and follow the minor road, past the school, for two miles to Keose Glebe. The loch is immediately north of the township.
Commentary Loch Keose is regarded by many as one of the loveliest lochs in the Hebrides. It is one mile north/south by up to 300yds wide and covers an area of 90 acres. There are two islands, the northern one being the ideal place for lunch. This easily accessible loch has an abundance of wildlife and is perfect for a family outing, something for everyone, angler and non-angler alike. Large baskets are the rule on Loch Keose, rather than the exception, and although the trout are not very large they fight well and give a good account of themselves. If you want to introduce someone to the 'gentle art', then this is the place to take them. They will catch fish.
Fish There are excellent stocks of brown trout which average 6-8oz and a few larger specimens of up to 1lb in weight as well.
Flies & Tactics Both boat and bank fishing bring good results and fish are taken from all round the loch. The south-east shore, the south bay, north-east bay, and north end are the most productive areas; also round the two islands. Loch Keose is joined to Loch nam Breac (OS14/367234) in the north and there are two additional lochs, further north, which are also worth a visit: Loch Cnoc Berul (OS14/382233) and Loch Coille Shuardail (OS14/378238), both of which can hold seatrout after heavy rain. Seatrout may also be encountered in the sea at OS14/383236, and to the north at OS14/371241 and OS14/371244 by Meavaig Island. Attract brown trout and seatrout with: Black Pennell, Soldier Palmer, Peter Ross.
Permission & Charges Apply to: Mr M Morrison, Handa, 10 Keose Glebe, Lochs, Stornoway, Isle of Lewis. Tel: (01851) 830334. Mr Morrison also offers first-class guest house accommodation and this is an ideal centre for exploring the surrounding area.

KINLOCH OUIRN, River See Lochan Tana (Glenside).
KINNEASTAL, Loch See Loch Criadha.
KINNEASTAL, River See Lochan Loch.
KINTARVIE, River See Loch Tiorsdam.

LACASDAIL, Loch
Location & Access 14/276065 See Loch an Eilein Bhig. Access to Loch Lacasdail is by foot, or by estate argo-cat.
Commentary A stunning loch in a very remote setting, guarded by Creag Mhuaiteseal (400m) to the east and Colla Sgarbh (291m) to the west. Loch Lacasdail is some 700 yds long, north/south, by up to 200 yds wide and exits south to the sea by the ruined shieling at Tob Smuaisibhig (14/273050). A good option, for those who enjoy a little pain before the pleasure of fishing, is a visit to Loch nan Uidhean (14/263073). The easiest way to approach this remote loch is to leave the track in Gleann Lacasdail at 14/274083 and follow the line of the outlet stream up to the loch, a distance of half a mile. After fishing Loch nan Uidhean, cross Colla Sgarbh and, carefully, descend to Loch Lacasdail.
Fish Loch Lacasdail is one of the principal sea-trout fisheries on the South Eishken Estate (see Loch Eishken for catch details); sea-trout may also be encountered at the mouth of the Abhainn Smuaisibhig burn, and, if you are minded to make the effort, further north at the head of sea Loch Claidh at 14/263065. Brown trout in little Loch nan Uidhean.
Flies & Tactics Few problems reading the water. As a general rule, stay close to the margins. The shallow, north end of the loch is perhaps the most productive area. Flies: Ke-He, Goat's Toe, Clan Chief.
Permission & Charges See Loch Eishken.

LADIES', Loch See Loch Chliostair

LAXADALE, Lochs
Location & Access 14/185020. Approach from Tarbert via the Scalpay road along the north shore of East Loch Tarbert.
Commentary The Laxadale System rises in Glen Laxadale, two miles north from its outflow in the sea at Urgha (14/182996). The principal loch is over one mile north/south by up to 350 yds east/west. There is a good foot track along the whole length of the west shore. The system used to be renowned for the quality and number of its sea-trout and salmon but over the years the Laxadale has declineed. Happily, this process is being reversed by the hard work of the fishery manager who is carrying out a well-planned re-stocking and management programme.
Fish Salmon and sea-trout in increasing numbers,

OS Map 14 — Tarbert & Loch Seaforth

including recent salmon of 14lb.
Flies & Tactics Improvement works to the lower lochs have made it easier for anglers to cover the water, whilst information on fishing the main body will be given to visiting anglers by Mr Sammy MacLeod. The north end of the loch, particularly near the old shielings where the Laxadale River enters, is a good place to begin your attack. With: Ke-He, Goat's Toe, Clan Chief.
Permission & Charges At the time of writing this fishery is in the process of changing hands. For the time being enquiries should be directed to: Harris Hotel (01859 502154), or Sammy MacLeod, The Anchorage, Ardhasaig (01859 502009).

LAXDALE, Loch See Laxdale River.

LAXDALE, River
Location & Access Source: Loch Bearesta Mor. Outflow: Traigh Luskentyre OS14/090974. The system flows for three and a half miles north-west from its source and is easily accessible throughout its entire length from the A859 Tarbert/Leverburgh road.
Commentary From its source in Loch Bearasta Mor to Loch Fincastle (OS14/093972), the Laxdale River is little more than a narrow burn, although there are one or two pools along the way. The upper lochs are Loch Bearasta Mor (OS14/124950) and Loch na Gairbhe (OS14/118957). One mile downstream from Loch na Gairbhe, the river enters Loch Laxdale (OS14/109963) where it is joined by the flow from Loch Bealach Stocklett (OS14/110954) which lies between West Stocklett (218m) and East Stocklett (175m). After leaving Loch Laxdale, and a further mile, the river reaches Loch Fincastle and the sea across the bright sands of Luskentyre.
Fish The principal interest here is seatrout and salmon, although the upper lochs all contain brown trout as well. Catches have declined in recent years but good numbers are still taken, depending upon water levels. An average season will produce up to 40 salmon and 150 seatrout. A seatrout weighing 10lb 8oz was caught in 1993.
Flies & Tactics Most of the action takes place on Loch Fincastle, which is man-made, and Loch Laxdale, adjudged to be the smallest salmon and seatrout loch in Britain. Fish begin running the river in late June and early July. Most seatrout are caught in Fincastle Loch. Loch Laxdale produces more salmon. The narrow river rarely yields fish, and although some fish undoubtedly reach the upper lochs they are infrequently tempted to take the fly; apart from Loch Bearasta Mor, which can be an excellent seatrout fishery. A good wind is needed for Loch Laxdale to produce of its best, and boat fishing is most productive. At low-tide, the Luskentyre seapool can also be give sport.
Permission & Charges Fishing is in the hands of the Borve Estate. Details from Gordon Cumming, 2 Seilebost, Isle of Harris, Outer Hebrides. Tel: 01859 550202 (day), 550317 (evenings). Day lets are sometimes available but may not be booked in advance. 2000 prices, subject to alteration without prior notice, are: Loch Fincastle £25 per rod per day, salmon and seatrout fishing; Loch Laxdale (including the river and Old Pool), £15 per rod per day, salmon and seatrout fishing; Loch Bearasta Mor, £4 per rod per day, seatrout and brown trout fishing; Luskentyre Sea Pool, £8 per rod per day, salmon and seatrout fishing; brown trout lochs, £4 per rod per day. Night fishing for salmon and seatrout is available for £15 per rod from 7pm until midnight. Day permits, when available, are issued from 10am until 5.30pm. Boats cost £5 per day and £5 for a night session. Flyfishing only, all seatrout under 12oz must be returned. No gaffs. Dogs on lead.

LEANA AN FHEOIR, Lochs See Loch Dubh Slettaval.
LEOSAID, Loch See Loch Chliostair.
LEOSAID, River See Loch Chliostair.

LIGHIGEAG, Loch
Location & Access 14/424243. Loch Lighigeag lies at the east side of the Aird Raerinish peninsula, to the south of Beinn-Mhor (104m). Approach from Quier (14/143246) at the end of the B897 road.
Commentary Apart from Loch Lighigeag, and Loch Sgeireach (OS14/417254) to the north, there are some 20 additional, small, unnamed lochs and lochans in the vicinity of Quier. A circuit of the peninsula makes a wonderful day out, as much for wildlife and scenery as for fishing.
Fish No difficulty in carrying fish home, they will not be large, but you will catch breakfast. Consider also a visit to the shore at OS14/409247, in the south, and near the school at Ranish, to the north at OS14/398532 where there is a chance of seatrout in the sea.
Flies & Tactics Fairly rough going and stay back from the edge of the cliffs. A compass and map are essential to find your way round. This is a full-day bank fishing expedition and all the waters are easily covered from the shore. Two other nearby locations should also be noted: Loch Hamarshader (OS14/394254), and the unnamed loch at OS14/406255 by Grimshader which can hold seatrout towards the end of the season. Flies: Loch Ordie, Grouse & Claret, Black Pennell.
Permission & Charges See Loch a'Ghruagaich entry.

LINNGRABHAIDH, Loch
Location & Access 14/347063 See Loch an Eilein Bhig. Very remote and best approached from the sea. Land by the ruined shieling at Mulhagery (14/367066).
Commentary Takes some organising to get to these lochs. The Eishken Estate boat is the easy way in. From the beach, follow the stream steeply up the hill to reach Loch Doimhne (14/356065), a circular loch of about 20 acres surrounded to the west and north by the crags of Beinn Doimhne (280m). Three streams enter the loch at the south end, near the two small islands. Hike the west stream 50m up the gully to locate Loch Linngrabhaidh, a wonderful corrie loch. Leave Loch Linngrabhaidh at the south end and, with the crags on your right, trek south for ten minutes to fish Loch nan Eilean (14/352057), the ideal place for lunch. Continue south, fishing the unnamed lochans to the south of Loch nan Eilean, to explore remote Loch a'Bhroduinn

135

Tarbert & Loch Seaforth — OS Map 14

(14/356048). Keeping to the high ground above the sea, return to the beach at Mulhagery, a distance of one mile, via Loch nan Eilein and Sgonnan (164m); and, hopefully, find transport back to civilisation.
Fish See Loch and Eilein Bhig.
Flies & Tactics It is important, for your own safety, that you carefully read the entry for Loch an Eilein Bhig. Do not wade. Try: Blue Zulu, Goat's Toe, Clan Chief.
Permission & Charges See Loch an Eilein Bhig.

LITE SITHINN, Loch See Loch nam Faoileag.
LOCHA DUBHA, Loch See Loch Dubh Slettaval.

LOCHAN, Loch
Location & Access 14/402109. No easy way in and a hard tramp. In Lemreway, leave the B8060 at 14/380120 and drive to the end of the road at 14/385112 overlooking the sea and Eilean Iubhard. Loch Lochan is a one mile hike east along the north shore of Caolas a'Tuath.
Commentary A day out in wild country with exciting wildlife and good fishing all the way. Angle round the cliff-top, keeping to the high ground. Descend to the outflow of Glen Kinneastal River at 14/391113 where there is the possibility of sea-trout. Climb round the south shoulder of Carnan Mor (143m), maintaining the high ground, to find Loch Lochan. There are three further lochs to the east which are worth a visit whilst you are in the parish: Loch Chrochaire (14/404104), Loch Cartach (14/408109) and the unnamed lochan at 14/407106 on the cliff above Grobrie.
Fish Nothing for the glass case but the chance of a few good trout in Loch Lochan. Otherwise, excellent quality, hard-fighting fish which average 6/8oz.
Flies & Tactics Compass and map country. Leave word of where you are going and when you expect to return. The north shore of Loch Lochan is high-banked and the water is deep. Do not wade. The unnamed lochan noted above is an idyllic place for lunch. Offer them: Black Zulu, March Brown, Dunkeld.
Permission & Charges See Loch a'Ghruagaich entry.

LOCHANAN MORA, Loch See Horsaclett River.
MAOLAIG, Loch See Loch Chliostair.
MEAVAIG, River See Loch Scourst.
MEURACH, Loch See Loch Aoghnais Mhic Fhionnlaidh.
MHANAIS, Loch See Loch Udromul.

MHIC NEACAIL, Loch
Location & Access 14/148919 Loch Mhic Neacail is easily accessible and lies adjacent to the minor road between Grosebay and Collam in South Harris.
Commentary The loch covers an area of some 35 acres and is joined by a short stream to the sea at Loch Chollaim near Eilean Duih Chollaim. There are a number of small hill lochs near by for those who like to hike to their fishing, including Loch an Rothaid (14/141917) on Carnan Mor (124m). Loch Mula (14/139909) is ideal for a cast before dinner, being right by the road at between Cluer and Kyles Stockinish.

Fish Given heavy rain and spate conditions, the chance of sea-trout and possibly salmon, particularly towards the end of the season. Brown trout in these lochs are not monsters, but happily fill a frying pan.
Flies & Tactics Loch Mhic Neacail is easily fished from the bank and wading is not necessary. Work the east shore which has a number of good points and little bays; and step over for a cast in the satellite lochan at the north end. Flies: Blue Zulu, Ke-He, Black Pennell.
Permission & Charges See Loch a'Ghruagaich entry.

MIRKAVAT, Loch See Loch nam Faoileag.

MOR AN TANGA, Loch
Location & Access 14/377195 Follow the B8060 south from Garyvard for one mile and park at 14/371189. Walk east up the outlet burn to reach the first, unnamed, loch of the day at 14/373191 after five minutes.
Commentary An expedition to ten named and unnamed lochs lying round Soval Mor (82m) to the east of Caversta. The first water is joined south-east to Loch Uaille Mhor (14/375189), with its small island off the north shore. Tramp the inlet burn from the north-east corner of Loch Uaille Mhor, over the hill, to reach Loch Mor an Tanga which is a headwater loch of the Caversta river. Fish Loch Mor an Tanga in an anti-clockwise direction, taking in the two unnamed lochans on the hill at the south end at 14/382195. After exploring the north shore of Loch Mor an Tanga, descend to the unnamed lochan at 14/373197, then climb north again to find two further unnamed lochans at 14/371201. Return south by the Caversta road to the south-west, stopping for a cast in the unnamed lochan to the left of the track (known locally as Caversta Lochan) at 14/369193. Consider also a tramp west, across the B8060, to have a look at the unnamed lochan on the Caversta river at 14/370181; little Loch Caol Eishal (14/380180), at the junction where the minor road runs north-east to Cromore, is also worth a look.
Fish Great sport with hard-fighting little trout which average 6-8oz.
Flies & Tactics Easy bank fishing and wonderful scenery all day. Compass and map country, and do not wade. Offer: Loch Ordie, Grouse & Claret, Silver Butcher.
Permission & Charges See Loch a'Ghruagaich entry.

MOR DUNTAHA, Loch See Loch nam Faoileag.
MOR DUNTAHA, Loch See Loch nam Faoileag.

MOR, Loch (Rhenigdale)
Location & Access 14/217033 Follow the road east from Tarbert, through Oban and Urgha Beag, along the north shore of East Loch Tarbert. Shortly after crossing Laxadale Lochs (14/184005), look out for the signpost to Rhenigdale.
Commentary Until recently, the only way in was on foot, but the road has been upgraded. Even so, this is still a remote place and the lochs which lie to the north of Rhenigdale are rarely visited. Loch Mor is the largest water here, draining Lochan an Fheoir

OS Map 14 — Tarbert & Loch Seaforth

(14/213039) to the north, then flowing south through Loch Beag (14/219028) to reach the sea at Gary-aloteger (14/221017). The best approach is from Rhenigdale, climbing north over Mulla (200m) to descend to Loch Beag, a journey of three quarters of a mile.

Fish Good sport with nice little trout which fight well and are great fun to catch.

Flies & Tactics This is rough country and you will need compass and map to be safe. Fish the west shore of the lochs on the way north and return from Lochan an Fheoir south, fishing the east shores along your way. The surrounding hills, Toddun (528m) to the west, and Toscaram (250m) to the east, often act as a wind-tunnel, so be prepared for hard casting work at times. Regardless, however, of the weather, these lochs will delight. Try: Black Zulu, Clan Chief, Peter Ross.

Permission & Charges See Loch a'Mhorghain.

MOR NA MUILNE, Loch
Location & Access See Loch Bhreacaich.

MOR STIOMRABHAIGH, Loch
Location & Access 14/338130 See Loch Eishken. Easily accessible via estate tracks to the east of the Eishken road.

Commentary Loch Mor Stiomrabhaigh, and its unnamed neighbour at 14/353134, is the principal fishery to the east of the Eishken road. The system exits south via a half mile long stream to the sea at Tob Stiomrabhaigh. The head of the long, narrow, sea-loch, is known as Lodan Stiomrabhaigh (14/343118). Loch Shaghachain (14/353123), on the hill to the east of Lodan Stiomrabhaigh, also feeds the system, flowing north to Loch Shanndabhat (14/348134) which is joined to Loch Mor Stiomrabhaigh by a substantial stream. Also of note is the tiny trout loch on the hill to the west of Lodan Stiomrabhaigh, Loch a'Chairn (14/343112).

Fish See Loch Eishken for details.

Flies & Tactics Boats on the principal waters, bank fishing on the others and bank fishing can often be just as productive as fishing from the boat. Loch Mor Stiomrabhaigh is a substantial body of water, extending almost half a mile north/south by up to 400 yds wide. The narrow, north bay, where a number of feeder streams enter, is a good place to start, and along the south-west shore. In high water conditions, the connecting burn to Loch Shanndabhat can be excellent, both with sea-trout and brown trout, whilst Loch Shanndabhat itself offers a full days sport, covering more than a mile and a half of shoreline fishing. Loch Shaghachain is reached after a fifteen minute walk south up the stream from the south shore of Loch Shanndabhat. On the way, have a cast in the unnamed lochan at 14/349127, an extension of the stream and also connected to Loch Shaghachain. The most productive area on Loch Shaghachain is the west and south shore, particularly in the vicinity of the small island near the west outlet stream. Flies that may tempt them include: Loch Ordie, Black Pennell, Blue Zulu, Ke-He, Soldier Palmer, Grouse & Claret, Clan Chief, Goat's Toe, Greenwell's Glory, Dunkeld, Peter Ross, Silver Butcher, Alexandra.

Permission & Charges See Loch Eishken.

MUILLEAN ATH AN LINNE, Loch See Loch Tiorsdam.
MULA, Loch See Loch Mhic Neacail.
NA BA RIABHAICH, Loch See Loch Beag Catisval.
NA BA RUAIDHE, Loch See Loch an Eilein Bhig.
NA BEINNE BUIDHE, Loch See Loch nan Stearnag.
NA BEIRIGHE, Loch See Loch Eishken.
NA BEISTE, Loch (Cromore) See Loch Cromore.
NA BUAILE DUIBHE, Loch See Loch a'Ghruagaich.
NA CARTACH, Loch See Loch Geimisgarave.
NA CISTE, Loch (Ceann an Ora) See Loch a'Mhorghain.
NA CRAOIBHE, Loch See Loch an Duin (Scalpay).
NA CRAOIBHE, Loch (Calbost) See Loch nam Faoileag.

NA CREIGE BRISTE, Loch
Location & Access 14/091897 The outlet stream for this system crosses under the South Harris east coast road just to the north of Flodabay (14/099888) and enters the sea at 14/110889.

Commentary Easily accessible, relatively speaking for South Harris, but still involves some bumpy tramping across a lunar-like landscape. The first loch, at 14/099891, is unnamed. Follow the inlet stream at the north end to reach Loch na Creige Briste after ten minutes. Loch na Creige Briste is linked to a number of other unnamed lochans to the west, fed by the Allt Cro Nan Gobhar burn which rises to the north on Bealach na Ciste. The most significant and attractive of these unnamed lochans is at 14/087898. The system is also fed by a substantial, unnamed loch at 14/094891, to the immediate south of the first loch at 14/099891. This loch is not so hard to reach and can often be productive.

Fish Seatrout and a possibility of salmon. Brown trout which average 8oz, and a few larger specimens.

Flies & Tactics You need a compass and map for this expedition, particularly if you propose to explore the unnamed lochans to the west. Bank fishing all the way, and it is easy to cover the lies from the shore without wading. Offer: Black Pennell, Soldier Palmer, Silver Butcher.

Permission & Charges See Loch Geimisgarave.

NA CRO, Loch See Loch Plocrapool.
NA H-AIBHNE RUAIDHE, Loch See Loch Tiorsdam.
NA H-AIBHNE GAIRBHE, Loch See Laxdale River.
NA H-AIRIGH, Loch (Gravir) See Loch nam Faoileag.
NA H-INGHINN, Loch See Loch Cnoc Iain Duibh.
NA H-IOLAIRE, Loch (Horsaclett) See Horsaclett River.

NA H-UIDHE, Loch
Location & Access 14/075861 An easily accessible loch to the south of Finsbay which flows into the sea at 14/081862.

Commentary The best way to approach this loch is

137

Tarbert & Loch Seaforth — OS Map 14

from the narrow, south-east branch road from Finsbay. Park at 14/076866 and climb the hill to the south to reach the unnamed lochan at 14/075864 within ten minutes. This loch is also joined to the sea and can hold migratory fish as well as Loch na h-Uidhe. After fishing the first water, continue south for a couple of minutes to find Loch na h-Uidhe.
Fish Seatrout, a chance of salmon, and brown trout which average 8oz.
Flies & Tactics These small lochs are easily fished from the bank and fish may be taken from all round the margins. Do not wade. It only scares the fish out into deeper water. Whilst in the parish, and if things are quiet on Loch na h-Uidhe, tramp further south for five minutes to explore the unnamed lochs on Cnoc Mor (55m), between Bayhead (18/069855) and Borsham (18/080859). Offer: Black Zulu, March Brown, Silver Butcher.
Permission & Charges See Loch Geimisgarave.

NA LARACH LEITHE, Loch See Horsaclett River.
NA MOINE, Loch See Loch Dubh Sletteval.
NA MUILNE, Loch (Keose) See Loch Cnoc Iain Duibh.
NA SGAIL, Lochan See Loch Brunaval.

NA SROINE, Loch
Location & Access 14/329040 See Loch an Eilein Bhig. No easy way in, other than by boat, and even then a long trip from either Eishken in the north or Tarbert in the south. Remember, should the weather suddenly change for the worse, you could face a long, difficult, dangerous overland journey back to safety.
Commentary Start from the small cove in the sheltered bay at Tob Bhrollum (14/321031) and follow the stream steeply up hill south east to the unnamed lochan at 14/324028. Cross east to fish Lochan Sgeireach (14/328029). Walk north now, over Cnoc a'Luig Mhoir (120m), to find Loch na Sroine after 20 minutes. Loch na Sroine is full of ragged bays and corners. Fish anti-clockwise round to the inlet stream at 14/330942 on the north shore. Climb the gully north west to the unnamed lochan at 14/329045 and descend to the unnamed lochan at 14/322050 in Gleann a'Loch Fheoir. Follow the stream down to Loch Aigheroil (14/315045) on the cliff above sea Loch Bhrollum. This is the largest of the lochs visited and it covers an area of approximately 15 acres. Tob Bhrollum and the cove is three quarters of a mile further south.
Fish See Loch an Eilein Bhig.
Flies & Tactics Carefully read the Loch an Eilein Bhig entry.
Permission & Charges See Loch an Eilein Bhig.

NAM BREAC, Loch (Eishken) See Loch Fhoirabhal Bheag.
NAM BREAC, Loch (Keose) See Loch Keose.
NAM BREAC, Loch (Rogavat) See Loch Rogavat.

NAM FAOILEAG, Loch
Location & Access 14/400157 Leave the B8060 Garyvard/Lemreway road at Gravir (14/376157) and follow the minor road east along the north shore of sea Loch Odhairn, signposted to Calbost. The road borders the west and north shore of Loch nam Faoileag.
Commentary This easily accessible loch is just under half a mile east/west and covers an area of 30 acres. In the past, it was used for rearing salmon smolts. It is joined to little Loch Feoir (14/406158) to the east of the minor road, and to Loch Mor Duntaha (14/398163) in the hills to the north. A number of other lochs in the area are worth a visit, as much for their beauty as for the chance of sport. Particularly, have a look at the series of unnamed lochans round Loch Mor Duntaha, starting at 14/397161, then working north to the six waters in the hills round 14/398169. Further adventure may be had by tramping east to visit Loch Lite Sithinn (14/420154), best approached from Loch Feoir; Loch na h-Airigh (14/408161), ten minutes east from the road, to the north of Loch Feoir; Loch Mirkavat (14/409169), and distant Loch na Craoibhe (14/420165) in the hills above the sea and approached from the end of the road at Bailie Phail (14/416170). The little unnamed lochan close to the road near Calbost (14/416172) is also worth a cast and is conveniently situated near a splendid beach at Camas Chalaboist (14/418172).
Fish There are reports of escapee smolts returning as grilse to Loch nam Faoileag and the loch also contains excellent trout, some of which are over 2lb in weight. However, be warned, they are not easy to catch. The Calbost loch can hold seatrout in high-water conditions and the other lochs noted above all have stocks of trout which average 6-8oz with the chance of a few larger specimens of up to and over 1lb in weight.
Flies & Tactics Bank fishing. Do not wade. You will need a compass to find your way round the smaller lochs, particularly the waters to the east of the road. Attack during May and early June. Some of these waters are badly affected by weed growth as the season advances. Offer: Black Pennell, Soldier Palmer, Peter Ross.
Permission & Charges See Loch a'Ghruagaich entry.

NAM FAOILEAG, Loch (Eishken)
Location & Access 14/315075 See Loch an Eilein Bhig entry. Start from Tob na Gile Moire (14/338099) on the south shore of Loch Sealg.
Commentary A long, eight mile day out in the hills, fishing four remote lochs between Gormol (470m) and Uisenis (371m). Compass and map land and rough going, but glorious country with more than a good chance of seeing golden eagle. Begin by climbing south west over Cleit a'Bhaile (104m) to find Abhainn Chorlabhaidh burn at 14/325090. Follow the stream south up the glen to the first loch, Loch Ruadh (14/3199080). After fishing Loch Ruadh, climb steeply west up the inlet stream to reach Loch Chumraborgh (14/309078) which lies below the north-east shoulder of Gormol. Walk south from Loch Chumraborgh for ten minutes to find Loch nam Faoileag. After exploring Loch nam Faoileag, climb round the north shoulder of Colla Cleit (271m) and descend to the north end of Loch Ucsabhat (14/326065). Walk the outlet stream

OS Map 14 — Tarbert & Loch Seaforth

north to return to Loch Ruadh. The start point at Tob na Giles Moire is one and a half miles north east from the loch.
Fish See Loch an Eilein Bigh entry. Loch Faoileag and Loch Ucsabhat hold some good fish of up to and over 1lb in weight.
Flies & Tactics It is important, for your own safety, that you carefully read the entry for Loch an Eilein Bigh. Loch nam Faoileag and Loch Ucsabhat are both more than quarter of a mile long. The south end and east shoreline of each loch is the most productive area. The other waters are easily read. Offer: Black Zulu, Soldier Palmer, Alexandra.
Permission & Charges See Loch an Eilein Bhig.

NAN CAOR, Loch See Loch Totaichean Aulaidh.
NAN CAOR, Loch (Diraclett) See Loch Diraclett.

NAN CAOR, Loch (Quidnish)
Location & Access 14/095875 Leave the South Harris east coast road at the head of Loch Finsbay at 4/082877 and drive east to the end of the road at Quidnish. The loch is a 15 min. walk to the north of the township.
Commentary Loch nan Caor can also be reached via a peat road from the north and this easily accessible, small island-clad loch is in a very attractive setting. There are several other unnamed lochans surrounding Quidinish which will repay a visit.
Fish Brown trout which average 6-8oz.
Flies & Tactics Bank fishing, and the north end of the loch, by the two islands is the place to start. Also have a look at the brackish loch immediately to the east of Quidnish, where there is a chance of sport with seatrout after heavy rain. Flies: Ke-He, Black Zulu, Alexandra.
Permission & Charges See Loch a'Ghruagaich entry.

NAN CNAMH, Lochan See Loch nan Stearnag.
NAN CRAOBHAG, Loch See Horsaclett River.
NAN EANG, Loch See Loch Tiorsdam.
NAN EILEAN, Loch (Garyvard) See Loch Totaichean Aulaidh.
NAN EILEIN, Loch (Mulhagery) See Loch Linngrabhaidh.
NAN EILEIN, Loch (Tom an Fhuadain) See Loch nan Stearnag.
NAN GILLEAN, Loch See Loch Brunaval.
NAN IOLAIREAN, Loch See Lochan Tana (Glenside).
NAN LUB, Loch See Loch nan Uidhean Beaga.
NAN RITHEANAN, Loch See Loch Cnoc Iain Duibh.

NAN STEARNAG, Loch
Location & Access 14/399135 Start from Loch Criadha (see entry). At the end of the peat road, walk south east, aiming for the high ground ahead. After ten minutes, at the stream, follow the flow up the glen to the tiny lochan at 14/398134 and there bear left. Loch nan Stearnag is five minutes east over the hill.
Commentary Golden plover country, and a magnificent day out in the moors exploring a series of lochs and lochans which rarely see an artificial fly from one season to the next. After fishing Loch nan Stearnag, continue south east for five minutes to find Lochan na Beinne Buidhe (14/404130), its satellite, unnamed lochan to the south west at 14/408124. Walk due east from the Shieling Lochan to fish the pretty, unnamed lochan with the small island at 14/413125. Track the outlet burn from 14/413125 south, then east, to explore a delightful series of unnamed waters leading north to Loch nan Eilean (14/419124), which lies on the cliffs above Lagan. This is the ideal place for lunch. Continue north east now, to fish Lochan nan Cnamh (14/421131), then march west to the last of the waters, Loch Caol (14/418130) and its surrounding unnamed lochans. A one and a half mile, rugged tramp west north-west, and accurate map reading, will bring you back to the start point at Loch Criadha.
Fish Splendid fun with bright little trout.
Flies & Tactics Careful map reading is the most necessary tactic - this is rough country and it is easy to become disorientated. No problem covering the water from the shore, these are small, intimate lochs. Offer: Ke-He, Goat's Toe, Alexandra.
Permission & Charges See Loch a'Ghruagaich entry.

NAN UIDHEAN BEAGA, Loch
Location & Access 14/328147 For access details see Loch Eishken entry. Park on the Eishken road at 14/324149.
Commentary A fine hill walk round a series of named and unnamed lochs and lochans lying, with the exception of the unnamed water at 14/321147, to the east of the road. Follow the outlet stream east to reach Loch nan Uidhean Beaga after ten minutes. Fish round the north and east shore, working south to explore the unnamed satellite lochans at 14/331145 and 14/332141. At the south end of the last lochan, climb gently rising ground to the east to find the unnamed lochan at 14/336143. Explore the west shore, working north, then follow the inlet stream over to Loch nan Lub (14/340145). Loch nan Lub is a straggling water, full of corners and fishy points. Proceed clockwise round Loch nan Lub to finish where you began. Return to the start point fishing the west shore of 14/346143, and the east shores of the other waters, back to Loch nan Uidhean Beaga. End the day with an assault on the lochan to the west of the road.
Fish Loch nan Uidhean Beaga flows north to the sea through Loch Sgibacleit (14/316170) and there is always the possibility, after heavy rain, of an encounter with sea-trout. This also applies to Loch nan Lub which flows south through Loch Shanndabhat (14/348134) to the sea to Tob Stiomrabhaigh. Otherwise, expect bright brown trout which average in the order of 8oz.
Flies & Tactics A round trip of some 3 miles and fairly rugged going. Avoid wading, fish tend to lie close to the margins and these lochs are mostly easily covered from the shore. The north east bank of the main part of Loch nan Lub is generally the most productive area, although fish are taken from all round the shore. Cast with confidence using Black Zulu, Goat's Toe, Clan Chief.
Permission & Charges See Loch Eishken entry.

Tarbert & Loch Seaforth — OS Map 14

NAN UIDHEAN, Loch (Brunaval) See Loch Brunaval.
NAN UIDHEAN, Loch (Horsaclett) See Horsaclett River
NAN UIDHEAN, Loch (Scadabay) See Loch Plocrapool.
OB LEASAID, Sea Loch See Loch Udromul.

OIL, Loch
Location & Access 14/303034. See Loch an Eilein Bhig entry. Access by boat from either Eishken in the north or Tarbert in the south. Otherwise, a marathon overland hike.
Commentary Go ashore by the ruined shielings at Bhalamus, a sheltered, sandy, well-protected bay. Walk north up the Abhainn Gleann Bhalamuis burn to begin a four mile round trip to seven named and unnamed lochs and lochans. After half a mile, follow the stream on the right, uphill to the unnamed lochan at 14/295031. From here, walk due east to reach the south end of Loch Oil. Fish clockwise round the loch, which, including its narrow north east arm, is some 700 yds long, and leave at the south end to tramp south east for 15 minutes to find tiny Loch Cleit an Aiseig (14/309025). Return west to explore the string of unnamed lochans on the way to Loch a'Gharaidh (14/300028). Follow the outlet stream from Loch a'Gharaidh down to Abhainn Gleann Bhalamuis and the start point.
Fish See Loch an Eilein Bhig entry. Possibility of sea-trout at the mouth of the burn at Bhalamus.
Flies & Tactics For your own safety, carefully read the Loch an Eilein Bhig entry.
Permission & Charges See Loch an Eilein Bhig.

PLOCRAPOOL, Loch
Location & Access 14/177935 Loch Plocrapool lies adjacent to the west side of the minor road from Diraclett to Scadabay, about 20 minutes drive south from Tarbert.
Commentary This is one of the most beautiful lochs in South Harris and requires more than a casual glance if the complicated nature and extent of this fine fishery is to be fully revealed. The loch is one mile north/south by up to quarter of a mile wide and it is accessible not only from the road, but also via a convenient track which runs the length of the west bank; beginning in the south near the church in Scadabay and ending by the post office at the north end. The south end of the loch, in particular, is very lovely, scattered with tree and scrub-covered little islands, whilst to the east of Loch Plocrapool, and hidden from view, is Loch Grannda (14/181930); guarded by Cleit a'Bhraigh (70m), another delightful water, well worth a visit. There are a number of other, easily accessible named and unnamed lochs and lochans in the vicinity: Loch Cul na Beinne (14/167944) and the unnamed lochan over the crag to the west at 14/165943; Loch Cnoc nan Sligean (14/161941), 500 yds north/south and flowing south into Loch Harmasaig (14/160934). The south shore of Loch Harmasaig touches the road. To the east of Loch Harmasaig is another 'classic' South Harris water, Loch nan Uidhean (14/165930), peat-stained, graced with perfect islands; and east again, Loch na Cro (14/169929) and the unnamed, roadside lochan at 14/166933. There is enough fishing here for several weeks, as well outstanding wildlife, flora and fauna. Those with non-fishing members in their party should despatch them to the magnificent sands at Luskentyre (14/070990).
Fish Brown trout which vary in size from 8oz up to 12oz, with the chance of some larger specimens, in all the lochs, and the possibility of sea-trout in the waters connected to the sea.
Flies & Tactics Not easy fishing, and some of these lochs might appear at first sight to be fishless. Have no doubt, however, that nothing could be further from the truth and cast with confidence. Avoid wading. Fish a short line. Trout tend to lie close to the shore, particularly on Loch Plocrapool and on Loch nan Uidhean. Flies to try: Blue Zulu, March Brown, Peter Ross.
Permission & Charges Contact: Dr Alasdair Fraser, 9 The Common, London W5 3TR. Tel: (0208) 567 1285; or at No 4 Cluer, Isle of Harris, Outer Hebrides. Tel: 530248.

RAOINABHAT, Loch See Loch Eishken

ROGAVAT, Loch
Location & Access 14/070899 A tough tramp. Park at the south end of Loch Huamavat (14/089870) on the South Harris east coast road. Follow the west shore of the loch north-west, climbing over rough ground, to reach Loch Rogavat after a hike of one and a half miles.
Commentary The loch has its source in Loch nam Breac (14/068922) on the west slopes of Heileasbhal Mor (384m). The Allt Uamh nam Ban burn flows south from Loch nam Breac to enter Loch Rogavat after one mile. Along the way, the stream collects in the waters from Loch Dubh mas Holasmul (14/06790) to the west.
Fish Brown trout in both lochs which average 8oz..
Flies & Tactics A compass and map is essential to find your way round this wilderness. There are so many unnamed lochs and lochans along the route that it is easy to become at least sidetracked, if not lost. Loch Rogavat is a substantial body of water covering an area of some 30 acres, Loch Dubh mas Holasmul is a smaller affair. Both are easily fished from the shore. The trout can be dour at times. Tempt them with: Blue Zulu, March Brown, Peter Ross.
Permission & Charges See Loch Geimisgarave.

RUADH, Loch (South Eishken) See Loch nam Faoileag.
RUAIRIDH, Loch See Loch Tiorsdam

SAILE, Loch
Location & Access 14/116929 Close to the sea at Bayhead at the head of Loch Stockinish and easily accessible from the minor east coast road from Diraclett on the A859 to Rodel and Leverburgh.
Commentary A brackish loch on a good migratory fish system which includes Loch Glumra Beag (14/125935), Loch Glumra More (14/119936), and Loch Creavat (14/116938) which is the largest loch on

OS Map 14 — Tarbert & Loch Seaforth

the system. Access is along a peat road which starts at Bayhead and reaches the west shore of Loch Creavat whithin half a mile. Loch Glumra Beag and Loch Glumra More are best approached via another peat track which leaves the minor road near Ardvey at 14/126930.
Fish Sea-trout and the odd salmon. Brown trout as well, but nothing for the glass case.
Flies & Tactics The most vital component of success is rain. The little stream has to be full for a few days to encourage fish into the upper lochs. However, Loch Saile generally hold fish from July onwards, dependent upon the state of the tide and upon who might be watching. Flies to offer: Blue Zulu, Kate MacLaren, Goat's Toe.
Permission & Charges See Loch Geimisgarave.

SCALADALE, River See Loch Tiorsdam.

SCOURST, Loch
Location & Access 14/100095 The headwater of the Meavaig River. See Loch Voshimid entry.
Commentary Loch Scourst has a reputation for being dour and it is often wild. The surrounding hills, Sron Scourst (491m) to the east and Oreval (662m) to the west, act as wind tunnel frequently making fishing conditions very difficult.
Fish Mostly noted for sea-trout, rather than for salmon, but, on its day, Loch Scourst can offer reasonable sport with salmon as well. Good water levels in the Meavaig River are vital to bring the fish into the system. Some very large sea-trout have been taken from the loch, including a fish of 11lb.
Flies & Tactics Loch Scourst is just under half a mile in length, north/south, by up to 200 yards wide. Do not wade, the loch is deep and wading only scares the fish out from the margins into the middle. The North end, where the water is shallow and the principal feeder stream enters from Caadale Ear (580m), is the place to start. Flies: Goat's Toe, Black Pennell, Peter Ross.
Permission & Charges See Loch Voshimid.

SEILEBOST, River See Loch Gleann na moine.
SGEIREACH, Loch (Quier) See Loch Lighigeag.
SGEIREACH, Loch (Tob Bhrollum) See Loch na Sroine.
SGEIREAGAN MOR, Loch See Loch a'Mhorghain.

SGIBACLEIT, Loch
Location & Access 14/316170 See Loch Eishken entry. Park near Seaforth Head at 14/300161. Loch Sgibacleit is a few moments east.
Commentary Easily accessible and the largest loch in the area; almost one mile east/west, with a narrow, one mile long, northern extension, referred to as North End. The Eishken Estate road borders the south shore of the loch. Where the road turns south, there is a small, unnamed loch at 14/323158 which is also worth a cast. Loch Sgibacleit is surrounded by hills which can act as a wind tunnel, but because of the configuration of the loch it is generally possible to find sheltered fishing somewhere. The river leading from the loch to the sea at Seaforth Head can be excellent in the right water

conditions, as can be fishing in the sea itself.
Fish Salmon and sea-trout. Salmon average 7/8lb, sea-trout 1lb. Larger fish are frequently taken, salmon of over 20lb have been landed in recent years. The annual average catch for the whole system, including other North Eishken and Scaliscro Lodge fishing, is in the order of 100 salmon, 150 sea-trout and 1000 brown trout. See also Loch Eishken entry.
Flies & Tactics Boat fishing brings best results, and helps to get around this large expanse of water. However, the south shore is easily accessible from the Estate road and North end, not too distant a tramp round the east end of the loch. The wide bay at the extreme north of North End, and in particular the east bank, is a good place to begin your assault. Offer them: Black Pennell, Ke-He, Soldier Palmer, Black Zulu, Blue Zulu, Grouse & Claret, Greenwell's Glory, Kate Maclaren, Clan Chief, Goat's Toe, Teal Blue & Silver, Alexandra, Peter Ross, Silver Butcher, Dunkeld.
Permission & Charges Fish rights are shared between two estates. Contact Scaliscro Lodge, Scaliscro, Uig, Isle of Lewis PA86 9EL. Tel: (01851) 672325. Fax: (01851) 672393. See also Loch Eishken entry. Costs, approximately, £60 per rod per day, July to September.

SGORR NI DHONNACHAIDH, Loch
Location & Access 14/389174 Park on the B8060 Garyvard/Lemreway road by the loch at 14/381169, known locally as the 'Square Loch'. Loch Sgorr Ni Dhonnachaidh lies to the east and is reached after a walk of about 30mins.
Commentary There are a number of exciting fishing possibilities in the vicinity, including the unnamed loch to the west of the road at OS14/379165, known locally as Loch Caol a'Gharaidh Mhoir. This is a headwater of the Caversta river. After fishing the Square Loch, walk due east to find the unnamed lochan at OS14/385169. Climb the hill to the east and descend to Loch Sgorr Ni Dhonnachaidh, 400yds north/south and covering approx. 30 acres. Return to the Square Loch from the north end of Loch Sgorr Ni Dhonnachaidh via the lunnamed lochan at OS14/387175. End the day with a few casts on Loch Caol a'Gharaidh Mhoir.
Fish The Square Loch holds excellent trout, with the possibility of fish over 2lb in weight, whilst Loch Caol a'Gharaidh Mhoir can hold seatrout (and perhaps salmon) towards the back end and after heavy rain. The other waters noted above contain good stocks of trout which average 8-10oz.
Flies & Tactics A super day out with easy bank fishing all the way. Do not wade. Fish the south shore of the Square Loch on the way out, the north shore on your return. The north end of Loch Sgorr Ni Dhonnachaidh is the most productive area, whilst on Loch Caol a'Gharaidh Mhoir, fish may be taken from all round the shore. Flies: Black Zulu, Grouse & Claret, Silver Invicta.
Permission & Charges See Loch Crois Ailein.

SHAGHACHAIN, Loch See Loch Stiomrabhaigh.
SHANNDABHAT, Loch See Loch Stiombraigh.
SHEEP, Loch See Horsaclett River

Tarbert & Loch Seaforth

OS Map 14

SHIELING, Lochan See Loch nan Stearnag.

SHROMOIS, Loch
Location & Access 14/257153. See Loch Sgibacleit entry. A croft road along the south shore of North Loch Seaforth, from Seaforth Head to Tob Mhic cholla (14/275158), makes access to this remote loch relatively easy. At the end of the track, walk south west between Dun Chonuill (143m) to the north and Cadha Cleit (210m) to the south to reach the loch in 30 minutes.
Commentary Until the advent of the new croft road this loch was rarely visited and, even now, few anglers venture this far. However, those who do are well rewarded, for the loch is very beautiful and lies amidst magnificent scenery. In the right conditions, it is also worth considering following the coastline south towards Chithish Bheag (120m). A number of streams flow into Loch Seaforth from Sidhean an Airgid (390m) and sea-trout frequently congregate at their mouth.
Fish Sport with sea-trout which average 1lb, brown trout of approximately 6/8oz and the chance of an occasional salmon.
Flies & Tactics Bank fishing and the water is easily covered from the shore. The east end of the loch produces best results, where five streams rush in, but fish are taken from all round the shore. This is a magical place to spend a day. Flies: Black Zulu, Soldier Palmer, Clan Chief.
Permission & Charges See Loch Sgibacleit

SKEAUDALE, River See Loch a'Mhorghain.
SOEIREACH, Lochan See Loch a'Ghruagaich.
SOVAL, Loch See Loch Cnoc Iain Duibh.
SQUARE, Loch See Loch Sgorr Ni Dhonnachaidh.
SRATH STEACHRAN, Loch See Laxdale River.
STIOCLETT, Loch See Loch Diraclett.
STIOMRABHAIGH, Lochan See Loch Stiomrabhaigh.

STULADALE, Loch See Loch Voshimid.

TANA, Lochan (Glenside)
Location & Access 14/371165 To the north of the township of Glenside on the B8060 Garyvard/Lemreway road. Park at 14/367159 and walk the outlet burn north to reach the loch after ten minutes.
Commentary The access point noted above is also a good start-point for a visit to the south end of Loch Totaichean Aulaidh (14/353170) and Loch nan Eilean (14/362175). Have a cast in Loch nan Iolairean (14/367162) and the unnamed lochan at 14/366166 whilst in the parish. The Kinloch Ouirn river flows to the south of the Glenside road and, in spate conditions, this can provide sport with migratory fish.
Fish Great fun with bright, little, brown trout which average 8oz. The Kinloch Ouirn river can produce seatrout and the odd salmon, given the right water levels. The south end of Loch Totaichean Aulaidh and Loch nan Eilean have some very good trout. Fish of over 2lb are not uncommon.

Flies & Tactics Easy bank fishing. The lochs are readily covered from the shore and there is really no need to wade. Offer them: Loch Ordie, Grouse & Claret, Alexandra.
Permission & Charges See Loch a'Ghruagaich entry.

TANA, Lochan (Aline) See Loch Tiorsdam.

TARBERT, Loch
Location & Access 14/094890 Immediately to the north of Flodabay (14/099888) on the tortuous, South Harris east coast road.
Commentary A small loch covering an area of a few acres, with a delightful, scrub-covered island. The loch exits to the south through a narrow stream and there are a number of adjacent, unnamed, lochs all of which contain trout.
Fish Seatrout and a possibility of salmon. Brown trout which average 6-8oz.
Flies & Tactics Easily fished from the bank and the chance of sport from all round the shoreline. Best after heavy rain when Black Zulu, Ke-He, Peter Ross can bring results.
Permission & Charges See Loch Geimisgarave.

TARSUINN, Loch See Loch an Duin, Scalpay.
TIDAL POND See Loch Dubh Slettaval.

TIORSDAM, Loch
Location & Access 14/218164. An easily accessible Aline Estate loch, close to the A859 road between Arivruaich to the north and Aline Lodge to the south.
Commentary Loch Tiorsdam is on the headwaters of the Kintarvie River system and it flows north to meet Allt nan Each burn at 14/226168. The stream crosses under the main road and enters the sea half a mile north at Tob Kintarvie (14/231173). To the east of the road, on Aird an Troim, are several other Aline Estate named and unnamed lochs, the principal ones being Loch an Rathaid (14/218150), Loch a'Bhoineid (14/2322165) and Lochan Tana (14/233155). There are good unnamed lochans at 14/238160, 14/232157 and 14/230155. The Aline Estate also have fishing on Loch na h-Aibhine Ruaidhe (14/217150) which is surrounded by commercial forestry, and Loch Cleit na Stiuire by the west side of the A859 road at 14/212145. These lochs feed into the Kintarvie River through Loch Tiorsdam. South from Loch Cleit na Stiure are three additional waters, all of which flow east into Loch Seaforth: the unnamed, roadside lochan at 14/212139, Loch Muillean Ath an Linne (14/210135), and little Loch Ille Chipain (14/205131).
Fish The principal interest is salmon and sea-trout, although Aline Estate also produces up to 1,000 brown trout each year. Approximately 80 salmon and 100 sea-trout are caught most seasons, depending upon water conditions. Salmon average 6/7lb, with a few fish in double figures, sea-trout 1lb.
Flies & Tactics There are boats on the principal migratory fish waters and advice on flies and tactics is available from the Fishery Manager. The lochs are small and easily 'read' and the river is very much salmon stalking country where a single handed rod and a

142

OS Map 14
Tarbert & Loch Seaforth

stealthy approach is all-important. The estate also have fishing rights on Loch Langavat (14/160170) and on the Langdale River which runs into the head of Loch Langavat (see entries). Access to these locations is by estate argocat or by foot. Sport may also be had at the mouths of two small streams to the south of Aline Lodge: Vigadale Bay at 14/190116 and Ardvourlie Bay at 14/190103. Those who appreciate a long hike to remote places will enjoy a visit to Loch Ruairidh (14/174111) at the head of the Vigadale River; and even longer and nicer, a tramp out to the headwaters of the Scaladale River to explore Loch Vistem (14/153089) and Loch nan Eang (14/146081) which lie in corries on the north slope of Clisham (799m), the highest peak in Lewis and Harris. The estate also offers a wide variety of other sport, including excellent shooting and stalking, and an inflatable boat for use on Loch Seaforth which could provide a means for visiting some of the small streams on the west shore of Loch Seaforth where sea-trout congregate after heavy rain. Flies: Loch Ordie, Ke-He, Soldier Palmer, Black Zulu, Blue Zulu, Black Pennell, Grouse & Claret, Greenwell's Glory, March Brown, Clan Chief, Goat's Toe, Kate McLaren, Teal Blue & Silver, Peter Ross, Alexandra, Silver Butcher, Silver Invicta.
Permission & Charges Sport (except for Scaladale and Vigadale) is let with Aline Lodge, a comfortable property on the shore of Loch Seaforth which accommodates 10/12 guests. For full details, contact Messrs Strutt & Parker, 13 Hill Street, Berkeley Square, London. Tel 0207 629 7282; Fax: 0207 499 1657 or Finlyson Hughes, Lynedoch House, Barossa Place, Perth PE1 5EP. Tel: (01738) 451600; Fax (01738) 451900. Day lets are sometimes available and range in price from £50 to £150 per day, depending upon numbers in the party. For availability and bookings, contact: The Fishery Manager, Aline Estate. Tel: (01859) 502006.

TOTA RUAIRIDH DHUIBH, Lochan See Loch Criadha.

TOTAICHEAN AULAIDH, Loch
Location & Access 14/353170. Leave the A859 Stornoway/Tarbert road at the head of Loch Erisort and follow the B8060 east to Garyvard. A peat road runs south from Garyvard at 14/356201 giving access to the lochs lying to the west of Sidhean Gorm (100m).
Commentary Three of the lochs in this series are close to the peat road mentioned above: Loch an Tairbeart (14/350198), Loch nan Caor (14/355195), and Loch a'Ghobhainn (14/362189). The other two, Loch Totaichean Aulaidh and Loch nan Eilean (14/362175) are a few minutes' walk south from the end of the peat track. Although easily accessible, the principal lochs (the last two noted above) are large waters, both covering an area of almost one mile north/south by up to 500yds wide. Consequently, exploring them involves a good hike so be properly prepared and take along a compass and map, just in case of bad weather.
Fish Trout average 8oz but there are larger fish as well, particularly in Loch Totaichean Aulaidh and Loch nan Eilean where trout of over 2lb in weight have been caught in recent years.
Flies & Tactics The peat road lochs are easily understood and covered from the shore. The larger lochs produce trout throughout their length, but the east bank of Loch nan Eilean is the most productive fishing area. This shore is a maze of bays and points, served by half a dozen inlet streams. On Loch Totaichean Aulaidh, concentrate on the wide, south bay, paying particular attention to the area round the two small islands in the south-west corner. It should also be noted that these lochs are surrounded by a number of small, unnamed lochans, generally within ten minutes of the main water. Some contain large trout. Visit the sea between Garyvard and Caversta to fish the mouth of the Caversta river at 14/364200. Given good conditions, there is always the chance of seatrout. Flies: Black Zulu, Soldier Palmer, Alexandra.
Permission & Charges For more information and local accommodation details, apply to Crois Ailein Lodge, Gravir, Stornoway, Isle of Lewis. Tel: (01851) 880409.

UAILLE MHOR, Loch See Loch Mor an Tanga.
UAMADALE, Loch See Loch Diraclett.
UCSABHAT, Loch See Loch nam Faoileag.

UDROMUL, Loch
Location & Access 14/102919 Approach from near the post office at Mill (14/111904) on the South Harris east coast road. Follow the Loch Geimisgarave outlet stream north into the hills. At the first junction (14/109912), climb across the saddle to the west and descend to Loch Udromul. The journey takes approx. 30mins.
Commentary Loch Udromul is the principal loch on a complicated little migratory fish system which draws its strength from both north and south. The northern source is from a tiny lochan on the grey crags of An Coileach (389m) which tumbles down the Allt a'Bhealaich Ghairbh to enter Loch Udromul amidst the finger-like bays and promontories at the north-west corner. From the south, the system flows from an unnamed lochan (14/109904) on the hill above Mill and collects in the water from Loch a'Gharaidh before joining Udromul. The loch exits to the south, winding its way through Loch Mhanais (14/097904) and Loch a'Chlachain (14/101899), reaching the sea near the church between Manish and Flodabay at 14/100895.
Fish Seatrout and a possibility of salmon. Brown trout which average 8oz, and a few larger specimens.
Flies & Tactics Good water levels are essential to bring fish into the system. Nae water, nae fish. The easiest approach to the lower lochs, Mhanais and a'Chlachain, is from the church, up the outlet stream. There is also the chance of seatrout sport in Ob Leasaid (14/109892) between Manish and Ardslave. Offer them: Blue Zulu, Grouse & Claret, Clan Chief.
Permission & Charges See Loch Geimisgarave.

UIDHEAN, Loch (Lacasdail) See Loch Lacasdail.
UISEADER, Loch See Loch Brunaval.

ULLADALE, Loch
Location & Access 14/080144 A four mile journey

143

Tarbert & Loch Seaforth — OS Map 14

north from the sea at Soya Sound along North Harris Estate roads from the weir on the B887 road at 14/053078.

Commentary The estate road passes round the west shore of Loch Leosaid (14/060085) past the power station on the River Eaval at 14/060092; climbing by Loch Chliostair (14/070106) to a watershed by the shieling at the north end of Loch Ashavat (14/072119). The track descends into the narrow glen between Tirga Beag (570m) to the west and Sron Ulladale (454m) to the east, following the line of the River Ulladale to reach the south shore of Loch Ulladale after a bumpy mile. The loch exits north as the Ulladale River, through Lochan an Fheoir (14/079152), Loch a'Cheivla (14/092157) and Loch A'Pheircil (095159), when it becomes the Housay River. The stream reaches the sea at Kinloch-resort in company with Abhainn Mhoir Ceann Resort, which drains the Voshimid system to the east.

Fish An excellent salmon and sea-trout fishery.

Flies & Tactics Good water levels and reasonable weather conditions are essential for best sport. The loch is up to half a mile long, north/south, by approximately 250 yards wide, shallow and naturally divided into two sections by a rock ledge. The northern section is favoured by sea-trout whilst the salmon seem to prefer the jagged, south end. Those who seek greater adventure can follow the stream one mile north to explore Loch a'Cheivla (14/092157), known locally as 'Reedy Loch', and the adjacent, famous 'Muggs Pool', where the flow exits from Loch a'Cheivla. Loch a'Pheircil (14/095159), the next extension of the stream is even more reedy than its northern neighbour and is almost impossible to fish. There is also the possibility of sport in the estuary at Kinloch-resort, where fish congregate prior to ascending both the Ulladale and the Voshimid systems, but it is a long, hard tramp north. Flies: Black Pennell, Invicta, Goat's Toe.

Permission & Charges See Loch Voshimid entry.

ULLADALE, River See Loch Ulladale.
VIGADALE, River See Loch Tiorsdam.
VISTEM, Loch See Loch Tiorsdam.

VOSHIMID, Loch

Location & Access 14/105130. Loch Voshimid is the premier fishery of the North Harris Estate and is located at the end of a 4 mile long estate track. The track runs north through Glen Meavaig by the Meavaig River from the sea at Meavaig (14/101063) on the shore of West Loch Tarbert. The track passes deep Loch Scourst (14/100095) at the head of the Meavaig River before crossing the watershed and descending for a further two miles to reach the south end of Loch Voshimid.

Commentary A legendary salmon and sea-trout fishery, flowing north for 3 miles from Loch Voshimid via the Abhainn Mhoir Ceann Resort river, to reach the sea at Kinloch-resort (14/105173). The loch is half a mile in length, north/south, by up to a quarter of a mile wide, shallow, and scattered with tiny islands and skerries. However, good water levels are all-important for the loch to give of its best, as is true for most Lewis and Harris migratory fish systems. To the south of Loch Voshimid, and draining into it, is Loch an Fheoir (14/104125), known locally as the 'Weedy Loch'. In high water conditions, when fish can ascend the intervening falls, this loch can also be very productive. Two main streams feed Loch Voshimid from the east. The most southerly, flowing down Glen Stuladale, enters Loch Voshimid at the north east corner. It rises in Loch Stuladale (14/124116), a remote, lovely trout loch lying in a high corrie between the north shoulder of Craig Stulaval (513m) to the south and Stulaval (579m) to the north. The second stream, Abhainn a'Chlair Bhig, enters Abhainn Mhoir Ceann Resort by the ruined sheiling at 14/114165 and rises from Loch Chleistir, blow the dark cliffs of Creag Chleistir (400m). Both lochs may be reached along a stalkers' path from the north end of Loch Voshimid. The track divides after half a mile, the north branch leading to Loch Chleistir after half a mile, and the right hand fork, leading south east for one mile to Loch Stulaval. This is rough country and the going is unrelentingly steep.

Fish For its size, Loch Voshimid is one of the most productive migratory fish waters in Europe. Some outstanding catches have been made in recent times from the North Harris Estate, with weekly returns in the order of 100 salmon and up to 100 sea-trout. Numbers have declined, but the fishery still averages approx. 200 salmon and up to 500 sea-trout most seasons. Salmon average 6-7lb, sea-trout 1.5-2lb. The brown trout lochs noted above have fish in the order of 8oz, but probably larger trout as well.

Flies & Tactics Loch Voshimid fish are taken throughout the loch from the margin to the middle. Boat fishing brings best results, although in adverse weather conditions, fishing from the shore can be just as productive. There are a number of noted hot spots, including Seal Rock, Sopwith's Bay, Green Bank, Mary Rose Island and Richard's Bay. Dapping is often excellent and the flies that do most damage are: Ke-He, Loch Ordie, Black Pennell, Goat's Toe, Clan Chief, March Brown, Invicta, Peter Ross, Silver Butcher. The same flies will do for the hill lochs. These hill lochs are very infrequently visited and information about how they perform is limited. However, they are small and easily understood and offer an exciting challenge amidst magnificent 'golden eagle' scenery.

Permission & Charges The North Harris Estate fishing is generally let by the week, including accommodation at Amhuinnsuidhe Castle. Sporting lets are arranged through Finlyson Hughes, Lynedoch House, Barossa Place, Perth PH1 5EP. Tel: (01738) 541600; Fax: (01738) 451900. Prices on application.

OS Map 15 — Loch Assynt

Loch Assynt

A'BHIRAILLE, Loch 15/130259 See Loch Beannach.

A'BHITH, Loch
Location & Access 15/328004 Approach from Lubcroy (15/355109) on the A837 Bonar Bridge/Ledmore Junction road. Follow the track on the north bank of the Allt Coire Ruchain burn for one mile, then cross the burn and walk south via a series of small waterfalls to reach the loch. 50 minutes from the road.
Commentary A very attractive little loch in a remote setting, rarely visited and great fun to fish. Far from the madding crowd country and magnificent surroundings.
Fish Nothing for the glass case, but good sport with pretty trout averaging 8oz.
Flies & Tactics Easily fished from the bank with action everywhere. First cast: Ke-He, Greenwell's Glory, Dunkeld.
Permission & Charges Oykel Bridge Hotel, Oykel Bridge, by Lairg, Ross-shire. Tel: (01549) 441218. £5 per rod per day.

A'BHRAIGHE, Loch
Location & Access 15/132307 A brief moorland canter from the end of the minor road leading south from the village of Nedd at 15/136320 on the B869 Unapool/Lochinver road.
Commentary Make a visit to Loch a'Bhraighe part of a longer expedition to include four lochs further south: Loch Tigh na h-Eige (15/127306), Loch Torr nan Uidhean (15/128300), Lochan Tolla Bhaid (15/119295) and Loch na Loinne (15/126290).
Fish All these lochs contain good stocks of small trout which average 8oz in weight. There are a few larger fish but anything of over 1lb in weight is unusual.
Flies & Tactics Bank fishing and a fair bit of scrambling along the way. Dark patterns of fly do well. Start with: Black Zulu, Grouse & Claret, Black Pennell.
Permission & Charges Bank fishing at £5 per rod per day, £25 per week, £45 per season. Drumbeg Post Office, Drumbeg, Sutherland. Tel: (01571) 833231; Tourist Office, Lochinver, Sutherland. Tel: (01571) 844330. A boat is available.

A'CHAORUINN, Loch
Location & Access 15/990138 To the north of the road, between Brae of Achnahaird (15/008134) and Altandu (15/984126). Park at 15/990136 and walk north for five minutes to reach the loch.
Commentary A very pleasant little hill loch, easily accessible and close to the road.
Fish Loch a'Chaoruinn trout average 6-8oz.
Flies & Tactics Comfortable bank fishing. An alternative venue is the little unnamed lochan at 15/981135.
Permission & Charges See Loch na Totaig entry

A'CHAPUIL, Loch
Location & Access 15/098178 See Loch a'Choin.

A'CHOIN, Loch
Location & Access 15/083185. Approach via the narrow minor road between Lochinver and Inverpolly. Park at 15/080187. Loch a'Choin ('the dog loch') is five minutes east.
Commentary An easily accessible little loch, quarter of a mile long by 200 yards wide, complete with small island off the south shore. There are two other lochs further east which, if included, make a good day out, hill walking and fishing: Lochan Fada (15/085179) and Loch a'Chapuil (15/098178).
Fish Loch a'Choin and Lochan Fada have trout averaging 8oz, but Loch a'Chapuil has larger fish, although they do not give themselves up easily.
Flies & Tactics All bank fishing with fish being taken from all round the shore. On Loch a'Chapuil, a long, straggling water, the south bay is perhaps the most productive area. Use: Ke-He, Woodcock & Hare-lug, Silver Butcher.
Permission & Charges For Loch a'Choin, see Loch na h-Innse Fraoich entry; for Lochan Fada and Loch a'Chapuil, see Loch Sionascaig entry.

A'CHOIRE DHEIRG, Loch 15/252272 See Loch Bealach a'Bhuirich.
A'CHOIRE DHUIBH, Loch (Glas Bheinn) 15/252281 See Loch Bealach a'Bhuirich.
A'CHOIRE DHUIBH, Loch (Suilven) 15/160188 See Loch na Gainimh.
A'CHOIRE GHUIRM, Lochan 15/261268 See Loch Bealach a'Bhuirich.

A'CHOIREACHAIN, Loch
Location & Access 15/112243 Immediately to the north of the A836 Inchnadamph/Lochinver road approached from 15/116240 near Brackloch. No dogs are allowed to accompany anglers fishing Assynt Angling Club lochs.
Commentary Another delightful, easily accessible Assynt loch which offers fine sport amidst splendid scenery. Loch a'Choireachain is partly shielded from north winds by the crags of Cnoc Bad a' Bhainne and often provides shelter when harsh winds howl.
Fish Very attractive little trout which give a good account of themselves.
Flies & Tactics Loch a'Choireachain is only a few acres in extent, narrow, and the water is easily covered from the bank. The loch is divided into two principal bays. The north bay is the most productive. First cast: Ke-He, Loch Ordie, Black Pennell.
Permission & Charges See Loch na h-Innse Fraoich entry.

A'CHRAOBHAIR, Lochan 15/323397 See Loch na Mucnaich.

A'CHREAGAIN DARAICH, Loch
Location & Access 15/170396 Close to the old A894 and easily accessible.
Commentary Enjoy a day out fishing Loch a'Chreagain Daraich first, then three lochs which lie to the east: Loch na Doire Duibhe (15/176394), Loch na Beiste Bric (15/184396) and the unnamed lochan at 15/182391.

Loch Assynt — OS Map 15

Fish Good trout which average 10oz, plus a few larger fish, particularly in Loch na Beiste Bric.
Flies & Tactics Bank fishing with fair bit of scrambling about. Fish the north shore of Loch a'Chreagain Daraich and then follow the inlet stream up to Loch na Doire Duibhe, and, again, the inlet stream onto Loch na Beiste Bric. Hike back via 15/182391. Useful flies: Loch Ordie, Greenwell's Glory, Alexandra.
Permission & Charges Scourie Hotel, Scourie, Sutherland. Tel: (01971) 502396. Permits at the village shop in Scourie at £5 per rod per day. Details of the angling club waters from the Secretary: Mrs R Mackay, Scourie, by Lairg, Sutherland. Tel (01971) 502425.

A'CHROISG, Loch 15/220155 See Lochan Fada, Canisp.
A'GHILLE, Loch 15/115165 See Loch Sionascaig.

A'GHILLE RUAIDH, Loch
Location & Access 15/230354 Approach by a track to the north of Kylstrome at 15/224359, a walk of about 15 minutes.
Commentary Not too far but far enough to give a sense of 'escape'. Sail Gorm (776m), the most northerly buttress of Quinag (808m), will be your day-long companion.
Fish Trout average 8oz and there are plenty of them, but if things are quiet walk on and explore the unnamed lochans at 15/240351, and, to the south of the track, the hill loch at 15/245349. They hold some nice trout.
Flies & Tactics Loch a'Ghille Ruaidh is shaped like a capital E facing the wrong way and there is a surprising amount of water, and ground, to cover in order to do it proper justice. Happy bank fishing, nevertheless, with action all round. Tempt them with: Blue Zulu, Greenwell's Glory, Kingfisher Butcher.
Permission & Charges The Reay Forest Estate, Estate Office, Achfary, by Lairg, Sutherland. Tel: (01971) 500221. £5 per rod per day.

A'GHLEANNAIN SHALAICH, Loch 15/149279 Enquiries to Reay Forest Estate (01971) 500221.
A'GHLINNE SGOILTE, Loch 15/106192 See Loch Bad na Muiriehinn.

A'GHLINNEIN, Loch
Location & Access 15/169233 Park near Little Assynt at 15/157250. Cross the field to a bridge over the River Inver at 15/156258. Follow the stalkers' path west (right) to cross the Allt an Tiaghaich burn at 15/151247 (wet feet). Walk the south bank of the burn up to the loch.
Commentary Climbing, rather than walking, to reach the loch, but the rewards are considerable. The burn is one of the most attractive in Assynt, a continual delight of secret waterfalls and dark pools. Few ever tramp this way and you will have the stream and the loch entirely to yourself all day.
Fish Mostly 8oz trout but a few much larger fish. Very pretty trout which fight superbly.
Flies & Tactics Start at the east end, where the inlet stream from Loch Feith an Leothaid (15/185224) forms an interesting delta. Good trout gather to feed in the flow. Elsewhere, trout may be taken from all round the shore. Stay on the bank. The fish lie close, waiting for: Black Pennell, Greenwell's Glory, Peter Ross.
Permission & Charges Inver Lodge Hotel, Lochinver, Sutherland IV27 4LU. Tel: (01571) 844496. £5 per rod per day; or from Assynt Estate (Tel. 01571 844203).

A'GHUIB AIRD, Loch 15/187240 See Loch Feith an Leothaid.
A'GLEANNAN A'CHOIT, Loch 15/160274 Enquiries to Reay Forest Estate. Tel: (01971) 500221.
A'MEALLARD, Loch 15/156337 See Loch an Torr Lochain.
A'MHADAIL, Loch 15/155144 See Loch Veyatie.

A'MHEALLAIN, Loch (Altnacealgach)
Location & Access 15/289108 Park at 15/288100 on the A837 Bonar Bridge/Ledmore Junction road. Follow the outlet stream up the hill to reach the loch after about 20 minutes.
Commentary A shallow hill loch, approximately 300 yards long by up to 150 yards wide. A very attractive loch to fish and the place to take hill loch fishing beginners.
Fish Good numbers of bright trout averaging 6-8oz.
Flies & Tactics No problems bank fishing and the east shore, particularly at the south end of the loch, should provide you with breakfast. Trout eagerly accept Soldier Palmer, Grouse & Claret, Silver Butcher. Whilst in the vicinity, walk over the hill to visit little Lochan Sgeireach (15/279116) which also holds good stocks of small trout, and a few larger specimens as well.
Permission & Charges Contact Forest Enterprise, 21 Church Street, Inverness (Tel: 01463 232811).

A'MHEALLAIN, Loch (Rubh Mor) 15/992110 See Loch Camas an Fheidh.
A'MHI RUNAICH, Loch 15/042295 See Loch Sgeireach.

A'MHINIDH, Loch
Location & Access 15/190379 Adjacent to the old A894 Scourie/Ullapool road and easily accessible.
Commentary Not so public, now the new road has been built, but the attraction of the Cnoc Chalbha Lochs further west is irresistible.
Fish An encouraging little loch full of pretty, little trout which average 6oz in weight.
Flies & Tactics Easy bank fishing and trout are not too particular about flies. Serve them: Black Zulu, Grouse & Claret, Dunkeld.
Permission & Charges Scourie Hotel, Scourie, Sutherland. Tel: (01971) 502396. Permits at the village shop in Scourie at £5 per rod per day. Details of the angling club waters from the Secretary: Mrs R Mackay, Scourie, by Lairg, Sutherland. Tel (01971) 502425.

A'MHUILINN, Loch 15/200242 See Loch Feith an Leothaid.

OS Map 15 — Loch Assynt

A'MHUILINN, Loch (Duartbeg)
Location & Access 15/165393 Easily accessible to the west of the A894 Scourie/Ullapool road at Duartbeg.
Commentary An attractive little loch, sheltered on the west bank by forestry.
Fish Trout average 8oz in weight.
Flies & Tactics Bank fishing using Blue Zulu, March Brown, Alexandra.
Permission & Charges Scourie Hotel, Scourie, Sutherland. Tel: (01971) 502396. Permits at the village shop in Scourie at £5 per rod per day. Details of the angling club waters from the Secretary: Mrs R. Mackay, Scourie, by Lairg, Sutherland. Tel (01971) 502425.

A'PHOLLAIN BHEITHE, Loch 15/090326 See Loch Donnaig.
A'PHOLLAIN DRISICH, Loch 15/080263 See Meall a'Chuna Mor.
A'PHOLLAIN, Loch 15/075261 See Meall a'Chuna Mor.
ABHAINN A'GHLINNE DHUIBH, Stream 15/287335 See Loch Beag, Sea Loch.
ABHAINN AN LOCH BHIG, Stream See Loch Beag (Sea Loch).
ABHAINN BAD NA H-ACHLAISE, River See Loch An Alltain Duibh.
ABHAINN NA CLACH AIRIGH, River See Loch An Alltain Duibh.

AILSH, Loch
Location & Access 15/315110 Leave the A837 Bonar Bridge/Ledmore Junction road at 15/297083. A rough forest track leads out to the loch and to Benmore Lodge (15/323114) at the north of Loch Ailsh.
Commentary One of the most attractive and productive lochs in Scotland, surrounded by magnificent scenery, dominated by Ben More Assynt (998m) to the north. The loch lies on the headwaters of the River Oykle and is shallow, three quarters of a mile long by up to half a mile wide. There is a delightful, scrub-covered island at the south end.
Fish Loch Ailsh is trout-user-friendly, with large stocks of fine little fish averaging 6-8oz which fight hard. Salmon and seatrout arrive from August onwards and the loch used to be particularly noted as a seatrout fishery.
Flies & Tactics The south end is very shallow, as is the area of the inlet stream at the north, but, generally trout are caught all over the loch, from the margins to the middle. This also applies to salmon and seatrout, and they can be encountered almost anywhere, although nearer to the shore rather than further out is best. Similar patterns of fly attract all species: Black Pennell, Grouse & Claret, Peter Ross and dapping can be very effective.
Permission & Charges Inver Lodge Hotel, Lochinver, Sutherland. Tel: (01571) 844496. Non hotel residents, Boat, £14 per day, bank fishing £5 per rod per

AIRIGH BLAIR, Loch 15/985170 See Loch na Totaig.
AIRIGH CHALUIM, Lochan 15/991159 See Clar Loch Beag.

ALLT MHIC MHUROHA DH GHEIR, River 15/242168 See Loch Awe.
ALLT NA H-AIRBE, Loch 15/205370 See Duart River.
ALLT NAN RAMH, Loch 15/211361 See Duart River.

AN ACHAIDH, Loch
Location & Access 15/029338 Approach from the B869 Lochinver/Unapool road along the minor road from Totag (15/041298) to Culkein (15/031333).
Commentary A small loch to the north of Culkein, east from Loch Cul Fraioch. Ideal for beginners.
Fish Brown trout average 6oz.
Flies & Tactics Room for a few casts using Black Pennell, March Brown, Silver Butcher. Stay well back from the shore.
Permission & Charges Bank fishing at £5 per rod per day, £25 per week, £45 per season. . Permits: Drumbeg Stores, Drumbeg, Sutherland. Tel: (01571) 843235; Drumbeg Post Office, Drumbeg, Sutherland. Tel: (01571) 843231; Culag Hotel, Lochinver, Sutherland. Tel: (01571) 844270; Tourist Office, Lochinver, Sutherland. Tel: (01571) 844330. Further details: P.N. MacPhail, Factor, North Assynt Estate, 216 Clashmore, Stoer, Sutherland. Tel: (01571) 5295.

AN AIGEIL, Loch 15/041280 See Loch Leathed a'Bhaile Fhoghair.
AN AIS, Lochan 15/185090 See Lochan Dearg a'Chuill Mhoir.

AN ALLTAIN DUIBH, Loch
Location & Access 15/147206 Approach as for Loch na Gainimh.
Commentary A special day out, hill-burn fishing, including Loch na h-Airigh Fraoich (15/133214) and Loch an Alltain Duibh.
Fish Good trout, averaging 8oz, and the chance of a few larger fish. Best tackled in July, after heavy rain.
Flies & Tactics Walk out to the head of the stream by the Shieling at Loch na Gainimh (15/170200) and fish back. The burn here is the Abhainn na Clach Airigh. Stop at the bothy at Suileag (15/150211) for lunch, the mid-point of the adventure, then continue west to Loch an Alltain Duibh and Loch na h-Airigh Fraoich. The burn now becomes the Abhain Bad na h-Achlaise, before entering into Loch Druim Suardalain at 15/119219. Use light tackle and offer them: Black Penel, March Brown, Grouse & Claret.
Permission & Charges Assynt Estate, Estate Office, Lochinver, by Lairg, Sutherland IV27 4YJ. Tel: (01571) 844203; Fax: (01571) 844666, or Inver Lodge Hotel, Lochinver, by Lairg, Sutherland IV27 4LU. Tel: (01571) 844496; Fax: (01571) 844395, at £5 per rod per day.

AN AON AITE, Loch
Location & Access 15/083282 Approach from the B869 Lochinver/Stoer road at 15/045270. A peat track leads east into the hills. After two miles, the track ends by the north shoulder of Creag Clais nan Cruineachd. Continue east for a further half mile to the loch.

Loch Assynt — OS Map 15

Commentary Sixteen for the price of one. A series of unnamed lochs and lochans lying between Creag Clais nan Cruineachd and Cnoc Daimh (192m). Loch An Aon Aite is the principal water, wonderfully situated at the centre of a splendid day out in the North Assynt Estate.
Fish Large stocks of very pretty little trout which average 6-8oz, with the chance of the occasional fish of up to 1lb from some of the smaller lochans.
Flies & Tactics Bank fishing. Loch An Aon Aite has two islands, east and west, and these areas are a good place to start. The surrounding hill lochs are all easily covered from the shore. Don't miss the beautiful lochan at 15/099285. Picnic paradise. Flies: Black Zulu, Grouse & Claret, Alexandra.
Permission & Charges See Crocach (North Assynt) Loch entry.

AN ARBHAIR, Loch
Location & Access 15/079189 Approach via the narrow, minor road from Lochinver to Inverpolly. Park at 15/080187. The loch is adjacent to the road on the west.
Commentary An excellent, easily accessible loch extending to over quarter of a mile east/west by up to 200 yards wide. Immediately to the west is another good water, Loch Rubha na Breige (15/072191).
Fish Trout in Loch an Arbhair ('the cat loch') average 6oz. Loch Rubha na Breige trout are smaller.
Flies & Tactics Bank fishing. On Loch an Arbhair, begin by the island on the south shore and work west. On Loch Rubh na Breige, the west end of the loch is most productive. Offer them: Blue Zulu, March Brown, Black Pennell.
Permission & Charges See Loch na h-Innse Fraoich entry.

AN CAORUINN, Loch 15/138281 Enquiries to Reay Forest Estate. Tel: (01971) 500221..

AN DOIRE DHUIBH, Loch
Location & Access 15/140108 Walk north over the hill from Linneraineach (15/127100) on the Drumrunie (15/167054) to Achiltibuie (15/024085) road to the Summer Isles. Reach Loch an Doire Dhuibh in 30 minutes.
Commentary Overlooked by Stac Pollaidh (618m), Cul Beag (769m) and Cul Mor (849m). Splendid fishing amidst spectacular scenery. Loch an Doire Dhuibh is joined to Lochan Gainmheich (15/140113) and flows west into Loch Sionascaig (15/120140). To the east, below Stac Pollaidh, is Loch Lon na h-Uamha (15/128110) which should be fished on the return journey to Linneraineach.
Fish Good stocks of trout which average about 8oz; but there are larger fish as well and trout of up to and over 2lbs are often taken. The inlet stream to Lochan Gainmheich, from 15/145106 down to the loch, is also worth exploring and contains excellent trout, particularly after heavy rain.
Flies & Tactics This is a five mile round trip, bank fishing along the way. The ruined house by the wood on the north shore of Loch Gainmheich is a good lunch spot, prior to crossing over the outlet stream to Loch Sionascaig and descending upon Loch Lon na h-Uamha. Offer them: Soldier Palmer, Greenwell's Glory, Dunkeld.
Permission & Charges Same as Loch Bad a'Ghaill.

AN DUIBHE, Lochan
Location & Access 15/219255 A ten minute scramble up the hill from Loch Assynt at 15/215251 on the A837 Inchnadamph/Lochinver road.
Commentary A good place to escape if the weather is wild on Loch Assynt. Also visit the unnamed lochan to the north, sheltered by Coire Riabach, at 15/219259.
Fish Small, beautiful trout averaging 6oz in weight.
Flies & Tactics Room for a few casts on both lochans and plenty of peace and quiet. Offer them: Loch Ordie, Greenwell's Glory, Black Pennell.
Permission & Charges Enquiries to Reay Forest Estate. Tel: (01971) 500221.

AN EASAIN, Loch 15/060299 See Loch nan Lub.

AN EICH UIDHIR, Loch
Location & Access 15/090292 Park on the B869 Drumbeg/Stoer road at 15/085313. Walk due south along the west shore of Lochan Fearna (private water), heading for Cona Chreag (171m). Climb the west shoulder, with Garbh Loch Mor (private water) to your right. Loch an Eich Uidhir is just over the hill, on the south side of Cona Chreag.
Commentary Loch an Eich Uidhir is a shallow loch, 400 yards long by up to 150 yards wide. Immediately to the east, is Loch na Buidheag (15/093291). South of Loch na Buidheig, there are three more unnamed lochans at 15/093290.
Fish All these lochs contain trout which average 8oz. Larger fish are rare, but the residents give a good account of themselves and are great fun to catch.
Flies & Tactics Start along the north shore of Loch an Eich Uidhir, then in the vicinity of the two tiny islands off the south shore. The other lochs in the series are all easily covered from the bank.
Permission & Charges See An Aon Aite, Loch entry.

AN EIRCILL, Loch 15/307275 See Loch nan Caorach.

AN FHEADAIN, Loch
Location & Access 15/003108 A small loch, unnamed on the OS map, to the north of Polbain (15/993102) in the Summer Isles. Park at 15/004100 and walk north via the peat track. After ten minutes, leave the track and walk north-west to find the loch below the summit of Meall an Fheadain (203m).
Commentary As much an excuse for exploring as fishing, and one of the best locations for a dramatic photograph of Stac Polly, Cul Beag and Ben Mor Coigach over Loch Oscaig (15/044120).
Fish Loch an Fheadain trout average 8oz.
Flies & Tactics A small lochan, easily covered from the shore. Use: Blue Zulu, March Brown, Peter Ross.
Permission & Charges See Loch na Totaig entry.

OS Map 15   Loch Assynt

AN FUATH, Loch 15/205356 See Loch Dubh a'Chnoic Ghairbh.
AN IASGAIR, Loch 15/198357 See Loch Dubh a'Chnoic Ghairbh.
AN INNEIL, Loch 15/228374 See Loch Clach a'Chinn Duibh.
AN LAOIGH, Loch 15/181105 See Lochan Dearg a'Chuill Mhoir.
AN LEATHAD RAINICH, Loch 15/063270 See Loch na Creige Leithe.

AN LEATHIAD BHUAIN, Loch
Location & Access 15/275360 From Lochmore at 15/300387 on the A838 Lairg/Scourie road. A stalkers' path leads into the Glendhu Forest via Bealach nam Fiann (15/273383). Bear south towards Loch an Leathiad Bhuain at 15/269370 and walk down the hill to the loch.
Commentary Breath-taking scenery with fine views south to Quinag (808m), Glas Bheinn (776m), Beinn Leoid (792m) and Ben More Assynt (998m). Loch an Leathiad Bhuain is the largest Glendhu Forest water, one and a half miles north/south, 500 yards east/west.
Fish Rarely fished and can be dour and unforgiving, but Loch an Leathiad Bhuain holds excellent trout. It all depends upon being there at the right moment. Late June/early July is a good time to try when you could be rewarded with fish of up to and over 3lb in weight.
Flies & Tactics Bank fishing is just as productive as boat fishing, but the boat makes it a lot easier to explore all the nooks and corners. The west shore, where the water is not so deep, is the place to concentrate, particularly as the loch narrows towards its exit. Also have a cast in the little satellite lochan at 15/267360. There are good fish waiting. Use: Black Zulu, Soldier Palmer, Silver Butcher.
Permission & Charges Scourie Hotel, Scourie, Sutherland. Tel: 01971 502 396. Bank fishing at £4 per rod per day.

AN LEOTHAID, Loch (Quinag)
Location & Access 15/173300 Approach from the B869 Unapool/Lochinver road via the stalkers path through Gleann Leireag that starts at 15/157313 and ends at Tumore on the A837 Inchnadamph/Lochinver road at 15/185268. The walk to the loch is a comfortable 30 minutes from the north, about one hour if you approach from the south.
Commentary One of the most dramatically situated lochs in an area crowded with dramatically situated lochs. The four-mile-long ridge of Quinag (808m) guards the east shore, the crags of Glas Chnoc sentinel the west shore. Including the satellite loch at the north end, Loch Uidh na h-Iarna (15/169305), the water extends for a distance of one mile south by up to half a mile east/west/
Fish A fine mixture of large and small, with the majority of trout being in the 8oz range. They are very pretty fish and fight hard.
Flies & Tactics Bank fishing and the west shore, in the vicinity of the small feeder stream that enters at the south end of the first bay (15/170296) is a good startpoint. Also, the far south end in the shelter of the little wood. Offer them: Ke-He, Greenwell's Glory, Peter Ross.
Permission & Charges The Inver Lodge Hotel, Lochinver, Sutherland. Tel: (01571) 844496. £5 per rod per day.

AN LEOTHAID, Loch (Suilven)
Location & Access 15/144226 Park near Little Assynt at 15/157250 on the A837 Ledmore Junction/Lochinver road. Walk south on a track across the field leading to a bridge over the River Inver at 15/156248. Follow the track round the north side of the hill to ford (wet feet) the Allt an Tiaghaich burn. Continue south, climbing between Cnoc an Leothaid (270m) at 15/144234 and An Leathad to the east. You see the loch, on your right, as you descend the bealach. The boat is moored at 15/142227.
Commentary A shallow, moorland loch, nearly half a mile long by up to 300 yards wide. Fantastic backdrop of Suilven (731m) to the south and Canisp (846m) to the east.
Fish Fine little fish which average about 8oz.
Flies & Tactics The margins of the loch tend to be soft and the water, dark and peaty, is not really conducive to wading. As the season advances, weed-growth can be a problem. The best fishing area is at the north end, down the west shoreline, and round the small islands. Offer them: Black Pennell, Grouse & Claret, Peter Ross
Permission & Charges Inver Lodge Hotel, Lochinver, by Lairg, Sutherland IV27 4LU. Tel: (01571) 844496; Fax: (01571) 844395. Free to hotel guests. Non-residents:- Boat: £14 per day; bank: £5 per rod per day.

AN ORDAIN, Loch
Location & Access 15/065260 An easily accessible roadside lochan to the north of the B869 Lochinver/Stoer road.
Commentary Dash here to catch breakfast, and don't miss also fishing the little unnamed satellite lochan to the north at 15/068262. Both waters are great fun.
Fish Trout average 6oz. A good place to introduce newcomers to the gentle art.
Flies & Tactics Loch an Ordain is more than half a mile long, narrow and easily fished from the shore. Fish are taken from all round the shore and there is little need to wade. Offer them: Loch Ordie, Greenwell's Glory, Dunkeld.
Permission & Charges Enquire Grosvenor Estate 01971 502220.

AN RUIGHEIN, Loch
Location & Access 15/155268 See Loch na h-Innse Fraoich.

AN RUIGHEIN, Loch (Duartmore)
Location & Access 15/187368 Park at the south end of the Duartmore Forest at 15/202363 and follow the edge of the plantation west. After 15 minutes, turn north at 15/191360 and follow the track to the loch.
Commentary A lovely little loch, surrounded by forestry and quite sheltered. After exploring Loch an Ruighein, fish Loch na Creige Ruaidhe (OS15/185362) to the west, also sheltered on the west

Loch Assynt — OS Map 15

shore by forestry. Complete your enjoyment by lunching at Duartmore Point overlooking sea-loch Loch Shark (OS15/180364).
Fish Not glass-case country, but great fun nevertheless with trout which average 8oz in weight
Flies & Tactics Easy bank fishing with Black Pennell, Invicta, Peter Ross.
Permission & Charges The Reay Forest Estate, Estate Office, Achfary, by Lairg, Sutherland. Tel: (01971) 500221 at £5 per rod per day.

AN TAIRBH, Lochan
Location & Access 15/085240 Park on the B869 Lochinver/Stoer road at 15/090241 and walk south on a good track. where the track swings west to a cottage, continue south over the moor for five minutes to reach Lochan an Tairbh, 'the loch of the bull'. Dogs are not allowed to accompany anglers to Assynt Angling Club lochs.
Commentary A small lochan (three acres), with two further, smaller lochans to the west, unnamed on the OS Map at 15/081241, but known locally as 'Ina's Lochs'. Reach Ina's Lochs by walking for ten minutes along the north side of Cnoc Braonach (113m).
Fish Brown trout which average 8-10oz.
Flies & Tactics All bank fishing. Offer them: Black Zulu, Woodcock & Yellow, Peter Ross.
Permission & Charges See An Achaidh Loch entry.

AN TUIR, Loch 15/118265 See Manse Loch.
AN TUIRC, Loch 15/115260 See Manse Loch.
AN-IASGAICH, Lochan See River Inver.

ASSYNT, Loch
Location & Access 15/200252 The north shore of Loch Assynt is adjacent to the A837 Ledmore junction/Lochinver road. The south shore is only accessible by foot or by boat.
Commentary Assynt is up to six miles long by three quarters of a mile wide and almost completely surrounded by mountains; including Quinag (808m) to the west and Ben More Assynt (998m), the highest peak in Sutherland, to the east. The loch is 280ft deep and can often be horrendously windy. Weather conditions alter within minutes here, so an outboard motor is essential if boat fishing and always wear a life-jacket.
Fish Salmon, brown trout and ferrox. Approximately 50-80 salmon are taken, mostly in August and September, by trolling. Ferrox are also caught whilst trolling and trout of 10lb are not uncommon. Brown trout are plentiful and average 8oz, but there are also good numbers of fish of over 1lb in weight.
Flies & Tactics Boat fishing brings best results, although bank fishing can also be productive. Concentrate your efforts in the shallows, particularly at the east end of the loch, and in the vicinity of the Ardvreck Castle shoreline. The southern bays by Eilean Assynt (15/196250) on the south shore, and the bays by Rubha an Doire Chuilinn (15/200247) to the north are also well worth a visit. Flies: Black Pennell, Soldier Palmer, Kingfisher Butcher.
Permission & Charges The Inchnadamph Hotel, Inchnadamph, Assynt, Sutherland. Tel: (01571) 822202. Boats on Loch Assynt, available when not required by hotel guests at £18 per day (two rods). Outboard motors cost £15 per day, including fuel. Bank fishing, £6 per rod per day.

AWE, Loch
Location & Access 15/247153 Easily accessible and adjacent to the A837 Ledmore Junction/Lochinver road.
Commentary One of the most productive and attractive lochs in Assynt, dominated by Canisp (846m). Also visit nearby Loch na Gruagaich (15/242159) and Loch na Saighe Duibhe (15/233159) and the unnamed lochan at 15/229158. They hold some nice trout. The inlet burn to Loch na Gruagaich, Allt Mhich Mhuroha Dh Gheir (15/242168), is a classic and very beautiful little limestone stream. Well worth a visit.
Fish Expect large baskets of trout averaging three to the pound, with a few larger specimens. Salmon also enter Awe, from June onwards, and are occasionally caught (1 x 8lb in August 1999).
Flies & Tactics Boat fishing is best, although bank fishing also produces good results. Concentrate your effort in the vicinity of the islands at the south end of the loch, offering them: Ke-He, March Brown, Alexandra.
Permission & Charges Inver Lodge Hotel, Lochinver, by Lairg, Sutherland IV27 4LU. Tel: (01571) 844496; Fax: (01571) 844395. Inchnadamph Hotel, Assynt, by Lairg, Sutherland. Tel: (01571) 822202. Boat: £18 per day (two rods); bank fishing, £6 per rod per day.

BAD A'CHIGEAR, Loch 15/169271 Enquiries to Reay Forest Estate. Tel: (01971) 500221.

BAD A'GHAILL, Loch
Location & Access 15/080100 Immediately to the south of and easily accessible from the Drumrunie (15/167054) to Achiltibuie (15/024085) road.
Commentary A deep, dark, somewhat intimidating loch. Bad a'Ghaill is two miles long by up to three quarters of a mile wide, guarded to the north by Stac Pollaidh (613m) and to the south by the mountains of Coigach.
Fish Large stocks of small trout averaging 8oz but undoubtedly some very much larger fish as well. Bad a'Ghaill is rarely fished and could well-reward more intensive exploration. Seatrout and Salmon from the River Garvie and Loch Osgaig, are also present although not often encountered.
Flies & Tactics Boat fishing allows you to get about more easily and is really essential for reaching the south shore, which is the best fishing area. An outboard motor is essential, as is wearing a life-jacket. There is a long, finger-like promontory, enclosing a shallow bay (15/070100) which offers good sport; as is the area to the west of the promontory, particularly by the small island. Offer them: Black Zulu, Soldier Palmer, Peter Ross.
Permission & Charges Estate Office, Inverpolly Estate, Ullapool, Wester Ross. Tel: (01854) 622452. Boat and two rods: £15 per day. Outboard hire: £10 per day inc

150

OS Map 15 — Loch Assynt

fuel. Life-jacket hire: £2 per day. Bank fishing: £5 per rod per day.

BAD AN OG, Loch
Location & Access 15/117314 Follow the peat track south from the north-west end of Loch Drumbeg at 15/109327 to reach the loch in about 20 minutes.
Commentary After fishing Loch Bad an Og, continue south to the end of the track to fish Lochan Fada (15/112304). Now, find the track at the north end of Lochan Fada that leads north uphill along the edge of the forest and climb to Loch nam Breac (15/107318). At the extreme north-west corner of Loch nam Breac, by the little island, walk due north to fish the unnamed lochan at 15/105324. From there, walk north-east to pick up the peat track back to the start point.
Fish Nothing for the glass case, but plenty of sport with trout averaging 8oz and the chance of the odd larger specimen, especially from Loch nam Breac.
Flies & Tactics Comfortable bank fishing all the way, and it is best to stay on the shore, rather than wade. The fish lie close. Offer them: Black Spider, March Brown, Silver Invicta.
Permission & Charges Bank fishing at £5 er rod per day, £25 per week, £45 per season. Permits: Drumbeg Stores, Drumbeg, Sutherland. Tel: (01571) 843235; Drumbeg Post Office, Drumbeg, Sutherland. Tel: (01571) 843231; Tourist Office, Lochinver, Sutherland. Tel: (01571) 844330.

BAD AN T-SLUIC, Loch
Location & Access 15/153218 Follow the same route as used for Loch an Leothaid and Loch Crom. Loch Bad an t-Sluic is to the east of track, just past Loch Crom, 45 minutes' walk from the road.
Commentary A very attractive loch in a dramatic setting, sheltered to the east by Creag Liath, 'The Grey Hill', and with a perfect, tree/scrub-clad island picnic site. Loch Bad an t-Sluic is approximately 300 yards across and generally circular in shape. If things are quiet on Loch Bad an t-Sluic, visit remote Loch Coire na Creige at 15/170214, at the head of the Allt Loch Coire na Creige burn. It is a stiffish climb, but there is a good track most of the way and this little loch is a gem of peace and solitude.
Fish A variety of good trout, from 6oz up to fish over 1lb in weight.
Flies & Tactics Both boat and bank fishing with boat-work bringing best results. The boat is moored at the west end of the loch, near to the island, at 15/150217. The north shore, where two streams tumble in, is a good place to begin. Start with: Kc-Hc, Soldier Palmer, Alexandra.
Permission & Charges See Loch an Leothaid entry.

BAD NA H-ACHLAISE, Loch
Location & Access 15/085090 Easily accessible from the Drumrunie (15/167054) to Achiltibuie (15/024085) road. Bad na h-Achlaise lies between Loch Bad a'Ghaill (15/080100) to the west, and Loch Lurgainn (15/100090) to the east.
Commentary Known locally as 'the Green Loch', half a mile long, shallow and rarely fished. Stunning surroundings, with Stac Pollaidh (613m) to the north and Ben Mor Coigach (743m) to the south.
Fish Great sport with small trout averaging 8oz and the chance of a few larger fish, and the odd seatrout.
Flies & Tactics Bank fishing, unless the water level in the adjoining lochs is high, when it is possible to haul a boat in. Offer them: Black Pennell, March Brown, Silver Butcher.
Permission & Charges Estate Office, Inverpolly Estate, Ullapool, Wester Ross. Tel: (01854) 622452. Bank fishing: £5 per rod per day.

BAD NA H-ACHLAISE, Loch (Ullapool) 15/155002
See Dam Lochs.

BAD NA MUIRIEHINN, Loch
Location & Access 15/095199. Park at 15/083203 on the road between Lochinver and Inverkirkaig. Walk south-east up the gully for 15 minutes to reach the loch.
Commentary Rarely visited. Suilven (731m) is the backdrop, and there is an excellent chance of encountering otters and divers. Continue east to visit four other lochs nearby: Loch Gleannan na Gaoithe (15/101192), Loch a'Ghlinne Sgoilte (15/106192), Loch Uidh na Ceardaich (15/114188), and the unnamed lochan at 15/103184.
Fish All contain good stocks of 6-8oz trout, but Bad na Muiriehinn has larger fish as well.
Flies & Tactics Bank fishing all the way, and the most productive area on Loch Bad na Muiriehinn is along the wooded south shore and in the bays at the east end. Tempt them with: Black Zulu, Soldier Palmer, Silver Butcher.
Permission & Charges Inver Lodge Hotel, Lochinver, by Lairg, Sutherland. Tel: (01527) 844496. Free to hotel guests. Non-residents bank fishing, £5 per rod per day.

BAD NAN AIGHEAN, Loch
Location & Access 15/132255 See Loch Beannach.

BEAG, Sea Loch
Location & Access 15/275290 For all practical purposes, only accessible by boat from Kylesku. Arrange transport with the Kylesku Hotel (see address below).
Commentary Very remote, amidst utterly splendid scenery, and worth a few casts on the way south to visit Loch nan Caorach (OS15/296275) and Loch an Eircill (OS15/308275).
Fish A chance of sport with seatrout in the tidal waters where the Abhain an Loch Bhig burn enters the sea at 15/275290. Another similar location is at the head of Loch Glendhu at 15/287335, where the Abhainn a'Ghlinne Dhuibh burn enters.
Flies & Tactics Fish two hours either side of low tide for best results. Fish are soft-mouthed and difficult to hook, but they fight spectacularly. Use: Black Pennell, Grouse & Claret, Peter Ross.
Permission & Charges Kylesku Hotel, Kylesku, by Scourie, Sutherland. Tel: (01971) 502231. £5 per rod per day.

Loch Assynt OS Map 15

BEALACH A'BHUIRICH, Loch
Location & Access 15/262280 Park by Loch na Gainmhich at 15/240292 on the A894 Skiag Bridge/Unapool road. A stalkers path leads round the north shore of Loch na Gainmhich up into the corries of Glas Bheinn (776m). Loch Belach a'Bhuirich is the first loch in a series of four, known locally as 'The Corrie Lochans'. The others are: Loch a'Choire Dhuibh (15/252281), Loch a'Choire Dheirg (15/252272) and Lochan a'Choire Ghuirm (15/261268).
Commentary This expedition should not be undertaken lightly, it is serious hill walking and in bad weather conditions can be dangerous. You must go prepared and be able to use a compass and map effectively. Otherwise, and particularly on a good day, this will be a walk in paradise amidst some of the most dramatic scenery in Scotland. You also have to the option of visiting the highest waterfall in UK, Eas a'Chual Aluinn, 'the maiden's tresses', at 15/2890278.
Fish The Corrie Lochans hold some of the best trout in Assynt and fish of up to and over 3lb are taken.
Flies & Tactics Classic bank fishing, where a cautious approach is best. Watch and wait before you cast and avoid wading. Offer them: Ke-He, Grouse & Claret, Silver Invicta.
Permission & Charges See Loch Assynt entry.

BEALACH A'MHADAIDH, Loch 15/310231 See Fionn Loch Mor.

BEALACH CORNAIDH, Lochan
Location & Access 15/209281 Park on the A894 Skiag Bridge/Unapool road at 15/233274 where there is a quarry for that purpose to the east of the road. A stalkers path leads west, towards the centre of the Quinag (808m) ridge, and the walk out to Loch Bealach takes about one hour.
Commentary One of the best of the Assynt lochs and certainly in one of the most dramatic settings. The huge buttress of Sail Gharbh towers north, sheer Spidean Coinich towers to the south. The loch extends to approximately 20 acres and there is a golden, sandy beach at the west end; the right spot for lunch and, in hot weather, for a cooling splash.
Fish Particularly pretty trout, brightly marked and hard fighting. A good mixture of sizes from 6oz up to fish of well over 1lb in weight.
Flies & Tactics Comfortable bank fishing. If the prospect of lugging waders up the hill is too much, just wade in and dry out later; the fish lie somewhat out from the generally shallow margins. Trout are taken all round the loch using; Soldier Palmer, Grouse & Claret, Alexandra.
Permission & Charges Enquiries to Reay Forest Estate. Tel: (01971) 500221.

BEALACH NA H-UIDHE, Loch
Location & Access 15/2632256 Park at Inchnadamph (15/261218) and follow the track up the north bank of the Traligill River. Past the cottages, this becomes a stalkers path leading steeply up the glen of Allt Poll an Droighinn burn, swinging north to Glas Bheinn (776m). Loch Bealach na h-Uidhe lies in a corrie to the left of the track. The walk out takes about an hour and a half.
Commentary This is serious hill walking and you must be reasonably fit before attempting the journey. You must also go well prepared for the worst weather. Even in late May it can snow in these remote hills. Loch Bealach na h-Uidhe is the first loch in a day-long hill walking and fishing expedition amidst the wilds of Assynt. Return down the stalkers path to fish Loch Fleodach Coire (15/273248), and, finally, on the way home, climb down to have a cast in the unnamed lochan at 15/270241 on the headwaters of the Allt Chalda Mor burn.
Fish You should not go back down the hill empty-handed. Although the average size of trout is only in the order of 8oz, be warned, there are also some seriously large specimens as well.
Flies & Tactics Avoid wading, it only scares the fish. Loch Fleodaich is my favourite, as much for the glorious ridge of Beinn Uidhe overshadowing the loch, as for the fishing. Offer them: Loch Ordie, Greenwell's Glory, Silver Butcher.
Permission & Charges See Loch Assynt entry.

BEANNACH BEAG, Loch 15/154265 See Loch na h-Innse Fraoich.

BEANNACH, Loch
Location & Access 15/140264 Park by the River Inver on the A837 Inchnadamph/Lochinver road at 15/142254. Walk north, passing between Loch Uidh na Geadaig, 'the grilse loch' (15/141257), to the east and Loch Bad nan Aighean, 'the loch of the grove of the hinds' (15/132255), to the west. Beannach, 'loch of the hillocks', is 15 minutes further north. No dogs are allowed to accompany anglers fishing Assynt Angling Club lochs.
Commentary One of the most attractive lochs in Assynt, extending for a distance of almost one and a half miles east/west, by up to half a mile north/south. There are 13 islands, the largest being delightfully wooded, and a seemingly unending succession of exciting bays and fishy promontories. The unnamed lochans to the north of Loch Beannach, at 15/132269 and 15/143272, are also well worth a cast or two or three.
Fish Predominantly 6oz trout, but also quite a few larger fish to keep you alert.
Flies & Tactics Fish are taken all round these lochs so cast with confidence. Try: Black Pennell, Greenwell's Glory, Grouse & Claret. At the north end of Loch Beannach, step over to little Lochan nan Liath Bhreac (15/123269), and on the way home, have an exploratory cast in Loch a'Bhiraille (15/130259) and in Lochan Guilc (15/128254), they also hold good fish.
Permission & Charges See Loch na h-Innse Fraoich entry.

BEINN DEIRG, Loch See Dam Lochs entry.

BEN STROME, Lochs
Location & Access 15/250363 In Kylestrome, follow a stalkers path north-east from 15/225348. Hard climb-

OS Map 15 — Loch Assynt

ing for 40 minutes brings you to the lochs which are to the west of track.
Commentary A delightful series of four unnamed lochs lying to the north of Ben Strome (426m) and surrounded by glorious scenery.
Fish Good brown trout with the chance of fish of up to and over 2lb in weight, but they can be difficult to move.
Flies & Tactics Begin at 15/252362, paying particular attention to the narrow, northern end. Walk west to 15/249363 (and the little satellite lochan to the south), and finally to 15/245363. Easy bank fishing and tempt them with: Ke-He, March Brown, Silver Butcher.
Permission & Charges The Reay Forest Estate, Estate Office, Achfary, by Lairg, Sutherland. Tel: (01971) 500221. About £5 per rod per day.

BORRALAN, Loch
Location & Access 15/265108 Adjacent to the A837 Oykel Bridge/Ledmore Junction road.
Commentary Gives you a first glimpse of Assynt with Suilven (731m) and Canisp (846m) dominating the western view. Close to the road, but nonetheless pleasant to fish. A shallow loch, one mile long by up to quarter of a mile wide.
Fish Lots of them, averaging 6-8oz, but also larger trout of up to and over 2lb in weight, as well as Arctic char.
Flies & Tactics Easy bank fishing, but boat fishing brings best results. Fish are taken all round the loch, using: Soldier Palmer, Grouse & Green, Silver Butcher.
Permission & Charges The Allt Bar, Altnacealagach, Elphin, by Lairg, Sutherland. Tel: (01854) 666220. Boat: £18 per day. Bank fishing: £5 per day.

BRAIGH A'BHAILE, Loch 15/069236 See Loch Dubh, Lochinver.
BUINE MOIRE, Loch 15/099155 See Loch Call an Uidhean.

CALL AN UIDHEAN, Loch
Location & Access 15/092145 An easily accessible loch on the east of the minor road from Lochinver to Inverpolly. Immediately to the west, at 15/089148, is the Black Loch, whilst just to the north is Loch Buine Moire (15/099155) both of which should also be thoroughly explored.
Commentary These lochs are peat-stained and deep close to the shore making casting uncomfortable and wading downright dangerous. Nevertheless, as they are but a step from the road, they are ideal for a couple of hours casting. Ideal if strong winds make launching a boat on nearby Loch Sionascaig (15/120140) impossible.
Fish Can be very dour but, and particularly Loch Call an Uidhean, they have the reputation of containing some excellent trout. There are plenty of small ones but, undoubtedly, monsters lurk in the dark depths.
Flies & Tactics The banks are steep and you will have to do a fair bit of scrambling to cover the water. Stay on terra firma at all times and be prepared to get snagged up on the back cast. First cast: Ke-He, March Brown, Silver Butcher.

Permission & Charges See Loch Bad a'Ghaill entry.

CAM, Loch
Location & Access 15/220139 Immediately adjacent and to the west of the A835 Ledmore Junction/Ullapool road.
Commentary The Cam Loch, 'Crooked Loch', is easily accessible and lies between Canisp (846m) and Cul Mor (849m). The loch is over 100ft deep, nearly two and half miles long by up to three quarters of a mile wide. Boats are moored near the cemetery at 15/220122.
Fish Large stocks of 8oz trout and good numbers of larger fish. Trolling is allowed on Cam Loch and was used to good effect by Gateshead angler, W. R. Clark, in July 1993, when he landed a 16lb ferox trout. The fish is displayed at the Birchbank Holiday Lodge at Knockan.
Flies & Tactics Boat fishing is best and allows access to Cam's nooks and crannies. Wading is dangerous because the banks shelve sharply. Be cautious, even boat fishing. The bow may be ashore, but the stern could be over 20ft of water. Best fishing areas: round Eilean na Gartaig (15/219123), and the south shore from 15/210131 west to the head of the loch. Flies: Ke-He, Woodcock & Hare-lug, Dunkeld.
Permission & Charges Assynt Estate Office, Lochinver, by Lairg, Sutherland IV27 4YJ. Tel (05714) 844203; Fax: (01571) 844666, or Inver Lodge Hotel, Lochinver, by Lairg, Sutherland IV27 4LU. Tel: (01571) 844496; Fax: (01571) 844395 or by arrangement with Birchbank Holiday Lodge, Knockan, Elphin, by Lairg, Sutherland IV27 4HH. Tel: (01854) 666203; Fax: (01854) 666215. Boat: £18 per day. Bank fishing: £5 per rod per day.

CAMAS AN FHEIDH, Loch
Location & Access 15/993117 Between Polbain (15/993102) and Altandu (15/983126), close to the circular road round the south of the Rubha Mor Peninsula.
Commentary An easily accessible roadside lochan sheltered from west winds by Meall Dearg (163m). Just to the north is another, simlarly accessible water, Loch a'Mheallain (15/992110) and both lochs provide good sport, particularly early in the season. Weed can become a problem after July.
Fish Good stocks of attractive trout which average 8oz.
Flies & Tactics Bank fishing only. Try the west bank of Loch Camas an Fheidh and east bank of its neighbour. Best cast: Black Zulu, March Brown, Peter Ross
Permission & Charges Same as Loch na Totaig.

CARN NAN CONBHAIREAN, Loch
Location & Access 15/345174 Approach via the A837 Bonar Bridge/Ledmore Junction road at 15/297083. A forest road heads north past Loch Ailsh (15/315110) to Benmore Lodge (15/322114). A path leads north following the course of the Upper Oykel and its tributary, Allt Sail an Ruathair. Bear right from the main track at 15/329130 and follow the stalkers track north. The loch lies in a corrie west of the track, four miles from Benmore Lodge.

Loch Assynt — OS Map 15

Commentary A long walk from Benmore Lodge, climbing steeply round the east shoulder of Meall an Aonaich (715m), 'the eagle's rock', but worth every inch of the way. Loch Carn nan Conbhairean lies in cathedral-like splendour surrounded on three sides by vast, black cliffs. There is a golden, sandy beach at the east shore by the outlet stream and this banks westward before dropping quickly into deeper, dark water.
Fish There are times you would swear there wasn't a fish in the loch, but, be assured, there are. Excellent trout lurk here and fish of over 1lb are not uncommon. Cast with confidence, but be prepared for blank days.
Flies & Tactics In high summer, wade the sandy east shore, casting onto the area between shallow and deep. The loch is half a mile long by 300 yards wide so there is plenty of water to fish; but start early because, as the day lengthens into afternoon, shadows from the cliffs at the west end extend quickly across the loch. Try: Black Pennell, Grouse & Claret, Alexandra.
Permission & Charges See Loch Ailsh entry.

CLACH A'CHINN DUIBH, Loch
Location & Access 15/240380 Approach along the stalkers path to the north of Kylestrome at 15/224348 taking the left-hand fork at the first junction. At 15/231378, bear right/east to reach the loch. The walk takes about one hour.
Commentary On the headwaters of the Duartmore River system and one of the best lochs in the area. North-east of Loch Clach a'Chinn Duibh is Loch Poll an Achaidh Bhuidhe (15/256382), which is well worth a visit. West of Loch Clach a'Chinn Duibh is a series of six excellent little lochans which should also be visited. They extend from 15/234374 to 15/227390. This latter lochan, which has two tiny islands, is particularly lovely and a haunt of red-throated diver.
Fish Trout average 10-12oz and fight well and there is the chance of much larger fish from some of the smaller waters.
Flies & Tactics The main loch covers an area of some 40 acres and is shaped like a boot. The north end, by the inlet stream, is a good area to start, as is the outlet stream that flows into the unnamed lochan at 15/237381. On your way home, stop for a few casts in Loch an Inneil (15/228374) and the unnamed lochan to the west of the track at OS15/229369. Try: Black Pennell, Greenwell's Glory, Alexandra.
Permission & Charges The Reay Forest Estate, Estate Office, Achfary, by Lairg, Sutherland. Tel: (01971) 500221 for Loch Clach a'Chinn Duibh. For the others contact: The Scourie Hotel, Scourie, by Lairg, Sutherland. Tel: (01971) 502396. Charges: £5 per rod per day.

CLAR BEAG, Loch (Knockan) See Clar Loch Mor.

CLAR BEAG, Loch (Rubha Mor)
Location & Access 15/991154 Visit Clar Loch Beag as part of an expedition to Loch na Totaig (see entry), including also Lochan Airigh Chaluim (15/991159), the unnamed lochan at 15/993162 and Clar Loch Mor (15/995150). After fishing Loch na Totaig, walk due east for ten minutes to reach Lochan Airigh Chaluim and the unnamed lochan, then south to Clar Loch Beag and Clar Loch Mor. The walk back to Reiff (15/966144) from Clar Loch Mor is two miles.
Commentary Four very attractive, small lochs in a remote setting on Rubha Mor. The walking is rough, but well within the capacity of most reasonably fit anglers, as well as little ones. Just about right for newcomers to hill loch fishing, a real 'adventure'.
Fish Mostly traditional 'breakfast-sized' trout but one or two surprises, particularly in Lochan Airigh Chaluim and the unnamed lochan to the north. Trout of over 2lbs are not infrequently encountered.
Flies & Tactics As always, when hill loch fishing, approach with caution. Trout often lie close to the shore and will be disturbed by a too vigorous approach. Offer them: Black Pennell, Grouse & Claret, Peter Ross.
Permission & Charges Same as Loch na Totaig.

CLAR MOR, Loch (Knockan)
Location & Access 15/178074 The largest of a series of six named and unnamed lochs lying to the west of the A835 Ledmore Junction/Ullapool road. Easily accessible from either the main road, or from a convenient stalkers' path which margins them to the west.
Commentary The other waters in this group are: Clar Loch Beag (15/181080), Loch Dhonnachaidh (15/176068) and the unnamed, surrounding satellite lochans.
Fish You will break no records here. Trout average 6-8oz, but they are nonetheless sporting and what they may lack in size they more than make up for by their fighting spirit.
Flies & Tactics Easy bank fishing and most flies produce results in all these waters. Begin with: Blue Zulu, March Brown, Silver Butcher.
Permission & Charges Birchbank Holiday Lodge, Knockan, Elphin, by Lairg, Sutherland. Tel: (01854) 666203 or 666205. The owner, Tom Strang, will provide all necessary information. The Factor, Assynt Estate, Estate Office, Lochinver, Sutherland. Tel: (01571) 844203. Bank fishing: £5 per rod per day.

CLAR MOR, Loch (Rubha Mor)
Location & Access 15/995150 See Clar Loch Beag.

CNOC CHALBHA, Lochs
Location & Access 15/174377. Start at Loch a' Mhinidh (15/189379), close to the old A894 Scourie/Ullapool road and walk due west for 20 minutes to reach the Calva Lochs.
Commentary I have a soft spot for these lovely lochs because my eldest son caught one of his first trout in a Calva loch. Quite apart from that, these moorland waters by the sea are absolutely lovely.
Fish Brown trout of ever size, from a few ounces up to fish of over 5lb in weight.
Flies & Tactics Exciting bank fishing and there are six lochs in the series, all unnamed on the OS map. Start at OS15/175375 and work north to OS15/175379. The water in this last loch is crystal clear and it has the reputation of producing the largest trout. Offer them: Ke-He, Loch Ordie, Silver Butcher.
Permission & Charges These waters are preserved by

OS Map 15 — Loch Assynt

the owner but access may be available from time to time. Further information from Mrs R Mackay, Scourie Angling Club, 12 Park Terrace, Scourie. Tel 01971 502425.

CNOC ODHAR, Lochs
Location & Access 15/211382. Approach from the stalkers path to the north of Duartmore Bridge at 15/220377. Climb steeply for 15 minutes to reach this unnamed loch which lies immediately to the east of the track.
Commentary Magnificent views south to Quinag (808m). Twenty minutes north brings you to a further series of lochans and pools, to the east of the track at OS15/222392, which are also worth fishing. On your way home, at OS15/211384, leave the track and walk west to visit the unnamed lochan at OS15/204383.
Fish Breakfast-sized trout which average 6-8oz.
Flies & Tactics Bank fishing, and the north end of the main loch is probably best. The steep east bank, near to the island, can also be very productive although it is awkward to fish. Offer: Black Zulu, Grouse & Claret, Peter Ross.
Permission & Charges Scourie Hotel, Scourie, by Lairg, Sutherland. Tel: (01971) 502396. £5 per rod per day.

COIRE A'BHAID, Loch
15/246294 See Loch na Gainmhich.

COIRE MHIC DHUGHAILL, Loch
Location & Access 15/350398. A long, hard walk in from Kinloch (15/348344) at the east end of Loch More (15/330370). Follow the stalkers track north-west from Aultanrynie (15/347361). Then climb north-east round the west shoulder of Meallan Liath Coire Mhic Dhuaghaill (801m) for 40 minutes to reach the loch.
Commentary Go here as much for the scenery and sense of 'escape' as for the fishing. Return via the small lochans below Meallan Liath Coire Mhic Dhughaill at OS15/347390 (unnamed on the map) and Lochan Dubh (OS15/351385). From Lochan Dubh, descend by following the outlet burn to the stalkers path at OS15/336384.
Fish Brown trout averaging 6-8oz.
Flies & Tactics Bank fishing, and a compass and map is all-important, even in good weather. Offer: Black Zulu, March Brown, Silver Butcher.
Permission & Charges The Reay Forest Estate, Estate Office, Achfary, by Lairg, Sutherland. Tel: (0971) 500221. £5 per rod per day.

COIRE NA CREIGE, Loch
15/170214 See Loch Bad an t-Sluic.

COIRE NA MEIDIE, Loch
Location & Access 15/314135. Approach via the A837 Bonar Bridge/Ledmore Junction road at 15/297083. A forest road heads north past Loch Ailsh (15/315110) to Benmore Lodge (15/322114). Walk north from Benmore Lodge and cross the River Oykel at 15/323119. Follow the tributary north-west climbing towards the summit of Sgonnan Mor, an outliner of Breabag (715m). The loch lies in a corrie between Sgnonnan Mor and the Black Rock (15/320137).
Commentary One and a half miles, climbing most of the way; but magnificent countryside and an adventurous day out.
Fish Nothing huge, but there are a few good fish.
Flies & Tactics Be prepared for all kinds of weather and take great care on the climb up to the loch. This is a tiny water which you can almost cast across, so approach cautiously and stay well back from the bank. Offer them: Loch Ordie, Grouse & Claret, Peter Ross.
Permission & Charges Assynt Estate (01571 844203). Access not encouraged during stalking season.

CRAGGIE, Loch (Glen Oykel)
Location & Access 15/324055. Immediately adjacent to the A837 Bonar Bridge/Ledmore Junction road, four miles west of Oykel Bridge.
Commentary A roadside loch, half a mile long by 200 yards wide.
Fish Brown trout which average 8-12oz and a few larger specimens.
Flies & Tactics Boat and bank fishing with best results coming from the boat. Craggie is a shallow water and fish are taken all over the loch. Offer them: Black Pennell, March Brown, Silver Invicta.
Permission & Charges Oykel Bridge Hotel, Oykel Bridge, by Lairg, Ross-shire. Tel: (01549) 441218. Boat with two rods: £15 per day

CROCACH, Loch (Duartmore)
Location & Access 15/197395. Lies in the hills to the east of the A894 Scourie/Ullapool road. Leave the new road at 15/1922380 and park 200 yards further south on the old road. Hike due north for 20 minutes to reach the loch. There is a locked gate on the old road. The key is available from Scourie Hotel.
Commentary The loch lies in a hollow and, because you are climbing, it is very easy to miss it by walking too far to the right. Save fishing time by using a compass and map. One of the most lovely lochs in the area, enticing and exciting, dotted with four small islands and interesting bays and fishy corners.
Fish Trout average 10oz but fish of over 2lb are also taken most seasons.
Flies & Tactics Boat fishing brings best results but if conditions are too wild to launch the boat fish the bank with confidence. Also carefully fish the adjacent lochans, no matter how small and fishless they might seem at first glance. Flies: Black Pennell, Woodcock & Hare-lug, Kingfisher Butcher.
Permission & Charges Scourie Hotel, Scourie, by Lairg, Sutherland. Tel: (01971) 502396. £5 per rod per day.

CROCACH, Loch (North Assynt)
Location & Access 15/100270. Park at Rhicarn (15/083253) on the B869 Lochinver/Stoer road. Follow the peat track north-east for one mile to reach the south end of the loch.
Commentary One of the most lovely and most

Loch Assynt   OS Map 15

productive lochs in the area. Crocach is one and a half miles long by up to half a mile wide across the middle bay, and 30ft deep at the north end. The most dramatic feature of the loch, apart from the surrounding countryside, are the bays and islands. There are 16 islands of varying size and their flora and fauna is representative of what Sutherland looked like, prior to the introduction of sheep.
Fish Large stock of excellent trout averaging 8-10oz, with good number of larger specimens of up to and over 2lb in weight.
Flies & Tactics The main bay, amongst the islands, is the most productive area and flies that do the damage include: Black Pennell, March Brown, Alexandra.
Permission & Charges See Loch Drumbeg entry. A boat may be available through Stoer Post Office.

CROM, Loch
Location & Access 15/148219. Take the same route as is used for Loch an Leothaid, and, as you descend from the bealach, continue south for ten minutes to reach Loch Crom.
Commentary A small, weedy loch, joined to Loch an Leothaid (north) and Bad an t-Sluic (south) at OS15/152217. A useful additional tramp may be made to the unnamed lochan at OS15/133222 which is always worth a few casts.
Fish Small, dark trout, averaging 6-8oz.
Flies & Tactics Loch Crom is really an expansion of the Allt na h-Airbhe burn, which drains the system into the River Inver. Bank fishing only and the loch is easily covered, although the margins are soft. Best to stay on the bank, rather than wade. Use: Black Pennell, Grouse & Claret, Silver Butcher.
Permission & Charges See Loch an Leothaid entry.

CUL A'MHILL, Loch
15/357310 See Meallan a'Chuail Lochs.

CUL FRAIOCH, Loch
Location & Access 15/025330. Approach from the B869 Lochinver/Unapool road along the minor road from Totag (15/041298) to Rubha Stoer (15/020321).
Commentary Loch Cul Fraioch, 'The Loch Behind the Heather', is three quarters of a mile long by up to 500 yards wide. It lies in a hollow, sheltered to the north by Sidhean Mor (162m), Meall Dubh Raffin (124m) to the west, and Cnoc Riabhach (100m) to the east. The loch is easily accessible and offers good sport in lovely surroundings.
Fish Brown trout averaging 10-12oz.
Flies & Tactics Safe and comfortable bank fishing all round the shore. The north, narrow end of the loch, and in the vicinity of the little island, from either shore, is a good place to start. Flies: Ke-He, Grouse & Claret, Silver Invicta.
Permission & Charges Bank fishing at £5 per rod per day, £25 per week, £45 per season. Permits: Drumbeg Post Office, Drumbeg, Sutherland. Tel: (015713) 833231; Tourist Office, Lochinver, Sutherland. Tel: (015714) 844330; Stoer PO 01571 855338.

CULAG, Loch
Location & Access 15/097217. Situated half a mile south of Lochinver on the minor road to Inverkirkaig.
Commentary Easily accessible and overlooked by both the road and Lochinver School.
Fish Brown trout averaging 8oz plus a few larger fish, and, after late June, salmon and seatrout.
Flies & Tactics Boat and bank fishing, with best results coming from the boat. Loch Culag is an early loch and can fish well during April and May. Trout are most cooperative in a good south-west breeze, but salmon seem to prefer a north wind. Dry fly is effective for trout, salmon like Jock Scott, Silver Grey, Black Doctor. Assault seatrout at dusk.
Permission & Charges Enquiries to Inver Lodge Hotel (01571 844496)

DAM, Lochs
Location & Access 15/155002. Approach via a narrow, tortuous hill road from 15/146007 on the A835 Ledmore Junction/Ullapool road. Drive with care and caution. Park at the dam.
Commentary A series of four lochs: Loch Beinn Deirg, Loch Maoile, Loch Bad na h-Achlaise, and the Dubh Loch, known collectively as the Dam Lochs. In spite of being in a remote setting they are easily accessible by car from the Power Station road.
Fish The local angling club have stocked Loch Beinn Deirg with rainbow trout and Loch Maoile with salmon. There are wild brown trout in all the waters. Do not expect large baskets, but excellent fish of up to and over 3lb are taken.
Flies & Tactics Bank fishing, with a fair bit of walking. The east end of Loch Maoile and the south end of Loch Beinn Deirg are the most productive fishing areas. Flies: Loch Ordie, Grouse & Claret, Kingfisher Butcher. Loch Dubh is dour.
Permission & Charges Mountainman, West Argyle Street, Ullapool, Wester Ross. Tel: (01854) 613383. Bank fishing only, £6 per rod per day.

DARAICH, Loch
Location & Access 15/1303320. Ten minutes up the hill from Ambraigh (15/124324) in the village of Drumbeg on the B869 Unapool/Lochinver road.
Commentary A small, 'evening' loch, easily accessible but with a fine feeling of remoteness. Ideal for a few after dinner casts or for introducing little ones to hill loch fishing.
Fish Traditional highland trout which average 6-8oz.
Flies & Tactics Easy bank fishing and Daraich Loch trout are not fussy and rise well to most standard patterns of flies. Begin with: Black Pennell, March Brown, Silver Butcher.
Permission & Charges See Loch Drumbeg entry.

DEARG A' CHUILL MHOIR, Lochan
Location & Access 15/158107. An adventurous day out, hill walking, scrambling and fishing on Cul Mor (849m). Start from the Visitor Centre at Knockanrock (15/190090) and follow the stalkers' path north. First stop, Lochan Fhionnlaidh (15/190102), then Loch an Laoigh (15/181105). From Loch an Laoigh climb

OS Map 15 — Loch Assynt

steeply due west aiming for between Creag nan Calman (15/160113) to the north and An Laogh (15/160102) to the south. Loch Dearg a' Chuill Mhoir is on the saddle. Now descend carefully to Gleann Laoigh and walk south-east to Lochan Dearg (15/167096). After paying your respects, continue east along a good track to visit the final three waters in the expedition: Lochan nan Ealachan (15/176090), Lochan an Ais (15/185090) and Lochan Fada (15/182084). This is a considerable journey, not so much in distance (five miles) but because the terrain is tough.
Commentary More hill walking than fishing, but the chance to visit and explore lochs which rarely see an artificial fly from one season to the next.
Fish Not too heavy to carry back.
Flies & Tactics Try to choose a good day for the journey and always go well-shod and well prepared. If you have any doubts, consult Tom Strang and accept his advice. Best flies: Black Zulu, Soldier Palmer, Peter Ross.
Permission & Charges See Cam Loch entry.

DEARG, Loch (Drumrinie) 15/167096 See Lochan Dearg a'Chuill Mhoir.
DEARG, Lochan (Coigach) 15/090571 See Loch Tuath.
DEARG, Lochan (Rubh Mor) 15/998128 See Loch na Beiste.
DHONNACHAIDH, Loch 15/176068 See Clar Loch Mor, Knockan.

DOIRE NA H-AIRBHE, Loch
Location & Access 15/105126). Approach form Inverpolly at 15/073131 on the minor road between Badnagyle (15/063112) and Inverkirkaig (15/091196). Follow the Polly River south-east and where the main stream turns north, continue up Gleann na Gaoithe to reach the loch after two miles.
Commentary Probably the most productive loch in the area and certainly one of the most lovely. Stac Pollaidh (618m) towers to the south, Cul Mor (849m) dominates the eastern horizon. There is a fine wood at the east end of the loch, by a sandy bay, ideal for snoozing, picnicking and summer swimming.
Fish Very pretty trout which average 10-12oz and good numbers of larger fish as well. On the way home, circle north from Loch Doire na h-Airbhe to visit the unnamed lochans at 15/102132 and 15/098137. The fish are not so large, but there are lots of them and they rise readily to the fly.
Flies & Tactics Exciting bank fishing and the south shore produces best results. From the narrows at the west end, wading is safe and comfortable, but as you progress east, high banks keep you ashore. Further east, wading is again safe and productive. First cast: Loch Ordie, Soldier Palmer, Black Pennell.
Permission & Charges Same as Loch Bad a' Ghaill entry.

DONNAIG, Loch
Location & Access 15/082317. Park by Loch Eileanach (private water) at 15/088315 on the B869 Unapool/Lochinver road and walk north-west for ten minutes to reach the loch.
Commentary This is a good loch set in rugged country.
Fish The hard-fighting little trout average 6-8oz, but be prepared for more savage tugs.
Flies & Tactics Exciting fishing in wonderful surroundings using: Black Zulu, Grouse & Claret, Peter Ross.
Permission & Charges Bank fishing £5 per rod per day, £25 per week, £45 per season. Permits: Drumbeg Post Office, Drumbeg, Sutherland. Tel: (01571) 833231; or Stoer P.O. Tel: (01571) 855338; or Tourist Office Lochinver, Sutherland. Tel: (01571) 844330.

DRUIM SUARDALAIN, Loch
Location & Access 15/115217. Accessible from the Inver Lodge Hotel via the Glencanisp Lodge road to the east of Lochinver.
Commentary A very attractive loch, a mile west of Lochinver, dominated by Caisteal Liath, 'The Grey Castle', the highest point of Suilven (731m). Loch Druim Suardalain is approximately three quarters of a mile long by about 200 yards wide, shallow, and graced by three, scrub-and-tree covered islets.
Fish Brown trout average 6-8oz and there are lots of them, particularly given a good wind. Salmon and seatrout enter the loch from late June onwards. Evening fishing for seatrout can be effective. Most salmon are encountered during September.
Flies & Tactics Boat fishing and strictly fly only. The north shore generally produces best results and favourite flies include: Loch Ordie, Mallard & Yellow, Silver Butcher.
Permission & Charges Contact Inver Lodge Hotel, Lochinver, by Lairg, Sutherland IV27 4LU. Tel: (01571) 844496

DRUMBEG, Loch
Location & Access 15/115325. Close to the B869 Unapool/Lochinver road at Drumbeg Village.
Commentary One of the most attractive lochs in the north. The main part of the loch is graced by four delightful little islands, a tree clad promontary guards narrows leading to two further bays west and south.
Fish Excellent stocks of trout averaging 8-10oz, and also fish up to 2lb.
Flies & Tactics Boat fishing is probably most productive. Approach from the peat track at the west end (15/111328) to explore the west shore. A track at the east end, by the school, gives access to the east shore. Try: Ke-He, Grouse & Claret, Silver Butcher.
Permission & Charges Bank fishing: £5, per rod per day, £25 per week, £45 per season. Permits: Drumbeg Post Office, Drumbeg, Sutherland (01571 833231). Stoer Post Office. Tel: (01571) 855338; Lochinver Tourist Information Office. Tel: (01571) 844330. A boat may be available from Drumbeg Post Office.

DRUMRUNIE, Loch
Location & Access 15/159041. Immediately adjacent and to the west of the A835 Ledmore Junction/Ullapool road.

Loch Assynt — OS Map 15

Commentary An easily accessible little loch in a delightful setting with splendid views.
Fish Good stocks of small trout which average in the order of 8oz.
Flies & Tactics Bank fishing only, and stay on the bank, wading is dangerous. Trout rise all round the loch. Offer them Blue Zulu, Woodcock & Hare-lug, Silver Butcher.
Permission & Charges Mountainman, West Argyle Street, Ullapool, Wester Ross. Tel: (01854) 613383. Bank fishing: £6 per rod per day.

DUART, River
Location & Access Source 15/240380 Ouflow 15/178369. Accessible from the A894 Scourie/Ullapool road at Duartmore Bridge (15/200376).
Commentary A modest salmon stream which offers the chance of a fish, providing there are good water levels. The lower section, to the west of the road, is slow moving, weedy and bounded south by a forestry plantation.
Fish In spate conditions, a few salmon are caught, but rarely more than 15-20 for the season. The lochs on the system do, however, produce some excellent trout, particularly Loch Duartmore (15/189374).
Flies & Tactics Loch Allt na h-Airbe (Loch Yucal) (15/205370) and Loch Allt nam Ramh (15/211361), and the stream that joins them (known as 'the salmon hole') are the most likely places. Boat fishing on Loch Allt na h-Airbe is best, for trout and salmon, bank fish the other waters. Use: Willie Gunn, Garry Dog, Silver Invicta, Black Pennell, Soldier Palmer.
Permission & Charges Scourie Hotel, Scourie, by Lairg, Sutherland. Tel: (01971) 502396.

DUARTBEG, Loch
Location & Access 15/167388. Easily accessible and to the west of the A894 Scourie/Ullapool road.
Commentary Very public and surrounded by more interesting waters in the hills, but useful if time is limited.
Fish Nice trout averaging 8oz in weight.
Flies & Tactics Comfortable bank fishing using Blue Zulu, March Brown, Alexandra.
Permission & Charges Scourie Hotel, Scourie, Sutherland. Tel 01971 502396. Permits at the village shop in Scourie at £5 per rod per day. Details of the angling club waters from the secretary: Mrs R Mackay, Scourie, by Lairg, Sutherland. Tel: (0971) 502425.

DUARTMORE, Loch 15/189374 See Duart River.

DUBH A' CHNOIC GHAIRBH, Loch
Location & Access 15/213352. Lies to the east of the old A894 Scourie/Ullapool road, one mile north from Kylestrome.
Commentary Sheltered north by Cnoc Garbh and to the east by forestry, easily accessible and ideal if time is limited. Make a longer day by also visiting the unnamed little roadside lochan at OS15/209353, and then, to the west of the old road, Loch an Fuath (OS15/205356) and Loch an Iasgair (OS15/198357).
Fish Lots of 6-8oz trout, but also a few larger fish of around 2lb.
Flies & Tactics If things are quiet to the east of the road, decamp rapidly to the west. Loch an Iasgair is very lovely and probably the best place to look for supper. Flies: Loch Ordie, March Brown, Silver Invicta.
Permission & Charges For all lochs other than Loch Iasgair, contact: The Scourie Hotel, Scourie, by Lairg, Sutherland. Tel: (0971) 502396. For Loch Iasgair, contact: The Reay Forest Estate, Estate Office, Achfary, by Lairg, Sutherland. Tel: (0971) 500221. Bank fishing, £5 per rod per day.

DUBH A'CHUAIL, Loch 15/347280 See Meallan a'Chuail Lochs.
DUBH LOCH BEAG, Loch (Ben More Assynt) 15/325165 See Loch Sail an Ruathair.

DUBH, Loch (Lochinver)
Location & Access 15/073240. Follow the minor road from Achadhantuir (15/083249) on the B869 Lochinver/Stoer road towards Achmelvich (15/058246) and park at 15/071249. Walk south, crossing the bridge over the narrows of Loch Roe. A track leads up to the loch. Dogs are not allowed to accompany anglers to Assynt Angling Club lochs.
Commentary Loch Dubh is the largest loch on the Ardroe Peninsula (approximately 15 acres), very pretty with small stands of woodland along the west and south shore. To the south-west, lie five other lochs, all of which should be fished as part of a super day out.
Fish A fine mixture, from 6oz trout up to fish of over 1lb in weight.
Flies & Tactics Bank fishing. Start at Loch Dubh, awkward in places due to steep sides. Follow the track east past Ardroe to fish the unnamed lochan at OS15/075233, known locally as 'The Sandy Loch'. Return over the hill, due west to Loch Braigh a' Bhaile, 'the loch above the village' (OS15/069236), and the 'Loch of the Peevish Creek' at OS15/069233. Now walk south to fish Loch nan Gobhair, 'the loch of the goats' (OS15/065231) and, finally Loch Thormaid, 'Norman's loch' at OS15/065235. Use: Black Pennell, March Brown, Alexandra.
Permission & Charges See Loch Drumbeg entry.

DUBH LOCH MOR, Loch (Ben More Assynt) 15/319189 See Loch Sail an Ruathair.
DUBH, Loch (Ullapool) 15/155002 See Dam Lochs.
DUBH, Lochan (Loch More) 15/351385 See Loch Coire Mhic Dhughaill.
DUBH MEALLAN MHURCHAIDH, Loch 15/215194 See Loch na Beinne Reidhe.

DUBHA, Lochan
Location & Access 15/979141. Drive north along the minor road from Achiltibue on the west side of the Rubha Mor Peninsula in the Summer Isles. Park at 15/970139 and follow the track to Blairbuie (15/974141). Lochan Dubha is ten minutes further east.
Commentary A quick scamper round a series of small lochans to the east of Blairbuie and Reiff. After

OS Map 15 Loch Assynt

Lochan Dubha, head north to OS15/979143 and OS15/972146. Return south to your car by the road.
Fish Small trout averaging 6oz.
Flies & Tactics You can cast across most of these lochans, so stay well back from the shore. Try: Black Zulu, Soldier Palmer, Silver Butcher.
Permission & Charges See Loch na Totaig entry.

EALLACH, Lochan 15/062093 See Lochan Sgeireach, Achiltibuie.

EILEAG, Loch
Location & Access 15/309063. A step south from the A837 Bonar Bridge/Ledmore Junction road at 15/312065.
Commentary A few acres in extent, shallow and bordered south by conifer plantations. Less exposed than its neighbour, Loch Craggie.
Fish Small fish which fight well. Average weight, 6-8oz.
Flies & Tactics Bank fishing and good sport all round the loch. Eileag trout are not fussy and take most patterns of fly. Start with: Black Zulu, Soldier Palmer, Alexandra.
Permission & Charges See Loch a' Bhith entry.

FADA, Lochan (Achiltibuie) 15/055092 See Lochan Sgeireach, Achiltibuie.

FADA, Lochan (Canisp)
Location & Access 15/206165. Start at Cam Loch and follow the well-marked stalkers'/walkers' track round the north shore of Cam Loch and up into the hills between Canisp (846m) and Suilven (713m). Branch right at 15/216154 to visit little Loch a' Chroisg (15/220155), prior to reaching Lochan Fada after a walk of about one hour.
Commentary Spectacular surroundings and a wonderful day out, perfectly suited for introducing beginners to the delights of both hill walking and flyfishing.
Fish Large numbers of very pretty little trout which fight hard, particularly in Lochan Fada.
Flies & Tactics Bank fishing, and Loch a' Chroisg, steep-sided, is best fished from the north-west shore. Depending upon wind direction, either shore of Lochan Fada (one mile long) produces great results. Include a visit to the scatter of lochans on the east shoulder of Suilven, centred on Loch Meall a' Mhutliaich (OS15/190166), a small piece of paradise. Begin with: Black Pennell, Woodcock & Hare-lug, Silver Butcher.
Permission & Charges Assynt Estate Office, Lochinver, by Lairg, Sutherland IV27 4YJ. (01571) 844203); or Inver Lodge Hotel (01571) 844496. Bank fishing, £5 per rod per day.

FADA, Lochan (Inverkirkaig) 15/085179 See Loch a'Choin.
FADA, Lochan (Knockanrock) 15/182084 See Lochan Dearg a'Chuill Mhoir.
FADA, Lochan (North Assynt) 15/112304 See Loch Bad an Og.

FEARNA, Loch
Location & Access 15/127249. Park on the A837 Inchnadamph/Lochinver road at 15/126244. Loch Fearna, 'the loch of the alders', is a ten minute hike north up the hill. No dogs are allowed to accompany anglers fishing Assynt Angling Club lochs.
Commentary Not too far to walk, easily fished from the bank.
Fish Lots of fine trout which average 6-8oz and fight well.
Flies & Tactics No need to wade and fish are caught from all round the shore. Offer them: Blue Zulu, Ke-He, Dunkeld.
Permission & Charges See Loch na h-Innse Fraoich entry.

FEITH AN LEOTHAID, Loch
Location & Access 15/185224 Park near Little Assynt at 15/157250. Cross the field to a bridge over the River Inver at 15/156258. Follow the track which leads east, along the hill overlooking Loch Assynt, to the Shieling at 15/198247. From the Shieling, fish little Loch a'Mhuilinn (15/200242), then return to the track and climb south by Gob Aird, leaving the track at 15/192238 to strike west to reach Loch a'Ghuib Aird (15/187240); then south-west to the unnamed lochan at 15/178237. Walk due south now to reach Loch Feith an Leothaid. After fishing Loch Feith an Leothaid, explore the inlet stream at the east end (Feith an Leothaid burn) and the unnamed lochan at 15/198232, before walking north-west to pick up the track back to Little Assynt.
Commentary This is a long day out, covering rough ground, but mostly on a good stalkers' path. You will visit waters that rarely see an artificial fly from one season to the next and the surrounding scenery is majestic.
Fish Mostly trout averaging 8oz, but a good chance of getting into some much larger fish, particularly on Loch Feith an Leothaid.
Flies & Tactics Loch Feith an Leothaid is a large water, almost three quarters of a mile long by up to 400 yards wide. The north shoreline is the most interesting, scattered with bays and points. The inlet burn can be very productive, particularly after heavy rain. Bank fishing all the way and the east end, where there is a sandy beach, is the ideal place for lunch. Tempt trout with: Ke-He, Invicta, Silver Butcher.
Permission & Charges See Loch an Leothaid (Quinag) entry.

FEITH AN LEOTHAID, Lochan 15/294308 See Loch nan Caorach.

FEUR, Loch (Ledmore)
Location & Access 15/270135 Park by the remains of the Neolithic chambered cairn at 15/250140 on the A837 Ledmore Junction/Inchnadamph road. Follow the Ledbeg River upstream for one mile to reach the loch, which is a small expansion of the main course of the river.
Commentary More a pleasant walk in the hills than a serious fishing expedition but nonetheless rewarding

Loch Assynt — OS Map 15

for being so. Marvellous countryside and a good chance of meeting greenshank along the way.
Fish A feature of Sutherland burns is their depth and the quality of trout some streams contain. Ledbeg River is connected to Cam Loch (15/220130), Urigill (15/244100) and Loch Borralan (15/263106) and can hold trout of considerable size, particularly towards the end of the season.
Flies & Tactics Stalking trout country. Keep well back from the bank and use light tackle and size 16 flies: Loch Ordie, Grouse & Claret, Black Pennell.
Permission & Charges Enquiries to Reay Forest Estate. Tel: (01971) 500221.

FHIONNLAIDH, Lochan 15/190102 See Lochan Dearg a'Chuill Mhoir.
FIONN BEAG, Loch 15/340228 See Fionn Loch Mor.

FIONN, Loch (Inverkirkaig)
Location & Access 15/134173 Park at Inverkirkaig (15/079195). Follow the track up the north bank of the River Kirkaig for three miles to reach the loch.
Commentary One of the finest and most lovely lochs in all of Scotland, two miles long by up to 300 yds wide and 40ft deep; guarded by Suilven (731m) to the north and Cul Mor (849m) to the west. Often windy, sometimes dour, but always exciting.
Fish Something for everyone: ferox trout, encountered trolling, good numbers of fish around the 2-3lb mark, and plenty of their smaller brethren averaging 8-12oz.
Flies & Tactics Bank fishing only on this narrow, scattered water. Fish are taken everywhere, but the most productive area is at the east end where the stream from Loch Veyatie enters. This stream is well worth exploring, particularly after heavy rain. It holds outstanding trout. Offer them: Loch Ordie, Woodcock & Hare-lug, Soldier Palmer.
Permission & Charges Inver Lodge Hotel, Lochinver, by Lairg, Sutherland. Tel: (01571) 844496. Free to hotel guests. Non-residents, £5 per rod per day.

FIONN MOR, Loch
Location & Access 15/335235 Approach from the A837 Bonar Bridge/Inchnadamph road at Glen Cassley (16/472023). Drive north up the glen on the minor road by the River Cassley to the road end at Duchally (16/388170). A four-wheel drive vehicle is required to drive further north to near the power station at 16/365206. Now walk north along the stalkers path past Loch na Sroine Luime (15/345217), one mile, and Fionn Loch Beag (15/340228) at two miles, to reach Fionn Loch Mor after two and a half miles. Follow the inlet stream north from Fionn Loch Mor for three quarters of a mile to reach Gorm Loch Mor (15/320245), one of the most remote lochs in Scotland.
Commentary Various options for exciting hill walking and fishing. Visit the lochs out to Fionn Loch Mor, returning via Loch nan Sgaraig (15/349248) crossing Creag Riabhach (379m); alternatively, head north from Fionn Loch Mor to fish round Gorm Loch Mor, returning by Loch Bealach a'Mhadaidh (15/310231) and the stalkers path, descending to Loch na Sroine Luime at 15/336219. After heavy rain, crossing the Upper Cassley could present problems; or take a tent and camp out for a few days.
Fish Great fun, with sport and action all the way. Trout average 8oz but there are fish of up to and over 1lb, particularly in Fionn Loch Mor and Gorm Loch Mor.
Flies & Tactics These remote lochs are rarely fished and some will not have seen an artificial fly for several seasons. Fionn Loch Mor alone, a wild maze of corners and inviting bays, is worthy of several days attention, and the tramp to Loch Bealach a' Mhadaidh takes you into one of the most magnificent corries in the north. Majestic bank fishing where Black Pennell, Greenwell's Glory and Peter Ross will supply lunch.
Permission & Charges Apply to Balnagowan Castle Properties, Balnagowan Estate, Kildary, Ross-shire. Tel: (01862) 842243.

FLEODACH COIRE, Loch 15/273248 See Loch Bealach na h-Uidhe.
GAINMHEICH, Lochan 15/140113 See Loch an Doire Dhuibh.
GARBH Loch Mor 15/088303 See Loch nan Lub.

GARVIE, River
Location & Access Source 15/039130 Outflow 15/040136. The River Garvie is a short, rocky stream flowing north from Loch Osgaig to reach the sea within half a mile in Garvie Bay. It is easily accessible from the Drumrunie (15/167054) to Achiltibuie (15/024085) road.
Commentary The principal fishing interest here is Loch Garvie, an extension of the river just before it enters Garvie Bay. This can offer excellent sport and is ideal for a family party, Garvie Bay being the perfect location for a beach-day out and a lazy picnic.
Fish Some great seatrout fishing with wonderfully fresh fish which average 1lb 8oz and the occasional fish of up to and over 5lb.
Flies & Tactics The west bank offers the best chance of sport with July producing most fish. Late-evening fishing is very exciting and don't forget to fish in the sea, close to the outlet stream. This can provide memorable action when the loch is quiet. First cast: Ke-He, Grouse & Claret, Alexandra.
Permission & Charges The west bank of the River Garvie is owned by Mr P M Rex, Badentarbat Lodge, Achiltibuie, Ullapool, Wester Ross. Tel: (01854) 622332. It is let on the basis of £25 per rod per day with a maximum of two rods fishing. Two rods are available on the east bank of the River Garvie through the Inverpolly Estate. Tel: (01854) 622454.

GILLAROO, Loch 15/277193 See Loch Mhaolach-Coire.
GLEANNAN A'MHADAIDH, Loch 15/160161 See Lochan Nigheadh.
GLEANNAN NA GAOITHE, Loch 15/101192 See Loch Bad na Muiriehinn.
GORM, Loch Beag 15/143289 See Gorm Loch Mor.
GORM LOCH MOR (Loch) 15/320245 See Fionn Loch Mor.

OS Map 15 — Loch Assynt

GORM LOCH MOR (Nedd)
Location & Access 15/143297 Drive south from the village of Nedd on the B869 Unapool/Lochinver road and park at 15/136312. Then walk south-east, passing Loch a'Bhraighe on your right, to reach Gorm Loch Mor within 15 minutes.
Commentary Whilst in the parish, walk south again to fish Gorm Loch Beag (15/143289) and two lochs to the east of Cnoc Gorm (251m) (15/150288), Loch na Tarraing (15/159290) and Loch Odhar (15/151297).
Fish Can be dour at times but usually generous, providing excellent sport with 8-10oz trout. Gorm Loch Beag has larger fish and the two other lochs noted also hold good trout.
Flies & Tactics The jagged west bay, with two small islands, is the place to begin, working south from there to the island at the south end of the loch. On Gorm Loch Beag, pay particular attention along the north shore and down to the promontory on the east bank.
Permission & Charges See Drumbeg Loch entry.

GUILC, Lochan 15/128254 See Loch Beannach.
INA'S, Lochs 15/081241 See Lochan an Tairbh.
INNIS THORCAILL, Loch 15/159280 Enquiries to Reay Forest Estate. Tel: (01971) 500221.

INVER, River (Upper)
Location & Access Source 15/230172 Outflow 15/095231. The main fishing on the River is from its exit point at Loch Assynt, down to the sea at Lochinver, a distance of about five miles; accessible from the A837 Inchnadamph/Lochinver road.
Commentary Water flow is regulated by sluices at the west end of Loch Assynt and the river has been much improved over the years by the construction of new pools and holding waters. The river is very attractive, surrounded by splendid mountain and moorland scenery, dominated by Quinag (808m) and Canisp (846m).
Fish Numbers of salmon caught have declined in recent years, from around 400 to between 100-200 fish. Seatrout have virtually vanished altogether. Salmon average 8-9lb, with double-figure fish most seasons. Spring salmon, caught in June, can weigh up to 20lb in weight.
Flies & Tactics There are a number of excellent pools, including Loch na Garbhe Uidhe and Lochan an-Iasgaich, which are extensions of the river, and famous pools such as Grassies, Deer, Whirl, Star, Pollan, Ladder, Battle Field and Flats. A 15ft rod is advisable but deep wading is not required. Flies: Green Highlander, Stoat's Tail, Jock Scott, Garry Dog, Willie Gunn, Hairy Mary.
Permission & Charges Inver Lodge Hotel, Lochinver, by Lairg, Sutherland. Tel: (01571) 844496. Upper River Inver. 26th June-15th October: £70 per rod per day. Non hotel residents pay a £5 surcharge.

KIRKAIG, River
Location & Access Source 15/123177, Outflow 15/079195. Accessible from the car park at Inverkirkaig, on the Sutherland/Ross-shire boundary at 15/086194. Two mile walk from this point, upstream, to the top of Beat 1.
Commentary One of the most attractive salmon streams in the north, but, in places, mountain goat country. Beat 1 in particular requires a deal of climbing, up and down to the river in order to explore all the pools. Beat 2 is more user-friendly, but also involves a fair bit of puffing and panting. Beat 3 is easily accessible being adjacent to the road.
Fish Salmon average 8lb and fish of over 20lb have been caught. Between 200-400 salmon are taken most seasons.
Flies & Tactics A 15ft rod is best, given the strong flow. When fishing Falls Pool, one of the most productive pools on the River, a second pair of hands is needed to land fish. Great care should be taken at all times. Little Falls Pool, downstream, is the best pool on the Kirkaig. On Beat 2, Hazel Pool always holds fish, and Middle Red is an excellent high-water pool. On Beat 3, Heather Pool is the most productive. Flies: Willie Gunn, Garry Dog, Green Highlander, Collie Dog, Jock Scott.
Permission & Charges Inver Lodge Hotel, Lochinver, by Lairg, Sutherland. Tel: (01571) 844496. 26th June-15th October: £24 per rod per day. Non hotel residents pay a £5 surcharge.

LEACACH, Lochan 15/055095 See Lochan Sgeireach, Achiltibuie.

LEXY'S, Loch
Location & Access 15/054280. Park at the end of the minor road from Stoer at 15/047281. Lexy's Loch is a couple of minutes west across the moor.
Commentary A good day out in the wilds, not taxing, and an easy introduction to hill loch fishing.
Fish Grand sport with little fish averaging 6-8oz.
Flies & Tactics Lexy's Loch is the largest loch in the vicinity, some 400 yards long by 200 yards wide. Fish are taken everywhere, but the east is perhaps the most productive. Poll an Droighinn lies north/south, a magnificent scattering of fishy bays and corners. Organise lunch by the island off the west shore. First cast: Loch Ordie, Grouse & Claret, Black Pennell.
Permission & Charges See Drumbeg Loch entry. A boat may be available from Stoer Post Office.

LOANAN, River
Location & Access Source 15/249159 Outflow 15/246219. Adjacent to and to the west of the A837 Ledmore Junction/Lochinver road. Access from this road at any point along the River.
Commentary The River Loanan is part of the Assynt/Inver System and flows for four miles between Loch Awe (OS15/247153) and Loch Assynt (OS15/200250). A pretty stream, full of small pools and tumbling runs, with Canisp (846m) dominating the western horizon.
Fish There are brown trout, and some surprisingly good ones, but the principal interest is in salmon and grilse, a few of which are taken most seasons.
Flies & Tactics Always worth a visit, but the best chance is after heavy rain with the River level falling. The lower section is most productive. Stalk the fish,

Loch Assynt — OS Map 15

keeping well back from the bank, using light tackle. Flies: Willie Gunn, Garry Dog, Stoat's Tail, Green Highlander.
Permission & Charges Contact: Assynt Estate, Estate Office, Lochinver, Sutherland. Tel: (01571) 844203. Fishing is only available to Inver Lodge Hotel residents or Estate guests.

LOCHAIN NAN EALACHAN, Lochs
Location & Access 15/323352. From Lochmore Side (15/318376) on the A838 Lairg/Scourie road. A stalkers' path climbs south over the west shoulder of Beinn Lice (470m) to reach the first loch (Lochain nan Ealachan) in about 40 minutes.
Commentary A long day out in the hills fishing a series of ten lochs and lochans to the north of Beinn Leoid (792m). For Loch nan Ealachan, walk south to OS15/328347 and its neighbour, OS15/330344. Rejoin the track and walk south to OS15/335333. South again on the track for ten minutes to pick up an inlet stream to Loch Srath nan Alainnin (15/320329). Follow it down to the main burn and the loch. At the west end of Loch Srath nan Alainnin, climb north-west to fish Lochain a' Mhill Dheirg, a series of lochans extending from OS15/315336 west to OS15/305339. After the last lochan, walk slightly north of east for 30 minutes to greet the stalkers' path back to Lochmore Side, or simply walk north north-east.
Fish Mostly modest-sized trout, but some of the lochs here contain larger fish as well.
Flies & Tactics A major expedition, not to be undertaken lightly. Make an early start and be well equipped and well prepared for all kinds of weather. You will cross difficult country and should be able to use a compass and map. Wonderful bank fishing and absolute isolation is the reward.
Permission & Charges The Reay Forest Estate, Estate Office, Achfary, by Lairg, Sutherland. Tel: (01971) 500221. £5 per rod per day.

LOCHANAN DUBH (Loch) 15/147055 See Loch Tuath.
LON NA H-UAMHA, Loch See Loch an Doire Dhuibh.
LOT-GHAOITH, Loch 15/359300 See Meallan a'Chuail Lochs.

LURGAINN, Loch
Location & Access 15/110090. Immediately to the south of and easily accessible from the Drumrunie (15/167054) to Achiltibuie (15/024085) road. Loch Lurgainn is the first in a series of three lochs extending eight miles west towards Rubh Mor and the Summer Isles.
Commentary For such a prominent, easily accessible loch, Lurgainn is infrequently fished. The loch is four miles long by up to half a mile wide and, on a sunny day, there are few more attractive settings. However, when the wind blows and the skies open, Lurgainn is a dangerous place to linger.
Fish Trout of over 5lb have been taken in recent years and Loch Lurgainn has always had a reputation for producing large trout, mostly caught by trolling. The bulk of the congregation, however, consist of trout which average 8oz. They can be hard to move at times, but at other times it is hard to avoid catching large numbers. Try: Black Pennell, Greenwell's Glory, Dunkeld.
Flies & Tactics Boat fishing brings best results, but you must wear a life jacket and have a reliable outboard engine. A boat gives you easy access to the south shore where there are a number of delightful bays and sandy corners which offer good sport. Boats are moored at 15/108094, below the Stac Pollaidh car park. An underwater rock shelf extends south-east from the boat mooring bay and this is a noted place for trolling.
Permission & Charges See Loch Bad a'Ghaill entry.

MAIDEN, Loch
Location & Access 15/050266 Lies adjacent to the north of the B869 Lochinver/Stoer road. Immediately to the north of Maiden Loch is another excellent water, Loch na h-Airighe Bige (15/062270).
Commentary The Maiden Loch is a popular water, easily accessible and offering exciting bank fishing. The loch is half a mile long by up to 200 yards wide at the east end. Loch na h-Airighe Bige, which drains into Maiden Loch, is centred by an attractive, scrub-covered island.
Fish Both waters contain good stocks of wild trout in the order of 8oz, but there are larger fish as well, particularly in h-Airighe Bige.
Flies & Tactics Bank fishing, and avoid wading. The water deepens rapidly in many areas. Offer trout: Black Pennell, Invicta, Silver Butcher.
Permission & Charges See Loch a'Bhraighe entry.

MANSE, Loch
Location & Access 15/095248 The Manse Loch lies to the north of Torbreck House on the B869 Lochinver/Stoer road and may be approached either from Rhicharn (15/083253) in the north, or from Loch an Ordain (15/091240) in the south. After visiting Manse Loch, follow the inlet stream up the glen to Loch an Tuirc (15/115260) and north to Loch an Tuir (15/118265). Then walk west to fish the unnamed lochan at 15/111266.
Commentary The Manse Loch is part of Roe System and for a number of years the local angling association carried on improvement works in an attempt to re-establish seatrout runs. They had some considerable success and this work is being continued by the North Assynt Estate.
Fish A few seatrout which average 1lb 8oz and brown trout averaging 8oz and the occasional larger fish as well. The other lochs hold good quality trout which average 8-10oz and also fish of up to 2lb.
Flies & Tactics Manse Loch is best fished from the boat because the banks are generally steep and uncomfortable to negotiate. At the time of writing, there is no boat, but the estate plan to place one on the loch in the future. The rest of the lochs in the series are easily fished from the bank. Spend less, rather than more time, at Manse Loch, the best of the fishing is further north. Offer them: Grouse & Claret, Woodcock & Hare-lug, Silver Butcher.

OS Map 15 — Loch Assynt

Permission & Charges See Drumbeg Loch entry.

MAOILE, Loch 15/155022 See Dam Lochs.

MEALL A'BHUIRICH, Loch
Location & Access 15/354120 Approach via the A837 Bonar Bridge/Ledmore Junction road at 15/297083. A forest road leads north past Loch Ailsh (15/315110) to Benmore Lodge (15/322114). Walk north-east from Benmore Lodge along the south shoulder of Meall a'Bhuirich (421m) for one and a half miles to reach the loch.
Commentary Loch Meall a'Bhuirich is a substantial, shallow loch lying in the shelter of Meall a'Bhuirich. The loch is half a mile long by up to 250 yards wide and is rarely fished.
Fish Good stocks of trout which average about 8-10oz.
Flies & Tactics Bank fishing. There are numerous bays and headlands. Concentrate in the vicinity of the inlet burns on the north-east and south-west shores. The outlet, where the loch flows down to Loch Ailsh, also produces excellent results. Offer them: Soldier Palmer, March Brown, Black Pennell.
Permission & Charges Assynt Estate (01571 844203) or Inver Lodge Hotel (01571 844496). Bank fishing, £5 per rod per day.

MEALL A'CHUNA MOR, Lochs
Location & Access 15/084270 Park at the end of the peat track at 15/071259 on the B869 Lochinver/Stoer road. Follow the track out to Pollan (15/074264). Walk north-east for 15 minutes to reach the first, unnamed, loch in the series at 15/082269.
Commentary This is a 'special' day out, exploring a series of eight lochs and lochans. Fish north from the start point, ending at the small lochan at 15/089274. Now walk due south, keeping the crags of Meall a'Chuna Mor to your right. Fish the Corrie Lochan at 15/086267. Continue south to the unnamed lochan at 15/082562, then west to Loch a'Phollain Drisich at 15/080263. Finally, fish Loch a'Phollain at 15/075261 prior to walking west to regain the peat track.
Fish Mostly breakfast-sized trout averaging 6-8oz, but there are larger fish, particularly in the first loch along the route.
Flies & Tactics Good bank fishing and no need to wade. All the water is easily covered from the shore. Offer them: Soldier Palmer, Invicta, Silver Butcher.
Permission & Charges See Drumbeg Loch entry.

MEALL A'MHUTLIAICH, Loch See Lochan Fada, Canisp.
MEALL NAN CAORACH, Loch 15/300230 See Loch nan Curran.
MEALLAN A'CHUAIL, Lochan 15/350296 See Meallan a'Chuail Lochs.

MEALLAN A'CHUAIL, Lochs
Location & Access 15/347292 Three and a half miles from the A838 Lairg/Scourie road. Park at 15/357334 and hike south up the track. Steep going all the way. At 15/350317 as the track turns west, leave the track and walk south for ten minutes to reach the first in this series of four lochans: Loch Cul a'Mhill (15/357310), then Loch Lot-Ghaoith (15/359300), Lochan Meallan a'Chuail (15/350296), and, finally, Loch Dubh a'Chuail (15/347280).
Commentary A long day out covering hard country. Beinn Leoid (792m) dominates the western horizon, Ben More Assynt (998m) to the south. After Loch Cul a'Mhill, the east face of Meallan a' Chuail (750m) embraces the next two lochs, with Dubh a'Chuail lying below its south shoulder.
Fish Great sport with trout which average 8-10oz.
Flies & Tactics In bad weather, stay off the hill. Bank fishing all the way. Offer them: Black Zulu, March Brown, Alexandra.
Permission & Charges Reay Forest Estate, Achfary, by Lairg, Sutherland. Tel: (01971) 500221. Bank fishing at £5 per rod per day.

MHAOLACH-COIRE, Loch
Location & Access 15/277193 Park at Inchnadamph (15/252218) on the A837 Ledmore Junction/Lochinver road. Follow the road up the north bank of the Traligill River (Norse meaning trolls, or giant's burn) and cross the River at 15/260220 to climb through Gleann Dubh. Stop along the way to visit the famous Inchnadamph limestone caves where human and animal remains dating back 8,000 years have been discovered. The track continues south over the hill the reach Loch Mhaolach-Coire after a walk of about one hour.
Commentary An splendid day out in the Inchnadamph National Nature Reserve, surrounded by the majesty of Conival (987m) and Ben More Assynt (998m), highest mountain in Sutherland. Apart from the limestone caves, look out for rare Alpine plants, nurtured by the lime-rich soil. As you approach the loch, the outlet river can be heard, deep underground, thundering through imestone tunnels, carved out over the centuries.
Fish Loch Mhaolach-Coire is also know as the Gillaroo Loch because in days past the trout resembled the famous Irish species. They have long-since disappeared, but the loch still contains excellent stocks of trout which average 8-12oz and also fish of up to and over 2lb in weight.
Flies & Tactics Bank fishing can be productive, but fishing from the boat generally brings best results on this thirty acre loch. Drift the west shoreline, about ten yards out, and look out for action. First cast: Ke-He, Greenwell's Glory, Kingfisher Butcher.
Permission & Charges See Loch Assynt entry.

MORE, Loch (Scourie)
Location & Access 15/325375 Lies immediately to the north of the A838 Lairg/Scourie road. The north shore of Loch More is only accessible by foot or by boat.
Commentary Loch More, linked to Loch Stack, is on the headwaters of the River Laxford, is four miles long, almost half a mile wide and 300 feet deep. The configuration of the surrounding hills expose the loch to north-west and south-east storms and More is sometimes very windy.

Loch Assynt OS Map 15

Fish A useful salmon and seatrout fishery, as well as producing specimen brown trout. Stack and More can produce 30-40 salmon and 500 seatrout each season. Loch More is the most productive water for salmon.
Flies & Tactics Boat fishing only and the shallow west and east ends of the loch are most productive. A gillie is essential, to keep the boat on station, near to the shore. Dapping works well on Loch More with Loch Ordie, Ke-He, Black Zulu, and Daddy Longlegs producing results. Wet fly patterns to try include: Soldier Palmer, Black Pennell, Grouse & Claret, Peter Ross.
Permission & Charges Reay Forest Estate, Estate Office, Achfary, by Lairg, Sutherland. Tel: (01971) 500221. Between £20 and £35 per boat per day depending upon the time of the season.

NA BARRACK, Loch 15/158189 See Loch na Gainimh.

NA BEINNE REIDHE, Loch
Location & Access 15/213216 Park on the A837 Ledmore Junction/Lochinver road near Stronchrubie at 15/248191. Walk down the moor to cross the River Loanan at 15/245181. Angle north across the hill to find the Alltan Beithe burn and climb west up Meall Liath Mor to reach Loch na Faoileige (15/214192) and Loch Dubh Meallan Mhurchaidh (15/215194) in 40 minutes. After fishing them, walk north to fish Loch nam Meallan-Liatha (15/221200). Finally, climb north-west again for 30 minutes to find Loch na Beinne Reidhe.
Commentary A major hill walking expedition, only to be undertaken in good weather and by those with experience of using a compass and map. You will visit four lochs involving a hard tramp during which you will climb 600m. Reward: some of the finest views in Sutherland, encompassing Ben More Assynt (998m), Canisp (846m), Suilven (731m), Quinag (808m), and mountains of Inverpolly. Because they are so remote, these lochs are rarely visited and trout are generally cooperative. Loch na Beinne Reidhe is the largest, being almost half a mile by up to 200 yards wide.
Fish As exciting as the scenery, although not so large. Trout average 8-10oz.
Flies & Tactics Bank fishing, with action all round the shores. Offer them: Black Zulu, Soldier Palmer, Peter Ross.
Permission & Charges See Loch an Leothaid (Quinag) entry.

NA BEISTE BRIC, Loch 15/184396 See Loch a'Chreagain Daraich.

NA BEISTE, Loch
Location & Access 15/004124 A most convenient road circles the south of Rubha Mor, and Loch na Beiste is contained within the circle. Approach from the peat track at 15/991122. The loch is reached after a walk of about 30 minutes.
Commentary Very rarely fished and set amidst superb scenery with wonderful views along the way. Two other lochs should be fished during the trip: Lochan Dearg, Rubh Mor (15/998128) to the north, and Loch na Creige Duibhe (15/004117) to the south. The surrounding hills provide welcome shelter here when storms howl elsewhere.
Fish Some very nice trout with fish of over 1lb, but predominately averaging 8-10oz.
Flies & Tactics No problems, just splendid bank fishing on all the lochs with fish being taken everywhere. First cast: Soldier Palmer, Woodcock & Hare-lug, Kingfisher Butcher.
Permission & Charges Same as Loch na Totaig.

NA BRUTHAICH, Loch
Location & Access 15/071316 Immediately adjacent and south of the B869 Drumbeg/Stoer road.
Commentary A roadside lochan, ideal for a few casts along the way to greater things, such as Loch na Lub (15/070300).
Fish Small trout averaging 6oz, but plenty of them and they fight well.
Flies & Tactics The roadside bank and the south-east shore is most conveniently fished. The south-west shore is backed by high banks. Offer them: Black Pennell, Invicta, Blue Zulu.
Permission & Charges See Loch Drumbeg entry.

NA BUIDHEIG, Loch 15/093291 See Loch an Eich Uidhir.

NA CLAISE, Loch (North Assynt)
Location & Access 15/035306 Approach from Clashmore. Loch na Claise lies just to the north of Balchladich (15/035304).
Commentary Loch na Claise is approximately 30 acres in extent, sheltered from east winds by the crags of Cnoc Ruigh a'Chairn. The south-west shoreline is damp and boggy but there is generally room to fish, regardless of weather conditions.
Fish Trout here average 8oz but there are larger fish as well. Can be dour, particularly in mid-summer.
Flies & Tactics The shallows tend to weed-up as the season advances but wading is safe and reasonably comfortable. The north and east shoreline offer the best chance of supper. Try: Red Palmer, Grouse & Claret, Dunkeld.
Permission & Charges See Drumbeg Loch entry. Boat may be available from Mr MacKenzie (01571) 855226.

NA CLAISE, Lochan (Scionascaig) 15/134138 See Loch Scionascaig.

NA CREIGE DUIBHE, Loch 15/004117 See Loch na Beiste.

NA CREIGE LEITHE, Loch
Location & Access 15/056265 On the north side of the B869 Lochinver/Stoer road and the start of a day hill loch fishing, visiting a series of five waters. Not far, but some tough-going over rough country.
Commentary From the north end of Loch na Creige Leithe, walk north-east to reach Loch an Leathad Rainich (15/063270), then due east to the unnamed lochan at 15/069269. Now, south-west to find two super little lochans at 15/065265 and 15/060263, then

164

OS Map 15 — Loch Assynt

back to the start-point.
Fish You will be welcomed all the way by splendid wild trout which average 8oz.
Flies & Tactics Best flies: Black Zulu, Greenwell's Glory, Peter Ross.
Permission & Charges See Drumbeg Loch entry.

NA CREIGE RUAIDHE, Loch 15/185362 See Loch an Ruighein.
NA DAIL, Loch See Polly Lochs.
NA DOIRE DUIBHE, Loch 15/176394 See Loch a'Chreagain Daraich.
NA DROIGHNICHE, Loch 15/159343 See Loch Torr an Lochain.
NA DUBH LEITIR, Lochan 15/174350 See Lochan Torr an Lochain.
NA FAOILEIGE, Loch 15/214192 See Loch na Beinne Reidhe.

NA GAINIMH, Loch
Location & Access 15/175186 A five mile walk out from the car park (15/107230) on the Glencanisp road, east from Lochinver. This is the most popular route for the ascent of Suilven (713m), so be prepared for company along the way.
Commentary Loch na Gainimh, enclosed by Suilen to the south and Canisp (846m) to the north, is one mile long by up to 300 yards wide.
Fish Loch na Gainimh trout tend to be of lesser quality than many of the surrounding lochs, but good baskets are the rule, rather than the exception. Of greater interest are the dozen or so little lochans on the north-west shoulder of Suilven, including Loch na Barrack (15/158189) and Loch a'Choire Dhuibh (15/160188). Trout here average 8oz, but some of these little lochans hold much bigger fish.
Flies & Tactics Visit Loch na Gainimh and then tramp uphill and over the moor to bank fish the North Suilven lochans. Flies for the plateau lochans: Blue Zulu, Loch Ordie, Ke-He.
Permission & Charges Assynt Estate (01571 844203) or Inver Lodge Hotel (01571 844496). Bank fishing, £5 per rod per day.

NA GAINMHICH, Loch
Location & Access 15/245278 To the east of the A894 Skiag Bridge/Unapool road. Park at 15/239284 where a stalkers path leads to the south shore of the loch.
Commentary An exposed roadside loch of considerable size, being half a mile long by up to quarter of a mile wide, dominated by Glas Bheinn (776m) to the east and Quinag (808m) to the west.
Fish Can be dour and rarely fished, but contains some good trout of up to and over 1lb in weight. The majority, however, average 8oz. During the course of the day, climb up to little Loch Coire a'Bhaid (15/246294), to the north of Loch na Gainmhich, which can also offer sport.
Flies & Tactics Stay on the bank. Wading can be dangerous. In an east wind, fish the south and south-east shore. Use: Black Pennell, March Brown, Silver Butcher.
Permission & Charges The Inchnadamph Hotel, Assynt, Lochinver, Sutherland. Tel: (01571) 822202. Bank fishing, £6 per rod per day.

NA GARBHE UIDHE, Loch See River Inver.
NA GRUAGAICH, Loch 15/242159 See Loch Awe.
NA H-AIRIGH FRAOICH, Loch 15/133214 See Loch Alltain Duibh.
NA H-AIRIGHE BIGE, Loch See Loch Maiden.

NA H-INNSE FRAOICH, Loch
Location & Access 15/161262 Park at 15/168257 on the A837 Inchnadamph/Lochinver road and walk north-west up the hill for ten minutes to reach Loch Torr an Lochain (15/163259). Walk round the west shore to find the outlet stream from Loch na h-Innse Fraoich, 'the loch of the heathery pasture', and follow it to the loch. No dogs are allowed to accompany anglers fishing Assynt Angling Club lochs.
Commentary After fishing Loch na h-Innse Fraoich and Loch Torr an Lochain, continue north-west for 15 minutes to fish Loch an Ruighein, 'the loch of the sheiling', at 15/155268 and Loch Beannach Beag, 'the little loch of the hillocks', at 15/154265.
Fish Sport with bright little trout averaging 8oz.
Flies & Tactics Comfortable bank fishing and no need to wade. On Loch na h-Innse Fraoich start north from the little wood on the east shore by the small island. On the way to Loch Ruighein have a cast in the unnamed lochan at 15/157263. Offer them: Black Zulu, Soldier Palmer, Kingfisher Butcher.
Permission & Charges Bank fishing: £5 per rod per day, £25 per week, £45 per season. Permits: Tourist Office, Lochinver, Sutherland. Tel: (01571) 844330; The Albanach, Baddidarroch; Caberfeidh Restaurant, Bridgend, Lochinver, Sutherland. Tel: (01571) 884321; Cruachan Guest House, The Old Manse Stoer. Tel: (01571) 855303; Inverbank Newsagents, Lochinver, Sutherland; Lochinver Fish Selling Co, Culag Square, Lochinver, Sutherland. Tel: (01571) 844228; Lochinver Holiday Lodges, Strathan, Lochinver, Sutherland. Tel: (01571) 844418. Further details from Hon President, S. McClelland. Tel: (01571) 844377.

NA H-UIDHE DOIMHNE, Loch
Location & Access 15/069285 Approach from the B869 Lochinver/Clashnessie road. Park at 15/040295 and walk east along a good peat track. After approximately 40 minutes, at 15/063290, by an un-named lochan, start fishing.
Commentary A splendid day out amidst the lochs and lochans of North Assynt Estate. There are five principal waters to explore beginning at the un-named lochan noted above. From there, walk south to the un-named lochan with twin islands at 15/065286. South again via the inlet stream to Loch na h-Uidhe Doimhne, a three-quarter mile long, narrow ribbon lying south-west/north-east. Half way up the east shore of Loch na h-Uidhe Doimhne, walk east to Lochan Ruadh (15/073288), again centred by a delightful island, then north to the largest loch, Loch Poll Dhaidh (15/077291). Loch Poll Dhaidh narrows quickly northwards from the main bay. At the end of this section, walk south to north end of Loch na h-Uidhe Doimhne

165

Loch Assynt — OS Map 15

and fish the west bank before re-joining the peat track for the walk home.
Fish The place to find breakfast, lunch and supper. Lots of fun with super little trout which average 8oz. Look out for larger specimens as well, fish of over 2lb are sometimes taken.
Flies & Tactics Bank fishing and a compass and map will help you find your way amongst this maze of lochs and lochans and is essential during misty conditions. First cast: Blue Zulu, Soldier Palmer, Alexandra
Permission & Charges See Drumbeg Loch entry.

NA LOINNE, Loch See Loch a'Bhraighe.

NA MUCNAICH, Loch
Location & Access 15/324390 Lies to the north of Loch More (15/330370). Access from the A838 Lairg/Scourie road at 15/300388 via a track, footbridge and vigorous hike of about 40 minutes.
Commentary Wild and inaccessible, surrounded by magnificent scenery, with Meallan Liath Coire Mhich Dhughaill (801m) towering to the east. The loch is almost one mile long by up to 400 yards wide, divided by narrows into two fine bays. Also visit Lochan a' Chraobhair (15/323397), to the north.
Fish Good stocks of excellent brown trout which average 8-10oz.
Flies & Tactics Bank fishing only, and the narrows, particularly from the north bank, is a good place to begin; also, east from there, in the vicinity of the feeder streams, and at the east end. Offer: Ke-He, Grouse & Claret, Alexandra.
Permission & Charges The Reay Forest Estate, Estate Office, Achfary, by Lairg, Sutherland. Tel: (01971) 500221. £5 per rod per day.

NA PLOYTACH, Loch 15/983177 See Loch na Totaig.
NA SAIGHE DUIBHE, Loch 15/233159 See Loch Awe.
NA SROINE LUIME, Loch 15/345217 See Fionn Loch Mor.
NA TARRAING, Loch 15/159291 Enquiries to Reay Forest Estate. Tel: (01971) 500221.
NA TARRAING, Loch 15/159290 See Gorm Loch Mor.

NA TOTAIG, Loch
Location & Access 15/980160 Leave the A835 Ullapool/Ledmore Junction road at Drumrunie (15/166055) and follow the minor road west to the Summer Isles. At 15/016096, by the tourist information board, turn right and drive north to the end of the road. Park at Reiff (15/966144). Follow a croft road, walking north-east for one mile to reach the loch.
Commentary Loch na Totaig is the largest loch on the Rubha Mor Peninsula, shallow, over half a mile north/south by up to 350 yards wide. This is desolate, infrequently visited territory, very lovely, rich in flora and fauna and trout.
Fish Good stocks of hard fighting fish averaging about 8oz.
Flies & Tactics Easy bank fishing all round Loc na Totaig, and the opportunity to walk north to explore Loch na Ploytach (15/983177) and Loch Airigh Blair (15/985170) and the unnamed lochans near Rubha Coigach, the extreme north of the peninsula. Pay particular attention to Loch na Ploytach. Flies: Ke-He, March Brown, Alexandra.
Permission & Charges Coigach Craft Shop, Polbain Tel: (01854) 622346 or Mr P Rex, Badentarbut Lodge, Tel (01854) 622225. Hill loch fishing at £6 per rod per day.

NA TRI, Lochan 15/133162 See Loch Sionascaig.
NAM BREAC, Loch (North Assynt) 15/107318 See Loch Bad an Og.
NAM BREAC MOR, Loch 15/322276 See Loch nan Caorach.
NAM MEALLAN-KIATHA, Loch 15/221200 See Loch na Beinne Reidhe.

NAN CAORACH, Loch
Location & Access 15/296275 One of the most remote lochs in the area. It is possible to walk in from Kylstrome (15/225435) following the north shore of sea-loch Loch Glendhu to the croft at 15/284337. Cross the Abhain a'Ghlinne Duibh burn and walk the south shore of Loch Glendhu, climbing Aird da Loch to reach a tract as 15/261324. This leads, eventually, pas the Stack of Glencoul via Glen Coul, to Loch an Eircill (15/307275). Loch nan Caorach lies to the west of Eircill. An alternative is to arrange a boat to drop you off at Glencoul (15/270303) and to walk in from there. Either way, reaching this area is not easy.
Commentary If you enjoy wild places, then this is for you, and even nicer if you are prepared to camp out for a couple of nights. Eas a'Chual Aluinn, the highest waterfall in Britain, is to the south, backed by a continuous range of mountains, none of which drop below 2,000ft in height. Beinn Leoid (792m) guards the northern horizon, and Loch nan Caorach and Loch an Eircill will keep you happy for hours. In the hills to the north, Lochan Feith an Leothaid (15/294308) is at the centre of a further series of six exciting waters whilst to the east in a Beinn Leoid corrie, Loch nam Breac Mora (15/322276) and the unnamed lochan at 15/316279 also offer great sport amidst spectacular surroundings.
Fish Reports of some excellent fish, but mainly more modest trout which average 8-10oz.
Flies & Tactics These lochs are rarely fished and some will not have seen an artificial fly for several seasons. All bank fishing and you will not go hungry. Caorach and Eircill are the most productive.
Permission & Charges Reay Forest Estate, Estate Office, Achfary, by Lairg, Sutherland. Tel: (01971) 500221. £5 per rod per day. Boat hire may be arranged through the Kylesku Inn, Kylesku, Scourie, by Lairg, Sutherland. Tel: (01971) 502231.

NAN CAORACH, Loch (Assynt) 15/300234 See Loch nan Curran.

NAN CREIGE DUIBHE, Loch
Location & Access 15/290367 From Lochmore at

OS Map 15 — Loch Assynt

15/300387 on the A838 Lairg/Scourie road. A stalkers path leads into the Glendhu Forest via Bealach nam Fiann (15/273383). Bear south towards Loch an Leathiad Bhuain at 15/269370 and walk down the hill to the loch. Skirt the north shore of Loch an Leathaid an Bhuain by Creag Dubh (15/279370) to reach Loch na Creige Dubhe.
Commentary Breath-taking scenery with fine views south to Quinag (808m), Glas Bheinn (776m), Beinn Leoid (792m) and Ben More Assynt (998m). The loch is three quarters of mile long by quarter of a mile wide and is often sheltered from north and south gales by the surrounding hills.
Fish Can be dour and unforgiving, but Loch na Creige Duibhe holds some very good trout. It all depends upon being there at the right time, when fish are in the mood. Then, expect action with fish of up to and over 2lb in weight.
Flies & Tactics Bank fishing and trout may be taken all round the loch. The east end is perhaps the most productive area and you should offer them: Blue Zulu, Greenwell's Glory, Dunkeld.
Permission & Charges Kylestrome Estate. Enquire at the Kylesku Hotel. Tel: (01971) 592231

NAN CURRAN, Loch
Location & Access 15/292239 Park at Inchnadamph (15/261218) and follow the track up the north bank of the Traligill River. Past the cottages, this becomes a stalkers path leading steeply up the glen of Allt Poll an Droighinn burn, swininging north to Glas Bheinn (776m) and Beinn Uidhe (740m). At the junction at 15/274240, turn right and climb the south slopes of Beinn Uidhe to reach Loch nan Curran. Allow an hour and a half for the walk.
Commentary A long day out in the hills. The hike up to Loch nan Curran is not for the faint-hearted. After fishing Loch nan Curran, walk south, having a cast in little Loch nan Caorach (15/300234) before climbing again to reach the last loch, Loch Meall nan Caorach (15/300230). Return via Loch nan Curran and the stalkers path.
Fish Trout averaging 8-10oz, but also the chance of larger fish.
Flies & Tactics Loch nan Curran is some 300 yards long by up to 200 yards wide and offers excellent bank fishing. Cast with confidence, anywhere. Start on Loch nan Curran, then walk south to lunch at Loch Meall nan Caorach, returning to finish the day back at Loch nan Curran. Flies: Soldier Palmer, March Brown, Alexandra.
Permission & Charges The Inchnadamph Hotel, Assynt, Lochinver, Sutherland. Tel: (01571) 822202. See also Loch Leitir entry. Bank fishing, £6 per rod per day.

NAN EALACHAN, Lochan 15/176090 See Lochan Dearg a'Chuill Mhoir.

NAN EUN, Loch (Lochinver)
Location & Access 15/109239 A small, roadside lochan two miles east from Lochinver on the A837 road. No dogs are allowed to accompany anglers fishing Assynt Angling Club lochs.
Commentary Worth a cast if time is limited, but better things await in less exposed surroundings.
Fish Trout average 8oz.
Flies & Tactics Easy bank fishing. Use: Loch Ordie, Invicta, Silver Butcher.
Permission & Charges See Loch na h-Innse Fraoich entry.

NAN EUN, Loch (Quinag)
Location & Access 15/231299 Park, carefully, on the A894 Unapool/Skiag Bridge road at 15/240291 by Loch na Gainmhich (15/245288). Cross the road and walk north-west over boggy moorland to reach Loch nan Eun in about twenty minutes.
Commentary Dramatic setting, overshadowed by the mighty buttress of Sail Gharbh, the highest point on Quinag (808m). A step to the south-east, at 15/227296, is another, unnamed lochan which should also be included in the expedition.
Fish These lochs are rarely fished, from one season to the next, but there are consistent reports of large trout being seen, hooked and lost. One such report, given to me by an irreproachable source, talked about a trout of over 6lb in weight.
Flies & Tactics No problem covering the water effectively from the bank, and it is best to stay well back to avoid announcing your presence. The best time to assault is early in the season, late April or May, when the residents might be grateful to see a well presented fly after long winter months. Try Messrs Loch Ordie, Ke-He and Peter Ross.
Permission & Charges Assynt Estate, Estate Office, Lochinver, by Lairg, Sutherland. Tel: (01571) 844003. Bank fishing, £5 per rod per day.

NAN GAD, Lochan
Location & Access 15/186335 A few minutes walk to the north of the B869 Unapool/Drumbeg road from 15/183333. Park carefully on this narrow, single-track road.
Commentary A tiny lochan, with two smaller waters to the east, sheltered by Gleann Arbhair. Time for a few casts before moving on to more notable waters further west.
Fish Trout here average 6oz.
Flies & Tactics Cast across the loch, using Soldier Palmer, Black Zulu, Peter Ross.
Permission & Charges J.G. Payne, Ardvar, Drumbeg, Sutherland (01571 833260)

NAN GOBHAIR, Loch 15/065231 See Loch Dubh, Lochinver.

NAN LIATH BHREAC, Lochan 15/123269 See Loch Beannach.

NAN LION, Loch
Location & Access 15/098275 Park at Rhicarn (15/083253) on the B869 Lochinver/Stoer road. Follow the peat track east for one mile to reach the south end of Loch Crocach (15/1007270). Walk the west shore of the loch for half a mile to pick up the outlet stream from Loch nan Lion at 15/099273.

Loch Assynt   OS Map 15

Follow the outlet stream up to the loch.
Commentary A full day out, fishing a series of six lochs surrounding Loch Crocach, including Loch na Uidhean Beaga (15/097279), the small lochans at OS15/112287, 15/113284, 15/111282 and Loch Preas nan Aighean (15/113274). After fishing Preas nan Aighean, return to the peat track by following the east shore of Loch Crocach. You will hike a total of seven miles through spectacular scenery.
Fish Expect mostly 8oz trout, but look out for a few much larger fish in Loch Preas nan Aighean and the unnamed lochans.
Flies & Tactics Traditional bank fishing and avoid wading. As important is a compass and map. If the mist descends, you will need it to find your way home. My favourite loch is Preas nan Aighean, particularly near the small island at the north end. Tempt them with: Blue Zulu, Greenwell's Glory, Kingfisher Butcher.
Permission & Charges See Drumbeg Loch entry.

NAN LUB, Loch
Location & Access 15/071300 Park by Loch na Bruthaich (15/071317) on the A869 Lochinver to Unapool road. Loch nan Lub is a 20-minute walk due south.
Commentary A dozen lochs and lochans lie waiting. Take a compass and map because it is easy to be come disorientated in this watery wilderness. The ideal solution is to use two cars, leaving one at 15/071317 in the north and the other on the B869 at 15/040295, the end of a peat track.
Fish Expect everything, from bright little 6oz trout up to vigorous fish of over 2lb in weight.
Flies & Tactics Loch nan Lub is a long, tortuous chain, lying east/west and covering a distance of more than two miles, rarely more than a few hundred yards north/south. The west end is Loch an Easain (15/060299), 'the loch of the waterfall', and the east end, Garbh Loch Mor (15/088303). My favourite area is the scattered bays and points round the island at 15/065301 and Garbh Loch Mor. Best flies: Ke-He, Woodcock & Hare-lug, Silver Butcher.
Permission & Charges See Drumbeg Loch entry.

NAN RAC, Loch See Lochan Nigheadh.
NAN SGARAIG, Loch See Fionn Loch Mor.
NAN UIDHEAN BEAGA, Loch See Loch nan Lion.

NIGHEADH, Lochan
Location & Access 15/182148 Approach by boat via Loch Veyatie (see Loch Veyatie entry,) and moor at 15/178144. Walk north to reach the loch in ten minutes. Otherwise, approach by walking four miles, round the north and west shore of Cam Loch, and following the Cam Loch feeder stream up past the ruined shieling (15/188140) to reach the lochs.
Commentary After fishing Lochan Nigheadh walk west to the unnamed lochan at 15/173151 and then on to fish Loch nan Rac (15/170159), which is joined to the last of the series, Loch Gleannan a'Mhadaidh at 15/160161. On the way back down Loch Veyatie, consider mooring at 15/193132 to visit the unnamed lochan at 15/192126.
Fish Trout average 6-8oz.
Flies & Tactics Most important, make sure you moor the boat securely on Veyatie, prior to setting off into the hills. Take compass and map and be well-shod. Classic bank fishing all the way with free-rising, hard fighting little fish. Offer: Black Zulu, Greenwell's Glory, Silver Invicta.
Permission & Charges See Cam Loch entry.

ODHAR, Loch 15/151297 See Gorm Loch Mor.

OSGAIG, Loch
Location & Access 15/045120 Immediately to the south of the minor road from Drumrunie (15/167054) to Achiltibuie (15/024085).
Commentary A dramatic place to fish, dominated by Ben Mor Coigach (743m), Stac Pollaidh (613m) and Cul Beag (769m). Loch Osgaig is one and a half miles long by up to three quarters of a mile wide and drops to a depths of more than 140ft at the south-east end. Often windy, always exciting.
Fish The principal quarry is seatrout, entering from Enard Bay via the Garvie River. In common with other northern seatrout fisheries, numbers have declined in recent years and Loch Osgaig produces approximately 100 fish each season. Average weight: 1lb 8oz.
Flies & Tactics Boat fishing only, from the boat house at 15/036130. The best drift is along the south shore, about six yards out from the bank and you really need a gillie to hold the boat in position. The north-east end of the loch, where the River Osgaig enters, can also produce good results. Flies: Black Pennell, Grouse & Claret, Peter Ross. Dapping is also effective.
Permission & Charges Summer Isles Hotel, Achiltibuie, Ullapol, Wester Ross. Tel: (01854) 622282. £24.50 per boat per day with two rods fishing.

OYKEL, Upper (River)
Location & Access Source 15/309190 Outflow 16/460013. The Inver Lodge Hotel Upper Oykel fishings extend from where the river exits from Loch Ailsh (15/318102) downstream to where the Allt Eileag burn enters at 15/324075. There after, the fishing is from the Oykle Bridge Hotel. Inver Lodge Hotel fishing is accessible from an estate road to Benmore Lodge and Loch Ailsh, and a forest track above the north bank of the River. The Oykel Bridge beats are accessible from the A837 Oykel Bridge/Ledmore Junction road and the same forest track along the north bank of the River.
Commentary Fishes best during July, August and September, dependent upon water levels. Inver Lodge is divided into two, two-rod beats. On Top Beat, best pools are Black Bank and Lazy Pool; on Lower Beat, Falls Pool, and Edmund's Pool. On the Oykel Bridge Hotel beats, productive pools include: Camus, Allt Eileag, Lower Stale Pool, Black Burn, Sallachy Bridge.
Fish Numbers of salmon caught fluctuate according to water conditions but most seasons generally produce in the region of 200 salmon for the Inver Lodge beats and about 300 for Oykel Bridge Hotel (700 in 1992,

OS Map 15 Loch Assynt

an exceptional year). Increasing numbers of seatrout are caught. Salmon average 8lb, with frequent double figure fish. A 17lb salmon was taken in Primrose Pool recently.
Flies & Tactics The Inver Lodge Hotel beats are salmon-stalking country, where stealth and skill are the pre-requisite of success. Use a strong trout rod, and, when the water is low, small flies and 5lb breaking strain nylon. There is rarely any need to wade. Stay back from the bank and fish fine and far off. The Oykel Bridge Hotel beats require a 12-15ft rod and thigh waders as least. Flies: Green Highlander, Jock Scott, Black Pennell, Willie Gunn, Garry Dog, Stoat's Tail, General Practitioner, Ally's Shrimp.
Permission & Charges Inver Lodge Hotel, Lochinver, by Lairg, Sutherland. Tel: (01571) 844496. Per rod per day, 22nd June-30th September, Top Beat: £70, Lower Beat: £40, per rod per day. Non residents pay a £5 surcharge. Oykel Bridge Hotel, Oykel Bridge, by Lairg, Sutherland. Tel: (01549) 441218. Oykel River fishing is always booked well in advance and rarely available. A three rod beat costs in the region of £1,500, plus VAT, per week.

PEEVISH CREEK, Loch 15/069233 See Loch Dubh (Lochinver).
POLL AN ACHAIDH BHUIDHE, Loch 15/256382 See Loch Clach a'Chinn Duibh.
POLL AN DROIGHINN, Loch 15/054288 See Loch Leathed a'Bhaile Fhoghair.
POLL DHAIDH, Loch 15/077291 See Loch na h-Uidhe Doimhne.

POLL, Loch
Location & Access 15/103309 Immediately to the south of the B869 Unapool/Lochinver road. Park at 15/097320 and walk south for ten minutes to reach the loch.
Commentary Loch Poll is over one mile long by up to half a mile wide across the south bay. The east shore is lined by high banks and a small forest, and the loch is connected to the sea by the River Oldany. Theoretically, therefore, salmon and seatrout could have access to Loch Poll but there are no records of them being caught.
Fish Good brown trout which average 10oz and fish of up to and over 2lb as well.
Flies & Tactics Boat fishing brings best results. Offer them: Ke-He, March Brown, Alexandra. Dry flyfishing on calm evenings also brings results.
Permission & Charges See Drumbeg Loch entry.

POLLY, Lochs
Location & Access 15/095139 Access from the minor, coastal road between Badnagyle (15/063112) in the south and Lochinver to the north.
Commentary Three, interlinked lochs on the headwaters of the Polly River, between Inverpolly and Loch Sionascaig: Loch Uidh Tarraigean, Loch na Dail are the Polly Lochs. In recent years, to improve access for migratory species, waterfalls have been bypassed and a salmon ladder built.
Fish Few salmon are taken which indicates they run straight through into Loch Sionascaig or Loch Doire na h-Airbhe. They are not caught there either. But the Polly Lochs hold excellent brown trout with fish of up to and over 3lb in weight.
Flies & Tactics Concentrate your attention on the margins, colse to the shore. The interconnecting streams also fish well and hold some really good trout. Flies: Black Pennell, Invicta, Peter Ross.
Permission & Charges Estate Office, Inverpolly Estate, Ullapool, Wester Ross. Tel: (01854) 622452. Bank fishing, £6 rod per day.

POLLY, River
Location & Access Source 15/089140 Outflow 15/062141. From the coastal road between Badnagyle (15/063112) in the south and Lochinver in the north.
Commentary The Polly River is fed by two lochs, vast Loch Sionascaig and its little neighbour, Loch Doire na h-Airbhe. The surrounding scenery is spectacular, Stac Polly (613m), Cul Mor (849m) and the peaks of Ben More Coigach (743m). In the recent past, the Polly was as well known for pearl fishing as it was for its salmon.
Fish Some 30/40 fish are taken most seasons and their average weight is about 8lb.
Flies & Tactics The Polly is very much a spate stream: no water no fish; but there are some good holding pools from the road bridge down to Sea Pool. Backing up fishes them effectively. Use a short rod. Stay away from the bank. Stalk the fish. Use: Stoat's Tail, Shrimp Fly, Willie Gunn, Garry Dog.
Permission & Charges Fishing is generally well-booked in advance, in conjunction with Inverpolly Lodge. Day lets are rarely available. For details, contact: Estate Office, Inverpolly Estate, Ullapool, Wester Ross. Tel: (01854) 622452.

PREAS NAN AIGHEAN, Loch 15/113274 See Loch nan Lion.
PRIVATE WATERS NAN EALACHAN, Loch (15/300394). This loch is private and may not be fished, even by its owners, The Reay Forest Estate. Fishing rights on Loch nan Ealachan have been gifted in perpetuity, exclusively to Reay Forest Estate staff. The waters to the east of the A835 Ledmore Junction/Ullapool road, in the Cromalt Hills and south to and including the River Kanaird are preserved by the owners. MEALL NAN GARBH Loch, Lochan FEARNA (15/087310), GARBH MOR, Loch (15/089300) and EILEANACH, Loch (Drumbeg) (15/090314) are preserved by the owner. AN ACHAIDH, Loch (15/029338); BAD AN OG, Loch (15/117314); NEIL BHAIN, Loch (15/040302); REIFF, Loch (15/927146); SGEIREACH, Loch (15/040290); AIRIGE NA BEINNE, Loch (15/219311); AN ALLTAIN DUIBH, Loch (15/147206); AN DUIBH, Lochan (15/219255); FEOIR, Lochan (15/270135); LEITIR EASAIDH (15/170266); LOANAN, River (15/249159); FHURAIN, Lochan (15/989128).

RAA, Loch
Location & Access 15/020120. Loch Raa lies to the

Loch Assynt
OS Map 15

west of the road from Achnahaird Bay (15/020127) to Achiltibuie (15/024085).
Commentary A popular, accessible road-side loch just to the south of Achnahaird sands. Park the bucket-and-spade brigade on the beach and have a few casts on Raa. The loch is three quarters of a mile long by up to almost half a mile wide, shallow and easily fished.
Fish Loch Raa contains good stocks of brown trout which average about 8-10oz.
Flies & Tactics Bank fishing only and south-west shoreline is the best place to start. Work north from there towards the inlet stream at 15/014126. Offer them: Blue Zulu, Greenwell's Glory, Silver Butcher.
Permission & Charges See Loch na Totaig.

RAPACH, Lochan 15/149324 See Loch Torr an Lochain.

RUADH, Loch
Location & Access 15/008140. Just to the north of Brae of Achnahaird (15/008134) on the road from Drumrunie (15/166055) on the A835 Ledmore Junction/Ullapool road to Achiltibuie (15/024085) in the Summer Isles.
Commentary Ruadh Loch covers about two acres and is easily accessible, perfect for a few pre-dinner casts and for little ones new to flyfishing. Close to the magnificent, golden sands of Achnahaird Bay.
Fish They will not be too heavy to carry home.
Flies & Tactics Safe, comfortable bank fishing all round the loch. Try: Loch Ordie, Grouse & Claret, Peter Ross.
Permission & Charges Same as Loch na Totaig.

RUADH, Lochan 15/073288 See Loch an h-Uidhe Doimhne.
RUBHA NA BREIGE, Loch 15/072191 See Loch an Arbhair.

RUIGHEAN A'AITINN, Loch
Location & Access 15/125327 At Drumbeg, immediately to the north of the B869 Unapool/Clashmore road.
Commentary Easily accessible and close to Drumbeg village.
Fish Good stocks of trout which average 6-8oz.
Flies & Tactics Bank fishing and the east shore produces best results. Offer the residents Loch Ordie, Grouse & Claret, Dunkeld.
Permission & Charges See Loch Drumbeg entry.

RUNIE, River
Location & Access Source 15/190057 Outflow 15/120006. Access is from Blughasary (15/135015), the layby on the A835 Ledmore Junction/Ullapool road at 15/158039, and from the layby south of the Drumrunie junction at 15/166054.
Commentary Only the lower half of the river, from Drumrunie to Blughassary, a distance of three miles, is fishable The Runie is a spate stream: no water, no fish.
Fish No accurate records of numbers of salmon taken, but unlikely to reach double figures. Sea-trout have all but disappeared

Flies & Tactics The Runie is divided into two 2-rod beats, alternating each day. Fly only, and vary the size according to water conditions. Try: Munro Killer, Green Highlander, Hairy Mary, Willie Gunn, Stoat's Tail.
Permission & Charges At the time of writing, the estate has been sold to Mr David Bulmer. Access details have not been announced. For further information contact the Tourist Office in Ullapool. Tel: (01854) 612135.

SAIL AN RUATHAIR, Lochs
Location & Access 15/333149 Approach via the A837 Bonar Bridge/Ledmore Junction road at 15/297083. A forest road heads north past Loch Ailsh (15/315110) to Benmore Lodge (15/322114). A path leads north following the course of the Upper Oykel at and its tributary, Allt Sail an Ruathair. Bear right from the main track at 15/329130 and follow the stalkers track north. The loch lies in a corrie west of the track, two miles from Braemore Lodge.
Commentary Having got to Loch Sail an Ruathair, climb north to visit Dubh Loch Beag (15/325165) and Dubh Loch More (15/319189), immediately below the summit of Ben More Assynt. The climb from Sail an Ruathair is straight-forward, although steep, but from Dubh Loch Beag to Dubh Loch Mor it is very steep and in bad conditions should be avoided. In both cases, exit at the north end of the lochs. Return from Dubh Loch Mor, the headwater of the River Oykel, by following the River down past the waterfalls and power station to pick up a stalkers path which leads back to Benmore Lodge. The round trip is nine miles and takes you into the very heart of the Benmore Forest.
Fish There are some excellent trout in these lochs.
Flies & Tactics The most important 'tactic' is to be well-prepared. Do not even think about going unless you know how to use a compass and map, regardless of weather conditions. Flies: Black Zulu, Soldier Palmer, Silver Butcher.
Permission & Charges See Loch Ailsh entry.

SAL, Lochan
Location & Access 15/071151 A coastal walk south from the minor road between Lochinver and Inverpolly, visiting two lochs. Park near Polly More at 15/076171, cross the bridge and walk south for one and a half miles to reach Lochan Sal; and stop at 15/075162 to fish the unnamed lochan along the way.
Commentary A wonderful day out in glorious scenery. Sea and moorland birds and rare wildflowers aplenty, and a perfect picnic spot on the cliffs overlooking Rubha Pollaidh bay.
Fish Small trout averaging 6-8oz.
Flies & Tactics Bank fishing with sport all round the shores of these little lochans. Try: Black Zulu, Woodcock & Hare-lug, Peter Ross.
Permission & Charges Estate Office, Inverpolly Estate, Ullapool, Wester Ross. Tel: (01854) 622452. Bank fishing: £6 per rod per day.

SANDY, Loch 15/075233 See Loch Dubh (Lochinver).

OS Map 15   Loch Assynt

SGEIREACH, Lochan (Achiltibuie)
Location & Access 15/049096 Approach from the Summer Isles in Achiltibuie at 15/027081. An up-hill slog, north-east from the road, for a distance of one and a half miles to reach the loch.
Commentary A sizeable hill loch, half a mile long by up to 200 yards wide. Glorious surrounding scenery with Ben Mor Coigach to the east, the Summer Isles and distant mountains of Skye to the west. Four adjacent satellite lochans should also be visited: Lochan Leacach (15/055095), Lochan Fada (15/055092), Lochan Smuirneach (15/055088) and Lochan Eallach (15/062093).
Fish Few monsters, but pretty, hard-fighting little trout which average 8oz.
Flies & Tactics A long day out, so be well-prepared for whatever the weather might do. It changes rapidly in this part of the world, take a compass and map. All bank fishing and trout rise readily to most standard patterns of fly. Begin with: Ke-He, March Brown, Silver Butcher.
Permission & Charges The Summer Isles Hotel, Achiltibuie, Ullapool, Wester Ross. Tel: (01854) 82282. £5 per rod per day.

SGEIREACH, Lochan (Altnacealgach) See Loch a'Mheallain.
SHARK, Loch 15/180364 See Loch an Ruighein.
SHIELING, Lochan Enquiries to Reay Forest Estate. Tel: (01971) 500221.

SIONASCAIG, Loch
Location & Access 15/120140 Park in a small quarry on the minor road between Inverpolly and Lochinver at 15/093151. A track leads east to reach Boat Bay in ten minutes. Sionascaig is boat fishing only and use the boat to reach two further lochs which offer great sport: Na Tri Lochan (15/133162) and Loch a'Ghille (15/115165). Moor the boat at 15/121155 and walk north. Lochan na Claise (15/134138) is also best visited by boat via Sionascaig.
Commentary Few lochs in Scotland match the beauty of Loch Sionascaig. The loch lies at the centre of the Inverpolly National Nature Reserve guarded by dramatic peaks: Stac Pollaidh (618m), Cul Beag (769m) and Cul Mor (849m). Sionascaig is three miles long by up to two miles wide, but the shoreline meanders round almost 18 miles of promontories and bays scattered with delightful islands. Take great care not to disturb nesting birds and do not land on the islands.
Fish Sionascaig is over 180ft deep and contains trout of all sizes, from 6oz up to fish in the teens of pounds. The largest trout caught in recent years, trolling, weighed 16lb 8oz and there is little doubt that there are even bigger fish in Sionascaig.
Flies & Tactics Safety is of paramount importance on this wild water and you must know how to handle a boat and outboard engine. Ask advice when booking. For instance, on the exit from Boat Bay (15/103150), at the narrows, there is a large, submerged rock which is a hazard in low water conditions. Similarly, the south-west bay (15/112132) is strewn with underwater boulders which could cost the unwary a sheer pin; and it is a long, dangerous row home. Ideally, have someone on the oars all the time, as much to hold the boat in position, close to the shoreline where most fish are caught, as for safety. Begin your attack in the north-east bay (15/134146), between the Shieling and Clais. Flies: Black Pennell, Grouse & Claret, Peter Ross.
Permission & Charges See Loch Bad a'Ghaill entry.

SMUIRNEACH, Lochan 15/055088 See Lochan Sgeireach, Achiltibuie.
THORMAID, Loch (Lochinver) 15/065235 See Loch Dubh (Lochinver).
TIGH NA H-EIGE, Loch 15/127306 See Loch a'Bhraighe.
TOLLA BHAID, Lochan 15/119295 See Loch a'Bhraighe.
TORR AN LochAIN, Loch (Little Assynt) 15/163259 See Loch na h-Innse Fraoich.

TORR AN LOCHAIN, Loch (Unapool)
Location & Access 15/151321 Approach from the B869 Unapool/Clashmore road. Park at Glenleraig (15/150314) and walk north to reach the loch in 15 mins.
Commentary After fishing Loch Torr an Lochain, walk north up the hill for five minutes to reach the tiny Lochan Rapach (15/149324), and then, to make a full day of it, strike north-east across the hill to visit Loch a'Meallard (15/156337) and Loch na Droighniche (15/159343) on the cliffs above Eddrachills Bay.
Fish These lochs are very rarely fished and offer good sport with trout which average 6oz. Loch a' Meallard, the most remote, is the most productive of these lochs.
Flies & Tactics Easy bank fishing all the way. The walking is less easy, rough going, but well worth the effort. The east end of Loch a'Meallard, by the little wood, is the ideal spot to rest from your labours. Explore the cliffs before returning to the start point. Look out for seals and even the odd passing whale. For trout, offer Ke-He, Greenwell's Glory, Black Zulu.
Permission & Charges Tourist Information Office, Lochinver, Sutherland (01571 844330). Bank fishing, £5 per rod per day.

TORR AN LOCHAIN, Lochan
Location & Access 15/181343 Leave the B869 Unapool/Drumbeg road at 15/177327 and walk out to Ardvar (15/172340). Walk east from Ardvar for 15 minutes to reach Lochan Torr an Lochain.
Commentary A wonderful round trip of the Cnoc na Bagh Choille peninsula with the opportunity of visiting the remote sands at Kerrachar Bay (15/180349) and sea loch Loch na Mola (15/172350). After fishing Lochan Torr an Lochain, walk north to Lochan na Dubh Leitir (15/174350), then west to explore the unnamed loch at OS15/170349 by Creag a'Phris.
Fish Ideal size for cooking over a beach fire, averaging about 8oz.
Flies & Tactics Comfortable bank fishing all the way. Chose a good day and you may decide just to stay there, forever. Best flies: Black Zulu, Woodcock & Yellow, Peter Ross.

171

Loch Assynt — OS Map 15

Permission & Charges J.G. Payne, Ardvar, Drumbeg, Sutherland (01571) 833260

TORR NAN UIDHEAN, Loch See Loch a'Bhraighe.

TUATH, Lochan
Location & Access 15/102056.
Commentary One of the most spectacular lochs in Wester Ross, dominated by the black crags of Sgurr and Fhidhleir (703m), the 'fiddler', much beloved of climbers. Choose a good day for this expedition and whilst in the parish, walk north from Lochan Tuath, round the bulk of Beinn an Eoin (618m), 'the mountain of the eagle', to visit lonely Lochan Dearg (15/095071).
Fish Small but beautiful trout.
Flies & Tactics Bank fishing with sport from all round the shore. Offer them: Blue Zulu, Invicta, Dunkeld.
Permission & Charges The Summer Isles Hotel, Achiltibuie, by Ullapool, Ross-shire (Tel: 01854 622282). Ban fishing, £5 per rod per day.

UIDH NA CEARDAICH, Loch
Location & Access 15/114188 See Loch Bad na Muiriehinn.

UIDH NA GEADAIG, Loch
Location & Access 15/141257 See Loch Beannach.

UIDH NA H-IARNA, Loch
Location & Access 15/169305 See Loch Leothaid.

UIDH TARRAIGEAN, Loch
Location & Access See Polly Lochs.

UNAPOOL, Loch
Location & Access 15/227320 Immediately to the east of the B869 Unapool/Drumbeg road. Park at 15/228315.
Commentary Wonderfully situated, dominated by Quinag (808m) and the mountains of the Reay Forest to the north.
Fish The place to catch supper. Good numbers of small trout which average about 6-8oz, and the occasional larger fish as well.
Flies & Tactics The east shore has steep banks but otherwise few problems bank fishing. The north end of the loch, and the large bay along the west shore, are generally welcoming. Start with: Black Zulu, Greenwell's Glory, Dunkeld.
Permission & Charges Kylestrome Estate. For further details, contact Kylesku Hotel, Kylesku, by Scourie, Sutherland. Tel: (01971) 502331.

URIGILL, Loch
Location & Access 15/244100 In the Cromalt Hills, to the east of the Ledmore Junction/Ullapool road. Easy access by forestry road at 15/253107.
Commentary A wonderful loch, one and three quarter miles long by half a mile wide, shallow, and a delight to fish. Sandy beaches for picnics and splashing. The ideal place to take beginners.
Fish Marvellous stocks of 6-8oz trout and fish of up to and over 2lb. Largest fish in recent years weighed 8lb 4oz. Be prepared.
Flies & Tactics Bank fishing is allowed, but boat fishing brings best results, particularly in the south-west corner, in the vicinity of the two small islands and where the main feeder streams enter. Dry fly works well on Urigill, and dapping. Otherwise, Black Pennell, March Brown, Silver Butcher never fail.
Permission & Charges Tom Strang, Assynt Guided Holidays, Birchbank Holiday Lodge, Knockan, Elphin, by Lairg, Sutherland IV27 4HH. Tel: (01854) 666215 or (01854) 666203. Boat: £16 per day. Bank fishing: £6 per rod per day. Gillie: £40 per day (including use of outboard motor).

VATACHAN, Loch
Location & Access 15/020110 Loch Vatachan lies to the west of the road from Achnahaird Bay (15/020127) to Achiltibuie (15/024085).
Commentary This roadside loch is one mile long by up to 300 yards wide, shallow, exposed and often windswept.
Fish Good stocks of trout which average 8-10oz.
Flies & Tactics Comfortable bank fishing all round the loch and action everywhere. The west shoreline, particularly in the vicinity of the principal feeder-stream (15/015111) is a good place to start. Flies: Blue Zulu, Woodcock & Hare-lug, Peter Ross.
Permission & Charges See Loch na Totaig.

VEYATIE, Loch
Location & Access 15/195125 Approach from the A835 Ledmore Junction/Ullapool road at Elphin (15/215120). A track leads west down to a fish farm (now defunct) and the boat mooring bay.
Commentary Loch Veyatie is dramatic, four miles long by up to 400 yards wide, and can be windy. The banks are steep and shelve quickly. The boundary between Sutherland and Ross-shire centres the loch and Veyatie is 'pinched' between Suilven (731m) to the north and Cul Mor (849m) to the south.
Fish Trout average 8oz but there are good numbers of much larger fish of up to and over 2lb in weight. Trolling is allowed on Veyatie and the largest fish caught in recent years weighed 9lb 8oz, taken on a Black Pennell.
Flies & Tactics Boat fishing, otherwise a long walk, and wading is dangerous. There is often a mayfly hatch (late June/early July) when sport can be fast and furious. The south-east shore is good, as is the far west end. An outboard motor is essential, and, when moving about the loch, take care - there are sub-surface rocks close to the shore. Loch a'Mhadail (15/155144), which can be joined to Loch Veyatie during high water conditions, is also excellent. The two unnamed lochans at 15/148151 and 15/152151 are also productive. Moor the boat at 15/159145 and walk over to investigate. Given the length of the loch, carry spare fuel for the outboard to avoid a long row home. Flies: Black Pennell, March Brown, Alexandra.
Permission & Charges See Cam Loch.

YUCAL, Loch 15/205370 See Duart River.

OS Map 16 — Lairg, Loch Shin & surrounding area

Lairg, Loch Shin & Surrounding Area

A'BHEALAICH, Loch See River Mallart.
A'BHEALAICH, Lochan See Loch Merkland.
A'BHROCHAIN, Loch See Loch na Claise Moire.
A'CHOIRE BHUIDHE, Lochan See Green Loch.
A'CHOIRE LEACAICH, Loch See Loch Fiag.
A'GARBH-UILLT, Loch See Loch Meadie.
A'GHIUBHAIS, Loch See Loch Eileanach (Crask).
A'GHORM-CHOIRE, Loch See Loch Fiag.
A'GHRIAMA, Loch See Loch Shin.
A'MHEALLAIN, Loch See River Blackwater (Ben Armine).

AN ALLTAN FHEARNA, Loch
Location & Access 16/750335. Approach from Badanloch Lodge (17/800331) and follow the track along the south shore of Loch Badanloch (17/770345) to reach the loch after two and a half miles.
Commentary A very attractive loch, circular in shape, and about three-quarters of a mile across.
Fish Good numbers of hard-fighting little trout which average in the order of 8oz.
Flies & Tactics Ideal for beginners, this shallow loch fishes as well from the bank as it does from a boat. Fish are taken all over the loch, particularly in the vicinity of the two inlet streams on the south shore. Try: Ke-He, Soldier Palmer, Peter Ross.
Permission & Charges See Loch Rimsdale.

AN ASLAIRD, Loch See Loch Merkland.
AN EOIN, Loch See Upper River Brora (Dalreavoch Lodge).
AN FHEOIR, Loch See Loch Eileanach (Crask).
AN FHREICEADAIN, Loch See Loch an Staing.
AN FLIUARAIN, Loch See River Mallart.
AN GLAS-LOCH, Loch See River Mudale.
AN LAOIGH, Loch See Loch an Staing.

AN STAING, Loch
Location & Access 16/523188. Approach from Loch Shin on the A838 Lairg/Scourie road. Park at the east end of the Sithean Dubh Mor plantation (16/512177) and walk north east for one mile over rising ground to the loch.
Commentary Remote and rarely visited, high on the moor above Loch Shin giving splendid views of the surrounding countryside. A further mile north-west brings you to Lochan an Laoigh (16/508200) and its little satellite which are also worth a cast or two.
Fish Nothing for the glass case but definitely something for breakfast.
Flies & Tactics An easy day out involving a non-taxing walk of about four miles. Bank fishing. Finish the day by having a look at Loch an Fhreiceadain (16/515168, just to the south of the A838 at 518167. Try: Blue Zulu, Soldier Palmer, Silver Butcher.
Permission & Charges Finlyson Hughes, 45 Church Street, Inverness. Tel: (01463) 224343; Fax: (01463) 243234. See also Loch Beannach.

AN T-SEILG, Loch See Loch Merkland.
AN T-SLUGAITE, Lochan See Upper River Brora (Dalreavoch Lodge).
AN TAIRBH, Loch See River Mudale. See Loch Merkland.
AN TUIRC, Loch See Loch Meadie.
AN ULBHAIDH, Loch See Loch Eileanach (Crask).
BAD AN LOCH, Loch See River Mudale.
BAD AN T-SEAN-TIGHE, Loch See Upper River Brora (Dalreavoch Lodge).
BEAG NA FUARALACHD, Loch See Loch Beannach (Lairg).
BEANNACH, Loch (East Dalreavoch) See Upper River Brora (Dalreavoch Lodge).

BEANNACH, Loch (Lairg)
Location & Access 16/600125. Approach from the A836 Lairg/Altnaharra road via a track which starts near the bridge over the Feith Osdail burn at 16/576139.
Commentary A first-class trout loch in attractive surroundings, well-managed by the Lairg Angling club and offering some of the best fishing in the area. There are two other lochs, to the north, on the Lairg Estate: Loch Beag na Fuaralachd (16/609157) and, in the forest, Loch na Fuaralachd (16/604163). Both are reputed to hold some nice fish and they may be approached from the same track as is used to reach Loch Beannach. At 16/600143, cross the Feith Osdail burn and climb north for one mile to find them. Bank fishing.
Fish Loch Beannach has excellent quality trout which average 1lb in weight. There are larger fish as well.
Flies & Tactics Boat fishing brings best results. The loch is just over half a mile north/south by up to 700 yds wide across the north bay. Trout rise and are taken throughout most of the loch, although the east shore, round the two small islands and where the inlet burn enters, is a good place to start. There is a long, finger-like, peninsula running south-west from the east shore. A drift about ten yards out from the bank, parallel to the shoreline, can produce results. Offer: Ke-He, March Brown, Peter Ross.
Permission & Charges The Sutherland Sporting Co, New Buildings, Lairg, Sutherland. Tel: (01549) 402239. £15 per boat per day, two rods fishing. No outboards. To obtain permission to fish the other two lochs mentioned, contact Finlyson Hughes, 45 Church Street, Inverness. Tel: (01463) 224343; Fax: (01463) 243234.

BEANNACH, Loch (West Dalreavoch) See Upper River Brora (Dalreavoch Lodge).
BEINN AN EOIN BHEAG, Loch See Loch na Claise Moire.
BEN HARRALD, Loch See River Mudale.

BLACKWATER, River (Ben Armine Lodge)
Location & Access Source: 16/673259. Outfall: 17/807110.
Commentary Ben Armine Lodge overlooks the River

173

Lairg, Loch Shin & surrounding area — OS Map 16

Blackwater, the principal tributary of the River Brora, and the setting of the lodge and the surrounding scenery is magnificent. Salmon fishing is let with the lodge and is not available for casual, day lets. Trout fishing may be available and it is worth contacting the factor to see if a booking is possible. The best trout fishing is in Glas-loch Mor (16/672196), which has a boat, and in Glas-loch Beag (16/660201) which is fished from the bank. There is also a boat on Lochan Dubh Cadhafuaraich (16/681183). Further north, up the Feith Dubh burn, is Loch nam Breac Beaga (16/651188), also known locally as the Dhli Loch. Return from Loch Breac Beaga by walking south along the west shoulder of Meallan Liath Mor (461m) and climb through the bealach to fish little Loch a'Mheallain Leith (16/660172). Follow the outlet burn from the loch down the hill to cross the Feith Dubh stream and regain the track back to Ben Armine Lodge. North from Ben Armine Lodge, there are two more splendid lochs, Gorm-loch Mor (16/713234), and Gorm-loch Beag (16/707273). A track continues north from the lodge, climbing the west shoulder of Meall an Fhrith-alltain (429m) and Bealach na Muic, reaching Gorm-loch Mor after a hike of two miles. The track continues north again for two miles, along the east side of Creag Mhor (713m), to reach Gorm-loch Beag. Reaching these lochs will tax both legs and lungs, but few places in Scotland offer such wonderful sport in such precious surroundings. The wildlife is outstanding with more than a good chance of seeing golden eagle and divers. A compass and map are essential, as is a reasonable degree of physical fitness.

Fish The River Blackwater holds salmon, sea-trout and brown trout. The five-year average for Ben Armine Lodge guests is in the order of 32 salmon per year. Glas-loch Mor has trout which average 10oz/12oz and a few fish of over 3lb in weight. There are also arctic char. Glas-loch Beag is the place to go for guaranteed breakfast and supper-sized trout. Large baskets are the rule, rather than the exception. The Gorm Lochs have smaller trout, in the 6oz/8oz class. Lochan Dubh Cadhafuaraich has similar-sized trout to Glas-loch Mor. Loch nam Breac Beaga and Loch a'Mheallain Leith trout average 8oz/10oz, with some larger fish as well.

Flies & Tactics Salmon fishing is entirely dependent upon there being good water-levels in the river. When conditions are right, there is always the chance of a fish throughout the three miles available to Ben Armine Lodge guests. There river is easily accessible and there is no need to wade. Offer them: Willie Gunn, Garry Dog, Green Highlander, Hairy Mary, General Practitioner, Munro Killer. Apart from Glas-loch Mor and Lochan Dubh Cadhafuaraich, where there are boats, all the other lochs are fished from the bank. Stay ashore and do not attempt to wade, particularly on the Gorm Lochs where the bottom shelves quickly along the west margins. Flies that work well include: Black Zulu, Blue Zulu, Loch Ordie, Black Pennell, Soldier Palmer, Woodcock & Hare-lug, Greenwell's Glory, Silver Invicta, Silver Butcher.

Permission & Charges The Factor, The Sutherland Estates Office, Duke Street, Golspie, Sutherland KW10 6RR. Tel: (01408) 633268; Fax: (01408) 633800. Ben Armine Lodge accommodates up to 9 people. Prices on application.

BRORA, Upper River (Dalreavoch Lodge)

Location & Access Source: 16/611219. Outfall: 16/754088. Dalreavoch Lodge overlooks the Upper River Brora and is approached from the A9 Inverness/Wick road, from Golspie (10 miles) or from Brora (12 miles). Salmon fishing on the Upper River Brora is let with the lodge and is not generally available for casual, day, lets. Trout fishing may be available and it is worth contacting the factor to see if a booking is possible.

Commentary The lodge is attractively situated and sleeps up to 15 people. The rental includes stalking and shooting, as well as salmon fishing and hill loch fishing. There are four principal lochs, with boats, accessed from an estate track which runs north from Dalreavoch to join the Ben Armine road. These lochs are, from south to north, Loch Grudaidh (16/744102), Loch Beannach (East Dalreavoch) (16/740114), Loch Dubh (16/745123), and Loch Bad an t-Sean-tighe (16/735133). Apart from them, there are other, remote lochs, on the moors around Meall Uaineil (342m) and Meall a'phiobaire (372m), which offer excellent hill loch fishing in superb surroundings. They are approached from the end of the Craigton track (16/676124), by crossing the Upper River Brora at Alltamhuilt (16/678128). Begin by walking east for one mile to reach Loch na Gaineimh (16/698125). From Loch na Gaineimh, continue north-north-east for one mile to find lovely Loch an Eoin (16/709142). Locate the inlet stream on the west shore of Loch an Eoin and follow it over the bealach between Meall Uaineil and Meall a'Phiobaire to reach the largest of the series, Loch Beannach (West Dalreavoch) (16/685145). Opposite the small island at the north end of Loch Beannach (West Dalreavoch), turn north, and walk over the hill and descend to little Lochan an t-Slugaite (16/678159) on the Coirefrois Burn. After fishing Lochan t-Slugaite, walk south-west for half a mile to fish Lochan Sgeireach (16/671155) and its adjacent satellite lochan. From there, a comfortable 1.5 mile walk south-east brings you back to the starting point at Alltamhuilt. Take along a compass and map and strong legs, but this is a super way to spend a day with good bank fishing all round.

Fish The Brora River produces about 800 salmon each season, as well as sea-trout. The lochs all contain good numbers of brown trout which average 8oz, and a few larger fish of up to and over 2lb in weight as well.

Flies & Tactics Four miles of double-bank salmon fishing is available to Dalreavoch Lodge tenants. There is no regular gillie, but the estate keeper will advise guests on fishing, and tell them where the boats are moored on the principal lochs. Success on the Upper River Brora depends upon good water levels. Commercial forestry and land drainage have reduced water-flow in recent years, as has extraction from Dalnessie (16/631153), where water is directed west to the Loch Shin hydro-electric scheme. The sand-bar at the north end of Loch Brora, and Balnacoil Falls, hold

OS Map 16 — Lairg, Loch Shin & surrounding area

fish back during drought conditions, but, generally, there are fish in the Upper River from May onwards. The river is easily fished from the bank and you should tempt the residents with: Willie Gunn, Garry Dog, Green Highlander, Hairy Mary, Munro Killer, Goat's Toe, General Practitioner. On Loch Beannach (East Dalreavoch), from the boat, concentrate your best effort in the vicinity of the small islands and the east bay. On Loch na Gaineimh, attack the south-west shore and the north shore. Fish the north-west end of Loch Beannach (West Dalreavoch), by the peninsula, islet and inlet stream. The other waters will provide sport everywhere. Flies: Blue Zulu, Soldier Palmer, Peter Ross.
Permission & Charges See River Blackwater (Ben Armine Lodge).

BUIDHE, Loch See Loch Meadie.
CAMASACH, Loch See Loch Eileanach (Crask).

CASSLEY, River
Location & Access Source: 15/318245. Outflow: 16/474010. Easily accessible from the minor road which leaves the A837 Bonar Bridge/Inchnadamph road at Rosehall near the Achness Hotel (16/473024) and runs north up Glen Cassley to Duchally (16/388170).
Commentary The principal source of the River Cassley is Gorm Loch Mor to the north of Ben More Assynt (998m). The river flows south from the loch, through Fionn Loch Mor (15/335235), Fionn Loch Beag (15/341229) and Loch na Sroine Luime (15/345217), before beginning its 25 mile journey down Glen Cassley to join the River Oykle in the Kyle of Sutherland. The best fishing is in the final 9 miles, below where the principal tributary, the Amhainn Gleann Muic, flows in at Glenmuick (16/397128). The falls above the confluence of the River Cassley and Amhainn Gleann Muic restrict access to the upper river, but a few fish are taken up to and beyond Duchally towards the end of the season and depending upon water levels. The late Neil Graesser was the acknowledged expert on fishing this little river and he spent much of his life working to improve Cassley salmon runs. The River Cassley is a classic Highland spate stream, a delight of tumbling rapids, foaming runs and deep pools, flowing past tree-lined banks and heather moorland. The principal obstacle to fish are the lower falls, three sections, centred by Fir Tree Island; with the famous tree which has withstood aquatic assault for more than 100 years. The falls act as a "temperature pool" and fish do not proceed upstream until water temperature reaches 48-52 degrees F, which generally occurs towards the end of April.
Fish Salmon, grilse, and a few sea-trout. The river produces in the order of 700/900 salmon each season. Average weight, 8lb.
Flies & Tactics Good water levels are all-important, although some pools, such as the Long Pool, which is nearly 1 mile long, hold fish in most conditions. There are about 100 named pools throughout the length of the river and these are described to fishing tenants in excellent detail in the information sheets which accompany bookings. Wading is not really necessary, although thigh-boots are useful for tackling some of the pools. Boats are provided at various points, to ease crossing the river, and there are comfortable fishing huts for lunch and relaxation. A 15ft rod will deal with most eventualities and a floating line is adjudged best. Neil Grasser always advised anglers to "strike" Cassley salmon, rather than waiting, and then tightening. He was also an advocate of "dibbling" the dropper fly in white water and claimed to have taken more than 100 fish to his own rod using this method. Small flies produce best results: Torrish, Hairy Mary, Shrimp Fly, and, the most consistently successful pattern, a Stoat's Tail, fished as a dropper.
Permission & Charges For the Upper Cassley Fishings, contact: Bell Ingram, Estate Office, Bonar Bridge, Sutherland IV24 3EA. Tel: (01863) 766683; Fax: (01863) 766736; for the Glenrossal Fishings, contact: Glenrossal Estate, Rosehall, by Lairg, Sutherland IV274BG. Tel: (01549) 441203; Fax: (01549) 441323. Rosehall Fishings, contact: Achness Hotel, Rosehall, by Lairg, Sutherland IV274BD. Tel: (01549) 441239. Duchally Fishing, contact: The Factor, Balnagowan Estate, Estate Office, Balnagowan, Ross-shire. Tel: (01862)843601. Prices vary, according to the beat and to the time of year but expect to pay between £100 and £600 per rod per week. Full details on application to those named above, and early booking is essential.

CHOIRE, Loch See River Mallart.
COIRE, Loch See Loch Merkland.
COIRE NA SAIDHE DUIBHE, Loch See Loch Fiag.
COIRE NAM FEURAN, Loch See Loch Naver.
CRACAIL BEAG, Loch See Loch Cracail Mor.

CRACAIL MOR, Loch
Location & Access 16/627020. Approach from the A9 Inverness/Wick road at Bonar Bridge. Coming north, immediately after crossing the bridge into Bonar, go north on the minor road directly in front of you signposted to Loch Buidhe (17/660984). After passing Loch an Lagain (17/660955), on your right, look for a gate on your left at 17/644966. Drive north up the track which leads to Garvary (17/639979), ignoring the left hand fork at 17/639979 which leads to Loch Laro (17/610994), and park off the track after the second gate past Garvary, a distance of two miles from the minor road. Hoof it from here, north again past Loch Cracail Beag (16/631009), which is preserved by the owner, to reach Loch Cracail Mor after a journey of approximately 30 minutes.
Commentary One of the best trout lochs in the area in a remote and dramatic setting, with Cnoc Cracail (297m) to the west and An Stoc-bheinn (336m) to the east. The small water on the hill to the east, Lochan na Faolaig (16/642010), is preserved by the owner and should not be fished.
Fish Quality brown trout which average 12oz in weight with the chance of larger fish of up to and over 2lb.
Flies & Tactics There is a boat on Cracail Mor, moored near the outlet stream at the south end of the

175

Lairg, Loch Shin & surrounding area — OS Map 16

loch (16/629015). Bank fishing is not allowed. The north and north-east shore, where three streams enter Cracail Mor, is a good place to launch your assault, although fish are taken from all over the loch. Hasten slowly in the boat and take particular care at the north end where rocks lurk just below the surface; and watch out for shallow skerries off the west shore approximately 250yds north from the boat mooring. Offer the residents: Soldier Palmer, March Brown, Alexandra.

Permission & Charges The loch is managed by the Dornoch & District Angling Association and a boat for the day costs £12, with two rods fishing. Permits from the Highlands of Scotland Tourist Board, The Square Dornoch, Sutherland IV25 3SD. Tel: (01862) 810400; Fax: (01862) 810644. Life jackets are also available at the tourist office, for those who require them, as well as a selection of local flies, a mixed pack of 10 for £3

CRAGGIE, Loch (Lairg)
Location & Access 16/625075. In Lairg, two hundred yards north of the road junction at the Sutherland Arms Hotel, turn right on the minor road signposted to Saval. At 16/594077, turn right along a track past Savalbeag cottage. The track passes Loch Dola (16/607080) on the left, then one branch heads north to Loch Tigh na Creige (16/615094), the other leads round the north shore of Loch Craggie to a parking place and boat mooring bay at the east end (16/630069).

Commentary Loch Craggie is one of the best trout lochs in the North of Scotland, three quarters of a mile east/west by up to 400 yds wide, and is certainly one of the most lovely to fish. Fine views west to Ben More Assynt and north over heather moorland. There is a bay near the old boathouse at the west end and this is a perfect place for a picnic and a splash on a hot day. Loch Dola is just as pleasant to fish, an intimate loch with room enough for one boat. Loch Tigh na Creige is smaller than Loch Craggie, with darker, peat-stained water, but none-the-less attractive.

Fish Loch Craggie trout average 12oz with fish of up to and over 2lb. Loch Dola has large numbers of 6oz/8oz trout. Loch Tigh na Creige also has good stocks of breakfast-sized trout, but larger specimens as well.

Flies & Tactics Fish Loch Dola along the north-east shore in the vicinity of the old boathouse. Fish anywhere on Loch Tigh na Creige. On Loch Craggie, start with a drift along the south-west bank, about 15 yds out from the woodland that margins the shore. There are numerous little corners here and barely submerged boulders which shelter excellent trout. The small island in the south-east is another favourite area. The loch shallows to the north, and the rock-strewn bay, where two burns feed in, can be productive. Offer them: Black Pennell, Soldier Palmer, Silver Invicta.

Permission & Charges Park House, Lairg, Sutherland. Tel: 01549 402208. Loch Craggie: £20 per boat per day; other lochs, £15 per boat per day. Outboard engines are not allowed and please remember to relock gates and boats after use. There is no bank fishing.

DOLA, Loch See Loch Craggie (Lairg).
DUBH CADHAFUARAICH, Lochan See River Blackwater (Ben Armine).
DUBH CUL NA CAPULICH, Loch See Loch Eileanach (Crask).
DUBH, Loch (Dalreavoch Lodge) See Upper River Brora (Dalreavoch Lodge).
DUBH, Lochan (Choire) See River Mallart .
EAS NA MAOILE, Loch See Loch Merkland.

EILEANACH, Loch (Crask)
Location & Access 16/483278. A long walk in from near the Crask Inn on the A836 Lairg/Altnaharra road. Follow the track west from 16/521258 past Loch Gaineamhach (16/514259) and Loch an Fheoir (16/510260), then hike north-west over Cnoc an Alaskie (312m) to reach the loch after a hard three miles.

Commentary The surrounding area here has been extensively afforested in recent years and access is difficult over boggy ground. To the west of Loch Eileanach is a further trout loch, Loch Camasach (16/473280), and to the south, Loch an Alaskie (16/479268), which drains via the Allt an Ulbhaidh burn into Loch an Ulbhaidh (16/492229). Loch an Ulbhaidh exits south-east in the River Tirry to enter Loch Shin near Dalchork (16/569100). The River Tirry offers some sport with brown trout near to Loch Shin, but forestry planting has contributed substantially to drying out this spate stream in all but heavy water conditions. Additional forestry now completely surrounds little Loch Dubh Cul na Capulich (16/529237), to the south of the Crask Inn, but Loch a'Ghiubhais (16/567237), to the south of the Strath a'Chraisg/Bealach Easach track, and known locally as the Sandy Loch, is worth a visit.

Fish All the lochs noted contain good stocks of brown trout which average in the order of 6oz/8oz.

Flies & Tactics Compass and map essential, to find your way around, and pints of midge-repellent in summer months. Bank fishing. Stay ashore and avoid wading. Flies: Black Zulu, Soldier Palmer, Silver Butcher.

Permission & Charges Very difficult to establish ownership since in recent years bits and pieces of this area have been sold on to various individuals in small lots; as is also the case with the land to the north of the forestry planting north from the Overscaig Hotel and including Loch Strath Duchally (16/423269) and Loch Suil a'Ghriama (16/412279). This area was recently offered for sale in "plots" of one acre. Best advice is to contact The Overscaig Hotel Tel: (01549) 431203, and the Lairg Angling Club Tel: (01549) 402239.

FEUR, Loch See Loch Merkland.
FIAG, Loch 16/450290. This loch, the Fiag River, Loch Poll a'Phac (16/462283), and the lochs to the north, Loch a'Ghorm-choire (16/44030), Loch a'Choire Leacaich (16/450344), and Loch Coire na Saidhe Duibhe (16/450360), are preserved by the owner and public fishing is not allowed.
FIAG, River See Loch Fiag.

OS Map 16
Lairg, Loch Shin & surrounding area

FLEET, River
Location & Access Source: 16/616006. Outfall: 21/774982. The river rises near Meall Dola (323m), to the east of Lairg, and is easily accessible throughout its entire length from the A839 Mound/Lairg road.
Commentary This small spate stream lies in very attractive countryside and empties into the Dornoch Firth through Loch Fleet at Mound on the A9 Inverness/Wick road. Loch Fleet is an important nature reserve, owned and managed by the Scottish Wildlife Trust, and is home to a wide variety of wildlife, as well as to the salmon and sea-trout which gather at the Mound sluice which opens under pressure from a spate. There are also a number of trout lochs in the area which are often available to the public through the Rogart Angling Association and through Tressady Estate when not required by Tressady Lodge guests. These lochs are: Loch Muidhe (16/667052), approached from Mule (16/672042) and Lochan Preas nan Sgiathanach (16/680000), accessed from Achnaluachrach at the end of the West Langwell road. Loch na Cinneamhuin (16/684069) and Lochan Preasnan Sgiathanach are exclusive to Tressady Estate and is reached up the line of Lettie River, a tributary of the River Fleet, but the angling club have access to Loch Salachaidh (16/759038) which is reached from the minor road from Rogart in the south to Dalreavoch in the north. Follow the track which runs east near the church at 16/739035.
Fish Salmon, sea-trout and brown trout in the river, brown trout in the lochs. Between 40 and 80 salmon are taken each season, depending upon water conditions. The angling club share is approximately 20/25 fish.
Flies & Tactics A very challenging stream, narrow, with wooded banks and best attacked using a single-handed rod and light tackle. The most productive part of the river is from the sea, upstream for the first four miles and the angling club have access to Polson's Beat and Coire Beat. A good wind on the surface helps to disguise evil intent and you should stay well back from the edge, stalking the fish, on hands and knees if necessary. Offer them: Willie Gun, Garry Dog, Green Highlander, Munro Killer. Trout fly patterns also work well, Black Pennell, March Brown, Grouse & Claret, Dunkeld. The trout lochs are easily understood and contain good stocks of trout which average 10oz in weight and also a few specimens of up to and over 2lb. Loch Preas nan Sgiathanach is the largest water, shallow and covering an area of some 50 acres. Bank fishing can be as productive as fishing from a boat, particularly down the north-east shoreline. Loch na Cinneamhuin, which is attacked from the shore, can only really be fished effectively in a south-west wind because of weed growth near the margin. Fish rise and are taken everywhere in the other lochs. Try Loch Ordie, Soldier Palmer, Alexandra to tempt them.
Permission & Charges For Tressady Lodge, contact Bell-Ingram, Estate Office, Bonar Bridge, Sutherland. Tel: (01863) 766683; Fax: (01863) 766736. The lodge is splendidly comfortable and sport costs in the order of £1,000 per week depending upon time of year. Sandy Mackenzie, Rogart Angling Club, c/o Rogart Post Office, Rogart, Sutherland. Tel: (01408) 641200. Salmon fishing, £10 per rod per session. There are three sessions in every 24 hour period on Monday, Wednesday and Saturdays. Trout fishing costs £10 per day.

GAINEAMHACH, Loch (Choire) See River Mallart.
GAINEAMHACH, Loch (Crask) See Loch Eileanach (Crask).
GLAS-LOCH BEAG, Loch See River Blackwater.
GLAS-LOCH MOR, Loch See River Blackwater (Ben Armine).
GORM-LOCH BEAG, Loch See River Blackwater (Ben Armine).
GORM-LOCH MOR, Loch See River Blackwater (Ben Armine).

GREEN, Loch
Location & Access 16/720393. Park at 16/724399 on the B871 Kinbrace/Syre road. Follow the track south for half a mile to reach the outlet burn from the loch. Walk west, up the outlet burn, to find the loch after ten minutes.
Commentary A small loch on the moorland between Loch Rimsdale (16/740355) and the Strathnaver Forest. Easy access and best fished in conjunction with a visit to Lochan a'Choire Bhuidhe (16/702386), one mile further west on the east slopes of Dalharrold Hill (190m). Also of interest is the unnamed loch immediately to the north of Lochan a'Choire Bhuidhe at 16/704390.
Fish Nothing of any great size, but good sport with trout which average three to the pound, and, towards the end of the season, the chance of the odd larger fish in the Green Loch which may have wandered up from Loch Rimsdale.
Flies & Tactics Comfortable bank fishing with sport from all round the shores. The round trip is four miles over rough ground. Excellent chance of meeting elusive greenshank. Flies: Soldier Palmer, March Brown, Alexandra.
Permission & Charges See Loch Rimsdale.

GRUAMA MOR, Loch See Loch Naver.
GRUDAIDH, Loch See Upper River Brora (Dalreavoch Lodge).
LETTIE, River See River Fleet.

MALLART, River
Location & Access Source 16/650306; Outflow 16/671378. Access to the lower river is via an estate road at the east end of Loch Naver (16/620370) which leaves the B873 Bettyhill/Altnaharra road at 16/670385. The middle and upper river are approached by a private estate road from the east end of Loch Badanloch (17/801330), from the B871 Kinbrace/Syre road out to Loch Choire Lodge, and by a track which borders the north bank of the river
Commentary The River Mallart is the principal tributary of the River Naver (see OS Map 10) and rises in Loch Choire (16/635290). This is a short, rocky stream, flowing north-east then north to reach the River Naver after six miles. There are a number of

Lairg, Loch Shin & surrounding area — OS Map 16

excellent pools along the way, including two Falls Pools and the Washing Pool. The Loch Choire Estate has first-class brown trout lochs, the principal water being Loch Choire itself; three miles long by up to half a mile wide and fed from Loch a'Bhealaich (16/600267) in the west. There are also good hill lochs, Loch nan Uan (16/567293), Loch an Fliuarain (16/582279), Loch Gaineamhach (16/583245), Loch Truderscaig (16/710328), Lochan Dubh (16/729329).

Fish Primarily salmon, although also a few sea-trout. Detailed catch statistics are not available but a reasonable estimate would be in the order of 50 fish per season. The trout lochs hold a wide variety of fish, from modest 8oz specimens, right up to glass case candidates, primarily from Loch Choire, where boat fishing brings best results.

Flies & Tactics Few fish are in the river until after April and thereafter the Mallart is entirely dependent upon good water-levels to give of its best. A single-handed rod is appropriate and wading is not required. Very much a case of stalking fish, keeping well back from the river bank. Lengthen line from one spot, rather than marching down the bank. Best Flies: Small, dark patterns, including trout flies such as Black Pennell; and Garry Dog, Willie Gunn, Hairy Mary. Apart from Loch Choire, the trout lochs are fished from the shore. Offer them: Loch Ordie, Soldier Palmer, Silver Butcher.

Permission & Charges Fishing on the Loch Choire Estate is rarely available on a casual basis, but may be occasionally available from the Altnaharra Hotel, Altnaharra, by Lairg, Sutherland. Tel: (01549) 411222. Sporting lets including Loch Choire Lodge, which accommodates parties of up to 12 people, are arranged through Finlyson Hughes, 29 Barossa Place, Perth PH1 5EP. Tel: (01738) 630926; Fax: (01738) 639017.

MEADIE, Loch

Location & Access 16/496397. Easily accessible from the minor road from Altnaharra to Hope. The boats are moored in the bay close to where the loch flows out under the road to join the River Mudale.

Commentary From the road, Loch Meadie looks a modest affair, but in fact the loch extends north for a distance of three miles, dominated to the west by Ben Hope (927m) and to the east by Ben Loyal (764m). This section of Loch Meadie can be found on OS Map 9. There are two, small, remote, trout lochs nearby, difficult of access, but well worth a visit: to the west Lochan Sgaothaichean (9/489443) and to the east Loch a'Bhuic (9/519418). Attack using the Loch Meadie boat. Take compass and map in case of bad weather. Loch Meadie is one of the prettiest lochs in Scotland and the islands in particular offer a wealth of wildflowers, unharmed by the attentions of grazing sheep or deer. Look, don't pick. The island in the narrows, one mile north from the mooring bay, is the perfect place for lunch.

Fish From time to time Loch Meadie produces large fish: a trout of 4lb was caught a few years ago at the north end and salmon are occasionally taken. However, Meadie is most famous for large baskets of 6oz/8oz trout and this is one of the best places in the north to introduce newcomers to the gentle art of fly-fishing.

Flies & Tactics Boat fishing is best and an outboard motor is essential if you are to explore the whole loch. But hasten slowly, because there are barely submerged rocks waiting to catch the unwary. Trout can be taken virtually anywhere, but the far north end is a favourite location. Meadie trout are not choosy about flies and readily take most patterns. Also occasionally available from the Altnaharra Hotel are the lochs to the west of the A836 Altnaharra/Tongue road: Loch Buidhe (16/570375), Loch a'Garbh-uillt (16/559378), and Loch an Tuirc (16/545393), to the north of Sron an Tuirc (226m), and the unnamed lochan at 16/558395). All hold breakfast-sized trout. Loch Buidhe is a ten-minute walk west of the A836 from 16/575375. Loch a'Garbh-uillt is best attacked from the Altnaharra/Hope road up the An Garbh-allt burn from the bridge at 16/55136. The other waters should be tackled by walking north-west for one mile from the north end of Loch a'Garbh-uillt. Bank fishing only.

Permission & Charges The Altnaharra Hotel, Altnaharra, by Lairg, Sutherland. Tel: (01549) 411222. £20 per day for boat.

MERKLAND, Loch

Location & Access 16/390315. Easy access to the east shore from the A838 Lairg/Scourie road. The west shoreline is trackless.

Commentary Loch Merkland is 2.5 miles north/south by up to 600 yds wide, a deep, somewhat depressing-looking loch. It is enclosed by Meallan Liath Mor (683m) to the east and and Creag nan Suibheag (465m) to the west and the glen is often in shadow.

Fish Brown trout which average 8oz/10oz and ferox trout in the depths.

Flies & Tactics The loch has a well-earned reputation for producing large ferox trout, but they are only to be caught by trolling - up and down and in the middle - which is not everyone's idea of a fun-day's fishing. Boat fishing brings best results and helps you to get around this large water. More than 40 small streams feed into Loch Merkland. The principal burns are the Garbh Allt, which enters by the north-west shore near the ruin of Garvault Cottage (16/384320), and the Allt nan Albhannach which flows in at West Merkland (16/385330). There is a small loch on the Garbh Allt, the Feur Loch (16/371312), which is worth the 1.5 mile hike it takes to reach. The Merkland Estate have a number of hill lochs, to the north of Loch Merkland, and these offer a chance of sport in stunning surroundings. Trout average 8oz, but there are good numbers of larger fish as well and trout of up to and over 2lb are not uncommon. Reaching these lochs is another matter, but a good stalker's path, starting from West Merkland, helps you on your way. The lochs are: Loch Eas na Maoile (16/372350), Loch Ulbhach Coire (16/379378), Lochan a'Bhealaich (16/386390), Loch na Mang (16/391395), Coire Loch (16/369395). A round trip of the above waters is a serious undertaking involving a walk of about ten miles, climbing steeply round the east shoulder of Carn Dearg (796m) to

OS Map 16 — Lairg, Loch Shin & surrounding area

reach the last three. Compass and map and climbing boot-country. Start from West Merkland and, after half a mile, bear west along the north edge of the forest, up the line of the Allt Beithe burn. Loch Eas na Maoile is a step west from the burn after the end of the plantation. The burn will lead you north for 1.5 miles to the marshy plateau containing Loch Ulbhach Coire. Find the inlet stream at the north-east end of Loch Ulbhach Coire, grit your teeth and climb steeply up the stream to gain Lochan a'Bhealaich and Loch na Mang. Coire Loch will tax you further and lies one mile west, below the north face of Carn Dearg. Return to West Merkland by retracing your outward journey. More user-friendly lochs lie close to the east of the West Merkland stalker's path, after a 2.5 mile tramp: Loch an Tuim Bhuidhe (16/409355), Loch an t-Seilg (16/416360), and Loch an Aslaird (16/422368). They are interlinked and extend north for a distance of two miles. If you must climb, then explore the lochans below Beinn Direach (688m), to the west of the stalker's track: Lochan na Creige Riabhaich (16/414378), and its satellite at 16/411373; and, to the north of Beinn Direach, remote Loch nan Rath (16/407393). The effort involved in reaching these distant waters is rewarding, not only for the chance of a fish or two, but also because of the matchless beauty of the surroundings. Attack all these waters using traditional Highland patterns of artificial fly: Black Pennell, Black Zulu, Blue Zulu, Ke-He, Loch Ordie, Soldier Palmer, Invicta, Woodcock & Hare-lug, Alexandra, Peter Ross, Dunkeld. Bank fishing on the hill lochs and do not wade.

Permission & Charges For Loch Merkland, contact the Overscaig Lochside Hotel, Overscaig, by Lairg, Sutherland. Tel: (01549) 431203. A boat with outboard engine costs £15 per day for two rods fishing. For the other lochs, contact Alan Walker, Head Keeper, Merkland Estate, Corriekinloch, by Lairg, Sutherland. Tel: (01549) 431222. Prices and access on application.

MOLACH, Loch See Loch Naver.

MUDALE, River

Location & Access Source 16/502390. Outflow 16/578355. Accessible from the minor road from Altnaharra to Hope.

Commentary The River Mudale rises in Loch Meadie (16/498395) and flows south-east for six miles through rough pasture and moorland to enter Loch Naver (16/620370) close to the township of Altnaharra. There are a number of pools and runs where salmon lie and the surrounding scenery is magnificent. The River Vagastie, which also flows into Loch Naver by Altnaharra (16/579349), is rarely fished, other than at the mouth. From May onwards, because of lack of water, most of the River Vagastie virtually disappears. There are, however, three, small trout lochs between the river and Ben Klibreck (961m) and they are reputed to hold some excellent trout of considerable weight: Loch an Tairbh (16/569312), Loch na Glas-choille (16/559305), and Loch Bad an Loch (16/550290). Loch na Glas-choille has the best fish and all these lochs can be reached from the A836 Lairg/Altnaharra road after a hike of about fifteen minutes.

Fish Salmon and brown trout. Salmon average 8lb, brown trout 8oz. The River Mudale is not fished regularly and few salmon are taken, perhaps a dozen fish each season.

Flies & Tactics Absolutely dependent upon water-levels and best fished after a heavy spate. Arrange to be dropped off near Mudale Farm (16/534358). A track leads down to meet the river where the waters from the Allt a'Ghlas-locha and the Allt an t-Srath a Dhuibh burns join the River Mudale. Both these substantial tributaries, in their lower reaches, can offer the chance of a fish, particularly towards the end of the season. Two excellent trout lochs lie on the headwaters of the Allt a'Ghlas-locha burn: Loch Ben Harrald (16/520330) and Loch An Glas-loch. They are reached, after a considerable walk south on a stalkers path by the stream. Fish the river back down to Altnaharra. After heavy rain, fish may be encountered throughout the system in the extended pools and runs created by a spate. Wading is not required but a 12ft rod is recommended to hold any fish hooked in the strong current. Stay well back from the bank and let the fly swing round, inviting salmon to "take" as the fly dangles at the end of the sweep. For salmon, offer: Willie Gunn, Garry Dog, Black Doctor, Green Highlander, General Practitioner. Brown trout: Ke-He, March Brown, Dunkeld.

Permission & Charges The Altnaharra Hotel, Altnaharra, by Lairg, Sutherland Tel/Fax: (01549) 411222. The hotel beat is 1.75 miles of double bank. Trout fishing on the lochs noted above may sometimes be arranged through the hotel, subject to availability.

MUIDHE, Loch See River Fleet.

NA CINNEAMHUIN, Loch See River Fleet.

NA CLAISE MOIRE, Loch

Location & Access 16/386050. Reaching Loch na Claise Moire involves a long, vigorous hike over rough ground to the north of the Oykel Bridge Hotel (16/385009). Miss the east edge of the forestry plantation by beginning your expedition at 16/397008 where the burn crosses under the A837 Bonar Bridge/Inchnadamph road.

Commentary This is compass and map country and you should maintain the high ground, striking north west up the burn to reach Loch a'Bhrochain and its satellite lochan after two miles (16/371031). Find the inlet stream on the north shore and continue north, climbing round the east shoulder of Fionn Bheinn Mhor (330m) to descend to Loch na Claise Moire. If you really want to make a day of it, fish round the south, east, and north shore of Loch na Claise Moire (to avoid a difficult crossing to the west), and locate the second inlet stream to the west. Tramp north up this stream to Loch Beinn an Eoin Bheag (16/381063) which lies in a small corrie at an altitude of 300m. Finally, and to complete your enjoyment, walk north-east from here, keeping the dark crags of Beinn an Eoin on your left, to fish remote Loch na Faic (16/398074). Return, happily downhill, to Loch na

179

Lairg, Loch Shin & surrounding area — OS Map 16

Claise Moire and, eventually, to the starting point on the A837.

Fish These lochs hardly see an artificial fly from one season to the next and they contain excellent numbers of wild brown trout which average 8oz in weight - and a few larger specimens as well.

Flies & Tactics This is a long, stiff walk which should not be undertaken lightly. Be well-prepared for whatever the weather may fling at you and let someone know where you are going and when you expect to return. Bank fishing all the way and it is safest to stay ashore. Do not wade. Loch na Claise Moire extends half a mile east/west and is almost one quarter of a mile wide. The north-west and west shore should provide breakfast, at least. After heavy rain, the narrow outlet stream which drains the loch west to the River Oykle is always worth a careful cast or two or three. The other waters noted above are easily understood and fish may be taken from all round their shorelines. This journey will take you 9 miles through splendid scenery with a good chance of seeing golden eagle, buzzard, golden plover and curlew along the way. Flies that tempt them are: Blue Zulu, Black Pennell, Peter Ross.

Permission & Charges The Oykel Bridge Hotel, Oykel Bridge, Rosehall, Sutherland. Tel: (01549) 441218. Cost: £5 per rod per day. Hotel guests have priority.

NA CREIGE RIABHAICH, Lochan See Loch Merkland.
NA FAIC, Loch See Loch na Claise Moire.
NA FAOLAIG, Lochan See Loch Cracail Mor.
NA FUARALACHD, Loch See Loch Beannach (Lairg).
NA GAINEIMH, Loch See Upper River Brora (Dalreavoch Lodge).
NA GLAS-CHOILLE, Loch See River Mudale.
NA MANG, Loch See Lock Merkland.
NAM BREAC BEAGA, Loch See River Blackwater (Ben Armine).
NAN CLAR, Loch See OS Map 17.
NAN RATH, Loch See Loch Merkland.
NAN UAN, Loch See River Mallart.

NAVER, Loch
Location & Access 16/620370. Easy access from the B873 Bettyhill/Altnaharra road which margins the north shore of the loch. The south shore is trackless and is best approached by boat.
Commentary Loch Naver, the headwater of the River Naver, is six miles east/west by up to half a mile wide. The loch is dominated to the south by Ben Klibreck (961m) which offers exciting hill walking for non-fishing companions. There is a caravan site by the shores of the loch at Grummore (16/610367). Note also the ruined broch here, and the remains of Grummore Township, cleared of its tenants in June 1814 at the start of the first of the two Strathnaver Clearances.
Fish Salmon, sea-trout and brown trout. Approximately 50/70 salmon are taken each season, mostly in the early months, March/April, and it can be cold, "savage entertainment". Fewer sea-trout these days, but plenty of sport with brown trout which average 8oz/10oz, and larger ferox, generally encountered whilst fishing for salmon.

Flies & Tactics Boat fishing brings best results and the shallow, west end of the loch, near Altnaharra, is the most productive area. Trolling is the preferred method, using various toby lures and Devons, but the extreme west end is restricted to fly only, between the post on the north shore and the large, flat, rock on the south shore. Your best opportunity for sport is to go out with a gillie. Failing that, keep within fifteen yards of the shore, fishing into the shallows. The salmon lie close in, other than near the mouth of the River Mudale, where they can be caught in the middle of the loch as well as at the margins. An outboard motor is essential. Loch Naver can often be a wild and dangerous water. Wear a life jacket at all times and stay seated whilst fishing. The boats are moored close to the road, in a little wood, at 16/59355. There are three further hill-lochs to the south of Loch Naver which also hold excellent brown trout: Loch Coire nam Feuran (16/665353) and Loch Ruigh nan Copag (16/649353), approached from the west end of Loch Naver by following the track past the old graveyard south into the hills for a distance of approximately 1.5 miles. The third, Loch Tarbhaidh (16/638360), lies in a magical glen between Beadaig (270m) and Cnoc Ruigh nan Copag (210m). The easiest way in to Loch Tarbhaidh is to have someone drop you off on the south shore of Loch Naver at 16/623367, then to climb due south for three-quarters of a mile to find the loch. Loch Tarbhaidh is one of the most attractive lochs in Sutherland. Three further lochs lie to the north of Loch Naver: Loch Molach (16/630392), Loch Gruama Mor (16/610395), and the unnamed lochan on Coire Buidhe (160m) at 16/614384. They are found by tracking the outlet burn uphill from near Grumbeg at 16/640387. Begin at Loch Molach, half a mile from the road, then continue up the inlet burn at the west end to find Loch Gruama after one mile. Return by hiking half a mile south to fish the unnamed lochan before angling along the north shoulder of Carn Gruama Beag (200m) to reach the road. All these lochs are fished from the shore, although a boat is sometimes available on Loch Tarbhaidh. For Loch Naver salmon try: Munro Killer, Willie Gunn, Garry Dog, General Practitioner, Green Highlander, Hairy Mary. For brown trout, offer Ke-He, March Brown, Willie Ross.

Permission & Charges The Altnaharra Hotel, Altnaharra, by Lairg, Sutherland IV27 4UE. Tel/Fax: (01549) 411222. Loch Naver: £20 per boat per day, two rods fishing. Outboard motor hire: £15 per day. Gillie: £35 per day. Fishing on the Loch Naver hill lochs is subject to availability and estate tenants have priority. Price: £15 per day.

OYKEL (LOWER), River
Location & Access The fishings begin to the west of Oykel Bridge at OS16/384013 and extend east for approximately 5 miles to the Kyle of Sutherland at 16/467012. Access is comfortably provided by the A837 Rosehall/Inchnadamph road to the north and a series of minor roads and tracks to the south of the stream.

OS Maps 16
Lairg, Loch Shin & surrounding area

Commentary The Lower Oykel fishings are divided into four beats and there are 64 named pools, including the pools on the River Einig which is a principal tributary of the River Oykel. The Oykel is a classic Highland spate river of great beauty flowing through wonderfully varied scenery; from the dramatic gorge and falls above the Oykel Bridge Hotel, to the fertile fields of Doune.

Fish The Oykel is one of Scotland's most productive salmon streams and the system has produced between 1,500 and 2,000 fish most seasons in recent years. The average weight of salmon is in the order of 7lb, but a fish of 18lb was taken from the Long Pool in June 1995.

Flies & Tactics The most difficult aspect of fishing the Lower Oykel is obtaining permission to do so. The river is invariably fully booked year after year by the same people. From the practical point of view, the fishing is straight forward with few technical problems. Even during the hot summer months anglers have good sport with a best day in a recent July of 32 fish and 142 for the month. A 15ft rod is advisable and the flies which do most damage include the Oykel General Practitioner, Munro Killer, Hairy Mary, Shrimp Fly, Willie Gunn, Stoats Tail, Garry Dog. Vary the size according to the water level and do not be afraid to experiment. Some of the most productive pools on the Lower Oykel are George, Sgolbach's Pool, Long Pool, Rock Pool, Lower George, Upper Farm Pool.

Permission & Charges To check on the unlikely chance of a vacant rod your best option is to contact Mr George Ross, c/o Oykel Bridge Hotel, Oykel Bridge, Rosehall, Sutherland. Tel: (01549) 441218. Prices on application.

OYKEL (Upper), River See OS Map 15.
POLL A'PHAC, Loch See Loch Fiag.
PREAS NAN SGIATHANACH, Lochan See River Fleet.
PRIVATE WATERS AIRIGH MHOR, Loch (16/692023); IAIN BHUIDHE, Lochan (16/689012); A'GHIBHAIS, Lochan (16/699011); NA GAOITHE, Lochan (16/663007); NA SAOBHAIDE, Loch (16/652016). These lochs all lie to the south of the River Fleet and the A839 Mound/Lairg road and they are preserved by the owner. The lochs which lie between Loch Shin to the east and Glencassley to the west are preserved by the owner. They are: NAFUARALAICH, Loch (16/487065), NA CAILLICH, Loch (16/517083), Loch (16/470112), DUBH MOR, Loch (16/440139), DUBH BEAG, Loch (16/421151), A'CHOIRE, Lochan (16/462134), LANGWELL, Loch (16/412130), SHEILA, Loch (16/455072), DOIR A'CHATHA, Loch (16/493039).

RIMSDALE, Loch
Location & Access 16/740355. Approach from 16/740399 on the B871 Kinbrace/Syre road. A track, which borders the western edge of the forestry plantation, reaches the shore of the loch and boats after one mile.
Commentary Loch Rimsdale is over three miles north/south by up to three-quartrs of a mile wide, joined through narrows to Loch nan Clar (16/755355) and Loch Badanloch (17/770345) east. Can be wild, windy, and unforgiving, but it is one of the most productive lochs in the area.
Fish Excellent stocks of brown trout, averaging 8oz/10oz and larger fish as well: best brown trout in recent years weighed 9lb 8oz.
Flies & Tactics Boat fishing brings best results and an outboard motor is essential if you are to explore the most productive areas: the south-west shoreline, by the inlet from Loch Trudersciag (16/7110326); the east bay, before Loch nan Clar, and the south-east shore. Give them: Black Pennell, Grouse & Claret, Dunkeld.
Permission & Charges Boat, £15 per day with two anglers fishing, outboard hire, £15 per day, including fuel. Bank fishing, £5 per rod per day. Contact: Brian Lyall, Badanloch, by Kinbrace, Sutherland. Tel: (01431) 831232. Tony Henderson, The Garvault Hotel, Badanloch, by Kinbrace, Sutherland. Tel: (01431) 831224.

RUIGH NAN COPAG, Loch See Loch Naver.
SALACHAIDH, Loch See River Fleet.
SGEIREACH, Loch (Dalreavoch) See Upper River Brora (Dalreavoch Lodge).

SHIN, Loch
Location & Access 16/500160. Park at the boathouse (16/570076) by the A836 Lairg/Altnaharra road, one mile north from Lairg.
Commentary One of the largest lochs in Scotland, some seventeen miles north/south by up to one mile wide and part of a hydro-electricity generating system. Often wild, windy and dangerous, but on a calm day, one of the most attractive waters in the north.
Fish A wide range of brown trout from 8oz specimens right up to ferox trout of 7lb and more.
Flies & Tactics Boat fishing is the fishing method, not only because there are soft margins, but also because it facilitates getting around this huge expanse of water. As a general rule, concentrate along the margins: if you can't see the bottom then you are fishing too far out. A good place to start is in the vicinity of Gull Island (16/530145), the bay at 16/500170, and off the mouth of the Fiag Burn (16/466204). At the north end, where Loch Shin is joined by Loch a'Ghriama (16/392260), work the narrow neck leading north-west to Corriekinloch and the mouth of the Abhainn a'Choire burn (16/370250). Loch a'Ghriama also holds good stocks of excellent brown trout of similar size and quality to the fish in Loch Shin. Offer them: Black Pennell, Invicta, Peter Ross.
Permission & Charges J M Ross, The Lairg Angling Club, St Murie, Lairg, Sutherland. Tel: (01549) 402010. Bank fishing at £5 per rod per day, £15 per week. Boat hire, £15 per day plus £15 for outboard motor (essential) hire, plus cost of extra fuel. Boats can't be pre booked. If you wish to obtain a boat, call at the Club Office at the loch between 9am and 11pm on the morning you wish to fish. The Overscaig Hotel has boats on both Loch Shin and on Loch a'Ghriama. Cost £15 per day for two rods, and £12 per day for outboard motor and fuel. Overscaig Hotel, by Lairg, Sutherland. Tel: (01549) 431203.

Strath of Kildonan — OS Map 16-17

SHIN, River See OS Map 21.
STRATH DUCHALLY, Loch See Loch Eileanach (Crask).
SUIL A'GHRIAMA, Loch See Loch Eileanach (Crask).
TARBHAIDH, Loch See Loch Naver.
TIGH NA CREIGE, Loch See Loch Craggie (Lairg).
TIRRY, River See Loch Eileanach (Crask).
TRUDERSCAIG, Loch See River Mallart.
ULBHACH COIRE, Loch See Loch Merkland.
VAGASTIE, River See River Mudale.

Strath of Kildonan

A'BHIDIDH, Loch See Loch Farlary.

AN RUTHAIR, Loch
Location & Access 17/865369 The loch lies adjacent to the A897 Helmsdale/Melvich road. A track, to Greamachary (17/851394) at 17/880378, gives easy access to the north and north west shoreline of the loch. The south end of the loch is close to the main road.
Commentary Loch an Ruthair is one and a half miles north/south by up to half a mile wide. The loch is a public water supply and rather featureless. Nevertheless, the surrounding scenery is very attractive, with the Ben Griam mountains to the west and Achentoul Hill (346m) to the east. Britain's highest Iron Age hill fort is situated at the top of Ben Griam Mor (590m). A number of smaller waters lie close by: Loch Culaidh (17/863390), adjacent to the Greamachary track, Lucy Loch (17/878397), near the railway line, Lochan Dubh (17/881371), to the north of Achentoul Lodge, and Loch Arichlinie (17/848350), a one mile tramp south-west from Loch an Ruthair. These waters drain south through Strath Beg into the Helmsdale River.
Fish With the exception of Loch an Ruthair, there is nothing really large in any of the lochs noted above, but the chance of a few trout of over 1lb in weight. Although Loch an Ruthair still has a vast stock of small trout, it has improved considerably in recent years, through purposeful management. In recent years, trout of up to 6lb 8oz have been caught.
Flies & Tactics There are three boats on Loch an Ruthair and two boats on Loch Arichlinie. Bank fishing can also be productive and when doing so it is best to stay firmly on terra firma. The north-west shore of Loch an Ruthair, below the bulk of Creag Sail a'Bhathaich (346m), is a good place to begin. On Loch Arichlinie, fish are taken all round the loch, but the vicinity of the inlet stream is the best place to start your attack. The other waters mentioned are easily understood and easily fished. Offer: Loch Ordie, Grouse & Claret and Dunkeld.
Permission & Charges Contact: Angus Ross, Head Keeper, Achentoul Estate, Kinbrace, Helmsdale, Sutherland. Tel: (01431) 831227. Bank fishing at approximately £6 per rod per day when not required for estate tenants.

ARICHLINIE, Loch See Loch an Ruthair.

ASCAIG, Loch
Location & Access 17/850255. Access from Borrobol Estate at 17/868265 via a well-maintained estate road.
Commentary One of the most attractive and productive trout lochs in the area. The surrounding scenery and wildlife is stunning, with a good chance of seeing golden eagle, peregrine, buzzard, hen harrier, black-throated diver, red deer and otter.
Fish Loch Ascaig contains excellent stocks of wild brown trout which average 10oz as well as good numbers of much larger fish and trout of over 2lb are not uncommon.
Flies & Tactics The loch is approximately three quarters of a mile east/west by up to 300 yards wide. There is rich feeding, particularly at the west end where there are extensive weed banks. Three boats are available, although bank fishing can be just as productive. The south-west shoreline is a good place to begin. Ascaig trout are non-discriminatory and rise readily to most patterns of artificial fly, but a Loch Ordie, somewhere on the cast, is a 'must'.
Permission & Charges The fishing is let in conjunction with comfortable estate cottages which sleep from four to six people. Costs vary from £226 to £339 per property, per week, including trout fishing on Loch Ascaig and salmon fishing on the River Frithe, which is a principal tributary of the famous River Helmsdale. For bookings, contact: Sir Michael Wigan, Borrobol Estate, Kinbrace, Helmsdale, Sutherland. Tel: (01431) 831264.

BAD NA H-EARBA, Loch See Lochan Dubh cul na h-Amaite.

BADANLOCH, Loch
Location & Access 17/770345 Loch Badanloch lies to the south of the B871 Kinbrace/Syre road. Leave the B871 at 17/800330 and follow the track to the boat mooring point at 17/788330 at the head of the loch.
Commentary Loch Badanloch is the eastern section of a series of lochs which feed the Helmsdale River. These lochs are interconnected and, to the west, include Loch nan Clar (17/765350) and Loch Rimsdale (16/740355). The system covers an area of approximately 6 square miles and is often exposed to high winds. The surrounding scenery is spectacular, with Ben Griam Mor (590m) to the north and Ben Klibreck (961m) to the west.
Fish Vast numbers of modest-sized, attractive, wild brown trout, some huge ferox trout, Arctic char, and the possibility of an occasional salmon.
Flies & Tactics An outboard motor is essential if you are to cover the loch effectively. Even then, you will need at least a full week in order to do so. Always wear a life-jacket and beware of barely-submerged rocks. Hasten about your business slowly and with care. Loch Badanloch and Loch-nan Clar are shallow, peat-stained waters, and you should concentrate your atten-

OS Map 17 — Strath of Kildonan

tion around the margins, about 10 to 20yards out from the bank. A good drift is from the island of Rubha Mor (17/770345), south to the jagged bay where the burn from Loch an Alltan Fhearna (16/750335) flows into Loch Badanloch. However, fish rise and are taken throughout the whole system. Most patterns of artificial fly produce results. Start with Black Pennell, Soldier Palmer and Silver Butcher. No need to cross the fingers. If the wind beats you off Loch Badanloch, bank fish, or hike south to the shelter and comfort of Loch na Gaineimh (17/767305) where good fish also lie.

Permission & Charges Boat, £15 per day with two anglers fishing. Outboard hire, £15 per day, including fuel. Bank fishing, £5 per rod per day. Tony Henderson, Garvault Hotel, Badanloch, by Kinbrace, Sutherland. Tel:(01431) 831224.

BADANLOCH, Water See River Helmsdale.
BANNOCK, Burn See River Helmsdale.

BERRIEDALE, Water

Location & Access Source 17/940345 Outflow 17/121225. Access to the Berriedale Estate is from the A9 Inverness/Wick road at 17/118226. The river, and its tributary, Langwell Water, are approached from estate roads which border their banks.

Commentary Both streams lie amidst spectacular scenery and are separated from each other by the Caithness mountains: Scaraben (626m), Maiden Pap (484m), Smean (509m), Morven (706m) and Small Mount (533m). The lower reaches of the rivers flow through magnificent woodlands, the upper reaches are enclosed by heather-clad moorland. Wildlife abounds: roe deer, red deer, badger, otter, fox, blue hare, pine marten, and a wide variety of birds and wild flowers. The estate has beautiful gardens and an excellent nursery garden which are open to the public.

Fish Returns for both rivers vary, year by year, according to water conditions and fishing effort, generally between 60 to 120 salmon and grilse each season. Most fish are taken from Berriedale Water and include a few sea-trout.

Flies & Tactics Berriedale Water is divided into three, two-rod beats, rotating daily. One beat is reserved throughout the season for the local angling association. The most productive pools on the river are Falls Pool and Lord Galway's Pool. Langwell Water, although smaller than Berriedale Water, also has a number of good holding-pools, including Parapet, Turnol, Lady's Tent, and Putting Stone Pool. Best months, depending upon weather and water conditions, are July, August and September. Stalk your salmon, keep well back from the river bank and use light tackle. Trout patterns, particularly Black Pennell, can be very useful. Otherwise, use Garry Dog, Green Highlander, Willie Gunn, Stoat's Tail, Hairy Mary. Stay clear of the dangerous, narrow gorge, where Langwell Water joins Berriedale Water. There are also two, small, remote, lochs which offer sport with modest wild brown trout: Loch na Stairne (17/961303), a group of four, tiny pools between Cnoc Chaorunn Bheag (400m) to the south and Creagan Liath (368m) to the north; and Loch Scalabsdale (17/964244), the source of Langwell Water, which lies on a plateau to the east of The Child's Seat (468m), Creag nan Gearr (516m) and Creag Scalabsdale (555m). The Estate also has Loch Borgue (17/120271) which holds some very fine trout. Access to the loch is via a rough track which leaves the A9 Inverness/Wick road at 17/133262. Bank fishing can be productive. Offer the trout: Blue Zulu, Soldier Palmer, Peter Ross.

Permission & Charges Fishing may occasionally be available to casual visitors and will cost in the order of £250/£300 plus VAT, per beat, per week. Applications, in writing only please, to: The Factor, Welbeck Estates, Estate Office, Berriedale, Caithness KW7 6HE.

BORGUE, Loch See Berriedale Water.
BRAIGH NA H-AIBHNE, Loch See Dunbeath Water.
BREAC, Loch (Dunbeath) See Dunbeath Water.

BRORA, Loch

Location & Access 17/852080 Easily accessible from the town of Brora on the A9 Inverness/Wick road via a public road which margins the north shoreline of the loch.

Commentary Loch Brora is three miles north/south by up to half a mile wide, divided into three distinct basins, known respectively, north to south, as Top Loch, Middle Loch and Bottom Loch. The loch is generally shallow with an average depth of 22ft and the dominant geological feature overlooking the water is the dramatic Carrol Rock (208m) by the west shore. The loch can be wild and windy, but the setting is spectacular. Loch Brora is one of the most productive fisheries in Sutherland.

Fish Primarily sea-trout, and in good numbers: approximately 300/400 each season. Salmon are also taken and the loch contains excellent brown trout as well as Arctic char.

Flies & Tactics Boat fishing only. The best fishing areas are, on Top Loch, round the margins; off the north shore, where the Upper Brora river enters (17/834097), eastwards and then south, round the area of the Luncheon Cottage and Jetty at 17/837098 which is also a noted salmon lie, then down to Salmon Point at 17/8410905. Miss the Gordonbush Burn bank, then work the southern section to where the flow empties into Middle Loch. On Middle Loch, fish the north and south ends, ignoring the east and west shoreline. On Bottom Loch, fish the Killin Narrows (17/855068) and all down the west shore. Flies: Black Pennell, Mallard & Claret, Loch Ordie, Blue Zulu and a 'dapped' daddy-long-legs.

Permission & Charges Guns & Tackle, Rossyln Street, Brora, Sutherland. Tel: (01408) 621373. A boat, with two rods fishing, costs £30 per day. The Golspie Angling Club also has a boat on Loch Brora (see Loch Horn entry), as do The Sutherland Estates (see Lower River Brora entry).

BRORA (Lower), River

Location & Access Source 17/861053 Outflow 17/910039. Easy access from a public road which margins the north bank of the river.

Strath of Kildonan — OS Map 17

Commentary The Lower River Brora is one of the most productive salmon streams in Sutherland and it extends for three miles, from Loch Brora to the sea. Rob Wilson, 'Mr Brora', is the most famous exponent of the stream and his booklet, 'Fishing the Lower River Brora', will greatly add, to your understanding of the river, and your enjoyment of fishing this wonderful stream.
Fish The Brora system, as a whole, generally produces approximately 800 salmon and grilse each season, as well as good numbers of sea-trout.
Flies & Tactics The River Brora has produced some huge salmon over the years, including a fish of 45lb Even in recent years, fish of over 20lb in weight are not uncommon. A 15ft rod is advised, not only to cover the lies effectively, but also to control any fish hooked. The river is divided into two beats, Upper and Lower. Each beat fishes 4 rods. Some of the most productive pools are: Ford Pool, Rallan, New Pool, Madman; and Bengie Pool, where Rob Wilson's brother, John hooked and landed a 40lb salmon on a size 8 Green Highlander whilst fishing with a 9ft trout rod. Flies: Green Highlander, Willie Gunn (named by Rob Wilson in honour of the Gordonbush Estate gillie, Willie Gunn), Garry Dog, General Practitioner, Brora Ranger, Stoat's Tail and Red & Black Waddingtons.
Permission & Charges The Factor, The Sutherland Estates, Estate Office, Duke Street, Golspie, Sutherland KW10 6RR. Tel: (01408) 633268; Fax: (01408) 633800. The Sutherland Estate has attractive, very well furnished and comfortable properties at Dalreavoch, Uppat and Ben Armine for let with sporting rights. Finlyson & Hughes, 29 Barossa Place, Perth PE1 5EP. Tel: (01738) 625134; Fax: (01738) 639017. Prices on application.

CATHERINE'S, Loch See Dunbeath Water.
CROSS REFERENCE For details and information on the following lochs see OS Map 11: Loch a'Cheracher, Loch Coire na Beinne and Lochan Airigh Leathaid.
CULAIDH, Loch See Loch an Ruthair.

DUBH CUL NA H-AMAITE, Lochan
Location & Access 17/760132 The majority of this loch appears on OS Map 16 but because it is accessed from Sciberscross (17/776101) on OS Map 17 and fished in conjunction with Loch Bad na h-Earba (17/767138) it is included here. Approach from Sciberscross Lodge on the Upper River Brora via a good track. Loch Dubh Cul na h-Amaite is to the right of the track, after 2.5 miles; Loch Bad na h-Earba is a short walk from the track to the north-east.
Commentary The fishing is in the hands of Sciberscross Lodge which may also have has access to salmon fishing on the River Brora and on Loch Brora and on other local waters.
Fish Excellent quality wild brown trout which average 10oz/12oz with good numbers of heavier fish as well.
Flies & Tactics All pretty straight-forward as fish rise and and are taken all round both lochs. Both boat and bank fishing and large baskets are the rule rather than the exception. The Lodge will advise on the fly of the moment, but a good start can be made with: Ke-He, March Brown, Dunkeld.
Permission & Charges Sciberscross Lodge, Strath Brora, Rogart, Sutherland IV28 3YQ. Tel: (01408) 641246; Fax: (01408) 641465 .

DUBH, Loch (Achentoul) See Loch an Ruthair.
DUBH, Loch (Dunbeath) See Dunbeath Water.
DUNBEATH WATER (River) There is no public access and all fishing on the river and on the estate lochs is preserved by the owner.

FARLARY, Loch
Location & Access 17/772050. Loch Farlary lies 5 miles up Dunrobin Glen, immediately adjacent to and to the west of the minor road from Golspie.
Commentary A great little loch for beginners.
Fish Modest brown trout which average 6oz/8oz. You will find larger trout in Loch a'Bhididh (17/820083) which is best approached from Kilbraur (17/823100) at the head of Loch Brora, but be prepared for a 'decent tramp' to get there.
Flies & Tactics Both lochs are easily fished from the shore, Loch Farlary trout will take most patterns of artificial fly. The inhabitants of Loch a'Bhidid and the unnamed lochan are more circumspect. Begin with Ke-He, Black Pennell and Dunkeld.
Permission & Charges The Factor, The Sutherland Estates, Duke Street, Golspie, Sutherland. KW10 6RR. Tel: (01408)633268; Fax: (01408) 633800. Estate tenants have priority, but casual lets are sometimes available at approximately £10 per rod per day.

FRITHE, River
Location & Access Source 17/762254 Outfall 17/872269. Access to the lower river is from Borrobol Farm at 17/867267 where there is a parking place and a ford across the stream. The upper river is accessed from the third quarry (17/859257) on the right of the track out to Loch Ascaig (17/850255). Park, then follow the fence north down to the river.
Commentary The River Frithe (pronounced 'Free') is a primary tributary of the famous River Helmsdale and the owner has recently completed a three-year plan to improve salmon access and spawning facilities. Fishing is from above Borrobol Railway bridge, just before the Frithe joins the Helmsdale, upstream for about two miles. Eleven new pools have been created.
Fish There has been no serious fishing effort on the river in recent years, therefore, catch returns have little meaning. A few salmon are always taken, but the effect of the improvements have yet to be put to the test. However, the 1999 season produced more than a dozen fish.
Flies & Tactics This is a spate river and sport is dependent upon good water levels. Given water, the river is delightful and easy to fish. Light tackle and 'fine and far off' is the method to use on the lower river. The upper reaches have deep, dark, peaty 'pots' which require skill and cunning for success. Vary the size of fly according to conditions. Try: Hairy Mary, Willie Gunn, Goat's Toe, Garry Dog and General Practitioner.

OS Map 17 — Strath of Kildonan

Permission & Charges The cost of salmon fishing is included in the cost of the rental of Borrobol Estate cottages, which also includes trout fishing on Loch Ascaig. See Loch Ascaig entry for details.

GLUTT, Loch
Location & Access See Dunbeath Water.

HELMSDALE, River
Location & Access Source 17/780340 Outfall 17/028153. The river is accessible from the A897 Helmsdale/Melvich road which parallels the east bank of the stream north to Kinbrace. Thereafter, access is via the B871 Kinbrace/Syre road.
Commentary The Helmsdale is a classic Highland stream which flows through wonderful countryside. The Helmsdale is also highly 'exclusive' and obtaining a rod on the main river is difficult. Those anglers fortunate enough to gain entry to a January week often have to wait years before being promoted to even a May week. However, the first mile or so of the river is open to the public. This is also true in regard to the upper river. The Badanloch Water, between the outfall from Loch Badanloch to Loch Achnamoine, and the Bannock Burn, from the outfall from Loch an Ruthair to its confluence with the main stream is often available for day lets.
Fish The Association Water (the first mile) produces upwards of 300 salmon each season. The upper river produces approximately 100 salmon. The Association water also offers excellent sport with sea-trout, particularly at night.
Flies & Tactics When other northern salmon streams suffer from lack of water, the Helmsdale system benefits from the metered flow from the catchment lochs: Loch Badanloch, Loch-nan Clar and Loch Rimsdale. Consequently, water levels are generally good throughout the season. The Association Water is restricted to eight rods per day, the upper river fishes two rods per day. A 15ft rod is advisable for the Association Water, but a strong single-handed rod is all that is required to tackle the smaller upper streams. After April, the rule is floating lines only and the use of treble hooks is not allowed. Small doubles work best. Try: Yellow Torrish, Green Highlander, Willie Gunn, Garry Dog, Stoat's Tail, General Practitioner, Hairy Mary and Black Doctor.
Permission & Charges For the Association Water, contact: Strathullie Crafts, Dunrobin Street, Helmsdale, Sutherland. Tel: (01431) 821343. From January to June, £17.65 per rod per day, July to September, £21.15 per rod per day. 8 daily tickets are available on a first-come first-served basis. For the Badanloch Water contact Brian Lyall, Badanloch, by Kinbrace, Sutherland. Tel: (01431) 831232. £15.00 per rod per day. For Bannock Burn contact Angus Ross, Head Keeper, Achentoul Estate, Achentoul, Kinbrace, Sutherland. Tel: (01431) 831227. £15 per rod per day.

HORN, Loch
Location & Access 17/797060 From Golspie on the A9 Inverness/Wick road, follow the minor road north east up Dunrobin Glen to Bridge of Horn (17/800048). Park, and climb steeply north up the line of the outlet burn to reach the loch after a tough half hour tramp.
Commentary Magnificent scenery and wildlife all the way. The loch lies on a shallow plateau between Ben Horn (521m) to the east and Meal Odhar (405m) to the west.
Fish Excellent brown trout which average 10oz to 12oz.
Flies & Tactics The angling club maintains a boat on Loch Horn, but bank fishing can be just as rewarding. When boat fishing, concentrate your efforts in the shallow margins. If you can't see the bottom, then you are too far out. Offer them: Black Zulu, Grouse & Claret and Dunkeld. In the evening and after dusk, try a dry fly.
Permission & Charges Golspie Angling Club, c/o Lindsay & Co, Main Street, Golspie, Sutherland. Tel: (01408) 633212. Access to the Golspie Angling Club waters is conditional upon joining the club. The annual subscription is £10. Use of boats costs £4, bank fishing £3. The use of the club boat on Loch Brora costs £6 per day.

LOCH NA GAINEIMH, Loch (Badanloch) See Loch Badanloch.
LOCH-NAN CLAR See Loch Badanloch.

LUNNDAIDH, Loch
Location & Access 17/785007. Turn north from the A9 Inverness/Wick road near Culmaily at 17/816994. Park at the end of the minor road and then follow a good track north west up Strath Lunndaidh for a mile and a half to reach the loch.
Commentary Loch Lunndaidh is approximately one mile long by up to 300 yards wide. The loch is often windy, lying as it does in a steep glen between Beinn Lunndaidh (446m) to the north and Aberscross Hill (275m) to the south. The Golspie Angling Club maintains a boat on Loch Lunndaidh.
Fish Good stocks of brown trout which average 8oz to 10oz.
Flies & Tactics Bank fishing can be just as productive as fishing from the boat. The south shore, where the burn tumbles in from Aberscross Hill, and the north end of the loch, in the vicinity of the inlet stream, are the most productive fishing areas. First cast: Ke-He, March Brown and Peter Ross.
Permission & Charges See Loch Horn.

MHADADH, Loch See Dunbeath Water.
NA STAIRNE, Loch See Berriedale Water.
NAM BO RIABHACH, Lochan See Dunbeath Water.
NAN CAORACH, Loch (Beinn a'Bhragaidh) See Loch Horn.
PRIVATE WATERS TUBAIRNAICH, Loch (17/877089); AN DUBH, Lochan (17/881078). These lochs are preserved by the owner.
SALACHAIDH, Loch See OS Map 16.
SCALABSDALE, Loch See Berriedale Water.

Sound of Harris

OS Map 18

Sound of Harris

Isles of Harris and North Uist Introduction
No matter where you fish in Harris and North Uist, permission must be obtained before doing so. At times, it is difficult to establish who owns the fishing rights and whether or not access is available. For Harris, a good place to seek advice is: Sportsworld, 1 Francis Street, Stornoway. Tel: (01851) 705464. For North Uist, you should consider becoming an Associate Member of the North Uist Angling Club. This will give you access to some very good trout lochs (with the chance of salmon and sea-trout in some cases). Contact Philip Harding, 1 Claddach, Kyles, North Uist HS6 5EW, Tel: 01876 580341. You should also, always, seek permission from the local crofter before crossing his land to reach a fishing location. Where access information is known, it is noted in the appropriate text. However, please double-check this information before fishing as details may change.

A' BHEALAICH, Loch See Loch Carran.
A'BHARPA, Loch See Loch nan Geireann entry.
A'BHUIRD, Loch See Loch Hunder.
A'CHAPULL, Loch See Loch Eashader.
A'CHARRA, Loch See Loch Horisary.
A'CHONNACHAIR, Loch See Loch Hunder.
A'PHOBUILL, Loch See Oban Irpeig.

AIRD AN DUIN, Loch
Location & Access 18/919768 A remote brown trout loch east of Newtonferry, best visited in conjunction with a number of other lochs along the way.
Commentary Park by the north shore of Loch an Sticir (18/89777) on the minor road before Newtonferry. Walk east over easy ground to reach Loch Camas-Duibhe (18/915777) after on mile. Walk south now for 15mins to find Loch Iosal an Duin (18/918771) with its Neolithic ruin on a tiny, man-made islet at the sound end. A step further south will bring you to Loch Aird an Duin and lunch. The return journey is absolutely splendid and one of the principal reasons for making this expedition. Follow the stream that feeds the Tidal Ponds uphill to Loch na Carnaich (18/910760), then continue through Gleann na Beiste to Loch Dubh na Moine (18/905762). Climb vigorously north-west from Loch Dubh na Moine to gain Bealach na Beine, between Beinn Bhreac (148m) to the north and Beinn Mhor (148m) to the south. Descend from the bealach down the line of the burn leading back to Loch an Sticir.
Fish Brown trout which average 8oz, seatrout of up to and over 3lb.
Flies & Tactics A wonderful, five-mile day out in North Uist, with magnificent views north across Bernery to the mountains of Harris. The lochs are easily 'read' and covered from the shore. Check the tide times before setting out. Flies: Black Pennell, Grouse & Claret, Silver Invicta.
Permission & Charges See Loch Scaapar.

ALATAIR, Loch See Loch na Criadhach.

AN ARMUINN, Loch See Loch an Duin, Laiaval.
AN DAIMH, Loch See Loch Hunder.
AN DUIN, Loch (Borve) See Borve Loch.
AN DUIN, Loch (Cheese Bay) See Loch na Cointich.

AN DUIN, Loch (Laiaval)
Location & Access 18/890735 Easily accessible from Lochportain road. Park at 18/894734 at the sound end where the angling club boat is moored and row north to reach Loch an Duin.
Commentary This is the principal North Uist Angling Club loch and it extends across the moor for almost one mile north/south by up to half a mile east/west. The system is complex and includes Loch Bru (18/897739) as its eastern arm. The north and north-west arm of Loch an Duin, known locally as 'Deadman's Loch' (18/892747), can also be reached from the main loch. However, the north-east section, Loch an Armuinn (18/901747), is accessible only on foot. Follow the inlet burn from Deadman's Loch. There are three other lochs here which are worth a visit: Loch na Creige at 18/884737, Cama-lochan at 18/901739 and Loch a Buaile, to the south of the Lochportain road at 18/900737. Apart from these waters, there are a number of unnamed lochans surrounding Loch an Duin which offer a good chance of sport. You should particularly note the lochs at 18/889744, to the west of Loch an Duin; 18/891748 and 18/894748 to the north of Deadman's Loch; and 18/899742 to the east of Loch an Duin.
Fish Good quality brown trout which average 8-10oz, but much larger fish as well, of up to and over 3lb in weight.
Flies & Tactics Dour, and boat fishing makes it easier to get about this scattered water, but bank fishing can bring just as rewarding results. On the main body of Loch an Duin, arrange a drift from the ruins of the Neolithic dun on the west shore which gives the loch its name, east through the small islands. Fish the west bay on Deadman's Loch and the north-east shore on Loch Armuinn. Flies: Blue Zulu, Soldier Palmer, Alexandra.
Permission & Charges See Loch Scaapar.

AN DUIN, Loch (Taransay)
Location & Access 18/021013. Getting here requires determination and organisation, but it is worth the effort. Loch an Duin is on the deserted island of Taransay, off the west coast of South Harris. Arrange transport in Leverburgh or through the Rodel Hotel.
Commentary Apart from Loch an Duin, there are four other significant lochs on the island: Loch na Gaoithe (18/024001), Loch Cromlach (18/025004), Loch Shinnadale (18/025012), and Loch Starabraigh (18/006007). The best course of action is to camp out near the site of Clach a Teampuill chapel at 18/014006, overlooking the sands by sea loch Na Uidhe. The island is 'pinched' here - the eastern section, where most of the lochs lie, being mountainous and craggy, whilst Loch Starabraigh, to the west, on Aird Vanish (99m), is in more gentle country.
Fish These little lochs are infrequently, if ever, fished and contain trout which average 8oz. Seatrout may be

186

OS Map 18 — Sound of Harris

encountered in Loch Starabraigh, and off the beach at Loch na h-Uidhe, and the beach to the north at Traigh a'Siar (18/009009).
Flies & Tactics The first essential is to be well-organised for your adventure, and to ensure that your transport understands when to return for you. Bear in mind that if adverse weather conditions arise, you could be marooned. Be provisioned, just in case. Loch an Duin drains through the eastern lochs to the sea at Paible by the remains of ruined shielings. Begin by climbing north from Clach an Teampuill to explore Loch an Duin, then follow the outlet stream south to the other waters. Return to the start round the west side of Beinn na h-Uidhe (137m), fishing little Loch na Gaoithe along the way. Flies: Black Pennell, March Brown, Silver Butcher.
Permission & Charges Taransay, now made famous by the BBC television series 'Castaway', belongs to Norman McKay, Horgabost, Harris. Tel: (01859) 550214. Prices on application.

AN EILEAN, Loch (Vallay) See Loch Scolpaig.
AN STICIR, Loch See Loch Aird an Duin.
AN STRUMORE, Loch See Loch Fada (Lochmaddy).
AN T-SAGAIRT, Loch See Aulasary (Upper Loch).
AN T-SEARRAICH, Loch See Loch Skealtar.
AN TOM, Loch See Loch nan Struban.

AONGHAIS, Loch
Location & Access 18/857738 Loch Aonghais is one of a number of accessible lochs lying adjacent to the A865, the circular road from Lochmaddy round the north of North Uist. The others are: Loch Nighe (18/855743), north of Loch Aonghais, and Loch na Morgha, (18/870743); Loch Steinavat (18/876742), Oban Trumisgarry (18/873746) and the unnamed brackish inlet at 18/878748 below the site of Tobar Chaluim Chille (18/879751) on the south shoulder of Laiaval (69m). These later lochs are approached from the B893 Newtonferry (18/895784) road.
Commentary A new, fast, road has been built on this section of the A865, replacing the old single-track carriageway. Park with care. As the season advances weed becomes a real problem, so visit them early in the season.
Fish Nothing much to shout about but you should catch breakfast.
Flies & Tactics Easy bank fishing on the freshwater lochs. The south shore of Loch Aonghais, near the Dun, is the most productive area. Take care with the tide on the others and seek local advice from the Angling Club before launching your attack. Flies: Black Pennell, Grouse & Claret, Peter Ross.
Permission & Charges See Loch Scaapar.

ARDENNISH, Loch See Loch Tergavat.

AULASARY, Upper Loch
Location & Access 18/937725. Visit Upper Loch Aulasary as part of a more extended day out fishing a number of named and unnamed lochs on the fertile, low-lying land to the north of Lochportain (18/942719).
Commentary Easy walking and bank fishing, with the most distant loch being one and a half miles north-west from the start point by the church at 18/947722. The largest loch here is Loch an t-Sagairt (18/948724), covering an area of approx. 20 acres. Cama-loch (18/942723), to the south, drains into Upper Loch Aulasary which flows north to reach the sea after quarter of a mile. There are five unnamed lochs further north and west, all of which are worth a visit, particularly the two at 18/932728 and 18/931730 which are also joined to the sea.
Fish Some nice brown trout of up to and over 1lb in weight.
Flies & Tactics Bank fishing, and stay ashore. Wading only moves the fish out into deeper water. Some of these lochs become very weedy as the season advances so plan an early assault. Also have a cast for seatrout in sea loch Aulasary, particularly between Orasay Island and where the little stream enters at 18/943733. Flies: Ke-He, Grouse & Claret, Black Pennell.
Permission & Charges See Loch Scaapar.

BEAG, Loch (Boreray) See Loch Bhruist.
BEAG NAN IAN, Loch See Loch Scolpaig.
BHIORAIN, Loch See Loch Vausary.

BHRUIST, Loch
Location & Access 18/918825 This is the principal loch on the Island of Berneray, off the north coast of North Uist. The other loch is Little Loch Borve (18/913818). Approach by the new causeway from the mainland.
Commentary Berneray is a wildlife paradise, with exciting flora and fauna and it is worth considering an extended stay in order to properly explore all this haven of tranquility has to offer. Less accessible is the Island of Boreray, to the west of Berneray, which was inhabited until the early 1960s. Boreray has one large, loch, Loch Mor (18/850811), and a smaller neighbour, Loch Beag (18/850806). You will have to arrange private transport from either Newtonferry or Berneray to visit them.
Fish Loch Bhruist and Little Loch Borve were recently stocked with brown trout which seem to have thrived mightily. Fish of up to and over 2lb in weight have been caught. The Boreray lochs are reputed to contain trout of 8oz/10oz, although it is very much unexplored territory and could hold a few surprises.
Flies & Tactics Loch Bhruist is a large water, almost half a mile north/south, shallow, and easily fished from the shore with safe wading. Little Loch Borve, to the south, is tiny and is best attacked back from the margin. Do not wade. Offer: Soldier Palmer, Greenwell's Glory, Silver Butcher.
Permission & Charges For details of fishing and excellent B & B accommodation contact: Mr D A MacKillop, Ferry Road, Ardmaree, Berneray, North Uist, Outer Hebrides. Tel:(01876) 540235.

BORVE, Loch
Location & Access 18/040950 Approach from the A859 Tarbert/Leverburgh. Turn left at 18/035953 and follow the track past the little forest to reach the loch after a drive of half a mile.

Sound of Harris — OS Map 18

Commentary An easily accessible, small loch which offers good sport in very attractive surroundings. There are additional fishing opportunities in the sea nearby, at the mouth of Gil Meodal in Glen Horgabost (18/046969) and at the mouth of the Borve river at 18/034952, near Borve Lodge. In the hills to the east of Borve, approached from the road by Heather Graham's craft centre, is Loch an Duin (18/035944), another, easily accessible, attractive seatrout and brown trout fishery, fed by a stream from Loch Eachkavat (18/033933) below the north face of Bleaval (398m). These hills, Heileasbhal Mor (384m), Bulabhall (354m), Slettaval (224m) and Bleaval, are scattered with small lochs and lochans, the principal two being Loch nam Breac (18/068921) and Loch na Caillich (18/053927). They are really tiny, rarely fished, and hold trout in the order of 6oz. Nevertheless, they offer good sport in perfect surroundings and there is always the possibility, because so little is known about them, that some of these unexplored waters could produce a candidate for the glass case.
Fish Seatrout in Borve Loch, Loch an Duin and in the sea. Brown trout in these lochs as well, and in the other waters noted above
Flies & Tactics If you venture out into the wilderness, be well-prepared and compass and mapped. The main lochs are fished from the boat and are easily 'read'. Check tide times and local advice for seatrout fishing in the sea. Flies: Blue Zulu, Soldier Palmer, Alexandra.
Permission & Charges See Laxdale River.

BORVE, River See Borve Loch.
BRU, Loch See Loch an Duin, Laiaval.
CAMA, Lochan See Loch an Duin, Laiaval.
CAMA-LOCH, Loch See Aulasary (Upper Loch).
CAMAS-DUIBHE, Loch See Loch Aird an Duin.
CHLADAICH, Loch See Loch na Eithir Eileana, OS Map 22.
CILLE, Loch See Loch nam Feithean.
CNOC CHOILICH, Loch See Loch na Cointich.
CROMLACH, Loch See Loch an Duin, Taransay.
CROSS REFERENCE The lochs lying to the south of sea-Loch Eport and to the south of the B894 Clachan/Locheport/Sidinish road are detailed on OS Map 22.
CUILCE, Loch (Scaapar) See Loch Scaapar.
DEADMAN'S, Loch See Loch an Duin, Laiaval.
DEORAVAT, Loch See Loch Hunder.
DUBH, Loch (Dusary) See Loch Dusary.
DUBH NA MOINE, Loch See Loch Aird an Duin.

DUSARY, Loch
Location & Access 18/773670. Loch Dusary lies immediately adjacent to and to the east of the A865 road 3 miles north from Clachan. A peat track runs the full length of the south shore and also gives access to Loch nan Athan (18/779668) which feeds Dusary at the north end.
Commentary There are two headwater lochs on the Dusary system: Loch Feirma (18/795688) and Loch Dubh (18/791683). These are best approached from the minor road between Ardeisker (18/768627) in the west and Botarua (18/789730)) in the north. Park at 18/783689 and walk west for ten minutes to reach these waters.
Fish Primarily sea-trout, but brown trout also. Sea-trout average 1lb 8oz, brown trout 6oz/8oz.
Flies & Tactics Good water levels are all important to bring fish into the system and through to the upper lochs. However, given these conditions, the Dusary System can provide great sport. Boat fishing brings best results and the most productive area on Loch Dusary is along the north shore, particularly in the vicinity of the small islands. Flies: Ke-He, March Brown, Peter Ross.
Permission & Charges See Loch nan Geireann.

EACHKAVAT, Loch See Borve Loch.

EASHADER, Loch
Location & Access 18/807727 Leave the A865 road round the north of North Uist at 18/805744 in Middlequarter, between Malaclete and Sollas. A peat road runs south and, with care, it may be followed almost right to the loch, past Loch a'Chapull (18/806730), a distance of one mile.
Commentary This is one of the most lovely lochs in North Uist and perfect for a family outing and picnic. The road continues south for a further half mile and ends at Loch Uisdein (18/808719) at the start of Strath Aulasary. For complete adventure, walk up the strath along the north shoulder of Marrival (230m) to fish the most remote loch in North Uist, little Loch Mousgrip (18/823709), golden eagle country. You may also wish to explore the small lochans round Locha Dubh at 18/820723. Reach them by following the fence line from the inlet burn at the north east corner of Loch Eashader for half a mile south east across Knock Mugary.
Fish In Loch Eashader, some excellent quality brown trout of up to and over 2lb in weight. They can be dour, but patience is generally rewarded. The other waters noted will all provide supper.
Flies & Tactics Loch Eashader is easily fished from the bank and, unlike in so many other Hebridean waters, wading is safe in a number of places: the sandy east bay, by headland and island on the south shore. The other waters are very much 'stand-back-and-cast' affairs where, because of the size of the lochs, wading will only scare the fish. Offer: Loch Ordie, Grouse & Claret, Black Pennell.
Permission & Charges See Loch nan Geireann entry.

EAVAL, Loch
Location & Access 18/725713. Easily accessible and immediately to the east of the A865 Clachan/Sollas road.
Commentary The contrast between the ragged peatlands by Loch Eaval and the fertile machair meadows to the west is remarkable, but this one mile long, narrow loch is just as attractive in its own right. It lies at the centre of the Hosta System and gathers in the flow from Loch na Beiste (18/744710) to the west and Loch nam Magarlan (18/727704) and Loch Bhiorain (18/739698) - see Loch Vausary entry - to the south. Loch Eaval exits north through Loch Grunavat (18/731714) via a narrow stream to Loch Hosta

OS Map 18 — Sound of Harris

(18/726728) before crossing under the A865 to reach the sea in Traigh Stir by Raikinish Point (18/718732). For a magnificent panorama of the Uists, Benbecula, and Barra, to the south and north to the Lewis and Harris hills, drive to the radar station on the top of South Clettraval. This is one of the most splendid view points in the Outer Hebrides. On a clear day, to the west, the stark, black, islands of St Kilda rear dramatically from a sea-blue, silver carpet.
Fish Loch Hosta is a superb brown trout loch. The other waters all contain stocks of pretty, brightly marked brown trout which average in the order of 6oz/8oz, with the odd larger specimen of up to 1lb in weight.
Flies & Tactics On Loch Hosta, boat fishing is the best method of attack, on the other waters, fishing from the shore is just as productive. There are short tracks at either end of Loch Eaval which give accass to the east shore and to Loch Grunavat, and to little Loch na Beiste. Flies: Loch Ordie, Black Pennell, Alexandra.
Permission & Charges See Loch nan Geireann entry.

EIK, Loch See Loch Scolpaig.
FADA, Loch (Kirkibost) See Loch nan Struban.

FADA, Loch (Lochmaddy)
Location & Access 18/875705. Park by Blashaval (18/894710 on the A865 road near little Loch Ialaidh (18/894709), two miles north from Lochmaddy. The east end of Loch Fada is reached after a ten-minute walk west over the moor.
Commentary Circumnavigating the shoreline of this loch would involve you in a vigorous five-mile hike and take at least a day to do all the fishing proper justice. Loch Fada exits south to the sea in Loch Houram through Loch Galtarsay (18/887705), Loch na Geadh (18/88706) and Loch an Strumore (18/900695), which can also offer great sport, and another full day's fishing. To the north of Loch Fada, and separated from it by Bogach Loch Fada, lie two further, excellent trout lochs: Loch Veiragvat (18/880720) and its smaller neighbour to the west, Loch Hungavat (18/872723). In strong north winds - a not infrequent occurrence in the Uists - these lochs can often be relatively sheltered, being protected by the heights of Crogary Beag (140m), Crogary Mor (180m) and Maari (171m). As well as fish, look out here for buzzard and golden eagle.
Fish Brown trout averaging 8oz in all the lochs, with a few fish up to and over 1lb as well. There is a chance of salmon and seatrout in Loch Strumore.
Flies & Tactics Boat fishing Loch Fada makes it a whole lot easier to get round this large expanse of water. The west end, amidst the small islands, is perhaps the most productive area, although fish are taken all over. Fish the other waters from the shore and approach Loch Veiragvat and Loch Hungavat from the old A865 road up the outlet stream at 18/886724. Flies: Black Pennell, Soldier Palmer, Alexandra.
Permission & Charges See Loch nan Geireann.

FADA NA GEARRACHUN, Loch See Loch Scolpaig.
FEIRMA, Loch See Loch Dusary.

GALTARSAY, Loch See Loch Fada, Lochmaddy.
GILLE-GHOID, Loch See Loch Scaapar.
GROGARY, Loch See Loch nam Feithean.
GROTA, Loch See Loch Scaapar.
GRUNAVAT, Loch See Loch Eaval.
HACKLETT, Loch See Loch Scaapar.

HORISARY, Loch
Location & Access 18/774686. Easily accessible from a peat track which leaves the A865 near Claddach-knockline at 18/756682, or from the minor road between Ardeiskar (18/791683) and Botarua (18/789730).
Commentary This is the principal North Uist sea-trout fishery and the system contains seven named and unnamed lochs. The largest water, and the most northerly, is Loch Mhic Gille-bhirde (18/772698) on the south slopes of Ben Ernakater (127m). This loch is best approached from the peat road which leaves the A865 near the church in Bayhead at 18/749684. Loch Mhic Gille-bhride exists south into Loch a'Charra (18/779689) and then enters Loch Horisary. The flow now becomes the Horisary River, continuing for approximately one mile south west to the reach Loch Trovasat. Along the way the river collects in the waters from unnamed lochan at 18/767695 and Loch Mhic a' Roin (18/758690). These assemble in Loch Trovasat before flowing under the A865 road to enter the sea in Oitir Mhor. The sands here are quite spectacular and perfect for non-fishing members of your party. Also, close by, is the Blaranald Nature Reserve, where the warden will direct visitors to the most significant ornithological residents and birds of passage.
Fish Substantial numbers of sea-trout most seasons and up to 200 in a good year. The average weight of fish is in the region of 2 1lb 8oz. Brown trout tend to be smaller, 8oz, and Loch Bruist (18/775681), to the east, contains only brown trout.
Flies & Tactics Most of the action is on Loch Trovasat, a small loch, easily fished either from the boat or from the shore; but this has as much to do with ease of access, as it has to do with quality of sport. The other lochs are less frequently fished, but, given good water levels, can be just as productive. When bank fishing Loch Trovasat, begin by the fence half way up the south shore. Newly arrived sea-trout are easily spooked so stay on the bank and do not wade. It only scares the fish out into deeper water. Flies: Loch Ordie, Black Zulu, Silver Invicta.
Permission & Charges See Loch nan Geireann entry.

HORISARY, River See Loch Horisary.
HOSTA, Loch See Loch Eaval.
HUNA, Loch See Loch Skealtar.
HUNDA, Loch See Loch Skealtar.

HUNDER, Loch
Location & Access 18/905655. Park by Loch an Daimh (18/860679) on the A897 Lochmaddy/Clachan road. Loch Hunder lies one and a half miles south-east towards South Lee (281m).
Commentary Nothing easy about getting to Loch Hunder. The moorland is rough and scattered with bog

Sound of Harris OS Map 18

pools and lochans which make travelling in a straight line virtually impossible and a compass and map essential. Either make a quick dash for Loch Hunder, or, much more fun, spend the whole day out exploring the other lochs along the way, including a visit to the sea-pool at head of Aird Bheag (18/900647). After a cast or two in Loch an Daimh, continue south-east via a series of unnamed lochans to find Loch a'Chonnachair (18/903663), another watery maze of points and narrow bays extending half a mile north/south over the moor. Cross the hillock to the east of Loch a'Chonnachair to visit Loch na Hostrach (18/911668) and its tiny neighbour, Loch Nighe (18/917668). From Loch Nighe, walk south along the lower slopes of North Lee and South Lee to reach Loch Hunder after 15mins. Loch Hunder is just over one mile north/south in length by up to quarter of a mile wide and is fed by a series of small streams from the North and South Lee hills. The south end of the loch touches the sea, where there is the chance of sport with seatrout. The unnamed lochans to the west should also be explored: at 18/898651, 18/890464, and at 18/890650. After doing so, walk north over Moinach Cainish to fish island-scattered Loch Deoravat (18/893660). End the day by returning to the A867 via Loch a'Bhuird (18/884669), another scattered, peat-stained loch which borders the road and offers great sport.
Fish Nice brown trout which average 8oz and the chance of some larger fish of up to and over 2lb in weight as well. Seatrout from sea loch Eport.
Flies & Tactics This is all bank fishing and it is best to stay ashore. Wading is dangerous. Keep moving. Don't make the mistake of spending too much time in one place unless, of course, the fish are rising. Cast and walk, constantly. The east shore of Loch Hunder is best, particularly towards the south end of the loch. For the rest, fish are taken from all round the shore, depending upon weather conditions and crossing the right fingers, but you should return with breakfast at least. These lochs are infrequently fished and lie in a very beautiful setting. Tempt the inhabitants with: Ke-He, Black Pennell, Alexandra.
Permission & Charges See Loch nan Geireann entry.

HUNGAVAT, Loch See Loch Fada, Lochmaddy.
IALAIDH, Loch See Loch Fada, Lochmaddy.
IOSAL AN DUIN, Loch See Loch Aird an Duin.

KIRKIBOST, Sea Pools
Location & Access 18/763666. Access is from the A865 road at a number of points between Claddach Kirkibost (18/780659) and Kyles-paible (18/754671) on the minor road running south from Bayhead (18/749685) along the west shore of Ceann a' Bhaigh (18/755678).
Commentary The opportunity of wonderful sport with sea-trout off the tide. This wide, sandy bay is protected from the full thrust of the Atlantic by Kirkibost Island and when the tide recedes, sea-trout may be caught in the brackish streams that empty the short river systems along the west coast of North Uist.
Fish Sea-silver sea-trout, from 1lb to anything over 5lb in weight.

Flies & Tactics All season sport, from March, if you are hardy, through to the end of the season in September. The best approach is from Claddach Kyles at 18/769664. Concentrate upon the area where the flow changes direction and turns from the south to the west. Even better, go there with a guide/gille. These sands can be dangerous. Be ever mindful of your safe return. Flies: Ke-He, Soldier Palmer, Teal Blue & Silver.
Permission & Charges See Loch nan Geireann entry.

LANGAVAT, Loch (Leverburgh) See Loch na Moracha.
LEODASAY, Loch See Oban Irpeig.
LITTLE BORVE, Loch (Berneray) See Loch Bhruist.
LOCHA DUBH, Loch See Loch Eashader.
MEALLA BRU, Sea Loch See Loch an Duin, Laiaval.
MHIC A'ROIN, Loch See Loch Horisary.
MHIC GILLE-BHRIDE, Loch See Loch Horisary.
MOR, Loch (Boreray) See Loch Bhruist.
MOUSGRIP, Loch See Loch Eashader.
NA BA CEIRE, Loch See Loch nan Struban.
NA BEISTE, Loch (Eaval) See Loch Eaval.
NA BEISTE, Loch (Scaapar) See Loch Scaapar.
NA BUAIL LOCHDRAICH, Loch See Loch na Struban.
NA BUAILE, Loch See Loch an Duin, Laiaval.
NA BUAILE, Loch See Loch Skealtar.
NA CAIGINN, Loch See Loch Scaapar.
NA CAILLICH, Loch See Borve Loch.
NA CARNAICH, Loch See Loch Aird an Duin.
NA CARTACH, Loch (Lochportain) See Loch Tergavat.
NA CARTACH, Loch (North) See Loch na Moracha.
NA CARTACH, Loch (South) See Loch Moracha.
NA CEARDAICH, Loch See Loch nan Geireann.

NA COINTICH, Loch
Location & Access 18/963721. Loch Cointich is the halfway point in a four-mile hill-walking and fishing expedition to a series of six lochs on the east side of North Uist. Start from 18/958729 on the road between Lochportain and Cheese Bay (18/960735).
Commentary Begin by walking east to reach Loch nan Smallag (18/959729) within five minutes. Climb due east from here to have a cast in tiny Loch Cnoc Choilich (18/963729) before continuing up Crogary na Hoe (154m) to find Loch na Creige (18/968724) which is joined to Loch na Cointich, the largest loch in the area. After exploring Na Cointich, descend along the outlet stream, via the little unnamed lochan at 18/959722, to fish Loch an Duin (18/954723) and, immediately to the north of Loch an Duin, Loch na Dubhcha (18/7954725).
Fish Nothing too heavy to carry home, but great sport with bright little trout which average 8oz in weight.
Flies & Tactics Hard-going, and compass and map country. Bank fishing all the way and stay on terra firma. The smaller lochs are easily read; on Loch na Cointich pay particular attention to the east shore, by the island and round the south bay. The steep-sided east end of Loch na Dubhcha should also be carefully fished. Offer: Black Zulu, Ke-He, Peter Ross.
Permission & Charges See Loch Scaapar.

190

OS Map 18 — Sound of Harris

NA CREIGE, Loch (Cheese Bay) See Loch na Cointich.
NA CREIGE, Loch (Laiaval) See Loch an Duin, Laiaval.

NA CRIADHACH, Loch
Location & Access 18/069860 To find the north end of the loch, turn left from the South Harris east coast road at 18/070864 just south of Finsbay. For the south end of the loch, and outlet stream, approach through Lingarabay and Bayhead where the system meets the sea (18/069855).
Commentary The system rises to the north in Loch Alatair (18/054871), below Creag Alatair and Bhoiseabhal (374m). Loch Alatair exits down Strath Litean into an unnamed lochan at 18/062864, before flowing under the road and into Loch na Criadhach. The planning application for a proposed super-quarry has been rejected, but at the time of writing an appeal is pending. A quarry of this size would profoundly affect this marvellous area.
Fish Sea-trout, some salmon, and some nice brown trout.
Flies & Tactics Sport is dependent upon high water levels and in the right conditions can be great fun with a good chance of a fish or two. Loch Alatair is best approached from the road at 18/055879 at the south end of Loch Langavat; a gentle, uphill hike of about half a mile. Concentrate on the north and south end. The unnamed lochan is easily covered from the shore and the west bank is best, particularly where the Abhain a' Choire stream enters. Loch na Criadhach is the most productive part of the system, fished from a boat, with sport all round. Offer them: Ke-He, Soldier Palmer, Clan Chief.
Permission & Charges See Loch Geimisgarave.

NA CRICHE, Loch (Lochportain) See Loch Tergavat.
NA DUBHCHA, Loch See Loch na Cointich.
NA GAOITHE, Loch See Loch an Duin, Taransay.
NA GARBH-ABHAINN ARD, Loch See Loch Skealtar.
NA GEARRACHUN, Loch See Loch Scolpaig.
NA H-IOLAIRE, Loch See Loch nan Struban.
NA HOSTRACH, Loch See Loch Hunder.
NA MAIGHDEIN, Loch See Loch Skealtar.

NA MORACHA, Loch
Location & Access 18/023885 An easily accessible roadside loch, lying to the north of Leverburgh adjacent to the South Harris east coast road.
Commentary Loch na Moracha is half a mile north/south by up to 300yds wide, with an additional quarter-mile long west bay. The loch drains its neighbour, Loch Langavat (18/045895), to the north, and flows south down Atha Dubh into Loch Steisavat (18/015875). The stream exits under the A859 road by the school in Leverburgh and enters the sea in The Obbe. The township by the shore used to be known as Obbe, but was renamed in honour of Lord Leverhulme who, between 1917 and 1925 spent one million pounds of his own money in an attempt to improve the island's commercial infrastructure.
Fish A first-class salmon and seatrout fishery, with exciting brown trout fishing as well. In a reasonable season up to 70 salmon and 250 seatrout are taken.
Flies & Tactics Migratory fish have ease of access into the system but heavy rain is required to get them into Loch Langavat which is, consequently, more noted as a brown trout fishery. Loch Langavat is the largest loch on South Harris, being almost two and a half miles north/south by up to half a mile wide. Boat fishing brings best results, particularly at the shallow, north end of the loch and amidst the tiny islands in the bay, mid-way down the east shoreline. Park at the north end of Loch Langavat and walk up the inlet burn to fish Loch na Cartach, North (18/040922). Loch na Moracha and Loch Steisevat are also best fished from the boat, and Loch na Moracha, also known as 'the top loch', is the most productive of the two. On Loch Steisevat, concentrate your effort at the west end and in the narrow bay along the north shore. The little loch on the hill between the pair, Loch na Cartach, South at 18/016881 is also worth an exploratory cast. Try: Blue Zulu, Loch Ordie, Peter Ross.
Permission & Charges For further information, contact Tom Jourdan, South Harris Fishery Ltd, The Dower House, Shipton-under-Wychwood, Oxfordshire OX7 6DZ. Tel: 01993 830179. Or the Keeper, David Rankin, 3 Lever Terrace, Leverburgh, Harris. Tel: 01859 520466 (evenings).

NA MORACHA, Loch See Loch Skealtar.
NA MORGHA, Loch See Loch Aonghais.
NAM BREAC, Loch (Borve) See Borve Loch.

NAM FEITHEAN, Loch
Location & Access 18/712703. This is one of a group of lochs within and close to the Balranald Nature Reserve to the east of the A865 road. The others are: Loch Scarie (18/718705), Loch Grogary (18/716717) and Loch Cille (18/718699).
Commentary Balranald is an important nature reserve and home to many varieties of resident and visiting species of birds. The reserve has a warden who will advise about what is happening on the reserve at any given time and for those who enjoy wildlife, flora and fauna, this is the ideal place for a respite from fishing.
Fish Most of these lochs are in private hands. In any case, leave the rod in the car and avoid disturbing the wildlife. There are dozens of other fishing opportunities on the island.
Flies & Tactics If you have to fish, try for sea-trout in the sea along the shore of Loch Paible at 18/719682; or have a cast or two for brown trout in Loch Sandary (18/735 683) and in tiny Loch Runavat (18/731694). Use: Black Pennell, Grouse & Claret, Silver Invicta.
Permission & Charges See Loch nan Geireann entry.

NAN ATHAN, Loch See Loch Dusary.
NAN CEITHIR EILEAN, Loch See Loch Scadavary, South.
NAN CLACHAN, Loch See Loch Scolpaig.
NAN EUN, Loch (Skealtar) See Loch Skealtar.
NAN GARNACH, Loch See Loch Scolpaig.
NAN GEADH, Loch See Loch Fada, Lochmaddy.

Sound of Harris — OS Map 18

NAN GEIREANN, Loch
Location & Access 18/846723 The north end of the loch is adjacent to the A865 road. When boat fishing Loch nan Geireann, park on the grassy area to the north of the road at 18/843737. The loch can't be seen from the road. Follow the track past the hatchery building for five minutes to reach the mooring bay. The easiest way to the west shore, when bank fishing, is via the peat track from Garry Skibinish at 18/928748.
Commentary This is one of the best lochs on North Uist and one of the most attractive. Nan Geireann is two miles north/south by up to half a mile wide. It is a scattered water, divided into three sections by substantial islands and the shoreline covers a distance of some four miles of bays, promontories and fishy corners. One of the islands was the site of a Neolithic pottery works which supplied most of the pottery used throughout the Uists. Just as exciting fishing may also be found to the north of Nan Geireann, in the sea-pool between Rubha Glas to the west and Clett to the east. At low tide the whole of this area is exposed and it is possible to walk out across the sands to fish this extraordinarily lovely tidal pool. It is best to go with a local angler. There are soft areas of sand along the way. Otherwise, not much longer, and much safer, walk out along the edge of the west machair shore.
Fish Something for everyone with seatrout, salmon and brown trout. Brown trout average 6-8oz, but there are also fish of over 1lb in weight. About ten salmon are taken most seasons and approximately 15/20 seatrout. Salmon and seatrout are caught in the tidal pool.
Flies & Tactics On Loch nan Geireann, boat fishing is most productive. The boat also makes it a lot easier to explore this large water. However, bank fishing is the best means of tempting salmon: fish tend to lie close to the margin, particularly at the north end of the loch, on the east bank. Look for seatrout between the islands of Aird Reamhar and Eilean Glas, and in the bay to the east where the stream flows in from Loch na Ceardaich at OSOS18/749754. Brown trout are taken everywhere. The tidal pool is fished from the shore and the rocks are seaweed-covered and slippery. Take great care. It is possible, just, to wade safely at the north-west corner. Walk out two hours before low tide. Flies to try include: Clan Chief, Loch Ordie, Black Zulu, Peter Ross, Soldier Palmer, Kate McLaren, Black Pennell.
Permission & Charges Lochmaddy Hotel, Lochmaddy, North Uist, Outer Hebrides. Tel: (01876) 500331; Brown trout, free to hotel guests. Non-residents, £6.00 per rod per day, £20 per rod per week. Use of boats, hotel guests and non-residents, £15 per day. Sea-trout and salmon, including use of boat. 25th February to 30th June. Hotel guests, £22 per beat per day (one rod fishing); £11 per each additional rod on the beat, Non-residents, £27 per rod per day. 1st July to 30th September. Hotel guests, £32 per beat per day (one rod fishing); £49 per beat per day (two rods fishing). Non-residents, £44 per rod per day (one rod fishing); £40 per rod per day for additional rods. 1st October to 31st October, Hotel guests, £32 per beat per day (one rod fishing); £49 per deat per day (two rods fishing). Non-residents, £44 per beat per day (one rod fishing) £44 per day for additional rods. Season: Brown trout - 15th March to 30th September; sea-trout - 15th March to 30th September; salmon - 25th February to 31st October.

NAN GEIREANN, Sea-Pool See Loch na Geireann.
NAN SMALAG, Loch See Loch Tormasad.

NAN STRUBAN, Loch
Location & Access 18/805646 An easily accessible loch to the east of the A865 Clachan/Claddach Kirkibost road. Park at 18/897642 and follow the outlet stream up to the loch.
Commentary Loch nan Struban is fed by Loch na Buail Lochdraich (18/801664) and Loch na h-Iolaire (18/800655). There is a small satellite loch, Loch na Ba Ceire at 18/809651, and good unnamed lochans which are joined to the system at 18/7800651, 18/806653, and at 18/799659.
Fish Primarily brown trout which average 8oz, but the chance of seatrout as well. The North Uist Estate are working to improve seatrout runs into the system. This also applies to the system to the west, based upon Loch an Tom (18/793659) and Loch Fada (18/792667) and the unnamed loch at 18/784661 by Claddach Kirkibost.
Flies & Tactics Few problems, with comfortable access from the main road and all the fishing easily covered from the shore. No one place is substantially better than another and fish are taken throughout the system. Offer them: Black Pennell, Greenwell's Glory, Silver Butcher.
Permission & Charges See Loch nan Geireann entry.

NIGHE, Loch (Aonghais) See Loch Aonghais.
NIGHE, Loch (South Lee) See Loch Hunder.
OBAN A'CHLEACHAIN, Sea Pool See Oban Irpeig.

OBAN IRPEIG, Sea Pool
Location & Access 18/806636. Close to the road at clachan on the A865. Follow the peat track that leads west from 18/814663.
Commentary All that is best in the sea-trout fishing from the shore with the chance of exciting sport. To the south, in Loch Leodasay (18/810631), sport with brown trout, and also on the east side of the road in Loch a' Phobuill (18/826631). Oban a' Chleachain (18/820640) and Oban na Curra (18/830635), approached from the B894 Clachan/Sidinish road, can also offer sport with sea-trout.
Fish Sea-trout of up to and over 5lb in weight have been taken here in recent years. Brown trout in the adjacent lochs are of more modest size, in the order of 6oz/8oz.
Flies & Tactics Fish these pools two hours either side of low tide for the best chance of sport. The rocks are slippery so take great care. Do not wade. Try: Black Pennell, Soldier Palmer, Peter ross.
Permission & Charges See Loch nan Geireann entry.

OBAN NA CURRA, Sea Pool See Oban Irpeig.
OBAN SPONISH, Sea Loch See Loch Scadavay, South.

OS Map 18 — Sound of Harris

OBAN TRUMISGARRY, Loch See Loch Aonghais.
OBBE, Loch See Loch na Moracha.
OLAVAT, Loch (Vallay) See Loch Scolpaig.
PAIBLE, Sea Loch See Loch nam Feithan.
ROISINISH BAY, Sea Loch See Loch Scadavay, South.
RUNAVAT, Loch See Loch nam Feithean.
SANDARY, Loch See Loch nam Feithean.

SCAAPAR, Loch
Location & Access 18/953696 Loch Scaapar lies on the north headland of Loch Maddy, close to the lighthouse at Weaver's Point. Park on the Lochportain road at 18/95723 by Loch an t-Sagairt (18/948724).
Commentary This is a five-mile round trip, visiting eight lochs on the east side of North Uist, of which Loch Scaapar is the most distant and the half-way point. After leaving the car, have a cast along the north shore of Loch na Caiginn (18/951718) before climbing between Beinn na Bile (100m) and Ben Hacklett (116m) to descending to Loch Gille-ghoid (18/959713). Find the inlet stream at the south end of Loch Gille-ghoid and follow it east round Bein an Fhaireachaidh (100m) to reach Loch Scalan (18/963708) on the cliff edge by Creag Scalan. Walk south now, to find Loch Scaapar, which is the ideal place for lunch. After fishing Loch Scaapar, angle west round the south slopes of Ben Scaapar (90m) for half a mile to little Loch Cuilce (18/949700) and its larger neighbour, Loch na Beiste (18/950702). Continue north along the outlet burn from Loch na Beiste to Loch Grota (18/950708) and Loch Hacklett (18/950712), which has the ruins of a prehistoric earth house on the west shore. Return to the start point along the south and east shore of Loch na Caiginn.
Fish Brown trout which average 8oz with a few fish of up to and over 1lb in weight.
Flies & Tactics This is fairly tough going, particularly after heavy rain, and you will need a compass and map in case a mist descends unexpectedly. You are unlikely to meet anyone else along the way, other than the occasional buzzard. All the lochs are easily fished from the shore. Do not wade. The margins deepen sharply and are difficult underfoot. There is the possibility of sport with seatrout where Loch na Caiginn enters the sea. Flies: Black Pennell, Soldier Palmer, Alexandra.
Permission & Charges Mr J Handyside, Stag Lodge, Lochmaddy, North Uist, Western Isles.(01876) 500364. 1994 charges: £5 per rod per day; £20 per rod per week; £35 per rod per season; boats, £10 per day.

SCADAVAY, Loch (North) See Loch Skealtar.

SCADAVAY, Loch (South)
Location & Access 18/878665 To explore the west shore of the loch, and if you intend to fish for seatrout at Oban Sponish (18/882645), park on the A867 Lochmaddy/Clachan road by Loch nan Ceithir Eilean (18/859665). To explore the north and east shore, park at 18/872672 and walk south for five minutes to reach the loch.
Commentary Loch Scadavay covers an area of one square mile, not as an entity, but in a wonderful, scattered madness of bays, narrows, necks and islands. A compass and map are essential in this wilderness, particularly if you are heading for Oban Sponish on Loch Eport; two, tough miles south from the road at Loch nan Ceithir Eilean.
Fish Brown trout from 6oz to over 1lb in weight. Seatrout of up to and over 3lb.
Flies & Tactics Start your journey about two hours before low tide. Walk straight to Oban Sponish; a long, narrow sea pool, with a rock ledge at the south end. The tide brings the fish over the ledge, into Oban Sponish, where they charge around the seaweed margins and, occasionally, can be tempted to take a fly. If Oban Sponish fish are uncooperative, have a look at Roisinish Bay (18/877640), to the west, where you might have better fortune. After Roisinish Bay, continue west to fish the unnamed lochans on the east shore of sea Loch Langass. Return to the road via Loch Tarruin an Eithir (18/874648) and the west shore of Loch Scadavay. Flies: Blue Zulu, Soldier Palmer, Peter Ross.
Permission & Charges See Loch nan Geireann entry.

SCALAN, Loch See Loch Scaapar.
SCARIE, Loch See Loch nam Feithean.

SCOLPAIG, Loch
Location & Access 18/732751 Easily accessible from the A865 road round the north of North Uist. Look for the loch to the west of the road with a square tower on a small, man-made, island in the middle.
Commentary There are a number of lochs in this area which are the perfect place for a family day out, particularly if you are burdened with non-fishing companions. All are close to the road and are ideal for a few casts if time is limited: Loch Skilivat (18/725749), to the south of Loch Scolpaig, and Loch Olavat (18/749754) and Lochan Eilean (18/749760) which are accessible from Griminish (18/751755). Little Loch nan Garnach (18/755752) and Loch Beag nan Ian (18/762749) to the north of the road; Loch Fada na Gearrachun (18/761746) and Loch na Gearrachun (18/766744) by Airigh Mhic Ruairidh; Loch Eik (18/762742) and Loch nan Clachan (18/769739) where the road touches the sea at Ceann nan Clachan. The beaches here are world-class. Even nicer is the tiny cove by Scolpaig. Drive past the twin lochs and park at the farm. Ask permission at the farmhouse, then walk west over the machair dune for five minutes to reach a secluded beach of breath-taking beauty. Continue north from the beach along the cliff top for half a mile to find the dramatic Sunken Caves of Hosta at 18/728761, and, half a mile north again, the ruins of a Pictish Fort at 18/730769. It is also possible to visit Vallay Island. The route starts at Claddach-Valley (18/781736) and runs close to the east shore of two smaller islands: Torogay and Stangram. Explore ruined Vallay House, visit the Monument, the site of a 13th century church and Neolithic standing stone at the east end of the island. Or, if the weather is fine, simply laze away a few hours in the peace and quite of one of the most beautiful places in the world. Keep an eye on the tide and remember to allow plenty of time for your return journey.

193

Sound of Harris — OS Map 18

Fish Very pretty brown trout in all the lochs. They average around 8oz in weight, although there are a few much larger specimens. Loch nan Clachan and Loch Eik also have a run of sea-trout, given good water levels.

Flies & Tactics There lochs are very easily understood and all the water can be covered with little difficulty from the shore. Stay ashore, do not wade. Look out also for outstanding flora and fauna, including rare orchids and the great raptors. Flies to try: Ke-He, Invicta, Dunkeld.

Permission & Charges See Locc nan Geireann entry.

SHINNADALE, Loch See Loch na Duin, Taransay.

SKEALTAR, Loch

Location & Access 18/895687 Easily accessible from the A867 Lochmaddy/Clachan road.

Commentary This is the principal salmon fishery on North Uist and Loch Skealtar was renowned for the quality and size of fish. Until recently, however, the system has been the site of a fish farming enterprise and this seems to to have had an adverse effect on fish runs. The fish farm no longer operates and salmon are now returning in increasing numbers. Loch Skealtar is fed from the west by a series of lochs, beginning with Loch Huna (18/812666), which flows into Loch nan Eun (18/840674). Loch na Moracha (18/847664), to the south of Loch nan Eun, is also joined to Loch nan Eun. These continue eastward into Loch Scadavay (18/860687) which has two small satellite lochs: Loch Hunda (18/832683) and Loch an t-Searraich (18/843703). The system is widely scattered over a distance of some 12 square miles of peat moorland and apart from the waters noted above there are also more than 20 additional unnamed lochs and lochans. Finding your way around involves some tough tramping and a compass and map are essential, not only whilst walking, but also when fishing from a boat. It is very easy to become disorientated and should a mist descend.

Fish Approximately 250 salmon and some 300 seatrout. Seatrout averaged 3lb, salmon 6-7lb. The heaviest salmon in recent years weighed 23lb 8oz. Brown trout are present in all these waters and average 8oz, but there are also good numbers of larger trout and fish of up to and over 1lb are not uncommon.

Flies & Tactics Given the right water conditions, salmon and seatrout may be encountered throughout the system, but most are taken in Loch Skealtar and its immediately adjacent neighbours, Loch na Garbh-Abhainn Ard (18/883683) and Loch na Buaile (18/889690). Loch na Maighdein (18/892681), by the A867, is purely a brown trout water. The services of an experienced gillie are essential if you are to get the best out of your visit. There are well-established lies and noted drifts on Skealtar, including from the small island at the south-west end towards the inlet burn from Loch na Garbh-Abhainn Ard, and from the island in the narrow, north neck, down the west shore. The gillie will keep you right. Excellent sport may also be had from the bank. Loch Skealtar exits in a narrow, rock-strewn stream, to an extension of the loch at 18/900685. Fish the inflow carefully, from the middle of the stream, extending line, rather than walking forward. The far bank, immediately opposite the inlet stream, can also be very productive. Loch Scadavay is a serious affair of several hundred acres; a maze of bays, corners, narrows and islands of endless delight. The north end, between Marrogh (160m) and Skealtraval (101m), is perhaps the most productive area, but fish may be taken anywhere. On Loch nan Eun, work the long, south shore, paying particular attention to the bay to the south of Eilean Buidhe Island. Loch Huna, the most remote of these lochs, offers perfect away-from-it-all peace and solitude, as well as great sport with good quality brown trout. Whilst there, visit the Pictish grave (18/808673) and Neolithic chamber cairn (18/800669) on Uneval (140m). If bank fishing, avoid wading. The margins are steep and often rocky, with deep water close to the edge. Stay safely on terra firma. For salmon and seatrout offer: Kate Maclaren, Clan Chief, Green Highlander, Goat's Toe, General Practitioner, Munro Killer, Garry Dog, Willie Gunn; for brown trout start with: Black Zulu, Soldier Palmer, Peter Ross.

Permission & Charges See Loch nan Geirann entry.

SKILIVAT, Loch See Loch Scolpaig.
SMALLAG, Loch See Loch na Cointich.
STARABRAIGH, Loch See Loch an Duin, Taransay.
STEAPHAIN, Loch See Loch Vausary.
STEINAVAT, Loch See Loch Aonghais.
STEISAVAT, Loch See Loch Moracha.
TARRUINN AN EITHIR, Loch See Loch Scadavay, South.

TERGAVAT, Loch

Location & Access 18/925735 A few minutes' walk east from Cnoc na Brathain (18/920733) on the Lochportain road.

Commentary An excellent, easily accessible loch which is linked to Loch na Criche (18/923729) to the east, and close to another good, little unnamed lochan at 18/926727. South from the unnamed loch, and accessible from Brae-callasay at 18/921723, is Loch na Cartach (18/924723) which is also worth a cast.

Fish Brown trout average 10-12oz with a few larger specimens as well, and the possibility of seatrout in the sea at the long bay of Aird nan Loach (18/749754).

Flies & Tactics Peat-stained water, deep margins and definitely bank fishing. Stay ashore at all times. Loch Tergavat is almost half a mile long, north/south, and the north end is the most productive area, particularly by the two islands at the narrows, and near the island in the east bay. There are two unnamed lochans, on the west shore at 18/922736, and on the east shore at 18/925735. Don't miss them. Also, walk north from Loch Tergavat, round the head of the sea loch, to have a cast in a very lovely, little, unnamed loch at 18/924742 which is known locally as Ardennish Loch; the perfect place for lunch with stunning views north to the hills of South Harris. The other waters noted above are easily covered from the bank and fish rise and are taken from all round the shore. Tempt them with: Ke-He, Invicta, Silver Butcher.

OS Maps 18-19 — Gairloch & Ullapool

Permission & Charges See Loch Scaapar.

THORSAGEARRAIDH, Loch
Location & Access 18/046840 This delightful little loch lies on the hill to the north of the A895 road through Glen Rodel, between Leverburgh and Rodel. It is approached in ten minutes from the Coast Guard look-out-point by the side of the road at 18/045839.
Commentary The loch exits to the sea in Rodel harbour through the unnamed, weedy, loch on the west side of the road at 18/045835. This loch can hold seatrout, given good water levels and high tides. The South Harris east coast road runs north from Rodel, where every scrap of useful ground is ridged with lazy-beds. Park at 18/053833 and climb east across Rodelpark to visit the most southerly loch on Harris, Loch Vallarip (18/0588833).
Fish A chance of seatrout, but primarily brown trout which average 8oz in weight.
Flies & Tactics Increase your chance of success by having a word with your Maker in St Clements Church at Rodel, before setting off. It is most noted for the magnificent tomb of Alexander Macleod, designed in 1528, in advance of his death, by the incumbent. The lochs are all easily covered from the shore. Do not wade. Also explore the unnamed lochs to the north near Uamh at 18/068843. Offer them: Black Zulu, Grouse & Claret, Peter Ross.
Permission & Charges See Loch na Moracha.

TIDAL PONDS, Sea Pools (Ardhainish) See Loch Aird an Duin.
TORMASAD BEAG, Loch See Loch Tormasad.

TORMASAD, Loch
Location & Access 18/821651 Easily accessible and immediately adjacent to the north side of the A867 Lochmaddy/Clachan road.
Commentary This is one of the best brown trout lochs in vicinity of the Langass Lodge and it covers and area of approx. half a mile north/south by up to 300yds wide at the south end. The loch exits through Loch nan Smalag (18/827645) to the sea at Barra-mhail (18/830641). Loch Tormasad Beag (18/826651) on the south side of the road is also worth a few casts. To the east of Loch Tormasad is Loch a'Bharpa (18/838662) which is the water supply for the North Uist Estate hatchery. There are a number of unnamed lochans to the north of Loch a'Bharpa which all have stocks of small brown trout. Non-fishing members in your party should visit the dramatic Neolithic burial mound on Ben Langass (90m) and the remains of the stone circle at 18/845651.
Fish Excellent quality brown trout in Loch Tormassad, smaller fish in the other lochs. The possibility of seatrout in Loch nan Smalag.
Flies & Tactics Boat fishing brings best results on Loch Tormasad, the other waters are all fished from the bank. Stay ashore and do not wade. Offer: Black Zulu, Grouse & Claret, Silver Butcher
Permission & Charges See Loch nan Geireann entry.

TROVASAT, Loch See Loch Horisary.

UISDEIN, Loch See Loch Eashader.
ULLAVEG, Loch See Loch Vausary.
VALLARIP, Loch See Loch Thorsagearraidh.

VAUSARY, Loch
Location & Access 18/750702. Turn east from the A865 at 18/728701, near the church at the south end of Loch nam Magarlan (18/727704). Loch Vausary is to the south of the track, after one and a half miles.
Commentary The Vausary System rises in Glen Drolla to the north, between Clettraval (133m) and Toroghas (101m). The stream flows south into Loch Steaphain (18/759701) and then into Loch Vausary. The Loch exists south via a narrow burn for one mile to reach the sea through a small, brackish pool by Bayhead (18/748686). Loch Bhiorain (18/739698), also approached from the Vausary road, is not joined to the system but flows north to Loch Eaval (18/725713). To the south is Loch Ullaveg (18/753695), best approached from the peat track near the post office on the A865 at 18/742687.
Fish The chance of sea-trout in Lochs Vausary, Steaphain and Bhiorain, modest brown trout in the other waters noted above.
Flies & Tactics Boat fishing brings best results on Loch Vausary and fish are taken from all over this small loch. If the wind is fierce, bank fish with confidence, particularly along the north west shore. On Loch Steaphain, concentrate on the west and south shore. Offer: Soldier Palmer, Grouse & Claret, Clan Chief.
Permission & Charges See Loch nan Geireann entry.

VEIRAGVAT, Loch See Loch Fada, Lochmaddy.

Gairloch & Ullapool

A'BHAID GHAINMHEICH, Loch See Loch na Doire Duinne.
A'BHAID SHAMHRAIDH, Loch See Loch an Iasgair.
A'BHAID-CHOILLE, Loch See Gruinard River.

A'BHAID-LUACHRAICH, Loch
Location & Access 19/895865. A good track leads out to the north end of the loch from the A832 Inverewe/Dundonnell road near the Drumchork Hotel at 19/880884.
Commentary Loch a'Bhaid-luachraich is known locally as the Goose Loch because its straggling shape resembles that of a goose. The loch is one and a half miles north/south by up to half a mile wide across the south bay and it is 'nipped' by narrows to form almost two separate waters. Immediately to the north of the Drumchork track is Loch na Claise Carnaich (19/901872), whilst a further mile south, round Carn Bad na h-Achlaise (243m), is little Loch Mhic'ille Riabhaich (19/905844). Both will reward a visit.
Fish Small wild brown trout which average 6oz/8oz but, in Loch a'Bhaid-luachraich, the chance of specimen fish as well.
Flies & Tactics A boat may be available on Loch a'Bhaid-luachraich and this is the easiest means of

Gairloch & Ullapool   OS Map 19

exploring the wide expanse of water. The shallow south bay is perhaps the most productive fishing area. When fishing the deeper north bay, you should hold the boat close the shore, a few yards out from the bank. When bank fishing, stay ashore and do not wade. It is dangerous to do so. Offer: Ke-He, Soldier Palmer and Peter Ross.
Permission & Charges Expect to pay in the order of £2 per rod per day for bank fishing. Contact: Francis Oats, Drumchork Hotel, Drumchork, Aultbea, Wester Ross. Tel: 01445 731242. The hotel will advise on access to hill loch fishing on other, adjacent, waters in the area.

A'BHAID-RABHAIN, Loch See Loch a'Mhadaidh.

A'BHEALAICH, Loch
Location & Access 19/865642 Loch a'Bhealaich lies at the very heart of the Shieldaig Forest at the end of a wonderful six and a half mile hike south from near Shieldaig Farm. The track leaves the B8056 Kerrysdale/Redpoint road at 19/807723 and passes along the way a number of other, first-class Shieldaig Lodge Hotel trout lochs on the line of the Badachro River.
Commentary Not for the faint-hearted, but utterly splendid fishing in unimaginably wonderful surroundings, dominated by the peaks and pinnacles of one of Torridon's most spectacular mountains, Beinn Alligin (985m). The other waters are, from north to south, Lochan Fuar (19/799709), Loch Braigh Horrisdale (19/798705), Loch Gaineamhaich (19/833670), Am Feur-loch (19/847668) and Loch a'Ghobhainn (19/854657). One further loch lies south of Loch a'Bhealaich, on a plateau below the towering heights of Sgurr Mhor (985m) at an altitude of 550m: Loch Toll nam Biast (19/869620). It is very rarely, if ever, fished and I have no first-hand information about any trout it may contain.
Fish Some specimen trout in Loch a'Bhealaich of over 3lb in weight and ferox in the depths. The other waters have excellent quality trout which vary from a few ounces up to the occasional fish of over 1lb.
Flies & Tactics Boat fishing on the principal waters, bank fishing on the rest, but either way, you are assured of good sport. Loch a'Bhealaich is almost 2 miles long by up to 400 yards wide and the most productive fishing area is at the north end. Loch Braigh Horrisdale is perfect for a family picnic and for beginners, where good baskets are the rule, rather than the exception. Flies: Black Pennell, Invicta and, Alexandra.
Permission & Charges See Lochan Sgeireach (Shieldaig) entry.

A'BHONNAICH, Loch See Loch Nan Clachan Geala.
A'BHRAGHAD, Lochan See Fionn Loch.
A'BHRAOIN, Loch See River Broom (OS Map 20).
A'BHRISIDH, Loch See Gruinard River.
A'CHAOL-THUIL, Loch See Loch an Daing.
A'CHLEIRICH, Lochan See Loch Bad an Saglaip.
A'CHOIR BHAIN, Loch See Loch na Teangaidh Fhiadhaich.
A'CHOIRE, Loch See Loch nan Clachan Geala.

A'CHOIRE MHOIR, Loch See Loch na h-Oidhche.
A'CHUIRN, Loch See Loch nan Dailthean.
A'GHAIRBHE, Loch See Kinlochewe River.

A'GHARBH-DOIRE, Loch
Location & Access 19/800792 Turn right from the B8021 Gairloch/Melvaig road at Strath (19/796773) and park at the end of the minor road in Mial (19/798784). The loch is half a mile to the north, on the other side of Meall na Dubh Chlaise (166m).
Commentary There are a number of other small lochs and lochans nearby which can be accessed either from Mial, or from the A832 Gairloch/Poolewe road via the quarry on the left hand side of the road, one mile north from Gairloch. These are: Loch Feur (19/809781), known locally as the Grass Loch, Lochan nam Breac (19/814784), tiny Loch Coire na h-Airigh (19/805784) and, to the north of Loch Tollaidh, Boor Loch (19/840795). Loch na Lairige (19/783789), to the west of Mial, is approached from the track at the end of the Lonemore road (19/785780).
Fish Expect bright little trout which average 6oz/8oz.
Flies & Tactics All the lochs noted above are readily accessible and are great for beginners. They are not too far for little legs to walk and offer a perfect introduction to hill lochs fishing. Flies: Black Zulu, Invicta and Silver Butcher.
Permission & Charges See Loch Sguod entry.

A'GHOBHAINN, Loch See Loch a'Bhealaich.

A'MHADAIDH, Loch
Location & Access 19/773833. Follow the B8021 west and north from Gairloch towards Melvaig. Park half a mile north of Peterburn at 19/741839 and hike the track that leads east up to Maol Breac (170m) (19/749839). From the end of the track begin a six mile day hill walking and fishing round four remote lochs and lochans.
Commentary The first water, Loch Meall a'Bhainne (19/754835), is very dour. Leave the loch at the south end and climb gently over the hill to the south east to find Loch a'Bhaid-rabhain (19/761829). Contour north east from Loch a'Bhaid-rabhain for half a mile to locate Loch a'Mhadaidh. Now walk across the side of the hill, south-east, for a further mile to fish the most remote water, Lochan Sgeireach (19/782822).
Fish Do not expect to fill the glass case here, but do be assured that you will return home with more than enough for supper.
Flies & Tactics A compass and map are essential and so are stout walking boots. All the lochs are easily covered from the shore and on your return journey from Lochan Sgeireach, catch the ones that got away on the route out. Flies: Blue Zulu, March Brown and Peter Ross.
Permission & Charges Free to guests at Sands Holiday Centre, otherwise, £5 per rod per day. Contact: W & M Cameron, Sands Holiday Centre, Big Sand, by Gairloch, Wester Ross. Tel: 01445 712125.

A'MHADAIDH MOR, Loch See Fionn Loch.
A'MHEALLAIN ODHAIR, Loch See Lochan Fada.

OS Map 19 — Gairloch & Ullapool

A'MHONAIDH-DHROIGHINN, Loch See Fionn Loch.
A'MHUILINN, Loch See Loch Airigh Mhic Criadh.
ABHAINN BRUACHAIG, Loch See Kinlochewe River.
AEROPLANE, Loch See Lochan Sgeireach (Shieldaig).
AIRIGH A'PHUILL, Loch See Loch Airigh Mhic Criadh.
AIRIGH AN EILEIN, Loch See Loch an Daing.

AIRIGH MHIC CRIADH, Loch
Location & Access 19/830765. Park just past the quarry on the A832 Gairloch/Poolewe road at 19/819780. Follow the outlet burn south, up the side of the waterfall, to reach Loch Airigh Mhic Criadh after a tramp of 40 minutes.
Commentary This is the first loch in a series of 5 named and unnamed waters which offer a full day's sport in the hills. You will cover 5 miles over rough ground, so be well prepared and carry a compass and map.
Fish Nothing for the glass case, but plenty of fun with lively little fish which average 4oz to 6oz and a few larger specimens of up to and over 8oz in weight.
Flies & Tactics Easy bank fishing and no need to wade. Fish round the north shore of Loch Airigh Mhic Criadh and then continue south east, through a perfect glen, for half a mile to fish Loch Airigh a'Phuill (19/844757). Work clockwise round the loch and then strike east round the south shoulder of Meall Fuaraidh (370m) to little Loch a'Mhuilinn (19/826760) above the Flowerdale Forest. Walk north from Loch a'Mhuilinn for 5 minutes to the last two waters, both of which are small and weedy and difficult to fish, but contain good stocks of little trout: Loch an t-Sabhailmhoine (19/821763) and Loch Clair (19/820765). Return north-east to the outlet burn of Loch Airigh Mhic Criadh via the unnamed lochan at 19/824769. Flies: Ke-He, Greenwell's Glory and Peter Ross.
Permission & Charges See Loch Garbhaig (Talladale) entry.

AIRIGH UILLEIM, Loch See Loch Clair.

ALLT EIGIN, Loch
Location & Access 19/131827. Approach from the A832 Braemore/Dundonnell road at 19/122813 near the bridge over the Dundonnell River. Walk north-east for forty minutes to reach the loch.
Commentary An exciting, beautiful, loch in a very attractive setting lying on the hill to the east of the Dundonnell River. Close by is Lochan Fraoich (19/134823) and a number of small, unnamed lochans, which are also well worth you attention.
Fish Wild brown trout which average 10oz in weight and also good numbers of fish of up to and over 2lb.
Flies & Tactics First-class bank fishing. Wading is not really necessary as fish lie close to the margins. Concentrate on the north end of Loch Allt Eigin. Lochan Fraoich is divided by narrows into two sections and fish may be taken from all round the shore. Offer the residents: Ke-He, March Brown, Silver Butcher.

Permission & Charges Mr Steve Potter, Factor, Estate Office, Dundonnell Estate, Dundonnell, Wester-Ross. Tel: 01854 633206. Expect to pay in the order of £5 per rod per day. Free to guests at The Sheiling Guest House, Garve Road, Ullapool, Wester-Ross IV26 2SX. Tel: 01854 612947.

ALLT EOIN THOMAIS, Loch See Loch an Daing.
AM FEUR-LOCH, Loch See Loch Bad an Sgalaig.
AM FEUR-LOCH (Shieldaig), Loch See Loch a'Bhealaich.
AN DAIMH, Loch See Gruinard River.

AN DAING, Loch
Location & Access 19/775905. Follow the B8057 road north from Poolewe past Mellanguan to park at 19/809898. Loch an Daing lies 2 miles north-west below the escarpment of An Cuaidh (296m).
Commentary Loch an Daing lies at the centre of a group of 20 named and unnamed lochs and lochans on the Inveran Estate, north of Poolewe. The only way in is by foot over rough ground. To circuit them all in a day is possible, but a major undertaking with more walking than fishing. Ideally, it would be best to split the expedition in two, by camping overnight at the ruins above Camas Mor beach at 19/761916. The total, round trip, involves approximately 9 miles and this is very much a compass and map, good-weather-expedition, not to be lightly undertaken. The rewards for effort, however, are outstanding, not only because of the fishing, but also because of the outstanding beauty of the surrounding scenery and wildlife along the way.
Fish All sizes, from modest three-to-the-pound trout, up to the occasional fish of over 1lb.
Flies & Tactics From the start point, follow the outlet stream up to the first water, Loch Allt Eoin Thomais (19/801898). Fish the larger, north bay, and then continue west via the unnamed lochan at 19/795899 to fish Loch Airigh an Eilein with its small island off the west shore. From the south-west corner of Loch Airigh an Eilein, pick up the outlet stream and track it west to Loch a'Chaol-thuil (19/787896). At this point, make a detour south to have a cast in Loch na Feithe Dirich (19/788888) which contains excellent trout. A good track leads north from here to the partly-wooded shores of Loch Ceann a'Charnaich (19/779895) and thence, north again, to Loch an Daing. This is the largest loch, nearly half a mile long by up to quarter of a mile wide and the north end of the loch, between the promontory and the small island, will always produce supper. Follow the outlet burn from the north of Loch an Daing to find Loch nan Eun (19/770914). At this point, if staying out overnight, continue north along the track to the ruins at Camas Mor. Otherwise, walk north east on a good track to locate Loch an t-Sean-inbhir (19/790920). Find the inlet stream at the north-east end and follow it south east to Loch na h-Uamhaidh Moire (19/799917) and its neighbour, to the west of Meall na h-Uamhaidh (200m), Loch na h-Uamhaidh Beag (19/800910). Descend to the village of Cove and the B8057 and walk south for half a mile to regain the start point. Flies: Blue Zulu, Invicta and Alexandra.

Gairloch & Ullapool   OS Map 19

Permission & Charges Bank fishing may be available at £6 per rod per day. Contact: Steven Younie, The Keeper's Cottage, Poolewe, Wester Ross. Tel: 01445 781274.

AN DOIRE CRIONAICH, Loch See Fionn Loch.
AN DUIBHE, Loch See Loch a'Chairn (OS Map 20).
AN DUN-CHAIRN, Loch See Loch na Doire Duinne.
AN EICH DHUIBH, Loch See Gruinard River.
AN EICH GHLAIS, Lochain See Loch Coire Chaorachain.
AN EILEIN (North), Loch See Fionn Loch.
AN EILEIN (South), Loch See Fionn Loch.
AN EILICH, Loch See Fionn Loch.
AN EILICH, Loch See Gruinard River.
AN FHAMHAIR, Loch See Fionn Loch.
AN FHEOIR, Loch
Location & Access See Loch an t-Slagain.

AN FHITHICH, Loch
Location & Access 19/851923 Leave the A832 Dundonnell/Gairloch road at Drumchork (19/878888) and drive north through Aultbea to park in Mellon Charles at 19/848918. Loch an Fhithich lies to the north of Creag an Fhithich Mor (121m) after a vigorous fifteen minute up-hill hike.
Commentary A group of eight small lochs clustered round Creag an Fhithich Mor which make an ideal day out in the hills overlooking Loch Ewe. Dramatic views east to An Teallach (1062m), south-east to Slioch (980m) and south to Beinn Eighe and the Torridon mountains.
Fish Trout average 8oz/10oz, with a few larger specimens as well.
Flies & Tactics Keep to the left side of Creag an Fhithich Mor and fish the west shore of Loch an Fhithich. At the first bay, step west to explore the three unnamed lochans, then west again to fish clockwise round Loch na Sgaireig Mor (19/847928). Turn east now and, skirting the south slope of the hill, locate little Loch na Leirg (19/856928). Loch Beinn Dearg (19/857922) is next, fifteen minutes south-east. If you are feeling terribly energetic, make a detour further east from Loch Beinn Dearg to examine the unnamed lochans between Loch Beinn Dearg and remote Loch Spogach (19/870924). Return via the unnamed lochan at 19/854923 to fish the east shoreline of Loch an Fhithich. Offer them: Black Zulu, Loch Ordie and Dunkeld.
Permission & Charges See Loch an t-Slagain entry.

AN GAINEAMH, Loch See Fionn Loch.

AN IASGAIR, Loch
Location & Access 19/804834 Approach from the B8057 Poolewe/Cove road at Naast (19/828834). Follow the line of the Allt nan Easan Bana burn due west for one and a half miles to reach the loch.
Commentary This loch lies in a remote location and is one of a series of nine named and unnamed lochs and lochans to the west of the B8057 road. You will need a compass and map to navigate your way round and expect to hike about six miles during the day.

Outstanding scenery all the way, with dramatic sea and mountain vistas. Also worth a separate expedition whilst in the vicinity is a visit to the little gem which is Loch a'Bhaid-shamhraidh (19/812847) on the hill above Brae (19/819850).
Fish Primarily pan sized trout in all the lochs, but a few fish of over two pounds in some of them.
Flies & Tactics Bank fishing only and it is best not to wade. After fishing Loch an Iasgair, walk due south for three quarters of a mile to find Loch nan Laigh (19/803816), which can often provide shelter in strong winds. Climb easily from Loch nan Laigh, north-east for half a mile, to descend to Lochain nan Seasgach (19/815819) and its unnamed partner to the north. Now walk south-east for another half mile to locate Lochan Sgeireach (19/823815) and weedy Loch na Cloiche (19/827817). Thereafter, climb due east for ten minutes to explore Loch Chriostina (19/834820) above sea-loch Loch Ewe. There are some really fine trout here. Descend to the road from Loch Chriostina and make your way back to the start point. Flies: Black Pennell, Soldier Palmer and Silver Butcher.
Permission & Charges Expect to pay £5 per day. Contact: The Keeper, Keeper's Cottage, Poolewe, Wester Ross. Tel: 01445781274.

AN IASGAIR, Loch See Fionn Loch.
AN NID, Loch See Gruinard River.
AN SGEIREACH, Loch See Lochan Fada.
AN T-SABHAIL-MHOINE, Loch See Loch Airigh Mhic Criadh.
AN T-SEAN-INBHIR, Loch See Loch an Daing.
AN T-SEANA-BHAILE, Loch See River Sand.

AN T-SLAGAIN, Loch
Location & Access 19/857939. Approach from Laide on the A832 Dundonnell/Gairloch road at 19/900918. Drive north towards Mellon Udrigle and leave the minor road at 19/888940. The track west may be followed, with care, to the ruins at Slaggan (19/845940) which is a good base for further exploration. Loch an t-Slagain is immediately to the south of the track.
Commentary There are a number of first-class trout lochs here, on the Rubha Mor peninsula, between Loch Ewe to the south and Gruinard Bay to the north. They all offer a wonderful chance to escape from dull care amidst glorious surroundings and the chance of a fish or two or three as well.
Fish Happy little brown trout which average 8oz, but a few larger fish as well with a couple of well-documented, uncatchable monsters.
Flies & Tactics Fish the east shoreline of Loch an t-Slagain, paying particular attention half way down the bank in the area where the stream flows in from the unnamed lochan on the hill. Follow the inlet burn south for a step to explore little Loch an Fheoir (19/862933) and, a quarter of a mile south-east again, its larger neighbour, Loch Caol na h-Innse-geamhraidh (19/872930). Return to the start fishing the west shore of the lochs. Offer them: Blue Zulu, March Brown and Silver Butcher.
Permission & Charges The Old Smiddy (Tel: 01445 731425) offers excellent accommodation and apres-

OS Map 19 — Gairloch & Ullapool

fishing food. Bridgend Stores, Altbea, Wester Ross. Tel: 01445 731204. Laide Post Office, Laide, Wester Ross. Tel: 01445 731252. Bank fishing at £5 per rod per day. Boats on Loch an t-Slagain and Loch na Beiste (19/884844). Contact the Old Smiddy for bookings.

AN TEAS (North), Loch See Loch an Teas (South).

AN TEAS (South), Loch
Location & Access 19/884912. Park by the viewpoint on the A832 Dundonnell/Gairloch road at 19/890900 and walk north for half a mile to reach the loch.
Commentary A small, moorland lochan, rarely fished, with a further tiny pool, Loch na h-Ard Eilig (19/884916) a few minutes north. Loch an Teas (North) lies to the west at 19/872915 and is easily accessed via a good track from Bualnaluib (19/869904).
Fish Trout average 8oz and there are plenty of them.
Flies & Tactics Easy bank fishing all round. Flies: Ke-He, March Brown and Peter Ross.
Permission & Charges See Loch an t-Slagain entry.

AN UILLT-GHIUBHAIS, Loch See Lochan Fada.
ATH GHAIRBH, Loch See Loch na Doire Duinne.
BAD A'CHREAMH, Loch See Loch na Curra.

BAD AN SGALAIG, Loch
Location & Access 19/850710 Immediately to the south of the A832 Kinlochewe/Gairloch road. Park at 19/850720.
Commentary The loch (Gaelic name - Loch of the Ploughman's Grove) has been enlarged by a hydro-electric scheme harnessing the River Kerry (see entry) and includes the Dubh Loch (19/845700) to the south and little Loch Am Feur-Loch (19/859720) to the west at Red Stable. All these waters are easily accessible and offer the chance of good sport with minimum effort. The principal waters extend for 2 miles north/south by up to half a mile wide. To the south of Loch Am Feur-Loch, approached via the track over the outlet burn, is an excellent beginner's water, Lochan a'Chleirich (19/876709).
Fish The Gairloch Angling Club stocks Loch Bad an Sgalaig from time to time and there are also native wild fish as well. The average weight of trout is a pound, but fish of over 3lb are taken regularly. All of these waters contain pike, some of which reach considerable proportions.
Flies & Tactics There are two boats on Loch Bad an Sgalaig and in suitable water conditions it is possible to navigate the narrows into the Dubh Loch. Bank fishing is also allowed, although wading is not recommended because of the unstable nature of some areas due to fluctuations in the water level caused by power generation. The trout lie close to the shore, so arrange your drift accordingly and expect sport all round, particularly near the waterfall and the burn leading to the Dubh Loch. Do not, however, expect large baskets: Loch Bad an Sgalaig can be dour and unforgiving. Try: Black Pennell, Invicta and, Silver Butcher.
Permission & Charges £10 per day for the boat with two rods fishing, £2 per rod per day bank fishing, £4 per day on Bad an Sgalaig. Book boat and bank via:

K Gunn, Newsagent, Strath, Gairloch, Wester Ross. Tel: 01445 712400; Gairloch Post Office issues permits at Anchorage Crafts, Pier Road, Gairloch, Wester Ross. Tel: 01445 712005. Gillie services and additional information from D W Roxborough, The Old Police Station, Gairloch. Tel: 01445 712057.

BAD NA H-ACHLAISE, Loch See Loch Clair.

BADACHRO, River
Location & Access Source: 19/892624 Outfall: 19/781737 Easy access from the B8056 Kerrysdale/Redpoint road near Badachro Farm at 19/785730.
Commentary This little river rises from Loch na Cabhaig (19/781737) below Beinn Dearg (914m) and flows north-west for eight miles through Loch a'Bhealaich and its attendant lochs (see Loch a'Bhealaich entry) to reach the sea in Loch Gairloch at Badachro. Loch Bad a'Chrotha (19/785729) is the principal migratory fish loch on the system since upstream passage is barred by impassable falls between Loch Bad a'Chrotha and Loch Braigh Horrisdale (19/798705).
Fish Few sea-trout, but about 30 to 40 salmon are usually taken which average 6lb 8oz. The best months are, depending upon water levels, July and September.
Flies & Tactics Boat fishing on Loch Bad a'Chrotha produces most of the fish, although some are taken in the slow-moving, canal-like, part of the river to the south and in the pool below the falls. Sport depends upon good water levels so that fish can safely negotiate the weir near the road and enter the loch. The south end, where the loch narrows in the vicinity of the small island, is a good place to begin. See Loch a'Bhealaich entry for commentary in regard to a proposed hydro-electric scheme which may adversely effect the flow of water and fishing conditions. Try: Kate McLaren, Goat's Toe, Ke-He, Willie Gunn, Green Highlander and Hairy Mary. Dapping can also produce results.
Permission & Charges Shieldaig Lodge Hotel guests have priority, but day lets may be available at £35 per day, two rods fishing. Contact: Shieldaig Lodge Hotel, Badachro, Gairloch, Wester Ross. Tel: 01445 741250; Fax: 01445 741305. Shieldaig Lodge Hotel also has two comfortable self cattering cottages for let.

BEAG, Loch See Fionn Loch.
BEANNACH BEAG, Loch See Fionn Loch.
BEANNACH MOR, Loch See Fionn Loch.
BEINN DEARG BAD CHAILLEACH, Loch See Lochan Feoir.
BEINN DEARG BHEAG, Loch See Lochan Feoir.
BEINN DEARG, Loch See Gruinard River.
BEINN DEARG, Loch See Loch an Fhithich.
BHANAMHOIR, Loch See Loch Allt an Daraich.
BOOR, Loch See Loch a'Gharbh-doire.
BRAIGH HORRISDALE, Loch See Loch a'Bhealaich.
CADH A'GHOBHAINN, Loch See Lochan Fada.
CAITIDHRIRIDH, Loch See Lochan Fada.
CAOL NA H-INNSE-GEAMHRAIDH, Loch See Loch an t-Slagain.
CARN NA FEOLA, Lochan See Loch na h-Oidhche.

199

Gairloch & Ullapool — OS Map 19

CEANN A'CHARNAICH, Loch See Loch an Daing.
CHRIOSTINA, Loch See Loch an Iasgair.

CLAIR, Loch
Location & Access 19/773718 Approach from Badachro Farm (19/785730) via a good track which arrives at the loch after a walk south-west for one mile.
Commentary Easily accessible and just about right for a beginner's introduction to the pleasures of hill loch fishing. Splendid scenery and wildlife all the way and the chance to explore six other named and unnamed lochs and lochans in the vicinity: Loch Doire nan Eala (19/779713) and Loch na Glaic Gille (19/765709), a step south from Loch Clair, and remote Lochan Sguat at 19/782693, a mile further south again. To the west of Loch Clair and best approached from South Erradale (19/749714) lie Loch Airigh Uilleim (19/755719) and Loch nam Breac Odhar (19/766720) both, of which are worth a visit. Two further lochs should be noted: Loch Bad na h-Achlaise (19/770736), the north shore of which borders the B8056 Kerrysdale/Redpoint road, and little Loch nan Eun (19/756732) which is reached in five minutes via a track from the B8056 at Port Henderson (19/753736).
Fish Loch Clair has excellent stocks of very pretty fish which average 10oz to 12oz in weight. Loch Bad na h-Achlaise has more modest trout, but also Arctic char. The surrounding smaller waters are dour, but are reputed to contain some specimen fish.
Flies & Tactics There is a boat on Loch Bad na h-Achlaise, but if you choose to bank fish stay ashore and do not wade. The narrow, south-east arm of the loch is the most productive area. The other lochs are easily fished from the shore. On Loch Clair, explore the south end and do not miss the unnamed lochan at 19/768717. A convenient peninsula on the north shore of Loch Airigh Uilleim will allow you to cover every inch of the loch. Flies: Soldier Palmer, Greenwell's Glory and Silver Butcher. Dapping can be effective of Loch Bad na h-Achlaise.
Permission & Charges See Loch Sgeireach (Shieldaig) entry.

CLAIR, Loch See Loch Airigh Mhic Criadh.
CNAPACH, Lochan See Fionn Loch.

COIRE CHAORACHAIN, Loch
Location & Access 19/107821. Approach from the A832 Braemore/Gairloch loch near the bridge over the Dundonnell River at 19/122813. Climb north-west for one mile to reach the south shore of the loch.
Commentary Utterly spectacular scenery, dominated by the bulk of An Teallach (1062m). Make a long day out by visiting a series of adjacent named and unnamed lochs in the surrounding area. After fishing Loch Coire Chaorachain, walk south for fifteen minutes to explore the unnamed lochans at 19/109812. Now cross the hill to the west for half a mile to find Lochain Dubh (19/098812) and its seven satellite lochans. Continue south-east, now, for half a mile, to reach Loch Fada (19/108799), and, if time and energy permit, south again to the unnamed lochan at 19/105793 below Carn nam Feithean (554m). The last loch here is Lochain Coir an Eich Ghlais (19/125786), a group of three small waters, but these are more easily approached directly from the A832 at Fain (19/139792).
Fish Good sport with attractive brown trout which average in the order of 8oz. However, there are some much larger specimens as well. Be prepared for a stronger than usual "tug".
Flies & Tactics This is a 4.5 mile round trip over tough ground, so be well-shod and take along a compass and map and know how to use them. Bank fishing all the way. On Loch Coire Chaorachain, begin near the two inlet streams and the island on the south shore. The other waters are small and easily "read" and fish may be taken from all round the banks. First cast: Blue Zulu, Invicta, Peter Ross.
Permission & Charges See Dundonnell River entry. Expect to pay £5 per rod per day.

COIRE MHIC FHEARCHAIR, Loch See Loch na h-Oidhche.
COIRE NA H-AIRIGH, Loch See Loch a'Gharbh-doire.
CROSS REFERENCES The following lochs are detailed on OS Map 24: LOCH A'MHULLAICH (19/810600); LOCHAN DUBH (West Diabaig) (19/789614); LOCH NAM BALL (19/787616); LOCH AIRIGH A'MHILL (19/788623); LOCH NAN GAMHNA (19/795620); LOCH A'CHAORAINN BEAG (19/802617); LOCH NA FEANNAIG (19/804614); LOCHAN DUBH (East Diabaig) (19/812616); LOCH FREUMHACH (19/814619); LOCH NA H-UAMHAIG (19/820624); LOCH ROAG (19/821611); LOCH AIRIGH EACHAINN (19/828610); LOCH MHEALLAIN (19/835619); LOCH GAINEAMHACH BEAG (19/838626); LOCHAN SGEIREACH (Diabaig) (19/804636); CRAIG RIVER (19/769639); LOCHAN DUBH (CRAIG) (19/776635); LOCHAN DUBH NA CAORACH (19/798650); LOCH NA H-UAMHA (Craig) (19/778661); LOCH A'BHAID-FHEARNA (19/759665)
DIAMOND, Loch See Lochan Sgeireach (Shieldaig).
DOIRE NA H-AIRIGHE, Loch See Loch nam Buainichean.
DOIRE NAN EALA, Loch See Loch Clair.
DRUIM NA FEARNA, Lochan See Lochan Sgeireach (Shieldaig).
DUBH A'PHLUIC, Loch See Loch na Teangaidh Fhiadhaich.
DUBH CAMAS AN LOCHAIN, Loch See Loch na Doire Duinne.
DUBH GEODHACHAN THARAILT, Loch See Loch Dubh na Maoil.
DUBH, Loch (Bad an Sgalaig) See Loch Bad an Sgalaig.
DUBH, Loch(Fionn) See Fionn Loch.
DUBH, Lochain See Loch Coire Chaorachain.
DUBH, Lochan See Fionn Loch.
DUBH NA CLAISE CARNAICH, Loch See Lochan Feoir.

OS Map 19 — Gairloch & Ullapool

DUBH NA MAOIL, Loch
Location & Access 19/891964 Approach from Laide on the A832 Dundonnell/Gairloch road and park at the beach by Mellon Udrigle. Follow the track north from the end of the metalled road to reach the loch in ten minutes.
Commentary Loch Dubh na Maoil and its northern neighbour, Loch Dubh Geodhachan Tharailt (19/892969) are in a delightful setting, close to an excellent sandy beach and well within range of little legs: the ideal location for introducing beginners to the gentle art.
Fish Nothing for the glass case, but decent, 8oz, trout which fight well and taste even better.
Flies & Tactics Easy to fish and few problems. Offer them: Black Pennell, Grouse & Claret and Silver Butcher.
Permission & Charges See Loch an t-Slagain entry.

DUBH NAN CAILLEACH, Lochan See River Kerry.

DUNDONNELL, River
Location & Access Source 19/102751. Outfall 19/090888. The river is adjacent to the A832 road at Dundonnell and is easily accessible.
Commentary The river rises on the north-east shoulder of Creag Rainich (807m) in the Fisherfield Forest and flows north-east as the Allt na Faine before swinging north to enter the sea at the head of Little Loch Broom. Because of impassable waterfalls, fish, and fishing, are confined to the lower reaches of the stream.
Fish Salmon and sea-trout. Approximately 50/80 salmon each season, depending upon water conditions Few sea-trout are caught now. Salmon average 6lb/7lb in weight, sea-trout 1lb 8oz. However, during one week in 1999, one rod had 6 salmon, the largest of which weighed 14lb..
Flies & Tactics This is very much a spate stream and good sport depends upon a good flow of water. A single-handed rod covers most eventualities and wading is not really necessary as most of the pools are easily, and better, covered from the bank. For conservation purposes the estate encourages a policy of catch-and-release. Flies: Try: Garry Dog, Hairy Mary, Black Doctor, Goat's Toe, Willie Gunn, Green Highlander.
Permission & Charges The Factor, Estate Office, Dundonnell Estate, Dundonnell, Wester-Ross. Tel: 01854 633206. Fishing is generally let with a comfortable estate cottage and the tenant has fishing priority. When otherwise available, day let salmon fishing costs £20 per rod per day.

EWE, River
Location & Access Source 25/975524 Outfall 19/858810. Easily accessible from the track which borders the north bank of the river.
Commentary A classic Highland river; two miles in length, from the outflow at Loch Maree to the sea in Loch Ewe, wide and swift-flowing. The most productive pool is probably Seapool, particularly in low water conditions. The other pools include such famous names as Macordies, Ken's Pool, the Tee Pool, Flats, Hen House Pool and The Narrows.
Fish The annual average catch is in the order of 100 salmon. Average weight of salmon is 8lb/9lb. The heaviest fish in recent years weighed 23lb 8oz and was taken from Seapool on an Ally's Shrimp by Alex Cochrane. Good numbers of sea-trout used to be taken but, sadly, they have all but disappeared because of the impact on wild fish of fish farm sea lice infestations.
Flies & Tactics A 15ft rod is required to cover the lies comfortably. Deep wading is not required, but thigh waders are useful. A few fish are taken during the early months, but autumn fishing, July onwards, now produces the best results. Escapee farmed salmon, from salmon farm cages in Loch Ewe, are an increasing problem and little seems to be being done to address the issue. Flies: Ally's Shrimp, Stoat's Tail, Silver Stoat, Munro Killer and Hairy Mary.
Permission & Charges Well-booked in advance, but, day rods are available from time to time. Contact: Steve Younie, The Keeper's Cottage, Poolewe, Wester Ross. Tel: 01445 781274. Expect to pay between £20 and £130 per rod per day, depending upon time of year.

FADA, Lochan
Location & Access 19/025710 No easy way in. The best approach is from a track which starts near Kinlochewe at Incheril (19/033626) and follows the north bank of the Kinlochewe River to Loch Maree. After crossing the Abhainn an Fhasaigh, turn north up Gleann Bianasdail. Lochan Fada is a stiff three mile hike through the glen, making the total journey, there and back, some eleven miles.
Commentary Lochan Fada lies at the heart of some of Scotland's most dramatic scenery, centred by the might of Slioch (980m) "The Spear". The loch is four miles long by up to half a mile wide and drops to a depth of 70m towards the west end. This is wild country where a compass and map and proper walking equipment is essential. To the south of Lochan Fada, on the plateaux between Slioch and Beinn Lair (860m) is Loch Garbhaig (19/000706), another outstanding water, one and a quarter miles east/west by quarter of a mile wide. To the north, tucked away in a dark corrie below the towering slopes of A'Mhaighdean (940m), lies remote Gorm Loch Mor (19/003740) which rarely sees an artificial fly. To the east of Lochan Fada, in the Kinlochewe Forest, lie a series of more than twenty additional named and unnamed lochs and lochans. These are approached via a private estate road from the cottage at the Heights of Kinlochewe (19/075642) at the junction of the Abhainn Gleann na Muice and the Abhainn Bruachaig, tributaries of the Kinlochewe River.
Fish In the smaller lochs and lochans, excellent stocks of traditional highland wild brown trout which average in the order of 3 to the pound. However, there are also larger specimens and, in some waters, Arctic charr. Lochan Fada and Loch Garbhaig hold splendid trout, as well as huge, hard-to-catch, ferox.
Flies & Tactics Do not go here unless you enjoy hill loch bank fishing and are prepared to do a lot of walking, some of it arduous. A private road runs from Heights of Kinlochewe cottage to the east end of Lochan Fada and this also gives access to the other hill

Gairloch & Ullapool — OS Map 19

lochs on the estate: Loch an Uillt-ghiubhais (19/055652), Loch na Guailne Idhre (19/064653), Loch Caitidhriridh (19/053682), Loch Cadh a'Ghobhainn (19/048679) with its small island and satellite lochans; the distant, tiny pools on the west shoulder of Meallan Chuaich (690m), Lochain Ceann na Moine (19/095674), Loch a'Mheallain Odhair (19/071686), Loch Meallan an Fhudair (19/062706l), which drains into Lochan Fada; Loch an Sgeireach (19/053695) and Loch Gleann na Muice (19/060688) which are an extension of the outlet burn from Lochan Fada at the head of Gleann na Muice. There is a lifetimes fishing here. Flies: Ke-He, Black Pennell, Silver Butcher.

Permission & Charges Outstanding value-for-money sport and self-catering accommodation at Heights of Kinlochewe cottage during May, June, July and early August. Approximately £420 per week, inclusive, for six people. Contact: Mrs Barbara Grant, Letterewe Estate, Loch Maree, Achnasheen, Ross-shire IV22 2HH. Tel: 01445 760207; Fax: 01445 760284.

FADA, Lochan (Fain) See Loch Coire Chaorachain.
FADA, Lochan (Strath Lungard) See Loch na h-Oidhche.
FAIRY, Loch See Lochan Sgeireach (Shieldaig).
FEITH MHIC-ILLEAN, Lochan See Fionn Loch.
FEITHE MUGAIG, Loch See Loch nam Buainichean.

FEOIR, Lochan

Location & Access 19/909887 Park by the viewpoint on the A832 Dundonnell/Gairloch road as 19/890900. Lochan Feoir is a tough one and a half mile hike south-east.

Commentary Lochan Feoir is the centre point for a long day out fishing a series of 11 named and unnamed lochs and lochans to the east of the main road. A compass and map are essential to find your way round and the total journey will involve you a six mile tramp over rough ground. Be prepared.

Fish Some first class trout of up to and over 2lb in weight and plenty of sport with their smaller brethren.

Flies & Tactics Begin on Loch Dubh na Claise Carnaich (19/893896) and them climb east to find Loch na Ba (19/904894). Don't miss the unnamed lochan adjacent to the west shore of Loch na Ba. Fish anti-clockwise round Loch na Ba and then continue up the inlet burn at the south end to locate Lochan Feoir. From Lochan Feoir, walk south for five minutes to the corrie loch, Loch Beinn Dearg Bheag (19/909883) below the crags of Beinn Dearg Bad Chailleach (273m). Now hike north, via the unnamed lochans at 19/912888 and 19/911894, to fish Loch Moine Sheilg (19/919897). Angle west from Loch Moine Sheilg round the slope of the hill towards the forest, half a mile distant, to visit Loch na Cathrach Duibhe (19/899902) and its unnamed neighbour, both of which lie on the south edge of the forest. Follow the edge of the plantation back to the start point. Easy bank fishing all round and no need for wading. Loch Moine Sheilg is perhaps the most productive water, but all give great sport. Show them: Blue Zulu, Invicta and Peter Ross.

Permission & Charges See Loch an t-Slagain entry.

FEUR, Loch See Loch a'Gharbh-doire.

FIONN, Loch

Location & Access 19/950785. Approach from Poolewe by following the track along the north bank of the River Ewe to Inveran and the Keepers Cottage at Kernsary (19/893794). This is a private, estate, road only accessible to four-wheel drive vehicles and there are locked gates along its length. The total distance, from Poolewe to the Fionn Loch is approximately five miles.

Commentary One of the most scenically magnificent lochs in all of Scotland and one of the most famous. On the 12th April 1851, Sir Alexander Gordon Cumming of Altyre caught 12 trout weighing 87lb 12oz. During June and July 1912, Mr F C Grady took 3,652 trout weighing 1,140lb, including eight fish of up to 8lb in weight. He noted that all trout under 6" were thrown back. The loch is five miles long by up to one mile wide at the north end and drops to a depth of 40m in the south. It is surrounded by a number of Munros (Scottish mountains over 3,000ft in height) and by a number of other, smaller, excellent trout lochs: to the west, Lochan Beannach Beag (19/948775), Lochan Beannach Mor (19/940774), Loch nan Clach Dubha (19/928782), Loch an Doire Crionaich (19/934770), Loch na Moine (19/924786), Loch an Gaineamh (920795), Loch nan Carn (19/935794, Loch Tholldhoire (19/897777), Loch na h-Airigh Molaich (19/920801), Loch an Eilein (South) (19/924808); to the north, Lochan Sgeireach (19/915814), Loch nan Uain (19/902827), Loch an Eilein (North) (19/909833), Loch na Moine Buige (19/920833), Loch an Eilich (19/926835), Loch an Iasgair (19/922844), Lochain Cnapach (19/928847), Loch nan Eun (19/932852), Loch Searrach (19/931862), Loch na h-Uidhe (19/930878), Loch a'Mhonaidh-dhroighinn (19/938885), Loch an Fhamhair (19/961879), Loch a'Mhadaidh Mor (19/964867), Lochan Dubh (19/955864); to the east, Loch Beag (19/948823), Loch Toll a'Mhadaidh (19/986812), Lochan na Bearta (19/999802); and to the south east, accessed by the stalker's path from the bothy at Carnmore (19/980769), Dubh Loch (19/985760), and a series of remote, high corrie lochans: Lochan Cnapach (19/005784), Lochan Feith Mhic-illean (19/005776), three inter-linked waters; Fuar Loch Mor (19/009760) which is approximately 120 acres in extent and Fuar Loch Beag (19/000761), a stiff climb up the inlet burn on the south west shore of Fuar Loch Mor; Lochan a'Bhraghad (19/025763) and its unnamed little satellite lochan with the small island immediately to the north.

Fish Super brown trout, and some Arctic Charr, with the chance of a salmon in the Fionn Loch. The trout vary in size from 4oz up to monsters of 10lb plus in the Fionn Loch.

Flies & Tactics Boat fishing only on the Fionn Loch and, be well-warned, this can be a very dangerous water. There a large number of barely-submerged rocks which are difficult to see, even during relatively calm

OS Map 19 — Gairloch & Ullapool

weather. Take great care. The best course of action, if you are unfamiliar with the water, is to arrange to go afloat with someone who knows the loch, preferably from the estate, or possibly with a member of the Gairloch Angling Club. The east shoreline is a good place to begin, as is the wide bay protected by Eilean Fraoch (19/945804) on the north-east shore. There used to be an inn here, on the line of a cattle drove-road. Old Boat House Bay (19/945782) is a noted salmon location and a good jump-off point for a visit to nearby hill lochs. All the hill lochs are fished from the shore. The lochs to the east and south-east are very remote and you will need good mountain-walking skills and physical fitness, to fish them safely. Never wade in any of these waters. It is highly dangerous to do so. Only kill the fish which you intend to eat. Return all others to fight another day. Offer the trout: Ke-He, Black Pennell, Blue Zulu, Black Zulu, Soldier Palmer, Peter Ross, Silver Invicta, and Dunkeld.

Permission & Charges All enquiries in regard to access and fishing in this area should be addressed to Mrs Barbara Grant, Letterewe Estate, Loch Maree, Achnasheen, Ross-shire IV22 2HH. Tel: 01445 760207; Fax: 01445 760284. Permission is entirely at the discretion of the Estate which also has a number of comfortable, self-catering, properties which are let with trout, sea-trout and salmon fishing. Details on application to Mrs Grant.

FRAOICH, Lochan See Loch Allt Eigin.
FUAR LOCH BEAG, Loch See Fionn Loch.
FUAR LOCH MOR, Loch See Fionn Loch.
FUAR, Lochan See Loch a'Bhealaich.
GAINEAMHAICH, Loch See Loch a'Bhealaich.
GAINEAMHAICH, Loch See Gruinard River.
GARBHAIG, Loch See Lochan Fada.

GARBHAIGH, Loch (Talladale)
Location & Access 19/900692 Approach from the A832 Kinlochewe/Gairloch road at 19/895714. A track winds south through woodlands signposted to Victoria Falls and Power Station, adjacent to the line of the outflow stream from the loch. Continue onto the hill and follow the forestry track to reach the small hydro-electric dam at the north end of the loch after an uphill hike of about 40 minutes.
Commentary Loch Garbhaig extends for over half a mile north/south and is up to 300yds wide. The east shore is steep, backed by Meall Garbhaig (410m) and this hill can provide some respite from strong south and east winds. A spectacular loch in glorious surroundings but now sadly degraded by a recent hydro-electric scheme.
Fish Brown trout with fish of up to and over 1lb in weight.
Flies & Tactics Bank fishing and they don't give themselves up easily. The best place to start is at the south end, in the vicinity of the three small inlet streams, working north again up the west shoreline. Try: Black Zulu, Grouse & Claret, Peter Ross.
Permission & Charges The Loch is leased by the Gairloch Angling Club. Prices vary, depending upon which loch you fish, but expect to pay in the order of £3 per rod per day for bank fishing and £10 for a boat with two rods fishing. Contact: K Gunn, Newsagent, Strath, Gair Loch, Wester Ross, Scotland.K Gunn, Newsagent, Strath, Gairloch, Wester Ross. Tel: 01445 712400; Taylor's Shop, Poolewe, Wester Ross. 01445 781240; Loch Maree Hotel, Loch Maree, Wester Ross. Tel: 01445 760288. Gairloch Post Office also issue permits at Anchorage Crafts, Oier Road, Gairloch, Wester Ross. Tel: 01445 712005. Gillie Services and additional information from D W Roxborough, The Old Police Station, Gairloch. Tel: 01445 712057.

GHIUBHSACHAIN, Loch See Gruinard River.
GHIURAGARSTIDH, Loch See Loch nan Dailthean.
GLEANN NA MUICE, Loch See Lochan Fada.
GORM LOCH MOR, Loch See Lochan Fada.
GORM LOCH NA BEINNE, Loch See Loch na Oidhche.
GRASS, Loch See Loch a'Gharbh-doire.
GROM-LOCH FADA, Loch See Loch na h-Oidhche.

GRUINARD, River
Location & Access Source 19/082744 Outflow 19/959920 Easy access from the A832 Dundonnell/Gairloch road via a private estate road. Also accessed from the A832 are five brown trout loch to the north of the Gruinard River: Loch a'Bhaid-choille (19/004914), Loch na-Cleire (19/009903), Loch an Eilich (19/995908), Lochan an Daimh (19/982928) and Lochan na Cairill (19/980914). These waters contain small brown trout which average 8oz but Loch an Eilich has larger specimens as well.
Commentary The headwaters of the Gruinard River lie amidst some of Scotland's grandest scenery, dominated by mighty An Teallach (1062m) in the heart of the Strathnasheallag Forest. The true source of the river is in Loch an Nid (19/081745), between Mullach Coire Mhic Fhearchair (1019m) to the west and Creag Rainich (807m) to the east. The river flows north for three miles as the Abhainn Gleann na Muice before turning west into Loch na Sealga by the climbers bothy at Shenavall (19/066810). Loch na Sealga is the principal feeder loch, nearly four miles in length by up to half a mile wide and dropping to 60m in depth. To the north of Loch na Sealga lie three excellent trout lochs, Loch Gaineamhaich (19/018876), Loch Mor Bad an Ducharaich (19/008862) and Loch an Eich Dhuibh (19/024854), all of which offer great bank fishing. To the south, on the line of the Allt Loch Ghiubhsachain, is Loch Ghiubhsachain (19/005820), a long, narrow water, and, south again, Loch Beinn Dearg (19/025789), both of which can hold sea-trout given good water conditions. Two other waters should be noted: Loch Toll an Lochain (19/074833) much-loved of climbers on hot days, and, perhaps the most difficult of access, Loch a'Bhrisidh (19/059758) on the north slopes of Sgurr Ban (989m) which is strictly for the angler who likes a really taxing hike with his fishing.
Fish The Gruinard produces approximately 80/100 salmon each season and a few of sea-trout, although sea-trout are greatly reduced in numbers now, compared to a few years ago. Although the average weight of brown trout is modest, some of the lochs contain very large trout.

Gairloch & Ullapool   OS Map 19

Flies & Tactics The Gruinard River is very much a spate stream and good sport depends upon adequate water levels. The river is easily fished with a strong, single-handed grilse rod and the principal pools include: Admiral's, Matheson's, Ghiubhsachain Runs & Flats, Craigower Stream, Tree, Middle and Lower Rockies, Bothy Flats, Miss Baring's, Upper, Middle and Lower Gibraltar, Otter, Iron House Flats, Bridge, Garden and Sea Pool. There is a boat on Loch na Sealga but all the other lochs noted are fished from the bank. Wading is dangerous and unnecessary because the fish tend to lie close to the margins. For salmon and sea-trout, offer: Green Highlander, Goats Toe, Willie Gunn, Hairy Mary, Stoat's Tail, Garry Dog. For trout: Black Pennell, Invicta, Alexandra.

Permission & Charges One beat of fishing is let in conjunction with Mungasdale House which is situated on the shores of Gruinard Bay. Lets are rarely available because the same tenants take the sport each year. Bookings through: Strutt & Parker, 13 Hill Street, Berkley Square, London W1X 8DL. Tel: 0171 629 7282; Fax: 0171 449 1657. Two beats are let by Eilean Darroch Estate, Anderson Strathearn WS, 48 Castle Street, Edinburgh EH2 3LX. Tel: 0131 220 2345 Fax: 0131 226 7788 (Accommodation, salmon fishing and unlimited trout fishing).

KERNSARY, Loch

Location & Access 19/880804. Approach from the A832 Poolewe/Dundonnell road. After cross the bridge over the River Ewe, heading north, park on the right hand side of the road at Srondubh (19/862813). A track leads south-east from here to reach the loch after an easy walk of about one mile.

Commentary One of the most scenically lovely lochs in Wester Ross, scattered over a wide area of bays, headlands and fishy corners, one and a half miles east/west by up to half a mile wide. The loch is 20m deep at the south end where the principal feeder burn enters. Loch Kernsary exits through Loch na h-Airde Bige to feed Loch Maree at Inveran (19/875785).

Fish Good stocks of wild brown trout and the occasional salmon and sea-trout. These are most often encountered towards the end of the season, in August and September.

Flies & Tactics Bank fishing only, at the north end of the loch, although there may be the chance of a boat from the Letterewe Estate to fish the south end. Contact Mrs Grant on 01445 760207. From the bank, fish the west shoreline and then Loch na h-Airde Bige. Offer the residents: Ke-He, Invicta and Alexandra.

Permission & Charges £6 per rod per day from: National Trust for Scotland, Inverewe Visitor Centre, Poolewe, Wester Ross. Tel: 01445 781229. Trust members pay £5 per rod per day.

KERRY, River

Location & Access Source: 19/902635 Outfall: 19/813739 One mile south from Gairloch and easily accessible from the A832 Kinlochewe/Gairloch road.

Commentary The true source of the river is Gorm Loch na Beinne (19/902635) to the south of Poca Buidhe in the Flowerdale Forest, but a hydro-electric scheme has impounded these waters behind a dam at the outlet of Loch Bad Sgalaig (19/850710). However, the river is guaranteed compensation flow and is often in fishable condition when other systems in the area are summer-dry. If the Kerry is not in condition, consider a hike out to a delightful, rarely visited, little loch on the hill to the west of the river: Lochan Dubh nan Cailleach (19/815734).

Fish Few sea-trout, but about 40 to 60 salmon each year, average 5lb/6lb in weight. Heavier fish are taken and most seasons produce 10lb plus specimens.

Flies & Tactics The river is divided into two beats by the road bridge on the B8056. There are 27 named and unnamed pools. Two rods fish each beat and the lower beat is the most productive with Bridge Pool, Kerrysdale Pool and Kerrysdale Glide being particularly notable. The New Pool, before the river enters the sea, is difficult to fish and should be approached with extreme caution. On the Upper River, Brigadier's Pool and the Corner Pool will often give a fish in decent conditions. Use a trout rod to tackle the stream and brush up on your roll and Spey casting in advance of your visit: the banks are lined with unforgiving trees. Best months, July, August and September. Offer: Kerry Blue, Munro Killer, Willie Gunn, Hairy Mary, Silver Wilkinson, and various Shrimp patterns.

Permission & Charges The river is managed by the Gairloch Angling Club and day tickets cost £12 per rod. Contact: Creag Mor Hotel, Gairloch, Wester Ross. Tel: 01445 712068.

KINLOCHEWE, River

Location & Access Source 25/975524 Outfall 19/014645. Access is from the A832 Dingwall/Gairloch road via Anancaun (19/025630) and from the track along the north bank of the river from Incheril (19/035621).

Commentary The source of the river is Lochan Uaine, between Sgorr nan Lochan Uaine (870m) and Beinn Laith Mhor (925m). The stream flows east for two miles down the Allt Coire Beine Leithe into the River Coulin and then north through Loch Coulin and Loch Clair (see OS Map 25) to become the A'Ghairbhe River. The flow is joined by the Abhainn Bruachaig at Kinlochewe and then flows west as the Kinlochewe River to enter the east end of Loch Maree after a further two miles.

Fish Approximately 60 to 90 salmon are taken each season, depending upon water conditions. The heaviest fish taken in recent years weighed 16lb and was caught in the Junction Pool. Sea-trout have declined in numbers.

Flies & Tactics The main river and the two tributaries, the Abhainn Bruachaig and the A'Ghairbhe River, are let with the rental of Kinlochewe Lodge which accommodates 18 guests. There are 5 rods on the rivers and two on the south end of Loch Maree, as well as trout fishing on Loch Fannich (see OS Map 20) and on other, adjacent, hill lochs. Salmon run up from Loch Maree as early as March, but the most productive fishing is generally in July and August. A single-handed rod is adequate for most eventualities and wading is not required. Flies: Green Highlander, Hairy Mary, Stoat's

OS Map 19 — Gairloch & Ullapool

Tail, Goat's Toe, Willie Gunn, Garry Dog, General Practitioner, Black Doctor and Ally's Shrimp.
Permission & Charges Finlyson Hughes, 29 Barossa Place, Perth. Tel: 01738 630926; Fax: 01738 639017. Expect to pay in the region of £2,500 for a July week.

LARAIG, Loch See Loch Tollaidh.

LITTLE GRUINARD, River
Location & Access Source: 19/950785 Outflow: 19/947899 Access is from Little Gruinard on the A832 Poolewe/Dundonnell road via a private estate road which margins the west bank of the stream.
Commentary The river flows out of the north end of the Fionn Loch (19/950785) and reaches the sea in Gruinard Bay after a journey of some four and a half miles. The upper reaches, Upper, Middle and Lower Flats, are good holding pools, deep and slow moving, whilst as the river progresses north its passage becomes more rapid; small, rocky pools and mountain-goat stumbling-country. From the main road to the sea, the river is less demanding to fish.
Fish Approximately 60/100 salmon each season, depending upon prevailing water conditions. Few sea-trout.
Flies & Tactics All the fishing is let on a strictly enforced policy of "catch-and-release". A single-handed rod is adequate for most situations, although when a heavy fish is hooked it may take some time to secure the salmon in a strong current such as is to be found in pool between the Major and the Garden Pool. Because of the nature of the river, you must be prepared to adopt an intuitive, non-standard approach, adapting your technique to the requirements of each pool. Flies: Willie Gunn, Green Highlander, Munro Killer, Garry Dog, General Practitioner, Hairy Mary.
Permission & Charges The river is let, along with a number of excellent, adjacent, wild brown trout lochs, with comfortable self-catering accommodation for up to 10 people. 5 rods each day salmon fishing. Inclusive cost: £1,500 per week. Contact: Mrs Barbara Grant, Letterewe Estate, Loch Maree, Achnasheen, Ross-shire. Tel: 01445 760207; Fax: 01445 760284.

LOCHAIN CEANN NA MOINE, Loch See Lochan Fada.
LOCHAIN CNAPACH, Loch See Fionn Loch.
LOCHAIN NAN SEASGACH, Loch See Loch an Iasgair.

MAREE, Loch
Location & Access 19/920730. Access from the A832 Gairloch/ Kinlochewe road at Talladale (19/915704) and from Kinlochewe (19/011642).
Commentary Very beautiful, 12 miles long and more than 2 miles wide across the north bay, scattered with romantic, tree-clad islands, dominated by Slioch (980m) to the north and Beinn Eighe (972m) to the south.
Fish In its glory days, Loch Maree boats used to catch upwards of 2000 sea-trout each season, but in recent years this has fallen at times to less than 50. Many anglers believe that this is due to sea lice infestation from Crown Estate licensed salmon farm cages in Loch Ewe. A substantial body of evidence indicates that this is indeed the case but neither government fishery scientists nor the fish farmers, seem to be prepared to do anything about it. In order to enhance stocks, the present policy is that all sea-trout are returned.
Flies & Tactics Fishing on Loch Maree is readily available, where once it was almost impossible to obtain a booking. For the best chance, go afloat with the resident gillie, Mick Markey. Dapping is the preferred fishing method and the loch is divided into rotating beats. Flies: Loch Ordie, Blue Zulu, Black Zulu, Ke-He, Clan Chief, Black Pennell and Grouse & Claret.
Permission & Charges For bookings, contact: The Loch Maree Hotel, Loch Maree, Wester Ross. Tel: 01445 760288. Mr MacDonald, Bridge House, Kinlochewe, Wester Ross. Tel: 01445 760256; H Davis, 'Sonas', Lechnaside, Gairloch, Wester Ross. Tel: 01445 741388; Shieldaig Lodge Hotel, Gairloch, Wester Ross. Tel: 01445 741250; Fax: 01445 741305. Kinlochewe Hotel, Kinlochewe, Wester Ross. Tel: 01445 760253. Expect to pay approximately £35 per day. Gillie, £35 per day plus gratuity.

MEALL A'BHAINNE, Loch See Loch a'Mhadaidh.
MEALLAN AN FHUDAIR, Loch See Lochan Fada.
MHIC'ILLE RIABHAICH, Loch See Loch 'Bhaid-luachraich.
MOINE SHEILG, Loch See Lochan Feoir.
MOR BAD AN DUCHARAICH, Loch See Gruinard River.
NA BA, Loch See Lochan Feoir.
NA BEARTA, Lochan See Fionn Loch.

NA BEINNE, Lochan
Location & Access 19/126961. Approach from the Ardmair/Ullapool road via a track which runs east at 19/115960 to Loch Dubh, which is one of the Dam Lochs (see OS Map 20).
Commentary This tiny lochan lies on the west shoulder of Creag na Feola (251m) and there are two, further, unnamed lochans to the north. North again, and also accessible from the same track, is Lochan Sgeireach (19/130980) with its unnamed satellite lochan and another lovely little unnamed lochan in the corrie below Creag na h-Iolaire (297m) at 19/136983.
Fish Nothing for the glass case, but plenty for supper.
Flies & Tactics Infrequently visited and offering wonderful hill walking and bank fishing with magnificent views south to the mountains of the Fisherfield Forest and north into Inverpolly and Assynt. Flies: Loch Ordie, Soldier Palmer, Black Pennell.
Permission & Charges The Mountainman, West Argyle Street, Ullapool, Wester-Ross. Tel: 01854 613383. Cost, £5 per rod per day.

NA BESTIE, Loch
Location & Access 19/884844. Easily accessible from the Laide Mellon Udrigle road. Close by, on the Slaggan track, is Loch na h-Innse Gairbhe another another little loch well worth a visit.
Commentary Both lochs are a step from the roadside and easily fished.

205

Gairloch & Ullapool — OS Map 19

Fish Small trout.
Flies & Tactics Loch na Bestie has a boat, but Loch na h-Innse Gairbhe is fished from the bank. There have been smolt cages in Loch na Bestie in the past. Offer them: Loch Ordie, Black Pennell and Peter Ross.
Permission & Charges See Loch an t-Slagain entry.

NA CABHAIG, Loch See Loch na h-Oidhche.
NA CAIRILL, Lochan See Gruinard River.
NA CATHRACH DUIBHE, Loch See Lochan Feoir.
NA CLAISE CARNAICH, Loch See Loch a'Bhaid-luachraich.
NA CLOICHE, Loch See Loch an Iasgair.

NA CURRA, Loch
Location & Access 19/823800 Park in the layby on the left of the A832 Gairloch/Poolewe road near Loch Tollaidh at 19/8367865. Loch na Curra is reached after a stiff walk north-west round the east shoulder of Meall Deise (230m). White posts, spaced approximately 300yards apart, should help to keep you on the right line.
Commentary A first-class loch in a wonderful setting. A step further north is another outstanding loch, Loch Bad a'Chreamh (19/818810), half a mile north/south by up to 600yards wide, and its little satellite water, Loch Sgeireach (19/813804).
Fish Loch na Curra has large stocks of brown trout which average 6oz/8oz. Loch Bad a'Chreamh has larger fish which average in the order of 8oz to 12oz.
Flies & Tactics There is a boat on each loch and although bank fishing is allowed in Loch na Curra, fishing is from the boat only on Loch Bad a'Chreamh. The south end of Loch na Curra is the most productive area, whilst when fishing on Loch Bad a'Chreamh, you should concentrate in the vicinity of the small islands at the south end and down the west shore of the loch. Flies: Soldier Palmer, Invicta and Peter Ross.
Permission & Charges It might be possible to arrange for Argo-cat transport. To do so, contact: Harry Davies, 'Sonas', Lechnaside, Gairloch, Wester Ross. Tel: 01445 741388. Also, The Post Office, Pier Road, Gairloch, Wester Ross. Cost approx £20 per boat.

NA DOIRE DUINNE, Loch
Location & Access 19/850967. Turn north from the A832 Dundonnell/Gairloch road at Laide (19/900918) and park at the end of the minor road at 19/877970. Loch na Doire Duinne lies at the end of a two mile walk due west from the parking place.
Commentary There are 14 named and unnamed lochs and lochans here, scattered over the moor from Meall a'Choire (141m) in the south, north to Greenstone Point. Spend a day visiting them in a six mile round trip amidst splendid scenery. Few people walk this way so you are guaranteed solitude and peace.
Fish The best fish caught in recent years weighed 4lb 8oz. The average weight is more modest, in the order of 8oz/10oz.
Flies & Tactics Begin with a cast on Loch Dubh Camas an Lochain (19/871972) and its tiny satellite lochan. Walk west for fifteen minutes to reach Lochan Sgeireach (19/864973), then follow the outlet stream south west to find Loch a'Bhaid Ghainmheich (19/857968). The unnamed lochan on the hill to the south at 19/864966 is worth a cast. Fish the north shoreline of Loch a'Bhaid Ghainmheich and then clockwise round Loch na Doire Duinne. After exploring Loch na Doire Duinne, return via the north shore of Loch a'Bhaid Ghainmheich to fish Loch an Ath Ghairbh (19/858972); then walk north to irk the inhabitants of Loch nan Eun (19/858979) and Loch an Dun-chairn (19/863982). Fish may be taken from all round the shores of these lochs and there is no need to wade. Lunch by the little island at the north end of Loch nan Eun on the cliff top overlooking the sea.
Flies: Blue Zulu, Soldier Palmer and Silver Invicta.
Permission & Charges See Loch an t-Slagain entry.

NA FAOILEIGE, Loch See Loch a'Chairn (OS Map 20).
NA FEITHE DIRICH, Loch See Loch an Daing.
NA FIDEIL, Loch See Loch na Teangaidh Fhiadhaich.
NA GLAIC GILLE, Loch See Loch Clair.
NA GUAILNE IDHRE, Loch See Lochan Fada.
NA H-AIRDE BIGE, Loch See Loch Kernsary.
NA H-AIRIGH MOLAICH, Loch See Fionn Loch.
NA H-ARD EILIG, Loch See Loch an Teas (South).
NA H-INNSE GAIRBHE, Loch See Loch na Bestie.

NA H-OIDHCHE, Loch
Location & Access 19/890654 Park on the A832 Kinlochewe/Gairloch road near the shed (known as the Red Stable) at 19/856721. A track crosses the outlet stream from Am Feur-Loch (19/859720) and leads south into the hills. Follow this track for four and a half miles to reach the north end of Loch na H-Oidhche (Gaelic name - The Loch of the Night). Allow two hours for the journey.
Commentary One of the 'great' fishing adventures of Wester Ross and one of the finest places to fish in all of Scotland. There is a boathouse at the north end of the loch where a boat and outboard engine are located. Use the boat to motor south down the loch (one and a half miles) to Poca Buidhe (19/899643), a well-furnished stone-built cottage which makes an ideal base from which to explore this magnificent wilderness area. The cottage sleeps four and is surrounded by a cathedral-like array of splendid mountains, guarded to the south by the 2,000ft high north wall of Liathach (1054m). Immediately south of Poca Buidhe lie the Gorm Lochs, Gorm-Loch Fada (19/899639) and Gorm-Loch na Beinne (19/902635). South again, scattered throughout an area covering 2 square miles or so at the head of Strath Lungard, is a splendid series of additional lochs and lochans all of which will provide great sport with hard-fighting small wild trout: Lochan Fada (19/921628), Loch Coire Mhic Fhearchair (19/942608) cradled in the hollow between Ruadh-stack Mor (1010m) and Sail Mhor (981m) guarding the famous Triple Buttress; Loch nan Caber (19/926605), Lochan Carn na Feola (19/920619), Loch a'Choire Mhoir (19/900609) below Beinn Dearg (914m) and Loch na Cabhaig (19/892624).
Fish The Gorm Lochs hold trout of over 3lb in weight. Loch na h-Oidhche trout average 12oz. The other

OS Map 19 — Gairloch & Ullapool

waters contain good stocks of beautiful half pound trout.

Flies & Tactics June is the perfect month for this expedition when it is possible to fish Loch na h-Oidhche almost right through the night, the best time, as the name implies, to launch your attack. The Gorm Lochs fish best during the day so you may, if you wish, have round-the-clock sport. Fish the margins of Loch na h-Oidhche, particularly in the vicinity of the stream which tumbles in from Baosbheinn (800m) (The Wizard's Mountain) half way down the west shoreline, and the shallow north and south ends. Bank fishing is just as productive as fishing from the boat. If you venture further south, into the wilderness, you must be well-prepared, able to use a compass and map and be ready for some tough walking. Flies: Ke-He, Grouse & Claret, Peter Ross.

Permission & Charges It may be possible to obtain the services of an Argo-cat to reach Poca Buidhe. For details and bothy-rental charges, contact: Harry Davis, 'Sonas', Lechnaside, Gairloch, Wester Ross. Tel: 01445 741388. Les Lamb, Post Office, Pier Road, Gairloch. Tel 01445 712402.

NA H-UAMHAIDH BEAG, Loch See Loch an Daing.
NA H-UAMHAIDH MOIRE, Loch See Loch an Daing.
NA H-UIDHE, Loch See Fionn Loch.
NA LAIRIGE, Loch See Loch a'Gharbh-doire.
NA LEIRG, Loch See Loch an Fhithich.
NA MOINE BUIGE, Loch See Fionn Loch.
NA MOINE, Loch See Fionn Loch.
NA SEALGA, Loch See Gruinard River.
NA SGAIREIG MOR, Loch See Loch an Fhithich.
NA-CLEIRE, Loch See Gruinard River.
NAM BREAC, Lochan See Loch a'Gharbh-doire.
NAM BREAC ODHAR, Loch See Loch Clair.

NAM BUAINICHEAN, Loch
Location & Access 19/854735. Park on the A832 Kinlochewe/Gairloch road at the Red Stable (19/857721). Find the outlet steam from Loch nam Buainichean immediately behind the building and walk north up the glen to reach the loch after half a mile.
Commentary The first loch in a series of 11 named and unnamed lochs and lochans which will provide an excellent day out in the hills covering approximately 5 miles. It is rough going and a compass and map are essential.
Fish The principal lochs contain trout which average 6oz/8oz. Some of the unnamed lochans, however, have fish of up to 1lb in weight.
Flies & Tactics Bank fishing all the way. The east end of Loch nam Buainichean is unfishable. Concentrate along the north shore, working east. Walk south-east for five minutes to reach the long, narrow, unnamed lochan at 19/863732; then climb steeply north-east over Creag Ruadh (320m) and descend to Loch Doire na h-Airighe (19/872740). Have a cast in the little, unnamed, lochans immediately to the south. Now walk north-west, round the side of the hill, for 15 minutes, to locate the long straggle of Loch Feithe Mugaig (19/860747). Return to the start point by following a track south, past the trout-filled unnamed lochan at 19/855741. First cast: Blue Zulu, March Brown and Silver Butcher.
Permission & Charges See Loch Garbhaig (Talladale) entry.

NAN CABER, Loch See Loch na h-Oidhche.
NAN CARN, Loch See Fionn Loch.
NAN CLACH DUBHA, Loch See Fionn Loch.

NAN CLACHAN GEALA, Loch
Location & Access 19/859953. See Loch an t-Slagain entry. Walk north from the Slaggan track, climbing easily over the moor to reach Loch nan Clachan Geala after 20 minutes. Along the way, stop for a throw in little Loch a'Bhonnaich (19/852948).
Commentary A five mile round hike centred on Meall a'Choire (141m) fishing five named and unnamed lochs and lochans. After examining Loch nan Clachan Geala, walk north west for ten minutes to reach Loch nan Uan. Return east to fish the north end of Loch nan Clachan Geala, then continue east via the unnamed lochan at 19/864955 to find Loch a'Choire (19/868954), the largest of the waters and covering an area of some 50 acres.
Fish Some nice trout, including a few fish of up to and over 1lb in weight.
Flies & Tactics The north end of Loch nan Clachan Geala can be very good, as can the narrow south section of Loch a'Choire. Otherwise, expect action all round with: Ke-He, Soldier Palmer and Dunkeld.
Permission & Charges See Loch an t-Slagain entry.

NAN DAILTHEAN, Loch
Location & Access 19/878830 Easily accessible from the A832 Poolewe/Dundonnell road at Tournaig (19/876835).
Commentary This delightful loch lies close to the road and extends for half a mile north/south by up to 250yards wide. South from Loch nan Dailthean, on Carn an Eich Dheirg (100m), is little Loch a'Chuirn (19/879818) and to the east, Loch Ghiuragarstidh (19/890812). Approach Loch Ghiuragarstidh from the same start point as for Loch Kernsary (see entry). Leave the Kernsary track at the stream at 19/885804 and walk north for 15 minutes to find the south end of the loch.
Fish Small brown trout in all the lochs, with the chance of a few fish of up to and over 1lb in weight. Loch nan Dailthean can also hold occasional salmon and seatrout.
Flies & Tactics Loch nan Dailthean is a shallow loch and fish may be taken from all round the shore. On Loch Ghiuragarstidh, concentrate your attack down the east shore, especially in the vicinity of the three small islands. Try: Black Pennell, Greenwell's Glory and Peter Ross.
Permission & Charges Permission to fish might be obtained from the estate upon written inquiry to: Sir John Horlick, Bt., Tournaig House, Poolewe, Wester-Ross.

Gairloch & Ullapool   OS Map 19

NAN EUN, Loch See Fionn Loch.
NAN EUN, Loch See Loch an Daing.
NAN EUN, Loch See Loch na Doire Duinne.
NAN EUN, Loch (Shieldaig) See Loch Clair.
NAN LAIGH, Loch See Loch an Iasgair.
NAN UAIN, Loch See Fionn Loch.
NAN UAN, Loch See Loch nan Clachan Geala.
PRIVATE WATERS ALLT AN DARAICH, Loch (19/990633); NA TEANGAIDH FHIADHAICH, Loch (19/935685); A'CHARNAIN BHAIN, Loch (19/133894); LAGAIDH, Loch (19/120897); NA H-AIRBHE, Loch (19/100924); NAM BADAN BOGA, Loch (19/099930); NA COIREIG, Loch 19/051932); NA H-UIDHE, Loch (19/045934); A'BHEALAICH, Loch (19/060939); CAMAS AN LOCHAIN, Loch (19/005981).

SAND, River
Location & Access Source: 19/790810 Outfall: 19/755785 Easily accessible from the B8021 Gairloch/Melvaig road.
Commentary The river rises from amongst the scattered, deserted, shielings on Meall Mor (244m) and flows west to enter the sea in Loch Ewe near the caravan site at Little Sands Farm.
Fish A few fish, both salmon and sea-trout, are taken most seasons.
Flies & Tactics Only worth fishing after a big spate, or at the mouth of the river at the top of the tide. This also applies to the mouth of the stream further north at Port Erradale (19/738811). There is trout fishing nearby in Loch an t-Seana-bhaile (19/763809) which is fished from the bank and is full of small trout. Offer them: Black Pennell, Grouse & Claret and Peter Ross.
Permission & Charges See Loch a'Mhadaidh.

SEARRACH, Loch See Fionn Loch.
SGEIREACH, Loch See Loch na Doire Duinne.
SGEIREACH, Loch (Loch Bad a'Chreamh) See Loch na Curra.
SGEIREACH, Lochan See Lochan na Beinne.
SGEIREACH, Lochan See Fionn Loch.
SGEIREACH, Lochan (Boor) See Loch an Iasgair.
SGEIREACH, Lochan (Meall Imireach) See Loch a'Mhadaidh.

SGEIREACH, Lochan (Shieldaig)
Location & Access 19/810708 Approach via the track leading south from near the Shieldiag Lodge Hotel (19/809724) on the B8056 Kerrysdale/Redpoint road. The journey takes approximately 40 minutes. Once off the path, the going is rough.
Commentary Lochan Sgeireach is adjacent to a series of lochs known locally as The Fairy Lochs'. These are unnamed on the OS Map, but are as follows: Fairy Loch (19/ 810713), Aeroplane Loch (19/808710), Spectacles (19/817705) and Diamond Loch (19/810702). East from the Fairy Lochs is another excellent water, Lochan Druim na Fearna (19/830703).
Fish The Fairy Loch itself has the best fish, trout of over 3 pounds. The other waters noted all contain excellent stocks of wild trout which average in the order of 10oz to 12oz, although larger specimens are taken from time to time.

Flies & Tactics First class bank fishing in splendid surroundings and no need to wade. Trout lie close to the shore and are easily covered. Fish may be taken almost anywhere round these small lochs and so cast with confidence. Flies: Soldier Palmer, Grouse & Green and Dunkeld.
Permission & Charges Hotel guests have priority, but occasional day lets may be available at £10 per rod per day. Contact: Gijs Lagerman, Shieldaig Lodge Hotel, Badachro, Gairloch, Wester Ross. Tel: 01445 741250; Fax: 01445 741305. Sheildaig Lodge Hotel also has two comfortable self catering cottages.

SGUAT, Lochan See Loch Clair.

SGUOD, Loch
Location & Access 19/810874 Leave the A832 Gairloch/Dundonnell road at Poolewe and follow the B8057 north signposted to Cove. Park at 19/819879. The loch is visible, to the west of the road, and is approached after a short walk over the moor.
Commentary Loch Sguod is a shallow water, approximately half a mile east/west by up to quarter of a mile wide and surrounded by peat moorland which should be walked with caution. The boat is moored just south of the outlet burn.
Fish This used to be a first class sea-trout loch but, in recent years, sadly, the numbers of fish have declined. Nevertheless, sea-trout can still be caught here, and good fish too, as well as bright little brown trout which average 6oz/8oz in weight.
Flies & Tactics Gairloch Angling Club members have first priority in use of the boat and boat fishing brings best results. Nevertheless, fishing from the bank can also be productive, particularly after heavy rain. The west shore, where there are extensive reed beds and three inlet streams, is the most productive area. Offer them: Black Pennell, Grouse & Claret and Peter Ross. Dapping can also be effective.
Permission & Charges £15 per day for the boat with two rods fishing, £5 per rod per day bank fishing. Book boat and bank fishing through Taylor's Shop, Poolewe, Wester Ross. Tel: 01445 781240. Also, bank fishing, via: K Gunn, Newsagent, Strath, Gairloch, Wester Ross. Tel: 01445 712400; Gairloch Post Office issue permits at Anchorage Crafts, Pier Road, Gairloch, Wester Ross. Tel: 01445 712005. Gillie services and additional information from D W Roxborough, The Old Police Station, Gairloch. Tel: 01445 712057.

SPECTACLES, Loch See Lochan Sgeireach (Shieldaig).
SPOGACH, Loch See Loch an Fhithich.
THOLLDHOIRE, Loch See Fionn Loch.
TOLL A'MHADAIDH, Loch See Fionn Loch.
TOLL AN LOCHAIN, Loch See Gruinard River.
TOLL NAM BIAST, Loch See Loch a'Bhealaich.

TOLLAIDH, Loch
Location & Access 19/840785 Easily accessible and immediately adjacent to the south of the A832 Gairloch/Poolewe road.

Beinn Dearg

Commentary Disfigured by fish farm cages at the west end. Approximately one mile east/west by up to 700 yards wide and 20m in depth. To the south lies little Loch Laraig (19/843772) and a number of unnamed, satellite lochans which will repay exploration.
Fish This is one of the Gairloch Angling Club's best waters and trout of up to and over 4lb in weight have been taken in recent years.
Flies & Tactics There are three boats available, moored at either end of the loch, and most fish are taken in the shallower water, a few yards out from the bank. The long, finger-like arm pointing south is also a noted 'hot-spot'. Bank fishing can be just as productive as fishing from the boat but do not attempt to wade. Flies: Black Zulu, Invicta and Alexandra.
Permission & Charges See Loch Garbhaig (Talladale).

Beinn Dearg

A'BHEALAICH, Loch See Loch Luichart.
A'BHEALAICH, Loch (Garve) See River Black Water.
A'BHRAOIN, Loch See River Broom.

A'CHAIRN MOR, Loch
Location & Access 20/148863. Approach from Letters at 20/162874 on the west shore of Loch Broom. Climb steeply west up the line of the outlet burn and past the waterfall to reach Locha'Chaien Beag (20/151867) after some forty minutes. Loch a'Chairn Mor is a step further west.
Commentary Glorious scenery and wildlife guaranteed. There are two, unnamed, lochans to the west of Loch a'Chairn at 20/140860 which should also be inspected, also Loch an Duibhe at 19/138874; and, to the north, a one-mile walk over the moor, Loch an Eilein (20/145877) and Loch na Faoileige (20/140878).
Fish Splendid trout, including fish of up to 5lb in weight.
Flies & Tactics Bank fishing only and wading is not really necessary because the fish, more often than not, lie close to the shore. The north shore of Loch a'Chairn, amongst the bays and promontories, is a good place to start. Flies: Black Zulu, Soldier Palmer, Alexandra.
Permission & Charges Steven Potter, Factor, Estate Office, Dundonnell Estate, Dundonnell, Wester-Ross. Tel: 01854 633206. Expect to pay in the order of £6 per rod per day. Fishing on a number of the lochs noted above is free to guests at The Sheiling Guest House, Garve Road, Ullapool, Wester-Ross IV26 2SX. Tel: 01854 612947.

A'CHOIRE BHUIG, Loch See Loch Achall entry.
A'CHOIRE DHUIBH, Loch See Loch Achall entry.
A'CHUILINN, Loch See Loch Luichart entry.
A'GHILLE, Loch See River Broom entry.
A'MHEALLAIN-CHAORAINN, Loch See Loch Luichart.

ACHALL, Loch
Location & Access 20/180951. Leave the A835 Ledmore Junction/Ullapool road on the outskirts of Ullapool, where the Ullapool River crosses under the main road at 19/129949. An estate road, which is private, leads out to the loch and to Rhidorroch Lodge.
Commentary Loch Achall is one and a half miles east/west by up to 650 yards wide. It drops to over 60ft deep near Rhidorroch Lodge but, otherwise, the loch is generally shallow. There are a number of delightful hill lochs to the north of Loch Achall, both named and unnamed, the principal waters being: Lochan Dearg (20/141954); Loch an Uidh (20/161963); Loch a'Choire Bhuig (20/169981); Lochanan an Uillt Mhoir (20/200976, the largest in a series of four, and Lochanan Aodann Beinn Donuill (20/209965). South of Loch Achall, on the north slopes of Beinn Eilideach (558m), are two more: Loch nan Cnaimh (20/160939) and Loch a'Choire Dhuibh (20/170937).
Fish Not a lot for the glass case here, but plenty for supper and for breakfast. Trout average 6oz/8oz with the odd chance of few larger specimens. Loch Achall, which lies at the head of the Ullapool River, also holds salmon and sea-trout from mid-June onwards.
Flies & Tactics A boat is available on Loch Achall and trout are encountered all round the loch. Salmon and sea-trout tend to lie close to the shore in shallow water and, more often than not, at the east of the loch in the vicinity of where the Rhidorroch River enters. The hill lochs noted above are all fished from the bank, after a hard hike and frequent consultation with the OS Map. Flies: For both trout and salmon, offer: Black Pennell, Grouse & Claret and Peter Ross.
Permission & Charges See Loch Beinn Dearg entry. Rhidorroch Lodge, which is superb and sleeps up to 10, is let along with sporting rights through Finlyson Hughes, 29 Barossa Place, Perth PH1 5EP. Tel: 01738 630926; Fax: 01738 639017. Good brown trout fishing in the nearby 'Chain Lochs' and the 'Gorge Lochs' goes with the Lodge. Prices on application.

ACHANALT, Loch See Loch Luichart entry.

AN ACHA, Loch
Location & Access 20/203915. No easy way in and a hard two and a half mile tramp up an estate track in Strath Nimhe, which leaves the A835 Ullapool/Braemore road at 20/169900.
Commentary There are a series of 25 named and unnamed lochs and lochans here, known collectively as the Leckmelm Hill Lochs. The principal waters are: Loch Sarraidh Mhoir (20/181923); Lochanan Fiodha (20/195925); Lochanan a'Mhuilinn (20/194918); Loch Coire na Ba Buidhe (20/200918); Loch Thormaid (20/211927) and Loch na Beinne Brice (20/218925).
Fish Nothing vast, but watch out for some surprises along the way.
Flies & Tactics A few of the lochs contain glass-case specimens and they invariably 'grab' when you are looking the wrong way and never grab again although you may be looking the right way all the time. Be prepared. Make this a long day out in the hills, starting in the north and then walking south, fishing the various lochs and lochans as you go. Pay particular attention to the unnamed lochan at 20/195911, at the north end,

Beinn Dearg OS Map 20

by the weed patch off the south shore.
Permission & Charges Contact: Donald Wyne, Navidale Farm, Helmsdale, Sutherland KW8 6JS. Tel/Fax: (01431) 821257. £5 per rod per day. These lochs are closed for fishing after 1st August.

AN AIRCEIL, Loch See River Broom entry.
AN EILEIN, Loch See Loch a'Chairn entry.
AN FHIONA, Loch See River Broom entry.
AN T-SIDHEIN, Loch See River Broom entry.
AN TIOMPAIN, Loch See River Broom entry.
AN TUIRC, Loch See River Black Water entry.
AN UIDH, Loch See Loch Achall entry.
BAD LEABHRAIDH, Loch See Loch Luichart entry.
BAD NA H-ACHLAISE (Ullapool), Loch See Loch Beinn Dearg entry.
BADAN NA MOINE, Loch See River Broom entry.

BEINN DEARG, Loch
Location & Access 20/153000. Access is from the A835 Ledmore Junction/Ullapool road near Strathkanaird at 15/146006. The road up to the loch is narrow and very steep, with blind summits and tight corners. Drive with extreme care. Park by the lochside.
Commentary Loch Beinn Dearg is the first water in a series known locally as the Dam Lochs. The other lochs are: Loch na Maoile (20/157999), Loch Bad na h-Achlaise (20/159995), Loch Dubh (20/147986), Loch Dubh Beag (20/149983) and Loch Ob na Lochain (20/155987). The system is impounded for electricity generation purposes and, as such, the water levels fluctuate.
Fish Brown trout and Arctic char. Fish average 10oz to 12oz in weight, but there are good numbers of much larger trout and fish of over 3lb are not uncommon.
Flies & Tactics Bank fishing only and upon no account attempt to wade. It is dangerous to do so. In any case, the trout lie close to the margins and are easily covered from the shore. Offer them: Black Pennell, Ke-He and Silver Butcher.
Permission & Charges The Mountainman, West Argyle Street, Ullapool, Ross-shire. Tel: 01854 613383. Expect to pay in the order of £6 per day for bank fishing.

BLACK WATER, River
Location & Access Source 20/320720 Outfall 26/478549. The river is paralleled by the A835 Garve/Ullapool road. See also OS Map 26.
Commentary The headwaters of the River Blackwater have been flooded by the construction of Loch Glascarnoch (20/320720) for hydro-electric power generation. The upper part of the stream, between Loch Glascarnoch and the Glascarnoch River, down to where it enters into Loch Garve (20/05600), is heavily wooded, and the life of the stream is entirely dependent upon heavy rain and compensation flow from Loch Vaich (20/348770).
Fish Brown trout only, and only in decent water conditions. Salmon are restricted from entering the upper river by a trap in Loch na Croic (26/429592).
Flies & Tactics Offer: Greenwell's Glory, Grouse & Claret, Silver Butcher. There are three, small, lochs on Carn Fearna (432m), which will take your mind off any lack of water in the river, and stretch your lungs and legs to reach. These are: Loch a'Bhealaich (20/425628), Loch na Gearra (20/429624), and Loch an Tuirc (20/415625). They make for a wonderful day out. Start at the car park on the A835 at 20/403640 and follow the track which climbs over the east shoulder of Beinn a'Ghuilbein (450m). Where the track turns south, continue to the top of the hill and then swing south to find the first loch, Loch a'Bhealaich, after a further ten minutes. Loch na Gearra is a step south, then Loch an Tuirc, 20 minutes hike further west.
Permission & Charges Free to guests staying at the Garve Hotel, Garve, Ross-shire. Tel: 01997 414205.

BRAN, River See Loch Luichart entry.

BROOM, River
Location & Access Source 20/200733 Outfall 20/175849. The river is easily accessible from the A835 Ullapool/Braemore road which parallels the east bank.
Commentary This little spate river flows north down Strath More for 5 miles before reaching the sea at the head of Loch Broom. The most noted aspect of the stream is the Falls of Measach in the Corrieshalloch Gorge, a popular tourist attraction, but since the headwaters of the river have been impounded for hydro-electric power generation, the falls are only impressive after heavy rain.
Fish Salmon and sea-trout. Most seasons produce in the order of 50/70 salmon. Few sea-trout are now taken, and even fewer of the 10lb+ fish for which the River Broom used to be famous.
Flies & Tactics A comfortable river to fish, with 25 named pools, the most productive of which lie between the Sea Pool and Kennel Burn. The river is entirely dependent upon rain to produce of its best, although some flow is maintained by compensation discharge from Loch Droma (20/261751). Fish are also taken from the lower reaches of the River Lael, including the odd sea-trout in the tidal waters of both the Lael and the River Broom. Best flies: Willie Gunn, Stoat's Tail, Goat's Toe, Garry Dog, Hairy Mary, General Practitioner. When the river is in poor condition, there are a number of first-class brown trout lochs, fished from the bank, in the hills nearby. All will stretch your legs and lungs to reach, but they offer splendid sport in magnificent surroundings. The inhabitants average 8oz in weight, but there are also good numbers of larger specimens. To the north of Inverbroom, in the Inverlael Forest, are Lochanan Deabharan (20/197879), Loch Reidh Creagain (20/190871) and Loch a'Ghille (20/198867). On the west side, towards the Dundonnell River and approached by hill tracks from Auchlunachan (20/180835), lie Loch an t-Sidhein (20/151802), Loch nan Eun (20/154817), Loch an Airceil (20/155830), Loch an Tiompain (20/155848) and Loch an Fhiona (20/163850). Loch a'Bhraoin (20/140748), which lies to the south of the A832 Braemore/Gairloch road, is the largest water. It is the source of the Abhainn Cuileig, the major tributary of the River Broom. The loch is 2.5 miles long by up to

OS Map 20 Beinn Dearg

400yds wide and is fished from the boat. Two, tiny, hill lochs feed into Loch a'Bhraoin from the north: Loch na h-Oidhche (20/154777) and Loch Badan na Moine (20/167782), both of which contain pretty little trout. First cast: Blue Zulu, March Brown, Dunkeld.
Permission & Charges The sport is let in conjunction with Inverbroom Lodge, a comfortable property for ten guests. Contact: Finlyson Hughes, 29 Barossa Place, Perth PH1 5EP for details. Tel: 01738 630926; Fax: 01738 639017. Trout fishing on a number of the lochs noted above is free to guests staying at The Sheiling Guest House, Garve Road, Ullapool, Wester-Ross IV26 2SX. Tel: 01854 612947.

COIRE NA BA BUIDHE, Loch See loch Acha entry.
DAIL FHEARNA, Loch See Loch Fannich entry.
DAM, Lochs See Loch Beinn Dearg entry.
DEABHARAN, Loch See River Broom entry.
DEARG, Lochan See Loch Achall entry.
DOUCHARY, River See Ullapool River entry.
DUBH BEAG, Loch See Loch Beinn Dearg entry.
DUBH MOR, Loch See Loch Luichart entry.
DUBH (Ullapool), Loch See Loch Beinn Dearg entry.

FANNICH, Loch
Location & Access 20/2105653. Access is from a private estate road to Fannich Lodge. Leave the A832 Garve/Gairloch road west of Lochluichart Station at 20/312626 and drive north up the line of the Gruide River to reach the loch.
Commentary Loch Fannich is part of the Conon Hydro-Electric scheme and the loch is impounded by a dam at the east end. Nearly eight miles east/west by up to three-quarters of a mile north/south, Loch Fannich can be an unforgiving, dour, windy place to fish. It is redeemed by the glory of the surrounding countryside which includes, to the north, no less the nine mountains of over 3,000ft (Munros). There is also excellent hill-loch fishing in a number of remote waters to the south of Loch Fannich: Loch na Curra (20/238637), Loch Dail Fhearna (20/218627), Loch na Moine Beag (20/1966270), Loch na Moine Mor (20/183633).
Fish In Loch Fannich, small brown trout which average 8oz in weight and large ferox trout in the depths, perch and voracious pike. The hill-lochs contain some good fish of up to and over 1lb in weight.
Flies & Tactics Boat fishing on Loch Fannich brings best results although bank fishing can be productive. However, it is dangerous to wade. The margins are unstable due to fluctuations in the water level. The west end, by the inlet burn from the Nest of Fannich and, to the south, the Abhainn a'Chadh Bhuidhe, are good places to begin. The bays and corners to the west of Fannich Lodge also offer good sport. Give them: Black Pennell, Grouse & Claret, Alexandra.
Permission & Charges The fishing on Loch Fannich is let in conjunction with accommodation and sport on the Kinlochewe & Lochrosque Estates. Details from Finlyson Hughes, 29 Barossa Place, Perth PH1 5EP. Tel: 01738 630926; Fax: 01738 639017. Expect rental charges of in the oder of £2,500/£3,000 for a week's fishing and accommodation.

GARVE, Loch See OS Map 26, Inverness.

GLASCARNOCH, Loch
Location & Access 20/310730. The south shore of the loch borders the A835 Garve/Ullapool road.
Commentary Loch Glascarnoch is 4.5 miles long by up to three-quarters of a mile wide at the west end. This is a hydro-electric water, dismal, dour and windy, much given to fluctuations in water level. A track runs for two miles along the north shore, ending by the bothy at 20/321727 below Meall an Torcain (536m), and gives access to less "public" fishing.
Fish Brown trout of modest proportions, although, undoubtedly, there must be ferox trout as well. Loch Glascarnoch also holds perch and pike of considerable size.
Flies & Tactics Bank fishing only. Do not wade. The margins are dangerously soft in many areas. The west end of the loch, in the vicinity of the inlet stream, is perhaps the most attractive fishing area, half a mile's walk from the hubub of the main road. Flies: Black Pennell, March Brown, Silver Butcher.
Permission & Charges Neither payment nor permit is required, but always check locally in case this changes.

GLASCARNOCH, River See River Black Water entry.

GLASS, Loch
Location & Access 20/510730. Approach from Evanton via the minor road which runs north-west up Glen Glass past Eileanach Lodge (21/545688).
Commentary Loch Glass is four miles long by up to half a mile wide and is 360ft deep. The surrounding mountains frequently funnel furious winds down the loch and it is often wild and stormy. An estate road, leading to Wyvis Lodge, margins the whole length of the south shore. The north shore is accessed by a forest track which extends for a distance of 1.75 miles.
Fish Brown trout average 8oz. Much larger fish inhabit the depths but they are rarely taken.
Flies & Tactics Bank fishing only. Wading is dangerous, stay ashore at all times. The east end of the loch is, generally, the most productive fishing area. Offer them: Black Pennell, Grouse & Claret, Silver Butcher.
Permission & Charges Novar Estate, Estate Office, Evanton, Ross-shire. Tel: 01349 830208. Bank fishing at £6 per rod per day.

GRUDIE, River See Loch Luichart entry.
LAEL, River See River Broom entry.
LOCHANAN A'MHUILINN, Loch See Loch Acha entry.
LOCHANAN AN UILLT MHOIR, Loch See Loch Achall entry.
LOCHANAN AODANN BEINN DONUILL, Loch See Loch Achall entry.
LOCHANAN FIODHA, Loch See Loch Acha entry.

LUICHART, Loch
Location & Access 20/350625. Access from Lochluichart Station (20/323626) on the A832 Dingwall/Gairloch road. Also see OS Map 26 where access may be obtained from the minor road which ends at Glenmarksie (26/389580).

Beinn Dearg   OS Map 20

Commentary This is a large, windswept, hydro-electric loch lying on the headwaters of the River Conon, 5.5 miles long by up to one mile wide across the north-west end. Loch Luichart is over 100ft deep at the south-east end, near the dam, and much of the shore-line is relatively inaccessible. There are two further lochs, to the west, in Strath Bran, Loch a'Chuilinn (20/290614) and Loch Achanalt (20/270610) which also offer sport, as does the River Bran which parallels the A832 for most of its fishable length. There are also a number of attractive trout lochs to the north of Loch Luichart. These are accessed by stalker's tracks: Lochan nam Breac (20/380665), Loch Bad Leabhraidh (20/364658), Loch Dubh Mor (20/343678), Loch a'Mheallain-chaorainn (20/331679), Loch na Salach (20/323672), Loch Mhic Iomhair (20/314668), Loch nam Faidh (20/317649), and, to the west of the River Gruide, little Loch na Beiste (20/278639). To the south of Loch Luichart is Loch a'Bhealaich (20/351603) which is accessed from the track along the south shore of Loch Luichart and thence by a stiff climb up to 450m. Loch Leabhraidh is the largest of these lochs and contains some fine trout.

Fish Brown trout which average 8oz, but good numbers of much larger fish as well. Trout of over 3lb are not uncommon in Loch Luichart and there are ferox as well. The River Grudie, which drains Loch Fannich (20/215652), has small brown trout.

Flies & Tactics Tactic & flies Bank fishing only and wading is dangerous. The area where the Allt Coire Mhuilidh enters Loch Luichart at 20/354627, and the shoreline east and west from this point, is a good place to begin. The south shore, approached from where the railway crosses the River Bran, is also productive, particularly in the bays and corners round the wood. The other lochs noted are also fished from the bank. Cross the River Bran by the bridge at 20/258615 to reach the south shore of Loch Achanalt. The river itself can produce good sport after heavy rain. Offer them: Ke-He, Soldier Palmer, Dunkeld.

Permission & Charges K S Bowlt, Chartered Surveyors, Barnhill, Pluscarden, by Elgin IV30 3TJ. Tel: 01343 890400. Expect to pay in the order of £15 per rod per day. Loch Achanalt and Loch Chuilinn may be fished via the Dingwall & District Angling Club. Contact: The Sports & Model Shop, 66 High Street, Dingwall. Tel: 01349 862346. The hill lochs should only be visited after consultation with the Head Keeper of the Lochluichart Estate, Jock Logie, who may be contacted on Tel: 01997 414224. Access may be restricted during the stalking season, from August onwards.

MHIC IOMHAIR, Loch See Loch Luichart entry.

MOIRE, Loch

Location & Access 20/530760. Approach from the A836 Struie road (see OS Map 21). Turn west at 21/639705 and follow the minor road north-west past Ballavoulen (21/570742) to reach the loch after a further 1.5 miles.

Commentary Loch Moire lies on the headwaters of the Alness River and is two miles long by half a mile wide.

The loch is over 300ft deep and lies in a "wind-tunnel" formed by the surrounding mountains. Access to the south shore is by an estate road leading to Kildermoire Lodge. The north shore is trackless.

Fish Brown trout, char and ferox trout. Ferox of over 15lb have been caught.

Flies & Tactics Bank fishing only. Stay ashore. It is dangerous to wade. The loch deepens very quickly and fish tend to lie close to the bank. The relatively shallow north end of the loch is perhaps the most productive fishing area. Flies: Black Zulu, Soldier Palmer, Dunkeld.

Permission & Charges Novar Estate, Estate Office, Evanton, Ross-shire. Tel: 01349 830208; Alness Angling Club, J & M Patterson, 33-35 High Street, Alness, Ross-shire. Tel: 01349 882286. Visitor's day ticket, £3.50.

NA BEINNE BRICE, Loch See Loch Acha entry.
NA BEISTE, Loch See Loch Luichart entry.
NA CURRA, Loch See Loch Fannich entry.
NA FAOILEIGE, Loch See Loch a'Chairn entry.
NA GEARRA, Loch See River Black Water entry.
NA H-OIDHCHE, Loch See River Broom entry.
NA MAOILE, Loch See Loch Beinn Dearg entry.
NA MOINE BEAG, Loch See Loch Fannich entry.
NA MOINE MOR, Loch See Loch Fannich entry.
NA SALACH, Loch See Loch Luichart entry.
NAM BREAC, Lochan See Loch Luichart entry.
NAM FAIDH, Loch See Loch Luichart entry.
NAN CNAIMH, Loch See Loch Achall entry.
NAN EUN, Loch See River Broom entry.
OB AN LOCHAIN, Loch See Loch Beinn Dearg entry.
PRIVATE WATERS The following lochs, to the north of Loch Fannich, are preserved by the owner: TOLL AN LOCHAIN, Loch (20/145720), SGEIREACH, Loch (20/232733), A'MHADAIDH, Loch (20/200732), AN FHUAR THUILL MHOIR, Loch (20/213708), LI, Loch (20/225707), AN EILEIN, Loch (20/231701), GORM, Loch (20/240696), ODHAR, Loch (20/241703), NAN EUN, Loch (20/250688). The following lochs are also preserved by their owners: A'CHAIRN, Lochan (20/517844) and CHUINNEAG, Loch (20/495848). The lochs to the north of Glascarnoch are preserved by the owner and are not available for fishing. These include: VAICH, Loch (20/348770), GORM, Loch (20/332799), ABAHAINN STRATH A'BHATHICH (20/369723), A'GHARBHRAIN, Loch (20/282760), COIRE LAIR, Loch (20/282785), NAN EILEAN, Loch (20/270792), FEITH NAN CLEIREACH (29/232792). The hill lochs in the Wyvis Forest and, north, in the Kildermoire Forest, are preserved by the owner. They are BAD A'BHATHAICH, Loch (20/538788), A'CHAORAINN, Loch (20/465790), FEUR, Lochan (20/449780), MAGHARAIDH, Loch(20/453770), NAN AMHAICHEAN, Loch (20/418762), GOBHLACH, Lochan (20/424743), COIRE BHEACHAIN, Loch (20/430729), FEUR, Lochan (20/439721), BEALACH CULAIDH, Loch (20/450720), NAN DRUIDEAN, Loch (20/462714), A'CHOIRE MHOIR, Loch (20/477693), MISIRICH, Loch (20/505690).

REIDH CREAGAIN, Loch See River Broom entry.

OS Maps 20-21 Dornoch Firth

RHIDORROCH, River See Ullapool River entry.
SARRAIDH MHOIR, Loch See Loch Acha entry.
THORMAID, Loch See Loch Acha entry.

ULLAPOOL, River
Location & Access Source 20/253858 Outfall 19/124946. The river is easily accessible from a private estate road which margins the south bank.
Commentary The river rises from Coire an Lochain Sgeirich (872m) in the Inverlael Forest and flows north as the River Douchary to Glen Achall. From there, west to Loch Achall, the stream is known as the Rhidorroch River. In the last 4 miles of its journey to the sea, it becomes the River Ullapool. At the Ness Pool the river flows through a very narrow cleft where, some years ago, a huge 40lb salmon reputedly got wedged. A cast of it now decorates the Rhidorrach Lodge.
Fish Salmon and sea-trout. Numbers vary, dependent upon water conditions, but most seasons produce in the region of 60/70 salmon. Sea-trout numbers, in common with most west coast systems, have declined/collapsed in recent years.
Flies & Tactics Fish enter the river from April onwards, given rain, and sport can be excellent from then until the end of the season in September. There are some 14 pools, including Loch Pool, Black Pool, Bridge Pool and Sea Pool. Because of the strength of the flow, a strong rod is required to hold onto any fish hooked. Flies: Willie Gun, Hairy Mary, Green Highlander, General Practitioner, Silver Wilkinson and Goat's Toe.
Permission & Charges The principal fishing is let by Finlyson Hughes along with Rhidorroch Lodge (see Loch Achall).

Dornoch Firth

A'GHIUBHAIS, Loch
Location & Access 21/717930. It is possible to drive to within 500 yards of the loch, from Evelix, via Astle (21/739918) and the forest track along The Crask (21/730924). From the parking place, follow the white marker posts, over a deer fence, to reach the loch.
Commentary A very attractive little loch, a few acres in extent, protected by Leathad nan Uan (183m) to the north and Creagan Asdale (192m) to the south, draining into the River Evelix.
Fish The Dornoch and District Angling Association stocks the water with brown trout and fish average approximately 1lb in weight. Larger fish, of up to and over 2lb, are taken most seasons.
Flies & Tactics Bank fishing only and the west end of the loch is inaccessible because of a treacherous marsh. Fish are taken from all round the remaining shoreline and may be tempted with: Ke-He, Soldier Palmer and Dunkeld.
Permission & Charges The Dornoch and District Angling Association (see Loch Buidhe entry) preserves the fishing on Loch a'Ghiubhais for club members only and visitors tickets are not available.

ALLT EILEACHAN, Burn See Kyle of Sutherland entry.
ALLT MUIGH BHLARAIDH, Burn See Kyle of Sutherland entry.

ALNESS, River
Location & Access Source 20/409809 Outfall 21/659680. Much of the course of the river is some distance from public roads and the fishing is accessed, mainly, via estate tracks from minor roads. Prior to fishing, anglers receive detailed directions.
Commentary The river rises from tiny Loch na Glass and flows east for ten miles amidst the mountain wilderness of the Kildermoire Forest before reaching 262ft-deep Loch Moire (20/533760) through the Gleann Mhuire and Ardross Forest. Loch Moire is dammed to provide additional flow for the river during low water conditions. From the loch, the Alness River continues south-east through an attractive wooded glen, finally reaching the sea in the Cromarty Firth near Dalmore. The Black Water is the principal tributary of the Alness and it joins its parent river to the west of Ardross Castle at 21/591746.
Fish Salmon and sea-trout, although sea-trout numbers have declined in recent years. The annual catch is in the order of 250 salmon and perhaps 80 sea-trout.
Flies & Tactics Most of the lies are readily covered without recourse to wading, although an ability to Spey, or roll cast, is frequently essential because of bank-side vegetation. The Alness is a spate river and good water levels are required for it to produce of its best. Some of the most noted pools on the river include: Raven Rock, Iron Bridge, Inchlumpie, Douglas, Falls, Stick Pool and Lady Pool. Offer them: Willie Gunn, Hairy Mary, Garry Dog, Munro Killer, Black Doctor and General Practitioner.
Permission & Charges The Novar Estates, Estate Office, Evanton, Ross-shire. Tel: 01349 830208; The Alness Angling Club, c/o George Ross, 127 Kirkside, Alness, Ross-shire. Tel: 01349 883726. Expect to pay between £10 and £35 per rod, per day, depending upon the time of the season.

AN LAGAIN, Loch
Location & Access 21/660955. Loch an Lagain lies to the east of the minor road, between Bonar Bridge in the south and Mound to the north. Leave the minor road at Bad Bog (21/642961) and follow a good track down to the east end of the loch where there is a parking area and the boat is moored.
Commentary Loch an Lagain is the source of the River Evelix and is approximately one mile west/east by up to 350 yards wide at its western end.
Fish Very pretty little brown trout which average 6oz in weight, with an outside chance of a few larger specimens: a 3lb trout was taken recently. There is also the possibility of salmon towards the end of the season.
Flies & Tactics Few problems, Loch an Lagain trout are very accommodating, all over the loch and they rise readily to most patterns of artificial fly. Begin with: Blue Zulu, Loch Ordie and Silver Butcher. Look out for salmon at the west end, in the vicinity of the inlet burn

213

Dornoch Firth — OS Map 21

at the south-west corner. The loch can be very windy and an outboard motor is recommended.
Permission & Charges See Loch Buidhe entry. The Kyle of Sutherland Angling Club also have fishing rights on Loch Lagain. Details from: M Brown, Kyle of Sutherland Angling Club, Balleigh Wood, Edderton, Ross-shire. Tel: 01862 821230.

BALNAGOWAN, River The river is preserved by the owner and fishing is not available to the public.

BUIDHE, Loch
Location & Access 21/660984 Loch Buidhe lies immediately adjacent to and to the north of the minor road between Bonar Bridge in the south and Mound in the north.
Commentary An easily accessible, attractive loch, approximately one and a quarter miles east/west by up to 400 meters wide.
Fish Wild brown trout which average 8oz, but always a chance of a few larger specimens. Depending upon water conditions, salmon and sea-trout, from Loch Fleet (21/790965), sometimes enter the loch towards the end of the season.
Flies & Tactics The Dornoch and District Angling Association maintains boats on Loch Buidhe, although bank fishing can be just as productive, particularly from the north shore in the vicinity of the little stream which flows down from Meal na Tulchainn (305m). Park at 21/674981. The boats are moored across the dam wall at 21/674983. Loch Buidhe can be wild and windy. An outboard motor is a great help. Offer them: Black Pennell, Grouse & Claret and Alexandria.
Permission & Charges Tickets to fish the Dornoch Angling Club Association waters, including a boat on Loch Brora (see OS Map 17), are available from: The Highlands of Scotland Tourist Board, The Square, Dornoch, Sutherland. Tel: 01862 810400; Fax: 01862 810644. Boat on Loch Brora, £15 per day; all other boats, £12 per day; bank fishing, £5 per rod per day; Littleferry bank fishing, £2 per rod per day. Life jackets are available on loan when making a booking, as is a mixed pack of 10 of the most successful patterns of artificial flies, at the bargain price of £3 per pack. Also, a mixture of 5 lures for £2

CARRON, River
Location & Access Source 20/284858 Outfall 21/608918 The river is easily accessible from minor roads on both banks as far west as Amat Lodge (20/475909) and thereafter by estate roads to Glencalvie Lodge (20/468891) and Deanich Lodge (20/369840).
Commentary Much of the River Carron system is on OS Map 20, but for ease of reference, the whole river is included in the OS Map 21 listings. The Carron rises to the south-west of the Kyle of Sutherland in the Freevater Forest and its principal tributaries are the River Alladale, Water of Glencalvie and the Black Water. The upper reaches of the river lie amidst spectacular scenery and the stream flows through a deep gorge before plunging over the dramatic Glencalvie Falls. Thereafter, there are two other, significant, falls on the river, Morrell and Gledfield, before the Carron enters the Kyle of Sutherland immediately opposite Bonar Bridge on the A9 Inverness/Wick road.
Fish The most productive months are August and September, although good numbers of spring fish are sometimes still taken.
Flies & Tactics The estates which own the river, Glencalvie, Amat, Braelangwell, Gruinards, Dounie, Cornhill, Gledfield and Invercharron, have excellent sport to offer, mostly linked with accommodation. The river is generally easily accessible, but where access is difficult, platforms, walk-ways and ladders have been installed. Some of the most noted pools include, Whirl Pool, Marge, Hiding Pool, Big Gorge, Gledfield, Falls Pool, Henderson, Glencalvie, Rock Pool and Vernon's Pool. You will need a 15ft, double-handed salmon rod. Flies: Willie Gunn, Garry Dog, Collie Dog, Stoat's Tail, Ally's Shrimp, Hairy Mary and Munro Killer.
Permission & Charges Finlyson Hughes, 29 Barossa Place, Perth PH1 5EP. Tel: 01738 630926; Fax: 01738 639017. Charges vary according to the time of year and accommodation. A lodge and fishing for 4 rods will cost in the order of between £2,000 and £7,000 per week, plus VAT.

EASTER FEARN, Burn See Kyle of Sutherland entry.
EDDERTON, Burn See Kyle of Sutherland entry.
EVELIX, River The Evelix river is preserved by the owner and there is no public access to the fishing. This also applies to Loch Evelix, which is the wide section of the river before it empties into Evelix Bay.
EYE, Loch 21/830798 Loch Eye lies to the south east of Tain and is noted for coarse fish, rather than for trout. However, it is an outstanding wildlife habitat and very lovely. For that reason alone, Loch Eye is well worth a visit.

FLEET, Loch (Littleferry)
Location & Access 21/805954 At the south end of The Mound causeway, on the A9 Inverness/Wick road, turn east and follow the minor road which parallels the sea. Park at the ruined pier at Littleferry (21/805954).
Commentary Loch Fleet is a wide, sandy, tidal bay and the fishing here is from the south shore of the loch as the flow narrows into the Dornoch Firth. The loch is also a National Nature Reserve, renowned for a wide variety of birdlife.
Fish Sea-trout, which can run up to 5lb in weight, but, in general, average 1lb 8oz/2lb. The larger fish arrive during May, followed thereafter by their small brethren, finnock.
Flies & Tactics Care and caution is most important when fishing a tidal reach. Watch out for sudden soft patches of sand and remember to keep an eye on the state of the tide. Launch your attack during the period immediately before or after high tide. Flies: Black Pennell, Grouse & Claret and Teal Blue & Silver.
Permission & Charges See Loch Buidhe entry.

GLASS (Evanton), River
Location & Access Source 20/418762 Outfall 21/626656 Access is from a minor road which parallels the north bank of the stream.

OS Map 21 — Dornoch Firth

Commentary The true source of the river is 15 miles to the north-west in Loch nan Amhaichean (20/418762), whence it flows through Loch Glass (20/510730), past Eileanach Lodge, into Glen Glass to reach the sea at the gravel beach at Balconie Point. The river is also known as the Allt Graad. The River Sgitheach, a near-neighbour of the River Glass, enters the Cromarty Firth half a mile south-west and both these streams are fished by the Evanton Angling Club.

Fish Not a lot, either of salmon or sea-trout, but there is a chance of sport after heavy rain.

Flies & Tactics Only the lower sections of these streams are fishable. The Black Rock Gorge (21/588667), on the River Glass, is impassable to migratory fish and severe floods have greatly damaged much of the usable fishing below this point. If there are fish about, try: Willie Gunn, Hairy Mary, Shrimp Fly and Black Doctor.

Permission & Charges Evanton Angling Club, c/o A & M Alcock, Newsagents, 16 Balconie Street, Evanton, Ross-shire. Tel: 01349 830672. £12 per rod, per day.

KYLE OF SUTHERLAND, Estuary

Location & Access Source 21/540989 Outflow 21/810860 Access to fishing throughout the Kyle of Sutherland is easy, from roads which parallel both the north and the south shores.

Commentary The Kyle of Sutherland covers a vast tidal area, extending from the confluence of the rivers Cassley and Oykel in the west, eastwards past Bonar Bridge and Wester Fearn Narrows (21/634883) to the Dornoch Firth, a distance of some 27 miles. There are endless, accessible, fishing opportunities throughout the length of the Kyle and it would take several angling seasons to do proper justice to all the sport which is available.

Fish The primary interest here is salmon and sea-trout, although, being tidal, many other species may also be caught. The Kyle of Sutherland Angling Club take approximately 400 salmon and 200 sea-trout most seasons.

Flies & Tactics Rainless, summer months hold salmon and sea-trout back in the Kyle, to the benefit of local anglers, if not to the benefit off anglers on the rivers Carron, Cassley, Oykel and Shin. However, knowing where to launch your attack is all-important and in this regard you should seek local guidance in the form of the excellent booklet, produced by the angling club, which fully describes the fishing. Generally, from the south shore, the most productive areas are where burns tumble into the Kyle: Allt Eileachan (21/604897), Wester Fearn Burn (21/635880), Easter Fearn Burn (21/644874), Allt Muigh bhlaraidh (21/702866), Edderton Burn (21/724846), and the River Tain (21/7786824). However, the best fishing is from a boat, in the middle of the Kyle, over the extensive areas of sand banks where the ebb and flow of the tide acts in the same fashion as a river. Offer them: Black Pennell, Teal Blue & Silver, Grouse & Claret, Mallard & Claret, Peter Ross, Alexandra and Silver March Brown.

Permission & Charges Expect to pay in the region of £15 per rod per day for fishing from the shore. Details: M Brown, Kyle of Sutherland Angling Club, Balleigh Wood, Edderton, Ross-shire. Tel: 01862 821230.

LANNSAIDH, Loch

Location & Access 21/738945. Leave the A9 Inverness/Wick road to the north of Evelix at 21/774917, turning west to follow the signpost to Birichen. After 2 miles, at 21/751939, on your left, you will find a good track which leads down to a car park at the lochside close to the boat mooring bay.

Commentary A pleasant, circular loch, covering an area of some 50 acres, surrounded by peat and heather moorlands. The loch is part of the local water supply system. Fishing is managed by the Dornoch and District Angling Association.

Fish Wild brown trout which average 6oz and stocked rainbow trout of about 2lb in weight.

Flies & Tactics Bank fishing can be just as productive as fishing from the boat, but the boat is required to 'explore' properly the 30ft deep hole which lies just out from the mooring bay. Trout tend to congregate in and around this hole during hot days and may often be tempted by: Loch Ordie, Woodcock & Hare-lug and Peter Ross.

Permission & Charges See Loch Buidhe entry and also Loch Lagain entry.

LAOIGH, Loch

Location & Access 21/731957. Turn west from the A9 Inverness/Wick road one mile north from the Trentham Hotel, opposite the telephone kiosk at 21/779941, and follow the minor road along the edge of the wood for one and a half miles to Ardshave at 21/760952. The track to the loch is on your left. With care, and preferably with a high wheel-base vehicle, you may drive to the loch, a distance of one and a half miles. The ground near the boathouse is boggy, so park and walk the last 50 yards.

Commentary Loch Laoigh, 'the loch of the calf', is half a mile long by up to 300 yards wide, sheltered from the worst of the weather by the surrounding hills: Creag Laith (283m), Meall an Eoin (306m), and Beinn Tarbhaidh (310m). To the north of Beinn Tarbhaidh is little Loch Tarbhaidh which contains good stocks of modest wild brown trout. This loch is best approached via a track which may be found to the west of the A9 at 21/771966.

Fish Wild brown trout which average 8oz in weight and a few much larger specimens of up to 3lb. The Dornoch and District Angling Association also stocks the water with hatchery-reared trout and these average between 1lb and 2lb.

Flies & Tactics Both boat and bank fishing is allowed and either can be effective. The small island at the south-west end of the loch is a good place to start and in the vicinity of the inlet burn from Loch Lannsaidh (21/738945). There is a boat house by the loch which is an ideal place for a picnic. Offer the trout: Black Pennell, Greenwell's Glory and Silver Butcher.

Permission & Charges See Loch Buidhe entry.

LARO, Loch

Location & Access 21/610994 Access is from the

Dornoch Firth OS Map 21

minor road between Bonar Bridge in the south and Mound to the north. The track begins on the west side of this road by the sheep pens at Sleasdairidh (21/645966). Park at the junction on the track at 21/639979 and walk the remaining mile and a half to the loch.
Commentary Loch Laro is three quarters of a mile east/west by up to 250 yards wide. The 40 minute walk to the loch is along a good track.
Fish Nothing for the glass case, although there probably are some monsters in the deeper areas of the loch. Expect a breakfast basket of 4 to 6 trout each averaging around 8oz in weight.
Flies & Tactics The Dornoch and District Angling Association maintain a boat on Loch Laro and bank fishing is not allowed. Carefully 'investigate' the margins of the deep channel which runs from east to west down the middle of the loch and offer the residents: Zulu, Soldier Palmer and Peter Ross.
Permission & Charges See Loch Buidhe entry and Loch Lagain entry.

LOSGAINN, Loch See Loch Migdale entry.

MIGDALE, Loch
Location & Access 21/640908. Loch Migdale lies to the north of Bonar Bridge and is easily accessible from the Golf Course road.
Commentary Loch Migdale is 2 miles long by up to 500 yards wide at the west end, narrowing to 200 yards in the east. The dominant feature is the dramatic thrust of Migdale Rock (243m), on the north east shore. The surrounding hills and the extensive forest plantations, give reasonable shelter in high winds. Consider also hiking out to Loch a'Ghobhair (21/660955), an easy 1 mile tramp along a good track past Badachuil from the main road at 21/637934. Few anglers fish the loch because it has a well-deserved reputation for being 'dour', but it holds some large trout. To the south and even less frequently fished, is little Loch Losgainn (21/667930) and the unnamed lochan between Cnoc Dubh Beag (286m) and Creag a'Bhealaich (334m) at 21/669924, both of which are worth a cast or three.
Fish Brown trout, which average in the order of 10oz, but trout of up to and over 2lb in weight are not uncommon.
Flies & Tactics Boat fishing brings best results and an outboard motor is essential in order to cover the best fishing areas. Start off in the south-west corner, near the site of the Neolithic hut circle (21/624914), then fish the south shore carefully eastwards to Creich Wood (21/644904), offering as you go, Ke-He, March Brown and Silver Butcher.
Permission & Charges In the order of £20 per day. Details from: M Brown, Kyle of Sutherland Angling Club, Balleigh Wood, Edderton, Ross-shire. Tel: 01862 821230.

MOIRE, Loch See Os Map 20
PRIVATE WATERS MUIGH-BHLARAIDH, Loch (21/636830); BEAG, Loch (Struie) (21/639839); SHEILAN, Loch (21/677782); ACHNACLOICH, Loch (21/665735); BAYFIELD, Loch (21/820718) AIRDE, Loch 21/700903; SAINE, Loch 21/697899; NAN GILLEAN, Loch 21/688920; A'BHIOCAIR, Loch 21/780994.
SGITHEAEN, River See River Glass (Evanton) entry.

SHIN, River
Location & Access Source 16/580060 Outfall 21/573967. Easy access from the B864 Inveran/Lairg road which parallels the west bank of the river, or from the A836 Bonar Bridge/Lairg road on the east bank. The Upper River Shin forms part of OS Map 16, but for ease of reference, the whole river is described in OS Map 21.
Commentary The River Shin is approximately 3 miles in length and draws its strength from Loch Merkland, Loch a'Ghriama and, finally, from 17 mile long Loch Shin. The outfall is in the Kyle of Sutherland, four miles west from Bonar Bridge. The character of the river has been much altered in recent years by the Loch Shin hydro-electric scheme, but the river still remains one of the most productive and attractive salmon streams north of Inverness.
Fish Upwards of 700 salmon and grilse are taken most seasons. The river is noted for its heavy fish and specimens of up to and over 20lb in weight are not uncommon. Depending upon weather conditions, July is usually the most productive month.
Flies & Tactics The river is divided into two beats, Upper and Lower, each fished by 3 rods. The spectacular Shin Falls (21/576994) act as a temperature pool and salmon rarely ascend to the Upper River in any great number until after mid-May. The river is fast flowing and areas of the banks are substantially tree-lined. An ability to roll cast is essential and a 15ft rod is recommended, as much to facilitate casting as to control any fish hooked. Noted pools on the river include: Little Falls, Piper, Fir Dam, Rocky Cast, Cromarty, Culag, Falls Pool, Lady Herbert and Meadow. Flies: Willie Gunn, General Practitioner, Collie Dog, Silver Wilkinson and Stoat's Tail.
Permission & Charges The River Shin is generally fully booked, but lets are sometimes available. For information contact: David Walker, Park House, Lairg, Sutherland. Tel: 01549 402208. Expect to pay in the region of £1,000 per beat week, depending upon the time of year.

TAIN, River See Kyle of Sutherland entry.
TARBHAIDH, Loch See Loch Laoigh entry.
WESTER FEARN, Burn See Kyle of Sutherland entry.

Benbecula

A'BHARPA, Loch See Loch Caravat, North Uist
A'BHURSTA, Loch See Loch nan Clachan
A'CHAFAIN, Loch See Loch Eilean an Staoir.
A'CHARRA, Loch See East Loch Ollay.

A'CHLACHAIN, Loch (Eynort)
Location & Access 22/760305. Easily accessible from various access points, the most convenient being, for the north shore, from the Loch Eynort road (see Loch Ceann a'Bhaigh entry). For the south shore of the loch, use the peat track which heads east from the A865 near Bornish General Stores (22/751295).
Commentary The loch was the site of a fish farm until recently and there are bits and pieces of equipment still scattered around. Nevertheless, they are soon left behind as you discover hidden corners and secret bays around this large, scattered, U-shaped loch. The shoreline meanders in and out round more than two miles, offering a full day fishing in attractive surroundings.
Fish Some fine trout with good numbers of fish of up to and over 1lb in weight.
Flies & Tactics The north west section, by Loch Eynort, is the most productive area, although the south shore can also produce excellent results. Bank fishing all round and a fair bit of scrambling to find a place to cast, particularly along the south shore where the bank is steep in places. Get the fly out as far as you can and don't be too quick to cast again. Stay ashore. Do not wade. Tempt them with Black Pennell, Soldier Palmer, Peter Ross.
Permission & Charges See Loch Ceann a'Bhaigh.

A'CHLACHAIN, Loch (Ormiclate) See Loch Roinich.
A'CHNOIC BHUIDHE, Loch See Loch a'Phuirt-ruaidh
A'CHNOIC MHOIR, Loch See Loch na Eithir Eileana
A'CHOIRE, Loch See Loch Spotal
A'GHEADAIS, Loch See Loch Obisary
A'GHLINNE-DORCHA, Loch See Loch Obisary
A'MHUILINN, Loch See Loch Bail-fhionnlaidh

A'PHUIRT-RUAIDH, Loch
Location & Access 22/768358 The east side of the loch borders the A865 road just south of Howmore and the road was recently up-graded and re-surfaced, much to the great disturbance of both fish and human residents.
Commentary There are three other small, roadside lochs nearby: Loch Eilein a'Ghille-ruaidh (22/769367) to the north, Loch a'Chnoic Bhuidhe (22/769353) and Loch Dobhrain (22/767344) to the south.
Fish The average weight of trout is about 6/8oz, plate-sized, and they are of good quality. Anything over 1lb is unusual.
Flies & Tactics The west and south shore of Loch a'Phuirt-ruaidh offers comfortable, safe wading and this is the best place to start. Do not wade in the other lochs. The fish are easily covered from the shore. Cast: Soldier Palmer, Invicta, Black Pennell.
Permission & Charges See East Loch Bee.

AIRIGH AMHLAIDH, Loch See Howmore River
AIRIGH ARD, Loch See Loch Caslub

ALTABRUG, Loch
Location & Access 22/745345. After passing the village of Howmore, turn west at 22/767346 by the red-roofed house, signposted to Howbeg and Peninerine. Follow the road past the north end of Loch Roag and the Howmore river (22/754356) and turn south across the machair. Park at 22/735345. Cross the field to the east to reach the boat mooring bay after a couple of minutes.
Commentary Two for the price of one, here, with the west section of the loch being 'machair' in character whilst the eastern end is 'traditional' and peaty. Either way there is plenty to keep everyone happy with over two miles of bank fishing in very lovely surroundings. The ruined broch (BC 200 - AD 100) on the north east shore is a dramatic place for lunch.
Fish Good quality trout throughout with the best fish being taken at the west end. Trout average in the order of 8oz but there are larger fish and specimens of up to and over 1lb are not uncommon.
Flies & Tactics Boat fishing makes it easier to cover all the corners of this 'tangled' loch, but bank fishing can be just as productive. Weed is a problem as the season advances, particularly at the west end. Persevere, the fish lie amongst the weeds and on the margins. The narrows between the two sections on the loch are very good as is the little bay to the north of the dun by Peninerine. The north section of the south bay is rocky and deep but can produce great sport. The south side of this bay is very shallow and is not so productive. Most flies will tempt the inhabitants and supper is assured on Loch Altabrug. Start with: Black Pennell, Ke-He, Silver Invicta.
Permission & Charges See East Loch Bee.

AN ATH RUAIDH, Loch See Lower Loch Kildonan.
AN ATHAIN, Loch See Loch Roinich.

AN DROMA, Loch
Location & Access 22/825618 Loch an Droma lies to the east of the A865 near Corunna (22/818618). Combine a visit to Loch an Droma with an assault on a number of other unnamed lochs in the vicinity to make a splendid, non-taxing, day out.
Commentary Begin with Loch nan Clach (2/821615) which touches the road at Corunna. Fish south down the east shoreline and cross to the little unnamed lochan with the island at 22/826611. Follow the inlet stream north from here to find Loch an Droma. After exploring Loch an Droma, step east for five minutes to the unnamed lochan, also island-clad, at 22/831617, before continuing north to find Loch an Iasgaich (22/825624) which is joined east to Loch Caravat (22/846615) (see separate entry).

Benbecula — OS Map 22

Fish Plenty of fun with attractive little trout. Anything over 1lb is unusual.

Flies & Tactics Easy access and easy bank fishing, but stay ashore and do not wade. Loch an Iasgaich is perhaps the most productive of these lochs. Pay attention along the north shoreline, particularly by the two small islands and in the bay at the north east end. Flies: Ke-He, Soldier Palmer, Silver Butcher.

Permission & Charges See Loch Caravat (North Uist) entry.

AN DUIN MHOIR, Loch See West Loch Bee
AN EILEIN, Loch See Loch Eilean an Staoir.
AN FHAING BHUIDHE See Loch an Droma
AN FHAING, Loch See Loch Caravat, Grimsay
AN FHEIDH, Loch See Loch Ba Alasdair
AN IASGAIR, Loch See Loch Toronish.
AN IONAIRE, Loch See West Loch Bee
AN OSE, Loch See West Loch Bee
AN T-SAILE, LOCH See West Loch Bee
AN T-SEASGAIN, Loch See Loch Colla

AN TAIRBH, Loch

Location & Access 22/845533 See Loch Ba Una entry. Follow the track east past Loch Hermidale (22/827525) which is to the south of the track, and up the hill past Loch na Dighe to Tuath (22/832536) which is to the north of the track. The track divides here. Take the left/north branch and walk on for half a mile to reach the loch which is immediately adjacent to and to the south of the track.

Commentary You are tramping in famous footsteps. Bonnie Prince Charlie walked this way with Flora Macdonald in June 1746, heading for Rossinish Point (22/823536) and the boat that was to carry him safely over the sea to Skye.

If the Prince had been a trout angler, no doubt he would have stopped by Loch an Tairbh and had a cast or two. Fish down the east bank, then track the burn south to cross the south branch of the Loch Ba Una track for a cast in the unnamed lochan at 22/835527. Return to the south branch and continue east for ten minutes to reach Loch Scarilode (22/846523), one of the most beautiful lochs in Benbecula. Lunch in the ruined shielings beyond the south shore, overlooking Oban Haka. People lived and worked here until the early 1960's.

Fish The trout in Loch Scarilode are not very big, averaging in the order of 8/10oz, but they are of a high quality, a classic shape, and perfectly marked.

Flies & Tactics Loch an Tairbh is easily understood and comfortably fished from the bank. Loch Scarilode is more difficult to fish, with high banks and deep water close to the margins.

The north end is readily approachable. At the north east end, there is a firm, large, underwater, rock outcrop which acts as a casting platform. It is possible, with care, to wade by the rowan tree on the side of the bay at the south end. Offer: Ke-He, March Brown, Peter Ross.

Permission & Charges See Loch Olavat (Gramsdale) entry.

AN TOMAIN, Loch See Loch Obisary

AN TUIRC, Loch See Loch Toronish.
AN UISGE-GHIL, Loch See East Loch Bee

ARD AN SGAIRBH, Loch See Lower Loch Kildonan.

BA ALASDAIR, Loch

Location & Access 22/857494 Approach via the B891 and take the minor road north by the telephone box at Hacklet (22/813483), signposted to Kilerivagh and Craigastrome. Park half a mile north from Craigastrome at 22/861490. Loch Ba Alasdair can't be seen from the road, but a five minute walk west will bring you to the south end of the loch.

Commentary One of the most beautiful lochs on Benbecula, scattered over a wide area and at different levels. The southern section is Loch an Fheidh (22/859485) and the outlet stream may be crossed here to climb the hill to the highest part of the system, known as Bluebell Loch at 22/850493.

On the way up the hill, have a careful look at two small, unnamed lochans. Both are dour but they have a long-standing reputation for holding some very large trout: 22/855488 and 22/852487. A round trip of Loch Ba Alasdair involves a splendid walk of some three miles.

For a less taxing expedition, explore the lochs on the Rarnish Peninsula. There are a number of good unnamed lochs, particularly the series centred on 22/876484, and Loch na Beiste, close to the road at 22/864491.

Fish Pretty brown trout which average 6/8oz. Sea-trout, fresh from the tide, at the north end of the loch and in the sea.

Flies & Tactics It is easy to become lost here, so take along a compass and map. Bluebell Loch will almost certainly provide supper, particularly at the narrow, south end or from the headland at 22/850495. Look for sea-trout at 22/859497, 22/855502, 22/852498. Offer them: Black Pennell, Loch Ordie, Peter Ross.

Permission & Charges See Loch Olavat (Gramsdale).

BA UNA, Loch

Location & Access 22/818529 Turn east from the A865 at Market Stance, by the local authority works depot, and follow the well-made track for three quarters of a mile to read the loch. Park and fish.

Commentary This is the ideal beginner's loch, and the perfect location for a family day out. The loch is very beautiful and the north shore is shallow, sandy and safe for wading and infant splashing on hot days.

This is also a good base for setting out to explore the superb lochs further to the east. Leave the less than dedicated members of your party by Loch Ba Una and follow the excellent track east for a wonderful adventure amidst marvellous, remote, scenery.

The track skirts the south shoulder of Rueval (124m), where Prince Charles Edward Stewart hid in June 1746, prior to his departure 'over the sea to Skye'. The first water to the south of this track is Loch Hermidale (22/827525), now sadly disfigured with smolt rearing cages, and it extends south over the moor for a distance of nearly three quarters of a mile.

OS Map 22 — Benbecula

A fine tour is to fish down the west shore of Loch Hermidale, taking in the useful unnamed lochan at 22/822521 along the way and then working up the east bank to about the mid-way point before striking east again to visit Loch Dubh Haka (22/835523). Follow the stream from the north end of Loch Dubh Haka north to Loch na Deighe fo Dheas (22/832520) and fish the east shoreline back to the track. The total route involves a tramp of some three miles.

Fish Loch Ba Una has small trout which average 6oz. The other lochs noted have similar trout, but there are also good numbers of much larger specimens as well, particularly in Loch na Deighe fo Dheas. As a bonus, there is the possibility of sea-trout after heavy rain and towards the end of the season.

Flies & Tactics Loch Ba Una will always produce sport. Away from the track, however, this is rough country. Be well-shod and carry a compas and map. Benbecula weather is fickle. Wading is not recommended. Stay safely ashore at all times. Fish are taken all round these lochs, so cast with confidence. Use: Black Zulu, Clan Chief, Silver Butcher.

Permission & Charges See Loch Olavat (Gramsdale) entry.

BAGH NAM FIADH, Loch See East Loch Bee
BAGH NAM FIADH, Loch See East Loch Bee

BAIL-FHIONNLAIDH, Loch
Location & Access 22/775537 Easily accessible from the minor road between Peinylodden (22/767544) on the B892 in the west to Market Stance (22/895536) on the A865 to the east.

Commentary Loch Bail-fhionnlaidh is one of a number of lochs accessible from either the north (see above), or from the south via another convenient minor road from the B892 at 22/766519 in the west to the Monument on the A865 at 22/801519 in the east. There are sixteen named and unnamed lochs between these two roads and they all offer a good chance of sport amidst very pleasant surroundings. The walking is easy, over gentle grasslands.

For those not so inclined, there is a magnificent crescent of golden sand at Culla (2/762536) for the bucket and spade brigade, and the ruins of a 13th century church and burial ground at Nunton to explore.

Fish Something for everyone. Trout range from a few ounces in weight right up to fish of over 2lb.

Flies & Tactics Plan your walk/attack from the map, either as a one day expedition, or over a more leisurely period. The other waters here are: the unnamed lochan at 22/780534, a small, narrow loch which is reputed to hold some very large trout, and three unnamed 'nursery' lochs immediately to the north. The unnamed lochan close to the road at Muir of Aird (22/78554) also has a reputation for large fish.

Walk east to find Loch Eilean Iain (North) (22/787535), linked to Loch Eilean Iain (South) (22/765531). West from the Loch Eilean Iain (South), across marshy ground, is Loch Borosdale (22/781529) with little Loch a'Mhuilinn (22/785523) south again; whilst to the east, is Loch Fada (Muir of Aird) (22/792530).

Additional lochs lie close to the sea and the B892 road: Loch Mor (Nunton) (22/770525); to the north, Loch na Lina Moire (22/765531) linked to the unnamed lochan with the Dun at 22/762531. South from Loch Mor (Nunton), across the road, is Loch Fada (Griminish) (22/774518) and the substantial, unnamed loch near the ruins of Borve Castle at 22/769510.

Finally, the chance of sea-trout in Oban Liniclate (22/785502) and near the Shell Bay Caravan Site at (22/796496). A number of these lochs weed up as the season advances so visit them in May or June to obtain the best results. Bank fishing. Flies: Blue Zulu, March Brown, Kingfisher Butcher.

Permission & Charges See Loch Olavat (Gramsdale).

BAIMALEE, Loch See Loch Eilean an Staoir.

BEE (EAST), Loch
Location & Access 22/785430 Easily accessible, at the north end of the Island of South Uist, adjacent to the A865 road, prior to crossing the South Ford causeway from North to South Uist. There is a parking place at 22/783433 where the boats are moored.

Commentary A large, peat-stained, shallow loch, rarely more than six feet deep and extending east for almost one mile. A narrow, very weedy, arm leads east again to a 50-acre extension at 22/805417 known locally as the Shell Loch. This is a famous gathering area for wild swans, both mute and whooper, and sometimes more than 100 birds may be counted.

A further south east channel brings you to a one mile long arm centred on 22/808409 at the sea end of which there are flood gates. Look out for the great raptors here: golden eagle, buzzard and harrier.

North from the Shell Loch is little Loch na Lice Baine (22/810423), whilst in the hills to the south, on the east shoulder of Rueval (87m), there are three excellent lochs, Loch Clach an Duilisg (22/789395), Loch Rueval (22/786399), and Loch an Uisge-ghil (22/791401).

These three lochs drain north into East Loch Bee through Bagh nam Fiadh (22/789414), a one mile long southern 'leg' of the main loch. To the west of Bagh nam Fiadh is Loch nan Sgeireag (22/800407) which can also offer great sport.

Further sport may be had in the small lochs to the north of East Loch Bee, Loch Dubh an Ionaire (22/790438) and Loch Druim an Iasgair (22/803434); have a cast in the tiny lochan by the west shore of Loch Druim an Iasgair - it holds some fine fish. There are other, unnamed and largely unexplored lochs between the two named lochs which can also produce a few surprises.

Fish East Loch Bee has brown trout of the highest quality. The average weight is in the order of 10oz but fish of up to 4lb are not uncommon. The surrounding lochs contain trout which vary in size from 6oz to a few of over the 1lb mark.

Flies & Tactics East Loch Bee is best fished from the boat. The most productive drift is from the main island in a direct line to the south shore. Although it is hard not to do so, don't finish the drift too quickly,

Benbecula — OS Map 22

simply because the water is shallow. Good trout lie in the shallows, waiting for the well-presented fly.

On the west shore, by the causeway, the vicinity of the inflow from West Loch Bee has cut a deep channel. This can be a highly productive fishing area, although the back cast could hook more passing cars on the causeway than trout in the loch.

High winds often make it impossible to launch the boat on East Loch Bee. That is the time to head for the hills and to explore the surrounding waters noted above. Bank fishing is not particularly effective on the main loch, but the narrow, weed-fringed, channel to the Shell Loch offers excellent sport from the shore.

The south east arm of East Loch Bee, towards the Flood Gate, holds some really serious trout and few anglers make the effort to tramp out and fish there. Do so, prepared with : Black Pennell, Bibio, Grouse & Claret, Ke-He, Soldier Palmer, Clan Chief, March Brown, Dunkeld, Peter Ross, Silver Butcher.

Permission & Charges Lochboisdale Hotel, Lochboisdale, Isle of South Uist, Outer Hebrides. Tel: (01878 700332). Approx. costs: Brown trout £25 per boat per day (2 rods fishing). Seatrout and salmon fishing 1-15 July, £35 per boat; 17 July-9 Sept £55 per boat. 11-23 Sept £35 per boat; 25 Sept-31 Oct, £30 per boat. Gillies are available if booked in advance at a cost of £35 per day, payable directly to the gillie. No more than than two rods per boat. All brown trout under 12oz and all seatrout under 1.5lb must be returned.

BEE (WEST), Loch

Location & Access 22/770440 West Loch Bee is at the north end of South Uist, divided from East Loch Bee by the A865 South Ford causeway, but joined to it by a conduit under the road.

Commentary The loch covers an area approximately two square miles and is linked to the sea at Clachan (22/769465) in the north. Indeed, only the Flood Gate at the south east end of East Loch Bee stops the whole system from being a separate island in its own right. West Loch Bee is predominantly brackish and, because of its size, difficult to fish. Local knowledge is really essential in order to find your way safely around this two mile long loch. However, there are several smaller lochs surrounding West Loch Bee which are easier to 'understand'.

They are, to the north: Loch an t-Saile (22/758462) near Ardknneth; Oban na Buail-uachdraich (22/765465); Loch an Ose (22/790457; little Loch Nid (22/809446) to the east of the A865 by Lochcarnan; Loch nam Breac Mora (22/787443) and Loch an Ionaire (22/763433), between West Loch Bee and the A865; and, to the south, Loch an Duin Mhoir (22/776415) and Loch Cille Bhanain (22/769414) at West Gerinish.

The west side of West Loch Bee is bordered by a military rocket firing range and access is prohibited when the red flag flies. For the rest, all these waters are easily accessible. West Bee is also popular with windsurfers and other non-angling water-sport addicts.

Fish Just about everything is possible in West Loch Bee, including a wide variety of sea fish. Sea-trout are present during most of the season and they are of the highest quality. There are also 'slob trout', brown trout which live on the margin between fresh and salt water, without becoming sea-trout. The other waters have brown trout which average in the order of 8/10oz.

Flies & Tactics West Loch Bee is very shallow and fishing is restricted mainly to the north west shore in the vicinity of the small islands and the narrows. The principal pool lies between the shore and the largest of these islands.

The brown trout lochs are fished from the bank and wading is not recommended. On Loch an Ose, concentrate your efforts at the south end. Loch Naid, on its day, can be very good, and you should also fish the two unnamed lochans immediately to the south and west of the main body of water. Flies: use something bushy, something sombre and something bright: Ke-He, March Brown, Teal Blue & Silver are about right.

Permission & Charges See Loch Olavat (Gramsdale) entry.

BEIN, Loch See Loch Spotal
BEIRE, Loch See Loch Dubh (Reuval)

BORNISH, Loch

Location & Access 22/733294. Turn west at Bornish General Stores (22/751295) and follow the road to Bornish Church (22/737296). The OS Map marks a definite road junction 22/740298. In fact, on the ground, the main road continues uninterrupted and it is easy to miss the left turn to Bornish Church. Park to the left of the church, making sure that you do not obstruct other traffic. Go through the gate in the wall and follow the track down to the loch and the boat mooring bay.

Commentary One of the most famous South Uist machair trout lochs and probably one of the finest trout lochs in Europe. Loch Bornish is shallow, lime-rich, three quarters of a mile north/south by up to quarter of a mile across. Quite apart from the quality of the fishing, Loch Bornish is also remarkable for the wide variety of wildflowers which adorn its banks: more than thirty different species can sometimes be found growing within the space of a few yards.

Fish Outstanding wild brown trout which average in the order of 12oz/14oz with good numbers of larger fish of up to and over 3lb in weight.

Flies & Tactics Loch Bornish is best fished from the boat, although in stormy weather bank fishing can also be productive and wading is safe. Fish rise and are taken all over the loch but the best drifts are from the west shore, east to the large island, then, progressively, south down the loch. Flies: Ke-He, Soldier Palmer, Peter Ross.

Permission & Charges See East Loch Bee entry.

BOROSDLAE, Loch See Loch Bail-fhionnlaidh
BUAILE GRAMASDALE, Loch See Loch Colla

CARAVAT, Loch (Grimsay)

Location & Access 22/858567. After crossing the causeway from North Uist to Grimsay, take the sec-

220

OS Map 22 — Benbecula

ond left from the A865 at Loch an Fhaing (22/844576) and follow the minor road signposted to Scotvein. Park at 22/852567, where the sea touches the road, and follow the outlet stream east over the moor to reach Loch Caravat after ten minutes.
Commentary Loch Caravat covers an area of approximately 30 acres and lies at the centre of the island of Grimsay. The little, unnamed, roadside lochan at Rudhadubh (22/852564) is also worth a few casts.
Fish Brown trout which average 6/8oz and the odd fish of up to 1lb.
Flies & Tactics Bank fishing, and stay ashore, wading is dangerous. The north west bay is the most productive, in the vicinity of the small island and on either side of the long promontory. Loch an Fhaing has similar fish. Flies: Black Zulu, March Brown, Dunkeld.
Permission & Charges See Loch Caravat (North Uist).

CARAVAT, Loch (North Uist)
Location & Access 22/846615. To reach the north shore of this large loch, leave the A867 road at 18/188645 and follow the B894 Locheport/Sidinish road to park at 18/835634 by Oban nam Fiadh. To visit the south shore, park at 22/837600 on the A865 and walk north east for half a mile to reach the loch.
Commentary Loch Caravat is spread over an area covering one square mile, with Beinn na Coille (64m) to the west. The loch is formed by two east/west arms, one to the north and the other to the south, joined by a quarter mile long 'waist' which is formed by the promontory of Aird nan Laogh.
The southern section is the deepest part of the loch, dropping to more than 40ft in the vicinity of the Pictish Dun. On the way to the south shore, have a cast in Loch a'Bharpa (22/835605) and the unnamed lochan to the south east at 22/842603, and the unnamed lochan just before Loch Caravat at 22/837609.
Fish Brown trout which average 8oz, but the loch does have a reputation for being dour and unproductive much of the time.
Flies & Tactics Bank fishing all round and be prepared for some heavy tramping if you propose to cover the whole loch during one visit: the shoreline is nearly six miles long. The north east shore, in the vicinity of the outlet stream, is a good place to start. The bay between Aird nan Laogh and the east bank can be rewarding, and don't miss the unnamed lochan at the head of the bay at 22/851618. The whole length of the south shore should produce sport, but concentrate by the small island. Wading is dangerous. Stay ashore. Offer: Black Pennell, March Brown, Alexandra.
Permission & Charges Fishing is in the ownership of the North Uist Estate and let to the Lochmaddy Hotel, Lochmaddy, North Uist, Outer Hebrides. Tel: (01876) 500331 and to Langass Lodge, Locheport, North Uist, Outer Hebrides. Tel (01876) 580285. Hotel and lodge guests have priority. Trout fishing is free to residents. Boat hire is £22 per day.

CASLUB, Loch
Location & Access 22/825416 Leave the A865 at 22/792451. Drive east on the minor road signposted to Lochcarnan and Sandwick. Park half a mile south from the Power Station at 22/834418. The loch is to the right of the road.
Commentary Not a particularly attractive loch, but nevertheless offering the opportunity of exciting fishing. Loch Caslub is one and a half miles east/west with a short 'foot' leading to the sea through the narrows of Strom Caltinish at 22/820412.
Along the way, park by the post box at Sandwick 22/830430 and have a cast in Loch Shnathaid (22/828427). Also, walk past Loch Shnathaid to visit the little unnamed lochan on the west at 22/821425. Another alternative to Loch Caslub is the Island Loch, unnamed on the OS Map at 22/830403. At the end of the road lie the East Gerinish lochs. There are six waters, the most significant of which is Loch Airigh Ard (22/843394). The others are unnamed on the OS Map, but are easily accessible from good peat tracks: one leads east past the burial chamber near Lon Dubh (22/844401) and the other runs south to Aird Horragay at 22/831390.
Fish Loch Caslub is reputed to contain some very large trout although they do not give themselves up easily. The Island Loch also has good trout, and fish of up to and over 2lb are taken here. The other waters noted above have smaller residents.
Flies & Tactics Caslub is fished from the boat. Do not wade anywhere in this steep sided loch. If you have to resort to bank fishing, then the best area is at the west end, and in the arm which exits to the sea. Stay on terra firma at all times.
The Island Loch also has steep banks, but plenty of room for casting. The south end is where the larger fish lie, amongst the islands, and, generally, close to the shore. The other waters are comfortably covered with: Black Zulu, Soldier Palmer, Dunkeld.
Permission & Charges See Loch Olavat (Grimsdale).

CEANN A'BHAIGH, Loch
Location & Access 22/765302. Also known as 'Bayhead'. Approach from the Loch Eynort road. Park by the telephone kiosk at 22/766298 and follow the track north for ten minutes to reach the loch.
Commentary The loch extends for a distance of nearly one mile east/west but in effect the best of the fishing is in the vicinity of where the stream flows in from East Loch Ollay (22/765312) from the north and where the stream exits south to sea-Loch Eynort. For further adventure, follow the inlet stream at the east end of Loch Ceann a'Bhaigh for one mile, east onto the lower slopes of Beinn Mhor to find the source at Loch Iarras (22/787309). This is a rough, soggy, tramp but it will take you into marvellous away-from-it-all country with a good chance of seeing golden eagle.
Fish In Loch Ceann a'Bhaigh, good quality small brown trout with a few of up to and over 1lb in weight as well. Salmon and sea-trout, particularly after the end of July. Sea-trout average 1lb 8oz, salmon 7lb. Loch Iarras: small trout and magical scenery.

Benbecula   OS Map 22

Flies & Tactics This brackish loch is fished from either boat or bank and is best attacked at low tide. Much improved during recent years. The north east bank is a good place to begin. Flies: Black Zulu, Ke-He, Goat's Toe.

Permission & Charges The Secretary, South Uist Angling Club, Ardmore, Eochar, South Uist. Tel: (01870) 610325 or Mrs A Kennedy, Bornish Stores, Bornish. Tel: (01878) 710366. £6 per rod per day bank fishing, the boat is a further £5 per day. £30 per week. Also from Campbell Sports Shop, Benbecula.

CILLE BHANAIN, Loch See West Loch Bee
CLACH AN DUILISG, Loch See East Loch Bee
CNOC A'BUIDHE, Loch See Lower Loch Kildonan.

COLLA, Loch
Location & Access 22/865607 Follow the minor road which leaves the A865 just before the start of the Causeway to Grimsay Island at Knock-cuien (22/841598) and park by Claddach-carinish (22/852590). Loch Colla is one and a half miles north east from the road, across the peat moorland.
Commentary Make this a full day out exploring a number of other waters along the way during the course of a five mile round trip. Begin with a cast in the unnamed lochan close to the road at 22/853593, then walk north east for half a mile to find Loch nan Garbh Chlachan (22/860300). Fish the west shore, north, then cross to Loch an t-Seasgain (22/861605). Loch Colla is immediately to the north of Loch an t-Seasgain. Work clockwise round the west shoreline, having a look at Loch Cuaile Gramasdale (22/860612) as you go. Continue along the north and east shore of Loch Colla and walk south to little Loch Fada (22/870600). Loch Fada exits to the sea at Oban nam Muca-mara where there is the chance of sea-trout in the vicinity of 22/873597.
Return by walking west, fishing the unnamed lochan at 22/871595, Loch nan Gealag (22/865594) and the sea at Oban an Innseannaich as you go. You should pick up a welcome track on the coast after crossing west from Oban an Innseanaich. This leads back to the minor road and the morning start point.
Fish There are some good fish waiting, but these lochs can be dour. The average weight is in the order of 8/10oz. The possibility of sea-trout in the sea.
Flies & Tactics This is rough going and you will most certainly require a compass and map to find your way safely round. Loch Colla is particularly attractive and the east shore should provide you with breakfast. Tempt the residents with: Blue Zulu, Ke-He, Silver Invicta.
Permission & Charges See Loch Caravat (North Uist).

CORODALE, Loch
Location & Access 22/832331 One of the most remote lochs in the Outer Hebrides and a long, hard walk, and a total distance of 10 miles if a visit to Loch Hellisdale (22/828310) is included. Start from the peat track that leads east from the A865 at 22/769341.

Commentary This is a serious expedition, not to be undertaken lightly by those inexperienced in basic hill walking techniques. A compass and map are essential, as is proper equipment and clothing.
After leaving the track by a small, peat-stained lochan at 22/778339 make for the hard ground on Moa Breac, the north shoulder of Beinn Mhor (608m). Climb Bealach Hellisdale and descend into Glen Hellisdale to reach the loch after a tough, three hour tramp.
Continue north from Loch Hellisdale, along the ragged coast, to find Prince's Cave (22/834313), where Bonnie Prince Charlie hid and held court during his stay in the Outer Hebrides in 1746 after the Battle of Culloden. Keeping to the high ground, circle north west round the hill to arrive at Loch Corodale in Glen Usinish.
Return by following the north branch of the inlet stream west up onto the bealach below Hecla (606m). A further three mile stiff trudge will bring you back to the peat track and the A865.
Fish Loch Corodale has large numbers of brown trout which average 6/8oz. Loch Hellisdale has a few specimen fish of up to and over 2lb in weight.
Flies & Tactics In view of the effort involved in reaching these remote lochs, you might imagine that the fish are going to throw themselves at you. Sadly, no, both lochs can be dour. Nevertheless, the sheer joy of these lonely places is reward enough in itself. A fish, regardless of size, is a bonus. Try them with: Blue Zulu, March Brown, Peter Ross.
Permission & Charges See East Loch Bee.

CROGAVAT, Loch See Loch Obisary
DOBHRAIN, Loch See Loch a'Phuirt-ruaidh

DRIMORE, Loch
Location & Access 22/772405 Loch Drimore is a small loch to the west of the A865, just south from Hugh Lormier's beautiful statue of Our Lady of the Isles, erected in 1957, on the west shoulder of Rueval.
Commentary An easily accessible loch, close to the road, and adjacent to three further, unnamed lochans where breakfast may be caught at 22/776402, 22/773403 and 22/775398.
Fish Trout average three to the pound.
Flies & Tactics Most patterns will tempt the residents. Begin with: Black Pennell, March Brown, Silver Butcher.
Permission & Charges See East Loch Bee.

DROLLAVAT, Loch See Loch Snigisclett.
DRUIDIBEG, Loch 22/790376 Loch Druidibeg, and its east extension, Loch Hamasclett (22/800386), is the largest freshwater loch on South Uist and it lies in the north of the island to the east of the A865 road. The loch is a Nature Reserve and important wildlife habitat. Although there are plenty of trout in the loch, fishing is restricted in order to avoid disturbance to flora and fauna.

DRUIM AN IASGAIR, Loch (South Uist) See East Loch Bee

OS Map 22 — Benbecula

DRUIM AN ISGAIR, Loch See Loch Langavat
DUBH AN IONAIRE, Loch See East Loch Bee
DUBH CNOC NA FILE, Loch See Loch na Eithir Eileana
DUBH HAKA, Loch See Loch Ba Una

DUBH, Loch (Rueval)

Location & Access See Loch Ba Una entry. From Loch Ba Una, follow the track east past the north shore of Loch Hermidale (22/827525). As the track rises, Loch na Deighe fo Tuath (22/832536) is on your left.
Commentary Loch na Deighe fo Tuath is the start point on the three mile round-trip visiting the lochs to the north of the Loch Ba Una track. Fish north up the west shore of Loch na Deighe fo Tuath to reach Loch Dubh after half a mile. Loch Dubh itself is half a mile long and the north end, round the island-clad bay, is the perfect away-from-it-all lunch location.
Work round the north end of Loch Dubh, then head south down the east bank. At the bay with two small islands, walk east again to fish Loch Beire (22/833542). Now walk south and return to the Loch Ba Una track having a cast in the unnamed lochans at 22/838538 and 22/837537 along the way.
Fish There are some serious trout in Loch na Deighe fo Tuath, but they are dour. The other lochs noted above also have some good fish, but the majority of the residents are of modest size.
Flies & Tactics Bank fishing. Do not wade. The trout tend to lie close to the margin, particularly on Loch na Deighe fo Tuath, so creep up on them from afar. First cast: Black Pennell, March Brown, Kingfisher Butcher.
Permission & Charges See Loch Olavat (Gramsdale).

DUBH MOR, Loch (Langavat) See Loch Langavat
DUN AN T-SIAMAIN, Loch See Loch Obisary

DUN MHURCHAIDH, Loch

Location & Access 22/795545 Also known as the 'Caravan Loch', Loch Dun Mhurchaidh lies between the B892 Balivanich road and the minor road from Knock Rolum (22/788550) in the west to Market Stance (22/895536) in the east. It is easily accessible from a number of paths around the shore.
Commentary This is a large, shallow, loch and one of the most exciting on Benbecula. It is readily accessible, and therefore it is very popular. The loch is surrounded by farmland - good for mushrooms - and Loch Dun Mhurchaidh is three quarters of a mile north/south by up to one quarter of a mile wide.
There are two other lochs in the immediate vicinity, also easily accessible, which could repay a visit: the unnamed loch near Uachdar at 22/800557 and Loch na Smalaig (22/795545), just to the south of Gramsdale.
Fish Trout in Loch Dun Mhurchaidh average 10oz and there are also fish of up to and over 4lb in weight. The other lochs noted above contain smaller specimens.
Flies & Tactics Easy bank fishing and the temptation is to wade. Resist this temptation. It is generally safe to wade, but the larger trout tend to lie in the shallow water, particularly in the evenings, and wading only scares them out into the middle of the loch.
Concentrate your attack along the north east arm, then down the east shore to the small island at the south end. Don't expect the residents to give themselves up easily, they can be extremely dour. The other waters are also fished from the bank and are easily covered. Flies: Black Pennell, Grouse & Claret, Silver Invicta.
Permission & Charges See Loch Olavat (Gramsdale).

EADARAY, Loch See Loch Roinich.

EAST OLLAY, Loch

Location & Access 22/765312. Follow the peat track that leaves the A865 at the south west corner of the loch. Park in the quarry hole and cross the outlet stream to find the boats moored at 22/765310.
Commentary East Loch Ollay is almost three quarters of a mile long by up to one quarter of a mile wide, rock-strewn and mercifully weed-free. The loch is used for fish rearing as part of the South Uist Estate fishery improvement programme. As such, it is 'disfigured' by cages but in spite of this East Loch Ollay is more than worth a visit and offers a wide variety of easily accessible sport.
Fish Something for everyone, including salmon, sea-trout and brown trout. Trout average 8oz, although I have seen a stray machair trout of 5lb taken by John Kennedy, the Fishery Manager; sea-trout, up to 3lb, salmon average 7lb.
Flies & Tactics Most anglers fish from the boat, personally, I prefer to attack from the shore. The south east corner, by the inlet burns is a good place to start. On the north bank, concentrate mightily where the Loch Beinn a'Charra (22/772314) joins East Loch Ollay. Salmon lie amidst the rocky shallows, well within casting distance. Indeed, wading will only scares the fish out into the middle so it is best to stay ashore. The large, shallow, bay half-way along the north bank also offers great sport. Vary your flies according to the wind conditions. Try: Ke-He, Clan Chief, Goat's Toe.
Permission & Charges See East Loch Bee entry.

EILEAN AN STAOIR, Loch

Location & Access 22/732260. Approach from the A865 at 22/745264 and drive west to Milton. The loch is immediately adjacent and to the south of the minor road.
Commentary This is one of a number of small, shallow lochs lying to the west and east of the A865 road between Milton in the north and Askernish to the south. They are all easily accessible from minor roads leading west from the A865, or from the track which borders the machair shore to the west. The other lochs are: the unnamed lochans to the south of Loch Eilean an Staoir at 22/738257 and 22/739259 and Loch Baimalee (22/741257); at Frobost, Loch nan Uan (22/739253) and Loch na Liana Moire (22/732249); at Askernish, Loch na Cuithe Moire (22/738235), Loch na Tanga (22/738231) and roadside Loch an Eilein (22/745238); and to the east of the A865, Loch a'Chafain (22/748242) and Loch Roinich

223

Benbecula   OS Map 22

(22/748248). For the most extraordinary game of golf in Scotland, have a few holes at Askernish. Green fees should be 'posted' in a box by the club shed - although the last time I tried I found the box otherwise engaged - acting as a nesting site for a pair of starlings.
Fish Plenty to feed the family, and the odd larger trout waiting to catch you unawares.
Flies & Tactics All of these lochs are fished from the shore. They are shallow and some almost disappear during dry weather. Weed is also a problem, so it is best to attack early in the season. They are great fun to fish and because so few bother to do so you will be assured of good sport. Flies: Black Zulu, Invicta, Silver Butcher.
Permission & Charges See Loch Ceann a'Bhaigh entry.

EILEAN IAIN, Loch (North) See Loch Bail-fhionnlaidh
EILEAN IAIN (South) See Loch Bail-fhionnlaidh
EILEIN A'GHILLE-RUAIDH, Loch See Loch a'Phuirt-ruaidh
FADA, Loch (Colla) See Loch Colla
FADA, Loch (Griminish) See Loch Bail-fhionnlaidh
FADA, Loch (Howmore) See Howmore River
FADA, Loch (Muir of Aird) See Loch Bail-fhionnlaidh
FADA, Loch (Spotal) See Loch Spotal

GROGARRY, Loch
Location & Access 22/762395 Access is by a military road from the A865 at 22/774397. Drive past Grogarry Lodge, in the trees on your left, and park at 22/762398 near the Rocket Range flag post. When the flag is flying, go no further. The boats are moored nearby.
Commentary This is one of the premier South Uist fisheries, a classic machair loch, circular in shape, shallow, and just under half a mile in diameter. Close by is little Loch nam Balgan at 22/762400, the ideal retreat if it is too windy to launch the boat on Grogarry. To the north of Loch nam Balgan, and joined to it, there is an excellent unnamed lochan at 22/766400 which should not be missed.
Fish The trout in all these lochs are of the highest quality and average 12oz in weight. Loch Grogarry also has fish of up to and over 3lb, as does the small unnamed lochan noted above.
Flies & Tactics Best results on Grogarry come from boat fishing, although bank fishing can also be productive. The west shoreline, between the sandy bottom and the darker water is a favourite drift, as is the edge of the large island at the north end. In truth, however, trout rise and are taken all over the loch so cast with confidence, everywhere.
Loch nam Balgan is very shallow and it is possible to wade across the north shore in thigh waders. The north and east bank produce the best results and this is where the larger trout lie, including fish of over 1lb. The unnamed loch can only be fished effectively from the north bank due to soft, marshy margins and thick weed along the south shore.

Weed becomes an increasing problem on the machair lochs as the season advances, so attack during the early months of the season. April, May, June and early July are best. Flies: Ke-He, Soldier Palmer, Alexandra.
Permission & Charges See East Loch Bee.

HAMASCLETT, Loch See Loch Druidibeg
HELLISDALE, Loch See Loch Corodale

HEOURAVAY, Loch
Location & Access 22/826510 Leave the A865 at 22/862510 at the north end of East Loch Olavat (22/804504). Park at the end of the track and walk east for half a mile to reach the loch.
Commentary A wonderful loch in a remote setting, consisting of a narrow, east/west arm extending for a distance of one mile, and a similar, north/south leg. There are a number of excellent, unnamed lochs close by, the most significant of which are at 22/829514 in the north, and at 22/833501 (with four small islands) in the south.
There is the chance of sea-trout at the head of Heouravay Bay, a minute west from the loch, and in the long, narrow, sea-loch at Lidistrome (22/839506).
Fish Brown trout average 8oz, sea-trout anything up to and over 4lb.
Flies & Tactics This loch is rarely visited and offers a glorious day out with good bank fishing. All the water is easily covered from the bank and you should avoid wading. Flies: Black Zulu, Loch Ordie, Alexandra.
Permission & Charges See Loch Olavat (Gramsdale).

HERMIDALE, Loch See Loch Ba Una

HORRARY, Loch
Location & Access 22/866572 Turn due east from the A865 at the school by Balaglas (22/848577) immediately after crossing the causeway from North Uist to Grimsay. Follow the minor road signposted to Baymore. Park at 22/869569. On your way over the causeway, glance west to note the old marker posts, showing the way across the sands before the building of the causeway in 1956.
Commentary Loch Horrary, with the island-Dun site, is on your left. The loch to the right is Loch na Faoileag (22/869567). Both are easily accessible, as are the unnamed roadside lochans one mile further south near Baymore, at 22/872560, 22/875554, and at 22/876556.
Another small, easily accessible Grimsay loch, which is worth a look is Loch Nighe (22/859582), on an islet off the north coast of Grimsay and reached by a causeway at Gearradubh (22/858579). If you visit these lochs during early June, watch out for the unforgettable sight of rafts of pink thrift by the sea-shore.
Fish Brown trout in the order of 8oz. There is always the chance of sea-trout in the salt-water inlets on the north and south coast of the island.
Flies & Tactics Few problems, provided you stay ashore and do not wade. All these lochs are easily covered from the bank and trout are taken from all round the shore. Offer: Black Pennell, Soldier Palmer, Peter Ross.

OS Map 22 — Benbecula

Permission & Charges See Loch Caravat (North Uist).

HOWMORE, River
Location & Access Source: Loch Roag 22/756354; Outflow: Bun na Feathlach 22/754363. East access to all parts of the system from the A865 via Howmore (22/758354) and Howbeg (22/761355).
Commentary The Howmore river is a short, sluggish stream draining four South Uist salmon and sea-trout fisheries: Loch an Eilein (22/763371), known locally as Castle Loch, Schoolhouse Loch (22/765364), Loch Roag (22/756354), and Loch Fada (22/757346). The true source is east of the A865. Loch Druidibeg feeds Castle Loch; Abhainn Roag, draining Loch Airigh Amhlaidh (22/791354), Loch nam Breac Ruadh (22/798359) and Loch nam Breac Peatair (22/789363) into Loch Roag; and the Abhainn Gheatry stream which feeds Loch Fada.
Non-anglers should visit the ruined 12th century chapel at Howmore, the birthplace of Neil MacEachan who helped Prince Charles Edward Stuart escape to France, and whose son, Jacques Etienne, became a Marshall of France and Duke of Taranto under Napoleon.
Fish Approximately 400 sea-trout and 205 salmon and grilse are taken most seasons. All sea-trout and finnock under 1lb 8oz are returned. The best month is August, but July, September and October can be just as productive.
Flies & Tactics The lochs are best fished under the direction of a gillie. They are often windy and a large part of your precious day could be wasted adjusting the drift, rather than fishing. Some very good baskets have been taken in recent years: Loch Fada, 2 sea-trout at 15lb 8oz, 4 sea-trout at 14lb 8oz. A 10½lb fish was taken in 2000.
Schoolhouse Loch also does well: 3 sea-trout at 10lb 8oz, 3 sea-trout at 14lb 8oz. Other notable catches included 3 sea-trout at 17lb and 1 sea-trout at 6lb from Loch Roag and a 5lb fish for Mr Cardno from Castle Loch. Flies that do the damage: Ke-He, Black Pennell, Blue Zulu, Soldier Palmer, Silver Invicta, Peter Ross, Clan Chief, Goat's Toe, Stoat's Tail.
These same patterns will suffice for the headwater lochs which contain brown trout of moderate size and are easily covered from the shore.
Permission & Charges See East Loch Bee.

IARRAS, Loch See Loch Ceann a'Bhaigh.
ISLAND, Loch See Loch Caslub

LANGAVAT, Loch
Location & Access 22/830490 Loch Langavat lies to the north of the minor road from the school at Kilerivagh (22/819486) to Craigastrome (22/857482) and is easily accessible from this road.
Commentary This is the longest loch on Benbecula, being almost two miles east/west by up to 250 yds wide. The loch can't be seen from the road and is a half mile tramp north over the moor. The quickest access is to the south end, from near Oban Uaine (22/846479).
There are two, unnamed lochs at the south end which you should also note, both of which have a reputation for containing good trout: 22/850481, and on Carnan-ard-Wiay at 22/849474. The Island of Wiay itself has good trout fishing, on Loch na Beiste (22/873456) and Lochan nan Lachan (22/875461) but access to the island is difficult to arrange.
Loch Uacrach nan Caorach (22/839494), to the north east of Loch Langavat, offers sport, as do the unnamed lochans to the south of Druim na Lice (25m) at 22/844491. At the north west end of Loch Langavat, there are a further series of unnamed lochans, at 22/821497, all of which hold nice trout. Three other small lochs in the vicinity are worth a visit: Loch Druim an Isgair (22/805494), the unnamed lochan at 22/801489, and Loch Dubh Mor (22/809477) to the south of Hacklet.
Fish Loch Langavat trout average 6/8oz, but there are larger fish. The other lochs noted above contain smaller fish, but Loch Druim an Isgair has 'specimen' residents, and there is the chance of sea-trout in Loch Dubh Mor and at Oban Uaine.
Flies & Tactics All bank fishing and rough walking. The middle and west end of Loch Langavat is a good place to start. Flies: Blue Zulu, Ke-He, Peter Ross.
Permission & Charges See Loch Olavat (Gramsdale).

LIDSTROME, Sea-loch See Loch Heouravay

LOWER KILDONAN, Loch
Location & Access 22/737276. For access see Upper Loch Kildonan entry.
Commentary This is one of the principal South Uist sea-trout and salmon fisheries and is linked to Mill Loch (22/747270), Loch an Ath Ruaidh (22/754264) and Loch Cnoc a'Buidhe (22/749260) to the east of the A865 road, and to Loch Ard an Sgairbh (22/733269) to the south of Lower Loch Kildonan. For those who wish to escape from view for a couple of hours, follow the peat track which runs south from Loch an Ath Ruaidh to little Loch nan Caorach (22/763257). Peace and quiet and fun with small brown trout await. The loch is guarded by the memorial marking the birthplace of Flora Macdonald (22/740269) who risked her life helping Prince Charles Edward Stewart to escape from the Hebrides in 1746.
Fish Most seasons produce sea-trout of up to and over 5lb in weight. Salmon average 6lb/7lb (see also Howmore River).
Flies & Tactics Lower Loch Kildonan and Mill Loch provide most sport and are best fished from the boat and with the services of a gillie; not only because of the local knowledge he provides, but also to hold the boat steady in the often windy conditions which prevail on the island. Flies: Clan Chief, Black Pennell, Goat's Toe.
Permission & Charges See East Loch Bee entry.

MID OLLAY, Loch
Location & Access Park at 22/761312 on the A865. The east end of Mid Loch Ollay touches the road, close to the boat mooring bay.

Benbecula — OS Map 22

Commentary Mid Loch Ollay is nearly one mile east/west by up to quarter of a mile wide, easily accessible and great fun to fish. An ideal beginners loch, full of bright little trout.
Fish Don't expect to break any records, but there are a few fish of up to and over 1lb in weight.
Flies & Tactics Boat fishing is most comfortable and helps getting around this extensive water. Fish are taken all round the loch, but the first bay to the south, protected by a small island, is always productive. The far west end of the loch is also good and contains larger, better quality trout. Cast: Blue Zulu, Invicta, Silver Butcher.
Permission & Charges See East Loch Bee entry.

MILL, Loch See Lower Loch Kildonan.

MOR, Loch (Baleshare)
Location & Access 22/791621 Leave the A865 road at 22/815628 and drive west across the causeway to the small island of Baleshare. Park by the school at 22/788619 and walk east for a couple of minutes to reach the loch.
Commentary A small, shallow loch, covering a few acres and surrounded by gentle machair fields.
There are five other lochans on Baleshare, the largest of which, near Teanamachar at 22/779619, can hold sea-trout. Baleshare beaches stretch for miles and are quite outstanding. There is a Youth Hostel, located in a renovated traditional, Hebridean 'black house'.
Fish Something for breakfast.
Flies & Tactics All the fishing is easily accessible and bank fishing is comfortable and safe. The water is readily covered from the shore but plan your attack in the early months because the waters become weedy and increasingly shallow as the season advances. Flies: Black Zulu, Ke-He, Peter Ross.
Permission & Charges See Loch Caravat (North Uist).

MOR, Loch (Nunton) See Loch Bail-fhionnlaidh
NA BEISTE, Loch (Rarnish) See Loch Ba Alasdair
NA BEISTE, Loch (Wiay) See Loch Langavat
NA BREAC PEATAIR, Loch See Loch nam Faoileann.
NA BUAILE DUIBHE, Loch See Loch na Eithir Eileana
NA CLEIBH, Loch See Loch Obisary
NA COINNICH, Loch See Loch na Eithir Eileana
NA CUITHE MOIRE, Loch See Loch Eilean an Staoir.
NA CURRAIDH, Loch See Loch Roinich.
NA DEIGHE FO DHEAS, Loch See Loch Ba Una
NA DEIGHE FO TUATH, Loch See Loch Dubh (Rueval)
NA DUCHASAICH, Loch See Loch Toronish.

NA EITHIR EILEANA, Loch
Location & Access Park on the B894 Clachan/Sidinish road by Loch Chladaich (18/860633), three quarters of a mile east from Locheport. Loch na Eithir Eileana is immediately to the south of the road.

Commentary Whilst it is perfectly possible to have a splendid day out exploring just Loch na Eithir Eileana and Loch Chladaich alone, it is even nicer to explore the adjacent lochs as well in a four mile hike across the heather.
Begin by working south down the west shore of Loch Chladaich to Loch na Eithir Eileana. Then cross to the north shore of Loch na Coinnich (22/856627). Fish anti-clockwise round Loch na Coinnich and return to the south west shore of Loch na Eithir Eileana, walking east to find the first inlet stream.
Follow the stream south for ten minutes to find Loch na Laire Baine (22/867619) and its unnamed neighbour at 22/864619. Cross due east now to fish Loch Dubh Cnoc na File (22/872617) and its unnamed neighbour at 22/871614.
Fish Brown trout which average 6/8oz. Sea-trout may be encountered throughout the system, particularly towards the end of the season and after heavy rain.
Flies & Tactics This is an arduous tramp and you should be well prepared and suitably dressed for the occasion. A compass and map are as vital as a fishing rod. Bank fishing all the way and do not wade. Offer them: Soldier Palmer, Invicta, Peter Ross.
Permission & Charges See Loch Caravat (North Uist).

NA FAOILEAD, Loch See Loch Horrary
NA H-ACHLAIS, Loch See Loch Spotal
NA LAIRE BAINE, Loch See Loch na Eithir Eileana
NA LIANA MOIRE, Loch See Loch Eilean an Staoir.
NA LICE BAINE, Loch See East Loch Bee
NA SMALAIG, Loch (Gramsdale) See Loch Dun Mhurchaidh
NA TANGA, Loch See Loch Eilean an Staoir.
NAID, Loch See West Loch Bee
NAM BALGAN, Loch See Grogarry Loch
NAM BREAC MORA, Loch See West Loch Bee
NAM BREAC PEATAIR, Loch See Howmore River
NAM BREAC RUADH, Loch See Howmore River
NAM BREAC RUADH, Loch See Howmore River

NAM FAOILEANN, Loch
Location & Access 22/798290 Leave the A865 at 22/757305 and follow the Loch Eynort road. After the telephone kiosk, take the left fork through North Lochynort and drive to the end of the road. Follow the track east to Arinambane (22/792284). The loch is a further ten minute walk north east.
Commentary Rarely fished and yet set amidst perfect surroundings, dominated by the grey shoulder of Beinn Mhor. Extend your day with a visit to the unnamed lochs to the north west, ending with a cast or two in Loch na Breac Peatair at 22/790295.
Fish Brown trout which average 8oz.
Flies & Tactics Bank fishing and few problems along the way provided you stay ashore. A compass and map is also a must, as are proper walking boots and clothing. Try: Black Zulu, Ke-He, Silver Invicta.
Permission & Charges See Loch Ceann a'Bhaigh entry.

OS Map 22 — Benbecula

NAN CAORACH, Loch See Lower Loch Kildonan.
NAN CLACH CORR, Loch See Loch nan Clachan
NAN CLACH, Loch See Loch an Droma

NAN CLACHAN, Loch
Location & Access 22/815520 Loch nan Clachan lies to the east of the A865 Gramsdale/Creagorry road and is the central loch in a days fishing expedition to a series of six accessible lochs. Begin the four mile adventure at Market Stance (22/805536).
Commentary Park on the track to the east of the road by the local authority works depot close to the north shore of the first water, Loch a'Bhursta (22/806535). Fish south down the east bank and then walk south east for fifteen minutes to reach Loch nan Clachan. Fish clockwise round Loch nan Clachan to the inlet stream at the west end of 22/811522. Follow the stream west to the unnamed loch with the small island by the main road at 22/808534. After exploring it, cross the road to the south end of Loch nan Clach Corr 22/810527.
Work north up the half mile long shoreline of Loch nan Clach Corr then cross to Loch nam Faoileinn (22/800534). Fish the west shore of Loch nam Faoileinn and finish with a few casts in the unnamed lochan at 22/806534, close to the road and your start point at Market Stance.
Fish Attractive, small brown trout in all these lochs but the chance of some much larger specimens of up to and over 1lb in weight in Loch nan Clachan and in the unnamed lochan at 22/808534.
Flies & Tactics Fairly easy going, but still off-road work and so you must be properly dressed and prepared. Do not wade in any of these lochs. Loch nan Clachan is the most remote water, and perhaps the most attractive. The east shore, by the small islands, is an ideal place for a picnic, and to catch supper. Flies: Loch Ordie, Soldier Palmer, Black Pennell.
Permission & Charges See Loch Olavat (Gramsdale).

NAN GARBH CHLACHAN, Loch See Loch Colla
NAN GEALAG, Loch See Loch Colla
NAN LACHAN, Lochan See Loch Langavat
NAN SGEIREAG, Loch See East Loch Bee
NAN UAN, Loch See Loch Eilean an Staoir.
NIGHE, Loch See Loch Horrary
OBAN AN INNSEANAICH Sea-loch See Loch Colla
OBAN LINICLATE Sea Loch See Loch Bailfhionnlaidh
OBAN NA BUAIL-UACHDRAICH Sea-loch See West Loch Bee
OBAN NAM MUCA-MARA, Sea-loch See Loch Colla
OBAN UAINE, Sea-loch See Loch Langavat

OBISARY, Loch
Location & Access 22/900620 Approach via the B894 Clachan/Locheport/Sidinish road (see OS Map 18). Park at the end of the road at 18/891631 and walk south for five minutes to reach the north end of the loch and the boat mooring bay.
Commentary This is one of the most beautiful lochs in North Uist, dominated to the east by the shapely tower of Eaval (347m) and its smaller neighbour to the north, Burrival (140m). The water is brackish at the north end, crystal clear, and drops to more than 80ft in depth near Eilean Mor.
Loch Obisary is a considerable affair, being two miles north/south by up to one and a half miles east/west across the north bay. The loch is a Site of Special Scientific Interest and is rich in flora and fauna. There are a number of adjacent lochs, the most important of which lie to the east of Eaval, and which may be approached by boat from Loch Obisary.
The satellite lochs are, from north to south: Loch Crogavat (22/920627), Loch a'Ghlinne-dorcha (22/915622), the three unnamed lochans to the east of Loch a'Ghlinne-dorcha at 22/923621, Lochan an Tomain (22/918610), Loch Surtavat (22/911605), Loch a'Gheadais (22/913595). There are further lochs to the south and west of Loch Obisary which will also repay a visit: Loch Dun an t-Siamain (22/885594) and Loch na Cleibh (22/877607).
In times gone by, this was a busy, well-populated area, as is evidenced by the ruins of the Duns on many of the Eaval lochs. There is reputed to be an execution place on an island in Loch an Tomain: the victim was plunged into a cone-shaped hole and left to die.
Fish Just about everything in Loch Obisary, including a range of salt-water species, but the brown trout are of exceptional quality: pink fleshed and silver bodied. Average weight of trout is in the order of 10/12oz.
Flies & Tactics Boat fishing makes it much easier to cover this large expanse of water, although bank fishing can produce good results as well. Be warned, however, that bank fishing can be dangerous. The water is deep close to the margins, backed by steep slopes.
Carefully fish the shores of the three main islands: Eilean Mor, Eilean Fada, and Eilean Leathann. Then organise a few drifts in the shallow waters of the east bay which is probably the most productive area on Loch Obisary.
To visit the Eaval lochs, moor the boat in the East Bay at 22/913611 and walk east. These are not inconsiderable waters in their own right: the shoreline of Loch an Tomain wanders in and out for almost three miles; Loch Crogavat is over half a mile east/west.
It is also possible to reach the Eaval lochs by hoofing it along the north shore of Loch Obisary and climbing the north slope from there to reach the other lochs, but be prepared for a vigorous day out. If you intend to visit Loch a'Gheadais, consider taking a tent and staying out overnight. There is a good pitch just below the cave on the east shoulder of Eaval at 22/907597.
All are fished from the bank and although the quality of fish is not as high as in Loch Obisary, they are very pretty trout, brightly spotted, and they fight well. On Loch Obisary, try: Loch Ordie, March Brown, Black Pennell; on the other lochs, offer Blue Zulu, Soldier Palmer, Silver Butcher.
Permission & Charges See Loch Caravat (North Uist).

OLAVAT, Loch (East) See West Loch Olavat

Benbecula — OS Map 22

OLAVAT, Loch (Gramsdale)
Location & Access 22/816545 An easily accessible loch lying close to the A868 road in the north of Benbecula.
Commentary This is the largest loch on Benbecula and it covers an area of one square mile. The shallow, peat-stained water is scattered with twenty seven scrub-covered islands, large and small, and the shoreline wanders in and out round bay and promontory for a distance of approximately four miles.
Fish Good quality brown trout which average 8oz, but with more than a strong possibility of a few fish of up to and over 1lb as well.
Flies & Tactics Both boat and bank fishing. The boat makes it easier to explore this large expanse of water and gives access to the islands around the margins of which fish feed. When bank fishing, stay ashore and do not wade. It is dangerous to do so. The north bank is perhaps the most productive shore, but fish may be taken from anywhere round the loch. Flies: Black Zulu, Grouse & Claret, Silver Invicta.
Permission & Charges Bank fishing costs £6 per rod per day. A boat about £5 per day. An outboard motor is a great boon, but you will have to provide your own since none are available for hire. If using an outboard, beware of sudden shallows and sunken rocks. Hasten slowly, everywhere.
Contact: Billy Felton, Secretary, South Uist Angling Association, 1 Ardmore, Eochdar, South Uist, Outer Hebrides. Tel: (01870) 610325; John Kennedy, Bornish Stores, Bornish, Isle of South Uist. Tel: (01878) 710366; Colin Campbell Sports, Balivanich, Benbecula. Tel: (01870) 602236; Shell Bay Caravan Site, Liniclate, Benbecula. Tel: (01870) 602447.

OLAVAT, Loch (West)
Location & Access 22/797513 West Loch Olavat, and its neighbour, East Loch Olavat (22/804504), lie close to the A865 road between the Memorial and Creagorry.
Commentary West and East Loch Olavat are considered to be the premier Benbecula fisheries. The combined lochs extend for a distance of one and a half miles north/south and are about 350 yrds wide. They are easily accessible and East Loch Olavat is particularly attractive, being scattered with scrub-covered little islands at the east end.
Loch na Faoilinn (22/803515), to the east of the Memorial (22/802519), is also worth a visit, although it is a bit 'public' being close to the A865. The long, narrow, unnamed loch by the peat track at 22/805510 should be thrashed, as well as the smaller lochans immediately to the south of the track at 22/814507 by Druim na Glaic Moire.
Fish Hard to say which is the better of the main lochs. Both contain excellent quality trout which average in the order of 10oz with plenty of much larger fish of up to and over 1lb. Loch na Faoilinn also has a reputation for holding large trout.
Flies & Tactics There are boats on the Olavats and whilst boat fishing makes progress easier, bank fishing, particularly on West Loch Olavat, can be just as productive. Trout rise and are taken throughout the system, although the east shoreline of West Loch Olavat seems to be the most productive bank.
On East Loch Olavat, concentrate your activities in the south bay. The other waters noted above are all easily covered from the shore. Do not wade. Offer: Ke-He, Soldier Palmer, Silver Butcher.
Permission & Charges See Loch Olavat (Gramsdale).

ROAG, Loch See Howmore River

ROINICH, Loch
Location & Access Turn west from the A865 at 22/766326 signposted to Stonybridge. After one mile, Loch Roinich is immediately to the north of the road.
Commentary This is one of a number of easily accessible named and unnamed lochs lying between Stonybridge to the north and Ormiclate to the south; the others are, to the west of Loch Roinich, the unnamed lochs at 22/746332 and 22/749333; south of the road, Loch na Curraidh (22/751323), Loch Vaccasary (22/759328) and its unnamed satellite at 22/760323. Also, and best approached from the A865, Loch an Athain (22/763325) and the unnamed lochan at 22/764322; long, narrow Loch a'Chlachain (22/756320) and its narrow neighbour immediately to the north; and two lochs at Market Stance, the unnamed loch to the west at 22/762318 and Loch Eadaray (22/765316) to the east.
Fish Some very good trout, but predominately breakfast-size fish which average 8oz.
Flies & Tactics These lochs are rarely fished, given their proximity to the more famous machair waters, but they are very attractive and offer a good alternative during high winds. All are fished from the bank and weed becomes a problem as the season advances. Loch na Curraidh and Loch Vaccasary are perhaps the most productive, but none of these waters should send you home empty handed. Flies to try: Ke-Ke, Invicta, Peter Ross.
Permission & Charges See East Loch Bee entry. Also, from The Secretary, South Uist Angling Club, 1 Ardmore, Eochar, South Uist. Tel: (01870) 610325; or Mrs A Kennedy, Bornish Stores, Bornish. Tel: (01878) 710366; £6 per rod per day, £30 per week.

ROINICH, Loch (Askernish) See Loch Eilean an Staoir.
RUEVAL, Loch See East Loch Bee
SCARILODE, Loch See Loch an Tairbh
SCHOOLHOUSE, Loch See Howmore River
SHIELING, Loch See Loch Spotal
SHNATHAID, Loch See Loch Caslub
SHURAVAL, Loch See OS Map 31

SNIGISCLETT, Loch
Location & Access 22/800252. Leave the A865 at 22/758305 and drive to the end of the South Locheynort road to park at 22/779275. Keeping to the high ground, walk south east for half a mile to find a stream on the east shoulder of Trinival (196m). Follow the stream due south, ignoring the west branch which flows in from Bealach Arnaval. Climb steeply over Ben Eallan (200m) and descend to the

OS Map 22 — Benbecula

loch. Allow approximately two hours for the journey.
Commentary One of the most remote and attractive lochs in South Uist, rarely visited because of the long hike. Splendid scenery and a good chance of an encounter with golden eagle and otters. Close to the west shore is another super little loch, Loch Drollavat (22/795252), the ideal place for lunch.
Fish Good stocks of brown trout which average 8oz/10oz.
Flies & Tactics You must be properly prepared, well-clothed and compass and mapped for this journey. The loch is almost one mile east/west by up to a quarter of a mile wide so there is plenty to keep you happy and active all day. The surrounding hills provide shelter from the prevailing winds and there is always a fishable bank. Stay on the bank and do not wade. The north shore, and in particular the north west bay, provide best sport. Flies: Blue Zulu, Soldier Palmer, Black Pennell.
Permission & Charges See East Loch Bee entry.

SPOTAL, Loch
Location & Access 22/834366 Leave the A865 road at Grogarry (22/774397) and follow the B890 east along the north shore of Loch Druidibeg (22/790376), signposted to Lochskipport. Park at Lochskipport at 22/828385.
Commentary Loch Spotal is one of the most lovely lochs in the Outer Hebrides, dominated by the towering, grey/blue mass of Hecla (606m) to the south. You can either hike straight there, a one mile tramp, or make a circular tour taking in six further named and unnamed lochs along the way.
The latter choice will give you a wonderful day out amidst dramatic scenery. From the road, follow the well-marked track that leads right, round the coast, past an attractive modernised cottage on the side of the hill to reach the Shieling Loch at 22/835379.
Continue south east from the Shieling Loch over rough, rising ground, to find Loch Bein (22/843372). Hill walkers should follow the inlet stream at the east end of Loch Bein up the glen to gain the north end of the Hecla Ridge on Moal Martaig at 22/850374.
Anglers should climb south west and then descend to the west shore of Loch Spotal after a journey of three quarters of a mile. Loch Fada (22/527368), a minute to the west of Loch Spotal, should also be explored, as should the unnamed lochan with the two small islands at 22/830370.
The tiny streams which flow down from Hecla to feed these lochs, and Loch a'Choire (22/818356), have some very attractive pools which contain pretty trout. Keep an eye out for the Hecla golden eagles and there is also a good chance of seeing otters.
Walk due north now to reach Loch an Eilein (22/829375). From Loch an Eilein, tramp half a mile north west to fish Loch Teanga (22/819383) before returning to the car. Also consider having a look at Loch na h'Achlais (22/809389) on the north of the B890, and its unnamed neighbour at 22/812389 to the south of the road, both easily accessible.
Notice also the remains of a Victorian formal garden, behind the wire fence to the south of the road.

Fish Nothing out in the hills is going to break your scales. The brown trout average about three to the pound and a fish of 1lb is remarkable, although Loch Teanga is reputed to hold sea-trout towards the end of the season. However, sea-trout most certainly reach Loch Spotal and they are an entirely different matter: hard-fighting fish of great quality and considerable size.
Flies & Tactics Bank fishing and do not wade. Loch Bein has steep sides and is tricky to fish. Concentrate on the north shore, opposite the island, and at the east end, by the sandy beach. On Loch Spotal, the west and south shore, by the inlet burns, are good places to begin. Loch Teanga also has high banks with deep water close in. Take great care. Flies: Loch Ordie, Black Zulu, Peter Ross.
Permission & Charges See East Loch Bee.

STILLIGARRY, Loch
Location & Access 22/765382 Leave the A865 at 22/770387. Follow the farm track west to park at 22/763386. Cross to the loch and the boat mooring bay via the gate on your left.
Commentary One of the finest lochs on South Uist, not only because of the quality of trout, but also because of outstanding wildlife. In the evenings, particularly in June, there is an excellent chance of at least hearing, if not seeing, corncrake. The loch is approximately half a mile east/west by up to 400 yds wide in the largest, north bay. The water is scattered with bays and delightful small, rocky islands upon which terns and black-headed gulls nest.
Fish Wonderful brown trout, perfectly marked and shaped, which average in the order of 14oz; but Loch Stilligarry is noted also for producing good numbers of fish of up to and over 3lb in weight.
Flies & Tactics Most anglers fish from the boat, and this does make it easier to get around and cover the water; but bank fishing can be just as productive, particularly along the north west and west shoreline where the wading is safe and comfortable.
The best drift in the north bay is from the mooring point directly south to the far shore. Look out for action about the middle of the drift. The extreme east bay offers easy bank fishing, as well as exciting boat fishing and large trout are frequently taken here. Flies to offer include: Soldier Palmer, Loch Ordie, Black Zulu, Bibio, Ke-He, March Brown, Invicta, Peter Ross, Kingfisher Butcher, Dunkeld.
Permission & Charges See East Loch Bee.

STULAVAL, Loch See OS Map 31
SURTAVAT, Loch See Loch Obisary
TEANGA, Loch See Loch Spotal

TORONISH, Loch
Location & Access 22/736305. Turn west at Bornish General Stores (22/751295) and follow the road towards Ormiclate. A junction is marked on the map at 22/740298 but in fact the main road is continuous. Park at 22/741308, the north end of the loch, which is on your left.
Commentary An excellent, easily accessible, little

North Skye — OS Maps 22-23

machair loch. Breakfast is almost assured. Non-fishing companions can bird watch or explore the machair wildflowers or beach-comb the yellow sands to the west. There are a number of other named and unnamed lochs in the vicinity which also offer good sport and are also easily accessible: Loch na Duchasaich (22/745313), Loch an Iasgair (22/750302), Loch an Tuirc (22/751293), behind Bornish General Stores, and the unnamed lochans at 22/744301, 22/741299, 22/744305 and at 22/743306.
Fish Loch Toronish has a large stock of exceptionaly pretty 8oz trout. The other lochs also contain trout which average 8oz, but some of them, particularly Loch Tuirc and Loch Iasgair, have a few more serious specimens of up to and over 1lb in weight.
Flies & Tactics Weed growth effects all these waters as the season advances. Indeed, Loch Toronish is hard to fish at the best of times and after July, virtually impossible. On Loch Toronish, concentrate your effort at the north end and in the north west bay. Attack during April, May and June, from the bank, using Soldier Palmer, Grouse & Claret, Alexandra.
Permission & Charges See Loch Ceann a'Bhaigh entry.

UACRACH NAN CAORACH, Loch See Loch Langavat.

UPPER BORNISH, Loch
Location & Access 22/743293 Turn west at Bornish General Stores (22/751295) and after half a mile take the narrow road on the left. Park after two hundred yards at the cattle grid. The boat mooring bay is on your left.
Commentary Not as spectacular as its larger namesake, but still a super loch to fish, easily accessible and offering great sport from either boat or bank.
Fish Trout average 8oz/10oz and are of excellent quality. There are a few fish of over 1lb, but they are the exception rather than the rule.
Flies & Tactics The loch is divided into two sections, with the boat confined to the southern area. Arrange your drift close to the shore and concentrate on the west bank, drifting past the site of the Dun to the south corner. The little bay in the south east corner invariably produces a fish or two. When bank fishing, start on the north shore of the boat mooring bay, good fish lie here, and work east towards the north section of the loch. The trout lie close so there is no need to wade. Offer them: Soldier Palmer, March Brown, Silver Butcher.
Permission & Charges See East Loch Bee entry.

UPPER KILDONAN, Loch
Location & Access 22/734285 Leave the A865 at Kildonan (22/744278) and drive west for half a mile to reach the loch which is to the north of the road. The boat is moored close to the parking area.
Commentary The road separates Upper Loch Kildonan from Lower Loch Kildonan, which is to the south of the road. Upper Loch Kildonan is half a mile north/south by up to quarter of a mile wide across the north bay. The loch is easily accessible, very attractive, and invariably hosts a group of mute swans. Non-fishing companions might care to visit the 2,000 year old Dun Vulan Broch at 22/713298 which is been excavated by a team from Sheffield University.
Fish Good quality brown trout which average 8oz/10oz with a few fish of over 1lb in weight.
Flies & Tactics Boat fishing brings the best results. Bank fishing is possible, but is uncomfortable due to the soft nature of the shallow margins. There is a deep channel running north/south up the loch and the edge of this channel always produces sport. The north bay is very shallow, but good trout lie around the small islands and near to where the inlet stream from Loch Bornish joins Upper Loch Kildonan. Flies to try: Bibio, March Brown, Alexandra.
Permission & Charges See East Loch Bee entry.

VACCASARY, Loch See Loch Roinich.

WEST OLLAY, Loch
Location & Access 22/740327 Turn west from the A865 at 22/766326 signposted to Stonybridge. After a mile and a half, bear left and park near the cattle grid at 22/746325. West Loch Ollay is on your right and the boat is moored close to the road.
Commentary One of the classic South Uist machair lochs, shallow, weedy and lime rich, half a mile north/south by up to half a mile east/west. Nearby, note the ruins of Ormiclate Castle, an ancient Clanranald stronghold destroyed by fire in 1715 - the day Clanraland was killed at the Battle of Sheriffmuir during the 1715 Jacobite Rebellion.
Fish Specimen country. Fine quality wild brown trout which average 2lb in weight and a very good chance of much larger fish as well.
Flies & Tactics Weed is always a problem and after mid-summer West Loch Ollay is almost impossible to fish. But the weed provides marvellous cover or the trout, so persevere. Fish may be taken all over the loch but the most productive areas are around the small islands and in the west bay. Boat and bank fishing, and bank fishing can be just as productive; although 'productive' is very much a relative phrase as far as West Loch Ollay is concerned, 'dour' being a more realistic description. Nevertheless, a great water to fish. Offer them: Loch Ordie, Black Pennell, Grouse & Claret.
Permission & Charges See East Loch Bee entry.

North Skye

A'BEALACH-BHIG, Lochan See Storr Lochs.
AN FHRIDHEIN, Loch See Hamara River.
AN-DUBH, Loch See Hamara River.
BEAG, Loch (Glen Hinnisdale) See River Hinnisdale.
BROGAIG, River See Kilmartin River.
BROGAIG, River See Loch na Luirginn.
CLEAP, Loch See Kilmartin River.
CLEAT, Loch See Loch na Luirginn.

OS Map 23 — North Skye

CONNAN, Loch
Location & Access 23/389430. Approach from the B885 Portree/Bracadale road at 23/394425. Walk north-west up the hill for ten minutes to reach the loch.
Commentary An excellent little loch covering approximately 20 acres, easily-accessible and the ideal place to introduce beginners to the pleasure of hill-loch fishing.
Fish Brown trout, but nothing for the glass case.
Flies & Tactics Easy bank fishing and best to stay ashore. The outlet burn at the south- west corner, which drains the loch into the River Ose, is a good place to begin; thereafter, work round the west shore-line to the inlet burn in the small north bay. Flies: Ke-He, March Brown, Dunkeld.
Permission & Charges See River Ose entry.

CONON, River
Location & Access Source 23/445636; Outflow 23/397637. Accessible from Uig, either from the A855 or from the two minor roads that lie to the north and south of the stream.
Commentary A spate river entirely dependent upon heavy rain to produce sport. The river is three miles in length from its source on the north slopes of Beinn Edra (611m) on the Trotternish Ridge, flowing west down Glen Uig to the sea in Uig Bay.
Fish Salmon average 5lb, sea-trout around 1lb 8oz.
Flies & Tactics It all depends upon being in the right place at the right time. August and September are best, providing that there is heavy rain. When there is, the first mile of the river expands into some delightful pools and runs.
A strong trout rod is all that is required. Offer them: Soldier Palmer, Clan Chief, Kate McLaren. Spinning and bait fishing is also allowed.
Permission & Charges See River Rha entry.

CORCASGIL, Loch See Kilmartin River.
CORLARACH, Loch See Loch Suardal.

CUITHIR, Loch
Location & Access 23/475597. Turn west from the A855 Portree/Staffin road just north of Lower Tote at 23/518605 and drive to Lealt (23/509609). Follow the line of the dismantled railway west up the Lealt River for two miles to reach the loch.
Commentary A small loch below Creag a'Lain (608m) and Flasvein (597m) on the Trotternish Ridge and a good starting point for climbers and hill walkers. The best trout loch here, however, is Loch Liuravay (23/485589), below Sgurr a'Mhadaidh Ruaidh, half a mile to the south of Loch Cuithir and covering approximately 20 acres.
Migratory fish are barred from access to the upper Lealt River by a waterfall. However, there is always the chance of encountering sea-trout and salmon in the gorge pool below the waterfall, before the river empties into the sea. The best time to mount your attack on the river is after heavy rain, particularly during August and September, and there is also a chance of sea-trout in the estuary at Inver Tote (23/520605) from about June onwards.
Fish Nothing to fill the glass case, but plenty of sport with brightly-marked trout which average 8oz. Salmon average 5lb, sea-trout in the order of 1lb 8oz.
Flies & Tactics Good bank fishing and few problems locating the fish: they are everywhere. Offer them Black Zulu, Soldier Palmer, Hardy's Gold Butcher. Spinning and bait fishing is allowed in the River Lealt.
Permission & Charges See Storr Lochs entry. Salmon fishing costs £10 per rod per session (dawn to 1pm, or from 2pm until dusk).

DROIGHINN, Loch See Loch Hasco.

DUAGRICH, Loch
Location & Access 23/397397. Approach along the track up Glen Bracadale from the minor road which leaves the A863 Broadford/Dunvegan road near the church at 23/359386. A distance of 2.5 miles.
Commentary Loch Duagrich lies in a steep-sided glen between Ben Duagrich (304m) to the south and Braon a' Mheallain (269m) to the north. The loch is almost one mile east/west by up to 300yds wide. Remote, isolated, and great for wildlife. Look out for sea eagles.
Fish A good stock of wild brown trout which average 8oz. Also, more than a fair chance of salmon and the odd sea-trout which enter up the outlet burn which drains Loch Duagrich into sea-Loch Beag.
Flies & Tactics Bank fishing only, with the possibility of salmon from anywhere round the shores. The most likely place, however, is at the west end of the loch, in the vicinity of the outlet. Stay ashore. Wading is dangerous and unnecessary. Salmon invariably lie very close, a few yards from the bank. Fish the shore onto which the wind is blowing, casting your line at an angle across the waves. Large, bushy trout flies, such as Ke-He, Loch Ordie, Soldier Palmer, work well.
Permission & Charges See River Ose entry.

DUBHAR-SGOTH, Loch See Kilmartin River.
DUNTULM, Loch See Kilmaluag River.
EISHORT, Loch See Hamara River.
ERGHALLAN, Sea Loch See Loch Suardal.
FADA, Loch (Braes) See River Varragill.
FADA, Loch (Quiraing) See Loch Hasco.
FADA, Loch (Storr) See Storr Lochs.

HAMARA, River
Location & Access Source 23/214435; Outfall 23/170500. Fishing on the Hamara River is preserved by the tenant and there is no public access. The lochs on the estate are also preserved: Loch Eishort (23/161459), Loch An Dubh Loch (23/199430), Loch Glen Iondal (23/193414), and Loch An Fhridhein (23/194398).
Commentary However, the lochs all contain large stocks of small trout and anyone passing that way (and reaching them involves a long, hard walk) with a trout rod, could apply to Mr Stevens of the Glendale Community Council (01470) 511375 for permission to have a cast or two. Loch Mor (23/146485), near Waterstein, can be fished, by application to Mr Sam Thornburn, 1 Borrodale, Glendale, Isle of Skye. Tel: (01470) 511315, but, in spite of attempts in recent

North Skye   OS Map 23

years to establish it as a fishery, the resident population of eels has been the only beneficiary.

HASCO, Loch
Location & Access 23/456701. Park by Loch Langaig (23/462708) on the A855 Portree/Kilmalug road. A track climbs south-west into the heart of the Quiraing, an amazing landscape of pinnacles and jagged peaks set amidst lime-rich, green-sward grassland.
Commentary Apart from Loch Hasco and Loch Langaig, noted above, there are two other little lochs which are worth a look: Loch Fada (23/458697) and, to the north, tiny Loch Droighinn (23/456712). A visit to all of these lochs will provide an excellent day out in a stunning landscape. Even without the benefit of a trout rod, this is one of the most-highly recommended expeditions in Skye.
Fish You will return with supper and it will not be too heavy to carry.
Flies & Tactics The round trip is only three miles and the going is not difficult. This would include a step south from Loch Fada to view the famous Quiraing rock-features known as The Table, The Needle and The Prison. Bank fishing all round and Loch Langaig can be very dour, but Loch Hasco and Loch Fada are full of small trout which are anxious to please. Try: Blue Zulu, Soldier Palmer and Black Pennell.
Permission & Charges See Storr Lochs entry.

HAULTIN, River
This river is preserved by the tenant and is not open for fishing to members of the public.

HINNISDALE, River (North Bank only)
Location & Access Source 23/469582 Outflow 23/384575. The Lower River is approached from Hinnisdale Bridge (23/398574) on the A856 Uig/Borve road. A minor road branches north-east from the bridge leading to Glenuachdarach (23/429586) and this road gives easy access to the north bank of the Upper River.
Commentary A very attractive little river which can offer sport after heavy rain. There are two hill-lochs to the north, Loch Beag (23/401596) and Loch Mor (406602), both of which offer good trout fishing should the river be out of condition.
Loch Beag is best approached from the Glen Hinnisdale road by following the outlet stream up the hill from Balmeanach (23/409582), a distance of three-quarters of a mile. Approach Loch Mor via the track to the north of the caravan site by the A856 at 23/391612; a stiff hike of approximately 30 minutes.
Fish Salmon and sea-trout in the river, small brown trout in the lochs.
Flies & Tactics The most important tactic for the river is being there at the right time, after heavy rain. August and September offer the best chance. Bank fishing on the trout lochs, stay ashore and avoid wading. Try: Invicta, Grouse & Claret, Dunkeld.
Permission & Charges See River Rha entry. Trout fishing costs £5 per rod per day. For further detail, speak to Mr Macdonald at Mackay's Building Supplies - see River Rha entry.

KILMALUAG, River
Location & Access Source: 23/414692; Outflow: 23/438749. The river rise from Loch Sneasdal (23/414692) which lies in a corrie below Creag Sneasdal (350m) four miles south from the outflow in Kilmaluag Bay by Port Gobhlaig. Access is from the A855 road at 23/435742 via a convenient minor road that borders the west side of the stream.
Commentary Very much a spate - stream and only worth fishing in the lower reaches towards the end of the season and after very heavy rain. Being in the right place at the right time is all-important. If you can manage to achieve this difficult feat you could have great fun in this delightful little river. The headwater loch, Loch Sneasdal, is in a very dramatic setting and is worth a visit as much for the small trout which inhabit its cold waters as for the splendid surrounding scenery. Approach from the A855 at 23/395719 and park at the end of the minor road near Heribusta (23/400708). Follow the track south-east up Glen Sneasdal to reach the loch after a hike of thirty minutes. Another, more accessible but equally attractive, option is a visit to the unnamed loch at Duntulm (23/416742) which has been stocked by the Portree Angling Club and contains excellent trout. For non-fishing companions there is the monument to Flora Macdonald and the museum at Omisgarry to visit.
Fish In the right conditions, grilse which average 5lb and a few sea-trout. In Loch Sneasdal, breakfast-sized trout, in Duntulm Loch, fish of up to and over 2lb.
Flies & Tactics Light tackle and a single-handed rod for the river. Keep well back and stalk your fish, extending line from one point, rather than marching down the bank. The trout-lochs are small and readily understood. Flies: for all species, try: Black Pennell, March Brown, Peter Ross. Vary the size according to prevailing conditions.
Permission & Charges See Storr Lochs entry. Bank fishing on Kilmaluag is £10 per day.

KILMARTIN, River
Location & Access Source: 23/475579 Outflow: 23/485683. The river has its true source in Loch Cuithir (23/475579) six miles south from the outflow in Staffin Bay by Stenscholl. The section to the east of the A855 road is known as the Stenscholl River, that to the west as the Kilmartin River.
Commentary Like all Skye streams, the system depends entirely upon heavy rain to give of its best. In dry weather the flow is very restricted and, at times, almost non-existent. However, the Kilmartin River has its moments and, providing you are in the right place at the right time, sport can be excellent.
Fish Mostly grilse and a few sea-trout from the end of July onwards, depending upon water levels.
Flies & Tactics The lower sections of the river offer the best chance of action, where, during spate conditions, there can be a number of sizeable pools and runs. Sea-trout may also be caught in the estuary. The system is easily accessible from a minor road that shadows the west bank of the stream for two miles. Another nearby stream which also offers the chance of the odd fish in high water conditions is the River

OS Map 23 — North Skye

Brogaig which flows into Staffin Bay across the beach at 23/475684. It is even more insignificant it terms of size than the Kilmartin River but can sometimes produce sport between the A855 and the sea. In low water conditions, consider abandoning the rivers and heading for the hills. There are three fine trout-lochs to the west, all of which will provide good sport and a good evening meal: Loch Cleap (23/468663) to the north and Loch Corcasgil (23/452643) and Loch Dubhar-sgoth (23/456640) to the south. The bad news is that reaching these waters involves a long, rough hike over broken ground. For Loch Cleap, start from near the house at 23/486665 on the road by the river. Walk due west over slowly-rising ground for one mile to find the loch.

For Loch Corcasgil and Loch Dubhar-sgoth, which contain the larger fish, park at the end of the road at Maligar (23/481646) and walk the stream south-west to the Trotternish Ridge for one and a half miles. The lochs are close to the base of the cliffs.

Flies: For the river, vary the size of the fly according to water levels, but, generally, you will find that size 8/10 trout patterns do fine. Try: Black Pennell, Grouse & Claret, Silver Invicta.

Permission & Charges See Storr Lochs entry. Salmon fishing costs £10 per rod per day.

KNOTT, Estuary See Loch Niarsco.
LANGAIG, Loch See Loch Hasco.
LEALT, River See Loch Cuithir.
LEATHAN, Loch See Storr Lochs.

LEUM NA LUIRGINN, Loch
Location & Access 23/447677. In Brogaig (23/469681) on the A855 Portree/Flodigarry road, turn west onto the tortuous, minor road that leads across the Trotternish Ridge to Idrigil near Uig on the West coast. Park at 23/447676 and walk south to find Loch na Luirginn.

Commentary This is a good 'jumping-off' point for those who wish to explore the Trotternish Ridge. The road crosses the ridge at the top of a 1 in 5, engine-heating climb, but there is easy access north to Meall na Suiramach (543m) and south to Biode Buidhe (466m). In high water conditions, also have a close look at the little River Brogaig, between the A855 road and the sea at Staffin Bay. There is always a chance of sport with salmon and sea-trout.

Fish Small trout which average 8oz. Salmon average 5lb, sea-trout in the order of 1lb 8oz.

Flies & Tactics After exploring Loch na Luirginn follow the inlet stream south for a few minutes to reach little Loch Cleat (23/447672). Both lochs are easily fished from the bank and wading is not advisable. Flies: Black Zulu, Soldier Palmer, Silver Butcher. Spinning and bait fishing is allowed in the River Brogaig, but the fly patterns noted above work just as well.

Permission & Charges See Storr Lochs entry.

LIURAVAY, Loch See Loch Cuithir.
LOCH GLEN IONADAL, Loch See Hamara River.

MEALT, Loch
Location & Access 23/595650. Easily accessible and immediately to the west of the A855 Portree/Flodigarry road at Elishader.

Commentary Loch Mealt covers an area of some 60 acres and is nearly half a mile north/south by over quarter of a mile wide. The surrounding scenery is stunning with wonderful views west to the Trotternish Ridge and east to the mountains of Gairloch and Fisherfield on Mainland Scotland.

Fish The attraction here is a unique species of arctic char: descendants of fish which have survived in Loch Mealt genetically intact since the end of the last Ice Age 10,000 years ago.

Flies & Tactics Bank fishing, and do not wade. The south end of the loch, where two feeder streams enter from Raisaburgh, is a good place to start. At the north end, concentrate in the vicinity of the broch ruins on the promontory at Dun Grianan. Barbless hooks are essential on Loch Mealt so that char caught can be returned undamaged to the water. Flies: Ke-He, March Brown, Silver Butcher.

Permission & Charges See Storr Lochs entry. All bank fishing is £8 per day.

MOR, Loch (Glen Hinnisdale) See River Hinnisdale.
MOR, Loch (Glendale) See Hamara River.
OSDALE, River See Loch Suardal.

OSE, River
Location & Access Source 23/370444; Outfall 23/315407. The lower river is easily accessible from the A863 Bracadale/Dunvegan road, where the road crosses the river close to the sea. Reaching the Upper River involves a vigorous hike up Glen Ose.

Commentary A pleasant little spate-stream in glorious surroundings, with more than three miles of pools, streams and glides, where even the upper reaches are eminently fishable; but only after heavy rain and towards the end of the season.

Fish Double-bank fishing, with an excellent chance of sea-trout and salmon, given high water. Salmon average 7lb, although occasionally fish of over 10lb are taken. Sea-trout average 2lb, and, from time to time, a few heavier specimens are caught as well.

Flies & Tactics Very much a question of stalking the fish, keeping well back from the river bank. The tidal section of the river, to the west of the road, can also give sport with sea-trout, an hour before and an hour after low tide. Offer: Goat's Toe, General Practitioner, Munro Killer, Hairy Mary for salmon, and for sea-trout, Black Pennell, Soldier Palmer, Peter Ross. Salmon will also take these patterns. Vary the size of fly according to water level.

Permission & Charges Ullinish Lodge Hotel, Struan, Isle of Skye. Tel: (01470) 572214. Hotel residents, £10 per rod per day. Ullinish Lodge Hotel also have good salmon fishing on the River Snizort (see entry). John Mulford, the proprietor is an experienced angler and advises guests on appropriate tackle and techniques.

PRIVATE WATERS NIARSCO, Loch (OS 23/391471), A'GHLINNE BHIG, Loch.

North Skye — OS Map 23

RAVAG, Loch
Location & Access 23/380450. Leave the A863 Bracadale/Dunvegan road by the ruined broch close to the sea at 23/310439. Follow the minor road east through Balmeanach (23/325435) along the track which ends at Glen Vic Askill (23/360443). Climb steeply through the pass directly to the east to reach the loch after twenty minutes. The loch may also be approached from Loch Connan (see entry) by walking north from the inlet burn at the north end of the loch for one mile.
Commentary A small, triangular-shaped loch in a very remote setting.
Fish Good quality, hard-fighting, little brown trout which average three to the pound.
Flies & Tactics Bank fishing and no need to wade, The trout lie close to the shore and are taken all round the loch. Offer them: Black Zulu, Soldier Palmer, Alexandra.
Permission & Charges See River Ose entry.

RHA, River
Location & Access Source 23/423692 Outflow 23/395640. Easily accessible from the minor road that crosses the Trotternish Ridge, joining Uig in the west to Brogaig in the east. The river margins the road throughout its four mile journey from Beinn a'Sga (414m) to the sea in Uig Bay.
Commentary A typical Skye spate-stream, with three waterfalls along its course, but offering a good chance of sport after heavy rain. The lower reaches are wooded and easily-accessible whilst the Upper River lies amidst mountain and moorland scenery.
Fish Mostly grilse in the order of 5lb in weight, with a few sea-trout averaging around 1lb 8oz.
Flies & Tactics Salmon-stalking country, and a strong trout rod will cope with most eventualities. The best sport is in the lower reaches of the stream. Plan your attack to coincide with a falling spate. Use trout patterns: Black Pennell, Grouse & Claret, Dunkled. Spinning and bait fishing is also allowed.
Permission & Charges The Ferry Inn, Uig, Isle of Skye. Tel: (01470) 542242; Mackay's Building & Home Improvements Supplies (01470) 542207. Cost: £15 per rod per day; £40 per rod per week. Uig Angling Association, Mrs I Nicholson, 2 Peinlich, Glenhinnisdale, Isle of Skye.

ROMESDAL, River
Location & Access This river is preserved by the tenant and is not open for fishing to members of the public.

SCAMADAL, Loch
Location & Access See Storr Lochs.

SNEASDAL, Loch
Location & Access See Kilmaluag River.

SNIZORT, River
Location & Access Source 23/425360 Outflow 23/414487. The lower river is accessible from the A850 at Skeabost Bridge (23/420484) and from the minor road between Carbost (23/431482) in the north and Uigshader (23/428464) to the south. The river meets the B885 at 23/421442 where there is also easy access both upstream and downstream. Reaching the Upper River is a far more vigorous affair involving a considerable hike, either from the point on the B885 noted above, or from Glen Bracadale and Loch Duagrich (23/400399) in the west. The journey takes about 45 minutes.
Commentary The River Snizort is the most productive Skye stream but like its neighbours it too requires a lot of rain to produce of its best. When conditions are right, however, sport can be very good indeed. During the first two weeks of September, recently, after good rain, five rods from Ullinish Lodge took 25 salmon and lost a further 9 fish.
Fish Salmon average 6lb/7lb, but larger fish are also taken most seasons. September to early October is best.
Flies & Tactics Salmon-stalking and crossed-finger country. Use a strong trout rod and stay well back from the bank. Spinning and bait fishing is also allowed. Flies: Green Highlander, Kate Maclaren, Garry Dog.
Permission & Charges The Lower River is available through Skeabost House Hotel and there is no fishing charge for guests staying for 3 or more days. Otherwise, the price is £15 per rod per day. The hotel has a resident casting instructor who will advise on techniques and tackle. Skeabost House Hotel, Skeabost Bridge, Isle of Skye. Tel: (01470) 532202. The Upper River is in the hands of Ullinish Lodge Hotel, a very comfortable sporting hotel run by John & Claudia Mulford. Ullinish Lodge also have fishing on the River Ose and three excellent trout lochs. Ullinish Lodge Hotel, Struan, Isle of Skye. Tel: (01470) 572214. Hotel guests have fishing priority. Cost: approximately £10 per rod per day.

STENSCHOLL, River
Location & Access See Kilmartin River.

STORR, Lochs
Location & Access 23/493495. The Storr Lochs lie 4 miles north from Portree, adjacent to the east side of the A855 Portree/Staffin road. Loch Fada (23/493495), to the south, and Loch Leathan (23/495515) to the north, are linked together and constitute the Storr Lochs. The system extends for 2.5 miles north/south by up to half a mile wide across the north bay of Loch Leathan. The lochs have been harnessed to provide power for an electricity generating station at the foot of the cliff at Bearreraig Bay - which has the only private railway in Scotland, used to take staff up and down the cliff. Members of the public access the beach by means of 600 invigorating steps.
Commentary One of the most famous Skye landmarks dominates the loch, 'the Old Man of Storr' (719m), a craggy pinnacle which is part of the Trotternish Ridge, very popular with hill-walkers and climbers. There is a limestone outcrop here which hosts an astonishing variety of wildflowers. There are two tiny waters, to the north and south of the Old Man, both of which contain modest-sized trout. However, if you wish to combine a wonderful Trotternish walk with a spot of fishing, then they are

OS Map 23-24 — Raasay and Loch Torridon

worth considering: Lochan a'Bhealach-Bhig (23/492527), and Loch Scamadal (23/501549).
Fish The average weight of fish in the Storr Lochs is 13oz but there are much larger fish and good numbers of trout of up to and over 3lb are taken most seasons. In recent years trout of between 5lb and 8lb 8oz have been taken and the heaviest trout ever caught from the loch weighed 11lb 4oz.
Flies & Tactics Boat fishing brings best results but the whole of the west shoreline is easily accessible from the A855 and in windy conditions can be very productive. The east shore of Loch Fada is best, particularly in the vicinity of the inlet stream and by the island at the south end. On Loch Leathan, four streams enter from the west and the mouths of these streams always provide sport. The north-east bay can also be good. Arrange your drift fairly close to the shore. As a general rule, if you can't see the bottom then you are fishing too far out. There is often a mayfly hatch. Use: Black Zulu, Greenwell's Glory, Alexandra. Most dark flies fish well.
Permission & Charges Jansports, Wentworth Street, Portree, Isle of Skye. Tel: (01478) 612559. Neil Cameron, Secretary, Portree Angling Association, 'Hillcroft', 2 Teraslane, by Portree, Isle of Skye, IV51 9NX. Tel: (01470) 582304. Bank fishing permits, which cover all the Portree Angling Association lochs, cost £8 per rod per day. Boat hire: £15 per boat per day, 9am until 4.30pm; £10 per boat per evening, 5.30pm until midnight; inclusive of 2 rods, keys from and permist from Jansports. No Sunday fishing. 6 trout per rod limit. Minimum size 10". Fly fishing only.

SUARDAL, Loch
Location & Access 23/240510. Drive north from Dunvegan Castle along the minor road for one mile. The road divides Loch Suardal and access is easy.
Commentary A shallow loch, almost one mile long, bordered on the east by a forestry plantation. Half a mile north again is Loch Corlarach (23/235520), an attractive little water on the moor between the road and Loch Dunvegan. The surrounding scenery is outstanding with views west across Loch Dunvegan to Healabhal Bheag (489m) and Healabhal Mhor (469m), 'MacLeod's Tables'. Follow the road north again to visit the famous White Coral Beaches opposite Lamprey Island.
Fish Brown trout, not many and not very large. The Estate have plans in hand to upgrade the fishing by stocking. Nevertheless, after heavy rain and on high tides, sea-trout and the occasional salmon can enter Loch Suardal.
South from Dunvegan, crossed by the B884, is the Osdale River, (outfall 23/248460) a good little spate stream which rises from the plateau between MacLeod's Tables. Towards the end of the season, and in high water conditions, look out for sea-trout and perhaps the odd salmon. 1.5 miles north again brings you to the fine sands of Loch Erghallan (23/228475) where, given the right water conditions, sea-trout may also be encountered.
Flies & Tactics The lochs are easily fished from the bank and are worth a cast or two, at present, as part of a day out exploring the area. Wait for heavy rain before chasing the migratory species. Flies: Blue Zulu, Soldier Palmer, Silver Invicta.
Permission & Charges MacLeod Estate, Estate Office, Dunvegan, Isle of Skye. Tel: (01470) 521206. Trout fishing: apply estate office for current prices; salmon and sea-trout fishing, per rod: from £10 per day to £ 50 per week.

TREASLANE, River See Loch Niarsco.
VARRAGILL, River Source 32/450340 Outfall 23/477412. The river is preserved by the owner and there is no public access. However, Portree & District Angling Club members have limited access to the fishing. The same applies to Loch Fada (23/502375) in Braes. For information and details about the angling club see Storr Lochs entry.

Raasay & Loch Torridon

A'BHAID-FHEARNA, Loch See Loch a'Mhullaich.
A'BHEALAICH, Loch See Loch na h-Airighe Riabhaich.
A'BHEALAICH MHOR, Loch See Loch a'Mhullaich.
A'CHADHA, Loch See Loch a'Mhullinn.
A'CHAISTEIL, Loch See Applecross River.
A'CHAORAIN (Kenmore), Loch See Loch na h-Airighe Riabhaich.
A'CHAORAINN BEAG, Loch See Loch a'Mhullaich.
A'CHAORAINN, Loch See Applecross River.
A'CHAORAINN, Loch See Loch Lundie.
A'CHAORAINN, Loch See Loch Thollaidh.
A'CHOIN DUIBH, Loch See Loch a'Mhullaich.
A'CHOIRE BHUIDHE, Loch See Loch na h-Airighe Riabhaich.
A'CHOIRE DHUIBH, Lochan See Applecross River.
A'GHLINNE DHUIRCH, Loch See Loch na Smeoraich.
A'GHOBHAINN, Loch See Applecross River.
A'MHUILINN, Loch See Applecross River.
A'MHUILINN, Loch See Loch na Creige (East Kenmore).

A'MHULLAICH, Loch
Location & Access 24/810600. Easily accessible via the minor road from Torridon to Lower Diabaig (24/790605). The road parallels the north shore of the loch.
Commentary Loch A'Mhullaich is the western section of Loch Diabaigas Airde (24/815597) and together the two waters extend for a distance of one and a half miles east/west by up to quarter of a mile north south. They are joined by narrows at Upper Diabaig (24/811600). There are a number of tiny lochans in the hills to the south, all of which contain small trout: Loch a'Bhealaich Mhor (24/801585), Lochan Dubh (South Diabaig) (24/799581), Loch a'Choin Duibh (24/818579) and Lochan Leirg (24/811588). These waters may be approached by following the track which leads south from the pier at 24/798599 on the

Raasay and Loch Torridon — OS Map 24

shores of sea-loch Diabaig, a long hard hike over rough terrain. There are a further twenty named and unnamed lochs and lochans lying to the north, again all involving a serious tramp to reach. The principal waters are: Lochan Dubh (West Diabaig) (24/789614), Loch nam Ball (24/787616), Loch Airigh a'Mhill (24/788623), Loch nan Gamhna (24/795620), Loch a'Chaorainn Beag (24/802617), Loch na Feannaig (24/804614), Lochan Dubh (East Diabaig) (24/812616), Loch Freumhach (24/814619), Loch na h-Uamhaig (24/820624), Loch Roag (24/821611), Loch Airigh Eachainn (24/828610), Loch Mheallain (24/835619), Loch Gaineamhach Beag (24/838626), Lochan Sgeireach (Diabaig) (24/804636), the Craig River (24/769639), Lochan Dubh (Craig) (24/776635), Lochan Dubh na Caorach (24/798650), Loch na h-Uamha (Craig) (24/778661), Loch a'Bhaid-Fhearna (24/759665), Loch nan Tri-eileanan (24/828599).

Fish Brown trout of various sizes, from 4oz up to fish of over 2lb. The possibility of sea-trout near the mouth of the Craig River during spate conditions, and in the estuary at Inveralligin (24/842573).

Flies & Tactics The most important requirements are strong lungs and legs and the ability to use a compass and map. This is serious hill-walking country in splendid surroundings, dominated by stark Beinn Alligin (985m), one of the most dramatic mountains in Torridon. Bank fishing all the way and it is best to avoid wading. Lochan Sgeireach should not be missed. Loch na h-Uamhaig and Loch Freumhach also hold better than average trout. Offer them: Black Pennell, March Brown, Peter Ross.

Permission & Charges Contact: Donnie Beaton, 1 Wester Alligin, Torridon, Wester Ross. Tel: 01445 791201. Expect to pay in the order of £5 per rod per day.

A'MHULLINN, Loch

Location & Access 24/553367. Loch a'Mhullinn, known locally as "The Home Loch", is in the Rassay Forest, to the north of Inverarish, and is easily accessible via the minor road from Clachan, and just to the north of Din Borodale (24/555365).

Commentary A very attractive, sheltered little loch. It drains south by the Inverarish Burn to reach the sea after one mile. A more serious expedition can be mounted by walking out to explore the lochs round Dun Caan (443m): tiny Loch Meall Daimh (24/576401), Loch na Meilich (24/574398), the loch water supply, Loch na Mna (24/579387), and, over the bealach to the east, remote, beautiful, Loch a'Chadha (24/585393). Return via Loch Storab (24/565387).

Fish All these lochs contain good stocks of trout which average 8oz: Loch a'Mhullinn and Loch na Meilich have trout of over 1lb. There is also the chance of sea-trout at the mouth of the Inverarish, in July and August, and brown trout in the pools in the river itself, particularly after heavy rain.

Flies & Tactics Approach the Dun Caan lochs from the road from Inverarish at 24/561405, turning south-east along a good track. Also consider a cast or two in Loch Eadar na Bhaile (24/558447) and Loch an Rathaid (24/555415), which is reached by following the outlet stream north from Loch Eadar na Bhaile for ten minutes. Rassay lochs are fished from the bank, and it is best to stay on terra firma whilst doing so, rather than wading. Busy flies work well. Try: Black Zulu, Red Palmer, Peter Ross.

Permission & Charges £2 per rod per day, £7 per week, from: Mrs Rebecca Mackay, 6 Oscaig, Island of Rassay, Skye. Tel: (01478) 660207. Mr Angus Gillies, Isle of Rassay Hotel, Isle of Rassay, Skye. Tel: (01478) 660222.

ABHAINN DUBH, River See Loch na Creige (East Kenmore).
ABHAINN THRAIL, River See River Balgy.
ACHAIDH NA H-INICH, Loch See Loch Lundie (Plockton).
AIRIGH A'MHILL, Loch See Loch a'Mhullaich.
AIRIGH ALASDAIR, Loch See Applecross River.
AIRIGH EACHAINN, Loch See Loch a'Mhullaich.
AN ARBHAIR, Loch See Loch Thollaidh.
AN DUBH-LOCH, Loch See Applecross River.
AN EILEIN, Loch See Applecross River.
AN FHEOIR, Loch See Applecross River.
AN FHEOIR, Lochan See Applecross River.
AN FHIDHLEIR, Loch See Loch Fada.
AN RATHAID, Loch See Loch a'Mhullinn.
AN T-SAGAIRT, Loch See Applecross River.
AN TURARAICH, Loch See Loch Coultrie.

AN UACHDAIR, Loch

Location & Access 24/583470. Loch an Uachdair lies immediately to the west of the road at the north end of the Island of Rassay, to the north of Brochel Castle and is easily accessible.

Commentary There are five good little lochs here, at the north end of the island, and another one on the adjacent island of Eilean Fladday: Loch an Uachdair, Loch na Broin (24/576465), Loch na Cuilce (24/574474), Loch Beag (24/586473), near Brochel Castle; north, by Torran, Loch Mallaichte (24/598494) and the adjacent unnamed lochans; and on Eilean Fladday, reached across Caol Fladda sands, Loch Mor (24/583513).

Fish Brown trout of varying sizes, mostly in the order of 8oz, but, on Loch an Uachdair, fish of up to and over 2lb in weight.

Flies & Tactics Bank fishing all round, with few problems, providing you stay ashore. Offer: Soldier Palmer, Grouse & Claret, Dunkeld.

Permission & Charges Cost: £2 per day, £7 per week. Contact: Mrs Rebecca Mackay, 6 Oscaig, Island of Rassay, Skye. Tel: (01478) 660207. Fishing rights to all lochs and burns on Rassay (except for Loch a'Mhuilinn) belong to Rassay Crofters' Association. Enquires to Mrs Mackay.

APPLECROSS, River

Location & Access Source 24/786460 Outfall 24/745456. Access to the river is from the village of Applecross where a stalkers' path borders the north bank of the stream.

OS Map 24 — Raasay and Loch Torridon

Commentary Sadly, because of a lack of salmon and sea-trout, the river has been closed for the past five years. The local fishery trust is examining the cause of the decline which has, at least in this writer's opinion, almost certainly been caused by sea-lice infestation from fish-farms in the vicinity. Until these fish-farms are either removed or more closely regulated, then it is unlikely that the fishing on this beautiful stream will recover. Apart from salmon and sea-trout fishing, the Applecross peninsula has outstanding fishing for brown trout on more than seventy named and unnamed lochs and lochans. The main waters to the south are accessed by a stalkers' path which starts at Toscaig (24/715385) and runs south-east for almost four miles to reach the sea at Loch Carron at Airigh-drishaig (24/7369). There is also the possibility of sport with sea-trout near the mouth of the Toscaig River. The principal lochs here are: Loch an t-Sagairt (24/744380) with its two, nearby, unnamed lochans, and, one mile north-east from the track, Loch Maol Fhraochach (24/755386) and Lochan Gobhlach (24/760389). To the south of the track, a good day out may be had by making a circuit of: Loch Airigh Alasdair (24/745369), walking south to explore the unnamed lochans round Meall Loch Airigh Alasdair (336m), working west to Loch Meall nam Feadan (24/730368) before returning to the track. Another adventure in both hill-walking and fishing may be experienced by leaving the track at 24/735376 and hiking north up the line of the Toscaig River to reach Loch Braigh an Achaidh (24/74440405), stopping along the way for a cast in Loch nan Slochd (24/739396) by Carn nan Uaighean (363m). Between Loch Braigh an Achaidh and the road from Tornapress (24/839432) on the A896 across the Bealach na Bo to Applecross village, there are a further series of lochs all of which will repay a visit: Loch nan Uaighean (24/734411) and its neighbours, Loch Leathann (24/741412) and Loch a'Chaisteil (24/730412). The lochs to the north of Loch a'Chaisteil are best approached from the Tornapress/Applecross road by walking south from where the Allt Beag burn cross the road at 24/745441. Have a long day out in the hills. Start at Loch Odhar (24/751432) and then walk south for half a mile to find Loch a'Chaorainn (24/749425). After fishing Loch a'Chaorainn, step west to have a look at Lochan Leathann (24/745425). Continue south to reach little Loch a'Ghobhainn (24/748419). Now walk north-west for one mile, passing a series of unnamed lochans on the way, to fish Lochan na Teanga (24/732425) and north-west again to Loch an Eilein (24/729431). Next is Loch na Larach (24/728434) which drains Loch an Eilein. Return to the start point via Lochan Sgeirach (24/735432) and Loch an Fheoir (24/735438). A less taxing cast may be had in Loch a'Mhuilinn (24/707436) which lies close to the roadside at Milton. The lochs between the Tornapress/Applecross road and the Applecross River are amongst the most remote in Wester Ross but are splendidly situated, surrounded by fine peaks: Beinn Bhan (896m), Coire Gorm Beag (712m) to the north and the long ridge of Carn Dearg (646m) to the south: Loch Coire Attadale (24/787460), Loch Dubh na Creige (24/781464), the headwaters of the Applecross River. These lochs are accessed along the stalkers' path on the north bank of the Applecross River, but, be warned, for the last two miles you are on your own. Little Lochan Dubh (24/750456) is less taxing to reach and should be approached from the road at 24/745411. Climb north for one mile to reach the loch. Considerable improvements have been made in recent years to the roads in Applecross and the village is now linked to Shieldaig in the north by a coastal route. Use this road to approach Loch nan Eun (24/704482) which lies at an altitude of 300m on Beinn a'Chlachain (626m) to the north of Applecross Village. Park near An Cruinn-leum at 24/685481 and follow the outlet burn, the Allt Tasabhaig, east, climbing steeply to reach the loch after a vigorous hike of forty minutes. You should also consider, having come this far, an additional half-mile tramp further east to the unnamed lochan at 24/719485. Loch nan Eun is the largest loch in the area and both these waters hold good trout. Another excellent Applecross day-out can be had by exploring the small lochs between Salacher (24/687511) on the coastal road and Meall na Fhuaid (518m), three miles east. This will involve you in a tough round trip of seven miles visiting ten named and unnamed waters along the way. Begin on Loch nan Eun (Salacher) and continue east, over rising ground, to find An Dubh-loch (24/731500) which is a superb little water in a deep corrie. Trek north from An Dubh-loch, following the outlet stream to locate Fiar Loch (24/721517) and its neighbour to the west, Lochan a'Choire Dhuibh (24/718512). Descend north-west from Lochan a'Choire Dhuibh for one mile to find Lochan Dubh (24/705522). After fishing Lochan Dubh, continue south to have a cast in Loch Dubh Deas (24/705519) and its tiny satellite lochan to the west, and, finally, to Lochan an Fheoir (24/704514) before returning to sanity at Salacher.

Fish The Applecross River used to produce upwards of 100 salmon and 50 sea-trout each season. Now, the salmon and sea-trout have almost completely vanished. Given the perilous plight of sea-trout stocks, they are best left in peace. The brown trout vary in size from 4oz right up to a few fish of over 2lb in weight.

Flies & Tactics Be well-prepared and accustomed and proficient in the use of a compass and map. The weather is fickle and you could easily become lost should a sudden mist descend. All the fishing is from the bank and you should avoid wading. Leave a note of where you intend to go and when you expect to return and it is best to go with a friend, rather than alone, in case of accidents. Flies: Black Zulu, Greenwell's Glory, Silver Butcher.

Permission & Charges Brown trout fishing permits are usually available at the Post Office in the village. Also contact Ken Griffin, Head Stalker, Applecross Estate, Applecross, Wester Ross. Tel: 01520 744247. Access will be limited during the stalking season, from late August onwards. All fishing on any Applecross river or bay for salmon or sea trout is subject to conditions laid down by the Estate Trust.

Raasay and Loch Torridon — OS Map 24

BALGY, River
Location & Access Source 24/899489 Outfall 24/847545. Approach from the A896 Gairloch/Shieldaig road. The river crosses the road at 24/846544.
Commentary Although the river drains a vast hinterland, the fishing interest is primarily confined to the one-mile section from Loch Damh (24/862510) to the sea. Falls below Loch Damh hold back fish during low water conditions. There are a number of productive pools on the river including Falls Pool, Rock Pool, Wall Pool, the Weir Pool and Sea Pool. Further sport is available on the loch, principally for sea-trout, and there are also good stocks of brown trout. The loch is four miles long by up to half a mile wide and drops to more than 50m in depth at the south end.
Fish Salmon enter the system from June onwards and average 7lb/8lb. Approximately 50/80 are taken most seasons. Sea-trout, for which Loch Damh used to be famous, are now scarce; caused, beyond reasonable doubt, by sea-lice infestation from nearby factory salmon-farms.
Flies & Tactics The river is narrow and fast flowing and a 14ft rod is required to hold the fish, and to keep the line away from the banks when casting. Dapping is the preferred fishing method on Loch Damh and the margins, particularly along the shallow, west shoreline, produce the best results. Bank fishing, for both brown trout and sea-trout, can be just as effective as fishing from a drifting boat. However, stay ashore and do not attempt to wade. There is a good track along the whole length of the east bank, the west shoreline is trackless. If you wish to explore the south end of the loch, the best approach is from the A896 at 24/850476 from whence a good track leads directly to the lochside. On the river, offer: Willie Gunn, Garry Dog, Stoat's Tail, Green Highlander, Hairy Mary, Shrimp Fly, General Practitioner. For the loch, use: Loch Ordie, Ke-He, Black Zulu, Black Pennell, Soldier Palmer, Peter Ross.
Permission & Charges There are a number of options: Tigh an Eilean Hotel, Shieldaig, Wester Ross, Tel: 01520 755251 have rods available on the River Balgy on Tuesday, Thursday and Saturday at a cost of £22.50 per rod per day; Loch Torridon Hotel, Torridon, Wester Ross, Tel: 01445 791242 offer bank fishing on Loch Damh at a cost of £6 per rod per day; Finlayson Hughes, 29 Barossa Place, Perth PH1 5EP, Tel: 01738 630926, Fax: 01738 639017 let Ben Damh Lodge and sporting rights on Ben Damh Estate on behalf of the owner. This includes accommodation for a party of 12 with salmon fishing on the Abhainn Thrail, a tributary of the River Torridon, and sea-trout and brown trout fishing on Loch Damh. The cost is in the order of £1,000 per party per week.

BEAG, Loch (Raasay) See Loch an Uachdair.
BHRAIGHAIG, Loch See Loch na h-Airighe Riabhaich.
BRAIGH AN ACHAIDH, Loch See Applecross River.
CEOPACH, Loch See Loch na h-Airighe Riabhaich.
COIRE ATTADALE, Loch See Applecross River.

COIRE NA POITE, Loch See Loch Lundie.

COIRE NAN ARR, Loch
Location & Access 24/809421. Park on the Tornapress/Applecross Village road where the Russel Burn crosses the road (24/814413). Follow the outlet burn north to reach the loch after an easy walk of ten minutes.
Commentary A very attractive loch, approximately 40 acres in extent.
Fish Lots of fun with bright little trout which average 6oz/8oz. There is also the possibility of sport with sea-trout in the estuary of the Russel Burn.
Flies & Tactics Easy bank fishing and no need to wade. The north end of the loch, where the feeder stream enters from Coire nan Arr, should provide you with supper. Offer them: Ke-He, Soldier Palmer, Silver Butcher.
Permission & Charges See Loch Lundie entry.

COULTRIE, Loch
Location & Access 24/853460. Ten minutes east from the A896 Lochcarron/Shieldaig road.
Commentary Loch Coultrie is the northern section of a one 1.5 mile long water, the southern section being Loch an Loin (24/854450). The two lochs drain north into Loch Damh. There are a number of small hill-lochs to the east, rarely fished, remote, and containing modest brown trout. They are: Loch an Turaraich (24/885491) on Meall na Saobhaidhe (368m), Loch na Suileig (24/898489) at the head of Strath a'Bhathaich; and to the south of the strath, Lochan Meall na Caillich (24/880439) and Loch na Caillich (24/863418) on Cearcall Dubh (410m).
Fish In the principal lochs, adequate stocks of brown trout which average 8oz/10oz.
Flies & Tactics Boat fishing brings the best results and most fish tend to be taken in the shallow water near the margins. The east shore of Loch Coultrie, by the finger-like promontory, is a good place to begin. On Loch an Loin, concentrate where the Allt a'Ghiubhais enters at the north-east corner. Try: Soldier Palmer, Greenwell's Glory, Peter Ross.
Permission & Charges Mr Pattinson, Couldoran, Kishorn, Wester Ross. Tel: 01520 733227. Cost: £20 per rod per day; boat with outboard motor, £20 per day.

CRAIG, River See Loch a'Mhullaich.
CUAIG, River See Loch Fada.
DAMH, Loch See River Balgy.
DIABAIGAS AIRDE, Loch See Loch a'Mhullaich.
DUBH (Craig), Lochan See Loch a'Mhullaich.
DUBH DEAS, Loch See Applecross River.
DUBH (East Diabaig), Lochan See Loch a'Mhullaich.
DUBH (Loch Lundie), Loch See Loch Lundie.
DUBH, Lochan See Applecross River.
DUBH NA CAORACH, Lochan See Loch a'Mhullaich.
DUBH NA CREIGE, Loch See Applecross River.
DUBH (Salacher), Lochan See Applecross River.
DUBH (South Diabaig), Lochan See Loch a'Mhullaich.

OS Map 24 — Raasay and Loch Torridon

DUBH (West Diabaig), **Lochan** See Loch a'Mhullaich.
DUBHA, Lochan See Loch nan Gillean.
DUGHAILL, Loch 24/827514. The loch is preserved by the owner, as is the short Shieldaig River which drains the loch north into sea-Loch Shieldaig.
EADAR NA BHAILE, Loch See Loch a'Mhullinn.
EOE, Loch See Loch Fada.

FADA, Loch
Location & Access 24/719598. Immediately adjacent to the minor road from Fearnbeg to Cuaig.
Commentary The largest of a series of easily-accessible lochs lying in the north of the Applecross peninsula. Loch Rubha Aird Choinnich (24/705601) and Loch nan Eun (24/710589) lie on the cliffs to the west of the road. The beach near Loch na Eun at the mouth of the Cuaig River (24/707587) is perfect for the bucket-and-spade brigade whilst you fish. To the east of the road, visit little Loch Eoe (24/724598) and its unnamed satellite, a step east again from Loch Fada. For a more adventurous expedition explore the two unnamed roadside lochans at 24/714590 before tramping half a mile south-east to find Loch nam Breac Beaga (24/721583) and its satellite lochan to the south at 24/721581. Fifteen minutes further east will bring you to Loch an Fhidhleir (24/728582) which is almost half a mile north/south by 100 yds east/west. There is one further loch worth a good look, Lochan Sgeirach (24/715575), and its satellite to the west at 24/717577. These are best approached from the Cuaig River.
Fish Brown trout most of the way with the chance of the odd fish of up to 1lb in weight and sea-trout at the mouth of the Cuaig River.
Flies & Tactics All these waters are very easily covered from the shore and there is no need to wade. As always, when walking in unfamiliar territory, take along a compass and map. Chuck them: Blue Zulu, March Brown, Alexandra.
Permission & Charges See Loch na h-Airighe Riabhaich entry.

FADA, Lochan 24/739555. This loch is now a smolt hatchery and is unavaible for fishing.
FIAR, Loch See Applecross River.
FREUMHACH, Loch See Loch a'Mhullaich.
GAINEAMACH, Loch See Loch Lundie.
GAINEAMHACH BEAG, Loch See Loch a'Mhullaich.
GAINEAMHACH, Loch (Kenmore) See Loch na h-Airighe Riabhaich.
GOBHLACH, Lochan See Applecross River.
INVERARISH, River See Loch a'Mhullinn.
KISHORN, River The river is not available to members of the public and the fishing is preserved for the sole use of the owner and his guests.
LEATHANN, Loch See Applecross River.
LEATHANN, Lochan See Applecross River.
LEIRG, Lochan See Loch a'Mhullaich.

LUNDIE, Loch
Location & Access 24/805490. Approach from near Tornapress (24/839432) on the A896 Lochcarron to Shieldaig road. Immediately after crossing the bridge over the River Kishorn river, look for a stalkers' track running north. This track ends after two and a half miles. Loch Lundie is a further mile and a half north.
Commentary Fantastic scenery, dominated by the dark crags and corries of Beinn Bhan (896m) to the west and An Staonach (513m) to the east. The loch is two miles long by up to half a mile wide and drains north into sea-Loch Shieldaig at Inverbain. There are four, subsidiary, lochs to visit along the way: Loch Gaineamach (24/820463), Loch Dubh (24/819468), Loch a'Chaorainn (24/817469) and, lastly, Loch Coire na Poite (24/818452) which lies at 380m below the summit of Beinn Bhan.
Fish Loch Lundie contains excellent stocks of brown trout as well as Arctic char. Trout average 8oz. Loch Gaineamach has a reputation for holding some large trout, but is considered to be "dour". The other waters will provide you with breakfast.
Flies & Tactics Bank fishing. Do not wade. It is dangerous to do so, particularly on Loch Lundie. Concentrate your efforts where the small feeder streams enter along the west shore. There are a series of "fishy" bays and the trout tend to lie close to the margin. Tempt them with: Loch Ordie, Black Pennell, Dunkeld.
Permission & Charges Contact Ken Griffin, Head Stalker, Applecross Estate, Applecross, Wester Ross. Tel: 01520 744247. Expect to pay in the order of £5 per rod per day. Access will be limited during the stalking season, from late August onwards.

LUNDIE, Loch (Plockton)
Location & Access 24/808318. Approach from Plockton along a forest road at 24/808326.
Commentary This is a substantial forest loch some 700yds north/south by up to 200yds wide. A mile to the south is another, similar water, Loch Achaidh na h-Inich (24/814308). Both waters are easily accessible.
Fish Loch Lundie has been stocked in the past, with rainbow trout and some Canadian brook trout, but these have long-since been fished out. The surviving population consists of small brown trout. Loch Achaidh na h-Inich contains voracious pike and a few anxious brown trout of up to and over 3lb in weight.
Flies & Tactics These lochs can be very dour. Bank fishing only and the roadside bank on Loch Lundie is as good a place as any to begin, as is the north shore on Loch Achaidh na h-Inich. Try: Black Pennell, Invicta, Silver Butcher.
Permission & Charges Permission not required.

MALLAICHTE, Loch See Loch an Uachdair.
MAOL FHRAOCHACH, Loch See Applecross River.
MEALL DAIMH, Loch See Loch a'Mhullinn.
MEALL NA CAILLICH, Lochan See Loch Coultrie.
MEALL NAM FEADAN, Loch See Applecross River.
MHEALLAIN, Loch See Loch a'Mhullaich.
MOR, Loch (Raasay) See Loch an Uachdair.

239

Raasay and Loch Torridon — OS Map 24

NA BROIN, Loch See Loch an Uachdair.
NA CAILLICH, Loch See Loch Coultrie.
NA CAORACH (East Kenmore), Loch See Lochan Fada.
NA CAORACH (West Kenmore) See Lochan Fada.

NA CREIGE, Loch (East Kenmore)
Location & Access 24/769557. Immediately adjacent to the Inverbain/Kenmore road.
Commentary A good start point for a longer expedition into the hills to visit Loch a'Mhuilinn (24/776547), a brisk half-mile hike to the south-east. There are also two, tiny, unnamed lochans to the east of Loch na Creige which are worth a cast or two.
Fish Small brown trout in the lochs and the chance of sea-trout, particularly after heavy rain, at the mouth of the outlet stream which enters sea-Loch a'Chracaich at 24/762566. Sea-trout may also be encountered at the mouth of the Abhainn Dubh near Inverbain at 24/788549.
Flies & Tactics Bank fishing and no need to wade. Offer the residents: Ke-He, Grouse & Claret, Peter Ross.
Permission & Charges See Loch na h-Airighe Riabhaich entry.

NA CREIGE, Loch (West Kenmore) See Lochan Fada.
NA CUILCE, Loch See Loch an Uachdair.
NA CURACH, Loch See Lochan Fada.
NA DOIRE MOIRE, Loch See Loch na Smeoraich.
NA DUBH-BHRUAICH, Loch See Lochan Fada.
NA FEANNAIG, Loch See Loch a'Mhullaich.

NA H-AIRIGHE RIABHAICH, Lochan
Location & Access 24/748514. The loch lies to the west of the stalkers' track which leads from Kenmore (24/75456) in the north to Applecross Village (24/719458) in the south. Walk four miles south from Kenmore and leave the track by the two unnamed lochans at 24/755520. Loch na h-Airighe Riabhaich is a further half a mile west.
Commentary There are two lochs here joined by a narrow stream, lying close to the east face of Meall na Fhuaid (518m). The stalkers' path also gives access to a number of additional waters which may be visited on the way home from Loch na h-Airighe Riabhaich or visited as a separate expedition. They are: Loch Gaineamhach (24/754534), the largest water, half a mile north/south by up to 400yds east/west and lying immediately adjacent to the track; Loch Ceopach (24/762537) and Loch a'Chaorain (24/769541), a mile east from Loch Gaineamhach on the north shoulder of Croic-bheinn (493m); Loch na h-Eangaiche (24/745543); Loch a'Bhealaich (24/750547) by Meall Dearg (279m); Loch a'Choire Bhuidhe (24/754555); and Loch Bhraighaig (24/754568), a few minutes from the minor road at 24/759568.
Fish Trout average 6oz/8oz.
Flies & Tactics You will cover at least 9 miles during the day so be properly prepared for whatever the weather brings. Take along a compass and map, fish from the bank, do not wade. Flies: Soldier Palmer, Grouse & Claret, Peter Ross.

Permission & Charges Contact Ken Griffin, Head Stalker, Applecross Estate, Applecross, Wester Ross. Tel: 01520 744247. Expect to pay in the order of £5 per rod per day. Access will be limited during the stalking season, from late August onwards.

NA H-EANGAICHE, Loch See Loch na h-Airighe Riabhaich.
NA H-UAMHA, Loch (Craig) See Loch a'Mhullaich.
NA H-UAMHAIG, Loch See Loch a'Mhullaich.
NA LARACH, Loch See Applecross River.
NA LARACH, Loch (Kenmore) See Lochan Fada.
NA LEITIRE, Loch See Loch nan Gillean.
NA LOIN, Loch See Loch Coultrie.
NA MEILICH, Loch See Loch a'Mhullinn.
NA MNA, Loch See Loch a'Mhullinn.

NA SMEORAICH, Loch
Location & Access 24/843303. Approach from Balmacara via Coillemore (33/806287). A track climbs steeply north east through Coille Mhor to Auchtertyre Hill (452m). At the end of the track, continue through the forest, keeping the cliff on your right, to reach Loch a'Bhealaich (33/830294) and then the south shore of Loch a'Ghlinne Dhuirch (33/837300). Loch na Smeoraich lies ten minutes to the north-east of Loch a'Ghlinne Dhuirch.
Commentary This expedition will stretch your legs and lungs a bit, but it makes for an unforgettable day out. There are four further waters to attack, whilst you are in the vicinity: Loch nam Breac Mora (24/838309), the two unnamed lochans at 24/832305, and, finally, Loch na Doire Moire (24/827304).
Fish Excellent trout which average in the order of 10oz and some fish of up to and over 2lb in weight as well.
Flies & Tactics The round trip is approximately 7 miles and the going is rough. You will need stout boots and a compass and map. Do not wade. Show them: Ke-He, Invicta, Black Pennell.
Permission & Charges See Loch Lundie (Plockton) entry.

NA SUILEIG, Loch See Loch Coultrie.
NA TEANGA, Lochan See Applecross River.
NAM BALL, Loch See Loch a'Mhullaich.
NAM BREAC BEAGA, Loch See Loch Fada.
NAM BREAC MORA, Loch See Loch na Smeoraich.
NAN EUN (Cuaig), Loch See Loch Fada.
NAN EUN, Loch See Applecross River.
NAN EUN (Salacher), Loch See Applecross River.
NAN GAMHNA, Loch See Loch a'Mhullaich.

NAN GILLEAN, Loch
Location & Access 24/838324. Approach from the Torr Mor road at 24/819321. Climb steeply east along a good track through Bealach Mor to reach the unnamed loch at 24/833321, the first in a series of six waters to be explored during the day.
Commentary The lochs are known locally as the Crag

OS Map 24-25   Glen Carron

Lochs and the first water leads to the south end of Loch nan Gillean which drains the largest water, Loch na Leitire (24/844321). Work round the tree-lined south shore of Loch na Leitire and then north to find the unnamed lochan at 24/844325 and back to the north end of Loch nan Gillean. Climb north-west from Loch nan Gillean for fifteen minutes to locate little Lochan Dubha (24/832329) on Creag nan Duilisg (150m). Descend south for half-a-mile to regain Bealach Mor and the start point.
Fish Brown trout which average 8oz/10oz and larger specimens as well.
Flies & Tactics Bank fishing all the way and do not wade. These lochs are easily covered from the shore and fish may be taken anywhere. Pay particular attention to Loch an Dubha: trout of over 5lb have been caught in this tiny water. Flies: Soldier Palmer, March Brown, Kingfisher Butcher.
Permission & Charges See Loch Lundie (Plockton) entry.

NAN SLOCHD, Loch See Applecross River.
NAN TRI-EILEANAN, Loch See Loch a'Mhullaich.
NAN UAIGHEAN, Loch See Applecross River.
ODHAR, Loch See Applecross River.
PRIVATE WATERS A'CHOIRE LEITH, Loch (24/872394); DUBHA, Lochan (24/834373); AN EICH-UISGE, Loch (24/836368); RERAIG, River (24/838362).
ROAG, Loch See Loch a'Mhullaich.
RUBHA AIRD CHOINNICH, Loch See Loch Fada.
RUSSEL, Burn See Loch Coire nan Arr.
SGEIRACH, Lochan See Applecross River.
SGEIRACH, Lochan See Loch Fada.
SGEIREACH, Lochan (Diabaig) See Loch a'Mhullaich.
SHIELDAIG, River See Loch Dughaill.
STORAB, Loch See Loch a'Mhullinn.

THOLLAIDH, Loch
Location & Access Loch Thollaidh lies at the end of a two mile hike east up Gleann Udalain. There is a good forest track which you should leave where the Allt an Lucha burn joins the main river at 24/879306. Follow the burn up to the loch.
Commentary Always worth a visit, not only because of the very pretty trout this loch contains, but also because of the outstanding serenity of the surrounding countryside. There are two other lochs, to the north of the forest, which can be accessed from the A890 road near to Stromeferry: Loch an Arbhair (24/883341) and Lochan a'Chaorainn (24/894348). Like Loch Thollaidh, these waters are rarely fished and lie amidst dramatic scenery.
Fish Loch an Arbhair has, in its day, produced brown trout of double figures. Loch Thollaidh trout are golden in colour, averaging 8oz; Lochan a'Chaorainn, and its satellite lochan will always provide supper.
Flies & Tactics Fish the north bank on Loch Thollaidh and round the small island at the east end. Approach Loch an Arbhair cautiously, to avoid scaring the residents. Lochan a'Chaorainn is easily covered. Offer them: Ke-He, Soldier Palmer, Silver Invicta.

Permission & Charges Not required, but check locally to be sure.
TOSCAIG, River
Location & Access See Applecross River.

Glen Carron

A'BHANA, Loch See Loch Mullardoch.

A'BHEALAICH, Loch
Location & Access 25/024213. Approach from the A87 Invergarry/Kyle of Lochalsh road at Morvich (25/959211). Drive to Dorusduain (25/981224) and cross the bridge over the Abhainn Chonaig. Find the track which climbs east, steeply, round the north shoulder of Sgurr a'Choire Ghairbh (870m) and up Gleann Choinneachair to Bealach an Sgairne before descending, steeply, to the south end of the loch. This is a stiff 2 miles walk.
Commentary Loch a'Bhealaich drains north down Gleann Gaorsaic into the River Elchaig (see separate entry) and is half a mile long by up to 400yds wide. There are are two other lochs on the course of the stream: Loch Gaorsaic (25/025224) and Loch Thuill Easaich (25/029232), both of which are worth a visit. A good day out would be to make a circuit of the three lochs before returning, foot-sore, to base at Dorusduain.
Fish Sport with bright brown trout which average 8oz.
Flies & Tactics Non-fishing companions may be despatched to visit the famous Falls of Glomach (25/019258), to the north of the lochs, whilst you get on with the real work of the day. Begin at the south end of Loch a'Bhealaich where the feeder burns enter and work north. The narrow connecting stream between Loch a'Bhealaich and Loch Gaorsaic can also produce fine sport after heavy rain, particularly at the outlet from Loch a'Bhealaich. Try: Loch Ordie, Ke-He, Black Pennell.
Permission & Charges Contact: Willie Fraser, National Trust for Scotland, Morvich, Inverinate, by Kyle of Lochalsh, Ross-shire. Tel: 01599 511231. There is no charge for trout fishing but access may be limited at certain times of the year for conservation purposes.

A'CHAORAINN, Lochan See Loch Coire na Caime.
A'CHLAIDHEIMH, Loch See Loch Monar.
A'CHLAIDHEIMH, Loch See Loch Affric.
A'CHOIRE BHIG, Loch See Loch Mullardoch.
A'CHOIRE DHOMHAIN, Loch See Loch Mullardoch.
A'CHOIRE DUIBH, Lochan See Loch Coire na Caime.

A'CHROISG, Loch
Location & Access 25/120585. Also known as Loch Rosque, the loch lies immediately to the south of the A832 Achnasheen/Gairloch road.
Commentary A dour, deep (50m), windy loch, 3.5 miles east/west by up to half a mile wide, close to the

Glen Carron — OS Map 25

road and easily accessible. It is fed by the Abhainn Dubh through little Loch Crann (25/090578) and the south shore is trackless and dominated by An Liathanach (508m).
Fish Pike, perch, brown trout, ferox, and, recently, the chance of salmon.
Flies & Tactics Bank fishing and it is dangerous to wade. You may, however, launch your own boat on the loch. The west end, approached from Lubmore (25/098586), is the most attractive fishing area where a good track crosses the inlet burn between Loch Crann and Loch a'Chroisg. After heavy rain this little burn, both below and above Loch Crann, can offer great fun with brown trout. Although there are undoubtedly salmon in the loch, so far, none have been caught. Loch a'Chroisg can be a wild place. If afloat, take care. Flies: Black Zulu, Greenwell's Glory, Silver Butcher.
Permission & Charges Contact: Ledgowan Hotel, Achnasheen, Ross-shire. Tel: 01445 720252. Fishing is free to hotel guests.

A'GHAIRBHE, River See Loch Coulin.
A'MHUILINN, Loch (Coulags) See Loch Coire Fionnaraich.
ABHAINN DUBH, River See Loch a'Chroisg.

ABHAINN THRAIL, River
Location & Access Source 25/943541 Outfall 25/905550. Access from the A896 Gairloch/Shieldaig road at the outfall (see above). A track borders the south bank of the stream.
Commentary This is a primary tributary of the River Torridon (see separate entry) and is fished by guests renting Ben Damph Lodge. The river rises from Lochan Neimha (25/943541) but a waterfall bars the passage of migratory fish to the loch. The loch may also be accessed via the track past the Ling Hut (25/958563) and Loch an Iasgair (25/959565). One mile past the Ling Hut, and just south of Loch na Frianach (25/954549), at 25/952541, locate the inlet stream and follow it down to the east end of the loch. If you continue to the end of the track, you may then climb the west shoulder of Beinn Liath Mhor to explore three corrie lochans lying at a height of 650m: Lochan Uaine (25/966527) - the Green Loch - and its unnamed neighbours. The trout lochs here are fished by Coulin Lodge guests.
Fish The chance of salmon and, perhaps, sea-trout, but only after heavy rain. The lochs all contain attractive brown trout which average 6oz/8oz.
Flies & Tactics For the river, see River Torridon entry. For the lochs, try: Loch Ordie, Soldier Palmer, Black Pennell.
Permission & Charges See Loch an Eion entry for Finlyson Hughes details. Coulin Lodge accommodates 12 guests. Cost: approximately £2,000 per week.

AFFRIC, Loch
Location & Access 25/160224. Continue west past the Glen Affric Hotel at Cannich (26/339318) on the minor road that borders the north bank of the River Glass (see OS Map 26). At the oppressive dam and power station (26/320294), bear right, signposted to Loch Affric. The road reaches Glen Affric Lodge after 9 miles, passing along the way the north shore of Loch Beinn a'Mheadhoin (see separate entry).
Commentary Loch Affric is one of the most perfect lochs in Scotland. The mountains of Kintail, the Five Sisters, dominate the western horizon, with Sgurr na Lapaich (1036m) towering to the north and Tigh na Seilge (929m) and Conbhairean (1109m) to the south. The lodge itself sits on a dramatic promontory overlooking the loch surrounded by native pine woods. The woodlands which line the south shore shelter a number of excellent hill-lochs: Loch Salach a'Ghiubhais (25/176217) and little Loch na Caillich (25/200219). There are eight further lochs between Loch Beinn a'Mheadhoin and the Tomich River (see OS Map 26) to the south: Loch a'Chlaidheimh (25/226235), Loch na h-Firidh (25/241223), Loch Pollain Buidhe (25/189224), Loch an Eang (25/249237), Loch na Gabhtach (25/261526), Loch an Amair (25/263261), Loch Innis Gheamhraidh (25/290269) and Coire Loch (25/294282). At the west end of Loch Affric, near Altnamulloch (25/134205), where the River Affric enters, is Loch Coulavie (25/132214) and Loch na Caimaig (25/139212), both of which will reward a visit.
Fish Brown trout which average in the order of 8oz but good numbers of larger trout as well. Loch Affric can produce fish of up to and over 5lb in weight. Loch Coulavie also has excellent stocks of larger fish although they do not give themselves up easily. Loch Affric generally produces about 1,000 trout each season.
Flies & Tactics Boat fishing only on Loch Affric and the west end of the loch is the most productive fishing area. The other lochs noted above are fished from the shore and are all, relatively, easily accessible. The Upper River Affric itself, where it enters the loch, can also give sport with brown trout, particularly after heavy rain. Don't underestimate Loch Affric, however, it is nearly three miles east/west by up to half-a-mile wide and 60m deep. On a fine day it looks magnificent, but should a storm catch you afloat it is an entirely different matter. Wear a life jacket, stay seated at all times, make sure you have a reliable outboard motor. Flies: Loch Ordie, Soldier Palmer, Black Pennell.
Permission & Charges The fishing is let with Glen Affric Lodge which accommodates a self-catering party of 12 guests in great comfort. Contact: Finlyson Hughes, 29 Barossa Place, Perth PH1 5EP. Tel: 01738 630926; Fax: 01738 639017. Prices: from £2,500 per week depending upon season.

AFFRIC (Lower), River See Loch Beinn a'Mheadhoin.
AFFRIC (Upper), River See Loch Affric.
AIRIGH LOCHAIN, Loch See Loch Beannacharain.
ALLT A'CHONAIS, River See River Carron.
ALLT AN LOIN-FHIODHA, Stream See Loch Calavie.
ALLT LOCH CALAVIE, Stream See Loch Calavie.

OS Map 25 — Glen Carron

AN AMAIR, Loch See Loch Affric.
AN DROIGHINN, Loch See Loch an Iasaich.
AN EANG, Loch See Loch Affric.

AN EION, Loch
Location & Access 25/924515. Leave the A896 Gairloch/Shieldaig road at 25/901548 and follow the stalkers' path south, climbing steeply round the east shoulder of Beinn na h-Eaglaise (737m). A 2.5 mile hike will bring you to the loch.
Commentary This is a wonderful, corrie loch, hemmed around by dramatic peaks: Meall Dearg (640m) to the east, Maol Chean-dearg (933m) to the south and Beinn na h-Eaglaise to the west. There are two other waters, reached shortly before Loch an Eion: Lochan Domhain (25/919519), to the right of the track, and Loch an Uillt-bheithe (25/920524) to the left. Those who relish further high adventure might chose to assault Meall Dearg to visit three tiny lochans on the 500m contour: Lochan Dearg (25/930522), Loch Meall a'Chuail (25/935527) and Lochan Dearg Beag (25/945524).
Fish The principal lochs contain excellent brown trout which average 10oz/12oz. The mountain lochans are rarely fished and they hold beautiful, 6oz trout but they are not always easy to catch.
Flies & Tactics Loch an Eion is a substantial water, circular in shape and some 700yds across. Bank fishing only and avoid wading. The north-east shore, near the two islands, is the place to begin. Work south to find the feeder stream at the south end of the loch and follow it up for five minutes to have a cast in Loch na Craoibhe-caorainn (25/928508) on the hill above Loch an Eion. This contains surprisingly good fish. The other waters noted are all easily covered from the shore. Best cast: Soldier Palmer, Woodcock & Hare-lug, Dunkeld.
Permission & Charges These waters lie within the Ben Damph Estate and the estate is factored by Finlyson Hughes, 29 Barossa Place, Perth. Tel: 01738 625926; Fax: 01738 639017. Sporting rights are let with Ben Damph Lodge which accommodates 12 guests and offers salmon fishing and sea-trout fishing as well as hill-loch fishing for brown trout. Cost: approximately £1,000 per week. Casual, day lets, for hill-loch trout fishing may be available through Alistair Holmes, Head Stalker, 2 Fuaran, Torridon, Wester Ross. Tel: 01445 791 252. Expect to pay in the order of £5 per rod per day.

AN FHAOIR, Loch See Loch an Iasaich.
AN FHIARLAID, Loch See Loch Coulin.
AN GEAD LOCH, Loch See Loch Calavie.
AN GORM-LOCH, Loch See Loch Fionnaraich.

AN IASAICH, Loch
Location & Access 25/952356. Accessed by a private estate road from the A890 Strathcarron/Kyle of Lochalsh road near to the mouth of the River Attadale at (25/924388).
Commentary Loch an Iasaich is the principal loch on the Attadale Estate; 35,000 acres of mountain and moorlands wilderness lying to the south of Loch Carron. The loch is approximately 600 yards north south by up to 300yds wide and is surrounded on three sides by forestry. There are a number of smaller lochs on the estate, remote and hard hiking to reach, but they will provide great fun with modest-sized brown trout.
They are: Loch an Droighinn (25/959365), Loch nam Forca (25/968361), Loch na Caillich (25/969369), approached from, and to the east of, Loch an Iasaich; and, to the west, a step from Loch an Iasaich, Loch Fuar (25/945351). Loch nam Breac Mora (25/932349), Loch nan Gillean (25/921354), Loch na Feithe-seilich (25/908348), Lochan Sgeireach (25/901341) and Loch na Sroine (25/901359) are best approached via a stalkers' track from the main road at Craigton (25/923385) and are reached after a stiff walk of four miles. To the north of Attadale, accessed via a stalkers' path at Achintee (25/941417), are four more, perfect, trout lochs round Creag Dubh Bheag ((270m): Loch nan Creadha (25/965408), Loch an Fhaoir (25/960400) and Lochan Dubha (25/943404) and its unnamed neighbour at 25/945405. A circuit of these lochs is a splendid way to spend the day, and to catch breakfast.
Fish Loch an Iasaich has been stocked and contains brown trout and rainbow trout which average 1lb in weight. The hill lochs contain wild trout which average 6oz/8oz. There is also the possibility of encountering salmon and sea-trout at the mouth of the River Attadale, particularly after heavy rain.
Flies & Tactics Boat fishing and bank fishing on Loch an Iasaich, bank fishing only on the other waters listed. Away from Loch an Iasaich, this is compass and map country. Be prepared. Offer: Ke-He, Woodcock & Hare-lug, Peter Ross.
Permission & Charges Contact Tom Watson, Attadale Estate, Strathcarron, Ross-shire. Tel: 01520 722308. Fishing is included in the cost of accommodation in self-catering cottages on the estate (£180/£325 per week). For details contact Susan Watson on Tel: 01520 722396.

AN IASGAIR, Lochan See River Torridon.
AN LAOIGH, Loch See River Carron.
AN TACHDAICH, Loch See Loch Calavie.
AN UILLT-BHEITHE, Loch See Loch an Eion.
ANNIE, Loch See Loch Calavie.
ATTADALE, River See Loch an Iasaich.
BEAG, Loch See Loch Monar.

BEANNACHARAIN, Loch (Scardroy)
Location & Access 25/230516. Approach from Little Scatwell (26/393572) via the minor road which leads west up Strathconon past Loch Meig (see separate entry) to the east end of the loch at Carnoch 25/250511).
Commentary Also known locally as Loch Scardroy, this is a substantial water, 1.5 miles long by up to 450yds wide. The loch is more than 50m deep and lies on the course of the River Meig and is part of the Conon Hydro-Electric scheme. The surrounding hills, principally Meall na Faochaig (660m) to the east and Bac an Eich (849m) to the west, form a wind tunnel

243

Glen Carron — OS Map 25

and Loch Beannacharain can often be wild and stormy.

Fish Good quality brown trout, descendants from Loch Leven fish. Average weight, 10oz, with good numbers of trout of up to and over 2lb. Arctic char and ferox in the depths.

Flies & Tactics Boat fishing brings the best results although reasonable sport may also be had from the shore. Most trout are caught in the shallow water, and the west end of the loch, where the River Meig enters, is a good place to begin. Work south and then east for a half a mile. The River Meig rises in the west from remote Lochan Gaineamhach (25/094451) and flows east down Gleann Fhiodhaig for six miles before reaching Loch Beannacharain. After exiting from the loch the river flows for a further four miles on OS Map 25 to near Strathanmore at 25/300551. The River Meig can produce excellent sport with brown trout throughout its length, providing there are good water levels. There are two, tiny, lochans on Meall nan Uan (840m) which will stretch your legs and lungs to reach but give you a superb excuse for hill-walking with a trout rod. They are: Loch Coire a'Mhuilinn (25/262550), best approached from Strathanmore, and Lochan na Croraig which may be reached by following the outlet stream up from near Carnoch. Further hill-loch adventure may be obtained south from Carnoch. Cross the River Meig to Inverchoran (25/261503) and climb through the wood on a good stalkers' path round the west shoulder of Cnoc Mall-lairig (440m). A 1.5 south-east, at 25/288489, you will find Loch Airigh Lochain on your right and, further up the hill to your left, Lochan Dubh nam Biast, both of which may provide you with breakfast. Flies: Soldier Palmer, March Brown, Kingfisher Butcher.

Permission & Charges Fishing is in the hands of the Loch Achonachie Angling Club. Tickets from: Urray Post Office, Marybank, Ross-shire. Tel: 01997 433201. A boat (with life jackets) and two rods fishing costs £16 until 4pm; evening session: £10 per boat (as above). Outboard hire, £8. Bank fishing costs £4 per day, £15 per week. The club offer a "rovers" ticket which includes fishing on Loch Meig and Loch Achonachie (see separate entries) as well as fishing on Loch Beannacharain; cost: £5 per rod per day, £20 per rod per week.

BEINN A'MHEADHOIN, Loch

Location & Access 25/240250. See Loch Affric entry.

Commentary Loch Beinn a'Mheadhoin, known locally as Loch Beneveian, is 5 miles east/west by up to half-a-mile wide and feeds the Beauly hydro-electric scheme. It is, nevertheless, a stunningly beautiful water. The Lower River Affric drains the loch through a tumultuous gorge into the River Glass (see OS Map 26) and is not fished.

Fish Brown trout which average 8oz.

Flies & Tactics Bank fishing is not allowed. The most productive boat-drifts are at the west end of the loch, close to where the stream enters from Loch Affric; the south-west shoreline; the small bays and promontories on the north-west shore, working east towards where the Abhainn Gleann nam Fiadh flows in from Tom a Choinich (1111m). Flies Try: Loch Ordie, March Brown, Alexandra.

Permission & Charges Contact: Peter Whitely, Glen Affric Hotel, Cannich, Inverness-shire. Tel: 01456 415214; Caledonian Hotel, Beauly, Ross-shire. Tel: 01463 01463 782278. Willie Armstrong, J Graham & Co, 37 Castle Street, Inverness. Tel: 01463 233178. Expect to pay in the order of £30 per day for a boat with two rods fishing.

BHARRANCH, Loch See Loch Coulin.
CADH AN EIDIDH, Loch See Loch Fionnaraich.

CALAVIE, Loch

Location & Access 25/050390. Loch Calavie lies at the end of an 8 mile long walk, east along a private estate track from Attadale (25/92438) on the A890 Strathcarron/Kyle of Lochalsh road.

Commentary Loch Calavie is one of a number of very remote lochs and lochans lying between Attadale in the west and Loch Monar (25/130405) (see separate entry) to the east. There is no easy way in to these waters and reaching them requires a considerable effort. An alternative means of access is by boat from the east end of Loch Monar to Pait Lodge (25/120401), a journey of some 5 miles followed by a hike along an estate path for another 4 miles. Consequently, these lochs are rarely fished. Loch Calavie drains north-east into Loch Monar via the Allt Loch Calavie, collecting together the waters of Lochan Gobhlach (25/084372) and its unnamed neighbour to the south, and Loch an Tachdaich (25/095380) and An Gead Loch (25/104387). A further series of lochs, south again, drain west into the River Ling (see separate entry) via the Allt an Loinfhiodha. The principal water is Loch Cruoshie (25/056364) which is fed by the Lub Chruinn burn. One mile south again from Loch Cruoshie is Loch na Maoile Buidhe (25/050345). Lochan Fuara (25/979387) is best approached from Achintee (25/940418) and lies to the south of the track, 3.5 miles east from Strathcarron.

Fish The last loch here, Loch Annie (25/000352), on the north slope of Faochaig (868m), is best approached from Killilan (25/947301) in the south. Hike 5 miles north up the line of the River Ling to the bothy at Coire-domhain (25/980344). Cross the bridge over the Allt Gleann a'Choire Dhomhain and continue steeply east up the waterfall to find the loch after a vigorous tramp of 30 minutes.

Flies & Tactics All shapes and sizes, including voracious pike in the lochs which drain into Loch Monar. The average weight of trout is in the order of 6oz/8oz. The most important requirement is to be thoroughly well prepared for all eventualities and a compass and map are essential. If you decide to approach via Loch Monar, by boat, remember that this can be a dangerous, wild loch. The connecting burns can provide sport after heavy rain. Lochan Gobhlach is very pretty and is perhaps the best place to begin. Flies: Black Pennell, Soldier Palmer, Dunkeld.

Permission & Charges Contact Tom Watson,

OS Map 25 Glen Carron

Attadale Estate, Strathcarron, Ross-shire. Tel: 01520 722308. Fishing is included in the cost of accommodation in self-catering cottages at £180/£325 per week. For details contact Susan Watson. Tel: 01520 722396.

CANNICH, River See Loch Mullardoch.
CARN MHARTUIN, Loch See Loch-Gowan.
CARRIE, Loch See Loch Mullardoch.

CARRON, River
Location & Access Source 25/125542 Outfall 25/935415. Access is from the A890 Achnasheen/Strathcarron road which borders the north bank of the stream.
Commentary The river runs through Glen Carron taking in the waters from Loch Sgamhain (25/100529) and Loch Dughaill (25/000475) and two principal feeder-streams, the River Lair, which enters Loch Dughaill near Achnashellach Lodge at 25/002479 and the Allt a'Chonais burn which enters the Carron at 25/048493. This is mountain country, graced by more than six Munros (mountains over 3,000ft in height), including Maolie Lunndaidh (1007m), Bidean an Eoin Deirg (1064m) and Sgurr a'Chaorachain (1053m).
Fish Salmon and sea-trout in the River Carron and the lochs, primarily brown trout in the burns although Allt a'Chonais can hold migratory fish as well depending upon water levels. Salmon and sea-trout numbers, particularly sea-trout, have declined drastically in recent years; probably due to the effect of lice infestation from factory-salmon farming in the vicinity. Smolt-rearing cages in the lochs do not improve the overall ambience of the fishing experience.
Flies & Tactics Tactics and flies The lochs on the River Carron used to be noted sea-trout fisheries but, sadly, are now but a poor shadow of their former glory. Some sea-trout are still taken and boat fishing brings the best results. The west end of Loch Sgamhain, near the islands, is the place to begin. On Loch Dughaill, concentrate along the south-west shore, in the shallow water round the two small islands. The river itself is entirely dependent upon heavy rain to produce of it best, but, given a good flood, salmon may enter the system from June onwards. The river is easily fished and there are some excellent holding pools where, in the right conditions, great sport may be had. Perhaps the most consistent sport with sea-trout is now to be found in the brackish, tidal water, at the estuary of the river, in Loch Carron itself. If water levels are unkind, there are a number of really first-class trout lochs in the hills, all of which will provide a memorable day out. Loch Croc na Mointeich (25/113512), 1.5 south from the main road in a corrie below Moruisg (928m), has wild trout of up to and over 3lb in weight. A step further southeast will bring you to little Loch Coireag nam Mang (25/120502) which is also worth a look. The lochans on Sgurr na Feartaig (863m) to the south of Loch Dughaill are very rarely visited but some contain arctic char and all will provide supper: Loch Sgurr na Feartaig (25/057460), Loch nan Gobhar (25/015453), Loch nan Caber (25/003460) and Loch an Laoigh (25/020415) which is a substantial water one mile north/south by 300yds wide. To the north of the A890 and Loch Sgamhain, on Carn Beag (550m), are two further trout lochs which will more than repay the effort involved in reaching them: Loch Meallan Mhic Iamhair (25/075544) and Lochan Sgeireach (25/094551). Start from the A890 at 25/088530 and follow the stalkers' track north with the forest on your left. At 25/075536, leave the track and climb steeply up the outlet burn to find the loch. Lochan Sgeireach is a mile east, round the north shoulder of Beinn na Feusaige (620m). Although these waters are remote, reaching them is eased by the presence of a series of stalkers' tracks. However, remember to pack a compass and map and be well shod and prepared for all kinds of weather along the way. Bank fishing only. Salmon flies: Willie Gunn, Garry Dog, General Practitioner, Black Doctor, Green Highlander, Shrimp Fly, Stoat's Tail. Dapping works well for sea-trout on the lochs. For sea-trout and brown trout, start with: Black Pennell, Soldier Palmer, Alexandra.
Permission & Charges Finlyson Hughes, 29 Barossa Place, Perth PH1 5EP. Tel: 01783 630926; Fax: 01783 639017. Sport is let in conjunction with Glencarron Lodge which overlooks the river. The lodge, which is self-catering, provides accommodation for up to 18 guests and costs from £2,000 per week depending upon the time of year booked.

CLAIR, Loch See Loch Coulin.
COIRE A'BHUIC, Loch See Loch-Gowan.
COIRE A'MHUILINN, Loch See Loch Beannacharain.
COIRE AN RUADH-STAIC, Loch See Loch Fionnaraich.

COIRE FIONNARAICH, Loch
Location & Access 25/974498. Approach from the A890 Achnashellach/Strathcarron road. Park near Coulags (25/962451) and follow the stalkers' path north up the east bank of the Fionn-a'bhainn (known locally as the Coulags River) to reach the loch after a three mile tramp.
Commentary There are, in addition to Loch Coire Fionnaraich, several other small, named and unnamed, waters in this magnificent wilderness which offer the chance of splendid fishing and splendid solitude. They are: Loch Coire an Ruadh-staic (25/921489) which is approached from the Coulags track at 25/949490. A subsidiary stalkers' path climbs steeply west between Meall nan Ceapairean (766m) and Maol Chean-Dearg (933m) and passes the north shore of the loch after a 2.5 mile slog. Two more, perfect, little lochs are approached from Tullich on the A896 road at 25/921422. A stalkers' path leads north round the east shoulder of Glass Bheinn (711m). Leave the track on the Bealach a'Ghlas-chnoic at 25/900449 and strike nort- east for one mile to reach Loch Cadh an Eididh (25/907461) and An Gorm-loch (25/901464).
Fish These lochs are rarely fished but they contain

Glen Carron — OS Map 25

brown trout which average 6oz. Loch Coire Fionnaraich has a few larger specimens but they are hard to tempt.

Flies & Tactics Although the Coulags stalkers' path is a right of way, check with the estate before setting out, particularly during the stalking season from late August onwards. June and July are the best months for trout fishing. All the lochs are easily covered from the shore and there is no need to wade. First cast: Black Zulu, March Brown, Dunkeld.

Permission & Charges John Fooks, Woodgate House, Beckley, Sussex TN31 6UH. Cost: £5 per rod per day. Christopher MacKenzie. Tel 01520 766266

COIRE, Loch See Loch Affric.
COIRE LOCHAN, Loch See Loch Mullardoch.

COIRE NA CAIME, Loch
Location & Access 25/922582. Park on the A896 Gairloch/Shieldaig road at 25/958569. Follow the stalkers' track north, climbing steeply up the west bank of the Allt a'Choire Duibh Mhoir between Liathach (1054m) to the west and and Beinn Eighe (972m) to the east. After four, hard miles, the track reaches Lochan a'Choire Duibh (25/930598) and then Loch Grobaig (25/922599) and tiny Lochan a'Chaorainn (25/908595). Loch Coire na Caime is a strenuous, additional, one-mile climb due south from Loch Grobaig, and the loch lies at an altitude of 550m below the dramatic crags of the north face of Liathach.
Commentary A serious nine mile round trip through some of the most stunning scenery in Scotland. Be prepared to use a compass and map.
Fish These small lochs contain lovely little trout which rise readily to the fly and fight much harder than their 4oz/6oz weight would suggest.
Flies & Tactics The temptation is just to sit and marvel at the surrounding scenery. However, make shift to catch your supper, from the shore, and to do so offer them: Ke-He, March Brown, Silver Butcher.
Permission & Charges See River Torridon entry. The estate do not charge for their hill-loch fishing.

COIREAG NAM MANG, Loch See River Carron.
COULAVIE, Loch See Loch Affric.

COULIN, Loch
Location & Access 25/015552. Approach from the A896 Kinlochewe/Shieldaig road. A private, estate, road leads south from the main road at 25/002581 along the east bank of Loch Clair (25/000570) to Coulin Lodge (25/003563).
Commentary Stunning scenery with magnificent views across Loch Clair and Loch Bharranch (25/979574) to Liathach (1054m) and Beinn Eighe (972m). Also, splendid hill loch fishing in a wide rage of remote waters which rarely see an artificial fly from one season to the next. These are, to the east of Coulin Lodge: Loch na Moine Moire (25/047560) and Loch an Fhiarlaid (25/051565), reached after a two mile hike along the stalkers' path from Torrancuilinn (25/024551). These lochs drain east into the River Bran and are joined by a narrow stream. They extend for one mile north/south across the moor and offer a full day's sport. To the north of Loch an Fhiarlaid, on Bidein Clann Raonaild (466m), are a further series of named and unnamed lochans, the principal waters being: Lochan nan Doirb (25/043576), Feith an Leothaid (25/042590) and Lochain Feith an Leothaid (25/044592).
Fish Salmon and sea-trout in Loch Clair, Loch Coulin and the A'Ghairbhe River, brown trout in the hill lochs. The River Coulin, which drains into Loch Coulin, holds some nice brown trout as well.
Flies & Tactics Tactics and flies The A'Ghairbhe River drains north into the Kinlochewe River and thence through Loch Maree to the River Ewe to the sea (see OS Map 19, Gairloch & Ullapool for details). Sport on the river is entirely dependent upon rain, but the lochs can hold good numbers of fish from June onwards. There are two boats on Loch Clair and fishing for six rods on the river. The hill lochs are fished from the shore and one of the most remote and challenging is tiny Lochan Gobhlach (25/981539), to the west of Coulin Lodge and reached only after an invigorating, steep, two mile climb via a stalkers' path over Coire an Leth-Uillt to a height of 580m. Flies for salmon and sea-trout include: Goat's Toe, Munro Killer, Shrimp Fly, Willie Gunn, Garry Dog, Hairy Mary. Dapping can also be effective. For brown trout, offer: Black Pennell, Soldier Palmer, Peter Ross.
Permission & Charges Finlyson Hughes, 29 Barossa Place, Perth. Tel: 01738 630926; Fax: 01738 639017. The lodge and fishing costs in the order of £2,000 per week, self-catering, for 12 guests.

COULIN, River See Loch Coulin.
CRANN, Loch See Loch a'Chroisg.
CROC NA MOINTEICH, Loch See River Carron.
CROE, River See OS Map 33.
CRUOSHIE, Loch See Loch Calavie.
DEARG BEAG, Lochan See Loch an Eion.
DEARG, Lochan See Loch an Eion.
DOMHAIN, Lochan See Loch an Eion.
DUBH NAM BIAST, Lochan See Loch Beannacharain.
DUBHA (Attadale), Lochan See Loch an Iasaich.
DUGHAILL, Loch See River Carron.
FEITH AN LEOTHAID, Loch See Loch Coulin.
FUAR, Loch See Loch an Iasaich.
FUARA, Lochan See Loch Calavie.
GAORSAIC, Loch See Loch a'Bhealaich.
GOBHLACH, Lochan See Loch Calavie.
GOBHLACH, Lochan See Loch Coulin.
GROBAIG, Loch See Loch Coire na Caime.
INNIS GHEAMHRAIDH, Loch See Loch Affric.
LAIR, River See River Carron.

LOCH-GOWAN, Loch
Location & Access 25/154565. Immediately adjacent to the east side of the A890 Achnasheen/Achnashellach road.
Commentary The loch lies on the headwaters of the River Bran (see OS Map 20) and is 1.5 miles long by up to 300yds wide at the south end. The loch is divid-

OS Map 25 — Glen Carron

ed into two sections, joined by a narrow stream at Inver (25/148561) where a bridge gives access to the east shore. There are two little lochs to the south of Loch-Gowan which offer perfect peace and solitude for the price of a 6 mile round trip: Loch Carn Mhartuin (25/179549) and Loch Coire a'Bhuic (25/165526). They are approached by following the track south from Inver for two miles to reach 25/169540 between Carn Mhartuin (538m) and the north east face of Carn Liath (857m). Loch Carn Mhartuin is half a mile to the east, Loch Coirc a'Bhuic approximately three-quarters of a mile to the west.
Fish Pike, perch, trout and ferox. Trout average 8oz.
Flies & Tactics Bank fishing only on Loch-Gowan and wading is dangerous. Hemmed in by the main road on one side and the railway line on the other, Loch-Gowan is a somewhat 'public' place to fish. Far better to head off to the hill lochs. Offer them: Ke-He, Black Pennell, Silver Butcher.
Permission & Charges Contact: Tommy Ross, Ledgowan, Achnasheen, Ross-shire. Tel: 01445 720209. Charges: £5 per rod per day.

LOCHAIN FEITH AN LEOTHAID, Loch See Loch Coulin.
LUB CHRUINN, Stream See Loch Calavie.
MEALL A'CHUAIL, Loch See Loch an Eion.
MEALLAN MHIC IAMHAIR, Lochan See River Carron.
MEIG, Upper River See Loch Beannacharain.
MHUILICH, Loch See Loch Monar.
MOIN A'CHRIATHAIR, Loch See Loch Coire Fionnaraich.

MONAR, Loch
Location & Access 25/130405. Loch Monar is approached from Struy (26/402404) on the A831 Lovat Bridge/Cannich road. Immediately before crossing the bridge over the River Farrar (see OS Map 26), a minor road leads west up Glen Strathfarrar and along the north shore of Loch Beannacharan (see OS Map 26) and Loch a' Mhuillidh (25/275380) (see separate entries) to arrive at the dam wall at 25/204394), 12 miles from Struy Bridge.
Commentary Loch Monar is a vast, hydro-loch, some 9 miles east/west by up to almost one mile wide. The surrounding scenery is magnificent and includes more than ten Munros, mountains over 3,00ft in height. A track borders the north shore of the loch for a distance of 5 miles but the south shore is trackless. There are a number of hill lochs to the north in the vicinity of Maoile Lunndaidh (1007m) and Bidean an Eoin Deirg (1046m). These are best accessed by boat from Loch Monar: Loch nam Breac Dearga (25/147458) and Loch a'Chlaidheimh (25/149466) are reached from 25/163424 where a stalkers' path leads north up the line of the Allt a'Choire Fhionnaraich towards the headwaters of the River Meig (see separate entry). Loch nam Breac Dearga lies to the west at an altitude of 640m and should be approached by a track which margins the outlet-burn from the loch at 25/158454 on the shore of Loch Monar. Loch a'Chlaidheimh is at 440m, also to the west of the track, reached from 25/159459. Loch Mhuilich (25/127430) is less distant and can be accessed from the shore of Loch Monar at 25/128414 via a good track which climbs north to reach the loch after a 30 minute hike. There are two further small waters to the south of Loch Monar which are less taxing to reach: Loch Mor (25/151352) and Loch Beag (25/147355), a step west from Loch Mor, which may be accessed by following the track up Glean Innis an Lochel, past the power station (25/183371) to a junction on the path at 25/151374. Hang a left and follow the track south, climbing steeply up into the corrie on the north face of Sgurr na Lapaich (1150m) to reach the lochs after about 40 minutes. Both lochs lie at an altitude of 650m and are utterly splendid.
Fish In Loch Monar, pike, perch, brown trout and huge ferox. In the surrounding hill lochs, brown trout which average 6oz/8oz.
Flies & Tactics Loch Monar is a dangerous, wild loch. When afloat always wear a life jacket and make sure that you have a thoroughly reliable outboard engine and reserve fuel. Fish the margins of the loch, where the bottom shelves into deeper water. The west end is perhaps the most productive area. The hill-lochs are all easily tackled from the shore and you should avoid wading. The north end of Loch Mhuilich, by the small island, is the perfect place for an away-from-it-all picnic. In the hills you must carry a compass and map and know how to use them. If in any doubt about the weather, don't set out. Flies: Black Zulu, March Brown, Silver Invicta.
Permission & Charges Contact: Peter Whitely, Glen Affric Hotel, Cannich, Inverness-shire. Tel: 01456 415214; Willie Armstrong, J Graham & Co, 37 Castle Street, Inverness. Tel: 01463 233178. Access may be restricted to the hill-lochs during the stalking season and you must seek appropriate advice before setting out. Expect to pay in the order of £25 per day for a boat with two rods fishing.

MOR, Loch
Location & Access See Loch Monar.

MULLARDOCH, Loch
Location & Access 25/160306. Approach from Cannich (26/338318). Immediately after crossing the River Cannich, before the Glen Affric Hotel, turn right on the minor road which parallels the stream. This leads, after eight miles, to the east end of the loch.
Commentary Loch Mullardoch is nearly 9 miles east/west by half-a-mile wide. The west section used to be a separate entity, Loch Lungard, but the two lochs were joined when the waters were impounded for a hydro-electric scheme in the 1950's. There are the remains of an old track along the middle of the north shore but, otherwise, the vast majority of this remote, wonderful loch is only accessible either by hoof or by boat. The hill-lochs to the north, Loch a'Choire Bhig (25/161332) and Loch Tuill Bhearnach (25/169343), and to the south, Loch a'Choire Dhomhain (25/139268) and Coire Lochan (25/124276) are amongst the most inaccessible in Scotland; indeed you require considerable experience

Glen Carron — OS Map 25

of hill-walking and compass-and-map work before considering an expedition in this direction. Just as inaccessible and just as wonderful are two small lochans between Carn Loch na Gobhlaig (715m) and Beinn a'Chairein (646m): Loch na Gobhlaig (25/263302) and Lochan na Cuidhe (25/292312). Much more accessible, however, are the lochs on the course of the River Cannich, Loch Sealbhanach 25/234316, Loch a'Bhana 25/225314 and the river itself. Loch Carrie (25/268334) is preserved by the owner.

Fish Some excellent brown trout which average 10oz and much larger specimens as well. The river can also hold excellent brown trout.

Flies & Tactics The margins and shallow water produce the best results, particularly at the west end of the loch. Make sure that you have a reliable outboard motor and a good reserve of fuel before setting off into the western sun because it is a long walk back. And remember that Loch Mullardoch can be as wild as the sea on a windy day, so also make sure that you have life jackets and take great care. There used to be a cottage at 25/140312 where the Allt Socrach burn enters on the north shore and this is a good bay for both fishing and a picnic. Flies: Ke-He, Greenwell's Glory, Silver Butcher.

Permission & Charges Contact: Peter Whitely, Glen Affric Hotel, Cannich, Inverness-shire. Tel: 01456 415214; Willie Armstrong, J Graham & Co, 37 Castle Street, Inverness. Tel: 01463 233178. Caledonian Hotel, Beauly, Ross-shire. Tel: 01463 782278. Access may be restricted to the hill lochs during the stalking season and you must seek appropriate advice before setting out. Expect to pay in the order of £30 per day for a boat with two rods fishing.

NA CAILLICH, Loch See Loch Affric.
NA CAILLICH, Loch See Loch an Iasaich.
NA CAIMAIG, Loch See Loch Affric.
NA CRAOIBHE-CAORAINN, Loch See Loch an Eion.
NA CRORAIG, Lochan See Loch Beannacharain.
NA CUIDHE, Lochan See Loch Mullardoch.
NA FEITHE-SEILICH, Loch See Loch an Iasaich.
NA FRIANACH, Loch See Abhainn Thrail.
NA GABHTACH, Loch See Loch Affric.
NA GOBHLAIG, Loch See Loch Mullardoch.
NA H-FIRIDH, Loch See Loch Affric.
NA MAOILE BHUIDHE, Loch See Loch Calavie.
NA MOINE MOIRE, Loch See Loch Coulin.
NA SROINE, Loch See Loch an Iasaich.
NAM BREAC DEARGA, Loch See Loch Monar.
NAM BREAC MORA, Loch See Loch an Iasaich.
NAM FORCA, Loch See Loch an Iasaich.
NAN CABER, Loch See River Carron.
NAN CREADHA, Loch See Loch an Iasaich.
NAN DOIRB, Lochan See Loch Coulin.
NAN GILLEAN, Loch See Loch an Iasaich.
NAN GOBHAR, Loch See River Carron.
NEIMHA, Lochan See Abhainn Thrail.
POLLAIN BUIDHE, Loch See Loch Affric.

PRIVATE WATERS All the rivers and lochs on the south-west quadrant of OS Map 25, including the River ELCHAIG and the River LING, Inverinate Forest, Killilan Forest and West Benula Forest, unless otherwise noted in the text, are private. They are in the ownership of an Arab Emirate Prince who does not allow public access for fishing.
TOLL A'MHUIC, Loch (25/230421); FHUAR-THUILL MHOIR, Lochan (25/240440); OIRE NA SGUILE, Loch (25/262439); AN GORM, Loch (25/225449); AN TUILL CHREAGAICH, Loch (25/285444); AM FIAR. Loch (25/247467); NA CAOIDHE, Loch (25/225465); TOLL LOCHAIN, Loch (25/231488); NA FRIANICH, Loch (25/262464). These lochs are generally preserved by the owner but occasional access is sometimes possible. For further information contact Paul Smith, Achlorachan House, Strathconon, Ross-shire. Tel: 01997 477207.

SALACH A'GHIUBHAIS, Loch See Loch Affric.
SEALBHANACH, Loch See Loch Mullardoch.
SGAMHAIN, Loch See River Carron.
SGEIREACH, Lochan See River Carron.
SGEIREACH, Lochan (Attadale) See Loch an Iasaich.
SGURR NA FEARTAIG, Loch See River Carron.
THRAIL, River See Abhainn Thrail.
THUILL EASAICH, Loch See Loch a'Bhealaich.

TORRIDON, River
Location & Access Source 25/959565 Outfall 24/898553. The river lies immediately adjacent to the A896 Gairloch/Shieldaig road.
Commentary This attractive spate stream is very easily accessible. The vast bulk of Liathach (1054m) towers to the north whilst Beinn Liath Mhor (925m) dominates the southern horizon. The river rises from Lochan an Iasgair (25/959565) and flows due west for four miles to reach the sea in Loch Torridon.
Fish Salmon, from July onwards, although not in any great numbers. A good season might produce 20/30 fish. Sea-trout are almost entirely absent now, probably destroyed by sea-lice infestation from near-by factory-salmon farms.
Flies & Tactics There are a few fine holding-pools but success depends entirely upon good water levels: no water, no fish. A single-handed rod will cover most eventualities. Loch an Iasgair used to be famous for large sea-trout. Sadly, not any more, although the loch still produces the occasional sea-trout of over 4lb. Boat fishing brings the best results on Loch an Iasgair. Flies: On the river: Willie Gunn, Garry Dog, Green Highlander, General Practitioner, Goat's Toe, Shrimp Fly. On the loch: Black Pennell, Soldier Palmer, Peter Ross.
Permission & Charges For information contact: Estate Office, Torridon House, Torridon, Wester Ross. Tel: 01445 791227. Cost: £15 per rod per day plus £10 per day for the boat on Loch an Iasgair.

TUILL BHEARNACH, Loch See Loch Mullardoch.
UAINE, Lochan See Abhainn Thrail.

Inverness

A'BHEALAICH (North), Loch See Loch an Eilein.
A'BHEALAICH (South), Loch See Loch an Eilein.
A'CHAIRN DUIBH, Loch See Loch an Eilein.
A'CHLACHAIN, Loch See Loch Duntelchaig.
A'CHLARAIN, Loch See Loch Eich Bhain.
A'CHOIRE LEITH, Loch See Loch an Eilein.
A'CHOIRE, Loch See Loch Ruthven.
A'CHOIRE RIDBHAICH (North), Loch See Loch Gruamach.
A'CHOIRE RIDBHAICH (South), Loch See Loch Gruamach.
A'CHRATHAICH, Loch See Loch ma Stac.
A'MHADAIDH, Loch See Orrin Reservoir.
A'MHUILINN, Loch See Loch Aradaidh.
A'MHUILINN (North), Loch See Loch ma Stac.
A'MHUILINN (South), Loch See Loch ma Stac.
A'PHUILL DHUIBH, Loch See Loch an Eilein.
ABBAR, Water See River Ness.

ACHILTY, Loch
Location & Access 26/434567. Approach from the A832 Contin/Gairloch road, turning left at 26/450567 onto the minor road which reaches the loch after one mile.
Commentary Loch Achilty is a very pretty loch, circular, approximately 100 acres in extent and 120 feet deep. It is surrounded by fine woodlands and there are resident ospreys. These graceful birds greatly enhance the pleasure of fishing here. There is also resident otter's.
Fish The loch is stocked every week with rainbow trout and brown trout of up to 7lb in weight. There is also a stock of pike and a few wild brown trout in the depths. There is also Arctic char and Orrin Blues.
Flies & Tactics There are 8 boats available for hire with four electric outboard motors. The shallow margins of the loch, particularly along the south and north shoreline, generally produce results. Traditional patterns of fly, such as Ke-He, March Brown, Soldier Palmer work well, as do reservoir lures on sinking lines. On calm evenings, dry fly can also bring results. Sedges as well as Invicta and Silver Butcher.
Permission & Charges Contact: Mark Butcher, Eilean View, Lochachilty, Contin, Ross-shire. Tel: 01997 421245 or 01997 421402. A four-hour session, including boat costs £10 per rod. Electric engines are available at £1.25 per hour. There is a bag limit of 2 fish per rod. Thereafter, anglers must fish with barbless hooks on a catch and release basis.

ACHONACHIE, Loch
Location & Access 26/444548. Approach from Marybank (26/480538) on the A832 Muir of Ord/Gairloch road. Follow the minor road west up the River Conon to reach the loch after two miles.
Commentary The loch is over one mile long by up to 400 yards wide, deep, dour, and featureless. It lies on the River Conon and is impounded as part of the Conon hydro-electric scheme.
Fish Brown trout which average 1lb, a few huge pike, and, from time to time, salmon.
Flies & Tactics Boat fishing brings the best results, particularly at the west end where the river enters, and along the north shore, in the shallows, by Torrachilty Forest. Flies to try: Black Pennell, Soldier Palmer, Silver Butcher.
Permission & Charges Fishing is in the hands of the Loch Achonachie Angling Club. Tickets from: The Post Office, Contin, Easter Ross. Tel: 01997 421351. A boat (with life jackets) and two rods fishing costs £12 per session until 4pm; evening session: £10 per boat (as above). The club offer a "rover" ticket which includes fishing on Loch Meig and Loch Beannacharain (see separate entries) as well as fishing on Loch Achonachie; cost: £5 per rod per day, £20 per rod per week.

AN ALLTAIN BHEITHE, Loch See Loch an Eilein.
AN DAIMH GHLAIS, Loch See Loch Gruamach.
AN DUBH-LOCHAN, Loch See Loch Ruthven.
AN DUBHAIR, Loch See Loch ma Stac.

AN EILEIN, Loch
Location & Access 26/305583. Park near the Post Office on the minor road by the bank of the River Meig at Milltown (26/307554). A track leads north through the wood to reach the loch after a distance of 2 miles.
Commentary Loch an Eilein is the first water in a series of 11 named and unnamed lochs and lochans lying on Creag Loch nan Dearcag (536m) to the north of Loch Meig (see separate entry). They provide the focus for a splendid day out in the hills which will take you on an 8-mile journey through wonderful scenery amidst outstanding wildlife. After fishing Loch an Eilein, have a cast in Loch Cul (26/306585), immediately to the north, then strike north east up the glen for 20 minutes to reach Loch Bhad Ghaineamhaich (26/325591) and its neighbour, Loch an Alltain Bheithe (26/319593). A step east brings you to Braigh Lochan (26/333591) from where you may consider climbing steeply up the burn to locate tiny Loch a'Bhealaich (North) (26/349594) which lies on the north shoulder of Sgurr Marcasaidh (580m) at an altitude of 440m. Descend to explore Loch a'Chairn Duibh (26/340586). South now, heading for the summit of Creag Loch nan Dearcag, to fish Loch nan Dearcag (26/337571) and then over the top to Loch a'Bhealaich (South) (26/330569). Follow the ridge north west for half a mile to Loch a'Choire Leith (26/322578) and return to the start point by hiking south-west down the hill via little Loch a'Phuill Dhuibh (26/309569).
Fish Mostly breakfast-sized brown trout, but Loch an Eilein and Loch an Alltain Bheithe hold larger fish of over 1lb in weight.
Flies & Tactics Allow a full day for this expedition and pack a compass and map in case of bad weather. Bank fishing all the way and the north shore of Loch an Alltain Bheithe, the largest water and covering an area of approximately 60 acres, is always kind. No need to wade, let the fish come to you. Best fishing time, June

Inverness OS Map 26

and July. Show them: Ke-He, Woodcock & Hare-lug, Alexandra.
Permission & Charges Contact Paul Smith, Achlorachan House, Strathconon, Ross-shire. Tel: 01997 477207. Expect to pay £5 per rod per day. Access may be restricted during the stalking season, from August onwards.

AN EOIN RUADHA, Loch See Loch Duntelchaig.

AN FHEOIR, Loch See Loch Aradaidh.
AN GORM, Loch See Orrin Reservoir.
AN SPARDAIN, Loch See Loch Gruamach.
AN UILLT-GHIUBHAIS, Loch See Loch Aradaidh.

ARADAIDH, Loch
Location & Access 26/379520. Approach from north of Loch Achonachie at 26/410555 on the banks of the River Conon. A track behind the school and post office climbs south through the forest round the east shoulder of Carn Sgolbaidh (409m) and reaches the loch after 3 miles.
Commentary This is a long day out in the hills, fishing a series of attractive small lochs during which you will cover distance of 7 miles. Begin by having a cast on the two lochs adjacent to the track: Loch an Fheoir (26/395) and Loch Sgolbaidh (26/392533). Walk on to reach Loch Aradaidh after a further 20 minutes. Walk north now, along the east slope of Carn na Claiche Moire (590m), climbing steadily to locate little Loch Carn na Cloiche Moire (26/380535), then north west for 10 minutes to Loch na Larach Blaire (26/372539) which is just big enough for a couple of exploratory casts. Descend following the outlet burn from Loch na Larach Blaire to Loch an Uillt-ghiubhais (26/378547) and Loch a'Mhuilinn (26/382549). End the day by walking east, skirting the south edge of the forest, to regain the outward path.
Fish Small brown trout with the possibility of a few fish of up to 1lb in weight.
Flies & Tactics Enjoy this day out as much for the magnificent scenery as for the fishing. Few bother to tramp this way and you will be assured of peace and quiet and breakfast for the following morning. Try: Blue Zulu, March Brown, Peter Ross.
Permission & Charges Contact: Mike Watt, Stalkers' Cottage, Little Scatwell, by Strathpeffer, Ross-shire. Tel: 01997 466221. Access may be restricted during the stalking season.

ASHIE, Loch See Loch Duntelchaig.

ASLAICH, Loch See Loch ma Stac.
BEAG, Loch See Orrin Reservoir.

BEAULY, River
Location & Access Source 26/408399 Outfall 26/555480. Accessible from the A831 Lovat Bridge/Cannich road and via estate roads bordering the river.
Commentary One of Scotland's finest salmon streams flowing through magnificent countryside. The catchment area is vast, extending almost to the west coast of Scotland. The river is divided into three sections and the principal beats are on the Lower Beauly; three miles of double-bank fly-fishing from below the Kilmorack dam downstream to Lovat Bridge. The Upper River is divided into two beats which are mostly fished from the bank. The river is in single ownership and in recent years the owners have carried out extensive improvements making the River Beauly one of the best-managed rivers in Scotland. The river is incorporated into the Beauly Hydro-electric scheme and, as such, is generally in excellent fishable condition regardless of the vagaries of the weather.
Fish The total annual catch is in the order of 1200 fish. The river also has good runs of sea-trout which average 2lb.
Flies & Tactics Each beat has an experienced gillie and his advice is an invaluable part of the Beauly fishing experience. There are comfortable lunch huts and access to all the pools is well-organised and managed. Luxurious self-catering accommodation is also available. On the Upper River there are 12 pools, including Junction Pool, where the River Glass and the River Farrar meet to form the Beauly, Jetties Pool, Boat Pool, Alder's Run, Green Gates, Green Patch and Stalkers. The most famous pool on the Lower River is probably Cruives but Back of the Castle is undoubtedly the most scenic. Some deep wading is required on the Lower River but boats are also available to help reach the more distant lies. The top flies during 1995 were: Shrimp Fly, Sheila, Stoat's Tail, Silver Stoat, Jamie's Fancy, Munro Killer, Greg's Glory. Green Braham, Martin's Fancy, Willie Gunn.
Permission & Charges Much of the river is syndicated/time shared but from time to time lets may be available. Cost per week, depending upon the time of year: Upper River (3 rods) from £400 to £1900; Middle River (3 rods) £700 to £1200; Lower River (5 rods) from £650 to £3,400. Priority will be given to those who take a complete beat or rent accommodation with the fishing. Prices shown are an average and may fluctuate significantly during the season. Contact: William Midwood, The River Beauly Fishing Company, Broomy Bank, Hampton Heath, Malpas, Cheshire. SY14 8LT. Tel: 01948 820393; Fax: 01948 820264. The tidal reaches of the river can also provide excellent sport and may be fished on a day-ticket basis. The beat extends from below Lovat Bridge on the A892 Inverness/Beauly road downstream to Wester Lovat (26/54463) and has some good pools: Below the Bridge, Teawig Pool and Malloch Pool. Recent in-river work has greatly enhanced the flow of water and improved the fishing. From Wester Lovat the fishing is restricted to spinning only. Contact: Messrs Morison, Ironmongers, West End, Beauly, Inverness-shire. Tel: 01463 782213. Cost: £10 per rod per day on the Lovat Bridge/Wester Lovat beat, £3.50 per rod per day for spinning on the estuary stretch. Fishing on Thursday and Saturday is reserved for members of the Beauly Angling Club.

BHAD GHAINEAMHAICH, Loch See Loch an Eilein.

BLACK WATER, River See River Conon.
BRAIGH LOCHAN, Loch See Loch an Eilein.
BRAN, River See River Conon.

OS Map 26 — Inverness

BUNAEHTON, Loch See Loch Duntelchaig.
CARN NA CLOICHE MOIRE, Loch See Loch Aradaidh.
CEOTHLAIS, Loch See Loch Duntelchaig.
COIRE NA RAINICH, Loch See Loch ma Stac.

CONON, River
Location & Access Source 26/355556. Outfall 26/555575. Access to the river is by public roads adjacent to the stream for most of its length.
Commentary The Conon is fed by four principal tributaries: the rivers Orrin, Black Water, Bran and Meig. The system was impounded during the 1950s by 9 dams feeding 6 hydro-electric power generating stations. The principal fishing is on the main river, although the Black Water is also a noted salmon steam. The other streams are now of limited salmon-fishing significance, although they can produce excellent results with brown trout. Dingwall Angling Club fish 2 miles of double bank up to the above the road bridge across the old A9 Inverness/Wick road. The three lower beats, Upper, Middle and Lower Brahan, are next and they are the most productive beats on the river. Above Brahan are the Fairburn and Coul Beats, extending to Torr Achilty Dam below Loch Achonachie (26/440548) (see separate entry). Above Loch Achonachie, upstream past Scatwell to the outfall from Loch Meig (26/360358) (see separate entry), the river is in the hands of the Loch Achonachie Angling Club which also has the fishing on Loch Meig. The Black Water has three owners: the lower beat is private, Lady Eliza Leslie Melville has the middle beat, which is considered to be the finest, and the Loch Achonachie Angling Club has the section of the stream above Rogie Falls (26/445584) up to Loch na Croic (26/432593) which is used for salmon-rearing purposes and is not fished.
Fish The system can produce upwards of 1,500 salmon and grilse each season. Sea-trout are mostly taken from the Dingwall Angling Club water but catches have drastically declined in recent years.
Flies & Tactics The river is fished either from the bank or from a boat and deep wading is required to cover some of the salmon lies. Fish enter the system in increasing numbers from March onwards. June and July can give outstanding sport and most fish are taken in July. Fishing above Tor Achilty Dam is best in Sept. Salmon average 8lb/9lb in weight but fish of up to and over 20lb are not uncommon. Details of the beats are given to visiting anglers prior to fishing, and the non-club waters have resident gillies to guide your efforts. Flies: Munro Killer, Willie Gunn, Stoat's Tail, Ally's Shrimp, Red Brahan, Black Brahan, Green Brahan, Waddingtons. Spinning is not allowed after 1 May.
Permission & Charges Fairburn Estates, (R Stirling), Tower of Fairburn, Urray, Muir of Ord, Ross-shire. Tel: 01997 433273; Fax: 01997433274. Coul House Hotel, Contin, by Strathpeffer, Ross-shire. Tel: 01997 421487; Fax: 01997 421945. Dingwall District Angling Club, The Sports & Model Shop, Tulloch Street, Dingwall, Ross-shire. Tel: 01349 862346. Loch Achonachie Angling Club, The Post Office, Contin, Ross-shire. Tel:01997 421351. Lady Eliza Leslie Melville, Lochluichart Lodge, by Garve, Ross-shire. Tel: 01997 414242. Prices range from £10 per rod per day on the club waters to up to £75 per day on the estate beats, depending upon the time of year. Advance booking is essential.

CROSS REFERENCES For details of the following lochs see OS Map 35: MHOR, Loch (26/555215); CONAGLEANN, Loch (26/587212); AN ORDAIN, Loch (26/554240); A'BHODAICH, Loch (26/552245); FARIGAIG, River (26/560259); NA CRAOIBHE-BEITHE, Loch (26/544235); DUBH (Ballaggan), Lochan (26/530246); RUAIRIDH, Loch (26/530214).

CUL, Loch See Loch an Eilein.
CULBOKIE, Loch 26/609589. Culbokie Loch lies in the north of the Black Isle. It contains pike and perch only.
DOCHFOUR, Loch See River Ness.
DROMA, Loch See Loch Eich Bhain.
DUBH-LOCHAN, Loch See Loch Ruthven.

DUNTELCHAIG, Loch
Location & Access 26/620315. Approach from the A862 Inverness/Fort Augustus road. The north end of Loch Duntelchaig is reached via a minor road which leaves the A862 at 26/608368. The south end is accessed from the A862 at Achnabat (26/599300).
Commentary There are a number of additional lochs in the vicinity of Loch Duntelchaig which also offer sport: Loch a'Chlachain (26/653321), immediately to the north east of Loch Duntelchaig, Loch nam Geadas (26/600307) which is in fact joined to Loch Duntelchaig, Loch Ashie (26/630350), Loch Bunaehton (26/676350), Lochan na Curra (26/605323), Loch an Eoin Ruadha (26/610321) and Loch Ceothlais (26/590289) which is adjacent to the A862 half a mile south from Loch Duntelchaig. Loch Duntelchaig is the largest water, 3 miles north/south by up to 1 mile wide across the north end. The loch is the Inverness water supply source and it is 60m deep.
Fish Brown trout and voracious pike. Trout average 8oz/10oz but there are much larger fish as well.
Flies & Tactics Bank fishing only and the water in these lochs is very clear. Do not wade. Fish may be taken from all round the shoreline of Loch Duntelchaig but the north end, which is relatively shallow, is the best place to begin. The east shore of Loch Ashie has a number of little bays and promontories which should be carefully examined. Lochan na Curra has a large stock of pike whilst Loch Ceothlais has a reputation for holding some specimen trout which are almost impossible to catch. Small flies are best, size 12/16 dressings. Offer: Black Pennell, March Brown, Silver Butcher.
Permission & Charges J Graham & Co, 37-39 Castle Street, Inverness IV2 3EA. Tel: 01463 233178; Fax: 01463 710287. Expect to pay £5 per rod per day.

ENRICK, River See Loch Meiklie.

FARRAR, River See River Glass.

FEURACH, Loch See Loch Gruamach.

GAOIREACH, Loch See Loch na Beinne Moire.

Inverness — **OS Map 26**

GLASS, River
Location & Access Source 26/310285 Outfall 26/408399. Access is from the A831 Lovat Bridge/Cannich road and associated side roads and the private road up Glen Strathfarrar.
Commentary The rivers Glass and Farrar merge near the village of Struy to form the River Beauly. The Culligran and Struy Estates have the fishing rights over most of the Farrar and the bottom section of the Glass. The Glen Affric Hotel has access to the upper section of the Glass. The middle section of the Glass mainly belongs to the River Glass Syndicate. The whole system, including the River Beauly, was incorporated into a hydro-electric generating scheme during the early 1950s and this provides the benefit of a constant flow of water. During dry summer months when other rivers are unfishable these waters are still capable of giving good sport.
Fish Salmon average 7lb 8oz in weight, grilse 5lb 8oz. Approximately 50 to 80 fish are taken each season from each river. The rivers also contain good brown trout.
Flies & Tactics Access to the river is well-maintained and most salmon lies can be covered wearing thigh waders. Fishing is by fly only and the Culligran Estate issue a map of the beats with the fishing permit. The Estate also offers first-class self-catering accommodation. The first salmon are usually taken in late June/early July and the most productive months are September and October. Strictly fly only, and the most successful patterns include: Shrimp Fly, Willie Gunn, Munro Killer, Stoat's Tail, Hairy Mary.
Permission & Charges Contact: Juliet & Frank Spencer-Nairn, Culligran Cottages, Struy, Nr Beauly, Inverness-shire. Tel: 01463 761285. Glen Affric Hotel, Cannich, Inverness-shire. Tel: 01456 415214. Cost: from £15 to £45 per rod per day, depending upon the time of year. Trout fishing costs £10 per rod per day all season. River Glass Syndicate: Tel 01463 761252.

GRUAMACH, Loch
Location & Access See Loch an Eilein entry. From Milltown, cross the River Meig and follow the stalkers' track south past Dalbreac Lodge to gain the hill. The track climbs steeply round the east shoulder of Creag Ghaineamach (580m) to access a group of lochs lying between Creag Ghaineamach to the north, Meall a'Bhogair Mor (666m) to the east and Carn na Coinnich (673m) to the south. Loch Gruamach lies to the west of the track, after two miles, adjacent to Loch Feurach (26/319520), Loch an Daimh Ghlais (26/317521), Loch a'Choire Ridbhaich (North) (26/316526), and to the east of the track, Loch na Cuillich (26/338519).
Commentary A visit to these lochs, fishing them all, is a full day expedition and a round trip of some 7 miles. There are three more lochs, further south from the Carn na Coinnich, and these also are splendid fun to fish. However, they should be treated as a separate entity because they will involve you in a taxing 11 mile day over rough ground. To reach them, walk south on the stalkers' path to 26/330500, overlooking Orrin Reservoir (see separate entry), then strike south west for half a mile to find Loch an Spardain (26/322496). After fishing Loch an Spardain, return east, crossing the track, and walk on for half a mile to locate Loch a'Choire Ridbhaich (South) (26/345502). Another mile further east, across the Allt Loch na Caillich burn, will bring you to Loch nan Clachan Dubha (26/358511). The shortest route home from Loch nan Clachan Dubha is by heading north west up the glen, back to Loch na Cuillich and Meall a'Bhogair Mor, to regain the stalkers' path back to Milltown.
Fish The weight of your catch will not over-burden you during this adventure.
Flies & Tactics This is an expedition for the serious hill loch angler. These lochs are rarely fished, because of the long walk required to reach them, and they hardly see an artificial fly from one season to the next. The lochs are easily covered from the shore and there is no need to wade. The best time to go is during June and July when the lochs have, relatively speaking, warmed up after winter. Flies: Black Zulu, Greenwell's Glory, Silver Invicta.
Permission & Charges See Loch an Eilein entry and remember that access will be restricted during the stalking season, from August onwards.

KINELLAN, Loch 26/470576. Loch Kinellan lies to the north of Strathpeffer, close to Loch na Crann (26/461583) and An Dubh-lochan (26/461585). They are preserved by their owners and not available to the public.

LIATH (East), Loch See Loch ma Stac.
LIATH (South), Loch See Loch ma Stac.

MA STAC, Loch
Location & Access 26/340215. Approach via the hill track leading north from the A887 Invermoriston/Loch Cluanie road at Bhlaraidh (34/380165) on the north bank of the River Moriston (see entry on OS Map 34). The distance from the main road is approximately 4 miles but the track may be negotiated with care using a high wheel-base vehicle.
Commentary This is the best loch in the area and one of a series of wild trout lochs centred around Meall a'Chrathaich (678m) above the village of Invermoriston. The others are: Loch a'Chrathaich (26/365215), Lochan Ruighe Dhuibh (26/381208), Loch an Dubhair (26/390201), Loch na Feannaig (26/396202), Loch Liath (South)(26/397210), Loch Coire na Rainich (26/400216), Loch nam Brathain (26/391219), Loch nam Meur (South) (26/391230), Loch a'Mhuilinn (South) (26/362230) and its unnamed lochans to the north, Loch na Leirisdein (26/370230), Loch Liath (East) (26/409221), Loch Aslaich (26/409236), Loch nam Meur (North) (26/391250), Loch a'Mhuilinn (North) (26/381249), Loch nan Eun (26/310210).
Fish Loch ma Stac holds fish of up to and over 3lb in weight. The other lochs contain more modest specimens, ranging from 6oz up to a few fish of over 1lb.
Flies & Tactics These lochs and lochans are scattered over an area of some 12 square miles. Once away from Loch Stac and Loch a'Chrathaich, both of which are approximately 1 mile north/south by up to 400 yds

OS Map 26 — Inverness

wide, you are on your own and the going is tough. A compass and map is essential to find your way around. Bank fishing only. On Loch ma Stac explore the south west shore, on Loch a'Chrathaich, concentrate in the vicinity of the islands at the south end and the bay half way up the west shore. The north east corner of Loch nam Meur (South), by the tiny islands, is a perfect place for lunch. Try: Ke-He, Loch Ordie, Peter Ross.

Permission & Charges Glenmoriston Lodge Estate, Invermoriston, Inverness-shire. Tel: 01320 351300; Fax: 01329 351301. Cost: £5 per rod per day. Boat for two rods: £20 per day. The estate also has a number of good self-catering properties as well as fishing on the River Moriston and Loch Dundreggan (see entries on OS Map 34).

MEIG, Loch

Location & Access 26/360558. Loch Meig lies three miles to the west of Loch Achonachie (see Loch Achonachie entry).

Commentary This is a long, narrow, hydro-electric loch lying on the River Conon and impounded by Curin Dam at the east end. Loch Meig is 2 miles east/west by 350yds wide and largely surrounded by forestry plantations.

Fish Brown trout which average 1lb in weight and some fish of up to and over 3lb.

Flies & Tactics Boat fishing only. The west end is the most productive fishing area. Concentrate your efforts in the shallow water, near the margins. Work the south shore, east to the bay where the feeder burn enters from Carn na Claiche Moire (590m). Offer: Black Zulu, Greenwell's Glory, Kingfisher Butcher.

Permission & Charges See Loch Achonachie entry.

MEIG, River See River Conon.
NA BEINNE BIGE, Loch See Loch na Beinne Moire.

NA BEINNE MOIRE, Loch

Location & Access 26/324263. Approach from Tomich (26/306272) via a private estate road which is best accessed by 4x4 vehicles. The estate will provide transport if required.

Commentary Loch na Beinne Moire is the central loch of the Tomich Fishings, the other waters being Loch nam Freumh (26/329269), known locally as the "Root Loch", and Loch Gaoireach (26/325272) which is to the north of Loch nam Freumh. South from Loch na Beinne Moire is Loch na Greidil (Loch Gretal) (26/319260), Loch na Luch (26/330256), Loch na Beinne Bige (26/328252), Loch nam Fiodhag (26/320236) and its unnamed neighbour at 26/319235, and, on the north shoulder of Leac nam Buidheag (549m), Lochan na Craoibhe (26/333235). There is also trout fishing on the Tomich Burn, close to the village, which drains east into the River Glass (see separate entry). The Tomich lochs are amongst the best in the area, cared for by Kyle Laidlay, one of Scotland's great fishing personalities.

Fish Just about everything, from 6oz trout up to specimen fish of over 7lb. Loch Beinne Bige is stocked with rainbow trout for beginners.

Flies & Tactics You will be pampered here and have the services of a gillie, not only to take you up the hill either by car or argo-cat, but also to direct your fishing efforts. Loch Greidil, approximately 7 acres in extent, is one of Scotland's most exciting trout lochs where a dry fly fished during the mayfly hatch in June is a magical and highly rewarding experience. Other patterns: Loch Ordie, Soldier Palmer, Dunkeld.

Permission & Charges A boat and two rods for a week, including 4 days gillie service, during June, the peak period, costs £262. August and September can be just as good and costs £80 per week with 1 day's gillie service. Details: Kyle Laidlay, Tomich, Strathglass, by Beauly, Inverness-shire IV4 7LY. Tel: 01456 415352. Early booking is essential. Excellent hotel and self-catering accommodation is available from Tomich Holidays (Tel: 01456 415332; Fax: 01456 415499).

NA CRANN, Loch See Loch Kinellan.
NA CRAOIBHE, Lochan See Loch Beinne Moire.
NA CROIC, Loch See River Conon.
NA CUILLICH, Loch See Loch Gruamach.
NA CURRA, Lochan See Loch Duntelchaig.
NA FEANNAIG, Loch See Loch ma Stac.
NA GREIDIL, Loch See Loch na Beinne Moire.
NA LARACH BLAIRE, Loch See Loch Aradaidh.
NA LEIRISDEIN, Loch See Loch ma Stac.
NA LUCH, Loch See Loch na Beinne Moire.
NAIRN (Upper), River Source 26/650200. Outfall 27/889571. The Upper River Nairn is preserved by the owners. See entry on OS Map 27 for details of access to the lower river, downstream from the A9 Perth/Inverness road to the sea at Nairn.
NAM BRATHAIN, Loch See Loch ma Stac.
NAM FIODHAG, Loch See Loch na Beinne Moire.
NAM FREUMH, Loch See Loch na Beinne Moire.
NAM GEADAS, Loch See Loch Duntelchaig.
NAM MEUR (North), Loch See Loch ma Stac.
NAM MEUR (South), Loch See Loch ma Stac.
NAN CLACHAN DUBHA, Loch See Loch Gruamach.
NAN CUILCEAN, Loch See Loch Eich Bhain.
NAN DEARCAG, Loch See Loch an Eilein.
NAN EILID, Loch See Loch Eich Bhain.
NAN EUN, Loch See Loch ma Stac.

NESS, Loch (North)

Location & Access 26/570320. The A82 Inverness/Fort Augustus road borders the north bank of the loch and the B852 Dores/Foyers road borders the south bank.

Commentary The northern part of the loch extends south from Loch Dochfour (see separate entry), through the narrows at Lochend down to Foyers (26/495210), a distance of 15 miles. Loch Ness is one and a half miles wide from Urquhart Bay (26/528295) in the west to Whitefield (26/555290) in the east and drops to a depth of over 750ft, the deepest point being just south from Urquhart Castle (26/530286). This is perhaps the best known loch in the world because of its reputation for being home to "monsters" and the loch is a major tourist attraction and always busy, both ashore and afloat. Nevertheless, and particularly in regard to the east shoreline, it is generally easy to

253

Inverness — OS Map 26

escape the madding crowd and find peace and seclusion.

Fish Salmon, sea-trout, brown trout, ferox, Arctic charr. Approximately 500 salmon are taken each season. The largest fish in recent years was a salmon of 35lb, caught by David Livingston. A brown trout of 12lb was caught off Foyers in 1995.

Flies & Tactics Unless you know the loch it is essential that you seek the services of an experienced gillie; not only to guide you to where the fish lie, but, and as important, to keep you safe on this vast expanse of water. Loch Ness can often be as rough and wild as the sea and great care is required when afloat. The majority of the fish caught are taken from the boat, trolling, close to the shore: in Loch Dochfour, at Aldourie (26/598370), Dores (26/590350), Inverfairgaig (26/519240), and Urquhart Bay. Dapping also brings results. However, bank fly-fishing for wild brown trout can be great fun and fish may be taken from almost any point along the shore. The loch has a run of spring salmon but catching them can be cold, savage, entertainment. Fish are frequently taken on opening day, 15th January, and these spring fish are often very large; salmon of over 20lb are common. After May, grilse and sea-trout enter the loch and the migratory fish are spread more evenly throughout the system. Offer salmon: Devons, Toby, Lukki, Rapala. Brown trout will take: Ke-He, March Brown, Silver Butcher.

Permission & Charges Jack Meredith, Highland Sports Fishing Ltd, Clunebeg House, Drumnadrochit, Inverness-shire. Tel: 01456 450387/450854. Cost: from £4 to £6 per hour per boat with gillie. Glenmoriston Lodge Estate, Invermoriston, Inverness-shire. Tel: 01320 351300 offer boats with outboard engine and gillie at approximately £70 per day for two rods. J Graham & Co, 37 Castle Street, Inverness. Tel: 01463 233178, Fax: 01463 710287 will also be able to arrange boat hire and the services of an experienced gillie.

NESS, River
Location & Access Source 26/603380. Outfall 26/663470. Public roads border both banks of the river.

Commentary One of the most productive salmon streams in the north, easily accessible throughout its 6 mile course from Loch Ness to the Moray Firth at Inverness. The top section is known as Loch Dochfour (26/605388) and is available for trout fishing from the north bank only. Abbar Water (26/600381), between the A82 Inverness/Fort Augustus road and the outflow of the river from Loch Ness, is heavily weeded and unfishable.

Fish Approximately 600/700 salmon are taken most seasons and some 200 sea-trout. Spring salmon average 15lb, summer and autumn fish, 12lb. Salmon of over 30lb are not uncommon. There are some excellent brown trout in Loch Dochfour but they are hard to catch. Average weight, 12oz/1lb.

Flies & Tactics This is a big river and serious wading is required to properly cover the lies. Boats are also used. A 15ft/16ft rod is essential. The stream is crystal clear and the Town Water, in the hands of the Inverness Angling Club, is the most readily accessible to visiting anglers. Salmon tend to run through the lower beats in the spring, but after May they linger in some delightful pools such as Little Island, General's Well and Red Braes. Upstream beats, Laggan and Ness-Side, also have excellent holding pools: Birch Tree, The Run, Holm Pool. Flies: Silver Stoat, Hairy Mary, Stoat's Tail, Munro Killer, Blue Charm, Willie Gunn, Ally's Shrimp, Black Doctor. Local anglers rarely use anything larger than a size 8, dropping to size 12 during low water summer months. Sea-trout fishing in the estuary is at its best from May until July: Clachnaharry (26/644464) and North Kessock (26/649480). Use: Black Pennell, Teal Blue & Silver, Peter Ross. Boats are not allowed on the estuary fishing.

Permission & Charges For the Town water and estuary sea-trout fishing, contact: J Graham, 37 Castle Street, Inverness. Tel: 01463 233178; cost ranges from between £10 per rod per day to £15 per rod per day; weekly lets from £50 to £75. Ladies and under 18 year-olds pay half price. Ness-Side Beat: Angus Mackenzie & Co, Redwood, 19 Culduthel Road, Inverness. Tel: 01463 234353; Fax: 01463 235171. Laggan Beat: Gordon Dawson, Prime Salmon Fishings Ltd, Red Brae, The Croft, Nether Blainslie, Galashiels. Tel/fax: 01896 860307. Prices for beats on application. For trout fishing on Loch Dochfour, contact: The Shop, Dochgarroch Locks, Inverness. Tel: 01463 861265. Cost: £4 per rod per day.

ORRIN, Reservoir
Location & Access 26/375497. The reservoir is accessed by an estate road from Aultgowrie.

Commentary Orrin Reservoir feeds water into the River Conon hydro-electric generating scheme and lies at the heart of the Corriehallie Forest. The loch is almost 5 miles long by up to half a mile wide and the surrounding scenery is majestic. There are two small hill lochs, to the south of Orrin Reservoir, and they also can offer great sport: An Gorm Loch (26/373464), Loch Beag (26/365466). Loch a'Mhadaidh (26/420490) is not thought to hold trout.

Fish Some good brown trout which average 8oz/10oz with a few much larger specimens in the depths.

Flies & Tactics Fishing is not generally available to the public, but the estate do allow occasional access. The far, west, end of the loch is the most productive fishing area, particularly where the loch narrows to receive the headwaters of the River Orrin. The hill lochs require a considerable effort to reach being some 2 miles south from Orrin Reservoir. Fishing is not allowed during the stalking season. Flies: Loch Ordie, Soldier Palmer, Kingfisher Butcher.

Permission & Charges For South bank permission, contact: Fairburn Estates, (R Stirling) Tower of Fairburn, Urray, Muir of Ord, Ross-shire. Tel: 01997 433273; Fax: 01997433274. The north bank is owned by Scatwell Estate; the Kirkbi Estate owns other parts of shore.

ORRIN, River See River Conon.

PRIVATE WATERS NAM BREAC DEARGA, Loch (26/454224); A'BHEALAICH, Loch (26/450208); AN

OS Maps 26-27   Nairn

T-SIONNAICH, Loch (26/432216); NAN EUN, Loch (26/451252); DUBH, Loch (26/470250); NA FAOLIEGE, Loch (26/434277); COILTIE, River (26/524295); FARR, Loch (26/686307). NAM BONNACH, Loch (26/480480); NAN EUN, Loch (26/464483); BALLACH, Loch (26/437471); NAN GOBHAR, Loch (26/441441); NAN CUILE, LOCH (26/432439); FADA, Lochan (26/428437); NA PLANGAID, Loch (26/428429); NA BEISTE, Loch (26/390423); LAIDE, Loch (26/545355); GLANAIDH, Loch (26/528325); BATTAN, Loch (26/539391); DUBH, Lochan (26/499338); NAM BAT, Loch (26/493333); NA BA RUAIDHE, Loch (26/499341); NAM FAOILEAG, Loch (26/495325); AN TORRA BHUIDHE, Loch (26/487322); GORM, Loch (26/481334); NAM BREAC DEARGA, Loch (26/473346); BAD NAN EARB, Loch (26/458340); NAN TUNNAG, Loch (26/456336); AN TAIRT, Loch (26/446337); BRUICHEACH, Loch (26/453365); GARBH BHREAC, Loch (26/435359); GARBH LOLACHAN, Loch (26/430359); NEATY, Loch (26/435368); RAINEACHAN, Loch (26/450384); A'MHUILINN, Loch (26/412383); NAN GOBHAR, Loch (26/416375); AN A'BHATHAICH, Loch (26/409361); NAM FAOILEAG, Loch (26/415357); CARN NAM BADAN, Loch (26/398345); MHAIRI, Lochan (26/392325); NA CRAOIBHE-FEARNA, Lochan (26/371329); DUBH, Lochan (26/370322); RIABHACHAIN, Loch (26/361310); MARBH, Lochan (26/381285); COMHNARD, Loch (26/361277); MEIKLIE, Loch (26/435300); AIGAS, Loch (26/454414)

RUIGHE DHUIBH, Lochan See Loch ma Stac.
RUIT A'PHUILL, Loch See Loch Eich Bhain.

RUTHVEN, Loch
Location & Access 26/620276. Turn west from the B851 Strathnairn road at East Croachy (26/651278). Follow the minor road past Elrig for one mile to reach the boat mooring bay at the east end of the loch (26/637284).
Commentary Loch Ruthven is easily accessible. Outboard motors are not allowed. Be prepared for some hefty oar-work when the wind howls or pack a strong friend. The loch is 2 miles east/west by up to half a mile wide and is a noted nature reserve, famous for the variety of its wildfowl which includes the rare Slavonian grebe.
Fish Excellent quality brown trout which average 12oz/14oz but fish of up to and over 4lb in weight are not uncommon.
Flies & Tactics Boat fishing only. Begin with a drift across the shallow east bay, concentrating particularly in the vicinity of the inlet stream from An Dubh-lochan (26/629285). An Dubh-lochan is rarely fished and it also contains some good trout which move there from Loch Ruthven in high water conditions. In the hills above Loch Ruthven is another fine trout loch, Loch a'Choire (26/628292) which is also fished from the boat. Loch a'Choire is a deep, cold loch and it contains arctic char as well as brown trout. Tramp half a mile north from Loch a'Choire to reach the Dubh-lochan (26/635304) on Stac na Cathaig (445m) which has

breakfast-sized trout. Flies: Black Zulu, Soldier Palmer, Silver Invicta.
Permission & Charges A. C. Humfrey, Balvoulin, Flichty, Inverness. Tel: 01808 521283. Boats on Loch Ruthven may also be booked through: J Graham & Co, 37 Castle Street, Inverness Tel: 01463 233178; Whitebridge Hotel, Stratherrick, Inverness. Tel: 01456 486272. Cost: £15 per boat per day with two rods fishing.

SGOLBAIDH, Loch See Loch Aradaidh.

TARVIE, Lochs (Trout Fishery)
Location & Access 26/424581. Approach from the A832 Contin/Gairloch road just north from Rogie Falls by turning left at 26/425590.
Commentary An Eich Bhain is the principal loch in a group of small hill-lochs known locally as the Tarvie Lochs. The other two lochs here are: Loch a'Chlarain (26/431581) and Loch Ruit a'Phuill (26/419583). There are three more lochs, to the south of the Tarvie Lochs: Loch nan Eilid (26/409573), Loch nan Cuilcean (26/411571) and Loch Droma (26/421575). These three are owned by the Forestry Commission and are not available for fishing.
Fish This is a commercial, put-and-take fishery, stocked predominantly with rainbow trout, but also containing brown trout. The fish are stocked at weights of between 1.5lb to 15lb.
Flies & Tactics Loch Eich Bhain, which is 25 acres in extent, is fished from a boat and is fly only. Loch Ruit a'Phuill and Loch a'Chlarain, each of about 7 acres, are fished from the bank. Trout rise well to flies such as Black Pennell, March Brown, Peter Ross and all sedges. Reservoir lures on sinking lines may also persuade the residents to grab.
Permission & Charges A full day (eight hours) for two rods, boat fishing on Loch Eich Bhain, costs £40 and there is a 4 fish per rod bag limit. Thereafter, it is strictly catch and release. There are also 4-hour sessions at half the above rate. Bank fishing costs £7.50 for a four-hour session, £15 for the day. Contact: Tarvie Trout Fishery, Tarvie, by Strathpeffer, Ross-shire. Tel: 01997 421250.

USSIE, Loch
Location & Access 26/505570. Loch Ussie lies to the south-east of Strathpeffer. It contains pike and perch only.

Nairn

A'CHAORAINN, Loch
Location & Access Location & Access 27/755374. Approach from the Auchnahillin Caravan Park (27/736385) which lies to the east of the main A9 Inverness/Perth road south from Daviot (27/724393).
Commentary This is a small, forest-girt, put-and-take fishery which lies between the railway and the minor road from Daviot to Moy (27/765345).
Fish Good quality brown trout which average 1lb. Much larger fish as well.

Nairn — OS Map 27

Flies & Tactics Boat and bank fishing, limited to 6 rods per day. The loch is approximately 10 acres in extent and fish are taken everywhere. Flies: Soldier Palmer, Greenwell's Glory, Black Pennell.

Permission & Charges Auchnahillin Caravan Park Reception, Daviot, Inverness-shire. Tel: 01463 772286. Cost: Per 4-hour session, £8 boat hire £8. OAP's and juniors (under sixteen) £4 per 4-hour session. There is a bag limit of 2 fish of over 12 " per rod. Tackle hire is available.

A'GHIUBHAIS, Lochanan See Loch Dallas (Altyre).

BLAIRS, Loch

Location & Access 27/032555 Two miles south from Forres, turn left onto a private estate road which leaves the A940 Forres/Grantown road at 27/021550. After a few hundred yards, turn left again and drive down to the boathouse by the loch.

Commentary A very lovely loch surrounded by mature woodlands and extending to approximately 50 acres. Prior to fishing, have a look at the astonishing array of graffiti on the wall of the shed next to the boathouse. Some inscriptions are more than 70 years old. Also look out for the resident osprey and other ducks and divers all of which make fishing here such a constant joy.

Fish This is a well-managed, put-and-take fishery, in the hands of the local council, and is regularly stocked with rainbow trout which average 1lb 8oz in weight.

Flies & Tactics Boat fishing only, and this shallow loch has clear water. Fish may be encountered throughout the length and breadth of the loch, but a favourite starting point is in the vicinity of the largest of the two islands off the west shore. There is a bag limit of 6 fish per rod. Show them: Loch Ordie, Soldier Palmer, Black Pennell. Reservoir lures also work well.

Permission & Charges Iain Grant, The Fishing Tackle Shop, 79D High Street, Forres, Morayshire. Tel: 01309 672936. Keys for the boathouse are issued with the permit. Cost: single angler in a boat, £11.80 per day; two anglers sharing a boat, £7.60 per rod per day. Over 60's and juniors (under 14 and accompanied by an adult), £6.50.

DALLAS, Loch (Altyre)

Location & Access 27/091475. Approach from the A940 Forres/Dava road at Glenernie (27/020465). Access is by a private estate road, only passable by a high wheel-base vehicle. The loch lies 5 miles to the east of the main road.

Commentary One of the most scenically perfect lochs in the north, lying at an altitude of 320m with stunning views south to the Grampian mountains. There are a number of smaller loch in the vicinity: Loch na Speur (27/099489) and Loch na Braan, small forest lochans to the north; Loch Noir (27/094453), 1 mile south from Loch Dallas, and Loch Trevie (27/095441) a further half-mile south from Loch Noir. Lochanan a'Ghiubhais (27/088449) and its unnamed neighbour at 27/083447 lie to the west of the track between Loch Noir and Loch Trevie.

Fish Loch Dallas has excellent brown trout which average 12oz/14oz in weight. The other waters contain smaller trout which average 8oz.

Flies & Tactics Boat fishing and bank fishing bring results on Loch Dallas and fish may be taken from all round the shore. The south-west and south shore, where the feeder streams enter, is the place to begin. There are three small, unnamed lochans immediately to the north and east of Loch Dallas which are also worth a throw. The remainder of the lochs noted above are easily fished from the bank and readily understood. Flies: Ke-He, March Brown, Peter Ross.

Permission & Charges Alastair Gordon Cumming, Altyre Estate, Forres, Morayshire IV36 0SH. Tel: 01309 672266; Fax: 01309 672270. Fishing on Loch Dallas and the other lochs noted is available from June onwards to tenants of Rochuln Cottage (27/073472). The estate will "design" a complete, mixed, sporting week for tenants including loch fishing for brown trout, salmon fishing on the River Findhorn, roe deer stalking, rough shooting and walked-up grouse shooting. Prices on application, depending upon tenants requirements, but generally in the order of £1,000 per party per week.

FINDHORN, River

Location & Access Source 35/653122 Outfall 27/030620. Access to the lower river is from the A940 Forres/Grantown road and the B9007 Logie/Carrbridge road. From Dulsie (27/932416) upstream to Drynachan (27/865397) access is by a minor road which ends at Daless (27/861383). Thereafter, access is either by a four-wheel drive vehicle or on foot. It should also be noted that immediate access to the famous 20-mile long Gorge Section of the river, from Dulsie downstream to Sluie, requires considerable caution. The Gorge is 200 ft high in places, sheer-sided and dangerous.

Commentary One of Scotland's most famous and scenically attractive salmon streams. The character of the river embraces a wide range of habitats, from the wild moorlands above Tomatin (35/803292) down to Drynachan, the wonderful natural woodlands of the Gorge, through to the rich arable pasture of the coastal plain where the river enters Findhorn Bay below the A96 Elgin/Inverness road.

Fish Approximately 800 salmon are taken each season. Sea-trout numbers have declined in recent years, although good fish may still be taken, particularly from the lower river and the estuary beats. The Tomatin beats can also produce sport with some surprisingly large brown trout.

Flies & Tactics Because of the strength of the current in the Gorge section of the river, a 15ft rod is required to quickly control any fish caught. The Drynachan beats are wide and a good cast is needed to cover all the lies. Again, use a 15ft rod. On the upper river, around Tomatin, a single-handed rod will suffice. Sport is dependent upon water levels; not helped by extensive commercial forestry planting in the upper reaches of the river which induces rapid run-off caused by forestry ploughing. The Gorge acts as a "temperature pool", holding fish back in the lower river until May when the water temperature rises. September generally produces the largest number of fish. Flies: Shrimp Fly, Willie Gunn, Stoat's Tail, Silver Stoat, General Practitioner, Munro Killer, Green Highlander, Garry Dog.

Permission & Charges Most of the fishing is in the hands of local estates and is let by the week, generally with accommodation. The same tenants take the beats each year so access is not readily available. The local angling association restrict access to members and guests only and visitor day tickets are not issued. However, day tickets can be had on a 1.5 miles section of the lower river, downstream from the A92 Elgin/Inverness road bridge, and in Findhorn Bay for sea-trout. Contact Iain Grant, The Tackle Shop, 97D High Street, Forres, Morayshire. Tel: 01309 672936. Cost: £10 to £50 per rod per day depending upon the time of year. For Findhorn Bay, contact: Moray Water Sports. The Old Fishery, Findhorn, Morayshire. Tel: 01309 690239. Cost: £1.10 per rod per day, £3.30 per week. For availability on the estate waters, contact: Lethen Estate, Lethen, Nairn. Tel: 01667 452247; Fax: 01667 456449 for the Daltra, Altnahara and Dunearn beats; Glenferness Fishings, Earl of Leven, Glenferness House, Nairn IV12 5UP.Tel: 01309 651202; Drynachan Beats, Cawdor Estates, Estate Office, Cawdor, Nairn. Tel: 01667 404666; Fax: 01667 404787. The price per beat, if available, will vary from approximately £400 to £1500, depending upon the time of year and the number of rods the beat fishes. For the Tomatin beats, contact: Glenan Lodge, Tomatin, Inverness-shire. Tel: 01808 511217; Cost: £20 to £35 per rod per day. Lodge guests have priority. Excellent summer sport may be had through the Englefield Estate, Theale, Redding RG7 5DU. Tel: 01734 302504. The estate has single bank fishing, either in conjunction with a self-catering cottage or by the day at £30 per rod per day. Priority is given to those renting accommodation as well as fishing.

LOCHINDORB, Loch

Location & Access 27/970360. From the south, approach via the B9007 Carrbridge/Forres road. At 27/950350, turn right onto the minor road which leads to Lochindorb Lodge (27/969355). From the north, turn right from the A939 Dava/Grantown road at 27/00383 to reach the north end of the loch.

Commentary Ease of access makes Lochindorb a popular fishery and advance booking is essential. The loch is 2 miles north/south by up to half a mile wide and the dominant feature is the ruined castle on the islet off the north-east shore; occupied by Edward 1, "Hammer of the Scots", in AD 1303 and therafter the lair of the Wolf of Badenoch who burned Elgin Cathedral in AD 1390.

Fish A large stock of modest brown trout which average in the order of 8oz, but some much larger specimens as well.

Flies & Tactics Boat fishing brings the best results and the south end of the loch, down to the inlet burn from Loch an t-Sidhein (27/973321) is the place to start. First cast: Black Pennell, Grouse & Claret, Silver Butcher.

Permission & Charges See Loch of Blairs entry; also Angus Stuart, Fishing Tackle, 60 High Street, Grantown-on-Spey. Tel: 01479 872612 or Caretakers Cottage, Lochindorb, Glenferness. Tel: 01309 651270. Three sessions. Cost per boat (two anglers fishing): £10 for one session, £16 for two sessions, £22 for three sessions.

MUCKLE Burn

Location & Access Source 27/858436 Outfall 27/019624 Muckle Burn may be accessed throughout its course from public roads.

Commentary Muckle Burn enters Findhorn Bay just to the north of the outfall of the River Findhorn. In days past the stream was a renowned sea-trout fishery but now, because of agricultural practices, it is but a poor shadow of its former self.

Fish Sea-trout and the chance of a salmon.

Flies & Tactics The lower section of the river, from the A96 Forres/Inverness road (27/980571) near Brodie Castle down to Findhorn Bay offers the best chance of sport, but only after substantial rain. Use a trout rod and small flies, size 10/12 dressings. Patterns: Ke-He, March Brown, Teal Blue & Silver.

Permission & Charges Iain Grant, 97D High Street, Forres, Morayshire. Tel: 01309 672936. Value for money sport at £3 per rod per day.

NA BRAAN, Loch See Loch Dallas (Altyre).
NA SPEUR, Loch See Loch Dallas (Altyre).

NAIRN, River

Location & Access Source 26/650200. Outfall 27/889572. The river is easily accessible from public roads which parallel its course from Daviot (27/721386) on the A9 Perth/Inverness road to where the stream enters the Moray Firth at the harbour in the town of Nairn. The Upper River, above Daviot, is preserved by the owners.

Commentary Fishing the River Nairn is as much an historical experience as it is an angling adventure: the stream passes Culloden Field where Prince Charles Edward Stuart's Jacobite army was defeated and massacred by government forces in April 1746. The Thane of Cawdor, infamous MacBeth, had his castle by the river and it is alleged to be the place where he murdered King Duncan in AD 1040. Despatch non-fishing companions to visit these sites whilst you enjoy this delightful little water.

Fish Salmon and sea-trout, although the number of fish caught, particularly sea-trout, has declined in recent years. The annual average catch is in the order of 80/100 fish.

Flies & Tactics The most important tactic is to be there at the right time, after heavy rain, because success depends very much upon good water levels. There are few problems fishing the stream and a single-handed rod will cover most eventualities. More often than not it is well into May before serious fishing begins, with July being the best month, but fish have been taken on opening day, 11th February. Sport can also be excellent in September. Flies: Smallish dressings, in doubles, size 10/12 do best. Try: Shrimp Fly, Munro Killer, Willie Gunn, Hairy Mary, General Practitioner, Stoat's Tail,

Elgin — OS Maps 27-28

When the water rises above certain levels livebait and spinning is permissable.
Permission & Charges Lower beat: The River Nairn Angling Association have 8 miles of double bank fishing and a further 1 mile of single bank fishing. Contact: P Fraser, TV & Radio, 41 High Street, Nairn, Nairnshire. Tel: 01667 453038. Cost: £13.50 per rod per day, £41 per rod per week. Juniors at half price. Upper beat: Calva Holiday Homes, Culloden Moor, Inverness-shire. Tel: 01463 790228/790405; Fax: 01463 790228. Calva Holiday Homes offer comfortable self-catering accommodation which includes the cost of salmon fishing in the rental. Day lets are also available at £6 per rod per day.

NOIR, Loch See Loch Dallas (Altyre).

PRIVATE WATERS FLEMINGTON, Loch (27/810520); LOY, Loch (27/933586); CRAN, Loch (27/945590); KIRKALDY, Loch (27/962417); TUTACH, Loch (27/984404); AN T-SIDHEIN, Loch (27/973321); ILLE MHOR, Loch (27/934320); DUBH, Lochan (27/958328); NA STUIRTEAG, Loch (27/001320); MOY, Loch (27/775345); FUNTACK Burn (27/783330); BOATH, Loch of (27/887451); CLUNAS Reservoir (27/860460).

SPEY, River See OS Map 28 Elgin
TREVIE, Loch See Loch Dallas (Altyre).

Elgin

AVON, River See River Spey.
DULIAN WATER, River See River Fiddich.
DULNAIN, River See River Spey.

FIDDICH, River
Location & Access Source 37/296286 Outfall 28/293454. The A941 Craigelachie/Dufftown road margins the west bank of the river; a minor road from Netherton on the A95 Craigelachie/Dufftown road follows the east bank. The upper river, above Dufftown is accessed from Coldhome (28/361398 on the A920 Dufftown/Huntley road and from Bridgehaugh (28/341357) on the A941 Dufftown/Rhynie road.
Commentary Famous for Glenfiddich whisky, the river rises far to the south near to the Elf House Cave (37/299292) and flows north through Dufftown to join the River Spey at Craigelachie. The River Fiddich has one, substantial, tributary, the Dulian Water, which supports another another fine whisky, the Dufftown Mortlach.
Fish The upper reaches of both streams can provide sport with brown trout whilst the lower River Fiddich holds salmon and sea-trout. Approximately 20 fish are taken most season, depending upon water conditions.
Flies & Tactics Be there after heavy rain for the best chance of sport. Use a single-handed rod and stalk the fish. July onwards is the best time to attack. Flies: small doubles, Willie Gunn, Shrimp Fly, Munro Killer, Stoat's Tail.

Permission & Charges TV Services, 1 The Square, Dufftown AB55 4AD. Tel: 01340 820527. Cost per seson: £12 (adults). £6 (juniors).

GLEN OF ROTHES, Loch
Location & Access 28/249543. To the east of the A941 Elgin/Rothes road, near Netherglen, two miles north from Rothes.
Commentary The Glen of Rothes Trout Fishery consists of a group of 4 small, man-made, lochs extending to 5.5 acres. They are fed by the Glen Burn and lie on the line of a disused railway. This is an attractive, easily accessible, put-and-take fishery which is a member of the Association of Scottish Stillwater Game Fisheries.
Fish Stocked with rainbow trout, brown trout, brook trout, blue rainbows, steelhead and charling. Best brown trout recently, 9lb 5oz, best rainbow, 15lb 11oz.
Flies & Tactics Bank fishing only and excellent facilities: heated fishing hut, snacks and sitting out area; tackle hire, large selection of lures and flies and free tuition for beginners every Saturday, April to October, 12 noon until 5 pm. Access for disabled anglers. Toilet facilities. Flies to use: Black Spider, Lake Olive, Bibio.
Permission & Charges Glen of Rothes Trout Fishery, Rothes, Morayshire. Tel: 01340 831888. Cost: Full day (8.30am until 10pm) with 4 fish limit, £18 per rod; 4 hour session with 2 fish limit, £10.50 per rod; full day, catch and release using barbless hooks, £8 per rod; 1 hour 1 fish session, £8. Concessions for OAP's, under 12's, groups and disabled. Open 7 days a week.

GLENLATTERACH, Reservoir
Location & Access 28/189530. Turn right from the A941 Elgin/Craigelachie road opposite the entrance to Millbuies Country Park at 28/236568. Follow the minor road south to reach the dam at Glenlatterach Reservoir after 3.5 miles.
Commentary Although this is a public water-supply source, the surrounding scenery is majestic and Glenlatterach Reservoir is a splendid place to escape to for a day. The loch is more than half a mile north/south by up to 200 yards wide, fed by the Leanoch Burn which enters on the south shore.
Fish Large stocks of wild brown trout which average 6oz/8oz.
Flies & Tactics Boat fishing and bank fishing, both of which will produce results. The present policy is to kill all fish caught in order to improve the average weight of the remaining trout. The south end is the most productive fishing area. In spate conditions have cast in Leanoch Burn. Flies: Black Zulu, Soldier Palmer, Silver Butcher.
Permission & Charges See Millbuies Loch entry.

ISLA, River See River Deveron (OS Map 29).

LOSSIE, River
Location & Access Source 28/100445. Outfall 28/28/240707 Apart from the section south from Dallas (28/123522), in Glen Lossie, the remainder of the river is easily accessible from the B9010

OS Map 28 — Elgin

Elgin/Dallas road for the middle river, and the B9103 Sheriffston/Lossiemouth road for the lower river to the sea.

Commentary The River Lossie rises to the south of Dallas from The Seven Sisters Springs and flows north through Dallas Forest to Elgin. From Elgin to its outfall, the stream is slow-moving and bounded by fertile agricultural land. The wide, tidal, bay, just before the river exits into the Moray Firth at Branderburgh is a very popular location for spinning for sea-trout.

Fish Salmon, sea-trout and brown trout. Approximately 100 salmon are taken most seasons, along with 400 sea-trout, mostly by spinning in the sea. The 1999 season was particularly good, with excellent quality sea-trout of up to and over 3lb in weight caught.

Flies & Tactics Few problems, other than being in the right place at the right time, that is, after heavy rain. The river is very much a spate stream. A single-handed rod covers most eventualities and wading is rarely required. When it is, then thigh waders are adequate. The river is narrow and the pools deep, so you should approach with caution to avoid "spooking" the fish. The banks are also heavily wooded in many places so you will require all your skill to tempt your quarry. The Elgin & District Angling Association have done much to improve the river and there are now more than 50 pools. The best time to launch your assault is from June onwards, depending upon rainfall. Give them: Willie Gunn, Shrimp Fly, Stoat's Tail, Munro Killer. For sea-trout, offer: Black Pennell, Grouse & Claret, Teal Blue & Silver.

Permission & Charges The lower river is fished by the Elgin Angling Association and day tickets are available from: The Angling Centre, Moss Street, Elgin, Moray IV30 1LT. Tel: 01343 547615; The Tackle Shop, 188 High Street, Elgin, Moray IV30 1BA. Tel: 01343 543129. Cost: £5 per rod per day, £20 per rod per week. OAP's and juniors at half price. The Dallas Angling Association have the upper river and day tickets are available from: The Dallas Hotel, Airel View, Dallas, Moray. Tel: 01343 890323. Cost: £5 per rod per day. The middle river is owned by the Kellas Estate, Pluscarden Lodge, Dallas, Moray. Tel: 01343 890219. Price on application.

MILLBUIES, Loch

Location & Access 28/242569. The loch lies to the east of the A941 Elgin/Craigelachie road in the Millbuies Country Park.

Commentary Millbuies Loch is managed by Moray District Council. There are two waters here, extending for almost half a mile, and they both offer excellent sport in very attractive surroundings.

Fish Stocked each year with 2,000 rainbow trout which average 1lb 4oz. Larger fish of up to and over 4lb in weight are caught most seasons. The loch also contains brown trout. All fish under 10 inches must be returned and there is a bag limit of 6 trout per angler.

Flies & Tactics Boat fishing only and there are four boats available for visiting anglers. Fish are caught throughout the system and no one place is substantially any better than another. Lochside facilities are excellent and include a good boathouse and landing-stage. Flies: Black Pennell, Greenwell's Glory, Silver Butcher.

Permission & Charges The Warden, Millbuies Country Park, Longmorn, Elgin, Moray. Tel: 01343 860234. Cost per day: Single angler, £11.80 two anglers sharing a boat, £7.60. OAP's, £6.50. Boathouse keys are issued with the permit at the time of booking.

NA BO, Loch

Location & Access 28/283600. Loch na Bo is immediately to the South of the A96 Elgin to Fochabers road to the south of Lhanbryde (28/275615).

Commentary This is an attractive, easily accessible, woodland loch covering approximately 35 acres. It is a popular fishery and advance booking is advisable. The trees provide welcome shelter in high winds and the loch is the haunt of a wide array of waterfowl.

Fish Brown trout which average 8oz/10oz.

Flies & Tactics Boat fishing only, with two sessions per day; from 8am until 2pm, 2pm to dusk. Fish rise and are taken all round the loch from the margins to the middle. Try: Ke-He, March Brown, Kingfisher Butcher.

Permission & Charges Mr D Kinloch, Keeper's Cottage, Loch na Bo, Lhanbryde, Elgin, Moray. Tel: 01343 842214. Cost: £8.50 per session bank fishing, £12 per session for 2 rods in boat.

PARK, Loch

Location & Access 28/355430. Immediately adjacent to the B9014 Keith/Dufftown road.

Commentary Loch Park is a long, narrow water, 1 mile east/west by up to 100 yards wide, approximately 356 acres in extent. It lies at the heart of the Loch Park Adventure Centre on the Drummuir Castle Estate which offers non-fishing companions plenty of other activities to keep them occupied whilst you fish: canoeing, kayaking, archery and gorge walking. The east shore is bordered by the railway line, the west shore by Lochend Wood.

Fish Stocked with brown trout which average 12oz/14oz.

Flies & Tactics Boat fishing only and fishing is divided into two sessions: 8am until 4pm and 4pm until midnight. Fish are taken all over the loch. Offer them: Invicta, Grouse & Claret, Dunkeld. Reservoir lures also work well.

Permission & Charges Drummuir Castle Estate, by Keith, Banffshire. Tel: 01542 810334. The Angling Centre, Moss Street, Elgin, Moray IV30 1LT. Tel: 01343 547615. One boat is available at a cost of £10 per single rod, £7.50 each for two rods fishing. Boat keys are issued at the time of booking.

PRIVATE WATERS Loch of the Cowlair; Lochs of the Little Benshalag.

SPEY, River

Location & Access Source 34/410975. Outfall 28/347652 The river is easily accessible throughout its entire length from both public and private estate roads.

Commentary The Spey is one of the most noted salmon rivers in Europe and rises from the slopes of

Elgin — OS Map 28

Glas Charn (790m) in the Monadhliath Mountains south of Loch Ness. It is over 100 miles in length with a catchment area of 1097 square miles. The Spey is the fastest-flowing river in Britain: in the first 48 miles of its journey north to the sea at Spey Bay the river drops 600ft. The principal tributaries are: the Mashie, Truim, Calder, Tromie, Feshie, Druie, Burn of Tulchan, Nethy, Dulnain, Fiddich, Avon (pronounced 'A'an') the two Rothes burns, Mulben Burn, Red Burn and the Burn of Fochabers. Some of these streams are major rivers in their own right: the Dulnain is 25 miles in length, the Avon is 40 miles. Much of the fishing is readily available to visiting anglers by the day or by the week through local angling associations, Speyside hotels and estates, generally in conjunction with accommodation. Few other salmon river systems of comparable excellence, anywhere in the world, offer such a wide range of access to members of the public. Numerous books are available which give precise detail of each part of the river, the best of which, in my opinion, is John Ashley-Cooper's definitive work "The Great Salmon Rivers of Scotland". Within the limited space available here, I can only give a general outline and direct you to the people who will be able to give you precise information. However, the River Spey is the most cosmopolitan of all Scottish salmon streams and, wherever and whenever you go, you will always find the chance of outstanding sport.

Fish Approximately 8,000 salmon and grilse and upwards of 2,000 sea-trout are taken most seasons. Salmon average 9lb/10lb although fish of over 20lb are not uncommon. The Spey is the premier Scottish sea-trout fishery: sea-trout average 2lb and fish of up 16lb have been caught. The river also contains some large brown trout and, in the upper reaches, pike, particularly in Loch Insh (see OS Map 35).

Flies & Tactics The upper Spey, from Spey Dam downstream to Loch Insh (described on OS Map 35), produces far fewer fish than the middle (described on OS Map 36) and lower river. The best of the sport is from Grantown-on-Spey downstream and includes, between Grantown and Rothes, such famous beats as: the Association Water, Castle Grant, Tulchan, Ballindalloch, Pitchroy, Knockando, Carron, Wester Elchies, Kinermony, Easter Elchies and Arndilly. The beats on the lower river are: Rothes, Aikenway, Delfur, Orton and Gordon Castle Water. The Strathspey Angling Association have 5 miles of double bank fishing with 21 pools, and 12 miles of fishing on the River Dulnain with 60 pools 30 named and 30 unnamed). The annual average catch is in the order of 400 salmon and grilse and upwards of 1000 sea-trout. This is first-class sport and outstanding value for money. Spinning is permitted on the Spey but the real joy of fishing here is fly fishing. Use a double-handed rod. This is a big river, often with tree-lined banks which induced the development of the Spey-casting technique. Remember, also, that the river is swift-flowing and wading can often be dangerous. Wear a floatation device and always use a wading stick. For the best chance of success, employ the services of a gillie. Sport with sea-trout is best at night and, prior to fishing, during daylight hours, you should walk the beat and 'test' out where you propose to fish. Ideally, stay in one place and let the sea-trout come to you. They generally run upstream after dusk. The most productive patterns of fly include: Munro Killer, Arndilly Fancy, Willie Gunn, Shrimp Fly, Stoat's Tail, Hairy Mary, Green Highlander, General Practitioner, Black Doctor, Waddingtons.

Permission & Charges Start at Grant Mortimer, 3 High Street, Grantown, Moray PH26 3HB. Tel: 01479 872684; Fax: 01479 872211. Mortimers have a wide knowledge of available fishing opportunities on the Spey and its tributaries and the staff are expert in meeting all the angling needs of visiting fishermen, including tackle hire and arranging gillies. They also issue tickets for the Association Water which includes fishing on the River Dulnain. Season ticket , £500; per seven days (excluding Sunday), £135. 3 day ticket, £80; 1 day ticket, £30. Aberlour Angling Association, c/o J A Munro, 93-95 High Street, Aberlour, Banffshire AB38 9PB. Tel: 01340 871428. Fishing is let to rods staying at the Aberlour Hotel (Tel: 01340 871287) and the Craigard Hotel (Tel: 01479 831206). Abernethy Angling Improvement Association, per/Allens, Deshar Road, Boat of Garten, Inverness-shire PH24 3BN. Tel: 01479 831372. Cost: £98 per rod per week, £28 per rod per day. Fishing on the other beats may be available but is often well-booked year after year by the same rods. Prices will be given on application, but expect to pay in the order of from £250 to £1200 per rod per week, depending upon the time of year. Orton Beats: Orton Management Company Ltd, Estate Office, Orton, Fochabers IV32 7QE. Tel:01343 880240. Craigelachie: Mr W Roy, Wollburn, Speyview, Aberlour AB38 9LT. Tel: 01340 871217. Delfur, Aikenway, Rothes, Upper Arndilly, Easter Elchies, Carron, Laggan: Messrs Bidwells, Etive House, Beechwood Park, Inverness. Tel: 01463 715585; Fax: 01340 831687. Lower Wester Elchies: Finlyson Hughes, 29 Barossa Place, Perth PH1 5EP. Tel: 01738 625134; Fax: 01738 639017. Delagyle: Messrs Savills, 12 Clerk Street, Brechin, Angus DD9 6AE. Tel: 01356 622187; Fax: 01356 625389. Castle Grant Water & Kinchurdy: Andrew Norval, Factor, Strathspey Estates, Estate Office, Heathfield, Grantown-on-Spey, Moray. Tel: 01479 872529; Fax: 01479 872901. Ballindalloch & River Avon: The Factor, Ballindalloch Estate, Ballindalloch, Banffshire. Tel: 01807 500205; Fax: 01807 500210. Upper Arndilly: G S Dawson, Prime Salmon Fishings Ltd, Red Brae, The Croft, Nether Blainslie, Galashiels. Tel: 01896 860307. Tulchan: Tulchan Sporting Estates Ltd, Estate Office, Tulchan, Grantown-on-Spey, Moray. Tel: 01807 510200; Fax: 01807 510234. Gordon Castle Estate Waters (Tel: 01343 820244): Fochabers Tackle & Guns, 91 High Street, Fochabers. Tel: 01343 820327; Knockando, 3 beats: R & R Urquhart, 117-121 High Street, Forres, Morayshire IV36 0AB. Tel: 01309 672216; Fax: 01309 673161. Mr Colin Whittle is the Clerk to the Spey District Fishery Board (01309 672216) although he points out that his Board is not empowered to grant fishing permissions for the individual beats listed above.

OS Map 28-29 Banff

WINDYRIDGE, Loch
Location & Access 28/233671. The loch lies close to the A941 Elgin/Lossiemouth road between the main road and the line of the old railway.
Commentary A small, easily accessible, put-and-take fishery in a pleasant situation between Elgin and Lossiemouth near to the ancient Palace of Spynie.
Fish Regularly stocked with both brown trout and rainbow trout which average 1lb in weight.
Flies & Tactics Fly fishing only, from bank and boat. Tackle hire is available and casting lessons can be arranged by prior appointment. Try: Black Pennell, Grouse & Claret, Peter Ross. Reservoir-type lures also produce results.
Permission & Charges A day-ticket costs £10. The bag limit is 3 fish, thereafter, catch-and-release using barbless hooks. The fishery is open 7 days a week. Contact: Dr Chalmers, Windyridge, Lossiemouth IV31 6RX. Tel: 01343 812001.

Banff

BLACK WATER, River See River Deveron.
BOGIE, River See River Deveron.
BOYNE, Burn of See Cullen Burn.

CULLEN BURN, River
Location & Access 29/505673. Access from the A98 Elgin/Portsoy road.
Commentary This is a short burn running into the Moray Firth in Cullen Bay at Seatown which is a popular holiday centre. To the east, and entering the sea at Portsoy (29/593662), and also accessed from the A98 road, is the Burn of Boyne.
Fish A chance of salmon, sea-trout and trout.
Flies & Tactics Both these little spate streams can give sport when conditions are right, after heavy rain. The best chance, however, is spinning in the brackish, tidal waters, where sea-trout may be taken. Try: Devon minnows, various Tobys and spoons.
Permission & Charges For the Cullen Burn, contact: Seafield Estates, Estate Office, York Place, Cullen. Tel: 01542 840777. Cost: £5 per day. There is a locked gate and the key for this gate is given to visitors upon payment of a deposit of £10; refundable on the return of the key and completed fishing return. No fishing during the hours of darkness. For the Burn of Boyne, contact: Mr Clark, Mount Pleasant, School Hendry Street, Portsoy AB45 2RS. Tel: 01261 842689. Cost: £6 per rod per day, no fishing during the hours of darkness.

DEVERON, River
Location & Access Source 37/365210. Outfall 29/695640. Public roads and private estate roads give easy access to all parts of the river.
Commentary The River Deveron rise on the north slopes of Glenbuchat at Roch Ford and flows north through Cabrach (37/385270), "the place of the antlers". The stream then swings east and north-east past Huntly (29/530400) and Turriff (29/725500) and then north again for a further 11 miles before entering the Moray Firth in Banff Bay between the towns of Banff and MacDuff. The length of the river is 48 miles and the principal tributaries are the Black Water, Bogie, Isla and the Idoch Water. The upper river is swift and fast-flowing, gathering in strength as it sweeps through the steep-sided gorge at Corinacy (37/380293). From Huntly to the sea, the stream meanders across fertile farmlands in a series of delightful, exciting, deep pools and glides which make the River Deveron one of Scotland's most attractive salmon streams.
Fish Salmon, sea-trout and brown trout. Upwards of 1,000 salmon and grilse and 1,500 sea-trout are taken most seasons. The record salmon for the river was a fish of 61lb caught by Mrs Morrison on October 21st 1924 and the river is noted for producing 20lb + fish. The average weight of salmon is 9lb/10lb. The River Deveron is equally famous as a sea-trout fishery: W B Sheret landed an 18lb specimen in 1969 and sea-trout of over 5lb are common. The whole river, and its tributaries, and particularly the River Bogie, can produce good sport with brown-trout and fish of up to and over 3lb are caught regularly. The River Bogie also has good catches of salmon and sea-trout. Escapee rainbow trout may sometimes be encountered.
Flies & Tactics The Deveron is a spate river and depends upon good water levels to give of its best. There are no lochs along its length and the water flow relies entirely on winter snow being metered out during the spring and early summer months, and post-rain floods. In low-water conditions, the river can look very sad indeed, but after rain there are few finer places to fish. Chest waders are useful on the lower river, to reach some of the lies, but, generally, thigh waders are all that is required. A 12ft rod covers most eventualities, fishing with a floating line, or, after rain, a sink-tip line. There are 40 beats on the river, some of which allow spinning, but the Deveron is classic fly water and it not really necessary to do anything other than fish with fly. Spring runs have shown signs of improvement in recent years, from March until early May, but the most productive months are September and October. Sea-trout fishing is at its peak during June and July. Patterns to try: for salmon, Shrimp Fly, Willie Gunn, Garry Dog, Munro Killer, General Practitioner, Stoat's Tail, Hairy Mary; for sea-trout and brown trout: Black Pennell, Grouse & Claret, Peter Ross.
Permission & Charges Fishing is widely available throughout the whole river, but the best beats, between Huntly and Turriff are generally booked well in advance by rods who return year after year. Nevertheless, cancellations and "natural wastage" often makes space for new rods. Check with the estates, or telephone the first-class Grampian Fishing Line service (Tel: 01891 881941) for an up-to-the-minute bulletin on available fishing. Costs vary from £4 per rod per day up to £50 per rod per day, depending upon the time of year and the beat booked. Also contact: for Banff & Macduff Angling Association Water: Banffshire Fishselling Company, 20 Shore

261

Fraserburgh & Peterhead
OS Maps 29-30

Street, Macduff Tel: 01261 832891 and Insports, 1 Carmelite Street, Banff Tel: 01261 818348. Huntly Angling Association Water, Bogie & Isla: J Christie Murdoch McMath & Mitchell, 27 Duke Street, Huntly Tel: 01466 792291. Turriff Water: Ian Masson Fishing Tackle, 6 Castle Street, Turriff. Tel: 01888 562428. Castle Hotel Water: Huntly Castle Hotel, Huntly Tel: 01466 792696. Rothiemay Fishing: Forbes Arms Hotel, Rothiemay AB5 5LT, Tel: 01466 711248. Mayen Beat: The Factor, Estate Office, Mayen Estate, Rothiemay Tel: 01466 711369 and R K Mann, Blencowe Hall, Blencowe, Penrith, Cumberland. Tel: 01768 483628. Marnoch Lodge Beat: E MacKenzie, Marnoch Lodge Fishings, Huntly AB54 5UE Tel: 01466 780872. Avochie Beat: (no longer Strutt & Parker - enquire locally). Lower & Upper Mountblairy and Yonder Bognie Beats: Mrs Joanne McRae, Estate Office, Forgue, Huntly Tel: 01464 871331. Carnousie Beat: J Mutch, Carnousie House, Turriff, Aberdeenshire. Tel: 01888 563321. Laithers Beat: Messrs Savills, 12 Clerk Street, Brechin, Angus DD9 6AE Tel: 01356 622187. Lynebain Fishings: Bell Ingram Rural, 42 Queens Road, Aberdeen AB15 4YE Tel: 01224 324282. Huntly Lodge Beat: H Eggington, Laureston Lodge, Newton Abbot, Devon. Tel: 01626 63081. Various Beats: Iain Forbes, Fishing Tackle, Gordon Street, Huntly Tel:01466 794251. Muiresk Beat: Guy Bentinck, Messrs Peterkins, 100 Union Street, Aberdeen AB9 1QQ Tel: 01244 626300.

FORGUE, Fish Farm
Location & Access 29/621453 Forgue Fish Farm is just to the north of the village of Forgue, where the Burn of Forgue is joined by Dronach Burn.
Commentary There are four little ponds, each approximately 2/3 acres in extent, easily accessible and stocked daily.
Fish Rainbow trout and brown trout. Average weight, 1lb 8oz, with fish of up to 8lb as well.
Flies & Tactics Fly-fishing only, from the bank. Use reservoir-type lures or March Brown, Grouse & Claret, Silver Butcher. Dry-fly fishing will also bring results.
Permission & Charges £18 per rod per day (5 fish limit), £13 per rod per day (2 fish limit), £10 per 4 hour session (2 fish limit), catch-and-release (barbless hooks), £8 per day. Trout may also be purchased at £1.60 per pound. Contact: Forgue Fish Farm, Boghead Bungalow, Inverkeithny, Aberchirder. Banff. Tel: 01466 730266.

IDOCH WATER, River See River Deveron.
ISLA, River See River Deveron.

STONEYHILL, Fish farm
Location & Access 29/645585. Stoneyhill is located by the A97 Aberchirder/Banff road at Bruntbrae.
Commentary Two small put-and-take ponds on a family-run fish farm which is easily accessible and open all year.
Fish Rainbow trout which average 1lb 4oz and some fish of up to 6lb.
Flies & Tactics The trout are not particular and take almost any pattern of fly offered to them.

Permission & Charges £12 per day (4 fish limit), £7 per day (2 fish limit). Thereafter, catch and release using barbless hooks. Trout may be purchased at £1.50 per pound.

YTHAN, River See OS Map 38.

Fraserburgh and Peterhead

BRUCKLAY, Loch
Location & Access 30/908499. To the north of the village of Maud (30/928480) in the grounds of Brucklay Estate. At the time of writing, the fishery has been leased to a private syndicate and is not available to the public. Future information from: Brucklay Estate, Estate Office, Shevado, Maud, Aberdeenshire. Tel: 01771 613623.

CRIMONMOGATE, Loch
Location & Access 30/040591. 6 miles south from Fraserburgh, immediately adjacent to the B9033 St Coombs/A952 road.
Commentary Two small, put-and-take fisheries in a quiet, woodland setting. Crimonmogate Loch is 6 acres, its neighbour, Loch of Logie, is 5 acres. There are excellent facilities, including car park and toilets, and parties and clubs are welcome by prior arrangement.
Fish Brown trout, rainbows and Canadian brook trout.
Flies & Tactics Fly fishing, from the bank only. Most anglers return the brown trout - these fish are all that remain of the Loch of Strathbeg species which have been virtually wiped out by pollution (see Loch of Strathbeg entry). Offer them: Ke-He, Loch Ordie, Silver Butcher, or reservoir lures.
Permission & Charges A day-ticket costs £20 half-day, £12. OAPs are £10 juniors (under 15), £8. Evening fishing costs £10 Contact: Crimonmogate Trout Fishery, Crimonmogate, by Fraserburgh. Tel: 01346 532203

FEDDERATE, Reservoir
Location & Access 30/865523. Approach from the minor road between Mill of Fedderate (30/890501) in the south and New Pitsligo (30/882560) in the north. Turn west at the school at 30/862534 on the road to Whitecairns Farm.
Commentary The reservoir lies on the headwaters of South Ugie Water and the fishing is in the hands of the Fraserburgh Angling Club (Secretary, R Birnie, 30 Saltoun Street, Fraserburgh. Tel: 01346 513861).
Fish Stocked with brown trout and rainbow trout which average 1lb 4oz.
Flies & Tactics Bank fishing only and fish are taken from all round the shoreline. Fly-fishing only and there is a bag limit of 4 fish per rod per day, thereafter fishing is catch-and-release using barbless hooks. Try:

OS Map 30 — Fraserburgh & Peterhead

Wickham's Fancy, Grouse & Claret, Dunkeld. Reservoir lures also produce results.
Permission & Charges Cost: £8 per rod per day. Contact: Mrs J Corbett, Whitecairns Croft, by New Deer, New Pitsligo. Tel: 01771 653235.

MEIKLE, Loch (30/030308) does not contain trout.

MILL OF ELRICK, Fish farm
Location & Access 30/936405. 7 miles north from Ellon on the A948 Ellon/New Deer road.
Commentary A commercial fish farm with 2 small, stocked ponds. One allows any fishing method, the other is fly-fishing only. There is access for disabled anglers. Casting tuition is offered at weekends. Tackle for hire and for sale, as well as fresh and smoked trout.
Fish Rainbow trout. In the all-methods pond, fish average 12oz, in the fly-only water trout range from 1lb up to fish of 9lb..
Flies & Tactics Bank fishing only and all fish landed must be killed. On the all-methods pond, these trout will be charged at £1.60 per pound. The fishery is closed on a Wednesday.
Permission & Charges All-methods pond: £5 per rod; on the fly-only pond, £20 per rod for a 6 fish limit. Contact: Mill of Elrick Fish Farm, The Bungalow, Mill of Elrick, Auchnagatt, Aberdeenshire. Tel: 01358 701628.

NORTH UGIE, Water See River Ugie entry.

PHILORTH, Water
Location & Access Source 30/964580 Outfall 30/028650. The mouth of the river is 2 miles east of Fraserburgh on the B9033 Fraserburgh/St Coombs road.
Commentary A small, spate stream, flowing into Fraserburgh Bay across the golf course.
Fish Primarily brown trout, and finnock in the early months, but also the chance of the occasional sea-trout and salmon.
Flies & Tactics Only the half-mile stretch between the road bridge on the B9033 and the sea is fished. The best chance of sport is after heavy rain when you should show the residents Soldier Palmer, Grouse & Claret, Peter Ross.
Permission & Charges G S Clark (Pets, Sports, Fishing), Frithside, 23 Hanover Street, Fraserburgh. Tel: 01346 514427. Cost, £6 per season.

PITFOUR, Loch
Location & Access 30/977488. Easily accessible from the A950 New Pitsligo/Mintlaw road, to the north of Old Deer Abbey.
Commentary A classic "architectural" estate loch in a woodland setting on the Pitfour Estate. Excellent facilities for anglers with seven boats available for hire.
Fish Primarily stocked-rainbow trout, but also good numbers of brown trout which are of a Loch Leven strain. Rainbow trout average 2lb 8oz with fish of up to 5lb not uncommon. Brown trout average 1lb 8oz..
Flies & Tactics Fly-fishing only and comfortable sport from good boats. This is a shallow water and fish are taken everywhere, from the middle to the margins. Offer them: Ke-He, Grouse & Claret, Dunkeld. Reservoir lures also produce results.
Permission & Charges £18 per rod per day (4 fish limit); £14 per rod per day (3 fish limit); evening £12 per rod (2 fish limit). Boat hire (2 rods): £6 per session, evening £3. Pitfour Fishery, Pitfour Estate, Mintlaw, Aberdeenshire. Tel: 01771 624448.

PRIVATE WATERS HADDO Lakes (30/882356 and 30/879347)

RED, Loch 30/990628. The loch lies 2.5 miles south from Fraserburgh. The Red loch used to be a good fishery but in recent years, probably because of the acidity of the water, stocked fish have died. The loch is no longer fished.

SOUTH UGIE, Water See River Ugie entry.

STRATHBEG, Loch of
Location & Access 30/078585. Situated between the A952 Peterhead/Fraserburgh road.
Commentary The Loch of Strathbeg used to be one of the premier trout fisheries in North East Scotland, famous for the quality of its trout which were a Loch Leven strain. Much of the loch and the surrounding area is now either owned or managed by the Royal Society for the Protection of Birds, and many anglers believe that the presence, and excrement, of upwards of 20,000 geese and other wildfowl has destroyed the trout fising on the loch. However a University of Aberdeen study showed that geese accounted for only 15-20% of the phospates - most of the incoming nutrients come from farming run-off. The loch is now very rarely fished.
Permission & Charges For further information, contact: RSPB, Loch of Strathbeg Reserve, Starnafin, Lonmay. Tel: 01346 532017.

UGIE, River
Location & Access Source 30/056486 Outfall OS30/120474. The river is easily accessible from public and farm roads along its course.
Commentary The Ugie is formed from the flow of North Ugie Water, which has its source near North Crawfords (30/880614), and the South Ugie Water which is impounded in its headwaters by the Fedderate Reservoir (see separate entry). The two streams meet to the east of Longside and enter the North Sea at Peterhead.
Fish Approximately 80/100 salmon and grilse most seasons and upwards of 300 sea-trout. Salmon average 8lb, sea-trout 2lb 8oz. Salmon of 20lb and 22lb have been landed in recent years.
Flies & Tactics Very much a spate stream. Agricultural drainage makes the river rise and fall quickly and being in the right place at the right time is all-important for success. The most noted pools are: Cruives Pot, Meadows, Pot Sunken, Scott's Pool and the Flats. Sea-trout are caught from June onwards, salmon are most abundant in September and October. All legal fishing methods are permitted other than shrimp or prawn. Wading is not really required and a single-handed rod

will do fine. Offer: Hairy Mary, Garry Dog, Willie Gunn, Ally's Shrimp, Stoat's Tail, Munro Killer, size 10/12 dressings.
Permission & Charges Visitor day-tickets at £15 per rod. Contact: Robertson's Sports, 1-3 Kirk Street, Peterhead. Tel: 01779 472584.

WAULKMILL, Fishery
Location & Access 30/885510. Approach from Mill of Fedderate (30/890504) on the minor road which leads north to the Fedderate Reservoir (see separate entry).
Commentary There are two small, put-and-take, lochs here, each about 4 acres in extent. They lie on the course of the Water of Fedderate which flows into South Ugie Water. The fishery has a comfortable fisherman's lodge and picnic area and fishing tackle is available for hire.
Fish Regularly stocked with rainbow trout which average approximately 2lb.
Flies & Tactics Tactics and flies Bank fishing, fly-only. Most patterns of trout fly and reservoir-type lures will produce results.
Permission & Charges £18 per rod per day (4 fish limit), £10 per rod per half-day (2 fish limit). Thereafter, catch-and-release using barbless hooks. Contact: Waulkmill Fishery, Waulkmill, by New Deer, Turriff. Tel: 01771 644357.

YTHAN, River
Location & Access Source 29/635384 Outfall OS38/009240. The estuary is easily accessible from the A975 Newburgh/Peterhead road and at Kirkton of Logie Buchan (38/990299). Public roads and estate roads give access to the remainder of the stream.
Commentary The river rises from the Wells of Ythan and meanders east for a distance of some 40 miles before reaching the North Sea through a four-mile-long, sand-dune-bordered estuary. The Udny Arms Hotel (Tel: 01358 789444) is a good centre for exploring the lower river, Gight House Hotel at Methlick (Tel: 01651 806389) for the upper river. The Sands of Forvie, to the north of the estuary, is an important nature reserve with a wide variety of birds and wildflowers.
Fish Salmon and sea-trout, but not as many of either as in days past. Approximately 80 salmon and between 1000 and 2500 sea-trout are taken most seasons. Salmon average 12lb, sea-trout 2lb. July is the peak sea-trout time but from May until the end of the season sport is generally excellent.
Flies & Tactics The Newburgh Fishings, in the estuary, is the most productive part of the river and is divided into 5 beats. Three are private, two are sometimes available on a day-ticket basis. At ebb tide, the water may be fished as one would fish a medium-sized river. When the tide is full, anglers fish from both boat and bank. The Ythan is a spate stream and the main river is often difficult to fish because of weed-growth caused by nitrogen-enrichment from surrounding farmland. However, there are a number of good holding pools, the best of which are the Machar Pools. Use a trout rod to fish them. The tidal Newburgh Fishings produce sport almost regardless of prevailing weather conditions. Details will be given when booking, as will details of tide-times, essential for safety when tackling the estuary section. Spinning is popular in the tidal reaches but fly-fishing also produces excellent results. Show them: Black Pennell, Teal Blue & Silver, Peter Ross. Streamer sea-trout flies also work well.
Permission & Charges For the Newburgh Fishings, contact: Mrs Audrey Forbes, 3 Lea Cottages, Newburgh, Ellon, Aberdeenshire, Tel: 01358 789297. Day-tickets, when available, £20 per rod. Private beats, when available, £440 in June to £605 per week in September (plus VAT) for 4 rods. Self-catering accommodation close to the fishing may be available through Mrs Forbes. Ellon fishing, from Buchan Hotel, Ellon, Aberdeenshire, Tel: 01358 720208; cost per rod per day in september, £15. Outwith that month, £7.50 per day. Methlick and Haddo Estate fishing, S French & Sons, Grocers, Methlick, Aberdeenshire, Tel: 01651 806213; cost per rod per day: February/August £6, August/October £15; Fyvie Estate (Tel: 01651 891630) have not issued tickets for the past two years because of a scarcity of fish. Fyvie Angling Association Water, J Mackie & Co, Lewes, Fyvie, Aberdeenshire, Tel: 01651 891209; cost: £10 per rod per day.

YTHAN VALLEY, Fishery
Location & Access 30/905338. The fishery lies to the right of the Ellon/Methlick road. 2 miles west of Ellon and is signposted from the top of the farm road.
Commentary A commercial, put-and-take, 11 acre fishery alongside the River Ythan. The loch has a large fishing lodge. Tackle for hire, flies etc for sale and tuition by prior arrangement. Troutmaster water and ASSF member.
Fish Regularly stocked with triploid rainbows trout to 6lb and a natural population of wild brown trout to 5lb plus. Record rainbow trout 13lb 1oz. Record brown 5lb 8oz. There is a small stretch of the river Ythan for two rods available.
Flies & Tactics Use small wet flies, nymphs and buzzers.
Permission & Charges Contact: Ythan Valley Fisheries, Ythanbank, Ellon, Aberdeenshire. Hours: 8.30am to dusk or 11pm (whichever comes first). Charges: Up to 5hrs £14, 3 fish limit; up to 8 hours £18, 4 fish limit; evening 6.30pm-11pm, £11, 2 fish limit.

Barra

A'BHARP, Loch
Location & Access 31/780210. Loch a'Bharp lies close to Lochboisdale and is easily accessible from the A865 road.
Commentary Loch a'Bharp is one of the principal South Uist sea-trout and salmon fisheries. It is joined to the sea by a half-mile-long narrow, brackish channel and the loch itself extends over an area of half a mile north/south and a similar distance east/west.

OS Map 31 — Barra

Fish Salmon and sea-trout from July until the end of the season in October. Sea-trout average 2lb, salmon 6lb/7lb. There are some good brown trout in the loch as well.

Flies & Tactics Boat fishing brings best results and the services of a gillies enhance the chance of sport. The loch is frequently windy and another pair of hands on the oars, holding the boat in position, is a great boon. Loch Gobhlach (31/784214), to the north of Loch a'Bharp and joined to it by a small stream, can also provide interesting sport from the bank. On Loch a'Bharp, the east shore and the north bay, where streams enter, are the most productive fishing areas. Tempt them with: Clan Chief, Kate Maclaren, Goat's Toe. Trout flies also work well.

Permission & Charges Lochboisdale Hotel, Lochboisdale, South Uist. Tel: (0878) 700332. 1st July/16th July - £25 per boat; 18th July/20th August - £35 per boat; 22nd July/17th September - £39 per boat; 19th September/1st October - £28 per boat; 1st October/31st October - £12 per boat. Two rods per boat. All sea-trout under 1lb 8oz must be returned.

A'CHOIRE, Loch See Loch Aisavat.
A'GHEARRAIDH DHUIBH, Loch See Loch Dun na Cille.

AISAVAT, Loch
Location & Access 31/757153. This is one of a series of nine named and unnamed lochs and lochans all lying close to the B888 road from Daliburgh to East Kilbride at the south end of South Uist. They are easily accessible from the B888 and from minor roads at South Boisdale, Garrynamoine and Smerclate.
Commentary The attraction here is accessibility, and the chance of loch-hopping: if the action is slow on one water, simply drive to the next. They are: Loch an Eilean (31/746169), Loch Trosaraidh (31/759170) and Loch nan Capull (31/755161) between South Boisdale and Garrynamoine; Loch na Bagh (31/750156), Loch Aisavat (31/757153), tiny Loch an Duin (31/746152) and Loch Smerclate (31/742153) near Smerclate; Loch a'Choire (31/767144) and the unnamed loch on the shore at 31/762142 near East Kilbride. If you have non-fishing companions, send them over to the lovely island of Eriskay whilst you fish. It is now joined by a causeway to South Uist. Better still, accompany them and tramp out to the only two lochs on Eriskay: Loch Crakavaig (31/795107) and little Loch Duvat (31/803113) on the slopes of Ben Scrien (185m) to the east of the Princes Strand (31/187105) by Coilleag; where Prince Charles Edward Stuart first set foot on Scottish soil in 1745.
Fish Modest brown trout all round.
Flies & Tactics Tactics and flies Bank fishing and the early months are the best time to attack. As the season advances weed becomes a problem. The lochs are easily understood and fish may be taken from all round the shore. The Eriskay lochs rarely see a fly from one season to the next, particularly tiny Loch Duvat. Sea-trout may also be encountered in the sea by Smerclate.
Permission & Charges See Loch Hallan entry.

AN DUIN, Loch (Daliburgh) See Loch Hallan.
AN DUIN, Loch (Smerclate) See Loch Aisavat.
AN EILEAN, Loch (South Boisdale) See Loch Aisavat.
BEINNE-RI-OITIR, Lochan See Loch Crogavat (Daliburgh).
BEOUIN MHOIR, Loch See Loch Crogavat (Daliburgh).
BUN SRUTH (SEA LOCH) See Loch Kearsinish.
CARTACH, Loch See Loch nam Faoileann.
CHILLEIRIVAGH, Loch See Loch nam Faoileann.
CORAGRIMSAIG, Loch See Loch Stulaval.
CRAKAVAIG, Loch See Loch Aisavat.

CROGAVAT, Loch (Daliburgh)
Location & Access 31/755221. Approach along the peat track that runs east at Garryheillie (31/752220) from the A865.
Commentary A group of eighteen small, named and unnamed lochs and lochans, lying to the east of the A865. Begin at the first loch to the north of the track, unnamed on the OS Map but known as Loch na h-Airigh Duibhe (31/756221). This leads north to Loch Crogavat (31/755225), the largest of the waters noted. Follow the inlet stream at the north-east corner of Loch Crogavat over to Loch Fada (31/763221) and work down the east shoreline of this narrow, half-mile-long loch. At the south end of Loch Fada, tramp east, crossing the Abhainn a'Bharp burn, and climb for ten minutes to reach Lochan Beinne-ri-Oitir (31/775222) and its satellite lochans to the south. Return west over the Abhainn a'Bharp burn exploring seven unnamed lochans along the way to locate the south end of Loch na Lice (31/765213). Fish north now to Loch Beouin Mhoir (31/762216) and end the day by having a cast in Loch na Capall (31/759219), unnamed on the OS Map. The north shore touches the Garryheillie track.
Fish Plentiful stocks of modest trout, with the chance of sea-trout.
Flies & Tactics Soggy going and easy to get lost amidst this tangle of bays, promontories and hidden corners. Take a compass and map. Loch Crogavat seems like three lochs, not one, and the north bank is best. The other waters are easily understandable and comfortably fished from the shore with: Blue Zulu, Grouse & Claret, Peter Ross.
Permission & Charges See Loch Hallan entry.

DUN NA CILLE, Loch
Location & Access 31/746190. Loch Dun na Cille lies to the south of Daliburgh close to the B888 road. Park at 31/753184 to fish the south and south-west shore. Attack the north end from Kilpheder at 31/743196.
Commentary This is the largest loch in the area and it extends one mile north/south by up to quarter of a mile east/west. The loch is peat-stained and often exposed to strong winds which stir up the bottom. To the west is Loch a'Ghearraidh Dhuibh (31/740188); a long, narrow strip of water divided into two sections by the B888, the south section being weedy and boggy.
Fish Loch Dun na Cille contains some of the largest trout in South Uist. The average weight is 2lb.
Flies & Tactics Bank fishing only and the trout are large because they are difficult to catch. Do not expect

to fill the glass case quickly, if at all. Your best chance of doing so, however, is at the south end, fishing near the two small islands. At the north end of the loch, concentrate your effort in the vicinity of the small island and down to the site of the ruined Broch. Do not wade. It is dangerous. Flies: Black Pennel, Invicta, Silver Butcher.
Permission & Charges See Loch Hallan entry.

DUVAT, Loch See Loch Aisavat.
FADA, Loch (**Daliburgh**) See Loch Crogavat (Daliburgh).

HALLAN, Loch
Location & Access 31/740220. Turn right from the A865 at Daliburgh (22/754214), past the north end of Loch nam Faoileann (31/752212). Turn right at the next junction and continue to where the road ends and the machair track begins. Turn north on the machair and drive to the cemetery (31/734220). Leave the track and drive down the field to park on the west shore of the loch, by the boat-mooring bay.
Commentary Although Loch Hallan is almost three-quarters of a mile north/south the only fishable areas are in the vicinity of the parking place; the narrows, immediately to the north, and in the south bay. Wearing thigh-boots, it is possible to wade the narrows. Nevertheless, Loch Hallan is attractive to fish, from the boat or from the bank, and the surrounding machair lands are rich in wildflowers and birds. Nearby, at 31/733202 amidst the sandy dunes, are the well-preserved remains of a 2,000 year-old Wheelhouse. Not easy to locate. The first time I looked, I found it only by stumbling into the ruin. There are three other little lochs in the vicinity, unnamed on the map, but known as: Loch an Duin (31/745223), Loch na h-Umha (31/745227), and Lochan Sgeireach (31/750226). These are best approached from Garryheillie (31/751220) on the A865. They will provide supper, but they weed-up as the season advances and should be visited in the spring.
Fish Very pretty trout indeed, pale silver in colour and averaging 10oz in weight.
Flies & Tactics Try: Invicta, Black & Peacock Spider, Black Pennell.
Permission & Charges Mr Bill Felton, Secretary, South Uist Angling Club, Eochar, South Uist. Tel: (0870) 610325; Mrs A Kennedy, Bornish General Stores, Bornish, South Uist. Tel: (0878) 710366. Boat: £5.00 per day, bank: £5.00 per day.

KEARSINISH, Loch
Location & Access 31/798169. Drive south from Daliburgh on the B888/West Kilbride road. At the mile-stone at 31/755180, turn left to North Glendale and park at 31/791177.
Commentary Not for the faint-hearted, but a splendid day out covering eight miles along a good track. The walk encompasses a visit to five perfect lochs in a remote setting at the southern-most tip of South Uist. From North Glendale, follow the track south-east to reach Loch Kearsinish (now despoiled with fish-cages)

after half a mile. Continue up North Glen Dale to Loch Marulaig (31/815163) after a hike of 20 minutes. Half a mile from the east end of Loch Marulaig, the track touches the sea at Eilean Dubh then swings south past an unnamed lochan at 31/829150 to climb gently to Loch Moreef (31/833168). Loch Moreef is joined to the sea at Bun Sruth (31/840144) and is fed from little Loch Ropach (31/829141) to the south. There is every chance of an encounter with golden eagle, buzzard and peregrine during the day, and the possibility of seeing otters.
Fish Something for everyone: bright little three-to-the-pound fish and more serious specimens in Loch Marulaig; the chance of sea-trout in Loch Moreef and at Bun Sruth.
Flies & Tactics Compass and map country. Be well-prepared and ready for all kinds of weather. Work anti-clockwise round Loch Kearsinish: the south and south-east bays are best. Fish the north shore of Loch Marulaig. The other waters are smaller and easily read. Try: Black Zulu, Ke-He, Peter Ross.
Permission & Charges See Loch Hallan entry.

MARULAIG, Loch See Loch Kearsinish.
MOREEF, Loch See Loch Kearsinish.
NA BAGH, Loch See Loch Aisavat.
NA CAPALL, Loch See Loch Crogavat (Daliburgh).
NA CARTACH, Loch (**Barra**) See Loch Tangusdale.
NA DOIRLINN, Loch See Loch Tangusdale.
NA DUIN, Loch (**Barra**) See Loch Tangusdale.
NA H-AIRIGH DUIBHE, Loch (**Chilleirivagh**) See Loch nam Faoileann.
NA H-AIRIGH DUIBHE, Loch (**Daliburgh**) See Loch Crogavat (Daliburgh).
NA H-UMHA, Loch (**Daliburgh**) See Loch Hallan.
NA LICE, Loch (**Daliburgh**) See Loch Crogavat (Daliburgh).

NAM FAOILEANN, Loch
Location & Access 31/755206. This easily-accessible loch lies close to Daliburgh and the A865 road. Loch nam Faoileann has roads all round, indeed, the B888 divides the loch into two sections, west and east, at the school.
Commentary Because of ease of access, Loch nam Faoileann is an attractive proposition for a few pre-dinner casts; as are the other waters which lie by the A865 and B88 roads, including Loch nan Clach-mora (31/756211) and Loch Nosinish (31/758197) which are marked on the OS Map.
The others, unnamed on the OS Map are: Loch Cartach (31/770208); Loch nan Crointean (31/770206); Loch na h-Airigh Duibhe (Chilleirivagh) (31/769203); Loch Chilleirivagh (31/765205); Loch nan Geadh (31/765208); Loch Thogail na Beiste (31/759204); Loch Sgeireach (South Daliburgh) (31/765205); Loch nan Siaman (31/756216).
Fish Brown trout abound, averaging 8oz/10oz in weight, but Loch nam Faoileann has the reputation of holding a few specimen fish of up to and over 2lb in weight.
Flies & Tactics Loch nam Faoileann is the largest water, extending for a distance of three-quarters of a

mile in a dog-leg, north to south-east. The west shoreline of the west section of the loch offers the best chance of sport. The other waters noted above all suffer from weed growth as the season advances and are best attacked in the spring, when, hopefully, the trout are more hungry and less discriminatory. Try: Ke-He, March Brown, Silver Butcher.
Permission & Charges See Loch Hallan entry.

NAM FAOILEANN, Loch See Loch Tangusdale.
NAN ARM, Loch See Loch Stulaval.
NAN CAPULL, Loch (South Boisdale) See Loch Aisavat.
NAN CLACH-MORA, Loch See Loch nam Faoileann.
NAN CROINTEAN, Loch See Loch nam Faoileann.
NAN GEADH, Loch See Loch nam Faoileann.
NAN SIAMAN, Loch See Loch nam Faoileann.
NAN SMALAG, Loch (North Lochboisdale) See Loch Stulaval.
NIC RUAIDHE, Loch See Loch Tangusdale.
NOSINISH, Loch See Loch nam Faoileann.
ROPACH, Loch See Loch Kearsinish.
SGEIREACH, Loch (South Daliburgh) See Loch nam Faoileann.
SGEIREACH, Lochan (Daliburgh) See Loch Hallan.
SHURAVAT, Loch (Benbecula) See Loch Stulaval.
SMERCLATE, Loch See Loch Aisavat.

STULAVAL, Loch
Location & Access 31/800228. Turn north from the A865 by the school building marked on the OS Map at 31/786201 and park at Lasgair. Follow the track to the footbridge over Clachan Arda at 31/786205 leading to Auratote. A good track rises north-east, reaching Loch nan Smalag (31/800208) after a hike of fifteen minutes. Descend north over boggy ground to cross the Abhainn nan Felein burn where an old fence line continues north to Loch Coragrimsaig (31/799223). Loch Stulaval is immediately to the north of Loch Coragrimsaig.
Commentary A six-mile round trip to a remote area of South Uist, fishing five lochs between Beinn-ri-Oitir (122m) to the west and Stulaval (374m) to the east. Apart from the lochs noted above, you should visit little Loch nan Arm (31/812225), unnamed on the OS Map, in a corrie to the east of Loch Stulaval, and Loch Shuravat (22/788241), the true source of the Loch a'bharp System, to the north-west of Loch Stulaval. Detour from Loch an Arm to explore the Iron Age burial chamber in Bealach a'Chaolais at 31/814227.
Fish The possibility of sea-trout and even salmon towards the end of the season, but hard-fighting, bright little brown trout at all times with the chance of a few good fish as well.
Flies & Tactics Loch Stulaval is the largest of these lochs, being almost one mile east/west by up to half a mile wide, 'pinched' into two sections by a long promontory from the north shore. The west section is the most productive area, particularly the north-west corner amidst the tiny outcrops. Also have a thrash where the inlet stream flows in from Loch Shuravat, and in the narrow neck on the north side of the promontory - and in the tiny lochan on the promontory itself. Loch Shuravat is only half a mile from Loch Stulaval and is worth extra effort to reach. On Loch Coragrimsaig, concentrate your expertise in the vicinity of the two small islands and finger-like bay at the west end. The east bay can also be good. Save your assault on Loch nan Smalag for the return journey and don't miss the little satellite lochan on the north shore. This holds some nice trout. Bank fishing all round. Do not wade. Offer them: Black Zulu, Soldier Palmer, Alexandra.
Permission & Charges Lochboisdale Hotel, Lochboisdale, South Uist. Tel: (01878) 700332. Bank fishing from £8 per rod per day.

TANGUSDALE, Loch
Location & Access 31/647997. This is the best trout loch on the Isle of Barra, easily accessible from the only road, the A888, which circles the island. Park by the stile at 31/651996 and walk down to the south end of the loch.
Commentary Although Barra has only nine lochs they offer a wide variety of fishing. The other waters are: Loch na Doirlinn (31/642003) by the white sands of Halaman Bay; the remote, unnamed lochan at 31/663000 on Cadha Mor (100m); Loch nam Faoileann (31/709014) and its two satellite lochans near Ruleos. Loch an Duin (31/692032) at the north of the island is the public water supply and a track along the south shore leads comfortably to tiny Loch na Cartach (31/695027) and Loch nic Ruaidhe (31/702018) with its ruined broch off the north shore. Barra is the perfect place for a family/fishing holiday.
Fish In Loch Tangusdale, trout average 2lb; in Loch na Doirlinn there are fish of over 5lb. The other lochs contain modest specimens which range in size from 8oz to a few of over 1lb in weight. Loch an Duin can sometimes produce sea-trout. There is also the chance of sea-trout from the sea near Borve at 31/655019.
Flies & Tactics Bank fishing, mostly, although it is possible to arrange for a boat to be put on Loch Tangusdale. It is possible to wade safely on Loch Tangusdale and you should start at the south-east corner, near the dramatic tower on the island, and work north. The north-west section frequently produces a good trout.
Loch na Doirlinn will break your heart. It is very small and weedy and there are only really a couple of places from which to cast. If the wind is in the wrong direction, forget it. Upon no account wade. Stay ashore when fishing the other lochs as well. No medals for wet bums. Flies: Ke-He, Invicta, Black Pennell.
Permission & Charges Tourist Information Office, Castlebay, Isle of Barra. Tel: (0871) 810336; Castlebay Hotel, Castlebay, Isle of Barra (0871) 810223. Bank fishing at £5 per rod per day.

THOGAIL NA BEISTE, Loch See Loch nam Faoileann.
TROSARAIDH, Loch See Loch Aisavat.

South Skye

OS Map 32

South Skye

A'BHAC-GHLAIS, Loch See River Eynort.
A'CHOIRE RIABHAIACH, Loch (North) See River Sligachan.
A'CHOIRE RIABHAIACH, Loch (South) See River Sligachan.
A'GHILLE-CHNAPAIN, Loch See Loch Fada (Borline).
A'GHLINNE, Loch See Loch Lamascaig.

A'GHROBAIN, Loch
Location & Access 32/440300. No easy way there. The loch lies near the summit of Sorn a'Ghrobain (250m) and drains north into the Drynoch River. The most direct route is from 32/433310 on the A863 Broadford/Struan road, fording the Drynoch River and climbing steeply over Bealach an Locha (32/437303). Otherwise, walk in from further west, taking a more gentle angle up the hill then circle east to approach the loch.
Commentary This is a very special little loch, as much for the spectacular views south to the Cullins as for the fishing. Loch a'Ghrobain is rarely visited and is worth the effort involved in getting to it. The boat there is kept locked - key from Gledrynoch Lodge for modest charge.
Fish Wild brown trout which average 8oz/12oz.
Flies & Tactics The loch covers an area of approximately 20 acres. Concentrate on the south shore, where the inlet burn enters the loch from Beinn Bhreac (370m). Offer them: Black Zulu, March Brown, Alexandra.
Permission & Charges See River Drynoch entry.

A'SGATH, Loch See River Sligachan.
ABHAINN CAMAS FHIONNAIRIGH, River See Loch na Creitheach.
AIRIGH NA SAORACH, Loch See Lochain Dubha.
ALLT DEARG MOR, River See River Sligachan.
ALLT GHLINNE, River See Loch Lamascaig.
ALLT NA GUILE, Burn See River Drynoch.
AN ATHAIN, Loch See Loch na Creitheach.
AN DROMA BHAIN, Loch See Lochain Dubha.
AN EILEIN, Loch (Suardal) See Loch Lonachan.
AN FIR-BHALLAICH, Loch See River Brittle.

AN IASGAICH, Loch
Location & Access 32/674143. Turn west from the A851 by the telephone box at 32/ 694166 and drive to Drumfearn (32/676156). Walk south from Drumfearn over broken, rising ground for half a mile to reach the north end of the loch. The loch may also be reached from the south by taking the track which leaves the A851 at 32/685120, up the Allt Duisdale burn and then north round the south shoulder of Meall Buidhe (160m).
Commentary A long walk, but worth the effort.
Fish Good brown trout which rise readily to the fly and average 8oz.
Flies & Tactics Although fish rise and are taken from all round the shore, the south end, and the east banks give best results. Try: Ke-He, Invicta, Black Pennell.
Permission & Charges See Loch Lonachan entry.

AN IME, Loch See Loch Baravaig.

AN LEOID, Loch
Location & Access Park by Loch Cill Chriosd at 32/614204 on the A881 Broadford/Elgol road. Follow the Suisnish track south, up the hill by the forest, to meet the Allt an Inbhire burn at 32/610190. A further, hard, two mile tramp will bring you to the outlet burn from Loch an Leoid. Follow it up to the loch. Also visit Loch Fada (32/603168), a ten minute tramp north of Loch an Leoid and its satellite lochan a further step north again. Return by striking north-east from Loch Fada for a distance of one mile, over Beinn a'Mheadhoin (250m), to find Loch Braigh Bhlair (32/618178). After fishing Loch Braigh Bhlair, descend east to the track by the Allt na Pairte burn and walk north to the A881. Another small loch on the Kilbride peninsula worth a visit is Loch nan Learg (32/594191) which is approached via the track that runs south from the site of the old chapel at Tobar na h-Annait (32/589202). When the track reaches the sea at Camus Malag (32/582193), climb east for half a mile to find the loch on the slopes of Beinn an Dubhaich (230m).
Commentary Reaching Loch an Leoid and exploring the other lochs involves a round trip of some 7 miles and should not be undertaken lightly. Skye weather is a fickle and you should always be prepared for the worst.
Fish Expect traditional hill-loch trout. But, be warned, there are some much larger fish as well, particularly in the smaller waters.
Flies & Tactics Bank fishing and, remember, in most hill-lochs the trout lie close to the margins. Approach with caution and offer them: Ke-He, March Brown, Gold Butcher.
Permission & Charges The sporting rights on the estate are let, and the present tenants, I Mackinnon and JTY Gillies, are not allowed to sublet by the owners, the Scottish Executive Rural Affairs Department, Highland Area Sub-Office, Estates Office, Portree IV51 9DH. Tel: (01478) 612516; Fax: (01478) 613128. Contact them for further details.

AN LETH-UILLT, Loch See River Brittle.
AN RUBHA DHUIBH, Loch See Loch Mor (Soay).
AN STARSAICH, Loch See Loch Lonachan.
AN T-SEILICH, Loch See Loch Lamascaig.
AN TUIM, Loch See Loch Dhughaill.
ARD, Loch See Loch Dhughaill.
ARDTRECK, Burn See Loch Fada (Borline).
ARUISG, Loch See Loch Lamascaig.
ASHIK, Loch See Lochain Dubha.

BARAVAIG, Loch
Location & Access 32/685098. Park by Loch nan Dubhrachan (32/676105) on the A851 Isleornsay/Armadale road. Loch nan Dubhrachan is a twenty minute walk south-east.
Commentary Start the day by fishing roadside Loch nan Dubhrachan, before hiking out to Loch Baravaig.

OS Map 32 — South Skye

On the way have a look at tiny Loch an Ime (32/679103).
Fish Fish which fight well and average 8oz.
Flies & Tactics Bank fishing, with sport from all round the shores. Best flies: Blue Zulu, Invicta, Dunkeld.
Permission & Charges See Loch Lonachan entry.

BIODA MOR, Loch See River Eynort.
BRAIGH BHLAIN, Loch
See Loch an Leoid.

BRITTLE, River
Location & Access Source 32/458245 Outfall 32/406209. Turn south at Merkadale (32/380310) on the B8009 Drynoch/Portnalong road and follow the minor road to Glenbrittle and the sea at Loch Brittle.
Commentary The River Brittle rises from Coir a'Tairneilear in the Cullin Hills, between Sgurr a'Ghreadaidh (973m) and Bruach Frithe (958m). It flows north-west down the Allt Coir a'Mhadaidh Burn over a spectacular waterfall before reaching the floor of the glen where it swings south to reach the sea after a journey of some 3 miles. The west bank is bordered by a forestry plantation but the east bank is easily accessible from the Glenbrittle road. There is an excellent camp-site by the shore of Loch Brittle and few rivers in the world have such a magnificent setting.
Fish Salmon in the river and the possibility of sea-trout in the estuary. The salmon are mostly grilse, weighing 6lb/7lb, sea-trout average 1lb 8oz.
Flies & Tactics As ever, on Skye, the river only produces sport after the skies have opened, but when you do manage to be in the right place at the right time, the fishing can be exciting. There are a number of pools, separated by streamy runs, and you should carefully explore them all. There is also a good trout loch, Loch an Fir-bhallaich (32/430209), on the south of the climbers' track out to Sgurr Alasdair (993m) from the Glen Brittle Hut. Even nicer, and not to be undertaken lightly, is remote Loch Coir a'Ghrunnda (32/452202), deep in the Cullin Hills, guarded by grey Sgurr Alasdair, Sgurr Sgumain and Sgurr Dubh Mor (944m). Taking a trout from these waters is an unforgettable experience. A less taxing day-out can be spent amidst the more modest hills to the west of the River Brittle and there is even a perfect little trout loch to encourage you to do so, Loch an Leth-uillt (32/365212), on the cliffs above Sgurr nam Boc. It is a five-mile round trip. Another away-from-it-all day can be planned by striking south from Glenbrittle Campsite, following the track that margins the east shore of Loch Brittle. This gives access to 3 lochs overlooking the island of Soay in sea-Loch Scavaig: Loch Meachdannach (32/439179), Lochan Coir a'Ghobhainn (32/417182), and the unnamed loch by the side of the track at 32/405177, close to Creag Mhor (124m). Choose the flies depending upon water conditions, but, and as a general rule, darker flies do best: Black Zulu, Black Pennell, Grouse & Claret, Silver Butcher.
Permission & Charges Sporting rights are owned by the MacLeod Estate, Dunvegan Castle, Dunvegan, Isle of Skye. Tel: (01470) 521206; Fax: (01470) 521205. Charges per rod: £10 per day, £50 per week. The estate have accommodation at Glenbrittle and fishing permits are also available from the Glenbrittle Campsite Shop.

BROADFORD, River
Location & Access Source 32/610205; Outfall 32/640236. The river rises from Loch Cill Chriosd and flows north down Strath Suardal, crossing the A850 Kyleakin/Portree in the town of Broadford itself to reach the sea in Broadford Bay. The total system is approximately 2.5 miles in length.
Commentary This is an easily-accessible river. Without rain, the Broadford can almost completely disappear, and the key to success is being there at the right time.
Fish Given appropriate water levels, sea-trout enter from late June onwards, and salmon run the river from late July through until the end of the season in October. Salmon average 7lb, sea-trout 2lb.
Flies & Tactics The river is narrow and the water clear. Keep well back from the banks and use light tackle. Vary the size of fly according to water conditions. Try trout patterns: Black Pennell, Grouse & Claret, Peter Ross.
Permission & Charges The Broadford Hotel has one bank of the first 1.5 miles of the stream and charges in the order of £8 per rod per day. Contact: Broadford Hotel, Broadford, Isle of Skye. Tel: (01471) 822204.

BUIDHE, Loch See Loch Lonachan.
CAMASUNARY, River See Loch na Creitheach.
CAOL, Loch (Sligachan) See River Sligachan.
CILL CHRIOSD, Loch See Broadford River.
COIR A'GHOBHAINN, Lochan See River Brittle.
COIR A'GHRUNNDA, Loch See River Brittle.
COIRE DOIRE NA SEILG, Loch See Loch Mor (Soay).
CORUISK, Loch See Loch na Creitheach.
CROSS REFERENCES The fishing on the Island of Raasay is detailed on OS Map 24.
The fishing on the Island of Rhum is recorded on OS Map 39.
CRUINN, Loch See Lochain Dubha.

DHUGHAILL, Loch
Location & Access 32/613082. Leave the A851 near Kilbeg (32/650061) and drive west along the minor road between Kilbeg and the beach at Gillean (32/587087). The loch lies beside the road after three miles.
Commentary Loch Dhughaill is easily accessible, but if you want to make a full day of it amidst some of the most stunning scenery in Scotland, plan a longer route to include a visit to Loch nan Uamh (32/633084), to the north-east of Loch Dhughaill. If still not satisfied, tramp further, on a superb round of the tiny lochs further north and west: Loch nan Breac Dubha (32/631089), then east to Loch Ard (32/640091), now a hard mile due west over rising moorland to find Loch an Tuim (32/624096). End the day by continuing south-west for half a mile to have a cast in Loch nan Clach (32/617095) before returning to the road over Sgurr na h-Iolaire (292m). An alternative, and just as attractive option, is to head south from Loch

South Skye — OS Map 32

Dhughaill to visit two very remote little waters by Sgurr Breac (249m): Loch Ic Iain (32/601070) and, at the end of a hard two mile tramp, Loch Nighean Fhionnlaidh, both of which will reward your efforts, not only with pretty little trout, but also with an unforgettable walk.
Fish The trout average three to the pound, with a few fish of up to and over 1lb in weight in the main lochs.
Flies & Tactics This is a stiff, four mile round trip so you should be properly prepared with compass and map, food and all-weather gear. Bank fishing all the way. Try: Black Zulu, March Brown, Dunkeld.
Permission & Charges Armadale Castle Gardens and Museum of the Isles, Armadale, Sleat, Isle of Skye IV43 8RS. Tel: (01471) 844305. A wide range of non-fishing attractions is also available, including museum, stable restaurant, study centre, gardens and Armadale Castle itself. There are also a number of excellent self-catering cottages for rent.

DOIRE A'CHREAMHA, Loch See Loch Mor (Soay).

DOIRE AN LOCHAIN, Loch See Loch Mor (Soay).

DRYNOCH, River
Location & Access Source 32/469307 Outfall 32/408314. Access to the whole river is obtained from the A863 Broadford/Struan road which margins the north bank through Glen Drynoch.
Commentary The River Drynoch is approximately 4 miles in length and runs west through steep-sided Glen Drynoch, with Sron a'Ghrobain (250m) to the south and Coire an t-Sagairt (300m) to the north. The river exits over wide sands into the sea at Loch Harport, mingling with the waters from the Vikisgill Burn and the Allt na Guile Burn.
Fish Salmon and sea-trout. Salmon are mostly grilse and average 5lb in weight, sea-trout average 1lb.
Flies & Tactics Like all Skye streams, the Drynoch is a spate river, entirely dependent upon rain to produce of its best. Sea-trout run the system from about June onwards, salmon appear towards the end of July. The first mile of the River Drynoch is the most productive part, given good water conditions, and the lower section of the Vikisgill Burn, before the waterfall, will also produce sport, as can fishing for sea-trout in the estuary of both streams. Use a single-handed rod and stay well back from the river bank. The water is very clear and fish are easily "spooked". Offer them: Green Highlander, Hairy Mary, Goat's Toe, Black Doctor, or size 10/12 trout flies: Black Pennell, Soldier Palmer, Silver Invicta.
Permission & Charges Sporting rights are owned by the Scottish Executive Rural Affairs Department and let to Drynoch & Borline Club secretary Commander W Peppe, Glendrynoch Lodge, Carbost, Isle of Skye. Tel: (01478) 640218. The club welcomes responsible fly-fishers and issues visitor permits at a modest cost for salmon and sea-trout fishing, and for hill-loch fishing for brown trout on the Drynoch and Borline Estates.

DUBH, Loch (Borline) See Loch Fada (Borline).

DUBH, Loch (Sligachan) See River Sligachan.

DUBH, Lochan (Meodal) See Loch Meodal.
DUBHA, Loch (Sligachan) See River Sligachan.

EYNORT, River
Location & Access Source 32/365280 Outfall 32/381265. Approach from Carbost, near the monument on the B8009 road at 32/385314. Turn west on the minor road and half a mile after the church, bear left to Eynort at the head of sea-Loch Eynort. The road borders the river.
Commentary The River Eynort is approximately 3 miles in length and rises from the east slopes of Beinn Bhreac (445m), flowing north-east through a forestry plantation before swinging south down the glen to reach the sea through the sands at Cnoc Loisgte. There are also three trout lochs here, in the south section of the Borline Estate, but none are easy of access. Two may be fished as part of a 4-mile hike. Start from Talisker (32/5301) and follow the line of the Sleadale Burn south up the hill. It will lead you to Loch a'Bhac-ghlais (32/341279), an excellent little water in wonderful surroundings. Climb south again from Loch a'Bhac-ghlais, almost to the summit of Beinn Bhreac (445m), to explore the unnamed lochan at 32/345273, rarely fished from one year to the next. Return north over rough ground to find Loch Sleadale (32/347290). The only other loch here is Loch Bioda Mor (32/370277) high on Biod Mor (383m), about which little is known. There are boats (locked) on Lochs a'Bhac-ghlais and Sleadale. Keys from Glendrynoch Lodge on payment of modest charge.
Fish Sea-trout and occasional salmon in the river, modest brown trout in the lochs.
Flies & Tactics As always on Skye, heavy rain is a must. No water, no fish. When conditions are right, however, this is a super little stream and can provide exciting sport. Only the lower river is fished, and 'fine and far off' gives the best chance of success. Offer: Black Pennell, Greenwell's Glory, Peter Ross.
Permission & Charges See River Drynoch entry.

FADA GHASGAIN, Lochan See Loch Meodal.

FADA, Loch (Meodal) See Loch Meodal.

FADA, Loch (Skye)
Location & Access 32/341318 Loch Fada is one of a group of seven lochs and lochans lying in the north of the Borline Estate. There are also a number of useful little burns where sea-trout may be encountered in the estuaries from April until the end of the season in October. The B8009 Carbost/Portnalong road, which borders sea-Loch Harport to the east, leads west via a minor road through Sabhail (32/324338) to a track south via Huisgill which starts at 32/323331. This track meets the minor road from Carbost in the east to Talisker Bay in the west and these routes give relatively, easy, access to all the lochs and streams in the area.
Commentary Something for everyone here, angler and non-angler alike: wonderful scenery, glorious, deserted beaches for the bucket-and-spade brigade, coastal walks, vigorous hikes into the hills, and, of course, a visit to the famous Talisker Distillery to sample one of the world's great single malts.

OS Map 32 — South Skye

Fish The chance of sea-trout at the mouths of the burns, and salmon and sea-trout in the Talisker River after heavy rain. Good sport also with pretty, red-speckled brown trout in the hill-lochs. Nothing for the glass case, but plenty for breakfast.

Flies & Tactics Park at 32/323331, at the start of the track south to Talisker. Climb over the north shoulder of Beinn Bheag (180m) to reach Loch a'Ghille-chna-pain (32/330329). Fish the east shore and follow the inlet stream round the hill to little Loch nan Uan (32/332328). Continue south now, with the crags of Lon Ban on your left, to reach Loch Lic-aird, a narrow water, 300 yds in length. At the south end, walk the inlet stream east, up the hill, to have a cast in the unnamed lochan at 32/338321 before walking south again to find Loch Fada. Return to the starting point fishing the west shores of the principal lochs. There are two further lochs to the east of the Huisgill track which are worth a visit: Lochan Sgurr Mhoir (32/312315) and tiny Loch Dubh (32/315328). For action with migratory fish, consider a visit to Talisker Bay, the Talisker River (32/315304), and Fiskavaig Bay (32/335346). Also, the mouth of the Ardtreck Burn (32/3403457) and the small bay between Sgurr nan Uan and Gob na h-Oa at 32/323344. Offer salmon, sea-trout and brown trout standard pattern flies. You will not go far wrong with a cast of Black Pennell on the "bob", Greenwell's Glory in the middle, and a Peter Ross on the tail.

Permission & Charges Sporting rights are controlled by Jonathan Wathen, Talisker House (Tel 01478 640245). Contact him before going.

FADA, Loch (Suisnish) See Loch an Leoid.
FISKAVAIG BAY, Estuary See Loch Fada (Borline).
HORAVEG, Loch See Loch Lamascaig.
IC IAIN, Loch See Loch Loch Dhughaill.
INVER AULAVAIG Estuary See River Ord.
INVER DALAVIL Estuary See Loch Lamascaig.
ISLAND OF SCALPAY Scalpay has a number of excellent trout lochs, the best of which is Loch an Leoid (32/617304), but fishing is not available to members of the public.
KILMARIE, River See Loch Creitheach.

LAMASCAIG, Loch
Location & Access 32/582038. The turning point on a long day out in the hills fishing a series of remote little lochs on the Aird of Sleat peninsula; in terms of miles, only five, but in terms of terrain, rough going and not to be undertaken lightly.

Commentary Park on the minor road to the west of Aird of Sleat at 32/589007. Angle uphill, north-west round the east shoulder of Sghurran Seilich (142m) to reach the first water, Loch Aruisg (32/575009), with its small island at the north end. Follow the inlet stream from Loch Aruisg, north and where it swings east climb the hill to find Loch Horaveg (32/57701). Track the inlet stream from Loch Horaveg to the Lochan an Dathaidh at 32/574022 between Sgurr an Easain Dhuibh (170m) to the west and Sgurr a'Chaise (190m) to the east. The next water, Loch an t-Seilich (32/57903), lies half a mile north from Loch an t-Seilich. Find the inlet burn in the north bay then walk north and east for ten minutes to locate Loch Lamascaig (32/582038). At this point, you have another, vigorous, option, of tramping a further mile north to visit Inver Dalavil beach. Otherwise, climb south-east up the inlet burn to Loch an t-Seilich to find Loch Sgurr na Caorach (32/589033). Return home over Sgurr na Caorach (280m) via an Loch Fada at (32/589027), following the outlet stream back down to Allt Mor. At 32/589011, bear west round the slope to visit the site of the old chapel at 32/584010.

Fish These lochs are very rarely fished and contain trout of various sizes. The tidal water at Inver Dalavil, and the Allt Ghlinne burn which feeds it from Loch a' Ghlinne (a Site of Special Scientific Interest and preserved), offer the opportunity of sport with sea-trout, given the right water conditions.

Flies & Tactics A major expedition requiring fitness and efficient use of a compass and map. Bank fishing all the way and no need to wade. The lochs are easily covered from the shore. Try: Loch Ordie, Greenwell's Glory, Black Pennell.

Permission & Charges See Loch Dhughaill entry.

LIC-AIRD, Loch See Loch Fada (Borline).
LOCHAIN A'MHULLAICH, Loch See Lochain Dubha.

LOCHAIN DUBHA, Loch
Location & Access 32/675208. Immediately to the west of the A851 Isleornsay/Broadford road. Park at 32/680208.

Commentary A group of three, easily-accessible, attractive roadside lochs. To the south is Loch Airigh na Saorach (32/683202), also close to the road. On Glac an Skulamus (140m), to the west, is little Loch an Droma Bhain (32/668200), whilst to the east of the A851 lie three small lochans which are also worth a cast: Lochain a'Mhullaich (32/690209), Loch Cruinn (32/681218), and Lochain Teanna (32/684219). South from the A850, and approached from Ashaig (32/690239), is Loch Ashik (32/691232).

Fish The main lochs have some good trout, as well as large numbers of 8oz fish. The hill-lochs have mainly small fish which average three to the pound.

Flies & Tactics Bank fishing and trout are easily covered from the shore. No need for wading. Early morning and late evening produce best results. Offer them: Blue Zulu, Soldier Palmer, Silver Invicta.

Permission & Charges See Loch Lonachan entry.

LOCHAIN STRATHA MHOIR, Loch See Loch na Sguabaidh.

LOCHAIN TEANNA, Loch See Lochain Dubha.

LONACHAN, Loch
Location & Access Loch Lonachan is the largest of a group of four remote lochs lying to the north of Beinn nan Carn (301m). They are best approached from the A881 Broadford/Torrin road. Park near Suardal at 32/622209 and follow the track south, round the shoulder of Ben Suardal (283m). A stiff tramp of approximately one mile brings you to the inlet burn to

South Skye — OS Map 32

Loch Lonachan. Walk the burn to the loch.
Commentary You will need a compass and map for this expedition and the round trip of all the lochs will take you over five rough miles. Fish the north shore of Loch Lonachan to the narrow east arm, then, tracking the inlet stream, climb steeply up the hill to locate Loch an Eilein (32/640187). Fish the south shore of Loch an Eilein to the east end, then walk north-east for ten minutes to find Loch an Starsaich (32/646190). At the north end of Loch an Starsaich, walk north-west to the last water, Loch Buidhe (32/639194). Descend to Loch Lonachan and fish the south shore back to the track.
Fish Great fun all the way with sparkling trout which average 8oz and the chance of a few larger specimens as well.
Flies & Tactics Comfortable bank fishing, provided you stay ashore and do not attempt to wade. The north shore of Loch Lonachan is the most productive area. On Loch an Eilein, fish in the vicinity of the three small islands. The other two waters are easily 'read'. Tempt trout with: Black Zulu, Soldier Palmer, Peter Ross.
Permission & Charges Hotel Eilean Iarmain, Eilean Iarmain, An t-Eilean Sgitheanach IV43 8QR. Tel: 01471 833266; Fax: 01471 833260. Charges: £7.50 per rod per day, £25 per rod per week.

MEACHDANNACH, Loch See River Brittle.

MEODAL, Loch
Location & Access 32/658111. Loch Meodal lies immediately adjacent and to the south of the minor road bordering the Ord River which leaves the A851 at 32/673104.
Commentary The minor road give access to a number of other lochs on Fearann Eilean Iarmain Estate. To the south lie Loch nan Dubhraichean (32/638108) and Loch Mhic Charmhiceil (32/645099). And to the north, for those who seriously want to disappear, Lochan Fada (32/658133), Lochan Dubh (32/659126), and Lochan Fada Ghasgain (32/64813).
Fish Brown trout which average 8oz and the chance of the odd larger fish.
Flies & Tactics Serious walking is involved and you should go well prepared with compass and map. All the lochs will delight, as will the surrounding wildlife: a wonderful day out. Take along: Black Pennell, Grouse & Claret, Silver Butcher to catch supper.
Permission & Charges See Loch Lonachan entry.

MHIC CHARMHICEIL, Loch See Loch Meodal.

MILL, Loch See Loch na Creitheach.

MOR, Loch (Soay)
Location & Access 32/454148. The only access is by boat, and it may be possible to arrange this at Elgol, being dropped off in the morning and then collected at the end of the day. If you do so, be well-prepared, because if the weather changes suddenly, as it frequently does in Skye, you could be stranded for days on the island.
Commentary Very rarely visited and very rarely fished. Not much is known about Loch Mor, or, indeed the other lochs on the Island of Soay: Loch Doire an Lochain (32/459147), Lochan na Teanga Riabhaich (32/447144), Loch Doir a'Chreamha (32/436132), Loch Coire Doire na Seilg (32/451126), Loch an Rubha Dhuibh (32/455131), and Loch na Doire Buidhe.
Fish There is no reason why Loch Mor and Loch Doire an Lochain should not hold sea-trout: Loch Coruisk (32/485205), once one of Scotland's most famous sea-trout waters, shares the same bay, Loch Scavaig. The only problem might be that sea lice infestation from fish-farm cages could have decimated sea-trout stocks in the area. The other lochs are all tiny hill-lochs and will contain small brown trout, but, perhaps, who knows, there could also be larger fish as well.
Flies & Tactics A track runs south from Camas nan Gall, bordering the shore, dotted with ruined crofts, and the hill-lochs are south and west of the track. Loch Mor and Loch Doire an Lochain are close to the beach at Camas nan Gall and are easily accessible - once you have found your way to Soay. Try: Loch Ordie, Soldier Palmer, Peter Ross.
Permission & Charges Very difficult to find out, in spite of extensive enquires on Skye. Best advice is to ask in Elgol, when making transport arrangements.

MOR NA CAIPLAICH, Loch See River Sligachan.

NA CREITHEACH, Loch
Location & Access 32/5772110. No easy way in. From Sligachan (32/488299) on the A850 Broadford/Portree road, it is a 5 mile hike south, although there is a good track all the way, bordering the Sligachan River. From the south-east, the loch may be approached from Kilmarie (32/545172) on the A881 Broadford/Elgol road, via a two mile track over the hill to near Camasunary where the track swings north, at 32/524189, reaching the loch after a further half a mile.
Commentary Loch na Creitheach is three-quarters of a mile north south by up to one quarter of a mile wide, completely surrounded by majestic Cullin peaks: Bla Bheinn (928m) to the east, Ruadh Stac (500m) to the north, Sgurr nan Eag (924m) west, and Sgurr na Stri (497m) to the south. The loch exits to the sea near Camasunary at 32/509188 via the Abhainn Camas Fhionnairigh river (Camasunary River). Walk west from the mouth of the Abhainn Camas Fhionnairigh to reach one of the most dramatic and exciting lochs in Scotland, Loch Coruisk (32/485205). However, be minded that to reach Loch Coruisk from Camasunary you must negotiate the infamous Bad Step (32/494192), a foot-narrow ledge above a precipitous plunge into the sea at Loch nan Leachd. Loch na Creitheach is fed from the north by Loch an Athain (32/512225) and the connecting burn is always worth a cast, particularly after heavy rain.
Fish The primary interest here is sea-trout, but, sadly, as throughout much of the West Highlands, sea-trout stocks have collapsed because of sea lice infestation from nearby fish-farms.
Flies & Tactics Fishing in the Abhainn Camas Fhionnairigh and Loch Coruisk is not available to the

OS Map 32 — South Skye

public. Neither is fishing available in the little Kilmarie River at 32/554173 or the Mill Loch at 32/545187. However, much of this area is now owned by the John Muir Trust, the Scottish conservation group, and fishing is available through the Trust on Loch na Creitheach and Loch an Athain. Fishing is from the bank and wading is not advisable. The north-west shore is best, in the vicinity of the inlet burn. Little Loch an Athain is easily understood. Flies: Loch Ordie, Camasunary Killer, Peter Ross, Black Pennell, Alexandra, Soldier Palmer, Grouse & Claret.
Permission & Charges Contact: Keith Miller, Strathaird, Broadford, Isle of Skye IV49 9AX. Tel: 01471 866260.

NA DOIRE BUIDHE, Loch See Loch Mor (Soay).

NA LERG, Loch See Loch an Leoid.

NA SGUABAIDH, Loch
Location & Access Approach from the bridge at Clach Oscar (32/564225) near Torrin on the A881 Broadford/Elgol road at the head of sea-Loch Slapin.
Commentary The source of the loch lies to the east, between the peaks of Beinn na Cro (700m) and Glas Bheinn Bheag (400m). The stream flows north, initially, before swinging south down Strath Mor to enter Lochain Strata Mhoir (32/564254). As Loch na Sguabaidh narrows, to the south, it forms an attractive little river, before entering Loch Slapin. A good track borders the whole system, from Clach Oscar in the south, north to Luib on the A850 Broadford/Portree road.
Fish Both lochs hold decent brown trout which average in the order of 8oz/10oz. There is a possibility of sea-trout and the occasional salmon, particularly after heavy rain and towards the end of the season.
Flies & Tactics Being there after a spate is the most important tactic, and keeping well back from the river bank to avoid spooking fish. The lochs are fished from the bank, and the south end of Loch na Sguabaidh is best. Fish lie close to the shore. Wading will only scare them out into deeper water. Try: Clan Chief, Goat's Toe, Willie Gunn, sizes 12 to 14.
Permission & Charges The Post Office, Torrin, Isle of Skye. Tel: 01471 822232. Costs: in the order of £8 per rod per day.

NA TEANGA RIABHAICH, Lochan See Loch Mor (Soay).

NAN BREAC DUBHA, Loch (Armadale) See Loch Dhughaill.
NAN CLACH, Loch See Loch Dhughaill.
NAN DUBHRACHAN, Loch See Loch Baravaig.
NAN DUBHRAICHEAN, Loch See Loch Meodal.
NAN EILEAN, Loch (Sligachan) See River Sligachan.
NAN UAMH, Loch See Loch Dhughaill.
NAN UAN, Loch (Borline) See Loch Fada (Borline).
NIGHEANN FHIONNLAIDH, Loch See Loch Dhughaill.

ORD, River
Location & Access Source: 32/645116; Outfall 32/617131. The river is easily accessible and lies on the south side of the road which runs from the A851 in the east to Ord, at the mouth of the river, in the west.
Commentary A significant little river, but only after heavy rain. When the rain gods dance, there is every chance of sport, particularly on the first few hundred yards of the stream. Sea-trout may also be taken in the sea at Inver Aulavaig (32/605127) where there are also excellent facilities for the bucket and spade brigade.
Fish Mostly sea-trout which average in the order of 2lb, but the odd salmon as well.
Flies & Tactics Stalk the fish, keeping well back from the bank, extending line from one spot, rather than marching down the river in the traditional fashion. The tidal reaches often produce results, even when river water levels are poor. Try: Black Pennell, Soldier Palmer, Peter Ross.
Permission & Charges See Loch Lonachan entry.

REIDH NAN, Loch
Location & Access 32/427332. Park near the View Point at 32/402321 on the A863 Broadford/Struan road. Keeping the Allt Coir a'Ghobhainn burn on your right, climb north for ten minutes, then cross the burn and walk north-east for one mile, still climbing, aiming for the craggy ridge ahead, to reach the loch.
Commentary Loch nan Reidh is the largest of a series of three lochans on the west shoulder of Coire an t-Sagairt (300m), nestling in a narrow, steep-sided glen, with the bulk of Roineval (439m) towering north. The surrounding views are splendid. There is a boat on the main loch (rowlocks from Glendrynoch Lodge for modest charge).
Fish Modest brown trout, but also the chance of a few larger fish, particularly in the two smaller waters to the north.
Flies & Tactics Bank fishing, and after exploring the main loch, walk north-east, up the line of the inlet burn, to find the first of the unnamed, satellite lochans. The last one is five minutes north east again. Bushy flies do the trick: Ke-He, Soldier Palmer, Black Zulu.
Permission & Charges See River Drynoch entry.

SGURR MHOIR, Lochan See Loch Fada (Borline).
SGURR NA CAORACH, Loch See Loch Lamascaig.
SLEADALE, Loch See River Enyort.

SLIGACHAN, River
Location & Access Source 32/470245 Outfall 32/490304. This is one of the longest rivers in Skye and it rises from Lota Corrie, below the summit of Sgurr nan Gillean (965m), sweeping down through Harta Corrie by Loch Dubha (32/498243) and Glen Sligachan to the sea in a journey of some seven miles. Access is from the Sligachan Hotel at the junction of the A850 and A863 roads. There is an excellent track bordering the river.
Commentary Breathtaking scenery and, occasionally, breathtaking sport. It all depends upon the weather and heavy rain is a pre-requisite for success. If the weather gods are unkind, console yourself with a visit to the surrounding hill lochs, both accessible and remote, and fish for brown trout instead. Two such waters, rarely fished and with the same name, lie in the mountains: Loch a'Choire Riabhaiach (32/497210), to

Loch Alsh & Glen Shiel — OS Map 32-33

the north of the track over to Loch Coruisk (32/4851205), at the end of a six mile hike, and tiny Loch a'Choire Riabhaich (32/479266) which is best approached from the climbers' path to Sgurr nan Gillean.

More accessible, and closer to Sligachan, are Loch Dubh (32/483281), Loch Caol (32/476301), Loch nan Eilean (32/471302), Loch Mor na Caiplaich (32/475310), and Loch a'Sgath (32/471320). The principal tributary of the River Sligachan, Allt Dearg Mor, which joins the main river just before it enters the sea, can also offer good sport - after a spate.

Fish All the lochs contain brown trout of varying size, including a few trout of over 1lb in weight. The river, and the tributary, hold sea-trout and salmon after heavy rain, particularly towards the end of the season.

Flies & Tactics When the river is in condition, fish fine and far off, using Green Highlander, General Practitioner, Munro Killer, Hairy Mary, Goat's Toe, Clan Chief. Trout patterns also work, depending upon water levels. The trout lochs are all fished from the bank and it is best to stay safely ashore. If you are minded to visit the remote, high lochs, take every precaution and make sure you leave a note saying where you are going and when you expect to return.

Permission & Charges See Storr Lochs entry on OS Map 23 for permit details from Jansports, Portree. Cost: salmon and sea-trout, per rod: £7.50 for a half day, £12 for a full day. Trout: £5 per rod per day. No half day permits. Full day £10. No Sunday fishing. Fishing 'any legal method'.

TALISKER, River See Loch Fada (Borline).
VIKISGILL, Burn See River Drynoch.

Loch Alsh & Glen Shiel

A'CHOIRE BHEITHE, Loch See Loch Quoich.
A'COIRE A'PHUILL, Loch See Inverie River.
A'MHAIM, Lochan See Loch Arkaig.
AN DUBH-LOCHAIN, Loch See River Inverie.
AN LAGAIN AINTHEICH, Loch See Loch Quoich.

ARKAIG, Loch

Location & Access 33/060916. The east end of Loch Arkaig (4 miles of the loch) is on OS34, Fort Augustus (34/140895). Approach from the B8005 Gairlochy/Achnasaul road, either via Achnacarry (34/176897) or the Mile Dorcha (the dark mile). A minor road runs along the north shore of the loch to the sheep farm of Strathan (33/979914).

Commentary The loch is 11 miles east/west by up to three-quarters of a mile north/south and is famous not only for its fishing, but also for its association with the Jacobite Rebellion of 1745. In July 1746 Cameron of Lochiel, who had raised Bonnie Prince Charles's Standard at Glenfinnan less than a year earlier, lay in the hills above Achnacarry and watched Government soldiers burn his fine house; gold from France, intended for the support of the Jacobite army, is reputed to have been thrown into the loch near Strathan; Prince Charles hid from his pursuers in the hills surrounding the loch. Loch Arkaig is one of Scotland's "special" places.

Fish Wild brown trout which average 8oz, but much larger fish as well, and some very large ferox lurking in the depths. Also, Arctic char, pike and the remote chance of sea-trout and salmon which enter the loch via the River Lochy (see separate entry) and the River Arkaig.

Flies & Tactics Loch Arkaig has long been one of the north's most popular fishing locations and, as such, has been heavily fished for many years. The building of the Caledonian Canal in the 19th century, the more recent Hydro-electric power developments constructed in the 1950's and fish farming in the loch has substantially altered the character of this lovely loch, and the quality of its fishing. Nevertheless, good sport may still be had, particularly towards the shallower, west end where two perfect streams, the River Dessarry and the River Pean, feed Loch Arkaig. An old track leads west up Glen Dessarry, climbing between Sgurr na h-Aide (867m) to the south and Sgurr na Ciche (1040m) to the north, dropping down to the ruined croft buildings at Finiskaig on the shores of sea-Loch Nevis (33/871944). This track passes Lochan a'Mhaim (33/902944) and its adjacent, unnamed neighbour, both of which hold wild trout which average 6oz; but it is a long way to hike for breakfast, unless you plan to camp out at Finiskaig. All the small lochs noted above are fished from the bank. On Loch Arkaig, the best results come from boat fishing, although bank fishing can be productive in the vicinity of many burn mouths. However, avoid wading since the water deepens quickly close to the shore in many places. There are no boats for hire, so if you wish to get afloat you must provide your own vessel. There is a small hill loch to the south of Loch Arkaig which is worth a cast, Loch Briobaig (34/111892) which is approached after a stiff climb north from Glen Mallie at 34/120880, and to the north of Loch Arkaig there are two further excellent waters, best approached from Caonich (33/063922). Climb north-west from the road for 1 mile to reach the first, and largest water, Loch Blair (33/056945) which is three-quarters of a mile north/south by up to quarter of a mile wide. A step further north from Loch Blair will bring you to its more modest neighbour, Lochan Dubh (33/ 061955). A circular tour, visiting both lochs makes a splendid day out in the hills and should send you happily home with supper. The River Arkaig can produce the occasional salmon and sea-trout and is also worth a visit, particularly in high water conditions. Offer trout: Black Pennell, March Brown, Silver Butcher. Salmon and sea-trout will also take trout patterns, as well as Ally's Shrimp, Stoat's Tail, Hairy Mary, Garry Dog.

Permission & Charges Contact: West Highland Estates, Estate Office, 33 High Street, Fort William, Inverness-shire. Tel: 01397 702433. Cost for river (fly only) and loch fishing (no live bait): £3.00 per rod per day. Boat launching charges: £10.00 per boat per day with two anglers fishing. Permits may also be obtained

OS Map 33 — Loch Alsh & Glen Shiel

from Mrs Yates, 2 Clunes, Achnacarry, by Fort William. Tel: 01397 712719 and from Rod & Gun Shop, 18 High Street, Fort William. Tel: 01397 702656.

ARKAIG, River See Loch Arkaig.
BEALACH NAN CREAGAN DUBHA, Loch See River Inverie.
BHRAOMISAIG, Loch See River Inverie.
BLAIR, Loch See Loch Arkaig.
BRIOBAIG, Loch See Loch Arkaig.
CARNACH, River See Inverie River.
CLUANIE, LOCH See OS Map 34.
COIRE CHAOLAIS BHIG, Loch See Loch Quoich.
COIRE NA CIRCE, Loch See Inverie River.
COIRE NAM CNAMH, Loch See Loch Quoich.
COIRE NAN CADHA, Loch See Loch Quoich.
COIRE SHUBH, Loch See Loch Quoich.

CROE, River
Location & Access Source 33/984157. Outfall 33/950212. Access is from the A87 Invermoriston/Kyle of Lochalsh road via the camp site and car park at Morvich (33/960211). A track, which parallels the south bank of the river, leads south-east from Morvich up Gleann Lichd to Glenlicht House (33/006174) and the headwaters of the system.
Commentary The river rises in a deep corrie between Sgurr Fhuaran (1068m) and Sgurr na Ciste Duibhe (1027m), two of the group of mountains known as the Five Sisters of Kintail. The stream is four miles in length and flows through spectacular scenery in a succession of smooth glides and deep, peat-stained pools.
Fish Few salmon and even fewer sea-trout due to sea-lice infestation from nearby factory-salmon farms.
Flies & Tactics Notable pools on the river include: Morvich Pool, Elbow Pool, New Pool and Road Pool.
Permission & Charges The river is jointly owned by the Inverinate Estate and the National Trust for Scotland. Because of the collapse of salmonid numbers the river is closed. For further information, contact: Willie Fraser, Warden, Morvich Farm, Inverinate, by Kyle of Lochalsh. Tel: 01599 511231.

CROSS REFERENCES All the waters on OS Map 33 which lie between Loch Morar (including Loch Morar) to the south and Loch Nevis to the north are described on OS Map 40. All the rivers and lochs in the Iverinate Forest (33/980253) and the West Benula Forest (33/085275) are described on OS Map 25. The lochs to the north of Kyle of Lochalsh (33/762273) and Balmacara (33/818272) and Dornie (33/883264) are described on OS Map 24.

All the waters on the Island of Skye that can be seen on OS Map 33 are described within OS Map 32.

DESSARRY, River See Loch Arkaig.
DOIRE MEALL AN EILEIN, Lochan See Loch Quoich.
DUBH, Lochan (Arkaig) See Loch Arkaig.
FEARNA, Loch See Loch Quoich.
GARRY, River See OS Map 34.
GLASCHOILLE, Loch See Inverie River.

GLENMORE, River
Location & Access Source 33/900130 Outfall 33/812199. The stream may be accessed from the tortuous, old Military Road which winds over the Bealach Ratagain from Shiel Bridge (33/935189) on the A87 Invermoriston/Kyle of Lochalsh road in the east to Galltair (33/811202) in the west.
Commentary In days past, this delightful little spate salmon stream was noted for the quality of its fishing and for its great scenic beauty. The latter is still the same, but, sadly, the salmon fishing is a poor shadow of its former glory. Nevertheless, the stream is still worth exploring, as are the ruins of Bernera Barracks (33/815197) and the famous Glenelg brochs, Dun Telve (33/829173) and Dun Troddan (33/834073), both of which are amongst the best preserved examples of these structures (100BC-200AD) in Europe.
Fish Salmon, but very few sea-trout due to sea lice infestation from factory-salmon farming and netting at sea. In a good year, perhaps 5/10 salmon are taken.
Flies & Tactics The primary tactic is to be there after heavy rain, preferably in late July. The lower half-mile of this little stream is the place to launch your assault. Offer them: Garry Dog, Hairy Mary, General Practitioner, Black Doctor; or size 12 trout flies such as Black Pennell, Greenwell's Glory, Grouse & Claret, Cinnamon & Gold.
Permission & Charges Apply to Mrs J Ellice, Scallasaig House, Glenelg, Inverness-shire. Tel: 01599 522217. Cost: £10 per rod per day.

GUSERAIN, River Source: OS33/788035. See Inverie River.

GUSERAN, River See Inverie River.

INVERIE, River
Location & Access Source 33/815004 Outfall 33/775989. The Inverie River is located on the Knoydart Peninsula, one of the most remote and wildly beautiful areas in all of Scotland. Access is by ferry from Mallaig (40/675970) to the Pier at Inverie (33/765000). The ferry then continues eastwards up sea-loch Nevis to Camusrory and the mouth of the Carnach River (33/862960). The route is much used by hill walkers and climbers to gain access to this wilderness land.
Commentary The Inverie River flows south-west from Loch an Dubh-Lochain (33/815004) for approximately 4 miles before reaching the sea in Inverie Bay. Loch an Dubh-Lochain is 1 mile east/west by up to 400 yards wide and it often produces sport with both salmon and sea-trout. Access to the river is from a track which margins the north bank of the stream. To the south of the river, below the summit of Sgurr nan Feadan (750m), lies Loch Bhraomisaig (33/785973) which is used as the local water supply for the Inverie community. Loch Bhraomisaig is a first-class trout loch with some really splendid fish which can weigh up to and over 4lb in weight. Immediately to the west of Loch Bhraomisaig is a smaller, unnamed loch (33/779973), which also holds excellent brown trout. The other notable, salmon and sea-trout river in Knoydart, the Abhainn Inbhir Ghuiserein, is known locally as the River Guserain. This

Loch Alsh & Glen Shiel
OS Map 33

enters the sea in the Sound of Sleat near Inverguserain (33/743074). Apart from these waters, there are a number of trout lochs, all difficult of access, but all containing wild brown trout. They are: Little Glaschoille Loch (33/738008) which lies close to the road from Inverie to Airor (33/715054); Loch a'Coire a'Phuill (33/730035) on the hill to the north-east of Sandaig (33/719020); Loch Coire na Circe (33/764080) between the crags of Meall na Coille Duibhe (339m) to the north and Na Cruachan (583m) to the south; and the tiny, distant, pools to the north east of Beinn na Caillich (785m) known collectively as Loch Bealach nan Creagan Dubha (33/810075).

Fish Salmon, sea-trout, wild brown trout and char. Approximately 40/50 salmon are taken from these rivers, depending upon prevailing water conditions. A 13lb 8oz salmon was taken from the Guserain in Sept 1996, but the average weight of fish is in the order of 6lb. Sea-trout, sadly, and probably because of sea lice infestation from near-by factory-salmon farms, are mostly noticeable by their absence, as they are throughout much of the West Highlands, but a few good fish are still taken each season. The brown trout, generally, average in the order of 8oz, but there are much larger fish as well.

Flies & Tactics The first requirement, if you are to reach some of the remoter trout lochs, is a high-wheel-based vehicle and this only eases you to the start of the long walks involved. The rivers are more accessible and may be readily fished with a single-handed rod. They are predominantly spate rivers: 'nae water, nae fish', although boat fishing on Loch an Dubh-Lochain can produce results, almost regardless of weather conditions. Bank fishing is not allowed. The other lochs are covered from the shore. Offer salmon and sea-trout: Munro Killer, Silver Stoat's Tail, Blue Charm, Hairy Mary, Willie Gunn, Garry Dog. For the hill lochs, try: Silver Invicta, Grouse & Claret.

Permission & Charges It is essential that you seek local advice before fishing any of the waters mentioned above. Further information may be obtained via: Iain Wilson, Inverguserain Farm, Knoydart, by Mallaig PH41 4PL. Tel: 01687 462844 or Mr Drew Harris, Kilhoan Estate, Knoydart, Mallaig PH41 4PL. Tel: 01687 462724.

MEALL NAN EUN, Lochanan See Loch Quoich.
NA CRUADHACH, Lochan See Loch Quoich.
NAM BREAC, Lochan See Loch Quoich.
PEAN, River See Loch Arkaig.

PRIVATE WATERS All the waters lying between the River Shiel in the East and Kyle Rhea in the West, and from Loch Alsh in the North South to Loch Huron, are private and not generally available. The only exception is the Glenmore River (see separate entry).

QUOICH, Loch

Location & Access 33/010023. The loch is accessed from Glen Garry. A minor road margins the north shore of the loch before the road climbs steeply north to drop down again to the east end of sea-Loch Huron near Kinloch Huron (33/955064). Along the way, the road passes 3 named and 1 unnamed lochs, all of which contain wild brown trout which average 6oz. These waters are, south to north: Loch a'Choire Bheithe (33/980036), Loch Coire nam Cnamh (33/974039), the unnamed lochan at 33/965046, and Loch Coire Shubh (33/961054). When the wind howls on Loch Quoich, as it frequently does, these small waters offer a good alternative. Less easily accessible, but very exciting to reach and to fish, is Loch Fearna (33/055031) which lies at an altitude of 550m in a corrie below Spidean Mialach (996m) to the north of the dam at the east end of Loch Quoich. Approach Loch Fearna from the small plantation at 33/0410022, keeping to the right of the Allt a'Mheil burn. After 1 mile, climb due east to drop down on the loch.

Commentary Loch Quoich is over 9 miles east/west by up to 1.5 miles north/south. There is an additional, 1.5 mile long "finger-like" extension to the north of the road which is fed by the River Quoich. Few lochs in Scotland display such an awesome presence; completely surrounded by intimidating peaks which are dominated by mighty Sgurr na Ciche (1040m) where Prince Charles Edward Stewart hid from his pursuers after the debacle of Culloden in 1746. The area is a noted venue for hill walkers and climbers, as much as it is noted for the excellence of its fishing. Those who enjoy both pastimes will be in their element. A Tomdoun Hotel boat will help you reach the mountains on the trackless south shore of Loch Quoich and allow you to fish little Lochan Doire Meall an Eilein (33/011009) at the east end of Quoich, and Lochan nam Breac (33/915996) and Lochan na Cruadhach (33/930992) at the west end. The outlet stream from Loch Quoich, east to Loch Poulary (see entry on OS Map 34, Fort Augustus) is not fished. There are also a number of very remote, tiny, hill lochans which may be accessed from the track which leads from the north shore of Loch Quoich at the outfall of Abhainn Chosaidh (33/959016) through Glen Barrisdale to the mountain rescue hut on the south shore of Loch Huron at 33/872049. These waters are rarely fished, because they are so inaccessible, but probably contain small brown trout and, perhaps, in the higher lochans, Arctic char. A visit to them could be combined with a serious walking expedition. They are: Loch an Lagain Aintheich (33/928028), Loch Coire nan Cadha (33/910025), Loch Coire Chaolais Bhig (33/901047) and Lochanan Meall nan Eun (33/902055) and its unnamed satellite lochan to the south.

Fish Brown trout which average 10oz and an endless stream of double-figure fish as well, huge ferox trout, caught by trolling. Fish of up to 19lb 9oz and 18lb 2oz have been taken from Loch Quoich in recent years. The loch also contains pike and Arctic char.

Flies & Tactics Boat fishing only, and the most vital thing to remember when fishing here is that the loch can, suddenly, become dreadfully wild and windy. Always wear a life jacket. Never stand up when fishing. Make sure your outboard engine is reliable and securely tied in. Tie in the oars. Take reserve fuel. There are myriad bays and corners to fish, the most productive being towards the west end of the loch. The Tomdoun Hotel will give you precise details. Above

OS Maps 33-34 Fort Augustus

all, if in doubt, don't go out. Try: Black Pennell, Soldier Palmer, Silver Butcher, or troll.
Permission & Charges At the time of writing, the Tomdoun Hotel is up for sale. For current information and access details, contact Tel: 01809 511218/244; Fax: 01809 511216. Previous charges were: boats, approximately £12.50 per day (two rods fishing), outboard motors £12.50 per day. Fishing was free to hotel guests.

QUOICH, River See Loch Quoich.

SHIEL, Loch (Duich) See River Shiel (Duich).

SHIEL, River (Duich)
Location & Access Source 33/044090. Outfall 33/935189. The whole length of the river is accessible from the A87 Invermoriston/Kyle of Lochalsh road which parallels the south bank of the stream.
Commentary The stream rises on the north slopes of the Maol Chinn-dearg ridge (981m) in the Cluaine Forest and flows north and then north-west to reach the sea in Loch Duich at Shiel Bridge after a turbulent journey of 10 miles. The surrounding mountains, the Cluaine peaks to the south and the Five Sisters of Kintail to the north, make this one of the most dramatic salmon fishing locations in the Highlands.
Fish Salmon and sea-trout. Meaningful catch numbers are not available because the river has been very lightly fished in recent years but under favourable conditions the river probably produces something in the order of 30/50 salmon each season. Sea-trout stocks have collapsed in recent years, as is the case throughout much of the West Highlands.
Flies & Tactics Fishing is confined to the lower 4 miles of the river and the best of the sport is to be had in the first 1.5 miles; particularly in the Bridge Pool which is the most productive pool on the river, and, to a lesser extent, in the Half Pool, Captain's Pool and the Inkpot Stream. Good sport depends very much upon good water levels. Salmon begin to run the river from July onwards and fresh fish may caught right through to the end of the season. Offer: Green Highlander, Hairy Mary, Willie Gunn, Garry Dog, Stoat's Tail, Ally's Shrimp, General Practitioner.
Permission & Charges Rods are most readily available to tenants of Shiel Lodge, a comfortable self-catering property close to the fishing. Enquires to The Hon Mrs A Hilleary, Greenhill House, Redcastle, Muir of Ord. Tel: 01463 870423. Prices on application.

Fort Augustus

A'BHAINNE, Loch See River Garry.
A'BHAINNE, Loch See Loch Liath.
A'CHINN MHONAICH, Loch See Loch Kemp.
A'CHOIN UIRE, Lochain
Location & Access See Loch Kemp.
A'CHOINIEH, Loch See Loch Loyne.
A'CHOIRE GHLAIS, Loch See Loch Lochy.
A'CHOIRE GHLAIS, Lochan See Loch na Stairne.

A'CHOIRE, Lochan
Location & Access 34/438882. Start from the Scottish Natural Heritage (SNH) building at Aberarder (34/479875) on the A86 Kingussie/Fort William road. A good track leads north and north-west to reach the lochan after a hike of about 3.5 miles.
Commentary Loch a'Choire is one of three waters on the Creag Meagaidh nature reserve which is owned and managed by SNH. The other lochs are: Lochan Coire Choille Rais (34/433867), unnamed on the OS Map. and, at the western end of the reserve, Lochan na Cailliche (34/412832). The deep cut in the ridge above Lochan a'Choire is known as 'The Window '(Bonnie Prince Charlie tramped this way, twice during his flight after the Battle of Culloden in 1746)
Fish A few small, white-fleshed, brown trout.
Flies & Tactics SNH have an open access policy and welcome responsible visitors. The lochs noted above are not really worth more than a passing cast. Take along a telescopic rod simply to say that you have wet a line on Creag Meagaidh. Flies: Blue Zulu, Invicta, Peter Ross.
Permission & Charges If you intend to have a cast during your walk you should seek prior permission by contacting: SNH, Creag Meadcaidh NNR, Aberarder, Kinlochlaggan, by Newtownmore, Inverness-shire. PH20 1BX Tel 01528 544265.

AN SGUID, Loch See Loch Loyne.
ARKAIG, Loch See OS Map 33.
ARKAIG, River See OS Map 33.
BAD AN LOSGUINN, Loch See River Garry.
BHLARAIDH, Reservoir See Loch Liath.
CARN A 'CHUILINN, Loch See Lochan Carn a' Chuilinn.

CARN A'CHUILINN, Lochan
Location & Access 34/431034 Start from 34/403090 on the B862 Whitebridge/Fort Augustus road at the south end of Loch Ness. A track leads south up Borlum Hill (400m), past unnamed lochan to the west of the path at 34/405080 which has some nice trout, climbing steeply into the heart of the Glendoe Forest. Lochan Carn a'Chuilinn (816m) and Creag an Fhireoin (775m).
Commentary The stalkers' path up Glendoe margins the Allt Doe burn and then swings north beneath the stark crags of Coire Doe. Leave the track at the 34/435051 and follow the little stream up to the obvious saddle in the crest ahead which leads through Coire an t-Seilich (34/430044). From this point, the loch lies 10 minutes further south. There are several other waters here spread over an area of 2 square miles which may also be include in the expedition. They are, from east to west: Lochan Carn a'Chuilinn (34/442040) and the unnamed lochan immediately to the east on the line of the inlet burn to Lochan Carn a'Chuilinn at (34/436038). Follow this burn, upstream, to reach the two sections of Lochan Carn a'Chuilinn itself; then Lochan nam Faoileag (34/428032) with its crooked bays and lovely little island. Five minutes west again will bring you to the long straggle of Lochan Dearg Uilit (34/420031), half

277

Fort Augustus — OS Map 34

a mile north/south in length, and its attendant, unnamed, tiny lochans.
Fish All these waters contain small wild brown trout which average 3 to the pound, but there are a few larger fish of up to 1lb in weight as well.
Flies & Tactics This is rough country and not an expedition to be lightly undertaken. Bank fishing and no need to wade: trout to lie close to the shore and rise readily, generally, to: Black Zulu, March Brown, Silver Invicta.
Permission & Charges See Lochan na Stairne entry.

CEANN, Loch See Loch Lochy.
CLUANIE, Loch See Loch Loyne.
COIRE LOCHAIN, Lochan See Loch Lochy.
COUR, River See River Spean.
DEARG LOCHAIN, Loch See Loch Kemp.
DEARG UILIT, Lochan See Lochan Carn a'Chuilinn.
DIOTA, Lochan See Loch Lochy.
DOIRE CADHA, Lochan See River Garry.
DUBH, Lochan See Loch na Stairne.
DUBHA, Lochain See River Garry.
DUNDREGGAN, Reservoir See River Moriston.
FHUDAIR, Lochan See Loch Lochy.

FOYERS, River
Location & Access Source 34/451046 Outfall 35/520239. The river rises to the south of Whitebridge in the Glendoe Forest and flows through Loch Mhor (see entry on OS Map 35) before joining Loch Ness by the village of Foyers.
Commentary The river is of very limited interest as a fishery now since its flows has been harnessed by a power-generation scheme. It is best-known for its spectacular falls, the upper one being 30ft in height, the lower, 90ft. However, even they have been mightily tamed and are only really worth a look after heavy rain.
Fish Brown trout in the upper reaches.
Flies & Tactics The upper river flows through a steep-sided gorge for much of its course and access is difficult, but some sport may be had in the section between Loch Mhor and Glenbrien Lodge (34/475120). Flies: Black Pennell, March Brown, Silver Butcher.
Permission & Charges Donald Campbell, Whitebridge Hotel, Stratherrick, Inverness IV1 2UN. Tel: 01456 486226; Fax: 01456 486413. Cost: £5 per rod per day.

FRAOCHACH, Loch See Loch na Stairne.

GARRY, River
Location & Access 33/000020. Outfall 34/320012 The Lower River Garry is accessible from the A82 Fort Augustus/Fort William road and the A87 Invergarry/Kyle of Lochalsh road. The Upper river is accessed from the minor road along the north shore of Loch Garry (34/230020) which leads to the hydro-dam at the east end of Loch Quoich (see OS Map 33).
Commentary Glen Garry is scenically outstanding, in spite of the ugly electricity pylons. However, the character of the river was greatly altered during the early 1950's when the stream was impounded for electricity generation. The River Garry used to be one of Scotland's most famous spring salmon rivers, noted for the size and quality of the fish it produced from opening day (15th January) until the end of April. These fish averaged 18lb. The hydro-electric scheme, although providing a fish pass, denies returning fish access to traditional salmon spawning grounds and the river is now but a poor shadow of its pre-hydro glory days. Above the dam at the head of the river, lie Loch Garry, Loch Inchlaggan (34/180015), the Upper River Garry and Loch Poulary (34/125013). In the hills to the north of Invergarry are Loch Lundie (34/298035), Lochan Doire Cadha (34/311029) which is very rarely visited and reputed to be fishless, and Loch a'Bhainne (34/276048). To the north of Loch Inchlaggan, lie Lochan Torr a'Gharbh-uillt (34/167020), Lochain Dubha (34/179042) which is full of small trout, and Loch Bad an Losguinn (34/159039) which is very weedy and home to some voracious pike.
Fish Approximately 100 salmon are taken most seasons from the lower river, the upper river and its attendant lochs also contain good numbers of salmon although most visitors concentrate on trying to catch "glass-case-size" brown trout and catch salmon more by accident than by design. Loch Garry and Loch Inchlaggan are noted for the size of their ferox trout: until recently, the British Record brown trout, a fish of 19lb 9oz, was held by a fish taken from Loch Inchlaggan. Loch Garry also contains pike, and Arctic charr, fish of up to 8lb in weight. The charr reach these proportions possibly by feeding on left-overs from the fish-farm cages in the loch. The hill lochs all contain modest wild brown trout which average 8oz.
Flies & Tactics A good tactic is to stay at the Tomdoun Hotel (See Loch Quoich entry) overlooking the upper River Garry. The hotel offers free fishing to guests and has boats on the principal lochs. Ardochy Lodge also fish Loch Garry and other waters in the area including the upper River Garry and Loch Ness. Loch Inchlaggan is generally shallow and the best fishing area is along the line of the old river bed, in the centre of the loch, and in the large, weedy bay by the little island at the south-east end. On Loch Garry, trolling is the favoured salmon fishing method and this sometimes produces double figure brown trout, particularly in September. The west end of the loch, in Greenfield Bay (34/204015), is the place to begin. The upper river, between Loch Inchlaggan and Loch Poulary can also produce some spectacular trout as well as the occasional salmon. Fishing is not permitted on the final stretch of the river, between Loch Poulary and the dam at Loch Quoich. Of the hill lochs noted above, Loch Lundie is the largest and most productive. The loch is stocked from time to time and contains good numbers of brown trout which average 8oz, but there are a few fish of up to and over 2lb in weight as well. The loch is accessed from Invergarry and involves a serious hike of about 2.5 miles. A good day out is to start on Loch Lundie and then continue round the north end of the loch to the ruins at 34/294044. From there, climb steeply north-west for 1 mile to find Loch a'Bhainne (permission to fish must be obtained from Mr Grant at the Faichem camp site prior to setting out) which is a beginner's paradise, full of small trout which rise read-

OS Map 34 — Fort Augustus

ily to the fly. Return to the start point by following the outlet stream from Loch 'Bhainne back to Faichem and Invergarry. The lower River Garry is 4 miles in length, from the dam across the gorge at the east end of Loch Garry down to Invergarry where the stream enters Loch Oich. There are 24 named pools and, because of the controlled water flow, salmon are held in the lower part of the river until 1st April when summer compensation water is released. The estuary beat can be excellent, especially in the spring, and there is also a boat available for trolling on Loch Oich. Col. Waddingtion, who designed the famous style of salmon fly which bears his name and is used by anglers throughout the world, has fished the River Garry with it for many years and has had great success. For salmon, try: Garry Dog, Willie Gunn, Ally's Shrimp, Munro Killer, Waddingtons various. Lures: Devon minnows, Tobies, Rapalas. For brown trout, offer: Ke-He, March Brown, Silver Butcher.

Permission & Charges Lower River Garry & Loch Oich: Invergarry Hotel, Invergarry, Inverness-shire PH35 4HG. Tel: 01809 501206; Fax; 01809 501236. Cost: weekly lets are preferred and these cost from between £400 and £1,800 per week, depending upon the time of year. When day lets are available (approximately 50% of the season), these cost £18 per rod per day. Brown trout fishing on Loch Oich is free to hotel guests. Upper River Garry and adjacent lochs, contact: Tomdoun Hotel, by Invergarry, Inverness-shire. Tel: 01809 511218/244; Fax: 01809 511 216. Fishing is free to hotel guests, boats cost approximately £12.50 per day (two rods fishing), outboard motors £12.50 per day. Ardochy Lodge, by Invergarry, Invernesshire. Tel: 01809 511232; approximate costs: day lets on Loch Garry at £18 per boat per day and £12 per day for the use of an outboard motor.

GORM, Lochan See Loch Loyne.

INCHLAGGAN, Loch See River Garry.

KEMP, Loch
Location & Access 34/470165. Loch Kemp is on the Dell Estate near Whitebridge and is accessed from the B862 Inverness/Fort Augustus road via a private estate road from Dell Lodge (34/486163).
Commentary Dell Lodge is an 18th century Laird's house between Loch Ness and Stratherrick and there are a number of other, smaller, waters on the estate which may be fished by lodge guests: Lochan Scristan (34/476178), Dearg Lochain (34/478182), Lochain a'Choin Uire (34/461165), Loch Paiteag (34/474156) and tiny Lochan a'Chinn Mhonaich (34/461156).
Fish Loch Kemp has the largest fish, trout which average 10oz; the other waters contain more modest specimens.
Flies & Tactics There is a boat on Loch Kemp and the opportunity for water sports other than fishing. The smaller lochs are all fished from the bank and require considerable leg-work to reach. Loch Paiteag is in a woodland setting and is particularly lovely, offering shelter during high winds. Show the residents: Loch Ordie, Grouse & Claret, Black Pennell.
Permission & Charges The lodge sleeps 12 people and is let on a self-catering basis. Contact: Finlyson Hughes, 29 Barossa Place, Perth PH1 5EP. Tel: 01738 625134; Fax: 01738 639017. Cost: approximately £2,000 per week. The estate may also be able to arrange additional sport, including stalking, walked up grouse shooting and salmon fishing.

KNOCKIE, Loch
Location & Access 34/455135 Turn west from the B862 Inverness/Fort Augustus road at Knockcarrach (34/469130) and follow the minor road towards Knockie Lodge Hotel (34/446133), one of the most comfortable hotels in the north. The loch and boat mooring bay is to the north of the road at 34/450128.
Commentary Loch Knockie is a long, straggling water, over 1 mile north/south by up to almost half a mile wide. There are numerous attractive bays, headlands and corners and the loch is an important nesting site for wildfowl and plays hosts to rare slavonian grebes. Immediately to the south of Knockie Lodge is Loch na Lann (34/442130), itself a substantial water of over half a mile in length, and in the surrounding hills 3 small lochans: to the north, Loch na Sgorthaick (34/448148) and Loch nan Nighean (34/455150), and to the south, Loch Mam-chuil (34/436112).
Fish Loch Knockie does not boast large fish but they are of excellent quality and average in the order of 10oz/12oz. There are also Arctic charr. Loch nan Lann has smaller fish but one or two very large trout as well. Loch na Sgorthaick contains pike. Loch Mam-chuil has the best fish, trout of up to and over 2lb in weight.
Flies & Tactics Loch Knockie is fished from the boat and the most productive area is at the north end of the loch and in the vicinity of the north-west headland. Arrange your drift about 10 yards out from the shore. The margins round the main island can also be productive. Loch nan Lann is easily fished from the shore and is ideal for a few post-supper casts. Getting to little Loch Mam-chuil involves a hike of approximately 45 minutes. Follow the track south along the edge of the forest to find the loch in a corrie on the east shoulder of Beinn a'Bhacaidh (655m). Flies: Black Zulu, Soldier Palmer, Dunkeld.
Permission & Charges Contact: Knockie Lodge Hotel, Whitebridge, Stratherrick. Tel: 01456 486276; Fax: 01456 486389. Hotel guests have priority, otherwise, expect to pay in the order of £25 per day for the boat. Hill lochs, £12 per rod per day. The Whitebridge Hotel (see Foyers River entry) also has a boat on Loch Knockie.

LAGGAN, Loch
Location & Access 34/475855. Easily accessible along the north shore which is bordered by the A86 Kingussie/Fort William road.
Commentary The loch is some 7 miles long by up to half a mile wide and is the headwaters of the River Spean (see separate entry). The river exits at Moy Lodge (34/440834) and flows into Loch Moy (34/410817). The system was impounded in the 1920's to provide water for the British Aluminium Company smelter in Fort William. This has severely effected the quality of fishing, not only in Loch Laggan and Loch

Fort Augustus   OS Map 34

Moy, but also in the rivers Spean, Roy and Lochy. In high water levels, Loch Laggan and Loch Moy become one continuous, 12 mile long, water. When the level drops, the connecting river regains its former character and can often offer good sport.

Fish Brown trout which average 10oz, but, undoubtedly, large ferox in the depths. There are also pike.

Flies & Tactics The north bank of both lochs is fished from the shore and wading is not recommended. The area where the Allt Coire Ardair burn enters near Aberarder (34/484872) is a good place to begin on Loch Laggan. Otherwise, simply park by the bay or promontory which takes your fancy and get on with it. Loch Moy, in particular, has many attractive little bays and corners along the north shore; the bay at 34/388816 and round Craigbeg (34/408818) should provide supper. Boats are available on Loch Laggan through the Ardverikie Estate (see Lochan na Hearba entry) which allow you to explore the south shore where there are many delightful, sandy, beaches and bays. The boat also gives the opportunity of trolling for ferox. Flies: Ke-He, March Brown, Silver Butcher.

Permission & Charges For Loch Laggan, contact: Laggan Stores, Laggan Bridge, by Newtonmore, Inverness-shire. Tel: 01528 544257. Cost: £6 per rod per day, bank fishing. For Loch Moy, contact: A Matheson, East Park Holiday Cottages, Roy Bridge, Inverness-shire. Tel: 01397 712370. Cost: £5 per rod per day. Mr Matheson is an expert angler and will also provide you with up-to-the-minute advice in regard to the best fishing areas.

LIATH, Loch

Location & Access 34/334198 The loch may be accessed by car, with care, but a high-wheel based vehicle is advised. Otherwise, it is a long hike (three and half miles) north from the A887. Invermoriston/Kyle of Lochalsh via a track which starts at Bhlaraidh (34/380165). This track also gives access to the Glenmoriston Estate hill lochs which are described on OS Map 26 (see Loch ma Stac entry).

Commentary Loch Liath (the grey loch) lies at an altitude of 450m and is surrounded by wonderful scenery with spectacular views west to the mountain group, 'The Five Sisters of Kintail'. On the way up the hill look out also for the wild goats which inhabit Levishie Forest. Loch a' Bhainne (34/362167), also will repay a visit.

Fish Loch Liath has some excellent brown trout and, in past times, this water was regularly stocked. Trout now average in the order of 10oz/12oz. The other waters noted above hold more modest specimens.

Flies & Tactics Bank fishing, and the best place to launch your assault on Loch Liath is down the west shore where three feeder streams enter. Offer them: Black Zulu, March Brown, Silver Butcher.

Permission & Charges See River Moriston entry.

LOCHY, Loch

Location & Access 34/230890. The A82 Inverness/Fort William road borders the east shore of the loch. Access to the west shore is by a forestry road from Kilfinnan (34/277958) in the north, or from Clunes (34/200886) in the south.

Commentary Loch Lochy is nearly 10 miles in length by up to 1 mile wide and drops to a depth of 150m between Altrua (34/242900) on the east shore and Glas Dhoire Mor (34/227905) on the west shore. The loch is part of the Thomas Telford's Caledonian Canal system which links the Moray Forth in the north to Loch Linnhe in the south, encompassing along the way Loch Ness and Loch Oich. Dramatic mountains, many of which rise to more than 700m, enfold the steel-grey waters. Consequently, the loch is frequently wild and stormy and anyone venturing out in a small rowing boat must be properly prepared. If in doubt, don't go out. There are a number of small, mountain, lochans to the west of Loch Lochy, rarely fished and difficult of access. These waters contain small, wild, trout. They are: Lochan na Beinne Brice (34/252991), Lochan Diota (34/269975), Loch a'Choire Ghlais (34/229951), Coire Lochain (34/221915), Lochan Fhudair (34/201951), Lochan na Gearr Leacainn (34/189967).

Fish In Loch Lochy, the possibility of salmon, although few are caught, brown trout which average 8oz, and good numbers of much larger specimens of up to and over 5lb in weight; escapee rainbow trout, Arctic charr and pike.

Flies & Tactics All legal fishing methods are permitted and most visitors fish Loch Lochy from the shore. Two areas are "out of bounds": the mouth of the River Arkaig (see Loch Arkaig entry on OS Map 33) at Bunarkaig (34/187878) and the stream to the power-station at Mucomir (34/185845). Otherwise, fish wherever you chose. The shallow, north end of the loch, known as Ceann Loch (34/285955), where the Kilfinnan Burn enters to the south of Laggan Locks, is one of the most productive areas, as is the bay at Clunes; but there are literally dozens of other attractive headlands and corners where you will have a chance of catching your supper. Whatever you do, avoid wading, stay safely on terra firma at all times. Flies: Black Pennell, Grouse & Claret, Silver Butcher.

Permission & Charges Loch Lochy has always been, to the best of my knowledge, free of charge. Boat hire is available from: Lochy Boat Hire, Tel: 01397 712257

LOCHY, River See OS Map 41.

LOYNE, Loch

Location & Access 34/160050. Approach from the A87 Invergarry/Kyle of Lochalsh road which parallels the south-east shore of the loch for 1 mile.

Commentary Loch Loyne is a hydro-electric loch, 7 miles long by up to half a mile wide. The east end, near the dam, is singularly uninviting and steep-sided. Getting to the more attractive west end is a mammoth hike for uncertain rewards, although the surrounding scenery is spectacular. This also applies to Loch Loyne's neighbour, Loch Cluanie, north over Coire Beithe (789m). Loch Cluanie is another dismal, dour hydro-electric loch, 7 miles long and bordered on its north shore by the A87 Invermoriston/Kyle of Lochalsh road.

Fish Loch Loyne is noted as the home of large pike;

OS Map 34 — Fort Augustus

one fish of over 50lb in weight is reputed to have been seen in recent years. There will, undoubtedly, be very large brown trout, ferox, both in Loch Loyne and Loch Cluanie, but the principal trout population average in the order of 8oz.

Flies & Tactics There are no boats on either loch and very few people fish them seriously. If you do stop for a cast, stay ashore and do not wade. Sections of the shoreline, because of fluctuations in the water level, are dangerously soft. Given the excellent fishing nearby, in Loch Inchlaggan and Loch Garry, (see separate entries) Loch Loyne and Loch Cluanie are left largely to their own devices. In the hills to the north of Loch Cluanie there are a number of small, very remote waters: Gorm Lochan (34/124133), Lochan Uaine (34/135145), Loch a'Choinieh (34/141169) and Loch an Sguid (34/172194). These are best explored during a hill-walking expedition when a telescopic or travel rod can be easily back-packed. A head for heights is required to reach Lochan Uaine and its unnamed neighbour and the Gorm Lochan, but the writer has seen fish rising in them. Flies: Black Pennell, Greenwell's Glory, Silver Invicta.

Permission & Charges Details are hard to obtain. Try Tel: 01320 340238; or Cluanie Lodge, Glenmoriston, Inverness-shire. Tel: 01320 340208. Also: Glenmoriston Estate Office, Invermoriston, Inverness-shire, Tel: 01320 357300.

LUNDIE, Loch See River Garry.
LUNDIE, Loch See River Garry.
MAM-CHUIL, Loch See Loch Knockie.

MORISTON, River

Location & Access Source 33/044090 Outfall: 34/428163 The river is easily accessible from the A887 Invermoriston/Kyle of Lochalsh road which parallels the north bank to Torgyle (34/ 310130) and the south bank to the hydro electric generating station at Ceannacroc (34/229109).

Commentary The river rises in the wilds of the Cluanie Forest. The headwaters have been impounded by two, major, dams built across the outlet streams of Loch Cluanie (34/145095) and Loch Loyne (34/160050) (see separate entries) for the purpose of hydro-electric power generation. Consequently, the Moriston is a poor shadow of its former glory, but the stream, when it flows, runs through an area of outstanding scenic beauty.

Fish Salmon, which average 10lb in weight, and some excellent brown trout, particularly in Dundreggan Reservoir (34/354156). Approximately 150 salmon are taken most seasons, depending on water conditions. The river has the reputation of producing excellent spring salmon. Most spring fish are double-figure in weight and some of them can be of up to and over 20lb. Spring salmon are caught from opening day, 15 January, onwards, generally when spinning in the estuary of the river.

Flies & Tactics The best of the salmon fishing is from below Dundreggan Reservoir to the estuary where the river enters Loch Ness (see OS Map 26). This lower beat, which fishes four rods per day, is a quarter of a mile in length and is easily accessible from the main road. The fish are confined to the lower river until May when compensation water is released into the stream as summer approaches. The upper river, from Torgyle downstream to the reservoir, fishes best on a falling water level which happens in the afternoons when power generation stops at Ceannacroc. Fish begin to reach the upper river from June onwards when sport can be good, given decent water levels. Brown trout of considerable size, probably having moved upstream from Loch Ness, are caught in Dundreggan Reservoir, fish of up to and over 6lb in weight. The loch is best fished from a boat. Concentrate your efforts down the east shoreline and in the vicinity of where the river enters. Salmon are also occasionally taken from Dundreggan. The most productive pools on the river are those immediately above and below the reservoir; Bobbin Pool, above, and the Alder Pool, below. The Upper River, from Torgyle to Ceannacroc, can also produce sport, particularly with brown trout. Offer salmon: Practitioner, Stoat's Tail. Spinning lures: Devon minnows, Toby spoon, Blair Spoon, brass tube flies; for trout, try Ke-He, Greenwell's Glory, Silver Invicta.

Permission & Charges Glenmoriston Lodge Estate, Invermoriston, Inverness-shire IV3 6YA; Tel: 01320 351300. Expect to pay, for salmon fishing, in the order of between £15-£35 per rod per day, depending upon the time of year; a boat with two rods fishing on Dundreggan Reservoir will cost approximately £20 per day; trout fishing, on the river and on the Glenmoriston Estate Hill lochs, £5 per rod per day. Trout and salmon fishing on the river between Torgyle and Ceannacroc may be had from Grant Harris, Balintombuie, Dalchreichart, Glenmoriston. Tel: 01320 340225. Cost: Brown trout, £6 per rod per day; salmon, £12 per rod per day.

MOY CORRIE, Lochan See Lochan a'Choire.
MOY, Loch See Loch Laggan.
NA BEINNE BRICE, Lochan See Loch Lochy.
NA CAILLICHE, Lochan See Loch a'Choire.
NA GEARR LEACAINN, Lochan See Loch Lochy.

NA HEARBA, Lochan

Location & Access Lochan na Hearba is on the Ardverikie Estate and is approached via private estate roads from Kinlochlaggan on the A86 Kingussie/Fort William road.

Commentary The loch is in two sections, joined by a short stream, and covers an area of 3.5 miles. The north loch is easily accessible from a road which circles the shoreline. The south loch, the larger of the two, is bordered by a road along the east shore but the north bank is trackless. Loch na Hearba lies in a wonderful glen, surrounded by majestic peaks: Binnein Shuas (746m), Binnein Shios (667m) to the north and Creag Pitridh (924m) and Creag a'Mhaigh (715m) to the south.

Fish Brown trout and some Arctic charr. Trout average 8oz/10oz, but there are much larger fish as well, particularly in the south loch which drops to over 70ft in depth.

Fort Augustus — OS Map 34

Flies & Tactics There is a boat on the north loch and the shallow, north end is the place to begin. Arrange a drift about 10 yards out from the bank. If you can't see the bottom then you are fishing too far out. Strong winds can be a problem and it is best to have someone on the oars to hold the boat in position. The south loch is fished from the shore and is dangerous to wade. The roadside bank is the most productive fishing area, and the south end of the loch where the Allt Coire Pitridh and Allt Coire a'Chlachair burns enter. There is an unnamed lochan to the south, at 34/455807, which is worth a few, well-considered, casts. After heavy rain the connecting stream between the north and south sections of Lochan na Hearba can also produce sport. Flies: Soldier Palmer, Greenwell's Glory, Alexandra.
Permission & Charges Fishing is available only to tenants of Ardverikie Estate holiday properties. These are highly recommended and vary in price from between £220 and £760 per property per week, according to the number of occupants and the time of year. For bookings, contact: Finlyson Hughes, 45 Church Street, Inverness IV1 1DR. Tel: 01463 224343; Fax: 01463 243234.

NA SGORTHAICK, Loch See Loch Knockie.

NA STAIRNE, Lochan
Location & Access 34/444059. A vigorous hike. Start from the B862 Whitebridge/Fort Augustus road by Loch Tarff (see separate entry) at 34/431099. A stalkers' path leads south, climbing steeply between Carn Clach na Fearna (483m) to the west and Carn Thomais (650m) to the east. The gradient eases after a mile and a half but Loch na Stairne is still another mile further south on the south shoulder of Creag Coire Doe (704m).
Commentary A serious hill-walking and fishing expedition amidst magnificent scenery giving wonderful views west to the Five Sisters of Kintail and adjacent peaks. The day will involve you in a round trip of approximately 6 miles during the course of which you will visit a series of 9 named and unnamed lochs and lochans. Upon reaching Loch na Stairne, walk the east shoreline to find the inlet burn half way down the bank. Follow this up to reach Lochan a'Choire Ghlais (34/449054). After exploring this lochan (which probably doesn't hold many fish), return to Loch na Stairne. From the outlet burn in the north-east corner, trek down to the Dubh Lochan (34/447066) and its unnamed neighbour, both of which you will have passed on the way up. Where the track ends, at the north shore of the Dubh Lochan, strike north-east for half a mile to fish the unnamed lochan on Cairn Vungie (700m). Now head north-east again for 10 minutes to locate Loch Fraochach (34/459081). Step north again to the little unnamed lochan at 34/455083, before returning south-west to regain the outward track near Loch Vungie at 34/450079. From here it is happy-downhill all the way back to the start point.
Fish Brown trout of modest proportions.
Flies & Tactics It is imperative to be fully prepared and equipped for whatever the elements might choose to throw at you. Stout boots, compass and map, wet weather gear and emergency rations are essential. Also, make sure that you leave word about when and where you are going and when you expect to return. On a fine day, there are few more lovely places in all of Scotland in which to walk and fish. Flies: Blue Zulu, March Brown, Black Pennell.
Permission & Charges See Loch Tarff entry.

NAM FAOILEAG, Lochan See Lochan Carn a'Chuilinn.

NAN EUN, Loch See Loch Tarff.
NAN LANN, Loch See Loch Knockie.
NAN NIGHEAN, Loch See Loch Knockie.
OICH, Loch See River Oich.

OICH, River
Location & Access Source: 34/337035 Outfall 34/383094. The river is accessible from private estate roads and forest roads which parallel both banks.
Commentary The River Oich lies in the Great Glen and links Loch Ness (see OS Map 26) with Loch Oich (34/327015) via the Caledonian Canal system. The river is 6 miles in length, flows through attractive countryside, and offers excellent value-for-money, day ticket, salmon fishing. Loch Oich, 4 miles long by up to 500 yards wide, is also great fun to fish although it can be an intimidating place on wild and windy days.
Fish Salmon, sea-trout and brown trout in the river, salmon, sea-trout, brown trout, rainbow trout and pike in the loch. Approximately 150 salmon are taken most seasons and these fish average 10lb in weight with good numbers of heavier fish of up to and over 20lb. The largest salmon taken from Loch Oich, by trolling, weighed 44lb 8oz and was landed by the famous gillie, the late "Wild" Jock Macaskill of Invergarry. Sea-trout catches have declined in recent years. Brown trout in Loch Oich average 10oz but there are large ferox in the depths.
Flies & Tactics The 2.5 miles of the river, from the road bridge over the A82 Fort Augustus/Fort William road down to the Invervigar Burn, are let by the Aberchalder Estate. This permit also includes permission to bank fish Loch Oich. The Glen Doe Estate have 3.5 miles of the north bank, from Coille Torr Dhuin down to Fort Augustus and Loch Ness. There are a number of excellent holding pools and runs including Kytra, Island Pool, Rock Pool, Camilon Pool, and, perhaps the most productive, Canada Pool. Adequate water levels are critical for good sport and it is wise to check first, before making a booking. Most salmon are caught whilst spinning, the most favoured lures being: gold, blue, black & orange, and silver Devon minnows. Flies which do the damage are: Ally's Shrimp, Willie Gunn, Silver Stoat's Tail, General Practitioner, Black Doctor.
Permission & Charges For the Aberchalder Estate, contact: W Wernham, Laragan, Aberchalder Estate, Invergarry, Inverness-shire. Tel: 01809 501373. Cost: £10 per rod per day, £40 per rod per week. Trout fishing only, £4 per rod per day. For accommodation on the Aberchalder Estate, contact: Miss Jean Ellice, Tighan-Lianach, Aberchalder Farm, Invergarry, Inverness-shire. Tel: 01809 501287. For the Glen Doe Estate

OS Map 34 — Fort Augustus

Beat, contact: George Watson, Glendoe Estate, Fort Fort Augustus, Inverness-shire. Tel: 01320 366234. Cost: approximately £15 per rod per day. Aberchalder Lodge, sleeping 10 people, is also let to sporting parties with fishing on the River Oich. For details, contact Finlyson Hughes, 29 Barossa place, Perth PH1 5EP. Tel: 01738 625134; Fax: 01738 639017.

PAITEAG, Loch See Loch Kemp.
POULARY, Loch See River Garry.

PRIVATE WATERS AN AONAICH ODHAIR, Loch 34/449997; IAIN, Lochan 34/485004; DUBH, Lochan 34/492000; SPEY, Loch 34/421938 and the upper river Spey on OS Map 34; A'BHANAIN, Loch 34/430923; ROY, Loch 34/417893; SGUADAIG, Loch 34/360876.

ROY, River
Location & Access Source 34/417893. Outfall 34/271805 Approach from Roybridge (34/270813) on the A86 Kingussie/Fort William road. The road north from Roybridge, into Glen Roy, parallels the river and ends at Brae Roy Lodge (34/338914).
Commentary The river rises from Loch Roy below the grey bulk of Creag Meagaidh (1130m) and flows north to the White Falls (34/398934). The stream then swings south-west down Glen Roy to join the River Spean at Roybridge; past the famous geological feature known as the "Parallel Roads": long "tide-marks" indenting the side of the hills, left when the glacier-filled glen warmed and the ice melted, 7,000 years ago at the end of the last Ice Age.
Fish Salmon, a few sea-trout, modest brown trout. Up until 1994 the 5-year average for the river was approximately 80/100 salmon each season, including a few seriously large fish of over 20lb in weight, but numbers have declined in recent years.
Flies & Tactics The lower beat, fished by visitors and the Roybridge Angling Club, is by no means busy. Nevertheless, 1999 managed to produced approximately 50 salmon. The river is narrow and rocky, with attractive, deep, holdings pools and tumbling runs. It is a "classic" Highland spate stream where worming produces the best results, although there is also good fly-fishing water.
Permission & Charges For the Roybridge Angling Club beat, contact Mr A Matheson, East Park Holiday Cottages, Roybridge, Inverness-shire. Tel: 01397 712370; four visitor permits are issued each day at a cost of £10 per rod. For the rest of the river and details of Braeroy Estate properties, contact: Strutt & Parker, 13 Hill Street, Berkeley Square, London W1X 8DL. Tel: 0171 629 7282; Fax: 0171 499 1657. Cost: for Braeroy Lodge, with 12 guests and the services of a cook and housekeeper and 6 rods fishing the river, you should expect to pay in the region of £5,000 per week.

SCRISTAN, Lochan See Loch Kemp.

SPEAN, River
Location & Access Source 34/441834 Outfall 34/178839. The river is accessed from the A86 Kingussie/Fort William road and from the minor road on the south bank from Spean Bridge (34/222815) to Corriechoille (34/251806).
Commentary The River Spean was, to all intents and purposes, terminally damaged during the 1920s when its head waters were impounded by the British Aluminium Company and fed to their smelter at Fort William. There is no "compensation" water and it is more likely than not that the majority of salmon now caught on the River Spean belong in fact to its major tributary, the River Roy.
Fish Salmon and a few sea-trout. Catch numbers are not available, but they are unlikely to amount to more than a couple of dozen fish each season.
Flies & Tactics Begin where the River Cour joins the River Spean at 34/248812. A few fish still run the River Cour which rises to the south of Spean Bridge below the intimidating, grey, heights of Aonach Beag (1236m). Work downstream from the Cour, fishing the pools as you go, to the railway bridge at 34/239817. The best time to assault is after a flood, when the water level is falling. The banks are awkward to fish and an ability to Spey cast is essential. Spinning is allowed. Flies: Garry Dog, Willie Gunn, General Practitioner, Stoat's Tail, Hairy Mary; lures: Devon minnows, Rapalas.
Permission & Charges Day tickets are available, on the day of fishing, from: Rod & Gun Shop, 18 High Street, Fort William, Inverness-shire. Tel: 01397 702656. Cost: £12 per rod per day.

TARFF, Loch
Location & Access 34/425100. Easily accessible and on the north side of the B862 Inverness/Fort Augustus road.
Commentary Loch Tarff is circular in shape, about half a mile across, and scattered with a series of 6 small islands. Close by, pinched between Carn an t-Suidhe (450m) to the north and Carn Clach na-Fearna (483m) to the south, is Loch nan Eun (34/453099) and this is best accessed from the B862 at 34/446102.
Fish Both lochs contain brown trout which average 10oz.
Flies & Tactics Bank fishing only and it is best to avoid wading. On Loch Tarff, begin by the roadside on the east shore and work north, paying particular attention in the vicinity of the headland promontory at the far north end. Loch nan Eun is steep-sided and awkward to fish but the east and west ends usually produce supper. Flies: Ke-He, Greenwell's Glory, Peter Ross.
Permission & Charges George Watson, Head Keeper, Upper Glendoe, by Fort Augustus, Inverness-shire. Tel: 01320 366 234. Cost: £5 per rod per day.

TORR A'GHARBH-UILLT, Lochan See River Garry.
UAINE, Lochan See Loch Loyne.
UAINE, Lochan See Lochan a'Choire.
VUNGIE, Loch See Loch na Stairne.

Kingussie

ALVIE, Loch See Loch Insh.
AN EILEIN, Loch See OS Map 36 Grantown and Cairngorm
BEAG, Loch See Loch Insh.

BRAN, Loch
Location & Access 35/509193. Approach from the B862 Inverness/Fort Augustus road at the south end of Loch Mhor (see separate entry) at 35/508180. Drive north along the minor road to reach the loch after 1 mile.
Commentary This is a very attractive, small (25 acre) forest loch which often provides welcome shelter when the wind howls down neighbouring Loch Mhor and Loch Ness.
Fish Brown trout which average 10oz, but fish of up to and over 3lb in weight as well.
Flies & Tactics Boat fishing, and the loch is splendidly varied in its configuration, with charming bays and corners. Fish rise and are taken everywhere. On a calm evening dry fly fishing can be very effective, otherwise offer them: Loch Ordie, Greenwell's Glory, Gold Butcher.
Permission & Charges See Loch Mhor entry.

CALDER, River See River Spey.
CONAGTEANN, Loch See Loch Mhor.
CROSS REFERENCES Loch RUTHVEN; Loch A'CHOIRE; Loch DUNTLECHAIG; Loch CEO GLAIS; River NAIRN; Loch NESS - see entries on OS Map 26.
DULNAIN, River See River Spey (OS Map 36).
E, River See Loch Mhor.
FECHLIN, River See Loch Killin.

FESHIE, River
Location & Access Source 43/827859 Outfall 35/842064. The lower river is accessed by a public road which runs south from the B970 Kingussie/Nethy Bridge road at Feshie Bridge (35/851043). The upper river is reached along private, estate roads which are blocked by locked forestry gates.
Commentary The river rises 16 miles to the south of the River Spey on the east slope of Leathad an Taobhain (902m). It flows north down Glen Feshie to join the Spey just below Loch Insh (see separate entry). The upper reaches of the glen have been adversely effected in recent years by hill-road construction work, the middle and lower reaches are heavily afforested. Trout fishing is available on two small forest lochs near the mouth of the river: Uath Lochan (35/836019) and Lochan Geal (35/852059), and on two further tiny waters near the head of the glen: Lochan nam Bo (35/861913) and Lochan an t-Sluie (35/829902). The estate may also be able to arrange salmon fishing on the River Spey.
Fish Salmon, sea-trout and brown trout in the river, small brown trout in the lochs. Depending upon the fishing effort, the river produces approximately 30 each season.

Flies & Tactics Water flow in the River Feshie is generally excellent and fish may be taken throughout the season, even in the high summer months. Fishing is by worm and fly and there are a number of first-class holding-pools which offer sport, particularity when the water level is high. A 4x4 vehicle is required to reach the upper river, which is crossed on several occasions by the estate track,. The estate can provide this facility for fishing guests, if required. Use a single-handed rod. Wading is not generally required, but thigh waders are useful in some sections of the stream. Flies: Garry Dog, Shrimp Fly, Willie Gunn, Stoat's Tail, Green Highlander, Hairy Mary; dressed on small (size 10/12) double hooks.
Permission & Charges The fishing is mostly let by the week to parties who book Glenfeshie Lodge, 4.5 miles up the glen. There is also a comfortable self-catering cottage which sleeps 8 guests. Cost: expect to pay in the order of £20/£30 per rod per day. Accommodation prices on application to the estate. Contact: Hugh S W Blakeney, Frognal, Woodside Avenue, Grantown, Inverness-shire PH26 3JR. Tel: 01479 972698.

FINDHORN, River See OS Map 27.
GAMHNA, Loch See OS Map 36.
GEAL, Lochan See River Feshie.

GYNACK, Loch
Location & Access 35/743022. The loch is accessed from Kingussie. Drive north up Glen Gynack from the centre of the town, signposted to the Golf Course, and then walk north-west for fifteen minutes to reach the loch.
Commentary A very attractive loch between Creag Mhor (660m) to the north and Creag Bheag (486m) to the south. The loch covers an area of approximately 80 acres.
Fish Stocked with good quality brown trout which average 1lb in weight. There are a few pike as well.
Flies & Tactics Boat and bank fishing, but boat fishing produces best results. The shallow, west end of the loch, is the place to begin. Offer them: Black Pennell, March Brown, Dunkeld.
Permission & Charges Messrs Cromarty's Fishing Tackle, 25 High Street, Kingussie, Inverness-shire. Tel: 01540 661565. Cost: £9 per rod per session. Sessions: 9am/5pm and 5pm - 10pm. Boat Hire: £7 per session. Cromarty's also issue tickets for the Badenoch Angling Association waters which include the River Spey and Spey Dam, Loch Ericht and Laggan and the Rivers Calder, Tromie and Truim (see separate entries).

INSH, Loch
Location & Access 35/830040. Easily accessible from the A9 Perth/Inverness road at Kincraig.
Commentary Loch Insh lies on the course of the River Spey. The loch is just over 1 mile north/south by up to half a mile wide. A wide variety of water sports are enjoyed here, not only angling, so be prepared for company when afloat. The loch is owned by the Alvie Estate and they have fishing on two adjacent waters, Loch Alvie (35/865095) and Loch Beag (35/863092). There is also a 2.5 acre put-and-take fishery which is

OS Map 35 — Kingussie

unnamed on the OS Map but is known locally as "Jock of the Bog" (35/839069).
Fish Loch Insh has salmon, sea-trout, brown trout, Arctic charr and pike. Loch Alvie and Loch Beag contain pike and brown trout. The average weight of brown trout is in the order of 8oz/10oz but these lochs are capable of producing a few fish of up to and over 4lb. Jock of the Bog is stocked with brown trout. The Alvie Estate also have fishing on the River Spey and on the River Feshie (see separate entries).
Flies & Tactics In recent years an increasing number of salmon are being caught on Loch Insh and boat fishing brings the best results. Concentrate your efforts at the shallow, south end of the loch where the Spey ambles in from the Insh Marshes. Loch Alvie is very beautiful but very dour and you will have to work hard for sport. The west and south-west bay, by the old church on the island, is the place to begin. Loch Beag is attacked from the shore and do not wade because the margins are soft in places. Jock of the Bog will quickly restore your self-confidence, if such a thing is required. Flies: Ke-He, Soldier Palmer, Peter Ross. Dapping is a useful ploy for bringing up Loch Insh sea-trout and salmon, as well as for tempting brown trout.
Permission & Charges A boat with an outboard motor with two rods fishing costs £40 per day on Loch Insh and £35 per day on Loch Alvie. Bank fishing costs £10 per rod per day. Jock of the Bog, which is fly-fishing only, costs £12 per rod for 3 fish, £3.20 per fish thereafter. Salmon fishing on the River Spey and the River Feshie costs £22 per rod per day, trout fishing £11 per rod per day. The Estate will arrange a gillie for you (£50 per day) and tackle hire is also available. Contact: Alvie Estate Office, Kincraig, Kingussie, Inverness-shire PH21 1NE. Tel: 01540 651255/651249; Fax: 01540 651380; or the Dalraddy Holiday Park, by Aviemore, Inverness-shire PH22 1QB. Tel: 01479 810330.

JOCK OF THE BOG, Loch See Loch Insh.

KILLIN, Loch
Location & Access 35/528102. Access is from the B862 Inverness/Fort Augustus road south of Whitebridge (35/485149). A narrow, tortuous road climbs south-east into the hills following the line of the River Fechlin (private fishing) to reach the loch after 4 miles. Drive with extreme care.
Commentary A wonderful little loch, easily accessible and ideal for beginners. Loch Killin is 1.5 miles north/south by up to 400 yards wide, surrounded by magnificent scenery and wildlife. The south end of the loch, where the River Killin enters, is shallow and has a sandy beach which is perfect for a lazy picnic. Respect the beauty of this lovely place and the privilege of being there: leave it as you would wish to find it, pristine.
Fish An enormous stock of small brown trout and the chance of a few Arctic charr as well.
Flies & Tactics Bank fishing only, from the east, roadside, shore, and at the south end of the loch. It is dangerous to wade. Stay on terra firma. Flies: Black Zulu, Grouse & Claret, Silver Butcher.

Permission & Charges Contact: Bill Brailsford, Head Keeper, Garrogie Estate, Estate Office, Gorthleck, Inverness-shire. Tel: 01456 486254. Cost: £5 per rod per day.

KILLIN, River See Loch Killin.
MARKIE, Burn See River Spey.

MHOR, Loch
Location & Access 35/545197. The B862 Inverness/Fort Augustus road parallels the north bank of the loch. the opposite shore may be approached from Farraline (35/566220), Wester Aberchalder (35/552199), Migovie (35/540189) and from Garthbeg (35/519170).
Commentary Loch Mhor was formed when the waters of Loch Farraline and Loch Garth were impounded to supply the power station at Foyers on the shores of Loch Ness. The loch-level is therefore subject to variations in height, particularly when water is drawn off during the hours of darkness to feed the Foyers turbines. Loch Mhor is four miles long by up to three-quarters of a mile wide at Wester Aberchalder.
Fish Brown trout which average 10oz, but fish of up to 4lb have been taken in recent years.
Flies & Tactics Boat fishing brings the best results and it is possible, with care, to pass through the narrows near Gorthleck which join the two bodies of water. The northern section, the old Loch Farraline, is the best fishing area, particularly along the north-east shore from the head of the loch to Ballindalloch. The wide bay at Wester Aberchalder, where the feeder burn enters from Loch Conagteann (35/587212) can also be productive; as is the extreme south-east corner of old Loch Garth where the River E enters at Garthbeg. Show the beasts: Black Pennell, Greenwell's Glory, Alexandra.
Permission & Charges Contact: Donald Campbell, Whitebridge Hotel, Stratherrick, Inverness-shire IV1 2UN. Tel: 01456 486226; Fax: 01456 486413. Cost: £15 per boat per day. Hotel guests have priority.

NAN REAMH, Loch See River Tromie.

PHONES & ETTERIDGE ESTATE, Lochs PHONES Loch (35/709949); Loch ETTERIDGE (35/691930); Lochan DUBH (35/7139530); Lochan AN DABHAICH (35/729962); Lochan ODHAR (35/736972). These waters contain large stocks of small brown trout and are only available to tenants of Phones Lodge or Etteridge Lodge.

PRIVATE WATERS BHODAICH, Loch (35/552245); AN ORDAIN, Loch (35/556240); NA CRAOIBHE-BEITHE, Lochan (35/545235); DUBH, Lochan (35/530246); RUAIRIDH, Loch (35/530214); FARIGAIG, River (35/522239); FEITH A'PHUILL, Loch (35/555089); NAN LOSGANAN, Loch (35/501155); BRAIGH BHRUTHAICH, Loch (35/885294); A'CHOIN DUIBH, Loch (35/816116); NA STUIRTEAG, Loch (35/730266); NA LAIRIGE, Loch (North) (35/565013); DEARG Lochan (35/544020); NAN SIDHEAN, Loch (35/509010); A'CHOIRE, Lochan (35/570986);

285

Kingussie — OS Map 35

CRUNACHDHAN, Loch (35/545928); NA LAIRIGE, Loch (South) (35/554917); DUBH, Loch (35/632013); UISGE, Loch (35/635039); SPEY, River (above Spey Dam);Loch GLAS-CHOIRE (35/630909).

SPEY DAM, Loch See River Spey.

SPEY, River

Location & Access On OS Map 35 the River Spey extends from Aviemore (35/900127) in the east to above Garva Bridge at 35/500950 in the west. There is no fishing above Spey Dam (35/570935). Access is from public roads on both banks of the stream (see also OS Maps 36 and 28).

Commentary The upper 13 miles of the Spey, between Loch Insh (see separate entry) and Spey Dam are managed by the Badenoch Angling Association. The principal tributaries on the Upper Spey are: Markie Burn, which flows into Spey Dam itself; the River Truim (made famous by John Inglis Hall in his book *Fishing a Highland Stream*) which enters at 35/687962 near Invertruim; the River Calder which joins the Spey near Newtonmore at Spey Bridge (35/709980); Allt Mor at Kingussie (35/759001) near Ruthven Barracks; the River Tromie which enters by the Dell of Killiehuntly at 35/780012; and, below Loch Insh, the River Feshie (35/842064). The Insh Marshes are notoriously prone to severe flooding and are a designated Site of Special Scientific Interest because of the wide range of flora and fauna which make it their home.

Fish Salmon and sea-trout, brown trout and pike. Not nearly as productive as the beats below Loch Insh and further downstream, but still a chance of sport. The Association Water produces about 8/10 salmon each season. However, the trout fishing is first-class.

Flies & Tactics The river here is slow-moving and sluggish as it wends its way north to Loch Insh. The best time to attack is after a spate, but even in normal conditions, because the river is deep, backing-up can often induce a salmon to "take". Wading is not really required and in some areas it is down-right dangerous. The tributaries also fish best after heavy rain. The brown trout are of excellent quality and there is some beautiful dryfly water. Spey Dam is an attractive alternative fishing location if the river is not in condition. The day is divided into 2 sessions on Spey Dam, from 9am until 5pm and from 5pm until dusk. Boat fishing brings the best results and the loch contains good stocks of brown trout which average in the order of 12oz/14oz. Flies: Salmon: Shrimp Fly, Munro Killer, Stoat's Tail, Hairy Mary, Willie Gunn, Garry Dog; trout and sea-trout: Black Pennell, Soldier Palmer, Peter Ross.

Permission & Charges Messrs Cromarty's Fishing Tackle, 25 High Street, Kingussie, Inverness-shire. Tel: 01540 661565. Alex Bennett, 113 High Street, Kingussie, Inverness-shire. Tel: 01540 661645. Spey Dam: cost: £9 per rod per session; boat hire: £7 per session. River Spey, and access to River Truim and River Calder for trout fishing: £5 per rod per day.

TROMIE, River

Location & Access Source 42/725800 Outfall 35/780012. Access to the lower river is from the B970 Kingussie/Nethy Bridge road at Tromie Bridge (35/790995). The middle and upper reaches of the stream are adjacent to the private estate road to Lynaberack Lodge (35/769949).

Commentary The majority of the river, both banks, lies within the Lynaberack & Ruthven Estate which extends south from Kingussie and covers an area of some 12,000 acres.

Fish Salmon, sea-trout and brown trout. Exact numbers are not given, perhaps in the order of 30 salmon may be taken each season.

Flies & Tactics Very much a spate stream and dependent upon the good grace of the elements. In the right conditions, a delightful stream to fish; deep holding-pools, swift, tumbling runs, fishy corners. A single-handed rod is best and wading is not really necessary. The estate also have 1 mile of single-bank fishing on the River Spey, and fishing on Loch an t-Seilich (42/759864) (see separate entry on OS Map 42) and little Loch nan Reamh (35/796983) near Killiehuntly can also give splendid sport with trout.

Permission & Charges Lynaberack Lodge is self-catering, sleeps up to 16 and costs from approximately £2600 per week. Stalking and shooting may also be available at an additional charge. Contact: Finlayson Hughes, 29 Barossa Place, Perth PH1 5EP. Tel: 01738 630926; Fax: 01738 639017.

TRUIM, River

Location & Access Source 42/608768. Outfall 35/688962. Accessible throughout its entire length from the A9 Perth/Inverness road.

Commentary The river rises from A'Mharconaich (975m), one of a cluster of Munros (Scottish mountains over 3,000ft in height) around Loch Ericht (see separate entry on OS Map 42) and Dalwhinnie, and flows north to join the River Spey at Invertruim. This little river is immortalised in John Inglis Hall's marvellous book, Fishing a Highland Stream, first published in 1960 and re-issued by Viking in 1987.

Fish Brown trout, which can be surprisingly large, and, very occasionally, the odd salmon and sea-trout.

Flies & Tactics Downstream from Dalwhinnie and upstream from the confluence with the River Spey is the best fishing area. Delicate work, stalking small pools and runs. High water conditions are essential for success. Inglis Hall suggested dry-fly, particularly the Iron Blue Dun, although wet fly patterns such as Black Pennell and Soldier Palmer also produce results.

Permission & Charges See River Spey entry.

UATH, Lochan See River Feshie.

OS Map 36 — Grantown & Cairngorm

Grantown and Cairngorm

A'BHAINNR, Lochan See River Avon.
A'GHARBH-CHOIRE, Loch See Loch Morlich.
ALIVE, Loch See OS Map 35, Kingussie.
ALLT BAN, Burn See Loch Morlich.
AN EILEIN, Loch This loch (36/895075), and Loch Gamhna (36/891068), lie within the Cairngorm National Nature Reserve and they are a very popular with visitors to Strathspey. Sadly, both waters are troutless and they are not fished.
AN LOCHAN UAINE, Lochan See Loch Morlich.
AN T-SEILACH, Loch See Loch Einich.
AVIELOCHAN, Loch See Loch Garten.
AVON, Loch See River Avon.

AVON, River
Location & Access Source 36/015023. Outfall 28/174370. (See also OS Map 28 for lower section of the river). Access is from the B9008 Bridge of Avon/Glenlivet road and the B9136 Glenlivet/Tomintoul road. The upper river is approached via estate roads.
Commentary The River Avon (pronounced A'an) is the longest tributary of the River Spey (see separate entry and also entries on OS Maps 28 & 35). The stream rises in the heart of the Cairngorm Mountains from Loch Avon (36/015024), a long, deep, narrow loch pinched between Cairngorm (1245m) to the north and Beinn Mheadhoin (1182m) to the south. Loch Avon contains Arctic charr and brown trout. There are five other lochs in the vicinity, all of which involve serious efforts to reach: Loch Etchachan (36/007004); Lochan Uaine (36/001981), a high corrie lochan on the east face of Ben Macdui (1309m); Dubh Lochan (36/038023), a step south from the Mountain Refuge Hut at Fords of Avon; and Lochan a'Bhainnr (36/047048) which lies one mile to the north of the hut. The higher lochs are frozen over for most of the year and do not hold trout. The lower level lochs contain a few small trout. Loch Builg (36/188035) and Lochan nan Gabhar (36/148037), to the east, are private.
Fish The River Avon produces upwards of 500 salmon and good numbers of sea-trout each season. The river also holds brown trout.
Flies & Tactics The best of the fishing is on the lower river where there are excellent holding-pools and exciting runs. This is a modest stream and a 12ft rod will cope with most fishing eventualities. Many of the pools, particularly during low water conditions in the summer months, are best approached on hands and knees to avoid "spooking" the residents. Where wading is required, thigh waders are adequate. The upper river, in the vicinity of Tomintoul, offers good fly-fishing for trout with the chance of an occasional salmon. The trout lochs noted above all contain small brown trout, but reaching these lochs, and fishing them, is reward enough in itself. The River Avon has four principal tributaries, the River Livet, Burn of Lochy, Chabet Water and Conglass Water and they also offer good sport in the right water conditions. Salmon flies: Garry Dog, Shrimp Fly, Stoat's Tail, Munro Killer, Goat's Toe, Willie Ross, Hairy Mary; for sea-trout and brown trout, try: Black Pennell, Greenwell's Glory, Peter Ross.
Permission & Charges Prices vary from between £8 per rod per day on the upper river to £400 per rod week on the lower river, depending upon the beat fished and the time of year. Ballindalloch Beats: The Factor, Ballindalloch Estate, Estate Office, Ballindalloch Estate, Banffshire AB37 9AX. Tel: 01807 500205; Fax: 01807 500210. The estate also has two first-class self-catering cottages available for rent with fishing. Delnashaugh Hotel, Ballindalloch, Banffshire AB3 9AS. Tel: 01807 500255; Fax: 01807 500389; Glenavon Water: The Factor, Eastridge Estate, Estate Offce, Ramsbury, Malborough, Wiltshire SN8 2RG. Tel: 01672 520042; Kylnadrochit Beat: Highland Sporting Estates, Kylnadrochit Lodge, Tomintoul, Banffshire AB37 9HJ. Tel: 01807 580230; Fax: 01309 690454; Tomintoul: Gordon Arms Hotel, The Square, Tomintoul, Banffshire AB37 9ET. Tel: 01807 580206; Fax: 01807 580488; Tomintoul Post Office, The Square, Tomintoul, Banffshire AB37 9ET. Tel: 01807 580201. The Post Office have 3 permits per day, available to anglers resident in Tomintoul. These are issued on a strictly first-come-first-served basis. The Post Office is open for business at 8.30am and a day ticket costs £8 per rod. Fishing is from 9am until 7pm. River Livet: For general information on the river and its tributaries, contact: Grant Mortimers, 3 High Street, Grantown, Moray PH26 3HB. Tel: 01479 872 684; Fax: 01479 872211; J A Munro, 93-95 High Street, Aberlour, Banffshire AB38 9PB. Tel: 01340 871428.

BEANAIDH, Lochan See Loch Einich.
BUILG, Loch See River Avon.
CHABET, Water See River Avon.
COIRE AN LOCHAIN, Loch See Loch Einich.
CONGLASS, Water See River Avon.

CRAGGAN, Fishery
Location & Access 36/017257. Easily accessible from the A95 Grantown/Dulnain Bridge road.
Commentary A small, put-and-take fishery, 2.5 acres in extent, visible from the main road. There are also two, small, bait-fishing ponds. The fishery offers light snacks for hungry anglers as well as suitable flies for hungry fish.
Fish Regularly stocked with rainbow trout and brown trout which average in the order of 1lb 4oz.
Flies & Tactics Bank fishing, and there are access facilities for disabled anglers. The fishery is open 7 days a week from April until October and rods are available for hire. Instruction will be given by prior arrangement. Most patterns of flies and lures catch fish.
Permission & Charges Cost: £9 for a 2 fish limit. Thereafter, anglers may catch 2 more fish (catch and release). If they wish to continue, they must purchase a new ticket. Otherwise, they may choose to have a round of golf on the 1,000 yard, 9-hole, course which surrounds the fishery. Cost per round, £6.

DALLAS, Loch See Loch Garten.

Grantown & Cairngorm — OS Map 36

DEE, River See OS Map 44, Braemar.
DERRY, River See OS Map 44, Braemar.
DON, River See OS Map 37, Strathdon.
DRUIE, River See Loch Einich.
DUBH, Lochan See River Avon.
DULNAIN, River See River Spey.

EINICH, Loch
Location & Access 36/914990. On the Rothiemurchus Estate and accessed from Coylumbridge (36/915108) along a private estate road.
Commentary The loch lies at the head of Glen Einich between Sgoran Dubh Mor (1111m) to the west and Braeriach (1296m) to the east. Loch Einich is over 1 mile north/south by up to a quarter of a mile wide. The water drops to a depth of 40m and is crystal-clear. A path leads steeply south up the west face of Einich Cairn (1237m) giving access to the summit plateau of Braeriach, passing along the way the source of the River Dee at the Wells of Dee (36/938988). There are a number of additional lochs in the vicinity: to the west, Loch Mhic Ghille-chaoil (36/921024), Lochan Beanaidh (36/911026) and Loch an t-Seilach (36/916006); to the south, on The Great Moss, Loch na Cnapan (36/918960) and Loch nan Stuirteag (36/941956). On Cairn Toul (1291m) at a height of 860m, is Lochan Uaine (36/960980) and on the north face of Braeriach, Loch Coire an Lochain (36/943004).
Fish The high lochs are frozen over for most of the year and do not contain fish. Loch Einich holds Arctic charr and brown trout. The other waters noted hold small brown trout which average a few ounces in weight.
Flies & Tactics Bank fishing only and it is dangerous to wade, particularly along the west shoreline of Loch Einich where the bottom shelves very quickly. Do not expect large baskets of trout but do expect a wonderful day out amidst magnificent scenery. Try: March Brown, Greenwell's Glory, Silver Butcher. For certain fishing success, if that is what pleases you, visit the Inverdruie Fish Farm (36/903113) just to the north of the B970 Aviemore/Coylumbridge road. This is an 8 acre stocked, put-and-take rainbow trout fishery complete with visitor facilities, rod hire, instruction and a farm shop. Feed the fish before you catch them. Fishing is also available on the 4 Rothiemurchus Estate beats of the River Spey (see separate entry) for salmon, sea-trout and brown trout, and on the River Druie which is a tributary of the Spey. Unique to the Estate, is a half mile long, man-made, stream which has been stocked with rainbow trout which is fly-only and fished by four rods.
Permission & Charges Access to Loch Einich and the remote hill lochs on the Rothiemurchus Estate is strictly controlled and is on foot only. The use of vehicles, mountain bikes, and other forms of transport is not permitted. The area forms part of the internationally important Cairngorm Nature Reserve and its conservation and protection is a major facet of the management policy of the estate. The 25,000 acre estate specialises in catering for corporate groups and provides clients with accommodation at Altnacaber Lodge and Drumintoul Lodge which has its own, private, stocked lochan for the use of guests. Prices and further information on application to: Visitor Service Department, Rothiemurchus Estate, Estate Office, by Aviemore, Inverness-shire PH22 1QH. Tel: 01479 810858; Fax: 01479 811778. Permission to fish at the Fish Farm, on Loch Pityoulish (see Loch Garten entry) and the River Spey and River Druie is available from the Fish Farm Shop at Inverdruie. Tel: 01479 810703. Approximate costs: Fish Farm Loch: £15 per rod per day with a 2 fish limit; Rainbow trout stream, £30 per rod per day with a 4 fish limit; River Spey, £35 per rod per day.

ETCHACHAN, Loch See River Avon.
FESHIE, River See OS Map 35.
GAIRN, River See OS Map 44.

GARTEN, Loch
Location & Access 36/975180. Approach from the B970 Nethybridge/Inverdruie road at East Croftmore (36/961195).
Commentary One of the most most frequently visited lochs in the north, not for its fish, but because it is home to Scotland's most famous resident anglers: the pair of ospreys which nest on a sparse tree by the loch. The RSPB owns the loch and the surrounding Abernethy Forest which is an important nature reserve, renowned for its ancient woodlands and wide variety of wildlife. To the south of Loch Garten, and accessed by forest paths, is little Loch Mallachie (36/965175). There are 5 more trout waters in the vicinity, all of which will repay a visit: Loch Pityoulish (36/920136), Loch Dallas (36/932159) Loch Vaa (36/914175), Avielochan (36/909165) to the south, and Loch Mor (36/962256) to the north adjacent to the A938 Carrbridge/Dulnain Bridge road.
Fish Quite a variety. Stocked rainbow trout and brown trout, and, in Loch Pityoulish, wild brown trout. The largest fish inhabit Loch Pityoulish where they are mightily harassed by voracious pike. Loch Dallas is probably the most productive water, where trout average 1lb and fish of up to 3lb are taken. Avielochan has stocked rainbow trout of up to 7lb in weight.
Flies & Tactics Avielochan is perhaps the least attractive water, being overlooked by the busy A9 Perth/Inverness road. Loch Vaa, to the north of Avielochan, is very attractive, secluded and surrounded by mature woodlands. The water is very clear and trout are easily "spooked". Loch Pityoulish is stunningly beautiful. All these lochs are fished from the boat and they vary in size from 8 acres up to Pityoulish which is half a mile long by up to quarter of a mile wide. Lochan Dubh (36/929163) immediately to the north of Loch Dallas, is private. Full details will be given on booking, but your should offer them: Ke-He, Soldier Palmer, Silver Butcher. Reservoir-type lures also produce results.
Permission & Charges Expect to pay in the order of £20 per day for a boat with two rods fishing. For Garten, Dallas, Vaa and Mor contact: Grant Mortimers, 3 High Street, Grantown, Moray PH26 3HB. Tel: 01479 872684; Fax: 01479 872211. Direct bookings for Avielochan from: Mrs Margaret MacDonald, Avielochan, by Aviemore, Inverness-shire. Tel: 01479 810847; For Pityoulish, contact Inverdruie Fish Farm Shop, Inverdruie, by Aviemore, Inverness-shire. Tel: 01479 810703.

OS Map 36 — Grantown & Cairngorm

GEAL, Lochan See OS Map 35, Kingussie.
INVERDRUIE, Fish Farm See Loch Einich.
LIVET, River See River Avon.
LOCHY, Burn See River Avon.
MALLACHIE, Loch See Loch Garten.
MHIC GHILLE-CHAOIL, Loch See Loch Einich.
MOR, Loch See Loch Garten.

MORLICH, Loch
Location & Access 36/965095. Approach from Coylumbridge (36/916108) along the minor road to the Glenmore Lodge National Outdoor Training Centre and the Aviemore ski slopes.
Commentary Loch Morlich lies at the heart of the Glen More Forest Park to the east of Aviemore. The loch is circular, about half a mile across, and popular as a water-sports centre. There is a campsite and caravan park on the east side of the loch so look out for company, both ashore and afloat. Non-angling companions will find a host of activities to keep them happily occupied whilst you fish.
Fish Modest brown trout which average approximately 8oz, but a few larger specimens and look out for pike as well.
Flies & Tactics Bank fishing and boat fishing, but boat fishing brings best results. This is a shallow loch and fish rise and may be caught almost anywhere, from the middle to the margins. The inlet burn, the Allt Ban, which enters the loch near to the campsite, also contains some useful brown trout. There are 3 other small waters in the vicinity, approached by forest paths, which may also be explored: Lochan na Beinne (36/006083), An Lochan Uaine (36/001105), and Loch a'Gharbh-choire (36/012111) near the Ryovan Bothy. Ask at the campsite for details. Flies: Soldier Palmer, Greenwell's Glory, Dunkeld. Dry fly can also be very effective in calm conditions.
Permission & Charges The Warden's Office, Glenmore Campsite, Glenmore, by Aviemore, Inverness-shire. Tel: 01479 861271. Cost: Bank fishing, £3.80 per rod per day, boats may be hired at approximately £16 per day.

NA BEINNE, Loch See Loch Morlich.
NA CNAPAN, Loch See Loch Einich.
NAN GABHAR, Lochan See River Avon.
NAN STUIRTEAG, Loch See Loch Einich.
NETHY, River See River Spey.
PITYOULISH, Loch See Loch Garten.
PRIVATE WATERS NA STUIRTEAG, Loch (36/002320); AN T-SIDHEIN, Loch (36/973321); DUBH, Lochan (36/957328); ILLE MHOR, Loch (36/934320); BRAIGH BHRUTHACH, Loch (36/885295).
ROTHIEMURCHUS, Stream See Loch Einich.

SPEY, River
Location & Access On OS Map 36, the River Spey extends from Wester Culfoich (36/118330) in the north to Ballindalloch March in the west and there is easy access to the river throughout the entire length from public and estate roads. See also OS Maps 28 and 35.
Commentary This section of the Spey, from Grantown upstream through Nethybridge and Boat of Garten to Aviemore, offers the best day-ticket salmon and sea-trout fishing anywhere in Scotland. Local angling clubs, hotels and private owners have a wide range of sport available and it is more often than not possible to make a booking on arrival, rather than in advance. The surrounding scenery is magnificent and there is a whole host of alternative activities for non-fishing companions to enjoy whilst you assault the Spey.
Fish One of the heaviest fish taken in recent years was a salmon of 35lb caught by Ms Elaine Schleiffer on Castle Grant No 1 Beat in 1994. Fish of over 20lb are not unusual. The Castle Grant beats produce approximately 600 salmon and 450 sea-trout each season; the Strathspey Angling Association Water and their River Dulnain fishings return an average of 300 salmon and 900 sea-trout (13lb sea-trout have been taken in recent years); Abernethy, 150 salmon and 700 sea-trout.
Flies & Tactics Working upstream, the first beats are the famous, and expensive, Tulchan beats, then 5.5 miles of Castle Grant fishing. Next is the Upper Castle Grant beat which ends at the new road bridge at Grantown on Spey. This leads on to the Strathspey Angling Improvement Association beat extending up to Nethybridge, followed by the Abernethy Angling Improvement Association Water with 6.5 miles of the river at Boat of Garten. Thereafter come the Aviemore, Kinchurdy, Kinrara, Kincraig and Rothiemurchus waters. The Spey is a big river, wide, deep and swift. Wading requires extreme caution. Use a 15ft rod, at least, and practice the Spey-cast before arrival. Spend your time fishing, not climbing trees to recover your flies. A gillie is a great comfort and can often make the difference between a blank day and one for the record book. The middle river fishes well throughout the entire season but the most productive months are generally June, July and September. Sea-trout fishing is superb in June and July, probably as good as anywhere in the world and quite outstanding. And don't forget the brown trout: there are some marvellous trout in the River Spey, fish of up to and over 3lb in weight. Encounter these brown trout in the lower reaches of the Spey's tributaries as they join the main stream: River Dulnain (36/002238), River Nethy (36/999224) and the River Druie (36/895119). Some very good brown trout haunt these areas, particularly after heavy rain. Salmon flies: Willie Gunn, Garry Dog, General Practitioner, Black Doctor, Munro Killer, Hairy Mary, Stoat's Tail, Waddingtons; for sea-trout and brown trout, try: Black Pennell, March Brown, Teal Blue & Silver, particularly after dusk.
Permission & Charges Expect to pay from between £30 per rod per day up to £250 per rod per day, depending upon the time of year and the beat fished. The Tulchan and Castle Grant waters are usually well-booked in advance by people who return every year but there are sometimes vacancies caused by cancellations. Tulchan: Tulchan Sporting Estates Limited, Estate Office, Tulchan, Grantown, Moray. Tel: 01807 510200; Fax: 01807 510234; Castle Grant, Upper Castle Grant and Kinchurdy beats: Strathspey Estate Office, Heathfield, Grantown on Spey, Moray. PH26 3LG Tel: 01479 872529 or Fax: 01479 873452; Strathspey Angling Association Water: Grant Mortimers, 3 High Street,

Strathdon — OS Maps 36-37

Grantown, Moray PH26 3HB. Tel: 01479 872684; Fax: 01479 872211; Abernethy Angling Improvement Association Water: Messrs Allen's, Deshar Road, Boat of Garten, Inverness-shire PH24 3BN. Tel: 01479 831372; Rothiemurchus Water: The Factor, Rothiemurchus Estate, Inverdruie, by Aviemore, Inverness-shire PH22 1QH. Tel: 01479 810647; Fax: 01479 810786; Kincardine Beat: Salmon Galore, Inverallan Road, 8 Georgeham Road, Camberley, Surrey GU15 4YR. Tel: 01344 750274; William Grant, Mountain Lodges, Beechgrove, Mains of Garten Farm, Boat of Garten, Inverness-shire. Tel: 01479 831551; Fax: 01479 831445. Mountain Lodges offer excellent accommodation and free brown trout fishing on the River Spey which is within easy walking distance of the lodges; Aviemore Fishing: Colin Sutton, Speyside Sports, 64 Grampian Road, Aviemore, Inverness-shire. Tel: 01479 810656: Fax: 01479873415. Speyside Sports day-tickets are only available to visitors staying in Aviemore, Coylumbridge or Rothiemurchus.

UAINE Loch (Cairn Toul), See Loch Einich.
UAINE, Lochan See River Avon.
VAA, Loch See Loch Garten.

Strathdon

BLACK WATER, River See River Deveron (OS Map 29).
BRAERADDACH, Loch 37/482002. This loch, together with Lochs KINORD (37/442994), DAVAN (37/441008) and Loch of ABOYNE (37/538998) contain few trout and are therefore more of interest to coarse fishermen.
BUCKHAT, Water of See River Don (Alford to Cockbridge).

DEE River (Trustach Cottage to Balmoral)
Location & Access On OS Map 37, the Dee extends from Trustach Cottage (37/650960) in the east to Balmoral Castle (37/250955) in the west. Easy access from the A93 Aberdeen/Braemar road along the north bank and the B976 Banchory/Crathie road on the south bank.
Commentary The Middle Dee, described here, is perhaps the most lovely part of this famous Scottish salmon stream. The river is confined between well-wooded banks, surrounded by spectacular, heather-clad hills. There are 45 beats throughout the river and the Middle Dee contains some of the most productive, and exclusive of them all: Balmoral, Invercauld, Abergeldie, Crathie, Birkhill, Glenmuick, Monaltrie, Cambus O'May, Dinnet, Glen Tanar, Aboyne Water, Aboyne Castle Water, Dess, Birse, Carlogie, Kincardine, Sluie, Woodend, Cairnton, Commonty and Blackhall. A H Wood, notable for his low-water, greased-line salmon-fishing technique, is reputed to have taken 3,490 fish on his own rod at Cairnton between 1913 and 1934. Those days have long-since gone, but reasonable sport may still enjoyed throughout the season. Rainbow trout fishing can also be obtained on Glen Tanar Loch (37/479952), a stocked loch with a boat on the Glen Tanar Estate to the west of Aboyne. See also OS Map 38.
Fish Some notable salmon have been landed during recent years. A fish of 29lb by Mrs Little; a splendid fish of 32lb for R Dalton from Lower Durris. See also OS Map 38.
Flies & Tactics The best of the Middle Dee fishing is from April until the end of May, depending upon weather conditions. A cold start to the season (see also OS Map 38) generally holds fish in the Lower River, but once the water temperature rises they run through the bottom beats very quickly and most of the Middle River is normally well-stocked with fish from mid-April onwards. A 15ft rod should be used. Wade cautiously, and remember that the river can sometimes be subjected to an unexpected "surge", causing a mini tidal wave which can catch you unawares. The principal tributaries, River Gairn, Girnock Burn, River Muick, Tullich Burn and the Water of Tanar are important salmon spawning burns and are not fished. See OS Map 38 for useful patterns of fly.
Permission & Charges See OS Map 38 for an indication of charges. For various beats, contact: J Somers 13-15 Bon Accord Terrace, Aberdeen. Tel: 01224 210008; Countrywear, 15 Bridge Street, Ballater, Aberdeenshire. Tel: 01339 755453; Kingcausie Water: The Factor, North Lodge Estate, Kingcausie, by Banchory, Aberdeenshire. Tel: 01224 732266; Aboyne Water: G S Dawson, Red Brae, The Croft, Nether Blainslie, Galashiels, Selkirkshire. Tel: 01896 860307; Middle Blackhall, Culter, and Glenmuick, Water: Messrs Savills, 12 Clerk Street, Brechin, Angus DD9 6AE. Tel: 01356 622187; Borrowston & Kincardine Water: The Factor, Kincardine Estates, Kincardine O'Neil, Aboyne, Aberdeenshire AB3 5AE. Tel: 013398 84225; Little Blackhall Water: The Factor, Auchnagathle House, Keig, Alford, Aberdeenshire AB33 8BQ. Tel: 019755 62525; Upper Blackhall: Messrs Smith Milligan, Chrtd Survyrs, 10 Golden Square, Aberdeen. AB9 1JA. Tel: 01224 638237; Glen Tanar, Cambus O'May, Craigendinnie, Deecastle; and Waterside: The Factor, Glen Tannar Estate, Brooks House, Glen Tanar, Aboyne, Aberdeenshire AB34 5EU. Tel: 01339 886451; for late availability, contact the DeeLine Information Service. Tel: 0891 88 1941.

DON, River (Alford to Cockbridge)
Location & Access See OS Map 38.
Commentary The River Don, from its source on Little Geal Charn (710m) downstream to Alford (pronounced A-ford), is much more " Highland" in character than the lower river. The upper river is surrounded by majestic mountains and its course down Strathdon is graced by some of Scotland's most dramatic castles: Corgarff, Glenbuckat, Towie, Kildrummy, Asloun and Castle Forbes. The Water of Buckhat meets the main flow at Bridge of Buckhat (37/401150) and is, in its own right, given good water levels, a super little trout stream; as is the Water of Nochty which joins the Don at Strathdon (37/355130). The contrast between the wild moorlands of Corgarff and the wonderful, mature, woodlands surrounding the stream at Castle Forbes are an angler's

OS Maps 37-38 Aberdeen

delight and offer great sport amidst outstanding scenery.
Fish The Upper River does not produce as many salmon as the beats below Alford (see OS Map 38), although the Castle Forbes Water and Kildrummy, in particular, are still two of the finest beats on the river. Spring salmon fishing can be good, but most fish are taken during September and October. Where the upper river excels, however, is in the quality and excellence of its brown trout fishing: superb fly water, from rocky, tumbling flows to perfect dry-fly pools such as the Dam Pool below Castle Forbes. Trout of up to and over 2lb are frequently caught.
Flies & Tactics During the early months of the season and in heavy water conditions, use a 12ft/15ft rod; not only to control the fish, but also to cover the lies as some of the pools are difficult to wade. In the summer months, and for trout fishing, a 10ft rod is more than adequate for most situations. For an account of useful patterns of flies, see OS Map 38.
Permission & Charges See OS Map 38 for Castle Forbes Water & Alford beats. For Edinglassie & Candacraig Beats, contact: Colquhonnie Hotel, Strathdon, Aberdeenshire. Tel: 019756 51210; Kildrummy Fishings, T R Hillary, Gateside, Milton of Kildrummy, Alford, Aberdeenshire. Tel: 019755 71208 and Kildrummy Castle Hotel, Kildrummy, by Alford, Aberdeenshire. Tel: 019755 71288; Upper Brux Fishing, enquire through Colquhonnie Hotel (above). Various beats, Forbes Arms Hotel, Bridge of Alford, Aberdeenshire. Tel: 019755 62108.

FIDDICH, River See River Spey (OS Map 28).
GAIRN, River See River Dee (Trustach Cottage to Balmoral).
GIRNOCK, Burn See River Dee (Trustach Cottage to Balmoral).
GLEN TANAR, Loch See River Dee (Trustach Cottage to Balmoral).
LIVET, River See OS Map 36 Grantown and Cairngorm
MUICK, River See River Dee (Trustach Cottage to Balmoral).
NOCHTY, Water of See River Don (Alford to Cockbridge).
TANAR, Water See River Dee (Trustach Cottage to Balmoral).
TULLICH, Burn See River Dee (Trustach Cottage to Balmoral).

Aberdeen

BISHOP'S, Loch See Corby Loch entry.

CORBY, Loch
Location & Access 38/925144. The loch lies to the north of Bridge of Don and is accessed from either the minor road at Causewayend (38/928124) on the B997, or from Newton of Shiehill (38/941141) on the B999.
Commentary Corby Loch is an attractive, shallow water, covering an area of some 54 acres. There are two additional lochs nearby, Lilly Loch (38/920414) and Bishops' Loch (38/912143) but both are heavily silted and over-grown and are not fished. Parkhill Loch (38/895141), near Mains of Dyce, is private.
Fish Stocked with brown trout which can reach double figures in weight and rainbow trout of up to 8lb.
Flies & Tactics Strictly fly-only and bank fishing. However, wading is comfortable and generally safe, using either thigh or chest waders, and trout are taken from all round the shores of the loch. Flies: Soldier Palmer, Grouse & Claret, Peter Ross. Dry-fly also works well, particularly on calm summer evenings.
Permission & Charges The loch is in the hands of an angling syndicate but day-tickets (4 in number) are issued at a cost of £10 per rod. Contact: Balgownie Sports Ltd, Bridge of Don, Aberdeen. Tel: 01224 826232.

COTEHILL, Loch 38/027293. The loch lies to the east of the A975 Aberdeen/Peterhead road at Collieston. Various attempts have been made in past years to stock Cotehill Loch, and its neighbour to the east, Sand Loch (38/035283), but to no avail. The beneficiaries have been the local cormorant population.

DEE, River (Hill of Cairnton to Aberdeen),
Location & Access Source 36/975007 Outfall. 38/962057 The section of the River Dee contained on OS Map 38, from Hill of Cairnton to Aberdeen, is easily accessible from public roads which border the north and south banks of the river. The south bank, from Banchory upstream to opposite the Hill of Cairnton, and the north bank at Cairnton itself, is accessed by estate roads. The remainder of the north bank, upstream from Banchory to Cairnton, is accessed from the A93 Aberdeen/Ballater road.
Commentary The Dee is one of the most famous and productive salmon streams in Europe and rises from the Pools of Dee in the Lairig Ghru between Ben Macdui (1309m) to the east and Braeriach (1296m) to the west. The silver stream flows south down Glen Dee before turning east through Royal Deeside to reach the sea at Aberdeen after a journey of some 90 miles. The lower river, described here, is wide and fast and contains some of the best of the early season fishing; beats such as Cairnton, Blackhall, Inchmarlo, Banchory Lodge, Crathes, Durris, Park, Drum, Tilbouries, Altries, Cutler, Ardoe and Banchory/Devenick. The Dee is essentially a spate river and it depends upon snow-melt from the Cairngorm mountains to maintain its flow. Harsh, cold weather, early in the year, holds the fish in the lower river, below Banchory; if the weather is mild, then fish tend to move quickly through the lower beats into the middle river between Banchory and Aboyne (see OS Map 37).
Fish Recent years have see a dramatic decline in the number of salmon and sea-trout caught throughout the year, particularly during the spring months. The river now produces approximately 5,000 salmon each year rather than, as in previous years, upwards of 9,000. At present, riparian owners, or most of them, delay the start of the season by one month until 1st March and

291

Aberdeen — OS Map 38

are seeking to make this statutory by application to the Scottish Secretary of State for an alteration to the opening and close times for rod-and-line fishing. There is a proposal to extend the season by two weeks, into October, which has angered many anglers because of the damage which might be done to pre-spawning fish. A fly-only rule is being applied and spring rods may only kill one salmon per rod per week. Thereafter, anglers may continue to fish on a catch-and-release basis. This "gentleman's agreement" has caused, and is causing, great concern throughout the whole river as some "do" and some "don't": a party of German anglers fishing the Banchory Lodge Beat recently are alleged to have killed every fish they caught, 30 salmon. Consequently, the situation is confused and likely to remain so into the foreseeable future.

Flies & Tactics In the early months of the season, a 15ft rod must be used, with at least a sink-tip line, in order to get the fly down to the fish. As the season progresses, a lighter rod may be used, with a floating line. Deep wading is frequently required on many of the beats and anglers should at all times wear a floatation device and use a wading staff. The Dee can rise dramatically and this could be dangerous for the unwary. Seek advice and guidance from the Beat gillie. The ability to Spey-cast is also essential, to avoid conflict with bankside vegetation. Flies: Shrimp Fly, Blue Charm, Logie, Munro Killer, General Practitioner, Willie Gunn, Mar Lodge, Stoat's Tail, Black Doctor, Silver Wilkinson.

Permission & Charges Access to many of the beats, because of the confusion outlined above, is less difficult than in times past. Many anglers have simply deserted the river for pastures new so there is a better-than-average chance of acquiring a rod on this most lovely of Scottish rivers. Expect to pay in the order of between £25 per rod per day to approximately £150 per rod per day, depending upon the time of year and the beat fished. Contacts: Banchory Lodge Hotel, Banchory, Aberdeenshire. Tel: 013302 822625; Bell-Ingram, 3 Rubislaw Terrace, Aberdeen, AB1 1XE. Tel: 01224 644272; Ian Black, Meadowhead Farm, Newmachar, Aberdeen. Tel: 01224 724286; Ardoe House Hotel, Blairs, South Deeside Road, Aberdeen. Tel: 01224 867353; Julie Nickols, Linc Holdings, Amber Hill, Boston, Lincs. Tel: 01205 290444; Fax: 01205 290237; 'Campbells', Altries, Maryculter, Aberdeen. Tel: 01224 733258; Carter Jonas, 20 Owen Street, Hereford HR1 2PL. Tel: 01432 277174; Tilbouries Fishing, 15 Kelsey Gate, Court Down Road, Beckenham, Kent BR3 6LT. Tel: 0181 6581754; Gordon Arms Hotel, Kincardine O'Neil, Aberdeenshire. Tel: 013398 84236; Dawn Ritchie, Marcliffe at Pitfodeles, North Deeside Road, Aberdeen AB15 9YA. Tel: 01224 869190; Howie Irvine, Sporting Factors, 62 Bon Accord Street, Aberdeen. Tel: 01224 580913; Turner Hall, Cambus O'May, Ballater, Aberdeenshire. Tel: 013397 55034; also the Deeline Late Availability Information Service. Tel: 0891 88 1941.

DON, River (Mill of Tillyfoure to Bridge of Don)

Location & Access Source 36/196067 Outfall 38/955095. The River Don is easily accessible throughout its entire length from public roads and via estate roads and river-side paths.

Commentary Unlike its near-neighbour, the turbulent River Dee, the Don is a moderately sedate affair. The stream rises from the Well of Don on the north face of Little Geal Charn (710m) and flows east through mainly agricultural land to reach the sea at Bridge of Don after a leisurely journey of some 68 miles. The different characteristics of these two famous rivers is best summed up by an Aberdeenshire farming phrase: "A mile of Don is worth twa o'Dee." In its lower reaches the river used to be badly effected by effluent from paper mills but this has now been curtailed. There are 63 beats along the river and the Don is unique amongst Scottish salmon streams in that the vast majority of these beats are readily available to visiting anglers, either on a day-ticket basis or by the week. The Don is joined by its principal tributary, the River Urie, just to the south of Inverurie (38/782190) and the lower beats of the Don include: Castle Forbes Fishings, Tillyfoure & Balquholly, Monymusk, Grandhome, Fintry, Kemnay Fishings, Inverurie Fishings, Keithhall, Balbithan, Fetternear, Kinellar, Pitmidden, Parkhill, Cruvies and Nether Don. As the river approaches the sea, downstream from Dyce (38/895125), the stream becomes enclosed between heavily-wooded, steep banks where some of the pools are more than 30ft in depth. Upstream, the river hosts a wide variety of varied pools all of which are a delight to fish, perhaps the most perfect being in the vicinity of Paradise Wood (38/678188).

Fish Salmon, sea-trout and brown trout. A composite total is not available but upwards of 1,000 salmon are taken most seasons. There is a reasonable spring run when some large fish are taken. A 27lb salmon was taken in April 1996 and early season fishing during 1996 was excellent. The Don is also the finest brown trout fishery in Europe and produces good numbers of top-quality fish. A brown trout of 7lb 12oz was caught on the Forbes Castle Water in 1985 and fish of over 3lb in weight are not uncommon.

Flies & Tactics Spinning produces most fish during the spring months but when the water level drops the Don is an outstanding fly water. The lower river is best tackled with a 15ft rod but take great care when wading. Some of the lies are awkward to cover and an ability to Spey-cast will greatly enhance the chance of a fish. The best of the brown trout fishing is probably on the Monymusk and Castle Forbes water and dry fly fishing in late May and June can be spectacular. Indeed, and unlike most Scottish salmon rivers, the Don offers the best of all worlds, almost regardless of water conditions: if the salmon are uncooperative, there is always more than a good opportunity of a brown trout of glass-case proportions. The River Urie is also an excellent salmon and trout stream and well worth a visit. Salmon flies, try: Stoat's Tail, Hairy Mary, Munro Killer, Shrimp Fly, General Practitioner, Willie Gunn, Waddingtons, Blue Charm; salmon lures: Green & Yellow Devons, Black & Gold Devons, Flying 'C', Abu Spoons, Rapala; for trout, use Greenwell's Glory, March Brown, Blue Dun, Cinnamon & Gold.

Permission & Charges Charges vary depending upon time of year and which beat you choose to fish. Expect to pay, per rod per day, from £6 to £10 for brown trout

OS Map 38 — Aberdeen

fishing and from £15 to £80 for salmon fishing. Hotel guests have priority on hotel beats. Contact: Upper & Lower Parkhill and Upper Fintray Beats, J Somers, 13-15 Bon Accord Terrace, Aberdeen. Tel: 01244 210008; Criche Beat, Balgownie Sports, 23 Scotstown Road, Bridge of Don, Aberdeen. Tel: 01224 826232; Keithhall, Ardmurdo, Inverurie Town Water, Manar Beat, J J Watson, 44-48 Market Place, Inverurie, Aberdeenshire. Tel: 01467 620321; Kintore, Inverurie Town Water & Don, Rod & Mary Sloan, DIY Supplies, 129 High Street, Inveruire, Aberdeenshire. Tel: 01467 625181; Grandhome Fishings, D Wardhaugh & Son, 38-40 East High Street, Forfar, Angus. Tel: 01307 463657; Kemnay Beats, F J & S L Milton, Kemnay Ho, Kemnay, Aberdeenshire. Tel: 01467 642220; Fetternear Beat, Richard Fyffe, Corsindae, Sauchen, by Inverurie, Aberdeenshire. Tel: 01330 833295; Alford Fishings, W & R Murray, Main Street, Alford, Aberdeenshire. Tel: 01975 562366 or The Warden, Haughton House, Alford, Aberdeenshire. Tel: 01975 562453; Monymusk, Colin Hart, Grant Arms Hotel, Monymusk, Aberdeenshire. Tel: 01467 651426; Castle Forbes Water, The Estate Office, Whitehouse, by Alford, Aberdeenshire. Tel: 01975 562524; Towie Beat, Messrs Strutt & Parker, 68 Station Road, Banchory, Aberdeenshire. Tel: 01330 824888; Tilliefoure Fishing, J Uren, Priory Farmhouse, Appledore Road, Teddington, Middx. Tel: 01833 331071. For late availability, also telephone the DonLine Information Service. Tel: 01891 881941.

FEUGH, River
Location & Access Source 44/505861 Outfall 38/702953. Access is from the B974 Banchory/Aboyne road.
Commentary The Water of Feugh is a major tributary of the River Dee (see separate entry) and rises from Tampie (723m) in the Forest of Birse. The stream flows north to Burnfoot (44/541907) before swinging east to join the Dee just downstream of the bridge in Banchory. There are substantial falls 1 mile upstream from the Feugh's confluence with the Dee and these are popular with tourists who gather there to watch fish leaping up the torrent.
Fish Salmon and sea-trout. Annual numbers caught are unknown.
Flies & Tactics Tactic & flies The fishing extends downstream from the Feughside Inn (44/641923) for 2.5 miles to Strachan (38/670920). The river is narrow, slow-moving, with several deep holding-pools where salmon lie. However, these are infrequently taken and the Feugh is better-known as a sea-trout fishery. Best results come on a falling spate. A single-handed rod is all that is required and you should 'stalk' the fish, keeping well back from the bank. Flies: Teal Blue & Silver, Goat's Toe, Silver Stoat's Tail, Munro Killer, Shrimp Fly, Peter Ross, Grouse & Claret.
Permission & Charges £3 per rod per day from the Feughside Inn, Strachan, by Banchory, Kincardineshire. Tel: 01330 850225.

LILLY, Loch See Corby Loch entry.

LORISTON, Loch
Location & Access 38/939011. It lies 4 miles south from Aberdeen, between the A92 and the A956 roads.
Commentary This easily accessible loch is almost half-a-mile north/south in length by up to 200 yards wide.
Fish Regularly stocked with rainbow and brown trout which average 1lb.
Flies & Tactics Bank fishing only and fish are taken from all round the shoreline. Depending upon wind direction, the west shore, furthest away from the main roads, is the most comfortable place to fish. Flies: Soldier Palmer, Ke-He, Dunkeld.
Permission & Charges £12 per rod per day (4 fish limit). Contact: J Somers, Fishing Tackle, 13-15 Bon Accord Terrace, Aberdeen. Tel: 01224 210008. Restricted to visitors residing more than 25 miles from Aberdeen city centre.

MILL OF STRACHAN, Fishery
Location & Access 38/655920. To the south of the B974 Banchory/Aboyne road, 1 mile west of the village of Strachan.
Commentary An easily accessible 5-acre loch in an attractive setting close to the River Feugh (see separate entry). This fishery is unique in that the charismatic owner has developed a first-class "pitch-and-putt" course around the loch and there is also an excellent gift shop and ladies boutique.
Fish Regularly stocked with rainbow trout, some of which reach considerable proportions.
Flies & Tactics Mostly bank fishing but a boat is also available. Reservoir lures, muddlers and the like, all catch fish.
Permission & Charges £12 per day (4 fish limit); evening session £6 (2 fish limit). Thereafter, catch-and-release using barbless hooks. Extra fish may be purchased at £2 each. Boat hire, £5.

PARKHILL, Loch See Corby Loch entry.
SAND, Loch See Cotehill Loch entry.
SKENE, Loch 38/785075. The loch lies to the south of the A944 Aberdeen/Huntly road and is more noted for pike and perch than for trout.
URIE, River See River Don (Tilliefoure to Bridge of Don) entry.
YTHAN, River 38/005255. The estuary beat of the River Ythan and the River Ythan is described on OS Map 30, Fraserburgh and Peterhead.

Loch Shiel — OS Map 39-40

Rhum & Eigg

CROSS REFERENCE
All the lochs on the Island of Skye which appear on OS Map 39 are detailed in this book in OS Map 32.

EIGG, Island of
Location & Access The Island of Eigg lies off the west coast of Scotland in the Inner Minch and is accessed by ferry from Mallaig on Mainland Scotland.
Commentary There are three principal lochs on this delightful little Hebridean island and they are: Loch nam Ban Mora (39/455852) with its ancient dun on the island in the middle of the loch; tiny Lochan Nighean Dughaill (39/451850) and Loch Beinn Tighe (39/449866).
Fish All the lochs contain modest wild brown trout which average in the order of 6oz/8oz.
Flies & Tactics The lochs lie to the west of the only road on the island, between Beinn Tigha (325m) in the north and An Sgurr (393m) to the south. Reaching them involves a stiff 2 mile hike over rough, rising ground, so be well shod and take along compass and map in case of bad weather. You should also consider a visit to the dramatic remains of An Sgurr hill fort (39/462846) on the summit of An Sgurr. The fort encloses an area of approximately 9 acres. Bank fishing only. Offer them: Black Zulu, March Brown, Silver Butcher.
Permission & Charges At the time of writing no details are available. However, on the advice of the incumbent of Eigg Post Office, if you want to fish, ask for permission from the crofters whose land you must cross to reach the lochs. At present there is no charge for fishing.

RUM, Island of
Location & Access The Island of Rum lies in the Inner Minch off the west coast of Scotland and is approached via ferry from Mallaig on Mainland Scotland.
Commentary The island is managed as a National Nature Reserve by Scottish Natural Heritage and the principal, indeed the only, population centre is at Kinloch on the east coast. Visitors are accommodated either on a campsite in self-catering cottages (Tel: 01687 462026) or in Kinloch Castle (Tel: 01687 462037). Rum has outstanding wildlife, including rare sea-birds and divers. The island was chosen as the most suitable location when sea-eagles were reintroduced to Scotland during the 1980's. Visit Rum as much for its flora and fauna as for its fishing. It is most convenient to simply list the various waters on the island, rather than giving individual details about each loch or river. They are, from north to south, as follows, including the status of each water in regard to fishing access: IAIN, Loch 405007 (not available for fishing); MITCHELL, Loch 39/389011 (not available for fishing); SHAMHNAN INSIR, Loch 39/379022 (not available for fishing); SGAORISHAL, Loch 39/349022 (not available for fishing); A'GHILLE REAMHRA, Loch 39/345997 (available for fishing); BEALACH MHIC NEILL, Loch 39/376990 (not available for fishing); GAINMHICH, Loch 39/380988 (not available for fishing); PRIOMH-LOCHS, Loch 29/369987 (not available for fishing); LONG, Loch 39/364985 (available); A'MHONAIDH, Lochan 39/413982 (closed to fishing); AN DORNABAC, Loch 39/355975 (available); COIRE NAN GRUNND, Loch 39/406958 (available); FIACHANIS, Loch 39/357947 (available); PAPADIL, Loch 39/364922 (not available for fishing); DUBH AN SGOIR, Loch 39/381915 (closed to fishing); KINLOCH, River 39/403997 (available); ABHAINN RANGAIL, River 39/341954 (available); GLEN SHELLESDER Burn 39/327020 (available).
Fish All the lochs contain modest wild brown trout which average 6oz/8oz in weight. Salmon and sea-trout run the streams, in particular the Kinloch River. Approximately 20/30 sea-trout are taken in a good year but there are no accurate records of the numbers of salmon caught. Anglers should not hold their breath in anticipation of marvellous sport with the King of Fish. Season: Salmon & sea-trout: 1st March/15th October; Brown Trout: 1st April/30th September.
Flies & Tactics A series of tracks and paths crisscross the island - nature trails - and these give access to most of the waters listed above. However, it must be remembered that access is by foot only and reaching the more remote waters will involve you in some serious expeditions. For instance, Loch Coire nan Grunnd, which contains some larger fish as well as good stocks of the 'little fellows', is a stiff 5-mile hike, there and back. Loch Fiachanis, another Rum loch which contains larger fish, is even nicer: 12 miles there and back. Access to some areas is restricted, particularly in the spring, because they are important bird breeding sites. Salmon and sea-trout can be caught, primarily in the Kinloch River, depending upon water conditions. Sea-trout may also be encountered in the brackish water at the mouth of the Abhainn Rangail in Glen Harris and at the mouth of the Glen Shellesder Burn. All the fishing is from the bank and you should offer the residents: Ke-He, Invicta, Dunkeld.
Permission & Charges For details, contact: Reserve Office, Isle of Rum, Inner Hebrides. Tel: 01687 462026 (office hours). Salmon fishing on the Kinloch River is restricted to 3 rods per day. Cost: £3 per rod per day, £12 per rod per week. Trout fishing: £2 per rod per day, £8 per rod per week. Returns of fish caught must be submitted to the Reserve Office.

Loch Shiel

A'BHADA DHARAICH, Loch See Loch an Nostarie.
A'BHRAGNAID, Loch See Gaskin Loch.
A'CHAIRN MHOIR, Loch See Loch na Bairness.
A'CHOTHRUIM, Lochan See River Carnoch.
A'CHUIN DUIBH, Loch See Lochan Stole.
A'GHILLE GHOBAICH, Loch See Loch an Nostarie.
A'MHEADHOIN, Lochan See Loch an Nostarie.
A'MHUILINN (North), Lochan See Loch nam Paitean.
A'MHUILINN (South), Lochan See River Moidart.
AILORT, River See Loch Eilt.

OS Map 40 — Loch Shiel

AN NOSTARIE, Loch
Location & Access 40/690955 Approach from Glasnacardoch (40/675960) on the A830 Arisaig/Mallaig road. A good track leads east from Glasnacardoch and reaches the north shore of the loch after an easy walk of about 15 minutes.

Commentary This is the largest of a series of hill lochs which lie to the north of Loch Morar (see separate entry). Loch an Nostarie is 1/2 a mile north/south by up to 1/2 a mile east/west across the north bay. At the south end of the loch narrows join it to Lochan a'Mheadhoin (40/693948) which in turn drains south again into Loch a'Bhada Dharaich (40/696945). The flow then exits via the Allt an Loin burn to reach Loch Morar at Bun an Loin (40/698932). The south end of the system may be approached by a track which leads north to Loch a'Bhada Dharaich from Bun an Loin. From the north shore of Loch an Nostarie, continue east along the track for a further mile and a half if you wish to fish Loch Eireagoraidh (40/720955); another excellent Morar hill loch which lies between Carn a'Ghobhair (548m) to the north and Carn Mhic Ghille-chaim (350m) to the south. You might also like to explore Loch a'Ghille Ghobaich (40/689940), 3/4 of a mile north/south by up to 250 yards wide, which lies to the east of Beoraidbeg (40/677935). Follow the outlet stream up the hill from the main road to reach the loch after a 20 minute hike.

Fish Nothing to weigh down your homeward journey, but sport with bright little fish that average 8oz - and the chance of a few larger specimens as well.

Flies & Tactics Bank fishing all the way and on Loch an Nostarie you should concentrate your efforts in the north-east corner of the loch, near to the small island and convenient promontory. The south bay can also be very productive, particularly near to where the stream exits into Lochan a'Mheadhoin. Loch a'Ghille Ghobaich is easily fished from the shore and trout may be taken from all round the loch. Do not wade in Loch Eireagoraidh. Flies: Soldier Palmer, Invicta, Alexandra.

Permission & Charges At present, no permission is required. However, prior to fishing, and as a matter of courtesy, you should check the position with Ewen Macdonald (Tel: 01867 462520), Chairman of the Morar Angling Club, or with Viv de Fresnes, the Superintendent at Loch Morar (Tel: 01687 462388).

AN OBAN BHIG, Lochan See Loch Morar.
AN ROPACH, Lochan See Lochan Stole.
AN TRI-CHRIOCHAN (East), Lochan See Loch Morar.
ARD A'PHUILL, Loch See Loch nam Paitean.
BAC AN LOCHAIN, Lochan See Loch Doilet.
BELLSGROVE, Loch See Loch Doilet.

CARNOCH, Loch
Location & Access Source: 40/895601. Outfall: 40/837607. Easily accessible from the A861 Corran/Acharacle road which borders the north bank of the stream.

Commentary This little spate river rises in Loch a'Chothruim (40/895601) and flows west down Glen Tarbert to reach sea-Loch Sunart after a journey of 4 miles. Great scenery, but somewhat exposed to public view. The River Strontian, which is similar in character to the River Carnoch, flows into Loch Sunart 1.5 miles to the west of Carnoch and is approached from the minor road from Strontian (good caravan site and accommodation) to Polloch.

Fish Salmon and sea-trout, although in greatly reduced numbers compared to days past (see Loch Shiel and Loch Eilt entries); caused by sea lice infestation from the plethora of factory-salmon farms which now litter Loch Sunart.

Flies & Tactics Tactics Absolute spate streams: nae water, nae fish. However, when conditions are right, and in spite of the factory-salmon farms, sport may sometimes be had, particularly with salmon. Flies: Garry Dog, Willie Gunn, Ally's Shrimp, Goat's Toe, Silver Stoat's Tail, Green Highlander, Clan Chief, Black Doctor.

Permission & Charges Cost: £5 per day. Contact: Strontian Angling Club, c/o Harry Whitney, Biggins End, Monument Park, Strontian, Argyll. Note that the season for salmon and sea-trout is from 1st June to 30th September. Catch and release only for sea-trout.

CROSS REFERENCES See OS Map 33 for the following: INVERIE, River; BHRAOMISAIG, Loch; CARNACH, River; QUOICH, Loch; NAM BREAC, Lochan; DESSARRY River; ARKAIG, Loch; PEAN, River.

DEARG, Loch See Loch nam Paitean.

DOILET, River
Location & Access 40/805677. Approach from Strontian (40/814616) on the A861 Corran/Acharacle road. A narrow, twisting, minor road on the west bank of the Strontian River (see separate entry) runs north to reach the loch after tortuous a journey of 6 miles.

Commentary Loch Doilet is an attractive loch surrounded by commercial forestry. The loch is almost 1.5 miles long by up to 350 yards wide and it exits to Loch Shiel through the Polloch River. There are a number of smaller lochs and lochans in the vicinity which will also repay a visit although some effort is required to reach them, apart from Lochan na h-Iubhreach (40/826688) in the Glenhurich Forest to the north of Loch Doilet which is not really worth fishing because of weeds; a group of 11 named and unnamed waters on Druim Garbh including Lochan Feith nan Laogh (40/839670) and Lochan Mhic Gille Dhuibh (40/857675); Bellsgrove Loch (40/845659), to the east of the minor road and the most easily accessible loch; and the rarely visited waters to the south of Ben Resipol (845m), Lochan Bac an Lochain (40/762650) and Lochan na Cuthaige (40/742639) which are best approached from Bunalteachan on the A861.

Fish Loch Doilet contains salmon and sea trout, although not nearly as many as in times past (see Loch Shiel and Loch Eilt entry), and modest brown trout. Salmon average 7lb, sea-trout 2lb, brown trout 8oz with the chance of a few larger fish of up to and over 1lb in weight. The hill lochs all contain very pretty little wild trout which average 6oz/8oz. Salmon and sea-trout may also be caught in the River Polloch.

295

Loch Shiel OS Map 40

Flies & Tactics Fishing is managed by the Strontian Angling Club who have boats on Loch Doilet (bank fishing is not allowed) and rods on the River Polloch. The river is very much a spate stream, dependent upon good water levels to give of its best, and is comfortably fished using a single-handed rod. On Loch Doilet, concentrate your activities at the outflow, and at the east end of the loch where the River Hurich enters. The hill lochs are small, intimate waters and are easily covered from the shore. For salmon and sea-trout, try: Goat's Toe, Clan Chief, Willie Gunn, Ally's Shrimp, Garry Dog, Stoat's Tail. For brown trout, show them: Ke-He, Grouse & Claret, Silver Invicta. Loch Doilet fish also respond to dapping.

Permission & Charges A boat with two rods fishing on Loch Doilet costs £10 per day. The River Polloch costs £5 per rod per day. The River Polloch ticket also allows anglers to fish the River Strontian and the River Carnoch (see separate entries) making this outstanding value-for-money salmon fishing, providing there is plenty of water in the streams. Hill loch trout fishing is generally free of charge, but you should check all these details with the Angling Club prior to setting out. Contact: Strontian Angling Club, c/o Harry Whitney, Biggans End, Monument Park, Strontian PH36 48Z. Tel: 01967 402480. Note: Salmon and sea-trout fishing is available from 1st June to 30th September. Catch and release only for sea-trout.

DUBH, Loch (Eilt) See Loch Eilt.
EANAICHE, Lochan See Loch Morar.

EILT, Loch
Location & Access 40/810820. Immediately adjacent to the A830 Fort William/Mallaig road.
Commentary Easily accessible and one of the most photographed lochs in Scotland. Very lovely and surrounded by magnificent mountains. The loch is 2 miles in length by up to 600 yards wide and exits via the River Ailort to reach the sea after approximately 2.5 miles in sea-Loch Ailort. Along the way, the flow passes through deep Lochan Dubh (40/789830) upstream of which is the famous "Fryingpan Pool". Sadly, Loch Eilt and the River Ailort, today, are barely worth fishing. The system was most famous as a sea-trout fishery and in the recent past upwards of 1,000 sea-trout were taken each season. Because of the collapse of West Highland sea-trout stocks, caused by sea lice infestation from factory-salmon farms, this system now struggles to produce 7 fish per season. The same is true in regard to salmon and very few fish are taken, even from Loch Dubh which used to be one of the most productive parts of the river.
Fish This once-famous sea-trout fishery has been ruined in recent years because of fish farm sea lice attack on wild salmonids. It is only worth fish for brown trout now.
Flies & Tactics The most obvious tactic would be to close down the factory-salmon farms in Loch Ailort. Otherwise, it seems that Loch Eilt sea-trout, as a distinct genetic species, will simply become extinct., if that has not already happened. To this end, anglers may feel compelled to express their concern to the First Minister, Scottish Parliament, St Andrews House, Edinburgh; although, on past showing, this is hardly likely to have any effect on the power the factory-salmon farming lobby seem to exert over Scottish politicians.
Permission & Charges If you decide to take a chance on finding sport on Loch Eilt or in the River Ailort, contact Colin Clarke, Tel: 01687 470327. Cost: Loch Eilt: £40 per boat (two rods fishing) per day, including outboard motor and fuel. River Ailort: £15 per beat per day, two rods fishing. Check prices, prior to booking, as these may change. There is no bank fishing on Loch Eilt.

EIREAGORAIDH, Loch See Loch an Nostarie.
FEITH NAN LAOGH, Lochan See Loch Doilet.
FORSIAN, Loch See River Moidart.

GASKIN, Loch
Location & Access 40/761919. No easy way in. Tramp east from Bracorina (40/725928) along the north shore of Loch Morar (see separate entry) on a good track to Brinacroy (40/754914) and then, at 40/750915, climb steeply north to the unnamed lochan at 40/755922. From here, strike due east and you will see Gaskin Loch below you after a hard 1/2 mile. Having come thus far, you should continue north-east again from Gaskin Loch to have a cast in Lochan nan Tri-chriochan (40/767923) and its surrounding satellite lochans, and then head south-east for 5 minutes to find Loch a'Bhragnaid (40/773921). Return to the Loch Morar track via Gaskin Loch. The round trip will take a full day and involve you in a hike of approximately 7 miles. Alternatively, and less taxing, approach Brinacroy by boat from Loch Morar (see Loch Morar entry for details).
Commentary This is a tough expedition and you should be well-prepared, with full hiking gear and compass and map in case the weather turns nasty. The scenery and wildlife along the way will more than compensate you for your effort.
Fish Wild brown trout which average 8oz in weight.
Flies & Tactics All the lochs are fished from the shore and are easily understood. Don't ignore the small lochans, they can, sometimes, produce outstanding fish. First cast: Black Pennell, Grouse & Claret, Silver Butcher.
Permission & Charges See Loch an Nostarie entry.

GORMA, Lochan See Loch na Bairness.
INNIS EANRUIG, Lochan See Lochan Stole.
MEALL A'MHADAIDH, Lochan See Loch nam paitean.
MHIC GILLE DHUIBH, Lochan See Loch Doilet.
MHIC LEANNAIN, Loch See Lochan Stole.
MOIDART, Loch See River Moidart.

MOIDART, River
Location & Access Source: 40/803768 Outfall: 40/708725. The river is easily accessible from both public and private Estate roads which margin the north shore of the stream.
Commentary The river rises on the west shoulder of Croit Bheinn (663m) and flows west down Glen Moidart for a distance of some 7 miles before reaching

296

OS Map 40 — Loch Shiel

the sea at Ardmorlich. Look out for the "Seven Men of Moidart", the trees in a field to the north of Kinlochmoidart which commemorate the seven men who accompanied Prince Charles Edward Stewart on his arrival in Scotland in 1745. On the river, look out for nothing other than splendid scenery and wildlife and the chance of a fish. In the hills to the south east of the river, on the Glenmoidart Estate, there are a number of remote hill lochs which require a considerable effort to reach. These are: Loch na Bioraich (40/790742), Lochan na Creige (north) (40/759722), tiny Loch Moidart (40/771725), Lochan na Creige (South) (40/752718), Lochan a'Mhuilinn (South) (40/751708) and Loch Forsian (40/762737) which is unnamed on the OS Map and is used as a water supply. Lochan nan Lochan (40/745727) is an extension of the River Moidart.

Fish Salmon and sea-trout, but very few of the later in recent years (see Loch Shiel and Loch Eilt entries). In a good year upwards of 50 salmon are taken. During the last 2 years the figure has been nearer 20 fish. However, this may not be a true reflection of the state of the river since much depends upon the fishing skill of those who wield the rods. The hill lochs all contain modest, pretty little wild brown trout, Loch Forsian is stocked and holds trout which average 12oz/14oz in weight.

Flies & Tactics The River Moidart is a narrow, spate stream which requires good water levels to give of its best. The lies are easily covered with a singled-handed rod, but are tree-lined in places. You should be able to either roll-cast or Spey-cast to avoid unnecessary scrambling about in branches. There are excellent holding pools and fast, streamy runs. Salmon begin to enter the river from May onwards and fresh fish may be taken right up to the end of the season. Offer them: Willie Gunn, Garry Dog, Green Highlander, General Practitioner, Goat's Toe, Stoat's Tail, Ally's Shrimp.

Permission & Charges For the lower river, contact: Mrs N D Stewart, Kinlochmoidart House, Kinlochmoidart, Lochailort, Inverness-shire. Tel: 01967 431609. Cost: £20 per rod per day; limited to 2 rods although more rods may be allowed to fish in high water conditions, at the discretion of the owner. Fishing on the Glenmoidart Estate waters is let with the Glenmoidart Estate cottage; a comfortable self-catering property, ideal for an away-from-it-all family holiday amidst glorious surroundings. For details, contact: Mrs Lees-Millais, Glenmoidart House, Glenmoidart, Lochailort, Inverness-shire. Tel: 01967 431254.

MORAR, Loch

Location & Access 40/770905. Approach from Morar (40/677930) via the minor road that margins the north west shore of the loch.

Commentary One of the most magnificent lochs in Scotland, surrounded by splendid scenery, 12 miles in length, east/west, by up to 1.5 miles wide. Loch Morar is also the deepest freshwater loch in Europe and plunges to a depth of over 1,000ft. The loch is drained by Scotland's shortest salmon stream, the River Morar (see separate entry) and is notorious as being the home of "Morag", a relation of the famous Loch Ness Monster.

Fish Salmon, sea-trout, brown trout, ferox trout, char. Few sea-trout are taken, because of the decline in West Highland sea-trout stocks caused by factory-salmon farm sea lice; but reasonable numbers of salmon are taken, depending upon prevailing conditions. As many as 100 fish have been landed during a season, but a more realistic average would be in the order of 20/30 fish. Salmon average 6lb but double-figure fish are not uncommon. Brown trout average 12oz/1lb, but good numbers of larger trout are taken each season, including fish of up to and over 5lb in weight. Surprisingly, few anglers troll for the huge ferox which undoubtedly inhabit the dark depths.

Flies & Tactics Pier with boat launching facilities near Bun an Lion Bay at 40/696932, and boat fishing is the most convenient way of exploring this vast loch. Most anglers ply the island-cladded shallow waters at the west end, but excellent sport may be had at the east end also, although it is a long way to go to fish. Should you decide to motor east, make sure you have reserves of fuel and that the weather is settled: Loch Morar can be as wild and windy as the open sea. The east bay, between Kinlochmorar (40/865910), where the Abhainn Ceann Loch-Morar burn enters, and in the vicinity of the small island off the north shore (40/860908), and south to Oban (40/864900) where another feeder stream enters, is always productive. From Oban, you may explore little Lochan an Oban Bhig (40/872899), or, if you wish a longer expedition, then follow the track north-east from Kinlochmorar to have a cast in Lochan Eanaiche (40/890920), a splendid tramp of 1.5 miles up Gleann an Lochain Eanaiche. There are further hill lochs to the north-east of South Tarbet Bay (40/800913), but they are hard to reach and, consequently, very rarely visited. The principal water is Lochan an Tri-chriochan (east) and it is surrounded by 5 other unnamed lochans. When fishing on Loch Morar itself, organise your drift close to the shoreline and carefully explore the many bays and corners: Camus Luinge Bay (40/788895 to 40/775895), Sworland Bay (40/789912), around Brinacroy Island (40/757909), Eilean Allmha (40/757897), Lettermorar Bay (40/730900) and between Rubha nam Fasaichean (40/725906) and Rubh Aird Cumnaich (40/710909). Bank fishing is allowed on Loch Morar and this can also produce excellent results. However, do not wade: it is extremely dangerous to do so. Flies: Black Pennell, Greenwell's Glory, Alexandra. For Morag, use barbless hooks.

Permission & Charges Boats with outboard engine and fuel, £35 per day, two rods fishing, from 0830hrs/1730hrs. Evening sessions cost £20 per boat. Bank fishing costs £4.50 per rod per day. Contact: Ewen Macdonald, 4 St Cumins House, Morar, by Mallaig. Tel: 01687 462520. The Morar Hotel, Morar, by Mallaig, have boats on Loch Morar which are available to hotel guests. Tel: 01687 462346. Morar Motors also issue fishing permits for Loch Morar. Tel: 01687 462118. For permission to fish the surrounding hill lochs, see Loch an Nostarie entry.

MORAR, River Fishing on the Morar River is private.

NA BA GLEISE, Loch See Lochan Stole.

Loch Shiel — OS Map 40

NA BAIRNESS, Loch
Location & Access 40/656759. Park by Seannlac (670761) 40/669760 on the A861 Lochailort/Acharacle road. Climb west for 1/2 mile on the line of the stream to reach the loch.
Commentary This is a lovely little loch, generally circular in shape and about 50 acres in extent. The south end is scattered with islands and Loch na Bairness is protected by the heights of Egnaig Hill (275m) from the effects of east winds. There is an unnamed, smaller, lochan to the west (40/651760), below Smirisary Hill (165m) which is also worth a visit. Further adventure lies in wait to the east of the road through Glenuig, around Glenuig Hill (300m), although reaching the lochs concerned involves a hard, compass and map hike. They are, from north to south, Loch a Chairn Mhoir (40/682774), Loch Bealach na Gaoithe (40/684765), Lochan na Cloiche Sgoilte (40/693757), Lochan Gorma (40/688755 and its surrounding, unnamed satellite lochans, and Loch na Draipe (40/674750) which lies on the crags just above the car park on the Bealach Carach (40/670752).
Fish Modest wild brown trout all round which average 8oz in weight. However, Loch na Draipe and Loch na Cloiche Sgoilte are reputed to contain a few larger specimens.
Flies & Tactics Tactics and flies All the lochs are easily fished from the shore. The going is tough and you should be well-equipped for whatever the weather decides to chuck at you. Chuck at the trout: Blue Zulu, March Brown, Alexandra.
Permission & Charges At present, the Estate do not require anglers to have prior permission to fish. Respect this courtesy, follow the countryside code, keep only the fish that you wish to eat.

NA BEALACH NA GAOITHE, Loch See Loch na Bairness.
NA BIORAICH, Loch See River Moidart.
NA CLOICHE SGOILTE, Lochan See Loch na Bairness.
NA CREIGE (North), Lochan See River Moidart.
NA CREIGE (South), Lochan See river Moidart.
NA CUTHAIGE, Lochan See Loch Doilet.
NA DRAIPE, Loch See Loch na Bairness.

NAM PAITEAN, Loch
Location & Access 40/724739. Approach from Brunery (40/727720). A track leads north past the feature know as "The Three Old Maids", between Coire Mor and Leachd Fheadanach, climbing steeply to a height of 300m. A stiff hike of approximately 1 hour 45 minutes will bring you to the south shore.
Commentary Loch nam Paitean is perhaps the best trout loch in Moidart, certainly one of the most scenic. The views from the hill are stunning and the effort involved in reaching the loch is worth every grunt and pant along the way. Further grunting and panting is required to explore the other waters in the vicinity, but, as with Loch nam Paitean, you will be rewarded by some of the most wonderful vistas and wildlife in the north. These waters are, from west to east: Loch Ard a'Phuill (40/690745), Lochan a'Mhuilinn (North) (40/700741), Lochan na Caillich (40/705747), Upper Lochan Sligeanach (40/716743), the unnamed lochan at 40/712748, Lochan Meall a'Mhadaidh (40/718750) and Loch Dearg (40/737742).
Fish Brown trout which vary in size from 8oz right up to specimen fish of up to and over 5lb in weight.
Flies & Tactics There is really a whole season's fishing here, there is so much water to explore. The going is rough, all the way, and you must always be well-prepared and used to taxing hill-walking expeditions. Loch nam Paitean in itself will take several visits before you begin to understand its undulating bays, promontories and fishy corners. The trout average just under 1lb and a good place to begin is at the island-clad bay to the north of the old boathouse at 40/722740. Follow the inlet stream at the north-west corner of the loch up the east side of Meall a Mhadaidh Beag to find Loch Meall a'Mhadaidh. This is where to look for something for the glass case. The trout average over 1lb in weight, but, be warned, they do not give themselves up easily. Tempt them with: Loch Ordie, Woodcock & Hare-lug, Black Pennell.
Permission & Charges Mrs N D Stewart, Kinlochmoidart House, Kinlochmoidart, Lochailort, Inverness-shire. Tel: 01967 431609. Cost: £5 per rod per day.

NAN LOCHAN, Lochan See Glen Shiel.
NAN TRI-CHRIOCHAN (West), Lochan See Gaskin Loch.
NAN UAN, Lochan See Lochan Stole.
POLLOCH, River See Loch Doilet.
PRIVATE WATERS All the waters between the south shore of Loch Morar and the A830 Fort William/Mallaig road are private. This also applies to the lochans on the Rhue Peninsula (40/650840) and to the lochs on the Ardnish Peninsula (40/720820).
All the waters on OS Map 40 which lie to the west of the A861 Acharace/Salen road are private. However, it may sometimes be possible to obtain access. For further information, contact: Mike Macgregor at the splendid visitor centre in Glenborrodale. Tel: 01972 500209. Lochan Dhonnachaidh (40/704606) in Morvvern is also private.

SHIEL (Loch & River) (Glenfinnan)
Location & Access 40/820730. The loch is accessible at the north end from Glenfinnan and at the south end from Acharacle. Otherwise, by foot. The river is bordered by public roads on both banks.
Commentary Loch Shiel lies to the west of Fort William on the 'Road to the Isles'. It is one of the longest lochs in Scotland, being 17 miles in length by up to half a mile wide. The loch is deepest by Meall na Creag Leac (775m) where it drops to over 400ft, although towards the south end, in the middle, there are areas barely 6ft in depth. The river is essentially slow moving, comfortable to fish, with many excellent pools and dramatic runs.
Fish Loch Shiel and the river Shiel used to be world-famous fisheries, particularly for sea-trout. But recent years have seen a catastrophic decline in salmonid numbers and today few bother to fish for these speices

Ben Nevis

in the loch. Catch numbers on the river are insignificant. Pollution and disease from fish farms on the migratory route of Shiel fish has been blamed for this disaster. The loch still holds reasonable stocks of brown trout, fish which average 8oz in weight.
Flies & Tactics The loch is really only worth fishing for brown trout, but there is always the remote possibility of encountering salmon and sea-trout as well. A sound boat and outboard motor is essential and you should concentrate your efforts close to the margins. Dapping used to be a favourite fishing method and will still work for brown trout, but for salmon and sea-trout the glory days have gone. Try: Black Pennell, Grouse & Claret, Dunkeld.
Permission & Charges D MacAukay, Dalilea Farm, Acharacle. Tel: 01967 431253; Glenfinnan House Hotel, Glenfinnan. Tel: 01397 722235. Prince's House, Glenfinnan. Tel: 01397 722246 (subject to availability). Expect to pay in the order of £35 per day for boat and outboard engine.

STOLE, Lochan
Location & Access 40/746935. Park at the end of the road along the north shore of Loch Morar (see separate entry) at Bracorina (40/725928). A track climbs steeply north-east from Bracorina and reaches the lochan after a distance of 1.5 miles.
Commentary There are 5 lochs here and they may be explored during the course of a vigorous day out in the hills. The first water you reach after climbing the hill from Bracorina is Lochan Innis Eanruig (40/737931). Lochan Stole is next and may be crossed by stepping stones at the south end, which separate it from its neighbour, Lochan an Ropach (40/747931). Immediately to the south of Lochan an Ropach is Loch a'Chuin Duibh (40/744927), whilst in the hills above Lochan Stole lies little Lochan nan Uan (40/753933). There are four further waters in the vicinity, between Carn Mhic Ghille-chaim (350m) to the north and Cruach Corrach (260m) to the south. They are difficult of access and rarely fished, but all offer the chance of sport with small wild trout: two unnamed lochans at 40/713935 and 40/711940, and Loch na Ba Gleise (40/715940) and Loch Mhic Leannain (40/713949).
Fish Wild brown trout which average 8oz, but good chance of some larger fish as well, particularly in Lochan Stole.
Flies & Tactics Bank fishing only and it is best not to wade. The fish lie close to the margins in most of these waters and wading only scares them out to the depths, and out of range. Fish are taken from all round the shorelines, so cast with confidence. Try: Black Zulu, Soldier Palmer, Silver Invicta.
Permission & Charges See Loch an Nostarie entry.

STRONTIAN, River See River Carnoch.
UPPER SLIGEANACH, Lochan See Loch nam Paitean.

Ben Nevis

A'CHUIM DHEIRG, Lochan See River Leven (Kinlochleven).
ACHTRIOTCHAN, Loch See River Coe.
BLACKWATER Reservoir See River Leven (Kinlochleven).
CHIARIAN, Loch See River Leven (Kinlochleven).
CIARAN Water See River Leven (Kinlochleven).

COE, River
Location & Access Source: 41/181539: Outfall: 41/099591. Access to the river is from the A82/Callander/Fort William road which margins the banks of the stream.
Commentary A dramatic little spate stream which tumbles busily through the bleak Pass of Glencoe, pausing briefly in Loch Achtriotchan (41/142567) before reaching the sea in Loch Leven at the village of Glencoe. Glencoe is always busy with climbers, hillwalkers and tourists, but the surrounding scenery is wonderful and justifies your attention at least as much as the fishing.
Fish Salmon and sea-trout, small brown trout in the loch. Salmon and sea-trout runs have collapsed in recent years. Few fish are even seen, let alone caught.
Flies & Tactics No water, no fish, otherwise, particularly after a spate, a chance of sport. Use a single-handed rod to cover the lies and offer them: Garry Dog, Hairy Mary, General Practitioner, Ally's Shrimp, Stoat's Tail.
Permission & Charges Because of the decline in the numbers of salmon and sea-trout in recent years the National Trust for Scotland, who own the upper river and Loch Achtriotchan, have closed their part of the river, and the loch, to fishing. For further information contact: The National Trust for Scotland Visitor Centre, Glencoe. Tel: 01855 811307. For information about the lower river, contact H S J MacColl, Ballachulish, Glencoe. Tel: 01855 811256.

COIRE AN LOCHAIN, Loch See River Leven (Kinlochleven).
COIRE NA MEINNE, Lochan See Loch Laidon.
CROSS REFERENCES For the following waters see OS Map 50: ETIVE, River; CRERAN, River; BA, Loch.
For the following waters see OS Map 34: Ben Nevis; Loch LOCHY; River SPEAN; River ROY; Loch SGUADAIG; Loch LAGGAN
For the following waters see OS Map 33: Loch ARKAIG; River ARKAIG; River MALLIE.
DOIRE AN DOLLAIN, Lochan See Loch Laidon.
DUBH, Lochan (Kingshouse) See Lochan Gaineamhach.
DUBH, Lochan (Laidon) See Loch Laidon.
EILDE BEAG, Loch See River Leven (Kinlochleven).
EILDE MOR, Loch See River Leven (Kinlochleven).

GAINEAMHACH, Lochan
Location & Access 41/303536 Approach from the A82 Callander/Glen Coe road. Park at 41/290523 and hike north east across the moor for 1 mile to reach the loch.
Commentary This is the largest (50 acres) of a series of

Ben Nevis — OS Map 41

attractive little lochs and lochans which lie between the Kingshouse Hotel in the north and Loch Ba (see OS Map 50) in the south. There is an unnamed lochan immediately to the north of Lochan Gaineamhach at 41/309539 which is also worth a few casts. The other waters here are Dubh Lochan (41/274538), with its 3 near, unnamed, neighbours close to the main road at 41/271534 and Lochan Mathair Eite (41/290542) between the Dubh Lochan and Black Corrie Lodge (41/299560). The track which wends north east from Black Corrie Lodge gives access to the most remote of the lochs, little Lochan Meall a'Phuill (41/311568).

Fish All the lochs contain excellent stocks of little wild brown trout which average 6oz/8oz.

Flies & Tactics It is possible to visit all the lochs noted above during single day. The round trip is approximately 5 miles and fishing is from the bank. Lochan Gaineamhach offers the best chance of a larger fish but regardless of size, this is a wonderful day out in the wilderness that is Rannoch Moor.

Flies: Black Zulu, March Brown, Dunkeld.

Permission & Charges At the time of writing local inquires suggest that permission is not required. However, check with the Kingshouse Hotel before setting out.

GARBH, Lochan See River Leven (Kinlochleven).

HOSPITAL, Lochan

Location & Access 41/104595 The loch is easily accessible and lies immediately to the north of Glencoe Village.

Commentary A very scenic, much-photographed little loch, dominated by the Pap Of Glencoe (742m) to the east and surrounded by woodlands and rhododendrons.

Fish Regularly stocked with rainbow trout which average 1lb in weight.

Flies & Tactics Bank fishing only and much of the vegetation surrounding the loch has been cut back to facilitate casting. Offer reservoir-type lures or traditional patterns such as Greenwell's Glory, March Brown, Butchers. All legal fishing methods are allowed.

Permission & Charges Mrs S Mortimer, Scorrybreac Guest House, Glencoe Village. Tel: 01855 811354. Cost £5 per rod per day. Use of boat, £10 per day. Facilities for disabled anglers.

LAIDON, Loch

Location & Access 41/390555. Easiest access is from Rannoch Station (42/422578) which lies at the end of the B846 road which runs west along the north shore of Loch Rannoch (see OS Map 42) from Kinloch Rannoch (42/661587). However, the majority of the loch is shown on OS Map 41 and access is possible from the A82 Callander/Glen Coe road via Loch Ba (see OS Map 50). Using this later approach involves you in hard 4 mile hike to reach the west end of Loch Laidon and has little to recommend it - unless you are packing a canoe, which is not uncommon.

Commentary Loch Laidon lies at the heart of Scotland on the bleak wilderness of Rannoch Moor (300m). The loch is 6 miles east/west by up to 1/2 a mile wide, but extending to almost two miles wide if you include the finger-like north west arm, half of which lies in Perthshire, the other half being in Argyll. The small lochs to the south of Loch Laidon, Dubh Lochan (41/397532), Lochan Coire na Meinne (41/398527) and Lochan Doire an Dollain (41/399401) at the west end of Laidon, and Lochan Caol Fada (42/411560), Lochan Ruighe nan-Sligean (42/405547), Loch Lochan a'Mhaidseir (42/413548), Lochan Ghiubhais (42/419545) and Lochan nam Breac (42/423539) at the east end, all contain small brown trout but as they lie in an area of Special Scientific Interest they are not fished. Lochan Dubh (42/415578), at the east end of Loch Laidon, is private. The River Gaur, which drains Loch Laidon into Loch Eigheach, offers good sport with brown trout and is a useful refuge when the wind howls across Rannoch Moor and launching a boat is impossible.

Fish Loch Laidon holds a vast stock of small, wild brown trout which average 6oz/8oz in weight. However, the loch also contains some very large, specimen, fish which can run to over 10lb in weight (see cast of 11lb trout in Moor of Rannoch Hotel). The heaviest fish taken in 1999 weighed 9lb 8oz.

Flies & Tactics Bank fishing is allowed and the north bank is best. A track margins the shoreline and gives easy access to a succession of delightful bays and corners where great sport may be had. However, a boat allows you to explore more of the loch, particularly the remote corners and bays at the west end. The wide bay on the north shore, protected by Iilean Iubhair (41/374538) is particularly productive, as is the small bay opposite, on the south shore at 41/383539. When motoring about this end of the loch take great care: there are numerous barely submerged rocks waiting to catching the unwary. Hasten slowly about your business. At the time of writing, no boats are available, but check with Moor of Rannoch Hotel as this position may have changed. Trout are not choosy on Laidon which makes it a great loch for beginners. Offer: Black Pennell, Grouse & Claret, Silver Invicta.

Permission & Charges Bank fishing, £4 per rod per day. Contact: John Harrisson, Moor of Rannoch Hotel, Rannoch Station, Perthshire. Tel: 01882 633238.

LEVEN, River (Kinlochleven)

Location & Access Source: 42/410602, Outfall 41/180622. Approach from the town of Kinlochleven via a track which margins the south side of the stream.

Commentary The true source of the stream is to the east of the Blackwater Reservoir (41/300600) in Lochan a'Chlaideimh (42/410602) on Rannoch Moor. In its infancy the river is known as the Black Water before it is swallowed up by the vast reservoir of the same name, constructed to supply the British Aluminium Company with water for their works at Kinlochleven. The Blackwater Reservoir is some 8 miles east/west by up to 1 mile wide; a dour loch, much given to water fluctuations which sometimes expose a tide-lined shore of as much as 50ft/80ft in height. No doubt it contains some huge fish but I cannot think of any other place less attractive to fish (with the possible exception of the British Aluminium Company's other water supply, Loch Treig -see separate entry). However,

OS Map 41 — Ben Nevis

there are a number of attractive hill lochs in the vicinity of Kinlochleven which are well worth a visit and the most accessible of these are Loch Eilde Mor (41/230639) and Loch Eilde Beag (41/255653). If you feel like having an adventure, follow the track from the north shore of Loch Eilde Mor (41/222638) up to Coire an Lochain (41/225654). This is a wonderful little lochan lying at a height of 725m, clutched between Sgurr Eilde Mor (1008m) and Binnein Mor (1128m). Loch Chiarian (41/291636), to the north of Blackwater Reservoir and drained into it by Ciaran Water, may be reached after a 4.5 hike along a stalkers' track which begins at the south-west end of Loch Eilde Mor (41/218632). In the hills between Loch Chiarain and Loch Eilde Beag are 3 further little lochans which rarely see an artificial fly from one season to the next: Lochan Tom Ailein (41/271641), cupped in the glen below Glas Bheinn (789m) to the west and Beinn na Cloiche (644m) to the east; Loch na Staoineig (41/293660), on the north east shoulder of Beinn na Cloiche and Lochan a'Chuim Dheirg (41/271663) on Ceann Caol na Glasbheinne (653m). Garbh Lochan (41/323592) and Lochan na Craoibhe (41/335593) which drain into the south shore of the Blackwater Reservoir, are just as difficult of access and are best approached from Black Corries Lodge (41/300560) after a 16 mile there-and-back tramp. Nevertheless, you will at least be guaranteed absolute peace and seclusion, and something for supper.

Fish Salmon and the chance of a sea-trout in the River Leven and brown trout in the hill lochs. In a good year, perhaps 20 salmon may be taken, depending upon water conditiions. The system is but a poor shadow of its former glory, prior to the arrival of the aluminium smelters. The siutation might improve, now that the smelter is closed, if Leven salmonids can survive fish farm pollution and disease.

Flies & Tactics This is a spate river and Dan Mackay's Falls, 1 mile upstream from the mouth is as far as salmon and sea-trout can go. Use a single-handed rod and stealth to try and catch them. The Canteen Pool is one of the best places to start. Boat fishing brings the best results on Loch Eilde Mor and makes it less difficult to explore this 2 mile long water. The Kinlochleven Angling Association has stocked the loch and the best sport is to be had at the shallow east and west ends, and by arranging a drift along the margins, about 10 yards out from the bank. To properly address the hill lochs noted above you will require stout walking boots, full hill-walking gear and a compass and map. Bank fishing only and avoid wading. It is dangerous to do so and help is a long way off. On the river, offer them: Black Doctor, Stoat's Tail, Hairy Mary, Garry Dog, Willie Gunn, Green Highlander. For trout, try: Ke-He, Woodcock & Hare-lug, Silver Butcher.

Permission & Charges Excellent value for money fishing. Prices for river lochs: £3.00 per day, junior, £6.00 per day adult, £10.00 per day family (2 adults and two children under 16 years of age). Catch returns must be filed at the end of fishing. All sea-trout under 12" to be returned. For further information and details contact: Jim McKinley, 1 Lochaber Road, Kinlochleven. Tel: 01855 831626.

LOCHY, River

Location & Access Source: 41/176842, Outfall: 41/110750. The river is easily accessible from Fort William (41/105742) and from the minor road which margins the east bank of the stream from Dalvenvie Farm (41/125774) in the south to Bridge of Mucomir (41/179838) in the north.

Commentary The River Lochy is one of the most attractive salmon streams in Scotland, dominated by the bulk of Ben Nevis (1344m), Britain's highest mountain. The river runs southwards from Loch Lochy (see OS Map 34) for a distance of 9 miles before entering the sea in Loch Linnhe near Fort William. There are more than 40 named pools, and casting is easy from the stony shores and gravel banks which border the clear waters of the stream.

Fish Salmon and sea-trout, although very few of the latter are now caught due to the deleterious effect of factory-salmon farming (see Loch Shiel and Loch Eilt entries on OS Map 40). Salmon numbers have also fallen, dramatically, in recent years. The five-year average for the main river for the months of July, August and September is 166 fish, although 1999 produced 231.

Flies & Tactics The river is divided into 4 principal beats, with the Mucomir Pool at the head of the stream being a separate let. The lower section of the stream is let to the Fort William Angling Association. The river offers classic fly-fishing, with deep pools, busy runs and calm glides. The main beats each have their own experienced gillie and they are always ready to share their expert knowledge with visiting rods. Amongst the most notable pools are: Sandy Haven and Golden Burn on Beat 1, Boat Pool, Loy Mouth and the Lodge Pool on Beat 2, Fank Pool and Rock Pool on Beat 3 and Big Rock Pool and Lundy Mouth on Beat 4. A 15ft rod is essential and deep wading is often required to cover some of the lies. Try: Ally's Shrimp, Willie Gunn, Goat's Toe, Silver Stoat's Tail, General Practitioner, Green Highlander, Garry Dog.

Permission & Charges Contact the Rod & Gun Shop in Fort William (Tel: 01397 702656) for information about the Association Beat. For details of charges and access to the main river, contact: Emma Jackson, Tel: 01722 782386. Also, Strutt & Parker, 13 Hill Street, Berkeley Square, London W1X 8DL. Tel: 0171 629782; Fax: 0171 4991657; Finlyson Hughes, 29 Barossa Place, Perth PH1 5EP. Tel: 01738 6630926 Fax: 01738 639017. Expect to pay in the order of £600 per 3/4 rod beat per week.

MATHAIR EITE, Lochan See Lochan Gaineamhach.
MEALL A'PHUILL, Lochan See Loch Gaineamhach.
NA CRAOIBHE, Lochan See River Leven (Kinlochleven).
NA STAOINEIG, Loch See River Leven (Kinlochleven).

NEVIS, River

Location & Access Source: 41/239692, Outfall: 41/108745. A minor public road, from Fort William in the north to the car park at Uamh Shomhairle (41/168691) in the south, margins the bank of the stream.

Loch Rannoch   OS Maps 41-42

Commentary The river runs through busy Glen Nevis where there is a caravan and camping site, a picnic area and a Youth Hostel. The glen is very lovely and popular with visitors, particularly with climbers and hill-walkers who use the glen to gain access to the surrounding mountains in the Mamore Forest. If you feel in need of a bit of peace and quiet, and a vigorous hike, consider a visit to Lochan Meall an t-Suidhe (41/144727). This corrie lochan is approached from the car park near Achintee House in Glen Nevis (41/125730) and lies at an altitude of 575m between Meall an t-Suidhe (711m) to the west and the broken crags of Carn Dearg (1212m) to the east. Although there is a good track all the way, reaching Lochan Meall an t-Suidhe is a serious expedition and the journey should not be undertaken lightly. Be thoroughly prepared. Tell someone where you are going and when you expect to return.

Fish Salmon and sea-trout although few of the latter in recent times (see River Lochy entry). In a good year upwards of 20 salmon may be taken, depending upon prevailing water conditions. There are also brown trout of modest size.

Flies & Tactics Migratory fish ascend the river as far as the Lower Falls (40/145864), approximately 4 miles from the sea, and the main run starts in June. This is very much a spate stream and good sport is entirely dependent upon high water levels. However, given the fact that the area has one of the highest rainfall levels in UK, conditions are frequently perfect. Use a single-handed rod and be prepared to stumble about a bit to reach the lies. There are 16 named pools, including Carlie's Pool, Roaring Mill, Long Pool, the Fank Pool and Lower Falls Pool. Trout fishing is not allowed below the Lower Falls but you may fish above the falls without a permit. Offer salmon and sea-trout: Stoat's Tail, Hairy Mary, Ally's Shrimp. Waddingtons, Garry Dog, General Practitioner, Willie Gunn. For trout, try: Soldier Palmer, Grouse & Claret, Dunkeld. Some trout also respond well to a carefully presented dry fly.

Permission & Charges The Rod & Gun Shop, 18 High Street, Fort William. Tel/Fax: 01397 702656. Cost, £5 per rod per day. Permits are limited in number and are issued on a first-come-first-served basis after 9am on the day they are required. Also note that the Rod & Gun Shop is the centre of angling excellence in the area and the staff will be able to advise you about all the fishing available in Lochaber.

PRIVATE WATERS OSSIAN, Loch (41/390680); NA SGEALLAIG, Loch (41/368658); NA LAP, Loch (41/397715); COIRE NA Lochain (41/365744).

TOM AILEIN, Lochan See River Leven (Kinlochleven).

TORLUNDY, Lochans
Location & Access 41/142782 Three miles north from Fort William on the Fort William/Inverness road, right from to Tomacharich. The fishery is 1 mile further on, on the right of the road.
Commentary Easily accessible sport on 2 small ponds.
Fish A stocked rainbow trout fishery where the fish average 12/0z14oz in weight.
Flies & Tactics Bank fishing only. Rod hire and casting instruction is available.
Permission & Charges Contact: Great Glen Holidays, Tomacharich, Fort William. Tel: 01397 703015. Cost: £15 per rod per day (9am/9.30pm) with a 3 fish limit. Additional fish charged at £2 each. Rod hire: £5 for a full day. Half day and evening sessions at a reduced price.

TREIG, Loch
Location & Access 41/335730. Approach from the A86 Spean Bridge/Kingussie road at Inverlair Falls (41/341805). A minor road leads to within 1/2 mile of the north end of the loch.
Commentary One of the most dismal and depressing-looking lochs in Scotland, the waters having been impounded to supply the British Aluminium Company works in Fort William. The last place in Scotland to fish.
Fish Undoubtedly huge ferox, small brown trout and voracious pike.
Flies & Tactics During 1995/1996 the water level in this 6 mile long water dropped by almost 80ft; leaving a vast, grey, mud and sand shingle tide mark, an absolute death-trap for bank anglers. There are no boats on the loch, neither are the facilities for launching your own, even if you wish to do so. Unless you are an angling masochist, give Loch Treig a miss.
Permission & Charges For information, contact: Rod & Gun Shop, 18 High Street, Fort William, Inverness-shire. Tel: 01397 702656.

Loch Rannoch

A'BHEALAICH LEAMHAIN, Loch See Loch Ericht.
CAOLDAIR, Loch See Loch Ericht.
CROSS REFERENCES See OS Map 52 for: TUMMEL, River; TUMMEL, Loch.
See OS Map 34 for: LAGGAN, Loch; NA EARBA, Lochan; A'CHOIRE, Lochan; ROY, Loch; NA CAILLICHE, Loch; DOIRE NAN SGIATH, Loch; COIRE CHUIR, Loch; AN TUIRC, Lochan;
See OS Map 35 for: TRUIM, River .
See OS Map 41 for: Loch LAIDON; RUIGHE NAN-SLIGEAN, Lochan; A'MHAIDSEIE, Lochan; GHIUB-HAIS, Lochan; NAM BREAC, Lochan.
See OS Map 43 for: GARRY, River (Perthshire);
See OS Map 52 for: TUMMELL, Loch.

CUAICH, Loch
Location & Access 42/695880. Approach from the A9 Perth/Inverness road via the hill track which begins near Cuaich (42/657870).
Commentary The loch lies 2.5 miles to the east of the A9 between Meall Chuaich (951m) and Creag Ruadh (658m). The setting is dramatic and Loch Cuaich is 1 mile long by up to 400 yards wide, dropping to a depth of over 70ft at the south end.
Fish Brown trout which average 10oz/12oz.
Flies & Tactics Bank fishing only and avoid wading. The margins shelve very quickly into deep water and it is dangerous to wade. The trout lie close to the shore so long casting is not required. The most productive areas

OS Map 42 — Loch Rannoch

of the loch are the shallower north and south ends, particularly where the Feith na Braclaich enters (42/701885).
Permission & Charges Contact: Michael Glass, Gamekeeper's House, Phones, Newtonmore, Invernesshire. Tel: 01540 673568. Cost: £5 per rod per day.

DUNALISTAIR WATER
Location & Access 42/700585. The loch is easily accessible and is situated close to the B846 Tummel Bridge/Kinloch Rannoch road.
Commentary Dunalistair Water lies between Loch Rannoch to the west and Loch Tummel in the east and was formed when Loch Rannoch and Loch Tummel were impounded for hydro-electric power generation purposes. Nevertheless, the loch looks entirely natural and maintains much of the characteristics of a wild fishery. The loch is approximately 1.5 miles long by up to half a mile wide and it is surrounded by attractive woodlands and dominated by the smooth slope of Schiehallion (1083m), one of Scotland's most famous mountains, which rises to the south.
Fish Stocked annually with brown trout which are reared in an Estate hatchery. Small fish are netted from feeder burns and released into the loch where they grow to considerable size. The average weight of fish is reputed to be 2lb and trout of over 5lb in weight are not uncommon. The loch also contains pike.
Flies & Tactics Dunalistair is a shallow water and fishing is from boats only. Outboard motors are not allowed and even when rowing, care should be taken to avoid the remains of tree stumps which still lurk below the surface. Trout rise and may be taken all over the loch with the west end perhaps being the more productive area. This is not an easy loch, so do not expect large baskets. A good day might send you home with a couple of fish, but, as we say in Scotland, they will be 'worth the hauding'. Flies that may tempt them: Black Pennell, Soldier Palmer and Dunkeld.
Permission & Charges Trout fishing only, at £17 per boat per day, 2 rods fishing. Contact: David Kerr, Loch Garry Cottage, Dunalistair Estate, Kinloch Rannoch PH16 5PD. Tel: 01882 632354.

EIGHEACH, Loch
Location & Access 42/450570. The north shoreline of the loch is accessible from the B846 Kinloch Rannoch/Rannoch Station road. The south shore may be reached via the track which crosses the outlet burn of the River Gaur at 42/465571 at the east end of the loch. The south west shore is accessed from the road bridge at 42/442572.
Commentary Loch Eigheach is 1 mile long by up to 1 mile wide, deep and somewhat forbidding. The loch is impounded by a dam at the east end where the flow exits into the River Gaur which in turn feeds Loch Rannoch (see separate entry).
Fish The vast majority of the residents average 6oz-8oz but there are much larger fish. Trrout of over 7lb have been taken in recent years.
Flies & Tactics Bank fishing only and upon no account wade. It is dangerous to do so. The north shoreline is probably the best place to concentrate your attack, working south to where the Garbh Ghaoir burn enters (42/440570). The Garbh Ghaoir burn itself, and the River Gaur, also offer the chance of sport with good brown trout, particularly after heavy rain. The River Guar is very pretty and extends for 2 miles, from the loch, down to Rannoch Barracks (42/500570). Offer them: Soldier Palmer, March Brown and Silver Invicta.
Permission & Charges Contact: Moor of Rannoch Hotel, Rannoch Station. Tel: 01882 633238. Cost: £3 per rod per day.

ERICHT, Loch
Location & Access 42/560750 Access is from the north, the Dalwhinne end, on foot via a private estate road along the west shore from the locked gate at 42/631844. A track also borders the east shore but this ends after 1 mile at the shielings at 42/624836. Thereafter, the east shore is trackless.
Commentary Loch Ericht is an intimidating water, 15 miles long by up to 1 mile wide at the south end. The loch is part of the Rannoch/Tummel Hydro-electric scheme and, consequently, Loch Ericht can look somewhat bleak at times, particularly when the water level is low. However, the surrounding scenery more than compensates for this starkness. The loch is dominated by Ben Alder (1148m) to the west and Beinn Udlamain (1010m) to the east and the area is very popular with climbers and hillwakers. The Ben Alder Estate operates an open access policy, both for walkers and anglers and allows access, on foot, to the more remote waters to the west of Loch Ericht. Reaching them involves a long hike, but they are amongst the most splendidly situated lochs in all of Scotland. They include: Loch Pattack (42/540790), Loch a'Bhealaich Leamhain (42/500800), tiny Lochan Mointeich (42/536802), Lochan na Doireuaine (42/585863) and Loch Caoldair (42/615895).
Fish Loch Ericht contains excellent stocks of wild brown trout which average in the order of 8oz. However, there are very much larger fish: ferox trout of up to and over 10lb, but they are rarely caught other than by trolling the depths from a boat. The hill lochs offer sport with modest trout and the chance of a few specimen fish as well. In high water conditions, also have a cast in Allt a'Chaoil-reidhe, the inlet burn to Loch Pattack, and in the River Pattack which drains Loch Pattack to the north.
Flies & Tactics Bank fishing only. When fishing Loch Ericht upon no account attempt to wade. It is dangerous! The banks, due to fluctuations in the water level, can be soft and treacherous, so take great care. The south end of the loch, in the vicinity of Alder Bay (McCook's Bay) (42/505670), is private fishing. On Loch Pattack, concentrate your efforts along the north shore in the area where the Allt Cam burn enters and around the promontory near the Ford (42/539787). Best flies: Black Pennell, Grouse & Claret and Silver Butcher.
Permission & Charges Contact: Loch Ericht Hotel, Dalwhinne, Inverness-shire. Tel: 01528 522257; Mr Williams, Tollhouse Shop, Dalwhinne, Inverness-shire. Tel: 01528 522274. Cost: £5 per rod per day. Prior to fishing the hill lochs, as a matter of courtesy, contact Ian Crichton, Ben Alder Estate, Dalwhinnie, Inverness-

Loch Rannoch   OS Map 42

shire. Tel: 01540 672000. During the stalking season, access to some areas may be restricted. Check, before setting out, to avoid unnecessarily disrupting the work of the estate.

ERROCHTY, Loch
Location & Access 42/685652 Approach from Trinafour (42/727645) on the B847 Kinloch Rannoch/Calvine road. Park within half a mile of the loch and walk the rest of the way.
Commentary Another hydro-electric water (see Loch Ericht & Loch Garry) but set in splendid scenery, particularly if you are prepared to make the 3 mile hike to the west end. The River Errochty, which drains the loch into the River Garry, is not fished.
Fish Some monsters, in the depths, which rarely rise to surface flies, and good numbers of smaller fish which average 8oz/10oz.
Flies & Tactics Bank fishing only. Do not wade: it is dangerous. There are tracks along both the north and south shores. Make a day out of the expedition and tramp west. There are a number of attractive corners, bays and promontories here where good sport may be had, particularly in the north west bay, in the vicinity of the small islands and where the Allt Steibh burn enters. Flies: Blue Zulu, Greenwell's Glory, and Silver Invicta.
Permission & Charges See Loch Garry (Perthshire) entry.

ERROCHTY, River See Loch Errochty.
GARBH GHAOIR Burn See Loch Eigheach.

GARRY, Loch (Perthshire)
Location & Access 42/633710. Access is from the the A9 Perth/Inverness road along the track which passes Dalnaspidal Lodge and the Keeeper's House at the head of the loch. Thereafter, a track borders the east, An Cearcall, shoreline to the bothy at the south end at the waterfall which cascades down from Meall Doire (732m).
Commentary The waters of Loch Garry have been diverted by a tunnel to Loch Ericht (see separate entry) and Loch Garry often displays all the unwelcome signs of fluctuations in water level associated with hydrolochs: bare, unstable, tide-marked margins. Apart from the surrounding scenery, Loch Garry is not a particularly pleasant place to fish.
Fish Some very large trout, including ferox trout, but they do not give themselves up easily and Loch Garry has a reputation for being 'dour'.
Flies & Tactics Bank fishing only and it is advisable not to attempt to wade. The south end, from both the east and west shore, is probably the best place to begin. Try: Loch Ordie, Soldier Palmer, Dunkeld.
Permission & Charges Contact: Highland Guns & Tackle, Blair Cottages, Blair Atholl, Perthshire. Tel: 01796 481303). Cost: £5 per rod per day.

GAUR, River See Loch Eigheach.

KINARDOCHY, Loch
Location & Access 42/777552 An easily accessible loch which lies between Tomphubil (42/779545) on the B846 road and the minor road to the west from Tomphubil to Kinloch Rannoch (42/663588).
Commentary A very pleasant little water, approximately 50 acres in extent, managed by the Pitlochry Angling Association. Park at the south end of the loch. The boats are moored at the boat house, a couple of minutes walk from the car park.
Fish Stocked with brown trout which average 10oz/12oz in weight, but also fish of up to and over 3lb.
Flies & Tactics Boat fishing only (or float tubes) and fish rise and are taken all over the loch. Strong winds can sometimes be a problem on this exposed water. Offer them: Black Pennell, Grouse & Claret, Silver Invicta.
Permission & Charges Mitchell's of Pitlochry, 23 Atholl Road, Pitlochry PH16 5BX. Tel: 01796 472613. Cost: £10 per boat per day (2 rods fishing).

MOINTEICH, Lochan See Loch Ericht.
NA DOIRE-UAINE, Lochan See loch Ericht.
PATTACK, Loch See Loch Ericht.
PRIVATE WATERS OSSIAN, Loch (42/400685); A'BHEALAICH, Lochan (42/451683); MEOIGEACH, Lochan (42/452641); SRON SMEUR, Lochan (42/449607); FINNART, Loch (42/523555); MONAGHAN, Loch (42/532552); MHEUGAIDH, Loch (42/532619); DUBH NA BEINNE BOIDICH, Lochan (42/569632); EOIN, LochAN (42447551); ABHAINN DUIBHE, River (42/468568); ALLT CHOMRAIDH, River (42/500569); ERICHT, River (42/521582); AN T-SEILICH, Loch (42/755860); BHRODAINN, Loch (42/747830); AN DUIN, Loch (42/724800); CON, Loch (42/690679); DUBH, Lochan (42/711674); MAUD, Loch (42/726650); BEOIL CHATHAICHE, Lochan (42/748569); AN DAIM, Lochan (42/719573)

RANNOCH, Loch Location & access 42/600580
Location & Access Loch Rannoch lies alongside The Road to the Isles, the B846 Tummel Bridge/Rannoch Station road which margins the north shore of the loch. Access to the south shore is via the minor road from Bunrannoch in the east to Rannoch Barracks in the west.
Commentary Although the waters of Loch Rannoch have been impounded by the Pitlochry Hydro Electric Scheme, the loch still looks entirely natural. The loch is over 10 miles east/west by up to 1 mile wide and drops to over 30m in depth at the east end. There are numerous camping sites and picnic areas beside the loch, the most scenic of which is perhaps the site at Carie (42/618570). The dominant feature here is graceful Schiehallion (1083m), one of Scotland's best-known and most-climbed mountains. The famous Black Wood of Rannoch, which contains remnants of the Caledonian pine forest which used to cover much of Scotland, lies to the west of Carie. The Forestry Commission have laid out a number of woodland walks, something for non-fishing members of your party to enjoy whilst you get on with more important matters.
Fish Loch Rannoch is most noted for its huge ferox trout, including fish of 22lb in 1867, 21lb in 1904, 23lb 8oz in 1905, 18lb 8oz in 1912. Even in recent years, dou-

ble-figure fish are caught and 1991 produced 4 ferox of up 12lb 10oz in weight. In 1999, a fish of 15lb 80z was caught. Apart from these specimen fish, the majority of trout in Loch Rannoch are of more modest proportions and average in the order 10oz, but good numbers of larger trout, of up to and over 2lb in weight, are taken most seasons. The loch also contains pike and perch.

Flies & Tactics Trout may be taken from virtually anywhere around the banks of the loch. In the early spring, and in the autumn, ferox trout are sometimes caught from the shore, particularly where streams enter the loch: Bridge of Ericht (42/521578), Crosscraig (42/550567), Dail Burn mouth (42/591568) Carie and Aulich (42/609589). However, boat fishing provides the most comfortable way of exploring this vast water and the most productive fishing areas are, generally, at the west end of the loch: the bay at Finnart (42/520574); drifting east from Finnart Lodge (42/525574); around the artificial island, Eilean nam Faoileag (42/531576) and the bay at Eilean Mor (42/553568). Flies: Ke-He, Wickham's Fancy, Silver Butcher.

Permission & Charges The loch is managed by the Rannoch Conservation Association and permission to fish may be obtained from a number of locations, including: P Legate, Glenrannoch House, Kinloch Rannoch, Perthshire. Tel: 01882 632307; Bunrannoch Hotel, Kinloch Rannoch, Perthshire. Tel: 01882 632367; Country Store, Kinloch Rannoch, Perthshire. Tel: 01882 632306; Dunalistair Hotel, by Kinloch Rannoch, Perthshire. Tel: 01882 632323. Cost: £4 per rod per day bank fishing; boat with outboard motor, approximately £30 per day (3 rods fishing).

Braemar

A'CHOIRE, Loch
Location & Access 43/949625 Loch a'Choire (also known locally as Ben Vrackie Loch) lies to the north of Pitlochry below the summit of Ben Vrackie (841m), a popular peak with climbers and hillwalkers. Park at Moulin (52/944592) on the A924 Pitlochry/Kirkmichael road. A stiff 2 mile climb will bring you to the loch.
Commentary A small loch in a big setting, offering magnificent views over the surrounding countryside. An exciting alternative return route from Loch a'Choire would be to follow the outlet stream from the loch, downhill, south east, to the little unnamed lochan at 43/955619, and, from there south again to explore the Settlements & Field Systems sites at 43/960608. A track from here leads back to the start point.
Fish Not many and averaging about 6oz. The loch has become very weedy in recent years, so, if you plan to fish, early season months are best.
Flies & Tactics An excellent day out amidst wonderful scenery. Flies: Solider Palmer, Greenwell's Glory, Dunkeld.
Permission & Charges No charge, but, as a matter of courtesy, if you intend to fish, you should ask permission from the keeper: D Seaton, Gamekeeper's House, Balsmund, Pitlochry. Tel: 01796 472273.

ALLT FEARNACH, Burn See Shee Water.
ARDLE, River See Shee Water.

BEANIE, Loch
Location & Access 43/160687 Park at Invereddrie Farm (43/138681). A good track leads east over easy ground and reaches the loch after a walk of approximately 1.25 miles. The loch is also known locally as Loch Shechernich.
Commentary A splendid introduction to hill loch fishing, Loch Beanie is set amidst glorious countryside and lies between Craigenloch Hill (738m) to the north and Mealna Letter Hill (702m) to the south. The loch is 700yds east/west by up to 300yds wide and the surrounding hills often provide shelter from harsh east winds.
Fish Large stocks of bright l wild brown trout which average 8oz. A few fish of up to and over 1lb are also taken most seasons. The heaviest trout caught in recent years weighed 2lb 4oz.
Flies & Tactics There is one boat on the loch and bank fishing is also allowed. Trout rise and are taken all round this shallow loch and no one place is substantial better than another. Cast with confidence, everywhere. Offer the residents: Ke-He, Black Zulu, Silver Butcher.
Permission & Charges Contact: Kevin Peters, Wester Binzian, Glenshee, Perthshire. Tel: 01250 885206. Cost: £7 per rod per day (including the use of the boat which may be booked in advance).

BHAC, Loch
Location & Access 43/822623 Loch Bhac (pronounced "Vaa") is approached via a forest track from the B8019 Garry Bridge/Tummel Bridge road. There is a locked gate and a key is required to gain vehicular access. Park at 43/818629 and walk down to the boathouse.
Commentary An attractive little loch in a sheltered, woodland setting. This is the ideal place to fish when the wind howls down the more exposed, large lochs in the area, such as Loch Rannoch and Loch Tummel.
Fish Stocked with brown trout, rainbow trout and book trout. Average weight, 12oz/14oz, with good numbers of trout of up to and over 4lb in weight. Fish of 7lb are not uncommon.
Flies & Tactics The loch is managed by the Pitlochry Angling Association and both boat and bank fishing is allowed. Loch Bhac is approximately 500yds long by 200yds wide and fish rise and are taken all over the loch from both bank and shore. Cast with confidence, using: Ke-He, Wickham's Fancy, Dunkeld.
Permission & Charges Mitchell's of Pitlochry, 23 Atholl Road, Pitlochry PH16 5BX. Tel: 01796 472613. cost: Bank fishing, £5 per rod per day, boat fishing, £15 per day (2 rods fishing).

BLACK, Water (Glenshee) See Shee Water.

BLAIR WALKER, Pond
Location & Access See Loch Valigan entry. 43/862661 An easily accessible, stocked pond within the grounds of Blair Castle.
Commentary Less than taxing fishing in Blair Walker pond, but ideal for newcomers to fly-fishing. Those

Braemar — OS Map 43

searching for a more rewarding experience might consider seeking permission to fish Loch Loch (43/985745), on the north east slopes of Beinn a'Ghlo (1121m) in Glen Loch. Loch Loch is best approached from the same track that is used to access Loch Valigan (see separate entry) and it will involve you in a tramp of some 16 miles. Check with Lude Estate before setting out, particularly during the stalking season.

Fish Trout in Blair Walker Pond average 12oz. Loch Loch has small brown trout which average 6oz/8oz in weight, although there are probably much larger fish as well: the loch is 80ft deep.

Flies & Tactics Bank fishing only on both lochs. There is a bag limit of 3 trout per angler on Blair Walker Pond. Loch Loch is 1 mile long, "nipped" by narrows into two equal sections. Do not wade in the loch, it is dangerous to do so. Fish lie close to the margins and may be taken from all round the shore. Flies: Black Zulu, Ke-He, Silver Butcher.

Permission & Charges The Highland Guns & Tackle, Blair Atholl, Perthshire. Tel: 01796 481303. Because of stalking, access to Loch Loch is restricted after 11th August. Highland Guns & Tackle is also the font of all fishing knowledge in the area and are happy to advise visiting anglers about what sport is available locally.

BRAUR, Water See River Tilt.
BRERACHAN, Water See Shee Water.
CROSS REFERENCE All the waters on OS Map 43, which lie to the north of Grid Line East 87 are described on OS Maps 35 and 36.
FENDER, Burn See River Tilt.
GARRY, River (Perthshire) See River Tilt.
ISLA, River See OS Map 53 Blairgowrie.
LOCH, Loch See Blair Walker Pond.
MORAIG, Loch See Loch Valigan.

NAN EUN, Loch
Location & Access 43/064780 Not for the faint-hearted. Approach from Spittal of Glenshee (43/109700). A track follows the north bank of Glen Lochsie Burn (good trout fishing in spate conditions and the chance of an occasional salmon) and climbs north through Glen Taitneach to the corrie between Creag Dallaig (750m) to the north and Glas Choire Bheag (930m) to the south. This is a tough, 6 mile hike over rough ground and you must be well prepared. A compass and map are essential.

Commentary An outstandingly beautiful loch in an outstandingly beautiful setting. Loch nan Eun is almost 1/2 a mile long by up to 300yds wide and it lies at an altitude of 800m. Magnificent wildlife along the way with more than good chance of seeing golden eagle.

Fish Reasonable stocks of wild brown trout which average 6oz/8oz. Because of stalking and shooting the loch may be closed after the 11th August. Check with the Estate Office before setting out.

Flies & Tactics Bank fishing only and the most productive are is at the north end, in the narrow bay near the two small islands. The promontory on the north east shore can also produce results. Offer them: Blue Zulu, Teal & Green, Black Pennell.

Permission & Charges Kevin Peters, Wester Binzin, Glenshee, Perthshire. Tel: 01250 885206. Invercauld Estates, Estate Office, Braemar, by Ballater, Aberdeenshire. Tel: 01339 741224. Cost: £7 per rod per day.

PRIVATE WATERS NA LEATHAIN, Lochan (43/841618); NAN NIGHEAN, Lochan (43/843613); CURRAN, Loch (43/048603); CRANNACH, Loch (43/056675); AUCHINTAPLE, Loch (43/197647); DRUMORE, Loch (43/165609); CALLATER, Loch (43/184840); PHADRUIG, Loch (43/177861)

SHEE, Water
Location & Access Source: 43/064782 Outfall: 53/149515 7. Easily accessible throughout its entire length from the A93 Bridge of Cally/Spittal of Glenshee road.

Commentary The river rises from Loch nan Euan (43/063781) (see separate entry), a remote loch cradled between the lower slopes of Mam nan Carn (986m) to the south and Beinn Iutharn Bheag (953m) to the north. The upper 7 miles of the stream, south to Blacklunans (43/149605), is known as Shee Water. From Blacklunans, downstream to where the Shee meets the River Ardle to form the River Ericht (see OS Map 53, Blairgowrie), the river is called the Black Water. The Ericht in turn joins the River Isla near Coupar Angus and, ultimately, the mighty River Tay at Isla Mouth (53/160375). The River Ardle, to the west of Shee Water, has less significance as a sporting river, although it is an important salmon spawning area. The River Ardle, however, and its major tributaries, can often offer sport with brown trout, given good water levels.

Fish Salmon, the occasional sea-trout and brown trout. Accurate catch records are not available, but it is probable that the system produces upwards of 250 fish each season. The average weight of salmon is approximately 6lb but double-figure fish are by no means uncommon. The largest salmon taken in recent years weighed 15lb.

Flies & Tactics Very much a spate stream, but when water conditions are "right", then Shee Water can provide outstanding sport. There are a number of good holding pools and attractive runs, all of which may be easily covered from the bank using a single-handed fly-rod. In high water conditions, spinning may be allowed. Fish arrive in Shee Water from late June onwards but the most productive months are September and October, depending upon water levels. Fresh fish are caught right up until the end of the season. Flies: Willie Gunn, Hairy Mary, Stoats Tail, Green Highlander, Shrimp patterns.

Permission & Charges Access to Shee Water may be obtained either on a day ticket or weekly basis. Dalnaglar Castle (43/146647) have a 4 rod beat which is let with the castle. Dalnaglar also have two attractive stocked trout fisheries which are available with the let. Cost: from £400 per party per night. Contact: William Bain, Dalnaglar Castle, Glenshee, Perthshire. Tel: 01250 882232. The west bank of the upper river (Finegand Estate) is divided into 2, 2 rod beats, and these may be accessed via Finegand Farm, Glenshee, Perthshire. Tel: 01250 885234. Cost: £40 per beat per day before August, £50 per rod per day thereafter.

OS Map 43 — Braemar

Anglers are limited to 2 salmon per day. Peter Cooper at the Spittal of Glenshee Hotel will also be able to advise anglers searching for sport, both on the river and on the trout lochs in the area. Contact: Spittal of Glenshee Hotel, Glenshee, Perthshire. Tel: 01250 885215. Also, Invercauld Estates, Estate Office, Braemar, by Ballater, Aberdeenshire. Tel: 01339 741224.

TARF, Water See River Tilt.

TILT, River
Location & Access Source: 43/993827 Outfall: 43/872651. Access is via the stalkers/walkers path from Blair Atholl (43/875682) in the south to White Bridge (43/019885) in the north.
Commentary The River Tilt rises from Loch Tilt (43/993827) and flows south for a distance of some 13 miles before joining the River Garry at Blair Atholl. There are four major tributaries: Tarf Water, An Lochain burn, which draws in the flow from distant Loch Loch (see separate entry), Allt Mhairc burn and the Fender Burn, The walk through Glen Tilt, north to Deeside, is one of the most attractive and notable long-distance paths in Scotland; Queen Victoria and Albert travelled this way in the mid-19th century; Mary Queen of Scots visited Glen Tilt in the 16th century when the Duke of Atholl arranged a vast hunting party for her amusement. The River Garry is less attractive now than in times past, having being robbed of much of its force by the diversion of its waters north into Loch Ericht as part of the Pitlochry Hydro-Electric scheme. Salmon no longer reach the principal tributary of the River Garry, Bruar Water, and a weir has been built across the river to stop fish from trying to do so in times of high water. However, the lower reaches of the river are still worth fishing, from Woodend (43/845659) down to the Pass of Killiecrankie (43/905630), although most salmon seem to prefer to run the River Tilt.
Fish Salmon in the rivers, modest brown trout in Loch Tilt. Thousands of fish are counted through the fish ladder at Pitlochry, but few are subsequently caught on rod and line. Depending upon water levels, perhaps 100/150 salmon may be taken during the course of a season.
Flies & Tactics For Loch Tilt, strong lungs and a strong desire for peace and quiet. The rivers are easily fished from the bank using a single-handed rod and the best time to attack is during the later months of the season, particularly in September and early October. Offer trout: Black Zulu, March Brown, Alexandra; for salmon, try: Garry Dog, Willie Gunn, Hairy Mary, Stoat's Tail, General Practitioner, Green Highlander.
Permission & Charges : Contact: The Highland Shop, Blair Atholl, Perthshire. Tel: 01796 481303. The Highland Shop factors 3 private beats on the River Tilt on behalf of Atholl Estates. Cost: in the order of £25/£30 per rod per day.

TUMMEL, Loch See OS Map 52.

VALIGAN, Loch
Location & Access 43/975694 A remote, wilderness, loch, located at the end of a long, hard, 4 mile tramp north east from Loch Moraig (43/905667) to the north of Blair Atholl (43/875682) on the old A9 Perth/Inverness road.
Commentary Loch Valigan is 400yds long by up to 100 yds wide and it lies to the south east of Beinn a'Ghlo (1121m) at the heart of the Atholl Forest. Leave the stalkers track at 43/958687 and follow the line of the Allt Loch Valigan burn up the glen to reach the loch after 1 mile. The surrounding mountains give the loch some shelter from prevailing winds. Loch Moraig is less stressful to reach, and offers an excellent alternative fishing venue for those in your party who may not inclined to make the longer expedition to Loch Valigan.
Fish Good stocks of hard fighting little brown trout which average 6oz/8oz in weight in Loch Valigan, Loch Moraig has larger fish of up to 1lb in weight.
Flies & Tactics Visit Loch Valigan as much for the marvelous scenery as for the fishing. This is a very special place, regardless of trout, and you will be well-rewarded for the effort involved in reaching it. There is a boat on the loch but unless you have a high wheel based vehicle, it a long way to carry oars and rowlocks. Bank fishing can be just as productive. The loch is closed to anglers after the 1 July. Loch Moraig has 2 boats and fishing is available from about mid-April until 12 August, from 9am until 5pm, Monday/Saturday. The small islands in the vicinity of the boat house is a good place to start, but fish may be taken from all round the loch. Flies: Blue Zulu, Soldier Palmer, Silver Invicta.
Permission & Charges Major A D Gordon, Lude, Blair Atholl, Perthshire. Tel: 01796 481240. Cost: from £25 per day, including the use of the boat (2 anglers fishing). The owner of this fishery advises that it is already over-subscribed and consequently, unlikely to be available for bookings.

VROTACHAN, Loch
Location & Access 43/123786 Start from the Ski-center on the A93 Rattray/Braemar road (43/139781). The chair-lift will take you, in comfort, to within 1/4 of a mile of the loch which lies at an altitude of over 2,000ft.
Commentary One of the highest hill lochs in Scotland, and probably the most productive. The surrounding scenery is magnificent and it is possible to stay out overnight in the well-equipped (bunk beds, calor gas stove) hut on the shores of the loch. For those who enjoy an adventure, it is possible to complete a fine high-level ridge walk from Loch Vrotachan to Loch nan Eun (see separate entry) and return, certainly foot-sore, but with something for breakfast the following morning.
Fish The average weight of trout is in the order of 1lb.
Flies & Tactics Flies & tactics The loch is cared for by the Ballater Angling Association who stocked it with brown trout in 1989. There has been no further stocking since then and the Association policy is to manage the resource as a wild fishery. A limestone outcrop gives the loch a high pH and the trout thrive, although they are notoriously hard to catch. Bank fishing only, and trout may be taken from all round the shore. The west end, where the feeder burn enters, is a good place to start. Flies: Black Pennell, Soldier Palmer, Black & Peacock Spider.

Ballater OS Map 43-44

Permission & Charges Contact: Martin Holroyd, Ballater Angling Association, 59 Golf Road, Ballater, Aberdeenshire. Tel: 01339 755454. Also, Countrywear, 15 &35 High Street, Ballater, Aberdeenshire. Tel: 01339 755453. Cost: £7.50 per rod per day.

Ballater

BACKWATER Reservoir
Location & Access 44/225610. Approach from the B951 Kirriemuir/Braemar road. Just west of where the road crosses Melgam Water, near Dykends (53/249576), turn north on the minor road that leads to the south end of the reservoir.
Commentary Backwater Reservoir is approximately 2 miles north/south in length by up to 700yds wide. The surrounded area is attractively wooded and there are numerous opportunities for rambling and hill walking. The wildlife is outstanding and there is a good possibility of spotting wildcat, particularly in the late evening and early morning. There is a comfortable fishing hut, well-manicured lawn and picnic area, all of which make Backwater Reservoir an ideal place of a family outing. To the west of Backwater Reservoir, there is another, delightful, little trout loch, Loch Shandra (44/219621) and this is accessed from the B951 road at East Mill (44/223603).
Fish Backwater Reservoir contains wild brown trout which average in the order of 8oz and reasonable numbers of larger fish as well. Trout of up to and over 1lb are not uncommon. Loch Shandra contains stocked brown trout which average 1lb in weight. Wild trout of 1lb 8oz are also taken, as well as large numbers of 6oz/8oz wild fish..
Flies & Tactics Bank fishing only on Backwater Reservoir, boat and bank fishing on Loch Shandra. The north end of Backwater Reservoir is the most productive fishing area, particularly in the bays and corners at the north east end. On Loch Shandra, the east shoreline is the place to start. Good fish may also be taken from the dam wall at the south end of the loch. Flies: Black Pennell, Grouse & Claret, Silver Invicta.
Permission & Charges For Backwater Reservoir contact: Jack Yule, Linthrathen Angling club, 61 Hillrise, Kirriemuir, Angus DD8 4JS. Tel: 01575 560327 (Loch); Tel: 01575 573816 (Home). cost: £10 per rod per day. For Loch Shandra, contact: Mr R Pate, Brelwands Cottage, Glen Isla, by Kirriemuir, Angus. Tel: 01575 582242. Cost: £12 per rod per day (9am/9pm) for boat fishing, £10 per rod per day bank fishing. There is a 2 fish limit for stocked fish, but no restriction on the numbers of wild fish which may be caught.

BRANDY, Loch See Loch Wharral.
CROSS REFERENCE All the waters on OS Map 44, to the north of Easting Grid Line 80 are described on OS Maps 36 and 37.

DEN OF OGIL Reservoir
Location & Access 44/435617 Approach from Tannadice (54/475582) on the B957 Finavon/Kirriemuir road. The reservoir lies to the north of Mains of Ogil (44/449615).
Commentary An easily accessible small reservoir stocked and managed by the Carnmore Angling Club.
Fish Stocked with brown trout which averaged between 1lb 8oz and 2lb in weight.
Flies & Tactics Den of Ogil Reservoir is approximately 1/2 a mile long by perhaps 100yds wide and fishing is from both boat and bank. Offer them: Ke-He, Greenwell's Glory, Alexandra.
Permission & Charges Contact: Charles Kerr, Sport Outfitters, 1-5 West High Street, Forfar, Angus. Tel: 01307 463347. Cost: £10 per day bank fishing, £8 for use of a boat. Further details from A Mackintosh, 30 Laurelbank, Forfar, Angus. Tel: 01307 465474

LEE, Loch
Location & Access 44/410795 Follow the minor road north west from Fettercarin on the B966 up the north bank of the River North Esk (see separate entry). At Invermark Castle (44/443804), at the end of the public road, continue west to reach the end of the loch after a further 1/2 mile.
Commentary A dramatic loch in a dramatic setting surrounded by wild mountains. Also, often, wild and windy.
Fish Wild brown trout which average 8oz/10oz, but also a few splendid fish of up to and over 5lb in weight. The largest fish taken in recent years weighed 9lb and was caught by an Arbroath angler on a size 12 Ace of Sapdes. Arctic char inhabit the depths and char of over 1lb are not uncommon.
Flies & Tactics Loch Lee lies on the headwaters of the River North Esk and fishing is from boats only. The loch is 1 and 1/2 miles east/west by up to 500yds wide and an outboard motor is essential, both for safety and for ease of exploring this large expanse of water. This is a deep loch and you should concentrate your efforts round the margins. The west end is perhaps the most productive fishing area, particularly where the Water of Lee enters (44/414797) and in the shallow bay on the Inchgrundle shore (44/414792). Flies: Black Zulu, Grouse & Claret, Kingfisher Butcher.
Permission & Charges Bookings, by letter only, to The Head Keeper, Invermark Estate, Tarfside, Glenesk, Angus. Tel: 01356 670208. Cost: approximately £20 per boat per day (three rods fishing). Outboard motors are not available, so you will have to supply your own. Also, during windy conditions, the Estate may, at their discretion, close the loch to fishing.

LEE, Water of See Loch Lee.

NORTH ESK, River
Location & Access Source 44/343801 Outfall 45/740625. The upper reaches of the River North Esk depicted on OS Map 44 (see also OS Map 45) are accessed from the minor road which runs north up Glen Esk from the B966 Fettercairn/Edzell road. Leave the B966 just after the bridge over the river at 45/601710. The River North Esk rises as the Water of Lee on the west slopes of Easter Balloch (834m) and drains into Loch Lee (see separate entry). After leaving Loch Lee

OS Map 44 — Ballater

the flow is joined by the Water of Mark and is then known as the River North Esk. The river continues south east for a distance of some 35 miles and enters the sea to the north of Montrose between Waterside and Charleton and Kinnaber Links.

Commentary Glen Esk is one of the most lovely of the Angus glens and the river in its upper reaches shows all the characteristics of a classic Highland spate stream: deep pools, handsome, gravel-bedded glides and heather-clad banks surrounded by magnificent moorlands and mountains.

Fish The River North Esk is primarily known as a salmon fishery although reasonable numbers of sea-trout are also taken. The river produces in the order of 1,000 salmon and grilse each season, depending upon prevailing water conditions. Fish begin to arrive in the upper river in considerable numbers after April.

Flies & Tactics Good sport is dependent upon good water levels. In the early months of the season a 12ft/13ft rod is required to fish the fly effectively, and to hold salmon in heavy water. A sink-tip line is most effective. As the season advances, a 10ft rod will cope with the majority of eventualities. Wherever possible, avoid wading. In some areas it is dangerous to do so and often only "spooks" the fish. The Millden fishing is divided into two beats (Upper & Lower) with a total of 48 named pools. Some of the most productive of these, working upstream from where the Burn of Rannoch enters (44/568763), are: Hillocks Pool, Nellies Pool, Menzies Pool, Falls Pool, Rannoch Pool, Ladder Pool, The Neuk Pool, Aspen Pool, Woodhaugh Runs and Top Pool. Downstream from the Millden Beats, before reaching the Loups of the Burn, the river hurries through the famous gorge where the exposed rock-slabs in the river are known as "The Rocks of Solitude". Spinning accounts for most of the early-running fish, but fly fishing can be just as effective. Try: Willie Gunn, Garry Dog, Munro Killer, Ally's Shrimp, Hairy Mary. Gold and Black Devon minnows are successful lures.

Permission & Charges For the Millden Fishings, contact: R M J Cooke, Factor, Dalhousie Estates Office, Brechin, Angus DD9 6SG. Tel: 01356 624566. Cost: day lets may be available at between £15 and £50, depending upon the time of year. Weekly lets are preferred and cost between £100 and £900 per 3 rod beat, again depending upon the time of year. The estate has comfortable self-catering cottages which may be let with the fishing. Gannochy: Head Keeper, Gannochy Estate, Edzell, by Brechin, Angus. Tel: 01356 647331, 2 miles of double-bank fishing, 4 miles of single. Cost: £300 per week per rod. Loups: The Factor, The Burn, Glen Esk, Edzell, Brechin, Angus. Tel: 01356 648281; 1 mile of single-bank fishing. Cost: £30 per rod per day. Edzell Beat: (see Dalhousie Estate above). Mrs Gray has fishing below Gannochy (44/599707) and this is let in conjunction with an excellent self-catering cottage close to the fishing. Inclusive cost: February, March, April, May, and September and October, £1022 per week (3 rods). During the summer months, June, July and August, Mrs Gray may have day lets available at a cost of £12 per rod per day. The beat produces in the order of between 50 and 70 salmon each season. For further information, contact: Mrs H Gray, Neuk Cottages, Edzell, Brechin, Angus DD9 7XU. Tel: 01356 648523. Messrs Savills, 12 Clerk Street, Brechin, Angus DD9 6AE, Tel: 01356 622187 may also be able to advise on access to fishing on the River North Esk. Also, contact: Joseph Johnston & Sons, 3 America Street, Montrose DD10 8DR. Tel: 01674 672666. Fax: 01674 677087.

PRIVATE WATERS MUICK, Loch (44/290830); MUICK, River (44/320883); DUBH, Loch (44/236828); NAN EUN, Loch (44/230854); SANDY, Loch (44/229864); LOCHNAGAR, Loch (44/252860); CARLOCHY, Loch (North) (44/411831); CARLOCHY, Loch (South) (44/397789); ESK, Loch (44/239793); PROSEN, Water (44/360624); GLENOGIL (RESERVOIR) (44/449644); NORAN, Water (44/451631).

SOUTH ESK, River

Location & Access Source 44/239793 Outfall 54/674578 Access to the upper reaches of the River South Esk is via the B955 road which circles both banks of the stream from Gella Bridge (44/373653) in the south to Clova Bridge (44/326728) in the north.

Commentary The upper river South Esk, on OS Map 44, (see also OS Map 54) is a modest stream, rising from Loch Esk and collecting in the flow of the White Water at Braedownie (44/287756) before heading off south towards Brechin and the sea at Montrose. Glen Clova, one of the famous five glens of Angus, is very lovely and, given good water conditions, this part of the river can provide excellent sport.

Fish Salmon and sea-trout. Salmon average 10lb, sea-trout 2lb. The best month are August, September and October.

Flies & Tactics A strong, single-handed, 10ft/11ft, rod will cover most eventualities. The river is narrow and care must be taken not to spook the fish. Stealth is the pre-requisite tactic here. Keep well back from the river bank and lengthen line from one casting position, rather than marching down the bank. Offer: Willie Gunn, Ally's Shrimp, Green Highlander, Silver Stoat's Tail.

Permission & Charges Anna & Graham Davie have 3 miles of double bank fishing available at a cost of £22 per rod per day - and excellent accommodation in the friendly Clova Hotel. Contact: Clova Hotel, Glen Clova, by Kirrriemuir, Angus. Tel: 01575 550222. The Kirriemuir Angling Club has a further 7 and 1/2 miles of fishing in Glen Clova, from Rottal (44/363700) downstream to Sawmill Dam near Cortachy. Cost from £15 per rod per day. The Secretary of the Kirriemuir Angling Club is Bill Dick, 49 Woodend Drive, Kirriemuir, Angus DD8 4TG. Tel: 01575 573277.

WEST, Water See OS Map 45.

WHARRAL, Loch

Location & Access 44/359745 Park at Wheen (44/362710) in Glen Clova on the B955. Walk north for 2 miles on a stalkers path up the slopes of Ben Tirran (896m) to reach the loch.

Commentary This small, corrie, loch lies below the Crags of Loch Wharral at an altitude of 600m, shel-

Stonehaven — OS Maps 44-45

tered from most of the prvailing winds by the surrounding hills. A smilar corrie loch, Loch Brandy (44/339755) lies to 1 mile to the west of Loch Wharral, but this loch is best approached from Clova (44/328731), via a track which starts from behind the Clova Hotel. Because they are difficult of access, these lochs are rarely fished. However, they offer splendid sport amidst magnificent scenery.
Fish Nothing to fill the glass case, but always something for supper.
Flies & Tactics Bank fishing only and the south and east shores are the most productive fishing areas. The water is very clear and wading is not really required. Flies: Blue Zulu, Greenwell's Glory, Silver Invicta.
Permission & Charges No charge is made to fish the lochs but anglers must obtain advance permission before setting out because the area is used for shooting and stalking. For furhter information, contact Sandy Mearns, Rottal Lodge Cottage, Glen Clova, Angus. Tel: 01575 550230; or Airle Estate Office, Cortach, Kiriemuir, Angus. Tel: 01575 540222.

Stonehaven

BERVIE, River
Location & Access Source 45/690850 Outfall 45/834725 Access to the river is from the B967 Inverbervie/Fordoun road.
Commentary A very attractive little spate stream which rises in the Dromtochty Forest to the west and enters the North Sea at the town of Inverbervie after a meandering journey of some 20 miles. There are 19 named pools on the lower section of the river and a detailed map is issued when making a booking. These pools include, working upstream from the sea: Donald's Hole, Little Dam, The Lade Pool, Gutherie's Dam, Long Pool and Castle Pot.
Fish Salmon, sea-trout and brown trout. Catch statistics are not available but probably amount to approximately 30 fish each season, depending upon water levels. Some very large salmon have been caught on the River Bervie in past years: in the 1930's, fish of 48lb and 50lb were landed.
Flies & Tactics The lower river is the most productive fishing area, from the estuary up to where Peattie Burn enters (45/818738) near Allardyce Castle. Sport is dependent upon good water levels and the "management" of a sand bar at the mouth of the stream. Few spring salmon are caught, but brown trout fishing can be excellent in the early months of the season. From July onwards, sea-trout run the stream and may be fished for using worm, spinning lures and artificial fly. The autumn months are the most productive months for salmon. Flies: trout: Black Gnat, Greenwell's Glory, Wickham's Fancy; sea-trout: Black Pennell, Peter Ross, Teal Blue & Silver; for salmon: small Silver Wilkinson, Stoat's Tail, Hairy Mary and sea-trout flies; lures: brown & gold Devon minnows, spoons and Rapalas.
Permission & Charges The Area Office, Church Street, Inverbervie, Kincardineshire, DD10 0RU Tel: 01561 361255 and Leisure Centre, Kirkburn, Inverbie Tel: 01561 361182. Cost: £2 per rod per day. Fishing between Midnight and 5am is prohibited. Night fishing is not allowed until 1st June. No fishing is allowed before 8am on Mondays. Permits to fish on the foreshore must be obtained in advance of fishing from Joseph Johnston & Sons (see River North Esk entry).

CARRON, Water See Cowie Water.

COWIE, Water
Location & Access Source 45/734866 Outfall 45/875862 Access to the river is from the A957 Stonehaven/Crathes road.
Commentary The river rises to the south of Monluth Hill (375m) from the Well of Monluth and flows east through the Forest of Fetteresso to reach the North Sea at the town of Stonehaven. Its neighbour, little Carron Water, enters Stonehaven Bay just to the south and both streams offer good fishing in the right water conditions. Stonehaven is a very attractive and popular sea-side town and there is plenty to keep non-fishing members of your party amused, including a visit to one of Scotland's most dramatic castles, Dunnottor, which lies to the south of the town.
Fish Salmon and sea-trout. Upwards of 100 sea-trout and 20 salmon may be taken from Cowie Water in a good year. Carron Water is not so productive but the Stonehaven & District Angling Club, who manage both streams, are currently engaged upon an improvement programme for Carron Water.
Flies & Tactics Spinning is allowed in spate conditions, but best results generally come from fly-fishing. The pools are easily accessible and a single-handed rod will cope with most eventualities. Night fishing can be excellent, particularly during the summer months, depending upon the level of your skill and stealth in presenting the fly to your quarry. The most productive pool on Cowie Water is perhaps the Estuary Pool but there are a further 5 pools available to visitors which, in the right conditions, can be just as user-friendly. Flies: try small patterns of Teal Blue & Silver, Stoat's Tail, Peter Ross, Black Pennell, Hairy Mary.
Permission & Charges Contact: David's Sport Shop, 31 Market Square, Stonehaven, Kincardineshire. Tel: 01569 762239. Visitor permits are available from 1st June until 30 September and cost in the order of £7 per rod per day. The Secretary of the Stonehaven & District Angling Club is David Macdonald, 93 Forest Park, Stonehaven, Kincardineshire AB39 2FF. Tel: 01569 764617.

CROSS REFERENCE On OS Map 45, Stonehaven, with the exception of Cowie Water and Carron Water, all the waters depicted on OS Map 45 which lie to the north of the easting gridline 80 are described on OS Map 38.

FASQUE, Lake
Location & Access 45/642746 Fasque Lake lies within the grounds of the Fasque Estate. Approach from the B974 Fettercarin/Stachan road and turn west 1mile north from Fettercairn.
Commentary An artificial lake constructed in 1840 and

extending to approximately 15 acres. Unnamed on the OS Map, Fasque Lake is an ornamental addition to the fields and gardens surround Fasque House, the home of the Gladstone family. The setting is magnificent and there is the added advantage of being able to send non-fishing members of your clan on a tour of the house and grounds whilst you go fishing.

Fish Stocked with brown trout and rainbow trout. The average weight of fish is in the order of 1lb but fish of up to and over 5lb in weight are by no means uncommon.

Flies & Tactics Boat fishing only and fish may encountered everywhere, from the middles to the margins. There is a bag limit of 3 fish per rod per day but trout of over 3lb 8oz, caught after the limit has been reached may be retained.

Permission & Charges Peter Gladstone, Fasque Estate, Estate Office, Fasque, Fettercarin, Kincardineshire. Tel: 01561 340202. Cost from £25 per rod per day. Fishing is in the hands of a local syndicate but casual lets are sometimes available. The estate also have a number of comfortable self-catering cottages.

LUTHER WATER See River North Esk.

NORTH ESK, River
Location & Access Source 44/343801 Outfall 45/740625 The river is easily accessible from public roads which margin both banks of the stream.

Commentary The last 10 miles of the River North Esk, shown on OS Map 45 (see also OS Map 44) flow through through well-cultivated agricultural land. The West Water, the most significant tributary of the river, meets the North Esk just to the north of Stracathro Hospital (45/623660) and this tributary also offers the chance of sport for visiting anglers. Cruick Water enters 1/2 a mile downstream from Stracathro, and Luther Water, from the Howe of Mearns, enters near Bridgend (45/660663). The principal fishing beats, downstream from Edzell, are: Stracathro, Inglismaldie, Pert, Balmakewan, Gallery, Hatton, Kirktonhill, Canterland, Craigo, and Morphie Dyke.

Fish The River North Esk produces approximately 1,000 salmon and grilse each season. The West Water averages approximately 80 fish per season, depending upon water conditions. Luther Water is of small significance as a fishery although a few fish are taken most seasons. Sea-trout are also caught, although not in such large numbers as are taken from the South Esk.

Flies & Tactics A double-handed rod is required when fishing the lower River North Esk, particularly in the early months of the season. Spring fishing, from opening day (16th February) onwards, can be excellent: February 1996 produced fish of 16lb 8oz and 15lb 8oz and a fish of 17lb which was caught by Derek Strachan on the Canterland Beat. Canterland has 9 named pools including Bridge Pool, Peter's Pot and Logie; The Galllery Beat has 11 named pools., including the famous Laird's Cast and the Hatton Pool. Most spring fish are taken by spinning (Black and Gold Devon minnows do great damage) and spinning is allowed up until 30th April, but fly can be just as effective. West Water has attractive holding pools and glides throughout it length and the Brechin Angling Club have access to 9 miles of fishing on this delightful spate stream. Flies: Garry Dog, Willie Gunn, Hairy Mary, Blue Charm, Shrimp Fly, Green Highlander.

Permission & Charges For the Brechin Angling Club waters contact: G Carroll, 15 Church Street, Brechin, Angus. Tel: 01356 625700. Mr Carroll has expert knowledge of most of the fishing in the area. Cost: West Water, February to August £10 per rod per day, September/October £17 per rod per day. Stracathro: Careston Estate, Estate Office, Brae of Pert, Laurencekirk, Kincardineshire AB30 1Q. Rods on Stracathro may sometimes be available during the season. Cost: up to approximately £2,000 per week, depending upon time of year (4 rods). Caterland & Kinnaber Beats: Joseph Johnston & Sons, 3 America Street, Montrose DD10 8DR. Tel: 01674 672666; Kinnaber,February & March, £70 per rod per day, April, £50 per day (Summer and autumn prices not available at time of writing); Canterland, February, March, April, £35 per rod per day, May-august, £25 per rod per day, September, £60 per rod per day, October, £65 per rod per day (all exclusive of VAT). For information on other beats, contact: Joseph Johnston & Sons (see above); Messrs Savills, 12 Clerk Street, Brechin, Angus. Tel: 01356 622187.

PRIVATE WATERS DUN'S DISH Loch (45/648610); ST JAMES'S Lochs (45/743711)

SAUGH, Loch
Location & Access 45/676788 Approach from the B974 Fettercarin/Strachan road at Clatterin Brig (45/665782). Follow the minor road east for 1 mile to reach the loch.

Commentary Loch Saugh lies adjacent to the road through Strath Finella from Clatterin Brig to Auchenblae. The loch is 1/2 mile long by 100yds wide, sheltered to the east be Strathfinella Hill (414m) and to the east by Birnie Hill (416m). The Brechin Angling Club manage the water and Loch Saugh is a popular venue with both local and with visiting anglers.

Fish The angling club stock Loch Saugh with brown trout. Average weight, 1lb 4oz..

Flies & Tactics Bank fishing only and no one place is really any more productive than another. Avoid wading and offer them: Black Zulu, Grouse & Claret, Dunkeld.

Permission & Charges Drumtochty Arms Hotel, The Square, Auchenblae, Kincardineshire. Tel: 01561 320210; Ramsay Arms Hotel, Laurencekirk, Tel: 01561 340334; G Caroll, Tackle Shop, 15 Church Street, Brechin, Angus. Tel: 01356 625700. cost: £10 per rod per day. There is a bag limit of 4 fish per rod per day.

WEST WATER See River North Esk.

Coll and Tiree

A'BHAIGH, Lochan See Loch Anlaimh.
A'CHROTHA, Loch See Loch Anlaimh.
A'GHRUIBE, Loch See Loch Anlaimh.
A'MHILL AIRD, Loch See Loch Anlaimh.

Coll and Tiree — OS Maps 46

A'MHILL, Loch See Loch Anlaimh.
A'PHUILL, Loch See Loch Bhasapoll.
AIRIGH MEALL BHREIDE, Loch See Loch Anlaimh.
AN DUIN, Loch See Loch Anlaimh.
AN T-SAGAIRT, Loch See Loch Anlaimh.

ANLAIMH, Loch

Location & Access 46/188558. Access is from the B8070. Park at Acha (46/186550) and follow the outlet burn north to reach the loch after an easy walk of half a mile.

Commentary This is perhaps the best of the trout lochs on the Island of Coll; a sparsely-populated Hebridean island where crofting is the main activity. Coll is a wonderful family holiday location: glorious, deserted, white-sand beaches, ancient Pictish forts and a dramatic ruined castle at Breachacha Cas (46/160539). There are a number of other trout lochs on the island, most of which contain excellent stocks of very pretty little trout: Loch nan Cinneachan (46/188566), immediately to the north of Loch Anlaimh, roadside Loch Ronard (South) (46/204555), little Loch Boidheach (46/202568), Loch Cliad (46/209587) the largest loch on the island, Loch an Duin (46/212578), and Loch Airigh Meall Bhreide (46/216565) to the west of Arinigour Farm. All these waters may be accessed from either the B8070 in the south or from the B8071 to the north. The north end of the island also holds more than 20 named and unnamed lochs and lochans and these are approached from the B8072 on the north-west coast or from the B8071 to the north of Arinigour, the principal township on Coll. The most remote of these waters lie along the north-east coastline and getting to them will involve you in a 5 mile round trip, there and back. However, the effort involved in reaching them will be more than rewarded, not only by the quality of the fishing, but also by the supreme beauty of the landscape along the way. Loch Fada (46/256620) is the best of these waters. The others include: tiny Lochan a'Bhaigh (46/252631), Loch a'Ghruibe (46/257626), the unnamed lochan at 46/265615 by Meall h-Iolaire (79m), Loch Ghillecaluim (46/258610) and its neighbours, Loch an t-Sagairt (46/2516100 and Loch a'Mhill (46/257604). South from these waters, on Druim Fishaig, are a number of other lochs which are well worth exploring: Loch na Cloiche (46/241611), linked to Loch Ronard (North) (46/238609), and Loch a'Mhill Aird (46/231609) to the west. The moor south from Loch Ronard (North) is scattered with a series of small, unnamed lochans. Loch a'Chrotha (46/236593) and its satellite lochans is best approached from the B8071. Arrange a boat passage across sea-Loch Eatharna from Arinigour to ease your way to Loch Urbhaig (46/231578) and Loch nan Geadh (46/239582).

Fish Island of Coll trout are not large. They average in the order of 8oz, but there are larger fish as well: the unnamed lochan at Meall nain Muc (46/240570) produced a fine specimen of 1lb 8oz in 1996. Attractive though it is, Loch Cliad is perhaps the least producitve of the Coll lochs.

Flies & Tactics All the lochs noted above are infrequently fished. Indeed, some may never see an artificial fly from one season to the next. Consequently, the great joy of fishing here is that nothing is absolute in terms of size or numbers of fish. Always be prepared for the unexpected. Bank fishing only, but the lochs are all of modest size and they are easily covered from the shore. Wading is generally safe and comfortable but you should carry a compass and map in case of bad weather. Flies: Loch Ordie, Soldier Palmer, Dunkeld.

Permission & Charges The islanders are pretty relaxed about access to their fishing but it is important that you always seek prior permission before walking across crofting lands. For further advice and information contact: K G Oliphant, The Isle of Coll Hotel, Arinigour, Argyll. Tel: 01879 230334. Fishing is generally without charge to anglers staying on the island.

BHASAPOLL, Loch

Location & Access 46/972470. Easily accessible from the B8068 road near Clachan Mor.

Commentary Loch Bhasapoll lies at the north-west end of the fertile Island of Tiree, often referred to as 'the granary of the highlands'. The island is famous for the fine quality of its horses, for its variegated coloured marble and for having more hours of sunshine each year then almost anywhere else in Scotland. The only other loch of any fishing consequence is Loch a'Phuill (46/958420) to the west of Balemartine. The other waters on the island, near Scarinish and Kirkapol, are all very shallow and, generally, fishless. The local angling club have made attempts at various times to improve the quality of these lochs but with little lasting benefit to anything other than local herons and otters. The island is unique in its wildlife and in its scenery. Tiree is the perfect location for a splendid Hebridean family holiday.

Fish Excellent quality brown trout which average 1lb and, but infrequently, sea-trout. The heaviest trout taken in recent years weighed 3lb 8oz.

Flies & Tactics Loch Bhasapoll fishes equally well from either boat or bank, and wading on both these lochs is safe and comfortable. On Loch Bhasapoll, the south shore and the south-west bay by Kilmoluag are the most productive areas. On Loch a'Phuill, concentrate your efforts down the west bank, about 100/150 yards out from the shore. Flies: Soldier Palmer, Woodcock & Hare-lug, Silver Butcher. Dry fly also produces results.

Permission & Charges Contact: Royal Bank of Scotland, Scarinish, Isle of Tiree, Argyll. Tel: 01879 220307. Cost: bank fishing, £5 per rod per day. Weekly, £20, Two weeks, £30, Monthly, £40.

BOIDHEACH, Loch See Loch Anlaimh.
CLIAD, Loch See Loch Anlaimh.
FADA, Loch See Loch Anlaimh.
GHILLE-CALUIM, Loch See Loch Anlaimh.
NA CLOICHE, Loch See Loch Anlaimh.
NAN CINNEACHAN, Loch See Loch Anlaimh.
NAN GEADH, Loch See Loch Anlaimh.
RONARD (North), Loch See Loch Anlaimh.
RONARD (South), Loch See Loch Anlaimh.
URBHAIG, Loch See Loch Anlaimh.

Tobermory

A'CHUMHAINN, Sea-Loch See River Bellart.

A'GHURRABAIN, Lochan
Location & Access 47/520538. This lochan (known locally as Aros Lake) lies 1 mile to the south of Tobermory, adjacent to the A848 Salen road.
Commentary A put-and-take fishery in an attractive woodland setting, easily accessible.
Fish Regularly stocked with rainbow trout. Fish of up to and over 9lb are sometimes taken. The average weight of trout is in the order of 2lb.
Flies & Tactics Bank fishing only and clearings have been cut in the surrounding woods to allow access to the bank. Flies: reservoir lures seem to be most favoured, designs such as Whisky Fly, Baby Doll, Ace of Spades, dog nobblers and muddler minnows various.
Permission & Charges See Loch Frisa entry.

A'MHADAIDH RIABHAICH, Lochan See Loch Mudle.
A'TUAIDH, Lochan See Loch Mudle.
ACHATENY Water See Loch Mudle.
AN IME, Lochan See Loch Mudle.

AN TORR, Loch
Location & Access 47/451530. Park at the south end of the loch at 47/453525 on the B8073 Tobermory/Dervaig road.
Commentary This attractive, easily accessible, loch drains north via the Mingary Burn to sea-Loch Mingary. A forest on the west shore, in Glen Gorm, often provides shelter in strong winds as do the heights of Sgulan Breac (231m) to the east.
Fish A large population of wild brown trout which average 8oz in weight. After heavy rain there is also the possibility of an occasional sea-trout.
Flies & Tactics An ideal beginners' loch, either from the boat or from the bank. Trout rise and are taken from all over this half mile long water so cast with confidence, from the middle to the margins. Offer them: Soldier Palmer, March Brown, Silver Butcher.
Permission & Charges See Loch Peallach entry.

AROS, River
Location & Access Source 47/511425 Outfall 47/560448. The river is accessible from the minor road through Glen Aros linking Aros in the east to Dervaig in the north-west.
Commentary The river rises from Loch Suil Bo on the slopes of Beinn nan Carn (333m) and flows north for 2 miles before swinging east down Glen Aros to reach the sea after 3 miles near Aros Castle. The Ledmore Burn, the outflow stream from Loch Frisa (see separate entry), joins the river at Achadh nan Each (47/522454) and upstream from this junction, on the Tenga Beat of the river, there are 2 substantial waterfalls which can impede the passage of the larger fish.
Fish Salmon and sea-trout. Salmon average 6lb/7lb, sea-trout, 2lb. The largest salmon taken from the river was a fish of 45lb, caught in the Ash Tree Pool by Edinburgh angler, James Greenhill, in 1911. Migratory fish numbers have declined in recent years but the river can still produce approximately 80 salmon and a similar number of sea-trout, given good water levels. The estuary of the Aros River can also produce good sport with sea-trout.
Flies & Tactics A classic spate stream and the all-important tactic is to be on the river after heavy rain. The lower beats, below the Ledmore Burn junction, are fly only, the Tenga Beat allows worm fishing and spinning in high water. This can often be a turbulent stream and exciting to fish. The best known pools include: Yellow Pool, Garden Pool, Bucket Pool, Ash Tree Pool and Corner Pool. Flies: Hairy Mary, General Practitioner, Silver Stoat's Tail, Willie Gunn, Garry Dog, Green Highlander.
Permission & Charges Tackle & Books, 11 Main Street, Tobermory, Isle of Mull, Argyll. Tel: 01688 302336; Fax: 01688 302140. Costs: Aros River estuary, £4 per rod per day, River Aros, up to June 30th, £10 per rod per day, thereafter, £14 per rod per day. The owners of the river may also be able to offer comfortable self-catering accommodation with the fishing. For details, contact: Mrs Ursula Bradley, Old Byre, Dervaig, Isle of Mull. Tel: 01688 400229. Mrs Bradley also has bank fishing rights on Loch Frisa. Mr & Mrs C Scott, Kilmore House, Kilmore, by Oban, Isle of Mull, Argyll PA34 4XT. Tel: 01631 770369. Traditional, well-equipped cottages at Glenaros Farm with fishing on the Aros River.

BA, River
Location & Access Source 47/570375 Outfall 47/537413. The river is adjacent to and accessible from the B8073 and B8035 roads.
Commentary The River Ba is a short (2.2 miles long) spate stream that rises in Loch Ba and flows into the head of sea-Loch na Keal near Killichronan House Hotel. The loch itself is of considerable proportions, being 3 miles in length by up to half a mile wide. The principal feeder streams are the Glencannel River (47/589363) which flows in at the south end of the loch, and the River Clachaig (47/571372) which enters from the south-east shore at the ruins of Knochantivore. Both these streams are sanctuary areas and neither is fished. Ben More (966m), Mull's highest mountain, towers to the south of Loch Ba, whilst Ben Talaidh (761m) guards the north shore.
Fish Salmon, sea-trout and, in the loch, brown trout. The system produces in the order of 80 salmon and perhaps 150 sea-trout, although in recent years the number of sea-trout running the river has declined drastically. Salmon average in the order of 7lb, sea-trout, 2lb. However, some much heavier fish have been taken, including a salmon of 22lb 8oz. Some very large sea-trout have been caught on Loch Ba, including a fish of 19lb, and double-figure sea-trout used to be the rule, rather than the exception. Sadly, this is no longer the case, although large sea-trout are still occasionally caught.
Flies & Tactics The river is easy to fish and there is no need to wade. A single-handed rod will suffice and the key to success is being in the right place at the right

Tobermory — OS Map 47

time, that is after heavy rain. There are no substantial barriers on the river to impede the progress of migratory fish, other than poor water conditions, and the most noted pools include: Sea Pool, Drumlang, Oak Tree, The Glide and the Corner Pool. The loch fishes best from a boat and dapping can be very effective. The south end of the loch produces the best of the sport, particularly in the bay where the River Clachaig enters and south through the large bays at Rubha Gainmhich (47/575370), An Dubh Aird (47/582366) and at the mouth of the Glencannel River. Flies: on the river, offer Dusty Miller, Garry Dog, Goat's Toe, Stoat's Tail, Willie Gunn; on the loch, dap large black, red or orange patterns, Loch Ordie, daddy-long-legs, or fish wet fly patterns such as: Black Pennell, Mallard & Claret, Peter Ross.
Permission & Charges Fishing on the river and the loch may be obtained by application to: John Lindsay, Knock House, Gruline, Aros, Isle of Mull, Argyll. Tel: 01680 300356. Day tickets are available, but tenants of the estate lodge have fishing priority. Expect to pay in the order of £20 per rod per day on the river. A boat, complete with outboard motor and the services of an experienced gillie, costs £75 per day (2 rods fishing). The river is also fished by guests staying at: Killiechronan House Hotel, Aros, Isle of Mull PA72 6JU. Tel: 01680 300403; Fax: 01680 300463. Cost: £8 per rod per day.

BEINNE BRICE, Lochain See Loch Mudle.

BELLART, River
Location & Access Source 47/478433. Outfall 47/432514 Access to the river is from the minor road from Aros in the south to Dervaig in the north.
Commentary An attractive little spate river which rises from Lochan Dubha on the north slopes of Beinn na Drise (424m) and flows north for a distance of 10 miles to reach the sea in sea-Loch a'Chumhainn.
Fish Salmon and sea-trout in the river and in the estuary. Approximately 10 salmon and 20 sea-trout may be taken during a good season, depending upon water conditions.
Flies & Tactics Sport is entirely dependent upon heavy rain. The river is narrow and there is no need to wade. Use a single-handed rod. The best chance of sport is on a high tide after heavy rain in little Loch na Cuilce (47/432515); an extension of the stream just before it flows under the B8073 and into the sea. Flies: trout patterns work well: March Brown, Mallard & Claret, Greenwell's Glory, Black Pennell, Peter Ross.
Permission & Charges Contact: Tackle & Books, 11 Main Street, Tobermory, Isle of Mull, Argyll. Tel: 01688 302336. Cost: up to June 30th, £8 per rod per day, thereafter, £10 per rod per day.

CARNAIN AN AMIS, Loch See Loch Peallach.
CHOINNICH MOR, Lochan See Loch Mudle.
CLACH NA BOITEIG, Lochan See Loch Mudle.
CLACHAIG, River See River Ba.
CREAG NAN CON, Lochan See Loch Mudle.
CROSS REFERENCE The waters on the Island of Coll are described on OS Map 46.

FRISA, Loch
Location & Access 47/490485. The loch is accessed via a forestry road which margins the east bank.
Commentary This is the largest and deepest freshwater loch on Mull, 5 miles north/south by over half a mile wide. The loch drops to a depth of more than 70m between Lettermore (47/496485) on the east shore and Coille na Dubh Leitire (47/484484) on the west shore. The surrounding hills act as a wind tunnel and Loch Frisa can be a wild place on a stormy day.
Fish Excellent stocks of brown trout, some of which are descended from a Loch Leven strain of fish. Although the overall average weight is modest, 10oz, there are some huge specimens lurking in the depths and trout of up to and over 5lb are by no means uncommon. There is also the chance of an occasional salmon or sea-trout.
Flies & Tactics Bank fishing only and wading is dangerous. The north end of the loch, where the water is shallower, is a good place to begin, and in the vicinity of the small islands, Eilean Dubh, at 47/480490. The large, sheltered bay at 47/488479 can also generally be relied upon to produce a brace for supper. Spinning, bubble-float and bait fishing, as well as fly fishing, is allowed. Flies: Ke-He, Grouse & Claret, Kingfisher Butcher.
Permission & Charges Tackle & Books, 11 Main Street, Tobermory, Isle of Mull, Argyll. Tel: 01688 302336; Fax: 01688 302140. Also, Archibald Brown & Son, 21 Main Street, Tobermory, Isle of Mull, Argyll. Tel: 01688 302020; Forest Enterprise, Aros, Isle of Mull, Argyll. Tel; 01680 300346. Cost: £3 per rod per day.

GLENCANNEL, River See River Ba.
LEDMORE, Burn See Aros River.
MEADHOIN, Loch See Loch Peallach.

MUDLE, Loch
Location & Access 47/544660. Loch Mudle lies immediately to the east of the B8007 road between Ardslignish (47/562616) and Kilchoan (47/490638) on the Ardnamurchan Peninsula, the most westerly point of Mainland Britain.
Commentary Loch Mudle is the largest of the Ardnamurchan lochs, three-quarters of a mile north/south by up to a quarter wide (87 acres) draining north via Alt an Doire Dharaich Burn and Achatene Water into the Sound of Sleat. The views from the surrounding hills and extinct volcanoes, are amongst the most dramatic in Scotland: the isles to the north, Skye, Rhum, Muck, & Eigg. Coll, Tiree and Outer Hebrides to the west and Mull south. A rover/camping permit is offered which will allow anglers who enjoy an adventure with their sport the opportunity to explore the lochs. Find the inlet stream at the north-east corner of the loch and climb over Beinn na Mointch Leathainn (193m) to locate the little unnamed lochan and Lochan na Carraige (47/569663). Having fished Lochan nan Sioman trek north west along the prominent ridge via the sanctuary lochan Creag nan Con (47/561674) to lochan Na Tudia (47/559678). Lochan an Ime (47/558684) the

OS Maps 47-48 — Iona & Ben More

smallest lochan holds some of the best wild brown trout. Finish by walking back down the forest road to Mudle.
Fish All the lochs have wild brown trout which average 8oz though 14 fish of between 3 and 4.5lbs were taken in 1995 - with 7 in 96. Loch Mudle also has sea-trout and the occasional salmon.
Flies & Tactics The estate will give anglers directions and guidance before they set off, and it has also produced a comprehensive leaflet describing the fishings. Apart from loch Mhdaidh Riabhaich, where all legal methods may be used, the rest of the fishing is by fly only, using barbless hooks. This is wild country and if you decide to visit the more remote waters you should be well-dressed and well-versed in the use of compass and map in the event of bad weather. A boat is available on the Mudle. Many of these little lochs are steep-sided and difficult to fish so do not be tempted to wade. Try: Blue Zulu, Woodcock & hare-lug, Silver Butcher. On calm evenings, Dry fly can work well - as can the midges - be prepared.
Permission & Charges Contact: N J Peake, Sithean Mor, Achnaha, Kilchoan, Argyll. Fax: 01972 510212 for details. Bank day permit £6. Some of the lochs noted above are bird sanctuaries. Details of these will be given when you purchase your permit.

NA CARRAIGE, Loch See Loch Mudle.
NA CUILCE, Loch See River Bellart.
NA GRUAGAICH, Lochan See Loch Mudle.
NAN DEARCAG, Lochan See Loch Mudle.
NAN GILLEAN, Lochan See Loch Mudle.
NAN SIAMAN, Lochan See Loch Mudle.

PEALLACH, Loch (Bottom Mishnish)
Location & Access 47/486533. Immediately adjacent to the B8073 Tobermory/Dervaig road.
Commentary This is the most northerly of an inter-linked chain of 3 lochs which are known locally as the Mishnish Lochs. The other 2 waters are: Loch Meadhoin (47/479527) (Middle Mishnish) and Loch Carnain an Amis (47/470523) (Top Mishnish). The complete system extends for 2 miles east/west and is up to 300 yds wide.
Fish Brown trout which average 10oz/12oz. The lochs are managed by the Tobermory Angling Association who stock them with fingerling trout at regular intervals. Good numbers of fish of up to 2lb are taken, as well as the occasional larger trout of up to 4lb in weight.
Flies & Tactics These are shallow lochs, between 2ft and 10ft in depth. Consequently, they are weedy and this provides an abundance of food upon which the residents thrive. In order to avoid being broken in the weeds, use at least 4lb breaking-strain nylon. Boat and bank fishing is allowed and Loch Peallach probably holds the largest fish - and the greatest weed growth - but, generally, trout rise and may caught throughout the whole system, with equal facility, from both boat and bank alike. Flies: Soldier Palmer, Teal & Green, Silver Butcher.
Permission & Charges See Loch Frisa entry. Costs: Bank fishing, £8 per rod per day. Boat hire, in addition to the bank permit, £12 per boat per day (2 anglers). Minimum age for hiring a boat is 16 years, outboard motors are not allowed. Lifejackets are available for hire when booking.

PRIVATE WATERS The hill lochs of Kilninan and Kilmore, between Loch Firsa (see separate entry) west to the sea, are private. Also: AIRDE BEINN, Lochans 47/472538; NA GUALLNE DUIBHE, Lochan 47/529521; NA CRITHE, Loch 47/514510; DEARG, Lochan 47/489509; CAOL, Lochan 47/515505; KILLUNDINE, River 47/580500; CHROIS BHEINN, Lochan 47/589546; GHLEANN LOCHA, Lochan 47/463639; DRUIM NA CLAISE, Lochan 47/425645; AN AODAIN, Lochan 47/459660; NA CRANNAIG, Lochan 47/465658; CAORACH, Loch 47/433656; GRIGADALE, Loch 47/431669; AN DOBHRAIN, Lochan 47/479701.
SUIL BO, Loch See Aros River.

Iona and Ben More

A'PHUILL, Loch See Loch Assapol entry.

ARM, Loch
Location & Access 48/419218. Approach from the A849 Pennycross/Bunessan road. Park at 48/414233 and follow the outlet stream south up Beinn Lighe (190m) to reach the loch after an easy walk of three-quarters of a mile.
Commentary Splendid hill-loch fishing, wonderful, panoramic, views over the Island of Ulva to Staffa and the Treshnish Isles. There are 2 additional lochs in the vicinity which may also be visited: tiny Loch a'Phuill (48/424221) and, 1 mile due east from Loch Arm, on the west slope of Cruachan Min (376m), Loch nan Learg (48/438219).
Fish Attractive little brown trout, although Loch Arm occasionally produces fish of up to 2lb in weight.
Flies & Tactics Comfortable bank fishing all the way. Do, however, take along a compass and map and be properly dressed to cope with any sudden change in the weather. Flies: Black Pennell, Mallard & Claret, Silver Invicta.
Permission & Charges James McKeand, Scoor House, Bunessan, Isle of Mull, Argyll. Tel: 01681 700297. Cost £5 per rod per day.

ASSAPOL, Loch
Location & Access 48/405206. Loch Assapol lies to the south of Bunessan in the Ross of Mull and is approached from the A849 by a lochside road which leaves the main road at 48/384219.
Commentary One of the most attractive lochs on the Ross of Mull, rich in wildlife and set amidst outstanding scenery. The loch is three-quarters of a mile north/south by up to 500 yds wide. From Scoor (48/419191), at the end of the road, tracks lead across fertile green pastures to marvellous cliff-top walks, cliffs which support an outstanding array of wild-

315

flowers and lead to hidden coves and beaches where solitude and peace is assured.
Fish Salmon, sea-trout and brown trout. Loch Assapol used to be one of the most prolific fisheries on Mull but, sadly, in recent years, the numbers of migratory fish reaching the loch has greatly diminished. Sea-trout are becoming increasingly scarce, 30/40 are taken in a good year. Brown trout average 8oz, although there are larger fish as well: a few years ago a brown trout of 7lb 8oz was landed.
Flies & Tactics The height of the loch has been raised by 2ft in 1996 by the construction of a weir at the outlet end. Boat fishing offer the best opportunity of sport. Noted fishing areas are: the Burn and the Flats, at the south end of the loch where there is considerable weed growth which provides good shelter for fish; the Wood and Saorphin on the west bank, and the Black Rock at the north-west corner where the loch begins to narrow. Flies: Ke-He, Invicta, Peter Ross.
Permission & Charges James McKeand, Scoor House, Bunessan, Isle of Mull, Agyll. Tel: 01681 700297. James McKeand knows the loch better than almost anyone else and is himself an expert angler. Scoor House also offer visitors comfortable self-catering accommodation linked to fishing on the loch. Cost: bank fishing, £5 per rod per day, a boat costs £8 per boat per day; also, the Assapol House Hotel, Bunessan, Isle of Mull, Argyll. Tel: 01681 700258; Fax: 01681 700445.

BEACH, River See Coladoir River entry.

COLADOIR, River
Location & Access Source 48/585268 Outfall 48/544290. The river is easily accessed from the A849 Lochdonhead/Bunessan road.
Commentary This short, spate stream, rises from Loch Fuaron, a substantial water of half a mile long by up to a quarter of a mile wide. The river is also fed by a number of streams which flow in from the south slopes of Ben More (966m) at Coire Clachach (49/615307). The River Coladoir flows north to Craig (48/585295) before swinging west for 3 miles to enter the sea in the shallow, enclosed, estuary of An Lethdunn. Two other, smaller, spate streams enter sea-Loch Scradain on the north coast of the Ross of Mull: the Leidle River (48/519264) and Beach River (48/465243). Although they used to give sport with sea-trout in their tidal reaches in times past, few fish are caught today.
Fish Salmon and sea-trout. The system produces in the order of 20 salmon and up to 30 sea-trout in a good year, but sport is entirely dependent upon heavy rainfall to induce the fish to run the river.
Flies & Tactics Pray for rain. If your prayers are answered, then great sport can be had on a falling spate using light tackle. Otherwise, hike out from Craig to bank fish Loch Fuaron for brown trout. The Pennyghael Estate has stocked a number of the small lochans above Glen Leidle and these can also offer a decent alternative to glowering at a dry river. Flies: trout patterns work well. Try: Grouse & Claret, Goat's Toe, Black Pennell, Silver Butcher, March Brown, Soldier Palmer.
Permission & Charges Fishing permission may be obtained from: John Lindsay, Knock House, Gruline, Aros, Isle of Mull, Argyll. Tel: 01680 300356; Pennyghael Estate, Pennyghael, by Oban, Isle of Mull, Argyll. Tel: 01681 704232. Expect to pay in the order of £20 per rod per day.

CROSS REFERENCES Loch BA (See OS Map 47); River BA (See OS Map 47); River CLACHAIG (See OS Map 47); GLENCANNEL River (See OS Map 47); Loch FRISA (See OS Map 47); AROS River (See OS Map 47); AROS Lake (See OS Map 47); FORSA River (See OS Map 49)
FUARON, Loch See Coladoir River entry.
LEIDLE, River See Coladoir River entry.
NAN LEARG, Loch See Loch Assapol entry.

POIT NA H-I, Loch
Location & Access 48/315225. Easily-accessible from the A849 Bunessan/Fionnphort road which margins the north shore of the loch.
Commentary A very attractive loch on the Ross of Mull, close to the ferry to the Island of Iona. The loch is triangular in shape, three-quarters of a mile north/south by up to 600 yds wide at the north end.
Fish Modest little brown trout which average 8oz/10oz and the occasional sea-trout.
Flies & Tactics Boat fishing is the most comfortable way to explore this loch, although bank fishing can be every bit as productive. Begin in the vicinity of the 3 small islets at the north end and work south down the east shoreline to the larger island where the loch begins to narrow. Offer: Soldier Palmer, Invicta, Silver March Brown.
Permission & Charges James Campbell, Fidden Farm, Fionnphort, Isle of Mull, Argyll. Tel: 01681 700427. Cost: Bank fishing, £5 per rod per day, boats £15 per boat per day.

PRIVATE WATERS FRAING, Loch 48/54525; NA GEIGE, Loch 48/522233; AN SGALAIN, Loch 48/345190; MOR ARDALANISH, Loch 48/363191.

Oban and East Mull

A'BHARRAIN, Loch See Soir Loch entry.
A'GHLEANNAIN, Loch See Loch Don entry.
ABHAINN CONNICH, River See Loch Uisge entry.
AIRDEGLAIS, Loch See Lussa River entry.

AIRIGH-SHAMHRAIDH, Lochan
Location & Access 49/953208. Approach as for Soir Loch (see separate entry) but at the quarry continue on down the hill to park at Musdale Farm (49/935220). Walk south-east from the farm on the line of the outlet-stream from the loch to reach Airighshamhraidh after a stiff hike of 1.5 miles.
Commentary If you enjoy wild scenery and complete

seclusion then this lovely little lochan will more than meet your expectations. The lochan lies on the moor to the south of the black crags of Beinn Dearg (482m). More than a good chance of seeing peregrine and buzzard.
Fish No glass-case specimens here, but very attractive trout which give a good account of themselves.
Flies & Tactics The lochan covers an area of approximately 12 acres and it is comfortably fished from the bank. On your way home, walk north round the crags to have a passing cast in the small, unnamed, pond in the bealach at 49/956214. Try: Loch Ordie, Grouse & Claret, Silver Invicta.
Permission & Charges See Soir Loch entry.

ALINE, River
Location & Access Source 49/661538 Outfall 49/698475. Access is from the A884 Corran/Lochaline road and from a private estate road that margins much of the east bank of the stream.
Commentary The River Aline is fed by two major tributaries, Abhainn a'Ghlinne Ghil (the White Glen) and the Black Water. These streams join the River Aline near Acharn (49/696505) and in high water conditions their force sometimes reverses the flow of the main river back to its source in Loch Arienas. This often means that a spate is prolonged, much to the enhancement of fishing on the lower river. Fishing is divided into 6, 2 rod beats which rotate during the day and rods fish 3 beats each day. The Black Water and the area between the lower falls on the White Glen (49/731499) and the footbridge at Uileann (49/747508) are not fished.
Fish In 1998 only 9 salmon and 48 sea-trout were caught, whereas prior to the advent of fish farming, upwards of 150 salmon and 300 sea-trout could be taken. The estate now have a strict catch-and-release policy.
Flies & Tactics This is one of the most delightful and accessible rivers in the west of Scotland. The water is crystal clear and the pools are well-defined and exciting to fish. Working downstream from the White Glen the most notable of these pools include: Ravens, Buxtons, Oak Tree Pool, Junction Pool, Suspension Bridge Pool, Rock Pool, the Larches and Macs Pool. All the water is easily covered from the bank and there is no need to wade. Best flies are: Green Highlander, Yellow Torrish, Blue Charm, Willie Gunn, Garry Dog.
Permission & Charges Generally let in conjunction with Ardtornish Estate self-catering accommodation (see Loch Arienas entry). Cost: £33 per day for two rods from July until the end of the season in October. £10,00 per day in May and June.

ALLT A'CHORMAIG, River See Loch Scammadale.
ALLT NAN DUBHA, Lochanan See Loch Tearnait.
AN DOIRE DHARAICH, Lochan See Lussa River entry.
AN EILEIN, Loch See Lussa River entry.
AN EILEN, Loch See Lussa River entry.
AN FHAING, Lochan See Loch Tearnait entry.

ARIEANS, Loch
Location & Access 49/685510 Leave the A884 Corran/Lochaline road at 49/696495 just south of Claggan Bridge and drive west on the minor road to reach the loch after 1 mile.
Commentary This easily accessible loch lies in the heart of Morvern, an area of outstanding natural beauty rich in flora and fauna with a wide range of alternative activities to amuse those not inflicted with the disease of angling. The loch is almost 2 miles east/west by up to 1/2 a mile wide and access to the south shore is directly from the minor road noted above. This road continues west to margin the north bank of Loch Doire nam Mart (49/660526). Thereafter, a private road, not accessible to vehicles, leads on to the wonderful sand and shingle beaches surrounding sea-Loch Teacuis in the Rahoy Nature Reserve.
Fish Good numbers of attractive brown trout, some of which reach considerable proportions: the largest trout taken in recent years weighed 6lb 14oz (1997) and a fish of 5lb 4oz was caught in 1998. Loch Doire nam Mart also contains brown trout which average 8oz/10oz in weight, but it has a few specimen fish as well.
Flies & Tactics Boat fishing and bank fishing on Loch Arienas, bank fishing only on Loch Doire nam Mart. There is a fish farm at the east end of Loch Arienas which spoils the ambiance of fishing. The water is very clear and bank fishing from the south shore is comfortable and easy. The north shoreline is best fished from the boat and this is where some of the larger fish are taken, particularly at the outlets of the 8 streamlets that flow in from the heights of Beinn na h-Uamha (464m). Avoid wading on Doire nam Mart, the margins are unstable in some places and it is dangerous to do so. Flies: Black Pennell, Soldier Palmer, Silver Invicta.
Permission & Charges Fishing is generally let in conjunction with Ardtornish Estate self-catering cottages and flats in Ardtornish House, all of which are very comfortable and furnished to a high standard. The diversity of trees, shrubs and plants in the polices of the house are reason enough for visiting Ardtornish, let alone the fishing. Contact: John Montgomery, Ardtornish Estate Office, Morvern, by Oban, Argyll PA34 5XA. Tel: 01967 421288; Fax: 01967 42`211. Web site: www.ardtornish.co.uk; email tourism@ardtornish.co.uk Cost: Accommodation charges on application. Fishing: Bank, £5 per rod per day, boat with outboard motor and fuel (2 rods fishing), £26 per day. Bank fishing on Loch Ternait and other hill lochs is £3.00 per rod per day. A boat is available on Loch Ternait at £8/00 per day (no engine). Visitors staying at the Ardtornish Estate self-catering properties can fish all lochs free, paying only for boat hire. All fishing is strictly fly only. Life jackets are available to estate tenants on receipt of a fully returnable deposit.

BAILE A'GHOBHAINN, Loch
Location & Access 49/850426. The loch lies on the Island of Lismore in Loch Linnhe, between

Oban & East Mull — OS Map 49

Benderloch in the east and Kingairloch to the west. Approach by ferry from Port Appin (49/904455).

Commentary Loch Baile a'Ghobhainn is the largest of the three lochs on the island. The other waters are: Loch Kilcheran (49/828393) and Loch Fiart (49/808375). Lismore is a fertile, green island and the perfect place for an away-from-it-all holiday. There are numerous, near-deserted, beaches for the bucket-and-spade brigade as well as exhilarating coastal walks; including a visit to the ruins of Castle Coeffin (49/854438) and Achadun Castle (49/804393). The modernised Parish Church (49/861435) is also well worth a visit and has the distinction of being the smallest Cathedral in Scotland. In times past it was the seat of the Diocese of Argyll.

Fish Excellent quality brown trout which average 8oz/10oz, but with fish of up to and over 1lb in Loch Baile a'Ghobhainn.

Flies & Tactics It is many years since sea-trout were caught in Lismore, but the fish in Loch Baile Ghobhainn display distinct sea-trout characteristics: small heads, deep-bodied, silvery in colour and with pink flesh. They fight well, as do the more traditional brown trout in the other 2 loch noted above. All the lochs lie adjacent to the main (only) road on the island and are comfortably fished from the bank. Loch Baile a'Ghobhainn is the largest loch, being half a mile north south by up to 150 yds wide. Permission will usually be given if you wish to launch your own boat.

Permission & Charges These lochs are private but permission to fish may be obtained by application to: John Carmichael, 3 Lorn Cottages, Lismore, by Oban, Argyll. Tel: 01631 760211. Generally, no charge is made for fishing.

BEARNACH, Loch See Lussa River entry.
CAOL, Lochan See Loch Tearnait entry.
DOIR NAM MART, Loch See Loch Arieanas entry.
DOIRE A'BHRAGHAID, Lochan See Lochan na Criche.

DON, Sea Loch

Location & Access 49/732333. Approach from the A849 Craignure/Bunessan road at Lochdon. A bridge across Leth-fhonn (49/726329) gives access to the south shore of Loch Don, and to Auchnacraig (49/747301). The north shore of the estuary may be accessed from Lochdon via the road which runs south-east to Gorten (49/746323). Auchnacraig Estate has a number of very comfortable self-catering properties on the south shore of Loch Don and they are the perfect location for a peaceful family holiday amidst outstanding surroundings. The estate also has the fishing rights on Loch a'Ghleannain (49/726314) which is a 15 minute hike south-west from Ardnadrochet Farmhouse (49/731319) on the road to Auchnacraig.

Fish Salmon and sea-trout in the estuary, brown trout in the loch. Migratory fish numbers have diminished in recent years, but a few good sea-trout are taken from the shore most seasons. Loch a'Ghleannain contains wild brown trout and a strain of Loch Leven trout and they average 8oz in weight.

Flies & Tactics The estuary extends from the private pier at Grass Point (49/748310), where the estate has converted the old ferryhouse into self-catering accommodation for 12 guests, east to the main road, a distance of approximately 2 miles. The loch then turns south into the 1 mile long, narrow, channel of Leth-fhonn. Fishing in the estuary is by fly only and the best time to attack is after heavy rain, where the tide and freshwater meet, or on either side of high tides. Loch a'Ghleannain, which covers an area of 30 acres, is easily fished from the shore, although as boat is also available. Flies: Black Zulu, Soldier Palmer, Peter Ross.

Permission & Charges Contact: Colonel M P dee Klee OBE, Auchnacraig Estate, Lochdon, Isle of Mull, Argyll. PA64 6AP.Tel: 01680 812486; Fax: 01680 812382. Prices on application.

DUBH, Loch (Seil) See Loch Scammadale entry.

DUBH MOR, Loch

Location & Access 49/949390. Approach from the B854 Barcaldine/Inversragan road. Park at 49/964404 and follow the forest track south west for 2 miles to reach the loch.

Commentary A pleasant walk with fishing, rather than a serious fishing expedition. The loch (also known as Glen Dubh Reservoir) is impounded as a water supply and drains north via the Learg Abhainn burn down Gleann Salach to the sea in Loch Creran.

Fish This is a Forestry Commission loch and, in the past, it has been stocked with rainbow trout. Few rainbow trout remain and the brown trout population now breed naturally and are the dominant species. They average 8oz with the occasional fish of up to 1lb in weight.

Flies & Tactics Bank fishing only and wading is not advisable. The loch covers an area of approximately 10 acres and fish may be taken from all round the shoreline. Try: Black Pennell, March Brown, Alexandra. The mouth of the river used to produce great sport with sea-trout, but, sadly, these days have long-since gone, probably due to the ill effects of factory salmon-farming in Loch Creran.

Permission & Charges J Lyon, Appin View, Barcaldine, Argyll. Tel: 01631 720469. Cost: £3.00 per rod per day.

DUBHA, Lochan See Soir Loch entry.
DUBHA, Lochanan See Loch Tearnait entry.
EUCHAR, River See Loch Scammadale entry.
FEOCHAN BHEAG, River 49/878243. See Loch Nell.
FIART, Loch See Loch Baile a'Ghobhainn entry.

FORSA, River

Location & Access Source 49/643343 Outfall 48/599433. The river is accessed via a private estate road which margins the west bank of the stream.

Commentary The River Forsa rises between the peaks of Sgurr Dearg (740m) to the east and Beinn Talaidh (761m) to the west. The stream flows quickly down Glen Forsa and reaches the sea in the Sound of Mull

318

OS Map 49 — Oban & East Mull

after a journey of 10 miles, 2 miles to the east of Salen.
Fish Salmon and sea-trout. Approximately 50/80 salmon, and similar numbers of sea-trout may be taken in a good season, depending upon water levels. Salmon average 6lb/7lb in weight, sea-trout, 2lb. Sea-trout run the river from April onwards, salmon do not arrive in any numbers until late May and early June..
Flies & Tactics Sport is almost entirely dependent upon water levels, and spate conditions are really required to encourage migratory fish over the falls at the mouth of the river. However, there are upwards of 30 pools on the river and the new owner of the system is currently engaged in a substantial improvement and stock-enhancement programme for the stream.
Permission & Charges At the time of writing the river is not available for public fishing. However, the position may change in the future and inquires as to the current status of the river should be made to: Tackle & Books, 11 Main Street, Tobermory, Isle of Mull, Argyll. Tel: 01688 302336.

GLEANN A'BHEARRAIDH, Loch
Location & Access 49/845270 Leave the A816 Oban/Kilninver road at 49/866272, signposted to Kilbride and Leargs. The loch is approached from the Barn Bar Cottages (49/854256) and is reached after an easy walk of about 1 mile.
Commentary This is the water supply for the town of Oban and the loch is 3/4 of a mile long by up to 1/4 of a mile wide. The surrounding countryside is attractive and welcoming, but the loch can be a wild place in windy weather. Immediately to the south west, and connected to Loch Gleann a'Bhearraidh, is Lochan na Croise which is also fished from the Barn Bar.
Fish Wild brown trout which average 10oz/12oz with a few fish of up to 2lb.
Flies & Tactics The banks are steep and the water deep and although there are a few places where bank fishing is possible, best results come from the boat. Concentrate your efforts at the south end of the loch, close to the margins, and do not expect spectacular results: the loch as a well-deserved reputation for being very dour. Flies: Black Zulu, March Brown, Kingfisher Butcher.
Permission & Charges The Barn Bar, Cologin, Leargs, by Oban, Argyll. Tel: 01631 564501. Cost: £6 per rod per day. The Barn Bar have excellent, self-catering, holiday cottages and tenants have fishing priority. Collect and return boat key and oars to the Barn Bar.

GLENGAMADALE, River See Loch Uisge entry.
KILCHERAN, Loch See Loch Baile a'Ghobhainn.

LUSSA, River
Location & Access Source 49/624285. Outfall 49/690309. Access to the river is from the A849 Lochdon/Bunessan road which margins the north bank of the stream. The headwater lochs, Loch Sguabain (49/630306), Loch an Eilein (49/623299), Loch an Eilen (49/623295) and Loch Airdeglais (49/623285), known locally as the Glen Lochs, are approached via a private estate track which leaves the main road at 49/621204.
Commentary This little spate stream is fed by the lochs noted above and runs north for 2 miles before swinging south-east to reach the sea in Loch Spelve after a further 3 miles. The lochs in the hills to the north of the estuary, Loch Bearnach, (49/690320) and Lochan an Doire Dharaich (49/717337) to the west of Lochdon, are private.
Fish Sea-trout, salmon and brown trout in the river, lochs and in the estuary. Sadly, however, not nearly as many migratory fish as in times past. Accurate catch statistics are not readily available, but approximately 20 salmon and perhaps the same number of sea-trout may taken from the whole system during the season, depending upon water levels. June and July are the most productive months on the river, but sport is entirely dependent upon there being sufficient rain to encourage the fish to run. The estuary of the river, and the shoreline of Loch Spelve, also used to produce good numbers of sea-trout but these have virtually completely disappeared in recent years.
Flies & Tactics A single-handed rod is adequate for the river and success with salmon and sea-trout is very much a matter of fishing 'fine and far off', stalking the fish, rather than marching down the river bank. The most noted pools, on the lower river, are the Sea Pool and the Pedler's Pool. On the Glen Lochs, boat fishing only on Loch Sguabain, for salmon and sea-trout, bank fishing on the other waters noted above. There are some excellent brown trout, particularly in Loch Airdeglais. Dapping is often productive and wet-fly trout fly patterns work just as well for salmon as they do for trout. Try: Black Pennell, Ke-He, Mallard & Claret, Peter Ross, March Brown, Teal Blue & Silver.
Permission & Charges For the River Lussa, contact: Christopher James, Torosay Castle, Craignure, Isle of Mull, Argyll. Tel: 01680 812421; Forest Enterprise, Aros, Isle of Mull, Argyll. Tel: 01680 300346. Cost: expect to pay in the order of £10 per rod day. For the Glen Lochs, contact: James Corbett, Laggan Farm, Lochbuie, Isle of Mull, Argyll. Tel: 01680 814214; also Tackle & Books, 11 Main Street, Tobermory, Isle of Mull, Argyll. Tel: 01688 302336; Fax: 01688 302140.

MACKAYS Loch
Location & Access 49/879300. A 10 minute drive east from the centre of Oban. Follow the signpost to the golf course and Glencruitten.
Commentary Unnamed on the OS Map, but an attractive, easily-accessible, little put-and-take fishery. The loch is enclosed on the west and north sides by the main railway line and on the east and south shores by woodlands.
Fish Stocked with rainbow trout and a strain of Loch Leven trout. Also a native population of brown trout. Trout average in the order of 1lb 8oz in weight.
Flies & Tactics Boats are available for hire and there is also bank fishing from the shore and from casting platforms. Flies: Loch Ordie, March Brown, Silver Invicta. Reservoir lures are also used.
Permission & Charges The Anglers Corner, 2 John Street, Oban, Argyll PA34 5NS. Tel: 01631 566374. Full-day sessions (5 fish bag limit), dawn to dusk, at

Oban & East Mull — OS Map 49

£22 per rod per day. Boat hire, £10 per boat per day (2 anglers). The Glencruitten Estate has comfortable self-catering accommodation and also offer guests a wide range of other outdoor activities including shooting, stalking, mountain-biking, and pony-trekking. For details, contact: Kevin Burnett, Glencruitten Estate, Oban, Argyll. Tel: 01631 565757.

MAM A'CHULLAICH, Lochan See Loch Tearnait.
NA CARRAIGEACH, Loch See Loch Nant entry.

NA CRICHE, Lochan
Location & Access 49/921574. The loch lies a quarter of a mile to the east of the B8043 Inversanda/Kingairloch road.
Commentary There are two other lochs here and they can all be explored during a single expedition involving an easy trek of about 2 miles. Begin the day at Lochan Doire a'Bhraghaid (49/925586), which is by the road, and then follow the outlet stream south for half a mile to find Lochan na Criche. After fishing Lochan na Criche, hike north for half a mile to visit Lochan Torr an Fhamhair (49/931583). This loch drains north into the River Tarbert which in turn enters sea-Loch Linnhe in Inversanda Bay.
Fish Brown trout average 8oz in Lochan Doire a'Bhraghaid and there are lots of them. . Loch na Criche has larger fish, some of which weigh up to and over 1lb, Lochan Torr an Fhamhair fish average 8oz/10oz. The River Tarbert offers the possibility of sea-trout and an occassional salmon.
Flies & Tactics The River Tarbert is very much a spate stream: no water, no fish, and in recent years the number of fish running the stream has diminished. However, after heavy rain, on a falling spate, there is always a chance of sport. Try: Ke-Ke, Grouse & Claret, Kingfisher Butcher.
Permission & Charges Contact: Harvey Phillips, Inversanda Farms, Inversanda, Ardgour, by Fort William. Tel: 01855 841305 or 841205. Cost: £5 per rod per day for the lochs and the river.

NA CROISE, Lochan See Loch Gleann a'Bhearraidh.
NA SULA BIGE, Loch See Loch Tearnait entry.
NA SULA MOIRE, Loch See Loch Tearnait entry.
NAN CLACH, LOCH See Loch Tearnait entry.
NAN CRAOBH, Lochan See Loch Tearnait entry.

NANT, Loch
Location & Access 49/999240. Approach from the B845 at 50/038240. A track leads west to reach the loch after 2 miles.
Commentary The loch has been impounded for hydro-electric generation purposes. The loch drains north, via the River Nant, to sea-Loch Etive, but the water is drawn off to serve a power station before being emptied into Loch Awe. Consequently, the River Nant is rarely fished, although the upper river does hold some good brown trout. Loch Nant is 1 mile east/west by up to 1.5 miles wide and the surrounding moorlands are somewhat bleak and forbidding. Loch Nant can be wild and windy, but on a summer day, with Ben Cruachan (1126m) as a back-drop, it is a pleasant enough place to spend a day.
Fish Brown trout which average in the order of 10oz.
Flies & Tactics Bank fishing only and it is dangerous to wade. The east end of the loch is a good place to begin, particularly amongst the bays and promontories to the west of Bealach Mor (258m) at 50/005234. A track continues west from here, along the south shore of the loch, and this gives access to the bay at 49/999230 which is also worth a visit. The long arm which runs north-east from the loch, at 50/010247, is unnamed on the OS Map but is known locally as Loch na Carraigeach and this loch is private. Flies: Black Pennell, March Brown, Alexandra.
Permission & Charges Fishing is available from the Oban & Lorn Angling Club via Anglers Corner, 2 John Street, Oban, Argyll. Tel: 01631 566374. Tel: 01866 833232. Cost: £5 per rod per day.

NANT, River See Loch Nant entry.

NELL, Loch
Location & Access 49/892274. Turn east at Kilmore, 3.5 miles south from Oban on the A816, signposted to Barran, Glen Lonan and Musdale. At the first T junction, turn left to reach the loch after a further quarter of a mile.
Commentary The loch is 1.5 miles long by up to 600yds wide and covers an area of some 150 acres, dropping to a depth of over 30m at the south end. The loch is drained by the River Nell, also known as Feochan Mhor, into the sea in Loch Feochan at 49/873245. Feochan Bheag, the principal tributary of the River Nell, joins the main flow in the tidal reaches of the river, but falls, 2 miles upstream from the sea, limit the further progress of any migratory fish running the river.
Fish Salmon, sea-trout, brown trout and arctic char. Salmon average 7lb but few are caught. However, a fish of 10lb 8oz was taken recently. Brown trout average 6oz/8oz, arctic char approximately 10oz/12oz.
Flies & Tactics The Oban and Lorn Angling Club have boats on the loch which are moored near the trees at the south end. Glenfeochan Estate also has fishing rights. Bank fishing is allowed but is restricted to an area south from the Angling Club hut and along the south and east shoreline. Sea-trout are present throughout most of the season, but salmon do not appear in any great numbers until well into June. The north end of the loch, which is relatively shallow, offers a good chance of sport, as does the bay at Kiliechainich (49/889276) on the west shore. The River Nell has a few good pools between the outlet from the loch and the road bridge at 49/877245, a distance of three-quarters of a mile. The most notable of these pools is the Bridge Pool, but the sea pools, downstream, can also produce results. However, sport is very much dependent upon heavy rain. Being in the right place at the right time is all-important. On Loch Nell, offer them: Black Pennell, Mallard & Claret, Silver Invicta. On the river, try Dusty Miller, Willie Gunn, Peter Ross, Garry Dog.
Permission & Charges For the angling club fishing, see Soir Loch entry.

OS Map 49 — Oban & East Mull

POND, Loch See Loch Uisge entry.
PRIVATE WATERS SONACHAN, Loch 49/940245; NAM BREAC REAMORA, Lochan 49/949263; A'CHAINNEACHAIN, Lochan 49/915255; CORR CHNOIC, Lochan 49/905265; DUBH, Lochan (Scammadale) 49/866223; FONTINALIS, Lochs 49/617211; AN DAIMH, Lochan 49/621213 ; NA CRAOIBHE-CAORUINN 49/639222; AN T-SIDHEIN, Loch 49/671235; A'BHEALAICH MHOIR 49/652237 ; A'CHAPUILL, Lochan 49/648240; NAN CAORACH, Lochan 49/636242; NA LEITREACH, Lochan 49/635245

The following waters are in a nature reserve and site of special scientific interest: BLACK Lochs 49/926315; LUSRAGAN, Burn 49/908328; LONAN, Loch 49/957280; NA BEITHE, Lochan 49/917352 (contains very small trout); NAN RATH, Lochan 49/921351 (contains very small trout); DUBH BEAG, Loch 49/939378; BARR, River 49/619567; SGURR NA GREINE, Lochan 49/656504; A'BHUINNA-SE, Lochan 49/660479; DUBHA, Lochan 49/702530; NAN LORG, Lochan or NA CANAICH, Lochan 49/683559; BAC AN Lochain 49/715588; CLACHAIG, Loch 49/744553; SALACHAN, Burn 49/980525; BLAR NAN Lochan 49/977499; A'CHOIRE DUHINN, Loch 49/969486; STEALLAIG, Loch 49/959482; DUBH BEAG, Loch (Barcaldine) 49/940378; UAINE, Lochan 49/967378.

RANNOCH, River See Loch Tearnait entry.

SCAMMADALE, Loch
Location & Access 49/890204. Approach from the A816 Kilninver/Lochgilphead road. Turn east at 55/840195 and follow the banks of the River Euchar up to the loch.
Commentary Loch Scammadale is 1.5 miles east-west by up to a quarter of a mile wide and drops to a depth of over 40m at the east end. The inlet burn, the Allt a'Choromaig, is private, although the mouth of the burn may be fished from the boat. The River Euchar, which drains Loch Scammadale into the sea in Loch Feochan, and the loch itself is popular with visitors because of the beauty of the surrounding countryside.
Fish Salmon, sea-trout and brown trout. Salmon now average in the order of 5lb/6lb, sea-trout, 1lb 8oz. The brown trout in both river and loch average 3 to the pound. Fish stocks have declined in recent years, due to the effects of intensive factory-salmon farming in the estuary.
Flies & Tactics Loch Scammadale used to produce good numbers of salmon and sea-trout but those days seem to have gone. This also applies to the river, the mouth of which is still netted by a local estate. In the recent past, upwards of 60 salmon and 150 sea-trout were taken from the system most years. Now, the sea-trout population has collapsed. Other owners of fishing rights on the River Euchar are coy about the precise numbers of fish caught. Therefore, it is hard to be enthusiastic about fishing here, in spite of the efforts made by Mrs Mary McCorkindale, who has fishing rights on both the loch and the river, to improve the situation. On the loch, try: Black Pennell, Mallard & Claret, Peter Ross. On the river, Dusty Miller, Green Highlander, Willie Gunn, General Practitioner.
Permission & Charges For Loch Scammadale and 1 mile of single-bank fishing immediately below the loch, contact: Mrs Mary McCorkindale, Glenann, Kilninver, by Oban, Argyll. Tel: 01852 316282. Cost: boat fishing (2 rods), £16 per boat per day; bank fishing on the loch and fishing the river costs £3 per rod per day. For other fishing on the River Euchar, contact: Mrs E Mellor, Barndromin Farm, Kilninver, by Oban, Argyll. Tel: 01852 316273. Andrew Sandilands, Lagganmore, Kilninver, by Oban, Argyll. Tel: 01852 316200. Expect to pay in the order of £5/£10 per rod per day, dependent upon the time of year. Comfortable self-catering cottages are available and estate tenants have fishing priority. Mrs Mellor also has fishing on Loch Seil (49/805204) and on Loch Dubh (49/801207). Loch Seil used to be an outstanding sea-trout loch but it is now almost completely devoid of fish, other than small brown trout. Loch Dubh also contains small brown trout

SEIL, Loch See Loch Scammadale entry.
SGUABAIN, Loch See Lussa River entry.

SOIR, Lochs
Location & Access 49/965230. Leave the A816 Oban/Kilmore road 3.5 miles south from Oban at 49/877254. Turn east at the signpost marked: Brran, Glen Lonan, Musdale. After a quarter of a mile, at the T junction, turn south and continue for 4 miles. Park in the quarry at 49/928233, just past the signpost to the footpath to Kilchrenan. Follow the footpath for three quarters of a mile, up the gully which contains the pipeline, to reach the Hydro-Board surfaced road out to the lochs.
Commentary Wild, remote country, with outstanding flora and fauna. The loch drains east into Loch Nant (see separate entry) and lies at the end of 4-mile-long hill track, passable with care by most vehicles. Originally, there were two lochs here which became one, now known as Soir Loch, when Loch Nant was impounded for hydro-electric generation purposes. The loch extends across the moor for a distance of approximately 1 mile and is some 300yds in width. Loch a'Bharrain (49/967241), to the north of Soir Loch, is a small peaty loch which is rarely fished, and neither is little Lochan Dubha (49/981214) to the south of Soir Loch.
Fish Excellent stocks of brown trout which average 3 to the pound.
Flies & Tactics Bank fishing only and it is advisable not to wade. The loch fishes well in the early months of the season but as summer advances, weed becomes a problem. Offer the residents: Black Zulu, Soldier Palmer, Silver Butcher.
Permission & Charges For further information, contact The Village Store, Kilmelford. Tel: 01852 200271. Also, Contact: Anglers Corner, 2 John Street, Oban, Argyll. Tel: 01631 566374; David Graham, 9-15 Crombie Street, Oban, Argyll. Tel: 01631 562069; Oban Sports Centre, 4 Craigard Road, Oban, Argyll. Tel: 01631 563845. Cost: approximately £10 per rod per day.

Oban & East Mull — OS Map 49

TARBERT, River See Lochan na Criche entry.

TEARNAIT, LOCH
Location & Access 49/747470 Approach from Achranich (49/705474) via a private estate track which borders the Rannoch River. The loch is reached after an easy walk of 2 and a 1/2 miles.
Commentary Loch Tearnait is approximately 1/2 a mile east west by up to 600yds wide. It lies to the north of the famous peak, An Dunan (479m), which also known as the Table of Lorn. The walk itself is reason enough for visiting this lovely loch and the bothy at Leacraithnaich (49/742471) which overlooks Loch Tearnait is a good base for exploring the other, more remote, lochs in the surrounding area. The 10 waters to the east of Loch Tearnait can be fished during a single day, but it will involve you a round trip, there and back from the bothy, of some 7 miles over some fairly rugged country. To reach them, continue east along the track from Leacraithnaich to Caol Lochan (49/781481) which lies on the south side of the path. Two lochs lie to the north, on the slopes of Caol Bheinn (425m): Lochan nan Craobh (49/775483) and, north again, Lochan an Fhaing (49/769488). After visiting them, return to Caol Lochan and climb the west shoulder of Beinn a Chaisil (436m) to find little Loch na Sula Bige (49/770468) and Loch na Sula Moire (49/777365). These flow into the largest of this group, Loch nan Clach (49/783464). From Loch nan Clach, climb round the west shoulder of Meall nan Clach (290m) and descend to Allt nan Lochanan Dubha (49/785454), Lochanan Dubha (49/780453) and is unnamed neighbour immediately to the west. Return to the south west corner of Loch Tearnait by walking north west from the unnamed lochan (see above) for approximately 1 and 1/2 miles. There is one other loch here which is worth a visit, Lochan Mam a'Chullaich (49/735430). This should be incorporated into a hike out to the Table of Lorn for lunch. The views from this "5-Star restaurant" are unforgettable.
Fish Falls bar the passage of migratory fish running the River Rannoch, but in the lower reaches there is the possibility of a salmon or a sea-trout after spate conditions. The lochs noted above all contain very handsome wild brown trout that average 8oz in weight.
Flies & Tactics The wildlife, flora and fauna along the way is outstanding and the long series of falls on the River Rannoch are very pretty. In high water conditions the River Rannoch, particularly where it exits from Loch Tearnait, and the little burns that flow in from the south, can give great sport with trout on light tackle. There is a boat on Loch Tearnait, the other lochs are all fished from the bank. The most productive area on Loch Terarnait is at the east end where 3 small feeder streams enter.
Permission & Charges See River Aline entry.

TORR AN FHAMHAIR, Lochan See Loch na Criche entry.

UISG, Loch
Location & Access 49/640252. Loch Uisg lies adjacent to the minor road from Lochbuie (49/610250) in the west to Kinlochspelve (49/658261) in the east.
Commentary The loch is approximately 1.5 miles east/west by up to a quarter of a mile wide and is drained by a short stream into sea-Lochbuie by Moy Castle in South-East Mull. Forests margin each bank and the heights of Creach Bheinn Bheag (457m) guard the north shore and Cnoc Shalachry (300m) the south shore. These hills act as a wind tunnel and this can make Loch Uisg a stormy place to fish.
Fish Loch Uisg used to contain salmon and sea-trout but in recent years they have drastically declined in numbers and few are now caught. There are, however, attractive, excellent quality, brown trout and they average in the order of 8oz/10oz.
Flies & Tactics Boat fishing brings the best results and, particularly after heavy rain, the shallower, east end of the loch is the best place to mount your attack - and to look for migratory fish. The south shore, at the mouths of the 5 streams that flow in from the forest, should provide you with a brace of trout for supper. Offer them: Ke-He, Invicta, Black Pennell.
Permission & Charges contact: James Corbett, Laggan Farm, Lochbuie, Isle of Mull, Argyll. Tel: 01680 814214.

UISGE, Loch
Location & Access 49/805550. Loch Uisge lies immediately adjacent to the south side of the B8043 Kingairloch/Lochuisge road.
Commentary The loch drains south via the Abhainn Coinnich river into sea-Loch a'Choire but fishing on the river itself is private. Nearby, to the north of Kingairloch, is a loch marked on the OS Map as Fish Pond (49/869542). This has been drained by breaching the dam at the south end and the loch no longer exists. The Glengamadale River, which drains this system, is preserved by the owner.
Fish Brown trout, but not very many and not very large.
Flies & Tactics Comfortable bank fishing and your best chance of sport is probably at the south end in the vicinity of the outlet stream. Flies: Black Zulu, Soldier Palmer, Silver Butcher.
Permission & Charges The loch is owned by the Kingairloch Estate. Local enquiries should be directed to Mr Davidson, Kenmore, Kingairloch, Ardgour, by Fort William. Tel 01967 411243.

Glen Orchy

AIRIGH NAN, Lochan See River Creran entry.
AN LAIR, Lochan See River Creran entry.
ARAY, River See River Shira entry.

AWE, Loch

Location & Access 50/100250. Easily accessible from the public roads which, generally, parallel the banks of the loch throughout its length.

Commentary Loch Awe (see also OS Map 55) is 26 miles long by up to 1 mile wide and drops to a depth of more than 300ft. The loch is by far the most popular fishery in the West of Scotland and it attracts hundreds of anglers during the season. It also attracts hundreds of other water-sport enthusiasts and, consequently, Loch Awe is invariably a busy place. Nevertheless, it is surrounded by spectacular scenery, dominated by the vast bulk of Ben Cruachan (1101m) to the north and the dramatic, much-photographed Clan Campbell castle, Kilchurn, which stands on a promontory (50/133275) near the mouth of the River Orchy (see separate entry).

Fish Brown trout, ferox trout, rainbow trout, salmon, a few sea-trout, Arctic char, pike and perch. Loch Awe is most famous for ferox trout: 1866 39lb 8oz, 1973 15lb 3oz, 1980 19lb 8oz, 1993 19lb 10oz, and, in April 1996, a new British Record brown trout which weighed 25lb 6oz, caught by caught by Andy Finlay from East Kilbride on a Rapala. Huge rainbow trout, escapees from fish farms, are also taken regularly: a rainbow trout weighing 30lb was caught and released during a recent survey; a rainbow trout of 19lb 4oz was caught by Steven Walker in 1996. Some of these rainbow trout are now sea-going and return as steelheads. The effect escapee rainbow trout are having on the native populations of fish is not known. Double-figure pike are also taken. However, the vast majority of Loch Awe brown trout are of more modest proportions and average 8oz/10oz in weight.

Flies & Tactics Bank fishing is allowed and can be very productive, particularly along the shoreline near Achlian (50/115245) on the east shore and in the bay near Auchachenna at 50/029211 on the west bank. Boat fishing, and trolling, produces the monsters, or might, and favoured areas are in the vicinity of Inishail Island (50/102244), the Black Islands (50/099242), Fraoch Eilean (50/109251) and Eilean Beith (50/109253). The mouth of Teatle Water (50/122252), Cladich River, (50/099231) and An t-Inbhir (50/005154) are also worthy of close inspection. The loch can often be very dangerous, wild and windy. If you are not confident skippering a boat, only go out with someone who is and who knows the fickle nature of the storms which frequently howl down this long, narrow, wind-tunnel of a loch. Always wear a life-jacket when afloat. A number of areas of the shoreline of the loch are preserved and not available for bank fishing. These are mainly in the immediate vicinity of houses and hotels and anglers are expected to respect the owners desire for privicy. Details are shown on the excellent map of the loch produced by Alan Chruch at Croggan Crafts (see below). This publication also contains a great deal of useful information for visiting anglers on other fishing locations in the area. Lures: Rapala, Tobbbies, Devon minnows, Kynoch Killer; flies: Black Pennell, Soldier Palmer, Dunkeld and reservoir lures.

Permission & Charges Loch Awe is designated under a Protection Order and fishing without proper permission is a criminal offence. Contact: Donald Wilson, Ardbrecknish House, by Dalmally, Argyll. Tel: 01866 833223; Portsonachan Hotel, by Dalmally, Argyll. Tel: 01866 833224; W A Church, Croggan Crafts, Dalmally, Argyll. Tel: 01838 200201. Cost: Bank fishing: £3 per rod per day, £6 for 3 days, £12 per week. Boat fishing: £26 per boat including outboard engine. Boat fishing from the Portsonachan Hotel is free (apart from the cost of fuel for the outboard) to hotel residents.

AWE, River

Location & Access Source 50/100250. Outfall 50/011325. Easily accessible from the A85 Dalmally/Taynuilt road.

Commentary This famous Scottish salmon stream flows west from Loch Awe (see separate entry) through the forbidding Pass of Brander and reaches the sea in Loch Etive after a brief journey of 3 miles. The river is dominated to the north by the Ben Cruachan (1101m) and to the south by the slopes of Creag an Aoineidh. This is Clan Campbell country and their ancient war cry is A Cruachan ! In 1308, during the Scottish Wars of Independence, Robert Bruce routed the MacDougalls of Lorne in the Pass of Brander but by tumbling a barrage of rocks down onto their unsuspecting heads as the passed through the narrow defile. A different kind of barrage controls the pass today: a 59ft-high concrete structure, built across the Awe at 50/046288 in late 1960's to impound the river for hydro-electric power generation purposes. This has greatly altered the character of the river and substantially tamed its previous, fiercesome flow.

Fish The River Awe used to be famous for the size and quality of its salmon. The most notable of these all fell to members of the Huntington family: A W Huntington had a 57lb fish in 1921, Mrs G B Huntington, a salmon of 55lb in 1927 and another of 51lb in 1930. Awe fish are of more modest size today and average 10lb, although fish of over 20lb are still occasionally taken. In a good year the river can produce upwards of 400 salmon. Sea-trout, which used to be abundant, are now few in number and are rarely caught.

Flies & Tactics All fishing is by fly only and the river is divided into 8 beats. There are a number of excellent pools and working downstream from the Barrage, they include: Colonel's Pool, Oak Pool, Castle Dubh (where Mr Huntington caught his monster), Red Bank, Gean Tree, Errachd Pool (Mrs Huntington) and Stepping Stones (Mrs Huntington). A stout 15ft rod with a 8/9 weight line is required and wading is uncomfortable in some of the pools. Take great care. Spring fishing can be good, dependent upon water

Glen Orchy — OS Map 50

conditions, and April and May often produce excellent sport. However, the best of the fishing is had in July and August. Flies: General Practitioner, Willie Gunn, Garry Dog, Hairy Mary, Black Doctor, Shrimp Fly, Waddingtons in various colours and guises.
Permission & Charges For the lower river, contact: Robert Campbell-Preston, Inverawe Fisheries, Taynuilt, Argyll. Tel: 01866 822446. Cost: according to the time of year, from £10 to £35 per rod per day, or £110 to £140 per rod per week. This beat takes approximately 25/35 salmon each season. For other beats, contact: Mr Lorne Nelson, Kilmaronaig, Connel, Argyll PA37 1PW. Tel: 01631 710223. Sir Charles McGrigor, Upper Sonachan, Dalmally, Argyll Tel: 01866 833229. Fishing is generally well booked in advance, but weekly lets for a 2 rod beat may sometimes be available. Cost: approximately £300 to £500 per beat per week.

BA, Loch
Location & Access 50/320498 Easily accessible from the A82 Tyndrum/Glencoe road.
Commentary Loch Ba is the largest of the group of waters that are divided by the main road. The system is fed by the River Ba (the source of the River Tummel) which rises 5 miles to the west on the east slopes of Aonach Mor (865m). Lochan Mhic Pheadair Ruaidh (50/282474) augments the flow near Ba Bridge and then the stream wends its way through Loch Buidhe (50/298482) and Loch na Stainge (50/302492) before passing under the main road and into Loch Ba. Immediately to the south of Loch Buidhe, is Lochan na h-Achlaise (50/312480) which also drains into Loch Ba. Loch Ba itself then flows east into Loch Laidon (see OS Map 41). The attraction of fishing here is not only the possibility of good sport, but also the great beauty of the surrounding mountains and moorlands. Within a 2 mile hike south east from Loch Ba, onto the edge of Rannoch Moor, there are three, additional, remote lochs where peace and solitude is also assured: Lochan Sithein Duibh (50/342485) with its lovely little island, Dubh Lochan (50/347481) and its unnamed neighbour to the north.
Fish All these lochs hold excellent stocks of small, wild brown trout, but Loch Ba has a reputation for producing much larger specimens as well. There is a cast of an 11lb trout, taken from Loch Ba, in the Kingshouse Hotel, and, in recent years, fish of up to and over 5lb in weight have been caught.
Flies & Tactics Bank fishing only, unless you have your own boat or canoe: it is possible to reach Moor of Rannoch by doing so. Loch Ba extends over an area 2 miles long by up to 1 mile wide and it would take several seasons to thoroughly investigate all the bays, promontories and fishy corners that beckon. If one includes the other lochs noted above, then the fishing opportunities are even nicer. Be careful if wading, the banks are soft and marshy in many places. And be prepared for bad weather, the climate is notoriously fickle in these arits. Flies: Black Zulu, Soldier Palmer, Silver Butcher.
Permission & Charges It has been accepted practice for many years that fishing here is free of charge, neither have I, ever, been able to establish from whom one should seek permission. My enquires, locally, have always produced the same response that permission is not required to fish the near-roadside lochs around Loch Ba.

BA, River See Loch Ba entry.
BAILE MHIC CHAILEIN, Loch See River Creran entry.
BUIDHE, Loch See Loch Ba entry.
CAIRN DIERG, Lochan See River Creran entry.
CAORAINN, Lochan See River Creran entry.
COARSE FISHERIES DUBH, Lochan (50/042260); TROMLEE, Loch (50/042250). These lochs may have a few trout, but they are most certainly full of pike.
COUPALL, River See River Etive entry.

CRERAN, River
Location & Access Source 41/090505 Outfall 50/008460. The river is accessed along a minor road the heads north up Glen Creran from 50/008460 on the A828 Glencoe/Oban road.
Commentary The River Creran is a short spate stream that rises from Lochan Caorainn on the north shoulder of Beinn Trilleachan (839m). The stream flows north down into Glen Creran before turning west on its 9 mile long journey to the sea. After a distance of 6 miles the river is joined by the River Ure which flows in from the east. Downstream from here, the water pauses in Loch Baile Mhic Chailein (known as Loch Fasnacloich), a substantial loch of 1/2 a mile long by up to 1/4 of a mile wide. There are a number of additional lochs in the area, on the headwaters of the River Ure and in the surrounding hills: Lochan an Lair (50/071439), Lochan na Saobhaidhe (50/089460), Airigh nan Lochan (50/082470) and its unnamed neighbour; Lochan na Fola (50/092483), the tiny pools of Lochan Cairn Dierg on Beinn Fhionnlaidh (959m) and Lochan na Maoile (50/012498) on Beinn Mhic na Ceisich (638m) to the north of Fasnacloich House. This is Robert Louis Stevenson country and the area is marvelously is depicted in his book *Kidnapped*.
Fish Salmon and a few sea-trout in the river, modest brown trout in the lochs. Accurate catch statistics are not available but, depending upon water conditions, the system produces in the order of 50/80 salmon most seasons.
Flies & Tactics Salmon run the river from May onwards but the best sport is had in September and October, providing that there has been rain. Nevertheless, the loch can always produce a fish, in spite of weather conditions and a boat provided for the purpose. Sadly, however, because of the impact of fish farms, wild fish numbers have collapsed in recent years. The hill lochs offer exciting wild brown trout fishing amidst magnificent scenery. Other than in high water, fishing is by fly only. Dapping can be productive on Loch Fasnacloich. Offer salmon: Hairy Mary, Silver Stoat's Tails, Willie Gunn, Garry Dog, Black Doctor, General Practitioner. For trout: Ke-He, Soldier Palmer, Dunkeld.

OS Map 50 — Glen Orchy

Permission & Charges Fasnacloich House, a comfortable, modern, property which sleeps 8 people, is let on a self-catering basis with 2 rods on the right bank of the river and 2 rods on the loch. The house is perfectly situated, in the midst of mature woodlands, overlooking the loch. An ideal base for a family holiday. Expect to pay in the order of £2,000/£2,500 per week, depending upon the time of year. For details contact: Finlyson Hughes, 29 Barossa Place, Perth PH1 5EP. Tel: 01738 630926; Fax: 01738 639017.

CROSS REFERENCES LOCH LOMOND (See OS Map 56); LOCH SLOY (See OS Map 56); LOCH NANT (See OS Map 49).
The following waters are described on OS Map 51: Loch LYON; River CONONISH; River FILLAN.
DOUGLAS, Water See River Shira entry.
DUBH, Lochan See Loch Ba entry.

ETIVE, River
Location & Access Source 41/186530 Outfall 50/115455. The river is easily accessible from the minor road which parallels the west bank of the stream.
Commentary The river rises in the Lairig Gartain between the vast bulk of The Shepherds, Bauchaille Etive Mor (1033m) Bauchaille Etive Beag (958m). The stream, then named the River Coupall, flows north east and, at Lagangarbh (50/221560), south east alongside the A82 Tyndrum/Glencoe road. The access road, to Dalness and Glenetive House, leaves the A82 1/2 a mile north from the Kingshouse Hotel at 41/246550 and ends at the head of sea-Loch Etive near the mouth of the Gualachulain Burn.
Fish Salmon and a few sea-trout. Approximately 80/100 salmon are taken most seasons, depending upon water levels. Salmon average 8lb in weight. However, because of the impact of fish farming, salmonid numbers have collaspsed in recent years. The upper reaches of the river and the River Coupall contain small brown trout. The loch at (50/513493), unnamed on the OS Map, is man-made and connected to the river, and it also has brown trout. Sea-fishing is also availbale on Loch Etive.
Flies & Tactics The falls at Dalness (50/171511) bar the upstream passage of migratory fish, but from the falls down to the sea there are 25 named salmon pools divided into 3 beats. The most productive of these are: Home Pool, Wall Pool, Luncheon Pool, Graveyard Pool, Big Pool, Fence Pool and the Master's Pool. Salmon rarely run the river in any numbers until early July, and even then it is very much a matter of praying for rain. Most fish, including good numbers of fresh fish, are caught in September and October. The river is easily fished from the bank and there is no need to wade. The best chance of sport with sea-trout is at the mouth of the river, particularly in the evenings during the summer months. A light, single-handed rod is adequate and flies that do the damage include: Ally's Shrimp, Willie Gunn, Garry Dog, General Practitioner, Hairy Mary, Green Highlander. For sea-trout, try: Black Pennell, March Brown, Teal Blue & Silver.

Permission & Charges Glenetive House and Dalness Lodge are let with 4/6 rods on the river. Both properties are very comfortable and are let on a self-catering basis. Glenetive House sleeps a maximum of 8 people, Dalness Lodge, 12. For details, contact: Strutt & Parker, 13 Hill Street, Berkeley Square, London W!X 8DL. Tel: 0171 6297282; Fax: 0171 4991675.

FASNACLOICH, Loch See River Creran entry.
FYNE, River For the time being, the River Fyne, and its neighbour, the Kinglass Water, have been closed to fishing because of an almost complete absence of stock. Up until 1989, the Fyne was capable of producing in the order of 200/250 salmon each season, in spite of the impoundment of its headwaters for hydro-electric power generation purposes. However, recent years have seen catastrophic collapse in salmon and sea-trout numbers; caused by the prevalence of factory-salmon farming in sea-Loch Fyne which have brought the wild stocks in these two stream to the point of extinction.
Permission & Charges For further and future information, contact: Peter Manson, Head Keeper, Ardkinglass Estate, Cairndow, Argyll. Tel: 01499 600244.

INVERAWE, Fishery
Location & Access 50/023315 Access is from the A85 Dalmally/Taynuilt road in the Pass of Brander. Turn right at 50/031299 and follow the minor road across the river and railway to reach the fishery after 1 mile.
Commentary A notable Argyll put-and-take rainbow trout fishery.
Fish Stocked with large rainbow trout, many of which run to double figures.
Flies & Tactics Bank fishing only on 3 pools, easily accessible and comfortable to fish. There is also a shop nearby which specialises in producing smoked salmon and trout and other delicacies. Anglers are restricted to the use of only one fly on a cast. Reservoir lures do most of the damage: Ace of Spades, Whisky Fly, Baby Doll, Dog Noblers.
Permission & Charges Contact Robert Campbell-Preston, Inverawe Fisheries, Taynuilt, Argyll. Tel: 01866 822446.

KINGLAS, RIVER See River Orchy entry.
KINGLASS WATER (Loch Fyne) See River Fyne entry.
LOCHY, RIVER (Argyll) See River Orchy entry.
MHIC PHEADAIR, Lochan See Loch Ba entry.
NA BI, LOCHAN See River Orchy entry.
NA FOLA, Lochan See River Creran entry.
NA H-ACHLAISE, Lochan See Loch Ba entry.
NA MAOILE, Lochan See River Creran entry.
NA SAOBHAIDHE, Lochan See River Creran entry.
NA STAINGE, Loch See Loch Ba entry.

ORCHY, River
Location & Access Source 50/295425 Outfall 50/138281. The river is accessed from the A85 Taynuilt/Tyndrum road at Dalmally (50/160271) and

Loch Tay
OS Maps 50-51

from the B8074 Dalmally/Bridge of Orchy Road which parallels the stream as it runs through Glen Orchy.

Commentary The river is fed from Loch Tulla and the streams that flow into Loch Tulla from the hills and mountains around Black Mount: Water of Tulla (50/355470), Linne nam Beathach (50/250423), Allt Coire Chailein (50/327340) and Allt Chonoghlais (50/350382) which is also known locally as the River Kinglas. The stream flows south west down Glen Orchy and enters the north east bay of Loch Awe (see separate entry) near the ruins of Kilchurn Castle. The River Lochy, which rises from Lochan na Bi (50/310313), is a major tributary of the River Orchy and it flows in at Inverlochy (50/191278). Just before its outfall into Loch Awe, the River Orchy collects in the waters of another major tributary, the River Strae, which is preserved by the ower. The Orchy is divided into 8 principal beats, from the outflow from Loch Tulla downstream to Loch Awe. There are a number of excellent holdings pools, some of the most notable being, working downstream from Loch Tulla: Junction Pool, Upper & Lower Otter Pool, Shepherds Pool, Upper Falls Pool, Dewar Pool, white Rocks Pool, Witches Pool, General's Rock, Yellow Flag and the Black Duncan Pool which produced a 35lb salmon in April 1961 for Mrs Chris McLauchlan.

Fish Salmon enter the River Orchy from sea-Loch Etive by way of the River Awe (see separate entry). Approximately 300 fish are taken most seasons, depending upon water conditions. On the River Lochy, falls bar the passage of migratory fish 1 mile upstream from its junction with the River Orchy and it is not fished. Sea-trout may also be encountered but most of them seem to prefer to run the River Strae. The river also hosts perch which descend from Loch Tulla. Perch of up to and over 3lb in weight, although not perhaps welcome, are not uncommon.

Flies & Tactics In recent years, afforestation has altered the water regimen and the river is now much more subject to flash-flooding than it was in the past, although the Orchy has always been known as a classic spate stream. In spate conditions, take great care when fishing: the river can be very wild indeed. Some of the pools are almost impossible to fish with fly, so bait fishing and spinning is allowed. However, fly fishing is the preferred fishing method and there are many delightful pools and glides, most of which can be effectively covered from the bank without any need to wade. A 13ft/15ft rod with a weight 9/10 line is appropriate and the flies that do the damage include: Ally's Shrimp, Silver Stoat's Tail, Willie Gunn, Shrimp Fly, Waddingtons orange/black/red, Garry Dog, Black Doctor.

Permission & Charges Prices vary according to the time of year and beat fished, but expect to pay in the order of £15 per rod per day in the spring months, rising to £50 per rod per day in the autumn. Mr W A Church, Croggan Crafts, Dalmally, Argyll. Tel: 01838 200201 will advise visiting anglers on availability and access. D M MacKinnon & Co, Station Road, Oban, Argyll. Tel: 01631 563014. L Campbell, Arichastilch, Glen Orchy, Dalmally, Argyll. Tel: 01838 200282.

West Highland Estates, 21 Argyll Square, Oban, Argyll. Tel: 01631 563617. Trout fishing is also available on the River Kinglas to guests staying with Mrs C MacDonald, Auch, By Tyndrum, Argyll. Tel: 01838 400233.

PRIVATE WATERS All the waters that lie to the south of Loch Awe on OS Map 50, and bounded to the east by Glen Shira and grid line easting 19, are preserved by the owners. Also preserved: CRUCHAN, reservoir 50/080285; NA CUAIG, Lochan 50/064268; A'MHILL BHIG, Lochan 50/224132; BEINN DAMHAIN, Lochan 50/291171; SRATH DUBH-UISGE, Lochan 50/282158; A'MHADAIDH, Lochan 50/269217; CREAG NAN CAORRUNN, Lochan 50/301219; DUIN, Lochain 50/315218; OSS, Loch 50/300251; A'CHAISTEIL, Lochan 50/342189; BEINN CHABHAIR, Lochan 50/352179; FALLOCH, River 50/330201; GREAT Loch 50/319162; AN LEOID, Loch 50/019244; AN DROIGHINN, Loch 50/021240; A'CHRION-DOIRE, Loch 50/006228; NA GEALAICH, Lochan 50/049233; A'CHREACHAIN, Lochan 50/368447; TULLA, Water of 50/354466; TULLA, Loch 50/300430; ALLT CHONOGHLAIS, River 50/348380; LINNE NAM BEATHACH, River 50/250421; DOCHARD, Loch 50/215420; NA SAOBHAIDHE, Lochan 50/200419; NA H-IURAICHE, Lochan 50/193417.

SITHEIN DUIBH, Lochan See Loch Ba entry.
SRON MOR, LOCHAN See River Shira entry.
STRAE, RIVER See River Orchy entry.
URE, River See River Creran entry.

Loch Tay

AN DAIMH, Loch See River Lyon entry.
CROSS REFERENCES The following waters are described on OS Map 42: Loch RANNOCH; Loch MONAGHAN; Loch FINNART; River GAUR; Loch EIGHEACH; DUBH Lochan; Lochan CAOL FADA; Lochan RUIGHE NAN SLIGEAN; Lochan A'MHAIDSEIR; Lochan GHIUBHAIS; Lochan NAM BREAC; Lochan AN EISG MHOIR; DUNALASTAIR Reservoir; Loch KINARDOCHY; Lochan BEOIL CHATHAICHE; Lochan AN DAIM. The following water is described on OS Map 41: Loch LAIDON. The following water is described on OS MAP 52: Loch TUMMEL; River TUMMEL; River TAY; UPPER RIVER EARN; River ALMOND (Perthshire); Water of RUCHILL; River LEDNOCK; DRUMMOND Trout Fishery. The following water is described on OS Map 57: Loch VOIL.

DOCHART, LOCH See River Dochart entry.

326

OS Map 51 — Loch Tay

DOCHART, River
Location & Access Source 50/277247 Outfall 51/584334 Easily accessible throughout its length from the A85 Aberfeldy/Crianlarich Road and, in its guise as the River Fillan, from the A82 Crianlaich/Glencoe road.
Commentary The River Dochart, which feeds Loch Tay, rises 21 miles to west of Killin amidst the corries of Ben Lui (1130m). The stream begins life as the Allt Coire Laoigh burn and then expands into the River Cononish. After it passes under the A82 Crianlarich/Glencoe road it is known as the River Fillan and, at Crianlarich (50/385255), where the stream turns east, it becomes the River Dochart. The most notable feature on the river are the spectacular Falls of Dochart, at Killin, a popular visitor attraction. There are two principal lochs on the course of the river, Loch Dochart (51/405256) and Loch Iubhair (51/425270). To the north of where the River Dochart flows into Loch Tay, another important feeder stream enters: the River Lochay, 15 miles from source to mouth and impounded for hydro-electric power generation purposes. The Allt a'Mhoirneas burn has also been impounded, creating Lochan na Lairige (51/599395) to the north of the National Trust Visitor Centre on the minor road from Edramucky (51/621363) to Bridge of Balgie (51/578467) in Glen Lyon. One further lochan in the vicinity should also be noted: remote Lochan nan Cat, cupped in the high corries of Ben Lawers and approached by hiking north up the Lawers Burn from the A827 Kenmore/Killin road at Machuim (51/680400).
Fish Accurate catch statistics for the River Dochart are not available but are likely to be in the order of 100 fish per season, most of them being taken downstream from the Falls of Dochart. The river also holds some good brown trout. Salmon may also be encountered in Loch Dochart and in Loch Iubhair. The River Lochay rarely produces salmon and is best fished for its modest brown trout. The other waters noted contain brown trout of 6oz.
Flies & Tactics Spinning accounts for most of the fish on the River Dochart and the Bridge Pool and the Garage Pool, downstream from the railway viaduct, are the most productive parts of the whole river. Fish are taken throughout the season but the early months are best. Few salmon ascend the falls until May, and, thereafter, sport on the upper river and in the headwater lochs is entirely dependent upon spate conditions. The river is easily fished from the bank and there are a number of pools and gravel runs; particularly on the River Fillan which can offer sport dry-fly fishing for brown trout. The River Lochay is regularly planted out with a salmon fry as part of a stock-enhancement programme for the River Tay system. On Loch Iubhair, concentrate your activities along the north bank where 6 feeder stream enter from Creag Liaragan (558m). Lochan Lairige and Lochan nan Cat are both fished from the bank.
Permission & Charges Prices: £5.00 per rod per day. Contact: Mr Rough, JR News, Main Street, Killin, Perthshire. Tel: 01567 820362. For other beats, contact: Group Captain D Dowling, Kinnell House, Killin, Perthshire FK21 8SR. Tel: 01567 820590; George Coyne, Head Keeper, Auchlyne Estate, Killin, Perthshire. Tel: 01567 820284; for Loch Dochart & Loch Lubhair, contact: Mr T Taylor, Portenellan Lodge, Crianlarich, Perthshire. Tel: 01838 300284. Prices on application. Portenellan Lodge will also arrange boats, outboard motors, gillies and fishing tackle hire. Lodge guests have priority.

EARN, Loch
Location & Access 51/640235 The loch is easily accessible along the north shore from the A85 Comrie/Lochearnhead road. A minor road parallels the south bank, from St Fillans (51/695240) in the east to Carstran (51/590228) in the west.
Commentary Loch Earn is 6 miles long by up to 3/4 of a mile wide and one of the most productive and popular waters in Scotland. The loch is covered by a Protection Order and managed by Loch Earn Fishings. Loch Earn is invariably busy, not only with anglers but also with other water-sport users.
Fish The loch is stocked with 7,500 brown trout (average weight between 10oz and 2lb 8oz) each year. The heaviest trout taken recently weighed 7lb 13oz. There is a native population of brown trout, occasional rainbow trout. Ferrox trout and good numbers of Arctic char Frequent the area close to the fish farm in the loch: char of over 3lb are frequently caught. There is also the chance of the occasional sea-trout and rare salmon.
Flies & Tactics This is an all methods fishery, spinning, bait and fly-fishing being allowed although the natural minnow is prohibited. Both boat and bank fishing is available and both methods do well. Drummond Estates have excellent, 15ft, loch style boats equipped with 4hp outboard motors, thole pin oars and life jackets. The west and east ends of the loch are perhaps the most productive fishing areas, but trout may be taken from almost anywhere around the shoreline. Rods are limited to 6 fish per day and the flies fish best include: Bibio, Kate McLaren, Black Pennell, Gosling, Mini Muddlers.
Permission & Charges Outstanding value-for-money fishing: Adults, £5, Under 16's, £1. Boat charges: 4 hour hire, £15, 6 hour hire, £22, 8 hour hire, £29 - including a full tank of petrol and an additional spare gallon for emergencies. Contact: Drummond Estates, Boat Hire, Loch Earn, Perthshire. Tel: 01567 830400. Also, St Fillans Post Office, St Fillans, Perthshire. Tel: 01764 685309 and Lochearnhead Post Office, Lochearnhead, Perthshire. Tel: 01567 830201. And the following places may provide permits in the evenings: 45 Bar & Restaurant, Lochearnhead, Perthshire tel 01567 830221; Clachan Cottage Hotel, Lochearnhead, Pethshire Tel 01567 830247; Four Seasons Hotel, St Fillans, Perthshire Tel 01764 685333; Drummond Arms Hotel, St Fillans, Perthshire Tel 01764 685212.

IUBHAIR, LOCH See River Dochart entry.
LAIRIGE, LOCHAN See River Dochart entry.
LOCHAY, River See River Dochart entry.
LYON, Loch See River Lyon.

Loch Tay   OS Map 51

LYON, River
Location & Access Source 50/382346 Outfall 51/794479. Access to the river is from the minor road from Keltneyburn (51/778492) to the dam at Loch Lyon (51/453417).

Commentary The River Lyon is born as the Allt Mhic Bhaidein burn on the west shoulder of Creag Mhor (1032) to the north of Tyndrum in Argyll. The headwaters of the stream have been impounded for hydro-electric power generation purposes, thus forming Loch Lyon (51/405415), Stronuich Reservoir (51/504419), an extension of the river itself, and Loch an Daimh (51/490468). After leaving Loch Lyon, the river flows east down Glen Lyon for a distance of some 30 miles before joining the River Tay (see OS Map 52) 2 miles downstream from the village of Killin. Glen Lyon is as noted for its beauty and history as it is for the quality of its fishing and deer stalking. Fortingall (the place of the strangers) is reputed to have been the birthplace of Pontius Pilate and in the churchyard here is the oldest tree in Europe, the famous 3,000 year-old Fortingall Yew.

Fish Fewer salmon now than in pre-hydro-electric days, but the river is still renowned for the quality of its spring fish: salmon of up to and over 20lb are regularly taken. Approximately 300 fish are landed most seasons. The River Lyon is also noted as a brown trout fishery. In recent years, the spawning habitat on the river has been improved by breaking up compacted gravel beds but there is no fish pass at the dam so spawning is restricted to the river itself and its small tributary streams: The hydro-lochs on the system have little to recommend them, being grim waters where bank fishing is difficult and dangerous and trout are of modest proportions. One small, hill lochan is of interest, Lochan nan Cat (51/487449), but more for its splendid location below the summit of Stuchd an Lochain (958m) rather than for its fish.

Flies & Tactics The best of the spring fishing is in the first 6 miles of the stream. Salmon are held in the lower river by the steep-sided, wooded, gorge above Fortingall which acts as a temperature pool and salmon rarely reach the upper beats until April, and, depending upon the severity of the winter, sometimes not until May. There are 60 pools on the river, most of them named by Peter Dewer (of Dewer's Whisky) who fished the river during the middle years of this century. Some of the most productive are: Junction Pool, Limekilns, Suspension Bridge Pool, Peter's Pool, Weaver's Pool (near MacGregor's Leap), Rock Pool, Invervar Bridge Pool, Still Waters, Roro Bridge Pool, Lower Wall and Wall Pool. The lower river is comfortable fished from the bank and by using thigh waders. In the gorge section of the river, fishing Platform Pool, it is often helpful to have a fellow angler "spot" the fish for you from the opposite bank. The wooden platform that gives the pool its name is unsafe and should be avoided. The upper river, Chesthill, Invervar, Innerwick and Meggerine, can be comfortably covered using a 12ft rod, and, in low water conditions, which, sadly, are all-too-frequent, a trout rod would be more appropriate. Salmon lures: Tobbies, Blair Spoon, Devon Minnows, Rapalas.

Salmon flies: Willie Gunn, Garry Dog, General Practitioner, Black Doctor, Ally's Shrimp, Hairy Mary, Green Highlander. For brown trout, try: Soldier Palmer, March Brown, Dunkeld. Dry flies: Greenwell's Glory, March Brown, Olives.

Permission & Charges Prices vary according to the time of year. In the spring, expect to pay in the order of £25 per rod per day and £50 per day in the autumn months. Sadly, much of the lower river, which used to be let through the Fortingall Hotel, has been taken back by the estate and is not now available to the general public. However, the Fortingall still has access to excellent fishing, including Peter's Pool and Platform Pool and at Roro. Contact: Fortingall Hotel, Fortingall, by Aberfeldy, Perthshire. Tel: 01887 830367. Also, Coshieville Hotel, Keltneyburn, by Aberfeldy, Perthshire. Tel: 01887 830319. Other fishing may be accessed through: Keeper's House, Innerwick, Glen Lyon, by Aberfeldy, Perthshire. Tel: 01887 886218; Post Office House, Bridge of Balgie, Glen Lyon, Perthshire. Tel: 01887 886221; Gregor Cameron, Keepers Cottage, Chesthill Estate, Glen Lyon, Perthshire. Tel: 01887 877207. Finlyson Hughes, 29 Barossa Place, Perth PH1 5EP. Tel: 01738 625134; Fax: 01738 639017, and Strutt & Parker, 13 Hill Street, Berkeley Square, London W1X 8DL. Tel: 0171 6297282; Fax: 0171 4991657 let fishing in conjunction with self-catering accommodation. For Loch Lyon and Lochan nan Cat, contact: The Keeper's Cottage, Lubreoch, Glen Lyon, Perthshire. Tel: 01887 886244. For Loch an Daimh, contact: W Mason, Croc-na-keys, Glen Lyon, Perthshire. Tel: 01887 886224 (Loch an Daimh is closed to anglers during windy conditions - check first). Cost: £5 per rod per day.

NAN CAT, LOCHAN See River Dochart entry.

NAN CAT, Lochan (Glen Lyon) See River Lyon.

PRIVATE WATERS
BELTACHAN, Loch 51/700262; NA CREIGE RUAIDHE, Lochan 51/679291; EAS DOMHAIN, Loch 51/661290; LEDNOCK , Reservoir 51/710300; BREACLAICH Lochan 51/621315; NAN GEADAS, Lochan 51/600297; FEURACH, Lochan 41/593285; MEALL NA CLOICHE, Lochan 51/591281; NAN DAMH, Lochan 51/324535; ESSAN, Loch 51/413284; MARAGAN, Loch 51/402278; CHAILEAN, Lochan 51/401302; ACHLLARICH, Lochan 51/433381; LEARG NAN LUNN, Lochan 51/450386; LAIRG EALA, Loch 51/559278 (reputed to be fishless); AN EIREEANNAICH, Lochan 51/515243.

TAY, Loch
Location & Access 51/670370 Loch Tay is accessed from the A827 Kenmore/Killin road along the north bank and from the minor road from Kenmore (51/775452) to Killin (51/572323) on the south bank.

Commentary Loch Tay is one of Scotland's most lovely and most popular lochs, not only with anglers but also with visitors who come to enjoy the wide variety of water-based sports which are available on the loch. Loch Tay is over 16 miles long by up to 1 mile wide and a range of accommodation providers, from excel-

OS Maps 51-52 — Aberfeldy and Glen Almond

lent hotels to self-catering chalets, meet the needs of anglers and their non-fishing companions. All this combines to make Loch Tay and its environs an ideal base for an exciting family holiday.

Fish The loch contains salmon, small numbers of sea-trout, brown trout, escapee rainbow trout and Arctic char. Approximately 400 salmon are taken most seasons and the average weight of Loch Tay salmon is in the order of 12lb. Brown trout vary in size from modest 8oz specimens right up to ferrox trout of over 10lb in weight. There have been a number of escapes from fish farms in recent years and rainbow trout of 14lb and 18lb have been landed.

Flies & Tactics Most salmon are taken by trolling and the early months of the season, from January until May, produce the best sport. Local knowledge is essential to find the fish, and to stay safe on this huge expanse of water, particularly in the spring when the weather can change with frightening rapidity. Some very large fish are taken from opening day (15th January) onwards. Fish of between 10lb and 20lb are common. During the summer months the loch fishes very well for brown trout, from both boat and bank, but, if bank fishing, avoid wading, it is dangerous to do so. From the boat, arrange your drift about 15 yards out from the bank and concentrate on the many bays and corners and where streams enter from the surrounding hills. On the north shore, try: the bay at Fearnan (51/722442), the outlet of Lawers Burn (51/685396), Milton Morenish and the shallow bay near Tirarthur (51/585345). Along the south shore, have a look at: Firbush Point (51/601336), Camusurich Bay (51/629349), Ardeonaig (51/666360), Ardtalnaig Bay (51/698392) and Acharn Point (51/756441). Remember, trout anglers are not permitted to troll. The most productive spinning lures are: Black & Gold Rapala, Blue & Silver Kynoch, Tobies and Devon Minnows. For trout, try: March Brown, Greenwell's Glory, Peter Ross.

Permission & Charges Salmon fishing charges vary according to the time of year, but expect to pay in the order of £30/£50 per day, 2 rods fishing, including boat, outboard motor and fuel and the services of a gillie. Bank fishing for brown trout costs approximately £4.00 per rod per day. Contact: Kenmore Hotel, Kenmore, Perthshire. Tel: 01887 830205; Loch Tay Highland Lodges, Milton Morenish, by Killin, Perthshire. Tel: 01567 820323; Fax: 01567 820581. Ardeonaig Hotel, Ardeonaig, South Loch Tayside by Killin, Perthshire. Tel: 01567 820400; Fax: 01567 820282. Mr Rough, JR News, Main Street, Killin, Perthshire. Tel: 01567 820362 (Mr Rough will also advise on other fishing available in the area). J Duncan Millar, Loch Tay Lodges, Remony, Acharn, by Kenmore, Perthshire. Tel: 01887 830209; Croft-na-Caber, Kenmore, Perthshire. Tel: 01887 830588.

Aberfeldy and Glen Almond

A'MHUILINN Lochan See River Braan entry.

ALMOND, River (Perthshire)
Location & Access Source 52/706325 Outfall 52/100268 Access to the lower reaches of the river is from public roads which parallel both banks. In the Sma Glen, a noted beauty spot, the stream runs adjacent to the A822 Crieff/Amulree road. The upper reaches of the river lie in Glen Almond and are approached via a track from Newton Bridge (52/885315) on the A822 which runs west up Glen Almond for a distance of nearly 10 miles to Dunan (52/740340).

Commentary The River Almond rises on the east shoulder of Creag Uchdag (879m) to the south of Loch Tay (See OS Map 51, Loch Tay) and flows quickly north to a stalkers bothy at Dunan. The stream then swings south east down Glen Almond past the disused weir at Dalreich (52/780333) and into the Sma Glen. After a jounrey of 24 miles the River Almond joins the River Tay a step upstream from the Fair City of Perth. The upper river lies amidst wild scenery rich with wildlife, particularly mountain hare, and there is more than a good chance of seeing a number of the great raptors. The lower river is a sadder affair, much afflicted in days past with the weirs which still impede the Almond's flow, particularly as the stream approaches the environs of Almondbank. Buchanty Spout (52/934284) also holds back fish but provides a popular viewing point for visitors and anglers alike who congregate here to watch the salmon attempt the falls.

Fish Salmon, sea-trout, brown trout, grayling and escappee rainbow trout in the lower river, small brown trout in the hills. Approximately 100 salmon and 200 sea-trout are taken each season.

Flies & Tactics The Almond is a spate river and good sport depends upon good water levels. Because the headwaters have been diverted to Lednock Reservoir (See OS Map 51, Loch Tay), low water levels are, sadly, the rule, rather then the exception. Much of the river can be fished without the necessity to wade and a 10ft rod will covery most of the lies. Salmon do not run the river in any numbers until the end of July and spinning accounts for the majority of fish caught. Devons, Rapala lures and Tobies do the damage. September and October are the most productive months. Popular salmon flies include: Hairy Mary, General Practitioner, Garry Dog, Ally's Shrimp. Sea-trout fishing is at its best in June and July and both sea-trout and brown trout will respond to: Black Pennell, March Brown, Peter Ross. Dry fly fishing for brown trout can also produce good results, particularly during the summer months.

Permission & Charges Contact: The Factor, Mansfield Estates, Scone Palace, Perth. Tel: 01738 552308. Cost: Salmon fishing, £10 per rod per day, trout fishing, £3 per rod per day. Brown trout fishing

Aberfeldy and Glen Almond

OS Map 52

permission on the upper river may be obtained from: Mr MacKenzie, Auchnafree Lodge Amulree, Perthshire. Tel: 01350 725233; T Muirhead, Corriemuckloch, Amulree, Perthshire. Tel: 01350 725206. Abercairny Estate, Estate Office, by Crieff, Perthshire (Tel: 01764 652706) offer salmon fishing at £15 per rod per day.

AN UAINE Lochan
See Loch Turret entry.

BRAAN, River
Location & Access Source 52/772369 Outfall 52/026424. The river is accessible from the A822 Dunkeld/Amulree road. Access to the upper river, above Amulree, is from the minor road between Amulree (52/900369) in the south to Kenmore (52/775452) at the east end of Loch Tay (See Os Map 51, Loch Tay) in the north.
Commentary The river rises on the north shoulder of Sron a'Chaonineidh (870m) and flows east and then south east down Glen Quaich, as the River Freuchie, through Loch Freuchie (52/865377) to Amulree. The Braan then swings north east down Strathbraan and joins the River Tay just upstream from Telford's Bridge in Dunkeld after a journey of 12 miles. In the hills to the south of Loch Freuchie, is another delightful little trout loch, Loch a'Mhuilinn (52/850359), which is accessed from a track that starts on the shores of Loch Freuchie at Croftmill (52/862369). The loch is reached after an easy walk of about 1 mile.
Fish Salmon in the lower river, below the Falls of Hermitage, pretty wild brown trout elsewhere. Loch Freuchie has brown trout which average 1lb and voracious pike and perch as well. Lochan a'Mhuilinn holds 8oz brown trout, but both these waters can produce much larger trout: the heaviest trout taken from Loch Freuchie in recent years weighed 6lb 8oz.
Flies & Tactics The River Braan is as famous for its natural beauty as it is for the quality of its fishing. The splendid falls at Hermitage are a very popular visitor attraction and are approached along a trail which winds its way through some of Scotland's most lovely woodlands.
The falls at Rumbling Bridge (52/998412) are also well worth a visit, as are the upper reaches of this perfect little Highland stream. Fishing the lower part of the river is fraught with difficulty from the surrounding trees. The upper river is easy to fish and great fun can be had using light tackle and a dry fly. Loch Freuchie may be fished either from the boat or from the bank and both methods can bring equal success. The north end of the loch, where the River Freuchie enters from Glen Quaich, is a good place to begin, although fish may be taken from almost anywhere round the shoreline, as is the case on Lochan a'Mhuilinn. Dapping is popular, and productive, on Loch Freuchie. Flies: Black Pennell, Grouse & Claret, Silver Invicta. On the river, dry fly fishing, offer them: Iron Blue Dun, Greenwell's Glory, March Brown, Partridge & Yellow.
Permission & Charges Salmon fishing on the River Braan is preserved. For trout fishing on the lower river, contact: Kettles of Dunkeld, Atholl Street, Dunkeld, Perthshire. Tel: 01350 727556. Cost: £5 per rod per day. For the Upper River Braan, contact: Bunnie's Tea Room & Post Office, Amulree, by Dunkeld, Perthshire. Tel: 01350 725200. Cost: £5 per rod per day. This ticket also allows you to bank fish on Loch Freuchie. For boat fishing on Loch Freuchie, contact: Graham Stewart, Amulree Hotel, Amulree, by Dunkeld, Perthshire. Tel: 01350 725218. Graham Stewart is an expert angler and he will give visiting anglers excellent advice on tactics and techniques. For Lochan a'Mhuilinn, contact: Finlyson Hughes, 29 Barossa Place, Perth PH1 5EP. Tel: 01738 625134; Fax: 01738 639017. Cost: £30 per boat per day, 2 rods fishing, from 8.30am until 9.30pm.

CROSS REFERENCE
LENDOCK Reservoir (See OS Map 51).
The following waters are described on OS Map 53, BLAIRGOWRIE: Loch BROOM; Lochan OISINNEACH MOR; OISSINNEACH BEAG, Lochan; NA BRAE, Loch; CHARLES, Loch; A'CHAIT, Lochan (Clunie); BENACHALLY, Loch; ORDIE, Loch; NA BEINNE, Loch; DOWALLY, Loch; ROTMELL, Loch; MILL DAM (Dunkeld); BUTTERSTONE, Loch of; LOCH OF CRAIGLUSH, Loch of; LOWES, Loch of the; SKIACH, Loch; LITTLE SKIACH Loch; STARE Dam; ROBIN'S Dam; MILL DAM (Murthly); TULLYBELTON, Loch; BERTHA, Loch; METHVEN, Loch; HUNTINGTOWER, Loch; TAY, River (from Ballinluig downstream to Perth). The following water is described on OS Map 58: DUPPLIN Lake. The following waters are described on OS Map 42: DUNALASTAIR Reservoir; AN DAIM, Lochan; BEOIL CHATHAICHE, Lochan; KINARDOCHY, Loch. The following waters are described on OS Map 51: TAY, Loch; LYON, River

DRUMMOND Trout Fishery
Location & Access 52/745212 Drummond Fish Farm lies 2 miles to the west of Comrie in the grounds of Aberuchill Castle. The fish farm is well-signposted from the A85 Comrie/St Fillans road.
Commentary A well-managed, popular, put-and-take fishery, open all year and offering tackle hire and free casting instruction for beginners during the summer months. There is also a farm shop which sells freshly prepared smoked trout and salmon and a range of venison and game products. Voted the Perthshire's most enjoyable visitor attraction in 1999.
Fish Stocked rainbow trout which average 2lb.
Flies & Tactics Bank fishing on 6 small ponds. 5 are "all methods" fisheries, 1 is reserved for fly fishing only. All fish caught are charged at £1.60 per pound and minimum parties of 10 anglers may book the exclusive use of the fishery. Prizes are awarded each month to adults and juniors for the heaviest fish caught and the heaviest catch.
Permission & Charges Adults: £3.50 per 2 hour session, £4.00 for 4 hours, £7 for 8 hours., £9 for 12 hours. Rod hire, £3.00 per session. Fish caught must be kept and will be charged at £1.60 per pound. Reductions for juniors and OAP's. Contact:

OS Map 52 — Aberfeldy and Glen Almond

Drummond Trout Fishery, Comrie, Perthshire. Tel: 01764 670500.

EARN (Upper), River (See also OS Map 58, Perth & Kinross)
Location & Access Source 51/640237 Outfall 58/197185 The River Earn on OS Map 52 begins by St Fillans Golf Course at the road bridge at 52/702241 and exits on to OS Map 58, Perth & Kinross to the south of Crieff near North Forr (52/870200). The stream is easily accessible throughout its length from the A85 Crieff/Lochearnhead road and the A822 Crieff/Dunblane road.
Commentary The River Earn is one of the major tributaries of the River Tay and it enters the Firth of Tay over Carpow Bank between Elcho Castle (58/165210) and Newburgh (58/235183). The upper river is quite different in character from the slower-moving lower river. From its beginnings at St Fillans to downstream from Comrie, the river flows through attractive, well-wooded farmlands in a series of fine, tumbling runs and deep holding pools. The Lower Strowan Beat, at the road bridge and church near Strowan House (52/821213), is particularly lovely, especially during the autumn months when the trees are myriad shades of red and gold. Crieff is a popular visitor centre and there is plenty for non-fishing members of yur party to do whilst you enjoy the river; including the excellent sport facilities available at the Crieff Hydro Hotel and splendid, non-taxing, walks round the Knock of Crieff (278m).
Fish Approximately 600 salmon and grilse are taken most seasons along with some 600 sea-trout, although the spring months also produce a few fish. October 1994 produced one of the heaviest salmon taken from the Earn for many years: a 35lb fish, landed at Freelands by Harry Dow. Sea-trout fishing, for which the River Earn was most famous, is not so good now as it was in days past. Sea-trout average around 2lb in weight but larger fish of up to and over 5lb in weight are occasionally caught. In recent years, escapee rainbow trout have invaded the river: Strathyre angler, Jim Stoddart, took a 16lb 4oz rainbow trout from the upper river in October 1994. Brown trout are also present and average 8oz and the river also holds some fine grayling: specimen fish of up to and over 3lb in weight are taken most years.
Flies & Tactics Much of the headwaters of the system have been impounded by reservoirs and water extraction also takes place in the lower river. Consequently, fishing can often be blighted by low water levels. The best sport is to be had after heavy rain, usually at the back end of the season. Spinning accounts for most early running fish, but there is some lovely fly water and, once the water temperature rises, fly-fishing is the preferred fishing method. Wading is generally user-friendly and a 15ft rod will adequately cover most of the lies. During the summer months, a strong trout is more appropriate and much of the river may then be covered without the need for wading. The most productive salmon flies include: Willie Gunn, Garry Dog, Hairy Mary, Stoat's Tail, Shrimp Fly. When spinning use Devon minnows in various colours, Tobies and Rapala lures. Sea-trout and brown trout will respond to: Black Pennell, March Brown, Peter Ross.
Permission & Charges The Comrie Angling Club have fishing on Dunira & Tomperran (where the River Lednock enters from the north), Aberuchill (immediately upstream from Comrie), amounting to approximately 2 miles on the Earn. They also have fishing on a short stretch of the Drummond Estate fishings on the Water of Ruchill, a major tributary of the River Earn which flows in from the south to join the River Earn at Comrie. Cost: £10 per rod per day salmon fishing, £4 per day for trout fishing. Further information may be had from J L Fraser, Secretary, Comrie Angling Club, Tiagh-na-h'Iasgair, St Fillans, Perthshire. Tel: 01764685305 (Country Membership is available for regular visitors). Crieff Angling Club have 6 miles of fishing divided into 3 beats for 20 rods. The fishing begins 1 mile downstream from Comrie and extends east to North Forr. The 3 beats average approximately 250 salmon and 400 sea-trout each year. Contact: Mr G F Penney, Adam Boyd, Newsagents & Tackle Shop, King Street, Crieff, Perthshire. Tel: 01764 653871. Also, the Tourist Information Office, High Street, Crieff, Perthshire. Tel: 01764 652578. Cost: from £10 to £20 per rod per day, depending upon the time of year. Trout fishing costs £5 per rod per day. Fishing on the Lower Strowan Beat, 1.36 miles of double bank with a small stretch of single bank fishing opposite Lochlane, is available from: Jim Henderson, Country Pursuits, 46 Henderson Street, Bridge of Allan FK9 4HS. Tel: 01786 834495; Fax: 01786 834210. The beat has 13 named pools and fishes a maximum of 6 rods. Cost: varies from between £30 and £50 per rod per day depending upon the time of year. The Lochlane & Laggan Fishings are also factored by Country Pursuits where the 4 year average catch for the month of October is 71 salmon. This includes 0.16 miles of the right bank of the Turret Burn. Upper Strowan Beats: Finlyson Hughes, 29 Barossa Place, Perth PH1 5EP. Tel: 01738 625134; Fax: 01738 639017. Cost: £50 per rod per day.

FARLEYER, Loch
Location & Access 52/810521 Approach from Camserney (52/817495) to the north of the B846 Aberfeldy/Keltneyburn road. A 4-wheel drive vehicle is required, otherwise, an invigorating 2 mile hike.
Commentary A lovely little loch, approximately 25 acres in extent, lying at an altitude of 400m. Access is strictly controlled and may be restricted after 12th August.
Fish Stocked with a Loch Leven strain of trout. Average weight 8oz/10oz.
Flies & Tactics Bank fishing only. Although fish may be taken from all round the shoreline, the most productive areas are where the two feeder burns enter, one at the north west corner of the loch, the other half way down the east shore. Flies: Ke-He, Woodcock & Hare-lug, Silver Butcher.
Permission & Charges Contact: David Campbell, The Square, Aberfeldy, Perthshire. Tel: 01887 829545.

Aberfeldy and Glen Almond
OS Map 52

Prior to setting out, report to: The Keeper, Farleyer Estate, Lurgan, by Aberfeldy. Cost: £10 per rod per day. David Campbell will advise visiting anglers on aditional fishing available in the area and also guide expeditions to some of the more remote waters.

FASKALLY, Loch See Lower River Tummel entry.
FREUCHIE, Loch See River Braan entry.
FREUCHIE, River See River Braan entry.
LEDNOCK, River See Upper River Earn entry.

MONZIEVAIRD, Loch
Location & Access 52/840233 The loch lies immediately to the north of the A85 Crieff/Comrie road at Ochtertyre.
Commentary The ideal place for a family holiday with something to keep every member of your tribe happily amused whilst you fish. There are 23 comfortably furnished self-catering chalets in the grounds of the estate and they all have superb views of this most attractive water. Loch Monzievaird covers an area of 80 acres and is approximately 1/2 a mile long by up to 200 yds wide. There are two tree-covered islands, one at either end of the loch, and a dominant promontory graced by the ruins of Monzievaird Castle.
Fish A healthy stock of native wild brown trout which average 10oz/12oz in weight.
Flies & Tactics Comfortable boat fishing and fish rise and are taken all round the loch. The margins of the islands is a good place to begin. Flies: Ke-He, March Brown, Dunkeld.
Permission & Charges Fishing is reserved for the use of guests staying in the Monzievaird chalets and costs in the order of £10 per rod per day. Boat fishing only. Additional fishing can also be arranged on other lochs and rivers in the area. Conatct: Loch Monzievaird Chalets, Crieff, Perthshire PH7 4JR. Tel: 01764 652586; Fax: 01764 652555.

PRIVATE WATERS MEALLBRODDEN, Loch 52/918252 KENNARD, Loch 52/906460; CREAGH, Loch 52/904443; SCOLLY, Loch 52/918478; GRANDTULLY, Loch of 52/915501; NA CRAIGE, Loch 52/882456 (NB This loch may become available in 1997. For information, contact Tourist Information Centre, The Square, Aberfeldy. Tel: 01887 820276 or Aberfeldy Angling Club. Tel: 01887 820385); HOIL, Loch 52/860435; FORMAL, Loch 52/863451; FENDER, Lochan 52/879414; DERCLUICH, Loch 52/864550; A'CHAIT Lochan 52/845561; LAIRG LAOIGH Lochan 52/829544; GLASSIE, Loch 52/851529 (Pike only); NA BA, Loch 52/884556; AN DUIN, Loch 52/890554; NAN EUN, Loch 52/890552; PITCASTLE Lochs 52/889558; SGARADH GOBHAIR Lochan 52/883570; CHUIR Lochan 52/912561; NA MOINE MOIRE Lochan 52/924558; CREAG A'MHADAIDH Lochan 52/708460.
RUCHILL, Water of See Upper River Earn entry.

TAY (Upper), River
Location & Access The section of the River Tay described here is from the outfall at the east end of Loch Tay (see OS Map 51) at Kenmore (52/772456), downstream to the River Tay's junction with the River Tummel (see separate entry) at Ballinluig (52/975512). Access to the river is from the A827 Ballinluig/Kenmore road and from other public roads which border both banks of the stream. (See also OS Map 53).
Commentary This 15 mile stretch of the river contains some of the most varied and attractive of the River Tay fishing beats, including Taymouth Castle, Bolfracks, Farleyer, Castle Menzies, Weem, Killiechassie, Cluny and Grandtully. The river here is far less intimidating to fish than the lower beats and most of the pools can be effectively covered from the bank. The River Lyon (See OS Map 51, Loch Tay), a major tributary of the Tay, flows in just downstream from Taymouth Castle at 52/795477. The river is also very popular with white-water rafters who float down from Loch Tay to enjoy the thrill of shooting the rapids at Grandtully. Amicable agreement has been reached between these interests and the interests of anglers over the time and frequency of rafting expeditions.
Fish The upper river beats are not as productive as the more famous, downstream beats, but they still manage to produce upwards of 1,000 salmon most seasons, the average number per beat being in the order of 80/120 fish depending upon prevailing water conditions. The river also contains some excellent brown trout as well as grayling and unwelcome, escapee rainbow trout.
Flies & Tactics Spring fishing can be good on the upper river, particularly in recent years when warmer weather has encouraged many fish entering the river to move quickly upstream. A 15ft rod is the best all-purpose rod for most of the season and you will need chest waders to reach some of the lies in high water. The river is approximately 45yds wide throughout much of its length and is easily manageable, but an ability to Spey-cast will greatly improve your chance of sport. There are some marvelous pools along the way, including: Miller's Bed, Twin Trees Pool, Bridge Pool, Cuil Pool, Island Pool, Rock Pool, The Pot, The Platform, Jubilee Pool, Church Flats and Junction Pool. Spinning accounts for most of the early running fish but after May the upper river offers some perfect fly water, particularly at Derculich. Tobies and Devon minnows are the most popular spinning lures, productive patterns of fly include: Stoat's Tail, Silver Stoat's Tail, Willie Gunn, Munro Killer, Garry Dog, Hairy Mary, General Practitioner, Ally's Shrimp and Waddingtons.
Permission & Charges Prices vary according to the time of year. Expect to pay in the order of £25/£50 per rod per day during the spring months, £30 per day in the summer and up to £60 per rod per day at the back end. Most beats can provide the services of an experienced gillie and his advice is invaluable if you are new to the water and when a boat has to be used. The rate per day for his services is approximately £35 (plus gratuity). For Taymouth, contact: Kenmore Hotel, Kenmore, Perthshire PH15 2NU. Tel: 01887 830205;

OS Map 52 — Aberfeldy and Glen Almond

Fax: 01887 830262; for Dercluich, Pitnacree, Balnabeggan, Lower Bolfacks, Findynate and Cloichfoldich, contact: Jim Henderson, Country Pursuits, 46 Henderson Street, Bridge of Allan FK9 4HS. Tel: 01786 834495; Fax: 01786 834210; Upper Grandtully & Edradynate, contact: Robert Cairns, Easter Cluny, Aberfeldy, Perthshire PH15 2JU. Tel: 01887 840228; Weem: Tom Sharpe, Station Road, Alcester, Warwickshire B49 5EQ. Tel: 01789 763938 and Weem Hotel, Weem, by Aberfeldy, Perthshire PH15 2LD. Tel: 01887 820381. Upper Farleyer: Michael Smith, Cuilaluinn, by Aberfeldy, Perthshire PH15 2JW. Tel/Fax: 01887 820302. Trout fishing is also available on the river via the above. Cost: approximately £10 per rod per day.

TUMMEL, Loch

Location & Access 52/820595. Easily accessible from the B8109 Killikrankie/Tummel Bridge road along the north shore and from the minor road which margins the south bank.

Commentary A splendid loch, immortalised in the song The Road to the Isles and very popular with visitors and anglers alike. The loch is 11 miles in length by up to 1 mile wide and is best appreciated from Queen's View (52/866595) where the Forestry Commission have a visitor centre. The view is named, not in honour of Queen Victoria, as most people imagine, but in honour of Mary Queen of Scots who paused here in about 1562. Loch Tummel is part of the Garry/Tummel Hydro-Electric scheme and the waters have been impounded by the Clunie Dam at the east end of the loch. The loch is fed from the west by Loch Rannoch and Dunalastair Reservoir (see Os Map 42, Loch Rannoch), and the Upper River Tummel, between Dunalastair Reservoir and Loch Tummel, is also available for fishing both above and below the hydro-dam at Tummel Bridge.

Fish In Loch Tummel, wild brown trout which vary in size from 8oz to fish of up to and over 5lb in weight. There are also very large ferox trout and voracious pike. Salmon enter the loch from the River Tummel (see separate entry) but they are rarely caught. In the river, modest brown trout, but the chance of larger fish on the lower river, particularly in the spring and autumn months of the season.

Flies & Tactics Fishing is from the bank only. Wading is dangerous and not really necessary since fish tend to lie in the shallow water, close to the bank. Fishing on Loch Tummel is strictly limited to the shoreline marked clearly on the reverse of the permits. Other areas are either sensitive because of re-stocking or the individual riparian owners do not allow fishing from their property. Contact Andrew MacKenzie, Secretary of the Riparian Association, on telephone 01882 634253.The north bank is the best option. Flies: Black Pennell, Soldier Palmer, Alexandra.

Permission & Charges For Loch Tummel, contact: Tourist Information Centre, 22 Atholl Road, Pitlcochry PH16 5BX. Tel: 01796 472215; Fax: 01796 474046. Mitchells of Pitlochry 01796 472613. Queen's View Visitor Centre, Forest Lodge, Strathtummel, by Pitlochry. Tel: 01350 727284. Tummel Valley Holiday Park, Strathtummel, by Pitlcohry. Tel: 01882 634221. For the Upper River Tummel, contact: Loch Rannoch Hotel, Kinloch Rannoch, Perthshire. Tel: 01882 632201. Tummel Valley Park (see above). Country Store, Kinloch Rannoch, Perthshire. Tel: 01882 632306. Cost: £3 per rod per day, £10 per rod per week, £25 per rod per season.

TUMMEL (Lower), River

Location & Access Source 50/235475 Outfall 52/978513 The east bank of the river is easily accessible from the A9 Perth/Inverness road. The west bank is accessed by a minor road that parallel's the stream.

Commentary The true source of the River Tummel lies in the mountains of Black Mount to the south of Glencoe. The stream rises from Coireach a'Ba and flows east as the River Ba, crossing under the A82 Tyndrum/Fort William road to reach Loch Ba and Loch Laidon (See Os Map 41, Ben Nevis). After leaving Loch Laidon, the river flows through Loch Eigheach as the River Gaur (See Os Map 42, Loch Rannoch). The stream becomes the River Tummel as it exits from Loch Rannoch and it eventually joins the River Tay at Ballinluig after a tortuous journey of some 58 miles in which it passes through Dunalastair Reservoir and Loch Tummel. The river is impounded for hydro-electric power generation and Loch Faskally, at Pitlochry, was formed when the most downstream dam was built. The dam is a popular tourist attraction because of the viewing windows built into the wall of the salmon ladder.

Fish Salmon, trout, grayling and the occasional seatrout. An unusual catch was a 9lb "steelhead" caught by Neil McGowan in March 1996. Salmon numbers have declined in recent years. Approximately 40 fish were taken during 1999. The brown trout average 8oz, although there are some specimen fish as well. Specimen grayling are also taken: a grayling of 3lb 6oz was landed in April 1996. Loch Faskally can produce large brown trout, fish of up to and over 10lb in weight, but it is most noted as a salmon fishery. Approximately 20 fish are taken each season, generally by trolling. Loch Faskally also contains pike and perch.

Flies & Tactics Few salmon are taken in the River Tummel above Loch Faskally, although there are good beats on the River Garry, and its tributary the River Tilt, which also flow into Loch Faskally. The best of the sport on the River Tummel is downstream from the dam to the junction with the River Tay. There is 5 miles of fishing in various beats, fished by a total of up to 20 rods per day. There are some 22 named pools, the best-known of which include: Sawmill Stream, Jimmy's Island, Tomdachoil, Rock Pool, Monument Pool and Junction Pool. The river is awkward to fish in the upper reaches and an ability to Spey-cast is a distinct advantage. Wading, particularly downstream from the dam, can be dangerous. Avoid the temptation of going a step to far by using thigh waders, rather than chest waders, and always wear a floatation jacket. Flies: Garry Dog, Willie Gunn, Stoat's Tail, Shrimp Fly, Munro Killer. On Loch Faskally, use

Blairgowrie OS Maps 52-53

Tobies, Devon minnows and Rapalas. Whilst it is possible to spin from the bank on Loch Faskally, boat fishing is more likley to produce results. Salmon do no enter the loch in any numbers until after June.

Permission & Charges Portnacraig Beat: Pitlochry Angling Club, per/Ross Gardiner, 3B Robertson Crescent, Pitlochry. Tel: 01796 472157 (evenings and weekends only); For information on private beats, contact: Mitchells of Pitlochry, 23 Atholl Road, Pitlochry. Tel: 01796 472613. Mitchells will also provide information and advice on the additional fishing available in the area. East House Hotel, by Pitlochry. Tel: 01796473121; Fax: 01796 472473. Costs vary, depending upon the time of year, from £6 to 35 per day on the Pitlochry Angling Club Water to up to £40/£50 on the private beats. Preference is given to anglers taking a weekly let, rather than a single day. Trout fishing on the River Tummel costs £3 per day or £10 per week. Loch Faskally: Dougal MacLaren, The Boat House, Loch Faskally, Pitlochry. Tel: 01796 472919. Cost: boat and outboard engine, £35 per day, 2 rods fishing, plus £5.75 per rod for a fishing permit.

TUMMEL (Upper), River See Loch Tummel entry.
TURRET Burn See Upper River Earn entry.

TURRET, Loch
Location & Access 52/810275 Loch Turret Reservoir lies to the north of Crieff. Approach from Hosh (52/855235), near the Glen Turret Distillery, via the minor road that margins the Turret Burn up to the dam at the south end of the loch.
Commentary The loch is 2 miles long by up to 1/2 a mile wide and lies between Choinneachain Hill (773m) to the east and Carn Chois (786m) to the west. These peaks act as a wind-tunnel and Loch Turret can often be a stormy place to fish. The source of the River Turret, which was dammed to form the loch, is Loch an Uaine (52/787309) and this is most easily accessed from Loch Turret. Moor the boat by the inlet stream and hike north up the glen to reach the loch after a rough tramp of about 1 mile. You will find splendid isolation here, and perfect peace.
Fish Trout average in the order of 8oz/10oz with a few of up to and over 1lb, but there must be some monsters lurking in the depths was well.
Flies & Tactics Bank fishing is allowed, but this can be taxing and most convenient way to explore this large water is by boat. Make sure that you have spare fuel for the outboard, before setting out, and always wear a life jacket. If in doubt, don't launch the boat. Best sport is had close to the shoreline, particularly at the north end of the loch and in the bay below Creag nan Uan and where the Allt nan Columamn burn enters (52/800286). Flies: Black Zulu, Grouse & Claret, Silver Butcher.
Permission & Charges Adam Boyd, Newsagents, 39 King Street, Crieff, Perthshire. Tel: 01764 653871. Cost: Bank fishing at £6 per rod per day, boat with outboard motor, 2 rods fishing, £18.00 per day. Proprietor: G.F. Penney. No Sunday fishing.

TURRET, River See Loch Turret entry.

Blairgowrie

BUTTERSTONE, Loch of
Location & Access 53/060450 The Loch of Butterstone lies adjacent to the A923 Dunkeld/Blairgowrie road, 3.5 miles east of Dunkeld.
Commentary Splendid scenery and always the chance of sharing your fishing with the resident ospreys from nearby Loch of the Lowes (see separate entry). The loch, which is circular (approximately 1/2 mile across), is entirely surrounded by mature woodlands and is a haven for wildlife.
Fish Rainbow trout and a few brown trout. Average weight is in the order of 1lb 8oz but fish of up to and over 7lb are taken.
Flies & Tactics Boat fishing only and there are 15 available for use each day. Day sessions are from 9am until 5pm, evening sessions from 5.30pm until dusk. Fish are taken all round the loch with the west end and the red-fringed south shore being particularly productive. Flies: reservoir-type lures, or try Black Pennell, March Brown, Dunkeld.
Permission & Charges For further information and bookings contact: R Knight, Butterstone Loch, Dunkeld. Tel: 01350 724238; Fax: 01350 724215. Cost: Day £30 per boat; evening £30 per boat. Three anglers per boat with a bag limit of 6 fish per angler.

COARSE FISHERIES HARE MYRE, Loch 53/182419; STORMONT, Loch (also known as Loch Bog) 53/193423; BLACK, Loch 53/175427; WHITE, Loch 53/170429; FINGASK, Loch 53/164430; RAE, Loch 53/159445; MARLEE, Loch (also known as Loch of Drumellie) 53/144444; CLUINE, Loch 53/114440.
CROSS REFERENCES BACKWATER Reservoir see OS Map 44; DUPPLIN Lake see OS Map 58; BRAAN, River see OS Map 52; TUMMEL, River see OS Map 52; ALMOND, River see OS Map 52.

DEAN, Water See River Isla.

ERICHT, River
Location & Access Source 53/148515 Outfall 53/239428 The River Ericht is easily accessible throughout its entire length from public roads.
Commentary An exciting, under-rated, salmon stream. The River Ericht is formed by the joining of the River Ardle and the River Blackwater which meet to the east of Bridge of Cally. The Blackwater is a continuation of the River Shee (see OS Map 43, Braemar) and all of these streams are important spawning grounds for Tay salmon. The Ericht, although a tributary of the River Isla (see separate entry), attracts more fish than its senior partner and has a substantial tributary of its own, the Lornty Burn, which flows in from Loch Benachally (53/070504) in the Forest of Clunie.
Fish No lack of salmon: several thousand fish pass through the counter at Blairgowrie each year. A few sea-trout, modest brown trout. Upwards of 300 salmon are taken most seasons.

OS Map 53 — Blairgowrie

Flies & Tactics The River Ericht is a classic spate stream and sport is very much dependent upon good water levels. Spring fishing has been much improved in recent years but the dry summer of 1996 was less exciting. Autumn months produce most fish. Although spinning is allowed on the Blairgowrie Angling Association water, most of the rest of the river is fly only. Indeed, fly-fishing is every bit as productive as spinning and, increasingly, anglers opt for the fly rod. In low water conditions, a single-handed rod is adequate and salmon may be tempted with flies as small as size 16 dressings. Above Blairgowrie, the river banks can be steep and daunting and care is required when wading. Downstream from Blairgowrie, the banks are overgrown in some places which makes casting interesting, but, generally, the river is user-friendly and most of the lies are easily covered. Try: Stoat's Tail, Hairy Mary, Shrimp Fly, Munro Killer, Garry Dog, Willie Gunn.

Permission & Charges See River Isla entry for Blairgowire Angling Association water. Day tickets at £20 per day, are available to visitors on Monday, Wednesday and Friday.

The Bridge of Cally Hotel have single bank and double bank fishing for 4 rods on some 3 miles of the Ericht, above Blairgowrie. The hotel also offers very comfortable accommodation for small, private, parties of anglers. Fishing cost: £30/£30 per rod per day. Fishing may also be available on the Craighall Beat via Finlayson & Hughes, 23 Barossa Place, Perth PH1 5EP. Tel: 01738 630926; Fax: 01738 639017. Also contact Kate Fleming (01250 873990) for trout permits (£5 per day) or salmon (£20 per day).

ISLA, River

Location & Access Source 43/177768 Outfall 53/160375 The river is easily accessible throughout most of its length from public roads. Upstream from Auchavan (43/191696) an estate road borders the stream and this is private.

Commentary The River Isla is one of the principal tributaries of the River Tay (see separate entry) and it rises on the east slope of Glas Maol (1068m) in the Caenlochan National Nature Reserve. The river flows south down Glen Isla through a spectacular gorge and over a 70ft-high waterfall at the Reekie Linn near Bridge of Craigisla (53/255537) and further falls at the Slug of Auchrannie, both of which are impassable to migratory fish. By Airlie Castle, the stream collects the waters from the Loch of Lintrathen and the Backwater Reservoir. South from Alyth, at Bridge of Crathies (53/281455), the Isla is joined by Dean Water which flows in from Strathmore. 3 miles downstream the River Ericht enters. From this meeting, the Isla wends its way through fertile farmlands in a 5-mile series of sluggish ox-bows to greet the Tay at the head of the famous Islamouth Beat.

Fish Salmon, a sea-trout, brown trout and grayling. Approximately 500 salmon are taken during the season.

Flies & Tactics The river is easily accessible and there are no problems in covering the slow moving stream with its deep pots and gentle glides. There are few clearly defined pools, so fishing the river is very much a case of carefully exploring every likely-looking nook and cranny. Spinning accounts for many salmon, using Rapalas, Tobies and Devon minnows, but fly fishing also produces results. Sea-trout fishing is best in July, depending upon water conditions. Grayling fishing, particularly in the autumn, can be outstanding and Grouse & Green, Green Peter and Invicta are popular patterns of flies. However, as with salmon, bait fishing is the most commonly used fishing method. Dean Water is also easy of access and a productive little stream, given good water levels. The upper reaches of the Isla contain small brown trout which often give good sport on the dry fly. For salmon, try: Willie Gunn, Garry Dog, Munro Killer, General Practitioner, Shrimp Fly, Stoat's Tail.

Permission & Charges Contact: Kate Fleming, 26 Allan Street, Blairgowrie. PH10 6AD. Tel: 01250 873990. Kate Fleming will also advise visitors on the wide range of additional fishing, both coarse and game, which is available in the area. Jas Crockart & Son, 28 Allan Street, Blairgowrie. Tel: 01250 872056. Mr Snip, Hairdressers, Coupar Angus. Tel: 01828 627148. Cost: £20 per rod per day for salmon fishing. The Athole Arms Public House (Tel: 01828 627205) issue trout fishing permits for the River Isla at £5 per rod per day and permits to fish Monk Myre Loch (see separate entry). Strathmore Angling Improvement Assoc. has a large amount of trout fishing between Airlie Castle and Erichtmouth including Dean Water. Limited number of salmon permits available for Balbrogie opposite Erictmouth. See Keithick A.C., Coupar Angus (ref Mr Snip) for information on several other beats including: Coupar Grange - Salmon permit (01828 627368), Grange of Aberbothrie (Salmon permit £20) includes Isla above Erichtmouth and lower stretch of Ericht.

LINTRATHEN, Loch of

Location & Access 53/277550 The Loch of Lintrathen lies to the east of the B954 Aylth/Dykends road. Leave the B954 at Bridge of Craigisla (53/255540) (pause to have a look at the famous Reekie Linn Waterfall) and follow the minor road east through Easter Peel to reach the lochside boathouse and parking area after 1.5 miles.

Commentary A splendid loch, surrounded by mature trees and host to a wide variety of wildlife. The loch is almost 1 and 1/2 miles north south by up to 3/4 of a mile wide and drops to a depth of 80 feet at the south end. There are excellent clubhouse facilities as well as facilities for disabled anglers.

Fish Regularly stocked with brown trout which average 14oz/15oz in weight.

Flies & Tactics Boat fishing only and the most favoured fishing areas are at the north end, round the tree-clad island, and in the shallow bay where the feeder burn enters from the Backwater Reservoir (See OS Map 44, Ballater). The south shoreline can also be productive. Arrange your drift to keep the boat about 15yds/20yds out from the bank. Flies: Black Pennell, Greenwell's Glory, Cinnamon & Gold.

Permission & Charges Lintrathen Angling Club, Tel:

Blairgowrie   OS Map 53

01575 560327. Cost: £32 per boat with up to 3 anglers fishing, with a 15 fish per boat bag limit. Anglers are required to wear a lifejacket when fishing (available for hire at boat house).

MILL DAM See Stare Dam entry.

MONK MYRE, Loch
Location & Access 53/210427 Approach from the A923 Coupar Angus/Blairgowrie road. At 53/200420, drive east on the minor road to reach the loch after 3/4 on a mile.
Commentary An easily accessible, put-and-take fishery. Monk Myre Loch is 14 acres in extent and the fishing is controlled by the local angling club whose Secretary is John Carrick.
Fish Regularly stocked with both brown and rainbow trout. Average weight, about 1lb. Fish of up to and over 3lb are also taken.
Flies & Tactics Boat fishing only and the centre of the loch generally produces best results. In the evenings, fish closer to the shore. There is a bag limit of 8 fish per rod per day. Flies: Grouse & Claret, Greenwell's Glory, Invicta.
Permission & Charges Atholl Arms Public House, Coupar Angus. Tel: 01828 627205. Cost: £20 per rod per session. Sessions: 9pm until 5pm and from 5.30pm until dusk.

MONTAGUE, Loch See Seamaw Loch entry.
NATURE RESERVE LOWES, Loch of the 53/050440; CRAIGLUSH, Loch of 53/043442

PIPERDAM, Fishery
Location & Access 53/318319 Piperdam lies to the north of the A85 Dundee/Perth road 2 miles west of Muirhead. Leave the A85 at Star Inn Farm 53/331305 and drive north for approximately 4 or 5 miles and turn left at A923. Piperdam is 1/2 mile from the road junction.
Commentary A popular put-and-take fishery which is open all the year round except for Christmas Day, Boxing Day and New Year's Day.
Fish Brown trout (average weight 12oz) rainbow trout (average weight 2lb 4oz) and grilse (average weight 4lb).
Flies & Tactics Boat fishing on the principal loch, which is 40 acres in extent, bank fishing on the 3 and 1/2 acre rainbow trout pond. Use rainbow trout lures and traditional patterns of trout flies. Dry fly fishing can also be productive, particularly in the evenings.
Permission & Charges Full day, half day and evening sessions are available. Day session (9.30am until 4.30pm), Evening session (5.00pm uintil dusk). Cost, with 2/3 rods fishing, £36 at weekends and £32 on weekdays. There is an 18 fish limit per boat. Contact: Piperdam Golf and Country Park, Broughty Ferry Road, Dundee DD4 6JS. Tel: 01382 580729.

PRIVATE WATERS REDMYRE, Loch 53/281335; LUNDIE, Loch 53/289371; LONG, Loch 53/289386; LEDCRIEFF, Loch 53/270371; LAIRD'S, Loch 53/259357; GLENDAMS Reservoir 53/199485; MHARALCH, Loch 53/119569; CHARLES, Loch 53/085542; SKIACH, Loch 53/951475; SKIACH, LITTLE LOCH 53/954468; BROOM, Loch 53/010580, BENACHALLY, Loch 53070504; ORDIE, Loch 53/035500; NA BEINNE, Lochan 53/033485; DOWALLY, Loch 53/019474; ROTMELL, Loch 53/023471; CALLY, Loch 53/027440; OISINNEACH MOR, Lochan 53/030549; OISINNEACH BEAG, Lochan 53/039559; TULLYBELTON, Loch 53/001349; OLD ENGLAND, Loch 53/123378; KING'S MYRE, Loch 53/113362; HUNTINGTOWER, Loch 53/074249; METHVEN, Loch 53/059258; BERTHD, Loch 53/080273.

ROBIN'S DAM See Stare Dam entry.

SEAMAW, Loch
Location & Access 53/313227 Seamaw Loch lies on the north edge of Pitmiddle Wood and is accessed from Tullach Ard on the B953 Balbeggie/Abernyte road.
Commentary An put-and-take fishery, sheltered from the wind and ideal for a few hours sport. The owners also have Montague Loch (53/192281), a more exposed water, which lies near Craigneb on the minor road between Redfield and Rait.
Fish Seamaw Loch is stocked with rainbow trout and brown trout, Montague Loch is stocked with rainbow trout and has a few native brown trout. Fish average approximately 2lb in weight.
Flies & Tactics These are small lochs, little more than 2 acres in extent, and fish rise and are taken everywhere. Seamaw is fished from the boat, bank fishing only on Montague Loch. Rods are limited to 4 fish per session.
Permission & Charges Contact; Mr James Watson, Mill of Montague, Balbeggie, Nr Perth. Tel: 01821 640271. Cost: £10 per rod per session bank fishing, £12 per rod per session from the boat. Sessions are: 9.30am until 5pm, and 5pm until dusk, May until September.

STARE, Dam
Location & Access 53/049388. Stare Dam lies adjacent to the A9 Perth/Inverness road about 3 miles north from Bankfoot (53/070351).
Commentary Stare Dam is a man-made loch in the grounds of Rohallion Lodge, the home of a former Chief Scout of the Boy Scout movement, Lord Rohallion. There are two small lochs here, joined together to form Stare Dam, and they lie in an attractive woodland setting. To the north of Stare Dam is Robin's Dam, and to the east, Mill Dam. Neither of these are available for public fishing.
Fish Stocked rainbow trout and a few native brown trout. Rainbow trout average 1lb in weight but there are much larger fish as well.
Flies & Tactics Boat fishing only and there is a boat on each section of Stare Dam. No one place is substantially better than another, so cast with confidence all over the loch. There is a 4 fish limit on rainbow trout, but no limit on the numbers of brown trout which may be retained. Flies: Ke-He, March Brown,

Blairgowrie

Kingfisher Butcher.

Permission & Charges Contact: Mr King, Factor, Murthly & Strathbraan Estate, Estate Office, Douglasfield, Murthly. Tel: 01738 710303. Cost: £16 per angler per day.

TAY, River

Location & Access The River Tay on OS Map 53, is described from Ballinluig, where the River Tummel enters (53/979512), downstream to its outfall in the Firth of Tay below Perth (53/128216). The River Tummel and the remainder of the River Tay, upstream from Ballinluig to Loch Tay, is described on OS Map 52. Access to the river is from public and private, estate, roads which margin either bank of the stream.

Commentary The River Tay is perhaps the most productive salmon stream in Europe and certainly one of the most famous salmon rivers in the world. The river drains a catchment area of over 2,500 square miles and, from source to mouth, west to east, is approximately 118 miles in length. This is a big river, in every sense, and, from Ballinluig down, because of its size, the Tay can be intimidating to fish. However, the beauty of the surrounding countryside and the enormous wealth of streams, pools and runs, make the Tay an angler's delight. Much of the best fishing is contained within this section of the Tay. Famous beats, including Upper and Lower Scone, Upper and Lower Redgorton, Islamouth, Cargill, Ballathie, Stobhall, Taymount, Catholes and Burnmouth, are rarely available on a casual basis. Such is their reputation that they are invariably booked in advance, often by the same people who return year after year. They are also extremely expensive. In recent years, much of the netting in the Tay estuary has been either closed down or bought out and there are signs that runs of fish are improving again, after many years of decline, and that spring fishing, for which the Tay used to be renowned, is recovering.

Fish Salmon, with approximately 9,000 salmon and grilse being taken most seasons. Considerable numbers of sea-trout also run the Tay but accurate catch statistics are not available. The Tay now hosts escapee farm rainbow trout and some run the river as steelheads. The river contains excellent brown trout with fish of over 5lb being taken in recent years. There are good stocks of grayling as well, with specimen fish of up to and over 3lb in weight. Species of coarse fish are also present. The Tay is famous for the size of its salmon, pre-eminent amongst which is Georgina Ballantine's famous 64lb fish, the British record rod-and-line caught salmon, taken on the Glendelvine Beat on 7th Oct.1922. T Stewart, fishing the Perth Town Water, had a salmon of 61lb 8oz in October 1907. Sir Stuart Coats had two fish of over 50lb: 7th Oct. 1913, a fish of 51lb from Ballathie, and, almost a year to the day after Miss Ballantine landed her monster, a 53lb salmon from Cargill. Even today fish of over 30lb in weight are not uncommon and double figure salmon are regularly taken from opening day on 15 January right through until the end of the season on 15th October. Salmon enter the river throughout the year and fresh fish may still be caught in October, although most of these are taken on the lower beats. There is a substantial summer grilse run which begins in June, then a further run of autumn fish from August onwards. The average weight of Tay salmon is now in the order of 11lb. Obviously, the annual catch per beat varies considerably, but, generally, it may be expected to range from between 150 to 800 fish per season.

Flies & Tactics Deep wading is part and parcel of fishing the middle and lower river. This can be dangerous and it is essential to have proper advice before setting a foot in the stream. This is readily available from those who know the river best: the local gillies. Always wear a flotation jacket and carry a wading staff. The river is fast-flowing, even in summer months, so let caution be your watchword. However, much of the early fishing on this part of the river is from boats, using the technique known as harling. Spinning lures are trolled from the stern of a boat as the gillie allows the boat to move downstream, covering the known salmon lies along the way. Boat fishing is also used at other times of the year, dependent upon water conditions. Spring fishing on the Tay is best during March, April and May, but, be warned, it can be savage, cold, entertainment. Thermal clothing is a must. When fly fishing, a sinking line is required to get the fly down to the fish and a rod of at least 15ft in length is essential. Summer months, and low water levels, sometimes allow for the use of a single-handed rod, but a 15ft rod is probably the most useful all-season rod and will cope with most eventualities. You should be sufficiently competent to cast at least 30yds if you hope to effectively cover many of the lies and the ability to Spey-cast, or roll cast, will give you a real advantage and increase your chance of sport. The Tay, in spite of what some might say, offers some of the best fly-fishing in Scotland and the most productive patterns are: Willie Gunn, Garry Dog, Silver Stoat's Tail, Munro Killer, Hairy Mary, General Practitioner, Black Doctor, Ally's Shrimp and Orange Red and Black Waddingtons. Vary the size of fly according to the time of year and water conditions. Spinning lures used include: Tobies, Devon minnows, Blair Spoons, Rapalas and Flying Cs. Worm fishing is allowed on some beats, and prawn and shrimp fishing, apart from during September and October. However, he use of these techniques is to be regretted when, essentially, fly-fishing can be just as productive and is far less damaging to any fish caught which have to be released.

Permission & Charges Many beat owners prefer not to publish details of the cost of their fishing. The least expensive fishing, and the most accessible to visitors, is on the Perth Town Water. From opening day until the of June, the cost is £10 per rod per day, thereafter, £15 per day. Tickets are available from the Department of Leisure and Recreation, 5 High Street, Perth. Tel: 01738 475000. Tickets are restricted to 20 per day. One the other beats, as a general rule, expect to pay in the order of £50 per rod per day for Spring salmon fishing and up to £300 per rod per day after August. Preference is given to anglers who take a rod for a week, or the whole beat for a week, rather than

Dundee — OS Maps 53-54

to those who are seeking only a single day's fishing. However, there are always bargain fishing weeks/days available during the summer months, even on the most famous beats. These cost considerably less than the more popular times and provide a wonderful opportunity of getting to know the river - and more than a good chance of a fish. For various beats, contact: Lower Scone, Waulkmill, Fishponds, Knowesbank: The Factor, Mansefield Estates, Estate Office, Scone Palace, Perth. Tel:01738 552308; Benchil, Pitlochrie, Catholes, Luncarty: Strutt & Parker, 13 Hill Street, Berkeley Square, London W1X 8DL. Tel: 0171 6297282; Fax: 0171 4092359. Ballathie: Ballathie Estates, Kinclaven, by Stanley, Perthshire PH1 4QN. Tel: 01250 883250; Fax: 01250 883275. Campsie & Burnmouth, Stobhall, Cargill, Lower Islamouth: Tay Salmon Fisheries Company, St Lenords Bank, Perth PH2 8ED. Tel: 01738 636407. Meiklour, Lower Islamouth, Upper Islamouth: Meiklour Hotels & Fishings. Tel: 01250 883206. Taymount: Taymount Fishings, Estate Office, Taymount Mains, Taymount, Perth PH1 4QH. Tel: 01738 828203. Upper & Lower Newtyle: Kinnard: Jim Henderson, Country Pursuits, Henderson Street, Bridge of Allan. Tel: 01786 834495; Fax: 01786 834210. Dunkeld: Stakis Dunkeld House Hotel. Tel: 01350 727771. Dalguise, Lower Kercock, Finlayson Hughes, 29 Barossa Place, Perth PH1 5EP. Tel: 01738 625134; Fax: 01738 630926. Upper Kercock & Delvine: Lethendy Estates Ltd., Tower of Lethendy, Meikleour, Perth PH2 6QE. Tel: 01250 884344. Upper & Lower Murthly: Mr King, Factor, Estate Office, Murthly & Strathbaan Estates, Douglasfield, Murthly. Tel: 01738 710303. Upper Kinnair

Dundee

BUDDON, Burn See Lunan Water entry.
COARSE FISHERIES FORFAR, Loch OS54/444505; FITHIE, Loch 54/490513; BALGAVIES, Loch 54/532510; NICHOLL'S Loch 54/649538; CLATTO Reservoir 54/368346

CROMBIE, Reservoir
Location & Access 54/525404 Approach from the A958 Carnoustie/Forfar road.
Commentary Crombie Reservoir is 1.5 miles long and surrounded by trees which provide shelter from cold east coast winds. It lies within a country park and is very popular, not only with anglers, but also with Dundonian countryside and wildlife lovers. Two miles to the south of Crombie is another put-and-take fishery, Monikie Reservoir (54/505382) which also lies within a country park and wildlife sanctuary. Monikie has 2 ponds, Island Pond and North Pond, approximately 1/2 mile square, divided by a walkway. Access to boats on both fisheries has been improved by the building of piers.
Fish Monikie and Crombie are managed by the Monkie Angling Club and are stocked with good quality brown trout which average in the order of 1lb. North Pond on Monikie also has rainbow trout. Fish of up to and over 2lb are also occasionally caught.
Flies & Tactics Boat fishing only. On Crombie, attack around the large island at the west end and in the vicinity of the "Cut", where the feeder burn enters. Fish are taken from all over Monkie and no one place is really any better than another. Flies: Black Pennell, Wickham's Fancy, Silver Invicta.
Permission & Charges March to Mid April, 9.30am until 7.00pm; Mid April until mid September, 9.30am until 4.30pm and 5.00pm until dusk; thereafter, 9.30am until 7,00pm.Cost, £26 per boat (2 anglers) per session. Single angler boat sessions when available, half price. For postal bookings, contact: William Bell, Monkie Angling Club, 12 Forfar Road, Dundee. Tel: 01382 459811. On-the-spot bookings, on a first come first served basis, from The Superintendent, Monikie Country Park, Monikie, Angus. Tel: 01382 370300,

DIGHTY, Burn See Lunan Water entry.
ELLIOT, Water See Lunan Water entry.

ESK (South), River
Location & Access On OS Map 54, the River South Esk is shown from Cortachy (54/393600) to its outfall in the Montrose Basin (54/675580). The river is easily accessible throughout its length via public roads. (See also OS Map 44).
Commentary The South Esk flows through the rich, arable, lands of Angus in a delightful variety of tree-lined banks, deep pools and gentle glides. The Airlie Estate beats, downstream from Cortachy Castle, include some splendid pools, including, on the Castle Beat, Upper Ben Hoose, Ben Hoose and the Factors Pool; Downiepark Beat begins with The Beech Tree Pool and has some superb water, such as Mackays, The Carity Mou and the three Kaimbridge pools. The Finavon Castle Fishings, 5 miles upstream from Brechin, is divided into three beats offering 2 miles of double bank fishing and approximately 2 and 1/2 miles single bank fishing. The beats are: Castle, Indes Beat and the Meadows & Balgarrock. There are 30 named pools including Bridge Pool, Volcano Glide, Melgund Pool, Marcus House Pool, Breadalbane Pool, Oaks Stream & Pool, March Stream and Bell Pool. The East Kintrockat Fishings, 2 miles upstream from Brechin, offers 1 mile of double bank fishing which is easily accessible from a farm track which borders the stream. Other famous South Esk beats include: Justinhaugh, Inshewan, Fortesk, Kinnaird and House of Dun.
Fish Salmon and sea-trout. One of the largest salmon ever taken in Scotland, a fish of 59lb, was caught on the South Esk. Today, salmon average in the order of 11lb/12lb but larger fish are not uncommon. Sea-trout, for which the South Esk is most noted, average 2lb 8oz with good numbers of much heavier fish as well, although in recent years sea-trout numbers have declined. Composite catch returns are not readily available, but are probably in the region of 800 salmon and 1,500 sea-trout each season.

OS Map 54 — Dundee

Flies & Tactics Water levels are critical. No rain, no fish, at least as far as salmon are concerned. However, even in low-water conditions, the South Esk can provide marvelous sport with sea-trout, particularly at night. Reconnoiter your beat, carefully, in daylight. During the early months of the season, when water conditions are generally favourable, a 12ft/13ft double-handed rod is required, but as the season advances, a single-handed rod is adequate. Wading is reasonably hazard-free, but seek local advice prior to fishing. If you can, avoid wading when sea-trout fishing at night, they are very easily spooked. Most of the fishing is fly only, although spinning is allowed on some beats in the spring. For salmon, offer: Red & Orange Waddingtons, Stoat's Tail, Willie Gunn, Hairy Mary, Garry Dog and Ally's Shrimp. Sea-trout should respond to: Black Pennell, Soldier Palmer, Teal Blue & Silver. Vary the size according to water conditions.

Permission & Charges Prices vary, widely, according to the time of year and beat, and much of the best of the fishing is well-booked in advance. Expect to pay between £100/£300 per rod week on the House of Dun Fishings, and, on the other beats, from £250/£1000 per rod per week. Day lets are not readily available and priority is given to those booking estate accommodation with their fishing. Contact: Airlie Estate, Estate Office, Crotachy, Kirriemuir DD8 4LY. Tel: 01575 540222; Fax: 01575 540400. South Esk Estate, Estate Office, Haughs of Kinnaird, Brechin DD9 6UA. Tel: 01674 810240. Colin Sandeman, East Kintrockat, Brechin DD9 6RP. Tel: 01356 622739. Finlayson Hughes, 29 Barossa Place, Perth PH1 5EP. Tel: 01738 630926; Fax: 01738 639017. Savills, 12 Clerk Street, Brechin DD9 6AE. Tel: 01356 622187. Inshewan Estate, Estate Office, by Forfar, Angus. Tel: 01307 860229. House of Dun Fishings, House of Dun, Montrose, Angus DD10 9LQ. Tel: 01674 810264; Fax: 01674 810722. Salmon Galore, Inverallan, 8 Georgeham Road, Owlsmoor, Camberley, Surrey GU15 4YR. Tel: 01344 750274.

KINGENNIE, Lochs

Location & Access OS54/466366 Kingennie Fishings lie adjacent to the B978 Broughty Ferry/Bankhead road, 3 and 1/2 miles north from Broughty Ferry.

Commentary An easily accessible, newly established put-and-take fishery in a woodland setting. There are 3 ponds, Woodside, Bankside Pool and the Specimen Pool. Kingennie also offer comfortable self-catering accommodation and will book additional fishing on your behalf on other lochs in the area.

Fish Mostly rainbow trout. Woodside fish average 1lb, Bankside Pool 1lb 12oz, Specimen Pool 5lb 8oz.

Flies & Tactics Bank fishing only and all the pools are easily covered. Reservoir lures and traditional patterns of fly all produce results. Try: G.R.H.E., Black Fritz, Cats Whisker, Black Spider, Grouse & Claret, Viva.

Permission & Charges Woodside: Any legal method may be used. £10 for 4 fish ticket, £6 for 2 fish ticket. Thereafter, fish caught cost £2 per lb. Bankside Pool: Fly only and catch-and-release after limit. £10 for 2 fish ticket, £16 for 4 fish ticket, £12 for 3 fish evening ticket. Specimen Pool: Fly only, no catch-and-release. £23 for 2 fish ticket (4 hours), £33 for 4 fish ticket (8 hours), £25 for 3 fish evening ticket. Half days sessions are from 9am until 1pm and from 1pm until 5pm. Full day sessions from 9am until 5pm. Evening sessions (May - September) 5pm until an hour after sunset. Bookings: Neil Anderson, Kingennie Trout Fishery, Kingennie, Broughty Ferry, Dundee. Tel: 01382 350777; Fax: 01382 350400.

KINNORDY, Loch (54/360542) Nature Reserve (no fishing).

LUNAN, Water

Location & Access Source OS54/490480 Outfall 54690511. Easily accessible from public roads between Lunan Bay and Friockheim (54/590495).

Commentary A small stream which rises at Silverhillock in the west and flows into the sea near Red Castle at Lunan Bay after a journey of 14 miles. The other small streams in the area, Buddon Burn, Pitairlie Burn, Dighty Burn and Elliot Water used to produce a few fish in times past but rarely do so now.

Fish Salmon, sea-trout and finnock, and small brown trout. In a good year approximately 10 salmon and up to 20 sea-trout are taken.

Flies & Tactics Flies & tactics The lower reaches of the river, below the road bridge by the church, produce most fish. On a high tide, fish congregate here and anglers may use all legal methods to try and tempt them to take. Upstream from the church, the river is a modest affair and only really fishes well after heavy rain. A new weir has been built at Boysack (54/623492) and this has created a useful holding pool. There is little fishing above Friockheim. Flies: Willie Gunn, Hairy Mary, Shrimp Fly, Green Highlander, Garry Dog. Sea-trout: Black Pennell, March Brown, Teal Blue & Silver.

Permission & Charges Two tickets are available: (1) Below the road bridge (2) upstream. Cost £10 per rod per day. Contact: T Clark & Son, 274 High Street, Arbroath. Tel: 01241 873467.

MONIKIE, Reservoir See Crombie Reservoir entry.
MORTON, Lochs (54/462265) Nature Reserve (no fishing).
PITAIRLIE Burn See Lunan Water entry.

RESCOBIE, Loch

Location & Access OS54/515516 Rescobie Loch lies 3 miles east of Forfar and is approached from the B9113 Forfar/Burnside road.

Commentary An attractive, well-managed, put-and-take fishery. The loch is just over 1 mile east/west by up to 500 yds wide and covers an area of some 190 acres.

Fish Regularly stocked with both brown and rainbow trout. The Rescobie Loch Development Association manage their own hatchery and all the brown trout are reared from native stock. The average weight of fish is approximately 2lb. The largest fish taken in 1999 was a rainbow trout of 11lb 13oz; the neaviest

Lochgilphead

brown trout weighed 7lb 4oz.
Flies & Tactics The boat house and landing stage are at the west end of the loch where there are excellent facilities for disabled anglers. Bank fishing is also allowed. Fish are taken all over the loch but a favourite area is at the east end and along the south east shoreline. Flies: Black Pennell, Wickham's Fancy, Dunkeld.
Permission & Charges Day tickets, 9am - 5pm, for a four fish limit. £10. Evening tickets, 5pm until 1 hour after dusk, £8 for a three fish limit. Boat hire: Day, with 2/3 rods fishing (four fish per rod limit), £25. A single rod boat costs £15. Evening boats, £18 for a three fish limit. Single rod evening boat, £12. For bookings, contact: Rescobie Boat House, Rescobie Loch, Clocks Brig, Forfar. Tel: 01307 830367. Further information from Ron Fordyce, Club Secretary, 5 Park Place, Lunanhead. Tel: 01307 465056.

Lochgilphead

A'BHRUIC, Lochan See Cam Loch (Loch Awe).
A'CHAORAINN, Loch See Feinn Loch.
A'CHAORAINN, Loch See Loch Gaineamhach.
A'CHEIGEIN, Loch See Feinn Loch.
A'CHLACHAIN, Loch See Loch an Losgainn Mor.
A'CHLAIGNN, Lochan See Loch Mhic Mhartein.
A'CHREACHAINN, Loch See Feinn Loch.
A'CRUAICHE, Loch See Loch an Losgainn Mor.
A'MHINN, Loch See Loch an Losgainn Mor.
A'MHINN, Loch See Cam Loch (Loch Awe).

A'PHEARSAIN, Loch
Location & Access 55/854137. Leave the A816 Oban/Lochgilphead road at the Post Office in Kilmelford (55/850130) on the road signposted to Loch Avich (see separate entry). Park at the top of the hill at 55/857129 and walk downhill to reach the loch within half a mile.
Commentary A pleasant, easily-accessible, well-managed loch in attractive surroundings. Loch a'Phearsain is approximately half a mile north/south by up to 300 yards wide and it drops to a depth of over 40 ft at the south end. The surrounding hills give some protection from the prevailing winds.
Fish The loch is managed by the Oban and Lorn Angling Club who have stocked it with brown trout which average 8oz. There are also a few fish up to and over 1lb in weight, as well as arctic char.
Flies & Tactics Mostly bank fishing, but the club sometimes have a boat on the loch. The most productive fishing areas, from both boat and bank, are at the relatively shallow north end, in the vicinity of the inlet stream in the north-east corner and around the island at the south end where another feeder stream also enters. Flies: Soldier Palmer, Grouse & Claret, Silver Butcher.

Permission & Charges See Oude Reservoir entry.

ABHAINN BHEAG AN TUNNS (Tunns River) See River Add.
ADD, Lochan See River Add.

ADD, River
Location & Access Source 55/966026 Outfall 55/805924. Access to the lower river is from the B841 road at Islandadd Bridge at the mouth of the river and the west end of the Crinan Canal. Also, from the A816 Kilmartin/Lochgilphead road at Bridgend (55/855926). Access to the upper river, from Bridgend to the commercial forestry planting (55/890950) is from a minor road that parallels the stream.
Commentary A variety of unfortunate circumstances have combined over the years to reduce the number of migratory fish running the system: water abstraction from the headwaters for hydro-electric power generation purposes, massive afforestation of the river catchment and factory-salmon farming off-shore. Against all odds, however, the River Add still offers the chance of sport. Loch Leathan (55/875982) which drains into the River Add, is full of pike and the small hill lochans to the west of Kirnan, Lochan an Torrnalaich (55/857955), Lochan na Curaich (55/861962) and Lochan Add (55/863977) are private.
Fish In the mid-19th century, more than 1,000 salmon and grilse could be taken during the course of a single season. By the 1950's this had dropped to 180 fish. Now, the system, in a good year might produce 10 salmon and grilse, depending upon prevailing water conditions. Salmon average 6lb/7lb in weight. Sea-trout are most noticeable by their absence.
Flies & Tactics Sport is entirely dependent upon spate conditions. After heavy rain the lower 2 miles of the stream, which are virtually at sea-level, become tidal and anglers tend to follow the tide, up or down stream, fishing the brackish water. The most notable pools on the river are downstream from Bridgend and they include: Horse Shoe Pool, Bert Lard's, Poacher's Pot, Weed Pool and Hardy's Pool. The upper river, from where it exits from the forest downstream to near the Standing Stone at Lechuary (55/876955), is a much more busy, turbulent, affair with deep pots, dark glides and small torrents. There are two main tributaries: the Abhainn Bheag an Tunns (Tunns River) which drains Loch Feorlin (55/957974) (private), and, joining the River Add at Tayintrath (55/824938), the Kilmartin Burn. Neither of these tributaries are fished. A single-handed rod is all that is required and the river is very easy to fish. On the lower section, the technique of backing-up is practiced, salmon on the upper section of the river are stalked, fine and far off. Flies to try: Shrimp Fly, Hairy Mary, Green Highlander, Munro Killer, Stoat's Tail.
Permission & Charges Access to the lower river, the most productive part of the system, may be obtained from Mr & Mrs John Breakell, Kirnan Country House, Kilmichael Glen, by Lochgilphead, Argyll PA31 8QL. Tel: 01546 605217. Cost: £10 per rod per day. Kirnan Country House offers comfortable self-catering accommodation in two cottages and estate

OS Map 55 — Lochgilphead

tenants have fishing priority. The upper river is fished by the Lochgilphead & District Angling Club who do not issue visitor permits.

AN ADD, Loch
Location & Access 55/806890. Approach from Daill (55/827908) on the B841 Cairnbaan/Barnlusgan road. A forest track leads south past Diall Loch (55/816898) to reach Loch an Add after 1.5 miles.
Commentary Loch an Add is a mile-long, narrow, forest, water, managed by the Lochgilphead & District Angling Club. There is a small forest loch close by: Loch na Bric (55/804893) and Loch McKay (55/799887) whilst to the east and south lie additional waters: Loch na Faoilinn (55/815886), Gleann Loch (55/814880), Dubh Loch (55/810879, Cam Loch (55/822878), Loch Clachaig (55/813870), Loch nam Breac Buidhe (55/817860) and Loch na Laimh (55/810855). The forest provides welcome shelter during high winds although the trees themselves often prevent access to the water.
Fish The majority of the lochs contain good stocks of bright little trout. Their average weight is 8oz/10oz but there are larger fish as well, particularly in Cam Loch and Loch Clachaig where fish of up to and over 1lb may sometimes be caught.
Flies & Tactics Most of the lochs noted above drain north into the Crinan Canal and reaching many of them involves walking on forestry roads. It is easy to become disoriented. Take along a compass and map to help in time of need. Bank fishing on Loch an Add is possible, with care, from the south-east shore. The other waters are all fished from the bank. On Loch Cam, concentrate your effort along the north shore: a promontory here gives you casting access to a wide area of water, as does the point at the north-east corner of the loch. The west bank of Loch Clachaig, in the vicinity of the 2 small islands and where the stream flows out to Gleann Loch should provide you with breakfast. Flies: Black Pennell, March Brown, Silver Butcher.
Permission & Charges See Loch Coille-Bharr entry.

AN COIRE, Loch See Loch na Druimnean.
AN CURRAIGH, Loch See Loch an Losgainn Mor.
AN DAIMH, Loch See Loch an Losgainn Mor.
AN LOSGAINN BEAG, Loch See Loch an Losgainn Mor.

AN LOSGAINN MOR, Loch
Location & Access Leave the A816 Oban/Lochgilphead road at the Post Office in Kilmelford (55/850130) and drive east along the road signposted to Loch Avich (see separate entry). The loch and car-parking area is on the right hand side of the road after a distance of 1 mile.
Commentary This easily accessible loch is approximately half a mile long by up to 300 yds wide at the west end. A grim place of a wild day, but, when the sun shines, great fun to fish. There are a number of additional lochs nearby which also offer the chance of sport. These are, to the north of Loch an Losgainn Mor, Loch an Losgainn Beag (55/860126), unnamed on the OS Map, Loch a'Mhinn (55/865128), Loch na Curraigh (55/864131) and Loch nam Ban (55/871125). To the south of Loch an Losgainn Mor, Loch an Daimh (55/861109) and Loch a'Chlachain (55/857115); also Loch Conastacih (55/869114) and Loch a'Cruaiche (55/854109) both of which are unnamed on the OS Map. All these lochs are accessed from the Loch Avich road and lie within half a mile of Loch an Losgainn Mor.
Fish A variety of excellent quality brown trout with the possibility of arctic char in Loch a'Mhinn. Loch an Losgainn Beag has a big fish reputation, but they tend to be dour and difficult to catch. Loch an Losgainn Mor trout average 12oz but are also reported to be dour. Loch a'Mhinn and Loch na Curraigh have been stocked with rainbow trout in the past but few if any of these fish now survive. The other waters noted above contain fish which average 8oz but Loch nam Ban can produce the occasional trout of up to 2lb in weight.
Flies & Tactics Bank fishing only, but generally comfortable fishing and it is possible to effectively cover much of the water from the shore. Loch na Curraigh becomes weedy as the season advances and the south end of this loch is very boggy and dangerous and should be avoided. This also applies to little Loch Conastaich and the Angling Club advise visitors only to visit Loch Conastaich after a prolonged spell of dry weather. First cast: Ke-He, Greenwell's Glory, Peter Ross.
Permission & Charges See Oude Reservoir entry.

AN SAILM, Loch See Feinn Loch.
AN TORRNALAICH, Lochan See River Add.
ANAMA, Lochan See Loch Gaineamhach.

AUCHNAHA, Loch
Location & Access 55/933820. Adjacent to the B8000 Otter Ferry/Kilfinan road and private.
Commentary This little loch, unnamed on the OS Map, does not contain fish. However, there are 2 hill lochs in Kilmordan, to the north of Otter Ferry (55/930845), which do: contain trout: Lochan Chuilceachan (55/984886) and Garbhallt Lochain (55/029945).
Fish Small wild brown trout in nearby hill lochs which average 8oz.
Flies & Tactics The estuary of the Kilail Burn at Otter Ferry used to be a useful place to fish for sea-trout as was the Strathlachan River (55/008951) but, since the advent of factory-salmon farming in Loch Fyne, sea-trout have vanished from the scene. Flies: Black Zulu, March Brown, Silver Butcher.
Permission & Charges For details of access, contact: Frank & Jennifer Coghill, Lairgemore Holiday Estate, Otter Ferry, by Tighnabruaich, Argyll PA21 2DH. Tel: 01700 821235; Fax: 01700 821235. Lairgemore have a number of well-furnished cedar chalets for rent and Frank Coghill, an enthusiastic angler himself, will advise visitors and guests on the various fishing opportunities available in the area.

Lochgilphead — OS Map 55

AVICH, Loch
Location & Access 55/940145. Loch Avich may be accessed either from the west or from the east. For the western approach, continue east from Loch an Losgainn Mor (see separate entry) for 2.5 miles and park in the quarry at the west end of Loch Avich. For the alternative approach, drive north from Barnaline Lodge (55/970139) on the shores of Loch Awe (see separate entry). A minor road here parallels the River Avich and reaches Drissaig (55/948157) on the north-east shore of Loch Avich after a distance of 1.5 miles.
Commentary Loch Avich is 3.25 miles long by up to half a mile wide across the eastern bay. The loch is over 50m in depth and water from Loch Scammadale and the headwaters of the River Euchar (see OS Map 49, Oban & East Mull) is redirected into Loch Avich for hydro-electric power generation purposes. Falls on the River Avich have been eased to allow the access of migratory fish from Loch Awe into Loch Avich but the river, other than for trout fishing, is preserved. However, presenting a fly to the river trout is very difficult because of the surrounding forest. There are only a few places where it is possible to cast effectively.
Fish Brown and rainbow trout which average 10oz in weight. Trout of over 4lb have been caught in recent years. There is also the possibility of a salmon.
Flies & Tactics The Oban and Lorn Angling Club have boats at the east end of the loch and also bank fishing for half a mile on the north bank and 1.5 miles on the south bank. Fishing and boats are also available at the east end, at Lochavich. Boat fishing is the best way to fish the loch as the banks are unstable in some areas and this can make wading dangerous. The north-west shoreline, from Duaig (55/908136) northwards through the bays by Castle Island (55/917137), Narrachan (55/920144) to near Lochavich House (55/929148) are perhaps the most productive fishing areas.
Permission & Charges For the Oban and Lorn Angling Club fishing and boats, see Oude Reservoir entry. For access to the east end of Loch Avich, and to the River Avich, and excellent advice on other fishing opportunities in the area, contact: Norman Clark, 11 Dalavich, by Taynuilt, Argyll. Tel: 01866 844209. Cost: Bank fishing: £3 per rod per day. Boat hire, with outboard engine and petrol, £30 per boat per day, £20. Boat only, £15 full day, £10 half day. Life jackets supplied free of charge. Own engines may be used.

AVICH, River See Loch Avich.

AWE, Loch
Location & Access 55/970110. Public roads on either shore give easy access to the loch. (See also OS Map 50).
Commentary Loch Awe is approximately 26 miles long by up to 1 mile wide. The southern 14 miles of the loch are shown on OS Map 55, Lochgilphead. Loch Awe is the subject of a Protection Order, granted under the terms of the 1976 Freshwater Fisheries (Scotland) Act and it is illegal to fish without permission. Loch Awe is a popular fishing venue with West of Scotland fishermen and is invariably busy, with both boat and bank anglers. Other water-sport enthusiasts also use the loch but, generally, everybody exists in reasonable harmony. Factory-fish farming is endemic in Loch Awe and escapes from farm cages have introduced thousands of rainbow trout into the loch in recent years. The full impact of these escapes has yet to be realised but there is little doubt that native populations of brown trout, sea-trout and salmon will be badly affected by the resultant increased competition for finite feeding and spawning resources.
Fish Brown trout, ferox, arctic char, rainbow trout, salmon, sea-trout (very few), pike and perch. Ferox of up to and over 15lb in weight are regularly caught. The new British Record brown trout (25lb 6oz) was taken in 1996 by East Kilbride angler, Andy Finlay. Rainbow trout of up to 30lb have been recorded. However, the average weight of the native population of brown trout is a more modest 10oz, although good numbers of larger fish are taken each season. Arctic char of up to and over 3lb are also caught.
Flies & Tactics Boat fishing is the most convenient way of covering this huge water but great care is required when afloat. Weather conditions can change with alarming suddenness. Always wear a floatation jacket, tie in the oars, make sure that your outboard motor is reliable, and pack spare fuel. On the north shore, fish Kames Bay (55/982140), Barr Phort (55/963105), around Innis Stiuire Island (55/942081), Rubha na Lic Moire (55/925070) and Arichamish Bay (55/908059). Along the south shore, try Innis Searamhach Island (55/975110), Eredine Bay (55/966095), Braevallich (55/953076) and Fincharn Castle Bay (55/903044). Reservoir-type lures, trolled Tobies, Rapalas, Devon Minnows and Spoons-various all take fish. Flies: Red Palmer, March Brown, Kingfisher Butcher.
Permission & Charges Bank fishing £3 per rod per day. Boats cost in the order of £30 per boat per day, including outboard motor and petrol. Contact: Ford Hotel, Ford, by Taynuilt, Argyll. Tel: 01546 810273; Fax: 01546810230. Norman Clark, 11 Dalavich, by Taynuilt, Argyll. Tel: 01866 844209. (See also OS Map 50). Croggan Crafts, Dalmally, Argyll (Tel/Fax: 01838 200201) offers visiting anglers a fishing information service, as well as a comprehensive range of flies, tackle and clothing. They also hire fishing tackle by the day.

BARNLUSGAN, Loch See Loch Coille-Bharr.
BEALACH GHEARRAN, Loch See Loch Glashan.
BLACKMILL, Loch See Loch Glashan.
BREAC-LIATH, Lochan See Loch Gaineamhach.
BUIE, Lochan See Loch an Add.
CAM, Loch (Ederline) See Loch Gaineamhach.
CAM, Loch (Loch an Add) See Loch an Add.

CAM, Loch (Loch Awe)
Location & Access 55/906094. Access is by forest tracks from the Loch Awe side.
Commentary Cam Loch is approximately 12 acres in extent and it is one of a number of delightful little

OS Map 55 — Lochgilphead

lochs and lochans which lie in the forest between Loch Avich to the north and Loch Awe to the south. The other waters here are: Eun Loch (55/916091) and its neighbour, Lochan Dubh (South) (55/910089), Loch Eireachain (55/928095), Lochan na h-Airigh Bige (55/932091), Lochan nam Breac Buidhe (55/90410), Lochan Dalach (55/915102), Lochan a'Bhruic (55/921104), Lochan Lus Dubha (55/931109), Lochan Mhic Earoich (55/941118), Lochan Dubh (North) (55/940131) and Loch a'Mhinn (55/892079).
Fish Wild brown trout which average 8oz in weight.
Flies & Tactics In pre-forestry days all these little lochs offered great sport to those prepared to make the effort to reach them. They still do, but now, however, they have been swallowed up by conifers and finding them can be difficult. Nevertheless, Elizabeth and Ken Hassall at the Ford Hotel will give you excellent directions, along with a permit, and these forest lochs provide an ideal fishing refuge when high winds make conditions on Loch Awe difficult. The River Liever, which enters Loch Awe at Liever Island (55/896050) is also now enclosed by forestry. Flies: Black Gnat, March Brown, Peter Ross.
Permission & Charges Ford Hotel, Ford, Argyll. Tel: 01546 810273; Fax: 01546 810230. Cost: £3 per rod per day. Boats and fishing on Loch Awe (see separate entry) are also available from Ford Hotel which is a comfortable, well-managed, anglers' retreat.

CHEALLAIR, Loch
See Feinn Loch.
CHUILCEACHAN, Lochan
See Auchnaha Loch.
CLACHAIG, Loch
See Loch an Add.

COILLE-BHARR, Loch
Location & Access 55/781900. Approach from the B841 Cairnbaan/Barnlusgan road. At Barnlusgan, continue south on the minor road for half a mile to reach the boat mooring point.
Commentary An easily-accessible and attractive forest loch, carefully managed by the Lochgilphead & District Angling Club. There are two further club waters close by: Loch Barnlusgan (55/792912) and Loch Linne (55/798910). Loch Fidhle (55/803910), immediately to the east of Loch Linne, is private. Loch Coille-Bharr is 1.25 miles long by up to 250 yds wide, Loch Linne is half that length and Loch Barnlusgan is a modest affair of approximately 6 acres.
Fish Brown trout which average 10oz/12oz.
Flies & Tactics Boat fishing only, because of the surrounding forest, and trout rise and may be taken from virtually anywhere on these waters. However, on Loch Collie-Bharr, the north end, by the promontory, is a good place to begin. Loch Barnlusgan is the most intimate of these waters, with fascinating, fishy, weed patches and likely-looking nooks and corners. Flies: Soldier Palmer, Grouse & Claret, Peter Ross.
Permission & Charges Archie McGilp, Fyne Tackle, 22 Argyll Street, Lochgilphead PA31 8NE. Tel: 01546 606878. Mr MacVicar, Tel: 01546 850210. Cost: Collie-Bharr: £6 per day for the boat plus £5 per rod.

Barnlusgan, £5 for boat, £4 per rod. Archie McGilp will advise on access to other fishing locations in the area, as well as arranging gillies, tackle hire and a full range of services for visiting anglers.

CONASTAICH, Loch See Loch an Losgainn Mor.
CROSS REFERENCE The waters on the Isle of Jura shown on OS Map 55, are described on OS Map 61.
CRUACH MAOLACHY, Loch See Feinn Loch.
DALACH, Lochan See Cam Loch (Loch Awe).
DIALL, Loch See Loch an Add.
DUBH, Loch (Black Loch) See Loch Gaineamhach.
DUBH, Loch (Duck Loch) See Loch Gaineamhach.
DUBH, Loch (Fincharn) See Loch Gaineamhach.
DUBH, Loch (Loch an Add) See Loch an Add.
DUBH, Loch (Loch Glashan) See Loch Glashan.
DUBH, Loch (Mhic Fhionnlaidh) See Loch Gaineamhach.
DUBH, Lochan (North) See Cam Loch (Loch Awe).
DUBH, Lochan (South) See Cam Loch (Loch Awe).
DUBH-BHEAG, Loch See Feinn Loch.
DUBH-MOR, Loch See Feinn Loch.
EDERLINE, Loch See Loch Gaineamhach.
EIREACHAIN, Loch See Cam Loch (Loch Awe).
EUN, Loch See Cam Loch (Loch Awe).
FADA, Loch See Loch Mhic Mhartein.

FEINN, Loch
Location & Access 55/870145. Start from the track at the north-west end of Loch an Losgainn Mor (see separate entry) at 55/555122. Walk due north keeping Loch a'Mhinn and Loch na Curraigh (see separate entry) to your right. After passing the ruined shieling in Gleann Mor (55/865135) cross the glen and climb the crags on the left hand side of the outlet burn from Feinn Loch. The journey should take approximately 1 hour, depending upon how fit you are and how fast you want to travel.
Commentary Big Feinn Loch, as it is known locally, is one of the Oban and Lorn Angling Club's most enigmatic lochs, and it lies in an area of outstanding beauty, surrounded by a series of additional waters, all of which will amply repay the effort involved in reaching them. Whilst it would be possible to visit them all during the course of a vigorous, 8 mile day-out, it is best to make two or three outings in order to be able to appreciate them fully. Wee Feinn Loch (55/869147) is unnamed on the OS Map but is immediately adjacent to, and 50 yds west and above, Big Feinn Loch. Ten minutes further north again will bring you to Loch Iasg (55/873150) and, to the west, Loch Cheallair (55/860152). To the east of Big Feinn Loch, bordered on 3 sides by forestry plantations, lie: Loch a'Chaorainn (55/883136), Loch Dubh-bheag (55/890139), Loch Cruach Maolachy (55/894139) (unnamed on the OS Map), Loch a'Chreachain (55/898143) and, to the north of Loch a'Chreachain and unnamed on the OS Map, the Gully Loch (55/890145). Loch Dubh-mor (55/893148) lies to the north of the Gully Loch. Return by walking south-west round the crags to find Loch na Sailm (55/877145), and south again to fish Loch a'Cheigein (55/876139).

343

Lochgilphead OS Map 55

Fish It is unlikely that you will return without supper at least, and there is a more than good chance of a specimen fish as well. Big Feinn has a reputation for holding dour monsters whilst its neighbour, Wee Feinn can produce trout of up to 2lb in weight, as can Loch a'Chaorainn. Loch Salim fish average 10oz and the other waters noted above all hold fish which vary in size from between 8oz and 1lb in weight.

Flies & Tactics Mostly bank fishing but the club often has boats on Loch Dubh-mor, Loch a'Chaorainn, Loch a'Cheigein and Big Feinn. The club also has an excellent fishing hut which is situated midway between Loch Dubh-bheag and the south end of Loch a'Chreachain at 55/889141 and this provides welcome shelter in stormy conditions. Bank fishing can be difficult, particularly on Loch Dubh-bheag which is steep-sided, and it is safest to avoid wading. The angling club has worked selflessly, and tirelessly, over the years to improve its fishing and the quality of trout in these lochs is a credit to the hard work of the members involved. Flies: Ke-He, Woodcock & Hare-lug, Kingfisher Butcher.

Permission & Charges See Oude Reservoir entry. The angling club publishes an excellent guide to their fishings and a copy of this guide (cost 50p) may be obtained from the ticket outlets.

FEORLIN, Loch See River Add.
FIDHLE, Loch See Loch Coille-Bharr.

GAINEAMHACH, Loch (Sandy Loch)
Location & Access 55/915010. Approach from the B840 on the south shore of Loch Awe (see separate entry) near Kilneuair Church (55/889038). A stalkers' track leads south into the hills and the loch is reached, in reasonable comfort, after a walk of 2.5 miles.
Commentary This is the largest of a group of more than 20 named and unnamed lochs and lochans lying in the hills around Sidh Mor (408m), Cruach Mhic Fhionnlaidh (458m) and Cruach a'Bhearraiche (262m). The other waters here are: Dubh Loch (55/913018), known locally as Duck Loch, and its unnamed, adjacent, neighbour; Loch Tunnaig (55/915015), and, to the south of Loch Gaineamhach, Lochan Anama (55/903989) and Lochan Breac-liath (55/913990). East from Loch Gaineamhach, the track passes between two small, unnamed lochans, the one the north side of the track (55/928012) being known as Windy Loch. The track now reaches Loch a'Chaorainn (55/930008) (Horseshoe Loch) and, half a mile further, Dubh Loch (55/940005) (Black Loch). The lochs to the north of Loch Gaineamhach are: Loch na Creige Maolaich (55/940017) (Doe Loch), Dubh Loch (55/944024 (Mhic Fhionnlaidh) and its 4 satellite lochans, followed by Loch nan Losgann (55/955031) (Frog Loch), Loch na Sgilleog (55/957039) (Shell Loch) and Loch Leachd (55/959046) the most northerly of the group. Return south to find Loch Geoidh (55/950034) (Narrow Loch), Loch nan Eilean (Island Loch), the Dubh Loch (55/937037) which drains into Fincharn Loch (55/930035). Due south from Fincharn Loch is a small, unnamed lochan (55/930018), which in the past has, surprisingly, been stocked with rainbow trout. To the east of the Rainbow Loch is Cam Loch (55/937018) (crooked loch). The last of the Ederline hill lochs lie on the north-west slope of Cruach a'Bhearraiche. They are: Loch na Ceard Mor (55/919022) (Big Tinker's Loch) and Loch na Ceard Beag (Wee Tinker's Loch).

Fish All these lochs and lochans, named and unnamed, contain good stocks of wild brown trout. The average size of fish is in the order of 8oz but there are larger specimens of up to and over 2lb in weight.

Flies & Tactics It will take several visits properly to explore all these lochs and, in order to reach the more remote waters, the expeditions will involve you in a round trip of up to 10 miles. Bank fishing all the way and you should take care when wading. Many of the waters are steep-sided where it is best to stay on terra firma, regardless of any temptation to do otherwise. Away from the stalkers' track, the going is rough to-very-rough so you should be appropriately shod and always carry a compass and map; not only to negotiate your way round this maze of waters, but also to see you safely home in the event of bad weather. However, the Ederline lochs offer some of the most exciting wild trout fishing in Argyll, and the surrounding scenery and wildlife is truly majestic. The most productive of the waters noted above, both in terms of size and number of fish, is probably Fincharn Loch, although Cam Loch can produce a few surprises, as can Loch nan Losgann and Loch Geoidh.

Flies: Blue Zulu, Grouse & Claret, Silver Invicta. Loch Ederline, at 55/870028, is a coarse fishery.

Permission & Charges Eddie Maclean, Head Keeper, Ederline Estate, Ederline, by Ford, Argyll. Tel: 01546 810215. Cost: £10 per rod per day. The Castle Riding Centre, Brenfield, Ardrishaig, Argyll PA30 8ER (Tel: 01546 603274; Fax: 01546 603225) can arrange accompanied fishing expeditions to the Ederline Lochs and to other fishing locations in the surrounding area. Contact David Hay-Thorburn for details of accommodation and other charges.

GARBHALLT (LOCHAIN) See Auchnaha Loch.
GEOIDH, Loch See Loch Gaineamhach.

GLASHAN, Loch
Location & Access 55/915930. Access is via a forestry road from the A83 Furnace/Lochgilphead road at Birdfield (55/960945).
Commentary A large, somewhat bleak expanse of water, entirely surrounded by commercial forestry. The loch has been impounded for hydro-electric power generation purposes and it is 2 miles long by up to half a mile wide. There are 2 other, significant, forest lochs to the north of Loch Glashan: Loch Bealach Ghearran (55/949949) and Blackmill Loch (55/950958). Little Loch Dubh (55/940935), on Asknish Hill (314m), is rarely visited and contains more frogs than fish.
Fish Brown trout and salmon smolts in Loch Glashan, brown trout in the other lochs. Brown trout average 8oz/10oz, salmon smolts, up to 12oz.
Flies & Tactics All these loch are now fished from the

OS Map 55 — Lochgilphead

shore, boats having been withdrawn in recent years. Extreme care must be taken and you should avoid wading, particularly on Loch Glashan where the banks can be unstable due to fluctuations in the water level. When fishing Blackmill Loch, concentrate on the south shore, where the feeder stream enters. On Loch Bealach Ghearran, the east shoreline brings best results. Loch Glashan must also contain ferox in the depths, but they are rarely caught and in recent years anglers have become exasperated by the large numbers of escapee salmon smolts which are hooked: 80,000 of the unfortunate beasts were released into the loch. Flies: Black Pennell, Grouse & Green, Silver Invicta.

Permission & Charges Forest Enterprise, West Argyll Forest District, Whitegates, Lochgilphead, Argyll PA31 8RS. Tel: 01546 602518; Fax: 01546 603381. Also, Mr A MacGilp, Fyne Tackle, 22 Argyll Street, Lochgilphead, Argyll. Tel: 01546 606878. Cost: £3.50 per rod per day.

GLEANN, Loch See Loch an Add.
GULLY, Loch See Feinn Loch.
IASG, Loch See Feinn Loch.
KILAIL, Burn See Auchnaha Loch entry.
KILCHOAN, Lochs See Loch na Druimnean.
KILDUSKLAND, Loch See Still Loch.
KILMARTIN, Burn See River Add.
LARAICHE, Lochan See Loch an Add.
LEACHD, Loch See Loch Gaineamhach.
LEATHAN, Loch (Kirnan) See River Add.
LINNE, Loch See Loch Coille-Bharr.
LOCHA MHADAIDH, Loch See Loch Mhic Mhartein.
LOSGUNN, Loch See Loch an Add.
LUS DUBHA, Lochan See Cam Loch (Loch Awe).
MCKAY, Loch See Loch an Add.
MHIC EAROICH, Lochan See Cam Loch (Loch Awe).

MHIC MHARTEIN, Loch
Location & Access 55/784033. Turn north from the B8002 Craigdhu/Aird road at Corranmore (55/798034). Follow the track to 55/788038. From here, Loch Mhic Mhartein is an easy 5 minute walk to the south-west.
Commentary This is the principal trout loch on the Craignish Peninsula, There are 6 other lochs in the area and they are: Loch Fada (55/789042) and Lochan Tigh Choinnich (55/790048), to the east of Dun Ailne, and Loch nah Ardlaraich (55/808054), Loch na Beiste (55/812059), Locha Mhadaidh (55/806061) and little Lochan a'Chlaignn (55/819058) to the west of Craigdhu (55/820054). All of the lochs are easily accessible from convenient tracks.
Fish Loch Mhic Mhartein has excellent-quality brown trout which are perhaps of Loch Leven origin. They are very pretty, well-shaped, fish, silver in colour and their flesh is salmon-pink. Average weight: 10oz/12oz. The other lochs have wild brown trout which average about 8oz in weight.
Flies & Tactics Easy access makes these waters perfect for a family fishing outing. They are all small lochs, from 6 to 10 acres in extent, and are readily covered from the shore; although, from time to time there may be a boat available on Loch Mhic Mhartein.
Permission & Charges Contact: Colin Lindsay-MacDougall, Lunga, Ardfern, by Lochgilphead, Argyll. Tel: 01852 500237; Fax: 01852 500639. Comfortable accommodation is also available (details and charges on request) and estate tenants have fishing priority. Cost: £10 per rod per day.

NA BEISTE, Loch See Loch Mhic Mhartein.
NA BRIC, Loch See Loch an Add.
NA CEARD BEAG, Loch See Loch Gaineamhach.
NA CEARD MOR, Loch See Loch Gaineamhach.
NA CREIGE MAOLAICH, Loch See Loch Gaineamhach.
NA CRUAICH, Loch See Loch na Druimnean.
NA CURAICH, Lochan See River Add.
NA FAOILINN, Loch See Loch an Add.
NA H-AIRIGH BIGE, Lochan See Cam Loch (Loch Awe).
NA LAIMH, Loch See Loch an Add.
NA SGILLEOG, Loch See Loch Gaineamhach.
NAH ARDLARAICH, Loch See Loch Mhic Mhartein.
NAM BAN, Loch See Loch an Losgainn Mor.
NAM BREAC BUIDHE, Loch See Loch an Add.
NAM BREAC BUIDHE, Lochan See Cam Loch (Loch Awe).
NAN CEARDACH, Lochan See Loch na Druimnean.
NAN EILEAN, Loch See Loch Gaineamhach.
NAN LOSGANN, Loch See Loch Gaineamhach.

OUDE, Reservoir
Location & Access 55/850161. The Oude Reservoir lies adjacent to the west side of the A816 Oban/Kilmelford road, 14 miles south from Oban.
Commentary This is the headwater loch of the Oude River and the waters have been impounded for hydro-electric generation purposes. The loch is approximately half a mile long by up to 200 yds wide, completely afforested along the west shore.
Fish Brown trout which average 3 to the pound.
Flies & Tactics Although bank fishing is allowed, because of fluctuations in the water level, this is not really to be recommended. The Oban & Lorn Angling Club sometimes place a boat on the loch and this is the safest, and the most productive, method of fishing Oude Reservoir. Try: Black Pennell, Grouse & Claret, Silver Butcher. Spinning is also permitted.
Permission & Charges Anglers' Corner, 2 John Street, Oban, Argyll. Tel: 01631 566374; David Graham, 9-15 Crombie Street, Oban, Argyll. Tel: 01631 562069; Oban Sports Centre, 4 Craigard Road, Oban, Argyll. Tel: 01631 563845. Prices on application.

OUDE, River See Loch na Druimnean.
PRIVATE WATERS NA H-AIRIGH, Lochan 55/829186; DUN DUBHAICH, Lochan 55/812180; NA GARBH-BHEINNE, Lochan 55/831179; BHAINNE, Lochan 55/801188; CAITHLIN, Loch 55/766189; ILITER, Lochan 55/749102; AIRIGH

345

Lochgilphead   OS Map 55

A'CHRUIDH, Lochan 55/700038; A'BHAILIS, Lochan 55/904158; NA SREINGE, Loch 55/928170; A'GHLINNE, Loch 55/939173; NAN CAORACH, Loch 55/959175; NA CRAITHRAICH, Loch 55/959199; OUDE, River 55/839140; BARBRECK, River 55/823053; MHIC CHUARAIG, Lochan 55/891097; A'GHILLE, Loch 55/899109; DUBH, Lochan 55/919126; FEARNHORM, Lochan 55/835036; DRUIM NA RATHAID, Lochan 55/825036; MIDHEAN, Lochan 55/803981, NA DRUIMNEAN, Loch 55/845140; AN COIRE, Lochan 55/813142; KILCHOAN, Lochs 55/798144; NA CRUAICH 55/821156; NAN CEARDACH 55/796158

The lochs to the east of Loch AWE and INVERARY, north from the EDERLINE HILL Lochs, are private. The lochs to the south of the LUSSA (55/780847) are private.

RUEL, River
Location & Access Source 56/053948 Outfall 55/012812. Access to the river is from the A886 Colintravie/Strachur road which parallels the stream through much of its length.
Commentary The river rises from the north slopes of Cruach an Lochain (508m) and a multitude of streams which flow in from Tom a'Bhiorain (476m) and Cruach nan Capull (481m) to the east. Impassable falls at Dunans (56/040913) limit the upstream passage of migratory fish, but downstream from these falls, the river has a number of excellent holding pools and runs where salmon lie. Sadly, in recent years, massive commercial afforestation in Glendaruel has altered the character of the river and it is subjected to flash-flooding. The lower river flows serenely through fertile farmlands past the Clachan of Glendaruel (55/996844) and Waulkmill (55/000828) to end its 14 mile journey to the sea in Loch Riddon (Loch Ruel).
Fish Salmon and sea-trout, but greatly reduced in number, particularly sea-trout, in recent years. In a good season, approximately 50/80 salmon and grilse may be caught. Salmon average 6lb/7lb, with a few double-figure fish.
Flies & Tactics Sport is almost entirely dependent upon water levels and the best time to fish is after heavy rain. The river is narrow and a single-handed rod will cover most eventualities, but you would be advised to stay well back from the river-bank to avoid alerting the beasts to your evil intent. Extend line, from one position, rather than marching down the bankside. Flies: Garry Dog, Willie Gunn, Stoat's Tail, Shrimp Fly, Munro Killer.
Permission & Charges The Dunoon & District Angling Club lease fishing rights on the river and, from time to time, visitor permits may be available ans £12 per rod per day. Contact: Purdie's of Argyll, 112 Argyll Street, Dunoon, Argyll. Tel: 01369 703232. Cost: £12 per rod per day. Also, for advance bookings, to: A H Young, Hon Sec, Dunoon & District Angling Club, Ashgrove, 28 Royal Crescent, Dunoon, Argyll PA23 7AH. Tel: 01369 705732. Access may also be obtained through the Glendaruel Hotel, Clachan of Glendaruel, Argyll PA22 3AA. Tel: 01369 820274. Cost: £15 per rod per day.

STILL, Loch
Location & Access 55/819858. Park at Glendarroch (55/850865) on the A83 Lochgilphead/Tarbert road. Climb west from the road, keeping the small forest on your right, up the line of the Kilduskland Burn to Kilduskland Loch (55/831864) which is a local water supply reservoir. Continue south-west, with the crags on your right, for a further half mile to reach the loch after a walk of 2 miles.
Commentary The Still Loch is a remote, sheltered, water to the west of Ardrishaig (55/851855). It is bounded to the south by commercial forestry whilst the heights of Cruach Breacain (360m) guard the north-west shore. The loch is approximately 15 acres in extent. Kilduskland Loch should also be examined, either on the way out or on your return journey.
Fish Both lochs contain native populations of wild brown trout which average 8oz in weight.
Flies & Tactics The Still Loch has been little fished in recent years and, consequently, the new tenant of the fishing has devised, and is currently implementing, a management strategy for this water. At present, fishing is restricted to bank fishing only, but the loch is very easy to cover from the shore and wading, particularly along the south-east shoreline is comfortable and safe. Offer the residents: Black Zulu, Greenwell's Glory, Dunkeld.
Permission & Charges For current details, contact: David Hay-Thorburn, The Castle Riding Centre, Brenfield, Ardrishaig, Argyll PA30 8ER. Tel: 01546 603274; Fax: 01546 603225. Cost: £5 per rod per day. David Hay-Thorburn can arrange accompanied fishing expeditions to the Ederline Lochs and to other fishing locations in the surrounding area.

STRATHLACHAN, River See Auchnaha Loch.
TIGH CHOINNICH, Lochan See Loch Mhic Mhartein entry.

TRALAIG, Loch
Location & Access 55/880165. Approach from Blaran (55/859173) on the A816 Oban/Kilmelford road. A track runs east to reach the loch after a distance of half a mile.
Commentary Loch Tralaig is a substantial water, 1.5 miles east/west by up to 1/2 a mile wide at the east end. The Braes of Lorn guard the north shore whilst to the south the crags of Eleraig (266m), Gleann Mor, Cruach (289m) and Cruach Maolachy (378m) crowd the horizon. The south-east shoreline of the loch is afforested and this can often provide shelter on windy days. More than a good chance of seeing golden eagle and buzzard, splendid hill-walking country and the ideal location for an invigorating holiday.
Fish Loch Tralaig contains adequate stocks of brown trout which vary in size from modest specimens of 8oz/10oz to fish of up to and over 1lb in weight.
Flies & Tactics Tactic & flies Both boat and bank fishing is allowed, although best results invariably come from the boat. Bank fishing can be awkward, the banks are steep in many places, and you should

OS Map 55-56 — Loch Lomond

not wade. It is dangerous to do so. The east end of the loch, in the vicinity of the small island (55/889163) is the place to begin your assault. Carefully explore the mouths of the 2 feeder streams which enter the loch here then work north to the bays and corners below the east end of the Braes of Lorn. Offer: Black Pennell, March Brown, Peter Ross.

Permission & Charges Fishing on the loch is free to the tenants of Eleraig Highland Chalets, comfortably-equipped properties which sleep 4/6 guests. For further information and details, contact: Robin and Anne Grey, Eleraig Highland Chalets, Kilninver, by Oban, Argyll PA34 4UX. Tel/Fax: 01852 200225. Bank fishing permits may be obtained from Peter Menzies, Corylorn Farm, Kilninver, by Oban, Argyll. Tel: 01852 200221. Cost: £5 per rod per day bank fishing.

TUNNAIG, Loch See Loch Gaineamhach.
WEE FEINN, Loch See Feinn Loch.
WINDY, Loch See Loch Gaineamhach.

Loch Lomond

ARKLET, Loch See Loch Katrine entry.
CHON, Loch See Loch Katrine entry.
CROE, Water (Arrochar) See Loch Restil entry.
CROSS REFERENCE Loch AWE: See OS Maps 50 and 55. River SHIRA, River ARAY, DOUGLAS Water, River FYNE and their associated lochs and lochans: See OS Map 50.
CUR, River See River Eachaig entry.
DOUGLAS, Water (Loch Lomond) See Loch Lomond entry.

EACHAIG, River
Location & Access Source 56/157999 Outfall 56/157828. Access is from the A815 Dunoon/Strachur road which margins the east bank of the river throughout its entire length.
Commentary The source of the River Eachaig is Curra Lochain on the north face of Cnoc Bheula (779m). The stream here is known as the River Cur and this flows west and then south into the head of Loch Eck (56/140920): a 6 mile long, narrow, expanse of water enclosed to the east by the mountains of the Glen Eck Forest and to the west by peaks and corries of the Benmore Forest. As the flow exits from Loch Eck, on its final 4 and 1/2 mile journey to the sea in Holy Loch, it becomes known as the River Eachaig. The principal tributary of the River Eachaig is the River Massan which rises in Garrachra Glen (56/100928) and joins the River Eachaig near Eckford House (56/140848). The Little Eachaig River flows into Holy Loch in the tidal waters to the south of Orchard (56/158827) and this stream is private.
Fish Salmon, sea-trout, brown trout as well as powan and Arctic char in Loch Eck. Approximately 300 sea-trout and 50 salmon are taken each season. Salmon average 7lb/8lb with the occasional fish of up to 20lb. Sea-trout average 2lb 8oz but good numbers of much larger specimens of up to and over 10lb in weight are regularly caught: a sea-trout weighing 17lb 8oz was landed during 1989. Eachaig is fly only.
Flies & Tactics The River Eachaig is most noted as a sea-trout fishery, although good runs of salmon are also present from July onwards. The peak time for sea-trout fishing is during June, July and August. Most of the salmon are taken in August, September and October. There are 35 named pools on the river, the most famous of these being perhaps, Cauld Pool, Ash Tree Pool, Hut Pool, Ballochyle Pool, Steamboat Pool and Cothouse Pool. The river is easily fished with a single-handed rod and thigh waders will allow you cover most of the lies. The bad news is that, because the river has been time-shared in recent years, access is strictly limited. Your best hope of a rod is to note your interest, in writing, to the fishery manager, Bobby Teasdale, Quarry Cottage, Rashfield, by Dunoon. Tel: 01369 840510. Bobby Teadale factors rods which the time-share owners do not wish to use and he also has, from time to time, availability for 3 year leases. Fishing on the River Cur, the River Massan and Loch Eck is more readily available through the good offices of the Dunoon & District Club. The Club's fishing on the River Cur include both banks of the river upstream for about 2 miles from the loch. The pools are easily accessible and there is some perfect fly water. Spinning and worming is allowed on the River Massan although some of the pools on the Upper River can be fished with the fly. On Loch Eck, be prepared for stormy weather, and for the presence of an increasing number of other water sports enthusiasts. Boat and bank fishing is allowed and the shallow, margins, of the loch are the most productive fishing areas, particularly along the west shore from Bernice (56/136916) south to where the Allt Corrach (56/139874) enters Loch Eck.
Flies: For sea-trout and salmon, offer: Ally Shrimp, Munro Killer, Hairy Mary, Black Doctor, Willie Gunn, Garry Dog and, surprisingly, for sea-trout, a reservoir lure, the Sweeny Tod. On Loch Eck, use: Soldier Palmer, Mallard & Claret, Peter Ross.
Permission & Charges Contact: Purdie's of Argyll, 112 Argyll Street, Dunoon. Tel: 01369 703232. River Cur & River Massan: £7.00 per rod per day. Loch Eck: bank fishing, £5.00 per rod per day. Bobby Teasdale (see above) also manages fishing rights on Loch Eck. Boats may be booked at: Coylet Hotel, Loch Eck, Dunoon, Tel: 01369 840322. Cost: £25.00 per boat per day.

ECK, Loch See River Eachaig entry.
ENDRICK, Water See Loch Lomond entry.
FALLOCH, River See Loch Lomond entry.
FINLAS, Water See Loch Lomond entry.

FINNART, River
Location & Access Source 56/159940. Outfall 56/189884. The river is accessible from a minor road which parallels the west bank to Larach Hill (187m).
Commentary A very attractive little spate stream that rises on the heights of Beinn Bhreac (623m) and flows

347

Loch Lomond   OS Map 56

south east down Glen Finnart to reach the sea in Loch Long just to the north of Ardentinny (56/188884).
Fish Mostly sea-trout, but also the occasional salmon. Sea-trout average 2lb and in a good year upwards of 40 fish may be taken.
Flies & Tactics All a matter of being there at the right time, that is, after heavy rain. The fishing is managed by the Dunoon & District Angling Club who have 1 mile of double bank fishing upstream, from the mouth of the river in Finnart Bay. Worming and spinning are the most effective and most oft-used fishing methods, but there are a few runs where a fly-fishing can be just as productive. Try: Black Pennell, Grouse & Claret, Alexandra.
Permission & Charges See Loch Tarsan entry.

FRUIN, Water See Loch Lomond entry.
GLENGYLE, Water See Loch Katrine entry.

GOIL, River
Location & Access Source 56/215045 Outfall 56/198015. The river is easily accessible from the B839 Lochgoilhead/Rest and be thankful road through Gleann Mor.
Commentary This stream rises in the high corries of Ben Donich (847m) and flows south west to Monevechadan (56/191052) before swinging due south past Pole Farm (56/191043) to reach the sea at Lochgoilhead after a journey of 5 miles. In recent years extensive commercial forestry has altered the landscape but the surrounding mountains and moorland still make this one of Scotland's most attractive fishing locations.
Fish Salmon and a few sea-trout. Approximately 30 fish are taken, depending upon water conditions. Salmon average 7lb in weight but double figure fish are caught most seasons.
Flies & Tactics The River Goil is a classic spate stream: no water, no fish. Being in the right place at the right time is all important, primarily, after heavy rain. There are about 30 named pools on the river, the most productive of these being Twin Tree Pool and the Minister's Pool. A single handed rod will cover most salmon fishing eventualities and wading is not required. Bait fishing is allowed in spate conditions. The most popular flies are: Munro Killer, Garry Dog, Stoat's Tail, General Practitioner, Willie Gunn, Ally's Shrimp.
Permission & Charges Contact: John Lamont, Shorehouse Inn, Lochgoilhead. Tel: 01301 703340. Cost: £15.00 per rod per day, £50.00 per rod per week.

INVERUGLAS, Water See Loch Sloy entry.

KATRINE, Loch
Location & Access 56/480095 Approach from Aberfoyle on the B829. At 56/397099 turn right to Stronaclachar (56/402103).
Commentary A wonderful loch at the heart of Clan Gregor country. Rob Roy MacGregor (1671-1734), the Highland outlaw romaticised by Sir Walter Scott, was born at Glengyle (56/387135) on the north west shore of the loch. A house still occupies the site to this day and a small, loch-side, graveyard nearby is peopled with the graves of MacGregor's descendants. Loch Katrine is 8 miles east/west by up to 1 mile wide and drops to a depth of over 150m at the east end near the Bealch nam Bo (the pass of the cattle). To the west of Loch Katrine, by the minor road from Stronachlachar to Inversnaid and Loch Lomond (see separate entry), lies Loch Arklet (56/380091), 2.5 miles long by 650 yards wide, enclosed in a dark glen bounded by Maol Mor (684m) to the north and Beinn Uamha (598m) to the south. South of Loch Katrine, surrounded on 3 sides by the Loch Ard Forest, is Loch Chon (56/424050) 1.5 miles long by 1/4 of a mile wide. These waters also have a close association with Clan Gregor, particularly Loch Arklet, where the MacGregors, on 3 occasions, attacked and destroyed the government fort guarding Inversnaid at the west end of the loch.
Fish Stocked with brown trout which average 8oz/10oz. Loch Chon also contains pike and perch. A hatchery is planned at Loch Arklet to rear native trout for restocking purposes.
Flies & Tactics Boat fishing only on Loch Katrine and Loch Arklet. The north west end of Loch Katrine is the place to concentrate your efforts, and exercise your arms - it is a 3 mile haul, there and back - particularly in the vicinity of Black Island (56/402118) where Rob Roy once incarcerated the Factor of the Duke of Montrose. The bays on the west shore, north from Black Island, can also be very productive, as can the flooded bay where Glengyle Water enters the loch (56/383134). On Loch Arklet, arrange a drift about 15 yards out from the bank, in relatively shallow water, along the south east shore west to Corrieachan (56/378087). Loch Chon is fished from the bank and the whole of the east shoreline is easily accessible from the B829 road. Fish the south east shore and the mouths of the 6 small feeder streams that tumble in from Stron Lochie (501m). Flies: Black Pennell, Grouse & Claret, Silver Invicta.
Permission & Charges Loch Katrine & Loch Arklet & Glen Finglas Reservoir (see Os Map 57, Stirling and The Trossachs): W. M. Meikle, 41 Buchany, Doune, Perthshire. Tel: 01786 841692. Cost: full-day boat: £20. electirc motors are now available for hire at £7 per day. There are concessions for OAP's and unemployed. For Loch Chon, contact: David Marshall Lodge, Queen Elizabeth Forest Park, Aberfoyle. Tel: 01877 382258. Cost: £3.00 per rod per day.

KINGLAS, Water See Loch Restil entry.
LITTLE EACHAIG, River See River Eachaig entry.

LOMOND, Loch
Location & Access 56/380935 The A82 Dumbarton/Crinlarich road borders the west shore of the loch. A minor road from Balmaha (56/417910) in the south to Rowardennan (56/360993) in the north margins the east shore. North from Rowerdennan, the West Highland Way, a long-distance footpath, may be used for access. The minor road along the north shore

OS Map 56 — Loch Lomond

of Loch Arklet (see separate entry) leads to Inversnaid (56/338090) also gives access to the West Highland Way and to the north east bank of Loch Lomond.

Commentary One of the world's most famous and best-loved lochs, immortalised in the song and story. Loch Lomond lies in an area of outstanding natural beauty and it is a major recreational centre for the population of Central Scotland. Not only for anglers, but also for many other water-sport enthusiasts. The loch is approximately 21 miles north/south by 1/2 a mile wide at the north end, opening up to some by up to 4 and a 1/2 miles wide at the south end. In its surface area of 17,500 acres it is the largest freshwater loch in Scotland. Ben Lomond (974m) guards the east shore whilst Ben Vorlich (943m) and the Arrochar Alps tower to the west. Although the loch is only 30m above sea level, it plunges to a depth of more than 150m between Tarbet (56/314045) in the west and Cailness (56/343063) in the east. The loch is fed by a number of significant tributaries, including: the River Falloch in the north (see separate entry) and, entering on the west shore, Inveruglas Water, Douglas Water, Luss Water, Finlas Water and Fruin Water. Apart from Fruin Water, the other streams noted above are salmon spawning sanctuaries and they are not fished. The stream from Loch Arklet and, the principal tributary, the Endrick Water, enter Loch Lomond on the east shore. Loch Lomond is drained by the River Leven which joins the Firth of Clyde at Dumbarton (63/399750).

Fish Salmon, sea-trout, brown trout, ferox, Arctic char, powan, pike, perch, roach, ruff, and gudgeon in Endrick Water. The whole system produces upwards of 1,500 salmon and 2,000 sea-trout most seasons, although, of course, much depends upon prevailing weather conditions. Salmon average 8lb, but double figure fish of up to and over 20lb are not uncommon. Sea-trout average 2lb 8oz with good numbers of heavier fish as well. Brown trout are a modest 8oz in weight, but larger specimens are taken, mostly whilst trolling for salmon rather than on the fly. Salmon and sea-trout enter the system from March onwards but the best of the fishing is generally from mid-June until the end of the season in October.

Flies & Tactics It really would take an angling lifetime to get to know the loch properly and visitors are advised to seek the services of a gillie in order to have the best opportunity of sport. Most of the angling activity is concentrated at the shallow, south end of the loch but many local anglers concentrate their efforts almost exclusively at the deeper north end. Fish the north east shore from where the River Falloch enters, down past Ardleish (56/327155) to Doune (56/332144). On the north west shore, try the bay to the south of Ardlui at 56/320150. The bays to the north and south of Inveruglas, and around Wallace's Isle, should also be carefully explored. The most popular drifts are to be found at the south end of Loch Lomond, out from Balloch (56/385823), where the River Leven leaves the loch on its 6 mile journey to the sea, and from Balmaha on the south east shore of the loch at the end of the B837 road from Drymen. Salmon lie close to the shore in shallow water and one of the best fly-fishing drifts is in the vicinity of Ross Priory (56/415877). Other notable drifts are: along the north west shore of Inchmurrin Island (56/376874), the north shore of Inchlonaig Island (56/382938) and the South shoreline of Inchfad Island (56/400907). A classic Loch Lomond drift is from the tiny island of Inchgalbraith (56/369903) north over the shallow sand banks at the west end of Inchmoan Island, then through "The Giggles" (56/384910) between Inchmoan and Inchcruin Island and along the south shore of Inchcruin Island (56/388908) to "Ladies Point" (56/389912). Most salmon are taken on spinning tackle during the early months of the season but spinning is not allowed after the 30th April. Spinning is also the most oft-employed fishing method on the River Leven. The River Endrick is mainly fly only. Both streams have some excellent fly water; on the River Endrick, this includes pools such as: Craigbell, Pot of Gartness and the Meetings Lynn, where Blane Water, a major tributary of the River Endrick joins the Endrick. The River Endrick is also well-renowned as a superb evening and night-time sea-trout fishery. Anglers new to Loch Lomond should be warned that this can be a very dangerous loch. On such a vast expanse of water waves can build up to very considerable proportions. You must seek local advice about weather conditions, before setting out, and always wear a life jacket. If in any doubt whatsoever, bank fish. However, even then, great care must be taken when wading: gravel banks can be notoriously unstable. Further information about fishing on Loch Lomond and the other waters noted above may be obtained from the Angling Association. Flies: brown trout: Ke-He, Soldier Palmer, Silver Invicta; sea-trout: Black Pennell, Grouse & Claret, Peter Ross; salmon: Hairy Mary, General Practitioner, Brown Turkey, Willie Gunn, Green Highlander, Stoat's Tail. Lures: Tobies, Rapalas, Devon Minnows.

Permission & Charges Fishing is controlled and managed by the Loch Lomond Angling Improvement Association and inquiries for membership should be made to the Hon Sec, P.O. Box 3559, Glasgow. Day tickets are widely available and cost £15 for the River Leven and £35 per week for River Leven and Loch Lomond. Boats may be hired, with outboard motors, for approximately £35 per boat per day. For day tickets, contact: Tulliechewan Caravan Park, Balloch. Tel: 01389 759475; Balloch Hotel, Balloch, Loch Lomond. Tel: 01389 752579; I & A Gibson, 225 Bank Street, Alexandria. Tel: 01389 752037; Macfarlane & Son, The Boatyard, Balmaha. Loch Lomond G63 OJG. Tel: 01360 870214; A Wallace, Flat-a-Float, Ardlui, Loch Lomond. Tel: 01301 704244; Rowardennan Hotel, Rowardennan, Loch Lomond. Tel: 01360 870273; Country Lines, 29 Main Street, The Village, East Kilbride. Tel: 013552 28952; Glasgow Angling Centre, 8 Claythorne Street, Glasgow. Tel: 0141 5524737; Cafaro Bros, 140 Renfield Street, Glasgow. Tel: 0141 3326224; W M Robertson, 61 Miller Street Glasgow. Tel: 0141 2216687; and local Tourist Information Offices at Balloch, Dumbarton and Helensburgh. Further details from Michael Brady, Chairman, LLAIA. Tel: 0141 423 2783

Loch Lomond   OS Map 56

LUSS, Water See Loch Lomond entry.
MASSAN, River See River Eachaig entry.
PRIVATE WATERS GEAL, Loch 56/318164; FALLOCH, River 56/318158; BEINN DAMHAIN, Lochan 56/292172; A'CHAISTEIL, Lochan 56/343188; BEINN CHABHAIR, Lochan 56/354179); SRATH DUBH-UISGE, Lochan 56/282158; A'MHADAIDH, Lochan 56/269218; CREAG NAN CAORRUNN, Lochan 56/312218; DUIN, Lochan 56/315218; NAN CNAIMH, Lochain 56/170975; CURRA, Lochain 56/156999; CORRAN, Lochan 56/217952; GHLAS LAOIGH, Lochan 56/220896; DUBH, Loch 56/403030; MHAIM NAN CARN, Lochan 56/399073; CRUACHAN, Lochan 56/351075; CALDARVAN, Loch 56/423838.

RESTIL, Loch

Location & Access 56/229080 Loch Restil is immediately adjacent to the west of the A83 Arrochar/Cairndow road.
Commentary An easily accessible loch by the side of the tortuous road from Loch Long to Loch Fyne. The loch lies in the Bealach an Easain Duibh near Rest and be thankful (56/230074) guarded by Beinn an Lochain (901m) to the west and Beinn Luibhean (857m) to the east. The present road is built along the line of an Old Military Road and soldiers were allowed to rest and be thankful by the shores of the loch after the steep ascent from either north or south.
Fish Modest wild brown trout which average 8oz in weight.
Flies & Tactics The loch is approximately 1/2 a mile north/south by 200 yards wide and both boat and bank fishing is allowed. The west shoreline, where 5 little burns tumble down into the loch from Beinn an Lochain, is the most productive fishing area from either boat or bank, but, generally, fish may be taken from all round the shores. Kinglas Water drains Loch Restil north, then west, into Loch Fyne (see Os Map 50, Glen Orchy), whilst Croe Water flows south from High Glencroe (56/233071) to reach Loch Loch at Ardgartan caravan and camp site (56/274030). Salmon and sea-trout numbers in Kinglas Water have declined in recent years, most probably due to the impact of salmon farming in Loch Fyne, but, given spate conditions, a few fish still run the stream. Croe Water rarely produces fish, although, no doubt, there will be the possibility of sport at the mouth of the stream after heavy rain. Flies for Loch Restil: Black Pennell, Grouse & Claret, Silver Butcher.
Permission & Charges For Loch Restil and Kinglas Water, contact: J M Turnbull, Strone House, Cairndow, Argyll PA26 8BQ. Tel: 01499 600284. Cost: Bank fishing at £5.00 per rod per day; boat hire: £10.00 per boat per day (plus a refundable deposit of £10.00 for the safe and sound return of the oars). Salmon fishing charges, when available, upon application.

SHIRA, RIVER

Location & Access Source 56/175207 Outfall 56/115100. The river is accessible via a private estate road that margins the east bank of the stream.
Commentary The headwaters of the River Shira have been impounded for hydro-electric generation purposes by a dam across the south end of Lochan Shira. The river flows south down Glen Shira through Lochan Sron Mor (50/161194) and past the site of Rob Roy's House, (50/150169). The stream reaches the sea in Loch Fyne through the tidal waters of the Dubh Loch (50/114110), a brackish water approximately 3/4 mile long by 300yds wide, and the Grearr Abhainn. Two other, delightful, little rivers run into Loch Fyne to the south of the River Shira: the River Aray at Inveraray Castle (56/098092) and the Douglas Water near the Caravan site at 56/072049.
Fish Because of the collapse in salmon and sea-trout numbers, these rivers have been closed for fishing.
Permission & Charges For further information and details contact: The Factor, Argyll Estates, Estate Office, Cherry Park, Inveraray, Argyll. Tel: 01499 302203.

SLOY, Loch

Location & Access 6/282120 approach from Inveruglas (56/320094) on the A82 Tarbert/Inveranrnan road on the west side of Loch Lomond (see separate entry). A hydro-road leads north west through the Arrochar Alps to reach the south end of the loch after a distance of 2 miles.
Commentary Loch Sloy has been impounded for hydro-electric power generation purposes and is 1 and 3/4 miles north/south by up to 400 yards wide. The loch is enclosed by Ben Vorlich (943m) to the east and Beinn Dhubh (773m) to the west and these mountains often make Loch Sloy a wild and windy place to fish. The landscape is considerably disfigured by the presence of pylons which margin both the east and the west shoreline.
Fish Brown trout which average 8oz but some larger fish as well as of up to and over 1lb 8oz in weight.
Flies & Tactics Bank fishing only and it is dangerous to wade. Stay safe on terra firma.The best chance of sport is north end of the loch and at the mouths of the burns that tumble down from Ben Vorlich, particularly along the north east shore. Flies: Invicta, Greenwell's Glory, Alexandra. Inveruglas Water, which drains Loch Sloy into Loch Lomond, is not fished.
Permission & Charges Vale of Leven Angling Club, Fisherwood, Balloch, Loch Lomond. Tel: 01389 757843. Cost: £6.00 per rod per day.

TARSAN, Loch

Location & Access 56/077840 The south end of the loch abuts the B836 Colintravie/ Dalinlongart road through Glen Lean.
Commentary Loch Tarsan lies between Loch Striven in the west and Holy Loch to the east. The loch is 1 and 3/4 miles long by up to 1 mile wide at the south end. The north end of the loch, which is surrounded by commercial forestry, narrows to about 100 yards and the water has been impounded by the construction of a dam at the south east corner near Glenlean (56/083838).
Fish Stocked with high quality brown trout which average 10oz in weight.

OS Map 56-57
Stirling & The Trossachs

Flies & Tactics the loch is managed by the Dunoon & District Angling Club and both boat and bank fishing is available. Do not wade, however, since in some areas the bottom is unstable due to fluctuations in the water level. The north end of the loch is the most productive fishing area. Flies: Ke-He, March Brown, Silver Butcher.
Permission & Charges Purdies of Argyll, 112 Argyll Street, Dunoon. Tel: 01369 703232. Cost: Bank fishing, £7.00 per rod per day. Boat hire, £10.00 per boat per day (plus a £5.00 returnable deposit on the keys).

Stirling and The Trossachs

ACHRAY, Loch See Loch Venacher entry.
ALLAN Water See River Teith.

ARD, Loch
Location & Access 57/470017 Easily accessible from the B829 Aberfoyle.Stronachlachar road.
Commentary Loch Ard lies on the headwaters of the River Forth (see River Teith entry) and is 2 miles long by up to 1/2 mile wide. The Trossachs are very popular with tourists and Loch Ard can be a busy place to fish.
Fish Brown trout which average 8oz in weight, pike and perch.
Flies & Tactics The loch has been badly effected by commercial forestry plantations in recent years when fish stocks diminished. Efforts are being made to restore the quality of fishing to pre-forestry days and there are encouraging signs that this is happening. Both boat and bank fishing is allowed. The south west corner of the loch, by Eilean Gorm (57/455015) is perhaps the best place to begin. Castle Bay (57/477012) also used to be a noted hot-spot. Flies: Blae & Black, Greenwell's Glory, Dunkeld.
Permission & Charges Altskeith Hotel, Kinlochard, by Aberfoyle, Perthshire. Tel: 01877 387266; Invesnaid Hotel, Inversnaid, by Aberfoyle, Perthshire. Tel: 01877 382223. Inverard Hotel, Lochard Road, Aberfoyle, Perthshire. Tel: 01877 382229. Cost: bank fishing, £5 per rod per day, boats at £15 per boat per day. Fishing is free to hotel guests.

BALVAG, River See Loch Voil entry.
BUIDHE, Lochan See Loch Lubnaig entry.
CALAIR, Burn See Loch Voil entry.
CARRON, River See Carron Valley Reservoir.

CARRON VALLEY, Reservoir
Location & Access 57/695835 Approach via the B818 Denny/Fintry road. A Water Board road (57/722839) leads to the Fishery Office at the east end of the loch.
Commentary Carron Valley can be an intimidating place to fish on a wild day, but when the sun shines it is all light and sweetness. The loch covers an area of 965 acres and is 3 miles east/west by up to 3/4 of a mile wide. The River Carron, which has its source in Carron Valley Reservoir and exits into the Firth of Forth near Grangemouth, used to be notoriously polluted. The river is recovering, slowly, thanks largely to the work of the Carron Angling Association. The Association also has excellent fishing on Loch Coulter Reservoir (57/765860) where a boat is reserved for visiting anglers. Loch Coulter trout average 1lb. To the north of Carron Valley Reservoir, on Cringate Muir, are the Earlsburn Reservoirs (57/700896) which are private. Touch Muir Reservoirs (67/727912) are also private. Easter Buckieburn Reservoir (57/740855) is not fished.
Fish Carron Valley Reservoir is stocked with brown trout which average 1lb in weight. 5,000 fish from the Howietown Farm are introduced throughout the season.
Flies & Tactics Boat fishing only and 16 are available for hire. An outboard motor is essential. Bring your own or hire one at the loch. The south shoreline offers the best fishing opportunities; the mouth of the River Carron (57/676845); Gartcarron Bay (57/674857) where the River Endrick flows out to the west; Burnhouse Bays, from Haugh Hill (57/687840) east to 57/705832. Flies: Loch Ordie, Grouse & Claret, Peter Ross.
Permission & Charges East of Scotland Water, Woodlands, St Ninnian's Road, Stirling FK8 2HB. Tel: 01786 458705 (Mon- Fri 9am to 4pm excluding public holidays). For 'on-the-day' bookings Tel: 01342 823698. Costs: boat with 2 anglers, £14. Outboard hire £8. The River Carron is generally reserved for Association members but day tickes may be available (£8 per day). For further information, contact James McGhee on Tel: 01324 815178. For Loch Coulter, contact: Alistair Steel, Topps Farm, Fintry, Carronbridge, Denny. Tel: 01324 822471. Expect to pay in the order of £24 per day.

CROSS REFERENCES Loch KATRINE (See OS Map 56, Loch Lomond); Water of RUCHILL (See OS Map 52); River EARN (See OS Map 52); River ENDRICK (See OS Map 56).
DOINE, Loch See Loch Voil entry.
DRUNKIE, Loch See Loch Venachar entry.
EARLSBURN, Reservoirs See Carron Valley Reservoir
EASTER BUCKIEBURN, Reservoir See Carron Valley Reservoir
ENDRICK, River See OS Map 56
FORTH, River See River Teith

GLEN FINGLAS, Reservoir
Location & Access 57/525090. Approach from Brig o'Turk (57/535066) on the A821 Trossachs/Callander road. Drive north for three-quarters of a mile to reach the south end of the loch.
Commentary The loch lies in a splendid setting with Ben Ledi (879m) towering to the east and the twin peaks of Ben Venue (727m) to the south.
Fish Stocked with good quality brown trout which average 8oz/10oz in weight. The largest trout taken in

351

Stirling & The Trossachs — OS Map 57

recent years weighed 2lb 8oz.
Flies & Tactics Boat fishing only and, at present, outboard motors are not allowed although this may change in the near future. In the meantime, be prepared for some vigorous oar work to reach the best fishing areas which lie at the north end of the loch, 1.75 miles distant. Also have a drift in the west bay by the small island (57/523808) and at the mouth of the Gleann Casig burn at 57/530092. Flies: Loch Ordie, March Brown, Dunkeld.
Permission & Charges W M Meikle, 41 Buchany, Doune, Perthshire. Tel: 01786 841692. Cost: See Loch Katrine entry on OS Map 56

ISHAG, Burn See Loch Voil entry.

KILLEARN, Fishery
Location & Access 57/505848. Approach from the A809 Bearsden/Drymen road or the A81 Milngavie/Killearn road. The fishery lies within the polices of Killearn House, on the south of the B834 road.
Commentary An easily-accessible 2.5 acre put-and-take fishery in a splendid situation amidst mature woodlands close to Killearn House.
Fish Rainbow trout which average 1lb 12oz. There are also fish of up to and over 6lb in weight.
Flies & Tactics Bank fishing only and wading is not allowed. The margins of the fishery are flat and this makes it a happy option for disabled anglers with good access to the bank. There is also a comfortable lodge on site where tea, coffee and snacks are available, as well as a good selection of flies for sale and tackle hire. Most reservoir patterns of lure produce results, as does dry fly fishing, particularly on warm summer evenings.
Permission & Charges Contact: David Young, Killearn Fishery, Killearn Home Farm, Killearn, Glasgow G63 9QH. Tel: 01360 550994. A 4-hour session (3 fish limit) costs £15 from 9am until 6.pm (5 fish limit) at £21 Catch-and-release after limit taken using barbless hooks.

KNAIK, River See River Teith.
LENY, River See Loch Lubnaig entry.
LOCH COULTER, Reservoir See Carron Valley Reservoir

LUBNAIG, Loch
Location & Access 57/580136. Loch Lubnaig lies adjacent to the west side of the A84 Callander/Lochearnhead road. The west shore of the loch may be accessed via forestry tracks.
Commentary Loch Lubnaig is surrounded by dramatic hills and mountains and is a classic Highland loch. The peak of Ben Vorlich (983m) towers to the east, immortalised in the song "Bonnie Strathyre", whilst graceful Ben Ledi (879m) guards the west shore. The loch is almost 4 miles north/south by up to 700 yds wide and it drops to a depth of more than 40m near Ardchullaire More (57/584136). Loch Lubnaig lies on the headwaters of the River Teith and is fed from the north by the River Balvag and the waters of Loch Voil

and Loch Doine (see separate entries). The loch exits south into the River Leny through the Pass of Leny and over its substantial falls.
Fish Brown trout, ferox trout, the chance of salmon and sea-trout, although these species are very rarely caught. Trout average 8oz in weight. Also, specimen perch, fish of up to and over 5lb in weight.
Flies & Tactics Both boat and bank fishing is allowed and the north, shallower, end of the loch is the most productive fishing area. As the season advances, substantial weed-beds develop near the mouth of the River Balvag and the inlet stream from little Lochan Buidhe (57/559155). Good fish lurk here, and down the north-west shore to the bays to the north and south of Laggan (57/563146). Fishing is also allowed on the first mile of the River Leny, to the falls, but this is only really worth exploring after heavy rain. Flies: Black Pennell, March Brown, Peter Ross
Permission & Charges I P R Winter, Laggan Farm, Strathyre. Tel: 01877 384614; Kings House Hotel, Balquhidder, Lochearnhead, Perthshire. Tel: 01877 384646; Munro Hotel, Strathyre, by Callander, Perthshire. Tel: 01877 384263; J Bayne, Fishing Tackle Shop, 76 Main Street, Callander, Perthshire. Tel: 01877 330218. Cost: bank fishing, £4 per rod per day.

MACANRIE, Loch See Lake of Menteith

MENTEITH, Lake of
Location & Access 57/580005 Approach from Port of Menteith on the B8034 Arnprior/Port of Menteith Road.
Commentary The Lake of Menteith is Scotland's only natural lake, as distinct from loch, and is a very popular fishing venue. The lake covers approximately 650 acres and is 1.5 miles east/west by up to 1 mile wide. Inchmaholm Island, in the centre of the lake (57/575005) contains the ruins of a 13th century priory which once was home to the infant Mary, Queen of Scots. Landing on any of the islands in the lake is forbidden. In winter months the loch is used for curling competitions, as it has been for more than 100 years. There are excellent facilities for anglers including a comfortable fishing pavilion with lounge, food preparation facilities and toilets. The little loch to the southwest of Lake of Menteith, Loch Macanrie (57/561994) has been stocked in recent years but has suffered from the unwelcome attention of poachers.
Fish Regularly stocked with rainbow trout. A few native brown trout still survive. Rainbow trout average 2lb in weight. There are much larger fish as well, including over-wintered fish. The quality of the stocked trout can vary considerably, from excellent to awful.
Flies & Tactics Boat fishing only. 28 boats are available and there are special boats for disabled anglers. The lake is shallow, with an average depth of 20ft, so fish rise and are caught everywhere. Flies: Bibio, Wickham's Fancy, Silver Butcher. Reservoir lures: Ace of Spades, Whisky Fly, Sweeney Todd.
Permission & Charges Costs: Day sessions: 1st April to 31st October. 9.30am -5.30pm (15 fish per boat)

OS Map 57
Stirling & The Trossachs

Mon - Fri £28 per boat, Sat, £32 per boat. Various other shorter options are available and cost between £10 per boat up to £32 per boat. Tackle hire, £6 per session. Contact: Lake of Menteith Fisheries, Port of Menteith, Stirling FK8 3RA. Tel: 01877 3885664.

MONACHYLE, Burn See Loch Voil.

NORTH THIRD, Reservoir
Location & Access 57/757890 From the south, approach via the minor road from Carron Bridge (57/742837) and turn left at 57/770874. The loch is a further 2 miles north. On the M80 Motorway, leave at Exit 9 and find the road signposted to Carron Bridge.
Commentary A attractive fishery fed by Robert the Bruce's Bannock Burn. The loch covers an area of 140 acres. 600 ft high cliffs dominate the eastern shoreline and beautifully frame the loch.
Fish Wild brown trout and rainbow trout. Stocked throughout the year with rainbow trout which average 1lb 8oz in weight. 20,000 fish are caught each year. 40/60 rainbow trout of over 10lb are caught each season. The record for the fishery stands at 19lb 13oz. During 1999 two fish each weighing 18lb 12oz were caught.
Flies & Tactics Boat fishing, bank fishing and tube floats. Fish rise and are caught everywhere, but the south end, in the vicinity of the two small islands is a favoured drift. Apart from the first two or three weeeks of the season, fishing is best using nymphs, buzzers or small imitative flies. Evening fishing, which can be particularly good with dry fly, is the best time to try for the large resident population of wild brown trout. They average 10oz, but the record brown trout caught weighed 9lb 3oz.
Permission & Charges Contact: George Holdsworth, Greathill House, Stirling FK7 9QS. Tel: 01786 471967; Fax: 01786 447388. Costs: Day Session (10am - 5pm) 15th March -31st October. Bank £15 10 fish limit; 1 Rod Boat £18 10 fish limit 2 Rod Boat £31 20 fish limit. Evening Sessions (6pm - 11pm) 1st May - 31st August. Bank £13 10 fish limit; 1 Rod Boat £16 10 fish limit; 2 Rod Boat £25 20 fish limit. Combined Permit (10am -11pm) 1st May - 31st August. Bank £18 no fish limit; 1Rod Boat £21 no fish limit; 2Rod Boat £34 no fish limit. Junior with adult. Only one junior per adult is allowed. Junior is free of charge and shares adult catch limit. Float Tubing. Charge is the same as per bank permit. Not available Sat/Sun day sessions. All tubers must supply and wear an approved life jacket before being allowed on the water. All prices include VAT @ 17.5%.

PRIVATE WATERS BALLOCH, Loch of 57/838191; A'CHROIN, Lochan 57/615167; TINKER, Loch 57/447069; BALLOCH, Lochan 57/591042; MUIR DAM, Loch 57/661024; DALDORN, Wester loch of 57/671035; MAHAICK, Loch 57/707069; WATSON, Loch 57/711003; LOSSBURN, Reservoir 57831990; WALTON, Loch 57/665866; LAGGAN, Loch (Stirling) 57/625925; MILL Dam 57/613919; MACARNIE, Loch 57/561994; SPLING, Lochan 57/501004; MUIR PARK, Reservoir 57/488920.

REOIDHTE, Lochan See Loch Venachar.

SWANSWATER, Fishery
Location & Access 57/782890 Leave the M80 Motorway at Exit 9 and follow the signs to Bannockburn Heritage Centre. Turn left at the Heritage Centre to Chartershall and follow the signs to the fishery.
Commentary A small, well-managed fishery consisting of three ponds: Swanswater (10 acres) Mill Pond (2 acres) and Meadow Pond (1 acre). The ponds are fed by Sauchie Burn, the site of the Battle of Sauchieburn (1488) which resulted in the murder of King James.
Fish Regularly stocked with rainbow trout, blue trout and steelheads. There are also a few wild brown trout. Average weight, 2lb 8oz. Largest rainbow in 1999 weighed 16lb 14oz, largest brown trout, 11lb 9oz.
Flies & Tactics Three boats are available and bank fishing is also allowed. Fish are taken everywhere. Use reservoir lures and buzzers.
Permission & Charges Contact: Alastair Lohoar, Swanswater Fisheries, Cultenhove, Nr Chartershall, Stirling. Tel: 01786 814805. Cost: Swanswater: £8 for a 2 hour two fish session; £18 for an 8 hour five fish session. Bank fishing on Mill and Meadow Ponds, between £6 and £15. Meadow Pond is ideal for beginners.

TEITH, River
Location & Access Source 56/374180 Outfall 57/699961. The river is easily accessible from public and private roads throughout its entire length; particularly from the A84 Stirling/Callander road which borders much of the north bank of the stream.
Commentary The River Teith rises to the west of Loch Doine (see Loch Voil entry) on the slopes of Beinn Chabhair (931m) and it is the most significant tributary of the River Forth. However, since the Forth's principal headwater, Loch Katrine, was impounded and redirected to supply the City of Glasgow with water, the Teith has become the main sporting river on the system. The Forth itself rises from Loch Ard (see OS 57 entry) and winds east across Flanders Moss past Stirling Castle in a series of lazy loops and ox-bows to reach the sea in the Firth of Forth at Alloa (58/880920). The other major tributary of the River Forth is Allan Water. This stream begins life on the east slopes of Creag Beinn na Eun (632m) as the River Knaik and only becomes Allan Water near the Inn at Greenloaning (57/840077). After flowing through Dunblane and Bridge of Allan, the stream joins the River Forth near Neatherton (57/788960).
Fish Salmon, sea-trout, brown trout and escapee rainbow trout. The whole system produces in the order of 1,000 salmon and a similar number of sea-trout each season. Fish run the river from opening day onwards and early season sport can be excellent. There is a grilse run during the summer months and autumn brings in good numbers of salmon which average 11lb in weight. Salmon of over 20lb are frequently taken. A salmon weighing 31lb was caught in 1997. Sea-trout average 2lb, brown trout 8oz.

353

Stirling & The Trossachs
OS Map 57

Flies & Tactics A 15ft double-handed rod is the best all-purpose rod for fishing the river. You will be able to cover most of the lies without difficulty or, frequently, the need to wade. Serious fishing starts around Callander and the principal beats are: Town Water, Roman Camp Hotel beat, Gart Farm, Cambusmore - 26 named pools producing approximately 200 salmon each season - Lanrick Castle with 3.5 miles single and double bank fishing including the famous Weir Pool; Deanston Angling Club Water with the Distillery Fishings; Doune Lodge and Doune Castle Pool; Blair Drummond Estate with Ardoch Pool, Chapel Pool, Horse Hole Pool, McLaren's Pool and the Beeches. Other beats include Ochtertyre, and Blue Banks where the Teith meets the River Forth. The best of the Forth fishings is from where the Teith flows in downstream to Stirling. The river here is 50yds/60yds wide, slow-moving, and is mostly fished by spinning. It is invariably busy, as is the case at Aberfoyle and Gartmore, the only other fishing of any note on the River Forth. Allan Water is very much a spate stream but given good water levels it can produce sport with salmon and sea-trout. Flies: Ally's Shrimp, General Practitioner, Munro Killer, Stoat's Tail, Silver Wilkinson. For sea-trout, try: Black Pennell, Mallard & Claret, Peter Ross.

Permission & Charges Callander & Stirfling Town Water: Stirling District Council, Beechwood House, St Ninnian's Road, Stirling. Tel: 01786 432348 and James Bayne, 74 Main Street, Callander. Tel: 01877 330218. Blue Banks Beat: Ross Muirhead, Unit 1, Kildean Market, Stirling. Tel: 01786 461597; D Crockart & Son, 47 King Street, Stirling. Tel: 01786 465517; Mitchell's Tackle Shop, 13 Bannockburn Road, Stirling. Tel: 01786 445587. Roman Camp Hotel Fishings is free of charge to hotel guests. Gart Farm, Cambusmore and Lanrick Castle Water: Jim Henderson, Country Pursuits, 46 Henderson Street, Bridge of Allan FK9 4HS. Tel: 01786 834495; Fax: 01786 834210. Country Sports also offer excellent fishing on the Tay and the Earn. Also, Lanrick Castle Estate, Broich Farm, Doune PK16 6HJ. Tel: 01786 841866; Strutt & Parker, 13 Hill Street, Berkeley Square, London. Tel: 0171 6297282; and Finlyson Hughes, 29 Barossa Place, Perth. Tel: 01738 630926. Aberfoyle & Gartmore: D Crockart (see above) and Visitor Centre, David Marshall Lodge, Queen Elizabeth Forest Park, Aberfoyle. Tel: 01877 382265. Fishing on the River Allan is restricted to 15 permits per day (excluding Saturdays). See Country Sports above. Fishing on the other beats noted is rarely available. For information, contact: Keir & Cawder Estates, Craigarnhall, Doune, Perthshire. Tel: 01786 833858. Prices vary widely, depending upon beat and time of year. Expect to pay in the order of £15 per rod per day, up to £3,000 for a good four rod beat for a week. Day rods on Cambusmore Fishings (see Country Sports above) cost: February - May £30; June - August £25; August £35; September £50; October £60 (all prices subject to VAT @ 17.5%). Gart Farm Fishings)also Country Sports) cost: February - April £25; May - July £20; August - September £40; October £50 (all prices subject to VAT@ 17.5%).

TOUCH MUIR, Reservoirs See Carron Valley Reservoir.

VENACHAR, Loch
Location & Access 57/570055. Easily-accessible from the A821 Callander/Trossachs road which margins the north shore.
Commentary Loch Venachar lies on the headwaters of the River Teith (see separate entry) and is 3.5 miles east/west by up to half mile wide. Loch Achray (57/515064) feeds Loch Venachar via the Black Water from the west, whilst to the south of Loch Venachar lie Loch Drunkie (57/545044) and little Lochan Reoidhte (57/521033) in the Queen Elizabeth Forest Park. Loch Venachar is often busy during the summer months but it is generally possible to find a quiet corner from which to practice the gentle art.
Fish Just about something for everyone in Loch Venachar and Loch Achray: brown trout, sea-trout, the chance of a salmon, huge pike and numerous perch. Loch Drunkie and Lochan Reoidhte contain only brown trout, although Lochan Reoidhte has been stocked with rainbow trout in the past. During 1996 approximately 400 pike were taken from Loch Venachar, the largest estimated to have been 42lb in weight. Brown trout average 8oz, but there are larger fish as well and trout of over 2lb are not uncommon.
Flies & Tactics Boat fishing brings the best results on Loch Venachar and helps you to effectively cover this large expanse of water. The west end of the loch, in the vicinity of Lendrick (57/545059), and the mouth of the Black Water will invariably produce fish; carefully explore the south shore from Invertrossachs (57/560054) east to West Dullater (57/583052). The other lochs noted above are fished from the bank. The north shore of Loch Achray is the most convenient fishing area, whilst on Loch Drunkie, the east shoreline offers the best chance of sport. Flies: Soldier Palmer, Greenwell's Glory, Silver Butcher.
Permission & Charges For Loch Venachar, contact: W M Meikle, 41 Buchany, Doune. Tel: 01786 841692 or J Bayne, 76 Main Street, Callander. Tel: 01877 330218. Bank fishing: £7 per rod per day, boat with outboard motor and fuel, £27 per day. Two sessions: 9.30am until 5.30pm and 6pm until 11 pm. For Loch Achray, contact: Loch Achray Hotel, The Trossachs, by Callander. Tel: 01877 376229 and Visitor Centre, David Marshall Lodge, Queen Elizabeth Forest Park, Aberfoyle. Tel: 01877 382258. Cost: £7 per rod per day. The Visitor Centre also issues a permit which includes fishing both Loch Drunkie and Lochan Reoidhte and costs £3 per rod per day.

VOIL, Loch
Location & Access 57/500197. Turn west from the A84 Callander/Lochearnhead road at Kingshouse (57/565203). The east end of the loch is reached at Balquhidder (57/535208) after 2 miles.
Commentary Loch Voil lies on the headwaters of the River Teith (see separate entry) and is 3.5 miles east/west by up to 600 yds wide. It is fed by the Ishag Burn which rises between the heights of Beinn Tulaichean (945m) to the east and Beinn a'Chroin

OS Maps 57-58 — Perth & Kinross

(946m) to the west. The burns flows past Inverlochlairg (56/439180), the site of Rob Roy MacGregor's house. The stream then enters Loch Doine (57/470192) before flowing through a narrow channel at Monachyle Tuarach (57/479192) into the west end of Loch Voil. The River Balvag drains Loch Voil east and then south into Loch Lubnaig (see separate entry) and this river, and its principal tributary, the Calair Burn which joins the River Balvag at Balquhidder, both offer an additional chance of sport for visiting anglers. Those not piscatorially inclined will find plenty of other things to do in the surrounding area, not the least of which is a visit to Blaquhidder where Rob Roy and two of his sons lie buried in the churchyard.

Fish Salmon, sea-trout, brown trout, ferox trout and arctic char. Approximately 20/30 salmon are taken most seasons, depending upon water conditions and these fish average 7lb/8lb. However, much larger salmon are also taken, including fish of up to 18lb in weight. Sea-trout average 2lb, but there are larger fish as well. Ferox trout of over 10lb are caught, mostly whilst trolling for salmon, and brown trout average 8oz/10oz but there are good numbers of heavier fish as well of up to and over 3lb. Arctic char are most often caught during the early months of the season and average approximately 1lb in weight, although char of up to 3lb have also been caught in recent years.

Flies & Tactics A public road along the north shore of Loch Voil and Loch Doine opens up nearly 5 miles of excellent bank fishing. Concentrate you efforts in the vicinity of Tulloch (57/518205), Balquhidder Lodge (57/506201), Craigruie (57/498198) where the Monachyle Burn enters the loch at Monachylemore (57/479196), and at the entrance and exit between Loch Doine and Loch Voil. The road along the south shore, past the caravan site to Muirlaggan, gives access to a further 2 miles of bank fishing. Thereafter, you are on your own along a trackless shore. It is not necessary to wade when bank fishing. The fish lie close to the shore and are only spooked out into deeper water by incautious wading. Boat fishing is perhaps the most convenient way to explore this large expanse of water and the services of a gillie will greatly enhance your opportunity of sport. The rivers noted above are very much spate streams and are only really worth fishing after heavy rain. This also applies to the Ishag Burn which can give splendid sport after a spate.. Lures: Kynoch Killer, Tobies, Rapalas, Devon Minnows. Flies: for salmon, try, Stoat's Tail, Goat's Toe, Garry Dog, Hairy Mary, Green Highlander, Clan Chief. These patterns will also attract sea-trout, as do Black Pennell, Mallard & Claret, Peter Ross. For brown trout, offer: Soldier Palmer, Greenwell's Glory, Silver Butcher. Dapping can also be a productive fishing method on Loch Voil.

Permission & Charges For Loch Voil and Loch Doine, contact: Mrs Catriona Oldham Muirlaggan, Balquhidder, Lochearnhead, Perthshire. Tel: 01877 384219; Stronvar Country House Hotel, Balquhidder, Lochearnhead, Perthshire. Tel: 01877 384688; C Marshall, Craigruie Farm, Balquhidder, Lochearnhead, Perthshire. Tel: 01877 384262. J Bayne, Fishing Tackle Shop, 76 Main Street, Callander, Perthshire. Tel: 01877 330218. Cost: bank fishing, £3 per rod per day; boats, £27 per boat per day. For the River Balvag, contact: Kings House Hotel, Balquhidder, Lochearnhead, Perthshire. Tel: 01877 384646 and Munro Hotel, Strathyre, by Callander, Perthshire. Tel: 01877 384263. Cost £4.00 per rod per day. The Kings House Hotel also has fishing on Loch Doine.

Perth and Kinross

BALLO, Reservoir
Location & Access 58/225050 Approach from Leslie on the A911 Leslie/Markinch road. Turn north at 58/251019 on the minor road to Falkland to reach the reservoir entrance (on your left) after a distance of 1 and 1/2 miles.

Commentary A substantial expanse of water, 3/4 of a mile long by up to 1/4 of a mile wide, exposed and often windy, but set amidst dramatic countryside and dominated by West Lomond (522m) to the north. Non-fishing companions should explore the Lomond Hills and visit to Falkland Palace, the favourite residence of the Stewart Kings of Scotland.

Fish Ballo Reservoir is a favourite residence of excellent quality brown and rainbow trout which average 1lb.

Flies & Tactics Boat fishing only and the north end of the reservoir, in the vicinity of the island and ragged promontory, is the place to begin. Electric outboard motors are available for hire and are highly recommended, otherwise pack a young friend with strong arms. Flies: Black Pennell, March Brown, Peter Ross.

Permission & Charges Richard Philp, Fishing Tackle Shop, 102 High Street, Kinross. Tel: 01577 862371. £28 per session (2 sessions per day). There is a bag limit of 16 fish per boat per session.

BLACK, Loch See Loch Glow.

CASTLEHILL, Reservoir
Location & Access 58/995036 Immediately adjacent to the A823 Yetts o'Muckhart/Auchterarder road in Glendevon.

Commentary Close to the road, easily accessible and very public.

Fish Stocked with good quality brown trout rainbow trout.

Flies & Tactics This small reservoir lies on the headwaters of the River Devon and offers bank and boat fishing (2 boats available). Fish are taken from all round the shore. Flies: Ke-He, Invicta, Black Pennell.

Permission & Charges See Holl Reservoir.

CRAIGLUSCAR, Reservoir
Location & Access 58/066904 Craigluscar Reservoir is 2 miles north from Dunfermline on the A823 Dunfermline/Powmill road. Turn west on the minor

Perth & Kinross — OS Map 58

road at 58/088901 to reach the reservoir entrance, on your right, after a distance of 1.5 miles.
Commentary A well-managed fishery, leased and cared for by the Dunfermline Artisans' Angling Club for the past 80 years. There is a comfortable club fishing hut at the reservoir and the surrounding countryside gives this water a natural, rather than a man-made look.
Fish Regularly stocked with both brown and rainbow trout. Fish of over 4lb are caught frequently and the largest specimen landed in recent years weighed 7lb 9oz.
Flies & Tactics Bank fishing only and fish may be taken from almost anywhere around the shoreline. There is an abundance of natural fly life which can make Craigluscar trout very choosy about what they select for supper. In the early months of the season, try: Black Spider, March Brown, Invicta. During summer, offer nymph's and dry fly, in the autumn try Ke-He, Wickham's Fancy, Kingfisher Butcher.
Permission & Charges Contact: The Club Hut, Craigluscar Reservoir, Dunfermline, Fife. Tel: 01383 732891. The Cost: 2 session daily, bank fishing, £11. There is a 6 fish per rod per session bag limit.

CROOK OF DEVON, Fishery
Location & Access 58/039004 close to the A977 Kincardine/Kinross road in Crook of Devon village.
Commentary A small, well-organised trout fishery covering an area of 4 acres and close to the banks of the River Devon. There are excellent facilities for visiting anglers: tackle hire, toilets, restaurant, access for disabled anglers and an adventure playground for children.
Fish Rainbow trout which average 1lb 8oz.
Flies & Tactics Bank fishing with reservoir lures does the business.
Permission & Charges Contact: Mr & Mrs Wallace, Crook of Devon Village Fishery, Crook of Devon, by Kinross. Tel: 01577 840297. Day permit: £5 per rod. Fish caught are charged at £2 per lb. If a greater weight than 10lb of trout is caught, the permit money is refunded.

CROSS REFERENCES
All the waters on OS Map 58 which lie to the north of a line between Crieff in the west and Perth in the east are described on OS Maps 52 or 53.

DEVON, River
Location & Access Source 58/890045 Outfall 58/909936 Easy access to the river from public roads: A91 Alva/Yetts o'Muckhart; A977 near Rumbling Bridge (58/017995); the A823 in Glendevon (58/990044).
Commentary A pretty stream in its upper reaches above Rumbling Bridge. The falls at Rumbling Bridge are impassable to migratory fish but the weir at Cambus now has a fish pass. Outwith spate conditions, the flow is dependent upon compensation water from Castlehill Reservoir in the headwater catchment area.
Fish Salmon, sea-trout and brown trout. There are positive signs that greater numbers of migratory fish are running the river each year. A fish-pass has been installed at Cambus to allow fish to pass upstream. In recent years the Devon Angling Association have stocked the river with upwards of 4,000 brown trout.
Flies & Tactics The river rises from Upper Glendevon Reservoir (see separate entry) and enters the Firth of Forth near Alloa after a journey of approx. 20 miles. Salmon and sea-trout run the river from mid-June onwards but the bulk of salmon do not arrive until September. Bait fishing and spinning are the most used fishing methods, although there are sections of the river where fly fishing is possible. Everything depends upon heavy rain. Lures: Devon Minnows, Tobys, Mepps. Flies: Stoat's Tail, GP. The Association also have the fishing rights on Glenquey Reservoir which is a very attractive headwater loch of the River Devon situated between Auchlinsky Hill (427m) and Innerdownie (611m) in Glendevon. The reservoir is approached by a water board road that leaves the A823 at 58/997033. The Association issue 5 visitor tickets per day (7 days a week), bank fishing for excellent quality brown trout which average 14oz. The largest trout taken in recent years weighed 4lb 8oz. Flies: Black Spider, Greenwell's Glory, Silver Invicta.
Permission & Charges For the River Devon, contact: Ronald Breingan, 33 Redwell Place, Alloa, Clackmanan FK10 2BT. Tel: 01259 215185. Scobie Sports, Primrose Street, Alloa, Clackmanan. Tel: 01259 722661; D W Black, The Hobby & Model Shop, 10-12 New Row, Dunfermline. Tel: 01383 722582. Cost: £6 per rod per day. For Glenquey Reservoir (fly only) contact: Yetts o'Muckhart Post Office, Yetts o'Muckhart, Clackmanan. Tel: 01259 781322; McCutcheons Newsagent, Dollar (Tel: 01259 742517). The Inn, Muckhart. Tel: 01259 781324. Cost: £9 per rod per day.

DOW, Loch See Loch Glow.

DRUMMOND, Pond of
Location & Access 58/855187 The loch lies 2 miles to the south of Crieff adjacent to the A822 Crieff/Muthill road.
Commentary An easily accessible, attractive, loch in a woodland setting covering an area of approximately 90 acres to the north of Drummond Castle. There is a convenient car park close by at the Ben y Beg Craft centre. The Crieff Angling Club manage the loch which is a Site of Special Scientific Interest.
Fish Stocked with good quality brown trout which average 12oz in weight.
Flies & Tactics Boat fishing only and club members have priority. Electric outboard motors are permitted but they are not available for hire. Anglers my use a drouge in windy conditions but may not fish from anchored boats. This is a shallow loch with excellent natural feeding and trout may be taken all round the loch, from the middle to the margins. Flies: Black Spider, Greenwell's Glory, Invicta.
Permission & Charges Contact: Bill Williamson,

OS Map 58 — Perth & Kinross

Strathearn Tyres, Crieff, Perthshire. Tel: 01764 654697. Cost: £25 per boat (2 rods) per session. There is a 6 fish per rod bag limit.

EARN, River
Location & Access On OS Map 58, the River Earn extends from Crieff (58/865215) in the West to its outfall in the Firth of Tay at 58/197185 in the east. (See also OS Map 52)
Commentary Downstream from Crieff, the River Earn becomes increasingly sluggish and canal-like on its journey the sea. It is also much given to flooding after prolonged rain and the lower reaches are effected by the tide and are often brackish as far upstream as Forgandenny (58/080196), a distance of some seven miles from the Firth of Tay.
Fish Salmon, sea-trout and brown trout. The whole system may produce in the region of 1,000 salmon and a similar number of sea-trout in a good year. Much, as always, depends upon prevailing water conditions. Salmon average 7lb/8lb, although double figure fish are taken most seasons, particularly during the autumn months when huge fish enter the river. Sea-trout average in the order of 2lb with a few specimen fish of up to 5lb/6lb in weight.
Flies & Tactics The most accessible fishing on the River Earn is in the Crieff/Comrie area, much of the lower river being preserved by the riparian owners. However, the Lower Aberuthven Beat, 1 mile of single bank fishing, is sometimes available on a day ticket basis and it fishes up to a maximum of 8 rods. Access is also often possible to the Trinity Gask Estate Water. The Mill of Gask Beat consists of 1 mile single bank fishing, bounded by fertile agricultural land, and there are 5 good pools, including Bank Pool, Grindles and the March Pool. Most fish are taken using bait or by spinning, at the back end, although flies such as Stoat's Tail, Willie Gunn, Garry Dog and Shrimp Fly can also produce results. The Dupplin Estate preserve the salmon fishing, but they do issue tickets for brown trout fishing
Permission & Charges For Lower Aberuthven, contact: James Haggart, Haugh of Aberuthven, Auchterarder, Perthshire. Tel: 01738 730206. For Trinity Gask, contact: Trinity Gask Estate, Old School House, Trinity Gask, Auchterarder, Perthshire. Tel: 01764. 663237. Expect to pay in the order of £15 to £30 per rod per day depending upon the time of year. For trout fishing on the Dupplin Estate Water, contact: The Factor, Dupplin Estate, Forteviot, by Perth. Tel: 01738 622757.

FITTY, Loch
Location & Access 58/120914 Loch Fitty lies 4 miles to the north of the A912 Dunfermline/Kelty road, close to the M80 Motorway (leave at Exit 3). Turn left at Lochend (58/131916) to reach the loch.
Commentary A well-established, very popular, put-and-take fishery covering an area of 160 acres. There are excellent facilities for visiting anglers, including club house, tackle shop, restaurant, rod hire and boats for disabled anglers.
Fish Regularly stocked with up to 20,000 brown and rainbow trout. Their average weight is 1lb 8oz and fish of up to and over 5lb are frequently taken.
Flies & Tactics 20 boats and bank fishing, so Loch Fitty can often be a busy place to fish. Trout rise and are taken throughout the system and no one place is any better than another. Reservoir lures do most of the damage: Fitty Black, Ace of Spades, Sweeney Todd, Viva. The fishery manager posts a daily bulletin of the most successful flies.
Permission & Charges Game Fisheries Limited, The Fishing Lodge, Loch Fitty, Kingseat, Dunfermline, Fife. Tel: 01383 620666. Cost: bank fishing for specimen trout. £20 for 2 trout (4 hours); £30 for 3 trout (5 hours); £38 for 4 trout (5 hours). Boat fishing (including outboard motor), £34 per two anglers per day, 8 trout per angler limit. The fishery is open from 25th February until 15th December each year.

GARTMORE, Dam
Location & Access 58/911941 Approach from either New Sauchie (58/904941) in the west or from the B9140 Fishcross/Coalsnaughton road in the north or the A907 Alloa/Clackmanan road in the south.
Commentary Gartmore Dam lies at the centre of a country park and Site of Special Scientific Interest. It was constructed in 1713 for the 6th Earl of Mar, Bobbing Johnnie, who, through masterly inactivity, neither lost nor won the Battle of Sheriffmuir (1715). The fishery is 1 mile east/west by up to 1/4 of a mile wide.
Fish Stocked with 20,000 brown trout and re-stocked during the season. Trout average 1lb in weight with a few fish of up to and over 4lb.
Flies & Tactics Boat and bank fishing. The area surrounding the island, including the adjacent north shore, and the north east end of the loch are not open for angling. Anglers are allowed to use spinning tackle from the shore, boat fishing is with fly only. Trout may be taken throughout the system and no one place is substantially better than another.
Permission & Charges Contact: Clackmanan District Council, Leisure Services Department, Spiers Centre, 29 Primrose Street, Alloa. Tel: 01259 213131 or Gartmore Dam Visitors Centre, by Alloa. Tel: 01259 214319. Cost: Day tickets, boat fishing £24, bank fishing, £7 per session. Electric motors are available at £7 per session. There is a limit of 5 fish per rod per session.

GLENFARG, Fishery
Location & Access 58/115099 Approach via the minor road from Milnathort (58/121047) past Middleton (58/124068) to Candy. The fishery is to the north of the small forestry plantation.
Commentary A busy put-and-take fishery in an attractive setting, open from March until December. There are good facilities for visiting anglers and numbers are limited to approx. 25/30 rods.
Fish Brown and rainbow trout which average 1lb 8oz. Also a few much larger specimens, including brown trout of up to 7lb and rainbow trout of 20lb in weight.
Flies & Tactics Bank fishing only. There are two small

357

Perth & Kinross — OS Map 58

ponds, one (4.5 acres) is reserved for fly-fishing, the other (2.5 acres) for bait fishing. On the fly-only pond, most reservoir lure patterns will produce the desired results.
Permission & Charges Contact: Ian Walker, Glenfarg Fishery, Kandy, by Glenfarg. Tel: 01577 830727. Charges vary from £8 for a 2 hour (2 fish) session to £18 for an 8 hour (8 fish) session.

GLENFARG, Reservoir
Location & Access 58/104112 From the M80 Edinburgh/Perth Motorway, leave at Exit 8 on the A91 to Cupar road. After 1/2 a mile, turn left to join the A90 to Glenfarg. In Glenfarg Village, turn left by the church and follow the road to Abbots Deuglie (58/120109) and the entrance to the reservoir.
Commentary Glenfarg lies in the Ochil Hills at an altitude of 200m and is just under 1 mile in length by up to 1/4 of a mile wide. The setting is dramatic although the reservoir can often be wild and windy. Little Loch Whirr (58/1190126), to the north of Glenfarg Reservoir, is private.
Fish Stocked with brown trout which average 12oz. Fish of up to and over 3lb in weight are also caught, particularly towards the end of the season.
Flies & Tactics Bank fishing is not allowed but there are 6 boats available for the use of visiting anglers. The north end of the reservoir, where it divides into 2 long narrow bays, is the most productive fishing area. Work the margins, about 15 yds out from the shore. Flies: Soldier Palmer, Woodcock & Hare-lug, Silver Butcher.
Permission & Charges See Holl Reservoir.

GLENQUEY, Reservoir See River Devon.

GLENSHERUP, Reservoir
Location & Access 58/964042 Access is from the A823 Yetts o'Muckhart/Auchterarder road in Glen Devon. Cross the bridge over the River Devon at Hunthall (58/967053) and drive south to reach the reservoir after 1/2 a mile.
Commentary Glensherup reservoir covers an area of approximately 50 acres and it is sheltered by commercial forestry to the east and the heights of Ben Shee (515m) to the west.
Fish Stocked with rainbow trout (2lb to 10lb) and brown trout which average 1lb 8oz.
Flies & Tactics Bank and boat fishing and either method can bring results. Fish rise and are taken everywhere but the forest shore (east) is the favoured drift. Flies: reservoir lures, Black Spider, March Brown, Silver Butcher.
Permission & Charges Richard Philp, Tackle Shop, 102 High Street, Kinross. Tel: 01577 862371. Cost: Bank fishing, £15 per rod (3 fish). Boat fishing, from £18 up to £38 for 3 rods. 5 fish per rod limit. Thereafter, catch-and-release using barbless hooks.

GLOW, Loch
Location & Access 58/087958 Approach from the minor road between Greenknowes (58/108932) in the south to Nivingston (58/101978) in the north. Turn west at 58/100954 to reach the loch after 1/2 a mile.
Commentary Loch Glow lies to the north of Dunfermline and is 3/4 of a mile east/west by up to 600yds wide and covers an area of 140 acres. Immediately to the north west is the Black Loch (58/076962), which contains excellent trout, and to the north, 2 small, shallow, puddles, Dow Loch and Lurg Loch which contain only a few coarse fish. Roscobie Reservoir (58/093934), to the south, is private.
Fish Brown trout average 12oz in weight and fish of up to and over 3lb are by no means uncommon: the Black Loch has produced a trout of 7lb 2oz.
Flies & Tactics The Black Loch, a small loch which is fished from the shore, does not give up its residents easily and has a well-deserved reputation for being dour. There are 4 boats on Loch Glow and bank fishing is also allowed. The south shore is the most productive fishing area, particularly at the mouths of the 7 feeders streams which enter from Tipperton Moss. Flies: Connemara Black, Greenwell's Glory, Kingfisher Butcher.
Permission & Charges The fishing is managed by the Sports Section of the Civil Service Angling Association. Contact: David Black, The Hobby & Model Shop, 10-12 New Row, Dunfermline, Fife. Tel: 01383 722582,. Jeff Barker, No 1 Wedderburn Street, Dunfermline, Fife KY11 4PT. Tel: 01383 723122/ Cost: bank fishing, £6 per rod per day.

HEATHERYFORD, Fishery
Location & Access 58/106021. Leave the M90 Motorway at Exit 6 and turn east onto the A977. Heatheryford is the signposted to the left, 500yds from Exit 6.
Commentary A small put-and-take fishery close to Loch Leven. There is a restaurant and art gallery attached to the complex and access to the ponds is across well-maintained grass parks.
Fish Stocked rainbow trout and brown trout minimum 1lb and also fish of up to and over 8lb in weight.
Flies & Tactics Bank fishing. Park and cast. The 4 ponds cover an area of approximately 10 acres and they are open for angling from March until December. Use reservoir lures or: Black Pennell, March Brown, Alexandra.
Permission & Charges Contact: John Cairns, Heatheryford Fishery, by Kinross, KY13 7NQ. Tel: 01577 864212. Cost: £12 for 4 hours (2 fish); £15 for 6 hours (3 fish); £18 for 8hours (4 fish).

HOLL, Reservoir
Location & Access 58/225036 Approach from the A911 Scotlandwell/Leslie road. Drive north at 58/232015 to reach the reservoir after a distance of 1 mile.
Commentary Holl Reservoir is owned and managed by East of Scotland Water and lies to the south of Ballo Reservoir (see separate entry) with the dramatic sweep of the Lomond Hills as a background.
Fish Stocked with brown and rainbow trout.
Flies & Tactics The reservoir covers an area of approximately 80 acres and there are 6 boats avail-

OS Map 58 — Perth & Kinross

able for hire. Bank fishing is not allowed. Concentrate your efforts at the west end of the reservoir, close to the shore. Flies: Loch Ordie, Grouse & Claret, Silver Invicta.
Permission & Charges East of Scotland Water, Fife Division, Craig Mitchell House, Flemmington Road, Glenrothes, Fife. Tel: 01592 614000. Boat and two anglers fishing, between £12 and £26 per day.

LEVEN, Loch
Location & Access 58/150015 Leave the M90 Motorway at Exit 6, signposted to Kinross. Turn south down the main street in Kinross and bear left by the church to reach the loch.
Commentary Once the most famous trout loch in Europe, now a just another put-and-take fishery - 3,500 acres in extent, 3 miles across and scattered with 7 small islands. The water of the loch had become so heavily phosphate-enriched that toxic blooms turned Loch Leven green and created a public health hazard. Consequently, native brown trout resorted to bottom feeding, to the dismay of anglers fishing traditional wet flies on the surface. Research shows that natural brown trout stocks are not abundant but they are healthy. The loch is an important bird sanctuary and site of the RSPB Vane Farm Nature Reserve (58/160990).
Fish Brown trout and rainbow trout. Brown trout average 1lb 6oz, rainbow trout are of a similar size. The heaviest brown trout taken in recent years was splendid fish of 8lb 3oz, caught in August 1991.
Flies & Tactics Boat fishing only and there are 50 available, complete with outboard motors. There are excellent facilities at The Pier (58/122017). Maps are available showing all the historic drifts but in essence, trout may be taken from almost anywhere around the loch. A favourite drift is along the south shore of Castle Island, from which Mary Queen of Scots famously escaped on 2nd May 1568, and around St Serf's Island with its ruined 13th century Priory. Flies: traditionally, anglers fishing Loch Leven used small double-hooked patters such as Dunkeld, Peter Ross, Greenwell's Glory, March Brown, Mallard & Claret, now, it is more usual to fling reservoir lures into the depths. There is a limit of 6 rainbow trout per angler but no limit on numbers of brown trout which may be caught and killed.
Permission & Charges April and May day boats, Monday to Friday, £25. April and September, 10am until 8pm, £36 per boat. May to August, 10am to 6pm, £30. Afternoon sessions, £17. Three anglers per boat. No limit on number of 10"+ brown trout caught. Rainbow trout, between 10" and 17", 12 per boat. Over 17", no limit. Contact: The Fishery Manager, Loch Leven Fisheries, The Pier, Kinross, Perthshire, KY13 7UF. Tel: 01577 863407.

LOCHMILL, Loch
Location & Access 58/222163 In Newburgh (58/230181) follow Woodruffe Road south towards Auchtermuchty to reach the loch after 1 mile.
Commentary A pleasant little loch to the east of Pitcairlie Hill (281m) and covering approximately 30 acres, 700 yds long by 200 yds wide.
Fish Stocked for many years with Loch Leven trout which now average 12oz in weight. Fish of up to and over 2lb are frequently caught.
Flies & Tactics The loch is managed by the Newburgh Angling Club and both boat and bank fishing is available. The west end of the loch is the preferred area, although trout may be taken from almost anywhere round the shoreline. Flies: Blae & Black, March Brown, Peter Ross.
Permission & Charges Contact: Edwin Young, Albert Bar, Newburgh, Fife. Tel: 01337 840439. £5 per rod, £6 per boat.

LOWER GLENDEVON, Reservoir
Location & Access 58/930049 Leave the A823 Yetts o'Muckhart/Auchterarder road at Glenhead Farm (58/949052). A water board road leads south west and reaches the loch after 1 mile.
Commentary Lower Glendevon Reservoir is approximately 1 mile long by up to 300yds wide and it lies in a dramatic setting at an altitude of 300m in the Ochil Hills. Lower Glendevon is fed from the west by Upper Glendevon Reservoir but of the two, Lower Glendevon is the most attractive fishery. Upper Glendevon is often subjected to water level fluctuations which leaves an unsightly tide mark round the shore.
Fish Stocked with brown trout which average 10oz.
Flies & Tactics Boat fishing (2 boats) and bank fishing on Lower Glendevon, bank fishing only on Upper Glendevon. It is dangerous to wade on Upper Glendevon. Don't be tempted. The west end of Upper Glendevon is the most productive fishing area. On Lower Glendevon work the north shore, particularly in the vicinity of the two streams that flow in from Weather Hill (520m). Flies: Black Zulu, Soldier Palmer, Alexandra.
Permission & Charges See Glensherup Reservoir entry.

LURG, Loch See Loch Glow.

ORCHILL, Loch
Location & Access 58/868117 Approach from minor road to Gleneagles which leaves the A827 just north of Braco at the site of the Roman Fort. Turn left before Seathaugh at 58/872107 to Orchill Home Farm. The loch is unnamed on the OS map.
Commentary A small (4.5 acre) put-and-take fishery in an attractive, woodland setting.
Fish Stocked with rainbow trout between 1lb 8oz and 12lb in weight.
Flies & Tactics Casting platforms have been placed round the shores of the loch and a boat is also available for hire. Flies: reservoir lures do most of the damage, in particular, Black and Green Fritz patterns and Cat's Whiskers.
Permission & Charges Mrs Elizabeth Jackson, South Lodge, Orchill Home Farm, Braco, Perthshire FK15 9LF. Tel: 01764 682287. Cost: day ticket £20 (5 fish); 4 hour session £12 (3 fish); boat hire £5 per session.

ORE, Loch
Location & Access 58/165955 Approach from Lochore (58/180967) on the B920 Lochgelly /Scotlandwell road.
Commentary Loch Ore is the central attraction of a country park, developed on the site of 2, disused, open-cast coal mining sites. They cover and area of approx. 1/2 a square mile and are complimented by a cafeteria, picnic area and golf course. The loch is also used for sailing and other water sport activities.
Fish Stocked with brown trout and rainbow trout which average 12oz in weight. Fish of up to and over 6lb are also taken.
Flies & Tactics Both boat and bank fishing are allowed but best results come from the boat. The fishery is open from March until November and fishing is by fly only until the end of May. Thereafter all legal methods are allowed. There is a Wheeley Boat for the use of disabled anglers. Best flies: Black Spider, Woodcock & Yellow, Kingfisher Butcher.
Permission & Charges Park Centre, Lochore Meadows Country Park, Crosshill, Nr Lochgelly, Fife. Tel: 01592 414312. Cost: from £7.50 for 8 hours bank fishing (5 fish) up to £42 for a boat and engine (3 rods fishing) for a full day.

PRIVATE WATERS CAMILLA Loch 58/220916; LUMPHINNANS Loch 58/170932; ARNOT Reservoir 58/208024; BALGILLIE Reservoir 58/239036; CARSBRECK Loch 58/869094; UPPER RHYND Loch 58/863101; LOWER RHYND Loch 58/858098; DUPPLIN Lake 58/033202; PITCARNIE Lake 58/029198; WHIT MOSS Loch 58/993142; HARPERLEAS Reservoir 58/211053. Harperleas used to be fished by a local angling club but because of unannounced fluctuations in the water level and a loss of stocked fish the club has disbanded itself and abandoned the water. LAICH Loch (58/958150) is a stocked fishery within the grounds of Gleneagles Hotel and is reserved for the use of hotel guests.
ROSCOBIE, Reservoir See Loch Glow.

SANDKNOWES, Fishery
Location & Access 58/141186 Approach from Bridge of Earn along the minor road to Wallacetown. The fishery is signposted, to the right, shortly after passing under the M80 Edinburgh/Perth Motorway.
Commentary An 8-acre put-and-take fishery in a woodland setting but sometimes over-loud with the sound of motorway traffic.
Fish Stocked with rainbow trout which grow to considerable proportions. There are also a few brown trout of up to 2lb 14oz in weight.
Flies & Tactics Bank fishing only and wading is prohibited. Fish are taken from all round the shore. The south bank has been cleared of trees to give easy of casting, whilst casting platforms allow access to the north shore. Flies: Pheasant Tail nymphs work well, as do reservoir lures and dry fly. Also: Soldier Palmer, Invicta, Alexandra.
Permission & Charges Contact: Fishery Manager, Sandyknowes Fishery, Collage Mill Trout Farm, Bridge of Earn. Tel: 01738 813033. Open 10am to 10pm. Cost: £10 per four hour session (4 fish limit).

UPPER GLENDEVON, Reservoir See Lower Glendevon Reservoir.
WHIRR, Loch See Glenfarg Reservoir.

St Andrews and Kirkaldy

CAMERON, Burn See Cameron Reservoir.

CAMERON, Reservoir
Location & Access 59/472112. Easy access from the A915 St Andrews/Upper Largo road. Turn west near Lathokar Cottage (59/487117) to reach the reservoir after 1/2 a mile.
Commentary A substantial reservoir, almost 1 mile east/west by up to 1/4 of a mile wide and situated 4 miles south from St Andrews. The reservoir impounds the water of the Cameron Burn which flows east from Cameron Reservoir to entry the sea near Boarhills (59/581143).
Fish Brown trout which average 10oz in weight. The mouth of Cameron Burn can also sometimes produce sport with sea-trout, depending upon water conditions.
Flies & Tactics Cameron Reservoir is managed by the St Andrew's Angling Club and both boat (no outboard motors) and bank fishing is allowed. This is a shallow water and it tends to become weedy as the season advances. After July, boat fishing brings the best results. Fish rise and are taken everywhere, from the middle to the margins and you should try: Black Spider, Wickham's Fancy, Dunkeld. The Cameron Demon, invented by D Hutchison, (gold body, jungle-cock eye, blue hackle) is also a popular pattern.
Permission & Charges The Fishing Hut, Cameron Reservoir, St Andrews, Fife. Tel: 01334 840236; St Andrews Angling Club, 54 St Nicholas Street, St Andrews, Fife. Tel: 01334 476347. Cost: charges vary from £12 per rod per day bank fishing, to £33 per boat per day (3 rods). There is a 6 fish per rod bag limit.

CARRISTON (Upper) Reservoir
Location & Access 59/328037 Approach from Star (59/315034) on the minor road to the north of Markinch between Newton in the west and Kennoway in the east.
Commentary A pleasant fishery fringed by woodlands and managed by the Methilhaven & District Angling Club. Unfortunately, in drought conditions, the water level drops drastically and this can produce problems for both fish and angler alike.
Fish Stocked with brown trout which average 1lb 8oz in weight. Fish of up to and over 3lb in weight are not uncommon.
Flies & Tactics Bank fishing only and the most productive fishing area is along the north dam wall and

OS Map 59 — St Andrews & Kirkaldy

the east shoreline. The natural feeding in the reservoir is excellent and the stocked trout grow rapidly. Consequently, they can be very choosy when it comes to selecting a meal and you will have to work hard for your sport. Try: Black Pennell, Wickham's Fancy, Dunkeld. Dry fly, particularly on a summer evening, can produce good results.
Permission & Charges The Village Store, Station Road, Windygates. tel: 01333 350319. Cost: £9 per rod per session. There is a limit of 4 fish per rod per session.

CERES, Burn See River Eden.

CLATTO, Reservoir
Location & Access 59/360079 Approach from Kame Bridge on the A916 Windygates/Cupar road. Turn west on the minor road and then first left to reach the dam wall at Clatto after a distance of 1.5 miles.
Commentary A reservoir covering an area of approximately 25 acres. Unlike many stocked fisheries, Clatto Reservoir manages to look almost entirely natural.
Fish Brown trout which average 1lb 4oz with good numbers of heavier fish as well of up to 3lb in weight.
Flies & Tactics The reservoir is managed by the Clatto & Strathden Angling Club. Fishing is from either boat or bank and both methods can bring equally excellent results. Avoid wading - it only scares the fish out into deeper water. The most productive months are late May, June and September and the south shore of the reservoir is a good place to begin. First cast: Black Pennell, Invicta, Dunkeld.
Permission & Charges Contact: The Waterman's Cottage, Clatto Reservoir, Pitlessie, Fife. Tel: 01334 652595. There are 2 sessions (9am until 4.30pm and 4.30pm until dusk) and access is on a first come first served basis. Cost: Bank fishing, £8 per rod per day, evening fishing, £10 per rod. The boat costs £4 per session (1 to 3 rods). There is a limit of 6 fish per rod.

COARSE FISHERIES KILCONQUHAR Loch (59/489018); BEVERIDGE PARK Loch (59/271909).
CUT, The (River) See River Leven.

EDEN, River (Fife)
Location & Access Source 58/155074. Outfall 59/452190. Easily accessible from public roads that margin the whole length of the stream.
Commentary The river rises near Southside, to the north of Loch Leven (see OS Map 58) and flows east through the Wee Kingdom of Fife to reach the sea at Guardbridge after a journey of some 20 miles. There is one major tributary, the Ceres Burn, which joins the River Eden near Kemback (59/415155). Falls on Ceres Burn at Dura Den, 1 mile upstream from where the Ceres Burn meets the River Eden, prervent the further passage of migratory fish. The wide estuary and sands are an important winter habitat for migratory birds, often disturbed by the activities of RAF Leuchars airbase on the north bank.
Fish Increasing numbers of salmon are being caught although sea-trout runs have been disappointing in recent years. The river also contains modest brown trout. Salmon average 6lb/7lb. Sea-trout run the river from June onwards. September and October are the most productive months for salmon.
Flies & Tactics In the past the river was badly effected by industrial pollution but the position has vastly improved in recent years. However, water is also extracted for agricultural irrigation and good sport is very much dependent upon spate conditions. The lower river, from Nydie Mill downstream to Guardbridge, is tidal. Bait fishing and spinning accounts for most of the fish taken but there are good runs and pools where fly-fishing can be just as effective. The most producitve part of the river is between Kemback and Nydie Mill. Offer them: Garry Dog, Shrimp Fly, Stoat's Tail.
Permission & Charges For further information, contact George Wilson, Franks Army Store, 10 Olympia Arcade, Kirkaldy, Fife. Tel: 01592 640402. Tickets from: J Gow & Sons, 12 Union Street, Dundee. Tel: 01382 225427; J Wilson & Sons, Ironmongers, 169 South Street, St Andrews, Fife. Tel: 01334 472477. J A Stewart, 31 Ladywynd, Cupar, Fife. Tel: 01334 652202. Cost: £6 per rod per day.

GOLDEN, Loch
Location & Access 59/259160 Approach from the Den of Lindores (59/252171). After the railway bridge take the first left through Grange of Lindores to Berryhill Farm.
Commentary A small (7 acre) put-and-take fishery to the west of Lindores Loch (see separate entry) on the side of Golden Hill (97m).
Fish Stocked with rainbow trout, but also a few brown trout as well. Rainbow trout average 1lb 8oz in weight, but fish of up to and over 5lb are also caught.
Flies & Tactics Boat and bank fishing. Reservoir lures are the most often used: Ace of Spades, Montana Nymphs, Orange Fritz, Whisky Fly, Sweeney Tod.
Permission & Charges Contact: Mrs Anne Nicol, Berryhill Farm, Newburgh, Fife. Tel: 01337 840355. Cost: £12 per angler, boat or bank.

LEVEN, River
Location & Access Source 58/150010 Outfall 59/380003. The river is accessible throughout most of its length from the A911 Windygates/Kinross road.
Commentary The River Leven drains Loch Leven (see OS Map 58, Perth & Kinross) and flows east via The Cut, a man-made channel constructed in the mid-19th century to lower the level of Loch Leven, to enter the North Sea between the Fife towns of Methil and Leven after a journey of some 14 miles. The river has suffered dreadfully from industrial pollution in days past, and, to some extent, still does: a major tributary, the River Ore, was reported to me recently as being coloured purple from some spillage accident. Nevertheless, matters are improving, thanks largely to the vigilance of the local angling club.
Fish Salmon, sea-trout and brown trout. Also, escapee rainbow trout, from Loch Leven and, possibly, from Loch Fitty (see OS Map 58, Perth & Kinross). Salmon

average 6lb/7lb, sea-trout, 1lb 8oz. Exact numbers of salmon caught are not available but are probably in the order of 20/30 fish.
Flies & Tactics All a matter of being in the right place at the right time, after spate conditions. Bait fishing accounts for most of the migratory fish taken, but fly fishing also produces results, particularly in The Cut. The little River Ore, again, given the right conditions, can produce some excellent trout of up to 2lb in weight. Flies: Wickham's Fancy, Grouse & Claret, Peter Ross.
Permission & Charges Contact Kircaldy Tourist Information Centre for details: Tel: 01592 267775. Cost: £5 per rod per day. For The Cut, contact: The River Leven Trust, The Sluice House, Kinross. Tel: 01592 840225. Cost: £5 per rod per day.

LINDORES, Loch
Location & Access 59/265164. Lindores Loch lies 2 miles to the south east of Newburgh and is easily accessed from the A913 Newburgh/Cupar road.
Commentary A well-managed put-and-take fishery in attractive surroundings, Lindores Loch is approximately 3/4 of a mile wide by up to 350 yds wide. The loch is bounded by the B937 road to the east and the main railway line to the west.
Fish Regularly stocked with rainbow trout which average 1lb 8oz in weight with fish of up to and over 5lb frquently taken. The loch also contains pike - a fish of 29lb was netted out a some years ago,
Flies & Tactics Boat fishing only and electric outboard motors are available for hire at the loch. This is a shallow loch and trout may be taken throughout its length, from the middle to the margins. Offer them reservoir lures, such as Sweeney Tod, Cat's Whiskers, Whisky Fly, or: Black Pennell, Teal & Green, Dunkeld.
Permission & Charges Contact: Mr Mitchell, Springfield, Cupar, Fife. Tel: 01334 654107; The Peir, Lindores Loch, Tel: 01337 810488 Cost per boat: single rod, £16 (5 fish), 2 rods, £32 (10 fish per boat), 3 rods, £36 (15 fish per boat).

NEWTON FARM, Fishery
Location & Access 59/401245 Follow the B946 south from Wormit (59/395260) for one mile and turn right onto the farm road immediately after passing under the railway bridge.
Commentary A small put-and-take fishery offering good sport in pleasant surroundings. There are excellent facilities for visiting anglers including access for disabled anglers and, at prior arrangement, casting instruction for beginners.
Fish Regularly stocked with rainbow trout and brown trout which average 1lb 8oz in weight.
Flies & Tactics Bank fishing only and the water is easily covered from the shore. Reservoir lures are most successful: Cat's Whiskers, Fritz patterns in various colours, Baby Doll, Ace of Spades.
Permission & Charges Contact: Mr & Mrs Gordon Crawford, Newton Farm, Wormit, Newport-on-Tay, Fife. Tel: 01382 542513. Cost: £11.50 for a 4 hour session (3 fish limit); £14 for a 6 hour session (4 fish);

day ticket (dawn to dusk) £19 (6 fish). Catch and release fishing is available at £7 for a 4 hour session.

ORE, River See River Leven.
PRIVATE WATERS MORTON Lochs 59/463265; CASH Loch 59/241905; COUL Reservoir 59/269039; DONALD ROSE Reservoir 59/329038; CARHURLIE Reservoir 59/395050.

RAITH, Lake
Location & Access 59/263914 Easily accessible and immediately adjacent to the B925 Kirkcaldy/Auchertoul road.
Commentary This is a man-made lake, constructed during the mid-19 century, completely surrounded by mature woodlands. In spite of being on the edge of a major population centre, Kirkcaldy, Raith Lake echoes with the grace of days past.
Fish Regularly stocked with rainbow trout and a few brown trout. The rainbow trout grow to considerable proportions: fish of up to 18lb have been taken, and their average weight is 2lb.
Flies & Tactics Boat fishing only on this shallow loch and fish may be taken from the margins to the middle. Dry fly can work well, particularly on warm summer evenings. Regulars use various reservoir lures, but more traditional patterns produce excellent results: Kate Maclaren, Wickham's Fancy, Dunkeld.
Permission & Charges Contact: Robert Duffy, Raith Lake Fisheries, Kircaldy, Fife. Tel: 01592 646466 (Lake) or 01592 643830 (Home). Costs: Monday to Friday, £10 per rod (3 fish) 10am to pm. Tuesday and Thursday, 2 man boat £16, 10am to 4pm. Weekends, single angler £15, 2 anglers £28, 3 anglers £36. 4 fish per rod, thereafter, catch and release using barbless hooks.

Islay

A'BHEALAICH AIRD, **Loch** See Loch Cam entry.
A'CHAORUINN, **Loch** See Loch Carn nan Gall entry.
A'CHLAIDHEIMH, **Loch** See Loch Cam entry.
A'CHNUIC BHRIC, **Loch** See Loch Cam entry.
A'CHURRAGAN, **Loch** See Loch Carn nan Gall entry.
AIRIGH NAN CAISTEAL, **Loch** See Loch Carn nan Gall.
ALLAN, **Loch** See Loch Ballygrant entry.
AN DHUBHAICH, **Loch** See Loch Carn nan Gall entry.
AN LEINIBH, **Loch** See Loch Cam entry.

ARDNAHOE, Loch
Location & Access 6/420715. The loch is approached from a narrow, single-track road which runs north from the A846 Port Askaig/Bridgend road. Leave the main road at 60/420688 and drive past Pearsabus and Loch nam Ban (60/419705) to reach Ardnahoe after a journey of 2 miles. Resist the temptation, if you can,

OS Map 60   Islay

to continue on to the end of the road and to Bunnahabhainn Distillery. On the other hand, why not? What would be so bad about a small dram before battle?
Commentary A lovely loch with stunning views east to the Paps of Jura (784m). Little Loch nam Ban is also worth a cast and is just as much fun to fish as its more illustrious neighbour.
Fish Brown trout which average 8oz.
Flies & Tactics Boat and bank fishing on Ardnahoe, bank fishing only on Loch nam Ban. Ardnahoe Loch is deep and boat fishing brings the best results. Arrange your drift a few yards out from the shore and cast in towards the shallow water. Use: Ke-He, March Brown, Silver Butcher.
Permission & Charges See Ardnave Loch entry.

ARDNAVE, Loch
Location & Access 60/284728. Approach from Aoradh (60/275673) along the minor road that runs north from the B8017 Uisgeantsuidhe/Loch Gorm road. The loch lies to the left of the road, 3.5 miles north from Aoradh.
Commentary An attractive little loch of about 15 acres, easily-accessible, with miles of nearby beach and coastline where any non-fishing members of your party will find plenty to do whilst you attack Ardnave. The nearby RSPB Loch Gruinart Nature Reserve is always worth a visit. There are 3 other waters here, to the west of Carn Mor (30m), which are approached from the end of the track that runs south from Ardnave to Sleidmeall (60/274722): Loch Laingeadail Beag (60/263718), Loch Laingeadail (60/265714) and Loch na Laithaich (60/272712).
Fish Brown trout all round. In Ardnave Loch they average 1lb, but there are also fish of up to and over 3lb in weight. The other lochs contain good stocks of more modest specimens.
Flies & Tactics Boat and bank fishing on Ardnave which has a well-deserved reputation for being "dour". The other lochs, which are fished from the shore, should all send you home with something for supper. Try: Black Pennell, Grouse & Claret, Silver Invicta.
Permission & Charges Contact: The Islay Estate Office, Bowmore on Tel: 01496 810221. Cost: bank fishing, £17 per season, £12 per week, £8 for 3 days, £3 per day; boat hire, £14 per boat per day and £10 after 5pm..

BALLYGRANT, Loch
Location & Access 60/405662. Turn south from the A846 Port Askaig/Bridgend road in Ballygrant. The loch is in the trees on your left after half a mile.
Commentary This is the largest of the Dunlossit Estate trout lochs and it extends for more than half a mile, tapering into a long, finger-like bay at the north-east end. Immediately to the north lies little Loch nan Cadhan (60/403669) whilst immediately to the south is Loch Lossit (60/409652). South again for 1.5 miles on an estate road lie Loch Fada (60/409636) and Loch Leathann (60/410632) to the east of the road and Loch Bharradail (60/393634) to the west. These lochs are accessed from 60/405635 after a walk of about 15 minutes. The last of the Dunlossit lochs, Loch Allan (60/425678) is best approached from Port Askaig along the estate road.
Fish Brown trout which average 8oz. Loch Ballygrant is reputed to hold larger trout, fish of up to and over 3lb in weight, but they are hard to catch.
Flies & Tactics Boat fishing brings the best results on Ballygrant and you should concentrate your piscatorial activities at the narrow, north-east end. On Loch Lossit, drift along the south bay by the 2 small islands. Loch Allan is also best fished from the boat and the south-west corner, where the feeder burn enters, is the place to begin. The other waters noted above are fished from the shore. Flies: Blue Zulu, Grouse & Claret, Peter Ross.
Permission & Charges Port Askaig Shop, Port Askaig, Island of Islay, Argyll, PA45 7QL. Tel: 01496 840245 or Dunlossit Estate, Estate Office, Ballygrant, Island of Islay, Argyll. Tel: 01496 840232. Cost: Boat fishing at between £10 and £15 per day, depending upon time of year, bank, £3 per day.

BARR, River See Laggan River entry.
BHARRADAIL, Loch See Loch Ballygrant entry.
BROACH, Loch See Loch Carn nan Gall entry.

CAM, Loch
Location & Access Leave the A846 Port Askaig/Bridgend road at 60/358640 and drive north to Balole (60/355661). Loch Cam is a further half a mile north-west.
Commentary Loch Cam is half a mile north/south by up to 300yds wide and is in itself sufficient for a good day's sport. However, this is also a convenient starting point for a 5 mile circuit of 8 named and unnamed lochs and lochans which lie to the north of Loch Cam: Loch Drolsay (60/331670), Loch a'Chnuic Bhric (60/323690), Loch a'Bhealaich Aird (60/330691), Loch a'Chlaidheimh (60/342691), Loch an Leinibh (60/342698), the unnamed lochan at 60/349691), Loch nan Caorach (60/334682), Loch Leathan (60/343680) and the unnamed lochan at 60/352679, beyond the Standing Stone on Beinn Cham (162m). A compass and map are essential to safely navigate your way round this watery wilderness and the going is rough to rugged, so be well shod and well prepared.
Fish All these lochs contain brown trout which average in the order of 8oz, but some of the waters noted above have specimen fish of up to and over 2lb in weight.
Flies & Tactics Bank fishing all the way and, in fishing terms, these lochs are easily understood. Trout may be taken from virtually anywhere round the shores. Flies that might tempt them: Ke-He, Greenwell's Glory, Kingfisher Butcher.
Permission & Charges See Ardnave Loch and Loch Smigeadail entry.

CARN NAN GALL, Loch
Location & Access 60/370705. Park at Staoisha Eararach (60/400726) to the west of Bunnahabhainn (see Ardnahoe Loch entry). This is the starting point

363

Islay OS Map 60

for a 7 mile day out in North Islay visiting a series of small hill lochs and lochans around Gleann a'Chapuill Bhain and Gleann Airigh an t-Sluic. You will require a compass and map, stout boots and wet weather gear. Islay weather is notoriously unpredictable.

Commentary A splendid hike with wonderful wildlife along the way and more than a good chance of seeing great raptors. An easy 10 minutes west from the starting point will bring you to the first cast, Loch an Dhubhaich (60/395724) and from there, after a gentle climb, you will find Loch Giur-bheinn (60/382728) below the summit of Giur-bheinn (316m). Work round the south shoulder of Giur-bheinn to locate tiny Loch a'Churragan (60/369721) and then walk due south across Airigh nan Sidhean (229m) to arrive at Loch Carn nan Gall. You now have the option of striking south-west for a further half mile to have a cast in Lochan Broach (60/359701). From Loch Carn nan Gall, tramp south-east for half a mile to fish Loch Airigh nan Caisteal (60/380698) from where you may make another 'dash' south-west to attack Loch a'Chaoruinn (60/380695). Now, head north east to arrive after 1.5 miles at the south end of the largest of today's waters, Loch Staoisha (60/407713). Fish the west shore. At the north end, follow the outlet burn for 600yds to where a little stream flows in from the west. Track this stream along the northern edge of the forestry plantation to regain Staoisha Eararach.

Fish Good stocks of modest brown trout but also a few surprises along the way.

Flies & Tactics All these waters are fished from the bank and it is best to avoid wading. Fish tend to lie close to the shore and splashing about in the shallows only scares them out into the depths. Loch Staoisha is perhaps the most productive loch and it contains some excellent fish. Flies: Blue Zulu, March Brown, Peter Ross.

Permission & Charges See Ardnave Loch and Loch Smigeadail entry.

CROSS REFERENCE For details of Jura fishing, see OS Map 61.
DROLSAY, Loch See Loch Cam entry.
DUBH, Loch See Loch Smigeadail entry.
DUICH, River See Laggan River entry.
FADA, Loch See Loch Ballygrant entry.

FINLAGGAN, Loch

Location & Access 60/387675. Approach from the minor road that runs north from the A846 Port Askaig/Bridgend road at 60/5401677.

Commentary Loch Finlaggan is one of the most famous lochs in Scotland, not because of its quality as a fishery, but because of its historical importance. Eilean na Comhairle, the Council Isles, at the north end of the loch, was the administrative base for Clan Macdonald; busy probably from the 5th century until the Clan Donald lands were forfeited to the Crown in 1493. A smaller island, linked to Eilean na Comhairle by an artificial causeway, housed a chapel and domestic buildings and these are now being excavated.

Fish Large stocks of small wild brown trout. Although Loch Finlaggan drains south-west into the River Sorn (see separate entry), only one salmon has ever been recorded as being taken from the loch: a fish caught in 1930 by the Scottish comedian, Harry Lauder.

Flies & Tactics Bank fishing and boat fishing and both methods can bring results. The boat has the advantage of making it easier to cover the water, the loch is over 1 mile long, but bank fishing is every bit as much fun. The east shore is the best fishing area, where 5 little burns tumble in from Robolls Hill (130m). Show the fish: Black Zulu, Soldier Palmer, Alexandra.

Permission & Charges See Ardnave Loch entry.

GIUR-BHEINN, Loch See Loch Carn nan Gall entry.
GLENASTLE, Loch See Loch Kinnabus entry.

GORM, Loch

Location & Access 60/230660. The loch lies in the north-west of the Island of Islay and is easily approached from various public roads which encircle the shoreline.

Commentary This is the largest and most significant trout loch on Islay, 1.5 miles east/west by up to 1.25 miles north/south. The loch is drained west into the sea by the little River Saligo. Migratory fish do not run this stream although they may be caught in the sea, at the mouth of the river, particularly after heavy rain (also the mouth of the Lossit Burn at 60/172562). The surrounding farmlands are low-lying and give Loch Gorm little protection from prevailing winds, consequently, Loch Gorm can often be stormy.

Fish Brown trout average in the order of 1lb but heavier fish, trout of up to and over 2lb in weight, are not uncommon.

Flies & Tactics Boat and bank fishing is available and both methods can be equally rewarding. However, a boat makes it easier to explore this large water and will allow you to carefully examine the margins of Eilean na Uan (60/222657) and tiny Castle Island (60/236654). When bank fishing, start at the north-east corner, between the promontory of Rubha Mor (62/234660) working south past the mouths of the burns that enter here, down to the outflow of the Allt na Criche (60/243658). However, wind direction will be the ultimate arbiter of where you fish, but cast with confidence because trout may be taken from all round the shore. A word of warning when boat fishing: the loch is generally shallow and there are numerous underwater outcrops and rocks waiting to catch the unwary. Hasten slowly and always take along spare sheer-pins for the outboard motor. Flies: Ke-He, March Brown, Peter Ross.

Permission & Charges Contact: Mrs Doyle, Foreland House, by Bridgend, Island of Islay, Argyll. Tel: 01496 850211. Foreland House offer bank and boat fishing, the services of an experienced boatman and tackle hire. Mr McHarrie, Ballinaby Farm, by Bridgend, Island of Islay, Argyll. Tel: 01496 850400. The Islay Estate Office in Bridgend on Tel: 01496 810221. Cost: expect to pay in the order of £3 per rod per day for bank fishing and £15 per day for boat hire (£10 after 5pm). An outboard engine is essential when fish-

OS Map 60 — Islay

ing Loch Gorm, but you will have to lug along your own because none are available for hire locally.

KILENNAN, River See River Laggan entry.

KINNABUS, Loch
Location & Access 60/302424. Approach from the minor road from Port Ellen to Lower Killeyan. Turn south at 60/2954429 to reach the Loch Kinnabus.
Commentary This is the largest of the Oa Peninsula waters all of which are easily accessible from the main road and adjacent tracks. East of Loch Kinnabus lie Loch nan Gillean (60/30931), known locally as School Loch, and its unnamed neighbour at 60/313428 on Maol Beag (152m). Further south, on the hill above Beinn Mhor (202m) is tiny Loch na Beinne (60/299412) which rarely sees an artificial fly from one season to the next. North of the road and approached from Risabus (60/315440) are Glenastle Loch (60/300448) and Lower Glenastle Loch (60/293450), perhaps the most productive of the Oa waters. The Oa Peninsula is outstandingly beautiful, rugged sea-bird cliffs to the west and the long, white sands of Laggan Bay to the north. There is also always the chance of spotting one of Islay's most famous ornithological residents here, the rare chough.
Fish Brown trout which average 5oz in weight with a few fish of over 8oz as well. The unnamed water contains arctic char.
Flies & Tactics Bank fishing only on these shallow, exposed lochs which are often wild and windy. Flies: Soldier Palmer, March Brown, Silver Butcher.
Permission & Charges Contact: Ian Laurie, Newsagents, 19 Charlotte Street, Port Ellen, Island of Islay, Argyll. Tel: 01496302264. Cost: bank fishing, £5 per rod per day and the one permit gives access to of all the lochs noted above.

LAGGAN, River
Location & Access Source 60/410632 Outfall 60/293554. The river is easily-accessible from public and private roads.
Commentary The River Laggan is the most significant of the Islay salmon streams and it rises from Loch Leathann to the west of Beinn Dubh (267m). It begins life as the Barr River and flows west for approximately 8 miles before entering the sea at Laggan Bay. The Laggan has 2 significant tributaries, the Torra/Duich River which joins the main stream at 60/299558 and the Kilennan River which greets the Laggan by Cnoc Amanta (60/355584).
Fish Salmon and sea-trout. The annual average catch varies, depending upon water conditions, but is probably in the order of 100 salmon. Salmon average 7lb. Sea-trout average 1lb 8oz.
Flies & Tactics The most productive part of the river is the 4 miles from Laggan Bridge (60/341573) downstream to the sea. The lower river is divided into 3 beats where there are a number of excellent holding pools and runs. The upper reaches of the river are more rugged in character. A single-handed rod is adequate and there is seldom any need to wade. Offer: Blue Charm, Goat's Toe, Willie Gunn, Garry Dog, Green Highlander, Hairy Mary, Stoat's Tail.
Permission & Charges The lower river is fished by Laggan Estate and is generally booked well in advance, the same tenants returning year after year. For availability, contact: Mrs Eva Hay, Laggan Estate, Bridge House, by Bowmore, Island of Islay, Argyll. Tel: 01496 810388. Cost: £850 per beat (2/4 rods) per week from 1st July until 15th October. No day tickets issued. Laggan Estate also have comfortable self-catering properties which are let in conjunction with the fishing. Access to other beats is sometimes available on a day ticket at £20 per rod. For bookings, contact: Dunlossit Estate (see Uisge an t-Suidhe River entry) and Islay Estate (see Ardnave Loch)

LAINGEADAIL BEAG, Loch See Ardnave Loch entry.
LAINGEADAIL, Loch See Ardnave Loch entry.
LEATHAN, Loch See Loch Cam entry.
LEATHANN, Loch See Loch Ballygrant entry.
LOSSIT, Burn See Loch Gorm entry.
LOSSIT, Loch See Loch Ballygrant entry.
LOWER GLENASTLE, Loch See Loch Kinnabus entry.
MARGADLAE, River See Loch Smigeadail entry.
MURCHAIDH, Loch See Loch Smigeadail entry.
NA BEINNE, Loch See Loch Kinnabus entry.
NA LAITHAICH, Loch See Ardnave Loch entry.
NA NIGHEADAIREACHD, Loch See River Laggan entry.
NAM BAN, Loch See Ardnahoe Loch entry.
NAN CADHAN, Loch See Loch Ballygrant entry.
NAN CAORACH, Loch See Loch Cam entry.
NAN GILLEAN, Loch See Loch Kinnabus entry.
PRIVATE WATERS FEUR, Lochain 60/249692; RUIME, Loch 60/240701; CORR, Loch 60/225697; CLACH A'BHUALIE, Loch 60/216643; DAM, Loch 60/253610; CANAIBHE 60/215600; GEARACH, Loch 60/227596; A'BHOGAIDH, Loch 60/225576; ARISH, Loch 60/270703; AN FHIR MHOR, Loch 60/265393; GRUNND, Loch 60/289573; AIRIGH DHAIBHAIDH, Loch 60/314556; MUCHAIRT, Loch 60/324473; NAN GABHAR, Loch 60/338484; TALLANT, Loch 60/335579; DHOMHNAILL, Loch 60/331537; LEORIN, Lochs 60/370485; LAOIM, Loch 60/377489; NA BEINNE BRICE, Loch 60/382482; SHOLUM, Loch 60/400491; IARNAN, Loch 60/420480; UIGEADAIL, Loch 60/404505; DEARG AN SGORRA, Loch 60/409520; LEATHANN AN SGORRA, Loch 60400521; BEINN URARAIDH, Loch 60/402534; NAM BREAC, Loch 60/409556; A'MHUILINN-GHAOITHE, Loch 60/420568; ALLALLAIDH, Loch 60/419580; DUBH, Loch 60/420591; NAN CLACH, Loch 60/428508; CARN A'MHAOIL, Loch 60/436507; NAN DIOL, Loch 60/431481; TALLANT, Loch 60/449505; MACHRIE, River 60/320503 (the mouth of the river is blocked by sand/silt); KINTRA, River 60/322484 (the river is badly polluted).
SALIGO, River See Loch Gorm entry.
SIBHINN, Loch See Loch Skerrols entry.

SKERROLS, Loch
Location & Access 60/341628. This easily-accessible loch lies 1 mile to the north of Bridgend (60/336624).
Commentary A pretty loch in a woodland setting, often sheltered when storms churn up its neighbours. This asset makes Loch Skerrols one of the most popular fisheries on Islay and, consequently, you are advised to book in advance. As an alternative, consider a tramp out to Loch Sibhinn (60/327653) an easy mile north-west from Loch Skerrols.
Fish Good quality brown trout in Loch Skerrols which average 8oz/10oz, but fish of up to and over 1lb as well. Attractive, 3 to the pound fish in Loch Sibhinn.
Flies & Tactics Boat fishing only on Loch Skerrols and fish may be taken from all over the loch. If anything, the north-east corner, where the burn flows in, may be the best place to begin. Bank fishing on Loch Sibhainn. Flies: Coch-y-Bondhu, Soldier Palmer, Black Pennell.
Permission & Charges See Ardnave Loch entry.

SMIGEADAIL, Loch
Location & Access 60/384754. Park to the north of Bunnahabhainn (see Ardnahoe Loch entry) at the end of the road on Boglach nan Tarbh (60/405735). Walk north-west on the line of the Margadale River (60/418735) to reach the loch after a tramp of 1.5 miles.
Commentary Loch Smigeadail is tucked away in a shallow, wide glen, cupped between Margadale Hill (255m) to the east and Cregan Corr (274m) to the west. After exploring Smigeadail, walk north-east for 1 mile to find tiny Loch Dubh (60/395770), the most northerly trout loch on Islay. Start your journey home by walking south from Loch Dubh to have a cast in Loch Murchaidh (60/399759). Continue south from here, round the east shoulder of Margadale hill to regain the course of the Margadale River. This expedition will involve you in a 5-mile day-out in the hills.
Fish Certainly breakfast, with very pretty, small, brightly-speckled brown trout.
Flies & Tactics Bank fishing and Loch Smigeadail is the largest of the waters here, approximately 15 acres in extent. The others can almost be covered with a single, long, cast. Try: Black Zulu, Soldier Palmer, Silver Invicta.
Permission & Charges See Ardnave Loch entry. One of the great pleasures of fishing on the Islay Estate is exploring the hill-lochs which lie to the north of the A846 Port Askaig/Bridgend road. This wonderful area is devoid of roads and the only way in is to hoof it over the heather. The estate policy is to encouraging responsible access and visitors, particularly anglers, are welcome. The early months, April through until July, are the most productive and also the time when the famous Islay midge is least active. When stalking is in progress, after the end of July, anglers, for their own safety, must seek advice from the Estate Office prior to setting out. All fishing is strictly by fly only.

SORN, River
Location & Access Source 60/387675 Outfall 60/334621. The A846 Port Askaig/Bridgend road margins the north bank of the stream.
Commentary The river draws its water from Loch Finlaggan to the north of the main road and from Loch Ballygrant to the south. The streams from these lochs meet at Emeraconart (60/371652) and form the main river which reaches the sea through Bridgend after a further 3 miles.
Fish Salmon and sea-trout. In a good year, depending upon water conditions, up to 50 salmon and sea-trout may be taken. But fish numbers have declined and anglers now have to work hard for sport in the recent prolonged, dry summers.
Flies & Tactics The water in the Sorn is very clear and fish are easily "spooked". It is essential to stay well back from the bank, off the skyline. A single-handed rod is all that is required and wading is seldom necessary. Fish arrive in the river from June onwards but the best chance of sport is at the back end in September and October. Flies: Garry Dog, Stoat's Tail, Blue Charm, Hairy Mary, Black Doctor, General Practitioner.
Permission & Charges Day-lets are sometimes available. Contact Islay Estate Office in Bowmore)(see Uisge an t-Suidhe River entry).

STAOISH, Loch See Loch Carn nan Gall entry.
TORRA, River See River Laggan entry.

UISGE AN T-SUIDHE, River
Location & Access Source 60/343680 Outfall 60/299631. Approach from the B8017 Uisgeantsuidhe/Eresaid road.
Commentary Uisge an t-Suidhe, 'the water of the thatch', rises from Loch Leathan (see separate entry) and flows south west and south for 5 miles to reach the sea at the head of Loch Indaal 2.5 miles west from Bridgend. It is known locally as the Grey River.
Fish Salmon and a few sea-trout. Salmon average 5lb in weight, sea-trout 1lb 8oz.
Flies & Tactics Only the lower mile of the river is fishable and that only after heavy rain. There are few identifiable pools and the stream is deep and fish seldom linger. It is very much a case of being in the right place at the right time, with your fly touching the nose of a running fish. Use: Willie Gunn, Blue Charm, Garry Dog, Hairy Mary, Black Pennell, Mallard & Claret, Peter Ross.
Permission & Charges Contact Islay Estate Office, Bowmore (see Loch Ardnave entry) Cost: £10 per rod per day.

OS Map 61 — Colonsay & Jura

Colonsay and Jura

A'BHALAICH, Loch
Location & Access See Loch Righ Mor entry.

A'BHURRA, Loch
Location & Access 61/669960. Drive north from Ardlussa (61/646878) towards Kinuachdrach (61/705986) - and the cottage in which George Orwell wrote 1984. Park at 61/687957 where the Allt Gharbh passes under the road. This is the starting point for a day out in the hills fishing a series of 8 named and unnamed lochs which will take you on an invigorating 5 mile tramp through glorious scenery with wonderful wildlife along the way.
Commentary Walk due west up the east shoulder of Glas Bheinn (276m) to find the first water, Loch Glasbheinn (61/679959). Head north from here for half a mile to reach Loch na Conaire (61/677968) and, a step north again, on Sgorr Mhor (288m) to Loch na Sgorra (61/676975). Descend south-west from Loch na Sgorra for 1 mile to explore delightful Loch nan Eilean (61/661967). This island-clad little loch is the perfect place for lunch. After lunch, have a cast in the unnamed lochan to the south of Loch nan Eilean before dropping down to fish Loch Doire na h-Achlaise (61/655957) and Loch a'Gheoidh (61/661954). Strike north-east now for half a mile to explore Loch a'Bhurra. Contour round the south shoulder of Glas Bheinn to regain the starting point.
Fish Splendidly marked, bright little brown trout which average 3 to the pound and the chance of the odd fish of up to 1lb as well.
Flies & Tactics Bank fishing only but all these small lochs are easily covered from the shore. Offer the residents: Ke-He, Soldier Palmer, Silver Butcher.
Permission & Charges See Lussa River entry. Ardlussa Estate does not generally charge for hill-loch brown trout fishing and the estate welcomes responsible access. However, it is essential that you seek permission prior to setting out particularly, for your own safety, during the stalking season.

A'CHINN GHAIRBH, Loch See Lochanan Tana entry.
A'GHARBH-UISGE, Loch See Loch Righ Mor entry.
A'GHEOIDH, Loch See Loch a'Bhurra entry.
A'MHILE, Loch See Loch Righ Mor entry.
A'MHUILLIN, Loch See Loch Righ Mor entry.
ABHAINN A'GHLEANN DUIRCH, Burn See Loch Righ Mor entry.
ABHAINN GHLEANN AOISTAIL, Burn See Loch Righ Mor entry.
AIRIGH NUALAIDH, Loch See Loch Righ Mor entry.
AN AOIMIDH DHUIBH, Loch See Loch Righ Mor entry.
AN ARCILL, Loch (Ardlussa) See Lochanan Tana entry.
AN SGOLTAIRE, Loch See Loch Fada (Colonsay) entry.
AN T-SITHEIN TARSUINN, Loch See Loch Righ Mor entry.
AN TUIM UAINE, Loch See Loch Righ Mor entry.
BARR A'BHEALAICH, Loch See Loch Iochdarach a'Chruaidh-Ghlinn entry.
BHEAG A'BHAILE-DOIRE, Lochain See Lochanan Tana entry.
CARN NAN GILLEAN, Loch See Lochanan Tana entry.
CATHAR NAN EUN, Loch See Loch Iochdarach a'Chruaidh-Ghlinn entry.
CHOLLA, Loch See Loch Fada (Colonsay) entry.
CROSS REFERENCE For details of Islay lochs see OS Map 62.
DOIRE NA H-ACHLAISE, Loch See Loch a'Bhurra entry.
DUBH, Loch (Ardlussa) See Loch Iochdarach a'Chruaidh-Ghlinn entry.
DUBH, Loch (Colonsay) See Loch Fada (Colonsay) entry.
DUBH, Lochain See Loch Righ Mor entry.
FAD A'CHRUIB, Loch See Loch Righ Mor entry.
FADA BEN GARRISDALE, Loch See Lochanan Tana entry.
FADA CUL A'CHRUIB, Loch See Loch Righ Mor entry.
FADA CUL NA BEINNE, Loch See Lochanan Tana entry.

FADA, Loch (Colonsay)
Location & Access 61/385957. Loch Fada is on the Island of Colonsay which is accessed via ferry from Oban on Mainland Scotland. The loch is divided by the A871 Scalasgaig/Kiloran road.
Commentary Colonsay is one of the least visited and yet one of the most lovely of all Hebridean islands. The beach at Kiloran Bay, Traigh Ban, rivals any beach in the world for its stunning beauty, as do the wide sands and dunes at the south end of the island separating Colonsay from its neighbour, Oronsay. Apart from Loch Fada, there are a number of other small lochs on the island, all of which will repay a visit. They are: Loch Tuiramain (61/392953), unnamed on the OS Map, Loch an Sgoltaire (61/387975), Dubh Loch (61/371946) and Loch Cholla (61/380919).
Fish Brown trout which average 12oz in weight.
Flies & Tactics These lochs are cared for by the Colonsay Fly Fishing Association and fishing is strictly by fly only. Boat fishing brings the best results on Loch Fada; a long, narrow water divided into 3 distinct sections and almost 2 miles in length. Loch Sgoltaire, which is fished from the bank, has the largest fish, and trout of up to and over 1lb in weight are not uncommon. Offer the trout: Soldier Palmer, March Brown, Kingfisher Butcher.
Permission & Charges Contact: Isle of Colonsay Hotel, Colonsay, Argyll PA61 7YP. Tel: 01951 200316; Fax: 01951 200353. Cost: £8 per rod per day bank fishing, £12 per day for the use of a boat. Self-catering cottages are available for rent.

GLAS-BHEINN, Loch See Loch a'Bhurra entry.

Colonsay & Jura — OS Map 61

GLEANN ASTAILE, Loch

Location & Access 61/475720. Approach from Inver Cottage (61/441714). The lochs lies 1.5 miles east of Inver, between Beinn a'Chaolais (734m) to the north and Aonach-bheinn (499m) to the south.

Commentary The loch is three-quarters of a mile long by up to 300yds wide and it is situated amidst some of the grandest scenery in Scotland, dominated by the Paps of Jura mountains. A vigorous 4 mile hike further north, along the western shoulders of the Paps of Jura, will bring you to splendid Loch an Arcill; locked in a corrie by the crags of Scrinadle (506m) and Beinn an Oir (784m), the highest of the Jura peaks. Those less inclined to walk will find more accessible sport in the Abhainn na h-Uainaire burn by Inver and its headwater loch, Loch a'Chnuic Bhric (61/445736) 1 mile to the north.

Fish Lochan Gleann Astaile contains good stocks of small brown trout which average 3 to the pound. Loch an Arcill has fewer but larger trout, fish of up to and over 2lb in weight. Salmon and sea-trout run the Abhainn na h-Uainaire and enter Loch a'Chnuic Bhric. Accurate catch statistics are not available and sport depends entirely upon spate conditions, but salmon of up to 20lb have been taken from this stream.

Flies & Tactics Loch an Arcill is the most exciting of these waters, not only to fish but also because of its remoteness and the effort involved in reaching its shores. All the lochs noted above are fished from the bank, the river with a single-handed rod and light tackle, and fish will respond to: Black Pennell, Mallard & Claret, Peter Ross. However, Loch a'Chnuic Bhric is somewhat spoiled by the presence for fish-farm cages.

Permission & Charges Contact: Mr Darroch, Inver Cottage, Isle of Jura, Argyll. Tel: 01496 820223. Cost: no charge for brown trout fishing, £10 per rod per day on the river and salmon loch.

IOCHDARACH A'CHRUAIDH-GHLINN, Loch

Location & Access 61/576903. Start from the A846 Craighouse/Ardlussa road at 61/628860. This loch lies on the west side of the Isle of Jura and reaching it involves a round trip of some 9 miles over rough terrain. Along the way you may visit a number of

Commentary other small waters including, to the north of Dubh Bheinn (477m), Loch Tigh-sealga (61/599897), the unnamed loch at 61/591901 in Cruaidh Ghleann, and, on your return from Loch Iochdarach a'Chruaidh-Ghlinn, Lochan Barr a'Bhealaich (61/577881) and its unnamed neighbour to the south at 61/585876. This is a considerable journey, not to be undertaken lightly. You will most certainly need a compass and map, in case of bad weather, and you should be well prepared for what is a major hill-walking expedition. Otherwise, consider having a few casts in Loch Shiffin (61/623862), Loch Cathar nan Eun (61/631869) and the Dubh Loch (61/629873) all of which are just a few minutes tramp west from the main road.

Fish Small brown trout, but the chance of larger fish as well, particularly in some of the unnamed waters.

Flies & Tactics Loch Iochdarach a'Chruaidh-Ghlinn drains west into the sea via the Abhainn na Corpaich (61/569915) and the raised beaches at the stream mouth are a perfect place to spend a day, regardless of fishing. To catch your supper, offer the trout: Blue Zulu, March Brown, Alexandra.

Permission & Charges See Lussa River entry.

LOCHANAN TANA, Loch

Location & Access 61/617936. Approach from Ardlussa (61/646878). Walk north past the Fishing Loch up the course of the Lussa River (see separate entry) to 61/627919. From this point you may choose between two, equally attractive options: a circuit north-east to visit a series of 11 waters, or north-west to visit 7 lochs and lochans and about a dozen small moorland pools.

Commentary For the first option, climb gently north-west up Gleann Airigh Mhic-cearra to find little Loch nan Caorach (61/637931) and then north again onto the summit of Ben Garrisdale (365m) to explore Loch Fada Ben Garrisdale (61/639941) and its satellite lochans. You have another option here, a visit to remote Loch Carn nan Gillean (61/651937), but this will add 2 more miles to your day. Otherwise, leave the summit of Ben Garrisdale by walking south-west, avoiding the steep west face of the mountain, down the broad slope to Loch nam Ba (61/620931). You will find Lochanan Tana a step north from Loch nam Ba. Fish Lochanan Tana and its unnamed neighbour to the north. Descend now to have lunch by the unnamed lochan (61/612941) on the cliffs to the west of Druim Airigh an t-Sluic (211m). Return to the head of the Lussa River via little Loch an Arcill (61/615930). For the alternative day, from Loch Arcill, climb north-west for 30 minutes to locate Loch Fada Cul na Beinne (61/601929) on the north slope of Ceann Min na Beinne Brice (325m). After exploring this loch, and its unnamed neighbours, continue south-west along the side of the hill, crossing the Garbh uisge nan Cad burn, to the 2 small waters that make up Lochain Bheag a'Bhaile-dhoire (61/586923). Climb steeply south from here up Beinn Bhreac (467m) to visit Loch a'Chinn Ghairbh (61/592910) and the unnamed lochs and pools by Corr Odhar Mor (61/600919). Descend east from the plateau to regain the Lussa River after an easy tramp of 1 mile.

Fish Nothing for the glass case, but great sport with very pretty little brown trout.

Flies & Tactics Both expeditions will involve you in a tough day out over rough country and each route is approximately 6 miles in length. Carry a compass and map and make sure that you let the estate know where you are going and when you expect to return. All these lochs are easily covered from the bank, indeed, many by a single, long cast, and breakfast is virtually guaranteed. Flies: Black Zulu, Soldier Palmer, Silver Invicta.

Permission & Charges See Lussa River entry.

LOCHDARACH AIRIGH NUALAIDH, Loch See Loch Righ Mor entry.

LUBANACH, Loch See Loch Righ Mor entry.

OS Maps 61 — Colonsay & Jura

LUSSA, River
Location & Access Source 61/620925 Outfall 61/644868. Approach from Killchianaig at the mouth of the river, and from Ardlussa (61/646878).
Commentary The river lies in the north of the Isle of Jura on Adlussa Estate. It rises from the north-east slopes of Beinn Bhreac (467m) and flows south-east down Gleann Bhaidseachan into the Fishing Loch (61/64288) before reaching the sea in Lussa Bay after a journey of 3.5 miles.
Fish Salmon and sea-trout. Salmon average 7lb, sea-trout 1lb 8oz. In a good year approximately 20 salmon and 40 sea-trout may be taken.
Flies & Tactics Fish begin to run the river from June onwards but the best chance of sport, depending upon water conditions, is during August and September. Only the lower river is fished seriously, from the Fishing Loch down to the sea, and then only after a spate. This is very much "stalking" salmon country using a single-handed rod and light tackle. When water levels are kind the Lussa is very exciting to fish. At other times, resort to the Fishing Loch which, even in high summer can produce excellent sport. Boat fishing only on the loch and fish rise and are taken from all over this attractive little fishery. Vary the size of flies according to water conditions in the river. Try: Goat's Toe, Stoat's Tail, Hairy Mary, Willie Gunn, Garry Dog, Green Highlander, Black Pennell, Mallard & Claret, Peter Ross. Dapping can also be effective on the Fishing Loch.
Permission & Charges Contact: Charles Fletcher, Ardlussa Estate, Ardlussa, Isle of Jura, Argyll. Tel: 01496 820323. Cost: £42 per rod per day on the river, £42 per boat per day on the Fishing Loch. The estate also have a number of comfortable self-catering properties availble for rental with (or without) fishing.

MOR BEALACH NA H-IMRICHE, Loch See Loch Righ Mor entry.
NA CAIME, Loch See Loch Righ Mor entry.
NA CONARIE, Loch See Loch a'Bhurra entry.
NA PEARAICH, Loch See Loch Righ Mor entry.
NA SGORRA, Loch See Loch a'Bhurra entry.
NAM BA, Loch See Lochnana Tana entry.
NAN CAORACH, Loch See Lochanan Tana entry.
NAN EILEAN, Loch See Loch a'Bhurra entry.
PRIVATE WATERS BRAIGH A'CHOIRE, Loch 61/591807; LOSGUINN, Loch 61/589797; LOCHANA, Loch 61/570806; TANA, Loch 61/569802; SGITHEIG, Loch 61/572797; NAN RON, Loch 61/559782; LESGAMAILL, Loch 61/571770; NAM BREAC, Loch 61/562763; NA CLOICHE, Loch 61/541757; CORRAN, River 61/545712; AN T-SIOB, Loch 61/515737; NA FUDARLAICH, Loch 61/532764; NA FUDARLAICH BEAG, Loch 61/529767; MAOL AN T-SORNAICH, Loch 61/549804; MHIC-A-PHI, Loch 61/532804.
RIGH BEAG, Loch See Loch Righ Mor entry.
RIGH MEADHGNACH, Loch See Loch Righ Mor entry.

RIGH MOR, Loch
Location & Access 61/542855. Start from the A846 Craighouse/Ardlussa road on the track to the south of Loch a'Mhuillin (61/607837).
Commentary Reaching Loch Righ Mor and the other lochs to the west of the road involves a serious hike. The most remote of the waters here, Loch an Tuim Uaine (61/533864), Loch an Aoimidh Dhuibh (61/519857) and Loch a'Mhile (61/5158490) involve a round trip of more than 12 miles across trackless moorland. There are 8 further lochs in the immediate vicinity of Loch Righ Mor, all of which are worth close examination. To the south, Loch Righ Meadhgnach (61/535843), Loch Righ Beag (61/529839), Loch na Caime (61/538836), Loch a'Gharbh-uisge (61/544832), Loch Lubanach (61/543838) and the Dubh Lochain (61/545844). To the east and north of Loch Righ Mor lie Loch Fada Cul a'Chruib (61/552855), Loch Lochdarach Airigh Nualaidh (61/548866) which drains the Shian River north-west through Loch an Tuim Uaine into Shian Bay (61/541874), Loch Airigh Nualaidh (61/559862) and Loch Mor Bealach na h-Imriche (61/569861). Apart from these lochs, there are more fishing opportunities between Cruib (305m) and the road: long Loch Fad a'Chruib (61/575855), Torr an Lochain (61/580850), Loch an t-Sithein Tarsuinn (61/596855), Loch na Pearaich (61/584833) and the most accessible water, Loch a'Bhalaich (61/609856) which is accessed by a good track directly from the main road.
Fish These lochs are the best brown trout waters on Jura and they contain a wide range of fish which vary in size from 4 to the pound to specimen fish of up to and over 3lb in weight. In spate conditions and after heavy rain salmon and sea-trout may also be encountered at the mouths of the burns: Abhainn Ghleann Aoistail (61/598842), Abhainn a'Ghleann Duirch (61/573834) and in Shian Bay (see above).
Flies & Tactics It would take years to properly explore all the lochs in this magical part of Jura. Loch Righ Mor itself is 1 mile north/south by up to half a mile wide and the sheer beauty of many of the others will keep you happy for days, regardless of whether or not the fish are rising. Bank fishing, and, as always when fishing our Highland lochs and lochans, it is best to avoid wading. There is seldom any need to do so because, in general, fish lie close to the shore and wading simply scares them out into deeper water. Flies: Ke-He, Grouse & Claret, Silver Butcher.
Permission & Charges Contact: John Connors, Craighouse, Isle of Jura, Argyll. Tel: 01496 820292. Fishing is generally let in conjunction with the estate lodge, but day-lets are sometime available at £5 per rod.

SHIAN, River See Loch Righ Mor entry.
SHIFFIN, Loch See Loch Iochdarach a'Chruaidh-Ghlinn.
TIGH-SEALGA, Loch See Loch Iochdarach a'Chruaidh-Ghlinn entry.
TORR AN LOCHAIN, Loch See Loch Righ Mor entry.
TUIRAMAIN, Loch See Loch Fada (Colonsay) entry.

North Kintyre

A'GHATHA, Loch See Loch Garasdale entry.

AN FHRAOICH, Loch
Location & Access 62/746473. Set off from Tavantaggart (62/702468) on the A83 Campbeltown/Tarbert road. A track climbs east through the forest and out onto the hill. Follow the Tayinloan Burn, the outlet burn of the loch, up past Lagloskine (62/728469) to reach Loch an Fhraoich after a pleasant hike of 3 miles.
Commentary A small water sheltered by Narachan Hill (285m) to the east and Cnoc nan Craobh (322m) to the south. Close by, and draining Loch an Fhraoich, is Loch Ulagadale (62/739467), whilst, to the south, is Loch Dirigadale (62/722459), known locally as the Reedy Loch.
Fish Brown trout which average 3 to the pound.
Flies & Tactics Bank fishing and it is best to avoid wading. The fish are easily covered from terra firma. Reedy Loch is the least productive water, but it lies in a perfect setting and is well worth a visit, if not for the fish, then for the wildlife. Flies: Blue Zulu, Soldier Palmer, Peter Ross.
Permission & Charges See Loch Garasdale entry.

ASGOG, Loch
Location & Access 62/949705. Approach from the B8000 Tighnabruaich/Kilfinan road at Auchoirk Cottages (62/955709). A track leads west and reaches the loch after half a mile.
Commentary A very attractive little loch covering an area of approximately 40 acres. The loch is dominated by Asgog Castle, in the woodlands surrounding the north-west shore, and Asgog is notable for its varied wildlife and tranquil setting. The loch is managed by the Kyles of Bute Angling Club who also have fishing on the 2 hill lochs known locally as Dam Lochs (62/950740) and on the Powder Dam (62/965740) all of which lie to the north of Tighnabruaich.
Fish Brown trout which average 10oz in weight. The club supplement this with additional rainbow trout which average 12oz. The Dam Lochs and Powder Dam contain brown trout and rainbow trout of similar proportions.
Flies & Tactics Bank fishing, fly only on Asgog and the Dam Lochs, fly and bait fishing on Powder Dam. Trout may be taken from all round the margins using: Ke-He, Soldier Palmer, Alexandra.
Permission & Charges Contact: Tom Andrews, Kames Hotel, Kames, Tighnabruaich, Argyll. Tel: 01700 811489; Kames Post Office, Kames, Tighnabruaich, Argyll. Tel: 01700 811366; Kyle of Bute Hotel, Tighnabruaich, Argyll. Tel: 01700 811674. For further information and the Angling Club's fishing, contact the Club secretary: A H Richardson, Allt Beag, Tighnabruaich, Argyll. Tel: 01700 811486. Cost: £5 per rod per day.

CIARAN, Loch
Location & Access 62/775543 Access is via a private estate road from Ronachan (62/748555) on the A83 Campbeltown/Tarbert road. The loch is reached from Talatoll after a journey of 1.5 miles.
Commentary A substantial body of water lying on the moor between Cruach Talatoll (242m) to the west and Creag Loisgte (201m) to the east. This loch is 1 mile long by up to half a mile wide. On the way out to Loch Ciaran, to the north of the track, is little Loch na Beiste (62/765547) which contains few fish.
Fish Good stocks of wild brown trout which average 3 to the pound.
Flies & Tactics Bank fishing only. Avoid wading. The best fishing is in the vicinity of the inlet burns at the east and south end of the loch. Flies: Black Pennell, Grouse & Claret, Silver Butcher.
Permission & Charges Contact: Mr J.D. Pollok, Ronachan Farmhouse, Clachan, Kintyre. Tel: 01880 740242. Cost: £5 per rod per day. Note: Mr Pollok owns about half the shore of the loch so can only grant permission to fish that area.

CROSS REFERENCE For details of the Island of Arran waters, see OS Map 69. CARRADALE WATER (See OS Map 68).
DAM, Lochs See Loch Asgog entry.
DIRIGADALE, Loch See Loch an Fhraoich entry.

GARASDALE, Loch
Location & Access 62/765510. Approach from Ballochroy (62/728522) on the A83 Campbeltown/Tarbert road. A track leads east up the north bank of the Ballochroy Burn, the outflow from Loch Garasdale, and reaches the loch after a distance of 2 miles.
Commentary The loch lies between the crags of Cnoc Laoighscan (226m) to the east and Cruach Mhic-Gougain (248m) to the west. Garasdale is approximately is half a mile long by half a mile wide and it drains little Loch a'Ghatha which lies a further 10 minute walk north-east.
Fish Brightly-speckled little brown trout which average in the order of 3 to the pound.
Flies & Tactics Bank fishing only and it is best not to wade. The fish lie close to the shore and wading only scares them out into the middle of the loch. Fish may be taken from all round the bank but the south end, with its bays and promontories, is where to make a start. Loch a'Ghatha has similar, but fewer fish. Flies: Ke-He, March Brown, Peter Ross.
Permission & Charges Contact: Point Sands Caravan Shop, Kilmory, North Kintyre. Tel 0158 441263 Cost: in the order of £5 per rod per day.

KILFINAN, Burn
Location & Access Source 62/978790 Outfall 62/923786. Approach from Kilfinan on the B8000 Tighnabruaich/Strachur road. A convenient track borders both banks of the stream.
Commentary The Kilfinan Burn rise from the west slopes of Bealach an Tobair (433m) as Eas nam Braighleag and flows due west for 3 miles, passing under the B8000 to reach the sea in Kilfinan Bay.
Fish Accurate catch records are not available but in a

OS Map 62-63 — Firth of Clyde

good year perhaps 20/30 salmon and sea-trout may be taken. The river is not fished until May and the most productive months are September and October.

Flies & Tactics Only the last mile of the river is fished, and then, only after heavy rain. Extensive commercial forestry planting has robbed this little stream of much of its water and sport is entirely dependent upon spate conditions. The section between the road and the outfall in Kilfinan Bay offers the best chance of a fish. Use a single-handed rod and stalk your prey, casting fine-and-far-off. Offer them: Blue Charm, Stoat's Tail, Willie Gunn, Hairy Mary, Garry Dog.

Permission & Charges Contact Kilfinan Hotel, Kilfinan, by Tighnabruaich, Argyll. Tel: 01700 821201. Cost: £15 per rod per day. For further information about fishing in the area, and excellent self-catering accommodation, contact: Frank & Jennifer Coghill, Largiemore Holiday Estate, Otter Ferry, by Tighnabruaich, Argyll PH21 2DH. Tel/Fax: 01700 821235.

MELDALLOCH, Loch

Location & Access 62/938745. Immediately adjacent to the B8000 Tighnabruaich/Kilfinan road.

Commentary A very pretty loch, easily-accessible and lying to the east of the main road. Melldalloch is a shallow water covering an area of approximately 40 acres and in recent years it has been considerably "developed". A new boathouse has been built as well as a walk-way out to the small island at the south end.

Fish In the past, large numbers of small wild brown trout; now stocked with rainbow trout.

Flies & Tactics Boat fishing and bank fishing from all round the shore and from the island. Fish rise and are caught almost anywhere and you may tempt them with: Soldier Palmer, March Brown, Kingfisher Butcher.

Permission & Charges There always seems to be problems finding out who has the fish rights, and they seem to change. The best I can come up with is to suggest you contact Neil Jack in the village of Kames.

MILL, Loch

Location & Access 62/644504. Mill Loch is on the Island of Gigha and may be accessed by ferry from either West Tarbert (62/844674) or from Tayinloan (62/693467) on the Mull of Kintyre.

Commentary Gigha is a popular holiday island with wonderful beaches and wildlife and Mill Loch is easily accessible from the minor road that serves the island. South-west of Mill Loch is another water, Upper Loch (62/639503), whilst to the west of Druimyeonbeg is a small, unnamed lochan (62/642497).

Fish Modest brown trout in all these lochs.

Flies & Tactics Mill Loch has had a checkered career in recent years. A previous owner dredged the loch and filled it with rainbow trout and Atlantic salmon. Neither prospered and the present owner, William Howden of the Gigha Hotel, is allowing the surviving wild brown trout to re-establish themselves, naturally.

Permission & Charges Contact: Gigha Hotel, Island of Gigha, Argyll. Tel: 01583 505254; Fax: 01583 505244. At present, no charge is made for fishing.

NA BEISTE, Loch See Loch Ciaran entry.
POWDER DAM, Loch See Loch Asgog entry.
PRIVATE WATERS SKIPNESS, River 62/900576; CLAONAIG, Water 62/871561 (Closed at present for fisheries reserarch purposes); CRAINN, Loch 62/832579; ROMAIN, Loch 62/822536; FRAOICH, Loch 62/815553; NAN GEADH, Loch 62/816530; NAN EUN, Loch 62/808529; AN EILEIN MOR, Loch 62/803538; AN EILEIN BEAG, Loch 62/799538; NAN GAD, Loch 62/784572; CHORRA-RIABHAICH, Loch 62/809560; LURACH, Loch 62/820578; FREASDAIL, Loch 62/812595; A'CHAOURINN, Loch 62/803504; NAM BREAC, Loch 62/794483; A'MHUILIN, Loch 62/797481; TANA, Loch 62/798472; CLACHAIG, Water 62/680403; MOR, Loch 62/730404; BEAG, Loch 62/733401; FEUR, Loch 62/890642; NA MACHRACH BIGE, Loch 62/888638; NA MACHRACH MOIRE, Loch 62/886631; DA CHEAN FHINN, Loch 62/851704; METILL MHOR, Loch 62/851737; A'GHILLE BHAIN, Loch 62/812754; CHAORUNN BEAG, Loch 62/812684 ; A'CHAORUINN, Loch 62/784666; RACADAL, Loch 62/768658; LIATH, Loch 62/813655; SGREAGACH, Loch 62/781672; A'BHAILLIDH, Loch 62/754633; CILL AONGHAIS, Loch 62/726619; A'BHARRA LEATHAIN, Loch 62/771622; A'BHAILLIDH, Loch 62/755632; NAN TORRAN, Loch 62/755685; ORMSARY, Water 62/733718; A'CHAORUINN, Loch 62/778750; NA CRAIGE, Loch 62/762748; A'GHILLE BHAIN, Loch 62/818754; BARANLONGART, Burn 62/763762; FUAR-BHEINNE, Loch 62/811784; ANMA, Loch 62/817791; DOBHRAIN, Loch 62/808795; ALLT CINN-LOCHA, Burn 62/766777; SITHEIN BHUIDHE, Loch 62/721744; ABHAINN MHOR, Burn 62/715738; MHIC EARLUIG, Loch 62/752788; NA FOLA, Loch 62/753790; NA BEISTE, Loch 62/75755788; NA H-EARRAINN, Loch 62/731790; ALLT OSSA, Burn 62/955670; AUCHALICK, River 62/914748; ABHAINN NA CUILE, Burn 62/800705.
ULAGADALE, Loch See Loch an Fhraoich entry.
UPPER, Loch See Mill Loch entry.

Firth of Clyde

ARDGOWAN, Fishery

Location & Access 63/251723. Approach from the A78 Greenock/Largs road along the minor past Dunrod (63/222733). Ardgowan Fishery is reached after 2 miles. To the south of Ardgowan Fishery is Daff Reservoir (63/215723). To reach Daff Reservoir, approach from Inverkip on the A78 Greenock/Largs road. Follow the minor road east from the village across the railway to Bogside (63/215723). Take the next right. This road leads to the fishery after a further 1 mile.

Commentary Ardgowan (noted as "Compensation

Firth of Clyde — OS Map 63

Reservoir" on the OS Map) is an attractive, well-managed, 40 acre put-and-take fishery offering a good range of facilities for visiting anglers, including tackle hire, tuition and hot and cold snacks served in a comfortable lodge. Fishing is by fly only. For non-anglers, there is an interesting Nature Trail which begins at the car park. Daff Reservoir is reserved for bait fishing. Sport is also available on the River Kip, unnamed on the OS Map, which is adjacent to the A78 Greenock/Largs road (63/218734).

Fish Ardgown and Daff Reservoir are stocked with brown trout and rainbow trout which average 2lb in weight. The river contains occasional salmon and sea-trout, although very few are taken, and small brown trout.

Flies & Tactics Boat fishing and bank fishing on Ardgowan, bank fishing only on Daff. On the river, sport is entirely dependent upon heavy rain. On Ardgowan, the usual reservoir lures are the most-used fly patterns and all produce results. Ground-baiting is not allowed on Daff Reservoir.

Permission & Charges Ardgowan Fisheries, Shielhill, by Greenock. Tel: 01475 522492; Mobile Tel: 07000 784775. Website: www.trout-fishery.co.uk. Cost: Ardgowan: £15 per day (5 fish), £10 per 1/2 day, any four hours (2 fish); plus £2 per angler for use of boat. Parent & child ticket £18 (6 fish). Catch and release permitted after limit has been attained. Daff Reservoir: £15 per day, 9am to 9pm (6 fish); £10 for any four hour period (3 fish). Parent & child ticket £18 (7 fish). River Kip: £7.50 per rod per day. Permits also from Brian Peterson, The Fishing Shop, 24 Union Street, Greenock PA16 8DD. Tel: 01475 888085.

ASCOG, Loch See Loch Fad entry.
BARR, Loch See Kilbirnie Loch entry.
BUSBIE MUIR, Reservoir See Mill Glen Reservoir entry.

CAAF, Reservoir
Location & Access 63/251502. Approach from Giffordland (63/269489) on the B780 Adrossan/Dalry road. Caaf Reservoir is 1 mile north-west.
Commentary This easily accessible reservoir is half a mile north/south by up to 400yds wide. It is managed by the Dalry Garnock Angling Club. The Club also have the nearby Auldmuir Reservoir (63/262505) which is approximately 8 acres in extent.
Fish Rainbow trout which average 1lb 8oz in weight.
Flies & Tactics Bank fishing only and wading is not permitted on Caaf Reservoir. Fish rise and may be taken from all round the shore, although the north end of Caaf Reservoir is probably the most productive fishing area. Most patterns of fly and reservoir-type lures will bring results.
Permission & Charges McGuigan's Newsagents, 43 New Street, Dalry. Tel: 01294 832360. Cost: £10 per rod per day (4 fish per rod limit). The Hon Sec of the Club is: Mr A Knox, 13 Courthill Street, Dalry. Tel: 01294 833975.

CALDER, Dam See Kilbirnie Loch entry.
CALDER, River See Kilbirnie Loch entry.

CAMPHILL, Reservoir See Muirhead Reservoir entry.
CASTLE SEMPLE, Loch See Kilbirnie Loch entry.
CROSS REFERENCES LEVEN, River (See OS Map 56); LITTLE EACHAIG River (See OS Map 56); RUEL, River (See OS Map 56); GRYFE, River (See OS Map 64); ISLAND OF ARRAN (See OS Map 69); ANNICK WATER (See OS Map 70).
DAFF, Reservoir See Ardgowan Fishery (Compensation Reservoir) entry.
DHU, Loch See Loch Fad entry.

DUNOON, Reservoir
Location & Access 63/159768. The reservoir is within walking distance of the centre of town, at the head of Bishop's Glen.
Commentary An easily accessible fishery in an attractive setting on the eastern, wooded, slopes of Bishop's Seat (504m) which is open all year round.
Fish Regularly stocked with rainbow trout of up to 4lb in weight.
Flies & Tactics Bank fishing only and the western end, where the reservoir narrows into an almost separate loch, is the most productive fishing area. Try: Ke-He, Grouse & Claret, Gold Butcher.
Permission & Charges Purdies of Argyll, 112 Argyll Street, Dunoon, Argyll. Tel: 01369 703232. Cost: £11 per rod per day.

FAD, Loch
Location & Access 63/073610. Approach by ferry from Wemyss Bay (63/193686) on Mainland Scotland to Rothesay (63/080648) on the Island of Bute in the Firth of Clyde.
Commentary Loch Fad is a highly-developed commercial, 175 acre, fishery on the Island of Bute and it lies adjacent to the B878 Rothesay/Straad road. The loch is 1.75 miles long by up to 400yds wide. Other lochs on the island, Loch Ascog (63/094624), Greenan Loch (63/069641) are coarse fisheries.
Fish In Loch Fad, brown trout and rainbow trout, stocked at between 1lb 4oz and 12lb. The other lochs noted above hold pike, carp, tench, roach and other coarse fish species. Sea-trout may be caught from the shore at Kilchattan Bay (63/100558).
Flies & Tactics Boat fishing brings best results on Loch Fad and, from the boat, it is fly fishing only. From the bank, anglers may bait fish at the north end, but the south end is restricted to fly only. There are 30 boats available for hire, most with outboard engines. Anglers may use their own outboards if they wish. Fish rise and are caught almost anywhere on Loch Fad. Flies: Most reservoir lure patterns work well.
Permission & Charges Loch Fad: contact Isle of Bute Trout Company Limited, Ardmaleish, Isle of Bute PA20 0QJ. Tel: 01700 504871. Cost: day permit £14 (10 fish limit); four hour prermit £9 (6 fish limit). Boats with outboards: Weekday, £11 per day, £8 per four hours. Tuition available. tackle for hire. Facilities for disabled anglers. Loch Quien costs: Day permit £8, boat £5 (three fish per angler limit).

GARNOCK, River
Location & Access Source 63/276625. Outfall

OS Map 63 — Firth of Clyde

63/303381. Easily accessible from the A737 Dalry to Kilwining road and the B780 Dalry to Kilbirnie road.
Commentary A greatly-improved stream in recent years due to pollution control and the consequent improvement in water quality. The river rises to the north-west of Kilbirnie from between West Grit Hill (522) and East Grit Hill (510m). It flows south for 20 miles before reaching the Firth of Clyde through a wide, tidal, estuary which also contains the outfall of the River Irvine (see separate entry).
Fish Accurate figures are not available but, dependent upon water conditions, Approx 80 salmon each year but sea-trout numbers have been disappointing. The heaviest salmon taken in recent years weighed 20lb.
Flies & Tactics The River Garnock is fed by Lugton Water and Rye Water, its principal tributaries, and good sport is very much a matter of being in the right place at the right time, after a heavy spate. The stream is narrow, but there are several excellent holding pools and attractive runs. Fish do not generally arrive until the end of July, but there are signs of an improving earlier run of fish. The most productive part of the river is the stretch between Kilbirnine and Dalry. A single-handed rod will cope with most eventualities and bait fishing is also allowed. Flies: Ally's Shrimp, Munro Killer, Garry Dog, General Practitioner, Silver Stoat's Tail.
Permission & Charges Kilbirnie Angling Club: R Russell, R & T Cycles, Glengarnoch, by Kilbirnie. Tel: 01505 682191. Cost: Day tickets at approximately £6 per rod per day. The Dalry Garnock Angling Club: McGuigan's Newsagents, 43 New Street, Dalry. Tel: 01294 832360; The Craft Shop, Main Street, Kilwinning, Largs. Tel: 01475 674237: Cost: £15 per rod per day. The Hon Sec of the Club is: Mr A Knox, 13 Courthill Street, Dalry. Tel: 01294 833975.

GLENBURN, Reservoir
Location & Access 63/217519. Turn east from the A78 Largs/Ardrossan road at Allan Wood (63/206530). Follow the minor road under the railway up the Glen to reach the reservoir after 1 mile.
Commentary Also known as Fairlie Moor Fishery, this is an attractive 10 acre put-and-take fishery, open all year round, on the west shoulder of Glentane Hill (265m).
Fish Stocked rainbow trout and a few native brown trout. Average weight of fish is 2lb.
Flies & Tactics There is only 1 boat, available free of charge on a first come first served basis. The south end of the reservoir is perhaps the most productive area, but, generally, fish are taken from all round the shoreline. Flies: Soldier Palmer, Wickham's Fancy, Peter Ross.
Permission & Charges £16.50 for a 6 fish limit down to £7 for a 2 fish limit. Father & son ticket, £14.50 for a 5 fish limit.

GOGA, Water See Muirhead Reservoir entry.

GREAT CUMBRAE, Island
Location & Access 63/170560. Great Cumbrae Island lies in the Firth of Clyde between Largs on Mainland Scotland and the southern end of the Island of Bute. Approach by ferry from Largs to Millport.
Commentary There are 2 small reservoirs in the south of the island managed by local anglers: Gowk Stone (63/159559) and Millport (63/161562).
Fish Stocked with rainbow trout and brown trout which average 1lb 8oz.
Flies & Tactics Fishing is generally preserved for local anglers but a limited number of day tickets may be available to visitors.
Permission & Charges Tourist Information Office, Millport, Great Cumbrae, Clyde, Scotland.

GREENAN, Loch See Loch Fad entry.

GRYFE, Reservoir
Location & Access 63/275719. Approach the north shore from Greenock via the road south past the golf course and Whinhill Reservoir (63/278747). Whinhill Reservoir contains trout and, according to local advice, permission to fish is not required. Gryfe Reservoir is 2 miles south from Whinhill. For access to the south shore of Gryfe Reservoir, approach from the A78 Greenock/Largs road via Dunrod (63/222733).
Commentary Gryfe Reservoir lies at the centre of a series of reservoirs which extend for a distance of nearly 2.5 miles east/west by up to 1.5 miles north/south. The other principal water here is Loch Thom (63/260720), to the west of Gryfe Reservoir.
Fish Small brown trout which average in the order of 6oz/8oz, but, from time to time, fish of up to and over 2lb are taken.
Flies & Tactics Bank fishing only and wading is not advised. Stay safely ashore. On Gryfe Reservoir concentrate your efforts at the narrow, west end. On Loch Thom you may catch fish from almost anywhere round the shoreline. Fly-fishing only. Try: Loch Ordie, Wickham's Fancy, Silver Butcher.
Permission & Charges Loch Thom: Contact Brian Peterson, The Fishing Shop, 24 Union Street, Greenock PA16 8DD. Tel: 01475 888085. Cost: £2 per rod per day. For Gryfe Reservoir, contact Archie MacKinlay, Dunrod Angling Association, 2 Kincaid Street, Greenock. Tel: 01475 636076. Cost: £5 per rod per day. The Association also have fishing on 3 small hill lochs, unnamed on the OS Map, close to Whinhill Reservoir. Brian Peterson at the Fishing Shop sells tickets for other waters in the area, including Harelaw Reservoir, Daff Reservoir and the River Gryfe (see separate entries). He is the best contact for further information about access to local fishing opportunities.

HARELAW, Reservoir
Location & Access 63/311733. Approach from the B788 Greenock/Kilmacolm road. The reservoir is immediately adjacent to the east side of the road on Devol Moor.
Commentary The fishing is managed by the Port Glasgow Angling Club who also look after nearby Knockairshill Reservoir.
Fish Both waters are stocked with brown trout which average 8oz.

Firth of Clyde   OS Map 63

Flies & Tactics Easy bank fishing with trout being caught from all round the shoreline of both reservoirs. Offer them: Black Pennell, Grouse & Claret, Alexandra.
Permission & Charges Brian Peterson, The Fishing Shop, 24 Union Street, Greenock PA16 8DD. Tel: 01475 888085. Cost: £5 per rod per day.

HAYLIE, Fishery
Location & Access 63/217581. Haylie Fishery lies adjacent to the north side of the A760 Largs/Kilbrinie road on the south slopes of Rigging Hill (387m).
Commentary An easily accessible, 3.8 acre put-and-take fishery a few minutes for the centre of Largs. Professional tuition is available, as well as tackle sale and rod hire.
Fish Stocked with brown trout, rainbow trout and Canadian brook trout. Average weight of fish is 2lb but fish of up to 10lb are also caught.
Flies & Tactics Bank fishing only and trout are taken from all round the shore. Offer them reservoir lures and standard wet fly and dry fly patterns.
Permission & Charges Contact: John Weir, Haylie Trout Fishery, Largs, Ayrshire. Tel: 01475 676005. Cost: £14.50 for a 4 fish limit, £11.50 for 3 fish, £8 for 2 fish. OAP's and juniors, £7.50 for a 2 fish limit. Thereafter, catch-and-release.

HOWWOOD, Fishery
Location & Access 63/397585. In Howwood, on the A737 Johnstone/Dalry road, turn left onto the B776 signposted to Uplawmoor. After 1 mile, before Barcraigs Reservoir (private fishery), turn left. The fishery is on your right after a quarter of a mile.
Commentary A popular, well-managed, put-and-take fishery in an attractive setting offering a full range of facilities to visiting anglers and to corporate entertainment parties and angling clubs; including tackle hire, instruction and catering.
Fish Regularly stocked with brown trout, rainbow trout and blue trout. Average weight of fish is 2lb. There are also fish of up to and over 20lb.
Flies & Tactics Boat and bank fishing. Trout are taken all round the loch. Reservoir lures, such as Cat's Whiskers, Whisky Fly, Ace of Spades, all take fish, as do traditional patterns of wet fly and, on calm evenings, dry fly patterns.
Permission & Charges Contact: John Cassells, Howwood Fishery, Bowfield Road, Howwood, Renfrewshire. Tel: 01505 702688. Cost: £15 per rod per day (5 fish); £10 per any four hour session (3 fish); £8 catch and release per rod per day. There are 3 boats.

KILBIRNIE, Loch
Location & Access 63/330545. Easily accessible and immediately to the east of the town of Kilbirnie.
Commentary An exciting fishery, 1 mile long by up to 650 yds wide, well-managed by the Kilbirnie Angling Club. The loch drains north-east via Dubh Burn into Barr Loch (63/353575) and Castle Semple Loch (63/362590) both of which are renowned coarse fisheries: pike of up to 25lb have been caught in Castle Semple Loch. The Club also has fishing on Camphill Reservoir (see separate entry) and the River Calder which drains into the north end of Barr Loch and contains small brown trout. There are 3 small waters on Queenside Muir (469m) at the head of the River Calder: Queenside Loch (63/292641) and Calder Dam (63/293655) and Pundavon Reservoir (63/296578). Queenside Loch is rearley fished, generally by those who enjoy a decent hike with their fishing, Pundavon Reservoir and Calder Dam are fished by members of the Kilbirnie Angling Club.
Fish Stocked on a monthly basis with rainbow trout which vary in size from 1lb 8oz to over 3lb. There are also ferox trout in Kilbirnie Loch, fish of over 7lb have been taken in recent years, and large stocks of roach upon which resident pike, voraciously feed.
Flies & Tactics Boat and bank fishing and the east shoreline, approximately, 15yds/20yds out from the bank, is a good place to start. Reservoir lures work well, as do traditional patterns of fly such as Black Pennell, March Brown, Silver Butcher. Dry fly also produces results, particularly on warm summer evenings.
Permission & Charges Contact: Victor Donati, Hon Secretary, 11 Briery Court, Kilbirnie. Tel: 01505 683923; R Russell, R & T Cycles, Glengarnoch, by Kilbirnie. Tel: 01505 682191. Cost: Day tickets at approximately £6 per rod per day.

KILCHATTAN, Bay See Loch Fad entry.
KIP, River See Ardgowan Fishery (Compensation Reservoir) entry.
KIRK, Dam See Loch Fad entry.
KNOCKAIRSHILL, Reservoir See Harelaw Reservoir entry.

LAWFIELD, Dam
Location & Access 63/379694. Follow the minor road east from Kilmacolm, across the golf course. The entrance to the fishery is on your left, at High Lawfield (63/379692).
Commentary A small, well-managed, put-and-take fishery on the outskirts of the village of Kilmacolm.
Fish Stocked with both brown and rainbow trout. Average weight, 2lb.
Flies & Tactics Bank fishing only. Trout rise to most patterns. Buzzers, and, particularly, Black & Peacock Spider and dry fly patterns, do very well during the summer months.
Permission & Charges Contact: Bill McFern, Lawfield Fishery, Kilmacolm, Renfrewshire. Tel: 01505 874182. Cost: £15 for eight hours (5 fish); £10 for four hours (3 fish). Catch-and-release thereafter.

LOSKIN, Loch
Location & Access 63/169787. The loch is on the east side of the A885 Dunoon/Sandbank road, 1 mile north from Dunoon.
Commentary An easily accessible fishery owned by the Dunoon & District Angling Club.
Fish There is a native population of brown trout and high quality stocked fish. Towards the end of the sea-

OS Map 63 — Firth of Clyde

son, there is also more than a good chance of sea-trout.
Flies & Tactics Boat fishing only, and fish rise and are taken everywhere. Offer them: Black Pennell, Greenwell's Glory, Silver Invicta.
Permission & Charges See Dunoon Reservoir entry. £10 per rod per day, boat hire included.

LUGTON, Water See River Garnock entry.

MAICH, Water
Location & Access 63/325583 (unnamed on OS Map). Approach from the minor road between Lochwinnoch (63/350585) in the north and Kilbirne (63/319549) in the south. At Auchenhain (63/325577), rive north for half a mile to reach the fishery.
Commentary A small (3 acre) put-and-take fishery lying on Ladyland Moor.
Fish Stocked with brown trout and rainbow trout which average 1lb 8oz in weight.
Flies & Tactics Boat and bank fishing, and fish are taken all over the loch. Reservoir lures are the most popular fly patterns.
Permission & Charges Contact: Maich Fisheries, Ladyland Moor, Ladyland Estate, Lochwinnoch, Ayrshire. Tel: 01505 842341. Cost: 5 fish limit, £18, boat, £3 per rod per day. Catch-and-release after limit has been reached.

MIDDLETON. Fishery
Location & Access 63/215625 The fishery lies to the north east of Largs to the east of the minor road between Largs and Loch Thom (see separate entry). From near the Lifeboat Station in Largs, take Douglas Street and follow the signpost for Brisbane Glen.
Commentary Easily accessible 5-acre put-and-take fishery sheltered by the wooded slopes of Craigton Hill (387m).
Fish There is a natural population of brown trout and the fishery is stocked on a daily basis with rainbow trout. Rainbow trout of between 1lb 8oz and 18lb in weight are caught. The heaviest brown trout in recent years weighed 10lb.
Flies & Tactics Boat and bank fishing. Float tubes are allowed in lieu of boat hire.The fishery has facilities for disabled anglers, toilets, car park, tackle hire and light snacks, tea and coffee are available. The most popular fly patterns include: Cats Whisker, GRHE, Green Fritz, Black Hopper, Bibio, Black Spider, Viva, Zonker, Montana.
Permission & Charges Contact: Iain McIntyre, Middleton Fishery, Brisbane Glen Road, Largs, Ayrshire. Tel: 01475 672095. Cost per rod: full day, 7am until 4pm, £13.50 for 4 fish; 5 hours for 3 fish £11; 4 hours for 2 fish £8; 1/2 day catch-and-release £4; full day catch-and-release £8. Rod are limited in number and advance booking is advisable.

MILL GLEN, Reservoir
Location & Access 63/239447. The reservoir lies on the east side of the B780 Adrossan/Dalry road, 1 mile north from Ardrossan.
Commentary Mill Glen Reservoir and, to the north, Busbie Muir Reservoir (63/242465) are managed by the Kilwinning & Eglinton Angling Club. Both are easily accessible and they lie amidst pleasant surroundings.
Fish Stocked with brown trout which average 10oz in weight.
Flies & Tactics Boat and bank fishing on both reservoirs, and trout rise and may be taken from anywhere on these 2 small waters. Offer them: Blae & Black, Wickham's Fancy, Alexandra.
Permission & Charges Contact: Alpine Stores, Dalry Road, Ardrossan, Ayrshire. Tel: 01294 467979. Cost: £8 per rod per day.

MUIRHEAD, Reservoir
Location & Access 63/257567. The east bank of Muirhead Reservoir borders the A760 Largs/Kilbirnie road.
Commentary This is an excellent fishery, managed by the Largs Angling Club. It drains south through Camphill Reservoir (63/270556) via Rye Water into the River Garnoch (see separate entry). The 2 reservoirs extend for a distance of 2 miles north/south and are up to a quarter of a mile wide. Kilbirnie Angling Club have access to Camphill, to Rye Water and to the upper reaches of the River Garnoch.
Fish The reservoirs are regularly stocked with brown trout which weigh between 1lb and 4lb. Rye Water contains occasional salmon, sea-trout and brown trout.
Flies & Tactics For visitors, bank fishing only on Muirhead Reservoir and wading is not permitted. The north end, sheltered from the main road by mature woodlands, is the place to start, particularly in the vicinity of the inlet burn and the wide bay below Brown Hill (344m). Camphill is fished from the boat and 2 are available for visitors. The north, narrow, end of Camphill is the most productive area, thereafter, down the west shoreline where 3 burns tumble in from Cock Law (356m). Arrange your drift close to the shore and cast towards the shallow, bankside water. Both reservoirs can be dour and you will have to work hard for success, but on their day Muirhead and Camphill offer some of the best sport in Ayrshire. In the early months, a single, black, tadpole-type lure, fished on a sinking line, should produce results. As the season advances, try Blae & Black, Claret Bumble, Gold Butcher.
Permission & Charges Muirhead Reservoir: Hasties of Largs, 109 Main Street, Largs. Tel: 01475 673104. Cost: £8 per rod per day. The Largs & District Angling Club also have fishing on Goga Water which flows into the Firth of Clyde through the town of Largs. In spate conditions there is the chance of connecting with migratory fish. Camphill Reservoir: R Russell, R & T Cycles, Glengarnoch, by Kilbirnie. Tel: 01505 682191. Cost: £15 per boat per day, 2 rods fishing.

PRIVATE WATERS NA LEIRG, Lochan 63/049785; ARDYNE, Burn 63/105710; KNAPPS, Loch 63/367685; AUCHENDORES, Reservoir 63/355723;

Firth of Clyde — OS Map 63

LEPERSTONE, Reservoir 63/352715; NEW YETTS, Reservoir 63/263739; CARWHIN, Reservoir 63/243709; KELLY, Reservoir 63/232685; COVES, Reservoir 63/249764 (There are only a few coarse fish in this water); KILMACOLM HIGH, Dam 63/312673; LADYMUIR, Reservoir 63/341639; BARCRAIGS, Reservoir 63/390570; CUFFHILL, Reservoir 63/388558; KIRKLEEGREEN, Reservoir 63/382557; KAIM Dam 63/341623; NODDSDALE, Water 63/225645; KNOCKENDON, Reservoir 63/243523; STEVENSTON, Loch 63/275443; CROSBIE, Reservoir 63/219505; MUNNOCH, Reservoir 63/252477 ; OUTERWARDS Reservoir 63/231654.

PUNDAVON, Reservoir See Kilbirnie Loch entry.
QUEENSIDE, Loch See Kilbirnie Loch entry.

QUIEN, Loch

Location & Access 63/065595. See Loch Fad entry. Loch Quien lies on the west coast of the Isle of Bute, adjacent to the A845 Rothesay/Kingarth road.

Commentary An attractive, completely natural loch, half a mile north/south by up to 500yds wide and covering an area of approximately 70 acres. The west end, between Loch Quien and the sea, has all the characteristics of the Hebridean machair lands: fertile, lime-rich, and host to a wide variety of wildflowers and birdlife. Whilst Loch Fad to the north is always busy, Loch Quien is invariably peaceful and offers visiting anglers exciting fishing in outstanding surroundings.

Fish Wild brown trout which average in the order of 12oz/1lb in weight. The heaviest fish caught in recent years weighed 4lb 8oz. There is also a possibility of sea-trout.

Flies & Tactics Both boat and bank fishing is allowed and bank fishing, particularly on warm, summer evenings, is just as productive as is fishing from a boat. The north-east shore, from the plantation working south, is a good place to begin. Also, in the vicinity of the small peninsula at the south-west end of the loch. Look out for the 2 rocky, weed-covered outcrops: they are in fact the remains of Pictish crannogs, artificial islands constructed more than 2,000 years ago. Flies: Black Pennell, Soldier Palmer, Silver March Brown. Dry-fly can also be very effective.

Permission & Charges See Loch Fad entry.

RYE, Water See Muirhead Reservoir entry.

SKELMORLIE, Fishery

Location & Access 63/202674. Approach from Skelmorlie on the A78 Greenock/Largs road. The fishery is to the east of the town, near the golf course.

Commentary An attractive 2.5 acre put-and-take fishery on the western edge of Ferret of Keith Moor (287m).

Fish Stocked mainly with rainbow trout which average 2lb in weight, but also, from time to time, with brown trout and golden trout. Brown trout of up to 1lb 8oz are caught.

Flies & Tactics Bank fishing only. Apart from the early, colder, months, when a sinking line is best, a floating line and small flies will bring results.

Permission & Charges Contact: Skelmorlie Fisheries, Skelmorlie, Ayrshire. Tel: 01475 520925. Cost: £13.50 for a 6 fish limit, £10 for a 4 fish limit, £5.50 for a 2 fish limit. Concessions are available for OAP's and juniors.

THOM, Loch See Gryfe Reservoir entry.
UPPER, Reservoir See Loch Fad entry.
WHINHILL, Reservoir See Gryfe Reservoir entry.

Glasgow

ALLANDER, Water See River Kelvin entry.
AVON, Water See River Clyde entry.

BANTON, Loch
Location & Access 64/739785. The loch lies on the outskirts of Kilsyth and is easily accessible from the town centre.
Commentary Banton Loch is unnamed on the OS Map but it lies on the southern edge of the Kilsyth Hills between Kilsyth and Banton, to the north of the A803 Bonnybridge/Kilsyth road. The loch is some 900yds east/west by up to 250 yds wide and the fishing is managed by the Kilsyth Fish Protection Association.
Fish Stocked with good quality brown trout which average 1lb in weight.
Flies & Tactics Primarily bank fishing for visitors, but boats may also be available. However, fish are taken from all round the shoreline and bank fishing can often be just as productive as boat fishing. Flies: Black Spider, Soldier Palmer, Silver Butcher.
Permission & Charges Tickets are available from Kilsyth Fish Protection Association committee members in attendance at the loch. Further information, contact: J&B Angling Centre, 37 Eastside, Kirkintilloch. Tel: 0141 7750083.

BURNFOOT, Reservoir See Craigendunto Reservoir entry.

CLYDE, River
Location & Access Source 78/022168. Outfall 64/450733. On OS Map 64, the River Clyde extends from Dalserf (64/800505) in the east to its outfall in the Firth of Clyde in Glasgow. (See also OS Maps 72 and 78).
Commentary The river is easily accessible from public roads throughout its length. In its lower reaches, the River Clyde flows through the heart of what was once industrial Scotland. Since the demise of so much of Scotland's heavy industry, water quality in the river has improved enormously. Great emphasis has also been placed upon restoring and improving the riverbank habitat and this work is continuing. The river is the subject of a Protection Order and conservation and management plans for fish stocks are being implemented. In its lower reaches, the Clyde gathers in the waters of a number of tributaries, the most important of which are the River Gryfe, Black Cart and White Cart Waters (see separate entries), North Calder Water, South Calder Water and Avon Water. The Calders are not very productive, although the Avon Water can produce some good brown trout. In spite of the urban background, it is still possible to find peace and quiet along the river banks and the stream is very popular with local anglers.
Fish After many years of absence, salmon and sea-trout are now returning in increasing numbers to the Clyde and there is substantial evidence to show that they are reaching adequate spawning grounds. Sadly, however, migrating smolts have a hard time escaping to the sea: there is a large, un-oxygenated "sink" in the Clyde estuary and many smolts, other than in spate conditions, fail to live through it. The Clyde has always contained excellent stocks of brown trout, some of which grow to considerable proportions, grayling, and other species of coarse fish.
Flies & Tactics The best of the fishing on the Lower Clyde is to be found upstream from Uddingston (64/689607) and all legal methods are allowed. The river is wide and slow-moving, often running between wooded banks, by the Livingstone Memorial at Low Blantyre, and the site of the Battle of Bothwell Bridge (1679) near Strathclyde Loch (see separate entry). The river can be very dangerous, particularly after heavy rain and it is safest to avoid wading. For the fly-fisherman, both wet and dry fly patterns bring results and some local anglers fish with a team of 5 or even 6 wet flies on one cast. Small flies are preferred and Partridge & Yellow, March Brown, Wickham's Fancy should produce results.
Permission & Charges Contact: Bruce MacMartin, Tackle & Guns, 920 Pollockshaws Road, Glasgow G41 2ET. Tel: 0141 6322005; The Anglers' Rendezvous, 18 Saltmarket, Glasgow. Tel: 0141 5524662; Wm Robertson & Co Ltd, 61 Miller Street, Glasgow. Tel: 0141 2216687. Cost: £5 per rod per day for adults, £3 per rod per day for OAP's and juniors.

COARSE FISHERIES HOGGANFIELD, Loch 64/643673; UNION Canal 64/750779; POSSIL, Loch 64/584701.

CRAIGENDUNTON, Reservoir
Location & Access 64/526457 Approach along the A719 Galston/Glasgow road at Amlaird (70/482443). Drive east up the reservoir road for 2 and 1/2 miles to reach the parking place at the dam wall.
Commentary This is an attractive, sheltered fishery, covering an area of approximately 50 acres, 700 yds east/west by 200 yds wide. Immediately to the north, and fed by Birk Burn, is a further reservoir of some 20 acres in extent. To the west of Craigendunton Reservoir, and approached from the A77 Kilmarnock/Glasgow road via minor road immediately north of Gardrum Mill (70/468449), is Burnfoot Reservoir (64/452450), most of which is shown on OS Map 70, Ayr & Kilmarnock.
Fish Both reservoirs hold good quality brown trout which average 12oz in weight although fish of up to and over 3lb are not uncommon.
Flies & Tactics Bank fishing only and trout may be taken from all round the shore. However, on Craigendunton, the north east bank is perhaps the most productive area. Avoid wading, it is dangerous to do so. Flies: Black Pennell, Teal & Green, Silver Invicta.
Permission & Charges Contact: P & R Torbet, 15 Strand Street, Kilmarnock. Tel: 01563 541734. Cost: Craigendunton, £15 per rod per day. There is a bag limit of 6 fish per rod. P & R Torbet will advise on Burnfoot Reservoir which is managed by the Kilmaurs

Glasgow — OS Map 64

Angling Club who also manage North Craig Reservoir (70/437413).

CROSS REFERENCE CARRON VALLEY Reservoir (See OS Map 57); River CARRON (See OS Map 57); BLANE Water (See OS Map 57).

GLASGOW (South), Reservoirs and Lochs PICKETLAW Reservoir 64/568513 (Eaglesham Angling Association Water); HIGH DAM, Loch 64/559509 (A put-and-take commercial fishery. W Bauld, South Kirktonmoor Farm, Eaglesham); DUNWAN Reservoir 64/552495 (J Lamont, 32 Riverside Rd, Waterfoot Glasgow G76 ODF. Tel: 0141 6443856; LOCH GOIN Reservoir 64/537476 (Eaglesham Angling Association Water); BENNAN, Loch 64/521502; CRAIG. Loch 64/534511; BROTHER, Loch 64/505527; BLACK, Loch 64/498513 (A Downie, 2 Teviot Avenue, Bishopbriggs, Glasgow G64 3LW. Tel: 0141 772629); CORSEHOUSE Reservoir 64/480500 (Eaglesham Angling Association Water); WHITE, Loch 64/489523; LONG, Loch 64/475525 (Newton Mearns Angling Club per G W Shearer, 21 Waterfoot Road, Newton Mearns, Glasgow); HARELAW Reservoir 64/475538 (St Mirin Angling Club Water, per W H Campbell, 68 Belford Crescent, Barrhead G82 5PS; COMMORE Dam 64/460545; CRAIGHALL Dam 64/471550; SNYPES Dam 64/481552; WALTON Dam 64/493555; GLANDERSTON Dam 64/499561; BALGRAY Reservoir 64/513571; RYLN LINN Reservoir 64/520572; WAULKMILL GLEN Reservoir 64/523579; LIBO, Loch 64/434556; CAPLAW Dam 64/434588; WHITTLEMUIR MIDTON, Loch 64/418589; GLENBURN Reservoir 64/477600; STANLEY Reservoir 64/465617; WHITEMOSS Dam 64/415719.

Note: The majority of the lochs and reservoirs noted above, with a few exceptions, and the other lochs and reservoirs noted under the 'Private Fishing' entry all contain trout. They are let to various angling clubs and private individuals and visitor access to them is not easy to obtain. Because they are situated in the most populous area of Scotland they often have to contend with the activities of poachers and this damages both the quality of the fishing and the financial input made by the clubs who manage and stock these waters. However, under the terms of most of the leases, it is incumbent upon the tenant that he does in fact make fishing available to members of the public. As such, if you wish to fish any of these waters you must apply to the local club secretaries or fishery managers in order to do so. The individuals concerned do not make it easy to find out how to make this approach and this, in my belief at any rate, compounds the problem of illegal fishing. The exceptions here are the waters of the Eaglsham Angling Club and the Busby Angling Club. For access to their waters and, indeed, advice on the other waters noted above and other fishing in the area, your best contact is: Bruce MacMartin, Tackle & Guns, 920 Pollockshaws Road, Glasgow G41 2ET. Tel: 0141 6322005. Cost: in the order of £10 per rod per day.

GLAZERT Water See Mount Dam entry.
GLAZERT Water See River Kelvin entry.

GRYFE, River

Location & Access Source: River Gryfe 63/260720; Black Cart Water 63/365590; White Cart Water 64/587522; Outfall 64/498691. Easily accessible from public roads close to the streams.

Commentary The River Gryfe rises from Gryfe Reservoir above the town of Greenock and flows north-east through Kilmacolm and Bridge of Weir to join Black Cart Water near Blackstone Mains Farm (64/461670). Black Cart Water has its birth in Castle Semple Loch (See OS Map 63). The White Cart Water, the longest of the 3 streams, is formed from the flow of Ardoch Burn and Threepland Burn which meet to the east of Eaglesham. White Cart Water the heavily populated suburbs of south Glasgow and meets the Black Cart Water on the outskirts of the town of Renfrew after a journey of 20 miles. The streams enter the River Clyde (see separate entry) after a further 1 mile. In the lower reaches the Black Cart and the White Cart border the north and south sides of Glasgow Airport.

Fish Salmon, sea-trout and brown trout. In a good year, up to 100 salmon may be recorded.

Flies & Tactics In recent years, because of the improvement of the water quality in the Clyde estuary and in the rivers themselves, salmon have returned to the system after being almost total by absent for 100 years. The rivers run, in general, through densely populated areas and fishing is a somewhat public affair, but none the less exciting for being so. High water levels are essential for sport, when light tackle and a cautious approach can bring excellent results.

Permission & Charges Fishing now reserved for club members. Contact: Bruce MacMartin, Tackle & Guns, 920 Pollockshaws Road, Glasgow G41 2ET. Tel: 0141 6322005.

KELVIN, River

Location & Access Source 64/758785 Outfall 64/558660. Easily accessible in Glasgow and in its upper reaches from public roads.

Commentary The River Kelvin rises from the east slopes of the Campsie Fells and flows south-west through Strathkelvin to join the River Clyde (see separate entry) in the centre of the City of Glasgow. The stream borders the Forth & Clyde Canal for much of its length and, also, the remains of the Roman's Antonine Wall. There are three principal tributaries, Glazert Water, Luggie Water and Allander Water.

Fish Modest brown trout and signs that salmon and sea-trout are returning. Few fish are taken from the Glazert and the Luggie.

Flies & Tactics In recent years there have been considerable improvements to both the water quality and the bankside habitat of these streams. However, success with salmonids depends entirely upon high waterlevels. For brown trout, light tackle and delicate presentation is essential. Dry fly patterns are most successful.

Permission & Charges Kelvin: Bruce MacMartin,

378

OS Maps 64-65 — Falkirk & West Lothian

Tackle & Guns, 920 Pollockshaws Road, Glasgow G41 2ET. Tel: 0141 6322005. Cost: £10 per rod per season. Kelvin, Glazert, Luggie: Contact: J & B Angling, 37 Eastside, Kirkintilloch. Tel: 0141 7750083.

LOCHEND, Loch
Location & Access 64/703662. Easily accessible and immediately to the east of the A752 Coatbridge/Muirhead road.
Commentary An attractive 50 acre put-and-take fishery on the outskirts of Coatbridge. Mature woodlands on the south shore, Coatbridge golf course to the north.
Fish Stocked by the District Council with rainbow trout which average 1lb in weight.
Flies & Tactics Bank fishing only and fish may be taken from all round the shoreline. Reservoir lures are the most popular fly patterns and bait fishing is also allowed.
Permission & Charges Permits issued by the Bailiff at the loch. Cost: £5 per rod per day.

LUGGIE, Water See River Kelvin entry.

MOUNT, Dam
Location & Access 64/645771. Mount Dam lies on the north side of the A891 Milton of Campsie/Lennoxtown road.
Commentary A small pond of approximately 2 acres adjacent to Whitefield Pond. Glazert Water, a tributary of the River Kelvin (see separate entry) runs by on the other side of the road.
Fish Brown trout which average 12oz in weight.
Flies & Tactics Bank fishing only, and Mount Dam is usually the more productive of these two waters. Avoid wading and offer them: Greenwell's Glory, March Brown, Dunkeld.
Permission & Charges For further information, contact: J&B Angling Centre, 37 Eastsde, Kirkintilloch. Tel: 0141 775 0083.

NORTH CALDER, Water See River Clyde.
PRIVATE WATERS DRUMBOWIE Reservoir 64/789811; LITTLE DENNY Reservoir 64/800814; EAST CORRIE Reservoir 64/697793; BRINKBURN Reservoir 64/674805; WOODBURN Reservoir 64/665780; GADLOCH, Loch 64/650710; ANTERMONY, Loch 64/669768; BISHOP, Loch 64/689669; WOODEND, Loch 64/705677; BARDOWIE, Loch 64/580736; ARDINNING, Loch 64/569775; MUGDOCK Reservoir 64/558759; CRAIGMADDIE Reservoir 64/565754; MUDOCK, Loch 64/554773; DEIL'S CRAIG Dam 64/560782; DUMBROCK, Loch 64/550783; CRAIGALLIAN, Loch 64/538784; GARBETH, Loch 64/535794; COCHNO, Loch 64/495760; BLACK, Loch 64/499767; KILMANHAN Reservoir 64/494781; BURNCROOKS Reservoir 64/485794; BURNBRAE Reservoir 64/475743; GREENSIDE Reservoir 64/475755; LILY, Loch 64/473779; HUMPHREY, Loch 64/457760; FYN, Loch 64/458773; BLACK LINN Reservoir 64/447771; CLADAVARN, Loch 64/423838; POWIE, Loch 64/424753; GARSHAKE Reservoir 64/424765; WHITNESS Dam 64/415718; CADZOW Reservoir 64/689519; WELLBRAE Reservoir 64/682537.
See also SOUTH GLASGOW Lochs and Reservoirs entry.

SOUTH CALDER, Water See River Clyde entry.

STRATHCLYDE, Loch
Location & Access 64/730570. Approach from Motherwell. There are car parks at 64/734575 on the east shore, at 64/719583 on the north shore and at 64/731562 on the south-west shore.
Commentary Strathclyde Loch lies within the Strathclyde Country Park and nature reserve between Motherwell and Hamilton. The loch extends for a distance of 1.5 miles north/south and is up to half a mile wide. The M74 Motorway borders the west bank so Strathclyde Loch is subjected to a considerable degree of noise pollution. The River Clyde lies between the Motorway and the west shore of the loch and this may also be fished.
Fish In Strathclyde Loch, brown trout which average 8oz/10oz in weight. In the River Clyde, brown trout, grayling, coarse fish and also the chance of salmon and sea-trout.
Flies & Tactics Bank fishing only and the whole shoreline of the loch is available for fishing apart from the bankside adjacent to the island which is a wildlife preserve. Fly fishing and bait fishing are allowed. Try: Wickham's Fancy, Grouse & Claret, Silver Butcher.
Permission & Charges Strathclyde Country Park, 366 Hamilton Road, Motherwell. Tel: 01698 266155. Cost: £1.80 per rod per day.

WHITEFIELD, Pond See Mount Dam entry.

Falkirk & West Lothian

ALLANDALE, TARN Fishery
Location & Access 65/024646. Turn north from the A71 Edinburgh/West Calder road in Polbeth (65/029640). Pass the school on your left and cross the West Calder Burn (see River Almond entry). The fishery is a few hundred yards further north, on the right, and just before Briestonhill House.
Commentary A 2.5 acre, put-and-take fishery, and a smaller man-made pond, lying on the outskirts of West Calder. Tackle hire, instruction and refreshments are available.
Fish Stocked with brown trout, rainbow trout, blue trout and golden trout. Average 2lb and there are the usual monsters in the teens of pounds.
Flies & Tactics Bank fishing from the shore and from casting platforms using reservoir lures.
Permission & Charges Contact: Margo Allan, Gavieside, West Calder, West Lothian EH55 8PT. Tel: 01506 873073. Cost: day ticket: £15 for 5 fish limit, half-day, £10 for 3 fish. Evening, £13 for 4 fish limit.

Falkirk & West Lothian   OS Map 65

There are various other options. Catch and release after limit, using barbless hooks.

ALMOND, River
Location & Access Source 65/877430 Outfall 65/189770. Access is from public roads which margin the banks for the entire length of the stream.
Commentary The river rises at Easter Hassockrigg close to the M8 Glasgow/Edinburgh Motorway and flows east through the heartland of industrial West Lothian to reach the Firth of Forth in the historic village of Cramond after a journey of some 24 miles. A number of little tributary burns add to the flow, particularly after heavy rain, and these are: How Burn, Cuttrig Burn, Bickerton Burn, Breich Water, Linhouse Water, West Calder Burn and Muireston Water.
Fish Primarily brown trout of modest proportions, from where Linhouse Water joins the Almond (65/077680) downstream to Cramond. Salmon and sea-trout run the river and recent reports (March 2000) suggest that increasing numbers are now running the river.
Flies & Tactics The river bank is very overgrown in many places which makes casting difficult, but dry fly fishing can bring results in the early morning and at dusk. Your best chance of sport with sea-trout or salmon is at the back end in the lower river. Flies: Partridge & Yellow, March Brown, Black Spider, Greenwell's Glory.
Permission & Charges Country Life, 229 Balgreen Road, Edinburgh. Tel: 0131 3376230. Cost: £5 per rod per day.

BEECRAIGS, Reservoir
Location & Access 65/010744. In Linlithgow, at the end of High Street, follow the road south signposted to Beecraigs Country Park. The loch is reached after 2 miles.
Commentary A small put-and-take fishery covering an area of some 20 acres, pleasantly situated within the confines of Beecraigs Country Park on the outskirts of Linlithgow. This loch is perhaps the most popular fishery in the Edinburgh area and boats are invariably booked in advance throughout the whole season.
Fish Stocked regularly from its own hatchery with rainbow trout. There are also a few brown trout and Canadian brook trout. The average weight of fish is in the order of 3lb and double-figure trout are taken regularly. The annual catch is approximately 14,000 fish.
Flies & Tactics Boat fishing only. The loch is spring fed and has a high pH and the trout grow rapidly. Reservoir lures, Ace of Spades, Whisky Fly and others, are the most popular patterns, although small dry fly and wet fly patterns also bring results: Black Pennell, Greenwell's Glory, Silver Invicta.
Permission & Charges Contact: Beecraigs Country Park, Linlithgow, West Lothian EH49 6PL. Tel: 01506 844516. Your best chance of a booking is to make a written request at the end of the season (October) for a booking the following year. Cost: Visitor permits, £38 per boat, with a 12 fish per boat limit, 2 rods fishing. Due to demand, night session are run between May and August, from 11pm until 7am.

BOWDEN SPRINGS, Fishery
Location & Access 65/972748. From the west end of Linlithgow, follow the A706 Linlithgow/Armadale road. Bowden Springs is on the left of the road near Easter Carribber (65/970751).
Commentary A very attractive put-and-take fishery consisting of 2 lochans totalling 7 acres in extent. Tuition is offered. Open all year.
Fish Stocked daily with and rainbow and blue trout. The average weight of fish is 2lb.
Flies & Tactics Both ponds are fished from the bank. Flies: Damsel Nymph, Black or White Cat's Whisker, Red Goldheads, Red Razzlers, Orange or Black Fritz patterns and fry imitations.
Permission & Charges Contact: Tony Coulson, Bowden Springs Trout Fishery, Carribber, Linlithgow EH49 6QE. Tel: 01506 847269. Day tickets: 8 hours, £17 for 4 fish. The fishery may be hired exclusively for the use of Corporate Entertainment parties. Prices on application. Advance booking essential

CROSS REFERENCES The following waters are detailed on OS Map 66: CULLALOE Reservoir; OTTERSTON Loch; UNION Canal; LEITH, Water of; CLUBBIEDEAN Reservoir; HARLAW Reservoir; THREIPMUIR Reservoir; LOGANLEA Reservoir.

CROSSWOOD, Reservoir
Crosswood Reservoir is closed at present. East of Scotland Water, Tel: 01786 458827

HARPERRIG, Reservoir
Location & Access The reservoir lies adjacent to the A70 Edinburgh/Lanark road. Approach via the track at the north end (65/098623). The car park is reached after half a mile.
Commentary In recent years, Harperrig has had its ups and downs, literally, being drained or lowered and then refilled on several occasions. The reservoir is very exposed and often wild and windy. It covers an area of 237 acres and is 1 mile long by up to half a mile wide with a maximum depth of 44ft.
Fish Stocked with brown trout which average 6oz/8oz in weight. Larger specimens are sometimes taken, including a few fish of up to and over 2lb in weight.
Flies & Tactics Bank fishing and boat fishing and trout may be caught from all round the shore. The small, triangular, southern section of the reservoir, cut by the road, is not fished. There are two dangerous areas of soft sand which should be avoided: on the south shore, approximately 100 yds west from Baad Park (65/100608) and on the north shore, at 65/090610. Flies: Black Pennell, Soldier Palmer, Silver Invicta.
Permission & Charges Permits are available from the ticket machine at the north end of the reservoir. The machine takes 50p, 10p and 5p coins. Also, Cairns Farm: Tel: 01506 881510. Cost: £7 per rod per day. Boat hire: £8. Boat with 2 anglers, £22.

HILLEND, Reservoir
Location & Access 65/835675. Hillend Reservoir lies

380

OS Map 65 — Falkirk & West Lothian

to the east of Caldercruix (65/822680) and is easily accessible from Eastfield (65/832682) on the north shore and from the A89 Blackridge/Caldercruix road which margins the south shore.
Commentary A large, exposed, water 1.25 miles east/west by up to half a mile wide and often wild and windy. The fishery is under the management of the Ardrie & District Angling Club who work tirelessly to maintain the best quality of sport for their members. Walkways have been built to give access for disabled anglers and five casting platforms have been installed.
Fish Stocked with brown trout. Average weight of fish, 2lb, but also fish of up to and over 5lb in weight. The heaviest fish taken during 1996 weighed 12lb 2oz. Rainbow trout been introduced (1999) and the heaviest landed weighed16lb.
Flies & Tactics Members have priority in the use of boats and they are generally booked in advance by members. However, when available, visitors may book a boat. Otherwise, bank fishing. The eastern, wooded bank of the loch, is reserved for members only and fishing is prohibited in the vicinity of the fish tanks near the dam. From April until May, boat fishing is restricted to between 9am and 5pm. Thereafter, until 15th August, there is an evening session from 5.30pm until 11pm. Spinning, bait fishing and fly-fishing, using one rod, is allowed. Reservoir lures are the most popular fly patterns.
Permission & Charges Cafaro Bros, 34 Dundas Street, Glasgow. Tel: 0141 3326224. Grants of Ardrie, 120 Stirling Street, Airdrie. Tel: 01236 755532. Cost: Outstanding value-for-money sport.Bank fishing, £5 per rod per session with a 4 fish limit; visitor boats, when available, cost an £10 per session including permit. The Secretary of the Club is: J Potter, 12 Sharp Avenue, Kirkwood, Coatbridge ML5 5RT. Tel: 01236 425576.

LILLY, Loch
Location & Access 65/821667. Approach from the A89 Blackridge/Caldercruix Road at 65/830670. The loch is half a mile south from the main road. Lilly Loch is not a commercial operation and is managed on a purely voluntary basis for the benefit of local anglers.
Commentary An easily-accessible, shallow, water covering an area of some 50 acres. Considerable improvement and landscaping work has been carried out during the past year.
Fish Stocked with brown trout and rainbow trout which average 1lb 8oz in weight.
Flies & Tactics Boat fishing and bank fishing is allowed. The main area of the loch may be fished with either bait or fly, but the south bay, crossed by a footbridge enclosing an area of approximately 2 acres, is reserved for fly fishing. There are casting jetties for disabled anglers. Reservoir lures are the most popular fly patterns.
Permission & Charges Contact: Sam Armstrong, 16 Luing, Ardrie NL6 8EB. Tel: 01236 769221. Cost: per session, day or evening, £6 per rod (£4 for juniors and OAP's). The bag limit is 5 fish per rod per session. 2 boats are available and they cost an additional £6 per boat per session, 2 anglers fishing.

LINLITHGOW, Loch
Location & Access 65/000775. In Linlithgow, at the Cross, turn north to reach the loch, car park and boathouse.
Commentary Linlithgow Loch is a well-managed put-and-take fishery, three-quarters of a mile east/west by up to a quarter of a mile wide. The loch is dominated by the magnificent ruins of Linlithgow Palace, birthplace of Mary, Queen of Scots in 1542, and although the loch is almost in the centre of the town it is still an exciting and attractive place to fish. There are facilities for disabled anglers.
Fish Regularly stocked with excellent quality brown trout and rainbow trout which average 2lb in weight. Much larger fish are frequently caught, including good numbers of 3lb trout and specimen fish of up to and over 7lb.
Flies & Tactics Both boat and bank fishing are available and no one place is really substantially any better than another on this lovely water, although boat fishing generally brings the best results. The trout tend to be bottom-feeders and, consequently, reservoir-type lures are much used to tempt them. However, when they rise to surface flies, dry fly patterns, dapping, and traditional wet flies (Soldier Palmer, March Brown, Alexandra) can be just as effective.
Permission & Charges Contact: Forth Area Federation of Anglers, PO Box 7, Linlithgow, West Lothian. Mobile Tel: 0831 288921. Cost: Full day, 9am until dusk, £32 for a 16 fish per boat limit with 2 rods fishing. Bank fishing, 9am until 4.15pm, £10.50 for a 4 fish per rod limit. There are day and evening sessions as well and concessions for OAP's and juniors.

MORTON, Fishery
Location & Access 65/074634. Approach from East Calder (65/084677) on the A71 Edinburgh/West Calder road. Pass under, and then over, railway lines to reach the fishery after further 1.5 miles.
Commentary One of the most popular Lothian fisheries where advance booking is essential. This 22 acre pond is attractively situated, surrounded by trees, and there is a comfortable clubhouse and a well-stocked tackle shop on site. Tackle hire available.
Fish Brown trout and rainbow trout which average 2lb in weight. Fish of up to and over 6lb are also caught. Arctic charr are being stocked this season (year 2000).
Flies & Tactics Boat and bank fishing, with 10 boat available. Fish may be taken anywhere and reservoir lures such as Ace of Spades, Whisky Fly and Baby Doll work well. Top fly last year was Juilie's Damscl, tide by the owner of the fishrery, Julie Hewitt. Traditional patterns, Black Pennell, Invicta, Silver Butcher also catch fish, as do dry flies, particularly on calm summer evenings.
Permission & Charges Contact: Ms Julie Hewitt, Morton Fishery, Morton, Mid Calder, West Lothian. Tel: 01506 882293 or 01506 880087. Cost: Bank fishing day ticket, £16.50 (6 fish limit), boat, £4. Evening or half-day ticket, £11 (3 fish limit), boat, £4. You may use your own, electric only, outboard motor.

Edinburgh — OS Maps 65-66

PARKLEY, Fishery
Location & Access In Linlithgow, at the station, turn south onto the B9080 Linlithgow/Winchburgh road. Half a mile after passing under the Union Canal, at Porterside (65/019769), turn right and drive to Parkley Farm, a further half mile. The fishery lies to the east of the farm in a disused quarry.
Commentary A 3 acre put-and-take fishery, attractively restored from the old quarry.
Fish Rainbow trout and some brown trout. Average weight, 1lb 8oz.
Flies & Tactics Bank fishing only, from the shore and from casting platforms, and 20 permits are available each day which is divided into various sessions. Reservoir lures and most fly patterns, wet or dry, will produce results.
Permission & Charges Contact: J Shanks, Parkley Fishery, by Linlithgow, West Lothian. Tel: 01506 842027. Cost: Day ticket, 9am until 4.30pm, £17 (4 fish limit), evenings, 5pm until 10pm, £13 (3 fish limit), 2-hour session, £8 (2 fish limit).

PRIVATE WATERS FORESTBURN Reservoir 65/865648 (Will open as a put-and-take fishery in 1998); REDMIRE, Loch 65/858566 ; GAIR RESERVOIR 65/859534; COBBINSHAW Reservoir 65/019580 (Members and their guests only); QUARREL BURN Reservoir 65/181589; BADDINSGILL Reservoir 65/129558; FANNYSIDE, Lochs 65/802736; LITTLE DENNY Reservoir 65/801813; ELLRIG, Loch 65/885749; PEPPERMILL Dam 65/950893; MOOR, Loch 65/945884; LOCHCOTE Reservoir 65/979737.

ROUGHRIGG, Reservoir
Location & Access 65/810640. Approach from near Peatpots (65/818624) on the B7066 Kirk O'Shotts/Airdrie road, or from Easter Dunsyton (65/805640) at the west end of the reservoir.
Commentary A substantial body of water covering an area of 165 acres, approximately 1 mile east/west by up to a quarter of a mile wide, exposed and often wild and windy. In the past year, a considerable amount of voluntary improvement work has been carried out, both to the fishery and to the bankside habitat.
Fish Stocked with good quality brown trout and rainbow trout which average in the order of 1lb 8oz. Also much larger specimens: a wild trout of 9lb 3oz was taken in 1996.
Flies & Tactics Bank and boat fishing is available. Reservoir lures are the most popular fly patterns and bait fishing is also allowed.
Permission & Charges J McLaughlin, 5 Hyslop Street, Airdrie. Tel: 01236 604238. Cost: First-class value-for-money sport. Bank fishing at £5 per rod per day, boats cost an additional £8 Tickets are also available from the fishing hut at the loch.

SELMMUIR, Fishery
Location & Access 65/086651). See Morton Fishery entry. Selm Muir is in the wood to the left, just after Blackraw (65/083651).
Commentary A 3 acre put-and-take fishery in an attractive woodland setting, sheltered from harsh Pentland Hills wind. There are good facilities for anglers, including a comfortable fishing lodge which offers hot food and tackle sale or hire.
Fish Stocked with brown trout, rainbow trout and Canadian brook trout. Average weight: 2lb 8oz.
Flies & Tactics Bank fishing only and most patterns of fly and reservoir lures will attract the residents. Open all year round.
Permission & Charges Contact: G Gowland, Selmmuir Fishery, nr Mid Calder, West Lothian. Tel: 01506 884550. Cost: 4-hour session, £12.50 (2 fish limit), 8-hour session, £14.50 (4 fish limit). After the limit has been reached, anglers may continue to fish their session on a catch-and-release basis using barbless hooks.

WEST WATER, Reservoir
Location & Access 65/117525. In West Linton, after crossing Lyne Water (see OS Map 72, Upper Clyde Valley), turn right towards West Linton golf course. After half a mile, at the clubhouse, turn left to reach the loch after a further 1.5 miles. This is a private road and you will need keys to open the locked gate which gives access to the parking place and the angling club boathouse. Keys are available from J & R Bell, Newsagent, Rothbury, Raemartin Square, West Linton, West Lothian. Tel: 01968 660407.
Commentary A small, exposed, 93 acre, reservoir lying at an altitude of 1,100ft on the eastern slopes of the Pentland Hills. West Water is in a Site of Special Scientific Interest, noted for over-wintering pink-foot geese and other resident and visiting birds. The reservoir can often be wild and windy.
Fish Wild brown trout which average 12oz with a few larger fish of up to 2lb in weight. To avoid undue disturbance to wild life, the season is curtailed to 1st May until 31st August.
Flies & Tactics Boat fishing only on this deep (90ft) reservoir. Begin at the north-west end, in the vicinity of the narrow neck where the reservoir is fed by the headwater stream of Lyne Water from Wolf Craigs (442m). The water is peat-stained and dark and West Water trout can be dour, so do not expect immediate action. However, the trout are of excellent quality and they fight well. Flies: Ke-He, Grouse & Claret, Black Pennell.
Permission & Charges East of Scotland Water, 55 Buckstone Terrace, Edinburgh. Tel: 0131 4456462. Cost: Boat with 2 anglers, £14.

Edinburgh

BEARFORD, Burn See River Tyne entry.
BIRNS & GIFFORD, Water See River Tyne entry.

BLACKWATER, Fishery
Location & Access 66/237594. In Penicuik, after crossing the bridge over the River North Esk (see separate entry) on the A701 Penicuik/Pebbles road, turn

OS Map 66 — Edinburgh

left at the end of the houses to reach the fishery.
Commentary The Blackwater Fishery lies on the course of the Black Burn and consists of 2, small, man-made ponds.
Fish Stocked with brown trout and rainbow trout from the nearby Penicuik Fish Farm. Trout average 2lb in weight.
Flies & Tactics Bank fishing only and reservoir lures catch fish.
Permission & Charges Contact: see Portmore Loch entry. Full day, £20 (5 fish limit), part day, £15 (3 fish limit).

BONALY, Reservoir
Location & Access 66/210662. Approach from Colinton Village along Woodhall Road and Bonaly Road. Pass the Boy Scout premises and park at 66/211672. A track leads due south from here and reaches the reservoir after a decent hike of 1 mile.
Commentary A small reservoir of approximately 10 acres lying in the shadow of Capelaw Hill (426m) to the east and Harbour Hill (420m) to the west.
Fish Brown trout which average 8oz and larger rainbow trout. Much heavier specimens are taken, including, in recent years 2 fish weighing 6lb and 8lb respectively.
Flies & Tactics Bank fishing only and it is best not to wade. Fish lie close to the margins. Offer them: Soldier Palmer, Wickham's Fancy, Silver Butcher.
Permission & Charges No charge and permission is not required.

CLUBBIEDEAN, Reservoir
Location & Access 66/200669. Approach from Colinton Village (66/215689) by way of Woodhall Road. Bear left onto Fernielaw Avenue and follow the road along the north shore of Torduff Reservoir (not fished) and the golf course to reach Clubbiedean after 1 mile. Park by the dam wall.
Commentary A small reservoir covering an area of 12 acres on the north edge of the Pentland Hills. Access is easy and there are two casting platforms on the north shore for use by disabled anglers.
Fish Regularly stocked with brown trout and rainbow trout which average 14oz in weight. Trout of up to and over 6lb have been caught in recent years.
Flies & Tactics Boat fishing only and the early months of the season, April and May, often produce the best results. Fish may be taken all over the loch. Offer them: Grouse & Claret, March Brown, Silver Butcher and reservoir lures.
Permission & Charges See Gladhouse Reservoir entry. Cost: Boat with two anglers, £26.

COARSE FISHERIES EDGELAW Reservoir 66/301581; KINGHORN, Loch 66/259874; DUDDINGSTON, Loch 66/283725; DUNSAPIE, Loch 66/281731; UNION, Canal 66/160702.
COLSTOUN, Water See River Tyne entry.
CROSS REFERENCES LEADER Water (See OS Map 73); GALA Water (See OS Map 73); LEITHEN Water (See OS Map 73); EDDLESTON Water (See OS Map 73); ALMOND, River (See OS Map 65)

ESK, River (North & South) (Lothian)
Location & Access North Esk source, 66/193504; South Esk source, 73/313484; Outfall 66/346734. Both streams, and the main river, are easily accessible from public roads throughout their entire length.
Commentary The North Esk rises from Auchencorth Moss (298m) and flows north-east through Penicuik (66/235595), Polton (66/290650) and Dalkeith (66/330676) to Castle Steads (66/339692) where it is joined by the South Esk. The South Esk rises on Blackhope Scar (651m) in the Moorfoot Hills and flows north past the ruins of Hirendean Castle through Galdhouse Reservoir (66/229535) and Rosebery Reservoir (66/308566) (see separate entries) to Dalkeith and its meeting with the North Esk at Castle Steads. The Glencorse Burn is the principal tributary of the North Esk, Redside Burn and Gore Water feed the South Esk. From Castle Steads, the Esk continues north to enter the Firth of Forth at Musselburgh after a further 4 miles.
Fish Salmon and sea-trout run the lower reaches of the river, up to Dalkeith, and, as water quality improves, migratory fish may eventually re-establish themselves in the stream. At present, few are caught, perhaps 10 in a good year. Both rivers contain brown trout. The North Esk is regularly stocked with brown and rainbow trout which average 12oz in weight and there are also good numbers of grayling. The tributary streams contain small brown trout which average 6oz.
Flies & Tactics The rivers are narrow and the banks often tree-lined and covered with thick vegetation. Casting is difficult and presenting the fly effectively to rising fish requires skill and patience. Although worm fishing is allowed, using a trout rod, dry fly fishing is probably more effective. Offer them: Greenwell's Glory, March Brown, Iron Blue Dun, Badge & Red, Partridge & Yellow.
Permission & Charges Contact: James Dickson, 3 Haddington Road, Musselburgh. Tel: 0131 6650211; Musselburgh Pet Centre, 81 High Street, Musselburgh. Tel: 0131 6654777; Mike's Tackle Shop, 46 Portobello High Street, Edinburgh. Tel: 0131 6573258; A & P Supplies, 24 The Square, Penicuik. Tel: 01968 678700. Cost: £8 per rod per day for salmon and sea-trout fishing, £4 per rod per day for trout fishing.

FALA DAM, Burn See River Tyne entry.

GLADHOUSE, Reservoir
Location & Access 66/229535. Approach from Mount Lothian (66/271570) on the B6372 Howgate/Temple road. At Upper Side (66/292557) follow the minor road south and turn first left to reach the car park and boat house after three-quarters of a mile.
Commentary Gladhouse Reservoir is the premier Lothian fishery and it lies on the edge of the Moorfoot Hills at an altitude of 274m. The reservoir covers an area of 400 acres and it is 1 mile east/west by up to 1.5 miles north/south. Gladhouse is one of the oldest of the Edinburgh reservoirs and it has an almost entirely natural look. The Reservoir is also an impor-

Edinburgh OS Map 66

tant nature reserve and hosts a wide variety of both resident and visiting birds throughout the year.
Fish Regularly stocked with excellent quality brown trout which average in the order of 12oz in weight. Fish of up to and over 3lb are not uncommon and most seasons produce upwards of 1,500 trout.
Flies & Tactics Boat fishing only and access is divided into day and evening sessions for part of the season. Anglers are not allowed to land on the south island (66/293532), but the larger, north, island (66/298538) has a shelter and toilets and is an ideal place for lunch. The reservoir is relatively shallow (maximum 10m) and fish may be taken almost anywhere. Perhaps the most productive areas are at the south end and along the east shoreline from where the South Esk River (see separate entry) enters round to the point at Mauldslie (66/303532). The area to the north of Mauldslie is a bird sanctuary and is not fished. Try: Black Pennell, Grouse & Claret, Cinnamon & Gold.
Permission & Charges Contact: East of Scotland Water, Comiston Springs, 55 Buckstone Terrace, Edinburgh. Tel: 0131 4456462. Cost: Boat with 2 anglers, £16.

GLENCORSE, Burn See River Esk (North & South) (Lothian) entry.

GLENCORSE, Reservoir
Location & Access 66/220637. Approach from the A702 Edinburgh/Biggar road. Turn right at Flotterstone (66/234630) to reach the reservoir after 1 mile.
Commentary A very popular and attractive reservoir, not only with anglers, but also with Pentland hikers who use the road along the north shore to access the surrounding hills. The road ends at The Howe and Loganlea Reservoir (66/195624), 18 acres which is rarely fished. On a number of ocasions in recent years Loganlea has been drained and this has discouraged attempts to manage the reservoir as a put-and-take fishery.
Fish Glencorse has been stocked with American brook trout, brown trout and rainbow trout. Brook trout of over 3lb in weight have been caught, rainbow trout of up to 4lb. The average weight is in the order of 12oz.
Flies & Tactics Boat fishing only on Glencorse Reservoir and you should concentrate your efforts in the shallow water along the north shoreline. Flies: Loch Ordie, Black Spider, Dunkeld, reservoir lures such as Cat's Whisker, Baby Doll and Whisky Fly.
Permission & Charges For Glencorse, see Gladhouse Reservoir entry. Cost: Boat with 2 anglers, £26.

GORE, Water See River Esk (North & South) (Lothian).

HARLAW, Reservoir See Threipmuir Reservoir entry.

HOPES, Reservoir
Location & Access 66/548621. Approach from Gifford (66/535681) along the minor road to Longyester (66/546653). Take the first right after leaving Longyester to reach the north end of the reservoir after 3 miles.
Commentary Hopes Reservoir lies at an altitude of 300m amidst the wilderness of the Lammermuir Hills, tucked between between Bleak Law (460m) to the west and Lowrans Law (497m) to the east. The reservoir covers an area of some 35 acres and it has a well-established look, complete with pseudo-Victorian water tower at the north end.
Fish Regularly stocked with brown trout which average 8oz/10oz in weight.
Flies & Tactics You will need keys for a locked gate and the boathouse. These may be obtained at the Water Manager's House on your way up to the loch. Boats are moored in the bay at (66/549618), near the beehives. Bank fishing is not allowed. The most productive fishing areas are along the south shore. The beehives are only there for about 4-6 weeks each year.
Permission & Charges Goblin Ha' Hotel, Gifford. Tel: 01620 810244 (Mon-Fri 8am to 5pm). cost: Boat with 2 anglers, £22.

HUMBIE, Water See River Tyne entry.

LEITH, Water of
Location & Access Source 65/080566 Outfall 66/271769. Easily accessible in Edinburgh, and, it its upper reaches, from the A70 Edinburgh/Lanark road.
Commentary The Water of Leith flows within a few hundred yards of Princes Street and Auld Reekie is one of the few world capitals which can boast of having an excellent trout stream just 5 minutes walk from its principal thoroughfare. The river begins life in the Pentland Hills as the West Burn and flows north through Harperrig Reservoir (see OS Map 65, Falkirk and West Lothian) to become the Water of Leith. The upper reaches, between Harperrig and Currie have the characteristics of a Highland moorland stream. Downstream from Currie, the river flows through the heart of the Capital of Scotland to reach the Firth of Forth in Leith Docks after a journey of about 23 miles.
Fishing concentrates the mind, and Water of Leith anglers quickly become oblivious to the stream's urban surroundings. Also, throughout much of its length the river runs through pleasant, often wooded, parks and dells, particularly at Colinton and at Powderhall. Never large or intimidating, the river has some good holding-pools, at Dean Bridge near the West End, and, at Powderhall and Bonnington where the stream is deep and slow moving, ideal dry fly water. In the past, the Water of Leith was heavily polluted by mills and industrial works along its banks, but, in recent years, most of these have closed and the water quality is greatly improved.
Fish The river is stocked every year with approximately 3,000 brown trout and there are also still wild fish upstream from Balerno which often migrate to the lower reaches. Some 450 trout are caught most seasons and an increasing number of anglers fish on a catch-and-release basis to improve and preserve the quality of sport. Large fish are not uncommon. Salmon and sea-trout sometimes enter the river, negotiating the locks at Leith Docks, and a 7lb fish was

OS Map 66 — Edinburgh

found, dead, at Bonnington Mill in 1996.
Flies & Tactics Considerable skill and patience is required to achieve the best results. The water level is often low and the slightest error in presentation will spook the fish. Use the lightest tackle you can manage, small, size 16/18 flies on 1lb/2lb breaking strain nylon. Early morning and dusk is the time to mount your attack, or after heavy rain when wet flies can be effective. However, dry fly is the most productive fishing method, provided you can cope with the surrounding vegetation. Offer them: Black Spider, March Brown, Greenwell's Glory, GRHE, Olives and Iron Blue Dun.
Permission & Charges Contact: City of Edinburgh Council, 17 Waterloo Place, Edinburgh. Tel: 0131 2299292; Balerno Post Office, 36 Main Street, Balerno, Midlothian. Tel: 0131 5297913; Currie Post Office, 280 Lanark Road West, Edinburgh. Tel: 0131 4496224; Colinton Post Office, 7 Bridge Road, Edinburgh. Tel: 0131 4411003; Juniper Green Post Office, 529 Lanark Road, Edinburgh. Tel: 0131 4533103; Water of Leith Conservation Trust, 24 Lanark Road, Slateford, Edinburgh. Tel: 0131 4557367. Cost: free of charge.

LOGANLEA, Reservoir See Glencorse Reservoir entry.

PORTMORE, Loch
Location & Access 66/260504. Approach from the A703 Edinburgh/Peebles road. Turn east at Waterheads (66/244510) and follow the winding, minor road for 1 mile up to Westloch (66/255515). Turn right here to reach the loch after a further mile.
Commentary A very attractive loch lying on the edge of the Moorfoot Hills at an altitude of 320m and covering an area of 100 acres. Mature woodlands margin much of the east and west shoreline and the surrounding area is noted for its diverse flora and fauna. An important, 2,000-year-old, Pictish Fort, Northshield Rings (73/258494) dominates the south end of the loch.
Fish Rainbow trout and brown trout. The brown trout are carefully reared from the indigenous stock.
Flies & Tactics Boat and bank fishing, but boat fishing invariably produces better results, as well as making it easier to explore the nooks and corners of this lovely loch. Fish may be taken from all over this shallow water (maximum depth, 10m), but begin your attack at the south end, where the feeder burn flows in from Dundreich Hill (622m), and along the south-east shore. Flies: Black Spider, Wickham's Fancy, Peter Ross. Also, reservoir lures.
Permission & Charges Contact: Steven McGeachie, 20 Avon Grove, Penicuik, Midlothian. Tel: 01968 675684; Mobile Tel: 0374 127467. Cost: Boat fishing: £34 per boat per day, 2 rods fishing (10 fish per boat limit). Bank fishing: £16 per day, £15 per evening, for a 4 fish limit per session.

PRIVATE WATERS OTTERSTON, Loch 66/167855; WHIM, Pond 66/218540; FALA FLOW, Loch 66/429585 (there are no fish in this loch);
STOBSHIEL Reservoir 66/501620; LAMMERLOCH Reservoir 66/513635; CULLALOE Reservoir 66/189876 (this reservoir has been drained).
REDSIDE, Burn See River Esk (North & South) (Lothian) entry.

ROSEBERY, Reservoir
Location & Access 66/307565. Approach as for Gladhouse Reservoir (see separate entry). Continue north from Upper Side (66/292557) for 1 mile to reach the reservoir. Alternatively, from Gorebridge (66/344606) on the A7 Edinburgh/Galashiels road, turn right to reach the reservoir through Temple (66/318587) on the B6372 Gorebridge/Mount Lothian road after 4.5 miles.
Commentary Rosebery Reservoir lies to the north of Gladhouse Reservoir and it is the most popular of the Edinburgh reservoir fisheries. The loch covers an area of 52 acres and is narrow and L-shaped, being almost half a mile long.
Fish Stocked with rainbow trout, brook trout and brown trout which average 12oz in weight. In recent years, rainbow trout of up to and over 5lb have been taken as well as brown trout of 4lb. There are also pike and perch in the reservoir. Pike of 15lb have been caught.
Flies & Tactics Boat and bank fishing, and, from July to September, spinning and worm fishing for pike and perch in the south-west bay. Bank fishing is restricted to the south-east shoreline. Flies: Ke-He, March Brown, Silver Butcher.
Permission & Charges Contact: Mrs Grant, Water Keeper's Cottage, Rosebery Reservoir, by Temple, Midlothian. Tel: 01875 830353. There is a bag limit of 6 fish per rod per day. Cost: Boat with 2 anglers, £26.

ROSSLYNLEE, Fishery
Location & Access 66/273596. Rosslynlee fishery lies immediately adjacent to the east of the A6094 Dalkeith/Howgate road 1 mile south from Newbigging (66/278603).
Commentary This is an easily accessible, well-managed, 7 acre put-and-take fishery acttractively situated on Cauldhall Moor to the north of Howgate Village.
Fish Stocked with brown trout, rainbow trout and blue trout which average 2lb in weight. Fish of over 8lb are not uncommon.
Flies & Tactics Boat fishing and daily bank fishing permits for up to 25 anglers. The fishery is open all-year-round and there are excellent facilities, including free tea and coffee during the winter months. Reservoir lures bring the best results.
Permission & Charges Contact: G R Scott, Rosslynlee, Newbigging Hill, Midlothian. Tel: 01968 679606. Cost: Day ticket, £18 for 4 fish (9-5), half day £15 for 3 fish (4 hours) or evening session (6pm to dusk). Thereafter, catch and release using barbless hooks. Boat, £4 per session.

STENHOUSE, Reservoir
Location & Access 66/211877. Stenhouse Reservoir lies to the south of the A907 Kirkcaldy/Aberdour road

Duns & Dunbar OS Map 66-67

and to the east of the A909 Burntisland/Bernard's Smithy road, 2 miles north from Burntisland.
Commentary An easily accessible fishery in an attractive setting. Stenhouse is approximately half a mile long by up to 200 yds wide covering an area of 35 acres.
Fish Stocked regularly with good quality brown trout which average 2lb in weight. Much larger fish are frequently caught, trout of up to and over 4lb, and the Club have stocked a number of specimen fish in the order of 8lb. Anglers who catch these trout, and return them to the water, receive a free day's fishing.
Flies & Tactics Boat and bank fishing and trout rise and are taken from all around the loch. During the early months of the season the lochs produces best results in the evening. As the season advances, the best catches are taken during the day. Flies: Bibio, March Brown, Silver Invicta.
Permission & Charges Contact: John Low, Tel: 01592 872267; Fax: 01592 874624. Permits may be obtained at the loch, from 9.45am until 11.30am, and again in the evening from 6.00pm onwards. Cost: Bank fishing ticket £12 per rod; Boat £14 per rod; Single rod boat, £16. (4 fish limit).

THREIPMUIR, Reservoir
Location & Access 66/175640. Approach from Balerno Village via Mansfield Road. After passing the Marchbank Hotel (66/506644), turn left to reach the car park. From there, a two minute walk brings you to the reservoir.
Commentary A large reservoir (246 acres), 2 miles east/west by up to half a mile wide and divided by road bridges into three sections. Access for visitors is to the east, and largest, section only. The other areas are reserved for local angling clubs. Immediately to the north of Threipmuir Reservoir, is Harlaw Reservoir, a deep, narrow water covering an area of 130 acres and extending north for half a mile. To find Harlaw Reservoir, turn left off Mansfield Road onto Harlaw Road and park near Harlaw Farm (66/179658). The reservoir is a 5 minute walk from the car park.
Fish Both waters are stocked with brown and rainbow trout. The average weight of fish is in the order of 10oz/12oz, but much larger fish, trout of up to and over 3lb in weight, are frequently taken.
Flies & Tactics Bank fishing only. Wading is generally safe on Threipmuir, where the bottom shelves down gently, but it is down-right dangerous on Harlaw where the shoreline deepens very quickly. Chest waders are banned on Threipmuir, stay firmly on terra firma when fishing Harlaw. The bank fishing area on Threipmuir is confined to the north shore only, a distance of approximately 1.5 miles from Black Springs (66/179643), along the dam wall, and down the north shore to the boathouse. The early months of the season can be very productive although it is often cold, finger-numbing work. Threipmuir and Harlaw Reservoir trout do not give themselves up easily, but they fight splendidly and are well worth the effort involved in their capture. Offer: Black Pennell, Wickham's Fancy, Alexandra.

Permission & Charges Day tickets may be purchased, from 7.00am onwards, but only on the day you intend to fish. They cost £8 for an adult and £6 for juniors and OAP's. Contact: A Fleming, 42 Main Street, Balerno, Edinburgh. Tel: 0131 4493833.

TYNE, River
Location & Access Source 65/393592 Outfall 67/625793. Major and minor public roads, particularly the A1 Edinburgh/Berwick-on-Tweed trunk road, margin both banks the stream throughout most of its length.
Commentary The river rises from the eastern slopes of the Moorfoot Hills and flows generally north-east through East Lothian to reach the Firth of Forth near Tyninghame House, 2 miles north of Dunbar, after a journey of 26 miles. Immediately to the south, in Belhaven Bay, bounded on the east by Dunbar Golf Course, Biel Water enters the Firth and this little stream can also produce sport after heavy rain. The River Tyne has a number of delightful tributaries, all of which are well worth exploring. Working downstream from the source of the Tyne, the most important of these tributaries are: Humbie Water, Birns & Gifford Water, Colstoun Water and Bearford Burn. They, in turn, have their own tributaries, such as Fala Dam Burn (66/432617). None of the waters noted above are over-fished, particularly the smaller streams, and they all offer good sport amidst peaceful, attractive surroundings.
Fish The River Tyne used to have a run of sea-trout and a few fish are still caught, but not nearly as many as in days past. There are good numbers of wild brown trout and the river is stocked with additional brown trout at the start of each season. Trout average 8oz/10oz in weight and there are larger specimens as well.
Flies & Tactics Delicate, demanding work with light tackle. The river is narrow and the banks are often tree-lined. Single flies, either wet or dry, are most commonly used, and bait fishing is also allowed. Sport is best in the early months of the season and after heavy rain. In the summer months, the water level drops, launch your attack either at dusk or dawn. The tributary streams and burns should be approached in the same way, with patience and caution. Some of them contain excellent trout of up to and over 1lb in weight. Flies: Iron Blue Dun, Partridge & Yellow, Ginger Quill, March Brown, Blae & Black, Black Spider, and, for any unsuspecting sea-trout you encounter, Peter Ross or Teal Blue & Silver.
Permission & Charges J S Main, 87 High Street, Haddington, East Lothian. Tel: 01620 882148. Charges: £5 per rod per day.

Duns and Dunbar

ALE, Water (Eyemouth) See Eye Water entry.
BLACKADDER, Water See Whiteadder Water entry.
BOTHWELL, Water See Whiteadder Water entry.

OS Map 67 — Duns & Dunbar

COLDINGHAM, Loch
Location & Access 67/896685. Approach from Coldingham (67/900661), to the east of the A1 trunk road. A minor road (dead-end) leaves the A1107 on the north outskirts of the village and reaches the loch after 1.75 miles.
Commentary One of Scotland's oldest put-and-take fisheries and the first to stock rainbow trout (1950). The loch covers an area of 22 acres, surrounded by mature woodlands, and is a haven for a wide variety of wildlife, particularly water fowl. If you can drag yourself away from the delights of the fishing, there are the dramatic remains of a 2,000-year-old Pictish settlement on the cliffs to the west of the loch at 67/892691.
Fish Regularly stocked throughout the season with brown trout and rainbow trout. The average weight of fish is 2lb. Brown trout fishing is from 15th March until 5th October, rainbow trout fishing is from 15th March until 31st October.
Flies & Tactics There are 5 boats and a limited number of bank fishing permits may also be available. Fish rise and are taken everywhere, from the middle to the margins, and the most productive flies include: Black Pennell, Greenwell's Glory, Black Spider, Wickham's Fancy and Soldier Palmer.
Permission & Charges Contact: Dr EJ Wise, West Loch House, Coldingham, Berwickshire. Tel: 018907 71270. Charges: Day session, £17 per rod (4 fish limit), evening session, £14 per rod (3 fish limit). Boats cost £4 per rod per day session and £3 per rod for an evening session. There are also very comfortable, well-equipped, self-catering cottages available for rent on the Estate, particularly the converted boat house which over-hangs the loch itself. Advance booking is essential.

CROSS REFERENCE TYNE, River (See OS Map 66); BIEL Water (See OS Map 66); TWEED, River (See OS Map 74).

DONOLLY, Reservoir
Location & Access 67/577686. Approach from Hornshill (67/571672) on the B6355 Gifford/Cranshaws road. Turn north at Hornshill, signposted to Garvauld, to reach the reservoir after 3/4 of a mile.
Commentary Donolly is an attractive little reservoir, tree-lined on the west shore, half a mile north/south in length and covering an area of approximately 16 acres. Sadly, the reservoir has been closed for fishing in recent years and there are no immediate plans for reopening it.

DYE, Water See Whiteadder Water entry.

EYE, Water
Location & Access Source 67/720684 Outfall 67/947645. Eye Water is accessible from the B6355 Eyemouth/Ayton road, the A1 Ayton/Granthouse road, and, in it its upper reaches, from minor roads.
Commentary The stream rises from Wightman Hill (351m) on Monynut Edge and flows south-east for 17 miles before reaching the North Sea through Eyemouth Harbour. Ale Water, the principal tributary of Eye Water, rises near Press Castle (67/870654) on Coldingham Moor and joins Eye Water at Old Linthill (67/939620) 1.5 miles upstream from the estuary.
Fish The occasional salmon and sea-trout, but mostly brown trout which average 6oz/8oz.
Flies & Tactics In times past, Eye Water and Ale Water used to have excellent runs of migratory fish, mostly sea-trout, but very few are caught now. However, there is still a chance of sport after heavy rain. Brown trout fishing on both streams is great fun, particularly dry-fly work, and skill and dexterity is required to present the fly properly to feeding fish in the confines of this stream. The best fishing is between Reston and Ayton. Offer them: Greenwell's Glory, Partridge & Yellow, Iron Blue Dun, March Brown.
Permission & Charges Mrs D McIntosh, Howburn, Reston, Berwickshire. Tel: 018907 61271. JAS Davidson & Sons, West Reston, Berwickshire. Tel: 018907 61672. Mr J Darling, Swinewood Mill, Reston, Berwickshire (written bookings only). Expect to pay in the order of £2 per rod per day.

FASENY, Water See Whiteadder Water entry.
KELL, Burn See Whiteadder Water entry.
MONYNUT, Water See Whiteadder Water entry.
PRIVATE WATERS PRESSMENNAN Reservoir 67/630733; DANSKINE, Loch 67/566677; THORTER'S Reservoir 67/608696; HEN POO, Loch 67/779549.
WATCH WATER, Reservoir See Whiteadder Water entry.
WHITEADDER, Reservoir See Whiteadder Water entry.

WHITEADDER, Water
Location & Access Source 67/626685 Outfall 75/972518. There river is easily accessible throughout its entire length from public roads.
Commentary Whiteadder Water is a major tributary of the River Tweed (See OS Map 74, Kelso, OS Map 73, Galashiels and Ettrick Forest and OS Map 72, Upper Clyde Valley). The river rises from Clints Dod (398m) on Dunbar Common and flows south for 3 miles before being impounded in Whiteadder Reservoir (67/655635). The main stream is joined here by Faseny Water, Bothwell Water, Monynut Water and Dye Water before flowing on to the delightful little hamlet of Abbey St Bathans. A further 8 miles brings the stream to Allanton (67/865544) where the Whiteadder is joined by its major tributary, Blackadder Water. After 5 miles, Whiteadder Water joins the tidal reaches of the River Tweed, in England, approximately 2.5 miles upstream from the town of Berwick.
Fish Salmon and sea-trout, brown trout and escapee rainbow trout. Brown trout average 8oz in weight. Whiteadder Reservoir, which is regularly stocked, contains larger trout of up to 1lb. In recent years the Tweed Foundation has carried out considerable improvement works to the river, easing obstructions which restricted access for migratory species and

South Kintyre — OS Maps 67-68

restoring their spawning habitat. This will increase the number of salmon and sea-trout running the river.

Flies & Tactics The best opportunity of sport with salmon or sea-trout is after heavy rain and most fish are taken during the autumn months. Whiteadder Water, Blackadder Water and the other burns and streams noted above, offer good fishing for brown trout which rise well to both dry and wet fly patterns. These streams, throughout their course, are easily fished and there is seldom any need for serious wading. The best sport, as with migratory fish, is had after heavy rain. Whiteadder Reservoir (193 acres) is a popular destination with local anglers and both boat and bank fishing is allowed. The reservoir can be wild and windy and the north end, where the Kell Burn enters (67/644640), and the bay to the south, where Faseny Water flows in (67/644635), are probably the most productive areas. There is one other reservoir on the headwaters of Whiteadder Water, Watch Water Reservoir (67/660563), which feeds into Dye Water. This is a well-managed, put-and-take fishery, stocked with both brown and rainbow trout which average 2lb in weight. The reservoir covers an area of 119 acres, bank fishing is allowed and 10 boats are available. There is also a comfortable fishing lodge supplying excellent meals, from breakfast onwards. For salmon and sea-trout, offer: Garry Dog, Dusty Miller, Green Highlander, Stoat's Tail, General Practitioner. For trout, Greenwell's Glory, Partridge & Yellow, March Brown, Iron Blue Dun, Grouse & Claret, Blae & Black, Black Spider.

Permission & Charges Whiteadder Water, Blackadder Water & Tributaries: D Cowan, Hon Secretary, Berwick & District Angling Association, 129 Etal Road, Tweedmouth, Berwick-upon-Tweed. Tel: 01289 306985. T Waldie, 26 East High Street, Greenlaw, Berwickshire. Tel: 01361 810542. Game Fare, 12 Marygate, Berwick-upon-Tweed. Tel: 01289 305119; Home Tel: 01289 302510. Cdr. Baker, Millburn House, Duns, Berwickshire. Tel: 01361 883086. R Welsh & Son, 28 Castle Street, Duns, Berwickshire. Tel: 01361 883466. R B Harrower, Blackadder Mount, Duns, Berwickshire. Tel: 01890 818264. R Carruthers, Bridgend House, 36 West High Street, Greenlaw, Berwickshire. Tel: 01361 810270. Charges vary from in the region of £1 per rod per day on Blackadder Water to £10 per rod per day on Whiteadder Water. Whiteadder Reservoir: Goblin Ha Hotel, Gifford, East Lothian. Tel: 01620 810244. Mrs E Graham, Cranshaws Smiddy, Cranshaws, Duns, Berwickshire. Tel; 01361 890277. The Water Keeper's House, Hungry Snout, Whiteadder Reservoir, East Lothian. Tel: 01361 890362. Cost: Bank fishing, £10 per rod per day. Boat with 2 rods fishing, £6 per boat per sesson. Bag limit, 6 fish per rod. Watch Water Reservoir: W F Renton, Watch Water Reservoir, Longformacus, Duns, Berwickshire. Tel: 01361 890331 or 01289 306028; Mobile Tel: 0860 868144; Fax: 01361 890331. Day ticket, £16 (6 fish limit), evening ticket £13 (4 fish limit). Boat, £4 per session. Catch-and-release using barbless hooks is permitted when limit bag has been achieved. For boats, telephone bookings are advised.

South Kintyre

AUCHA LOCHY, Loch
Location & Access 68/726226. Approach from the A83 Campbeltown/Westport road at 68/717218. A minor road leads north to the loch after a distance of 1 mile.
Commentary An attractive, easily-accessible loch to the north of Campbeltown with another, just as attractive little water, Knockruan Loch, immediately to the east. These waters are managed by the Kintyre Fish Protection Association, as is Crosshill Loch (68/717193) unnamed on the OS Map and lying to the south of Campbletown.
Fish Stocked with brown trout which average 8oz/10oz. Aucha Lochy Loch, however, does contain larger fish as well and trout of up to and over 2lb in weight are occasionally taken.
Flies & Tactics Bank and boat fishing. Club members have priority over the use of boats. These small waters are easily "read" and fish rise may be taken from virtually anywhere. Offer: Black Pennell, Wickham's Fancy, Cinnamon & Gold.
Permission & Charges See Lussa Loch entry.

BACK, Water See Machrihanish Water entry.
BREACKERIE, Water See Machrihanish Water entry.

CARRADALE, Water
Location & Access Source 62/745479 Outfall 68/803372. Access is from the B8001 Carradale/Whitehouse road which runs adjacent to the north bank of the stream.
Commentary The source of the river is on Narachan Hill (285m), 10 miles from its outfall in Carradale Bay. The surrounding hills and moors are heavily afforested and this has affected water-levels in the stream, as does water-extraction from the river for the local communities' needs. Nevertheless, given a good spate, this can be a very exciting little stream to fish.
Fish Salmon and diminishing numbers of sea-trout. Approximately 20/30 salmon and perhaps 40/50 sea-trout may be taken in a good year. The heaviest salmon caught last season weighed 12lb 13oz, best sea-trout, 4lb 8oz.
Flies & Tactics Work has been done recently on dams and pools, improving the river, and the most notable pools include, from the sea working upstream: Kennel, Bowling Pool, Dump, Post Office and Cemetery. There is a water gauge on the hut by the road bridge. Over 3ft on the gauge allows all legal fishing methods, otherwise, it is fly only. No need to wade, use a single-handed rod and offer them: Garry Dog, Blue Charm, Stoat's Tail, Goat's Toe, Hair Mary, Black Pennell, Peter Ross.
Permission & Charges See Lussa Loch entry. Also from David Oman, General Merchants, The Pier, Carradale. Tel: 01583 431228. Cost: £8 per rod per day.

CONIE, Water See Machrihanish Water entry.
CROSS REFERENCE For details of the Island of Arran, see OS Map 69.

OS Maps 68 — South Kintyre

CROSSHILL, Loch See Aucha Lochy Loch.

GLENLUSSA, Water
Location & Access Source: 68/710345 Outfall: 68/764255. The river is accessible from the minor road which margins the north bank of the stream.
Commentary Glenlussa Water rises from the west slopes of Cnoc Reamhar (329m) and flows east and south into Lussa Loch (see separate entry). The river then flows for 5 miles down Glen Lussa and reaches the sea in Ardnacross Bay after passing under Peninver Bridge on the B842 Campbeltown/Carradle road. The stream has been tamed in recent times by its use for hydro-electric power generation at Gartgreillan (68/735260). The upper reaches, between the dam on Lussa Loch and the power station, are more often than not dry throughout the summer months. Fishing on the river is in the stretch between the power station and the sea where there are a number of decent pools and runs.
Fish Salmon and sea-trout, although not many of the latter in recent years. Approximately 80 salmon may be taken in a good season. Salmon average 7lb, with a few double-figure fish as well, sea-trout weigh in the order of 2lb.
Flies & Tactics This is a comfortable river to fish and there is seldom need to wade. A single-handed rod will do fine and be prepared to 'stalk' your fish, keeping below the skyline, covering the pools from one casting position, rather than marching down the bank. Fish run the river from June onwards but the best sport is at the back end, in August and September, depending upon God's good rain. Flies: Garry Dog, Willie Gunn, Hairy Mary, Silver Stoat's Tail, General Practitioner, Blue Charm.
Permission & Charges This loch is privately owned. Cost: £5 to £10 per day depending upon the time of year. Permits can usually be obtained from the Water Bailiff's caravan at the river.

KNOCKRUAN, Loch See Aucha Lochy Loch entry.

LUSSA, Loch
Location & Access 68/710300. Approach via the forest track (5 miles to the loch) from Kildonan (68/779280) on the B842 Campbeltown/Carradle road or from near Drumore on the A83 at 68/711218, a journey of 4 miles to the south end of Lussa.
Commentary Lussa Loch is the principal trout fishery in the area, 2 miles north/south by up to half a mile wide. It is sheltered in the west by Cnoc Buidhe (312m) and, to the east, by Sgreadan (397m), both of which hills are heavily afforested. Nevertheless, Lussa Loch can still be a wild and windy place to fish and care is required when afloat. The loch has been impounded as part of a hydro-electric power generation scheme and it drains southeast to the sea through Glenlussa Water (see separate entry). Tangy Loch, to the south-west of Lussa Loch, is approached from the A83 at 68/655279. Follow the minor road past Tangy Farm to Gartgunnel (68/6792821) and walk east from there for half a mile to reach the loch.
Fish Brown trout which average 10oz, but good numbers of larger fish as well.
Flies & Tactics The fishing is managed by the Kintyre Fish Protection Association and both boat and bank fishing is available. On Lussa Loch, a convenient track borders the whole of the west shoreline; however, avoid wading because bankside margins can be dangerously soft in places due to fluctuations in water levels caused by power generation. The north-east shore and the north end of Lussa Loch are good places to begin, particularly in the vicinity of the bay to the north of Stramollach (68/716307). On Tangy Loch, concentrate your efforts round the little island and in the south bay. Tangy Loch can become weedy as the season advances. Flies: Blae & Black, Grouse & Claret, Kingfisher Butcher.
Permission & Charges A P. MacGrory, Main Street, Campbeltown, Kintyre. Tel: 01586 552132. Cost: approximately £8 per rod per day for bank fishing, an additional £12 per day for the use of a boat. Further information about South Kintyre fishing may be obtained from the club secretary: S Martin, Kilkerran Road, Campbeltown, Kintyre. Tel: 01586 552835. For Tangy Loch Carradale Angling Club (Sec. D Paterson), 4 Tormore Carradale, Argyll.

MACHRIHANISH, Water
Location & Access Source 68/675263 Outfall 68/645211. Easily accessible from the Links of Machrihanish.
Commentary The river rises to the north, near Largiebeg, and in its upper reaches is known as Back Water. After passing under the road to the airfield it becomes known as Machrihanish Water where it flows across the golf course to enter the sea to the north of the village. There are three other modest salmon streams to the south, at the tip of the Mull of Kintyre: Breackerie Water and Strone Water which enter the sea in Carsker Bay (68/660075), and, to the east, Conie Water which gets afloat by Southend through the golf course near Dunaverty (68/690075).
Fish The chance of a salmon or sea-trout after heavy rain. There are no accurate catch statistics.
Flies & Tactics All legal fishing methods are used and sport is entirely dependent upon rain.
Permission & Charges As far as I can establish, no permission is required to fish Machrihanish Water and there is no charge. For the other waters, which are cared for by the angling club, see the entry for Lussa Loch.

PRIVATE WATERS BARR, Water 68/661358; SADDLE, Water 68/790315; DUBH, Loch 68/713399; SKEROBLIN, Loch 68/702262; BLACK, Loch (North) 68/737245; BLACK, Loch (South) 68/717177; KILLYPOLE, Loch 68/648179; ARNCILE, Loch 68/712355.
STRONE, Water See Machrihanish Water entry.
TANGY, Loch See Lussa Loch entry.

Isle of Arran

OS Map 69

CLOY, Water See Loch Garbad entry.
CROSS REFERENCE For details of the waters on the Mull of Kintyre, see OS Map 68.
DUBH, Loch See Iorsa Water entry.

GARBAD, Loch
Location & Access 69/019239. Approach from Whiting Bay (96/046253). Park at the end of the road and then walk the last 2 miles along a forest track to reach the loch.
Commentary This small forest loch is managed by the Arran Angling Association (AAA). The AAA also have the fishing on a number of modest spate streams throughout the island, including Sliddery Water (96/934220), Kilmory Water (96/953208), Cloy Water (96/01363) and Sannox Water (96/015465).
Fish Stocked brown trout in Loch Garbad, sea-trout and the chance of an occasional salmon in the streams. Accurate records of numbers of salmonids caught are not available but, in an exceptional year, are probably in the region of 30 sea-trout and 50 salmon. The island is now heavily afforested and water drains off the hill very quickly. This, coupled with dry summers, has made sport increasingly hard to find in recent years.
Flies & Tactics The loch is fished from the shore and anglers are limited to 2 fish per rod per day. Sport on the streams is entirely dependent upon rain and most fish are caught using bait, rather than fly, although fish-fishing on a falling spate can be just as effective. Sliddery Water is the most productive of the AAA streams. Try: Teal Blue & Silver, Grouse & Claret, Peter Ross, Goat's Toe, Clan Chief, Black Pennell, Soldier Palmer.
Permission & Charges Contact: Tourist Information Centre, Brodick Pier, Brodick, Isle of Arran. Tel: 01770 302140. Cost: Trout fishing: £7.50 per rod per day; Sliddery Water, £10 per rod per day; all other AAA waters, £7.50 per rod per day. For further information about the AAA fishing contact: Ms Celia Sillars, Secretary, AAA, Catriona, Ross Burn, Brodick, Isle of Arran. Tel: 01770 302327.

IORSA, Water
Location & Access Source 69/960430 Outfall 69/883370. Access to the island is via ferry from Adrossan on mainland Scotland to Brodick on Arran. Iorsa Water is on the west coast of Arran and is approached via a private estate road that borders the north bank of the stream.
Commentary Iorsa Water is a short, 6 mile long, spate river which rises from the west shoulder of Beinn Tarsuinn (825m) and Cir Mhor (798m). The stream flows south through a confined glen to 69/935403 where it collects in the waters from little Dubh Loch (96/914426) and Loch Tanna (69/921430); both of which contain small, 4oz/6oz wild brown trout. The river hesitates in Loch Iorsa (69/915380) before continuing its journey south-west to reach the sea by the jetty at Dougaire.
Fish Sea-trout and a few salmon. Approximately 50 sea-trout are taken most seasons and perhaps up to 10 salmon. Sea-trout average 2lb 8oz in weight, salmon, 6lb/7lb.
Flies & Tactics The river between Loch Iorsa and the sea contains 16 pools and these are divided into 2 beats, the upper of which includes Loch Iorsa where there is a boathouse and boat for the use of fishing tenants. Fishing is by fly only and a single-handed rod will effectively deal with most eventualities. When the river is low, the best chance of sport is on the loch. On a falling spate, however, this delightful little stream can be great fun and very exciting to fish. Flies: Goat's Toe, Mallard & Claret, Teal Blue & Silver, Peter Ross, Black Pennell, Clan Chief, Silver Butcher.
Permission & Charges Contact: Estate Office, Dougarie Estate, Isle of Arran KA27 8EB. Tel: 01770 840259. Charges: between £125 and £160 per rod per week depending upon the time of year. Day tickets may occasionally be available at £35 (plus VAT) per rod per day but weekly lets are preferred. The estate has a number of comfortable self-catering cottages and a lodge which may be rented with fishing.

KILMORY, Water See Loch Garbad entry.

MACHRIE, Water
Location & Access Source 69/965379 Outfall 69/892335. The river is easily accessible from public and private estate roads along its length.
Commentary This short stream rises from the south slopes of Beinn Tarsuinn (825m) and flows south-west for 7 miles to reach the sea at Machriewater Foot on the A841 road. The upper river journeys through wild, mountainous country and it is only after passing Monyquil Farm (69/938349) that it becomes fishable. The best of the sport is had in the last 4 miles where there are some 25 pools including the famous Sea Pool and Factor's Pool.
Fish Salmon and sea-trout. Fish numbers have declined in recent years but the annual catch is in the order of 60 salmon and 40 sea-trout. Salmon average 7lb in weight, sea-trout 3lb.
Flies & Tactics The river is divided into 3 beats each offering excellent fly fishing water. A part of the river is reserved for worm fishing, but spinning and the use of spinning tackle is not allowed. Spate conditions are required for the Machrie to give of its best: nae water, nae fish. A single-handed rod is appropriate and be prepared to 'stalk' your quarry, fine-and-far-off. Flies: Willie Gunn, Garry Dog, Blue Charm, Garry Dog, Green Highlander, Hairy Mary, Teal Blue & Silver, Mallard & Claret, Peter Ross, Black Pennell. These patterns will attract both salmon and sea-trout.
Permission & Charges Contact: Mrs Margo M Wilson, 10 Leysmill, by Arbroath DD11 4RR. Tel: 01241 828755. Cost: Expect to pay in the region of between £110 and £200 per rod per week, depending upon the time of year. Weekly beat (2 rods) bookings are preferred although some day tickets may be available. Accommodation is also available in conjunction with fishing lets. The Machrie Water Bailiff may be contacted on 01770 840241.

OS Map 69-70 — Ayr & Kilmarnock

PORT NA LOCHAN, Fishery
Location & Access 96/903270. The fishery lies adjacent to the A841 road at Kilpatrick near Blackwaterfoot.
Commentary A small, easily-accessible put-and-take fishery.
Fish Rainbow trout which average 1lb 8oz.
Flies & Tactics Bank fishing only and, at specified times, bait fishing is allowed. The residents are not too particular about what they will grab. Try: Black Pennell, March Brown, Peter Ross.
Permission & Charges Kinloch Hotel, Blaekwaterfoot, Isle of Arran. Tel: 01770 860444. Cost: £10.50 for a 4 hour 2 fish session. The hotel has fishing tackle for hire. For further information, contact the proprietors, Mr & Mrs C Bannatyne, Fairhaven, Catacol, Isle of Arran. Tel: 01770 830237.

PRIVATE WATERS A'MHUILLIN, Loch 69/940497; COIRE FHIONN, Loch 69/902459; NUIS, Loch 69/939380; UIRE, Loch 69/002281; NA LEIRG, Loch 59/020271; CNOC AN LOCH, Loch 69/935288.
SANNOX, Water See Loch Garbad entry.
SLIDDERY, Water See Loch Garbad entry.
TANNA, Loch See Iorsa Water entry.

Ayr and Kilmarnock

ANNICK, Water See River Irvine entry.

AYR, River
Location & Access Source 71/758286 Outfall 70/337226 The River Ayr is easily accessed from public and private, estate, roads which border its banks throughout most of its length. (See also OS Map 71).
Commentary On OS Map 70, the Ayr extends from the bridge over the river on the B743 Mauchline/Muirkirk road at 70/549269, downstream to the sea near St Nicholas Rock at Ayr Harbour. A number of important tributaries feed the Ayr, including Lugar Water (70/494253) which flows in at upstream from Old Barskimming, and the Water of Coyle (70/396215) which joins the river near Bridgend Mains on the outskirts of the town of Ayr, famous "for honest men and bonnie lassies". It is impossible to travel anywhere in this area without being reminded of its association with Scotland's bard, Robert Burns; from the Globe Tavern in Ayr where Burns seduced Anna Park, a barmaid, to Mauchline, where he set up house in an apartment overlooking the churchyard after marrying Jean Armour.
Fish Salmon and a few sea-trout. Approximately 500 fish may be taken in a good season but everything depends upon there being sufficient water. For instance, the Annbank beat, can produce up to 100 fish in the right conditions. Large numbers of brown trout have been introduced into the river, to compensate for the low numbers of salmon, and there are some fine fish to be caught, trout of up to and over 2lb in weight. Spring salmon are rare, now, and the main run of fish occurs in July, if there is rain, with the best fishing being in September and October.
Flies & Tactics The Ayr used to be impoverished by pollution from coal mines but, in recent years, with the demise of the Ayrshire coal mining industry, water quality has greatly improved and the local angling improvement association stocks the river on a regular basis from their own, well-run, hatchery. Although the river is generally of modest width, a 12ft rod is required to effectively fish many of the pools. Perhaps the most attractive of the fishing is to be found between Ballochmyle (70/523261) - sing Burns' song "The Bonnie Lass o' Ballochmyle" whilst casting - downstream to Clune (70/449248). The river here runs through a steep-sided gorge where there are some excellent pools and runs. Leaving the gorge, the Ayr meanders west in a series of loops and ox-bows past Stair (70/438235) and the East of Scotland Agricultural Collage at Auchincruive (70/387230) before sweeping down to the sea through the middle of Ayr. Most fish are taken by spinning (Devon minnows) or on bait, but fly-fishing can be just as effective and, indeed, is the only allowable method on some of the beats. Try: Ally's Shrimp, Munro Killer, Stoat's Tail, Willie Gunn, General Practitioner.
Permission & Charges For Ayr Town Water, Failford & Craige Park, contact: Alfi Coli, Game Sport of Ayr, 60 Sandgate, Ayr KA7 1BX. Tel/Fax: 01292 263822; for the Mauchline area, contact: Linwood & Johnstone, Newsagents, The Cross, Mauchline, Ayrshire. Tel: 01290 550219 (including fishing on Lugar Water); at Auchinleck, contact: J Gibson, General Store, Main Street, Auchinleck, Ayrshire. Tel: 01290 420396; Auchinleck Anglers' Association, per G McClue, 61 Coal Road, Auchinleck, Ayrshire. Tel: 01290 423491. Cost: £3 per rod per day for the Town Water and between £6 and £20 per rod per day on other beats, depending upon the time of year.

BELSTON, Loch
Location & Access 70/477169 The loch lies immediately to the south of the B7046 Drongan/Skares road at Sinclairston.
Commentary A pleasant, easily accessible, stocked fishery which drains east through Burnock Water into Lugar Water, a tributary of the River Ayr (see separate entry).
Fish Rainbow trout which average 1lb 8oz.
Flies & Tactics The loch covers an area of approximately 20 acres and both boat and bank fishing is available. Trout rise and are taken with equal facility from shore or boat and most reservoir lure patterns will produce results. On calm summer evenings dry fly fishing can also be rewarding.
Permission & Charges Contact: Alfi Coli, Game Sports of Ayr or Linwood & Johnstone (see River Ayr entry).

BURNOCK, Water See Loch Belston entry.
CARMEL, Water See River Irvine entry.
CESSNOCK, Water See River Irvine entry.

Ayr & Kilmarnock   OS Map 70

COARSE FISHERIES MARTNAHAM, Loch 70/393174; SNIPE, Loch 70/385174; FERGUS, Loch 70/392182; LINDSTON, Loch 70/372162.

COLLENNAN, Reservoir
Location & Access 70/351332 Approach from the A78 Irvine/ Loans road. Turn east at 70/342326 and follow the road up the west end of the reservoir (1/2 a mile).
Commentary A well-managed and well-policed little reservoir covering an area of approximately 8 acres.
Fish Regularly stocked with fingerling brown trout, and, on a weekly basis, with rainbow trout. Trout of up to and over 4lb are frequently taken.
Flies & Tactics Bank fishing only and the south east shore is the place to begin. Black flies seem to do best: Black Pennell, Black & Peacock Spider, Connemara Black.
Permission & Charges Contact: Torbets Outdoor Leisure, Troon, Ayrshire. Tel: 01292 317464.

COYLE, Water of
See River Ayr entry.

CROSS REFERENCES BURNFOOT Reservoir (See OS Map 64); NORTH CRAIG Reservoir (See OS Map 64).

DALVENNAN, Fishery
Location & Access 70/385106 The fishery lies on the minor road between Patna (70/418105) in the east and Kirkmichael (70/344089) in the west.
Commentary A 1 acre pond which is part of a country sports centre which includes falconry, clay pigeon shooting and archery.
Fish Regularly stocked with brown trout, rainbow trout and also grilse which 3lb 8oz average weight.
Flies & Tactics Bank fishing and most reservoir lures will produce results. Only barbless hooks may be used. Excellent facilities for visitors, including clubhouse, restaurant, tackle hire and facilities for disabled anglers.
Permission & Charges Contact: Dalvennan Country Sports Fishery, Dalvennan, by Patna, Ayrshire. Tel: 01292 531134. Full day (8 hours) £16 for 4 fish limit; half day (4 hours) £8 for 2 fish limit; catch-and-release only: £5 for 4 hours, £7.50 for 8 hours.

DOON, River
Location & Access Source 77/490990 Outfall 70/325194 The river is easily accessible throughout its entire length from public and private, estate, roads.
Commentary The 'Banks and Braes O' Bonnie Doon' are amongst the best known in the world, thanks to the poems and songs of Robert Burns. The river rises from Loch Doon (see OS Map 77, New Galloway & Glen Trool) but draws in the waters for a vast additional catchment in the "Little Highlands" if Scotland, the Galloway Hills. The river is some 23 miles in length and, after passing Alloway, the birth place of Burns and Brig O'Doon, where Tam O'Shanter almost came to grief, it flows into the sea to the south of Ayr. There are no major tributaries along its course and the river depends for its life upon heavy rainfall and compensation water from Loch Doon. It its upper reaches, the river runs through dramatic Ness Glen before entering Bogton Loch (see OS Map 77, New Galloway & Glen Trool) which is noted for the size and quantity of pike it contains. Thereafter, north from Dalmellington, the Doon flows swiftly through lovely countryside and some excellent fishing beats, the best known being Smithston, Swallow Braces and Skeldon.
Fish A wonderfully successful river in recent years, largely due to an improvement in water quality and the hard work of the River Doon Angling Improvement Association. Approximately 1,500 salmon and grilse are taken most seasons. The heaviest salmon taken in recent years was caught in 1995 by Carlos Van Heddegem of Dalrymple, a fish of 24lb. A few sea-trout also run the river. The best of the fishing is had in September and October, but, given rain, the earlier months can also be productive.
Flies & Tactics A 12ft double-handed rod is perhaps the most effective, all-purpose rod for fishing the Doon although during the summer months, and in the upper reaches, a 10ft, single-handed rod is adequate. The river is not wide and most of the lies are easily covered from the bank without the need to wade. However, in some areas, there is bankside vegetation waiting to catch the unwary, so an ability to Spey-cast is an valuable asset. Notable pools on the river, starting downstream from Patna (70/418105), include: Whisky Hole, Pump House Pool, Thorn Tree Pool, Ken's Cast, Clach Pool, Ailsa Craig, Willows, Lang Pool, Turn Wheel, Rumbler Bridge, Swallow Braes and Tidal Pool. Fly-fishing is the preferred fishing method although spinning and bait fishing is allowed on some of the beats. Flies: Garry Dog, Willie Gunn, Stoat's Tail, Ally's Shrimp, Munro Killer, Hairy Mary, Blue Charm.
Permission & Charges Upper River: Craigengillan Estate, Dalmellington, Ayrshire. Tel: 01292 550237; Craigengillan Farm, Dalmellington, Ayrshire. Tel: 01292 550366; Drumgrange & Keirs Angling Club, per B McHattie, Corserine Terrace, Dalmellington, Ayrshire. Tel: 01292 550173; Patna Angling Club: contact Mrs Sheila Campbell, Parsons Lodge, Patna, Ayrshire. Tel: 01292 531306. Smithston Fishing Club: occasional lets are available, for details, contact Gordon Dawson, Prime Salmon Fishings Limited, Red Brae, The Croft, Nether Blainslie, Galashiels TD1 2PR. Tel/fax: 01896 860307. Skeldon Estate : contact: Mrs Campbell, Skeldon Estate, Dalrymple, Ayrshire. Tel: 01292 560656. Cost: on the upper river, expect to pay in the order of between £10 and £20 per rod per day depending upon the time of year. On the prime beats, from July onwards, think in terms of between £125 and £425 per rod per week.

GLEN, Water
See River Irvine entry.

IRVINE, River
Location & Access Source 71/577355 Outfall 70/302379 Easy access from public roads bordering the river.
Commentary The river rises to the south of Darvel (71/570374) and flows west through Newmilns

OS Maps 70 — Ayr & Kilmarnock

(70/530372), Kilmarnock (70/430382) and Irvine (70/333389) to reach the sea over Irvine Bar after a journey of 26 miles. In the past, the river was heavily polluted but in recent years the water quality has improved due to the closure of coal mines, the reduction in industrial activity in the area and the hard work of the River Irvine Angling Improvement Association. There are a number of important tributaries including: Glen Water (71/569374), Cessnock Water (70/482375), Carmel Water (70/361377) and Annick Water (70/324376). The river is owned by the Crown Estate Commissioners who let the fishing rights to 7 angling clubs and two satellite angling clubs.

Fish Salmon and a few sea-trout run the river from July onwards. The most productive months are September and October. Catch statistics are almost impossible to obtain. Officially, perhaps 80/100 salmon are taken in a good year. Salmon average in the order of 7lb but the largest fish of recent years weighed 17lb 8oz. The river, and its tributaries, have been regularly stocked with brown trout from Yorkshire since 1948 and these fish offer excellent sport both with wet and dry fly.

Flies & Tactics The Irvine is very much dependent upon spate conditions to produce of its best. The most productive fishing is between Kilmarnock and Darvel and spinning (Devon minnows) is the preferred method. There is always the chance of a salmon or two, particularly after heavy rain. Flies: salmon: General Practitioner, Yellow Dog, Blue Charm, Silver Butcher, Teal Blue & Silver, Stincher Stoat's Tail. Trout: Red & Black, Murray Blue Bottle Spider, Dark Olive, Greenwell's Glory (with yellow tail).

Permission & Charges Contact: T C McCabe, 8 East Park Crescent, Kilmaurs. Tel: 01563 538652; P & R Torbet, 15 Strand Street, Kilmarnock. Tel: 01563 541734; J Steven, 25 New Road, Galston. Tel: 01563 822096. George Finlay, 19 Keith Place, New Farm, Kilmarnock, Ayrshire KA3 7NS. Tel: 01563 528084. Cost: between £8 and £20 per rod per day, depending upon the time of year.

LUGER, Water See River Ayr entry.

MOCHRUM, Loch

Location & Access 70/270092 Approach from the B7203 Pennyglen Maybole road near West Enoch. Turn south at 70/277104 along the farm road to Mochrum. Park at 70/271097 and walk down to the loch (5 minutes).

Commentary Mochrum Loch covers and area of 24 acres and it lies on the Cassillis Estate in an attractive moorland setting to the south of Mochrum Hill (270m).

Fish Stocked with brown trout and rainbow trout. Brown trout average 1lb in weight, rainbow trout 1lb 8oz.

Flies & Tactics Boats are reserved for the use of club members but bank fishing is available for visitors. Bank fishing can be just as effective as boat fishing and the north shore is the place to begin. Offer: Black Pennell, Soldier Palmer, Kingfisher Butcher.

Permission & Charges Contact: R Shannon, 12A Kennedy Drive, Dunure, by Ayr. Tel: 01292 500665. Cost: £12 per rod per day (5 fish). Evening, £8 for 3 fish.

PRESTWICK, Reservoir

Location & Access 70/395272 The reservoir lies to the east of Prestwick Airport adjacent to the B739 Raith/Monkton road.

Commentary An easily accessible, well-managed 12 acre put-and-take fishery although, at times, somewhat noise-polluted by the sound of the activities of the nearby busy airport. To the south of Prestwick Reservoir, is another little put-and-take fishery, Raith (70/387269) which also welcomes visiting anglers.

Fish Stocked on a regular basis with rainbow trout which average 1lb 4oz in weight. Trout of up to and over 4lb in weight are not uncommon.

Flies & Tactics Fish rise and are taken from all over the loch. Cast with confidence using reservoir lures or: Black Pennell, March Brown, Silver Butcher.

Permission & Charges Contact: Alfi Coli, Game Sport of Ayr (see River Ayr entry) and W & A Newall, Newsagents, 29 Main Street, Monkton, Ayrshire. Tel: 01292 479175. Further information, by letter, from: John Murphy, The Secretary, Prestwick Reservoir Angling Club, 5 Raith Terrace, Prestwick, Ayrshire.

PRIVATE WATERS WHIRR, Loch 70/516228; SWAN, Loch (Auchinleck) 70/506226; SWAN, Loch (Culzean) 70/224098; KERSE, Loch 70/425144; SPALLANDER, Loch 70/390080; SHANKSTON, Loch 70/394119; BARNSHEAN, Loch 70/380115; CROOT, Loch 70/379120; DRUMORE, Loch 70/339098; CRAIGDOW, Loch 70/262064; RED MOSS, Loch 70/269125; DRUMSHANG, Loch 70/272139; LOCHSPOUTS, Loch 70/289058; BLACKTOP HILL, Loch 70/277151.

RAITH, Fishery See Prestwick Reservoir entry.

SPRINGWATER, Fishery

Location & Access 70/371152 Springwater Fishery lies close to the B742 Coylton/Dalrymple road, just before where the old railway viaduct cross the road near Burnton.

Commentary There are 3 ponds, the largest of which has been recently extend to cover an area of 5 and 1/2 acres. 2 artificial islands are connected to the bank by bridges and there is a long promontory with casting platforms.

Fish Rainbow trout which average 1lb 8oz and also "jumbo" fish of up to 22lb.

Flies & Tactics The fishery is re-stocked on a daily basis and is open all year round (except for New Year's Day). There is a substantial club house with a log fire for cold days and snacks, coffee and tea are available as required. Tackle hire and casting instruction by prior arrangement. Most reservoir lure patterns bring results. Bank fishing only.

Permission & Charges Daniel Wilson, Springwater Fishery, Drumgabs Farm, by Dalrymple, Ayrshire. Tel: 01292 560343.

Lanark & Upper Nithsdale — OS Map 71

Lanark and Upper Nithsdale

AYR, River
Location & Access Source 71/758286 Outfall 70/337226. (See also OS Map 70). Access to the river is from the A70 Douglas/Muirkirk road and from the B743 Muirkirk/Sorn Road.
Commentary The source of the Ayr is in Glenbuck Loch (dam) and the river flows west from here to reach the sea through Ayr after a journey of 39 miles. On OS Map 71, the Ayr extends for a distance of 15 miles, from Glenbuck to Sorn (71/550270). Glenbuck Dam used to be fished by a syndicate but, in 1996, when an island appeared in the middle of the loch due to falling water levels, it passed to the Muirkirk Angling Association. In its upper, moorland, reaches, the Ayr gathers in the waters from a number of small burns and 2 significant tributaries: Carpel Water (71/682263), downstream from Muirkirk, and Greenock Water (71/629269), which flows in at Greenock Mains.
Fish Salmon, sea-trout and brown trout. Approximately 30/50 salmon and sea-trout may be taken from the upper river in a good year but it all depends upon water conditions. For a description of the more productive, downstream, beats, see OS Map 70, Ayr & Kilmarnock.
Flies & Tactics Everything depends upon good water levels and recent dry summer have not been conducive to sport with migratory fish. Brown trout fishing, is, however, always possible and some excellent fish are taken, mostly using dry fly. The river is very easy to fish and wading is not required. Most of the salmon and sea-trout that are taken using bait but fly fishing can also bring results. For trout, offer: March Brown, Greenwell's Glory, Soldier Palmer.
Permission & Charges See River Ayr, OS Map 70. Cost: between £5 and £10 per rod per day depending upon the time of year.

BLACK, Loch See River Nith entry.
CARPEL, Water See River Ayr entry.
CREOCH, Loch See River Nith entry.
CROSS REFERENCES DOUGLAS Water (See OS Map 72); LOCHYLOCH Reservoir (See OS Map 72); CLEUCH Reservoir (See OS Map 72); RIVER CLYDE (See OS Map 72); RIVER NETHAN (See OS Map 72); AVON Water (See OS Map 64); ELVAN Water (See OS Map 72); POTRAIL Water (See OS Map 72); DUNEATON Water (See OS Map 72); AFTON Water (See OS Map 77).

GLENGAVEL, Reservoir
Location & Access 71/662345 Immediately adjacent to the A723 Strathaven/Muirkirk road.
Commentary Park near the dam wall at the north end of the reservoir.
A substantial, easily accessible reservoir 3/4 of a mile long by up to 1/4 of a mile wide. Exposed and often windy.

Fish Wild brown trout which average 10oz in weight.
Flies & Tactics Bank fishing only and wading is not advised. Fluctuations in the water level make the bottom unstable and it is possible to get into difficulties. Stay safe on terra firma. The rocky south west shoreline is the most productive area. Concentrate your efforts around where the Spoutloch Burn enters (71/662342). Offer: Black Spider, Soldier Palmer, Silver Butcher.
Permission & Charges Contact Glengavel Fly-Fishing Club, per Chris Crozier, Duchess Road, Rutherglen. Tel: 0141 6477303. Cost: £10 per rod per day.

GREENOCK, Water See River Ayr entry.
KYPE, Reservoir See Logan Reservoir entry.

LOGAN, Reservoir
Location & Access 71/742360 Turn south on the A726 Kirkmuirhill/Strathaven road at Juanhill (71/750417). After 2 and a 1/2 miles, at 71/772384, turn right towards Auchrobert. This road leads to the dam wall at the east end of the reservoir. Kype Reservoir (71/737385), to the north of Logan Reservoir, is accessed directly from the A726 at Yardbent (71/740419). Turn south here and follow the road for 2 miles, past Hareshawhead, to reach the dam wall at the north end of the reservoir.
Commentary Both reservoirs lie in a moorland setting and, as such, can often be wild and windy places to fish.
Fish Logan Reservoir is stocked with brown trout which average 10oz/12oz in weight, Kype Reservoir has rainbow trout which average 1lb.
Flies & Tactics Logan Reservoir is managed by the Wellbrae Angling Club and boats are reserved for the use of members and their guests. Bank fishing, however, can be just as productive, particularly at the south end. Kype Angling Club have 1 boat on their reservoir and it is available on a first-come-first-served basis. Bank fishing is also allowed on Kype. Flies: Black Pennell, Grouse & Claret, Kingfisher Butcher.
Permission & Charges For Logan Reservoir, contact: J B Soutter & Sons & Main, 63 Almada Street, Hamilton, Lanarkshire. Tel: 01698 286131. Cost: visitor permit: £8 per rod per day. Fishing permits for Kype Reservoir are available from the bailiff at the loch at £6 per rod per day for a 3 fish limit. Further details from from Kype Angling Club, per Duncan McDougal, 34 Millburn Way, East Kilbride G75 8AB. Tel: 013552 65639.

LOWES, Loch O' Th' See River Nith entry.

NITH, River
Location & Access Source 70/539092 Outfall 84/995683. The A76 Sanquhar/Cumnock road borders the river.
Commentary The section of the River Nith shown on OS Map 71 (see also OS Maps 78 and 84) extends from House of Water (71/550120) in the west, downstream to Burnmouth (71/850050), a distance of approximately 20 miles. For a description of the river below Kirkconnel and Sanquhar, see OS Map 78,

394

OS Maps 71-72 — Upper Clyde Valley

Nithsdale and Lowther Hills. The upper reaches of the Nith, between Kirconnel and New Cumnock, including the headwaters which are shown on OS Map 70, suffer greatly from low water levels during the summer months and, even after a spate, the extensive commercial afforestation of recent years means that the river drops far more rapidly than in pre-forestry days. However, there are a number of pools and glides, all of which can give sport and the river is easily accessible throughout its entire length. The New Cumnock Anglers Association have trout fishing on Creoch Loch (71597151), to the north of New Cumnock, which they stock. Loch o' the Lowes (71/603146) is private.

Fish For a full description of Nith salmon and sea-trout, see the other OS Maps noted above. Serious sea-trout and salmon fishing does not really begin until downstream from Sanquhar. The upper reaches of the river, from Marchbank (71/672131) to the source, are controlled by the New Cumnock & District Angling Association and they have, in the interests of conservation of migratory fish stocks, imposed a complete ban on salmon and sea-trout fishing in their water. However, the upper river contains brown trout which give a good account of themselves and they average in the order of 8oz. There are also excellent grayling in the river. Loch Creoch has rainbow trout which average 1lb in weight. .

Flies & Tactics Very much a question of being in the right place at the right time, that is after heavy rain. Nevertheless, local experts do well with dry fly, particularly on warm summer evenings. Try: Greenwell's Glory, March Brown, Partridge & Yellow, Snipe & Purple and well as Black Pennell, Grouse & Claret and Peter Ross. Bait fishing or spinning also allowed.

Permission & Charges T Basford, Burnbrae Cottage, 1 Pathhead, New Cumnock. Tel: 01290 332654. or the Tackle Shop, New Cumnock. Cost: if you are in the area for a few days, buy a season permit for £10. Otherwise, a day ticket costs £6. Loch Creoch costs £3 per rod per day bank fishing, plus an additional £5 for the use of a boat. There is a 3 fish per rod bag limit.

PRIVATE WATERS BOGHEAD Reservoir 71/765409; DUNSIDE Reservoir 71/747374.

Upper Clyde Valley

BIGGAR, Water See River Tweed entry.

CLYDE, River
Location & Access Source 78/023168 Outfall 64/450733. Easily accessible from both major and minor roads that margin the banks of almost the entire river. See also OS Map.
Commentary The River Clyde extends for a distance of more than 20 miles on OS Map 72 and this section contains the best of the fishing, from Crawford (72/967200) in the south downstream to Brownlee House (72/800513) near Hamilton. The upper reaches of the river, which are shown on OS Map 78, Nithsdale and Lowther Hills, also give good sport and take in water from Daer Reservoir (See OS Map 78, Nithsdale and Lowther Hills) as well as the flow from Potrail Water and Elvan Water which meet the Clyde near Elvanfoot (78/955715). Although overlooked for much of its length by busy roads, the Clyde, particularly in its upper reaches, maintains the characteristics of a fine moorland stream and it is a delight to fish. Where the river wanders away from public roads, between Lamington (72/975315) and The Meeting (72/974443), where Medwin Water flows in, the Clyde is even nicer and offers the peace and solitude that anglers prize. The Clyde has a number of significant tributaries, including: River Nethan (72/825472), Mouse Water (72/867440) which flows in at Lanark, Douglas Water (72/896395) entering just upstream from Bonnington Linn, Duneaton Water (72/935260), Glengonnar Water (72/931223) and Midlock Water (72/959212) which joins the Clyde at Crawford. (The Forth & District Angling Club have fishing on Mouse Water for trout and grayling. Contact: I Morrison, 121 Cloglands, Forth. Tel: 01555 812338)

Fish Salmon, sea-trout, brown trout and grayling. Migratory fish have returned to the Clyde in recent years as water quality in the lower river and in the Clyde estuary has improved. Salmon run the Clyde from about June onwards, the main run being in September. Sea-trout also arrive in June. Approximately 80/100 fish may be recorded in a season, most of which are returned to spawn and thus increase overall stocks. Their average weight is in the order of 7lb. Sea-trout of up to 4lb have been caught. Brown trout are plentiful and average 1lb but there are good numbers of larger fish as well: trout of up to and over 3lb in weight are taken most seasons. Grayling are numerous and average 10oz.

Flies & Tactics All legal methods are allowed on the river and its tributaries but there is an increasing preference for fly fishing. The Clyde has always been noted for the quality of its indigenous trout and dry fly fishing on the Clyde is a highly refined art. Wading is often required and those doing so should take great care, particularly in the lower, more slow moving parts of the river. The Clyde suffers from bank erosion in places and this can make wading dangerous. In the upper river, and on the tributaries, however, there are miles of wonderful fly fishing on smooth, deep pools and delightful runs. Most anglers spin for salmon using Devon minnows, but standard pattern salmon flies, such as Garry Dog, Willie Gunn and Hairy Mary also bring results. For trout, offer: Partridge & Orange, Partridge & Yellow, Medium Olive, Greenwell's Glory, Black Spider, March Brown, Invicta or traditional Clyde flies.

Permission & Charges The United Clyde Angling Protective Association hold a lease from the Crown Estate Commissioners in respect of the rights to fish for salmon and sea-trout in the Clyde upstream of Bothwell Bridge to Stonebyries Falls in the lower reaches. The Association manage the River Clyde in 3

Upper Clyde Valley OS Map 72

areas: The Upper Reaches: Dear Water, River Clyde and its feeder burns, downstream to Roberton Village; The Middle Reaches: From Thankerton Bridge to Easter Sills Farm, upstream from Hyndford Bridge; The Lower Reaches: From Kirkfieldbank, downstream to Bothwell Bridge. Reserved areas are noted on the permit. The 'Salmon Permit' covers the stretch of water between Motherwell Bridge and Stonybyres Power Station. Lamington Angling Association and Hozier Angling Club issue their own permits for water under their control. Further information is available from the Secretary of the Association, J Quigley, 39 Hillfoot Avenue, Branchalwood, Wishaw ML2 8TR. Tel: 01698 382479. Day tickets for the Association water are readily available. Contact: Post Offices at: Leadhills, Abington, Crawford, Motherwell (Civic Square); Tourist Information Offices at: Motorway Service, Albington; Biggar; Lanark and then from the following River Wardens: David Blacklock, 9 Bridge End Road, Wandel, Abington; Jim Fullarton, 40 Bankhead Terrace, Lanark; John Gauld, 109 Strawfrank Road, Carstairs Junction; George Jack, 16 Forrest Place, Crossford; Ian & Neil Miller, 15 Coronation Street, Crawford; Clive Shotton, 55 Sommerville Drive, Carnwath; Robert Ritchie, 33 Mian Street, Leadhills. Cost: Annaul permit (adult) £21 (Juvenile) £6; Annual (Senior Citizen) £6; Day Permit (trout) £5. Season, salmon and sea-trout, £25.

CROSS REFERENCE ENTRIES LYNE Water (See OS Map 73); MEGGET Water (See OS Map 73); BADDINSGILL Reservoir (See OS Map 65); WEST WATER Reservoir (See OS Map 65); NORTH ESK Reservoir (See OS Map 65); CROSSWOOD Reservoir (See OS Map 65); COBBINSHAW Reservoir (See OS Map 65)
DOUGLAS, Water See River Clyde entry.
DUNEATON, Water See River Clyde entry.
FRUID, Reservoir See Talla Reservoir entry.
GLENGONNAR, Water See River Clyde entry.
HOLMS, Water See River Tweed entry.
MEDWIN, Water See River Clyde entry.
MIDLOCK, Water See River Clyde entry.
MOUSE, Water See River Clyde entry.
NETHAN, River See River Clyde entry.

NEWHOUSE PARK, Fishery
Location & Access 72/925453 The fishery is at Ravenstruther, close to the junction of the A70 Uddington/Carstairs and the A743 Lanark/Carstairs roads.
Commentary A put-and-take trout fishery and caravan park in an attractive setting.
Fish Stocked with brown trout and rainbow trout which average 1lb. Trout of up to 7lb are also taken.
Flies & Tactics The fishery covers an are of 2 acres and is restricted to boat fishing only for 4 anglers per session. Tackle hire available. Most reservoir-type lures produce results.
Permission & Charges Contact: Newhouse Park Trout Fishery, Ravenstruther, by Lanark. Tel: 01555 870228. Cost: Full day (8 hours), £18 per rod for a 3 fish limit; half day (4 hours), £12 per rod for a 2 fish limit.

NEWMILL DEER FARM, Fishery
Location & Access 72/915454 Approach from the A706 Lanark/Forth road 2 and 1/2 miles east from the centre of Lanark. Turn right at 72/915464, just past the site of the Roman Camp.
Commentary A stocked fishery combing fishing on a small loch, a pond and on the River Mouse (see River Clyde entry), a tributary of the River Clyde. There is a smoke-house, cafe and shop and tackle is available for sale and for hire.
Fish Regularly stocked with rainbow trout which average 1lb 12oz in weight. From time to time, grilse may also be stocked.
Flies & Tactics There are 32 boats which are used on a first-come-first-served basis. Bank fishing is also allowed. On the River Mouse rainbow trout now outnumber brown trout by a ratio of 5 to 1. Most flies and lures work, but the Scots Dancer, devised at Newmill and similar in style to the Ace of Spades, is the favoured pattern.
Permission & Charges Contact David Buchanan, Newhouse Trout & Deer Farm, Cleghorn, by Lanark. Tel: 01555 870730. Cost: £16 per rod per day for a 6 fish limit, £11.30 per rod per day for a 4 hour, 3 fish, limit.

PRIVATE WATERS REDMIRE, Loch 72/859566; WHITE, Loch 72/962471; RED, Loch 72/957475; COULTER WATERHEAD Reservoir 72/040724; COWHILL UPPER Reservoir 72/010280; COWHILL LOWER Reservoir 72/009291; LYOCH Reservoir 72/933357; CLEUCH Reservoir 72/938353; CAMPS Reservoir 72/010225 (in the process of being let to a private angling club); SPRINGFIELD Reservoir 72/905520 (at present, not fished).

TALLA, Reservoir
Location & Access 72/120214 Leave the A701 Broughton/Moffat road at Tweedsmuir (72/097245) and follow the minor road signposted to St Mary's Loch (See OS Map 73 Galashiles and Ettrick Forest). Talla Reservoir dam wall is reached after 1 mile.
Commentary Talla Reservoir is 2 and 1/2 miles long by up to 1/4 of a mile wide and lies on the headwaters of Talla Water, a tributary of Tweed (see separate entry). The reservoir covers an area of 300 acres it is enfolded on either side by steep, green hills, Mathieside (690m) to the east, Garelet Hill (680m) to the west. Close by, and also approached from Tweedsmuir, is Fruid Reservoir which is similar in size and surroundings. Fruid is drained into Tweed by Fruid Water.
Fish Brown trout which average 8oz/10oz in weight.
Flies & Tactics Boat and bank fishing on Talla, bank fishing only on Fruid. Bank fishing on Talla is restricted to the east side of the reservoir and access is from the convenient road which margins the whole length of the loch. The south end is the most productive fishing area, particularly where Talla Water flows in at Talla Linnfoots (72/135205). Fish rise and may be taken from all round Fruid's shore. Flies: Soldier Palmer, March Brown, Alexandra.
Permission & Charges Contact: Crook Inn,

OS Maps 72-73 — Galashiels & Ettrick

Tweedsmuir, Broughton. by Biggar. Tel: 01899 880272. Cost: bank fishing, £6 per rod per day, boat hire, £12 per boat (2 rods fishing).

TWEED, River
Location & Access Source: 78/053146 Outfall: 75/000523. The river is accessible from the B712 Drumelzier/Peebles road and the A710 Broughton/Moffat road.
Commentary Some 17 miles of the Upper Tweed are shown on OS Map 72 (see also OS Maps 73 and 74) from near Glenbreck (72/050200) downstream to Stobo (72/200399). The most important of the Tweed's tributaries here are: Biggar Water, and its own tributary Holms Water, which join Tweed at 72/133353, Talla Water (72/102247) and Fruid Water (72/086232). Both of these later named waters have been impounded by reservoirs (see separate entries) and this has constrained the flow of the main river to a very considerable extent; as has the extensive commercial afforestation that has taken place in Tweed's headwaters during recent years. The final few miles of Tweed, shown on OS Map 78, Nithsdale and Lowther Hills, are of little fishing significance, but those who love and admire Tweed should, at some time during their fishing career, pay their respects to the source of their pleasure at Tweed's Wells.

In many ways, the Upper Tweed is more attractive than the lower river. The growing stream bustles through perfect countryside surrounded by wild hills and moorland bordered by red-berried rowan and yellow gorse; hesitating for a moment in fine pools, dashing through narrow gorges and long glides, all of which are a fly-fishers delight.
Fish Salmon and sea-trout, mostly taken during September, October and November. Approximately 35/45 are caught most seasons but it all depends upon water levels. Some of these fish are red and ready for spawning but even here fresh fish are still encountered. Brown trout are relatively abundant although in recent years their numbers have declined. Trout average 8oz in weight, but there are fish of up to and over 2lb in weight as well.
Flies & Tactics A single handed rod will adequately deal with most angling eventualities and it is rarely necessary to wade. Indeed, you would be well-advised to keep back from the bank to avoid "spooking" the fish, trout or their larger cousins. Dry fly fishing, particularly during May and June, can be very rewarding. The best chance of sport, however, is after a spate when you will find miles of river that provide some of the most pleasant fishing in the borders. At the back end, if you should encounter red salmon or sea-trout, return them careful to fight another day. For salmon and sea-trout try small, size 8/10 patterns such as Munro Killer, Garry Dog, Hairy Mary, Willie Gunn. For trout offer: Partridge & Yellow, Iron Blue Dun, March Brown, Greenwell's Glory, Snipe & Purple, Silver Butcher.
Permission & Charges The primary source of trout fishing on Tweed in Peeblesshire, whether above or below Stobo, is on water controlled by the Peeblesshire Trout Fishing Association. Although most of the Association Water is below Stobo, the Association still have approx. 5 miles of fishing on Tweed above Dawyck Estate. Fishing on the Association Water can be booked through Tweedale Tackle Centre, Bridgate, Peebles. Tel: 01721 720979. Cost: approx. £8 per day for trout fishing. Stobo & adjacent waters; contact: Derek Hathaway, Horseshoe Inn. Eddleston, by Peebles. Tel: 01721 730225 or 01721 730306. Horseshoe Inn have 9, two rod, rotating salmon beats. Rods change at noon each day. Salmon fishing costs £35 per rod per day. Weekly lets vary from between £80 per rod and £110 per rod. Trout fishing costs in the order of £8 per rod per day. Horseshoe Inn residents have priority, but day lets are generally available throughout the season. At Tweedsmuir, contact: Mr Ferguson, Crook Inn, Tweedsmuir, Broughton, by Biggar. Tel: 01899 880272 and Tweedale Tackle Centre, Bridgegate, Peebles. Tel: 01721 720979. Cost: expect to pay in the order of £8 per rod per day for trout fishing and £30 per rod per day for salmon fishing. There are some parts of the river which are private. For further information, contact: D.G. Fyfe, Blackwood & Smith, 39 High Street, Peebles. Tel: 01721 720131.

Galashiels and Ettrick

CADDON, Water See River Tweed entry.
CROSS REFERENCES GLADHOUSE Reservoir (See OS Map 66); RIVER NORTH ESK (Lothian) (See OS Map 66); PORTMORE Loch (See OS Map 66); ROSEBERY Reservoir (See OS Map 66); EDGELAW Reservoir (See OS Map 66); FALA FLOW Loch (See OS Map 66); ACKERMOOR Loch (See OS Map 79); ALE Water (See OS Map 74); RIVER TEVIOT (See OS Map 74)
EDDLESTON, Water See River Tweed entry.
ETTRICK, Water See River Tweed entry.
GALA, Water See River Tweed entry.

HEADSHAW, Loch
Location & Access 73/460237 Approach from the A7 Selkirk/Hawick road near Ashkirk (73/474227) via the minor road that leads to Headshaw Farm. The loch lies to the north of the farm.
Commentary An attractive 17 acres loch in a moorland setting on the slopes of Stobshaw Hill (296m). Headshaw is fed by the Loch Sike burn and drains south into Ale Water, a tributary of the River Teviot (see OS Map 74).
Fish Regularly stocked with brown trout and rainbow trout which average 2.5lb in weight. The loch is open for fishing from 1st March to 28th November.
Flies & Tactics Boat and bank fishing and most reservoir patterns produce results. There are good lochside facilities for anglers, including free tea and coffee and a lodge with a cooker.
Permission & Charges Contact: D Beattie, Manager, Headshaw Loch, Ashkirk, by Selkirk. Tel: 01450

Galashiels & Ettrick   OS Map 73

376809; Mobile: 0374 287762 or Mrs Hunter at Farmhouse 01750 32233. Cost: Boat fishing: £14 per boat (2 rods); Bank fishing, £12. Fishing is from 9am until dusk and there is a limit of 3 rainbow trout and 1 brown trout per rod. Thereafter, catch-and-release using barbless hooks.

LEADER, Water See River Tweed entry.
LEITHEN, Water See River Tweed entry.

LINDEAN, Reservoir
Location & Access 73/501291 Turn south east from the A7 Galashiels/Selkirk road at 73/481309. Follow the minor road to Linden Moor (1 and 1/2 miles). The reservoir is to the right of the road.
Commentary This pleasantly situated reservoir is managed as a fishery by the Selkirk & District Angling Association and it covers an area of 35 acres.
Fish Stocked with brown trout and rainbow trout which average 1lb in weight. Fishing is open from 1st April until 15th October.
Flies & Tactics Boat fishing only and trout are taken from all over, from the margins to the middle. Offer: Soldier Palmer, Grouse & Claret, Silver Butcher.
Permission & Charges Contact: P & E Scott, High Street, Selkirk. Tel: 01750 20749. Cost: £14 per boat per day (3 rods). There is a boat limit of 12 fish. Further information from: Mr A Wilson, Secretary, Selkirk & District Angling Association, 2 Hillview Crescent, Selkirk. Tel: 01750 20907.

LOWES, Loch of the (Yarrow) See St Mary's Loch entry.
LYNE, Water See River Tweed entry.
MANOR, Water See River Tweed entry.

MEGGET, Reservoir
Location & Access 73/215230 Turn west from the A708 Selkirk/Moffat road at Cappercleuch (73/240231) by St Mary's Loch (see separate entry). After 1 mile, you will see Megget reservoir is on your left.
Commentary Megget is the most recently constructed of the border reservoirs and it is not shown on the Landranger Series of OS Maps. The reservoir is 2 and 1/2 miles long by up to 1/2 mile wide and it covers an area of approximately 640 acres. It is drained by Megget Water into St Mary's Loch at Cappercleuch. This is a bleak, featureless water, often wind-swept and wild.
Fish brown trout which average 10oz in weight.
Flies & Tactics Boat and bank fishing. The fishing hut and boat mooring point is at the west end of the reservoir. Bank fishing is restricted to the north shore only. The reservoir is very deep, dropping to 180ft, and you best chance of a fish is close to the shore. Try: Invicta, Grouse & Claret, Silver Butcher.
Permission & Charges Contact: Tibbie Sheil's Inn (See St Mary's Loch entry). Cost: bank fishing £6 per rod per day, boat hire, £20 per boat (3 rods fishing).

MEGGET, Water See St Mary's Loch entry.
PRIVATE WATERS EDDY, Loch 73/281309;

CAULDSHIELS, Loch 73/513323; ESSENSIDE, Loch 73/451207
QUAIR, Water See River Tweed entry.

ST MARY'S, Loch
Location & Access 73/250230 The loch lies immediately adjacent to the A708 Selkirk/Moffat road.
Commentary St Mary's loch lies on the headwaters of Yarrow Water (see separate entry), a tributary of Ettrick Water, and the loch is 3 miles long by up to 1/2 a mile wide. A narrow causeway separate St Mary's Loch from its sister water to the south, Loch of the Lowes, and Tibbie Sheil's Inn, one of Scotland's best known hotels overlooks them both. Tibbie Sheil, who died in 1878 at the age of 96, met most of Scotland's literati during her long life when they came to St Mary's to fish; Sir Walter Scott, James Hogg, Thomas Tod Stoddart, John Lockhart and John Wilson (Christopher North). The loch is as popular today with both anglers and visitors who come to admire St Mary's beauty and enjoy the simple pleasures of Tibbie Sheil's famous inn.
Fish Brown trout, pike and perch.. St Mary's trout average 8oz, but there are larger fish as well, Loch of the Lowes trout are bigger and average in the order of 1lb.
Flies & Tactics Boat and bank fishing on St Mary's, bank fishing only on Loch of the Lowes. On St Mary's, try Cappercleuch Bay (73/244230) and where Megget Water flows in (73/242225). On Loch of the Lowes, fish the roadside bank. You may use your own outboard motor, provided that it is not more than 5hp. Fishing is from 9am until 1 hour after sunset and a special boat seat for disabled anglers is available on prior booking through the Keeper (see below). Flies: Blue Zulu, Black Spider, Kingfisher Butcher. Bait fishing is also allowed, but only after 1st May.
Permission & Charges Contact: Henry Brown, The Keeper, Henderland East Cottage, Cappercleuch, St Mary's, Yarrow, Selkirk. for permits and only he can rent our boats (01750 42243). Or from: Tibbie Sheil's Inn, Yarrows, by Selkirk. Tel: 01750 42231. Boats may be hired from: The Keeper, Henderland East Cottage, Cappercleuch, St Mary's, Yarrow, Selkirk. Tel: 01750 42243. Cost: Fly fishing: £5 per rod per day; bait fishing £8 per rod per day; boat hire, £20 (3 persons) per boat per day.

STANTLING CRAIG, Reservoir See River Tweed entry.

TRIPONDIUM, Fishery
Location & Access 73/586303 Tripondium fishery immediately to the west of the A68 Edinburgh/Jedburgh road, 1/2 a mile south from St Boswells.
Commentary A small put-and-take fishery at Mainhill Farm on the line of the disused railway. The new owners are making improvements to the fishery, including making wheelchair access to most parts of the fishery.
Fish Stocked with good quality triploid rainbow and brown trout. Some large fish double-figure trout were caught in 1997.

OS Map 73 — Galashiels & Ettrick

Flies & Tactics Bank fishing only. All day ticket: £12 (2 fish kill, up to 3lb each); half day ticket (10am to dusk): £8 (1 fish kill). Catch and release is permitted. Most patterns of reservoir lure will produce results.

Permission & Charges Contact: Mark Fouracres, Mainhill, St Boswells, Selkirkshire. Tel: 01835 823628. Cost: £10 per day, catch and release only.

TWEED, River

Location & Access Source: 78/053146. Outfall: 75/000523. OS Map 73 shows 28 miles of Tweed (see also OS Maps 72 and 74), from where Lyne Water enters (73/210400), downstream to Dryburgh (73/600321). The river is easily accessible throughout its entire length from public roads which margin both banks.

Commentary This is a very lovely part of the river, particularly in its upper reaches between Innerleithen (73/335365) and Lyne Water. A number of important tributaries feed Tweed here: Leader Water (73/578346), by the dramatic, disused, redstone railway viaduct at Leaderfoot, Ettrick Water and its tributary, Yarrow Water (73/489323) at Sunderland Hall, Caddon Water (73/449349) which drains Stantling Craig Reservoir (73/431394), Leithen Water (73/337362) and Quair Water (73/332357) near Innerleithen, Eddleston Water (73/249404) in Peebles, Manor Water (73/230396) upstream from the gaunt ruins of Neidpath Castle (73/237404) and, finally, Lyne Water. As salmon fisheries, only Ettrick Water is of any real consequence, producing approximately 80 fish in a good year, depending upon water levels, but most of them give sport with brown trout, particularly Lyne Water. However, they all suffer dreadfully in drought conditions and intensive agriculture and commercial afforestation aggravates the situation. Nevertheless, they are very pretty little waters and, after a heavy spate, will produce fish, even the occasional salmon or sea-trout. They should be fished using light tackle, stalking the pools and runs from the bank. The best of the sport is generally found in their lower reaches as they hurry towards Tweed. There is also plenty here to keep non-fishing companions amused and happy: Melrose and Dryburgh Abbeys, the Eildon Hills and Sir Walter Scott's home at Abbotsford and Traquair House, the oldest inhabited house in Scotland with its famous Bear Gates; closed after Prince Charles Edward Stewart left Traquair in 1745 and never to be reopened until a Stewart king reigns in Scotland. The principal salmon fishing beats on Tweed here include: Lyne, Hay Lodge & Park, Kailzie, Horsburgh Castle, King's Meadows, Cadrona, Glenmoriston, Traquair, Caberston, Holylee, Eilbank, Thornilee, Ashiesteel, Peel, Caddonlee, Yair, Fainrilee, Sunderland, Boleside, Drygrange, Ravenswood, Bemersyde and Dryburgh. The lower beats, downstream from Innerleithen, are the most productive and the river at Melrose and Dryburgh is extraordinarily lovely: guarded by mature, deciduous woodlands which are flame with colour during the autumn months. Anglers who visit this area should make a pilgrimage to the Tweed Valley Hotel to pay their respects to Cannon William Greenwell who devised the Greenwell's Glory, one of our most outstanding trout flies. The hotel has a fine portrait of the great man, displayed in splendour in the conservatory overlooking his beloved river.

Fish For a description of salmon and sea-trout numbers and runs, see OS Map 74, Kelso. In recent years, with the decline of the spring run, salmon rarely arrive in any number in this section of Tweed until after August. The prime months are October and November. Bemersyde returns 60/70 salmon in October. Fairnilee can produce 40/50 fish in November. Traquair, above Innerleithen, can produce 30/40 November fish. However, the beats upstream from Innerleithen offer good trout fishing although in recent years there has been a serious and worrying decline in trout numbers; on the New Water, Red Yetts, Cadrona, King's Meadows, Neidpath, Manor and Lyne. The average weight of trout is in the order of 8oz, but fine fish of up to and over 3lb are frequently taken, mostly by local anglers fishing dry fly during April, May and June.

Flies & Tactics The Lower Beats require the use of a 15ft double-handed rod and, in many cases, a well-developed Spey-casting skill. Wading is often required and it can be difficult: take along the "third leg" a wading staff provides and wear a life-jacket. Some pools are fished from the boat, others from the shore. Boats are also used to cross the river in order to reach appropriate casting positions. In inclement weather, you will find comfortable fishing huts and the beats generally employ the services of a gillie/boatman who will show you the water if you are new to the river. The are some very attractive pools throughout this part of the river. On Holylee Water: Burnfoot Pool and the Boat Pool. On Peel & Caddonlee: The Rampy. The Policemen and Caddonfoot Pool. On Fairnilee & Sunderland Hall: Bogie Stream, Cauld Pool, Yair Gullet, Russell's Rock, Arpes Putt, Black Strand and the Doocotes. On Traquair: Boat Pool, New Water, Long Stream and Jawstane Pool.

For the trout angler, there is easy access to excellent fishing at 73/314370. The pool at the end of the wood on the opposite bank holds some large trout. Further upstream, park near the old bridge over Manor Water (73/231394). Start below the new bridge over Tweed and work downstream to where the river swings right-handed through a deep, gravely pool. This pool invariably produces fish. At Lyne, start at the footbridge on the north bank and work downstream. Flies: for salmon: Willie Gunn, Garry Dog, Munro Killer, General Practitioner, Black Doctor, Ally's Shrimp, Waddingtons. For trout try: Ke-He, Greenwell's Glory, Partridge & Yellow, Silver Butcher.

Permission & Charges For fishing on Tweed at St Boswells contact: The Factor, Mertoun Estate, St Boswells. Tel: 01835 823236; Euan McCorquodale, Crossflat Farm, St Boswells. Tel: 01896 823700. For Bemersyde & Gledswood: J H Leeming, ARICS, Stichill House, Kelso, Roxburghshire TD5 7TB. Tel; 01573 470280; Fax: 01573 470259. J H Leeming also lets Glenmoriston, Traquair, Peel Water, Fairnilee, Boleside, Netherbarns and Ravenswood and a number of top-class beats on in the Kelso area (see entry on OS Map 74, Kelso). At Melrose and Galashiels, contact: Ted Hunter, Anglers' Choice, 23 Market Square, Melrose. Tel/Fax: 01896 823070. Sunderland Hall Beat: R Smyly, Sunderland Hall, Galashiels. Tel: 01750 21298. Yair: W Thyne, Yair, Selkirk. Tel: 01750 21298. Tweed Valley Hotel, Walkerburn, nr Peebles EH43 6AA. Tel: 01896 870636; Fax: 01896 870639; (e-mail: 101325.2515@compuserve.com). The hotel has access to a number of beats as well as excellent trout fishing Stantling Craig Reservoir. They also run salmon and trout fishing courses for both beginner and expert alike. Innerleithen: Traquair Arms Hotel, Innerleithen EH44 6PD. Tel: 01896 830229; Fax: 01896 830260. At Peebles, contact: A W Dickson, Peebles Angling School, 10 Dean Park, Pebbles. Tel: 01721 720331 (Andy Dickson runs fishing courses including casting instruction). Tweedale Tackle Centre, 1 Bridgegate, Peebles. Tel: 01721 720979; Peebles Town Water: Tweedale District Council, Direct Services Organisation, Dovecot Depot, Peebles. Tel: 01721 723354. For up-to-date information on Tweed, use the Tweed Hot Line: Fishing Reports: 0891 666 410; River Heights: 0891 666 411; Vacancies: 0891 666412. Cost: the further downstream you go, the more expensive and difficult it becomes to obtain fishing. Peebles Town Water will cost in the order of £5 per rod per day. Elsewhere, expect to pay between £25 and £250 per rod per day depending upon when and where you wish to fish. Trout fishing will cost between £3 and £8 per rod per day. Fishing on Ettrick Water and Yarrow Water is available from: The Factor, Buccleuch Estates, Estate Office, Bowhill, Selkirk. Tel: 01750 20753. There are 30 named pools along 13 miles of double bank fishing and rods cost £20 per rod per day in the spring, rising to £40 per day in the autumn months. Also, Ettrickshaws Hotel, Ettrickbridge, Selkirk. Tel: 01750 52229 (free to hotel guests). Selkirk & District Angling Association issue 4 visitor permits daily for the Ettrick at £22 per rod per day. Contact: P & E Scott, Newsagents, 2 High Street, Selkirk. Tel: 01750 20749. Access to the tributaries is as follows: Gala Water: Galashiels Angling Association per J & A Turnbull, 30 Bank Street, Galashiels. Tel: 01896 753191; Anglers' Choice (see above); Kingsknowe Hotel, Galashiels. Tel: 01896 758375. Leader Water: Lauderdale Angling Association per Anglers

UPPER BOWHILL, Loch

Location & Access 73/428277 Approach from the A708 Selkirk/Yarrow road. The loch lies within the polices of Bowhill House, between the Etrrick Water and Yarrow Water (see separate entries).
Commentary A very attractive, sheltered, little water covering an area of approximately 10 acres and surrounded by mature woodlands.
Fish Stocked with brown trout and rainbow trout which average 1lb in weight.
Flies & Tactics Boat fishing only and trout rise and are taken from all over the loch. Offer: Black Pennell, Greenwell's Glory, Kingfisher Butcher.
Permission & Charges The Factor, Buccleuch Estates, Estate Office, Bowhill, Selkirk. Tel: 01750 20753.

Cost: £40 per boat per day (2 rods fishing) with a 4 fish per rod limit. Advance booking is advisable.

YAIR, Water See River Tweed entry.
YARROW, Water See River Tweed entry.

Kelso

ALE, Water See River Teviot entry.
BOWMONT, Water See River Tweed entry.
CROSS REFERENCES WHITEADDER Water (See OS Map 67); BLACKADDER Water (See OS Map 67); HEN POO Loch (See OS Map 67); WATCH WATER Reservoir (See OS Map 67); LEADER Water (See OS Map 73).
EDEN, Water See River Tweed entry.
JED, Water See River Teviot entry.
KALE, Water See River Teviot entry.
LEET, Water See River Tweed entry.
PRIVATE WATERS HIRSEL, Lake 74/815402; HULE MOSS, Loch 74/714491; YETHOLM, Loch 74/803280; HOSELAW, Loch 74/809319.

TEVIOT, River (See also OS Map 79, Hawick & Eskdale)

Location & Access The River Teviot, as shown on OS Map 74, Kelso begins at Menslaws (74/585200) in the south west and flows north east by Ancrum (74/631245) and Roxburgh (74/702302) to join the River Tweed (see separate entry) in the famous Junction Pool at Kelso (74/726339). The river is easily accessible from the A698 Hawick/Kelso road on the east bank and by minor roads which parallel the west bank.
Commentary The river flows through rich, fertile, agricultural land, margined in many places by mature, deciduous woodlands. Two kings of Scotland died near here: James 11, killed by an exploding canon during the siege of Roxburgh Castle in 1460 and, on Flodden Field in 1513, his grandson, James 1V. The area is redolent with memories of Scotland's long wars with its powerful neighbour, England.
Fish Salmon, sea-trout, brown trout and grayling. Few salmon are caught before June but there are encouraging signs that the spring run is improving. Approximately 700 salmon may be taken during the season and their average weight is 9lb. Depending upon water conditions, sea-trout fishing is at its best in July and August. There are some excellent brown trout, fish of up to and over 3lb in weight. April, May and June provide the best chance for a meeting with them.
Flies & Tactics The most productive Teviot salmon fishing is in this, lower, section of the river and, although more modest in size than its illustrious patron, Tweed, a 12ft/14ft rod is the most convenient means of covering the lies. In the summer months, however, a single-handed rod is more than adequate and the river is very dependent upon good water levels to produce of its best. Three important tributaries

OS Map 74 — Kelso

join the Teviot between Menslaws and its meeting with Tweed: Ale Water (74/630235), Jed Water (74/660244) and Kale Water (74/709275). These tributaries are important spawning habitats for migratory fish and a considerable amount of work has been, and is being, undertaken to improve and sustain their quality. Notable pools on the lower river include: Foghouse Nick, Castle Pool, Kay Braes, Cottage Pool and Teviot Bridge. For salmon, offer: Willie Gunn, Garry Dog, Silver Wilkinson, Black Doctor, General Practitioner, Ally's Shrimp, Waddingtons in various hues. Sea-trout will respond to: Black Pennell, Mallard & Claret, Peter Ross. For brown trout, try: Soldier Palmer, Partridge & Yellow, Silver March Brown. There is some delightful dry fly: Iron Blue Dun, Greenwell's Glory, Snipe & Purple. Spinning is allowed on some beats but fly fishing is the preferred technique.

Permission & Charges Contact: Roxburghe Estates, Estate Office, Kelso, Roxburghshire TD5 7SF. Tel: 01573 223333; Fax: 01573 226056. (Sunlaws House Hotel, Tel: 01573 450331, have rainbow trout fishing available on a stocked lake. W Wright, Teinside Lodge, Hawick. Tel: 01450 850252. A H Graham, Lochkeeper, Eckford, by Kelso. Tel: 01835 850255. Lothian Estates, Estate Office, Jedburgh. Tel: 01835 862201 (excellent self-catering cottages are available with the fishing). Jedforest Angling Association Waters: The Country Sports Shop, 6-8 Canongate, Jedburgh. Tel: 01835 863019. Further details about the Jedforest Angling Association are available from the Secretary: Jim Tait, 9 Boundaries, Jedburgh. Tel: 01835 863871. Tweedside Tackle, 36-38 Bridge Street, Kelso. Tel: 01573 225306. Forrest & Sons, 35 The Square, Kelso. Tel: 01573 224687. Kelso Angling Association, per Euan Robson, Secretary, 33 Tweedsyde Park. Kelso. Tel: 01573 225279. For salmon fishing, expect to pay between £15 and £100 per rod per day depending upon where and when you fish. Trout fishing will cost approximately £8 per rod per day.

TILL, River See River Tweed entry.

TWEED, River
Location & Access Source: 78/053146. Outfall: 75/000523. Tweed is easily accessible from public and private roads which margin both banks of the river throughout almost its entire length. (See also OS Maps 72 and 73).

Commentary The river is born at Tweed's Well on the west shoulder of Foal Burn Head (509m) close to the source of two other great Scottish rivers, the Clyde and the Annan. Tweed flows north and north east to reach Drumelzier before swinging east to begin its long journey to the sea at Berwick. The river is 100 miles in length and the character of the stream changes constantly, from moorland burn in the upper reaches to a mighty river downstream from Kelso. The lower part of the Tweed shown on OS Map 74 is in England. Thereafter, from Gainslaw (74/948520), upstream to near Carham (74/790379), the centre of the river forms the boundary between Scotland and England. Tweed is affectionately known as "the Queen of Scottish rivers" and is one of the most famous river in the world; not only because of its beauty but also because of the place it has played in Scottish history: constant disputes, border raids and battles, hundreds of years of strife between England and Scotland as the two countries struggled to establish a boundary line acceptable to both nations. The first of the many tributaries to feed Tweed flow in a few miles above the tide: from the south, the River Till, an outstanding sea-trout stream and entirely in England, and, from the north, Whiteadder Water (see OS Map 67, Duns & Dunbar) which, apart from its last miles, is entirely in Scotland. Bowmont Water, a tributary of the River Till, begins its life in Scotland but after passing Kirk Yetholm (74/822280) is lost to its native land in Northumberland. Leet Water flows into Tweed by the caravan park in Coldstream (74/846398). Eden Water (74/766376) joins Tweed 2 miles downstream from Kelso and, at Kelso itself, the River Teviot meets Tweed in Junction Pool which is regarded by many as being the finest salmon pool in Europe. From Kelso, upstream to where Tweed exits OS Map 74 at Leaderfoot (74/570348), the river runs through superb countryside, often bordered by ancient beech and oakwoods which in their autumn colours make fishing here a constant, unforgettable, pleasure. This pleasure is not only confined to fishing, because, should you have non-fishing companions with you, then there is a wealth of other activities to keep them fully amused whilst you concentrate on the river: marvelous walks, visits to the famous abbeys at Melrose, Jedburgh, Dryburgh and Kelso, Sir Walter Scott's home at Abbotsford, ancient castles and border peel towers.

Fish The Tweed System produces approximately 10,000 salmon each season as well as substantial numbers of sea-trout. In recent years there are signs that the spring run is improving but summer months can be difficult if rainfall is low; many of the headwater streams are now impounded by reservoirs and commercial afforestation has substantially affected the flow regimen. However, there is a useful run of summer grilse and, unique to Tweed, a run of back-end, fresh fish, many of which weigh over 20lb in weight. The average weight of Tweed salmon is in the order of 8lb/10lb but 20lb plus fish are taken most seasons. During 1996 over 70 salmon of between 20lb and 34lb were taken by Tweed rods. Sea-trout can also run to a prodigious size and fish of up to and over 10b in weight are not infrequently taken. In the lower reaches of the river, and particularly around Ladykirk (74/891474) and Coldstream (74/844398), there are considerable numbers of coarse fish: roach, dace, gudgeon, eels, and perch. There are also brown trout in the river but the best of the brown trout fishing is to be found in further upstream. In recent years, however, and sadly, the brown trout for which the Tweed was once so famous have declined in numbers.

Flies & Tactics Fishing on the Lower and Middle river is from both boat and bank. Some of the pools, particularly in heavy water, and because of their size, can only be effectively covered from a boat; either

Berwick & Girvan — OS Map 74-76

"dropped" downstream by the boatman as the angler covers the lies, or by the boatman on the shore, "roping down" the angler who fishes alone in the boat. Wading is conveniently practiced on many of the beats but chest waders are essential, as are wading staff and life-jacket. Although the days of the infamous 18ft-long, heavy greenheart and cane rods are over, a 15ft/16ft rod is still advisable in order to get the fly to where the fish are, and to control how the fly is presented to them. You must be competent in the use of the rod. In the spring and when the water level is high, expect to be engaged in some hard work with sinking lines and large flies. An ability to Spey-cast is a considerable advantage, not only in fishing the pools, but also in keeping you safe from hooking yourself. It would require a book in its own right to properly describe all the beats, Tweed has 128 riparian owners, but the most famous of the Lower and Middle river beats include: Pavillion, Drygrange, Bemersyde, Dryburgh, Maxton, Mertoun, Makerstoun, Floors, Junction, Hendersyde, Sprouston, Birgham, Carham, Wark Lees, Learmouth, Cornhill, Twizel and Ladykirk. In recent years, the netting stations that used to operate as far upstream as Border Bridge at Coldstream, have been bought out and closed. Consequently, some of the lower beats, such as Ladykirk and Horncliffe are only now being managed as rod and line fisheries. In low water conditions, during the summer months, these beats, on the top of the tide, can produce excellent sport and they are often more readily available than are their more illustrious upstream cousins. Nevertheless, it is possible to have a day on the better known beats during the summer months and even Junction Pool can be fished for a very modest charge at that time. The Tweed Foundation, a charitable Trust, supervises the overall management of the river and their dedication and hard work, year by year, is bringing valuable improvements to Tweed: habitat regeneration, bankside protection, monitoring the movement of fish and a host of other projects all with the single aim of improving, preserving and protecting the quality of the river and its fish stocks for the benefit of anglers now and in the years to come. Fly fishing is preferred but spinning is allowed between the 15th February and 14th September. Devon minnows in various colours are the most popular spinning lures, for flies, try: Willie Gunn, Garry Dog, Silver Wilkinson, Jock Scott, Dusty Miller, Ally's Shrimp, Munro Killer, Black Doctor, General Practitioner, Waddingtons. Sea-trout often take these patterns also as well as Black Pennell, March Brown, Peter Ross.

Permission & Charges On the Middle River, for the majority of anglers, prices are heart-stopping: up to £4,000 per rod per week. Even then, regardless of whether or not you are willing and able to pay that price, vacancies are few and far between. Many anglers book a spring week on a "gentleman's" understanding that when an autumn week becomes available, they may be given an opportunity of booking it as well. However, excellent fishing can be obtained at a reasonable cost on much of the river. In the spring and summer months expect to pay in the order of £25 to £60 per rod per day. In the autumn, think in terms of between £60 to £600 per rod per day, and bear in mind that weekly lets are preferred. For availability on 16 first-class Tweed beats, including Upper, Middle and Lower River beats, contact: James Leeming, ARICS, Tweed Salmon Fishing Agent, Stichill House, Kelso. Tel: 01573 470280; Fax: 01573 470259; Freephone: 0800 387 675. For Lower Mertoun and Maxton: contact: Euan McCorquodale, Crossflat Farm, St Boswells. Tel: 01835 823700. Drygrange/Leaderfoot Water: contact: Ted Hunter, Anglers' Choice, 23 Market Square, Melrose. Tel/Fax: 01896 823070l. Birgham Dub: contact: Douglas & Angus Estates, per Tweedside Tackle, 36-38 Bridge Street, Kelso. Tel: 01573 225306; Fax: 01573 223343. The Lees: contact: Mrs Jane Douglas-Home, The Lees, Coldstream. Tel/Fax: 01890 882706 (and James Leeming - see above). Horncliffe: A Robinson, Bri

WOODEN, Loch
Location & Access 74/709254 Approach from Eckford (74/709262) or from the A698 Hawick/Kelso road at Eckfordmoss (74/704258).
Commentary A small put-and-take fishery close the River Teviot in a pleasant situation on the west side of Wooden Hill (198m).
Fish Stocked with rainbow trout which average 1lb 8oz in weight.
Flies & Tactics Boat fishing only and there is only one boat so advanced booking is essential. Trout are taken all over the loch and no one place is substantially any better than another. Offer them: Black Spider, Invicta, Dunkeld.
Permission & Charges Contact: A H Graham, Lochkeeper, Eckford, by Kelso. Tel: 01835 850255.

Berwick Upon Tweed

TWEED, River See OS Map 74
WHITEADDER Water See OS Map 67

Girvan

BLACK, Loch (Ochiltree) See Loch Ochiltree entry.
COARSE FISHERIES GOOSEY, Loch (76/300825); CRONGART, Loch (76/280826)
CROSS REFERENCES MOAN, Loch (See OS Map 77); River BLADNOCK (See OS Map 82).

DRUMLAMFORD, Loch
Location & Access 76/280776. The loch lies to the east of the B7027 Barrhill/Newton Stewart Road. Approach via the estate road at 76/274775.
Commentary Closed for public fishing in recent years, the estate have now re-opened the fishery, as well as allowing access to two adjacent waters, Loch Dornal

OS Map 76 — Girvan

(76/294762) and Loch Nahinie (76/280771). Loch Maberry (76/285759) to the west of the B7027 road, is a pike fishery. The estate also have salmon and trout fishing on the west bank of the River Cree (see separate entry) from Dalnaw Bridge down the Three Counties Pool.
Fish Drumlamford Loch has wild brown trout and is also stocked with brown trout. Loch Dornal is a stocked rainbow trout fishery. Loch Nahinie has wild brown trout.
Flies & Tactics Drumlamford Loch is fished from either boat or bank, as is Loch Dornal, but Loch Nahinie is bank fishing only. These are all shallow waters and fish rise and are taken virtually everywhere. Fly-fishing only and start with a Blae & Black, Wickham's Fancy and Silver Butcher.
Permission & Charges Trout permits are £15 per rod per day with a 3 fish limit for rainbow trout and a 2 fish limit for brown trout. Salmon fishing on the Cree beat costs £20 per rod per day. Contact: The Lodge, Drumlamford Estate, Barrhill, Girvan, Ayrshire KA26 0RB. Tel 01465 821243. Further information from the estate factor, Andrew Crompton, Tel: 0131 4515154

DUISK, Water of See River Stincher entry.
FYNTALLOCH, Loch of See Loch Ochiltree entry.

GIRVAN, Water of
Location & Access Source: 77/412926 Outfall: 76/183982. The river is easily accessible from the B741 Girvan/Straiton road and from the B7045 Rowanston/Straiton road.
Commentary The Girvan rises from tiny Loch Girvan Eye on the east slopes of the Shalloch of Minnoch. The stream flows north into Loch Bradan (see OS Map 77 New Galloway & Glen Trool) and then north-west through the forestry village of Straiton (77/380050) to Clancaird Castle (77/355075). From Clancaird, the Girvan swings south-west and reaches the sea at Girvan after a journey of some 25 miles opposite 'Paddy's Milestone', Ailsa Craig rock in the Firth of Clyde. The river has no significant tributaries and it relies for its life upon water from the Galloway Hills, now largely impounded for hydro-electric generation purposes. This flow-limitation is further complicated by the commercial forestry plantations that cover almost 45% of the land area South-West Scotland and which have had the effect of lowering the pH level of the water and creating flash-flood conditions. The problems of water abstraction and the impact of forestry are being addressed by the owners of the river, and by other concerned orgnaisations.
Fish Salmon, a few sea-trout and modest brown trout. Salmon numbers have declined in recent years and the river now rarely produces more than 100 salmon and grilse each season. The average weight of salmon is in the order of 7lb. The principal run of fish is in July and, provided that there is sufficient water, the river produces of its best during September and October. A few fish are taken in the early months of the season.
Flies & Tactics The upper reaches of the river are moorland in character, and waterfalls at Tairlaw (77/402010) are impassable to migratory fish. The most attracitve fishing is between Straiton and Crosshill (76/324069), on the Blairqhaun Beat, where there are some lovely pools and runs including: Black Wheel Pool, Witch Wheel Pool, O'Malley's Pool, Sir David's Pool and Kirstie's Pool. Downstream for here, on the Kilkerran Water (76/3000370), the river is more sluggish and slow moving. The Bargany Estate Water, from Dailly Bridge (76/266014) downstream to Cairnhill (76/234001), is more interesting to fish and has some excellent holding pools and glides such as: the Colonel's Pool, Lady Wheel, Stepping Stones Pool, the Laird's Cast and Allan's Stream. Most of the lies can be adequately covered using a single-handed rod and wading is rarely necessary. What is really necessary is a lot of rain, otherwise the river becomes a sad affair and it is much affected by weed growth. In drought conditions the most likely chance of a salmon or sea-trout is to be had on the lower river, above the tide. Spinning is allowed on some beats but fly-fishing is preferred. Offer: Hairy Mary, Stoat's Tail, Garry Dog, Willie Gunn, General Practitioner, Black Doctor.
Permission & Charges Blairquhan Estate: contact: Mr Galbraith, Head Keeper, Blairquhan Estate, Straiton, Ayrshire. Tel: 01655 770259. Blairquhan also have fishing of a stocked loch, The Approach Loch. Coast, including use of boat, £13 per rod per day for a four fish bag limit). Kilkerran Estate: contact: The Factor, Kilkerran Estate, Crosshill, Ayrshire. Tel: 01655 740278. Cost: expect to pay in the order of between £12 and £25 per rod per day. Further information from the Secretary of the Carrick Angling Club: Peter Noble, Alex Noble & Sons, Newton Kennedy, Girvan, Ayrshire. Tel: 01465 712223.

OCHILTREE, Loch
Location & Access 76/315745. Turn north from the B7027 Newton Stewart/Pinwherry road at 76/322709. Loch Ocihltree is on your left, 2 miles from the road junction.
Commentary The loch is almost 1 mile north/south by up to half a mile wide and, because of its exposed position, it can be a wild and windy place to fish. Close by, and joined to Loch Ochiltree, is Loch of Fyntalloch (76/313740) and both waters are managed by the Newton Stewart Angling Association. The Black Loch, to the north of Loch Ochiltree, is not fished.
Fish Brown trout and rainbow trout in Loch Ochiltree, as well as a few pike and perch; rainbow trout only in Loch of Fyntalloch. Trout of 5lb have been taken in Ochiltree but the average size is a more modest 1lb. Fyntalloch rainbow trout are larger and average 14oz/1lb.
Flies & Tactics Boat and bank fishing on Loch Ochiltree, bank fishing only on Loch of Fyntalloch. Fish rise and are taken all round both waters but the north end of Loch Ochiltree is perhaps the most productive bank fishing area. When boat fishing, concentrate your efforts near the margins of the small islands and the promontory at the south-east end of the loch. Flies: Black Pennell, Invicta, Dunkeld.
Permission & Charges Galloway Gun & Tackle Shop,

Girvan   OS Maps 76

36a Arthur Street, Newton Stewart, Wigtownshire. Tel: 01671 403404. Cost: £15 per rod per day, boat hire, £8 per day. There is a bag limit of 2 fish per rod per day on each water.

OCHILTREE, Loch 76/315745

PENWHAPPLE, Reservoir
Location & Access 76/260970. The reservoir lies immediately adjacent to the B734 Girvan/Barr road.
Commentary This easily-accessible fishery is three-quarters of a mile long by up to a quarter of a mile wide.
Fish Regularly stocked with brown trout in the past and now containing rainbow trout as well. The heaviest trout caught recently were two fish which weighed 9lb 8oz and 8lb 6oz respectively.
Flies & Tactics Boat (5 boats) and bank fishing is available but bank fishing can be every bit as productive as fishing from the boat. The south end of the loch is perhaps the most rewarding fishing area, from both boat or bank; but, in reality, fish may be taken from almost anywhere around the loch. Wading is safe but not really necessary as fish lie close to the margins. Take care, however, in the area directly opposite the spawning burn where the margins are soft and boggy. Flies: Blae & Black, Greenwell's Glory, Kate Maclaren and gold head lures.
Permission & Charges Mr Stewart, Wee Lanes Farm, Barr, Girvan, Ayrshire. Tel: 01465 861663. Cost: £15 per rod per day, £10 for the evening. There is a 6 fish per rod limit. Further information from the club secretary: Alistair Scobie, 7 Golf Course Road, Girvan. Tel: 01465 714538.

PRIVATE WATERS GOWER, Loch 76/289771; MABRENNIE, Loch 76/275760; DERRY, Loch 76/252735; BLACK, Loch (Drumlanford) 76/263842; ROTTEN, Loch 76/249844; NEAR EYES, Loch 76/254843; KNOCKY SKEAGGY, Loch 76/252845; FARROCH, Loch 76/254850; BLACK, Loch (Darnarroch) 76/197830 ; KIRKIE, Loch 199828; COW, Loch 76/239770; LONG, Loch 76/239764; CRAIGIE, Loch 76/243764; MARTLE, Loch 76/243762; SCALLOCH, Loch 76/283890; LIG, Loch 76/2018841; KILANTRINGAN, Loch 76/090790; APP, Water of 76/050727; SWAN, Loch 76/224097 (in the grounds of Culzaean Castle and not fished); CRAIGDOW, Loch 76/263065

STINCHER, River
Location & Access Source: 77/389930 Outfall: 76/080818. The river is easily accessible throughout its entire length. The lower river is accessed from the B7044 Ballantrae/Colmonell road on the north bank and by a convenient minor road on the south bank. Thereafter, upstream, access is from the A765 Colmonell/Girvan road and the B734 Glenburnie/Barr road. The upper river is approached from the minor road running east from Barr (76/274941).
Commentary As with the Water of Girvan (see separate entry), the River Stincher has suffered much in recent years from the twin evils of water abstraction and commercial forestry. Nevertheless, the Stincher is perhaps the most attractive salmon stream in Ayrshire, running through wild countryside and in many places bordered by pleasant, natural woodlands. The river rises from the north slopes of Shalloch on Minnoch (769m) and flows north through the Carrick Forest before turning south-west at Aldinna (77/350953). After Aldinna the stream meanders past the village of Barr to Pinwherry (76/197870) where it collects in the waters from its most significant tributary, Duisk Water. After a further 8 miles the river reaches the sea through the nature reserve to the south of Ballantrae. Ballantrae is a popular holiday resort and famous, amongst other things, for its association with Robert Louis Stevenson and his book "The Master of Ballantrae".
Fish Salmon and sea-trout, but not nearly so many today as in times past. The Bardrochat Beat produces approximately 40/50 salmon and grilse each season and up to 20 sea-trout. Knockdolian, the most productive beat, in a good year might produce up to 500 fish. Dalreoch Water alone, in the 1960s, used to produce 300 sea-trout; now, a good season might give up 20 fish. The average weight of salmon is in the order of 8lb but larger fish are often taken: one of the heaviest caught recently was a salmon of 25lb, taken from the Dalni Pool in 1995. A few fish are caught in the early months of the season but the best of the fishing is now from July onwards. It all depends upon good water levels after heavy spates.
Flies & Tactics A 12ft/14ft double-handed rod will deal with most angling situations and chest waders are necessary to effectively cover many of the lies. The river-bottom is gravel and wading is generally safe although care is required in high water when less-compacted gravel could cause you to loose your footing. Some of the most notable pools on the Knockdolian Water include: Minister's Pool, Corbie Stairs, Shaksiston Pool, Mermaid Pool, Twins and Sallachan. Noted pools on Bardrochat Water are: Willow Pool, Duhbanee Pool, Rory's Pool and Oaknowe Bridge. Salmon flies: Silver Stoat's Tail, Munro Killer, General Practitioner, Black Stincher, Garry Dog, Willie Gunn. Sea-trout flies: Black Pennell, March Brown, Teal Blue & Silver.
Permission & Charges Dalreoch Water: contact: Douglas Overend, Dalreoch Lodge, Colmonell, Ayrshire. Tel: 01465 881214; Knockdolian Water: contact: The Factor, Knockdolian Estate, Alderside, Colmonell, Ayrshire. Tel: 01465 881237; Bardrochat Water: Robert Anderson, Bardrochat Estate, Oaknowe, Colmonell, Ayrshire. Tel: 01465 881202; Hallow Chapel: contact: Donald Telford, Colmonell, Ayrshire. Tel: 01465 881249; Almont Beat: contact: Donald Love, Almont, Pinwherry, Ayrshire. Tel: 01465 841637; Kirkhill Water: Mrs Shankland, Colmonell, Ayrshire. Tel: 01465 881220. Cost: expect to pay, per rod per day, £15 during the opening months of the season, £20 in June, £25 in July, £35 in August and from £40 to £90 in September and October. Priority is given to weekly lets in the autumn months, but day lets may also be available. The best of the fishing is booked well in advance and is rarely

OS Map 76-77 — New Galloway & Glen Trool

available. Alasdair Ash at the Boar's Head Hotel in Colmonell (Tel: 01465 881371) will guide your efforts if you have problems in finding a vacancy.

New Galloway and Glen Trool

AFTON, Reservoir
Location & Access 77/634042. Drive south from New Cummnock at Afton Bridgend (71/617132) on the minor road up the banks of Afton Water (see Os Map 71, Lanark and Upper Nithsdale). The reservoir is at the end of the road, 8.5 miles from New Cummnock.
Commentary Glen Afton and Afton Water are famous for their beauty, immortalised in the song, 'Flow Gently Sweet Afton', and the reservoir lies in a remote setting between Cannock Hill (594m) to the east and White Knowles (541m) to the west. Afton Reservoir is approximately 1 mile long by up to 400 yds wide and it is fed by Montraw Burn and Afton Water both of which rise from the north slopes of Alwhat Hill (629m).
Fish The New Cummnock Anglers' Association stock the reservoir with brown trout and the average weight of fish is in the order of 10oz.
Flies & Tactics Bank fishing only and avoid wading: it is dangerous to do so. The most productive fishing area is at the south end, where the feeder burns enter, and along the south-west shore. Offer the residents: Black Spider, Grouse & Claret, Gold Butcher. Spinning also allowed.
Permission & Charges Contact: T Basford, Burnbrae Cottage, 1 Pathhead, New Cummnock, Ayrshire. Tel: 01290 332654. Tickets are also available at the reservoir from Association committe members. Cost: £8 per rod per day.

BARSCOBE, Loch
Location & Access 77/669813. Access is either from the A712 Balmacllan/Dumfriess road in the south or via a forest track from Corriedoor (77/680830) on the A702 St John's Town of Dalry/Thornhill road in the north.
Commentary A very attractive little loch covering an area of some 13 acres, surrounded by outstanding scenery. To the west of Barscobe is another small water, Loch Brack (77/684821). Brack is enclosed on 3 sides by forestry and it also offers good sport in a perfect setting. Moss Roddock Loch (77/632816), 8 acres in extent and lying to the north of the A702 half a mile east from St John's Town of Dalry, is also available for fishing.
Fish Barscobe Loch is stocked with excellent quality brown trout, rainbow trout and brook trout. The average weight of fish is 1lb but trout of up to and over 4lb in weight are not uncommon. Trout in the other waters noted above are smaller.
Flies & Tactics Boat fishing only on Barscobe Loch,

boat and bank fishing on Loch Brack and bank fishing on Moss Roddock Loch. Fish are taken from all over these lochs, from the margins to the middle, so cast with confidence everywhere. All fishing is by fly only. Try: Soldier Palmer, Black Spider, Cinnamon & Gold.
Permission & Charges Contact: Milton Park Hotel, St John's Town of Dalry. Tel: 01644 430286. Barscobe Loch is reserved for hotel guests (£15 per boat per day - 2 rods fishing), Loch Brack and Moss Roddock Loch are sometimes available on a day-ticket basis at £17 per rod per day. Milton Park Hotel guests also have access to Earlstoun Loch (77/615830), a productive fishery on the River Dee system where there is the chance of the occasional salmon. Cost £15 per rod per day.

BLACK, Loch (Clatteringshaws) See Clatteringshaws Loch entry.
BOGTON, Loch See Loch Doon entry.
BRACK, Loch See Barscobe Loch entry.

BRADAN, Loch
Location & Access 77/425972. Approach from Straiton (77/381049) on the B741 Dalmellington/Dailly road. In the village, follow the minor road south by the River Girvan (see separate entry) to reach the west end of the loch after a distance of 4 miles.
Commentary Loch Bradan lies on the headwaters of the River Girvan (see separate entry) in the Carrick Forest and it is 2 miles long by three-quarters of a mile wide. The loch is administered by the Forest Enterprise and Ayr Angling Club and there is a further Forest Enterprise loch here which is also available for anglers: Loch Breckbowie (77/432960). Approach Breckbowie along a marked track from the forest road.
Fish Loch Bradan is stocked and contains brown trout which average 8oz/12oz. A few larger fish are taken, trout of up to and over 3lb in weight.
Flies & Tactics Bank fishing only and great care should be taken because of the unstable nature of some of the margins; on Loch Bradan, particularly, to the east of the dam where underwater tree stumps are an unexpected hazard. A strong wind, indeed a gale, can often provide the best fishing conditions on Loch Bradan and fish are taken close to the shore. The south-west bay on Loch Bradan is the place to begin but you will catch trout all over these lochs. Show them: Black Pennell, Grouse & Claret, Peter Ross. Fish of over 5lb in weight should be returned to the water "to retain the genetic capability to produce large fish.
Permission & Charges Contact: Caldons Campsite, Bregrennan, Newton Stewart, Wigtownshire. Tel: 01671 840218; Forestry Commission, Creebridge, Newton Stewart, Wigtownshire. Tel: 01671 402420; Forestry Commission, 21 King Street, Castle Douglas, Kirkcudbrightshire. Tel: 01556 503626; Talnotry Caravan Park, Newton Stewart, Wigtownshire. Tel: 01671 402170; Clattreringshaws Forest Wildlife Centre, New Galloway, Ayrshire. Tel: 01644 2285; Kirrieoughtree Visitor Centre. Tel: 01671 402165.

New Galloway & Glen Trool — OS Map 77

Cost: £6.50 per rod per day. Under 16, £3.00 per rer day.

BRECKBOWIE, Loch See Loch Bradan entry.

CARSFAD, Reservoir

Location & Access 77/606860. Immediately adjacent to the east side of the A713 St John's Town of Dalry/Carsphairn road.

Commentary Carsfad is an impounded section of the River Ken Hydro-electric generation scheme and is half a mile long by up to 400 yds wide. The reservoir is surrounded by fields and access is easy. Park in the roadside lay-by.

Fish Brown trout, rainbow trout, brook trout, pike and the chance of the occasional salmon (approximately 3 each season) and sea-trout. Trout average 10oz, a pike of 10lb was caught recently.

Flies & Tactics Bank fishing only and wading can be dangerous due to unstable margins caused by water-level fluctuations. Also beware of sudden rises in the water-level due to power-station operations. Seek advice when obtaining your ticket. The west bank is the most productive fishing area, particularly at the north end where the River Ken flows in. Fishing is by fly only until 1st June, thereafter spinning and worm fishing is permissible. The use of natural minnow, live or dead bait, is prohibited at all times. Night fishing, between midnight and one hour before sunrise, is also prohibited. Flies: Soldier Palmer, March Brown, Silver Butcher.

Permission & Charges Contact: Clachan Inn, 10 Main Street, St John's Town of Dalry. Tel: 01644 430241. Cost: £10 per rod per day, Juniors half price.

CLATTERINGSHAWS, Loch

Location & Access 77/5443770. The loch lies adjacent to the north side of the A712 Newton Stewart/New Galloway road.

Commentary On a wild day Clatteringshaws lives up to its name and can be a forbidding, dour place, but when the sun shines the loch is a delight. Just as delightful are the wide range of facilities awaiting any non-anglers with whom you may be encumbered: The King's Stone, marking the site of one of Robert Bruce's battles in 1307, the Clatteringshaws Forest Wildlife Centre and, a few miles down the road towards Newton Stewart, the Wild Goat Park, Murray's Monument and pleasant walks by the waterfalls along the Grey Mare's Tail Burn. There are 3 other, small, lochs in the vicinity which can offer excellent sport: Loch of the Lowes (77/469705), The Black Loch (77/497728), Lillie's Loch (77/517747). Salmon, sea-trout and brown trout fishing is also available from the west bank of the Palnure Burn upstream from Craignine Bridge (83/460664).

Fish Clatteringshaws contains brown trout, pike and perch, the other lochs excluding Lillie's Loch have been stocked with brown trout. The average weight of fish is in the order of 10oz but there are larger fish as well.

Flies & Tactics Bank fishing only. Clatteringshaws was impounded in the 1930's as part of the Doon Hydro-electric generating scheme. It has a shore-line that extends for more than 5 miles and, because of fluctuations in the water-level, wading is not advised. The way of the wind will dictate where you fish but the north end of the loch is generally the most productive area; and the wide bay to the north of The King's Stone. The other lochs are easily understood and fish are taken everywhere, depending upon their mood and your ability. Palnure Burn requires masses of water before it produces sport.

Permission & Charges See Loch Bradan entry. Lillie's Loch costs: £3 adult; under 16 £1.50. Palnure Burn costs: trout, March to June, £3 per rod per day; salmon, July to October, £6.50 per rod per day. Permits for Clatteringshaws Loch may also be obtained from: Galloway Gun & Tackle Shop, 36 Arthur Street, Newton Stewart, Kirkcudbright. Tel: 01671 403404; Merrick Camp Site, Glentrool Village, Newton Stewart, Kirkcudbright. Tel: 01671 840280.

COARSE FISHERIES LINFERN, Loch 77/367980 ; MOAN, Loch 77/350860 ; GRANNOCH, Loch 77/544705; FLEET, Loch 77/560700; HOWIE, Loch 77/695834.

CROSS REFERENCES EUCHAN Water (See OS Map 78); KELLO Water (See OS Map 78); AFTON Water (See OS Map 71); SCAUR Water (See OS Map 78); DOON, River (See OS Map 70); SPALLANDER Loch (See OS Map 70); GIRVAN, Water of (See OS Map 70); STINCHER, River (See OS Map 76); CREE, River (See OS Map 83); DEE, River (See OS Map 83).

DEE, Loch

Location & Access 77/468790. Reaching Loch Dee involves a 5 mile forest drive from the south end of Clatteringshaws Loch (see separate entry) to Bruce's Wa's (77/503782) and thereafter by forest road by the Blackwater of Dee around the north side of Cairngarrock (557m). Loch Dee is just over 1 mile long by half a mile wide and it is perhaps the best trout loch in the area.

Fish The loch has a considerable population of indigenous trout and this has been augmented with stocking. The average weight of fish is in the order of 1lb 8oz and the largest trout caught in recent years was a fish taken in 1993 which weighed 10lb 4oz.

Flies & Tactics Bank fishing only and wading is not recommended. The wind will dictate where you fish, but the south shore, in the vicinity of the long peninsula (77/471791), is a good place to begin. The promontory on the north shore (77/472795) should also be carefully explored and the south end of the loch where Dorgall Lane flows in. Flies: Blae & Black, Mallard & Claret, Cinnamon & Gold.

Permission & Charges See Loch Bradan entry.

DOON, Loch

Location & Access 77/49990. Approach from Dalmellington (77/475060). Drive south on the minor road past Bogton Loch (77/470053) (contains pike) and Wee Berbeth Loch (77/471035), which is private, and the dramatic gorge of Ness Glen to reach the

OS Map 77 — New Galloway & Glen Trool

north end of Loch Doon after a distance of 3 miles.
Commentary Loch Doon, on the headwaters of the River Doon (see separate entry), is the largest expanse of water in Ayrshire and it is 6 miles long by up to 1.5 miles wide. The loch has been impounded for hydro-electric power generation purposes and, consequently, the water-level fluctuates considerably, by up to 40ft, according to this need. Because of massive afforestation in the surrounding area the loch water is now very acid. Prior to being impounded, Doon Castle (77/484949), an ancient Douglas Family stronghold at the south end of the loch, was dismantled, stone by stone, and rebuilt on its present site above the new water-level. The "banks and braes o' bonnie Doon" are very popular with visitors, and the minor, shore-side road gives convenient access to many fine walks amidst the Rhinns of Kells, particularly to Corseine (814m).
Fish Brown trout, arctic charr, perch and some huge pike. Although salmon, in theory, can enter the loch, very few are either seen or hooked. Brown trout average 8oz and there are vast numbers of them, but some very large fish are also taken, trout of up to and over 15lb in weight.
Flies & Tactics Take great care when bank fishing. Some areas of shoreline are very unstable due to water fluctuations. Fish may be taken from almost anywhere but the south end is perhaps the most productive fishing area. All legal fishing methods are allowed. Flies: Black Spider, Greenwell's Glory, Peter Ross.
Permission & Charges No permissions is required.

EARLSTOUN, Loch See Barscobe Loch entry.

KEN, Loch
Location & Access 77/654735. Major roads mirror both banks of the loch. Access to the east bank is from the A713 St John's Town Dalry/Castle Douglas road. The west bank is accessed from the A762 New Galloway/Kirkcudbright road.
Commentary Loch Ken lies at the heart of the Doon Hydro-electric power generation system and the main loch is 4 miles long by up to 700 yds wide. The west shore is bordered by the Cairn Edward Forest, the east shoreline by fertile fields. Fish stocks in the loch have been badly effected by a reduction in the pH level of the water due to increased acidification from commercial plantations. In recent years, a great deal of work has been undertaken to reverse the situation and this effort appears to be having the desired effect. Fishing is also available on Stroan Loch (77/644703), to the south-west of Loch Ken and on Earlstoun Loch (77/614830) to the north of St John's Town Dalry. There is one further fishing location here, ideal "if all else fails": Mossdale Loch (77/657710), by the side of the A762. Mossdale Loch is managed by the New Galloway Angling Association. The tributaries of the Water of Ken, the Black Water (77/615885), Water of Deugh (77/580927), Polharrow Burn (77/604844), Polmaddy Burn (77/600880) and the upper reaches of the Water of Ken and their attendant streams, can produce sport with brown trout, but only in high water conditions and these burns are rarely fished.

Fish Loch Ken is reputed to have produced the most famous pike in Scotland: a fish weighing 72lb allegedly caught in 1771. Huge pike still inhabit the loch, as well as brown trout, rainbow trout, arctic charr and the occasional salmon and sea-trout. Brown trout average 14oz but a trout of 17lb was caught in 1993. The heaviest salmon in recent years weighed 17lb, and a 22lb fish has been taken from the Water of Ken. Stroan Loch has mostly coarse fish, but there are good brown trout as well, whilst Earlstoun Loch contains fish stocks similar to Loch Ken. Mossdale Loch is stocked with both brown trout and rainbow trout which average 1lb 8oz in weight.
Flies & Tactics Any legal fishing method may be used on Loch Ken and both boat and bank fishing is available. Most salmon are taken from the Water of Ken (approximately 12 a year), rather than from the loch, and these are invariably caught by local anglers. Fishing on the river is from the west bank only, from Ken Bridge (77/640783) downstream to where the river flows into the north end of Loch Ken. Power generation operations often "adjust" the level of both river and loch and anglers should seek local advice in regard to these matters, particularly if they are tempted to wade. Be warned also that the margins of the loch in some areas, because of fluctuating waters levels, are unstable and dangerous. In general, the north end of the loch fishes best, but, by and large, fish may be taken from almost anywhere around the shore. Earlstoun Loch is boat fishing, fly only, and anglers are not allowed to land anywhere other than at the boathouse. Those using boats on Earlstoun Loch are warned of the danger of approaching the intake canal on the West Bank of the reservoir and of approaching the dam structure, particularly in high water conditions. Bank fishing only on Stroan Loch, from the east shore, fishing on Mossdale Loch is by boat only.
Permission & Charges Contact: For Loch Ken, Water of Ken, (and Moss Roddock Loch and Clatteringshaws Loch - see separate entries): Kenmure Arms Hotel, High Street, New Galloway DG7 3RL. Tel: 01644 420240. Cost: from £2 per rod per day. Boat hire on Loch Ken, £30 per boat per day (2 rods fishing). For Earlstoun Loch (£5 per rod per day), Stroan Loch and the other waters noted above, contact the Clachan Inn (see Carsfad Reservoir entry). For Mossdale Loch, contact: Jim Blore, Mossdale Post Office, Laurieston, by New Galloway. Tel: 01644 450281. Cost: £10 per rod per day (£5 for boat) for a 3 fish limit. Kenmure Arms Hotel offers excellent facilties for anglers, including all-day snacks for fishermen and freezer space for their catches. Further details from angling association treasurer is Mr Hopkins, Tel: 01644 420229.

KIRRIEREOCH, Loch
Location & Access 77/365865. Approach from Glentrool Village (77/361784) via the minor road that runs north through the Glentrool Forest to Laglanny (77/353907). The loch is on the east of the road and drains into Minnoch Water, a tributary of the River Cree (See OS Map 83).
Commentary Kirriereoch Loch is managed by the

OS Maps 77-78

Newton Stewart Angling Associaton and lies in the heart of the Glentrool Forest almost completely surrounded by trees. Salmon and trout fishing is also available on Minnoch Water (for permission see Loch Bradan entry: cost: trout, March to June, £3 per rod per day, salmon, July to October, £6.50 per rod per day), upstream from the marker-posts above Kirrereoch Bridge.
Fish Stocked each year with brown trout which average 12oz in weight. A few fish of up to 3lb are taken most seasons.
Flies & Tactics Bank fishing only and trout are taken from all round the shore, although the treeless west bank is perhaps the most productive area. Minnoch Water needs a heavy spate (a rare occurrence) to produce of its best. Flies: Soldier Palmer, Mallard & Claret, Teal & Black. Worm fishing is allowed after the 1st June and there is a bag limit of 4 fish per rod.
Permission & Charges Galloway Gun & Tackle Shop, 36 Arthur Street, Newton Stewart, Wigtownshire. Tel: 01671 403404; Merrick Camp Site, Glentrool Village, Newton Stewart, Kirkcudbright. Tel: 01671 840280. Cost: £12 per rod per day.

LILLIE'S, Loch See Clatteringshaws Loch entry.
LOWES, Loch of the (Clatteringshaws) See Clatteringshaws Loch entry.
MINNOCH Water See Kirriereoch Loch entry.
MOSS RODDOCK, Loch See Barscobe Loch entry.

MUCK, Loch
Location & Access 77/511009. By the side of the A713 Dalmellington/Carsphairn road.
Commentary An easily-accessible loch of approximately 35/40 acres lying between Loch Doon and the A713 at Little Eriff Hill (329m). This is an exposed little water and it can often be swept by unforgiving winds, but it is a very attractive palce to fish when conditions are right.
Fish The loch has been limed and stocked with brown trout which average 8oz/10oz. There are a number of very much larger fish.
Flies & Tactics Bank fishing only, but anglers may use their own float-tubes if they wish. Trout rise and are taken everywhere and a convenient track margins the whole length of the west shore. Flies: Soldier Palmer, March Brown, Peter Ross.
Permission & Charges Mr Swan, Factor, Eriff Estate, Eriff Farm, Carsphairn, Dalmellington. Tel: 01292 550340. May be let to a private syndicate - check with Mr Swan for details.

PALNURE Burn See Clatteringshaws Loch entry.
PRIVATE WATERS LURKIE, Loch 77/730709; FALBAE, Loch 77/739719; ARVIE, Loch 77/741758; SKAE, Loch 77/710837; CRAIG, Loch 77/689757; TROQUHAIN, Loch 77/682799; KNOCKSTING, Loch 77/6998; FINLAS, Loch 77/468978; DERCLACH, Loch 77/445990; CORNISH, Loch 77/408940; RIECAWR, Loch 77/430935; GOOSIE, Loch 77/440950 ; BALLOCHLING, Loch 77/455946; ALDINNA Loch 77/365939; SLOCHY, Loch 77/425924 ; GIRVIN EYE, Loch 77/412926;

MACATERICK, Loch 77/440910; TROOL, Loch 77/410800; WATER OF TROOL, River 77/390785; ENOCH, Loch 77/445850 (not fished); ROUND LOCH OF THE DUNGEON, Loch 77/466846 (not fished); LONG LOCH OF THE DUNGEON, Loch 77/466840 (not fished); NELDRICKEN, Loch 77/445830 (not fished); VALLEY, Loch 77/440816 (not fished); LONG LOCH OF GLENHEAD, Loch 77/445806 (not fished); ROUND LOCH OF GLENHEAD, Loch 77/450803 (not fished); HARROW, Loch 77/530867; KNOCKMAN, Loch 77/667837; MINNOCH, Loch 77/530858; DUNGEON, Loch 77/520845; KENDON, Loch 77/610905 ; REGLAND, Loch 77/692858; MIDDLE, Loch 77/396741; LOCHINVAR, Loch 77/658854.
Note: Many of the lochs noted above and around Merrick (843m), the highest mountain in the Southern Uplands of Scotland, have lost their native fish populations. The most probable reason for this is increased acidification of their habitat, caused by air-borne pollution, and exacerbated by the extensive afforestation that has taken place throughout much of Galloway & Dumfriesshire in recent years. This has also reduced the ability of lochs and river systems in the region to sustain natural populations of salmon, sea-trout and brown trout and has led to re-stocking programmes, for reasons of environmental probity as well as in order to provide sport for anglers. The West Galloway Fisheries Trust is leading this effort, in conjunction with the Forestry Commission and the Freshwater Fishery Research Laboratory in Pitlochry. The saddest aspect of the whole affair is that there was sufficient prior evidence of the probable damage that factory-tree-farming would cause to fish stocks but little attention was paid to that evidence by the authorities concerned.

SKELLOCH, Loch See Loch Bradan entry.
WEE BERBETH, Loch See Loch Doon entry.

Nithsdale and Lowther Hills

AE, Water See River Annan entry.

ANNAN, River
Location & Access Source: 78/060129 Outfall 85/192643. (See also OS Map 85). The river is easily accessible from major and minor roads throughout its entire length.
Commentary In its infancy, the Annan is in exalted company: the source of both the River Tweed and the River Clyde lie close by; the Tweed, at Tweed's Well (78/052146), the Clyde on Clyde Law (546m) (78/023168). The Annan flows south through Annandale and reaches the sea in the Solway Firth after a journey of some 40 miles at Barnkirk Point Lighthouse. A number of substantial tributaries join

OS Map 78

Nithsdale & Lowther Hills

the Annan in its upper reaches and near Lochmaben: Moffat Water and Evan Water (78/095021), Kinnel Water and the Water of Ae (78/099836), Dryfe Water (78/108821) the Water of Milk (85/149732) and Mein Water (85/185725). The upper river flows through wild, mountainous scenery, but after Threewater Foot (78/095021) the stream is bordered by fertile agricultural lands. The Annan is particularly lovely to fish during the autumn months, when gold-decked trees nod by the river and salmon surge upstream to their headwater spawning-grounds.

Fish Approximately 700/800 salmon and upwards of 1,500 sea-trout are taken most seasons. Salmon average 10lb, sea-trout 2lb. However, the Annan is famous for the size of some of its autumn fish, known locally as "greybacks", and although they are not so plentiful today as they were in days of yore, salmon of up to and over 30lb are still occasionally taken. The river also hosts good brown trout (a fish of 5lb 4oz was caught during 1995), grayling and, in some areas, excellent chub.

Flies & Tactics The lower beats are described on Map 85. Because of extensive afforestation in the catchment area, the Annan has become much more of a spate stream than in days past. There are no large lochs on the headwaters and the opportunity of good sport is increasingly dependent upon heavy rain. This occurs, sometimes, in abundance, and the lower river often breaks its banks and floods large areas of the surrounding land. There is a reasonable run of spring salmon but the most productive fishing time is at the back end, September, October and November, when fresh fish may still be caught. Sea-trout run the river from April onwards and the peak time for sea-trout fishing is in June and July. Chest waders and care is required on some of the beats and a 12ft/15ft double-handed rod to cover more distant lies. Further upstream a single-handed rod is adequate. Spinning and bait fishing is allowed on most beats, but fly-fishing is the preferred fishing method. For many anglers, the most exciting sport is night fishing for sea-trout. Reconnoitre your beat, carefully, during daylight hours, and, thus prepared, look out for great afterdark action. There are a number of delightful pools and runs, including: Corgies Pool, Orchard Pools, Woodend, Annanbank, Girthhead Pothole, Trough Pool and the Minister's Pool. Salmon flies: Brown Turkey, Blue Charm, Ally's Shrimp, Garry Dog, Willie Gunn, Munro Killer. Sea-trout flies: Black Pennell, Mallard & Claret, Silver March Brown, Peter Ross, Teal Blue & Silver. Most spinning lures produce results, although Devon minnows are most popular.

Permission & Charges Starting at the top of the river and working downstream: the Upper Annandale Angling Association have 10 miles of fishing on the Annan and its tributaries. The Association water, interjected with private beats, extends from Threewater Foot downstream to the mouth of Kinnel Water. Contact: A Dickson, Braehead, Woodfoot, Beattock, Dunfriesshire DG10 9PL. Tel: 01683 300592; Red House Hotel, Wamphray, Moffat, Dumfriesshire DG10 9NF. Tel: 01576 470214. Sport & Tackle Shop, 52 High Street, Lockerbie, Dumfriesshire DG11 2AA. Tel: 01576 202400. Cost: February to August, £8 per rod per day, thereafter, £45 per rod per week (5 days only). Johnstonebridge Water (6.5 miles): contact: The Factor, Annandale Estate, Estate Office, St Ann's, Lockerbie, Dunfriesshire DG11 1HQ. Tel: 01576 470317. Cost, from £8 per rod per day in the early months up to £50 per rod per week in the autumn. Jardine Hall & Millhouse Fishings (2 miles): contact: Anthony Steel, Kirkwood, Lockerbie, Dumfriesshire GD11 1DH. Tel: 01576 510200. Hallheaths Water: (3.5 miles): contact: McJerrow & Stevenson, 55 High Street, Lockerbie, Dumfriesshire DG11 2JJ. Tel: 01576 202123. Three visitor-permits are issued each week. Dryfeholm Water (1.5 miles): season tickets only on Dryfeholm Water at approximately £120 per rod. Contact: G M Thomson & CO 35 Buccleuch Street, Dumfries DG1 2AB. Tel: 01387 252689. Royal Four Towns Water (4 miles). The towns in question are Hightae, Greenhill, Heck and Smallholm and they were granted fishing rights by King Robert Bruce as a reward for the support he had received from them during the Scottish Wars of Independence that culminated in the Battle of Bannockburn (1314). Contact: Mrs K Ratcliffe, Jay-Ar, Prestonhouse Road, Hightae, Lockerbie, Dumfriesshire DG11 1JR. Tel: 01387 810220. Expect to pay in the order of from £8 per day up to £150 week, depending upon time of year and location of beat.

BARONY, Loch
Location & Access 78/020870. Turn east from the A701 Dumfries/Beattock road at Kirkmichael Mains (78/018875). The loch is within the grounds of Barony Agricultural College.
Commentary A small put-and-take fishery in an attractive woodland setting. Good facilities for disabled anglers.
Fish Stocked with brown trout and rainbow trout which average 1lb 12oz in weight. Fish of up to 5lb are also taken.
Flies & Tactics Bank fishing only with dry fly, nymphs, damsel patterns and Black Spider.
Permission & Charges Contact: Ae Inn, Parkgate, Dumfries DG1 3NE. Tel: 01387 860222 fro details.

CAMPLE, Water See River Nith entry.
CARO, Water See River Nith entry.
COARSE FISHERIES UPPER Loch (78/071834); MILL Loch (78/079832); BLIND Lochs (78/062838); KIRK Loch (78/078826); CASTLE Loch (78/089815); HIGHTAE MILL Loch (78/086805); HIGH DAM (78/820020); DABTON Loch (78/877968); MORTON Pond (78/887995).
CRAWICK, Water See River Nith entry.
CROSS REFERENCES FRUID Reservoir (See OS Map 72); CLYDE, River (See OS Map 72).

DAER, Reservoir
Location & Access 78/977080. Approach from the A702 Carronbridge/Elvanfoot road. Follow the minor road south-east at Watermeetings (78/950133) to reach the dam wall after a further 4 miles.

409

Nithsdale & Lowther Hills — OS Map 78

Commentary Daer Reservoir lies on the headwater system of the River Clyde (see OS Map 72, Upper Clyde Valley and OS Map 64, Glasgow). The reservoir is 2 miles north/south by up to 1 mile wide and it is very exposed both to prevailing and every other kind of wind. The fishing is let to the Kilbryde Angling Club.
Fish Brown trout which average 10oz, but there are much larger fish lurking in the depths.
Flies & Tactics Boat fishing only and an outboard motor is essential - as is a life-jacket and a good knowledge of boat work and safety-afloat procedures. Concentrate your efforts in the shallow waters close to the shore and in the north-east bay where the Shiel Burn enters (78/987079). Flies: Black Pennell, Invicta, Alexandra.
Permission & Charges Contact: Alex Thomson, 3 Moffat Place, Mossneuk, East Kilbride. Tel: 01355 232824; Fax: 01355 266479. Cost: £25 per day (3 rods). Advance booking essential. Bring your own outboard.

DRYFE, Water See River Annan entry.

ETTRICK, Loch
Location & Access 78/946938. Approach from the A76 Dumfries/Thornhill road. Turn east at Kirkpatrick (78/904907), cross the railway and follow the minor road, signposted "Ettrick & Ae", through Gilchristland to reach the loch after 4 miles.
Commentary Loch Ettrick is an easily-accessible roadside water on the northern edge of the Forest of Ae. It covers an area of 19 acres and lies in attractive countryside, sheltered by the forest to the south and Dollard Hill (339m) to the north.
Fish A stocked fishery offering sport with rainbow trout and a few indigenous brown trout. Average weight of fish is 1lb, but fish of up to and over 3lb in weight are also taken.
Flies & Tactics Fish are caught all over the loch and no one place is really any better that another. Boat and bank fishing using Black Pennell, Soldier Palmer, Silver Butcher.
Permission & Charges Contact: John Crofts, Blawbrae, Ettrick, Thornhill, Dumfriesshire DG3 5HL. Tel: 01848 330154. Tickets also from: Closeburn Post Office, Closeburn, by Thornhill, Dumfriesshire. Tel: 01848 331230. Cost: £15 per day (4 fish limit). Boat: £10 per session (2 rods fishing).

EUCHAN, Water See River Nith entry.
EVAN, Water See River Annan entry.

JERRICHO, Loch
Location & Access 78/990810. Immediately to the west of the A701 Dumfries/Beattock road at Lochanbriggs.
Commentary A put-and-take fishery with a substantial reputation. Jerricho covers an area of 12 acres and is open 7 days a week for fishing from April until the end of October. Can be a very busy place to fish.
Fish Stocked with rainbow trout, brook trout and brown trout. Average weight of fish is in the order of 2lb.

Flies & Tactics Bank fishing only and fish are taken from all round the shore. There are good facilities for anglers including tackle shop, kitchen, hot & cold drinks. Easy access for disabled anglers. Most flies and reservoir-type lures will produce results.
Permission & Charges David McMillan, Fishing Tackle Shop, 6 Friars' Vennel, Dumfries DG1 2RN. Tel: 01387 252075; Patties of Dumfries, 109 Queensberry Street, Dumfries. Tel: 01387 252891; R M Currie, Glenclova Caravan Park, Amisfield, Dumfries. Tel: 01387 710447. Cost: £15 per day (4 fish limit).

KETTLETON, Reservoir
Location & Access 78/899003. See Morton Castle Loch entry. The reservoir is immediately to the north of Morton Mains Farm. There is a car park at the lochside.
Commentary A small, remote, reservoir enfolded between Parr Hill (423m) to the east and East Morton Hill (328m) to the west. Kettleton is half mile north/south by up to 150 yds wide. Because of its situation it can often be a wild and windy place to fish. Nevertheless, Kettleton offers good sport in dramatic surroundings.
Fish Stocked with rainbow trout which average 1lb 2oz. The heaviest rainbow trout taken in recent years weighed 7lb 8oz. There are a few wild brown trout as well.
Flies & Tactics Bank fishing only and the north end, where the feeder burn enters from Nether Hill (393m) is perhaps the most productive fishing area. Fishing is from 8am until one hour after sunset. Try: Black Pennell, Grouse & Claret, Silver Invicta - and Viva, Muddlers, Daddy-long-legs, Buzzers.
Permission & Charges Mid Nithsdale Angling Association, 110 Drumlanrig Street, Thornhill, Dumfriesshire. Tel: 01848 330555. Cost: £15 per rod per day. There is a 4 fish limit on rainbow trout, catch as many brown trout as you can. Barbless hooks to be used after taking your limit.

KINNEL, Water See River Annan entry.
MENNOCK, Burn See River Nith entry.

MOFFAT, Fishery
Location & Access 78/090045. A few hundred yards from the centre of Moffat, on the A708 Moffat/Selkirk road, look out for the fishery signpost on your right.
Commentary A popular put-and-take fishery open all year round, apart from Christmas Day and Boxing Day. Excellent facilities for anglers including restaurant, tackle shop, "Family Pond" for beginners and casting instruction and fly-tying instruction by a resident expert.
Fish Rainbow trout, brown trout and brook trout. Average weight of fish, 3lb. Also, occasionally, stocked with "monsters" of up to and over 20lb in weight.
Flies & Tactics Bank fishing only on this spring-fed water and fish respond to most artificial flies and reservoir lure patterns.

OS Map 78 — Nithsdale & Lowther Hills

Permission & Charges Contact: Shaun Ottewell, Fishery Manager, Moffat Fishery, Moffat, Dumfriesshire DG10 9QL. Tel: 01683 221068. Cost: 3 fish limit, £20 per rod, 2 fish limit, £15 per rod. Catch-and-release, £10 full day (until 5pm), £6 half day.

MOFFAT, Water See River Annan entry.

MORTON CASTLE, Loch

Location & Access 78/891992. Leave the A702 Carronbridge/Elvanfoot road at Drumshinock (78/875000). Follow the minor road east to Morton Mains Farm to reach the loch after 2 miles.
Commentary Morton Castle Loch is dominated by the dramatic ruins of Morton Castle, the ancestral home of the Earls of Morton. The loch is owned by the Buccleuch Estates and covers an area of 8 acres. Buccleuch Estates have two other attractive trout fisheries, Starburn Loch (78/851980), 4.25 acres on the south edge of Drumlanrig Woods, and Slatehousse Loch (2.7 acres) within the Drumlanrig Policies. Both these lochs offer visiting anglers excellent fishing in peaceful surroundings.
Fish Stocked throughout the season with rainbow trout. There are also good populations of wild brown trout. Fish average 1lb in weight, but fish of up to 5lb have been caught in recent years.
Flies & Tactics Boat fishing and bank fishing (no wading) and trout are taken everywhere. Dry fly can be particularly effective, as is dapping. Preferred patterns: Daddy-long-legs, nymphs, Invicta, Ace of Spades. Tenants have exclusive use of the loch, limited to 3 rods per day. The fishing season extends from 1st of April until 30th September on Morton Castle Loch and from 1st April until 16th August on Starburn Loch. Barbless hooks must be used and all brown trout must be carefully released.
Permission & Charges The Factor, Buccleuch Estates Ltd. Drumlanrig Mains, Thornhill, Dumfriesshire DG4 3AG. Tel: 01848 600283; Fax: 01848 600244. Cost: 2/3 rods for the day, £40 +VAT, three trout per rod per day. Starburn Loch, 2/3 rods, £30.50 +VAT. Slatehouse Loch: £12.50 +VAT per rod per day. Should a loch not be booked for the day, evening tickets (2 fish limit) will be available from 4.30pm. These can be booked by contacting the Estate Office by telephone after 2pm on the day in question.

NITH, River

Location & Access The River Nith rises approximately 50 miles to the north of Dumfries in the commercial forests surrounding Nith Lodge (70/536093). The section of the river shown on OS Map 78 (see also OS Maps 71 and 84) extends from Knockenjig (78/75011) in the north to Carnsalloch (78/969800) in the south. Access is from the A76 Dumfries/Cumnock road and from minor roads which margin the entire length of both banks of the river.
Commentary The River Nith is one of Scotland's most productive salmon and sea-trout streams, and, also, one of the most attractive rivers to fish. The character of the river is widely varied, from steep-sided, rocky, tree-covered gorges and moorland glides in the upper reaches, to wide, swiftly flowing pools and runs bounded by rich agricultural land further downstream. There are no major lochs on the system and the life of the river depends upon heavy rainfall and the strength of it principal tributaries: Afton Water (71/620140), Crawick Water (78/771103), Euchan Water (78/780091), Mennock Burn (78/809080), Caron Water (78/868976), Cample Water (78/869938), Scaur Water & Shinnel Water (78/874925) and Cairn Water (See OS Map 84, Dumfries). Given good water levels, few other Scottish rivers match the quality of sport that the Nith can produce and the majority of this fishing is readily available to visiting anglers.
Fish Outstanding sea-trout fishing, with upwards of 2,000 fish being taken most seasons. Sea-trout average 2lb 4oz in weight but larger fish, fish of up to and over 5lb in weight, are also caught. The Nith produces between 1,800 and 2,500 salmon which average 8lb/9lb. Some heavier fish, the autumn "greybacks", for which the Solway rivers are renowned, are still taken. The largest salmon caught in recent years weighed 35lb. The upper river and the tributary waters also contain brown trout and grayling. The Dumfries & Galloway Angling Association stocks Cairn Water (see OS Map 84, Dumfries) with brown trout.
Flies & Tactics The Nith Fishing's Improvement Association, in cooperation with the West Galloway Fisheries Trust, have instigated a management plan for the river and a considerable amount of habitat improvement work has been carried out on a number of spawning burns in recent years. The Upper Nithsdale Angling Club has 11 miles of water which contains 35 named pools from Sanquhar downstream to Enterkinfoot (78/859040) including: Crawick Foot, Euchan Foot, Willow Pool, Scaur Pool, Birk Bush, Mennock Foot, Butter Hole, Round Horse, Slunks Pool, Burn Mouth and Black Joe. The Ryehill Beat (78/795084) has 5 excellent pools: Woodend, Big Rock, Gutter Pool, Mill Pool and Ellers Pool and this beat produces about 100 salmon and 200 sea-trout each season. Drumlanrig Castle Fishings, the most productive of the Nith Beats, near Thornhill (78/880954) extends for 7.5 miles and is divided into four beats: Lower, Middle, Upper and Nith Linns. Some of the most notable pools here are: Bell's Pool, Mermaid's Stone, Isla Home Stream, Willowholm Pool, Quarry Pool and Doctor's Pool. Nith Linns Beat will test your casting ability, and your stamina. The pools are reached by steps cut into the steep-sided hill, but this is superb water and when levels are right the beat offers great sport in dramatic surroundings. The Mid Nithsdale Angling Association Water imposes a catch limit of 6 sea-trout and 3 salmon per rod per day. There are 20 named pools on 3 .5 mile beat and it produces approximately 300 sea-trout and between 250 and 350 salmon most seasons. The heaviest salmon taken from the beat in recent years was caught in 1992 and weighed 25lb. The Association also has excellent fishing on Scaur Water which is available to

411

sitors if they are accompanied by a local angler. However, sport on Scaur Water is entirely dependent upon there being high water levels and most visitors opt to fish the Nith itself, rather than the tributaries. For much of the rest of the river access is easy, as is the wading, although you should check details of your beat before setting out. Chest waders are used during the spring and autumn months, thigh waders will suffice for summer. A 12ft rod deals with most eventualities, although in high water a 15ft rod will give you more control of the fly. Spinning and some bait fishing is allowed, but fly-fishing is the preferred fishing method. The use of natural minnow, artificial or natural prawns or shrimps, is prohibited at all times. Salmon flies: Stoat's Tail, Hairy Mary, Yellow Dog, Blue Charm, Brown Turkey. Sea-trout flies: Black Spider, Greenwell's Glory, Peter Ross. Devon minnows are the most popular lures.

Permission & Charges For Upper Nithsdale Angling Club waters: contact: Pollock & McLean, 61 High Street, Sanquhar, Dumfriesshire DG4 6DT. Tel: 01659 50241. Cost: £15 to £30 per day depending upon the time of year. Further information from William Laidlaw, Water Bailiff, 22 Renwick Place, Sanquhar, Dumfriesshire. Tel: 01659 50612. Ryehill: contact R Hyslop, Glenholm, Kirkconnel, Dumfriesshire DG4 6YL. Tel: 01659 67460. Cost: between £15 and £50 per rod per day. Drumlanrig Castle Fishing's: The Factor, Buccleuch Estates, Drumlanrig Mains, Thornhill, Dumfriesshire DG4 3AG. Tel: 01848 600283; Fax: 01848 600244. Cost: Weekly lets are preferred, but day tickets may be available at between £10 and £56 +VAT per rod per day. Weekly lets on Castle Beats, (2 rods) range from £122 +VAT to £893 +VAT per beat. Nith Linns beat, costs per rod per week, from £41 +VAT to £255 +VAT. Day rods, when available, from £9 +VAT to £41+ VAT. The estate also have very comfortable self-catering cottages for rent along with their fishing. Mid Nithsdale Angling Association Water (3 miles double bank fishing, half mile single bank): contact: Mid Nithsdale Angling Association, 110 Drumlanrig Street, Thornhill, Dumfriesshire. Tel: 01848 330555. Cost: weekly and 3-day lets are preferred but day tickets are sometimes available: June to August, £20 per rod per day; August onwards, £35 per rod per day. Barjarg Fishings: contact: Andrew Hunter-Arundell, Newhall, Auldgirth, Dumfriesshire DG2 OTN. Tel: 01848 331342. Cost: £35 per rod per day until the end of August, thereafter, fingers crossed, apply for vacancies. There is a self-catering cottage for rent with the fishing. Blackwood Estate Water (2 miles double bank at 78/907872): contact: Mrs Mathews, Blackwood, Auldgirth, Dumfriesshhire DG2 0UA. Tel: 01387 740256. Cost: approximately £400/500 per week. Friars Carse Water (1 mile, 2 excellent pools): contact: Friars Carse Country House Hotel, Auldgirth, Dumfriesshire DG2 0SA. Tel: 01387 7400388. Cost: £15 to £40 per rod per day (hotel guests have priority). Dalswinton Water (2 miles left-bank fishing - near Ellisland Farm (78/929839) where Robert Burns wrote his epic poem, 'Tam O'Shanter'): contact: Mrs Sylvia Blacklock, The Colt House, Dalswinton Estate, Dalswinton, Dumfriesshire DG2 0XZ. Tel: 01387 740279. Cost: between £40 and £60 per rod per day. Rosehill Beat (78/961812): contact Smiths Gore, 28 Castle Street, Dumfries DG1 1DG. Tel: 01387 263066. Rare cancellations only. See OS Map 84 for other, lower beats.

PRIVATE WATERS CARRICK, Loch 78/044913; DALSWINTON, Loch 78/944844; HEATHERY Dam 78/920933; URR, Loch 78/760845; GAMESHOPE, Loch 78/130166; LEADHILLS, Reservoir 78/890135.
SCAUR, Water See River Nith entry.
SHINNEL, Water See River Nith entry.
STARBURN, Loch See Morton Castle Loch entry.

Hawick and Eskdale

ACREKNOWE, Reservoir See Hellmoor Loch entry.
ALEMOOR, Loch See Hellmoor Loch entry.
ALLAN, Water See River Teviot entry.

BLACK ESK, Reservoir
Location & Access 79/204967. Approach from Sandyford (79/205938) on the B723 Lockerbie/Eskdalemuir road. Turn north and follow the signs to Kilburn to reach the south end of the reservoir after 1.5 miles.
Commentary The Black Esk Reservoir lies in an impounded gorge in the midst of the Castle O'er Forest. It is the source of Black Esk Water which feeds into the Border Esk River (see separate entry). The reservoir is 1 mile in length by up to 500 yds wide and is sheltered from the prevailing winds by the surroundings trees. There are forest walks of various lengths nearby to keep any non-fishing companions amused whilst you lower the level of the loch by the removal of fish.
Fish Excellent stocks of native wild brown trout which average 8oz in weight.
Flies & Tactics Bank fishing only. It is dangerous to wade. Stay safely on terra firma. The west shoreline is easily accessible and is the most productive fishing area. Offer: Black Pennell, March Brown, Peter Ross. Spinning is also allowed.
Permission & Charges Tickets may be obtained at the 1st cottage on the right on the B723, opposite the road up to the reservoir. If nobody is at home, then use the "Honesty Box" provided to deposit your fee. Further details of the fishing may be obtained from R P D'Souza, Kamala, 3B The Crescent, Skelmorlie, Ayrshire PA17 5DX. Tel: 01475 520073. Cost: £5 per rod per day.

BLACK ESK, Water See Border Esk entry.

BORDER ESK, River
Location & Access The Border Esk is formed by two principal feeder streams: the Black Esk (Source: 79/205969) and the White Esk (Source: 79/238053). These two streams meet half a mile upstream from

OS Map 79 — Hawick & Eskdale

Bailiehill at 79/254909 to form the Border Esk. The river then flows south-west and south down Eskdale, through Langholm (79/362845), Canonbie (85/394763) and Longtown (85/379690) to reach the sea in the Solway Firth after a journey of approximately 45 miles. The A7 Longtown/Hawick road borders the river to Langholm. Thereafter, the B709 Langholm/Eskdalemuir road and other minor roads give easy access to the stream and to its tributaries.

Commentary The Border Esk is one of the most lovely of all the South-West of Scotland rivers. It is fed by a number of tributaries which are, in their own right, excellent fisheries. The most significant include: Meggat Water (79/298912), Ewes Water (79/362849), Wauchope Water (79/362846), Tarras Water (79/374807), Liddle Water (85/391738) and Lyne Water (85/360652). Liddle Water is the most important tributary. It rises from Windy Knowe (329) near Saughtree (80/563966) which was a station on the old Waverly Line, the railway from Edinburgh to Carlisle which was closed in 1969. The main tributary of Liddle Water is Hermitage Water, an attractive, busy, clear stream that flows past the dramatic ruins of Hermitage Castle (79/498960), a gaunt, square, impregnable fortress which was historically known as The Strength of Liddisdale. The first few miles of Liddle Water lie on the boundary between Scotland and England and the last few miles of the Esk, before it enters the Solway Firth. The ownership of this area was a source of constant dispute between the two countries for centuries and it was known as 'the Debatable Lands' - a lawless jungle where almost every inch of soil is soaked in the blood of feudal dispute. The catchment of the Border Esk and its attendant streams has been heavily afforested in recent years and this has brought with it the usual raft of problems associated with increasing water acidity, siltation, flash-flooding, loss of wildlife and diminishing juvenile fish stocks. These matters are now being addressed by those responsible for the health of the river.

Fish Primarily sea-trout and finnock, but good numbers of salmon and brown trout as well. In its hey-day, the Border Esk could produce upwards of 8,000 sea-trout each season. Today, the number is in the region of 2,500. Sea-trout average 2lb in weight with a few fish of up to and over 5lb being taken most seasons. Sea-trout run the river from March onwards but the peak time for sea-trout fishing is June, July and August. Approximately 1,500 salmon are taken and they average 9lb, but fish of over 20lb are also caught. The spring run of salmon has virtually disappeared and most fish are now taken during September, and October. Season ends in October. These fish are fresh run, although, of course, there will be some red fish amongst them which should be returned. Brown trout fishing is best on the upper reaches of the Esk and on Liddle Water. Brown trout average 8oz in weight but some much larger specimen fish are taken most seasons.

Flies & Tactics Many parts of the river are tree-lined and this can make casting interesting. An ability either to roll cast or Spey cast is essential to effectively cover a number of the lies. This is most true of the river between Langholm and Canonbie but any problems experienced are more than offset by the beauty of the surroundings, particularly during the back-end months when the tress are red and gold in autumnal splendour. Wading is generally reasonably safe, provided that you seek local advice before setting out. Many of the pools are very deep, over-hung with under-water rock shelves, and an ill-considered step could place you in great danger. When the river is low it can also become weedy, but weed is quickly washed out after a good spate. Night fishing for sea-trout is perhaps the most exciting aspect of fishing on the Border Esk. Reconnoitre your beat carefully, during daylight hours, and choose you fishing positions. Let the fish come to you, rather than splashing around in search of them. Some anglers use a 15ft double-handed rod, but a 10ft/11ft, single-handed rod will more than adequately deal with most fishing eventualities. Spinning and bait fishing is allowed on some of the beats, but fly-fishing is preferred. Most of the smaller tributaries are preserved as spawning areas and they are not fished. Sea-trout flies: Black Pennell, Grouse & Claret, Mallard & Claret, Soldier Palmer, Invicta, Peter Ross, Teal Blue & Silver. Salmon flies: Blue Charm, Munro Killer, Brown Turkey, Willie Gunn, Garry Dog, Ally's Shrimp, Silver Stoat's Tail, General Practitioner. Trout flies: March Brown, Greenwell's Glory, Silver Butcher. Dry fly also produces good results.

Permission & Charges Much of the river is available to the public, mainly through the Esk & Liddle Fisheries Association. They offer a range of options, from an All Ticket Water to tickets for specific beats: Canonbie, Langholm, Lower Liddle Ticket and the Newcastleton Ticket. Precise details of the extent of the fishing, and location maps, are noted on the tickets. The Buccleuch Estate lets fishing on beats upstream from Byreburnfoot (85389778) upstream to Broomholm (85/371818): including Gilnockie, Glencartholm, Irvine House Lower, Irvine House Mid and Irvine House Upper (right bank only). There are a number of excellent pools and runs here including, and working upstream from the end of the Gilnockie Beat, Bridge Pool, Mill Stream, Caul Pool, Crooked Pool, Peats Hole, Stone End, Boat Pool, Carrot Bed and Scar Pool. Contact: for the Esk & Liddle Fishery Association Waters: George Graham, The Old School, Hagg-on-Esk, Canonbie, Dumfriesshire DG14 0XE. Tel: 01387 371416, or Stevenson & Johnstone WS, Bank of Scotland Buildings, Langholm, Dumfriesshire DG13 0AD. Tel: 01387 380428. Cost: All Waters Ticket: from £61 to £119 per rod per week. Day tickets on some beats may be available, from £7 to £38 per rod. Ask for details when booking. Buccleuch Estate Beats: Contact: The Factor, Buccleuch Estates, Estate Office, Ewesbank, Langholm, Dumfriesshire DG12 0ND. Tel: 01387 380202 (Prices on application). White Esk Fishing: Contact: Hart Manor Hotel, Eskdalemuir, by Langholm, Dumfriesshire DG13 0QQ. Tel: 01387 373217. Cost: £10 per rod per day. Tanlawhill Beat (79/239912): Contact: J D Jewitt, Lyneholm House, Westerkirk, by Langholm,

Hawick & Eskdale — OS Map 79

Dumfriesshire DG13 0PF. Tel: 01387 370228. Meggat Water: Contact: W Briggs, Georgefield, Westerkirk, by Langholm, Dumfriesshire DG13 0NJ. Tel: 01387 370227 (let with B & B accommodation). Westerhall Beat (79/319893): Contact: K Irving, Westerhall, by Langholm, Dumfriesshire DG13 0NQ. Tel: 01387 370257. Burnfoot Beat (79/336887): Contact: Mr Lavericks, Burnfoot House, Burnfoot, by Langholm, Dumfriesshire DG13 0HJ. Tel: 01387 370611. Broomholm Beat (79/371818): Contact: Mrs Anne Collett, Broomholm House, Langholm, Dumfriesshire DG13 0LJ. Tel: 01387 380448. Mrs Collett lets fishing in conjunction with excellent self-catering cottages, each sleeping six, at between £250 - £920 per week depending upon the time of year, including 3 rods fishing the Esk. Other estate beats: expect to pay in the order of between £100 and £800 per rod week. For details of fishing on the Border Esk in England, contact: The March Bank Hotel, Longtown, Cumbria CA6 5XP. Tel: 01228 791325.

BORTHWICK, Water See River Teviot entry.
CLEARBURN, Loch See Ettrick Water entry.
CROSS REFERENCES DRYFE Water (See OS Map 78); MILK, Water of (See OS Map 85); CORRIE Water (See OS Map 85); MOFFAT Water (See OS Map 78); LOCH OF THE LOWES (See OS Map 73); ALE Water (See OS Map 73)

ETTRICK, Water
Location & Access Source: 79/174066 Outfall: 73/489349. The section of Ettrick Water shown on OS Map 79 (see also OS Map 73) extends for a distance of 15 miles, from its source at Ettrick Head on Capel Fell (678m), downstream to just north of Tushielaw. The stream is easily accessible from the B7009 Tushielaw/Selkirk road and from the B709 Ramseycleuch/Eskdalemuir road.
Commentary Ettrick Water is a major tributary of the River Tweed (see OS Maps 73 and 74) and, on OS Map 79, Ettrick Water also has its own substantial tributaries: Tima Water (79/274145) and Rankle Burn (79/304176). The stream flows through magnificent scenery, wild moorlands and gentle, rounded hills although in recent years the landscape, and the river habitat, have been badly effected by ill-planned commercial forestry. James Hogg (1770-1835), the Ettrick Shepherd, sheep-farmer and poet and author was born by the stream at Ettrickhill (79/263144) and he, like many of his literary contemporaries, was a skilled angler. To the north of Rankle Burn, on the B711 Tushielaw/Greenbank road, is Clearburn Loch (79/341155) and this offers a pleasant alternative fishing venue in low water conditions. A great deal of habitat improvement work is being carried out by the Tweed Foundation on the uppper reaches of Ettrick Water and the status of fish stocks in the river is improving year by year.
Fish Fewer today than in Hogg's time, but still a good chance of salmon and the occassional sea-trout. Ettrick Water can produce approximately 80 to 100 salmon in a good year but sport is entirely dependent upon heavy rainfall. Salmon average in the order of 8lb, although those caught during the early months of the season tend to be smaller. The tributaries are not fished as they are significant spawning areas. Brown trout average 6oz/8oz in weight.
Flies & Tactics Being there after a spate is the most important tactic, otherwise, tempting fish to take can be difficult. The river is easily covered with a single-handed rod and wading is not required. Clearburn Loch is boat fishing only and this water contains excellent stocks of wild trout which rise readily to the fly. The east end of the loch, in the vicinity of the 2 small islands is the most productive fishing area. On the river, small flies should be used: Garry Dog, Willie Gunn, Dusty Miller, Silver Wilkinson, or even trout fly patterns such as Black Pennell, Grouse & Claret, Silver Invicta.
Permission & Charges The salmon fishing is largely owned by the Buccleuch Estates, trout fishing is let to the Selkirk Angling Club. For details and advice, contact: The Factor, Buccleuch Estates, Bowhill, Selkirk TD7 5ES. Tel: 01750 20753. Also, Steve Osbourne, Tushielaw Inn, by Selkirk. Tel: 01750 62205. Cost: Salmon fishing, between £20 and £40 per rod per day dependent upon the time of year; trout fishing, £5 per rod per day; Clearburn Loch, £15 per rod per day (including the use of the boat). Trout fishing is free to Tushielaw Inn residents.

EWES, Water See Border Esk entry.

HELLMOOR, Loch
Location & Access 79/385170. Approach from Hawick on the B711 Martinhouse/Tushielaw road. 150yds after passing across the south end of Alemoor (97/400155), look for the double gate on the right of the road. Pass through (keys from Hawick Angling Club - see address below) and follow the track north through the forest. At the junction, bear right and continue until you see the loch ahead. Park in the quarry on the left of the road and hoof it for the last 200 yds to reach the loch.
Commentary Alemoor Loch, which you cross on the way to Hellmoor, is primarily a coarse fishery containing pike and perch, although the Hawick Angling Club have in the past stocked it with brown trout. A few remain and it is always worth a cast or two on your way either to or from Hellmoor Loch. The loch covers an area of 60 acres and it lies on a damp plateau on the edge of the forest sheltered by surrounding hills: Bleak Law (370m), Broadgair Knowe (378m) and White Knowe (360m). The club also has fishing on two smaller waters to the south of Hawick: Williestruther Loch (79/492115), approximately 8 acres, and Acreknowe Reservoir (79/495106) which is 14 acres.
Fish Brown trout in Hellmoor, and some enormous pike - a pike of 28lb has been caught here - brown trout and rainbow trout in the other waters.
Flies & Tactics Apart from Acreknowe, where there is 1 boat, all fishing is from the bank. Spinning, bait or fly-fishing on Williestruther, fly only on Acreknowe, bait, spinning and fly-fishing on Hellmoor. On Williestruther and Acreknowe there is a bag limit of 2

OS Map 79 — Hawick & Eskdale

rainbow trout and 4 brown trout per rod per day and on Hellmoor, 4 brown trout per rod per day.
Permission & Charges Contact: The Pet Shop, I Union Street, Hawick, Roxburghshire. Tel: 01450 373543. Cost: Hellmoor Loch & Williestruther Loch, Acreknowe Reservoir and other club waters, including the river, £7 per day. For further information about the club's fishing contact: The Secretary, Hawick Angling Club, 6 Sandbed, Hawick, Roxburghshire. Tel: 01450 373771. Robert Johnson (Tel: 01450 372266) is Club President.

LIDDLE, Water See Border Esk entry.
LYNE, Water See Border Esk entry.
MEGGAT, Water See Border Esk entry.
PRIVATE WATERS KINGSIDE, Loch 79/342134; CROOKED, Loch 79/355139; GOOSE, Loch 79/351142; WINDYLAW, Loch 79/361142; BACK, Loch 79/369157; SHAWS UNDER, Loch 79/386195; SHIELSWOOD, Loch 79/454191; ASHKIRK, Loch 79/477192; BRANXHOLME EASTER, Loch 79/435118; BRANXHOLME WESTER, Loch 79/422111.
RANKLE, Burn See Ettrick Water.

SKEEN, Loch

Location & Access 79/173165. Access is from the A708 Moffat/Selkirk road. There is a car park at the foot of the spectacular, 200ft high 'Grey Mare's Tail' waterfall. Park here and enjoy a spectacular hike up the side of the waterfall to reach the loch.
Commentary Loch Skeen lies in a dramatic corrie at the head of the waterfall and the loch is dominated by the dark crags of White Coomb (822m) and Lochcraig Head (800m). Take great care when making the climb up from the road, particularly in wet weather. After a vigorous 45 minutes you should be catching your first fish.
Fish A wild brown trout haven amidst the storm of Lowland put-and-take, commercial, fisheries. Loch Skeen trout are very pretty, fight hard and average 8oz in weight. From time to time larger fish of up to 2lb are taken. Vendace (a species of Arctic char) have been introduced to Loch Skeen by Scottish Natural Heritage.
Flies & Tactics This is a considerable expedition, more so if you fish all round the shoreline: Loch Skeen is 1 mile long by 350yds wide. If you can bear to pack thigh waders, they are a great help. Trout may be taken from all round the bank but the north end of the loch is perhaps the most productive fishing area. Flies: use black flies, such as Black Pennell, Black Zulu, Black Spider as well as Peter Ross, Silver Butcher and March Brown.
Permission & Charges Permission is not required.

SLITRIG, Water See River Teviot entry.
TARRAS, Water See Border Esk entry.

TEVIOT, River

Location & Access Source: 79/340986 Outfall: 74/724339. The section of the River Teviot shown on OS Map 79 (see also OS Map 74) extends from its source between Black Burn Head (471m) and White Hope Edge (475m) and extends north-east, passing through Hawick (79/504150), for a distance of 17 miles to Ashybank (79/550180). The river is accessed from the A698 Hawick/Kelso road and from the A7 Langholm/Hawick road. The upper reaches of the river may be reached via the minor road that runs south-west from Teviothead (79/405053) to Commonbrae (79/375019).
Commentary The River Teviot is one of the principal tributaries of the River Tweed (see OS Map 74, Kelso and OS Map 73, Galashiels and Ettrick Forest) and it greets the Tweed in the waters of the famous Junction Pool at Kelso after a journey of 35 miles. The River Teviot on OS Map 79 has 3 principal tributaries of its own: Allan Water, which flows in at Newmill (79/455106), Borthwick Water, which joins the Teviot at Martinshouse (79/480134) and Slitrig Water which meets the Teviot in Hawick. Even in its upper reaches the River Teviot is a considerable stream and it grows in size as it bustles along through Upper Teviotdale past ancient battlefields and ruined castles.
Fish Salmon, sea-trout and brown trout. Although spring runs have diminished in recent years, a few salmon may still be caught during the early months of the season. However, the best of the sport is to be had at the back-end. Approximately 100/150 salmon may be taken during a good year. The average weight of fish is in the order of 8lb/9lb. Sea-trout numbers have also diminished, but the Teviot has always been the principal sea-trout fishery on the Tweed System and good numbers of sea-trout can still be taken today. The Tweed Foundation is hard at work improving the spawning habitat on all their rivers and this should, eventually, vastly improve the health and numbers of fish in the river and its tributaries. Brown trout in the Teviot are of modest size, 6oz/8oz, but a few larger fish are caught most seasons.
Flies & Tactics The upper river is adequately fished with a single-handed rod and there are few bankside obstructions to impede casting. Downstream from Hawick, a longer rod is useful, to effectively swim the fly over the lies. Recent mass-afforestation of the headwaters of the river has made the Teviot even more of a spate stream, and heavy rainfall is required before the river will produce of its best. Thigh waders are useful, although many of the pools are best tackled fine and far off to avoid spooking the fish. Trout respond well to dry fly and give great sport, particularly in the tributaries. These streams are, however, awkward to fish in many places because of bankside vegetation and they will fully test your casting skills. Salmon Flies: Willie Gunn, Garry Dog, Silver Wilkinson, Munro Killer, Ally-s Shrimp, Black Doctor, General Practitioner. Sea-trout flies: Black Pennell, Mallard & Claret, Peter Ross. Brown trout flies: Partridge & Yellow, Greenwell's Glory, Iron Blue Dun, March Brown, Silver Butcher.
Permission & Charges The Hawick Angling Club may have day tickets available, Monday to Friday only. Contact: The Pet Shop, I Union Street, Hawick, Roxburghshire. Tel: 01450 373543. Cost: £20 per rod per day. Trout fishing tickets, which also include fish-

ing on the Ale, Borthwick, Rule and Slitrig waters, cost £4 per rod per day. For further information about the club's fishing contact: The Secretary, Hawick Angling Club, 6 Sandbed, Hawick, Roxburghshire. Tel: 01450 373771. (See also Hellmore Loch entry).

TIMA, Water See Ettrick Water entry.
WAUCHOPE, Water See Border Esk entry.
WHITE ESK, Water See Border Esk entry.
WILLIESTRUTHER, Loch See Hellmoor Loch entry.

The Cheviot Hills

CROSS REFERENCE ENTRY All the Scottish waters on OS Map 80 are described on OS Map 74, Kelso.

Alnwick & Morpeth

The game fishing within OS Map 81 is not relevant to this publication.

Stranraer & Glen Luce

BLACK, Loch (Balminnoch)
Location & Access 82/280655. The Black Loch lies on the south side of the minor road between Glassoch (82/335695) on the B7207 Newton Stewart/Barhill road in the north and Glenluce (82/200575) on the A747 to the south.
Commentary An attractive 6 acres forest fishery close to the Three Lochs Caravan Park at Balminnoch. The other two lochs, Loch Ronald and Loch Heron, are coarse fisheries. The Black Loch is a very popular fishery and advance booking is essential.
Fish Stocked with brown trout (1lb 8oz to 3lb) and rainbow trout (3lb to 10lb).
Flies & Tactics Boat fishing only on this 14ft deep loch. Flies that work well include Pheasant Tail Nymphs, Daddy Long-Legs, Orange & Black Buzzers.
Permission & Charges Contact: The Water Bailiff, Mark of Ronald, by Newton Stewart, Wigtownshire. Tel: 01671 830202. Cost: £15 per day for a 3 fish limit. There is also an evening ticket at £8 for a 1 fish limit.

CHESNEY, Loch
Location & Access 82/336540
Commentary At the time of writing this water did not contain fish.

CLUGSTON, Loch
Location & Access 82/345574. Approach from Spittal Croft (83/357579) on the B733 Wigtown/Kirkcowan road. Turn west along the minor road to reach the loch after 1.5 miles.
Commentary A pleasant loch lying on the course of the Craigdow Burn, approximately 23 acres in extent, sheltered by forestry planting to the east.
Fish Wild brown trout and rainbow trout of up to 6lb in weight.
Flies & Tactics Boat fishing only and trout rise and may be taken all over the loch. Offer them: Ke-He, Greenwell's Glory, Gold Butcher.
Permission & Charges Contact: Peter McDougal, Corsemalzie House Hotel, Port William, Newton Stewart, Wigtownshire. Tel: 01988 860254; Fax: 01988 860213. Cost: £16 per rod per day including the use of the boat. Hotel guests have priority.

COARSE FISHERIES GARWACHIE, Loch 82/344690; ROBIN, Loch 82/247559; WHITFIELD, Loch 82/235555; RONALD, Loch 82/265645; HERON, Loch 82/274650; BARFAD, Loch 82/325663.
CONNELL, Loch 82/018682 At the time of writing this water did not contain fish.
CROSS REFERENCE BLADNOCH, River (see OS Map 83).

DINDINNIE, Reservoir
Location & Access 82/022606. Turn left from the A718 Stranraer/Kirkcolm road at Auchneel (82/038625) 1.5 miles north from Stranraer. Follow the minor road west for a further 1 and 1.25 mile to Dindinnie Farm. Park at the farm and walk a quarter mile to reach the reservoir.
Commentary A small (15 acre) reservoir managed by the Stranraer & District Angling Association and drained by the Piltanton Burn. The burn flows south-east for 10 miles to reach the sea through Luce Sands between Ringdoo Point in the west and the golf course to the east (82/170565).
Fish Dindinnie Reservoir is stocked with brown trout which average 1lb in weight. The Piltanton Burn contains salmon and sea-trout - depending upon water levels - from June onwards. The most productive months are September and October.
Flies & Tactics On Dindinnie, begin at the south end of the reservoir where the 2 feeder burns enter. There is a bag limit of 3 fish per rod per day. Offer: Black Spider, Greenwell's Glory, Silver Butcher. The fishing on Piltanton Burn is the 2 mile stretch in the vicinity of Dunragit. Approach from the road bridge on the A715 at 82/145565. There are 2 beats, each of approximately 800m in length, containing 16 pools. Use light tackle and the best fishing is had at dusk or in the early morning. Try: Ally's Shrimp, Munro Killer, Garry Dog, Stoat's Tail, Black Pennell, Grouse & Claret, Teal Blue & Silver.
Permission & Charges Eric MacLean, The Sports Shop, 90 George Street, Stranraer. Tel: 01776 702705. Cost: £15 per rod per day. After September, Piltanton Burn costs £15 per rod per day.

DRUMNESCAT, Loch 82/338498. At the time of

OS Map 82 — Stranraer & Glen Luce

writing this water did not contain fish.

DUNSKEY, Loch
Location & Access 82/004565. Adjacent to the west side of the A764 Portpatrick/Little Goldenoch road. Park next to the boathouse and fishing hut.
Commentary Two small lochs, attractively situated within the grounds of the Dunskey Estate. Upper Dunskey is 11 acres, Dunskey is 5 acres. The lochs are the exclusive preserve of the 2 rods per loch permitted to fish each day.
Fish Stocked with good quality brown trout and rainbow trout which average 1lb. Fish of up to and over 3lb in weight are also frequently taken.
Flies & Tactics Boat fishing by fly only and there is a bag limit of 3 fish per rod per day and 2 fish per rod for evening sessions. Trout may be taken all over the loch. Flies: Bibio, Grouse & Claret, Black Pennell. On warm, summer evenings small dry flies also work well, particularly a Black Spider.
Permission & Charges Philip C Hoyle, The Kennels, Dunskey Estate, Portpatrick, Wigtownshire DG9 8TJ. Tel: 01776 810364. Cost: £15 per rod per session, including the use of the boat.

GOWER, Loch
82/327547. At the time of writing this water did not contain fish.

KNOCKQUHASSEN, Reservoir
Location & Access 82/020594. Approach from Stranraer via the old Portpatrick road to Knockglass. At the foot of Auchterlure Hill (82/048596) turn right to Greenfield Farm. The reservoir is a mile to the west.
Commentary Knockquhassen lies on Broad Moor and it can often be a wild and windy place to fish. The reservoir is half a mile east/west by up to 180 yds wide and is drained by the Crailloch Burn into Piltanton Burn (see separate entry).
Fish Brown trout which average 10oz in weight.
Flies & Tactics Bank fishing only. The north-west shoreline is the place to begin, amidst the small bays and promontories. There is a bag limit of 3 fish per rod per day. Flies: Ke-He, Grouse & Claret, Alexandra.
Permission & Charges See Dindinnie Reservoir.

LENNOWS, Loch
82/332536. At the time of writing this water did not contain fish.

LOCHNAW CASTLE, Loch
Location & Access 82/993632. Approach from Leswalt on the B7043 road. The loch lies adjacent to the south side of the road, 2 miles west from Leswalt.
Commentary A pretty little loch covering an area of 46 acres, complete with small island and ruined castle, surrounded by mature beech woods and rhododendron bushes.
Fish Stocked with Loch Leven trout which average 12oz in weight. Also, the occasional fish of up to 3lb.
Flies & Tactics Boat fishing only and trout may be taken all round the loch, but the margins of the island is the place to begin. Flies: Black Spider, Invicta, Gold Butcher.

Permission & Charges Contact: Lochnaw Castle, Leswalt, by Stranraer, Wigtownshire. Tel: 01776 870227. Cost: £15 per rod per day.

LUCE, water of
Location & Access Source: Cross Water of Luce 76/200818; Main Water of Luce 76/135782. Access is from a convenient minor road and from estate roads which border the stream.
Commentary The Water of Luce is formed by the meeting of two streams: Main Water of Luce and Cross Water of Luce. Cross Water rises from the commercial forestry plantations that smother Knockshin Hill (202m), in Ayrshire, whilst Main Water of Luce has its source on the south slopes of Beneraird Hill (439m). The streams meet at New Luce (82175646) to form the Water of Luce which flows into the Solway Firth by St Helena Island (82/197557). The West Galloway Fishery Trust, riparian owners and other interested parties have introduced a number of conservation and management measures which will improve the numbers of the salmonid population in the Luce, and in other rivers throughout the region.
Fish Salmon, sea-trout and small brown trout. Precise details of the number of migratory fish caught are not available. Fish are fewer than in years past, particularly sea-trout. Depending upon water conditions, a good year might produce in the region of 100 fish.
Flies & Tactics Both streams are noted for rapid variations in water levels and this fact has been made worse by blanket afforestation on the headwaters. Spate water, upon which sport depends, drains off very quickly. Salmon congregate in the estuary and, when conditions are suitable, run upstream to New Luce more-often-than-not without pause. Therefore, the best of the fishing is to be found above New Luce. - on Cross Water of Luce, upstream to the footbridge at Dalnigap (76/133710), and on Main Water of Luce, upstream to where the flow from Penwhirn Reservoir joins the stream (82/137697). A single-handed rod will cover most eventualities and keeping a low profile, off the skyline, to avoid spooking the fish. Flies: Ally's Shrimp, General Practitioner, Stoat's Tail, Silver Stoat's Tail, Munro Killer, Garry Dog.
Permission & Charges Rods are not generally available of a day basis. Beats are let, to the same tenants, for the whole season. For further information, contact: Stair Estates, Estate Office, Rephad, Stranraer, Wigtownshire. Tel: 01776 702024. At the time of writing there are no vacancies. However, there is an exception in regard to access to the Cross Water of Luce. A limited number of day tickets for visitors may be had through application to: Jim Greenhill, 20 Challoch Crescent, Leswalt, Stranraer, Wigtownshire. Tel: 01776 870638. Cost: £15 per rod per day.

PENWHIRN, Burn
See Penwhirn Reservoir entry.

PENWHIRN, Reservoir
Location & Access 82/124696. Approach from the minor road at New Luce (82/172648). Pass under the railway and follow the road north-west beside the Main Water of Luce (see separate entry) to reach the

Stranraer & Glen Luce   OS Maps 82

reservoir after a distance of 3.5 miles. Park near the dam at the east end of the reservoir.
Commentary This is an excellent fishery in a dramatic, moorland and forest setting lying to the north of Diddles Hill (200m). Penwhirn is 1 mile east/west by up to quarter of a mile wide and the reservoir is fed by the Penwhirn Burn which rises on Drumcargo (209m) and Loch Ree. Loch Ree (82/104699), to the west on Penwhirn, is reached via Awies (82/115695) after an easy walk of approximately half a mile.
Fish Wild brown trout which average 10oz.
Flies & Tactics Bank fishing only and the north shore produces the best results. The area of the inlet burn at 82/120698 is a good place to start. Penwhirn Burn, and the stream connecting Penwhirn to Loch Ree, also hold good trout and they fish well after a heavy spate. On Loch Ree, fish may be taken from all round the shore. There is a bag limit for 4 fish per rod per day. Flies: Black Pennell, Greenwell's Glory, Silver Butcher.
Permission & Charges See Dindinnie Reservoir entry.

PILTANTON Burn See Dindinnie Reservoir entry.
PRIVATE WATERS STRANRAER & DISTRICT ANGLING ASSOCIATION reserves the following lochs: BLACK, Loch (82/113615); WHITE, Loch (82/104610); LOCH MAGILLIE (82/098596)
The following are all private waters: LOGAN MAINS, Loch 82/102431; CULTS, Loch 82/121604; CASTLE, Loch 82/280534; MOCHRUM, Loch 82/300530; BLACK, Loch (Mochrum) 82/300545; FELL, Loch 82/310550; HEMPTON, Loch 82/307547; WAYOCH, Loch 82/302562; BLACK, Loch (Drumblair) 82/283510; DOON, Loch (Drumblair) 82/286511; BLACK, Loch (Gass Moor) 82/329569; BARHAPPLE, Loch 82/260592; DERNAGLAR, Loch 82/263582; ELDRIG, Loch 82/254694; ELRIG, Loch 82/325491.
REE, Loch See Penwhirn Reservoir entry.

RYAN Sea-loch (North Channel & Luce Bay)
Location & Access KIRCLACHIE, Burn (82/082632); BEOCH, Burn (82/080647); SEVERAL, Burn (82/076659); CLADDY HOUSE, Burn (82/071674); GLEN, Burn (82/061690); KIRKCOLM, Burn (82/040685); SOLEBURN BRIDGE (82/035644); PORT KALE (82/985552); PORT OF SPITTAL BAY (82/020520); DRUMBREDDAN BAY (82/078436); PORT LAGAN BAY (82/095405); KILSTAY BAY (82/129383); TERALLY BAY (82/124411); ARDWELL (82/111454); SANDHEAD BAY (82/098493); SANDMILL, Burn (82102508); CLAYSHANT (82/113524); MILLON, Burn (82/209538); AUCHENEMAIG BAY (82/235518); CRAIGNARGET Burn (82/261511); PORT WILLIAM (82/336436)
Commentary There is always a good chance of encountering sea-trout where burns enter Loch Ryan, the North Channel off the west coast of the Mull of Galloway.
Fish Sea-trout
Flies & Tactics Fish around the shore of Luce Bay. They are present throughout year but are most likely to be caught from March until June. The best time to launch your attack is after heavy rain when the burns are in spate. Take great care when fishing and seek local advice about the safety and stability of the sands prior to setting out. Remember to wash your tackle at the end of the day. Sea water is highly corrosive. Flyfishing can be just as effective as spinning. Offer: Black Pennell, Silver Invicta, Peter Ross.

SOULSEAT, Loch
Location & Access 82/100590. Turn south from the A75 Stranraer/Glenluce road near the church at 82/101603. Follow the minor road for 1 mile to reach the loch.
Commentary A popular loch with both local and visiting anglers. Soulseat is half a mile long by up to a quarter of a mile wide and covers an area of 72 acres. The loch is easily accessible and offers excellent sport in very attractive surroundings. There is an access area for disabled anglers.
Fish Managed by the Stranraer & District Angling Association and regularly stocked with both brown and rainbow trout. The average weight is 1lb 8oz and fish of up to and over 5lb are not uncommon.
Flies & Tactics Boat fishing and bank fishing and both methods can be equally successful. This is a shallow water and fish may be taken almost anywhere, but the promontory by the roadside at the south-west end is not a bad place to begin, as it is in the vicinity of where the Soulseat Burn enters at the south end of the loch. There is a bag limit of 3 fish per rod per day. Flies: Soldier Palmer, Grouse & Green, Gold Butcher. Reservoir lures also produce results, as does dry fly on calm evenings.
Permission & Charges See Dindinnie Reservoir entry.

TORWOOD, Loch
Location & Access 82/245642. See Black Loch (Balminnoch) entry. Torwood Loch is at the Torwood House Hotel, 100 yards north from Gass.
Commentary A pleasant, shallow (2' 9"deep) put-and-take fishery of 1.5 acres.
Fish Stocked with between 500 and 1,000 brown trout and rainbow trout each year. Average weight of fish, 1lb. Fish of up to 6lb are taken.
Flies & Tactics Easy bank fishing using leaded nymphs, daddy long-legs and dry flies. The chef at the hotel will be delighted to cook your catch to order.
Permission & Charges Contact: David Canning, Torwood House Hotel, Gass, Glenluce, Newton Stewart, Wigtownshire. Tel: 01581 300469. Cost: £6 for catch release per session, £10 per session for a 3 fish limit.

WHITE, Loch 82/343560. At the time of writing this water did not contain fish.

Kirkcudbright

BARLAY, Burn See Water of Fleet entry.
BIG WATER OF FLEET, River See Water of Fleet entry.
BLACK, Burn See River Bladnoch entry.
BLACK WATER OF DEE, River See River Dee entry.

BLADNOCH, River
Location & Access Source 76/286750 Outfall 83/440547. Access to the upper reaches of the river is from the B7027 Newton Stewart/Barrhill road and from Shennanton (82/343632) on the A75 Newton Stewart/Glenluce road. The middle and lower river is easily accessed from the B733 Wigtown/Kirkcowan road and the B7005 Bladnoch/Spittal road.
Commentary The river rises from Maberry Loch (see OS Map 76, Girvan) in Ayrshire and flows south-east to reach the sea in Wigtown Bay after a journey of approximately 7 miles. A number of tributary streams add to the flow of the main river and the most significant of these are: Black Burn, which joins the Bladnoch near Carsebuie (82/339659), Tarf Water, at The Holm (82/348603) and the Water of Malzie near High Barness (83/379544). Blanket afforestation of the headwaters, carried out during the 1970's and 1980's has degraded the water quality and increased the speed and at which spates clear the river, as well as increasing water acidity and damaging the spawning habitat. The river is also affected by peat-sediment which is washed into the stream from forestry ploughing furrows. The West Galloway Fishery Trust, riparian owners and other interested parties, are now addressing these matters in an attempt to bring the river back to its former state.
Fish Salmon, a few sea-trout, excellent brown trout and voracious pike. Accurate catch statistics are not readily available, but are probably in the order of 200 fish each season depending upon water conditions. The average weight of fish is 10lb. The heaviest salmon taken was a 34lb fish, caught in 1972. More recently, in August 1992, a 28lb salmon was landed and most seasons produce fish of up to 20lb. Brown trout of up to and over 4lb in weight are also caught. The Bladnoch still maintains a good spring run of salmon and these fish arrive from late February onwards. Indeed, almost 35% of the total catch from the river is taken between February and May. Thereafter, September and October are the most productive months, but much depends upon heavy rainfall.
Flies & Tactics The upper reaches of the river, from Maberry Loch downstream to the Linn of Barnoise and Barhoise Dam (82/340617) is primarily a trout fishery and very few salmon are caught here now. The best of the fishing is from below the dam, downstream to where the Crows Burn enters (83/372560). Thereafter, until it reaches Wigtown Bay, the steam meanders sluggishly through flat farm lands and rough grazings. Although the river is generally narrow and wading is not required, a 12ft double-handed rod is advised in order to properly present the fly; and to hold fish, particularly spring salmon, in a strong current. Backing up can be very effective in the slow-moving sections when a strong wind disguises evil intent by ruffling the surface of the stream. The most productive of the many pools on the Bladnoch include: the 2 Crouse Pools, High Bank, Ash Trees, 40-Footer Pool, Nut Pool, The Pot, Bridge Pool, Ivy Tree, Plantation Pool, McLellans and the Junction Pool. The Water of Tarf can also produce excellent sport, both in its lower and upper reaches, and there are some fine holding pools on the river. The other tributaries are not fished. Flies: General Practitioner, Shrimp Fly, Garry Dog, Thunder & Lightning, Silver Stoat's Tail, Hairy Mary, Black Doctor.
Permission & Charges Upper River: Newton Stewart & District Angling Association, per Galloway Guns & Tackle, 36a Arthur Street, Newton Stewart DG8 6DE. Tel: 01671 403404. Upper Tarf: David Canning, Torwood House Hotel, Glenluce, Newton Stewart. Tel: 01581 300469; A Brown, Three Lochs Holiday Park, Kirkcowan, Newton Stewart, Wigtownshire. Tel: 01671 830304. Middle and Lower River: Jonathan Haley, Mochrum Park Sporting Holidays, Riverview Cottage, Spittal Bridge, Nr Kirkcowan, Wigtownshire DG8 0DG. Tel: 01671 830471 or 01422 822148; Peter McDougal, Corsemalzie Hotel, Port William, Newton Stewart, Wigtownshire DB8 9RL. Tel: 01988 860254; Fax: 01988 860213 (also five miles of fishing on the Water of Tarf and trout fishing on Malzie Burn and Clugston Loch); Peter McLaughlan, Bladnoch Inn, Bladnoch, Wigtown. Tel: 01988 402200; Galloway Sporting Agents, Wyncherry Yard, North Corar, Newton Stewart, Galloway DG8 8EJ. Tel: 01850 733670 or 01860 553584; Fax: 01532 813056; Sue & Garry Pope, Church End, 6 Main Street, Kirkcowan, Wigtownshire. Tel: 01671 830246 (also fishing on Water of Tarf); Creebridge Hotel, Newton Stewart, Galloway. Tel: 01671 402121 (also fishing on Cree and Minnoch). Cost: Upper Bladnoch and Upper Water of Tarf, in the order of £5 per rod per day; main river, depending upon the time of year, from between £15 and £25 per rod per day. The river is very popular so book well in advance. There are excellent self-catering properties available with rods. Inquire when booking.

BRUNTIS, Loch
Location & Access 83/445654. Leave the A75 Newton Stewart/Gatehouse of Fleet road near Craig Hall (83/435648) and drive north on the forest track to the top of the hill. The loch is reached after an easy half mile hike.
Commentary Managed by the Newton Stewart Angling Club, the loch covers an area of 10 acres and lies at the heart of the Auchlannochy Forest. Consequently, on wild days, Bruntis is invariably sheltered and eminently fishable.
Fish Stocked with brown trout and rainbow trout which average 12oz in weight.
Flies & Tactics Bank fishing only and there is a limit of 2 fish per rod per day. Flies: Dry fly patterns, particularly black flies, also weighted nymphs, buzzers and sedge patterns.

Kirkcudbright — OS Map 83

Permission & Charges Galloway Guns & Tackle, 36A Arthur Street, Newton Stewart. Tel: 01671 403404. Cost: £15 per rod per day.

BURNFOOT, Burn See Water of Fleet entry.
CADOON, Burn See Water of Fleet entry.

CALLY, Lake
Location & Access 83/600555. Immediately to the south of Gatehouse of Fleet and within the grounds of the Cally House Hotel.
Commentary A small (6 acre) man-made lake in a very attractive setting, noted for its wildlife which includes resident swans and visiting otters.
Fish Stocked with excellent quality brown trout which average 1lb in weight. The largest fish taken in recent years weighed over 3lb. There are also carp.
Flies & Tactics Boat fishing only and Cally Lake fishes best in the early morning or at dusk.
Permission & Charges Fishing is reserved solely for the use of hotel guests. Contact: Cally House Hotel, Gatehouse of Fleet, Kirkcudbright. Tel: 01557 814341.

CASTRAMONT, Burn See Water of Fleet entry.
CLEUGH, Burn See Water of Fleet entry.
COARSE FISHERIES ERNCROGO, Loch 83/745678; MURRAY, Loch 83/473578; ELDRIG, Loch (Penninghame) 83/352666; WOODHALL, Loch 83/674670

CREE, River
Location & Access Source 76/345857 Outfall 464600. Easily accessible from the A714 Newton Stewart/Girvan road.
Commentary The river rises from Loch Moan (see OS Map 76, Girvan) in the Glentrool Forest and in recent years commercial forestry operations have dramatically affected both water quality and flow rates. Because of deep forestry ploughing, spates run off very quickly and the water has become more acid, and, consequently, less able to sustain fish life. The West Galloway Fishery Trust, in conjunction with the riparian owners and other interested parties, is addressing these problems in an attempt improve the river habitat and reverse the decline in fish numbers. Apart from modest brown trout, the upper reaches of the river, which used to hold good numbers of salmon, are now virtually fishless. Sport is essentially confined to the lower 8 miles of the stream; from Clachaneasy (77/356748) near where the Water of Minnoch enters, downstream to the outfall in Wigtown Bay. The other principal tributaries are: Cordorcan Burn, Penkiln Burn, Palnure Burn and Moneypool Burn. The river is tidal almost up to Newton Stewart.
Fish Salmon, sea-trout, herling, brown trout and pike. Catch statistics for the Galloway Estate waters show the decline in fish numbers: 1988 - 414, 1992 -179, 1995 -136, 1996 - 85 (low water year). The total catch for the whole river, in a good year, is now probably in the region of 200 salmon. Records of sea-trout catches are not available. The most productive months are September and October when between 50%/60% of all the fish are caught. One of the heaviest salmon in recent years was a fish of 27lb (1986), taken from the Palnure Burn. Palnure has also produce a sea-trout of 13lb 8oz.
Flies & Tactics The character of the stream varies considerably throughout it course, fast flowing in its upper reaches and slowing to a wide, deep, channel as it passes Larg. Indeed, the local name for the river here is "Loch Cree." Downstream, as the river passes Penninghame Open Prison, the flow increases and there are a number of very attractive pools including: House Pool, Leek Pool, Garden Pool and Linloskin, this last named being perhaps the most productive pool on the whole river. Some of the pools are best fished from a boat, others require the use of chest waders and a 15ft rod to effectively cover the lies. Spinning and bait fishing is allowed, depending upon the height of the water, and most fish are caught by these methods, rather than by fly. The Palnure Burn offers a completely different challenge, being narrow and, in many places, tree-lined. Worming in low water conditions requires particular skill. There are some excellent pools, given water, the most notable of which are: Will's Home, Upper Bridge Pool, Alder Hole, Cunningham's Ford and Lady's Pool. The other tributaries noted above can also provide sport but, again, it all depends upon there being good water levels. Flies: Ally's Shrimp, Stoat's Tail, Blue Charm, General Practitioner, Garry Dog, Thunder & Lightning - but mainly bait fishing.
Permission & Charges Contact: Newton Stewart & District Angling Association, per Galloway Guns & Tackle, 36a Arthur Street, Newton Stewart. Tel: 01671 403404 (also access to the Water of Minnoch and Penkiln Burn); Jonathan Haley, Mochrum Park Sporting Holidays, Riverview Cottage, Spittal Bridge, Nr Kirkcowan, Wigtownshire DG8 0DG. Tel: 01671 813471 (and Palnure Burn); Galloway Sporting Agents, Wyncherry Yard, North Corar, Newton Stewart DG8 8EJ. Tel: 01850 733670 or 01860 553584; Fax: 01532 813056; Galloway Estates, G M Thomson & Co, 10 Victoria Street, Newton Stewart DG8 6NH. Tel: 01671 402887; Fax: 01671 402650. Palnure Burn: Jonathan Bradburn, Bargaly House, Newton Stewart, Wigtownshire DG8 7BH. Tel: 01671 402392. Mochrum Park and Bargaly have first-class self-catering properties available with fish. Details on request. Cost: from between £15 per rod per day to £800 per week for a 3 rod beat in October.

CROSS REFERENCES KEN, Loch (See OS Map 77); GRANNOCH, Loch (See OS Map 77); FLEET, Loch (See OS Map 77).

DEE, River
Location & Access Source 77/470790 Outfall 83/690532. Access from the A711 Tongland/Cairney Hill road, the A75 Ringford/ Castle Douglas road, from minor roads to the north of Bridge of Dee (83/833 601) and from the B795 road at Glenlochar (83/731644).
Commentary The river rises from Loch Dee and flows south-west through the Cairn Edward Forest as the

420

OS Map 83 — Kirkcudbright

Back Water of Dee via Clatteringshaws Loch and Loch Stroan to enter Loch Ken (see OS Map 77, New Galloway & Glen Trool) near Hensal House (83/685700). From Loch Ken, the river flows south and enters Kirkcudbright Bay after a journey of 8 miles. Tarff Water, a subsidiary stream, enters the bay to the west of Tongland at 83/685541. The River Dee is part of a hydro-electric power generation scheme which has radically diminished its status as a migratory fish system. This situation has been compounded by the damaging effects of the blanket afforestation that covers so much of the headwaters of the river. Loch Ken was formed when the River Dee was impounded.

Fish Predominately a coarse fishery, famous for the size of its pike, although there are signs that salmon are returning. No accurate records exist of the number of salmon caught, but they are unlikely to exceed 20 fish in a good year.

Flies & Tactics All legal methods are allowed. The stream is wide, deep and essentially sluggish other than in times of spate. Most anglers spin and bait fish. It is dangerous to wade.

Permission & Charges Contact: Mrs Neil, Braefoot, Glenlochar, by Crossmichael. Tel: 01556 670249. Cost: £5 per rod per day for coarse and trout fishing, £15 per rod per day for salmon fishing. Tarff Water is private.

DRUMCLEUGH, Burn See Water of Fleet entry.

FLEET, Water of

Location & Access Source Little Water of Fleet 83/560699, Big Water of Fleet 83/540699; Outfall 83/588547. The river is accessed from the B796 Gatehouse of Fleet/Upper Rusko road and, thereafter, upstream, by riverside tracks.

Commentary Both tributaries rise from lochs surrounded by commercial forestry plantations around Craigwhinnie Hill (417m): Little Water of Fleet, to the east, from Loch Fleet, Big Water of Fleet, to the west, from Loch Grannoch (see OS Map 77 New Galloway & Glen Trool for details both lochs). The streams flow south to meet at Aikyhill (83/587609) where they become the Water of Fleet. After a further 3.5 miles the stream enters Wigtown Bay through a channel constructed in 1924 to allow access for shipping. The Water of Fleet has been dramatically altered by the effects of blanket afforestation on its headwaters: flash flooding, river bank erosion, increased acidity, low pH levels, siltation of pools, degradation of the spawning habitat. The principal tributaries on Big Water of Fleet are: Cadoon Burn, Russon Burn and Upper Rusko Burn. On Little Water of Fleet, the tributaries are: Burnfoot Burn, Cleugh Burn and Castramont Burn. Water of Fleet is fed by: Drumcleugh Burn, High Creach Burn and Barlay Burn from the east and Pulcree Burn from the west. There is also the chance of sport with sea-trout at the outfall of the Skyre Burn which flows into Wigtown Bay to the south-west of Gatehouse of Fleet at Drummuckloch (83/572546) on the A75 Gatehouse/Creetown road.

Fish Mainly sea-trout, although a few salmon and grilse are taken as well. The average weight of salmon is 8lb but heavier fish are not uncommon: the heaviest fish caught in recent years weighed 20lb. However, sea-trout numbers have declined in recent years. Sea-trout average 1lb 8oz and eyed ova are now planted out in the headwaters. All sea-trout under 12oz must be returned. The season does not open until 1st June.

Flies & Tactics The best of the fishing is on the middle section of the stream, from where the two tributaries join, downstream for 2 miles to where the Pulcree Burn enters (83/594575). The most noted pools include: Barbara Pool, Standing Stone Pool and the Stranger's Pool. On the Big Water of Fleet, the best pool is Pool of Ness (83/559643). Fishing in October is by fly only. Spinning is allowed in high water conditions. Full details are given on the permit. A single-handed rod will deal with most eventualities. Flies: Hairy Mary, Jock Scott, Silver Doctor, Brown Turkey, Blue Charm. Night fishing for sea-trout can give great sport. Try: Brown Turkey, Coachman, Peter Ross, Bloody Butcher, Teal Blue & Silver. For non-angling companions, a visit to Castramont Wood (83/592605) is a must. This ancient oak woodland is renowned for its wildflowers, particularly the bluebells which carpet the forest floor in the Spring.

Permission & Charges Contact: Murray Arms Hotel, Gatehouse-of-Fleet DG7 2HY. Tel: 01557 814207; Fax: 01577 814370. Cost: from £8 per rod per day on Pool of Ness up to £20 per rod per day on the middle stretch of the river. Tickets are not transferable and must be paid for on booking. No refund will be made in the event of the tickets not being used.

HIGH CREACH, Burn See Water of Fleet entry.

JORDIELAND, Loch

Location & Access 83/715536. Approach from Tongland (83/701536) via Culdoach Farm. The loch is to the north of the small wood.

Commentary A small loch of 20 acres lying on Culdoach Moor surrounded by bracken, heath and rough grassland.

Fish Brown trout which average 8oz in weight.

Flies & Tactics Bank fishing only, day session and evening session. Flies: Black Pennell, March Brown, Silver Butcher.

Permission & Charges B West, Jordiebank, Kirkcudbright. Tel: 01557 330118. Cost: £8 per rod per day, £5 per evening.

LITTLE WATER OF FLEET (River) See Water of Fleet.

LOCHANBRECK, Loch

Location & Access 83/640658. Approach via the minor road from Laurieston (83/681648) on the A762 New Galloway/Ringford road to the east or from Gatehouse of Fleet (83/603565) in the south.

Commentary Lochanbreck Loch lies within the Laurieston Forest, sheltered from the wind and surrounded by outstanding wildlife. The loch is carefully managed by the Kirkcudbright & Gatehouse Angling Association and it covers an area of about 70 acres.

Kirkcudbright   OS Map 83

Fish Stocked with good quality brown trout and rainbow trout which average 12oz/14oz in weight. Fish of up to and over 3lb are not uncommon and the largest fish taken in recent years weighed over 8lb.
Flies & Tactics There are 5 boats available and bank fishing is also allowed. The bays at the south-east and south-west end are a good place to start, and in the vicinity of the inlet burns at the north-west corner of the loch. Black flies work well. Try: Black Spider, Blae & Black, Black Pennell.
Permission & Charges Contact: M & E Brown, Newsagents, 52 High Street, Gatehouse of Fleet, Kirkcudbright. Tel: 01557 814222; Watson McKinnell, Ironmongers, 15 St Cuthbert Street, Kirkcudbright. Tel: 01557 330693. Cost: £10 per rod per day, £3 for a boat. There is a bag limit of 4 fish per rod (prices will probably rise in 2001).

MALZIE, Water of See River Bladnoch entry.

MANNOCH, Loch (Lairdmannoch)
Location & Access 83/664600. Approach from near Twynholm (83/661545) on the A75 Castle Douglas/Gatehouse of Fleet road. Look for the signpost, on the north side of the road, to Glengap. Follow this minor road for 3.5 miles. The road ends at a parking place 500 yards from the loch.
Commentary Also known as Lairdmannoch Loch, this splendid, 72 acres water is 1 mile north/south in length by up to 350 yds wide.
Fish Good population of wild brown trout which average 8oz. Most seasons produce upwards of 1,200 fish. The estate policy is to kill all trout caught in order to increase the overall size of the remaining stock.
Flies & Tactics Boat fishing, fly or dapping only. Outboard motors are not allowed. Fish are taken from all over the loch and no one place is substantially any better than another. The trout are not fussy about patterns of fly, and Loch Mannoch is an ideal place to introduce beginners to the gentle art.
Permission & Charges Contact: G M Thomson & Co, 27 King Street, Castle Douglas DG7 1AB. Tel: 01556 504030 or 502973; Fax: 01556 503277. Cost: £22.50 per boat per day (2 rods fishing).

PRIVATE WATERS WHITE LOCH OF MYRTON 83/357434; BLAIRBUIE, Loch 83/364416 ; WHITE LOCH OF RAVENSTONE 83/400440; DORNELL, Loch 83/704658); LACHENGOWER, Loch 83/695660; GLENTOO, Loch 83/700625; BARGATTON, Loch 83/695620; WOODHALL, Loch 83/674670; BLATES MILL, Loch 83/680672; SKERROW, Loch 83/605680; ERSOCK, Loch 83/370436; LOW MAINS, Loch 83/453388; CULCAGRIE, Loch 83/664576 (no fish in this loch).

ROAN, Loch
Location & Access 83/743690. Approach from Crossmichael (83/730670) on the A713 Ayr/Castle Douglas road. Turn east at the church and follow the minor road for 1.5 miles to Walbutt (83/749685). Take the first left immediately after Walbutt to reach the loch after half a mile.

Commentary A sheltered loch in a peaceful setting, almost completely surrounded by forestry. The loch covers an area of 66 acres and drops to a depth of 70ft/80ft. The loch is managed by the Castle Douglas Angling Association.
Fish Stocked with brown trout and rainbow trout which average 1lb in weight. Fish of up to and over 4lb are not uncommon.
Flies & Tactics Boat fishing only. Fishing is most productive around the margins, in the shallower water, and in the two bays at the south end. There is a bag limit of 8 fish per boat per day. Flies: Soldier Palmer, Teal & Green, Silver Invicta.
Permission & Charges Contact: Tommy's Sport Shop, 178 King Street, Castle Douglas. Tel: 01556 502851. Cost: £25 per day for boat, 2 rods fishing. Bag limit, 8 fish. Evening fishing is reserved for club members only.

RUSSON, Burn See Water of Fleet entry.
SKYRE, Burn See Water of Fleet entry.
TARF, Water of See River Bladnoch entry.
TARFF, Water See River Dee entry.
UPPER RUSKO, Burn See Water of Fleet entry.

WEE GLENARMOUR, Loch
Location & Access 83/431664. Approach from the A712 Newton Stewart/New Galloway road at 83/440672.
Commentary A tiny loch on the northern edge of Auchlannochy Forest. Easy access and good facilities for disabled anglers.
Fish Stocked with brown trout and rainbow trout which average 1lb in weight.
Flies & Tactics Bank fishing only and rising fish are easily covered from the shore. There is a bag limit of 2 fish per rod per day. Offer them reservoir lures, and, on calm days, dry fly patterns.
Permission & Charges See Bruntis Loch entry.

WHINYEON, Loch
Location & Access 83/625610. See Lochanbreck entry. The track to the loch leaves the minor road at Laghead (83/609606). Park, and walk east to reach the loch after an easy hike of three quarters of a mile.
Commentary Loch Whinyeon lies on the western edge of the Glengap Forest, protected from the worst of cold east winds. The loch covers an area of 104 acres and it is managed by the Kirkcudbright & Gatehouse Angling Association.
Fish There is a natural population of wild brown trout, augmented by limited stocking. Average weight, 10oz, but fish of up to 2lb are also taken.
Flies & Tactics Boat and bank fishing. Begin at the north end and work the shore west to where the inlet burn enters from Mc Ghie's Seat (250m). There is a bag limit of 4 fish per rod per day. Try: Ke-He, Grouse & Claret, Dunkeld.
Permission & Charges Watson McKinnell, Ironmongers, 15 St Cuthbert Street, Kirkcudbright. Tel 01557 330693. Cost: approx. £6 per rod per day, boat, £3 (2 rods fishing).

Dumfries

CASTLEFAIRN, Water See Cluden Water entry.
CLUDEN, Water (Cairn Water) See River Nith entry.
COARSE FISHERIES EDINGHAM, Loch 84/838634; DUFF'S Loch 84/854560; BAREAN, Loch 84/858557; CLONVARD, Loch 84/857545; WHITE, Loch 84/865536; ARTHUR, Loch 84/900690; CORSOCK, Loch 84/755755; AUCHENREOCH, Loch 84/820715; LOCHRUTTEN, Loch 84/899735; BAREND, Loch 84/880550; CARLINGWARK, Loch 84/765615.
CROSS REFERENCES For details of the following waters see OS Map 83: ROAN, Loch; ERNCROGO, Loch; WOODHALL, Loch; DORNELL, Loch; GLENTOO, Loch; BARGATTON, Loch; MANNOCH, Loch; CULCRAIGRIE, Loch; JORDIELAND, Loch; DEE, River; TARFF Water. For details of the following waters see OS Map 77: ARVIE, Loch; FALBAE, Loch; MOSSDALE, Loch; LOWES Lochs; KEN, Loch.

CULDRAIN, Loch
Location & Access 84/860640. At Congeith (84/872662), 4 miles north from Dalbeattie on the A711 Dalbeattie/Dumfries road, drive south on the minor road. The entrance to the fishery is on your left after 1.5 miles.
Commentary Culdrain Loch is not shown on the OS Map, but it is about 2 acres in extent and lies close to Culdrain Farm.
Fish Stocked with rainbow trout which average 1lb 8oz. Fish of up to and over 5lb are also taken.
Flies & Tactics Bank fishing, but there is 1 boat available free of charge on a first-come-first-served basis. Most patterns of fly and reservoir lures produce results.
Permission & Charges Contact: See Dalbeattie Reservoir entry. Cost: £14 for 8 hours (4 fish limit), £7 for 4 hours (2 fish limit).

DALBEATTIE, Reservoir
Location & Access 84/804616. Turn north from the A745 Dalbeattie/Castle Douglas road, I mile west from Dalbeattie at Buttle Church (84/816618).
Commentary A small, easily-accessible fishery, 10 acres in extend, lying to the south of Barskeach Hill (182m) and managed by the Dalbeattie Angling Association.
Fish Stocked with brown trout and rainbow trout which average 12oz in weight. Stocking takes place in March, May, July and August during which time approximately 250 brown trout and 750 rainbow trout are introduced.
Flies & Tactics Boat and bank fishing are allowed. Bank fishing from 6am until 11pm, boats, from 9am until 4.30pm and from 5.30pm until 10pm. There is a bag limit of f fish per rod and wading is not allowed, unless it is in order to reach the small island at the north end. Boats are not allowed to fish to the north of the island. Dalbeattie Reservoir trout do not give themselves up easily and there are some very large fish which are often seen but rarely caught. Try: Black Pennell, Grouse & Claret, Peter Ross.
Permission & Charges Contact: M McCowan & Son, 43 High Street, Dalbeattie, Kirkcudbrightshire. Tel: 01556 610270. Cost £14 per rod, boats, £5 extra (2 rods fishing). Outboard motors are not allowed. Further information on the Dalbeattie Angling Association waters may be obtained from: J Moran, 12 Church Crescent, Dalbeattie, Kirkcudbrigh. Tel: 01556 502292.

GLENESSLIN, Burn See Cluden Water entry.

GLENKILN, Reservoir
Location & Access 84/840785. Approach from Shawhead (84/872760). Follow the minor road north-west up the line of the Old Water to reach the reservoir after 2 miles.
Commentary A substantial water, constructed in 1934, over half a mile long by up to 400yds wide, sheltered to the east by Carnless Hill (392m) and to the west by Bennan Hill (398m). The minor road margins the west shore line, the east bank is trackless.
Fish Last stocked with brown trout and rainbow trout in 1995. Average weight, 10oz. The largest fish caught in recent years weighed 7lb 2oz. There are still a few wild brown trout as well.
Flies & Tactics Boat fishing and bank fishing, but take care wading, the bottom can be unstable in places. The most productive area is the north end, where the Shalloch Burn and the Muil Burn enter, although fish rise and may be caught all over the reservoir. Flies: Soldier Palmer, Grouse & Green, Silver Invicta. There is a 6 fish per rod per day limit.
Permission & Charges Contact: Customer Services, South West of Scotland Water, Marchmount House, Moffat Road, Dumfries DG1 1PW. Tel: 01387 250000. Cost: £2.75 per rod per day; £3 per rod per day for the hire of the boat, £1.50 after 6pm. Free of charge to OAP's and under-16-year-olds if accompanied by an adult.

JARBRUCK, Burn See Cluden Water.

NITH, River
Location & Access The river rises 50 miles to the north of Dumfries, to the west of New Cummnock in Ayrshire. The section of the Nith shown on OS Map 84 (see also OS Maps 71 & 78) extends from the estuary by Glencaple (84/995683), upstream to Over Broomrigg Farm (84/969799).
Commentary In its lower reaches the Nith flows by fertile farmlands through the town of Dumfries, famous, amongst other things, for its connection with Scotland's bard, Robert Burns. The Nith's most significant tributary, Cluden Water (more commonly known as Cairn Water) joins the stream by Collage Motte (84/965780) and, in its own right, is a significant sporting river with its own important tributaries: Old Water, Glenesslin Burn, Jarbruck Burn and Castlefairn Water. The care of the river is in the competent hands of the Nith Fishings Improvement Association and affiliated organisations and it is

Carlisle & Solway Firth — OS Maps 84-85

entirely due to their commitment and hard work that the river is in such good heart today.
Fish The Nith is one of the most prolific salmon and sea-trout rivers in Scotland. Recent years have produced between 1,800 and 2,500 salmon and grilse, and upwards of 2,000 sea-trout most seasons. Salmon average 8lb/9lb whilst sea-trout average 2lb. Salmon of up to and over 30lb are not uncommon as well as double-figure sea-trout. The river also hosts brown trout and grayling as does Cairn Water which is stocked by the Dumfries & Galloway Angling Association (D&GAA). Cairn Water now also contains escapee rainbow trout. June, July and August are the prime sea-trout months, most salmon are taken during September, October and November.
Flies & Tactics You will need a 15ft double-handed rod to deal with the Nith and although spinning is allowed, the use of prawn and shrimp is prohibited. Cairn Water will respond, under most conditions, to a single-handed rod. There are a number of other important rules and regulations governing the fishing and these are detailed on the permit. The D&GAA water on the Nith, both banks, extends from Carnsalloch (78/961812) downstream to Lincluden (84/977777), a distance of 3 miles. The Association also have 14 miles of fishing on Cairn Water, from Moniaive (78/780910) through Dunscore (78/860840), downstream to New Bridge (84/949791), again, mostly double bank. There are some first-class pools and runs on Cairn Water, including: Snade Mill, Dun's Pool, Lady's Pool, Hannah's Pool, Viaduct Pool and Six Mile Corner. The River Nith and Cairn Water, within the burgh boundaries (Dumfries Common Good Fishings), is let by the local council. As always, good sport is very much dependent upon favourable water levels. Chest waders are required on the Nith to cover some of the lies, thigh waders should suffice during the summer months. Night fishing for sea-trout, even in low water conditions, can be splendid. Flies: Salmon: Brown Turkey (devised specially for the Solway rivers), General Practitioner, Ally's Shrimp, Blue Charm, Black Doctor, Garry Dog, Willie Gunn. For sea-trout, try: Black Pennell, Greenwell's Glory, Peter Ross. Spinners: Devon minnows, Rapalas, Mepps spoons, Flying Condom.
Permission & Charges Contact: David McMillan, Tackle Shop, 6 Friars Vennel, Dumfries DG1 2RN. Tel: 01387 252075 (also state-of-the art information on other local fishing opportunities); Dumfries & Galloway Council, Housing Services, High Street, Dumfries DG1 2AD. Tel: 01387 253166. Cost: depending upon the time of year, between £15 and £30 per rod per day. Visitor tickets are available Mon-Sat, but if a day ticket is required for a Saturday, it must be purchased during week. (Council Offices closed on Saturdays. Further information in connection with the D&GAA may be obtained (Mon-Fri only) from: L. Chalmers, Secretary, D&GAA, 50 Brooms Road, Dumfriess DG1. Tel: 01387 267647 (enclose s.a.e.).

OLD, **Water** See Cluden Water entry.

PRIVATE WATERS FERN, Loch 84/864626; MILTON, Loch 84/840710; KINDAR, Loch 84/970640; LOCHENKIT, Loch 84/800757; LOWES, Loch 84/705785; BENGRIAN, Loch 84/788522; FELLCROFT, Loch 84/785504; FLOORS, Loch 84/775613; PARTICK, Loch 84/788708; BLACK, Loch 84/784720; SOLWAY Fishery 84/941661.

URR, Water
Location & Access Source 78/760845 Outfall 84/834565. Public roads margin both banks of the stream throughout almost its entire length.
Commentary Urr Water rises from the south slopes of Craes Hill (345m), approximately 30 miles north from its outfall in Rough Firth near Kippford Sands. The principal tributaries are: Craigenputtock Burn, Crogo Burn, Knarie Burn and Drumhumphry Burn. In its upper reaches Urr Water is a delightful moorland stream, as it reaches the sea south of Dalbeattie it becomes much more sluggish and slow-moving.
Fish Salmon, brown trout, but very few sea-trout. Accurate catch statistics are not available but are unlikely to be more than 60 fish in a good year. The average weight of salmon is 7lb/8lb but much larger fish (the famous Solway "greybacks") are sometimes taken during September and October.
Flies & Tactics The best of the fishing is from the Old Bridge of Urr (84/776677) on the B794 Dalbeattie/Drumhumphry road, downstream to the estuary, and include a number of useful pools: Well Pool, Step End, Cauls Pool, Davie Craig, Spottes Dam, Jean's Pool and Grange Water. However, sport depends entirely upon heavy rain. In this connection, commercial forestry in recent years has made the river much more flashy as well as degrading the upstream spawning habitat. Fishing is fly only, other than in high water levels when spinning is allowed. The upper reaches can offer great sport with small brown trout, particularly on dry fly. For salmon, try: Ally's Shrimp, Stoat's Tail, Hairy Mary, Garry Dog, Blue Charm.
Permission & Charges Contact: M McCowan & Son, 43 High Street, Dalbeattie, Kirkcudbrightshire. Tel: 01556 610270; Tommy's Sports Shop, 178 King Street, Castle Douglas, Kirkcudbrightshire. Tel: 01556 502851. Cost: £15 per rod per day. Visitor tickets are not available on Saturday. Also, J Haley, Mochrum Park Sporting Holidays, Riverside Cottage, Spittal Bridge, Nr Kirkcowan, Wigtownshire. Tel: 01671 813571.

Carlisle & Solway Firth

ANNAN, River
Location & Access The River Annan rises from the bleak, moorland, wilderness of the Devil's Beef Tub at Annanhead (78/065132). The stream flows south from its source to reach the sea in the Solway Firth after a journey of 35 miles. The section of the River Annan shown on OS Map 85 (see also OS Map 78)

OS Map 85 — Carlisle & Solway Firth

extends from Greenhill (85/105800) in the north, downstream through the town of Annan, to its outfall at Barnkirk Point Lighthouse (85/190645). The river is easily accessible from public roads which margin both banks along almost its entire length.

Commentary In its lower reaches the Annan is considerable width, flowing between grasslands and pasture, wooded banks and fertile fields. The river is joined here by one of its principal tributaries, Water of Milk, which flows in near Hoddom Mill (85/149732). Mein Water, another tributary, meets the Annan at Meinfoot (85/185725). The Annan is cared for by the River Annan Improvement Association.

Fish Salmon, sea-trout, finnock, brown trout, grayling and coarse fish species, particularly chub. Approximately 700/800 salmon and grilse and upwards of 1,500 sea-trout are taken most seasons. The principal salmon run occurs in the autumn, but a few spring fish are also taken. The river used to be famous for enormous autumn fish (greybacks) and even today salmon of up to and over 20lb are not uncommon: the largest fish in recent years weighted 34lb 8oz and was taken on the last day of the season in 1984 from the Cauld Pool. The average weight of salmon is in the order of 10lb. Sea-trout fishing is best during June, July and August and their average weight is 2lb. Catch statistics for the Newbie Beat, considered to be the most productive beat on the river, show an average of 130 salmon and grilse and 100 sea-trout each year. The Hoddom Castle Beat, upstream from Newbie, averages 80 salmon and about 120 sea-trout.

Flies & Tactics Fly fishing is preferred on most beats but spinning and, on a limited number of beats, bait fishing may also be allowed. As ever, good water levels are required for the river to produce of its best. Given such circumstances, the summer months can be excellent, offering the chance of sport with grilse and excellent, after dark, sea-trout fishing. Thigh waders will suffice in most water conditions, but, to effectively cover some of the lies, chest waders are required. A 12ft double-handed rod will deal with most fishing eventualities, a single-handed rod is adequate for summer work. A floating line is a good all-rounder, carry a sink-tip and/or a sinking line for high water fishing. There are a number of first-class pools and runs, including: Manse Pool, Jimmie's Pool, Milk Foot, Dukes, Banks of Hoddom, Island Pool, the famous Cauld Pool, Pat's Bridge, Mill Pool, The Flats and Spittal Pool. Salmon flies: Silver Stoat's Tail, Silver Wilkinson, Blue Charm, Brown Turkey, Willie Gunn, Garry Dog, Munro Killer, Ally's Shrimp, General Practitioner. Sea-trout flies: Black Pennell, Mallard & Claret, Peter Ross, Dunkeld, Teal Blue & Silver. Most spinning lures will produce results. Brown trout fishing is more productive further upstream, but good fish may be caught using the same patterns as are used for sea-trout.

Permission & Charges Contact: Annan & District Anglers' Club, 63-65 High Street, Annan, Dumfriesshire DG12 6AD. Tel: 01461 202616; Newbie & Distillery Beat: Michael Aprile, Newbie Fisheries, Newbie Mill, Annan, Dumfriesshire. Tel: 01461 202608; A Lynn, Northfield House, Annan, Dumfriesshire. Tel: 01461 202064 (self-catering accommodation with fishing adjacent to the river); Warmanbie Hotel, Annan, Dumfriesshire DG12 5LL. Tel: 01461 204015 (The outstanding fishing hotel in the area. Private fishing and access may be arranged to most other beats on the river. Excellent advice, accommodation and support); Cleughead Water: N Harris, Roddick & Laurie, 20 Murray Street, Annan, Dumfriesshire DG12 6EG. Tel: 01641 202575 (good for sea-trout). Hoddom Castle Beat: D Rothwell, Factor, Hoddom & Kinmount Estates, Estate Office, Hoddom, Lockerbie, Dumfriesshire. Tel: 01576 300244 or 01576 300417; Fax: 01576 300757; Kirkwood Beat: Anthony Steel, Kirkwood, Lockerbie, Dumfriesshire DG11 1DH. Tel: 01576 510212 (also, trout fishing on 12 miles of the Water of Milk. Self-catering cottages available with the fishing). Castle Milk Water: Castle Milk Estates, Norwood, Lockerbie, Dumfriesshire DG11 2QX. Tel: 01576 510203. Royal Four Towns Water: Mrs K Ratcliffe, The Clerk, "Ja-Ar", Prestonhouse Road, Hightae, Lockerbie, Dumfriesshire DG11 1JR. Tel: 01387 810220 Cost varies, depending upon time of year, less expensive during the spring months, more expensive for autumn fishing, but excellent value-for-money-fishing throughout the season. Expect to pay from between £5 and £50 per rod per day.

COARSE FISHERIES ASHYARD Ponds 85/245758; KELHEAD QUARRY 85/146692

CROSS REFERENCE BORDER ESK, River: OS Map 85 contains only a small part of the river (although some of the best fishing). Nevertheless, for simplicity of access, the Border Esk is described in full on OS Map 79.

MEIN, Water See River Annan entry.

MILK, Water of See River Annan entry.

PRIVATE WATER TORBECKHILL Reservoir 85/232797

PURDOMSTONE, Reservoir

Location & Access 85/215775. Approach from the B725 Ecclefechan/Waterbeck road. Turn north in Middlebie. The reservoir is a further half a mile, first right and then first left to reach the south end.

Commentary A very attractive, easily-accessible, little reservoir surrounded by gentle hills which give some shelter from the prevailing winds.

Fish All wild brown trout which average 10oz in weight.

Flies & Tactics Reserved for the use of Annan Anglers Association. Day tickets no longer avavilable.

Permission & Charges Contact: The Factor, Hoddom & Kinmount Estates, Estate Office, Hoddom, Lockerbie. Tel: 01576 300244; Fax: 01576 300757 or Dickie Graham, Hoddom Bridge, Ecclefechan. Tel: 01576 300417.

Index

A

A' BHEALAICH, Loch 108, 125, 173, 186, 196, 208-209, 235, 241, 254, 367
A'BEALACH-BHIG, Lochan 230
A'BHAC-GHLAIS, Loch 268
A'BHADA DHARAICH, Loch 294
A'BHADAIDH DARAICH, Loch 54
A'BHAGH GHAINMHICH, Loch 52
A'BHAID GHAINMHEICH, Loch 195
A'BHAID SHAMHRAIDH, Loch 195
A'BHAID-CHOILLE, Loch 195
A'BHAID-FHEARNA, Loch 235
A'BHAID-LUACHRAICH, Loch 195
A'BHAID-RABHAIN, Loch 196
A'BHAIGH, Lochan 311
A'BHAILE, Loch 29, 153
A'BHAILE, Loch (Tolsta Chaolais) 29
A'BHAINNE, Loch 205, 277
A'BHAINNR, Lochan 287
A'BHALAICH, Loch 367
A'BHANA, Loch 241
A'BHARP, Loch 264
A'BHARPA, Loch 186, 217
A'BHARRAIN, Loch 316
A'BHEALAICH (North), Loch 249
A'BHEALAICH (South), Loch 249
A'BHEALAICH AIRD, Loch 362
A'BHEALAICH LEAMHAIN, Loch 302
A'BHEALAICH MHOR, Loch 235
A'BHEALAICH, Loch 108, 125, 173, 186, 196, 208-209, 235, 241, 254, 367
A'BHEALAICH, Loch (Garve) 209
A'BHEALAICH, Lochan 173, 304
A'BHEANNAICH, Loch (Uig) 107
A'BHEANNAIN, Loch (Ardroil) 107
A'BHEANNAN MHOIR, Loch 125
A'BHIDIDH, Loch 182
A'BHIRAILLE, Loch 145
A'BHITH, Loch 145
A'BHLAR BHUIDE, Loch 29
A'BHOINEID, Loch 125
A'BHONNAICH, Loch 196
A'BHRAGHAD, Loch 107
A'BHRAGHAD, Lochan 196
A'BHRAGHAIL, Loch 29
A'BHRAGNAID, Loch 294
A'BHRAIGHE, Loch 145
A'BHRAOIN, Loch 196, 209
A'BHRISIDH, Loch 196
A'BHROCHAIN, Loch 173
A'BHRODUINN, Loch 125
A'BHROMA, Loch 107
A'BHRUIC, Lochan 340
A'BHUALAIDH, Loch 74
A'BHUIC, Loch 54, 245
A'BHUIRD, Loch 186
A'BHUNA, Loch 29
A'BHURRA, Loch 367
A'BHURSTA, Loch 217

A'CERACHER, Loch 96
A'CERIGAL, Loch 96
A'CHADHA, Loch 72, 235
A'CHAFAIN, Loch 217
A'CHAIRN DUIBH, Loch 249
A'CHAIRN MHOIR, Loch 294
A'CHAIRN MOR, Loch 209
A'CHAIRN, Loch 29, 96, 125
A'CHAISTEIL, Loch 235
A'CHAM ALTAIN, Loch 52
A'CHAMA, Loch 107
A'CHAOL-THUIL, Loch 196
A'CHAORAIN (Kenmore), Loch 235
A'CHAORAINN BEAG, Loch 235
A'CHAORAINN, Loch 65, 212, 235, 255, 340, 344
A'CHAORAINN, Lochan 241
A'CHAORUINN, Loch 74, 145, 362, 371
A'CHAPHAIL, Loch 29, 107
A'CHAPHAIL, Loch (Scaliscro) 107
A'CHAPUIL, Loch 145
A'CHARRA, Loch 186, 217
A'CHAS BHRAIGHE RUAIDH, Loch 107
A'CHEIGEIN, Loch 340
A'CHEIVLA, Loch 125
A'CHINN GHAIRBH, Loch 367
A'CHINN MHONAICH, Lochan 277
A'CHITEAR, Loch 29
A'CHLACHAIN, Loch 29, 125, 217, 249, 340
A'CHLACHAIN, Loch (Creed) 29
A'CHLACHAIN, Loch (Eynort) 217
A'CHLACHAIN, Loch (Ormiclate) 217
A'CHLAIDHEIMH, Loch 241, 362
A'CHLAIGNN, Lochan 340
A'CHLARAIN, Loch 249
A'CHLEIRICH, Lochan 196
A'CHLEITE TUATH, Loch 107
A'CHNOIC BHUIDHE, Loch 217
A'CHNOIC MHOIR, Loch 217
A'CHNUIC BHRIC, Loch 362
A'CHNUIC, Loch 107
A'CHOIN BHAIN, Loch 125
A'CHOIN DUIBH, Loch 235, 285
A'CHOIN UIRE, Lochain 277
A'CHOIN, Loch 107, 145
A'CHOINIEH, Loch 277
A'CHOIR BHAIN, Loch 196
A'CHOIRE BHEITHE, Loch 274
A'CHOIRE BHIG, Loch 241
A'CHOIRE BHUIDHE, Loch 235
A'CHOIRE BHUIDHE, Lochan 173
A'CHOIRE BHUIG, Loch 209
A'CHOIRE DHEIRG, Loch 145
A'CHOIRE DHOMHAIN, Loch 241
A'CHOIRE DHUIBH, Loch 145, 209
A'CHOIRE DHUIBH, Loch (Glas Bheinn) 145
A'CHOIRE DHUIBH, Loch (Suilven) 145
A'CHOIRE DHUIBH, Lochan 235
A'CHOIRE DUIBH, Lochan 241

A'CHOIRE GHLAIS, Loch 277
A'CHOIRE GHLAIS, Lochan 277
A'CHOIRE GHUIRM, Lochan 145
A'CHOIRE LEACAICH, Loch 173
A'CHOIRE LEITH, Loch 241, 249
A'CHOIRE MHOIR, Loch 196, 212
A'CHOIRE RIABHAIACH, Loch (North) 268
A'CHOIRE RIABHAIACH, Loch (South) 268
A'CHOIRE RIDBHAICH (North), Loch 249
A'CHOIRE RIDBHAICH (South), Loch 249
A'CHOIRE, Loch 196, 217, 249, 265, 305, 369
A'CHOIRE, Lochan 181, 277, 285, 302
A'CHOIREACHAIN, Loch 145
A'CHONNACHAIR, Loch 186
A'CHOTHRUIM, Lochan 294
A'CHRAOBHAIR, Lochan 145
A'CHRATHAICH, Loch 249
A'CHREACHAINN, Loch 340
A'CHREAGAIN DARAICH, Loch 145
A'CHREAGAIN THET, Loch 52
A'CHROISG, Loch 146, 241
A'CHROTHA, Loch 311
A'CHUILINN, Loch 209, 277
A'CHUIM DHEIRG, Lochan 299
A'CHUIN DUIBH, Loch 294
A'CHUIRN, Loch 196
A'CHUMHAINN, Sea-Loch 313
A'CHURRAGAN, Loch 362
A'COIRE A'PHUILL, Loch 274
A'CRUAICHE, Loch 340
A'FHRAOICH, Loch 107
A'GARBH-UILLT, Loch 173
A'GEODHA BEAG, Loch 107
A'GHAINMHICH, Loch 29
A'GHAIRBHE, Loch 196
A'GHAIRBHE, River 242
A'GHARAIDH, Loch 107, 125
A'GHARAIDH, Loch 107, 125
A'GHARAIDH, Loch (Udromul) 125
A'GHARBH-BHAID BEAG, Loch 52
A'GHARBH-BHAID MOR, Loch 52
A'GHARBH-CHOIRE, Loch 287
A'GHARBH-DOIRE, Loch 196
A'GHARBH-UISGE, Loch 367
A'GHATHA, Loch 370
A'GHEADAIS, Loch 217
A'GHEARRAIDH DHUIBH, Loch 265
A'GHEODHA RUAIDH, Loch 53
A'GHEOIDII, Loch 107, 125, 367
A'GHILLE GHOBAICH, Loch 294
A'GHILLE RUAIDH, Loch 108, 146
A'GHILLE RUAIDH, Lochan 29
A'GHILLE, Loch 146, 209, 346
A'GHILLE-CHNAPAIN, Loch 268
A'GHIUBHAIS, Loch 173, 213, 248
A'GHIUBHAIS, Lochanan 256
A'GHIUTHAIS, Loch 125
A'GHLEANNAIN SHALAICH, Loch 146

427

Index

A'GHLEANNAIN, Loch 316
A'GHLINNE DHUIRCH, Loch 235
A'GHLINNE SGOILTE, Loch 146
A'GHLINNE, Loch 107, 268, 346
A'GHLINNE-DORCHA, Loch 217
A'GHLINNEIN, Loch 146
A'GHOBHAINN, Loch 126, 196, 199, 235, 317
A'GHOBHAINN, Loch 126, 196, 199, 235, 317
A'GHOBHAINN, Loch (Garyvard) 126
A'GHOIRTEIN, Loch 107
A'GHORM-CHOIRE, Loch 173
A'GHRIAMA, Loch 173, 182
A'GHROBAIN, Loch 268
A'GHRUAGAICH, Loch 125
A'GHRUIBE, Loch 311
A'GHUIB AIRD, Loch 146
A'GHURRABAIN, Lochan 313
A'GLEANNAN A'CHOIT, Loch 146
A'LEADHARAIN, Loch 29
A'MEALLARD, Loch 146
A'MHADAIDH MOR, Loch 196
A'MHADAIDH RIABHAICH, Lochan 313
A'MHADAIDH, Loch 152, 160, 196, 208, 212, 249
A'MHADAIDH, Loch 152, 160, 196, 208, 212, 249
A'MHADAIL, Loch 146
A'MHAIDE, Loch 107, 123
A'MHAIDE, Loch (Soval) 107
A'MHAIM, Lochan 274
A'MHAIRT, Loch 107
A'MHEADHOIN, Lochan 294
A'MHEALLAIN ODHAIR, Loch 196
A'MHEALLAIN, Loch 146, 173
A'MHEALLAIN, Loch (Altnacealgach) 146
A'MHEALLAIN, Loch (Rubh Mor) 146
A'MHEALLAIN-CHAORAINN, Loch 209
A'MHI RUNAICH, Loch 146
A'MHILE, Loch 367
A'MHILL AIRD, Loch 311
A'MHILL DHEIRG, Loch 53
A'MHILL, Loch 156, 236, 312
A'MHINIDH, Loch 146
A'MHINN, Loch 340
A'MHINN, Loch 340
A'MHONAIDH, Loch 126
A'MHONAIDH-DHROIGHINN, Loch 197
A'MHORGHAIN, Loch 126
A'MHUILINN (North), Loch 249
A'MHUILINN (North), Lochan 294
A'MHUILINN (South), Loch 249
A'MHUILINN (South), Lochan 294
A'MHUILINN Lochan 329
A'MHUILINN, Loch 53, 74, 146-147, 197, 211, 217, 235, 242, 245, 249, 255
A'MHUILINN, Loch (Coulags) 242
A'MHUILINN, Loch (Duartbeg) 147
A'MHUILINN, Loch (Tongue) 74
A'MHUILLIN, Loch 367, 391

A'MHUINEAN, Lochs 53
A'MHUIRT, Loch 53
A'MHULA, Loch 107
A'MHULLAICH, Loch 235, 271
A'MHULLINN, Loch 236
A'PHEALUIR MOR, Loch 107
A'PHEARSAIN, Loch 340
A'PHEIRCIL, Loch 126
A'PHOBUILL, Loch 186
A'PHOLLAIN BHEITHE, Loch 147
A'PHOLLAIN DRISICH, Loch 147
A'PHOLLAIN, Loch 147
A'PHREASAIN CHALLTUINE, Loch 53
A'PHREASAN CHAILLTEAN, Loch 53
A'PHUILL BHUIDHE, Loch 54
A'PHUILL DHUIBH, Loch 249
A'PHUILL, Loch 197, 255, 274, 285, 295, 312, 315
A'PHUIRT-RUAIDH, Loch 217
A'ROTHAID, Loch 108
A'SGAIL, Loch 29, 108, 126
A'SGATH, Loch 268
A'SGEIL, Lochan 29
A'SGUAIR, Loch 108
A'TUAIDH, Lochan 313
A'TUATH, Loch (Morsgail) 108
ABBAR, Water 249
ABHAINN A'GHLEANN DUIRCH, Burn 367
ABHAINN A'GHLINNE DHUIBH, Stream 147
ABHAINN AN LOCH BHIG, Stream 147
ABHAINN BAD NA H-ACHLAISE, River 147
ABHAINN BHEAG AN TUNNS (Tunns River) 340
ABHAINN BRUACHAIG, Loch 197
ABHAINN CAMAS FHIONNAIRIGH, River 268
ABHAINN CONNICH, River 316
ABHAINN DUBH, River 236, 242
ABHAINN DUBH, River 236, 242
ABHAINN EADAR, River 126
ABHAINN GEIRAHA (River Garry) 29, 44
ABHAINN GHLEANN AOISTAIL, Burn 367
ABHAINN NA CLACH AIRIGH, River 147
ABHAINN THRAIL, River 236, 242
ABHAINN THRAIL, River 236, 242
ACHAIDH NA H-INICH, Loch 236
ACHALL, Loch 209
ACHANALT, Loch 209
ACHATENY Water 313
ACHILTY, Loch 249
ACHONACHIE, Loch 249
ACHRAY, Loch 351
ACHRUGAN, Loch 74
ACHTRIOTCHAN, Loch 299
ACREKNOWE, Reservoir 412
ADD, Lochan 340
ADD, River 340

AE, Water 408
AEROPLANE, Loch 197
AFFRIC (Lower), River 242
AFFRIC (Upper), River 242
AFFRIC, Loch 242
AFTON, Reservoir 405
AHALTAIR, Loch 108
AHAVAT BEAG, Loch 29
AHAVAT MOR, Loch 29
AIGAS, Loch 255
AIGHEROIL, Loch 126
AILORT, River 294
AILSH, Loch 147
AIRD AN DUIN, Loch 186
AIRD, Loch (Grimersta) 29
AIRD, Loch (Scaliscro) 108
AIRDEGLAIS, Loch 316
AIRIGH A'BHAIRD, Loch 54
AIRIGH A'BHEALAICH, Loch 108
AIRIGH A'GHILLE RUAIDH, Loch 108
AIRIGH A'MHILL, Loch 236
AIRIGH A'PHUILL, Loch 197
AIRIGH ALASDAIR, Loch 236
AIRIGH AMHLAIDH, Loch 217
AIRIGH AN EILEIN, Loch 197
AIRIGH AN SGAIRBH, Loch 29
AIRIGH AN T-SAGAIRT, Loch, Orasay 29
AIRIGH AN UISGE, Loch 108
AIRIGH ARD, Loch 217
AIRIGH BLAIR, Loch 147
AIRIGH CHALUIM, Lochan 147
AIRIGH EACHAINN, Loch 236
AIRIGH FHEARCHAIR, Loch 108
AIRIGH IAIN OIG, Loch 126
AIRIGH LEATHAID, Lochan 93
AIRIGH LOCHAIN, Loch 242
AIRIGH MEALL BHREIDE, Loch 312
AIRIGH MHIC CRIADH, Loch 197
AIRIGH MHIC FHIONNLAIDH, Loch 29
AIRIGH NA BEINNE, Loch 54
AIRIGH NA CEARDAICH, Loch 108
AIRIGH NA CREIGE, Loch 74
AIRIGH NA H-AIRDE, Loch 108
AIRIGH NA LIC, Loch 29
AIRIGH NA SAORACH, Loch 268
AIRIGH NAN CAISTEAL, Loch 362
AIRIGH NAN GLEANN, Loch 29
AIRIGH NAN, Lochan 323
AIRIGH NUALAIDH, Loch 367-368
AIRIGH RIABHACH, Loch 30
AIRIGH SEIBH, Loch 30
AIRIGH THORMAID, Loch 126
AIRIGH UILLEIM, Loch 197
AIRIGH-SHAMHRAIDH, Lochan 316
AISAVAT, Loch 265
AISIR MOR, Loch 55
AISIR, Loch 54
AITH, Loch 20
AITHSNESS, Loch 6
AKRAN, Loch 93

428

Index

ALATAIR, Loch 126, 186
ALE, Water 386, 400
ALE, Water (Eyemouth) 386
ALEMOOR, Loch 412
ALINE, River 317
ALIVE, Loch 287
Allan Water see River Teith. 351
ALLAN, Loch 362
ALLAN, Water 412
ALLANDALE, TARN Fishery 379
ALLANDER, Water 377
ALLAVAT, Loch 30, 36
ALLT A'CHONAIS, River 242
ALLT A'CHORMAIG, River 317
ALLT AN LOIN-FHIODHA, Stream 242
ALLT BAN, Burn 287
ALLT DEARG MOR, River 268
ALLT EIGIN, Loch 197
ALLT EILEACHAN, Burn 213
ALLT EOIN THOMAIS, Loch 197
ALLT FEARNACH, Burn 305
ALLT GHLINNE, River 268
ALLT LOCH CALAVIE, Stream 242
ALLT LON A'CHUIL, River 74
ALLT MHIC MHUROHA DH GHEIR, River 147
ALLT MUIGH BHLARAIDH, Burn 213
ALLT NA GUILE, Burn 268
ALLT NA H-AIRBE, Loch 147
ALLT NAM BEARNACH, Loch 126
ALLT NAN DUBHA, Lochanan 317
ALLT NAN RAMH, Loch 147
ALLTNASUILEIG, Lochs 55
ALMAISTEAN, Loch 30
ALMOND, River 329, 334, 380, 383
ALMOND, River (Perthshire) 329
ALNESS, River 213
ALTABRUG, Loch 217
ALVIE, Loch 284
AM FEUR-LOCH (Shieldaig), Loch 197
AM FEUR-LOCH, Loch 197
AMAR SINE, Loch 30
AMHASTAR, Loch 30
AN ACHA, Loch 209
AN ACHAIDH, Loch 147, 169, 238
AN ADD, Loch 341
AN AIGEIL, Loch 147
AN AIRCEIL, Loch 210
AN AIS, Lochan 147
AN ALLTAIN BHEITHE, Loch 249
AN ALLTAIN DUIBH, Loch 147, 169
AN ALLTAN FHEARNA, Loch 173
AN AMAIR, Loch 243
AN AOIMIDH DHUIBH, Loch 367
AN AON AITE, Loch 147-148
AN ARBHAIR, Loch 148, 236
AN ARCILL, Loch (Ardlussa) 367
AN ARMUINN, Loch 186
AN ASLAIRD, Loch 173
AN ATH RUAIDH, Loch 108, 217

AN ATH RUAIDH, Loch 108, 217
AN ATHAIN, Loch 217, 268
AN ATHAIN, Loch 217, 268
AN CAORUINN, Loch 148
AN COIRE, Loch 341
AN CURRAIGH, Loch 341
AN DAIMH GHLAIS, Loch 249
AN DAIMH MOR, Loch 55
AN DAIMH, Loch 126, 186, 197, 326, 341
AN DAIMH, Loch (Marvig) 126
AN DAIMH, Loch, Aird Skapraid 30
AN DAING, Loch 197
AN DEASPOIRT, Loch 108
AN DHUBHAICH, Loch 362
AN DOIRE CRIONAICH, Loch 198
AN DOIRE DHARAICH, Lochan 317
AN DOIRE DHUIBH, Loch 148
AN DROIGHINN, Loch 169, 243, 326
AN DROMA BHAIN, Loch 268
AN DROMA, Loch 217
AN DRUNGA, Loch 108
AN DUBH, Loch 55
AN DUBH-LOCH, Loch 236
AN DUBH-LOCHAIN, Loch 274
AN DUBH-LOCHAN, Loch 249
AN DUBHAIR, Loch 249
AN DUIBHE, Loch 198
AN DUIBHE, Lochan 148
AN DUIN MHOIR, Loch 218
AN DUIN, Loch 30-31, 126, 186, 190, 265, 304, 312, 332
AN DUIN, Loch (Borve) 186
AN DUIN, Loch (Carloway) 30
AN DUIN, Loch (Cheese Bay) 186
AN DUIN, Loch (Daliburgh) 265
AN DUIN, Loch (Laiaval) 186
AN DUIN, Loch (Lower Bayble) 31
AN DUIN, Loch (Scalpay) 126
AN DUIN, Loch (Smerclate) 265
AN DUIN, Loch (Taransay) 186
AN DUIN, Loch, Aird 30
AN DUN-CHAIRN, Loch 198
AN DUNA, Loch 31
AN DUNA, Loch (Orasay) 31
AN DUNAIN, Loch 31
AN EANG, Loch 243
AN EARBALL, Loch 31, 108
AN EAS GHAIRBH, Loch 55
AN EASA GHIL, Loch 108
AN EASAIN UAINE, Loch 55
AN EASAIN, Loch 148
AN EICH DHUIBH, Loch 198
AN EICH GHLAIS, Lochain 198
AN EICH UIDHIR, Loch 148
AN EILEAN CHUBHRAIDH, Loch 31
AN EILEAN LIATH, Loch 108
AN EILEAN, Loch (Eishken) 127
AN EILEAN, Loch (Grimersta East) 108
AN EILEAN, Loch (South Boisdale) 265
AN EILEAN, Loch (Vallay) 187

AN EILEIN (North), Loch 198
AN EILEIN (South), Loch 198
AN EILEIN BHIG, Loch 127
AN EILEIN CHOINNICH, Loch 108
AN EILEIN DUIBH, Loch (Glenside) 127
AN EILEIN, Loch 31, 75, 108, 197, 210, 212, 218, 236, 249, 268, 284, 287, 317
AN EILEIN, Loch (Scaliscro) 108
AN EILEIN, Loch (Suardal) 268
AN EILEN, Loch 317
AN EILICH, Loch 198
AN EILICH, Loch 198
AN EION, Loch 243
AN EIRCILL, Loch 148
AN EOIN RUADHA, Loch 250
AN EOIN, Loch 173
AN FHADA BHIG, Loch 31
AN FHAING BHUIDHE 218
AN FHAING, Loch 218
AN FHAING, Lochan 317
AN FHAMHAIR, Loch 198
AN FHAOIR, Loch 243
AN FHEADAIN, Loch 148
AN FHEIDH, Loch 50, 153, 218
AN FHEIDH, Lochan 56
AN FHEOIR BHEAG, Loch 31
AN FHEOIR MHOIR, Loch 32
AN FHEOIR, Loch 31-32, 75, 108, 173, 198, 236, 250
AN FHEOIR, Loch 31-32, 75, 108, 173, 198, 236, 250
AN FHEOIR, Loch (Habost) 108
AN FHEOIR, Lochan 127, 236
AN FHEOIR, Lochan (Ulladale) 127
AN FHEOIR, Lochan (Voshimid) 127
AN FHIARLAID, Loch 243
AN FHIDHLEIR, Loch 236
AN FHIONA, Loch 210
AN FHIR MHAOIL, Loch 32, 108
AN FHITHICH, Loch 198
AN FHORSA, Loch 108
AN FHRAOICH, Loch 32, 370
AN FHREICEADAIN, Loch 173
AN FHRIDHEIN, Loch 230
AN FIR-BHALLAICH, Loch 268
AN FLIUARAIN, Loch 173
AN FUATH, Loch 149
AN GAINEAMH, Loch 198
AN GEAD LOCH, Loch 243
AN GLAS-LOCH, Loch 173
AN GORM, Loch 248, 250
AN GORM-LOCH, Loch 243
AN IAR, Loch 108
AN IASAICH, Loch 243
AN IASGAICH, Loch 268
AN IASGAIR, Loch 149, 198, 218, 222
AN IASGAIR, Lochan 243
AN IME, Loch 268
AN IME, Lochan 313
AN INNEIL, Loch 149
AN IONAIRE, Loch 218, 223

429

Index

AN LAGAIN AINTHEICH, Loch 274
AN LAGAIN, Loch 213
AN LAIR, Lochan 323
AN LAOIGH, Loch 149, 173, 243
AN LAOIGH, Loch, Beinn Ghreinaval 32
AN LAOIGH, Loch, Pentland Road 32
AN LEATHAD RAINICH, Loch 149
AN LEATHIAD BHUAIN, Loch 149
AN LEINIBH, Loch 362
AN LEOID, Loch 268, 326
AN LEOTHAID, Loch (Quinag) 149
AN LEOTHAID, Loch (Suilven) 149
AN LETH-UILLT, Loch 268
AN LOCHAN UAINE, Lochan 287
AN LOSGAINN BEAG, Loch 341
AN LOSGAINN MOR, Loch 341
AN NID, Loch 198
AN NIGHE LEATHAID, Loch 56
AN NOSTARIE, Loch 295
AN OBAN BHIG, Lochan 295
AN OIS GHUIRM, Loch 32
AN OIS, Loch (Beinn Tulagaval) 32
AN OIS, Loch (River Creed) 32
AN ORDAIN, Loch 149, 251, 285
AN OSE, Loch 218
AN RATHAID, Loch 127, 236
AN ROPACH, Lochan 295
AN ROTHAID, Loch 127
AN RUBHA DHUIBH, Loch 268
AN RUIGHEIN, Loch 149
AN RUIGHEIN, Loch (Duartmore) 149
AN RUTHAIR, Loch 182
AN SAILM, Loch 341
AN SGATH, Loch 108
AN SGEIREACH MHOIR, Loch 32
AN SGEIREACH, Loch 198
AN SGOLTAIRE, Loch 367
AN SGUID, Loch 277
AN SPARDAIN, Loch 250
AN STAING, Loch 173
AN STARSAICH, Loch 268
AN STICIR, Loch 187
AN STRUMORE, Loch 187
AN T- SIDHEIN, Loch 32
AN T-SABHAIL-MHOINE, Loch 198
AN T-SAGAIRT, Loch 187, 236, 312
AN T-SAILE, LOCH 218
AN T-SEAN-INBHIR, Loch 198
AN T-SEANA PHUILL, Loch 56
AN T-SEANA-BHAILE, Loch 198
AN T-SEARRAICH, Loch 187
AN T-SEASGAIN, Loch 218
AN T-SEILACH, Loch 287
AN T-SEILG, Loch 173
AN T-SEILICH, Loch 268, 304
AN T-SIDHEIN, Loch 109, 210, 258, 289, 321
AN T-SITHEIN TARSUINN, Loch 367
AN T-SLAGAIN, Loch 198
AN T-SLIOS, Loch 108

AN T-SLUGAITE, Lochan 173
AN TACHDAICH, Loch 243
AN TAIRBEART NAN CLEITICHEAN, Loch 32
AN TAIRBEART, Loch (South Cleitshal) 32
AN TAIRBEIRT, Loch 127
AN TAIRBH DUINN, Loch 127
AN TAIRBH, Loch 127, 173, 218
AN TAIRBH, Lochan 150
AN TAOBH SEAR, Loch 108
AN TEAS (North), Loch 199
AN TEAS (South), Loch 199
AN TIGH SHELG, Loch 56
AN TIGH-CHOIMHID, Loch 75
AN TIOMPAIN, Loch 210
AN TIUMPAN, Loch 32
AN TOBAIR, Loch 32
AN TOM, Loch 187
AN TOMAIN, Loch 108, 218
AN TORR, Loch 313
AN TORRNALAICH, Lochan 341
AN TRI-CHRIOCHAN (East), Lochan 295
AN TRUIM, Loch 127
AN TUIM AIRD, Loch 32
AN TUIM UAINE, Loch 367
AN TUIM, Loch 32, 60, 112, 268
AN TUIM, Loch (Pentland Road) 32
AN TUIR, Loch 150
AN TUIRC, Loch 150, 173, 210, 218
AN TURARAICH, Loch 236
AN UACHDAIR, Loch 236
AN UAINE Lochan 330
AN UIDH, Loch 210
AN UILLT-BHEITHE, Loch 243
AN UILLT-GHIUBHAIS, Loch 199, 250
AN UILLT-GHIUBHAIS, Loch 199, 250
AN UISGE MHAITH MOR, Loch 127
AN UISGE-GHIL, Loch 218
AN ULBHAIDH, Loch 173
AN UMHLAICH, Loch 32
AN-DUBH, Loch 230
AN-IASGAICH, Lochan 150
ANAMA, Lochan 341
ANLAIMH, Loch 312
ANNAN, River 408, 424
ANNICK, Water 391
ANNIE, Loch 243
AOGHNAIS MHIC FHIONNLAIDH, Loch 127
AONGHAIS, Loch 187, 371
AORAIDH, Loch 32
APPLECROSS, River 236
ARADAIDH, Loch 250
ARAY, River 323
ARBHAIR, Lochan 75
ARCHRIDIGILL, Loch 75
ARD A'PHUILL, Loch 295
ARD AN SGAIRBH, Loch 218
ARD, Loch 33, 42, 191, 217, 268, 351
ARDENNISH, Loch 187

ARDGOWAN, Fishery 371
ARDLE, River 305
ARDNAHOE, Loch 362
ARDNAVE, Loch 363
ARDTRECK, Burn 268
ARICHLINIE, Loch 182
ARIEANS, Loch 317
ARKAIG, Loch 274, 277, 295
ARKAIG, River 275, 277
ARKLET, Loch 347
ARM, Loch 267, 315
ARNOL, Loch 32
ARNOL, River 33
AROS, River 313
ARUISG, Loch 268
ASCAIG, Loch 182
ASCOG, Loch 372
ASHAVAT, Loch 128
ASHIE, Loch 250
ASHIK, Loch 268
ASLAICH, Loch 250
ASSAPOL, Loch 315
ASSYNT, Loch 150
ASTA, Loch 20
ATH GHAIRBH, Loch 199
ATTADALE, River 243
AUCHA LOCHY, Loch 388
AUCHNAHA, Loch 341
AULASARY, Upper Loch 187
AVICH, Loch 342
AVICH, River 342
AVIELOCHAN, Loch 287
AVON, Loch 287
AVON, River 258, 287
AVON, Water 377
AWE, Loch 150, 323, 342
AWE, River 323
AYR, River 391, 394

B

BA ALASDAIR, Loch 218
BA UNA, Loch 218
BA, Loch 205, 299, 324, 332, 369
BA, River 313, 324
BAC AN LOCHAIN, Lochan 295
BACAVAT ARD, Loch 33
BACAVAT CROSS, Loch 33
BACAVAT IORACH, Loch 33
BACAVAT, Loch (Gress) 33
BACAVAT, Loch (Shader) 33
BACAVAT, Loch, Barvas Moor 33
BACK, Water 388
BACKWATER Reservoir 308, 334-335
BAD A'BHOTHAIN, Loch 75
BAD A'CHIGEAR, Loch 150
BAD A'CHREAMH, Loch 199
BAD A'GHAILL, Loch 150
BAD AN FHEUR-LOCH, Loch 56, 68
BAD AN LOCH, Loch 173

Index

BAD AN LOSGUINN, Loch 277
BAD AN OG, Loch 151, 169
BAD AN SGALAIG, Loch 199
BAD AN T-SEABHAIG, Loch 56
BAD AN T-SEAN-TIGHE, Loch 173
BAD AN T-SLUIC, Loch 151
BAD LEABHRAIDH, Loch 210
BAD NA H-ACHLAISE (Ullapool), Loch 210
BAD NA H-ACHLAISE, Loch 57, 151, 199
BAD NA H-ACHLAISE, Loch (Ullapool) 151
BAD NA H-EARBA, Loch 182
BAD NA MUIRIEHINN, Loch 151
BAD NAM MULT, Loch 57
BAD NAN AIGHEAN, Loch 151
BADACHRO, River 199
BADAIDH NA MEANA, Loch 76
BADAN NA MOINE, Loch 210
BADANLOCH, Loch 182
BADANLOCH, Water 183
BAGH NAM FIADH, Loch 219
BAIL-FHIONNLAIDH, Loch 219
BAILE A'GHOBHAINN, Loch 317
BAILE MHIC CHAILEIN, Loch 324
BAIMALEE, Loch 219
BALACLAVA, Loch 23
BALGY, River 238
BALIGILL, Loch 76
BALLO, Reservoir 355
BALLYGRANT, Loch 363
BALNAGOWAN, River 214
BALVAG, River 351
BANNISKIRK, Loch 97
BANNOCK, Burn 183
BANTON, Loch 377
BARAVAIG, Loch 268
BARAVAT, Loch 33, 108-109
BARAVAT, Loch (Great Bernera) 108
BARAVAT, Loch (Uig) 109
BARDISTER, Loch 6
BARLAY, Burn 419
BARNLUSGAN, Loch 342
BARONY, Loch 409
BARR A'BHEALAICH, Loch 367
BARR, Loch 372
BARR, River 321, 363
BARSCOBE, Loch 405
BARVAS River 33, 38
BASTA, Loch 1
BAYS Water 6, 13
BAYWEST, Loch 23
BEA Loch 23-25
BEACH, River 316
BEAG A'CHOCAIR, Loch 33
BEAG A'GHRIANAIN, Loch 33
BEAG AIRIGH NAN LINNTEAN, Loch 109
BEAG AN STAIRR, Loch 33
BEAG CATISVAL, Loch 128
BEAG EILEAVAT, Loch 33

BEAG GAINEAMHAICH, Loch 33
BEAG LEIG TADH, Loch 33
BEAG NA BEISTE, Loch (Grimersta) 109
BEAG NA CRAOIBHE, Loch (Orasay) 34
BEAG NA FUARALACHD, Loch 173
BEAG NA MUILNE, Loch 109
BEAG NAN IAN, Loch 187
BEAG RUADH, Loch (Gisla) 109
BEAG SANDAVAT, Loch 34
BEAG SGEIREACH, Loch 34
BEAG SHEILABRIE, Loch 109
BEAG THOMA DHUIBHE, Loch 34
BEAG, Loch 29, 33, 43, 48, 52, 77-78, 83, 86-87, 107, 116, 122, 128, 133, 152, 154, 158, 160, 175, 177, 181, 187, 195, 199, 203, 207, 211-212, 216, 230, 235, 238-239, 243, 250, 284, 299, 321, 341, 345, 365, 369, 371
BEAG, Loch (Arnish) 33
BEAG, Loch (Boreray) 187
BEAG, Loch (Glen Hinnisdale) 230
BEAG, Loch (Raasay) 238
BEAG, Loch (Rhenigdale) 128
BEAG, Lochan (Eaval River) 128
BEAG, Sea Loch 147, 151
BEALACH A'BHUIRICH, Loch 152
BEALACH A'MHADAIDH, Loch 152
BEALACH AN EILEIN, Lochs 57
BEALACH CORNAIDH, Lochan 152
BEALACH GHEARRAN, Loch 342
BEALACH NA H-UIDHE, Loch 152
BEALACH NA SGAIL, Loch 34
BEALACH NAN CREAGAN DUBHA, Loch 275
BEALACH STOCKLETT, Loch 128
BEANAIDH, Lochan 287
BEANIE, Loch 305
BEANNACH BEAG, Loch 152, 199
BEANNACH MOR, Loch 199
BEANNACH, Loch 152, 173
BEANNACH, Loch (East Dalreavoch) 173
BEANNACH, Loch (Lairg) 173
BEANNACH, Loch (West Dalreavoch) 173
BEANNACHARAIN, Loch (Scardroy) 243
BEARASTA MOR, Loch 128
BEARFORD, Burn 382
BEARNACH, Loch 126, 318
BEAULY, River 250
BEE (EAST), Loch 219
BEE (WEST), Loch 220
BEECRAIGS, Reservoir 380
BEIG NA BEISTE, Loch 34
BEIN, Loch 220
BEINN A'MHEADHOIN, Loch 244
BEINN AN EOIN BHEAG, Loch 173
BEINN BHREAC, Loch (Arnish) 34
BEINN DEARG BAD CHAILLEACH, Loch 199
BEINN DEARG BHEAG, Loch 199
BEINN DEARG, Loch 199, 210
BEINN DEIRG, Loch 152, 156

BEINN IOBHEIR, Loch 34
BEINN NA GAINMHEICH, Loch (Orasay) 34
BEINN NAN SGALAG, Loch 34
BEINN NAN SGALAG, Loch (West) 34
BEINNE BRICE, Lochain 314
BEINNE-RI-OITIR, Lochan 265
BEIRE, Loch 220
BELLART, River 314
BELLISTER, Loch 6
BELLSGROVE, Loch 295
BELMONT, Loch 1
BELSTON, Loch 391
BEN HARRALD, Loch 173
BEN STROME, Lochs 152
BENISVAL, Loch 109
BENSTON, Loch 7
BEOSETTER, Lochs of 20
BEOUIN MHOIR, Loch 265
BERRARUNIES, Loch 7
BERRIEDALE Water 93, 183, 185
BERRIEDALE, Water 183
BERVIE, River 310
BHAC, Loch 305
BHAD GHAINEAMHAICH, Loch 250
BHANAMHOIR, Loch 199
BHARRADAIL, Loch 363
BHARRANCH, Loch 244
BHASAPOLL, Loch 312
BHEAG A'BHAILE-DOIRE, Lochain 367
BHLARAIDH, Reservoir 277
BHRAIGHAIG, Loch 238
BHRAOMISAIG, Loch 275, 295
BHREACAICH, Loch 128
BHREAGLEIT, Loch 34
BHRUIST, Loch 187
BHRUTHADAIL, Loch 34
BIG WATER OF FLEET, River 419
BIGGAR, Water 395
BIODA MOR, Loch 269
BIRKA Water 1-5
BIRNS & GIFFORD, Water 382, 386
BIRRIER, Loch 1
BIRRIESGIRT, Loch 1
BISHOP'S, Loch 291
BLACK ESK, Reservoir 412
BLACK ESK, Water 412
BLACK Loch 7, 19, 98, 358, 406, 416, 418
BLACK Water 7, 209-214, 251, 300, 306, 317, 354, 407, 419
BLACK WATER OF DEE, River 419
BLACK WATER, River 210, 250, 261, 290
BLACK, Burn 419
BLACK, Loch 334, 355, 378-379, 389, 394, 402, 404-405, 416, 418, 424
BLACK, Loch (Balminnoch) 416
BLACK, Loch (Clatteringshaws) 405
BLACK, Loch (Ochiltree) 402
BLACK, Water (Glenshee) 305
BLACKADDER, Water 386
BLACKMILL, Loch 342

Index

BLACKWATER Reservoir 299-301
BLACKWATER, Fishery 382
BLACKWATER, River 34, 173
BLACKWATER, River (Ben Armine Lodge) 173
BLADNOCH, River 416, 419
BLAIR WALKER, Pond 305
BLAIR, Loch 147, 275
BLAIRS, Loch 256
BLAR A'BHAINNE, Lochan 76
BLARLOCH MOR, Loch 57
BOARDHOUSE, Loch 25
BODAVAT, Loch 109
BOGIE, River 261
BOGTON, Loch 405
BOIDHEACH, Loch 312
BONALY, Reservoir 383
BOOR, Loch 199
BORASDALE, Loch 34
BORDER ESK, River 412, 425
BORDIGARTH, Loch 7
BORGIE, River 76
BORGUE, Loch 183
BORNISH, Loch 220, 230
BOROSDLAE, Loch 220
BORRALAN, Loch 153
BORRALIE, Loch 57
BORTHWICK, Water 414
BORVE River 31, 35, 188
BORVE, Loch 187, 190
BORVE, River 188
BOSQUOY, Loch 23, 25
BOSQUOY, Loch 23, 25
BOTHWELL, Water 386
BOWDEN SPRINGS, Fishery 380
BOWMONT, Water 400
BOYNE, Burn of 261
BRAAN, River 330, 334
BRACK, Loch 405
BRADAN, Loch 405
BRAERADDACH, Loch 290
BRAIGH A'BHAILE, Loch 153
BRAIGH AN ACHAIDH, Loch 238
BRAIGH AN T-SIDHEIN, Loch 109
BRAIGH BHEAGARAIS, Loch 109
BRAIGH BHLAIN, Loch 269
BRAIGH HORRISDALE, Loch 199
BRAIGH LOCHAN, Loch 250
BRAIGH NA H-AIBHNE, Loch 183
BRAIGH NA H-IMRICH, Loch 128
BRAIGH NAN RON, Loch 128
BRAIGHE GRIOMAVAL, Loch 109
BRAIGHE, Lochan 77
BRAN, Loch 212, 284
BRAN, River 210, 250
BRANAHUIE, Loch 35
BRANDY, Loch 308
BRAUR, Water 306
BREAC, Loch (Dunbeath) 183
BREAC-LIATH, Lochan 342

BREACKERIE, Water 388
BREACLETE, Loch 109
BREASCLETE, River 35
BRECK, Loch 7
BRECKBOWIE, Loch 406
BRECKON, Loch 7
BRECKSIE, Loch 1
BREI Water (Lunnasting) 7
BREI Water (Mangaster) 7
BREI Water of Nibon 7
BREIVAT, Loch (Carloway) 35
BRENISH, River 109
BRERACHAN, Water 306
BREUGACH, Loch 35
BRINDISTER, Loch 20
BRINNAVAL, Loch 109
BRIOBAIG, Loch 275
BRITTLE, River 269
BROACH, Loch 363
BROADFORD, River 269
BROCH OF CUSTWICK Loch 20, 23
BROCKAN, Loch 26
BROGAIG, River 230
BROO Loch 20-21
BROOM, River 210
BRORA (Lower), River 183
BRORA, Loch 183
BRORA, Upper River (Dalreavoch Lodge) 174
BROUGH, Loch 1, 20
BROUSTER, Loch of 7
BROUSTER, Upper Loch 8
BRU, Loch 188
BRUCKLAY, Loch 262
BRUE, Loch 23
BRUICHE BREIVAT, Loch 109
BRUNAVAL, Loch (Eadar) 128
BRUNAVAL, Loch (Resort) 128
BRUNTIS, Loch 419
BUAILE BHIG, Loch 35
BUAILE GRAMASDALE, Loch 220
BUAILE MIRAVAT, Loch 109
BUAILE NAN CAORACH, Loch 110
BUCKHAT, Water of 290
BUDDON, Burn 338
BUIDHE BEAG, Loch 77
BUIDHE MOR, Loch 77
BUIDHE, Loch 63, 77, 88, 137, 175, 211, 214, 222, 248, 269, 273, 324, 345
BUIDHE, Lochan 71, 345, 351
BUIE, Lochan 342
BUILG, Loch 287
BUINE MOIRE, Loch 153
BUN SRUTH (SEA LOCH) 265
BUNAEHTON, Loch 251
BURGA Water, Lunnasting 8
BURGA Water, Mousa Vords 8
BURKI Waters 8, 10
BURNATWATT, Loch 8
BURNESS, Loch 23

BURNFOOT, Burn 420
BURNFOOT, Reservoir 377
BURNOCK, Water 391
BURRALAND, Loch 8
BURWICK, Loch 20
BUSBIE MUIR, Reservoir 372
BUTTERSTONE, Loch of 330, 334

C

CAAF, Reservoir 372
CADDON, Water 397
CADH A'GHOBHAINN, Loch 199
CADH AN EIDIDH, Loch 244
CADOON, Burn 420
CAIRN DIERG, Lochan 324
CAISE, Loch 97
CAITIDHRIRIDH, Loch 199
CALADAIL, Loch 58
CALAIR, Burn 351
CALAVIE, Loch 244
CALDER, Dam 372
CALDER, Loch 97
CALDER, River 284, 372
CALL AN UIDHEAN, Loch 153
CALLY, Lake 409
CAM NAN EILIDEAN, Loch 36
CAM, Loch 153, 342, 363
CAM, Loch (Ederline) 342
CAM, Loch (Loch an Add) 342
CAM, Loch (Loch Awe) 342
CAMA, Lochan 188
CAMA-LOCH, Loch 188
CAMAS AN FHEIDH, Loch 153
CAMAS-DUIBHE, Loch 188
CAMASACH, Loch 175
CAMASORD, Loch (Ardroil) 110
CAMASORD, Loch (Crowlista) 110
CAMASUNARY, River 269
CAMERON, Burn 360
CAMERON, Reservoir 360
CAMPHILL, Reservoir 372
CAMPLE, Water 409
CAMSTER, Loch 97
CANNICH, River 245
CAOL A'GHARAIDH MHOIR, Loch 129
CAOL A'GHARAIDH MHOIR, Loch (Glenside) 129
CAOL DUIN OTHAIL, Loch 36
CAOL EISHAL, Loch 129
CAOL NA H-INNSE-GEAMHRAIDH, Loch 199
CAOL NORTH, Loch 77
CAOL SOUTH, Loch 77
CAOL, Loch (Gisla) 110
CAOL, Loch (Lemreway) 129
CAOL, Loch (Scaliscro) 110
CAOL, Loch (Sligachan) 269
CAOL, Loch (Tom an Fhuadain) 129
CAOL, Lochan 315, 318

Index

CAOL-LOCH BEAG, Loch 78
CAOL-LOCH CREAG NAN LAOGH 78, 86
CAOL-LOCH MOR 78
CAOL-LOCH, Loch (Meadie) 78
CAOLDAIR, Loch 302
CAORAINN, Lochan 324
CARAVAT, Loch (Grimsay) 220
CARAVAT, Loch (North Uist) 221
CARLOWAY, River 36
CARMEL, Water 391
CARN A 'CHUILINN, Loch 277
CARN A'CHUILINN, Loch 277
CARN A'CHUILINN, Lochan 277
CARN MHARASAID, Loch 58
CARN MHARTUIN, Loch 245
CARN NA CLOICHE MOIRE, Loch 251
CARN NA FEOLA, Lochan 199
CARN NAN CONBHAIREAN, Loch 153
CARN NAN GALL, Loch 363
CARN NAN GILLEAN, Loch 367
CARNACH, River 275, 295
CARNAIN AN AMIS, Loch 314
CARNOCH, Loch 295
CARO, Water 409
CARPEL, Water 394
CARRADALE, Water 388
CARRAN, Loch 129
CARRIE, Loch 245
CARRISTON (Upper) Reservoir 360
CARRON VALLEY, Reservoir 351
CARRON, River 214, 245, 351
CARRON, River See Carron Valley Reservoir 351
CARRON, Water 310
CARSFAD, Reservoir 406
CARTACH, Loch 36, 117, 129, 137, 190, 265-266
CARTACH, Loch (Lemreway) 129
CASGRO, Loch 36
CASLUB, Loch 221
CASSLEY, River 175
CASTLE SEMPLE, Loch 372
CASTLEFAIRN, Water 423
CASTLEHILL, Reservoir 355
CASTRAMONT, Burn 420
CATHAR NAN EUN, Loch 367
CATHERINE'S, Loch 184
CATISVAL, Loch 128-129
CAVERSTA, River 129
CEANN A'BHAIGH, Loch 221
CEANN A'CHARNAICH, Loch 200
CEANN ALLAVAT, Loch 36
CEANN HULAVIG, Sea-loch 110
CEANN, Loch 278
CEOPACH, Loch 238
CEOTHLAIS, Loch 251
CERES, Burn 361
CESSNOCK, Water 391
CHABET, Water 287
CHAOLARTAN, Loch 110

CHEALLAIR, Loch 343
CHEARASAIDH, Loch 36
CHESNEY, Loch 416
CHIARIAN, Loch 299
CHILLEIRIVAGH, Loch 265
CHLACHAN DEARGA, Loch 129
CHLADAICH, Loch 188
CHLEISTIR, Loch 129
CHLIOSTAIR, Loch 129
CHOILLEIGAR, Loch 110
CHOIN, Loch (Allt na Muilne) 36
CHOINNICH MOR, Lochan 314
CHOIRE, Loch 175, 196, 217, 249, 265, 305, 369
CHOLLA, Loch 367
CHON, Loch 347
CHRAGOL, Loch 110, 118
CHRIOSTINA, Loch 200
CHROCHAIRE, Loch 129
CHUILCEACHAN, Lochan 343
CHULAIN, Loch 36
CHULAPUILL, Loch 37
CHUMRABORGH, Loch 129
CIARAN Water 299
CIARAN, Loch 370
CILL CHRIOSD, Loch 269
CILLE BHANAIN, Loch 222
CILLE, Loch 188, 265
CLACH A'CHINN DUIBH, Loch 154
CLACH AN DUILISG, Loch 222
CLACH NA BOITEIG, Lochan 314
CLACH NA H-IOLAIRE, Loch 110
CLACHAIG, Loch 321, 343
CLACHAIG, River 314
CLACHARAN, Loch 37
CLAIR, Loch 200, 245-246
CLAIS NAN COINNEAL, Loch 58
CLAISEIN, Loch 78
CLAR BEAG, Loch (Knockan) 154
CLAR BEAG, Loch (Rubha Mor) 154
CLAR LOCH MOR, Loch 58
CLAR MOR, Loch (Knockan) 154
CLAR MOR, Loch (Rubha Mor) 154
CLAR, Loch 93, 129, 180
CLAR, Loch, Scourie 58
CLAR-LOCH MOR, Loch 78
CLATTERINGSHAWS, Loch 406
CLATTO, Reservoir 361
CLEAP, Loch 230
CLEARBURN, Loch 414
CLEAT, Loch 230
CLEIT A'GHUIB CHOILLE, Loch 129
CLEIT AN AISEIG, Loch 129
CLEIT DUASTAL, Loch 110
CLEIT EIRMIS, Loch 37
CLEIT NA STIUIRE, Loch 129
CLEIT STEIRMEIS, Loch 37
CLEUGH, Burn 420
CLIAD, Loch 312
CLIASAM CREAG, Loch 37

CLIBH CRACAVAL, Loch 110
CLIFF, Loch of 1
CLINGS Water 8, 10
CLODIS Water 9
CLOUSTA, Loch 9
CLOY, Water 390
Cluanie, Loch 275, 278
CLUANIE, Loch 275, 278
CLUBBA Water 9, 15
CLUBBIEDEAN, Reservoir 383
CLUDEN, Water (Cairn Water) 423
CLUGSTON, Loch 416
CLUMLIE, Loch 20
CLUMMLY, Loch 23, 26
CLYDE, River 377, 395, 409
CNAPACH, Lochan 200
CNOC A'BUIDHE, Loch 222
CNOC BERUL, Loch 129
CNOC CHALBHA, Lochs 154
CNOC CHOILICH, Loch 37, 188
CNOC IAIN DUIBH, Loch 129
CNOC NAN SLIGEAN, Loch 110
CNOC ODHAR, Lochs 155
CNOC THORMAID, Lochs 58
CNOC THULL, Lochs 59
COAL LOCH A' MHIND, Loch 59
COAL, Lochan 59
COARSE FISHERIES 324, 334, 338, 361, 372, 374, 377, 383, 392, 402, 406, 409, 416, 420, 423, 425
COE, River 299
COILL A'GHORM LOCHA, Loch 59
COILLE SHUARDAIL, Loch 130
COILLE-BHARR, Loch 343
COIR A'GHOBHAINN, Lochan 269
COIR A'GHRUNNDA, Loch 269
COIRE A'BHAID, Loch 155
COIRE A'BHUIC, Loch 245
COIRE A'MHUILINN, Loch 245
COIRE AN LOCHAIN, Loch 287, 299
COIRE AN RUADH-STAIC, Loch 245
COIRE ATTADALE, Loch 238
COIRE CHAOLAIS BHIG, Loch 275
COIRE CHAORACHAIN, Loch 200
COIRE DOIRE NA SEILG, Loch 269
COIRE FIONNARAICH, Loch 245
COIRE LOCHAIN, Lochan 278
COIRE LOCHAN, Loch 246
COIRE MHIC DHUGHAILL, Loch 155
COIRE MHIC FHEARCHAIR, Loch 200
COIRE NA BA BUIDHE, Loch 211
COIRE NA BEINNE, Lochan 97
COIRE NA CAIME, Loch 246
COIRE NA CIRCE, Loch 275
COIRE NA CREIGE, Loch 155
COIRE NA H-AIRIGH, Loch 200
COIRE NA MEIDIE, Loch 155
COIRE NA MEINNE, Lochan 299
COIRE NA POITE, Loch 238
COIRE NA RAINICH, Loch 251

Index

COIRE NA SAIDHE DUIBHE, Loch 175
COIRE NAM CNAMH, Loch 275
COIRE NAM FEURAN, Loch 175
COIRE NAM MANG, Loch 79
COIRE NAN ARR, Loch 238
COIRE NAN CADHA, Loch 275
COIRE SHUBH, Loch 275
COIRE, Loch 160, 175, 182, 246, 341
COIREAG NAM MANG, Loch 246
COIRGAVAT, Loch 110
COIRIGEROD, Loch 111
COLADOIR, River 316
COLDINGHAM, Loch 387
COLL, River 37
COLLA, Loch 222
COLLASTER, Loch (Twatt) 9
COLLAVAL, Loch 37, 111
COLLENNAN, Reservoir 392
COLLUSCARVE, Loch 130
COLSTOUN, Water 383
CONAGTEANN, Loch 284
CONASTAICH, Loch 343
CONGLASS, Water 287
CONIE, Water 388
CONNAN, Loch 231
CONON, River 231, 251
CONON, River 231, 251
CORAGRIMSAIG, Loch 265
CORBY, Loch 291
CORCASGIL, Loch 231
CORLARACH, Loch 231
CORMAIC, Loch 79
CORODALE, Loch 222
CORRASAVAT, Loch 37
CORUISK, Loch 269
COTEHILL, Loch 291
COULAVIE, Loch 246
COULDBACKIE Lochan 79
COULIN, Loch 246
COULIN, River 246
COULTRIE, Loch 238
COUPALL, River 324
COUR, River 278
COWIE, Water 310
COYLE, Water of 392
CRACAIL BEAG, Loch 175
CRACAIL MOR, Loch 175
CRAGACH, Loch (Morsgail) 111
CRAGACH, Lochanan 111
CRAGGAN, Fishery 287
CRAGGIE, Loch (Glen Oykel) 155
CRAGGIE, Loch (Lairg) 176
CRAGGIE, Loch (Tongue) 79
CRAIG, River 238
CRAIGENDUNTON, Reservoir 377
CRAIGLUSCAR, Reservoir 355
CRAISG, Loch 79
CRAKAVAIG, Loch 265
CRANN, Loch 246, 253
CRASGACH, Loch 80

CRAWICK, Water 409
CREAG FORTHILL, Loch 111
CREAG NAN CON, Lochan 314
CREAGACH, Loch 111
CREAVAT, Loch 130
CREE, River 406, 420
CREED, River 37
CREOCH, Loch 394
CRERAN, River 299, 324
CRIADHA, Loch 111, 130
CRIDHA, Loch*****
CRIMONMOGATE, Loch 262
CRO CRIOSDAIG, Loch 111
CRO WATER, South Yell 9, 11
CRO Waters 2-3, 5
CROC NA MOINTEICH, Loch 246
CROCACH, Loch 59, 80, 111, 155
CROCACH, Loch (Duartmore) 155
CROCACH, Loch (North Assynt) 155
CROCACH, Loch (Rhiconich) 59
CROCACH, Loch (Scaliscro) 111
CROCACH, Loch (Strathtongue) 80
CROE, River 246, 275
CROE, River 246, 275
CROE, Water (Arrochar) 347
CROGAVAT, Loch 222, 265
CROGAVAT, Loch (Daliburgh) 265
CROIS AILEIN, Loch 130
CROISPOL, Loch 59
CROISTEAN, Loch 111
CROM, Loch 156
CROMBIE, Reservoir 338
CROMLACH, Loch 188
CROMORE, Loch 130
CROOK OF DEVON, Fishery 356
CROSS Lochs 80
CROSS REFERENCE 93, 184, 188, 294, 306, 308, 310, 314, 330, 343, 347, 364, 367, 370, 378, 387-388, 390, 396, 416, 425
CROSS REFERENCE ENTRIES 396
CROSS REFERENCE ENTRY 416
CROSS REFERENCES 38, 111, 200, 251, 269, 275, 284, 295, 299, 302, 316, 325-326, 334, 351, 356, 372, 380, 383, 392, 394, 397, 400, 402, 406, 409, 414, 420, 423
CROSSHILL, Loch 389
CROSSWOOD, Reservoir 380
CRUACH MAOLACHY, Loch 343
CRUINN, Loch 269
CRUOSHIE, Loch 246
CUAICH, Loch 302
CUAIG, River 238
CUIL AIRIGH A'FLOD, Loch 111
CUILC, Loch 38
CUILCE, Loch (Scaapar) 188
CUILCEACH, Loch 130
CUITHIR, Loch 231
CUL A'MHILL, Loch 156
CUL FRAIOCH, Loch 156
CUL NA BEINNE, Loch 130, 367
CUL NA CREIGE, Lochan 60

CUL UIDH AN TUIM, Loch 60
CUL, Loch 251
CULAG, Loch 156
CULAIDH, Loch 184, 212
CULBOKIE, Loch 251
CULDRAIN, Loch 423
CULLEN BURN, River 261
CULLIVOE, Loch 2
CULTERYIN, Loch 9
CUPPA Water 9, 12
CUR, River 347
CURE Water 9, 16
CUT, The (River) 361
CUTHAIG, Loch 111

D

DA LOCH FUAIMAVAT 38, 50
DA LOCHAN FHEIDH, Loch 38
DAER, Reservoir 409
DAFF, Reservoir 372
DAIL FHEARNA, Loch 211
DAILL, River 60
DALACH, Lochan 343
DALBEATTIE, Reservoir 423
DALBEG, Loch 38
DALLAS, Loch 256, 287
DALLAS, Loch (Altyre) 256
DALSA Waters 9, 15
DALVENNAN, Fishery 392
DAM Loch (Unst) 2
DAM, Lochs 156, 211, 370
DAMH, Loch 238
DANEY'S, Loch 9
DARAICH, Loch 54, 145, 156, 208
DEABHARAN, Loch 211
DEADMAN'S, Loch 188
DEAN, Water 334
DEARG A' CHUILL MHOIR, Lochan 156
DEARG BEAG, Lochan 246
DEARG LOCHAIN, Loch 278
DEARG UILIT, Lochan 278
DEARG, Loch 157, 199, 210, 295
DEARG, Loch (Drumrinie) 157
DEARG, Lochan 157, 211, 246, 315
DEARG, Lochan (Coigach) 157
DEARG, Lochan (Rubh Mor) 157
DEE River (Trustach Cottage to Balmoral) 290
DEE, Loch 406
DEE, River 288, 291, 406, 419-420, 423
DEE, River (Hill of Cairnton to Aberdeen), 291
DEIBHEADH, Loch 60
DEIREADH BANAIG, Loch 111
DELL River 38
DEN OF OGIL Reservoir 308
DEORAVAT, Loch 188
DERRY, River 288
DESSARRY, River 275

434

Index

DEVERON, River 261
DEVON, River 356
DHOMHNUILL BHIG, Loch 111
DHONNACHAIDH, Loch 141, 157
DHU, Loch 372
DHUGHAILL, Loch 155, 269
DIABAIGAS AIRDE, Loch 238
DIALL, Loch 343
DIAMOND, Loch 200
DIBADALE, Loch 38, 111
DIGHTY, Burn 338
DINDINNIE, Reservoir 416
DIONARD, Loch 60
DIONARD, River 60
DIOTA, Lochan 278
DIRACLETT, Loch 130
DIRIGADALE, Loch 370
DJUBA Water, Longa 9
DJUBA Water, Norby 9
DOBHRAIN, Loch 222, 371
DOCHART, LOCH 326
DOCHART, River 327
DOCHFOUR, Loch 251
DOILET, River 295
DOIMHNE, Loch 131, 165
DOINE, Loch 351
DOIR NAM MART, Loch 318
DOIRE A'BHRAGHAID, Lochan 318
DOIRE A'CHREAMHA, Loch 270
DOIRE AN DOLLAIN, Lochan 299
DOIRE AN LOCHAIN, Loch 270
DOIRE CADHA, Lochan 278
DOIRE MEALL AN EILEIN, Lochan 275
DOIRE NA H-ACHLAISE, Loch 367
DOIRE NA H-AIRBHE, Loch 157
DOIRE NA H-AIRIGHE, Loch 200
DOIRE NAN EALA, Loch 200
DOLA, Loch 176
DOMHAIN, Lochan 246
DON, River 288, 290, 292
DON, River (Alford to Cockbridge) 290
DON, River (Mill of Tillyfoure to Bridge of Don), 292
DON, Sea Loch 318
DONNAIG, Loch 157
DONOLLY, Reservoir 387
DOOMY, Loch 24
DOON, Loch 406, 418
DOON, River 392, 406
DOUCHARY, River 211
DOUGLAS, Water 325, 347, 396
DOUGLAS, Water (Loch Lomond) 347
DOW, Loch 356
DRIDEAN, Loch 38
DRIMORE, Loch 222
DRINISHADER, Loch 131
DROIGHINN, Loch 169, 231, 243, 326
DROLLAVAT, Loch 38, 222
DROLSAY, Loch 364
DROMA, Loch 217, 251

DRUIDIBEG, Loch 222
DRUIE, River 288
DRUIM A'CHLIABHAIN, Loch 80
DRUIM A'GHRIANAIN, Loch 38
DRUIM AN IASGAIR, Loch (South Uist) 222
DRUIM AN ISGAIR, Loch 223
DRUIM NA COILLE, Loch 61
DRUIM NA FEARNA, Lochan 200
DRUIM NAM BIDEANNAN, Loch 131
DRUIM NAN GOBAN RAINICH, Loch 131
DRUIM NAN SGORACH, Loch 38
DRUIM SUARDALAIN, Loch 157
DRUMBEG, Loch 157
DRUMCLEUGH, Burn 421
DRUMLAMFORD, Loch 402
DRUMMOND Trout Fishery 326, 330
DRUMMOND, Pond of 356
DRUMNESCAT, Loch 416
DRUMRUNIE, Loch 157
DRUNKIE, Loch 351
DRYFE, Water 410
DRYNOCH, River 270
DUAGRICH, Loch 231
DUAIL, Loch 61
DUART, River 158
DUARTBEG, Loch 158
DUARTMORE, Loch 158
DUBH (Craig), Lochan 238
DUBH (East Diabaig), Lochan 238
DUBH (Loch Lundie), Loch 238
DUBH (Salacher), Lochan 238
DUBH (South Diabaig), Lochan 238
DUBH (Ullapool), Loch 211
DUBH (West Diabaig), Lochan 239
DUBH A' CHNOIC GHAIRBH, Loch 158
DUBH A'CHLEITE, Loch 38
DUBH A'CHUAIL, Loch 158
DUBH A'GHOBHA, Loch 38
DUBH A'PHLUIC, Loch 200
DUBH AIRIGH, Lochan (Skelpick) 81
DUBH AN DUINE, Loch 38
DUBH AN IONAIRE, Loch 223
DUBH BEAG, Loch 181, 211, 321
DUBH BEUL NA FAIRE 78, 81
DUBH CADHAFUARAICH, Lochan 176
DUBH CAMAS AN LOCHAIN, Loch 200
DUBH CNOC NA FILE, Loch 223
DUBH CUL NA CAPULICH, Loch 176
DUBH CUL NA H-AMAITE, Lochan 184
DUBH DEAS, Loch 238
DUBH EAST, Lochan (Borgie) 81
DUBH GEODHACHAN THARAILT, Loch 200
DUBH GORMILEVAT, Loch 38
DUBH HAKA, Loch 223
DUBH Loch (Tamanavay) 111
DUBH LOCH BEAG, Loch (Ben More Assynt) 158
DUBH LOCH MOR, Loch (Ben More

Assynt) 158
DUBH MAS HOLASMUL, Loch 111
DUBH MEALLAN MHURCHAIDH, Loch 158
DUBH MOR, Loch 181, 211, 223, 318
DUBH MOR, Loch (Langavat) 223
DUBH NA CAORACH, Lochan 238
DUBH NA CLAISE CARNAICH, Loch 200
DUBH NA CREIGE, Loch 238
DUBH NA MAOIL, Loch 201
DUBH NA MOINE, Loch 188
DUBH NAM BIAST, Lochan 246
DUBH NAN CAILLEACH, Lochan 201
DUBH NAN GEODH, Loch 98
DUBH SKIASGRO, Loch 38
DUBH SLETTEVAL, Loch 131
DUBH SUBHAL, Loch 111
DUBH THURTAIL, Loch 38
DUBH WEST, Lochan (Borgie) 81
DUBH, Loch (Achentoul) 184
DUBH, Loch 38, 55, 111, 131, 158, 176, 184, 188, 190, 200, 223, 255, 270, 286, 296, 309, 318, 343, 350, 364-365, 367, 389-390
DUBH, Loch (Ardlussa) 367
DUBH, Loch (Bad an Sgalaig) 200
DUBH, Loch (Black Loch) 343
DUBH, Loch (Borline) 270
DUBH, Loch (Breasclete) 38
DUBH, Loch (Colonsay) 367
DUBH, Loch (Dalreavoch Lodge) 176
DUBH, Loch (Duck Loch) 343
DUBH, Loch (Dunbeath) 184
DUBH, Loch (Dusary) 188
DUBH, Loch (Eilt) 296
DUBH, Loch (Fincharn) 343
DUBH, Loch (Habost) 111
DUBH, Loch (Lemreway) 131
DUBH, Loch (Loch an Add) 343
DUBH, Loch (Loch Glashan) 343
DUBH, Loch (Lochinver) 158
DUBH, Loch (Mhic Fhionnlaidh) 343
DUBH, Loch (Morsgail) 111
DUBH, Loch (Rueval) 223
DUBH, Loch (Seil) 318
DUBH, Loch (Shiltenish) 111
DUBH, Loch (Sligachan) 270
DUBH, Loch (Stornoway) 38
DUBH, Loch (Ullapool) 158
DUBH, Loch(Fionn) 200
DUBH, Lochain 200, 367
DUBH, Lochan 81, 111, 131, 158, 176, 185, 200, 238, 255, 258, 270, 275, 278, 283, 285, 288-289, 299, 304, 321, 324-325, 343, 346
DUBH, Lochan (Arkaig) 275
DUBH, Lochan (Choire) 176
DUBH, Lochan (Kingshouse) 299
DUBH, Lochan (Laidon) 299
DUBH, Lochan (Loch More) 158
DUBH, Lochan (Loch Suirstavat) 111

435

Index

DUBH, Lochan (Maivaig) 111
DUBH, Lochan (Meodal) 270
DUBH, Lochan (North) 343
DUBH, Lochan (South) 343
DUBH, Lochan (Tom an Fhuadain) 131
DUBH-BHEAG, Loch 343
DUBH-LOCHAN, Loch 249, 251
DUBH-MOR, Loch 343-344
DUBHA (Attadale), Lochan 246
DUBHA, Loch (Sligachan) 270
DUBHA, Lochain 65, 278
DUBHA, Lochan 158, 239, 241, 318, 321, 345
DUBHA, Lochanan 317-318
DUBHAR-SGOTH, Loch 231
DUGHAILL, Loch 239, 246
DUICH, River 364
DUINTE, Loch 81
DUISK, Water of 403
DULIAN WATER, River 258
DULNAIN, River 258, 284, 288
DUN AN T-SIAMAIN, Loch 223
DUN MHURCHAIDH, Loch 223
DUN NA CILLE, Loch 265
DUNALISTAIR WATER 303
DUNBEATH Water (River) 93, 184
DUNBEATH WATER (River) 93, 184
DUNDONNELL, River 201
DUNDREGGAN, Reservoir 278
DUNEATON, Water 396
DUNNET HEAD, Lochs 98
DUNOON, Reservoir 372
DUNSKEY, Loch 417
DUNTELCHAIG, Loch 251
DUNTULM, Loch 231
DUNVIDEN Lochs 75, 81
DUSARY, Loch 188
DUVAT, Loch 266
DYE, Water 387

E

E, River 284
EACHAIG, River 347-348
EACHKAVAT, Loch 188
EADAR NA BHAILE, Loch 239
EADARAY, Loch 223
EADY, Island 24
EAGASGRO, Loch 38
EALACH MOR, Lochan 93
EALACH, Lochan 81
EALAIDH, Loch 111
EALLACH, Lochan 159
EANAICHE, Lochan 296
EARACHA, Loch 82
EARLSBURN, Reservoirs 351
see Carron Valley Reservoir 351-352, 354
EARLSTOUN, Loch 407
EARN (Upper), River (See also OS Map 58, Perth & Kinross) 331, 361

EARN, Loch 327
EARN, Loch 327
EARN, River 357
EAS NA MAOILE, Loch 176
EASHADER, Loch 188
EAST LOCH OF SKAW 5-6
EAST OLLAY, Loch 223
EAST YELL, Loch 9
EASTAPER, Loch 111
EASTER BUCKIEBURN, Reservoir see Carron Valley Reservoir 351
EASTER FEARN, Burn 214
EASTER Loch 1-3
EAVAL, Loch 188
EAVAL, River 131
ECK, Loch 347
EDDERTON, Burn 214
EDDLESTON, Water 397
EDEN, River (Fife) 361
EDEN, Water 400
EDERLINE, Loch 343
EELA Water 9
EGILSAY, Island 24-25
EIDHBHAT, Loch 38
EIGG, Island of 294
EIGHEACH, Loch 303
EIK, Loch 189
EILASTER, Loch 38
EILDE BEAG, Loch 299
EILDE MOR, Loch 299
EILEAG, Loch 159
EILEAN AN STAOIR, Loch 223
EILEAN IAIN (South) 219, 224
EILEAN IAIN, Loch (North) 224
EILEAN NA CRAOIBHE MOIRE, Lochs 61
EILEANACH, Loch 61-62, 82, 98, 169, 176
EILEANACH, Loch (Ardmore) 61
EILEANACH, Loch (Ben Auskaird) 61
EILEANACH, Loch (Ben Stack) 61
EILEANACH, Loch (Bettyhill) 82
EILEANACH, Loch (Crask) 176
EILEANACH, Loch (Druim na h-Aimhne) 61
EILEANACH, Loch (Rhiconich) 62
EILEATIER, Loch 38
EILEAVAT, Loch 33, 38, 44
EILEIN A'GHILLE-RUAIDH, Loch 224
EILLAGVAL, Loch 38
EILT, Loch 296
EINICH, Loch 288
EIREACHAIN, Loch 343
EIREAGORAIDH, Loch 296
EISHKEN, Loch 132
EISHKEN, River 132
EISHORT, Loch 231
ELLIOT, Water 338
ELVISTER, Loch 9
ENDRICK, Water 347
ENRICK, River 251
EOE, Loch 239

ERERAY, Loch 38
ERERAY, River 39
ERGHALLAN, Sea Loch 231
ERICHT, Loch 303
ERICHT, River 304, 334
ERRAID, Loch 39
ERROCHTY, Loch 304
ERROCHTY, River 304
ESK (South), River 338
ESK, River (North & South) (Lothian) 383-385
ETCHACHAN, Loch 288
ETIVE, River 299, 325
ETTRICK, Loch 410
ETTRICK, Water 397, 414
EUCHAN, Water 410
EUCHAR, River 318
EUN, Loch 94, 167, 191, 208, 212, 240, 253, 255, 282, 306, 309, 332, 343, 367, 371
EVAN, Water 410
EVELIX, River 214
EVRA Loch 2, 4
EWE, River 201
EWES, Water 414
EYE PENINSULA, Lochs 39
EYE, Loch 214, 408
EYE, Water 387
EYNORT, River 270

F

FAD A'CHRUIB, Loch 367
FAD ORAM, Loch 39
FAD, Loch 372
FADA BEN GARRISDALE, Loch 367
FADA CAOL, Loch 39
FADA CUL A'CHRUIB, Loch 367
FADA CUL NA BEINNE, Loch 367
FADA GHASGAIN, Lochan 270
FADA NA GEARRACHUN, Loch 189
FADA NAM FAOILEAG, Loch 39
FADA, Loch 111, 189, 203, 224, 231, 239, 266, 270-271, 312, 343, 364, 367
FADA, Loch (Braes) 231
FADA, Loch (Colla) 224
FADA, Loch (Colonsay) 367
FADA, Loch (Daliburgh) 266
FADA, Loch (Griminish) 224
FADA, Loch (Howmore) 224
FADA, Loch (Kirkibost) 189
FADA, Loch (Laxay) 111
FADA, Loch (Lochmaddy) 189
FADA, Loch (Meodal) 270
FADA, Loch (Muir of Aird) 224
FADA, Loch (Quiraing) 231
FADA, Loch (Skye) 270
FADA, Loch (Spotal) 224
FADA, Loch (Storr) 231
FADA, Loch (Suisnish) 271
FADA, Lochan 159, 201-202, 239, 255
FADA, Lochan (Achiltibuie) 159

Index

FADA, Lochan (Canisp) 159
FADA, Lochan (Fain) 202
FADA, Lochan (Inverkirkaig) 159
FADA, Lochan (Knockanrock) 159
FADA, Lochan (North Assynt) 159
FADA, Lochan (Strath Lungard) 202
FADAGOA, Loch 112
FAIRY, Loch 202
FALA DAM, Burn 383
FALLOCH, River 326, 347, 350
FANGMORE, Lochs 62
FANNICH, Loch 211
FAOGHAIL AN TUIM, Loch 112
FAOGHAIL CHARRASAN, Loch 39, 112
FAOGHAIL CHARRASAN, Loch 39, 112
FAOGHAIL KIRRAVAL, Loch 112
FAOGHAIL NAN CAORACH, Loch 112
FAOILEAG, Loch 39, 88, 118-119, 138, 255
FARLARY, Loch 184
FARLEYER, Loch 331
FARRAR, River 251
FASENY, Water 387
FASGRO, Loch 39
FASKALLY, Loch 332
FASNACLOICH, Loch 325
FASQUE, Lake 310
FATH, Loch 132
FEARNA, Loch 67, 159, 275
FECHLIN, River 284
FEDDERATE, Reservoir 262
FEINN, Loch 343, 347
FEIRMA, Loch 189
FEITH AN LEOTHAID, Loch 159, 246-247
FEITH AN LEOTHAID, Lochan 159
FEITH MHIC-ILLEAN, Lochan 202
FEITH NAN LAOGH, Lochan 296
FEITHE MUGAIG, Loch 202
FENDER, Burn 306
FEOCHAN BHEAG, River 318
FEOIR, Loch 132
FEOIR, Lochan 169, 202
FEORLIN, Loch 344
FESHIE, River 284, 288
FETLAR FISHING LOCATIONS 5
FEUGH, River 293
FEUR, Loch 159, 176, 202, 371
FEUR, Loch (Ledmore) 159
FEUR, Lochan 62, 212
FEURACH, Loch 251
FEUSAIGE, Loch 82
FHIONNAICH, Loch 82
FHIONNLAIDH, Lochan 160
FHOIRABHAL BHEAG, Loch 132
FHORSA, River 112
FHRAOICH, Loch 32, 39, 107, 310
FHREUNADAIL, Loch 112
FHUDAIR, Lochan 278
FIAG, Loch 176
FIAG, River 176

FIAR, Loch 239
FIART, Loch 318
FIDDICH, River 258, 291
FIDHLE, Loch 344
FINCASTLE, Loch 132
FINDHORN, River 256, 284
FINLAGGAN, Loch 364
FINLAS, Water 347
FINNART, River 347
FIONN MOR, Loch 160
FIONN BEAG, Loch 160
FIONN, Loch 160, 202
FIONN, Loch (Inverkirkaig) 160
FIONNACLEIT, Loch 39
FISKAVAIG BAY, Estuary 271
FITTY, Loch 357
FLATPUNDS, Loch 9
FLEET, Loch (Littleferry) 214
FLEET, River 177, 419
FLEET, Water of 421
FLEODACH COIRE, Loch 160
FLUGARTH, Loch 2
FOISNAVAT, Loch 39
FORGUE, Fish Farm 262
FORSA, River 318
FORSE Water 8, 10
FORSIAN, Loch 296
FORSS, River 98
FORTH, River see River Teith 351
FOYERS, River 278
FRAMGORD, Loch 10
FRAOCHACH, Loch 278
FRAOICH, Lochan 203
FREESTER, Loch 10
FRESWICK, Burn 99
FREUCHIE, Loch 332
FREUCHIE, River 332
FREUMHACH, Loch 239
FRISA, Loch 314
FRITHE, River 184
FRUID, Reservoir 396
FRUIN, Water 348
FRYING PAN, Loch 39
FUAR LOCH BEAG, Loch 203
FUAR LOCH MOR, Loch 203
FUAR, Loch 246
FUAR, Lochan 203
FUARA, Lochan 246
FUAROIL, Loch 112
FUARON, Loch 316
FUGLA Water 2-3, 10-11, 15, 18
FYNE, River 325
FYNTALLOCH, Loch of 403

G

GAINEAMACH, Loch 239
GAINEAMHACH BEAG, Loch 239
GAINEAMHACH, Loch (Choire) 177
GAINEAMHACH, Loch (Crask) 177

GAINEAMHACH, Loch (Kenmore) 239
GAINEAMHACH, Loch (Sandy Loch) 344
GAINEAMHACH, Lochan 299, 344
GAINEAMHAICH, Loch 33, 39, 132, 203
GAINEAMHAICH, Loch (Lemreway) 132
GAINEIMH, Loch (Bettyhill) 82
GAINEIMH, Loch (Forsinard) 82
GAINEIMH, Loch, Westerdale 99
GAINMHEACH NAM FAOILEAG, Loch 39
GAINMHEICH, Lochan 160
GAINMHICH, Loch (Gisla) 112
GAINMNICH, Loch 83
GAIRN, River 288, 291
GALA, Water 397
GALAVAT, Loch 40
GALTA Water 8, 10
GALTARSAY, Loch 189
GAMHNA, Loch 89, 240, 284
GAOIREACH, Loch 251
GAORSAIC, Loch 246
GARASDALE, Loch 370
GARBAD, Loch 390
GARBH GHAOIR Burn 303-304
GARBH Loch Mor 148, 160, 168
GARBH, Loch 99
GARBH, Lochan 300
GARBHAIG, Loch 203
GARBHAIGH, Loch (Talladale) 203
GARBHALLT (LOCHAIN) 344
GARNOCK, River 372
GARRY, Loch (Perthshire) 304
GARRY, River 275, 278, 302, 306
GARRY, River (Perthshire) 302, 306
GARTEN, Loch 288
GARTH, Loch 2, 15, 20
GARTMORE, Dam 357
GARVAIG, Loch 40
GARVE, Loch 211
GARVIE, River 160
GASKIN, Loch 296
GAUR, River 304
GEAL, Loch (Great Bernera) 112
GEAL, Lochan 284, 289
GEIMISGARAVE, Loch 132
GEOIDH, Loch 344
GERDIE, Loch 10
GERIA Water 7, 10
GERSHON, Loch 20
GHILLE-CALUIM, Loch 312
GHIUBHSACHAIN, Loch 203
GHIURAGARSTIDH, Loch 203
GIL SPEIREIG MHOR, Loch 40
GILL BREINADALE, Loch 112
GILLAROO, Loch
GILLE-GHOID, Loch 189
GILSA Water 8, 10, 14-15, 18
GIRLSTA, Loch 10
GIRNOCK, Burn 291
GIRSIE, Loch 10

437

Index

GIRVAN, Water of 403, 406
GISLA, River 112
GIUR-BHEINN, Loch 364
GLADHOUSE, Reservoir 383
GLAS-BHEINN, Loch 367
GLAS-LOCH BEAG, Loch 177
GLAS-LOCH MOR, Loch 177
GLASCARNOCH, Loch 211
GLASCARNOCH, River 211
GLASCHOILLE, Loch 275
GLASGOW (South), Reservoirs and Lochs 378
GLASHAN, Loch 344
GLASS (Evanton), River 214
GLASS, Loch 211
GLASS, River 252
GLAZERT Water 378
GLEANN A'BHEARRAIDH, Loch 319
GLEANN ASTAILE, Loch 368
GLEANN NA MOINE, Loch 133
GLEANN NA MUICE, Loch 203
GLEANN, Loch 29, 345
GLEANNAN A'MHADAIDH, Loch 160
GLEANNAN NA GAOITHE, Loch 160
GLEN FINGLAS, Reservoir 351
GLEN OF ROTHES, Loch 258
GLEN TANAR, Loch 291
GLEN, Water 392
GLENASTLE, Loch 364-365
GLENBURN, Reservoir 373
GLENCANNEL, River 314
GLENCORSE, Burn 384
GLENCORSE, Reservoir 384
GLENESSLIN, Burn 423
GLENFARG, Fishery 357
GLENFARG, Reservoir 358
GLENGAMADALE, River 319
GLENGAVEL, Reservoir 394
GLENGONNAR, Water 396
GLENGYLE, Water 348
GLENKILN, Reservoir 423
GLENLATTERACH, Reservoir 258
GLENLUSSA, Water 389
GLENMORE, River 275
GLENQUEY, Reservoir 358
GLENSHERUP, Reservoir 358
GLINNAVAT, Loch 40
GLOUP Lochs 2, 4
GLOUP VOE Sea Loch 2
GLOW, Loch 358
GLUMRA BEAG, Loch 133
GLUMRA MORE, Loch 133
GLUSS Water 10-11, 14-15
GLUSSDALE Water 11
GLUTT Loch 94
GLUTT, Loch 185
GOBHLACH, Loch 112
GOBHLACH, Lochan 212, 239, 246
GOBHLAICH, Loch 40
GOBHLOCH, Loch 62

GOBLACH, Loch 40
GOGA, Water 373
GOIL, River 348
GOLDEN, Loch 361
GONFIRTH, Loch 11
GORE, Water 384
GORM LOCH MOR (Loch) 160
GORM LOCH MOR (Nedd) 161
GORM LOCH MOR, Loch 203
GORM LOCH NA BEINNE, Loch 203
GORM, Loch 62, 160, 212, 248, 250, 255, 364
GORM, Loch Beag 160
GORM, Lochan 279
GORM-LOCH BEAG, Loch 177
GORM-LOCH MOR, Loch 177
GORMA, Lochan 296
GORMAG MOR, Loch 40
GOSSA Water 2-3, 9, 11-12, 20
GOSSA Water (North Nesting) 11
GOSSA Water (Unst) 2
GOSSA Water (Yell) 2
GOSSA Water, Burraview 11
GOSSA Water, Yell 3-4, 11
GOSSA Waters, Mus Wells 11
GOSTER, Loch 11
GOWER, Loch 404, 417
GRAEMSHALL LOCH 28
GRAEMSTON LOCH 28
GRANNDA, Loch 133
GRASS Water 9, 11-12
GRASS, Loch 203
GRASSAVAT, Lochan 40
GREAT CUMBRAE, Island 373
GREEN, Loch 177
GREENAN, Loch 373
GREENOCK, Water 394
GREIVAT, Loch 113
GRESS, Loch 40
GRESS, River 40
GREY EWE, Loch of the 3
GRIAN-LOCH BEAG, Loch 83
GRIAN-LOCH MOR, Loch 83
GRIESTA, Loch of 21
GRIMERSTA, River 113
GRIMSETTER, Loch 21
GRINAVAT, Loch 40
GRINNAVAT, Loch 40
GRINNAVAT, Loch (Gress) 40
GRINNAVAT, Loch, Stornoway 40
GROBAIG, Loch 246
GROGACH, Loch 40
GROGARRY, Loch 224
GROGARY,Loch 189
GROM-LOCH FADA, Loch 203
GROSAVAT, Loch 40
GROSEBAY, Loch 133
GROSVENOR, Loch 62
GROTA, Loch 189
GRUAMA MOR, Loch 177

GRUAMACH, Loch 252
GRUD Waters 3
GRUDAIDH, Loch 177
GRUDIE, River 63, 211
GRUINARD, River 203, 205
GRUNAVAT, Loch 40, 113, 189
GRUNAVAT, Loch (Leurbost) 40
GRUNNAVOE, Loch 11
GRUTING, Loch 11
GRUTWICK, Loch 11
GRYFE, Reservoir 373
GRYFE, River 372, 378
GUILC, Lochan 161
GULLY, Loch 345
GUNNA, Loch 40
GUNNISTA Lochs 20-21
GUSERAIN, River 275
GUSERAN, River 275
GUTCHER, Loch 3
GYNACK, Loch 284

H

HACKLETT, Loch 189
HADD, Loch 3, 17
HAGGRISTER, Loch 11
HAKEL, Loch 83
HALLADALE, Loch 114, 125
HALLADALE, River 83, 114
HALLADALE, River 83, 114
HALLADALE, Upper Loch 114
HALLAN, Loch 266
HAMARA, River 231
HAMARI Water 11-13
HAMARSHADER, Loch 133
HAMARSLAND, Loch 12
HAMASCLETT, Loch 224
HAMASORD, Loch 114
HAMNA VOE, Estuary, South Yell 12
HARELAW, Reservoir 373
HARLAW, Reservoir 384
HARMASAIG, Loch 133
HARPERRIG, Reservoir 380
HARRAY, Loch 26
HASCO, Loch 232
HATRAVAT, Lochan 41
HATRAVAT, Lower Loch 41
HATRAVAT, Upper Loch 41
HAULTIN, River 232
HAYLIE, Fishery 374
HEADSHAW, Loch 397
HEATHERYFORD, Fishery 358
HEILAN, Loch 99
HEILEASBHAL, Loch 133
HEILIA Water, Bridge of Walls 12
HELDALE WATER 28
HELLIERS Water 3
HELLISDALE, Loch 224
HELLISTER, Loch 12
HELLMOOR, Loch 414

438

Index

HELMSDALE, River 185
HEMPRIGGS, Loch 99
HEOURAVAY, Loch 224
HERMIDALE, Loch 224
HEVDADALE Water 3
HIGH CREACH, Burn 421
HILL OF GIRLSTA Lochs 9-10, 12, 14
HILLEND, Reservoir 380
HINNISDALE, River (North Bank only) 232
HOGLINNS WATER 28
HOLAVAT, Loch 133
HOLL, Reservoir 358
HOLLORIN, Loch 12
HOLMASAIG, Loch 133
HOLMS, Water 396
HONAGRO, Loch 41
HOPE, Loch 63
HOPE, River 63
HOPES, Reservoir 384
HORAVEG, Loch 271
HORISARY, Loch 189
HORISARY, River 189
HORN, Loch 185
HORRARY, Loch 224
HORSACLETT, Loch 133
HORSACLETT, River 133
HORSE Water 12, 16
HOSPITAL, Lochan 300
HOSTA, Loch 189
HOSTIGATES, Lochs 12
HOULL, Loch 5
HOULLAND, Loch 12, 21
HOULLAND, Loch (South Nesting) 12
HOULLS Water 2-3, 13
HOULLS Water (Yell) 3
HOULMA Water 13-14
HOUSA Water 21-23
HOUSAY, River 133
HOUSETTER, Loch 3
HOUSTER, Loch 13
HOVERSTA, Loch 3
HOWMORE, River 225
HOWWOOD, Fishery 374
HUAMAVAT, Loch 133
HULK Water 2-3
HULMA Water 13, 17
HUMBIE, Water 384
HUNA, Loch 189
HUNDA, Loch 189
HUNDER, Loch 189
HUNDLAND, Loch 26
HUNGAVAT, Loch 190
HUXTER, Loch 6

I

IALAIDH, Loch 190
IARRAS, Loch 225
IASG, Loch 345

IBHEIR, Loch 114
IC IAIN, Loch 271
IDOCH WATER, River 262
ILLE CHIPAIN, Loch 134
INA'S, Lochs 161
INCHLAGGAN, Loch 279
INNIS EANRUIG, Lochan 296
INNIS GHEAMHRAIDH, Loch 246
INNIS Loch 3
INNIS NA BA BUIDHE, Loch 63
INNIS THORCAILL, Loch 161
INNIS, Loch 41
INNISCORD Lochs 3-5
INNSEAG, Loch 41
INSH, Loch 284
INSHORE, Loch 64
INVER AULAVAIG Estuary 271
INVER DALAVIL Estuary 271
INVER, River (Upper) 161
INVERARISH, River 239
INVERAWE, Fishery 325
INVERDRUIE, Fish Farm 289
INVERIE, River 275, 295
INVERUGLAS, Water 348
IOBHAIR, Loch 41
IOCHDARACH A'CHRUAIDH-GHLINN, Loch 368
IONADAGRO, Loch 41
IONAIL, Loch 109, 114
IORSA, Water 390
IOSAL AN DUIN, Loch 190
IRVINE, River 392
ISBISTER, Loch 6, 26
ISBISTER, Loch 6, 26
ISHAG, Burn 352
ISLA, River 258, 262, 306, 335
ISLAND OF SCALPY 271
ISLAND, Loch 25, 225, 312, 372
IUBHAIR, LOCH 327

J

JAMIE CHEYNE'S Loch 21
JARBRUCK, Burn 423
JED, Water 400
JERRICHO, Loch 410
JOCK OF THE BOG, Loch 285
JOHNNIE MANN'S Loch 13, 15
JORDIELAND, Loch 421, 423

K

KALE, Water 400
KATRINE, Loch 348
KEARSAVAT, Loch 42
KEARSINISH, Loch 266
KEARSTAVAT, Loch 42
KEARTAVAT, Loch 42
KEARVAIG, River 64
KEBISTER, Loch 21

KEISGAIG, Loch 64
KELL, Burn 387
KELLISTER, Loch 13
KELVIN, River 378
KEMP, Loch 279
KEN, Loch 407, 420, 423
KEOSE, Loch 134
KERNSARY, Loch 204
KERRY, River 204
KETTLESTER, Loch 13
KETTLETON, Reservoir 410
KILAIL, Burn 345
KILBIRNIE, Loch 374
KILCHATTAN, Bay 374
KILCHERAN, Loch 319
KILCHOAN, Lochs 345-346
KILDUSKLAND, Loch 345
KILENNAN, River 365
KILFINAN, Burn 370
KILIMSTER, Loch 100
KILKA Water 13, 16
KILLEARN, Fishery 352
KILLIN, Loch 285
KILLIN, River 285
KILMALUAG, River 232
KILMARIE, Loch 271
KILMARTIN, Burn 345
KILMARTIN, River 232
KILMORY, Water 390
KINARDOCHY, Loch 304, 330
KINELLAN, Loch 252
KINGENNIE, Lochs 339
KINGLAS, RIVER 325
KINGLAS, Water 348
KINGLASS WATER (Loch Fyne) 325
KINLOCH, River 64, 84, 294
KINLOCHEWE, River 204
KINNABUS, Loch 365
KINNEASTAL, Loch 134
KINNEASTAL, River 134
KINNEL, Water 410
KINNORDY, Loch 339
KINTARVIE, River 134
KIP, River 374
KIRBISTER, Loch 26
KIRK Loch 3, 5, 409
KIRK, Dam 374
KIRKABISTER, Loch 13
KIRKAIG, River 161
KIRKHOUSE Water 9, 13, 18
KIRKIBOST, Sea Pools 190
KIRKIGARTH, Loch 13
KIRRIEREOCH, Loch 407
KISHORN, River 239
KNAIK, River see River Teith. 352
KNOCKAIRSHILL, Reservoir 374
KNOCKIE, Loch 279
KNOCKQUHASSEN, Reservoir 417
KNOCKRUAN, Loch 389
KNOTT, Estuary 233

Index

KUSSA Waters 2-5
KYLE OF DURNESS Sea Loch 64
KYLE OF SUTHERLAND, Estuary 215
KYLE OF TONGUE (Sea Loch) 84
KYPE, Reservoir 394

L

LACASDAIL, Loch 134
LADIES', Loch 134
LADY, Loch 64
LAEL, River 211
LAGGAN, Loch 279, 302, 353
LAGGAN, River 365
LAIDON, Loch 300
LAINGEADAIL BEAG, Loch 365
LAINGEADAIL, Loch 365
LAIR, River 246
LAIRCHEARD, Loch 65
LAIRDS, Loch 14
LAIRIGE, LOCHAN 327
LAIRIGE, LOCHAN 327
LAIRO Water 23-25
LAMADALE, Loch 114
LAMASCAIG, Loch 271
LAMBA Water 13-15, 19
LANG CLODIE Loch 1, 4
LANG, Loch 14
LANGADALE, River 115
LANGAIG, Loch 233
LANGAMAY, Loch 24
LANGAVAT, Loch 42, 114, 190, 225
LANGAVAT, Loch (Amhuinnsuidhe) 114
LANGAVAT, Loch (Carloway) 42
LANGAVAT, Loch (Central) 114
LANGAVAT, Loch (Gress) 42
LANGAVAT, Loch (Leverburgh) 190
LANGAVAT, Loch (North Lewis) 42
LANLISH, Loch 65
LANNSAIDH, Loch 215
LAOIGH, Loch 149, 173, 215, 243
LARAICHE, Lochan 345
LARAIG, Loch 205
LARO, Loch 215
LATHAMUL, Loch 42
LAWFIELD, Dam 374
LAXADALE, Lochs 134
LAXAVAT ARD, Loch 42
LAXAVAT IORACH, Loch 42
LAXAY, River 115
LAXDALE, Loch 135
LAXDALE, River 135
LAXFORD, River 65
LAXO Water 14
LEA SHUN Loch 24
LEACACH, Lochan 161
LEACHD, Loch 345
LEADER, Water 398
LEALT, River 233
LEANA AN FHEOIR, Lochs 135

LEATHA, Loch (Morsgail) 115
LEATHAID NAN CRUINEACHD, Loch 65
LEATHAIN, Loch 115, 371
LEATHAN, Loch 233, 345, 365
LEATHAN, Loch (Kirnan) 345
LEATHANN, Loch 239, 365
LEATHANN, Lochan 239
LEDMORE, Burn 314
LEDNOCK, River 332
LEE, Loch 308
LEE, Water of 308
LEET, Water 400
LEIDLE, River 316
LEINAVAT, Loch 42
LEINISCAL, Loch 42
LEIR, Loch 94
LEIRAVAY, River 43
LEIRG, Lochan 239, 375
LEISAVAT, Loch 43
LEITH, Water of 380, 384
LEITHEN, Water 398
LEITIR, Loch 43
LENNOWS, Loch 417
LENY, River 352
LEODASAY, Loch 190
LEOSAID, Loch 135
LEOSAID, River 135
LERGEO Water 10, 14
LETTIE, River 177
LEUM NA LUIRGINN, Loch 233
LEVEN, Loch 359
LEVEN, River 300, 361, 372
LEVEN, River (Kinlochleven) 300
LEXY'S, Loch 161
LIATH (East), Loch 252
LIATH (South), Loch 252
LIATH, Loch 108, 280, 371
LIC-AIRD, Loch 271
LIDDLE, Water 415
LIDSTROME, Sea-loch 225
LIGHIGEAG, Loch 135
LILLIE'S, Loch 408
LILLY, Loch 293, 381
LINDEAN, Reservoir 398
LINDORES, Loch 362
LINGAVAT BEAG, Loch 43
LINGAVAT MOR, Loch 43
LINISH, Loch 116
LINLITHGOW, Loch 381
LINNE, Loch 45, 137, 345
LINNGRABHAIDH, Loch 135
LINTRATHEN, Loch of 335
LITE SITHINN, Loch 136
LITTLE BORVE, Loch (Bernerary) 190
LITTLE EACHAIG, River 348
LITTLE GRUINARD, River 205
LITTLE LUNGA Water 4
LITTLE WATER OF FLEET (River) 421
LITTLESTER, Loch 14
LITTLURE, Loch 14

LIURAVAY, Loch 233
LIVET, River 289, 291
LIVISTER, Loch 6
LOANAN, River 161, 169
LOCH COULTER, Reservoir 352
see Carron Valley Reservoir 351-352, 354
LOCH GLEN IONADAL, Loch 233
LOCH, Loch 34, 36, 39, 46-47, 84, 93, 107, 115-116, 118, 121, 128, 138, 165, 167, 173, 176, 187-188, 192, 202, 206, 210, 229, 232, 243, 255, 269, 306, 308, 310, 330, 368, 391
LOCH-GOWAN, Loch 246
LOCH-NAN CLAR 182, 185
LOCHA DUBH, Loch 190
LOCHA DUBHA, Loch 136
LOCHA MHADAIDH, Loch 345
LOCHAIN A'CHAORAINN, Loch 65
LOCHAIN A'MHULLAICH, Loch 271
LOCHAIN CEANN NA MOINE, Loch 205
LOCHAIN CNAPACH, Loch 205
LOCHAIN DOMIHAIN Lochs 65
LOCHAIN DUBHA, Loch 271
LOCHAIN FEITH AN LEOTHAID, Loch 247
LOCHAIN NA CREIGE DUIBHE Lochs 66
LOCHAIN NA CREIGE GILE, Loch 66
LOCHAIN NAN EALACHAN, Lochs 162
LOCHAIN NAN SEASGACH, Loch 205
LOCHAIN STRATHA MHOIR, Loch 271
LOCHAIN TEANNA, Loch 271
LOCHAN, Loch 90, 136, 246, 250
LOCHANAN A'MHUILINN, Loch 211
LOCHANAN AN UILLT MHOIR, Loch 211
LOCHANAN AODANN BEINN DONUILL, Loch 211
LOCHANAN DUBH (Loch) 162
LOCHANAN FIODHA, Loch 211
LOCHANAN MORA, Loch 136
LOCHANAN TANA, Loch 368
LOCHANBRECK, Loch 421
LOCHAVAT, Loch 43
LOCHAY, River 327
LOCHDARACH AIRIGH NUALAIDH, Loch 368
LOCHEND, Loch 379
LOCHINDORB, Loch 257
LOCHMILL, Loch 359
LOCHNAW CASTLE, Loch 417
LOCHY, Burn 289
LOCHY, Loch 280, 388
LOCHY, River 280, 301, 325
LOCHY, RIVER (Argyll) 325
LOGAN, Reservoir 394
LOGANLEA, Reservoir 385
LOMASHION, Loch 100
LOMHAIN, Loch 116
LOMOND, Loch 348
LON NA H-UAMHA, Loch 162
LONACHAN, Loch 271

440

Index

LONG, Loch 14, 294, 336, 378, 404
LONGA Water 4, 9, 13-15, 19
LONGA Water, West Burrafirth 14
LONGNECKED, Loch 14
LORGA Water 7, 14
LORISTON, Loch 293
LOSGAINN, Loch 216
LOSGUNN, Loch 345
LOSKIN, Loch 374
LOSSIE, River 258
LOSSIT, Burn 365
LOSSIT, Loch 365
LOT-GHAOITH, Loch 162
LOWER GLENASTLE, Loch 365
LOWER GLENDEVON, Reservoir 359
LOWER KILDONAN, Loch 225
LOWER SETTER, Loch 4
LOWES, Loch O' Th' 394
LOWES, Loch of the (Clatteringshaws) 408
LOWES, Loch of the (Yarrow) 398
LOYAL, Loch 84
LOYNE, Loch 280
LUB CHRUINN, Stream 247
LUBANACH, Loch 368
LUBNAIG, Loch 352
LUCE, water of 417
LUGER, Water 393
LUGGIE, Water 379
LUGTON, Water 375
LUICHART, Loch 211
LUMBISTER, Loch 4
LUNAN, Water 339
LUNDIE, Loch 239, 281, 336
LUNDIE, Loch (Plockton) 239
LUNGA Water 4-5, 14, 21
LUNGA Water (Mid Yell) 4
LUNGAWATER, Loch 15
LUNKLET, Loch 15
LUNNDAIDH, Loch 185
LUNNISTER, Loch 15
LURG, Loch 359
LURGAINN, Loch 162
LUS DUBHA, Lochan 345
LUSS, Water 350
LUSSA, Loch 389
LUSSA, River 319, 369
LUTHER WATER 311
LYNE, Water 398, 415
LYON, Loch 327
LYON, River 328, 330
LYTHE, Loch 28

M

MA STAC, Loch 252
MAA Water, Loch 15
MAADLE SWANKIE Water 4
MAAMIE of Garth, Loch 15
MACANRIE, Loch 352
see Lake of Menteith 352

MACHRIE, Water 390
MACHRIHANISH, Water 389
MACKAYS Loch 319
MAEA Water 4
MAGGIE BLACK'S Loch 21
MAICH, Water 375
MAIDEN, Loch 162
MAINLAND FISHING LOCATIONS 6
MALLACHIE, Loch 289
MALLAICHTE, Loch 239
MALLART, River 177
MALZIE, Water of 422
MAM A'CHULLAICH, Lochan 320
MAM-CHUIL, Loch 281
MANNOCH, Loch (Lairdmannoch) 422
MANOR, Water 398
MANSE Loch, Egilsay 24
MANSE, Loch 162
MANY CROOKS Loch 4
MAOILE, Loch 156, 163, 176, 212
MAOL FHRAOCHACH, Loch 239
MAOLAIG, Loch 136
MARAVAT, Loch 43
MAREE, Loch 205
MARGADLAE, River 365
MARKIE, Burn 285
MARL, Loch 100
MARROFIELD Water, Loch 15
MARULAIG, Loch 266
MASSAN, River 350
MATHAIR A'GHARBH UILT 66
MATHAIR EITE, Lochan 301
MAW, Loch 15
MCKAY, Loch 345
MEACHDANNACH, Loch 272
MEADAIDH, Loch, Durness 66
MEADHOIN, Loch 314
MEADHONACH, Loch 66, 121
MEADHONACH, Lochan 43
MEADIE, Loch 66, 78, 84, 100, 178
MEALA, Loch 84
MEALL A'BHAINNE, Loch 205
MEALL A'BHUIRICH, Loch 163
MEALL A'CHUAIL, Loch 247
MEALL A'CHUNA MOR, Lochs 163
MEALL A'MHADAIDH, Lochan 296
MEALL A'MHUTLIAICH, Loch 163
MEALL A'PHUILL, Lochan 301
MEALL DAIMH, Loch 239
MEALL NA CAILLICH, Lochan 239
MEALL NAM FEADAN, Loch 239
MEALL NAN CAORACH, Loch 163
MEALL NAN EUN, Lochanan 276
MEALLA BRU, Sea Loch 190
MEALLAN A'CHUAIL, Lochan 163
MEALLAN A'CHUAIL, Lochs 163
MEALLAN AN FHUDAIR, Loch 205
MEALLAN MHIC IAMHAIR, Lochan 247
MEALT, Loch 233
MEAVAIG, River 136

MEDWIN, Water 396
MEGGAT, Water 415
MEGGET, Reservoir 398
MEGGET, Water 398
MEIG, Loch 253
MEIG, River 253
MEIG, Upper River 247
MEIKLE Water, Stronsay 23-24
MEIKLE, Loch 263
MEIN, Water 425
MELAVAT, Loch 116
MELDALLOCH, Loch 371
MENNOCK, Burn 410
MENTEITH, Lake of 352
MEODAL, Loch 272
MERKLAND, Loch 178, 216
MEURACH, Loch 136
MEY, Loch 100
MHADADH, Loch 93, 185
MHANAIS, Loch 136
MHAOLACH-COIRE, Loch 163
MHARCOIL, Loch 43, 116
MHEACLEIT, Loch 116
MHEALLAIN, Loch 146, 173, 239
MHIC A'ROIN, Loch 190
MHIC CHARMHICEIL, Loch 272
MHIC EAROICH, Lochan 345
MHIC GHILLE-CHAOIL, Loch 289
MHIC GILLE DHUIBH, Lochan 296
MHIC GILLE-BHRIDE, Loch 190
MHIC IOMHAIR, Loch 212
MHIC LEANNAIN, Loch 296
MHIC MHARTEIN, Loch 345
MHIC NEACAIL, Loch 136
MHIC PHEADAIR, Lochan 325
MHIC'ILLE RIABHAICH, Loch 205
MHOR, Loch 40, 48, 120, 143, 181, 235, 251, 258, 285, 289, 365, 371
MHUILICH, Loch 247
MID OLLAY, Loch 225
MIDDLETON. Fishery 375
MIDLOCK, Water 396
MIGDALE, Loch 216
MILK, Water of 414, 425
MILL DAM 330, 336, 353
MILL GLEN, Reservoir 375
MILL Loch 3-5, 10, 12, 15-16, 19-21, 24, 225, 273, 371, 409
MILL Loch (Mid Yell) 4
MILL Loch (Muckla Moor) 15
MILL Loch (North Roe) 4
MILL Loch, Island of Eady 24
MILL LOCHS OF SANDVOE 4
MILL OF ELRICK, Fish farm 263
MILL OF STRACHAN, Fishery 293
MILL POND Loch 21
MILL, Loch 15, 226, 272, 371, 422
MILL, Loch (Lunnasting) 15
MILL, Loch (Unifirth) 15
MILL, Lochs 15

441

Index

MILL, Lochs of Okran 15
MILL, North Loch (Lunna Ness) 15
MILL, South Loch (Lunna Ness) 15
MILLBUIES, Loch 259
MILLEHO, Loch 43
MINNOCH Water 408
MIRKA Water 3-4, 7
MIRKA Water, Loch 15
MIRKAVAT, Loch 136
MOCHRUM, Loch 393, 418
MODSARIE, Loch 84
MOFFAT, Fishery 410
MOFFAT, Water 411
MOGLAVAT, Loch 116
MOHAL BEAG, Loch 116
MOIDART, Loch 296
MOIDART, River 296
MOIN A'CHRIATHAIR, Loch 247
MOINE SHEILG, Loch 205
MOINTEICH, Lochan 304
MOIRE, Loch 117, 122, 153, 179, 207, 212, 216, 226, 240, 248, 251, 253, 320, 371
MOLACH, Loch 85, 179
MONACHYLE, Burn 353
MONAR, Loch 247
MONIKIE, Reservoir 339
MONK MYRE, Loch 336
MONTAGUE, Loch 336
MONYNUT, Water 387
MONZIEVAIRD, Loch 332
MOO Water, Loch 15
MOORA Waters 13, 15, 18
MOOSA Water 4
MOR A'CHRAISG, Loch 67
MOR A'CHROTAICH, Loch 43
MOR A'GHOBA, Loch 43
MOR A'GHRIANAIN, Loch 43
MOR AIRIGH NAN LINNTEAN, Loch 116
MOR AN FHADA MHOIR, Loch 116
MOR AN IARUINN, Loch 116
MOR AN STAIRR, Loch 44
MOR AN TANGA, Loch 136
MOR BAD AN DUCHARAICH, Loch 205
MOR BEALACH NA H-IMRICHE, Loch 369
MOR BRAIGH AN TARAIN, Loch 116
MOR CONNAIDH, Loch 43
MOR DUNTAHA, Loch 136
MOR EILEAVAT, Loch 44
MOR GHRIANAIN, Loch 44
MOR LEIG TADH, Loch 44
MOR NA CAIPLAICH, Loch 272
MOR NA CAORACH, Loch (Skelpick) 85
MOR NA CLIBHE, Loch 116
MOR NA MUILNE, Loch 137
MOR SANDAVAT, Loch (Clistul) 44
MOR SANDAVAT, Loch (Tolsta) 44
MOR SGEIREACH, Loch 44
MOR SOVAL, Loch (Arnish) 44
MOR STIOMRABHAIGH, Loch 137

MOR, Loch 29, 40, 43-45, 48-49, 52, 55, 57-58, 77-78, 83, 85-86, 88, 107, 116, 127-128, 136, 141, 154, 158, 160, 166, 169, 175, 177, 181, 190, 196, 199, 203, 207, 209, 211-212, 223, 226, 233, 239, 247, 269, 272, 289, 299, 318, 341, 345, 369, 371
MOR, Loch (Baleshare) 226
MOR, Loch (Bettyhill) 85
MOR, Loch (Boreray) 190
MOR, Loch (Glen Hinnisdale) 233
MOR, Loch (Glendale) 233
MOR, Loch (Melvich) 85
MOR, Loch (Nunton) 226
MOR, Loch (Raasay) 239
MOR, Loch (Rhenigdale) 136
MOR, Loch (Soay) 272
MORAIG, Loch 306
MORAR, Loch 297
MORAR, River 297
MORE, Loch 100, 133, 163
MORE, Loch (Scourie) 163
MOREEF, Loch 266
MORISTON, River 281
MORLICH, Loch 289
MORSGAIL, Loch 116
MORSGAIL, River 117
MORTON CASTLE, Loch 411
MORTON, Fishery 381
MORTON, Lochs 339
MOSHELLA Lochs 1, 4
MOSS RODDOCK, Loch 408
MOUNT, Dam 379
MOUSA Water 15
MOUSAVORD, Loch 15
MOUSE, Water 396
MOUSGRIP, Loch 190
MOY CORRIE, Lochan 281
MOY, Loch 258, 281
MUAVAT, Loch 45
MUCK, Loch 408
MUCKLA Water 10, 15
MUCKLE Burn 257
MUCKLE LUNGA Water 4
MUCKLE VANDRA Water 5
MUCKLE WATER, Rousay 26-27
MUDALE, River 179
MUDLE, Loch 314
MUICK, River 291, 309
MUIDHE, Loch 179
MUILLEAN ATH AN LINNE, Loch 137
MUIRHEAD, Reservoir 375
MULA, Loch 137
MULLARDOCH, Loch 247
MURCHAIDH, Loch 365
MURRASTER, Loch 16
MUSKRA Loch 4-5
MUSSEL, Loch 16

N

NA AIRICH, Loch 118
NA AIRIGH BIGE, Loch 85
NA BA CEIRE, Loch 190
NA BA GLEISE, Loch 297
NA BA RIABHAICH, Loch 45, 137
NA BA RIABHAICH, Loch 45, 137
NA BA RUAIDHE, Loch 137, 255
NA BA, Loch 205, 332
NA BAGH, Loch 266
NA BAIRNESS, Loch 298
NA BARRACK, Loch 164
NA BEALACH NA GAOITHE, Loch 298
NA BEARTA, Lochan 205
NA BEINNE BIGE, Loch 45, 253
NA BEINNE BRICE, Loch 212, 365
NA BEINNE BRICE, Lochan 281
NA BEINNE BUIDHE, Loch 137
NA BEINNE MOIRE, Loch 253
NA BEINNE REIDHE, Loch 164
NA BEINNE, Loch 54, 130, 169, 203, 289, 330, 365, 367
NA BEINNE, Loch 54, 130, 169, 203, 289, 330, 365, 367
NA BEINNE, Lochan 97, 205, 336
NA BEIRIGHE, Loch 137
NA BEISTE BRIC, Loch 164
NA BEISTE, Loch 34, 45, 109, 117, 137, 164, 190, 212, 226, 255, 267, 345, 371
NA BEISTE, Loch (Carloway) 45
NA BEISTE, Loch (Cromore) 137
NA BEISTE, Loch (Eaval) 190
NA BEISTE, Loch (Grimersta) 45, 109, 117
NA BEISTE, Loch (Grimersta) 45, 109, 117
NA BEISTE, Loch (Rarnish) 226
NA BEISTE, Loch (Scaapar) 190
NA BEISTE, Loch (Wiay) 226
NA BESTIE, Loch 205
NA BI, LOCHAN 325
NA BIORAICH, Loch 298
NA BO, Loch 259
NA BRAAN, Loch 257
NA BRAISTE, Loch 45
NA BRATHAN MOR, Loch 45
NA BREAC PEATAIR, Loch 226
NA BRIC, Loch 345
NA BROIN, Loch 240
NA BRUTHAICH, Loch 164
NA BUAIL LOCHDRAICH, Loch 190
NA BUAILE DUIBHE, Loch 137, 226
NA BUAILE GHARBHA, Loch 45
NA BUAILE, Loch 190
NA BUIDHEIG, Loch 164
NA CABHAIG, Loch 206
NA CAIGINN, Loch 190
NA CAILLICH, Loch 67, 117, 181, 190, 240, 248
NA CAILLICHE, Lochan 281
NA CAIMAIG, Loch 248
NA CAIME, Loch 246, 369

Index

NA CAIRILL, Lochan 206
NA CAIRTEACH, Loch 45
NA CAISE LUACHRAICH, Loch 67
NA CAORACH (East Kenmore), Loch 240
NA CAORACH (West Kenmore) 240
NA CAORACH, Loch 85, 273
NA CAPALL, Loch 266
NA CARNAICH, Loch 190
NA CARRAIGE, Loch 315
NA CARRAIGEACH, Loch 320
NA CARTACH, Loch 117, 137, 190, 266
NA CARTACH, Loch 117, 137, 190, 266
NA CARTACH, Loch (Barra) 266
NA CARTACH, Loch (Lochportain) 190
NA CARTACH, Loch (North) 190
NA CARTACH, Loch (South) 190
NA CATHRACH DUIBHE, Loch 206
NA CEANNAMHOIR, Loch 117
NA CEARD BEAG, Loch 345
NA CEARD MOR, Loch 345
NA CEARDAICH, Loch 85, 108, 172, 190
NA CINNEAMHUIN, Loch 179
NA CISTE, Loch 45, 117, 137
NA CISTE, Loch (Ceann an Ora) 137
NA CISTE, Loch (Habost) 117
NA CISTE, Loch (Langavat) 117
NA CISTE, Loch (Scaliscro) 117
NA CISTE, Loch (Soval) 117
NA CISTE, Loch (Uig) 117
NA CLAISE CARNAICH, Loch 67, 200, 206
NA CLAISE FEARNA, Loch 67
NA CLAISE MOIRE, Loch 179
NA CLAISE, Loch (North Assynt) 164
NA CLAISE, Lochan (Scionascaig) 164
NA CLEAVAG, Loch 117
NA CLEIBH, Loch 226
NA CLEITH, Loch 45
NA CLIBHE, Loch 116-117
NA CLOICH AIRDE, Loch 117
NA CLOICH, Loch 45
NA CLOICHE SGOILTE, Lochan 298
NA CLOICHE, Loch 94, 206, 312, 369
NA CNAPAN, Loch 289
NA COINNICH, Loch 226
NA COINTICH, Loch 190
NA COIRNISH, Loch 117
NA COIS, Loch 45
NA COIT, Loch 86
NA CONARIE, Loch 369
NA CRANN, Loch 253
NA CRAOBHAIG, Loch 45, 117
NA CRAOBHAIG, Loch (Great Bernera) 117
NA CRAOBHAIG, Loch (Tamanavay) 117
NA CRAOBHAIGE MOIRE, Loch 117
NA CRAOBHE, Loch 34, 45, 117, 137
NA CRAOBHE, Loch (Calbost) 137
NA CRAOBHE, Loch (Glen Ordale) 45
NA CRAOBHE, Loch (Shiltenish) 117

NA CRAOIBHE, Lochan 253, 301
NA CRAOIBHE, Lochan 253, 301
NA CRAOIBHE-CAORAINN, Loch 248
NA CREIGE (North), Lochan 298
NA CREIGE (South), Lochan 298
NA CREIGE BRISTE, Loch 137
NA CREIGE DUIBHE, Loch 164
NA CREIGE FRAOICH, Loch 118
NA CREIGE GUIRME, Loch 45
NA CREIGE LEITHE, Loch 164
NA CREIGE MAOLAICH, Loch 345
NA CREIGE RIABHAICH, Loch 67
NA CREIGE RIABHAICH, Lochan 180
NA CREIGE RUAIDHE, Loch 165
NA CREIGE, Loch (Cheese Bay) 191
NA CREIGE, Loch (East Kenmore) 240
NA CREIGE, Loch (Laiaval) 191
NA CREIGE, Loch (West Kenmore) 240
NA CREITHEACH, Loch 272
NA CRIADHACH, Loch 191
NA CRICHE, Loch (Lochportain) 191
NA CRICHE, Loch (Scaliscro) 118
NA CRICHE, Lochan 320
NA CRO, Loch 137
NA CROIBHE, Loch (Soval) 118
NA CROIC, Loch 253
NA CROISE, Lochan 320
NA CRORAIG, Lochan 248
NA CRUADHACH, Lochan 276
NA CRUAICH, Loch 345
NA CUIDHE, Lochan 248
NA CUILCE, Loch 240, 315
NA CUILCE, Lochan 86
NA CUILLICH, Loch 253
NA CUITHE MOIRE, Lochan 226
NA CURACH, Loch 240
NA CURAICH, Lochan 345
NA CURRA, Loch 206, 212
NA CURRA, Lochan 253
NA CURRAIDH, Loch 226
NA CUTHAIGE, Lochan 298
NA DAIL, Loch 165
NA DEIGHE FO DHEAS, Loch 226
NA DEIGHE FO TUATH, Loch 226
NA DOIRE BUIDHE, Lochan 273
NA DOIRE DUIBHE, Loch 165
NA DOIRE DUINNE, Loch 206
NA DOIRE MOIRE, Loch 240
NA DOIRE-UAINE, Lochan 304
NA DOIRLINN, Loch 266
NA DRAIPE, Loch 298
NA DROIGHNICHE, Loch 165
NA DUBH LEITIR, Lochan 165
NA DUBH-BHRUAICH, Loch 240
NA DUBHCHA, Loch 191
NA DUCHASAICH, Loch 226
NA DUIN, Loch (Barra) 266
NA EILEAN, Loch, Arnish 45
NA EITHIR EILEANA, Loch 226
NA FAIC, Loch 180

NA FAING, Loch 45, 118
NA FAING, Loch (Morsgail) 118
NA FAING, Loch (Scaliscro) 118
NA FAOILEAD, Loch 226
NA FAOILEIGE, Loch 165, 206, 212
NA FAOILEIGE, Lochan 68
NA FAOILINN, Loch 345
NA FAOIRBH, Loch 118
NA FAOLAIG, Lochan 180
NA FEANNAIG, Loch 240, 253
NA FEANNAIG, Loch 240, 253
NA FEITHE DIRICH, Loch 206
NA FEITHE-SEILICH, Loch 248
NA FIDEIL, Loch 206
NA FOLA, Loch 45, 371
NA FOLA, Lochan 325
NA FREAGAIRT, Lochan 68
NA FRIANACH, Loch 248
NA FUARALACHD, Loch 173, 180
NA GABHTACH, Loch 248
NA GAINEIMH, Loch 180, 185
NA GAINIMH, Loch 68, 71, 165
NA GAINIMH, Loch (Sandwood) 68
NA GAINMHICH, Loch 45, 68, 165
NA GAINMHICH, Loch (Achmore). 45
NA GAINMHICH, Loch (Breasclete) 45
NA GAOITHE, Loch 160, 191, 298
NA GARBH-ABHAINN ARD, Loch 191
NA GARBHE UIDHE, Loch 165
NA GEADH, Loch 45
NA GEARR LEACAINN, Lochan 281
NA GEARRA, Loch 212
NA GEARRACHUN, Loch 189, 191
NA GLAIC GILLE, Loch 206
NA GLAIC TARSUINN, Loch 68
NA GLAIC, Loch 86
NA GLAMHAICHD, Lochan 68
NA GLAS-CHOILLE, Loch 180
NA GOBHLAIG, Loch 248
NA GREIDIL, Loch 253
NA GRUAGAICH, Loch 165
NA GRUAGAICH, Lochan 315
NA GUAILNE IDHRE, Loch 206
NA H-ACHLAIS, Loch 226
NA H-ACHLAISE, Lochan 325
NA H-AIBHNE GAIRBHE, Loch 137
NA H-AIBHNE RUAIDHE, Loch 137
NA H-AIRDE BIGE, Loch 206
NA H-AIRDE, Loch 45, 108
NA H-AIRIGH BIGE, Lochan 345
NA H-AIRIGH DUIBHE, Loch (Chilleirivagh) 266
NA H-AIRIGH DUIBHE, Loch (Daliburgh) 266
NA H-AIRIGH FRAOICH, Loch 165
NA H-AIRIGH MOLAICH, Loch 206
NA H-AIRIGH SLEIBHE, Loch 69
NA H-AIRIGH UISGE, Loch 45
NA H-AIRIGH, Loch (Gravir) 137
NA H-AIRIGHE BIGE, Loch 165

443

Index

NA H-AIRIGHE RIABHAICH, Lochan 240
NA H-ARD EILIG, Loch 206
NA H-ATH, Loch 69
NA H-EAGLAISE BEAG, Loch 86
NA H-EAGLAISE MOR, Loch 86
NA H-EANGAICHE, Loch 240
NA H-EARAIG, Loch 45
NA H-FIRIDH, Loch 248
NA H-IMRICHE, Loch 87, 369
NA H-INGHINN, Loch 118, 137
NA H-INNSE FRAOICH, Loch 165
NA H-INNSE GAIRBHE, Loch 206
NA H-IOLAIRE, Loch 110, 118, 137, 191
NA H-IOLAIRE, Loch (Horsaclett) 137
NA H-IOLAIRE, Loch (Soval) 118
NA H-OIDHCHE, Loch 206, 212
NA H-OLA, Loch 118
NA H-UAMHA, Loch (Craig) 240
NA H-UAMHAIDH BEAG, Loch 207
NA H-UAMHAIDH MOIRE, Loch 207
NA H-UAMHAIG, Loch 240
NA H-UIDHE DOIMHNE, Loch 165
NA H-UIDHE, Loch 137, 152, 207-208
NA H-UMHA, Loch (Daliburgh) 266
NA HEARBA, Lochan 281
NA HOSTRACH, Loch 191
NA LAIMH, Loch 345
NA LAIRE BAINE, Loch 226
NA LAIRE DUIBHE, Loch 69
NA LAIRIGE, Loch 207, 285
NA LAITHAICH, Loch 365
NA LARACH BLAIRE, Loch 253
NA LARACH LEITHE, Loch 138
NA LARACH, Loch 69, 240
NA LARACH, Loch (Kenmore) 240
NA LEAC, Loch (Beinn Tulagaval) 45
NA LEAMHAIN, Loch 45
NA LEARGA, Loch 118
NA LEIRG, Loch 207, 391
NA LEIRISDEIN, Loch 253
NA LEITIRE, Loch 240
NA LERG, Loch 273
NA LIANA MOIRE, Loch 226
NA LICE BAINE, Loch 226
NA LICE, Loch (Daliburgh) 266
NA LINNE, Loch 45
NA LOIN, Loch 240
NA LOINNE, Loch 166
NA LUCH, Loch 253
NA MAIGHDEIN, Loch 191
NA MANG, Loch 180
NA MAOILE BHUIDHE, Loch 248
NA MAOILE, Loch 176, 212
NA MAOILE, Lochan 325
NA MEILICH, Loch 240
NA MNA, Loch 240
NA MNATHA, Loch 69
NA MOINE BEAG, Loch 212
NA MOINE BUIGE, Loch 207
NA MOINE MOIRE, Loch 248

NA MOINE MOR, Loch 212
NA MOINE, Loch 87, 133, 138, 188, 205, 207, 210
NA MOINEACH, Loch 45
NA MORACHA, Loch 191
NA MORGHA, Loch 191
NA MUCNAICH, Loch 166
NA MUILNE, Loch 45, 109, 118, 137-138
NA MUILNE, Loch (Arnol) 45
NA MUILNE, Loch (Bosta) 118
NA MUILNE, Loch (Gisla) 118
NA MUILNE, Loch (Grimersta) 45, 118
NA MUILNE, Loch (Grimersta) 45, 118
NA MUILNE, Loch (Keose) 138
NA MUILNE, Loch (Loch nan Geadraisean) 118
NA MUILNE, Loch (North Shawbost) 45
NA MUILNE, Loch (Shiltenish) 118
NA MUILNE, Loch (South Shawbost) 45
NA MUILNE, Loch (Stiapavat) 45
NA MUILNE, Loch (Tamanavay) 118
NA MUILNE, Loch (Tolsta Chaolais) 45
NA NIGHEADAIREACHD, Loch 365
NA PEARAICH, Loch 369
NA PLAIDE, Loch 45, 118
NA PLOYTACH, Loch 166
NA SAIGHE DUIBHE, Loch 166
NA SALACH, Loch 212
NA SAOBHAIDHE, Loch 87
NA SAOBHAIDHE, Lochan 325-326
NA SCARAVAT, Loch 45
NA SEALGA, Loch 207
NA SEAMRAIG, Loch 69
NA SEILG, Loch 69, 269
NA SEILGE, Loch 70, 87, 94
NA SEILGE, Loch (Ben Stack) 70
NA SEILGE, Loch (Creagan Meall Horn) 70
NA SGAIL, Lochan 138
NA SGAIREIG MOR, Loch 207
NA SGEULACHD, BEALACH Loch 87
NA SGILLEOG, Loch 345
NA SGORRA, Loch 369
NA SGORTHAICK, Loch 282
NA SGUABAIDH, Loch 273
NA SMALAIG, Loch (Gramsdale) 226
NA SMEORAICH, Loch 240
NA SPEUR, Loch 257
NA SROINE LUIME, Loch 166
NA SROINE, Loch 138, 248
NA STAINGE, Loch 325
NA STAIRNE, Loch 185
NA STAIRNE, Lochan 282
NA STAOINEIG, Loch 301
NA STIOMA GILE, Loch 70
NA SUILEIG, Loch 240
NA SULA BIGE, Loch 320
NA SULA MOIRE, Loch 320
NA TANGA, Loch 226
NA TARRAING, Loch 166
NA TEANGA RIABHAICH, Lochan 273

NA TEANGA, Lochan 240
NA THULL, Loch 70
NA TOTAIG, Loch 166
NA TRI, Lochan 166
NA TUADH, Loch 70
NA-CLEIRE, Loch 207
NAH ARDLARAICH, Loch 345
NAID, Loch 226
NAIRN (Upper), River 253
NAIRN, River 257
NAM BA, Loch 369
NAM BALGAN, Loch 226
NAM BALL, Loch 240
NAM BAN, Loch 345, 365
NAM BO RIABHACH, Lochan 185
NAM BO UIDHRE, Loch 87
NAM BRAC, Loch 70
NAM BRATHAIN, Loch 253
NAM BREAC BEAG, Loch 87
NAM BREAC BEAGA, Loch 180, 240
NAM BREAC BEAGA, Loch 180, 240
NAM BREAC BUIDGE, Loch 88
NAM BREAC BUIDHE, Loch 88, 345
NAM BREAC BUIDHE, Lochan 71, 345
NAM BREAC BUIDHE, Lochan (Cape Wrath) 71
NAM BREAC DEARGA, Loch 248, 254-255
NAM BREAC MOR, Loch 88, 166
NAM BREAC MORA, Loch 226, 240, 248
NAM BREAC ODHAR, Loch 207
NAM BREAC PEATAIR, Loch 226
NAM BREAC RUADH, Loch 226
NAM BREAC, Loch 36, 46, 88, 118, 138, 166, 191, 365, 369, 371
NAM BREAC, Loch (Borve) 191
NAM BREAC, Loch (Druim a'Botha Chlach) 46
NAM BREAC, Loch (Eishken) 138
NAM BREAC, Loch (Fionn Allt Beag) 46
NAM BREAC, Loch (Keose) 138
NAM BREAC, Loch (Laxay) 118
NAM BREAC, Loch (North Assynt) 166
NAM BREAC, Loch (Rogavat) 138
NAM BREAC, Loch (Stornoway) 46
NAM BREAC, Loch (Stornoway) 46
NAM BREAC, Lochan 100, 207, 212, 276, 295, 302
NAM BUAINICHEAN, Loch 207
NAM BURAG, Lochan 88
NAM FAIDH, Loch 212
NAM FALCAG, Loch 46
NAM FAOILEAG, Loch 39, 88, 118, 138, 255
NAM FAOILEAG, Loch (Eishken) 138
NAM FAOILEAG, Lochan 282
NAM FAOILEANN, Loch 226, 266-267
NAM FEITHEAN, Loch 191
NAM FIASGAN, Loch 46
NAM FIODHAG, Loch 253
NAM FORCA, Loch 248

Index

NAM FREUMH, Loch 253
NAM GEADAS, Loch 253
NAM MEALLAN-KIATHA, Loch 166
NAM MEUR (North), Loch 253
NAM MEUR (South), Loch 253
NAM PAITEAN, Loch 298
NAN ALLT RUADH, Lochan 118
NAN ARM, Loch 267
NAN ATHAN, Loch 191
NAN BREAC DUBHA, Loch (Armadale) 273
NAN CABER, Loch 207, 248
NAN CADHAN, Loch 365
NAN CAOR, Loch 139
NAN CAOR, Loch (Diracleit) 139
NAN CAOR, Loch (Quidnish) 139
NAN CAORACH, Loch 46, 110, 112, 163, 166, 185, 227, 230, 346, 365, 369
NAN CAORACH, Loch (Assynt) 166
NAN CAORANN, Loch 46
NAN CAORANN, Loch (Ben Hulabie) 46
NAN CAORANN, Loch (Ben Mholach) 46
NAN CAPULL, Loch 46, 267
NAN CAPULL, Loch (South Boisdale) 267
NAN CARN, Loch 267
NAN CAT, LOCHAN 328
NAN CAT, Lochan (Glen Lyon) 328
NAN CEARDACH, Lochan 345
NAN CEITHIR EILEAN, Loch 191
NAN CINNEACHAN, Loch 312
NAN CLABAN, Loch 46
NAN CLACH CORR, Loch 227
NAN CLACH DUBHA, Loch 207
NAN CLACH GEALA, Lochan 94
NAN CLACH, Loch 46, 89, 227, 273, 320, 365
NAN CLACH, LOCH 46, 89, 227, 273, 320, 365
NAN CLACH, Loch (Stornoway) 46
NAN CLACH-MORA, Loch 267
NAN CLACHAN DUBHA, Loch 253
NAN CLACHAN GEALA, Loch 101, 207
NAN CLACHAN, Loch 191, 227
NAN CLAR, Loch 180
NAN CLEITICHEAN, Loch 32, 46
NAN CNAIMH, Loch 212
NAN CNAMH, Loch 46, 89
NAN CNAMH, Lochan 139
NAN CRAOBH, Lochan 320
NAN CRAOBHAG, Loch 139
NAN CREADHA, Loch 248
NAN CREAGANAN GROID, Loch 118
NAN CREIGE DUIBHE, Loch 166
NAN CROINTEAN, Loch 267
NAN CUILCEAN, Loch 253
NAN CULAIDHEAN, Loch 46
NAN CURRAN, Loch 167
NAN DAILTHEAN, Loch 207
NAN DEARCAG, Loch 253
NAN DEARCAG, Lochan 315
NAN DEAREAG, Loch (Arnish) 46

NAN DOIRB, Lochan 248
NAN DUBHRACHAN, Loch 273
NAN DUBHRAICHEAN, Loch 273
NAN EALACHAN, Lochan 167
NAN EANG, Loch 139
NAN EILEAN, Loch 46, 118-119, 139, 212, 273, 345, 369
NAN EILEAN, Loch (Achmore). 46
NAN EILEAN, Loch (Garyvard) 139
NAN EILEAN, Loch (Langavat) 119
NAN EILEAN, Loch (Roineval) 119
NAN EILEAN, Loch (Sligachan) 273
NAN EILEIN, Loch (Mulhagery) 139
NAN EILEIN, Loch (Tom an Fhuadain) 139
NAN EILID, Loch 253
NAN EUN (Cuaig), Loch 240
NAN EUN (Salacher), Loch 240
NAN EUN, Loch 167, 191, 208, 212, 240, 253, 255, 282, 306, 309, 332, 367, 371
NAN EUN, Loch (Lochinver) 167
NAN EUN, Loch (Quinag) 167
NAN EUN, Loch (Shieldaig) 208
NAN EUN, Loch (Skealtar) 191
NAN FAOILEAG, Loch (Morsgail) 119
NAN GABHAR, Lochan 289
NAN GAD, Lochan 167
NAN GALL, Loch 89, 363
NAN GAMHNA, Loch 89, 240
NAN GAMHNA, Lochan 89, 240
NAN GARBH CHLACHAN, Loch 227
NAN GARNACH, Loch 191
NAN GEADH, Loch 46, 191, 267, 312, 371
NAN GEADH, Loch (Stacashal). 46
NAN GEADRAISEAN, Loch 119
NAN GEALAG, Loch 227
NAN GEIREANN, Loch 192
NAN GEIREANN, Sea-Pool 192
NAN GILLEAN, Loch 139, 216, 240, 248, 365, 367
NAN GILLEAN, Lochan 315
NAN GOBHAIR, Loch 167
NAN GOBHAR, Loch 248, 255
NAN IOLAIREAN, Loch 139
NAN LACHAN, Lochan 227
NAN LAIGH, Loch 208
NAN LANN, Loch 282
NAN LAOGH, Loch (Orasay) 46
NAN LEAC, Loch (Ceann Allavat) 46
NAN LEAC, Loch (Cliastul) 46
NAN LEAC, Loch (Gress) 46
NAN LEARG, Loch 316
NAN LEARGA, Lochan 119
NAN LIATH BHREAC, Lochan 167
NAN LION, Loch 167
NAN LOCHAN, Lochan 298
NAN LOSGANN, Loch 345
NAN LUB, Loch 139, 168
NAN LUIG, Loch 46
NAN NIGHEAN, Loch 282
NAN RAC, Loch 168
NAN RAMH, Loch (Tamanavay) 119

NAN RATH, Loch 180
NAN REAMH, Loch 285
NAN RITHEANAN, Loch 139
NAN SGARAIG, Loch 168
NAN SGEIREAG, Loch 227
NAN SGIATH, Loch 46, 302
NAN SIAMAN, Loch 267
NAN SIAMAN, Lochan 315
NAN SLOCHD, Loch 241
NAN SMALAG, Loch 192, 267
NAN SMALAG, Loch (North Lochboisdale) 267
NAN STARR, Loch 46
NAN STEALL, Loch 46
NAN STEARNAG, Loch 46, 139
NAN STEARNAG, Loch (Stacashal) 46
NAN STRUBAN, Loch 192
NAN STUIRTEAG, Loch 289
NAN TRI-CHRIOCHAN (West), Lochan 298
NAN TRI-EILEANAN, Loch 241
NAN UAIGHEAN, Loch 241
NAN UAIN, Loch 208
NAN UAMH, Loch 273
NAN UAN, Loch 180, 208, 227, 273
NAN UAN, Loch (Borline) 273
NAN UAN, Lochan 298
NAN UIDH, Loch 71
NAN UIDHEAN BEAGA, Loch 139, 168
NAN UIDHEAN BEAGA, Loch 139, 168
NAN UIDHEAN, Loch (Brunaval) 140
NAN UIDHEAN, Loch (Garynahine) 46
NAN UIDHEAN, Loch (Horsaclett) 140
NAN UIDHEAN, Loch (Scadabay) 140
NAN UIDHEAN, Loch (Tamanavay) 119
NAN UIDHEAN, Loch (Uig) 119
NANT, Loch 320
NANT, River 320
NASAVIG, Loch 119
NATURE RESERVES 26, 171, 191, 222, 264, 277, 287-288, 294, 317, 321, 335-336, 339, 359, 363, 379, 384, 404
NAVER, Loch 75, 180
NAVER, River 89
NEADAVAT, Loch 46
NEAPABACK, Loch 16
NEIL BHAIN, Loch 46, 169
NEIMHA, Lochan 248
NELL, Loch 320
NESHION Water 16-17
NESS, Loch (North) 253
NESS, River 254
NETHAN, River 396
NETHY, River 289
NEVIS, River 301
NEWHOUSE PARK, Fishery 396
NEWMILL DEER FARM, Fishery 396
NEWTON FARM, Fishery 362
NIC DHOMHNUIL, Loch 46
NIC RUAIDHE, Loch 267
NIGHE, Loch 192, 227

445

Index

NIGHE, Loch (Aonghais) 192
NIGHE, Loch (South Lee) 192
NIGHEADH, Lochan 168
NIGHEAN SHOMHAIRLE, Loch 46
NIGHEANN FHIONNLAIDH, Loch 273
NIOSAVAT, Loch 41, 46
NISHAVAT, Loch 119
NISREAVAL, Loch 46
NITH, River 394, 411, 423
NOCHTY, Water of 291
NOIR, Loch 258
NORTH CALDER, Water 379
NORTH ESK, River 308, 311
NORTH GALSON, River 47
NORTH Loch, Sanday 24
NORTH RONALDSAY, Island 24
NORTH THIRD, Reservoir 353
NORTH UGIE, Water 263
NORTH-HOUSE, Loch 16
NOSINISH, Loch 267
NOTTINGHAM MILL DAM, Loch 94
NUCKRO WATER 6

O

OB AN LOCHAIN, Loch 212
OB LEASAID, Sea Loch 140
OBAN A'CHLEACHAIN, Sea Pool 192
OBAN AN INNSEANAICH Sea-loch 227
OBAN IRPEIG, Sea Pool 192
OBAN LINICLATE Sea Loch 227
OBAN NA BUAIL-UACHDRAICH Sea-loch 227
OBAN NA CURRA, Sea Pool 192
OBAN NAM MUCA-MARA, Sea-loch 227
OBAN SPONISH, Sea Loch 192
OBAN TRUMISGARRY, Loch 193
OBAN UAINE, Sea-loch 227
OBBE, Loch 193
OBISARY, Loch 227
OCHILTREE, Loch 403-404
ODHAR, Loch 168, 207, 212, 241
ODHAR, Loch 168, 207, 212, 241
OICH, Loch 282
OICH, River 282
OICHEAN, Loch 47
OIL, Loch 140
OLAVAT, Loch (East) 227
OLAVAT, Loch (Gramsdale) 228
OLAVAT, Loch (Vallay) 193
OLAVAT, Loch (West) 228
OLD, Water 424
OLIGINEY, Loch 101
OLLAS Water, Loch 16
ORASAY, Loch 47
ORCHILL, Loch 359
ORCHY, River 325
ORD, River 273
ORDAIS, Loch 47
ORE, Loch 360

ORE, River 362
ORRIN, Reservoir 254
ORRIN, River 254
ORWICK Water 13, 16
OSDALE, River 233
OSE, River 233
OSGAIG, Loch 168
OUDE, Reservoir 345
OUDE, River 345-346
OYAVAT, Loch 119
OYKEL (LOWER), River 180
OYKEL (Upper), River 181
OYKEL, Upper (River) 168

P

PAIBLE, Sea Loch 193
PAITEAG, Loch 283
PALM, Loch 90
PALNURE Burn 406, 408, 420
PAPIL Water (Fetlar) 5
PAPIL, Loch of (Yell) 5
PARK, Loch 259
PARKHILL, Loch 293
PARKLEY, Fishery 382
PATTACK, Loch 304
PEALLACH, Loch (Bottom Mishnish) 315
PEAN, River 276, 295
PEEVISH CREEK, Loch 169
PENWHAPPLE, Reservoir 404
PENWHIRN, Burn 417
PENWHIRN, Reservoir 417
PERRIE WATER, Mainland 27
PERRIE WATER, Rousay See Muckle Water, Rousay 27
PETTA Water 16
PETTADALE Water 3, 5
PHILORTH, Water 263
PHONES & ETTERIDGE ESTATE, Lochs 285
PILTANTON Burn 416-418
PIPER, Loch 47
PIPERDAM, Fishery 336
PITAIRLIE Burn 339
PITFOUR, Loch 263
PITYOULISH, Loch 289
PLOCRAPOOL, Loch 140
POIT NA H-I, Loch 316
POLL A'PHAC, Loch 181
POLL AN ACHAIDH BHUIDHE, Loch 169
POLL AN DROIGHINN, Loch 169
POLL DHAIDH, Loch 169
POLL, Loch 169
POLLA, River 71
POLLAIN BUIDHE, Loch 248
POLLOCH, River 298
POLLY, Lochs 169
POLLY, River 169
POND, Loch 321
PORT NA LOCHAN, Fishery 391

PORTMORE, Loch 385
POULARY, Loch 283
PREAS AN LOCHAN, Loch 90
PREAS NAN AIGHEAN, Loch 169
PREAS NAN SGIATHANACH, Lochan 181
PRESTWICK, Reservoir 393
PUNDAVON, Reservoir 376
PUNDS Water 7, 9, 16, 18-19
PUNDS, Lochs 16
PURDOMSTONE, Reservoir 425

Q

QUAIR, Water 398
QUASSAWALL, Loch 16
QUEENSIDE, Loch 376
QUIEN, Loch 376
QUINNI, Loch 16
QUINNIGEO, Loch 16
QUOICH, Loch 276, 295
QUOICH, River 277
QUOY, Loch 5

R

RAA, Loch 169
RAHACLEIT, Loch 47
RAITH, Fishery 393
RAITH, Lake 362
RAMALACH, Loch 119
RANGAG, Loch 101
RANGAVAT, Loch (Ardroil) 119
RANKLE, Burn 415
RANNOCH, River 321
RAOINABHAT, Loch 140
RAOINAVAT, Loch 47
RAONASGAIL, Loch 119
RAPACH, Lochan 170
RAVAG, Loch 234
RED, Loch 263, 396
REDSIDE, Burn 385
REE, Loch 418
REIDH CREAGAIN, Loch 212
REIDH NAN, Loch 273
REOIDHTE, Lochan 353
RESCOBIE, Loch 339
RESTIL, Loch 350
RHA, River 234
RHICONICH, River 71
RHIDORROCH, River 213
RHIFAIL, Loch 90
RIBAVAT, Loch 120
RIFA-GIL, Loch 90
RIGH BEAG, Loch 369
RIGH MEADHGNACH, Loch 369
RIGH MOR, Loch 369
RIMSDALE, Loch 181
RISORD, Loch 48
ROAG, Loch 228, 241

446

Index

ROAN, Loch 422-423
ROBBIE GLEN'S, Loch 17
ROBIN'S DAM 330, 336
ROER Water 1, 5
ROGAVAT, Loch 140
ROINEVAL, Loch 120
ROINICH, Loch 228
ROINICH, Loch (Askernish) 228
ROISINISH BAY, Sea Loch 193
ROISNAVAT, Loch 48
ROMESDAL, River 234
RONARD (North), Loch 312
RONARD (South), Loch 312
RONAS Hill Lochs 17
ROOS Loch 25
ROPACH, Loch 267
ROSAIL, Loch 90
ROSCOBIE, Reservoir 360
ROSEBERY, Reservoir 385
ROSSLYNLEE, Fishery 385
ROTHIEMURCHUS, Stream 289
ROUGHRIGG, Reservoir 382
ROUSAY, Island 25
ROY, River 283
RUADH A'DEAS, Loch (Langavat) 120
RUADH GHEURE DUBH MHOR, Loch 48, 120
RUADH MEADHONACH, Loch 121
RUADH, Loch 109, 120-121, 140, 170, 226
RUADH, Loch (North Scaliscro) 120
RUADH, Loch (South Eishken) 140
RUADH, Loch (South Scaliscro) 121
RUADH, Lochan 91, 118, 170
RUAIDH EITSEAL BHEAG, Loch 48
RUAIRIDH, Loch 121, 140, 251, 285
RUAIRIDH, Loch (Morsgail) 121
RUARD, Loch 101
RUBHA AIRD CHOINNICH, Loch 241
RUBHA NA BREIGE, Loch 170
RUCHILL, Water of 332
RUEL, River 346, 372
RUEVAL, Loch 228
RUFF, Loch 21
RUIG SANDAVAT, Loch 121
RUIGH NAN COPAG, Loch 181
RUIGHE DHUIBH, Lochan 255
RUIGHEAN A'AITINN, Loch 170
RUIGLAVAT, Loch 48
RUISAVAT, Loch 48
RUIT A'PHUILL, Loch 255
RUM, Island of 294
RUMMIE, Loch 25
RUMSAGRO, Loch 48
RUMSDALE, Loch 95
RUMSDALE, Water 95
RUNAGEO, Loch 48
RUNAVAT, Loch 193
RUNIE, River 170
RUSSEL, Burn 241
RUSSON, Burn 422

RUTHVEN, Loch 255
RYAN Sea-loch (North Channel & Luce Bay) 418
RYE, Water 376

S

SAE Water, Loch 17
SAIL AN RUATHAIR, Lochs 170
SAILE, Loch 140
SAINTEAR, Loch 25
SAL, Lochan 170
SALACH A'GHIUBHAIS, Loch 248
SALACHAIDH, Loch 181, 185
SALACHAIDH, Loch 181, 185
SALIGO, River 365
SAND VATN Loch 20-21
SAND Water 4-5, 7, 13, 16-17, 21, 23
SAND Water (Culswick) 21
SAND Water (Mid Yell) 5
SAND Water, Lamba Scord 17
SAND Water, Loch (Garderhouse) 17
SAND Water, Loch (Hulma) 17
SAND, Loch 102, 293
SAND, River 208
SANDARY, Loch 193
SANDAVAT, Loch 34, 44, 48, 121
SANDAVAT, Loch (Brenish) 121
SANDAVAT, Loch (Carloway) 48
SANDAVAT, Loch (Glen Tolsta) 48
SANDAVAT, Loch (Mangersta) 121
SANDAVAT, Loch (Orasay) 48
SANDAVAT, Loch (Pentland Road) 48
SANDAVAT, Lochan 48
SANDKNOWES, Fishery 360
SANDS WATER, Hoy 28
SANDWICK, Loch 21
SANDWOOD, Loch 72
SANDY WATER 1, 3, 28
SANDY, Loch 21, 170, 309
SANNOX, Water 391
SAORACH, Loch 102, 268
SARCLET, Loch 102
SARRAIDH MHOIR, Loch 213
SAUGH, Loch 311
SCAAPAR, Loch 193
SCADAVAY, Loch (North) 193
SCADAVAY, Loch (South) 193
SCALABSDALE, Loch 185
SCALADALE, River 141
SCALAN, Loch 193
SCAMADAL, Loch 234
SCAMMADALE, Loch 321
SCANADALE, Loch 121
SCARF Water 21-22
SCARIE, Loch 193
SCARILODE, Loch 228
SCARMCLATE, Loch 102
SCARRASDALE, Loch 48, 51
SCATTLAND, Loch 5

SCAUR, Water 412
SCHOOL, Loch 121
SCHOOLHOUSE, Loch 228
SCOLPAIG, Loch 193
SCORA Water 15, 17
SCOURST, Loch 141
SCRABSTER, Loch 102
SCRISTAN, Lochan 283
SEA-TROUT FISHING LOCATIONS 17, 23, 27, 28
SEALBHANACH, Loch 248
SEAMAW, Loch 336
SEARRACH, Loch 208
SEIL, Loch 321
SEILEBOST, River 141
SELMMUIR, Fishery 382
SEMBLISTER, Loch 17
SETTER, Loch 4, 22
SGAILLER, Loch 121
SGAIRE, Loch 48, 121
SGAIRE, Loch 48, 121
SGAMHAIN, Loch 248
SGAOTHAICHEAN, Lochan 72
SGARAVAT BEAG, Loch 48
SGEIRACH, Lochan 241
SGEIRACH, Lochan 241
SGEIREACH A'GHLINN MHOIR, Loch 48
SGEIREACH MOR, Loch 48
SGEIREACH NA CREIGE BRIST, Loch 48
SGEIREACH, Loch 34, 44, 48, 141, 169, 181, 198, 208, 212, 267
SGEIREACH, Loch (Dalreavoch) 181
SGEIREACH, Loch (Loch Bad a'Chreamh) 208
SGEIREACH, Loch (North Lewis) 48
SGEIREACH, Loch (Quier) 141
SGEIREACH, Loch (South Daliburgh) 267
SGEIREACH, Loch (Springcorrie) 48
SGEIREACH, Loch (Stornoway) 48
SGEIREACH, Loch (Tob Bhrollum) 141
SGEIREACH, Lochan 72, 122, 171, 208, 241, 248, 267
SGEIREACH, Lochan (Achiltibuie) 171
SGEIREACH, Lochan (Altnacealgach) 171
SGEIREACH, Lochan (Attadale) 248
SGEIREACH, Lochan (Boor) 208
SGEIREACH, Lochan (Daliburgh) 267
SGEIREACH, Lochan (Diabaig) 241
SGEIREACH, Lochan (Great Bernera) 122
SGEIREACH, Lochan (Meall Imireach) 208
SGEIREACH, Lochan (Shieldaig) 208
SGEIREACH, Lochanan 122
SGEIREADH, Loch 91
SGEIREAGAN MOR, Loch 141
SGIATHANAGH, Loch 91
SGIBACLEIT, Loch 122, 141
SGIBACLEIT, Loch 122, 141
SGIER A'CHADHA, Loch 72
SGITHEAEN, River 216
SGOLBAIDH, Loch 255
SGORR NI DHONNACHAIDH, Loch 141

Index

SGRIACHACH, Loch (Aird Skapraid) 49
SGUABAIN, Loch 321
SGUAT, Lochan 208
SGUOD, Loch 208
SGURR MHOIR, Lochan 273
SGURR NA CAORACH, Loch 273
SGURR NA FEARTAIG, Loch 248
SHADER, Loch 49
SHAGHACHAIN, Loch 141
SHANNDABHAT, Loch 141
SHAPINSAY, Island 27
SHARK, Loch 171
SHEE, Water 306
SHEEP, Loch 141
SHIAN, River 369
SHIAVAT, Loch 49
SHIEL (Loch & River) (Glenfinnan) 298
SHIEL, Loch (Duich) 277
SHIEL, River (Duich) 277
SHIELDAIG, River 241
SHIELING, Loch 122, 228
SHIELING, Loch (Great Bernera) 122
SHIELING, Lochan 142, 171
SHIFFIN, Loch 369
SHIN, Loch 181
SHIN, River 182, 216
SHINARY, River 72
SHINNADALE, Loch 194
SHINNEL, Water 412
SHIRA, RIVER 347, 350
SHNATHAID, Loch 228
SHROMOIS, Loch 142
SHURAVAL, Loch 228
SHURAVAT, Loch (Benbecula) 267
SHURRERY, Loch 103
SIAN, Loch 72
SIBHINN, Loch 365
SIONASCAIG, Loch 171
SITHEIN DUIBH, Lochan 326
SKAIL, Loch 27
SKAPRAID, Loch 49
SKAVAT, Loch 49
SKEALTAR, Loch 194
SKEAUDALE, River 142
SKEEN, Loch 415
SKELLISTER, Loch 17
SKELLOCH, Loch 408
SKELMORLIE, Fishery 376
SKENE, Loch 293
SKERRAY, Loch 91
SKERROLS, Loch 366
SKEUN, Loch 122
SKILIVAT, Loch 194
SKORASHAL, Loch 49
SKULA Water 8, 18
SKYLINE, Loch 103
SKYRE, Burn 422
SLAIM, Loch 91
SLEACH, Water 95
SLEADALE, Loch 273

SLEITIR, Loch 49
SLETILL, Loch 95
SLIDDERY, Water 391
SLIGACHAN, River 273
SLITRIG, Water 415
SLOY, Loch 350
SMA, Lochs 18
SMALLA Waters 12, 18
SMALLAG, Loch 194
SMERCLATE, Loch 267
SMERLA Water, Loch 18
SMIGEADAIL , Loch 366
SMINIG, Loch 49
SMUAISAVAL, Loch 49, 122
SMUIRNEACH, Lochan 171
SNEASDAL, Loch 234
SNEHAVAL BEAG, Loch 122
SNEHAVAL, Loch 122
SNIGISCLETT, Loch 228
SNIZORT, River 234
SOEIREACH, Lochan 142
SOIR, Lochs 321
SOOLMISVIRD Water 15, 18
SORN, River 366
SOTERSTA, Loch 22
SOULSEAT, Loch 418
SOUTH CALDER, Water 379
SOUTH ESK, River 309
SOUTH RONALDSAY, Island 28
SOUTH STOFAST, Loch 18
SOUTH UGIE, Water 263
SOVAL, Loch 44, 122, 142
SPAGACH, Loch 122
SPEALDRAVAT MOR, Loch 49
SPEALTRAVAT, Loch 49
SPEAN, River 283
SPECTACLES, Loch 208
SPEIREACH, Loch 49
SPEIREAG, Loch 49, 122
SPEIREIG, Loch 40, 122
SPEY DAM, Loch 284, 286
SPEY, River 258-259, 286, 289
SPIGGIE, Loch 22
SPOGACH, Loch 208
SPOTAL, Loch 229
SPRINGWATER, Fishery 393
SQUARE, Loch 142
SRATH STEACHRAN, Loch 142
SROINE MOIRE, Loch 122
SRON MOR, LOCHAN 326
ST JOHN'S, Loch 103
ST MARY'S LOCH 28, 396, 398
ST MARY'S, Loch 398
ST. TREDWELL, Loch 25
STACK, Loch 72
STACSAVAT, Loch 122
STAING, Loch 91, 173
STANES Water 15, 18
STANEVATSTOE, Loch 18
STANTLING CRAIG, Reservoir 398

STAOISH, Loch 366
STARABRAIGH, Loch 194
STARBURN, Loch 412
STARE, Dam 336
STAVANESS, Loch 18
STEAPHAIN, Loch 194
STEINAVAT, Loch 194
STEISAVAT, Loch 194
STEISHAL, Loch 122
STEMSTER, Loch 103
STENHOUSE, Reservoir 385
STENNESS, Loch 27
STENSCHOLL, River 234
STIAPAVAT, Loch 49
STILL, Loch 346
STILLIGARRY, Loch 229
STINCHER, River 404, 406
STIOCLETT, Loch 142
STIOMRABHAIGH, Lochan 142
STOLE, Lochan 299
STONEYHILL, Fish farm 262
STORAB, Loch 241
STORR, Lochs 234
STRAE, RIVER 326
STRAND, Loch 22
STRANDAVAT, Loch (Balallan) 122
STRATH DUCHALLY, Loch 182
STRATH, Burn 104
STRATHBEG, Loch of 263
STRATHCLYDE, Loch 379
STRATHLACHAN, River 346
STRATHMORE, River 73
STRATHY, Loch 92
STRATHY, River 92
STRIAMAVAT, Loch 49
STROM, Loch 18
STROMNESS,Loch 27
STRONE, Water 389
STRONTIAN, River 299
STUBBA Water 16, 18
STULADALE, Loch 142
STULAVAL, Loch 229, 267
SUAINAGADAIL, Loch 49
SUAINAVAL, Loch 123
SUARDAL, Loch 235
SUIL A'GHRIAMA, Loch 182
SUIL BO, Loch 315
SUIRSTAVAT, Loch 123
SUIRSTAVAT, River 123
SULMA Water 18
SULMA-NESS, Loch 18
SUNG, Loch 18
SURTAVAT, Loch 229
SWANNAY, Loch 27
SWANSWATER, Fishery 353
SWARTMILL, Loch 25
SWORDALE, Loch 50

T

Index

TA, Loch 50
TAIN, River 216
TALISKER, River 274
TALLA, Reservoir 396
TALLAHEEL, Loch 95
TANA NA GILE RUAIDHE, Loch 123
TANA NAN LEAC, Loch 50
TANA, Loch 50, 123, 368-369, 371
TANA, Loch (Aird Skapraid) 50
TANA, Loch (Garynahine) 50
TANA, Loch (Great Bernera) 123
TANA, Loch (Skapraid) 50
TANA, Lochan (Aline) 142
TANAR, Water 291
TANAVAT, Loch 50
TANGI, Loch 18
TANGUSDALE, Loch 267
TANGY, Loch 389
TANKERNESS, Loch 28
TANNA, Loch 391
TARAVAT, Loch 50
TARBERT, Loch 142
TARBERT, River 322
TARBHAIDH, Loch 73, 182, 216
TARF, Water 307, 422
TARF, Water of 422
TARFF, Loch 283
TARFF, Water 422
TARRAS, Water 415
TARRUINN AN EITHIR, Loch 194
TARSAN, Loch 350
TARSTAVAT, Loch 50
TARSUINN, Loch 68, 142, 367
TARVIE, Lochs (Trout Fishery) 255
TAY (Upper), River 332
TAY, Loch 328, 330
TAY, River 330, 337
TEANGA, Loch 229
TEARNAIT, LOCH 322
TEITH, River 353
TERGAVAT, Loch 194
TEVIOT, River 400, 415
TEVIOT, River (See also OS Map 79, Hawick & Eskdale) 400
THOGAIL NA BEISTE, Loch 267
THOLLAIDH, Loch 241
THOLLDHOIRE, Loch 208
THOM, Loch 376
THORMAID, Loch 104, 126, 171, 213
THORMAID, Loch (Lochinver) 171
THORSAGEARRAIDH, Loch 195
THOTA BRIDEIN, Loch 50
THRAIL, River 236, 242, 248
THREIPMUIR, Reservoir 386
THUILL EASAICH, Loch 248
THULACHAN, Lochan 104
THURSO, River 96
TIDAL POND 131, 142
TIDAL PONDS, Sea Pools (Ardhainish) 195
TIGH CHOINNICH, Lochan 346

TIGH NA CREIGE, Loch 182
TIGH NA H-EIGE, Loch 171
TIGH-CHOIMHID, Lochan 92
TIGH-SEALGA, Loch 369
TILL, River 401
TILT, River 307
TIMA, Water 416
TINGWALL, Loch 22
TIORMACHD, Lochan 92
TIORSDAM, Loch 142
TIRRY, River 182
TODALE, River 123
TOFTINGALL, Loch 104
TOLL A'MHADAIDH, Loch 208
TOLL AN LOCHAIN, Loch 208, 212
TOLL NAM BIAST, Loch 208
TOLLA BHAID, Lochan 171
TOLLAIDH, Loch 208
TOM AILEIN, Lochan 302
TOM AN FHEIDH, Loch 50
TOM AN RISHAL, Loch 51
TOM LIAVRAT, Loch 51
TOM NAN AIGHEAN, Loch 51
TOM, Loch (Springcorrie) 51
TOMA DUBHA, Loch 51
TORLUNDY, Lochans 302
TORMASAD BEAG, Loch 195
TORMASAD, Loch 195
TORONISH, Loch 229
TORR A'GHARBH-UILLT, Lochan 283
TORR AN FHAMHAIR, Lochan 322
TORR AN LOCHAIN, Loch 171, 369
TORR AN LochAIN, Loch (Little Assynt) 171
TORR AN LOCHAIN, Loch (Unapool) 171
TORR AN LOCHAIN, Lochan 171
TORR NAN UIDHEAN, Loch 172
TORRA, River 366
TORRIDON, River 248
TORWOOD, Loch 418
TOSCAIG, River 241
TOTA RUAIRIDH DHUIBH, Lochan 143
TOTAICHEAN AULAIDH, Loch 143
TOUCH MUIR, Reservoirs see Carron Valley Reservoir 354
TOWN, Loch 18
TRAIGHIDH, Loch 123
TRALAIG, Loch 346
TREALAVAL, Loch 123
TREASLANE, River 235
TREBISTER, Loch 22
TREIG, Loch 302
TRENA LOCH 28
TREVIE, Loch 258
TRIALAVAT, Loch (Valtos) 123
TRIPONDIUM, Fishery 398
TROLLADALE Water 15, 18
TROMIE, River 286
TROSARAIDH, Loch 267
TROVASAT, Loch 195

TRUDALE Water 18
TRUDERSCAIG, Loch 182
TRUGGLES Water 14, 19
TRUIM, River 286, 302
TUAMISTER, Loch 51
TUATH, Lochan 172
TUILL BHEARNACH, Loch 248
TUIRAMAIN, Loch 369
TUIRSLIGHE, Loch 92
TULAGAVAL, Loch 51
TULLICH, Burn 291
TUMMEL (Lower), River 333
TUMMEL (Upper), River 334
TUMMEL, Loch 302, 307, 333
TUMMEL, Loch 302, 307, 333
TUNGAVAT, Loch 124
TUNNAIG, Loch 347
TURRET Burn 331, 334
TURRET, Loch 334
TURRET, River 334
TURRI Water 22-23
TWEED, River 387, 397, 399, 401-402
TYNE, River 386-387

U

UACRACH NAN CAORACH, Loch 230
UAILLE MHOR, Loch 143
UAINE Loch (Cairn Toul), 290
UAINE, Lochan 248, 283, 287, 290, 321
UAMADALE, Loch 143
UAMASBROC, Loch 124-125
UAMASBROC, Loch (Uig) 125
UAMH DHADHAIDH, Loch 73
UANALAIR, Loch 51
UATH, Lochan 286
UCSABHAT, Loch 143
UDROMUL, Loch 143
UGIE, River 263
UIDEMUL, Loch 125
UIDH NA CEARDAICH, Loch 172
UIDH NA GEADAIG, Loch 172
UIDH NA H-IARNA, Loch 172
UIDH TARRAIGEAN, Loch 169, 172
UIDHEAN, Loch (Lacasdail) 143
UISDEIN, Loch 195
UISEADER, Loch 143
UISG AN T-SOLUIS, Loch 51
UISG, Loch 322
UISGE AN T-SUIDHE, River 366
UISGE, Loch 45, 108, 286, 322
ULADALE, Loch (Brenish) 125
ULAGADALE, Loch 371
ULAPOLL, Loch 125
ULBHA, Lochan 73
ULBHACH COIRE, Loch 182
ULLADALE, Loch 143
ULLADALE, River 144
ULLAPOOL, River 213
ULLAVAT A'CLITH, Loch 51

Index

ULLAVAT A'DEAS 32, 51
ULLAVEG, Loch 195
ULSTA, Loch of 19
UNAPOOL, Loch 172
UPPER BORNISH, Loch 230
UPPER BOWHILL, Loch 400
UPPER GLENDEVON, Reservoir 360
UPPER HALLADALE, Loch 125
UPPER KILDONAN, Loch 230
UPPER RUSKO, Burn 422
UPPER SLIGEANACH, Lochan 299
UPPER, Loch 371
UPPER, Reservoir 376
URAVAL, Loch (Garynahine) 51
URBHAIG, Loch 312
URE, River 326
URIE, River 293
URIGILL, Loch 172
URR, Water 424
URRAHAG, Loch 51
USSIE, Loch 255
USTANESS, Loch 22

V

VAA, Loch 290
VAARA, Loch 19
VACCASARY, Loch 230
VAGASTIE, River 182
VALIGAN, Loch 307
VALLARIP, Loch 195
VALTOS, Loch 125
VARRAGILL, River 235
VATACHAN, Loch 172
VATACOLLA, Loch 51
VATALEIOS, Lochan 52
VATANDIP, Loch 52
VATS-HOULL, Loch 6
VATSETTER, Loch 22
VATSTER, Loch 19
VAUSARY, Loch 195
VEIRAGVAT, Loch 195
VENACHAR, Loch 354
VEYATIE, Loch 172
VIGADALE, River 144
VIKISGILL, Burn 274
VIRDI Water 2, 5
VISTEM, Loch 144
VIVILIE Loch 23
VOE, Loch 19
VOIL, Loch 354
VOSHIMID, Loch 144
VOXTERBY, Loch 19
VROTACHAN, Loch 307
VUNGIE, Loch 283

W

WABISTER, Loch 28

WARD OF CULSWICK Lochs 21, 23
WAREHOUSE, Loch 104
WARENDER, Loch 92
WASDALE, Loch 28
WATCH WATER, Reservoir 387
WATENAN, Loch 104
WATSNESS, Loch 19
WATTEN, Loch 105
WATTEN, Loch, Egilsay 25
WAUCHOPE, Water 416
WAULKMILL, Fishery 264
WEE BERBETH, Loch 408
WEE FEINN, Loch 347
WEE GLENARMOUR, Loch 422
WELLAND, Loch 25
WEST Loch 6-7, 10, 12, 19, 126, 131, 134, 144, 158, 218, 220, 222, 226-228, 230, 269, 387
WEST LOCH OF SKAW 6
WEST MILL LOCH OF HAMAR 16, 19
WEST OLLAY, Loch 230
WEST WATER 311, 382, 396
WEST WATER, Reservoir 382
WEST, Water 309
WESTER FEARN, Burn 216
WESTER Water 19
WESTER, Loch 105, 415
WESTER, River 105
WESTERWICK, Loch 23
WESTYRE Loch 24-25
WHARRAL, Loch 309
WHEELHOUSE, Lochans 73
WHINHILL, Reservoir 376
WHINYEON, Loch 422
WHIRLS Water, Loch 19
WHIRR, Loch 360, 393
WHITE ESK, Water 416
WHITE, Loch 334, 378, 396, 418, 423
WHITEADDER Water 386-388, 400-402
WHITEADDER, Reservoir 387
WHITEADDER, Water 387
WHITEBRIGS, Loch 19
WHITEFIELD, Pond 379
WHITELAW, Loch 19
WICK, River 106
WILLIESTRUTHER, Loch 416
WINDY, Loch 347
WINDYRIDGE, Loch 261
WINLESS, Loch 106
WOODEN, Loch 402
WORMADALE, Water 23

Y

YAIR, Water 400

YARROW, Water 400
YARROWS, Loch 106
YELL FISHING LOCATIONS 6
YTHAN VALLEY, Fishery 264
YTHAN, River 262, 264, 293
YUCAL, Loch 172

450